A HISTORY OF PRIVATE LAW IN SCOTLAND

Volume 1

A HISTORY OF PRIVATE LAW IN SCOTLAND

Volume 1
Introduction and Property

Edited by

KENNETH REID

and

REINHARD ZIMMERMANN

OXFORD
UNIVERSITY PRESS

This book has been printed digitally and produced in a standard specification in order to ensure its continuing availability

OXFORD
UNIVERSITY PRESS

Great Clarendon Street, Oxford OX2 6DP

Oxford University Press is a department of the University of Oxford.
It furthers the University's objective of excellence in research, scholarship,
and education by publishing world-wide in

Oxford New York

Auckland Bangkok Buenos Aires Cape Town Chennai
Dar es Salaam Delhi Hong Kong Istanbul Karachi Kolkata
Kuala Lumpur Madrid Melbourne Mexico City Mumbai Nairobi
São Paulo Shanghai Taipei Tokyo Toronto

Oxford is a registered trade mark of Oxford University Press
in the UK and in certain other countries

Published in the United States
by Oxford University Press Inc., New York

© Kenneth Reid, Reinhard Zimmermann, and several contributors 2000

The moral rights of the author have been asserted

Database right Oxford University Press (maker)

Reprinted 2003

All rights reserved. No part of this publication may be reproduced,
stored in a retrieval system, or transmitted, in any form or by any means,
without the prior permission in writing of Oxford University Press,
or as expressly permitted by law, or under terms agreed with the appropriate
reprographics rights organization. Enquiries concerning reproduction
outside the scope of the above should be sent to the Rights Department,
Oxford University Press, at the address above

You must not circulate this book in any other binding or cover
And you must impose this same condition on any acquirer

ISBN 0-19-826778-9 (Vol. 1)

Printed in Great Britain by
Antony Rowe Ltd., Eastbourne

Acknowledgements

The arduous task of ensuring a uniform practice on citations and other matters was undertaken at the University of Regensburg, first by Christian Eckl and later by Phillip Hellwege. They deserve our gratitude and the gratitude of the other contributors. We also wish to record our thanks to Niall Whitty for his encouragement, advice, and practical help.

Kenneth Reid and Reinhard Zimmermann
Edinburgh/Regensburg, April 2000

Summary of Contents

Table of Contents	x
List of Contributors	xxiii
List of Abbreviations	xxiv
Table of Cases	xxxiv
Chronology of Scottish Legal History	xcii
Table of Kings and Queens	xcvii
John W. Cairns	
A Note on Law Reporting	xcviii
Kenneth Reid	

1. The Development of Legal Doctrine in a Mixed System — 1
   Kenneth Reid and Reinhard Zimmermann

2. Historical Introduction — 14
   John W. Cairns

3. Property Law: Sources and Doctrine — 185
   Kenneth Reid

4. The Romanization of Property Law — 220
   Grant McLeod

5. Accession by Building — 245
   C. G. van der Merwe

6. Transfer of Ownership — 269
   D. L. Carey Miller

7. Servitudes — 305
   M. J. de Waal

8. Rights in Security over Moveables — 333
   Andrew J. M. Steven

9. Leases: Four Historical Portraits — 363
   Martin Hogg

10. Assignation — 399
    Klaus Luig

11.	Water Law Regimes *Niall Whitty*	420
12.	Trusts *George Gretton*	480
Index of names		519
Index of subjects		527

Table of Contents

List of Contributors	xxiv
List of Abbreviations	xxv
Table of Cases	xxxiv

CHRONOLOGY OF SCOTTISH LEGAL HISTORY	**xcii**
TABLE OF KINGS AND QUEENS	**xcvii**
John W. Cairns	

A NOTE ON LAW REPORTING	**xcviii**
Kenneth Reid	
I. COURT OF SESSION	xcviii
II. HOUSE OF LORDS	ciii
III. SHERIFF COURT	civ
IV. DIGESTS	civ

1. **THE DEVELOPMENT OF LEGAL DOCTRINE IN A MIXED SYSTEM** — **1**
   Kenneth Reid and Reinhard Zimmermann

I. MIXED LEGAL SYSTEMS AND THE PLACE OF SCOTS LAW	**1**
1. Civil law and common law	1
2. Mixed legal systems	3
3. South African Law	4
4. Scots Law	6
II. DOCTRINAL HISTORY IN SCOTLAND	**8**
1. Challenges	8
2. Justifications	10
3. Emerging themes	12

2. **HISTORICAL INTRODUCTION** — **14**
   John W. Cairns

I. INTRODUCTION	**14**
II. THE RISE OF THE SCOTTISH COMMON LAW, 1000–1286	**15**

1.	The creation of the kingdom	15
2.	New directions	18
	(a) Universities and *utrumque jus*	18
	(b) Norman influence	19
	(c) Feudal tenures	20
	(d) Royal justice	21
	(e) The justiciar	22
	(f) The sheriff	23
	(g) The burgh	23
	(h) The Lords	24
	(i) The suitors of the court	25
	(j) Procedure and proof	26
3.	The Scottish common law	27
	(a) Royal justice and Lords' justice	28
	(b) Canon law and ecclesiastical discipline	29
	(c) Canon lawyers	30
	(d) Common law and local practice	31

III. THE LATER MIDDLE AGES, 1286–1424 — **33**

1.	The Great Cause, the Edwardian occupation, and the succession of the Stewarts	33
	(a) The succession of Margaret	33
	(b) The Great Cause	34
	(c) The Edwardian occupation	35
	(d) The Edwardian administration and the law	36
	(e) Bruce, independence, and the Stewart succession	37
2.	Institutional continuities and changes	38
	(a) The new regime	38
	(b) Parliament and Council	38
	(c) Justiciars	39
	(d) Baronies and regalities	39
	(e) Conservatism and innovation	39
3.	Law reform	40
	(a) Politics, problems, and law reform	40
	(b) The development of heritable rights	41
4.	Legal literature and the men of law	42
	(a) *Regiam Majestatem*	42
	(b) *Quoniam Attachiamenta*	44
	(c) Tradition and reconstruction	44

Table of Contents xi

- 5. Common law and *jus commune*   45
  - (a) Litigation and learned law   45
  - (b) The influence of the Church's lawyers   46
  - (c) *Jus commune* in Scotland   46
- 6. Common law and social order   47
  - (a) Violence, order, and law   47
  - (b) Affirmation of the common law   48

IV. **FROM THE MIDDLE AGES TO THE RENAISSANCE**   **50**

- 1. The Stewarts, politics, and government   50
  - (a) Royal authority   50
  - (b) Consolidation of the dynasty   51
- 2. Continuity and development   52
  - (a) Kingship and justice   52
  - (b) Parliaments and courts   54
  - (c) Burghs, free and unfree   55
  - (d) Barons and tenants   55
  - (e) New directions   56
- 3. Continuity and crisis   57
  - (a) The Sessions   57
  - (b) Council, Session, College of Justice   58
  - (c) The failure of the ordinary courts   59
  - (d) The decline of process on brieves   61
  - (e) Rational procedure and learned law   62
  - (f) Romano-canonical procedure   63
- 4. Common law, statute, and *jus commune*   64
  - (a) Statutes   64
  - (b) The 'Auld Lawes'   65
  - (c) The law commissions   66
  - (d) The attraction of the *jus commune*   67
- 5. Lawyers and learning   68
  - (a) Men of law   68
  - (b) Academic education   68
  - (c) The legal profession and the *jus commune*   70
- 6. *Jus proprium* and *jus commune*   71
  - (a) Litigation and the *jus commune*   71
  - (b) The blend of *jus commune* and *jus proprium*   73
  - (c) Continuity and change   74

V. FROM THE REFORMATION TO THE RESTORATION — 74

1. Government, religion, and political thought, 1542–1651 — 74
   - (a) Limited monarchy, absolute monarchy — 74
   - (b) Reformation of the Kirk — 76
   - (c) The Jacobean state — 77
   - (d) Union projects — 78
   - (e) The problems of multiple monarchy — 79
   - (f) The covenanting revolution — 80
   - (g) Civil war and Cromwellian conquest — 81
2. Consolidation and innovation — 82
   - (a) The impact of the Session — 82
   - (b) New consistorial courts — 83
   - (c) Improving the Session — 85
   - (d) Appointment of Senators — 86
3. The legal profession and legal education — 86
   - (a) Advocates before the Session — 86
   - (b) Procurators, writers, and notaries — 88
4. University study of law in Scotland — 89
5. Common law and social order — 91
   - (a) The problem of order — 91
   - (b) Extending royal authority — 91
6. Common law, codification, reason, and justice — 93
   - (a) Reforming the common law — 94
   - (b) The texts of the law — 95
   - (c) The law commissions — 96
   - (d) *Jus divinum, jus naturale, jus gentium* — 98
7. Common law and *jus commune* — 99
   - (a) Learned law and legal practice — 99
   - (b) The strength of the *jus commune* — 101
8. Scotland under the Commonwealth and Protectorate, 1652–1659 — 101
   - (a) A new legal system — 101
   - (b) The effectiveness of the new courts — 103
   - (c) Continuities — 104

VI. FROM THE RESTORATION TO UNION AND THE END OF THE STEWART DYNASTY — 105

1. Politics, religion, and government, 1660–1690 — 105
   - (a) The restored polity — 105

	(b) Struggles in Kirk and state	108
	(c) The succession of James VII	109
	(d) The Claim of Right	110
	(e) The new regime	111
2.	Relations with England and proposals for union, 1660–1715	112
	(a) Political tensions and Union proposals	112
	(b) The problem of the succession	113
	(c) Negotiating Union	114
	(d) The aftermath of Union	116
3.	The institutions of the common law	118
	(a) Heritable jurisdictions	118
	(b) Justices of the peace	119
	(c) The operation of the courts	120
	(d) The development of written pleadings	121
	(e) The new Justiciary Court	122
	(f) Protestations and appeals	123
4.	The development of the legal profession	124
	(a) The Lords of Session	124
	(b) The independence of the advocates	125
	(c) The admission of advocates	126
	(d) Status, 'breeding', and civil law	127
	(e) The education of the advocates	128
	(f) The development of Scottish law faculties	129
	(g) Advocates, writers, and procurators	130
5.	Liberty and property: codification, legislation, and the common law	130
	(a) Procedure and substantive law	130
	(b) Improving the sources of the law	132
	(c) The statute book	133
	(d) The decisions of the Lords	134
6.	Pleading, common law, and *jus commune*	135
	(a) *Jus commune, jus proprium*, and interpretation	135
	(b) *Jus naturale, jus gentium*, and interpretation	137
	(c) *Jus commune* in practice	138
7.	The development of a Scottish law library	140
	(a) Sources, general works, and treatises	140
	(b) *Jus commune*, libraries, and English law	141

VII. UNION, INTEGRATION, AND REFORM, 1716–1832 — 142

1. From patronage to party, 1707 to 1832 — 142
   - (a) New administrative structures — 142
   - (b) The politics of patronage — 143
   - (c) The 'Dundas Despotism' — 145
   - (d) The Whigs and reform — 145
2. Reform and continuity in the institutions of the common law — 147
   - (a) Legislative neglect and pressures for reform — 147
   - (b) Heritable jurisdictions and the criminal courts — 148
   - (c) Criticism of the Session — 149
3. The creation of the modern court system — 151
   - (a) The division of the Session — 151
   - (b) The Jury Court — 152
   - (c) Outer House, Inner House, and reformed procedure — 152
   - (d) Rationalization and amalgamation of jurisdictions — 153
   - (e) The sheriff court — 154
   - (f) Local courts and central courts — 154
4. The legal profession and legal education — 155
   - (a) The growth of the legal profession — 155
   - (b) Tensions in the Faculty of Advocates — 155
   - (c) The Faculty's examinations — 156
   - (d) Agents before the Court of Session — 156
   - (e) The rise of local faculties and societies — 157
   - (f) The education of writers and procurators — 158
5. The development of a law for a commercial society — 159
   - (a) The importance of natural jurisprudence — 159
   - (b) Statutory reform of property and commercial law — 160
   - (c) The courts and English law — 161
6. History, common law, and *jus commune* — 162
   - (a) *Jus commune* and Scots law — 162
   - (b) Moral sense, history, and English law — 163
   - (c) Roman law in the Scottish Enlightenment — 165
   - (d) Roman law, English law, and completing the Union — 166
7. Courts, legislation, and common law — 168
   - (a) The authority of statutes — 169
   - (b) Common law: authoritative and other writings — 170
   - (c) Common law: case reports — 172
   - (d) Scots law as an autonomous national law — 175

VIII.	EPILOGUE—AFTER 1832	**177**
	1. General themes	177
	2. The Scottish Office and the Parliament	178
	3. Courts and procedure	178
	4. Trends in the law	179
	5. The legal profession	181
	6. Scots law, civil law, and the future	182

3. PROPERTY LAW: SOURCES AND DOCTRINE — **185**
Kenneth Reid

I. SOURCES AND INFLUENCES — **185**

1. Feudal law — 185
   - (a) Chronology — 186
   - (b) Influence — 189
   - (c) Effects — 190
2. Roman law — 192
3. Canon law — 193
4. English law — 193
   - (a) Receptions — 193
   - (b) Borrowings — 194
5. Native invention — 196

II. TEXTS AND THEORIES — **198**
1. Reading the texts — 198
2. Which texts? — 199
   - (a) Before Stair — 199
   - (b) From Stair to Erskine — 199
   - (c) Hume and Bell — 204
   - (d) Breaking through the Roman wall — 206
3. The strange death of property law — 208

III. TWO DOCTRINES — **210**
1. Possession — 210
   - (a) Meaning of possession — 211
   - (b) Spuilzie — 212
   - (c) The decline of possession — 214
2. Law of the tenement — 216

4.	**THE ROMANIZATION OF PROPERTY LAW** *Grant McLeod*	**220**
	I. INTRODUCTION	220
	II. STAIR: ROMAN LAW RISES AS EQUITY	224
	III. BANKTON: THE HIGH NOON OF ROMAN LAW	229
	IV. ERSKINE: THE LONG AFTERNOON OF ROMAN LAW	235
	V. HUME: THE TWILIGHT OF THE IDOLS	239
	VI. CONCLUSIONS	242
5.	**ACCESSION BY BUILDING** *C. G. van der Merwe*	**245**
	I. INTRODUCTION	245
	II. ROMAN LAW	246
	III. INSTITUTIONAL WRITERS	247
	IV. BEFORE 1820: THE DOMINANCE OF SUCCESSION LAW	248
	V. 1820–1876: TRADE AND ITS FIXTURES	250
	1. The industrial revolution	250
	2. *Fisher* v. *Dixon* (1835–1845)	252
	3. From *Fisher* to *Brand's Trs*	253
	4. Outside influences	255
	VI. THE LAW TURNS: *BRAND'S TRS* v. *BRAND'S TRS* (1874–1876)	257
	VII. THE LEGACY OF *BRAND'S TRS*	260
	1. The two rules in *Brand's Trs*	260
	2. *Brand's Trs* ignored	261
	3. *Brand's Trs* misunderstood	262
	4. *Brand's Trs* applied	263
	VIII. CODA: THE EFFECT OF HIRE-PURCHASE	264
	IX. CONCLUSION	267

Table of Contents xvii

6. TRANSFER OF OWNERSHIP — 269
D. L. Carey Miller

   I. INTRODUCTION — 269

   II. A UNITARY SYSTEM? — 271

   III. THE FEUDAL CONTEXT — 272

   IV. CONVEYANCING IN THE FEUDAL CONTEXT — 274
      1. The conveyancing template — 274
      2. Infeftment — 276
      3. Role of superior — 277
      4. Alternative forms in development of conveyancing — 278

   V. SASINE — 282
      1. The actuating event — 282
      2. Real/personal rights dichotomy — 284
      3. Respective roles of natural and symbolic possession — 285
      4. Scots and English sasine distinguished — 286
      5. Inherent civilian factor — 289

   VI. PRESCRIPTION — 289

   VII. THE MODERN SYSTEM — 292

   VIII. CONSEQUENCES OF TRANSFER — 297

   IX. CONCLUSION — 301

7. SERVITUDES — 305
M. J. de Waal

   I. INTRODUCTION — 305

   II. NATURE AND DEFINITION — 307
      1. The Roman law basis — 307
      2. Reception into Scots law — 308

   III. CLASSIFICATION — 310
      1. Rural and urban — 310
      2. Positive and negative — 312
      3. Other classifications — 313

   IV. AN OPEN OR CLOSED STRUCTURE? — 314
      1. The function of requirements in an open structure of servitudes — 314
      2. The position in Scots law — 315

V.	THE REQUIREMENTS FOR THE ESTABLISHMENT OF SERVITUDES	**317**
	1. Introduction	317
	2. Specific requirements	317
	(a) Two tenements separately held	317
	(b) *Vicinitas* (vicinity or locality)	318
	(c) *Utilitas* (utility)	321
	(d) *Perpetua causa* (permanent cause)	325
	(e) *Servitus in faciendo consistere nequit* (passivity)	326
	(f) Known to the law	329
VI.	DEVELOPMENT AND CHANGE	**329**
	1. Creation of new servitude types	329
	2. Flexibility within the traditional types	331
VII.	CONCLUSION AND EVALUATION	**332**

8. RIGHTS IN SECURITY OVER MOVEABLES   **333**
Andrew J. M. Steven

I.	INTRODUCTION	**333**
II.	PLEDGE	**334**
	1. Systems prior to Scots law	334
	2. Early Scots law	335
	(a) The *Regiam Majestatem*	335
	(b) *Leges Quatuor Burgorum*	337
	3. The fifteenth century	338
	4. The sixteenth century	338
	(a) Wad-wives	338
	(b) The Burgh Records	339
	(c) Balfour's *Practicks*	339
	5. The seventeenth century	340
	(a) Hope's *Major Practicks*	340
	(b) Stair's *Institutions*	341
	6. The eighteenth century	341
	(a) Institutional writings	341
	(b) Case law	342
	7. The nineteenth century	343
	(a) Institutional writings	343
	(b) Case law	343
	(c) The development of pawnbroking	344
	8. The modern period	345

III. HYPOTHEC		**345**
1. The civilian background		345
2. The Anglo-Norman period		346
3. The institutional period		347
4. The modern period		349
IV. LIEN		**350**
1. The civilian and English background		350
(a) Civil law		350
(b) English law		351
2. The seventeenth century		353
3. The eighteenth century		354
(a) Institutional writings		354
(b) Case law		355
(c) Terminology		356
4. The nineteenth century		357
(a) Bell		357
(b) Other nineteenth-century developments		359
5. The modern period		360
V. CONCLUSION		**361**

9. LEASES: FOUR HISTORICAL PORTRAITS   **363**

Martin Hogg

I. INTRODUCTION		**363**
II. TERMINOLOGY		**364**
1. Main terms		364
(a) Tack		364
(b) Assedation		364
(c) Maills		364
(d) Lease		365
2. Civilian terminology: *Locatio conductio*		365
3. Other types of tenure with similarities to the lease		366
4. *Emphyteusis*		366
5. Rentals		366
6. Kindly tenants		368
7. Leases and feudal tenure		369
(a) Origins of tenure at ferme		369
(b) Comparison of lease and feu farm		369
8. Conclusion on terminology		371

III.	THE EARLY ORIGINS OF LEASES	**371**
	1. Comparison of Roman and Scots leases	372
	2. Views of jurists	374
	(a) Robert Bell	375
	(b) Walter Ross	376
	(c) Robert Hunter	377
	3. Evidence of finite leases for short terms	377
IV.	PORTRAIT ONE: A LEASE FROM THE LATE FOURTEENTH CENTURY	**377**
	1. Form of the lease: unilateral grant	380
	2. Security of tenure	381
	3. Other statutory development	382
V.	PORTRAIT TWO: A LEASE FROM THE SIXTEENTH CENTURY	**383**
	1. Legal literature	385
	2. Statutes	386
	3. Duration of leases	386
VI.	PORTRAIT THREE: A LEASE FROM THE MID-EIGHTEENTH CENTURY	**388**
	1. Background to leases of the period	391
	(a) Stair	391
	(b) Bankton	392
	(c) Erskine	392
	(d) Robert Bell	392
	2. Statute	393
	3. Duration of leases	393
VII.	PORTRAIT FOUR: A LEASE FROM THE LATE NINETEENTH CENTURY	**394**
	1. Statutes	396
	2. Legal literature	396
VIII.	CONCLUSIONS	**397**

10. ASSIGNATION   **399**

Klaus Luig

I.	THE BEGINNINGS	**399**
	1. Uses of assignation	399
	2. *Causa*	402
	3. Intimation	403

(a) Payment to the cedent		403
(b) Competitions		404
(c) Conclusion		406
II. LEGAL LITERATURE BEFORE STAIR		**407**
1. Balfour's *Practicks*		407
2. Skene's *De Verborum Significatione*		407
3. Craig's *Jus Feudale*		407
4. Hope's *Major Practicks*		408
III. DECISIONS OF THE COURT OF SESSION 1633–1681		**410**
IV. STAIR		**412**
V. JURISTS OF THE EIGHTEENTH CENTURY		**414**
1. Bankton		414
2. Erskine		416
3. Kames		417
VI. THE NINETEENTH CENTURY: GEORGE JOSEPH BELL		**418**
VII. SOME FINAL REMARKS		**419**

11. WATER LAW REGIMES — 420
Niall Whitty

I. INTRODUCTION		**420**
II. EXTERNAL SOURCES		**421**
1. Water rights and the influence of medieval English law		421
2. Glanvill, *Regiam Majestatem*, and purpresture		421
3. The possessory brieves of novel dissasine and *de aqueductu*		423
4. The end of medieval English influence		425
5. The influence of the *jus commune*: the *regalia* and the classification of real rights		426
III. THE SEA, THE SEABED, AND THE FORESHORE		**429**
1. The concept of *res communes omnium* in Roman law		429
2. The *res communes* doctrine and the freedom of the seas		429
3. The withering of the concept of *res communes omnium*		431
4. The foreshore		432
5. The sea-bed (*fundus* or *solum maris*)		436

IV. RIVERS — 438

1. The criteria for classifying 'public' and 'private' rivers — 438
   - (a) Overview — 438
   - (b) The Roman classification of watercourses and rivers — 438
   - (c) The institutional period: navigability as the test of public rivers — 440
   - (d) Reception of the English concept of tidality as the test of public rivers — 441
     - (aa) Tidality and ownership of the *alveus* of rivers — 441
     - (bb) Public rivers and the conflict between public and private rights of fishing — 443
   - (e) *Perennitas* as the test of riparian common interest — 446
   - (f) Common interest and tidal rivers — 448
   - (g) Public rights of passage — 448
   - (h) The modern law — 449

2. The development of the Scottish doctrine of riparian common interest — 450
   - (a) The Scottish regime of riparian common interest — 450
     - (aa) Overview — 450
     - (bb) Roman influence: the interdict *uti priori aestate* — 451
     - (cc) The evolution of doctrine of riparian common interest: the main developments — 452
     - (dd) The idea of 'natural flow' — 458
     - (ee) Primary and secondary purposes — 459
   - (b) River pollution, common interest, and nuisance — 460
   - (c) The comparative law context — 461
     - (aa) 'Prior appropriation' and 'riparian rights' theories of rights in watercourses — 461
     - (bb) Forms of riparian rights theories: 'natural flow' or 'reasonable use' — 462
   - (d) The role of economic and social factors — 463

V. LOCHS AND STANKS — 465

1. Introductory — 465
2. Ownership of the *alveus* — 466
3. The change from common ownership to several ownership. — 467
4. Common interest — 467
5. Public rights of navigation and fishing in lochs — 468

Table of Contents xxiii

    VI. CASUAL WATERS **468**

    VII. REMEDIES **471**

    VIII. THE STATUTORY PUBLIC LAW ON WATER **472**

    IX. THE SECOND RECEPTION OF ENGLISH LAW **473**

    X. CONCLUSION **478**

12. TRUSTS **480**

George Gretton

    I. INTRODUCTION **480**
        1. Defining the trust   480
        2. The influence of English law 484

    II. ORIGINS **485**
        1. Nineteenth- and twentieth-century ideas as to origins   485
        2. The seventeenth century and before   486
        3. Pre-seventeenth century private arrangements 486
        4. *Fideicommissum* and Roman law   490
        5. The seventeenth century   491
        6. Proof of trust   496

    III. HISTORY SINCE THE SEVENTEENTH CENTURY **496**
        1. Some uses of the trust   496
        2. Proof of trust   498
        3. Immunity to creditors   499
        4. Powers   501
        5. English influence after 1700 502
        6. Conceptualizations 506
        7. Mortification, charities, public trusts, and foundations   508
        8. Constructive trusts 512
        9. *Frog's Creditors* v. *His Children*   513
        10. Resulting trusts and the doctrine of the radical right 513
        11. Executry   514

    IV. CURRENT LAW **516**

INDEX OF NAMES   519

INDEX OF SUBJECTS   527

List of Contributors

JOHN W. CAIRNS is Professor of Legal History in the University of Edinburgh.

D. L. CAREY MILLER is Professor of Property Law in the University of Aberdeen.

M. J. DE WAAL is Professor of Private Law in the University of Stellenbosch.

GEORGE GRETTON is Lord President Reid Professor of Law in the University of Edinburgh.

MARTIN HOGG is a Lecturer in Law in the University of Edinburgh.

KLAUS LUIG is Professor of Private Law and Roman Law in the University of Cologne.

GRANT MCLEOD is a Lecturer in Law in the University of Edinburgh.

KENNETH REID is Professor of Property Law in the University of Edinburgh.

C. G. VAN DER MERWE is Professor of Civil Law in the University of Aberdeen.

ANDREW J. M. STEVEN is a Lecturer in Law in the University of Edinburgh.

NIALL WHITTY is a Visiting Professor of Law in the University of Edinburgh.

REINHARD ZIMMERMANN is Professor of Private Law, Roman Law, and Comparative Law in the University of Regensburg.

List of Abbreviations

ABGB	*Allgemeines Bürgerliches Gesetzbuch* (Austria)
ABI	Association of British Insurers
AC	Law Reports, Appeal Cases
AcP	*Archiv für die civilistische Praxis*
AD	South African Law Reports, Appellate Division
ADA	T. Thomson (ed.), *Acta Dominorum Auditorum: The Acts of the Lords Auditors of Causes and Complaints 1466–1494* (1839)
Ad & El	Adolphus and Ellis's Reports, King's (later Queen's) Bench
ADC	*Acta Dominorum Concilii*
Afr.	Africanus
AJCL	American Journal of Comparative Law
AJIL	American Journal of International Law
AJLH	American Journal of Legal History
Aleyn	Aleyn's Reports, Kings Bench
ALI	American Law Institute
All ER	All England Reports
All ER Rep	All England Law Reports Reprint
ALR	Argus Law Reports
	Australian Law Reports
Am Rep	American Reports
App Cas	Law Reports, Appeal Cases, House of Lords
APS	Acts of the Parliament of Scotland
art(s).	article(s)
AS	Acts of Sederunt
Atk	Atkyn's Reports, Chancery
B & Ad	Barnewall and Adolphus's Reports, King's Bench
B & Ald	Barnewall and Alderson's Reports, King's Bench
B & C	Barnewall and Cresswell's Reports, King's Bench
B & PNR	Bosanquet & Puller's New Reports
B & S	Best & Smith's Reports, Queen's Bench
Balfour, *Practicks*	Peter G. B. McNeill (ed.), *The Practicks of Sir James Balfour of Pittendreich*, Stair Society, vol. 21 (1962); vol. 22 (1963)
Bankton	Andrew McDouall, Lord Bankton, *An Institute of the Laws of Scotland in Civil Rights: With Observations upon the Agreement or Diversity between them and the Laws of England*, 1751–3, reprinted Stair Society, vols. 41–3 (1993–5)

List of Abbreviations

Beav	Beavan's Reports, Rolls Court
Bell App	S. S. Bell's Appeals, House of Lords
Bell Fol Cas	R. Bell's Folio Cases, Court of Session
Bell Oct Cas	R. Bell's Octavo Cases, Court of Session
Bell, *Commentaries*	George Joseph Bell, *Commentaries on the Law of Scotland and on the Principles of Mercantile Jurisprudence*, 7th edn. (1870)
Bell, *Principles*	George Joseph Bell, *Principles of the Law of Scotland*, 10th edn. (1899)
Bes Thes	Christoph Besold, *Thesaurus Practicus* (Nuremberg, 1666)
BGB	*Bürgerliches Gesetzbuch* (Germany)
Bing	Bingham's Reports, Common Pleas
Blackstone's Reports	William Blackstone's Reports, King's Bench
Bligh	Bligh's Reports, House of Lords
Bos & P	Bosanquet and Puller's Reports, Common Pleas
Broun	Scottish Judiciary Reports (1842–5)
Brown Ch	Brown's Reports, Chancery
Brown's Supp	Brown's Supplement to Morison's Dictionary of Decisions, Court of Session
Brown's Syn	Brown's Synopsis of Decisions, Court of Session
BS	Books of Sederunt
Bull Civ	Bulletin des arrêts de la Chambre Civile de la Cour de Cassation
Bulst	Bulstrode's Reports, King's Bench
Burr	Burrow's Reports, King's Bench
C.	*Codex Iustiniani*
c(c).	chapter(s) (legislation)
CA	Court of Appeal
California LR	California Law Review
Call.	Callistratus
Can Bar Rev	Canadian Bar Review
Can SC	Canadian Supreme Court
cap.	caput
Cass Civ	Arrêt de la chambre civile de la Cour de Cassation
CB	Common Bench Reports by Manning, Granger, & Scott
CB (NS)	Common Bench, New Series
CC	*Code Civil* (France)
Cels.	Celsus
Ch	Law Reports, Chancery Division
Ch App	Law Reports, Chancery Appeals
Ch D	Law Reports, Chancery Division

CILSA	The Comparative and International Law Journal of Southern Africa
Cl & Fin	Clark and Finnelly's Reports, House of Lords
CLJ	Cambridge Law Journal
CLP	Current Legal Problems
Cmnd.	Command Paper
col(s).	column(s)
Columbia LR	Columbia Law Review
Com	Comyn's Reports, King's Bench
concl.	conclusio
condictio c.d.	*condictio causa data causa non secuta*
condictio t.i.	*condictio ob turpem vel injustam causam*
consil.	*consilium*
Co Rep	Coke's Reports, King's Bench
Cowp	Cowper's Reports, King's Bench
CPD	Law Reports, Common Pleas Division
	South African Law Reports, Cape Provincial Division
Cr & M	Crompton & Meeson's Exchequer Reports
Craig	Thomas Craig, *Jus Feudale* (3rd edn., 1732 and tr. Lord Clyde, 1934)
Cro Eliz	Croke's King's Bench Reports *tempore* Elizabeth (1 Cro.)
Cro Jac	Croke's King's Bench Reports *tempore* James I (2 Cro.)
Cun	Cunningham's Reports, King's Bench
D	Dunlop's Session Cases
D (HL)	House of Lords Cases in Dunlop's Session Cases
D.	Justinian's *Digest*
De G M & G	De Gex, Macnaghten, & Gordon's Chancery Reports
Dirl	Dirleton's Decisions, Court of Session
disp.	disputatio
DLR	Dominion Law Reports
Dow	Dow's Reports, House of Lords
Drew	Drewry's Chancery Reports *tempore* Kindersley
Durie	Durie's Decisions, Court of Session
E & I App	Law Reports, English and Irish Appeals, House of Lords
East	East's Term Reports, King's Bench
ECR	European Court of Justice Reports
EDC	Eastern District Court Reports, Cape of Good Hope
Edinburgh LR	Edinburgh Law Review
EGD	Estates Gazette Digest

List of Abbreviations

El Bl & El	Ellis, Blackburn, & Ellis's Queen's Bench Reports
Elchies	Elchies' Decisions, Court of Session
Eng Judg	Decisions of English Judges during the Usurpation
Eq Abr	Abridgment of Cases in Equity
Eq Cas Ab	Abridgment of Cases in Equity
ER	English Reports
Erskine	John Erskine, *An Institute of the Law of Scotland*, 8th edn. (1871)
Esp	Espinasse's Nisi Prius Reports
Exch	Exchequer Reports
Ex D	Law Reports, Exchequer Division
F	Fraser's Session Cases
F (HL)	House of Lords cases in Fraser's Session Cases
F (J)	Justiciary cases in Fraser's Session Cases
FC	Faculty Collection, Court of Session
Fed Cas	Federal Cases
Flor.	Florentinus
fo.	folio
Fol Dic	Folio Dictionary of Decisions, Court of Session, by Lords Kames and Woodhouselee
Forbes	Forbes's *Journal of the Session*
fos.	folios
Fount	Fountainhall's Decisions, Court of Session
FSR	Fleet Street Reports
GA	General Assembly
Gai.	Gaius
	Gaius' *Institutes*
Georgia LR	Georgia Law Review
Guth Sh Cas	Guthrie's Select Sheriff Court cases
GWD	Greens Weekly Digest
Had	Haddington's Reports, Court of Session
Hailes	Hailes' Decisions, Court of Session
Harv LR	Harvard Law Review
HC	House of Commons
Herm.	Hermogenianus
HL	House of Lords
HLC	Clark's House of Lords Cases
HL Cas	Clark's House of Lords Cases
Holt KB	Holt's Reports, King's Bench
Hope, *Practicks*	Lord Clyde (ed.), Hope's *Major Practicks*, Stair Society, vol. 3 (1937); vol. 4 (1938)
Hume	Hume's Decisions, Court of Session
Hume, *Lectures*	G. C. H. Paton (ed.), *Baron David Hume's Lectures*

1786–1822, Stair Society, vol. 5 (1939); vol. 13 (1949); vol. 15 (1952); vol. 17 (1955); vol. 18 (1957); vol. 19 (1958)

Iav.	Iavolenus
ICLQ	International and Comparative Law Quarterly
ICR	Industrial Cases Reports
IH	Inner House
insp.	inspectio
Inst.	Justinian's *Institutes*
IRLR	Industrial Relations Law Reports
IR	Irish Reports
Ir Rep CL	Irish Common Law Reports
Iul.	Iulianus
J.	Judge
JBL	Journal of Business Law
JC	Justiciary Cases
JLH	Journal of Legal History
J Juris	Journal of Jurisprudence
J L & Econ	Journal of Law and Economics
JLS	Journal of Legal Studies
JLSS	Journal of the Law Society of Scotland
JR	Juridical Review
Jur	Jurist Reports
JuS	Juristische Schulung
Kames Sel Dec	Kames's Select Decisions, Court of Session
K & W Dic	Lords Kames's and Woodhouselee's Folio Dictionary of Decisions, Court of Session
KB	Law Reports, King's Bench Division
Keb	Keble's King's Bench Reports
Kilk	Kilkerran's Decisions, Court of Session
LA	Lord Advocate
Lab.	Labeo
La LR	Louisiana Law Review
Law Com	Law Commission
LC	Lord Chancellor
LCJ	Lord Chief Justice
Ld Raym	Lord Raymond's Reports, King's Bench
Leo	Leonard's Reports
Lev	Levinz's Reports, King's Bench and Common Pleas
L Hist Rev	Law and History Review
lib.	liber
LJ	Lord Justice
L J-C	Lord Justice-Clerk

List of Abbreviations

LJ Ex	Law Journal, Exchequer
LJ KB	Law Journal, King's Bench
LJ NS	Law Journal Reports, New Series
LJ QB	Law Journal, Queen's Bench Division
Ll L Rep	Lloyd's List Law Reports
Lloyd's Rep	Lloyd's Law Reports
LMCLQ	Lloyd's Maritime and Commercial Law Quarterly
Louisiana LR	Louisiana Law Review
LQR	Law Quarterly Review
LR App	Law Reports, Appeal Cases
LR CP	Law Reports, Common Pleas
LR Eq	Law Reports, Equity
LR Exch	Law Reports, Exchequer
LR HL	Law Reports, House of Lords
LR Ir	Law Reports, Ireland
LR QB	Law Reports, Queen's Bench
LR QBD	Law Reports, Queen's Bench Division
M	Macpherson's Session Cases
M (HL)	House of Lords cases in Macpherson's Session Cases
Macl & R	Maclean and Robinson's Appeals, House of Lords
Maclaurin	Arguments and Decisions in Remarkable Cases before the High Court of Justiciary and Other Supreme Courts in Scotland Collected by Mr Maclaurin (1774)
Macph	Macpherson's Session Cases
Macq	Macqueen's Appeals, House of Lords
M & Cr	Mylne and Craig's Chancery Reports
M & S	Maule and Selwyn's Reports, King's Bench
M & W	Meeson and Welsby
M'F	Macfarlane's Jury Trials
Marc.	Marcianus
March NR	March's New Cases, King's Bench
Mason	Mason, United States Circuit Court Reports
Mer	Merivale's Reports, Chancery
Michigan LR	Michigan Law Review
Minn LR	Minnesota Law Review
Miss LR	Missouri Law Review
MLR	Modern Law Review
Mod	Modern Reports
Mod.	Modestinus
Moo PCC	Moore's Privy Council Cases
Moore KB	Moore's Reports, King's Bench
Mor	Morison's Dictionary of Decisions, Court of Session
Mor Synopsis	Morison's Synopsis, Court of Session

MS(S)	manuscript(s)
Murr	Murray's Jury Court Cases
NAS	National Archives of Scotland
NBW	*Nieuw Burgerlijk Wetboek* (Netherlands)
n.d.	no date
Ner.	Neratius
NILQ	Northern Ireland Legal Quarterly
NLS	National Library of Scotland
no(s).	number(s)
Noy	Noy's Reports, King's Bench
obs.	*observatio*
OH	Outer House
OJLS	Oxford Journal of Legal Studies
OPD	South African Law Reports, Orange Free State Provincial Division
OR	*Obligationenrecht* (Switzerland)
Owen	Owen's Reports, King's Bench & Common Pleas
Palm	Palmer's Reports, King's Bench
Pap.	Papinian
Pat App	Craigie, Stewart, & Paton's Appeals, House of Lords
Paul.	Paulus
PC	Judicial Committee of the Privy Council
PLM	Poor Law Magazine
Pomp.	Pomponius
pr.	*principium*
PS	*Pauli Sententiae*
P Will	Peere William's Chancery Reports
QB	Law Reports, Queen's Bench Division
quaest.	*quaestio*
R	Rettie's Session Cases
R (HL)	House of Lords cases in Rettie's Session Cases
r	*recto*
Raym	Lord Raymond's Reports, King's Bench
Res.	resolution
RIDA	Revue internationale des droits de l'antiquité
RLR	Restitution Law Review
RMS	J. M. Thomson et al. (ed.), *Regestrum Magni Sigilli Regum Scottorum: The Register of the Great Seal of Scotland* (1822–1914)
Rob	Robinson's Appeals, House of Lords
Robert	Robertson's Appeals, House of Lords
Robin	Robinson's Appeals, House of Lords
Roll Rep	Rolle's Reports, King's Bench

Ross LC	Ross's Leading Cases in the Law of Scotland (Land Rights)
RPC	Reports of Patents, Designs and Trade Marks Cases J. H. Burton et al. (ed.), *Register of the Privy Council of Scotland* (1877–1970)
RRS	G. W. S. Barrow (ed.), *Regesta Regum Scottorum I: The Acts of Malcolm IV King of Scots, 1153–1165* (1960); *Regesta Regum Scottorum II: The Acts of William I King of Scots, 1165–1214* (1971); A. A. M. Duncan (ed.), *Regesta Regum Scottorum V: The Acts of Robert I King of Scots 1306–1329* (1988); B. Webster (ed), *Regesta Regum Scotturum VI; The Acts of David II King of Scots, 1329–1371* (1982)
S	Shaw's Session Cases (NE indicates New Edition)
S & D	Shaw & Dunlop's Session Cases
S & M	Shaw & Maclean's Appeals, House of Lords
SA	South African Law Reports
SA Merc LJ	South African Mercantile Law Journal
SALJ	South African Law Journal
Salk	Salkeld's Reports, King's Bench
SAL Rev	(Butterworth's) South African Law Review
Saund	Saunders' Reports, King's Bench
SC	Session Cases
SC (HL)	House of Lords cases in Session Cases
SCCR	Scottish Criminal Case Reports
SCLR	Scottish Civil Law Reports
Scot Hist Rev	Scottish Historical Review
Sess Cas	Session Cases
Sh & Macl	Shaw and Maclean's Appeals, House of Lords
Sh App	Shaw's Appeals, House of Lords
Sh Ct Rep	Sheriff Court Reports
Shaw	Shaw's Justiciary Reports
Show	Shower's Reports, King's Bench
Sim & St	Simon & Stuart's Reports, Chancery
SJ	Scottish Jurist
SLM	Scottish Law Magazine and Sheriff Court Reporter
SLPQ	Scottish Law & Practice Quarterly
SLR	Scottish Law Reporter
SL Rev	Scottish Law Review and Sheriff Court Reporter
SLT	Scots Law Times
SLT (Notes)	Notes of Recent Decisions in Scots Law Times
SLT (Sh Ct)	Sheriff Court Reports in Scots Law Times
SN	Session Notes

List of Abbreviations

SRO, GD	Scottish Record Office, Gifts and Deposits
Stair	James Dalrymple, Viscount Stair, *Institutions of the Law of Scotland* (tercentenary edn. by D. M. Walker, 1981)
Stair Rep	Stair's Reports, Court of Session
Stellenbosch LR	Stellenbosch Law Review
Strange	Strange's Reports, King's Bench
s.v.	*sub voce*
Term Rep	Term Reports
THRHR	Tydskrif vir Hedendaagse Romeins-Hollandse Reg
tit.	title
	titulus
TLR	Times Law Reports
TPD	South African Law Reports, Transvaal Provincial Division
TR	Tijdschrift voor rechtsgeschiedenis
	Taxation Reports
TSAR	Tydskrif vir die Suid-Afrikaanse Reg
Tul LR	Tulane Law Review
Ulp.	Ulpian
Univ of Chic LR	University of Chicago Law Review
v	*verso*
Vern	Vernon's Chancery Reports
Ves Jun	Vesey Junior's Reports, Chancery
W & S	Wilson and Shaw's Appeals, House of Lords
Wils KB	Wilson's Reports, King's Bench
WLR	Weekly Law Reports
WN	Law Reports, Weekly Notes
Yale LJ	Yale Law Journal
Y. B(B).	Yearbook(s)
ZEuP	Zeitschrift für Europäisches Privatrecht
ZfRV	Zeitschrift für Rechtsvergleichung
ZGB	*Zivilgesetzbuch*
ZSS (RA)	Zeitschrift der Savigny-Stiftung für Rechtsgeschichte, Romanistische Abteilung
12mo	Duodecimo edition of the Acts of Parliament of Scotland

Table of Cases

A v. *B* (1540) Mor 843 403, 404, 418
A v. *B* (1589) Mor 10717 290
A v. *B* (1677) Mor 14751 213
Abercorn *(Marquis of)* v. *Jamieson* (1791) Mor 14285, Hume 510 447, 453, 456
Aberdeen *(Bishop of)* v. *Lord Dunlagery* (1622) Mor 828 408
Adam v. *Adam* 1962 SLT 332 499
Adamson v. *McMitchell* (1624) Mor 859 404, 406, 411, 413
Agnew v. *Lord Advocate* (1873) 11 M 309 325, 434, 435, 437, 475
Aiken v. *Caledonian Railway Company* 1913 SC 66 504
Alexander v. *Butchart* (1875) 3 R 156 329
Alexander v. *Lundies* (1675) Mor 940 413
Allan v. *MacLachlan* (1900) 2 F 699 327
Allan's Trustees v. *Lord Advocate* 1971 SC (HL) 45 486
Anderson v. *Anderson's Tr* (1898) 6 SLT 204 499
Anderson v. *Dickie* 1914 SC 706 329
Anderson v. *Robertson* 1958 SC 367 313
Anderson v. *Yorston* (1906) 14 SLT 499
Anderson, Petitioner (1857) 19 D 329 509
Anderson's Tr v. *Fleming* (1871) 9 M 718 359
Anstruther v. *Black* (1626) Mor 829 410
Arbuthnot *(Viscount)* v. *Scott* (1802) 4 Pat App 337 460
Arbathnot v. *Morison (1716)* 162
Argyle *(Earl of)* v. *Lord McDonald* (1676) Mor 842 411
Arkwright v. *Billinge* 3 Dec. 1819 FC 249, 250, 256
Armour v. *Thyssen Edelstahlwerke AG* 1989 SLT 182, 1990 SLT 891 301
Assessor for Dundee v. *Carmichael & Co. Ltd* (1902) 4 F 525 262
Assessor of Fife v. *Hodgson* 1966 SC 30 262
Attorney-General v. *Chambers* (1854) 4 De G M & G 206 476
Auld v. *Hall and Co.* 12 Jun. 1811 FC 344
Axis West Developments Ltd v. *Chartwell* 1999 SLT 1416 219
Ayton v. *Colville* (1705) Mor 6247 355
Aytoun v. *Douglas* (1800) Mor Appendix, 'Property' no. 5 453
Badenhorst v. *Joubert and Others* 1920 TPD 100 311
Baillie v. *Lady Saltoun* (1821) Hume 523, 1 S 227 440, 454
Bain v. *Cunningham McMillan* (1679) Mor 863 405, 411
Baird v. *Fortune* (1861) 23 D (HL) 5 325
Bairdie v. *Scartsonse* (1624) Mor 14529 452, 453, 460, 463
Baird's Trustees (1888) 15 R 682 505
Balmernock v. *Coutfield* (1620) Mor 3007 279

Table of Cases xxxv

Bank of Lisbon and South Africa Ltd v. *De Ornalas* 1988 (3) SA 580 (A) 351
Banks and Co. v. *Walker* (1874) 1 R 981 313
Bannatyne v. *Cranston* (1624) Mor 12769 452, 453, 463, 464, 472, 477
Bannerman v. *Masters of Queen's College* (1710) Mor 16187, Forbes 420 500
Barclays Bank v. *Quistclose Investments* [1970] AC 567 506
Bealey v. *Shaw* (1805) 6 East 208, 102 ER 1266 461
Beaumont v. *Lord Glenlyon* (1843) 5 D 1337 325
Bedwells & Yates v. *Tod* 2 Dec. 1819 FC 419
Begg v. *Begg* (1665) Mor 6304 414
Berkley v. *Poulett* [1977] EGD 754 245
Bermans and Nathans Ltd v. *Weibye* 1983 SLT 299 358
Best (In re) [1904] Ch 354 505
Beveridge v. *Beveridge* 1925 SLT 234 499
Binning v. *Brotherstones* (1676) Mor 13401 354, 361
Black v. *Pitmedden* (1632) Mor 201 278
Blair v. *Hunter Finlay and Co.* (1870) 9 M 204 469
Blanchard v. *Miller, 8 Greenleaf American Reports,* 268 477
Blantyre (Lord) v. *Dunn* (1848) 10 D 509 451, 454–6, 475
Bonthrone v. *Downie* (1878) 6 R 324 450
Boucher v. *Crawford* 30 Nov. 1814 FC 434
Bowie v. *Marquis of Ailsa* (1887) 14 R 649 432, 445
Boyd v. *Shorrock* (1867) LR 5 Eq 72 255
Boylstoun v. *Robertson* (1672) Mor 15125, 2 Stair Rep 54 500
Braid v. *Douglas* (1800) Mor Appendix, 'Property', no. 2 453, 456
Braid Hills Hotel Co. Ltd v. *Manuels* 1909 SC 120 318, 329
Brand's Trs v. *Brand's Trs* (1874) 2 R 258, (1876) 3 R (HL) 16 253–8, 261–4, 267
Breadalbane (Marquis of) v. *West Highland Railway* (1895) 22 R 307 450
Brechin Town Council v. *Arbuthnot* (1840) 3 D 216 282, 284
Brodie v. *Cadel* (1707) 4 Brown's Supp 660 460, 472
Brown v. *Best* (1747) 1 Wilson KB 174, 95 ER 557 457
Brown v. *Miller* (1820) 3 Ross LC 29 359
Brown v. *Sommerville* (1844) 6 D 1267 359, 360
Bruce v. *Buckie* (1619) Mor 207, 10415 409
Bruce v. *Rashiehill* (1711) Mor 9342 434
Buccleuch (Duke of) v. *Cowan* (1866) 5 M 214 440–2, 464
Buccleuch (Duke of) v. *Cunynghame* (1826) 2 Ross LC 338 291
Buccleuch (Duke of) v. *Tod's Trustees* (1871) 9 M 1014 253
Buchanan and Another v. *Buchanan's Trustees* (1908) 16 SLT 421 505
Burgess v. *Brown* (1790) Hume 504 454, 456
Burnet v. *Burnets* (1701) Mor 2284 139
Bush (Ex parte) (1734) 2 Eq Cas Ab 109 pl 4, 22 ER 93 352
Cairnis v. *Leyis* (1533) Mor 827 407

Calder v. *Stewart* (1806) 3 Ross LC 250 298
Camille & Henry Dreyfus Foundation v. *IRC* [1956] AC 39 486
Campbell v. *Arkison & Clark* 445
Campbell v. *Brown* 18 Nov. 1813 FC 434
Campbell v. *Bryson* (1864) 3 M 254 469, 470
Campbell v. *Campbell* (1752) Kames Sel Dec 35, Mor 16203 509
Campbell of Edderline (1801) Mor Appendix, 'Adjudication', no. 11 514
Carmichael v. *Colquhoun* (1787) Mor 9645 444
Carnegy v. *Creditors of Cruikshanks* (1729) Mor 14316 282
Carron & Co. v. *Ogilvie* (1806) 5 Pat App 61 440
Carstairs v. *Brown* (1829) 7 S 607 325
Cathcart (Lord) v. *Laird of Gadzat* (1585) Mor 10716 290
Central Regional Council v. *Ferns* 1979 SC 136 328
Chalmer's Tr v. *Dick* 1909 SC 761 262
Charity v. *Riddell* (1808) Mor Appendix, 'Public Police', no. 6 465
Chase v. *Westmore* (1816) 5 M & S 180, 105 ER 1016 352
Christie v. *Magistrates of Edinburgh* (1774) Mor 5755 510
Christie v. *Ruxton* (1862) 24 D 1182 343
Christie v. *Smith's Exrs* 1949 SC 572 260, 262
Clerk v. *Napier* (1614) Mor 835 410
Cliffplant Ltd v. *Kinnaird* 1981 SC 9, 1982 SLT 2 261, 262, 265
Cobb v. *Cobb's Trs* (1894) 21 R 638 505
Cochran v. *Fairholm* (1759) Mor 14518 311, 322
Cochrane v. *Black* (1855) 17 D 321 503
Cochrane v. *Stevenson* (1891) 18 R 1208 257, 263
Cockburn v. *Wallace and Governors of Heriot's Hospital* (1825) 4 S 128 320
Cocks [1871] LR 12 Eq 574 505
Coggs v. *Bernard* (1703) 2 Raym 909, 92 ER 107 342
Cokburn v. *Twedy of Drumelior* (1478) ADA 65 338
Colquhoun's Trs v. *Orr Ewing & Co.* (1877) 4 R (HL) 116 441, 445, 448–9, 460, 462, 468, 474, 477
Corser v. *Cartwright* (1875) L.R. 7, E. and 1 App 781 506
Couts v. *Straiton* (1683) 2 Brown's Supp 30 139
Cowan v. *Lord Elphingstoun* (1636) Mor 202 278
Craig v. *Carbiston* (1677) Mor 16174, 2 Stair Rep 571 497
Craig v. *Edgar* (1674) Mor 838 411
Craill (Town of) v. *Gresill Meldrum* 24 May 1549, reported in Balfour, *Practicks*, 626 432–3
Crawford v. *McMichen* (1729) 2 Ross LC 112 291
Creditors of Lord Ballenden (1707) Mor 865 406
Crichton v. *Bandoun* (1613) Mor 13443 408
Crichton v. *Turnbull* 1945 SC 52 309, 318
Crichton's Case (1828) 3 W & S 329 505

Table of Cases

Crown Estate Commissioners v. *Fairlie Yacht Slip Ltd* 1979 SC 156 433, 435, 437, 475
Cruikshank v. *Aberdeen Lime Co. Ltd* 1927 SLT (Sh Ct) 39 453
Cruikshanks v. *Henderson* (1791) Hume 506 458
Cuningham v. *Kennedy* (1713) Mor 12778 453
Cunningham v. *Montgomerie* (1879) 6 R 1333 506
Cuninghame v. *Assessor for Ayrshire* (1895) 22 R 596 437
Cuthberts v. *Ross* (1697) 4 Brown's Supp 374 354
Dalton v. *Angus* (1881) 6 AC 740 327
Davidson v. *Balcanqual* (1629) Mor 2773 414
Dewar v. *Fraser* (1767) Mor 12803, Hailes 177 431
Dick v. *Earl of Abercorn* (1769) Mor 12813 457, 466, 474
Dicksons v. *Trotter* (1776) Mor 873 406, 417
Dixon v. *Fisher* (1843) 5 D 775 245, 251–3, 255–6, 258–9, 265
Dougal v. *Gordon* (1795) Mor 851 407
Douglas (Elspeth of) v. *Wach of Dawik* (1484) ADA * 149 338
Douglas v. *Menzeis* 1 Mar. 1569, reported in Balfour, *Practicks*, 196, c. 7 340
Dowall v. *Miln* (1874) 1 R 1180 253–4
Drummond v. *McKenzie* (1758) Mor 16206, Kames Sel Dec 203 502
Drummond v. *Milligan* (1890) 17 R 316 309
Drummond v. *Muschet* (1492) Mor 843 403, 407, 417
Dun (Lady) v. *Lord Dun* (1624) Mor 6217 347
Duncan v. *Blair* (1900) 3 F 274, (1901) 4 F (HL) 1 505
Dundas v. *Blair* (1886) 13 R 759 313
Dunipace v. *Sandis* (1624) Mor 859 404, 405, 411
Durham v. *Lady Winton* (1622) Mor 855 406
Dyce v. *Hay* (1849) 11 D 1266, (1852) 15 D (HL) 14 316–7, 322–3
Edinburgh (Town of) v. *Town of Leith* (1630) Mor 14500 309, 331
Edinburgh Entertainments Ltd v. *Stevenson* 1926 SC 363 191
Edmonstone v. *Lanark Twist Co.* (1810) Hume 520 453
Elibank v. *Hamilton* (1827) 6 S 69 499
Elliot v. *Conway* (1915) 31 Sh Ct Rep 79 345
Ellis v. *Laubscher* 1956 (4) SA 692 (A) 313
Ellis v. *Selby* (1836) 1 M & Cr 286 505
Elphingston (Lord) v. *Ord* (1624) Mor 858 402, 405
Embrey v. *Owen* (1851) 6 Exch 353, 155 ER 579 457, 461, 462, 477
Emerald Stainless Steel Ltd v. *South Side Distribution Ltd* 1982 SC 61 301
Faculty of Advocates v. *Dickson* (1718) Mor 864 402, 406
Fairly v. *Eglinton* (1744) Mor 12780, Kilk 452, Elchies, 'Property', no. 7, Hume 506 454, 472
Farquharson v. *Farqhuarson* (1741) Mor 12779, 5 Brown's Supp 688, Elchies, 'Property', no. 5 453
FC Finance Ltd v. *Brown & Son* 1969 SLT (Sh Ct) 41 213

Ferguson v. *Paul* (1885) 12 R 1222 263
Ferguson v. *Tennant* 1978 SC (HL) 15 310, 317, 325
Ferguson and Stuart v. *Grant* (1856) 18 D 536 360
Fergusson v. *Shirreff* (1844) 6 D 1363 444, 451, 468
Ferme, Ferme & Williamson v. *Stephenson's Trs* (1905) 13 SLT 236 505
Fisherrow Harbour Commissioners v. *Musselburgh Real Estate Co. Ltd* (1903) 5 F 387 432, 476
Fleeming v. *Howden* (1868) 6 M (HL) 113 485, 512
Fleming v. *Lord Crechton* (1479) ADA 87 338
Forbes' Trustees v. *Davidson* (1892) 19 R 1022 328
Forth Bridge Railway v. *Assessor of Railways* (1890) 1 PLM (NS) 147 437
Foulis v. *Cognerlie* 6 Apr. 1566, reported in Balfour, *Practicks*, 195, c. 6 340
Fraser v. *Secretary of State for Scotland and Others* 1959 SLT 36 325
Fraser's Trs v. *Cran* (1879) 6 R 451 464
Frog's Creditors v. *His Children* (1735) Mor 4262 513
Gadzeard v. *Sheriff of Ayr* (1781) Mor 14732 213
Gammell v. *Commissioners of Woods and Forests* (1851) 13 D 854, (1859) 3 Macq 419 476
Garden Haig Scott & Wallace v. *White* 1962 SLT 78 361
Garscadden v. *Ardrossan Dry Dock Co. Ltd* 1910 SC 178 360
Gay v. *Malloch* 1959 SC 110 448
Gemmell v. *Bank of Scotland* 1998 SCLR 144 213
Gib v. *Hamilton* (1583) Mor 16080 213
Gibson v. *Hunter Home Designs Ltd* 1976 SC 23 196, 296
Gilchrist v. *Assessor for Lanarkshire* (1898) 25 R 589 263
Gilmour v. *Gilmours* (1876) 11 M 853 514
Glasgow Corporation v. *Barclay, Curle & Co. Ltd* 1922 SC 413 423
Glenlee (Lord) v. *Gordon* (1804) Mor 12834 453, 456, 464, 465
Gordon (Duke of) v. *Duff* (1735) Mor 12778 454
Gordon v. *Cheyne* 5 Feb. 1824 FC, (1824) 2 S 675 500
Gordon v. *Gordon's Tr* (1866) 4 M 501 483
Gould v. *McCorquodale* (1869) 8 M 165 313
Govan New Bowling-Green Club v. *Geddes* (1898) 25 R 485 196
Grant v. *Duke of Gordon* (1781) Mor 12820, (1782) 2 Pat App 582 440, 449
Grant v. *Henry* (1894) 21 R 358 445, 448, 451
Gray v. *Ferguson* (1792) Mor 14513 313
Gray Petitioner (1856) 19 D 1 505
Green v. *Farmer* (1768) 4 Burr 2214, 98 ER 154 352
Grier v. *Maxwell* (1621) Mor 828 401
Grierson v. *School Board of Sandsting and Aithsting* (1882) 9 R 437 318, 325
Grimond's Trs (1904) 6 F 285, (1905) 7 F (HL) 90 505
Hagan v. *Duff* (1889) 23 LR Ir 516 505
Haliburton v. *Rutherford* (1541) Mor 14739 213

Table of Cases

Halkerton v. *Falconer* (1628) Mor 765 414
Hall v. *Corbet* (1698) Mor 12775 217
Hallett's Estate (Re) (1880) 13 Ch D 696 512
Halsey v. *Esso Petroleum Co. Ltd* [1961] 1 WLR 683 471
Hamilton (Duke of) v. *Douglas* (1762) Mor 4358, (1779) 2 Pat App 449 293
Hamilton v. *Bogle* (1819) 1 Ross LC 22 273
Hamilton v. *Boyd* (1610) Mor 7188 409
Hamilton v. *Edington & Co.* (1793) Mor 12824 425, 453, 455–7, 464, 472
Hamilton v. *Hamilton* (1629) Mor 830 410
Hamilton v. *Macdowal* 3 Mar. 1815 FC 294
Hamilton v. *Western Bank of Scotland* (1856) 19 D 152, (1861) 23 D 1033 343, 344
Hamilton v. *Wood* (1788) Mor 6269 348, 356
Hariot v. *Cuninghame* (1791) Mor 12405 342
Harper v. *Flaws* 1940 SLT 150 310, 324
Harper's Creditors v. *Faulds* (1791) Bell Oct Cas 440 355, 358–360
Harris v. *Abbey National plc* 1997 SCLR 359 213
Harris v. *Magistrates of Dundee* (1863) 1 M 833 318, 328, 331
Harrowar's Trustees v. *Erskine* (1827) 5 S 284 325
Harvey v. *Lindsay* (1853) 15 D 768 317, 323, 329
Harvie v. *Stewart* (1870) 9 M 129 318, 325
Hay v. *Feuars* (1677) Mor 1818 453
Hay v. *Keith* (1623) Mor 6188 347
Hay v. *Ker* (1622) Mor 828 410
Hay's Trs v. *Baillie* 1908 SC 1224, (1907) 15 SLT 494 505
Henderson v. *Selkrig* (1795) 294
Heritable Reversionary Co. Ltd v. *Millar* (1891) 18 R 1166, (1892) 19 R (HL) 43 195, 210, 500, 507
Hewett v. *Bishop of Glasgow's Fund Committee* (1898) 4 Sh Ct Rep 95 261
Higgins v. *Callander* (1696) Mor 16182 496
Hill v. *Burns* (1826) 2 W & S 80 505
Hill v. *Hunter* (1766) Mor 16207 498
Hislop v. *Anderson* (1919) 35 Sh Ct Rep 116 345
HMA v. *Fraser of Belladrum* (1758) Mor 15196 382
Hobson v. *Gorringe* [1892] 1 Ch 182 260, 265
Holland v. *Hodgson* (1872) LR 7 CP 328 255
Home v. *Pringle* (1841) 2 Rob 384 504
Home & Elphingston v. *Murray* (1674) Mor 863 405, 411
Hood v. *Williamsons* (1861) 23 D 450
Horn v. *Horn* (1825) 2 Simon and Stuart 448 506
Howard v. *Chaffer* (1863) 32 L.J. Ch 686 506
Howie's Trs v. *McLay* (1902) 5 F 214 263–4
Hume v. *Hume* (1632) Mor 848 402, 404

Hunter v. *Fox* 1964 SC (HL) 95 313
Huntly (Marquis of) v. *Nicol* (1896) 23 R 610 324
Hyslop v. *Hyslop* 18 Jan. 1811 FC 249
Incorporated Trades of Aberdeen v. *The Magistrates, Council and Guildry of Aberdeen* (1793) Mor 1797 511
Inglis v. *Clark* (1901) 4 F 288 313
Inglis v. *Robertson and Baxter* (1898) 25 R (HL) 70 344
Inland Revenue v. *Clark's Trs* 1939 SC 11 196, 506, 508
Innes v. *Downie* (1807) Hume 552 434
Innes v. *Stewart* (1542) Mor 3081 318
International Banking Corporation v. *Ferguson, Shaw & Sons* 1910 SC 182 210
Irvine Knitters Ltd v. *North Ayrshire Co-operative Society Ltd* 1978 SC 109, 1978 SLT 105 318
Irving v. *Leadhills Mining Co.* (1856) 18 D 833 469
James v. *Allen* (1817) 3 Mer 17 505
Jamieson v. *Clark* 1872 10 M 399 515
Jarman's Estate (In re) (1878) 8 Ch D 584 505
Johnston v. *MacRitchie* (1893) 20 R 539 310, 313
Johnstone v. *Dobie* (1783) Mor 5443 248
Johnstone v. *Ritchie* (1822) 1 S 327 453
Johnstone v. *Spevin* (1682) Mor 864 406
Jopp v. *Johnston's Tr* (1904) 6 F 1028 512
Kaur v. *Singh* 1999 SLT 412 215
Kelso v. *Boyds* (1768) Mor 12807, Hailes 224 447, 453, 458, 460
Kemp v. *Youngs* (1838) 16 S 500 355
Kennedy v. *Begg Kennedy & Elder Ltd* 1954 SLT (Sh Ct) 103 504
Ker v. *Scot's Creditors* (1702) Mor 14310 282
Kirkpatrick's Trustees v. *Kirkpatrick* (1874) 1 R (HL) 37 294
Kilsyth Fish Protection Association v. *McFarlane* 1937 SC 757 467
King (The) v. *Laird of Seafield* 29 July 1500 reported in Balfour, *Practicks*, 626 433
Kinloch Petitioner (1859) 22 D 175 501
Kinloch v. *Finlayson* (1629) Mor 847 402, 404, 405
Kinnoull (Earl of) v. *Keir* 18 Jan. 1814 FC 453
Kintore (Earl of) v. *Pirie & Sons* (1906) 8 F (HL) 16 464
Konstanz Properties (Pty) Ltd v. *WM Spilhaus (WP) Bpk* 1996 (3) SA 273 (A) 267
Laird v. *Laird* (1858) 20 D 984 503
Lanark Twist Co. v. *Edmonstone* (1810) Hume 520 456, 464
Laurie v. *Black* (1831) 10 S 1 359
Laurie v. *Denny's Tr* (1853) 15 D 404 359, 360
Lawder v. *Goodwife of Whitekirk* (1637) Mor 1692 411

Lawrie v. *Hay* (1696) Mor 849 404–6
Leith v. *Garden* (1703) Mor 865 406, 416–7, 419
Leith-Buchanan v. *Hogg* 1931 SC 204 468
Leslie v. *Cumming* (1793) Mor 14542 325, 331
Leslie and Black Petitioners 8 June 1819 FC 509, 510
Lidderdale's Creditors v. *Nasmyth* (1749) Mor 6248 355
Liggins v. *Inge* (1831) 7 Bing 682 693, 131 ER 263 461
Liquidator of Grand Empire Theatres v. *Snodgrass* 1932 SC (HL) 73 361
Livingston v. *Forrester* (1664) Mor 191 and 10200, 1 Stair Rep 232 494, 499, 500
Livingston v. *Lindsay* (1626) Mor 860 404, 411
Lockhart v. *Duke of Hamilton* (1890) 192
Logan v. *Hunter* (1628) Mor 13542 293
Logan v. *Wang (UK) Ltd* 1991 SLT 580 471
Lord Advocate v. *Clyde Trs and Hamilton* (1849) 11 D 391, (1852) 1 Macq 46 431, 440, 441, 466
Lord Advocate v. *Clyde Navigation Trs* (1891) 19R 174 434, 437, 468, 476
Lord Advocate v. *Lord Blantyre* (1879) 6 R (HL) 72 434
Lord Advocate v. *Maclean of Ardgour* (1866) 2 SLR 25 434, 476
Lord Advocate v. *Sprot's Tr* (1901) 4 F (HL) 11 505
Lord Advocate v. *Wemyss* (1899) 2 F (HL) 1 431, 437, 476
Luke v. *Dundass* (1695) 4 Brown's Supp 258 217
Lutea Trustees Ltd v. *Orbis Trustees Guernsey Ltd* 1 Mar. 1996 504
Lyon v. *Fishmongers Co.* (1876) 1 App Cas 662 442, 448
Macalister v. *Campbell* (1837) 15 S 490 434
Macbraire v. *Mather* (1871) 9 M 913 448
McCartney v. *Londonderry & Lough Swilly Railway Co. Ltd* [1904] AC 301 450
McGrie's Trs, Petitioners 1927 SC 556 509
McCrone v. *Ramsay* (1901) 9 SLT 118 464, 472
McDonald's Trustee v. *Aberdeen City Council* 2000 SC 185 297
MacDonald Ltd v. *Radin NO & The Potchefstroom Dairies & Industries Co. Ltd* 1915 AD 454 267
Macdonnell v. *Caledonian Canal Commissioners* (1830) 8 S 881 440, 468
McDowal and Gray v. *Annand and Colhoun's Assignees* (1776) 2 Pat App 387 356
McGibbon v. *Rankin* (1871) 9 M 423 313, 317, 319, 320, 329
McGill v. *Hutchison* (1630) Mor 860 405, 410, 411
McGill v. *Laurestoun* (1558) Mor 843 403, 407
McGregor v. *Tolmie* (1860) 22 D 1183 254
Mackalzean v. *Mackalzean* (1586) Mor 854 403
Mackenzie v. *Bankes* (1877) 5 R 278, (1878) 5 R (HL) 192 467
Mackenzie v. *Carrick* (1869) 7 M 419 318, 328
Mackenzie v. *Watson* (1678) Mor 10188, 2 Stair Rep 607 494, 499, 500

McKichen v. *Muir* (1849) Shaw 223 359
Mackinnon v. *Avonside Homes Ltd* 1993 SCLR 976 213
Macklonaquhen v. *Carsan* (1632) Mor 830 411
McKnight v. *Irving* (1805) Hume 412 249
McLean v. *Marwhirn Developments Ltd* 1976 SLT (Notes) 47 329
McLeish's Trs v. *McLeish* (1841) 3 D 914 514
McMillan v. *Conrad* (1914) 30 Sh Ct Rep 275 345
McTaggart v. *McDouall* (1867) 5 M 534 325, 331
Magistrates of Aberdeen v. *Menzies* (1748) Mor 12787 453, 454, 471, 472
Magistrates of Aberdeen v. *University of Aberdeen* (1877) 4 R (HL) 48 509
Magistrates of Ardrossan v. *Dickie* (1906) 14 SLT 349 446, 448, 451, 466, 467
Magistrates of Culross v. *Earl of Dundonald* (1769) Mor 12810, Hailes 291 433
Magistrates of Dumfries v. *Water of Nith Heritors* (1705) Mor 12776 471, 472
Magistrates of Edinburgh v. *Binny* (1694) 1 Fount 635, Mor 9107 501, 509
Magistrates of Edinburgh v. *Magistrates of Leith* (1877) 4 R 997 323
Magistrates of Linlithgow v. *Elphinstone* (1768) Mor 12805, 5 Brown's Supp 935, Hailes 203 446, 448, 451, 453, 454, 457, 458, 467, 472, 477
Malcolm v. *High* (1909) 25 Sh Ct Rep 264 261
Malloch v. *McLean* (1867) 5 M 335 249
Mansfield (Earl of) v. *Walker's Trs* (1835) 1 S & M 203 471
Marshall v. *Tannoch Chemical Co. Ltd* (1886) 13 R 1042 261
Mason v. *Hill* (1833) 5 B & Ad 1, 110 ER 692 461, 477
Mayor of Berwick v. *Lord Hayning* (1661) Mor 12772, 2 Brown's Supp 292 459, 460
Mayor of Bradford v. *Pickles* [1895] AC 587 476
Meikle and Wilson v. *Pollard* (1880) 8 R 69 359
Melrose and Co. v. *Hastie* (1851) 13 D 880 360
Melville (Lord) v. *Denniston* (1842) 4 D 1231 450
Mendelssohn v. *The Wee Pub Co Ltd* 1991 GWD 26–1518 330
Menzies v. *Earl of Breadalbane* (1828) 3 W & S 235 454, 456, 458, 472, 475
Menzies v. *Macdonald* (1854) 16 D 827 467
Mercantile Credit Co. Ltd v. *Townsley* 1971 SLT (Sh Ct) 37 213
Mercedes-Benz Finance Ltd v. *Clydesdale Bank plc* 1997 SLT 905 506
Merchant Company of Edinburgh v. *Governors of Heriot's Hospital* 9 Aug. 1765 FC, Mor 5750 501, 510
Metcalfe v. *Purdon* (1902) 4 F 507 309, 313, 318
Millar v. *Black's Trs* (1837) 2 S & M 866 505
Miller v. *Muirhead* (1894) 21 R 658 264
Miller v. *Stein* (1791) Mor 12823, Bell Oct Cas 334 459, 460, 465
Miller's Trs v. *Miller* (1848) 10 D 765 505
Milton v. *Glen-Moray Glenlivet Distillery Co. Ltd* (1898) 1 F 135 469

Miner v. *Gilmour* (1858) 12 Moo PCC 131 450
Mitchell v. *Burnet and Mouat* (1746) Mor 4468 342
Mitchell v. *Ferguson* (1781) Mor 10296, 3 Ross LC 120 284
Moncreiffe v. *Perth Police Commissioners* (1886) 13 R 921 448
Montgomerie v. *Buchanan's Trs* (1853) 15 D 853 470
Montgomery v. *Hamilton* (1548) Mor 14731 213
Montgomery v. *Watson* (1861) 23 D 635 444, 451, 467–8
Morice v. *Bishop of Durham* (1804) 9 Ves Jun 399 505
Morris v. *Bicket* (1864) 2 M 1082, (1866) 4 M (HL) 44 450, 454–8, 477
Morrison v. *Watson* (1883) 2 Guth Sh Cas 502 359
Morrisson v. *Robertson* 1908 SC 322 210
Mortensen v. *Peters* (1906) 8 F(J) 93 431
Mudiall v. *Frissal* (1628) Mor 14749 213
Muir's Trs v. *Jameson* (1903) 10 SLT 70 504
Murdoch v. *Carstairs* (1823) 2 S 159 325
Murphy v. *Ryan* (1867) Ir Rep 2 CL 143 445
Murray v. *Durham and the Lady Winton* (1622) Mor 855 404
Murray of Philiphauch v. *Cuninghame* (1668) 1 Brown's Supp 575 341
Nairn Magistrates v. *Brodie* (1738) Mor 12779 454
National Commercial Bank of Scotland v. *Liquidators of Telford Grier Mackay & Co. Ltd* 1969 SC 181 350
National Homecare Ltd v. *Belling & Co.* 1994 SLT 50 360
Neill v. *Scobbie* 1993 GWD 13–887 330
New v. *Jones* (1 Hall and Twells 632) 505
Newlands v. *Newlands' Creditors* (1794) Mor 4289 513
Nicolson v. *Mellvill* (1708) Mor 14516 218, 328
Niven v. *Pitcairn* (1823) 2 S 204, 3 Mar. 1823 FC 249, 250
Nordic Travel Ltd v. *Scotprint Ltd* 1980 SC 1 515
North British Railway Co. v. *Park Yard Co. Ltd* (1898) 25 R (HL) 47 318
North Western Bank v. *Poynter, Sons and Macdonald* (1894) 22 R (HL) 1 344
Officers of State v. *Smith* (1846) 8 D 711 434–5
Ogilvie v. *Lyon* (1729) Mor 16200, 2 K & W Dic 477 497
Ogilvie v. *Mercer* (1793) Mor 3336 293
Ogilvie v. *Ogilvie* (1681) Mor 863 405, 411
Ogilvy v. *Kincaid* (1791) Mor 12824, Hume 508 450, 453
Oliver & Boyd v. *Marr Typefounding Co.* (1901) 9 SLT 170 210
Parson of Dundee v. *Inglish* (1687) Mor 14521 328
Paterson v. *Douglas* (1705) 2 Ross LC 78 293
Paton v. *Wyllie* (1833) 11 S 703 359
Patrick v. *Napier* (1867) 5 M 683 309, 317, 318, 320, 323, 324
Pattison's Trs v. *Liston* (1893) 20 R 806 333
Peebles (Town of) v. *The Lady Halton* (1628) Mor 6885 279
Pemsel's Case [1891] AC 531 505

Peter v. *Eccles* (1686) Mor 14515 309
Pickard v. *Glasgow Corporation* 1970 SLT (Sh Ct) 63 360
Poole's Case (1703) 1 Salk 368 255
Pringle v. *Gribton* (1710) Mor 9123 342
Proprietors of Royal Exchange Buildings, Glasgow, Limited v. *Cotton* 1912 SC 1151 310, 318
Provenhall's Creditors (1781) Mor 6253 355, 356, 361
Purnell v. *Shannon* (1894) 22 R 74 497
Purves v. *Strachan* (1677) 2 Ross LC 140 276, 279
Queen, The v. *George Cranston of Corsbie* (1566) Mor 3007 279
Ramsay (Elizabeth) v. *Ker of Westnisbet* (1667) Mor 203 278
Rebbech, In re, 1894, 63, L. J. Ch. 596 506
Redelinghuis v. *Bazzoni* 1976 (1) SA 110 (T) 311
Redfearn v. *Somervail* 22 Nov. 1805 FC, (1813) 1 Dow 50, 5 Pat App 707 419, 507
Regina v. *Keyn (The Franconia)* (1876) LR 2 Ex D 63 436–7
Reid's Exrs v. *Reid* (1890) 17 R 519 262
Renton (Lady) v. *Her Son* (1629) Mor 14733 213
Richardson v. *Goss* (1802) 3 Bos & P 119, 127 ER 65 353
Rilands (In re) (1881) WN 173 505
Robertson v. *Baxter and Inglis* (1897) 24 R 758 344
Robertson v. *Scottish Union and National Insurance Co.* 1943 SC 427 328
Robertson's Tr v. *Royal Bank of Scotland* (1890) 18 R 12 359
Robins & Co. v. *Gray* [1895] 2 QB 501 358
Robinson v. *Lord Byron* (1785) 1 Brown Ch 588, 28 ER 1315 461
Rodger (Builders) Ltd v. *Fawdry* 1950 SC 483 298, 504
Rogano Ltd v. *British Railways Board* 1979 SC 297 328
Rollock v. *Hamilton* (1560) 487
Ross v. *Allan's Trs* (1850) 13 D 44 503
Ross v. *Powrie and Pitcaithley* (1891) 19 R 314 448
Roxburghe (Duke of) v. *Waldie* (1881) Hume 524 453
Rubislaw Land Co. Ltd v. *Aberdeen Construction Group Ltd* 1999 GWD 14-647 13
Rugby Joint Water Board v. *Walters* [1967] 1 Ch 397 462
Rushforth v. *Hadfield* (1805) 6 East 519, 102 ER 1386 353
Russell v. *Haig* (1791) Mor 12823, Bell Oct Cas 338, 3 Pat App 403 459, 460, 465
Safeway Food Stores Ltd v. *Wellington Motor Co. (Ayr) Ltd* 1976 SLT 53 310, 318
St Barbe Tregonwell v. *Sydenham* (1815) 3 Dow 194 514
Sandeman v. *Scottish Property Investment Co.* (1885) 12 R (HL) 67 372
Sanderson v. *Lees* (1859) 22 D 24 323
Schaw (1622) Mor 829 410

Schooler v. *Lawson* (1890) 6 Sh Ct Rep 110 261
Scot v. *Drumlanrig* (1628) Mor 846 405
Scot v. *Elliot of Stobs* (1636) Mor 201 278
Scott v. *Miller* (1832) 11521 499
Scottish Discount Co. v. *Blin* 1985 SC 216, 1986 SLT 123 263, 264, 266, 268
Scottish Highland Distillery Co. v. *Reid* (1877) 4 R 1118 328
Scott's Hospital Trs Petitioners 1913 SC 289 511
Seamen of 'Golden Star' v. *Miln* (1682) Mor 6259 354
Secretary of State for India v. *Chelikani Rama Rao* (1916) 32 TLR 652 437
Seton v. *Pitmeddon* (1717) Mor 4425 491
Shank (*Ex parte*) (1745) 1 Atk 234, 26 ER 151 352
Sharp v. *Thomson* 1995 SC 455, 1995 SLT 837, 1997 SLT 636, 1997 SC (HL)
    66,1997SCLR328 196,210,283,285,289,295,296,297,301,302,303,350; 512
Shelfer v. *City of London Lighting Co.* [1895] 1 Ch 287 470
Shelley's Case (1581) Co Rep 93b, 76 ER 206 513
Shetland Islands Council v. *BP Petroleum Development Ltd* 1990 SLT 82 265
Shetland Salmon Farmers Association v. *Crown Estate Commissioners* 1991
    SLT 166 437, 438
Sinclair v. *The Magistrates and Town Council of Dysart* (1779) Mor 14519 310
Sivright v. *Borthwick* (1828) 7 S 210 313
Skinner v. *Paterson* (1823) 2 S 554 359
Skinner v. *Upshaw* (1702) 2 Raym 752, 92 ER 3 352
Smith v. *Earl of Stair* (1849) 6 Bell App 487 434, 437, 476
Smith v. *Kenrick* (1849) 7 CB 515 470
Snee & Co. v. *Anderson's Trs* (1734) Mor 1206 514
Soar v. *Ashwell* [1893] 2 QB 390 504
Southall v. *Cunninghamhead* (1657) Eng Judg 49 491
Southern Cross Commodities Property Ltd v. *Martin* 1991 SLT 83 504
Sowman v. *City of Glasgow DC* 1985 SLT 65 360
Spittell v. *Urquhart* (1532) Balfour, *Practicks*, 198 488, 489
Stanipath (Lady) v. *Her Son's Relict and Bairns* (1624) Durie 141 487, 492
Stephens v. *Creditors of the York Building Company* (1735) Mor 9140 201
Stevinson v. *Craigmiller* (1624) Mor 858, 1 Fol Dic 64, Durie 102 403
Stewart v. *Stewart* (1803) 294
Stewart's Trs v. *Robertson* (1874) 1 R 334 467
Stirling v. *White & Drummond* (1582) Mor 7127 411
Strachan v. *Creditors of Strachan* (1754) 5 Brown's Supp 814 167
Strachan v. *Gordons* (1671) Mor 1819 213
Strathmore (Earl of) v. *Earl of Strathmore's Trs* (1830) 8 S 530 503
Street v. *Hume* (1669) Mor 15122, 1 Stair Rep 616 500
Strong v. *Phillips & Co.* (1878) 5 R 770 359
Sutherland (Duchess of) v. *Watson* (1868) 6 M 199 431
Sutherland (Earl of) v. *Coupar* (1738) Mor 6247 355

Sutton (In re) (1885) 28 Ch D 464 505
Syme v. *Harvey* (1861) 24 D 202 251, 253, 254, 255, 258
Tailors of Aberdeen v. *Coutts* (1840) 1 Rob 296 197, 359
Tait v. *Cockburn* (1780) Mor 14110 356
Taylor & Ferguson Ltd v. *Glass's Trs* 1912 SC 165 516
Thome v. *Thome* (1683) 403
Tod's Trs v. *Finlay* (1872) 10 M 422 254
Trade Development Bank v. *Warriner & Mason (Scotland) Ltd* 1980 SC 74 191
Trotter v. *Farnie* (1831) 5 W & S 649 471
Trotter v. *Hume* (1757) Mor 12798 472
Troup v. *Aberdeen Heritable Securities Co.* 1916 SC 918 327
TSB Scotland plc v. *James Mills (Montrose) Ltd (in receivership)* 1991 GWD 39-2406 266
Turnbull v. *Blanerne* (1622) Mor 14499 309
Turnbull v. *Stewart* (1751) Mor 868 406
Turwin v. *Gibson* (1749) 3 Atk 720, 26 ER 1212 352
Tyler v. *Wilkinson* (1827) 4 Mason 397 457, 462
University of St Andrews v. *Creditors of Newark* (1762) Mor 10171 509
Wallace v. *Edgar* (1662) Mor 837 410
Walton Brothers v. *Magistrates of Glasgow* (1876) 3 R 1130 318
Wardlaw v. *Mitchell* (1611) Mor 6187 347
Warnock v. *Anderson* (1633) Mor 2787 284
Watkins v. *Cheek* (1825) 2 Simon and Stuart 199 506
Wauchop v. *Borthwik* 13 Dec. 1537 reported in Balfour, *Practicks*, 398, c. 9. 347
Webb v. *Webb* [1994] ECR 1-1717 481
Westraw v. *Williamson & Carmichael* (1626) Mor 859 401, 404, 406, 411, 413, 417
White (J.) & Sons v. *J. & M. White* (1905) 8 F (HL) 41 464
Whitmore v. *Stuart and Stuart* (1902) 10 SLT 290 218
Williams v. *Kershaw* (1835) 5 Cl & Fin 111 505
Williams v. *Morland* (1824) 2 B & C 910, 107 ER 620 458, 461
Williamson v. *Law* (1623) Durie 54 492, 496
Willoughby de Eresby (Lady) v. *Wood* (1884) 22 SL Rep 471 475
Wills' Trs v. *Cairngorm Canoeing and Sailing School Ltd* 1976 SC (HL) 30 441, 445, 448, 449, 451
Wilmot v. *Wilson* (1841) 3 D 815 360
Wilson v. *Fraser* (1824) 3 Ross LC 23 359
Wishart v. *Arbuthnot* (1573) Mor 3605 213
Wolifson v. *Harrison* 1977 SC 384 365
Wood v. *Waud* (1849) 3 Exch 748, 154 ER 1047 457, 461, 462
Workman v. *Crawford* (1672) Mor 10208, 2 Stair Rep 121 497
Wright v. *Howard* (1823) 1 Sim & St 190, 57 ER 76 458, 461

Wright v. *Wright* 1712 Mor 16193 504
Wylie v. *Duncan* (1803) Mor 10269, 3 Ross LC 134 500
Wyper v. *Harveys* (1861) 23 D 606 344, 359, 360
Yeaman v. *Crawford* (1770) Mor 14537 316
Yeoman v. *Moncreif* (1669) Mor 14740 213
York Buildings Co. v. *Mackenzie* (1795) 3 Pat App 378 504
Young v. *Leith* (1844) 6 D 370, (1847) 9 D 932, 2 Ross LC 81 214, 284, 285, 293
Young & Co. v. *Bankier Distillery Co.* (1893) 20 R (HL) 76 450, 477
Yuille v. *Laurie* (1823) 2 S 155 349

Chronology of Scottish Legal History

JOHN W. CAIRNS

843	Accession of Kenneth
1016	Battle of Carham
1066	Norman invasion of England
1068	Malcolm III marries Princess Margaret
c.1100–30	Irnerius active in Bologna
c.1140	*Decretum* of Gratian
1124–53	Start of spread of feudal tenures and lordships with the introduction of Norman governmental institutions
1192	Bull *cum universi* recognizes special status of Scottish Church
1194	First evidence of the Bishop's Official
1230	Introduction of brieves of mortancestry and novel dissasine
1245	Start of criminal procedure by dittay (indictment) before the justiciar
1264	First surviving reference to Scottish common law
c.1270	Berne MS (oldest MS containing Scottish legal material)
1286	Death of Alexander III
1291	Great Cause and award of throne to John Balliol
1295	Edwardian occupation
1306	Robert Bruce crowned King of Scots
1318	First entail settling throne on Robert Stewart
c.1318–71	*Regiam Majestatem* and *Quoniam Attachiamenta* composed
1318	Parliament at Scone enacts important legislation, especially concerning heritage and brieves
1326	First evidence of burgesses in Parliament
1326	Second entail settling throne on Robert Stewart
1357	First reference to the Three Estates
1371	Robert Stewart succeeds as Robert II
1401	Parliament at Scone enacts important legislation on land tenures
1406–24	James I in captivity in England
1426	Parliament emphasizes authority of common law of Scotland
1426	Law Commission to examine *Regiam* and *Quoniam*
1426	Institution of the Sessions
1469	Parliament declares James III to possess 'ful jurisdictioune and fre Impire'

1469	Proposal to 'codify' Scots law, especially *Regiam* and *Quoniam*
1472	See of St Andrews becomes Archbishopric
1473	Proposal to codify the law
1496	Education Act
1504	Authority of King's common law asserted, especially over the Isles
1507	Royal Patent to Chepman and Millar covers printing of the books of the laws and Acts of Parliament
1532	Parliamentary foundation of College of Justice
1535	Papal erection of College of Justice
1541	Parliamentary ratification of College of Justice
1541	First printed collection of Scottish legislation
1560	Reformation Parliament
1564	Creation of the commissary courts
1566	Law commission draws up and prints collection of statutes from James I to Mary
1574–83	Compilation of Balfour's *Practicks*
1575	Law commission appointed to revise the law
1578	Law commission appointed to revise the law
1582	First mention of the Dean of the Advocates
1587	Small barons and freeholders called to Parliament
1592	Law commission appointed, including Skene
1596	Regulation of 'Informations' to the Lords
1597	Skene publishes *Lawes and Actes* from 1424 onwards
1599–1600	Craig writes bulk of *Jus Feudale*
1603	James VI inherits English throne
1604	Union negotiations
1609	Skene publishes Latin and Scots editions of *Regiam* and the 'auld lawes'
1609	Introduction of the Justice of the Peace
1611	'Foreign laws' no longer to be used in Orkney and Shetland
1617	Register of Sasines established
1628	Law commission appointed to examine statutes
1630	Law commission appointed to examine statutes, customary laws, and 'auld lawes'
1633	Law commission appointed to examine statutes, customary laws, and 'auld lawes'
1638	National Covenant signed at Greyfriars in Edinburgh
1640	Covenanting Parliaments embark on major constitutional reform
1649	Law commission appointed to 'codify' the laws
1651	Charles II crowned at Scone

Chronology of Scottish Legal History

1651	Cromwellian conquest and occupation
1652	Cromwellian Commissioners for Administration of Justice appointed
1655	First edition of Craig's *Jus Feudale* (written c.1599–1600)
1660	Restoration of Charles II and old institutions
1662	Early version of Stair's *Institutions* largely completed
1669	Union Negotiations
1670	Report of law commission (appointed 1669) to examine functioning of the courts
1672	Courts Act reforms functioning of Court of Session and establishes a reconstructed Court of Justiciary
1678	Mackenzie, *Laws and Customes of Scotland, in Matters Criminal*
c.1680	Foundation of the Advocates' Library
1681	Test Act
1681	Commission to revise the laws
1681	Glendook folio edition of the statutes
1681	First edition, Stair's *Institutions of the Law of Scotland* (written c.1660–5)
1682–3	Glendook duodecimo edition of the statutes
1683	Stair publishes first printed volume of decisions of the Session
1684	Mackenzie, *Jus Regium* in favour of *iure divino* kingship
1686	Mackenzie, *Observations on the Statutes*
1689	Claim of Right
1690	Establishment of Presbyterianism
1693	Real Rights Act
1693	Register of Sasines Act
1695	Commission to revise the laws
1701	Criminal Procedure Act
1703	Act of Security
1706	Union Negotiations
1707	Act of Union
1707	Chair of Public Law and the Law of Nature and Nations in Edinburgh
1708	Treason Act
1708	New Exchequer Court established
1710	Chair of Civil Law in Edinburgh
1712	Patronage Act
1712	Toleration Act
1714	Chair of Civil Law in Glasgow
1715	Clan Act
1722	Chair of Scots Law in Edinburgh
1732	Third edition (by Baillie) of Craig, *Jus Feudale*

1741	Kames, *Dictionary of Decisions*
1747	Heritable Jurisdictions (Scotland) Act
1747	Tenures Abolition Act
1754	First publication of Balfour's *Practicks* (written *c.*1574–83)
1772	Bankruptcy law reformed
1773	Erskine's *Institute of the Law of Scotland* (posthumously) published
1786–1822	David Hume, Professor of Scots Law, University of Edinburgh
1797	Hume's *Commentaries of the Law of Scotland Respecting the Description and Punishment of Crimes*
1800	Hume's *Commentaries on the Law of Scotland, Respecting Trial for Crimes* (in subsequent editions, combined with earlier work into *Commentaries on the Law of Scotland, Respecting Crimes*)
1800–4	Bell's *Treatise on the Law of Bankruptcy* published (later editions *Commentaries on the Law of Scotland*)
1801–8	Morison's *Dictionary of Decisions*
1808	Court of Session split into two divisions
1813	Permanent Outer House
1815	Establishment of Jury Court
1819	Jury Court made permanent
1823	Local commissary jurisdiction merged with that of sheriff courts
1825	Court of Session and its procedure further reformed
1830	Jury Court merged into Court of Session
1830	Consistorial jurisdiction of Edinburgh Commissaries granted to Court of Session
1832	Scottish Reform Act
1836	Edinburgh commissary court abolished
1856	Exchequer Court merged into Court of Session
1857–91	*Journal of Jurisprudence* published
1865	Procurators Act establishes uniform educational and training requirements
1868	Court of Session Act
1885	Secretary for Scotland established
1886	Crofters Holdings (Scotland) Act
1887	Major reform of criminal procedure
1889	Foundation of *Juridical Review*
1897	Creation of roll of Queen's Counsel
1926	Secretary for Scotland becomes a Secretary of State
1949	Law Society of Scotland established
1949	Legal Aid introduced

1965	Scottish Law Commission established
1979	Land Registration (Scotland) Act
1999	New Scottish Parliament begins to sit.

Table of Kings and Queens of Scots (or of Scotland) (to 1707), thereafter of Great Britain (to 1801), and thereafter of the United Kingdom

Kenneth I: 843–58
Donald I: 858–62
Constantine I: 862–77
Aed: 877–8
Eochaid: 878–89
Donald II: 889–900
Constantine II: 900–43
Malcolm I: 943–54
Indulf: 954–62
Duff: 962–6
Cullen: 966–71
Kenneth II: 971–95
Constantine III: 995–7
Kenneth III: 997–1005
Malcolm II: 1005–34
Duncan I: 1034–40
Macbeth: 1040–57
Lulach: 1057–8
Malcolm III (Malcolm Canmore): 1058–93
Donald III: 1093–4
Duncan II: 1094
Donald III (restored): 1094–7
Edgar: 1097–1107
Alexander I: 1107–24
David I: 1124–53
Malcolm IV: 1153–65
William I: 1165–1214
Alexander II: 1214–49
Alexander III: 1249–86
Margaret: 1286–90
(Interregnum: 1290–2)
John: 1292–6
(Interregnum: 1296–1306)
Robert I (Robert the Bruce): 1306–29

David II: 1329–71
Robert II: 1371–90
Robert III: 1390–1406
James I: 1406–37
James II: 1437–60
James III: 1460–86
James IV: 1486–1513
James V: 1513–42
Mary I: 1542–67
James VI: 1567–1625 (from 1603 James I of England)
Charles I: 1625–49
Charles II: 1649–54
(Interregnum: 1654–60)
Charles II (restored): 1660–85
James VII: 1685–8 (James II of England)
(Interregnum: 1688–9)
Mary II: 1689–94 (jointly with William II)
William II: 1689–1702 (William III of England)
Anne: 1702–14
George I: 1714–27
George II: 1727–60
George III: 1760–1820
George IV: 1820–30
William IV: 1830–7
Victoria: 1837–1901
Edward VII: 1901–10
George V: 1910–36
Edward VIII: 1936
George VI: 1936–52
Elizabeth II: 1952–

A Note on Law Reporting

KENNETH REID

I. COURT OF SESSION

The Court of Session is the supreme court in Scotland in civil matters although, since the union with England in 1707, subject to a final appeal to the House of Lords in London. The Court of Session was founded in 1532, evolving out of earlier institutions.[1] There were fifteen Lords of Session, headed by a Lord President. For much of its history the Court of Session was a unitary court, with questions of importance being determined by all fifteen judges sitting together, or at least by a majority of such judges. Certain preliminary matters, however, including evidence from witnesses, were heard by a single judge in the 'Outer House' of the court. Judges sat in the Outer House by rotation. The full court sat in the 'Inner House'. The names reflect the geography of the building.[2]

In 1808, after many years of discussion, a process of reorganization began which was completed by 1830. This inaugurated the modern court. Only eight judges now sat in the Inner House, in two divisions of four judges. The First Division was chaired by the Lord President and the Second Division by the Lord Justice-Clerk.[3] The remaining judges sat as Lords Ordinary in the Outer House. Cases at first instance were heard by a single Lord Ordinary, and the Inner House was transformed into a court of appeal. Appeals might be heard by either Division, and each had equal status. Today an ad hoc Extra Division often sits due to pressure of business. The modern practice is for Divisions of the Inner House to sit with three judges.

No systematic law reporting was undertaken until the eighteenth century. Before that time decisions of the Court of Session were collected privately, by judges or advocates. The reports are generally brief and sometimes difficult to understand, and there are a number of gaps, particularly in the early period. The first collection is Sinclair's *Practicks* which begins in 1540, some eight years after the Court of Session was established.[4] Many of the collections circulated only

---

[1] The story is a complex one: see Chapter 2.
[2] Or rather of two buildings, for before Parliament House the Court met in the Tolbooth. The names were already in use for the earlier building.
[3] For a list of Lords President and Lords Justice-Clerk, see G. C. H. Paton (ed.), *An Introduction to Scottish Legal History*, Stair Society, vol. 20 (1958), 459.
[4] A. L. Murray, 'Sinclair's Practicks', in A. Harding (ed.), *Lawmaking and Lawmakers in British History* (Royal Historical Society, 1980), 90 sqq. For the role of practicks in law reporting, see Hector McKechnie, 'Practicks', in Hector McKecknie (ed.), *An Introductory Survey of the Sources and Literature of Scots Law*, Stair Society, vol. 1 (1936).

in manuscript and either remained unpublished, or were not published until long after they were first prepared. Balfour's *Practicks*, for example, which was completed in 1579, was not published until 1754.[5] The publication of Lord Elchies's collection of decisions, which covers the period from 1733 to 1754, had to wait until 1813.[6] Sinclair's *Practicks* remains unpublished to this day although his cases often found their way into later works.[7] No decision of the Court of Session appeared in print before 1683,[8] and it was not until the following century that a substantial programme of publication was undertaken.[9] An indispensable guide to the early collections of reports, both published and unpublished, is the notes appended to Tait's *Index to the Decisions of the Court of Session* (1823).[10] The Stair Society's volume on *The Sources and Literature of Scots Law*[11] gives a complete list of the printed law reports.

In the private collections decisions were sometimes arranged by subject matter, as in the *Practicks* of Balfour and Hope. More usually the arrangement was chronological, with the result that decisions on particular topics were difficult to trace. It was partly to remedy this difficulty that Henry Home, later Lord Kames, published in 1741 *The Decisions of the Court of Session from its first Institution to the Present Time, Abridged, and Digested under proper Heads, in Form of a Dictionary* (cited as 'Fol Dic' or 'K&W Dic'). The work was in two volumes and brought together many of the cases from existing collections, both published and unpublished. Two supplementary volumes, by Alexander Fraser Tytler (later Lord Woodhouselee), were published in 1770 and 1797. Shortly thereafter Kames's *Dictionary* was superseded by a much more ambitious work of the same name prepared by William Maxwell Morison.[12]

---

[5] The 1754 edition was reproduced as vols. 21 and 22 in the Stair Society series (1962–3).

[6] It was published as Appendix II, Branch I of Morison's *Dictionary*.

[7] A provisional text of Sinclair's *Practicks* was prepared by Professor Gero Dolozalek, now of the University of Leipzig, in 1996. This is based primarily on a transcription by Dr A. L. Murray from the manuscript at Edinburgh University Library La. III 488a, with some supplementary case reports.

[8] The first volume of Stair's *Decisions of the Court of Session* was pubished in 1683, and the second in 1687.

[9] For law reporting in the 18th century, see David M. Walker, *A Legal History of Scotland*, vol. 5 (1998), 5–17.

[10] W. Tait, *Index to the Decisions of the Court of Session, Contained in all the Original Collections and in Mr Morison's Dictionary of Decisions* (1823), 499 sqq. This includes incidental information of considerable interest, such as the current prices of the various collections, and (on p. 511) an account of which volumes a lawyer would need in order to have proper coverage of the decisions of the court.

[11] J. S. Leadbetter, 'The Printed Law Reports 1540–1935', in Hector McKechnie (ed.), *An Introductory Survey of the Sources and Literature of Scots Law*, Stair Society, vol. 1 (1936), 47–58. And see also David M. Walker, *The Scottish Legal System* (7th edn., 1997), 474–80.

[12] Tait (n. 10), 518 explains the relationship thus: 'He [Morison] has given at full length what they [Lords Kames and Woodhouselee] have abridged: In every other respect, his Dictionary is just a new edition of Kames' Dictionary, with Woodhouselee's and McGrugar's Supplements, and the Faculty Decisions up to 1808, incorporated.' By Tait's time (1823), nearly 750 copies had been sold (Tait, 525), an impressively high figure. The price by then was £52 10s. (Tait, 527).

Morison's *Dictionary* (cited as 'Mor') was published between 1801 and 1804, but with a later appendix which included cases up to the reorganization of the Court of Session in 1808.[13] It comprises nineteen substantial volumes,[14] and even today is the main published source for cases up to 1808. A *Synopsis*, also prepared by Morison, continued the work as far as 1816.[15] The *Dictionary* reproduced the reports contained in all existing collections of decisions and was intended to replace them. Many were previously unpublished, the title-page describing the *Dictionary* as being one 'in which all the decisions in manuscript in the Library of the Faculty of Advocates are published for the first time, and those formerly printed are corrected'. Nonetheless there were numerous and important omissions, not least the 1,500 decisions collected in Fountainhall's printed reports.[16] Tait's estimate was of 10,000 omitted decisions, from both published and unpublished collections.[17] These omissions were substantially repaired by Mungo P. Brown's five-volume *Supplement to the Dictionary of Decisions of the Court of Session* (1826) (cited as 'Brown's Supp')[18] and by a *Supplemental Volume* published in 1815 by Morison himself. Tait's *Index* (1823) has the important merit of collecting together all reported interlocutors pronounced in the same case, which under pre-1808 procedure might be numerous as well as contradictory. That sometimes these are contained in different collections emphasizes the dangers of relying only on Morison's *Dictionary* or other single source.

Private reporting continued into the nineteenth century,[19] but in 1752 the Faculty of Advocates, after several false starts, succeeded in inaugurating a series of law reports which came to be published with reasonable regularity. This *Faculty Collection* (cited as 'FC') ran from 1752 to 1825, and was succeeded in 1825 by the more elaborate *Faculty Decisions* (cited as 'Fac Dec'). The coverage, however, was far from complete, particularly in the early years. The growth in law reporting was accompanied, and no doubt in part caused, by an increasing tendency for judges to elaborate on the reasons for their decisions. In turn this was due both to the reorganization of the Court of Session, mentioned earlier, and also to a more developed concept of precedent.[20]

---

[13] This is sometimes known as Appendix I, but the *Dictionary* is usually bound in such a way that the relevant parts of the appendix appear after each title.

[14] As normally bound today. Originally it was issued in 38 volumes.

[15] This should not be confused with Morison's other *Synopsis*, published as volumes 20 and 21 of the *Dictionary*, which is a digest of the cases in the *Dictionary*.

[16] Fountainhall's *Decisions*, which were published in two volumes in 1759 and 1761, cover the period 1678–1712.

[17] For the details, see Tait (n. 10), 516 sqq. See also the preface to M. P. Brown's *General Synopsis of the Decisions of the Court of Session* (1829).

[18] In this volume. It is also commonly cited as 'BS'.

[19] The last collection along traditional lines was by Baron Hume, published in 1839 and covering the period 1781–1822.

[20] G. Maher and T. B. Smith, 'Judicial Precedent', in *The Laws of Scotland: Stair Memorial Encyclopaedia*, vol. 22 (1987), § 249 sqq.

For a time, *Faculty Decisions* ran in parallel with a new series of reports which, beginning in 1821, was to become known as *Session Cases*. At first the aim was the modest one of providing a brief summary of cases which could act as an index to the full collections of papers (known as session papers) which were lodged in the Advocates' Library. There was no intention to compete with the much fuller reports contained in *Faculty Decisions*:

> They [the authors] do not pretend to offer either a selection or a detailed report of the cases,—that being the duty of the Gentlemen appointed to collect the Decisions. They have given neither the arguments of the parties, nor even the authorities; but have confined themselves to a short notice of each case, which they hope may convey an intelligible account of it, enabling those who wish to inquire farther to consult the Collection itself. Occasionally they have also briefly introduced those observations which were made on the Bench, tending to illustrate the decision, or to explain or correct former cases.[21]

Before long, however, the reports in *Session Cases* rivalled in length those in *Faculty Decisions*,[22] and the latter ceased publication in 1841. Today *Session Cases* remains the leading series of reports of decisions of the Court of Session. A volume has been published for every calendar year since 1821. For the period until 1906 the volumes are cited by the names of the principal reporter, as follows:

Shaw	16 vols. 1821–38	(cited e.g. (1831) 10 S 443)
Dunlop	24 vols. 1838–62	(cited e.g. (1840) 3 D 291)
Macpherson	11 vols. 1862–73	(cited e.g. (1872) 10 M 71)
Rettie	25 vols. 1873–98	(cited e.g. (1891) 17 R 272)
Fraser	8 vols. 1898–1906	(cited e.g. (1906) 8 F 365)

From 1907 onwards, when the series was taken over by the Faculty of Advocates, the annual volumes are cited simply as 'SC' (e.g. '1932 SC 21'). Since 1957 Session Cases have been published by the Scottish Council of Law Reporting.

The 1820s also saw the launch of a third series of reports, the *Scottish Jurist* (cited 'SJ'), with the ambitious programme of a fresh issue every Monday during court term containing 'authentic information regarding the judicial occurrences of the week immediately preceding'.[23] The series eventually ran to forty-five annual volumes and covers the years between

---

[21] Introduction to the first volume ((1822) 1 S), ii–iii.
[22] The first five volumes were reissued in 1834 (cited e.g. '(1821) 1 S 235 (NE)'). In recognition of the fact that the early reports had been 'exceedingly brief' (p. xi of the reissued vol. 1), the first three volumes incorporate fuller reports.
[23] *Scottish Jurist*, vol. 1 (1829), 1. More than law reporting was offered: 'To render this work as inviting as is possible, in consistency with its leading objects, to the general reader, the proprietors have likewise resolved to introduce, as often as space and opportunity are afforded, the temperate and dispassionate discussion of legal questions . . .'

1829 and 1873. The transformation of law reporting during the 1820s was indeed remarkable. At the start of the decade there was only *Faculty Collection*, which appeared irregularly, and was usually several years in arrears. The first volume of the decade, published in 1821, reported cases from as long before as November 1815. By the decade's close, this leisurely approach to law reporting had been challenged, first by Patrick Shaw's *Session Cases*, with its prompt annual volumes, and later by the weekly parts of the *Scottish Jurist*. Nor was this all. In 1826 Patrick Shaw launched a separate series of reports of House of Lords appeals.[24] Tait's *Index* was published in 1823, Brown's *Supplement* in 1826, and the same author's *Synopsis* in 1829. 'Such as devote themselves seriously to the *Profession* of the Law', proclaimed the *Scottish Jurist* in 1829,[25] require immediate access to the decisions of the court: 'Not unfrequently a question may be decided to-day, establishing legal doctrines or points of form never previously considered, which, before a fortnight has elapsed, may be used as precedents in judging or regulating the most important analogous cases.' The situation was exaggerated, no doubt, for a new publication needs subscribers. Nonetheless the impression is of a legal system in a process of rapid change.

Newspapers also contained law reports, and in 1865 the *Scottish Law Reporter* (cited 'SLR') was launched mainly with the purpose of printing cases which had already appeared in the *Edinburgh Courant*. This was also a weekly publication, and seems to have won the circulation battle against the *Scottish Jurist*, which ceased publication, in mid-sentence, on 5 November 1873, part of the way through its forty-sixth volume.[26] In 1893 the *Scottish Law Reporter* was joined by another weekly publication, the *Scots Law Times* (cited 'SLT') which quickly flourished[27] and remains today a leading series of law reports, now available on CD-ROM.[28] The *Scottish Law Reporter*, however, ceased publication in 1924.

Session Cases and the *Scots Law Times* were joined in 1987 by *Scottish Civil Law Reports* (cited 'SCLR'), which included commentaries on some of the cases. Since the beginning of *Session Cases* in 1822, therefore, there have always been two, and sometimes three, series of law reports running concurrently. The reports issued in weekly parts have usually reported a wider range

---

[24] Discussed below.   [25] *Scottish Jurist*, vol. 1 (1829), 1.

[26] The unfinished sentence, on p. 80 of the 46th volume, is: 'The correspondence thus makes it plain that the purchaser who proposed the clause understood and stated when he pro-'. The *Scots Revised Reports* (1907), which reprint, sometimes selectively, the earlier volumes of *Session Cases* and of House of Lords reports, include a most useful volume of cases reported only in the *Scottish Jurist*.

[27] The Prefatory Note to the first bound volume refers to 'the steady and flattering increase in the circulation as the year has gone on' with the result that the financial success of the enterprise was placed 'far beyond doubt'.

[28] For a review, see Eric Clive, 'A Hundred Years of the SLT', 1993 *SLT* 171.

of cases than *Session Cases*, and where the same cases are reported in more than one series there are sometimes small discrepancies.[29]

Greens Weekly Digest (cited 'GWD') was started in 1986 to give early notice of decisions of the court, not all of which are later reported. The full text of Court of Session opinions from September 1998 onwards is available on the Scottish Courts' Web Site: www.scotcourts.gov.uk/

II. HOUSE OF LORDS

Although appeals from the Court of Session to the House of Lords began with the Union, in 1707, they went virtually unreported until the beginning of the nineteenth century. David Robertson, a barrister of the Middle Temple who in 1807 published the first volume of a projected series of reports covering appeals made 100 years earlier, attributed this neglect in part to 'the jealousy that was entertained by the Courts and by the Practitioners of the Law of Scotland, of the new appellate Jurisdiction'.[30] One result was that a decision relied on in argument might, unknown to both parties, turn out to have been overturned on appeal.

Contemporaneous reporting was initiated by Patrick Shaw, who was also responsible for the early volumes of *Session Cases*. The first volume of Shaw's reports, covering the period 1821–3, was published in 1826 and inaugurated a series which lasted until 1865. The volumes are cited by the names of the reporters, as follows:

Shaw	2 vols. 1821–6	(cited e.g. (1821) 1 Sh App 43)
Wilson & Shaw	7 vols. 1825–35	(cited e.g. (1828) 3 W & S 230)
Shaw & Maclean	3 vols. 1835–8	(cited e.g. (1836) 2 Sh & Macl 431)
Maclean & Robinson	1 vol. 1839	(cited e.g. (1839) Macl & R 22)
Robinson	2 vols. 1840–1	(cited e.g. (1840) 1 Rob 296)
Bell	7 vols. 1842–50	(cited e.g. (1848) 5 Bell App 325)
Macqueen	4 vols. 1851–65	(cited e.g. (1852) 1 Macq 237)

Reports of some Scottish appeals also appeared in a collection begun by an English barrister, Dow, in 1814. Dow published six volumes altogether which covered the period 1813–18. Another barrister, Bligh, followed this with three volumes reporting appeals from 1819 to 1821. There were later volumes, although they are not generally used in Scotland.[31]

---

[29] Some examples of discrepancies are given in William W. McBryde, 'The Citation of Cases in Court', in Hector L. MacQueen (ed.), *Scots Law into the 21st Century: Essays in Honour of W. A. Wilson* (1996), 178.

[30] *Reports of Cases on Appeal from Scotland decided in the House of Peers* (1807), xv. See also A. Dewar Gibb, *Law from over the Border* (1950).

[31] They are listed in Leadbetter (n. 11), 57.

Session Cases began to include reports from the House of Lords from volume 13 of Dunlop's reports in 1850 (cited 'D (HL)', later 'SC (HL)') and these came to replace the separate series. There remained the question of filling the gap beween 1707 and the beginning of Shaw's first volume in 1821.[32] As already mentioned, David Robertson had published a single volume in 1807 (cited 'Robert') which covered appeals from 1707 to 1727. Much later, between 1849 and 1856, Thomas S. Paton[33] produced six volumes of reports (cited 'Pat App') covering the period from 1726 to 1821. Since 14 November 1996 new judgments of the House of Lords have been available on the House of Lords Website: www.parliament.the-stationery-office.co.uk/pa/ld/ldjudinf.htm

III. SHERIFF COURT

The sheriff court is the local court in Scotland, with jurisdiction in both criminal and civil matters.[34] The first printed collection of reports from the sheriff court appeared under the editorship of Sheriff William Guthrie in 1879.[35] By the time that Guthrie's second (and final) volume appeared, in 1894, a series of annual *Sheriff Court Reports* (cited 'Sh Ct Rep') had been launched. These were published from 1885 to 1963 as part of the *Scottish Law Review* (cited 'SL Rev'). Later, sheriff court reports were included in the *Scots Law Times*, where they were (and are) paginated separately (cited as 'SLT (Sh Ct)'), and in *Scottish Civil Law Reports*.

IV. DIGESTS

Law reports were (and are) usually arranged chronologically, with the result that cases on particular topics could (and can) be traced only through the use of digests. M. P. Brown's *A General Synopsis of the Decisions of the Court of Session from its Institution until November 1827*, published in 1829 in four volumes, is a digest of the main collections of decisions of the Court of Session, including Morison's *Dictionary*, Brown's *Supplement*, and *Faculty Collection* after 1808 (when Morison's *Dictionary* finished). From a slightly earlier period, Halkerston's *Compendium* (1819) digested *Faculty Collection*

---

[32] Some coverage of this period was provided at the beginning of the 19th century in the *Abstract of the Judgements of the House of Lords in Appealed Cases, from 1708 to 1773* compiled by Archibald Swinton and continued, as far as 1814, by Morison. For the shortcomings of this *Abstract*, see Tait (n. 10), 528 sqq.
[33] The first volume was produced with John Craigie and John Shaw Stewart.
[34] For the jurisdiction of the sheriff court, see Walker (n. 11), 273 sqq.
[35] *Select Cases Decided in the Sheriff Courts of Scotland* (1879) Cited as 'Guth Sh Cas'.

from its inception in 1752. The *Scots Digest*, published in 1908 in four volumes, covered all reported decisions of the years 1800 to 1873 as well as decisions of the House of Lords from 1707. Supplementary volumes continued the digest to 1947. A parallel publication, *Faculty Digest*, was published by the Faculty of Advocates in 1924 and covered the period 1868 to 1922.[36] Thereafter a number of supplementary volumes appeared, covering periods of ten years, the most recent being the volume for the 1980s.[37] The *Sheriff Court Digest*, in five volumes, covers the period 1885–1944, and there is a separate *Digest of Sheriff Court Cases Selected from the Scots Law Times 1893–1943* (1944). *Scottish Current Law*, which began in 1948 and is now available on CD-ROM, digests both cases and statutes. Case reports which are held electronically are searchable by computer. Scottish case reports are held on the Lexis database, and it is understood that they are shortly to be held on the Westlaw database.

[36] This was viewed as a continuation of Shaw's *Digest* which covered the period 1800–68.
[37] Published in 1999.

1

The Development of Legal Doctrine in a Mixed System

KENNETH REID and REINHARD ZIMMERMANN

I. MIXED LEGAL SYSTEMS AND THE PLACE OF SCOTS LAW

1. Civil law and common law

Private law scholarship in Europe has been, for about 150 years, predominantly national in substance, outlook and approach.[1] In continental Europe, it has tended to accept the *lex positiva* as an immovable boundary of its intellectual endeavours and to solve all legal problems on the basis, and within the conceptual confines, of a national codification. This state of affairs has repeatedly been criticized.[2] But it is only today that we see the age of more or less autonomous systems of national law gradually drawing to its close. The directives enacted by the Council of the European Union, the case law emanating from the European Court of Justice,[3] the legal problems arising from the application of the United Nations Convention on Contracts for the International Sale of Goods:[4] they all increasingly affect the legal condition in most Western European countries. Private law in Europe is in the process of reacquiring a transnational character.[5] The first textbooks have appeared

---

[1] On the *jus commune* prevailing before the period of legal nationalism see Helmut Coing, *Europäisches Privatrecht*, vol. 1 (1985); Manlio Bellomo, *The Common Legal Past of Europe 1000-1800* (1995); Reinhard Zimmermann, 'Das römisch-kanonische ius commune als Grundlage europäischer Rechtseinheit', 1992 *Juristenzeitung* 10 sqq.

[2] See Reinhard Zimmermann, 'Savigny's Legacy: Legal History, Comparative Law, and the Emergence of a European Legal Science', (1996) 112 LQR 576 sqq. (with further references).

[3] On the importance and character of which, see, for instance, the contributions by David A. O. Edward and Lord Mackenzie Stuart, both in David L. Carey Miller, and Reinhard Zimmermann (eds.), *The Civilian Tradition and Scots Law: Aberdeen Quincentenary Essays* (1997), 307 sqq., 351 sqq. For general background on legal unification by means of appeal courts decisions in states with several legal systems, see the symposium edited by Klaus Luig, (1997) 5 *ZEuP* 762 sqq.

[4] The Convention has been adopted by close to fifty states, among them ten member states of the European Union. Concerning Great Britain, see Barry Nicholas, *The United Kingdom and the Vienna Sales Convention: Another Case of Splendid Isolation?* (1993).

[5] See, e.g., the contributions in Nicolò Lipari (ed.), *Diritto Privato Europeo* (1997); Thomas G. Watkin (ed.), *The Europeanization of Law* (1998) (also covering other areas of the law); Arthur Hartkamp, Martijn Hesselink, et al. (eds.), *Towards a European Civil Code* (2nd edn., 1998); Peter-Christian Müller-Graff (ed.), *Gemeinsames Privatrecht in der Europäischen Gemeinschaft* (2nd edn., 1999). On contract law, see Reinhard Zimmermann, 'Konturen eines Europäischen

which analyse particular areas of law under a European perspective and deal with rules of English, French, or German law as local variations of a common theme.[6] Several legal periodicals are competing for the attention of lawyers interested in the development of European private law; and a number of international groups of academics are busy drafting 'Restatements' or 'Principles' of European contract,[7] tort,[8] or trust law.[9] We are living in an age of post-positivism.[10] The narrowness, but also the security, of a national system of private law is increasingly left behind and we are moving towards a new *jus commune*.[11]

It has sometimes been contended that all efforts aimed at the creation of a new *jus commune*, and of a European legal scholarship supporting and sustaining it, are doomed to failure in view of a deeply entrenched and irreducible chasm between the civil law and common law traditions.[12] This contention is exaggerated. On the one hand, it greatly overstates the insularity, or isolation, of the common law and its development. Roman law, canon law, indigenous customary law, feudal law, natural law theory, the law merchant: these were the most important ingredients in the development of continental law. All of them, in various ways, also shaped the English common law.[13] Protagonists of this development, on both sides of the Channel,

---

Vertragsrechts', 1995 *Juristenzeitung* 477 sqq.; Hans-Leo Weyers (ed.), *Europäisches Vertragsrecht* (1997); Jürgen Basedow, 'The Renascence of Uniform Law: European Contract Law and its Components', (1998) 18 *Legal Studies* 121 sqq.

[6] See the programme sketched by Hein Kötz, 'Gemeineuropäisches Zivilrecht', in *Festschrift für Konrad Zweigert* (1981), 498, and now implemented in Hein Kötz, *Europäisches Vertragsrecht*, vol. 1 (1996) (English translation by Tony Weir, 1997); Christian von Bar, *Gemeineuropäisches Deliktsrecht*, vol. 1 (1996) (an English translation appeared in 1998), vol. 2 (1999).

[7] Ole Lando and Hugh Beale (eds.), *Principles of European Contract Law* (1999) (incorporating a previously published part 1 (1995)).

[8] See now Jaap Spier and Olav A. Haazen, 'The European Group on Tort Law ("Tilburg Group") and the European Principles of Tort Law', (1999) 7 *ZEuP* 469 sqq.

[9] D. J. Hayton, S. C. J. J. Kortmann, and H. L. E. Verhagen (eds.), *Principles of European Trust Law* (1999).

[10] See Jürgen Basedow, 'Rechtssicherheit im europäischen Wirtschaftsrecht: Ein allgemeiner Rechtsgrundsatz im Lichte der wettbewerbsrechtlichen Rechtsprechung', (1996) 4 *ZEuP* 570 sqq.; Eugen Bucher, 'Recht—Geschichtlichkeit—Europa', in Bruno Schmidlin (ed.), *Vers un droit privé européen commun?—Skizzen zum gemeineuropäischen Privatrecht* (1994), 23.

[11] This new *jus commune* will have to be built around shared values and generally recognized legal methods as well as common principles and guiding maxims. See Jürgen Basedow, 'Anforderungen an eine europäische Zivilrechtsdogmatik', in Reinhard Zimmermann, Rolf Knütel, and Jens Peter Meincke (eds.), *Rechtsgeschichte und Privatrechtsdogmatik* (2000) 79 sqq.; Reiner Schulze, 'Allgemeine Rechtsgrundsätze und europäisches Privatrecht', (1993) 1 *ZEuP* 442 sqq.; Reinhard Zimmermann, *Roman Law, Contemporary Law, European Law: The Civilian Tradition Today* (forthcoming), 107 sqq.

[12] e.g. Pierre Legrand, 'Legal Traditions in Western Europe: The Limits of Commonality', in R. Jagtenberg, E. Örücü, and A. J. de Roos (eds.), *Transfrontier Mobility of Law* (1995), 63 sqq.; idem, 'European Legal Systems are Not Converging', (1996) 45 *ICLQ* 52 sqq.

[13] For an attempt to summarize the intellectual connections between civil law and common law, see Reinhard Zimmermann, 'Der europäische Charakter des englischen Rechts: Historische Verbindungen zwischen civil law und common law', (1993) 1 *ZEuP* 4 sqq.

have been Parliament, courts, and academic writers.[14] English law was an integral part of the 'Western legal tradition'.[15] On the other hand, any attempt to analyse the Western legal world in terms of a civil law/common law dichotomy is in danger of underrating the diversity within the civil law systems. The differences between French and German law may sometimes be as great, or even greater, than those between French and English, or German and English law; and this is true even in areas where both French and German law are based on Roman law.[16] This is attributable to the specific nature of the Roman sources as well as to the dynamic nature of the civilian tradition. The European legal landscape resembles a painting in many different shades and colours rather than a simple monochrome snapshot.

2. Mixed legal systems

Nonetheless, of course, it remains true that continental legal systems are codified whereas the English common law is not. Moreover, it is also true that the ideology of English lawyers is as much shaped by the nationalist historiography that originated in the nineteenth century[17] as that of their continental counterparts; and that the myth of being quite distinct has grown deep roots. If, therefore, the establishment of an intellectual connection between civil law and common law is regarded as an important prerequisite for the emergence of a genuinely European legal scholarship,[18] it should be of the greatest interest to see that such connection has already been established, on an intellectual as well as practical level, in a number of 'mixed' legal systems. Such systems provide a wealth of experience of how civil law and common law may be accommodated within one legal system. Comparative lawyers have indeed started to pay attention to mixed legal systems as potential models for 'procuring a gradual approximation of Civil Law and Common Law'.[19] First attempts are even being made to compare mixed legal systems with each other,[20] to explore their similarities and differences and to present them as a distinctive legal family.[21] Some members of that family have codified their

---

[14] On these protagonists of legal development in Europe see, in general, R.C. van Caenegem, *Judges, Legislators and Professors*, (1987); idem, *An Historical Introduction to Private Law* (1988), 170 sqq.   [15] Harold J. Berman, *Law and Revolution* (1983), 18.
[16] The argument is developed in Reinhard Zimmermann, 'The Civil Law in European Codes', in Carey Miller/Zimmermann (n. 3), 259 sqq. Cf. also the remarks in (1996) 112 *LQR* 590 sqq.
[17] Berman (n. 15), 17.
[18] For recent statements to that effect, see Axel Flessner, 'Die Rechtsvergleichung als Kundin der Rechtsgeschichte', (1999) 7 *ZEuP* 518 sq.; Mathias Reimann, 'Towards a European Civil Code: Why Continental Jurists Should Consult their Transatlantic Colleagues', (1999) 73 *Tul LR* 1341 sq.
[19] Konrad Zweigert and Hein Kötz, *An Introduction to Comparative Law* (3rd edn., 1998, tr. Tony Weir), 204.
[20] See e.g. Esin Örücü, Elspeth Attwooll, and Sean Coyle (eds.), *Studies in Legal Systems: Mixed and Mixing* (1996).
[21] Vernon V. Palmer (ed.), *Mixed Jurisdictions of the World: A Comparative Study* (forthcoming).

private law.[22] Others are still largely based today on common (in the sense of uncodified) law. They thus present the particularly fascinating picture of courts and legal writers still having to grapple with the historical sources of the *jus commune* and of the common law and thus being faced with the specific problems and challenges arising from a living interaction between civil law and common law.

3. South African Law

A few years ago, the first large-scale attempt was made to trace the history of legal doctrine in South African law: one of the two major uncodified mixed legal systems in the world. *Southern Cross*[23] provides stimulating insights into how a modern legal system with its own peculiar flavour emerged from civilian as well as common law roots.[24] It shows how the Dutch variant of the European *jus commune* that was transplanted to the Cape of Good Hope in the seventeenth century came under the influence of English law in the course of the nineteenth and early twentieth centuries and, in the process, acquired an identity which is neither purely Roman-Dutch nor purely English.[25] Of course, there are entire areas of the law where the balance has been tilted very much in one direction. The law of evidence, procedural law, and large parts of commercial law (especially those governed by statute) are mainly English. The law of things (property law) and succession, on the other hand, remain largely Roman-Dutch.

But even here we do not usually find the one strand of legal tradition continuing to exist in clinical purity. The law of procedure provides a good example. For, on the one hand, a particularly characteristic aspect of the English procedural model, the distinction between courts of law and courts of equity and the concomitant distinction between two distinct bodies, or levels, of law, was never received in South Africa.[26] On the other hand, the superimposition of a judicial and procedural framework of common law

---

[22] On the history of codification in Louisiana, and on Louisiana's mixed legal system in general, see Joachim Zekoll, 'Zwischen den Welten: Das Privatrecht von Louisiana als europäisch-amerikanische Mischrechtsordnung', in Reinhard Zimmermann (ed.), *Amerikanische Rechtskultur und europäisches Privatrecht: Impressionen aus der Neuen Welt* (1995), 11 sqq.; and now the essays in Vernon V. Palmer, *Louisiana: Microcosm of a Mixed Jurisdiction* (1999); for Quebec see e.g. H. Patrick Glenn, 'Québec: Mixité and Monism', in Örücü/Attwooll/Coyle (n. 20), 1 sqq.

[23] Reinhard Zimmermann and Daniel Visser (eds.), *Southern Cross: Civil Law and Common Law in South Africa* (1996).

[24] See, from a Scottish perspective, the reviews by George Gretton, (1997) 4 *Edinburgh LR* 501 ff. and Hector MacQueen, (1997) 17 *Legal Studies* 346 ff.

[25] For a general account, see Reinhard Zimmermann, *Das römisch-holländische Recht in Südafrika* (1983), 1 sqq.; Eduard Fagan, 'Roman-Dutch Law in its South African Historical Context', in Zimmermann/Visser (n. 23), 33 sqq.

[26] See Reinhard Zimmermann, 'Good Faith and Equity', in Zimmermann/Visser (n. 23), 217 sq.

origin upon the Roman-Dutch law had a decisive influence on South African judicial style which, in turn, could not fail to colour the way in which substantive rules of law were perceived and applied, even where they were of Roman-Dutch origin.[27] The law of obligations is probably that part of the law where the most complex process of blending of the two traditions has occurred. Here too, of course, there has sometimes been a competition of approaches, resulting, ultimately, in the rejection of one of them. Thus, South African law recognizes contracts in favour of third parties[28] and penalty clauses,[29] and it has rejected the doctrine of consideration.[30] In all three respects, the development of South African law has foreshadowed that of modern European private law.[31] More often, however, we find a complex process of interaction. One may think, by way of example, of the doctrine of offer and acceptance,[32] the analysis of the problem of mistake,[33] the impact of the doctrine of innocent misrepresentation,[34] the adoption of the notion of undue influence,[35] the development of the concept of anticipatory repudiation of a contract,[36] cancellation as a remedy for breach of contract,[37] the problems surrounding the right to specific performance,[38] the emergence of a generalized delictual liability for patrimonial loss caused wrongfully and culpably,[39] or the development of a refined body of rules dealing with the protection of personality rights.[40]

---

[27] For details, see the analysis by H. J. Erasmus, 'The Interaction of Substantive Law and Procedure', in Zimmermann/Visser (n. 23), 141 sqq.

[28] See David Joubert, 'Agency and Stipulatio Alteri', in Zimmermann/Visser (n. 23), 335 sqq.

[29] See Schalk van der Merwe, L. F. van Huyssteen, M. F. B. Reinecke, G. F. Lubbe, and J. G. Lotz, *Contract: General Principles* (1993), 315 sqq.

[30] The story of the rejection of the doctrine of consideration is told by Dale Hutchison, 'Contract Formation', in Zimmermann/Visser (n. 23), 166; cf. also Reinhard Zimmermann and Philip Sutherland, '"... a true science and not a feigned one": J. G. Kotzé (1849–1940), Chief Justice der Südafrikanischen Republik (Transvaal)', (1999) 116 *ZSS (RA)* 175 sqq.

[31] See, as far as the *Principles of European Contract Law* are concerned, Arts. 6:110 (Stipulation in Favour of a Third Party), 9:509 (Agreed Payment for Non-Performance) and 2:101 (Conditions for the Conclusion of a Contract); cf. also the comparative analysis (on the first two issues) presented in 1995 *Juristenzeitung* 483 and 487 sq.   [32] See Hutchison (n. 30), 173 sqq.

[33] Hutchison (n. 30), 180 sqq.; for general background see, most recently, Martin Josef Schermaier, 'Europäische Geistesgeschichte am Beispiel des Irrtumsrechts', (1998) 6 *ZEuP* 60 sqq.

[34] See Gerhard Lubbe, 'Voidable Contracts', in Zimmermann/Visser (n. 23), 264 sqq., 294 sqq.; Zimmermann (n. 26), 229 sqq.   [35] Lubbe (n. 34), 286 sqq., 294 sqq.

[36] Alfred Cockrell, 'Breach of Contract', in Zimmermann/Visser (n. 23), 314 sqq.; Zimmermann (n. 26), 251 sqq.   [37] Cockrell (n. 36), 320 sqq.

[38] Cockrell (n. 36), 325 sqq.; Zimmermann/Sutherland, (1999) 116 *ZSS (RA)* 166 sqq.

[39] See Dale Hutchison, 'Aquilian Liability II (Twentieth-Century)', in Zimmermann/Visser (n. 23), 595 sqq.

[40] See Jonathan M. Burchell, 'The Protection of Personality Rights', in Zimmermann/Visser (n. 23), 639 sqq.; Helge Walter, *Actio iniuriarum: Der Schutz der Persönlichkeit im südafrikanischen Privatrecht* (1996).

4. Scots law

The present volume may be seen, in many respects, as a companion volume to *Southern Cross*. It attempts to provide a doctrinal history of two core areas of Scots private law: the law of property and obligations. There are a number of interesting parallels in the development of Scots law and South African law.[41] Both may be classified as mixed jurisdictions today since they have received elements both from the English common law and from the continental civil law. Like South African law, Scots law has developed, since its inception, without codificatory intervention. Just as South African law has its old authorities (*ou skrywers*),[42] so Scots law has its 'institutional writers'.[43] The Scots Grotius was James Dalrymple, Viscount Stair. For in the same way that Hugo Grotius' *Inleydinge tot de Hollandsche Rechtsgeleertheyd* laid down Roman-Dutch law in the mid-seventeenth century,[44] the publication of Stair's *Institutions* some fifty years later constituted Roman-Scotch law.[45] The second half of the nineteenth century saw the ascendancy of English legal influence both in South Africa and in Scotland;[46] as in South Africa, a backlash occurred in Scotland towards the middle of this century against what was perceived to be an English intrusion. In both countries nationalistic sentiments have played their part.[47] But there are also very obvious differences in the legal development in both countries. Thus, in particular, neither the

---

[41] The parallels between Scots law and South African law as mixed legal systems were first pointed out by T. B. Smith, 'Scots Law and Roman-Dutch Law: A Shared Tradition', in *idem*, *Studies Critical and Comparative* (1962), 46 sqq. Contacts between private lawyers from both jurisdictions (first established by T. B. Smith and J. C. de Wet) were revived in the middle of the 1990s; see, in particular, Reinhard Zimmermann, 'Roman Law in a Mixed Legal System: The South African Experience', in Robin Evans-Jones (ed.), *The Civil Law Tradition in Scotland* (1995), 41 sqq.; Niall R. Whitty, 'The Civilian Tradition and Debates on Scots Law', 1996 *TSAR* 227 sqq., 442 sqq.; Alan Rodger, 'The Use of the Civil Law in Scottish Courts', in Carey Miller/Zimmermann (n. 3), 225 sqq.; Daniel Visser, 'Placing the Civilian Influence in Scotland: A Roman-Dutch Perspective', in Carey Miller/Zimmermann (n. 3), 239 sqq.; Hector MacQueen, 'Mixture or Muddle? In Defense of Revisionism in Scottish Legal History', (1997) 5 *ZEuP* 369 sqq.; Jacques du Plessis, 'The Promises and Pitfalls of Mixed Legal Systems: The South African and Scottish Experiences', 1998 *Stellenbosch LR* 338 sqq.

[42] See J. C. de Wet, *Die Ou Skrywers in Perspektief* (1988).

[43] See *The Laws of Scotland: Stair Memorial Encyclopedia*, vol. 22 (1987), §§ 443 sqq.; John W. Cairns, 'Institutional Writing Reconsidered', (1983) 4 *JLH* 76 sqq.; Peter Birks, 'More Logic and Less Experience: The Difference between Scots Law and English Law', in Carey Miller/Zimmermann (n. 3), 171 sqq.

[44] See Reinhard Zimmermann, 'Römisch-holländisches Recht- ein Überblick', in Robert Feenstra and Reinhard Zimmermann (eds.), *Das römisch-holländische Recht: Fortschritte des Zivilrechts im 17. und 18. Jahrhundert* (1992), 9 sqq., 26 sqq.

[45] On the term 'Roman-Scotch law', see John W. Cairns, 'The Civil Law Tradition in Scottish Legal Thought', in Carey Miller/Zimmermann (n. 3), 211.

[46] See Ben Beinart, 'The English Legal Contribution in South Africa: The Interaction of Civil and Common Law', 1981 *Acta Juridica* 7 sqq.; T. B. Smith, 'English Influences on the Law of Scotland', in *idem*, *Studies Critical and Comparative* (1962), 116 sqq.

[47] For South Africa, see Fagan (n. 25), 60 sqq.; for Scotland, see in particular T. B. Smith, *Studies Critical and Comparative* (1962).

reception of the civil law nor that of the common law ousted what may be termed an indigenous, Scottish common law.[48] South Africa, on the other hand, saw a complete transplantation of Roman-Dutch law in the seventeenth century; the indigenous, African customary law developed quite separately from the general law of the land.[49] Scots law, therefore, constitutes an even more complex *mélange* of different elements than South African law.

As in South Africa, vigorous debates have taken place about the proper sources and the true nature of Scots private law and about the way in which it has developed.[50] The relative importance of civil law and common law has been, and to some extent remains, a matter of keen controversy.[51] Equally controversial is the approach to be adopted towards the civilian sources of Scots law: should courts and legal writers attempt to explore Justinianic and classical Roman law as constituting the basis of the civilian tradition or should they turn their attention to the medieval and early modern *jus commune* of which Scots private law, for some time, was a province?[52] Is continuity of legal development one of the outstanding features of the history of Scots law,[53] or is it characterized by a record of 'false starts and rejected experiments'?[54] Is it a good thing or a bad thing to be a mixed legal system?[55] Obviously, the very open-ended texture of both South African and Scots law, and the nearly infinite variety of potentially relevant sources, can be a cause either of chaos or of perfection.[56] Scots law may be seen as a muddled system,[57] or, through other eyes, as a potential model for a European *jus commune*.[58] And indeed, like its Roman-Dutch counterpart in South Africa, the

---

[48] See e.g. W. D. H. Sellar, 'The Resilience of the Scottish Common Law', in Carey Miller/Zimmermann (n. 3), 149 sqq.

[49] See Reinhard Zimmermann and Daniel Visser, 'Introduction: South African Law as a Mixed Legal System', in Zimmermann/Visser (n. 23), 12 sqq.

[50] On the South African 'bellum juridicum', see Zimmermann (n. 41), 50 sqq. with references; for Scotland, see the assessment by MacQueen, (1997) 5 *ZEuP* 375 sqq.

[51] T. B. Smith, 'Strange Gods: The Crisis of Scots Law as a Civilian System', in *idem*, *Studies Critical and Comparative* (1962), 72 sqq.; Angelo D. M. Forte, 'A Great Future Behind it? Scottish Commercial Law and the Millennium', (1994) 2 *European Review of Private Law* 375 sqq.; Alan Rodger, 'Thinking about Scots Law', (1996) 1 *Edinburgh LR* 3 sqq.

[52] Alan Rodger, 'Roman Law Comes to Partick', in Evans-Jones (n. 41), 198 sqq.; *idem* (n. 41), 225 sqq.; Robin Evans-Jones, 'Civil Law in the Scottish Legal Tradition', in Evans-Jones (n. 41), 3 sqq.; *idem*, 'Unjust Enrichment, Contract and the Third Reception of Roman Law in Scotland', (1993) 109 *LQR* 663 sqq.

[53] See W. D. H. Sellar, 'A Historical Perspective', in M. C. Meston, W. D. H. Sellar, and Lord Cooper, *The Scottish Legal Tradition* (1991), 29 sqq.

[54] Lord Cooper, 'The Scottish Legal Tradition', in Meston/Sellar/Cooper (n. 53), 65 sqq. (70).

[55] This is the question asked by du Plessis, (1998) 9 *Stellenbosch LR* 338 sqq., 342 sqq.

[56] See Zimmermann (n. 41), 66 sqq.

[57] Robin Evans-Jones, 'Receptions of Law, Mixed Legal Systems and the Myth of the Genius of Scots Private Law', (1998) 114 *LQR* 228 sqq.

[58] See John Blackie and Niall Whitty, 'Scots Law and the New Ius Commune', in Hector L. MacQueen (ed.), *Scots Law into the 21st Century: Essays in Honour of W.A. Wilson* (1996), 65 sqq.; Hector MacQueen, 'Scots Law and the Road to the New Ius Commmune', *Ius Commune Lectures in European Private Law* 1/2000 (2000).

modern Scots law of obligations shares a number of characteristic features with other civilian legal systems: it recognizes the contract in favour of third parties (*jus quaesitum tertio*), it accepts an order for specific performance ('specific implement') as the primary right of a creditor, and it does not have a doctrine of consideration. But we also find at least an equal number of rules and institutions that Scots law shares with English law: an essentially unified concept of breach of contract, breach of contract by repudiation, or the doctrine of the unidentified principal in the law of agency. Hector MacQueen has drawn attention to the fact that in all these cases Scots law has anticipated the position eventually adopted by the European Contract Law Commission.[59] It is equally interesting to see that both Scotland and South Africa have developed, in different ways, civilian versions of the trust[60] and that the Scots model has exercised considerable influence on a first set of 'Principles of European Trust Law'.[61]

II. DOCTRINAL HISTORY IN SCOTLAND

1. Challenges

The history of legal doctrine in Scotland has been a subject of study since at least the eighteenth century,[62] and in recent years in particular much valuable work has been accomplished.[63] An overview account appeared in volume 20 of the Stair Society series,[64] a pioneering work in its day. More recently, David Walker has provided a fuller picture in his multi-volume *Legal History of Scotland*.[65] Nonetheless our view of the past remains strikingly incomplete.

---

[59] MacQueen (n. 58).
[60] See Tony Honoré, 'Trust', in Zimmermann/Visser (n. 23), 847 sqq.; George Gretton, 'Trusts', in this volume. For a comparison between South African and Scots trust law, see Tony Honoré, 'Obstacles to the Reception of Trust Law? The Examples of South Africa and Scotland', in Alfredo Mordechai Rabello (ed.), *Aequitas and Equity* (1997), 793 sqq.
[61] D. J. Hayton, S. C. J. J. Kortmann, and H. L. E. Verhagen (eds.), *Principles of European Trust Law* (1999); cf. K. G. C. Reid, 'National Report for Scotland', ibid. 68 sqq.
[62] Notable works from this period include Lord Kames, *Historical Law Tracts* (1759), and Walter Ross, *Lectures on the History and Practice of the Law of Scotland Relative to Conveyancing and Legal Diligence* (1792; 2nd edn., 1822). This, however, was very much the beginning, Ross (p. xvii) complaining that 'We have no history proper to our Law, but some loose unconnected hints, thrown out by Sir Thomas Craig, and Lord Stair'.
[63] For example, the two recent collections of essays edited by Evans-Jones (n. 41) and Carey Miller/Zimmermann (n. 3) examine doctrinal developments with reference to the civil law tradition and contain much material of value. The studies on European doctrinal history being published under the auspices of the *Gerda Henkel Stiftung* contain contributions on Scots law. Two of these (on negligence and on trusts) are reproduced in this volume. In addition, some of the leading texts on modern law contain historical material.
[64] G. C. H. Paton (ed.), *An Introduction to Scottish Legal History*, Stair Society, vol. 20 (1958).
[65] David M. Walker, *A Legal History of Scotland* (first vol., 1988). The most recent volume to be published was the fifth (1998) which deals with the 18th century. Each volume has a number of chapters on the subject of doctrine.

Often it seems a matter of chance which areas of law have and which have not been investigated, and there are many gaps.

The two volumes which comprise this work are an attempt to engage in doctrinal history in a more systematic way than has previously been possible. A team of contributors was assembled from a number of different countries and, at a preliminary meeting held in the University of Regensburg in January 1997, a common approach was discussed and agreed upon. Each contributor was then asked to prepare a paper on a selected area. An obvious model was *Southern Cross,* the companion volume on South African law.[66]

The result is not, of course, a full history of legal doctrine in Scotland. The coverage is confined to private law, and within private law to selected topics from the law of property and the law of obligations. A more comprehensive treatment, however desirable, would have required several volumes and a much longer period of preparation. Furthermore, the findings are, in one sense, provisional, for it would be the work of many lifetimes to do full justice to the sources on Scottish law. Published sources alone go back to the medieval period, including a substantial number of manuscript sources rendered into print and published by the Stair Society and other learned societies. Behind the published sources lies a rich body of material which is unpublished but yet readily available to the scholar: court records, protocol books, public registers, session papers, and so on.[67] It is an exciting, but also a daunting, prospect. If this work stimulates further research it will have achieved an important part of its purpose.

History is not objective truth. Faced with too much documentation, the historian must select, not only his sources, but also the material from within those sources. That which is discarded must await rediscovery at other hands; and in Scotland, at least, the wait is likely to be a long one. After selection there is interpretation. Indeed the two go hand in hand, for the main criterion of selection is likely to be an assessment of significance. Here there are obvious traps. The historian is separated from his material by the passage of time; and the fact that he knows how the story stands at present is bound to affect the way in which he describes its earlier stages. If that were not so it would not be necessary for each generation to rewrite its history. The historian can acknowledge the problem and fight against it, but it is unrealistic to expect complete success. Sometimes hindsight is even to be welcomed. If a doctrine flourished for a brief few years in the middle of the seventeenth century only to disappear without trace thereafter, it would be extravagant to dwell too

---

[66] Zimmermann/Visser (n. 23).

[67] The foundation text on the sources of Scots law remains *An Introductory Survey of the Sources and Literature of Scots Law* (1936) which was published as the first volume of the Stair Society series. An indispensable guide to the public records is the *Guide to the National Archives of Scotland* (1996), published jointly by the Scottish Record Office and the Stair Society.

long on it. A treatment of the law of servitudes which is historically balanced would be largely taken up with thirlage.[68]

The historian is trapped, not only by his knowledge of the present, but also by his hopes for the future. If the historian of law seems particularly vulnerable here, this is nowhere more true than in Scotland, where the relative importance of civil law and common law has been, and to some extent remains, a matter of keen controversy. Naturally, the contributors to this work have their own views on how the law should develop. There is an obvious temptation to use the past as a means of legitimizing the future.

If we have not avoided these traps in this work, we have at least been aware of them. This work does not set out to prove, or to disprove, any particular theory. Of course in one sense legal history seems always on the side of those who argue for the civil law tradition in Scots law. For, even allowing for a survival of Anglo-Norman law from the medieval period,[69] it can hardly be disputed that the main reception of English law did not occur until the nineteenth century. Hence, if priority of time determines priority of right, civil law (supplemented of course by homegrown law) can be presented as the 'true' law of Scotland, later to be polluted by the unwelcome attentions of English law. 'The common law cuckoo', wrote T. B. Smith, has 'laid too many eggs in the eagle's nest';[70] and, as the metaphor implies, the eagle was there first. This outlook may explain why civil law has received the greater attention from legal historians. There has been no book celebrating the common law tradition in Scots law.[71]

We take no sides in these debates. The two receptions, first of the civil law and then of English law, are fascinating, and complex, historical processes. In this work we seek to observe rather than to apportion credit or blame.

2. Justifications

'The history of law', wrote Lord Kames, 'in common with other histories, enjoys the privilege of gratifying curiosity'.[72] But quite apart from its intrinsic

---

[68] Thirlage was an obligation to take corn from particular land to a particular mill to be ground. Long since obsolete, it was formally abolished by the Abolition of Feudal Tenure etc. (Scotland) Act 2000, s. 55.

[69] Itself a controversial subject on which see e.g. W. D. H. Sellar, 'The Common Law of Scotland and the Common Law of England', in R. R. Davies (ed.), *The British Isles 1100–1500: Comparisons, Contrasts and Connections* (1988), 82; Whitty, 1996 *TSAR* 230 sqq.; MacQueen, (1997) 5 *ZEuP* 369; W. D. H. Sellar, 'Scots Law: Mixed from the Very Beginning? A Tale of Two Receptions', (2000) 4 *Edinburgh LR* 3.

[70] T. B. Smith, 'The Common Law Cuckoo', in *idem, Studies Critical and Comparative* (1962), 89.

[71] In contrast, there have been two volumes celebrating the civil law tradition: see above, n. 63.

[72] Lord Kames, *Historical Law Tracts* (4th edn., 1792), v. Ross (n. 62), xvi saw history as an aid to study, and later to practice: 'Would it not be better to give him [the student] some employment for his acquirements, to excite his recollections by historical allusions, to awaken his attention by pictures of ancient manners, and to surprise him now and then with a flower of the Belles

interest as part of the intellectual and cultural history of a nation, the history of legal doctrine is of obvious and special value to the lawyer. Two justifications in particular may be mentioned.

First, a study of history gives context and texture to contemporary law. The present law grows out of the past, and the future out of the present. A knowledge of legal history seems an indispensable guide both to the present law and to decision-making as to its future.

Secondly, an uncodified system makes no break with history, so that ancient history remains part of the living law. For the modern lawyer, however, the interpretation of historical sources is problematic. A fragment of law cannot be detached from the legal world in which it was created without violence to its meaning and significance, and the proper use of historical sources presupposes, in the user, a degree of historical sensitivity which in practice is often not attained.[73] The difficulty can be seen in case law.[74] The doctrine of precedent holds that a decision of the year 1800 is as valuable as a decision of the year 2000. But this seems to imply that the law has remained constant in the intervening 200 years or, in other words, that there has been no doctrinal development. Sometimes that may be true, but quite often it is not true. The elderly decision, or *obiter dictum*, relied upon may flow into a tributary of the law which has since dried up. In order to know whether this is so, decisions must be read against the background of the law as it was at the time they were pronounced and of subsequent doctrinal development. That this ideal is often not achievable is a weakness which seems inherent in the system.

Similar issues arise with the institutional writers. Modern Scots law has tended to canonize certain jurists while, until recently at least,[75] paying little attention to most others. While this mixture of regard and disregard may be further evidence of the 'mixed' nature of Scots law,[76] it leads to the

Lettres, amidst the brambles of his profession? ... Is it not a shame to see people, during the whole course of their lives, writing words, nay whole clauses of Deeds, they do not understand; and going gravely, like horses in a mill, the round of Forms, without knowing one iota of their origin, their progress, or even their present importance? The only reason they have to give for doing any thing is, that it has been done before. The least deviation, then, from practice, confounds and distracts them.'

[73] Hume, *Lectures*, I, 8: '[History] is necessary for enabling us to estimate, with accuracy, the weight we should allow the older decisions to have, in questions relative to the same subjects, when they occur in our own days.'

[74] The same is of course true of statutes. Thus Kames (n. 72), vi–vii: 'A statute, or any regulation, if we confine ourselves to the words, is seldom so perspicuous as to prevent errors, perhaps gross ones. In order to form a just notion of any statute, and to discover its spirit and intendment; we ought to be well informed how the law stood at the time, what defect was meant to be supplied, or what improvement made. These particulars require historical knowledge; and therefore, with respect to statute-law at least, such knowledge appears indispensable.'

[75] For the modern position see K. G. C. Reid, 'The Third Branch of the Profession: The Rise of the Academic Lawyer in Scotland', in MacQueen (ed.) (n. 58), 39.

[76] Until the mid-20th century much the same pattern was evident in South Africa. Since then the courts have taken note of contemporary academic writers. See Zimmermann/Visser (n. 49), 11.

awkwardness that the main juristic sources are historical treatises and, like all such sources, easily misunderstood. Furthermore, this canonization has led to a lack of curiosity about the institutional texts, which are read at face value, almost in the way that a statute might be read.[77] David Walker suggests that a dictum of an institutional writer carries the same weight, in the system of precedent, as a decision of the Inner House of the Court of Session.[78] Viewed historically, this is puzzling. The institutional texts are valuable accounts of the law of their time. They are scholarly, and also practical, guides. Stair's *Institutions* is, by any standards, a work of dazzling brilliance. But like all such texts they are likely to be derivative to some degree, and also prone to error. Neither topic has been much investigated by historians. In volume 2 of this work John Blackie shows that, in the field of defamation at least, Bankton borrowed heavily from Voet, so that in reading Bankton we are, unknowingly, reading Voet. Studies of Stair's *Institutions* have found examples of unacknowledged use of earlier works by Craig, Grotius, Vinnius, and Gudelinus.[79] Only careful textual study would show how often such patterns are repeated, in Stair and Bankton and in other writers. As for error, it is clear that their contemporaries regarded the institutional jurists as fallible. Stair, for example, was quite frequently not followed by the courts.[80] It was only later, in the early nineteenth century, that the idea of institutional writers emerged. Of course the more historians probe, the less secure the pedestal on which the institutional writers rest. There is an unresolved tension here between legal history and the methodology of the legal system.

3. Emerging themes

The chapters that follow reveal a rich and varied pattern of development. In the face of such diversity, general conclusions seem hazardous, but it is possible to identify some emerging themes. One is the crucial role of the civil law. Of the different influences which have combined to make modern Scots law, none endured so long, nor became so firmly entrenched. Already an important source of law in the later medieval period, civil law continued to provide new ideas and solutions until the end of the eighteenth century. By contrast, English law arrived all in a rush. Although there were already signs of English influence in the eighteenth century,[81] routine citation of English

---

[77] To this Stair's *Institutions* is a partial exception. See in particular D. M. Walker (ed.), *Stair Tercentenary Studies*, Stair Society, vol. 33, (1981); W. M. Gordon, 'Stair, Grotius and the Sources of Stair's Institutions', in J. A Ankum, J. E. Spruit, and F. B. J. Ankum (eds.), *Satura Roberto Feenstra Sexagesimum Quintum annum aetatis complenti ab alumnis collegis amicis oblata* (1985), 571.

[78] D. M. Walker, *Scottish Legal System* (7th edn., 1997), 457.

[79] Gordon (n. 77); Cairns (n. 45), 204 sqq.

[80] John Blackie, 'Stair's Later Reputation as a Jurist', in Walker (n. 77), 207 especially at 218 sq.; Cairns (1983) 4 *JLH* 76 sqq.

[81] This, of course, was the second reception of English law. The shared law of the Anglo-Norman period was mentioned earlier.

authority in the courts dates mainly from the second half of the nineteenth. By the end of the twentieth century there were signs that it was not always welcome.[82] Whether the influence of the common law hare exceeded that of the civil law tortoise is difficult to determine, and varied from topic to topic.

A second theme is the importance of period. In many of the areas covered by this work, the law was in a state of continuous, if not always rapid, change. Over time a doctrine might alter beyond recognition. When that occurred, authority from an earlier phase could no longer be treated as reliable, a fact which the modern lawyer may be apt to overlook. In some cases, a change in doctrine followed on from a change in sources. John Blackie's study of the law of defamation, for example, charts a gradual shift from *jus commune* to *Corpus Juris Civilis* to English law. Along the way, there was substantial doctrinal development, not all of it linked to the pattern of receptions.

Finally, there is the role of native thought and invention. It would be quite wrong to present the law in Scotland as a mere patchwork of the laws of other countries. A great deal of Scots law was made in Scotland, and even doctrine imported from elsewhere was generally assimilated and developed in a distinctive manner. If the law was incoherent, as often it was, this was not usually the result of different influences pulling in different directions. For the state of Scots law, the blame, and the credit, must go mainly to those lawyers who practised it and wrote about it.

[82] See e.g. *Rubislaw Land Co. Ltd* v. *Aberdeen Construction Group Ltd* 1999 GWD 14-647.

2

Historical Introduction

JOHN W. CAIRNS*

I. INTRODUCTION

In 1999, a Parliament with law-making powers once again began to sit in Edinburgh. As a devolved legislature, its competency to reform Scots law is not total, as certain areas are reserved to the Westminster Parliament. The new body's authority is sufficiently great, however, that the highly symbolic term 'Parliament' is appropriate to describe it. The direction in which this new legislature will ultimately take Scots law is unknown, although it will be unable to legislate contrary to the European Convention on Human Rights and will have to take into account the requirements of the European Union.[1]

In 1944, the late Lord Cooper of Culross wrote: 'There is a sense in which it is true to say that Scots Law has no history.' By this he meant that Scots law had no *continuous* history: 'its story is a record of false starts and rejected experiments'.[2] This is an overly dramatic way to conceptualize Scottish legal history. David Sellar has presented the strongest argument against Cooper and in favour of viewing the history of Scots law as essentially continuous.[3] Development of an appropriate model to explain the dynamic of continuity

---

* The author is much indebted to Mr Donald Jardine, Professor Hector MacQueen, Mr W. David H. Sellar, Professor Alan Watson, and Mr Niall Whitty for assistance and criticism. He gratefully acknowledges the permission of the Keeper of the Records of Scotland, of the Trustees of the National Library of Scotland, of the Brititsh Library Board, of the Keeper of the Muniments of the University of St Andrews, of the Librarian of Glasgow University, of the Royal Faculty of Procurators, and of the Librarian of Edinburgh University Library to cite and quote from unpublished manuscript material in their respective custodianship. Mr Angus Stewart, QC, Keeper of the Advocates' Library kindly granted a similar permission for law manuscripts in the collection of the Advocates' Library lodged for safekeeping in the National Library of Scotland (Adv. MSS). The author also benefited from kind access to a number of unpublished Ph.D. theses and permission to draw on material from a number of them. In this respect he is grateful in particular to Professor Hector MacQueen, Dr Alan Borthwick, Dr Trevor Chalmers, Dr John Finlay, Dr Mark Godfrey, Dr Clare Jackson, Dr Lesley Smith, and Dr Michael Wasser. This historical introduction derives from the author's forthcoming book. *A History of Scots Law* (2000). All dates are given as if the year started on 1 January. Original spellings have generally been preserved in quotations, while abbreviations have been expanded.

[1] Scotland Act 1998. See generally, C. M. G. Himsworth and C. R. Munro, *Devolution and the Scotland Bill* (1998).
[2] T. M. Cooper, *Select Scottish Cases of the Thirteenth Century* (1944), lxi.
[3] W. D. H. Sellar, 'The Common Law of Scotland and the Common Law of England', in R. R. Davies (ed.), *The British Isles 1100–1500: Comparisons, Contrast and Connections* (1988), 82–99.

and change in the history of any topic considered over a lengthy period of time is difficult; in the history of Scots law it has proved particularly so. This is partly because the source material for certain periods is scarce and partly because such source material as survives has not always been subjected to the careful scrutiny it deserves.

The following account will attempt to trace the changing nature of Scots law, focusing on its main institutions and taking into account the history of politics, social and economic life, and philosophy. The story will be told from the emergence of the Scottish kingdom to 1832. By this date, the basic architecture and much of the sculptural detail of Scots law was in place. An epilogue will review some subsequent developments. The picture that emerges is not one of 'false starts'. Nor is it one of simple continuity. In fact, the historical reality is too complex to reduce to simple descriptions or metaphors.

II. THE RISE OF THE SCOTTISH COMMON LAW, 1000–1286

1. The creation of the kingdom

Geography and people must be the starting point. The formation of the medieval kingdom was gradual. The original Scots were migrants from Ireland who, from around AD 500 settled in the west, creating their kingdom of Dalriada. To their east and north they encountered another Celtic people known as the Picts. By the ninth century, after a period of contact and intermarriage, the king of Scots, in the person of Kenneth mac Alpin, had also become king over the Picts, begetting the new kingdom of Alba or Scotia north of the Forth. The expansionist kings of Scots now looked south. The old British kingdom of Strathclyde, whose kings latterly had been clients of the mac Alpin dynasty, became incorporated into the kingdom of the Scots in the eleventh century. Contrariwise, the strongly Gaelic region of Galloway in the far south-west remained largely independent, until it recognized the sovereignty of David I (1124–53), although it did not come under direct Scottish control until subdued in 1160 by Malcolm IV (1153–65). South of the Forth, the area known as the Lothians had been settled by Angles and become part of the kingdom of Northumbria. The Scots started to occupy the Lothians as far south as the Lammermuir hills, perhaps even to the Tweed in the ninth and tenth centuries. The territory was finally acquired in 1018 after the battle of Carham. Aspects of the boundary with the emerging kingdom of England could vary or be debatable, but modern, mainland Scotland was now largely fixed.[4] The western isles were acquired under Alexander III

---

[4] See, generally, A. A. M. Duncan, *Scotland: The Making of the Kingdom: The Edinburgh History of Scotland*, vol. 1 (1975), 1–116; Michael Lynch, *Scotland: A New History* (1991), 1–50.

(1249–86), their repossession from the Norsemen symbolized by the defeat of the Norwegian king, Haakon IV, at the battle of Largs in 1263.[5] The northern isles came later, by treaties in 1468 and 1469, in wadset (security) for the payment of the (unpaid) dowry of Princess Margaret of Denmark, who married James III (1460–88) in 1469.[6]

Geographical divisions remained of immense importance and caused problems in the government of the country. A major division was between Scotland north and south of the Forth, a barrier made even more significant by the mosses and peat bogs west of Stirling. The Stirling area acted as a buffer between Scotia and the Lothians. North of the Forth, Scotia proper could be divided into areas such as Fife, Menteith, the Lennox, Gowrie, the Mearns, Mar, Buchan, Moray, and Ross, often corresponding to older administrative areas, lordships, and earldoms. To the south and the west were other distinct areas such as Strathclyde and Galloway.[7] It was to be of crucial importance, however, that the focus of the united realm in the later Middle Ages was the fertile lowlands, especially of the eastern seaboard. Their rich agricultural land and ports convenient for trade across the North Sea and to the Baltic allowed them to dominate, especially when the Norseman's occupation of the Western Isles for long reduced continuing Gaelic influence from Ireland. As the kings of Scots expanded their kingdom, they inevitably changed its nature.

In European terms, Scotland was thus a precocious kingdom, if not the most ancient kingdom in the world, as many writers were to claim in the seventeenth century.[8] By the eleventh century, something close to modern Scotland as a geographical entity can be recognized in the polity united under

---

A. P. Smyth, *Warlords and Holymen: Scotland AD 80–1000. The New History of Scotland*, vol. 1 (1984) has attracted some criticism because of the views expressed on the Picts and on certain other topics, such as the kingdom of Strathclyde: see W. D. H. Sellar, 'Warlords, Holy Men and Matrilineal Succession', (1985) 36 *Innes Review* 29–43. Alan MacQuarrie, 'The Kings of Strathclyde, *c.* 400–1018', in Alexander Grant and K. J. Stringer (eds.), *Medieval Scotland, Crown, Lordship and Community: Essays Presented to G. W. S. Barrow* (1993), 1–19; RRS, I, 12–13; RRS, II, 7–8, 13–14. See the maps showing the development of the frontier and the various parts of northern England held from to time by the Kings of Scots in P. G. B. McNeill and H. L. MacQueen (eds.), *Atlas of Scottish History to 1707* (1996), 79–80.

[5] Lynch (n. 4), 88–90.

[6] Ranald Nicholson, *Scotland: The Later Middle Ages. The Edinburgh History of Scotland*, vol. 2 (1974), 413–17; see also Gordon Donaldson, 'Problems of Sovereignty and Law in Orkney and Shetland', in W. D. H. Sellar (ed.), *Miscellany Two*, Stair Society, vol. 35 (1984), 13–40.

[7] See RRS, I, 36–44; RRS, II, 39–40. The starting point for a discussion of Galloway and the kingdom of the Scots must now be K. J. Stringer, 'Acts of Lordship: The Records of the Lords of Galloway to 1234', in Terry Brotherstone and David Ditchburn (eds.), *Freedom and Authority, Scotland c.1050–c.1650: Historical and Historiographical Essays Presented to Grant G. Simpson* (2000), 203–34.

[8] See Colin Kidd, *Subverting Scotland's Past: Scottish Whig Historians and the Creation of an Anglo-British Identity, 1689–c.1830* (1993), 25–7.

the kings of Scots. Their kingdom was diverse, but essentially Celtic, though all its early peoples have left their traces. But the evidence of its institutions and laws is slight, and, as Professor Duncan reminds us, we ought not to attempt 'by a wholesale importation of Irish institutions to fill out the exiguous evidence for the dark ages'.[9] What is clear is that reciprocal relationships of dependency held the society together in a land, much of which was divided into 'shires' or 'thanages' under the direction of an officer known as 'thane' or 'mair' or 'toiseach'. Larger divisions of the country were entrusted to 'mormaers' (later earls), one of whose functions was to raise the army.[10] Knowledge of the law was guarded by an official known as the *brithem* (in Latin *judex*) or dempster.[11] An officer known as the *toieaschdeor* perhaps had duties similar to those of the feudal sergeant and may have been concerned with the supervision of the dewars who guarded the sacred relics used in certain legal procedures.[12] It seems fair to assume that the later plentiful evidence of Celtic secular marriage and the practice of fostering sons with other families, thereby creating continuing ties of kinship, also reflects the practice of this era.[13] Indeed, the significance of kinship is underlined by the survival into the early modern period of the requirement that one seeking a remission of slaughter obtain a 'letter of slains' from the family of the victim: the root of 'slains' is the Gaelic technical term 'sláinte' meaning guarantee.[14] Later Scottish evidence also points to further elements of Celtic law as practised in Scotland.[15]

The diversity of the kingdom of the Scots left its traces, however. Anglo-Saxon terms such as 'shire', 'thane', 'moot' and 'hamsocn' entered Scottish practice, the last lasting as a term of art until the nineteenth century, while

---

[9] Duncan (n. 4), 106.

[10] McNeill/MacQueen (n. 4), 183–8; G. W. S. Barrow, *The Kingdom of the Scots: Government, Church and Society from the Eleventh to the Fourteenth Century* (1973), 7–68; idem, *Kingship and Unity: Scotland 1000–1306* (1981), 1–22; Alexander Grant, 'Thanes and Thanages, from the Eleventh to the Fourteenth Centuries', in Grant/Stringer (n. 4), 39–81.

[11] Barrow, *Kingdom* (n. 10), 69–82; W. D. H. Sellar, 'Celtic Law and Scots Law: Survival and Integration', [1989] 29 *Scottish Studies* 1–27 at 3–4; W. C. Dickinson (ed.), *The Sheriff Court Book of Fife, 1515–22*, Scottish History Society, Third Series, vol. 12 (1928), lxvi–lxix; D. S. Thomson, 'Gaelic Learned Orders and Literati in Medieval Scotland', (1968) 12 *Scottish Studies* 57–78; John Bannerman, 'The Lordship of the Isles', in J. M. Brown (now Wormald) (ed.), *Scottish Society in the Fifteenth Century* (1977), 209–40 at 227; Jean Munro and R. W. Munro (eds.), *The Acts of the Lords of the Isles, 1336–1493*, Scottish History Society, Fourth Series, vol. 22 (1986), xliii–xliv. The modern Gaelic term is *breitheamh*.

[12] W. C. Dickinson, 'The *Toschederach*', (1941) 53 *JR* 85–109; Sellar, [1989] 29 *Scottish Studies* 8–10.

[13] W. D. H. Sellar, 'Marriage, Divorce and Concubinage in Gaelic Scotland', (1981) 51 *Transactions of the Gaelic Society of Inverness* 464–95.

[14] Jenny Wormald, 'Bloodfeud, Kindred and Government in Early Modern Scotland', (1980) 87 *Past and Present* 54–97 at 62; Sellar, [1989] 29 *Scottish Studies* 11.

[15] Sellar, [1989] 29 *Scottish Studies* 15–17. See further below.

the third even became a loanword in Scots Gaelic.[16] Moreover, the Anglo-Saxon concept of the king's peace was later to play a major role in the development of Scots law.[17] The procedure of symbolically delineating the area of a court—known as fencing—was of Scandinavian origin, as were the birlawmen who dealt with issues of good neighbourhood.[18]

2. New directions

The law and institutions of this Celtic kingdom on the western fringe of Europe were to be dramatically shaken up by three events that took place within the space of a hundred years. In 1066, William of Normandy invaded England. Around 1100, Irnerius started to teach Roman law from Justinian's *Corpus Juris Civilis* in Bologna. Some forty years or so later, the basic text of the *Decretum* (or *Concordia Discordantium Canonum*) of Gratian was established, providing the first major collection of the canon law of the Catholic Church.[19]

William's invasion of England was significant in initiating the spread of feudal tenures and the reform of the mechanisms of government in England—developments that were to lead to the creation of a distinctive English common law by around 1200.[20] The causes of the evolution in England of a common law marked by a progressive monopolization of secular justice by the King remain controversial;[21] but, by the end of the twelfth century, with its system of royal writs, inquests, and juries, it had been summed up in the work known as Glanvill.[22]

(a) *Universities and* utrumque jus

By the end of the thirteenth century, universities teaching the *jus civile* had spread across much of southern Europe and had even reached England.

---

[16] Barrow, *Kingdom* (n. 10), 7–68; Grant (n. 10); Sellar, [1989] 29 *Scottish Studies* 6; J. W. Cairns, 'Hamesucken and the Major Premiss in the Libel, 1672–1770: Criminal Law in the Age of Enlightenment', in R. F. Hunter (ed.), *Justice and Crime: Essays in Honour of the Right Honourable The Lord Emslie M.B.E., P.C., LL.D., F.R.S.E.* (1993), 138–79.

[17] See Alan Harding, 'The Medieval Brieves of Protection and the Development of the Common Law', (1966) 11 *JR* 115–49.   [18] Duncan (n. 4), 106.

[19] See e.g. J. A. Brundage, *Medieval Canon Law* (1995), 44–69; Stephan Kuttner, 'The Revival of Jurisprudence', in *idem, Studies in the History of Medieval Canon Law* (1990), III (=R. L. Benson and G. Constable (eds.), *Renaissance and Renewal in the Twelfth Century* (1982), 299–323); *idem, Gratian and the Schools of Law, 1140–1234* (1983); Manlio Bellomo, *The Common Legal Past of Europe 1000–1800* (1995, tr. L. G. Cochrane), 58–70.

[20] See e.g. J. G. H. Hudson, *The Formation of the English Common Law: Law and Society in England from the Norman Conquest to Magna Carta* (1996).

[21] See e.g. S. F. C. Milsom, *The Legal Framework of English Feudalism* (1976); J. G. H. Hudson, *Land, Law, and Lordship in Anglo-Norman England* (1994); P. A. Brand, *The Making of the Common Law* (1992).

[22] See R. V. Turner, 'Who was the Author of *Glanvill*? Reflections on the Education of Henry II's Common Lawyers', (1990) 8 *Law and History Review* 97–127.

Study of the Roman texts made possible the compilation of an authoritative commentary in the *Glossa Ordinaria* of Accursius (died 1263), while many independent works were also produced.[23] It is telling that Gratian probably completed the first version of his *Decretum* in Bologna, where civil law was already taught, so that the canon law, from its beginning, was influenced by the civilian learning of the legists.[24] Study of both the laws, the *utrumque jus*, was common, although there were attempts to discourage the clergy from studying the civil law, which could require that those wishing to do so gain a dispensation.[25] The rapid development of canon law was an important part of the Church's attempt to enforce ecclesiastical discipline from the eleventh century onwards. Thus, popes issued decretals for the government of the Church, while Councils, such as the Third Lateran of 1179 and Fourth Lateran of 1215, issued decisions. Around 1230, Gregory IX commissioned the great canonist Raymond de Peñafort to compile the collection known as the *Liber Extra* or *Decretales Gregorii IX*. Subsequent decretals were gathered in the *Liber Sextus* promulgated in 1298 by Boniface VIII, while in 1317 came the *Clementinae* issued by John XXII, though planned by Clement V.[26]

(b) Norman influence

By 1070, the Norman invader had secured England as far north as the river Tees. The claimant to the English throne, Edgar, along with his sisters Margaret and Christina, had fled to Scotland in 1068, where Malcolm III (1058–93) (Canmore, *ceann mor*—probably meaning chief, but perhaps 'big head'), whose wife Ingibjorg was dead, had insisted on marrying the Princess Margaret. Malcolm and Ingibjorg had two sons, Duncan and Donald; Malcolm and Margaret were to have six sons and two daughters, three of the sons—Edgar (1097–1107), Alexander I (1107–24), and David I (1124–53)—eventually ruling as kings of Scots. In 1072, William of Normandy invaded Scotland, getting as far as Abernethy on the Tay. This invasion was ultimately inconsequential, but Malcolm may have offered homage to William, giving rise to a claim that was to plague the kings of Scots for centuries. The complex history of events after the death of Malcolm need not concern us, although it is worth noting that the English who had been with Malcolm

---

[23] See e.g. Bellomo (n. 19), 126–48, 169–74.

[24] On the development of the early law faculties, see Antonio García y García, 'The Faculties of Law', in H. de Ridder-Symoens (ed.), *A History of the University in Europe. Volume 1: Universities in the Middle Ages* (1992), 388–408.

[25] The prohibition was initiated by the constitution *Super Speculam* issued by Pope Honorius III in 1219; this was extended to Scotland in 1253 by the Bull *Dolentes*: see Walter Ullmann, 'Honorius III and the Prohibition of Legal Studies', (1948) 60 *JR* 177–86 (=George Garnett (ed.), *Law and Jurisdiction in the Middle Ages* (1988), XIII); Stephan Kuttner, 'Papst Honorius III. und das Studium des Zivilrechts', in *Festschrift für Martin Wolff* (1952) 79–101 (= *idem*, *Gratian and the Schools of Law 1140–1234* (1983), X).

[26] See e.g. Brundage (n. 19), 190–200; R. H. Helmholz, *The Spirit of Classical Canon Law* (1996), 15–17.

(presumably including his children) at one point were expelled; suffice it to say that, with the support of the English king, Wiliam Rufus, Edgar acquired the throne in 1097.[27]

In 1100, Matilda, the sister of Edgar, King of Scots, married Henry I of England; in 1102, Mary, his other sister, married the Count of Boulogne (her daughter, another Matilda, was to marry King Stephen). Taken together with the flight of the children of Malcolm and Margaret to England, these marriages (though probably designed to bolster the legitimacy of the claim of the Norman usurpers in England) indicate an increasing trend of English influence in the kingdom of the Scots.[28] Thus, David I, King of Scots, was educated as a knight in England, where he had even served as a royal justice. In 1113, he had been granted the double Earldom of Huntingdon and Northampton in the English Midlands as the husband of Maud de Senlis.[29]

During the successive reigns of the sons of Malcolm and Margaret, especially during that of David I, the institutions of Scottish government were transformed by the selective borrowing of the mechanisms used by the Normans in England. This development was intensified in the reigns of David's grandsons Malcolm IV (1153–65) and William I (1165–1214) and consolidated in those of William's son Alexander II (1214–49) and grandson Alexander III (1249–86).[30]

(c) Feudal tenures

Drawing on his English experience, David I started to grant land out on feudal tenure. In his reign, such grants had not spread north of the Forth; in those of his grandsons, feudal tenures are found beyond the Forth and Tay, though still confined to Lowland areas of Scotland.[31] The new knights' fees were generally awarded to men brought in from outwith Scotland, such as Normans, Bretons, Flemings, and French; some of these men came to Scotland from England, while others were recruited direct from continental Europe.[32] If some grants, such as that to Robert de Brus in Annandale for the service of ten knights, were large,[33] many in the Lothians, Fife, and the Mearns were granted in return for a single knight. Large grants were frequently subject to subinfeudation, creating, in conjunction with the fre-

---

[27] See Duncan (n. 4), 117–26; *idem*, 'The Earliest Scottish Charters', (1958) 37 *Scot Hist Rev* 103–35; Lynch (n. 4), 74–8.   [28] Duncan (n. 4), 126.
[29] K. J. Stringer, *Earl David of Huntingdon 1152–1219* (1985), 1–5; Barrow, *Kingdom* (n. 10), 280–3.
[30] See G. W. S. Barrow, *The Anglo-Norman Era in Scottish History* (1980), *passim*; *idem*, *Kingdom* (n. 10), 279–310; *idem*, *Kingship* (n. 10), 43–59.
[31] McNeill/MacQueen (n. 4), 412–13, 417.   [32] Barrow (n. 30), 61–117.
[33] G. W. S. Barrow (ed.), *The Charters of King David I: The Written Acts of David I King of Scots, 1124–1153 and of his Son Henry Earl of Northumberland, 1132–1152* (1999), 61–2 n. 16; A. C. Lawrie (ed.), *Early Scottish Charters Prior to A.D. 1153* (1905), 48–9 no. 54; RRS, II, 178–9 no. 80.

quent small royal grants, the large class of lairds that was to be such a distinct feature of later medieval and early modern Scotland.

There can be little doubt that the granting out of land as knights' fees was part of a policy of reinforcing royal control in the country. The new fiefs can be traced through the spread of mottes across the nation, as the innovation of castle building expressed a new dominance and power in the localities.[34] Where it was possible, the traditional earldoms were turned into feudal grants. Thus, William I appointed his brother David as Earl of Lennox in the 1170s for the service of ten knights in order to increase royal authority in this rich and strategic area.[35] As part of a strategy of feudalization of Moray after the defeat of the last mormaer, William also awarded the Lordship of Garioch to his brother.[36] David I not only granted lands in Midlothian to Duncan, Earl of Fife, on knight service, he also made a feudal grant to him of the earldom itself, probably in the 1130s.[37]

Such royal and other grants of land soon took on relatively standard forms, suggesting that, at least by the thirteenth century, there was a general understanding as to the main practices relating to land grants. These assumed tenure from a superior lord with set forms of service, such as knight service, burgage, blench, and free alms, and inheritance by a system of male primogeniture in which, failing sons, females could succeed.[38] Land one inherited (heritage) was also distinguished from land one acquired (conquest). Widows had legal rights of terce and widowers rights of courtesy.[39] All of this was borrowed from Anglo-Norman England. It is evident, however, that some aspects of tenures from Celtic Scotland were assimilated into this new mode of landholding, since certain Celtic terms for services and payments for land survived into the Scottish feudal system, emphasizing the force of customary norms in a largely oral system, even when faced with such massive innovation.[40]

(d) Royal justice

Other institutions were adapted from Anglo-Norman England to aid the kings of Scots impose their authority over their diverse realm and its peoples. Alongside the familiar mormaers (or earls), thanes, and mairs, on whom earlier kings of Scots had relied, came justiciars and sheriffs, while those to

---

[34] McNeill/MacQueen (n. 4), 430. [35] Stringer (n. 29), 14–18.
[36] Ibid. 30–55. [37] Barrow, *Kingdom* (n. 10), 283.
[38] G. W. S. Barrow, 'The Scots Charter', in H. Mayr-Harting and R. I. Moore (eds.), *Studies in Mediaeval History Presented to R. H. C. Davis* (1985), 149–64; P. R. Hyams, 'The Charter as a Source for the Early Common Law', (1991) 12 *Journal of Legal History* 173–89; H. L. MacQueen, *Common Law and Feudal Society in Medieval Scotland* (1993), 248–9.
[39] Sellar (n. 3), 89–90. Alexander II is found adjudicating on an issue of terce, demonstrating its general acceptance by his reign: APS, I, 401–2; Cooper (n. 2), 52–3 no. 39.
[40] Sellar, [1989] 29 *Scottish Studies* 15–17; C. J. Neville, 'A Celtic Enclave in Norman Scotland: Earl Gilbert and the Earldom of Strathearn, 1171–1223', in Brotherstone/Ditchburn (n. 7), 75–92. A major debate on 'feudalism', has been stimulated by Susan Reynolds, *Fiefs and Vassals: The Medieval Evidence Reinterpreted* (1994). I cannot comment on this here.

whom land had been granted were also generally given the right and duty to hold courts to exercise a delegated royal authority over their tenants. Moreover, while the primary motive for the promotion of settlements as burghs must have been economic, their erection created a new centre of authority and jurisdiction. These institutions need to be considered separately, although it should be noted that the evidence is far from complete.

The primary source of royal justice was the king in his *curia regis*, although evidence for its early existence is sparse. Access to the king directly for justice was restricted, however, and only arose either on the king's own initiative or as a favour to an individual or group.[41] The king regularly granted protections to individuals or bodies; should such protections be breached, he would intervene, while he would also act should there be failure of justice by another.[42] In this vein, he could issue orders to individuals to act in such a way that there would 'be no further complaint for default of right'.[43] The king also had the duty to ensure the keeping of the peace; from this developed the notion of the pleas of the Crown, those violations of public peace that were so heinous that the king had the responsibility of punishing them.[44]

(e) The justiciar

The king normally delegated his judicial functions to his justiciar, an office first recorded in the twelfth century, which was always held by men of the highest rank. The justiciar had general administrative functions, but the title suggests—although the evidence is unclear before the thirteenth century, but thereafter ample—that the office always involved the exercise of jurisdiction. The office was split on geographical lines, with a justiciar north of the Forth (who came typically to be described as of Scotia) and a justiciar of Lothian south of the Forth. Sometimes a separate justiciar of Galloway can be traced. In theory, the justiciar went on ayre (circuit) through his regions twice each year, holding courts at the head burgh of every sheriffdom.[45]

After 1245, at least in Lothian and probably also in Scotia, criminal proceedings before the justiciar were by indictment (or dittay). This procedure, borrowed directly from English practice, required suspects to be arrested and brought before the justiciar for trial. An accused was now to be indicted by a jury of presentment and then have his guilt or innocence established by an assize (visnet); in future, no one was to be attached by the king's sergeants ('*servientes domini Regis*') on the sole accusation of one man. Galloway, however, '*que leges suas habet speciales*' was specifically exempted from the legislation.[46] In 1292, the duties of the justiciars were described as '[to] know and

---

[41] MacQueen (n. 38), 42–3, 47–8.   [42] Harding, (1966) 11 *JR* 115–41.
[43] MacQueen (n. 38), 194–5.   [44] RRS, II, 178–9 no. 80; APS, I, 374–5 (c. 12).
[45] Barrow, *Kingdom* (n. 10), 83–139.
[46] APS, I, 403 (c. 14). John Stuart George Burnett (ed.), *Exchequer Rolls of Scotland* (1878–1908), I, 34 demonstrates that procedure by dittay was in use in Scotia by 1266.

be able to give law and right to poor as well as rich, and to preserve and control the right of the king in all points which belong to his crown'. This was to be done 'so that no complaints should be presented to the king, except for those only, which, because of the default of justices or sheriffs, cannot be remedied except in the presence of the king himself'.[47]

(f) The sheriff

Sheriffs can first be traced in the reign of David I.[48] By the death of Malcolm IV in 1165, they had replaced the thanes as royal administrators in centres of royal demesne in southern and eastern Scotland; north of the Forth, the spread of sheriffs was slowed by the large lordships, powerful earldoms, and large number of thanages. Their duties on behalf of the king will have been loosely defined, but included helping to collect the king's revenue, although there is no evidence of their holding courts at this early period.[49] By 1214, there is some ambiguous evidence that sheriffs may have started to hold courts; their remit had definitely widened, however, to include enforcement of teinds and recovery of fugitive serfs on behalf of the king's subjects, while sheriffdoms had spread further north to Moray.[50] By 1300, there was a relatively full network of sheriffdoms over Scotland, although the highest density was in the eastern and lowland areas; one of the most important functions of the sheriff was now to hold what was considered to be a royal court.[51]

(g) The burgh

From the early twelfth century, a number of Scottish urban settlements started to be given the rank of 'burgh', central to which was the granting of special status to those inhabitants who were burgesses, with privileges over trading, tenure, and jurisdiction. The early inhabitants were of diverse origin, many coming from Flanders, northern France, the Rhineland, and eastern England.[52] By 1210, there were around forty burghs in Scotland, no less than thirty of which were in the eastern half of the country.[53] Early government of the burgh was in the hands of the *prepositus* and *ballivi*, perhaps under the supervision of the local sheriff. By the early thirteenth century they can be found presiding over a burgh court: an obscure development perhaps related to freeing the burghs from the supervision of the sheriffs.[54] Though chosen by

---

[47] 'The Scottish King's Household', in *Miscellany of the Scottish History Society (Second Volume)*, Scottish History Society, First Series, vol. 44 (1904), 3–43 at 36–7.
[48] See Dickinson (n. 11), 347–68.   [49] RRS, I, 45–49; McNeill/MacQueen (n. 4), 192.
[50] RRS, II, 39–43; Duncan (n. 4), 204–8; McNeill/MacQueen (n. 4), 193.
[51] Duncan (n. 4), 596–9; MacQueen (n. 38), 49; McNeill/MacQueen (n. 4), 194.
[52] Barrow, *Kingship* (n. 10), 84–97; Duncan (n. 4), 463–501; Michael Lynch, Michael Spearman, and Geoffrey Stell (eds.), *The Scottish Medieval Town* (1988).
[53] Barrow, *Kingship* (n. 10), 87. For the spread of burghs up to 1300, see McNeill/MacQueen (n. 4), 196–8.
[54] H. L. MacQueen and W. J. Windram, 'Laws and Courts in the Burghs', in Lynch/Spearman/Stell (n. 52), 208–27 at 213.

the burgh community, the *prepositus* and *ballivi* were royal officers, which meant that the burgh court, as well as representing the burgh community, was a royal court. It had a jurisdiction that was in some respects limited, however, since it could not try very serious crimes; these had to be dealt with by the justiciar.[55] The chamberlain, an important member of the king's household, was supposed to travel to burghs once a year on ayre to investigate their proper administration and to ensure proper accounting for the king's revenue from his burghs; he also could hear appeals from their courts. Further, he presided over the Court of the Four Burghs (Berwick, Edinburgh, Roxburgh, and Stirling). This obscure body, first encountered in 1292, seems to have settled doubtful points of law and acted as a forum for appeal from the chamberlain ayre.[56]

The special privileges of the burghs, by the early thirteenth century, were judged to form a relatively homogeneous body of law, of which the most distinctive aspect was tenure *in burgagio*.[57] By 1270, the burgh laws had been collected as the *Leges burgorum*.[58] These require further study; it is worth stressing, however, that the privileges enjoyed by burgesses 'were introduced to Scotland by royal legislation, by the continuation of the settled customs and usages amongst burgesses outwith Scotland and perhaps by specific grants to individuals'.[59] The differences between the laws applied in the burgh courts and those applied in the sheriff courts should not be exaggerated.

(h) The Lords

For most Scots, secular justice was delivered by their lord and the developed baron court is a familiar institution of later medieval and early modern Scotland.[60] From the start of the Normanization of the Scottish administration, it became a regular practice for those to whom land was granted also to be awarded jurisdiction. Thus, both Dunfermline Abbey and St Andrews Priory had the right to hold courts bestowed on them, while David I's Abbey of Holyrood had the right of holding the *examen duelli, aque et ferris caldi*

---

[55] MacQueen/Windram (n. 54), 215.

[56] See W. C. Dickinson (ed.), *Early Records of the Burgh of Aberdeen 1317, 1398–1407*, Scottish History Society, Third Series, vol. 49 (1957), cxlii–cxlv; idem, 'A Chamberlain's Ayre in Aberdeen 1399 X 1400', (1954) 33 *Scot Hist Rev* 27–36; G. S. Pryde, 'Burgh Courts and Allied Jurisdictions', in G. C. H. Paton (ed.), *An Introduction to Scottish Legal History*, Stair Society, vol. 20 (1958), 384–95 at 392–4.

[57] See RRS, II, 437 no. 475 where William I grants to his burgesses of Inverness 'all the laws and right customs which all my other burgesses have living in my burghs in Scotland'.

[58] The earliest text is in the Berne MS: National Archives of Scotland (formerly Scottish Record Office), PA 5/1, starting at fo. 62ʳ. See MacQueen/Windram (n. 54), 209–11.

[59] MacQueen/Windram (n. 54), 212.

[60] See generally W. C. Dickinson (ed.), *The Court Book of the Barony of Carnwath 1523–1542*, Scottish History Society, Third Series, vol. 29 (1937). On the somewhat obscure origins of the barony in Scotland and its link with thanage, see R. R. Reid, 'Barony and Thanage', (1920) 35 *English Historical Review* 161–99 at 179–83; D. Roffe, 'From Thanage to Barony: Sake and Soke, Title, and Tenants-in-Chief', (1990) 12 *Anglo-Norman Studies* 157–76.

(that is to try by battle and the ordeals of water and iron), as indeed did those of Scone and Arbroath.[61] The Abbot's Court was also declared equal to the courts of the Bishop of St Andrews and the Abbots of Dunfermline and Kelso.[62] Early grants of knights' fees often did not specify jurisdictional rights, since it was common for charters to specify rights simply by comparison with the holdings of another.[63] Styles developed, however, until, during the reign of William I, the majority of infeftments for knight service bestowed grants of 'sac', 'soke', 'toll', 'team', and 'infangthief'. (The first two of these basically denoted a general police jurisdiction, including breach of the grantee's peace, bloodshed, civil cases involving the ordeal, and the right to take the profits of justice; 'toll' permitted the grantee to buy and sell on his land and require payment from any who did the same; 'team' concerned warranty of sales, especially of cattle, and to determine disputes arising out of that warranty; 'infangthief' entitled trial and execution of thieves taken on the land either red-handed or in possession of the stolen goods.) Some grants, probably in the case of larger estates, also awarded the right of *'furca et fossa'* ('pit and gallows'), a higher capital criminal jurisdiction, later to be the near-essential indicator of baronial jurisdiction in Scotland.[64] In its charter, Dunfermline Abbey was granted a particularly wide jurisdiction, of the type that would, in the fourteenth century, come to be described as that of a 'regality'.[65] The rights granted to a lord of regality would vary according to the charter, but could include the pleas of the Crown, thereby excluding the criminal jurisdiction of the justiciar, so that possessors of such rights would hold their own justice ayres and chamberlain ayres.[66] Whatever the precise nature of these grants, the reality is clear: those infeft with such rights had the duty to keep the peace on their holdings and ensure justice was done; failure would result in action by the king's servants.

(i) The suitors of the court

Central to the functioning of these new courts was the offering of suit by those who held land in the area of the court's jurisdiction: the king's tenants-in-chief at the sheriff court; burgesses at the burgh court; those holding land on feudal tenure at the court of their feudal superior; those who held land in a lordship at the court of their lord. In the early period, the king's tenants-in-chief and other important men were expected to attend the justice ayre. From the thirteenth century, suit of court was normally specified in a charter of infeftment, the nature of the suit (which could sometimes be offered by proxy)

---

[61] Barrow (n. 33), 70–2 no. 53, 122–5 no. 147, 114–15 no. 126; Lawrie (n. 33), 61–3 no. 74, 116–19 no. 153, 126–8 no. 163; RRS, I, 263–5 no. 243, 267 no. 247; RRS, II, 136 no. 27, 250–2 no. 197.   [62] RRS, II, 48.
[63] Ibid.   [64] See Reid, (1920) 35 *English Historical Review* 174–5; RRS, II, 48–50.
[65] J. M. Webster and A. A. M. Duncan (ed.), *Regality of Dunfermline Court Book 1531–1538* (1953), 3–6.   [66] Dickinson (n. 60), xxxix–xliv.

being set out in the charter; but the norm covered at least the three head courts of Michaelmas, Yule, and Pasch (Easter). Some individuals had to offer suit at intermediate courts, although there was a general practice of holding important business over for the head courts when the most important suitors attended. Absent suitors were fined, after the court and its peace had been formally fenced, marking its bounds and the limits of its peace. The sheriff or other officer of the king or lord presided; it was the suitors, however, who returned the judgment. This judgment (or doom) was delivered by the dempster whose presence was necessary for the proper constitution of the court; he might be one of the suitors, perhaps offering this service in return for his landholding.[67]

(j) Procedure and proof

The most significant way of initiating actions was by royal letters or brieves, which the litigant had to purchase from the royal chapel or writing house. The history of the development of the variety of brieves used in medieval Scotland is complex.[68] While, presumably, such an invocation of royal authority in a dispute between subjects had been exceptional and granted as a favour on an ad hoc basis, by the end of the thirteenth century, some brieves had already become *de cursu* or 'coursable', that is of standard form; others remained *de gratia*, that is, fashioned for a specific purpose. Some brieves were 'retourable', which meant that the sheriff had to hold an inquest and then return (retour) a reply to the royal chapel, where further steps would be taken: examples are brieves of inquest (to serve heirs to land) and tutory (to determine who had the right to act as tutor to a fatherless child). Another class was that of pleadable brieves, where a court would reach a decision on an issue identified by the parties through a procedure of pleas and exceptions; there would be no retour, as the court would itself implement the decision reached by an assize. Brieves of 'right' to recover land, of 'novel dissasine' to recover land from an individual who had put one out of it, and of 'mortancestry' to recover land on a right of inheritance were of this nature. There were other non-retourable brieves that were not, however, pleadable; these delimited boundaries, such as perambulation, or division, such as terce (where a widow was allocated a liferent of a third of her deceased spouse's lands). As the system developed, jurisdictional rules evolved, such as that

---

[67] Dickinson (n. 11), xv, lxvi–lxix, lxxii–lxxxvi; Dickinson (n. 56), cxvii, cxix, cxxii, cxxxviii; Dickinson (n. 60), lxxv–lxxvi, lxxxviii–xci; I. D. Willock, *The Origins and Development of the Jury in Scotland*, Stair Society, vol. 23 (1966), 75–6, 89–90; Duncan (n. 4), 405–7; Webster/ Duncan (n. 65), 6–7; P. Hamilton-Grierson, 'Fencing of Court', (1924) 21 *Scot Hist Rev* 54–62.

[68] For styles, see Lord Cooper (ed.), *The Register of Brieves as Contained in the Ayr MS., the Bute MS. and Quoniam Attachiamenta*, Stair Society, vol. 10 (1946).

brieves of mortancestry and novel dissasine had to be taken to the justiciar and brieves of right to the sheriff or burgh court.[69]

Most suits, however, will not have been initiated by brieve. Such suits of 'wrang and unlaw' will have been instituted by a complaint (perhaps either oral or by 'bill') to the relevant court; the pursuer probably had to find some caution or security before the court would execute a summons on a defender.[70] This must have been the normal method of bringing suits before a lord's court and is well attested for the early fourteenth century;[71] earlier practice will have been similar.

While there is little direct evidence of early procedure, proof could originally be by battle, ordeal, and compurgation (wager of law). The brieve of right initially led to trial by battle, which, though found in charter evidence, had become rare by the end of the thirteenth century.[72] Already by the time of William I, burgesses were being exempted from trial by battle and instead being tested by compurgation.[73] In the course of the thirteenth century, however, battle and ordeal started to give way to the empanelling of a jury or assize to determine issues of fact (as we have noticed for criminal procedure before the justiciar);[74] the newer brieves of novel dissasine and mortancestry had always assumed such a mode of proof.[75] At the Lateran Council of 1215, the Church had found against the use of the ordeal; although it is likely that such modes of proof were probably only used when there was no other way to determine an issue of fact.[76] However this may be, the jury must have been seen as offering an apparently more rational and satisfactory form of proof.

3. The Scottish common law

Inference of what happened in this early, formative period based on later evidence probably gives an overly formal picture of the operation of courts. In essence, they remained gatherings of the important men of the neighbourhood to settle disputes. Customary practices will have been enforced.

---

[69] See now, above all, MacQueen (n. 38), 105–214; *idem*, 'Pleadable Brieves, Pleading and the Development of Scots Law', (1986) 4 *Law and History Review*, 403–22; *idem*, 'The Brieve of Right Re-Visited', in R. Eales and D. Sullivan (eds.), *The Political Context of Law* (1987), 17–25; *idem*, 'Dissasine and Mortancestor in Scots Law', in Albert Kiralfy and H. L. MacQueen (eds.), *New Perspectives in Scottish Legal History* (1984), 21–49 (= (1983) 4 *Journal of Legal History*, 21–49); *idem*, 'The Brieve of Right in Scots Law', (1982) 3 *Journal of Legal History*, 52–70. See also, Willock, (n. 67), 105–32; Hector McKechnie, *Judicial Process upon Brieves, 1219–1532* (1956), *passim*; and Harding, (1966) 11 *JR* 115–49.   [70] Dickinson (n. 56), cxxvi.

[71] See T. D. Fergus (ed.), *Quoniam Attachiamenta*, Stair Society, vol. 44 (1996), 106–7, 117–9.

[72] RRS, I, 263–5 no. 243, 267 no. 247; RRS, II, 136 no. 27, 250–2 no. 197; MacQueen (n. 38), 197–9; W. D. H. Sellar, 'Courtesy, Battle and the Brieve of Right, 1368—A Story Continued', in *idem* (n. 6), 1–12. See generally, George Neilson, *Trial by Combat* (1890).

[73] RRS, II, 379–80 no. 388. See also Willock (n. 67), 29.   [74] Duncan (n. 4), 539–41.

[75] Willock (n. 67), 31–7; MacQueen (n. 38), 199.

[76] See generally Robert Bartlett, *Trial by Fire and Water: The Medieval Judicial Ordeal* (1986), 34–102.

Royal intervention by brieve will have been exceptional, though of growing significance. Hints of a measure of continuity with the Gaelic past are provided by the presence in courts of the dempster, an office deriving from that of the Gaelic *judex*. Likewise, when a lord repledged a man under his jurisdiction from another court to his own for trial, the surety he had to give was termed 'culrath', a Gaelic legal term.[77]

(a) Royal justice and Lords' justice

Scottish kings, however, were prepared to intervene in lords' exercise of a disciplinary and proprietary jurisdiction over their tenants. Charters of David I granting franchise jurisdiction state that royal justice would take effect in the event of a failure of lords' justice.[78] Justiciars were commanded to ensure that sheriffs carried out their duties, such as compelling payment of teind.[79] Justiciars and sheriffs are found attending lords' courts and an assize of William I required the sheriff to be present when a judicial duel was held in such a court.[80] It is likely that the brieves of mortancestry and novel dissasine were introduced by royal act in 1230, with the latter aimed at controlling lords who dissaised their tenants.[81] All of this followed from the royal duty of ensuring peace and protection.[82]

This emphasizes that the king's duty to ensure that justice was enforced could lead to interference between lords and tenants, thereby subordinating feudal justice to that of the king. By the end of the twelfth century, he is found dispensing justice in his *curia regis*. In the next century, he is also found doing so *in colloquio*, the forerunner of Parliament.[83] He was thus deciding what was the law of the land if a general principle was at stake, just as he could lay down general laws, as Alexander II did, in 1230, in an important series of 'statutes' on remedies and procedure.[84]

In 1264, a royal brieve of Alexander III referred to usage throughout Scotland 'according to ancient approved custom and common law [*jus commune*]'.[85] The accidental survival of this usage 'common law' suggests a wider currency of what was later to become a very familiar term.[86] Its use was as in

---

[77] Sellar, [1989] 29 *Scottish Studies* 3–4, 15–17.

[78] Barrow (n. 33), 70–2 no. 33, 129–30 no. 159, 136–8 no. 172; Lawrie (n.33), 61–3 no.74, 140–1 no.179, 167–71 no.209.   [79] MacQueen (n. 38), 42.

[80] Ibid. 42–7.   [81] Ibid. 137–40, 169–70.   [82] Harding (1966) 11 *JR* passim.

[83] RRS, II, 192–4 no. 105; A. A. M Duncan, 'The Early Parliaments of Scotland', (1966) 45 *Scot Hist Rev* 36–58 at 36–8; MacQueen (n. 38), 47–9.

[84] See H. L. MacQueen, 'Canon Law, Custom and Legislation: Law in the Reign of Alexander II', (forthcoming); Duncan (n. 4), 538–41. J. M. Gilbert, *Hunting and Hunting Reserves in Medieval Scotland* (1979), 244 surmizes that assizes were used to issue forest regulations.

[85] *Liber Sancte Marie de Melros: Munimenta Vetustiora Monasterii Cisterciensis de Melros*, Bannatyne Club, vol. 56 (1837), vol. I, 273 no. 309.

[86] See Sellar (n. 3), 86–7; *idem*, 'The Resilience of the Scottish Common Law', in D. L. Carey Miller and Reinhard Zimmermann (eds.), *The Civilian Tradition and Scots Law: Aberdeen Quincentenary Essays* (1997), 149–64 at 151.

contemporary England—the law applied in the royal courts as distinct from local usage and custom. In Scotland the term referred above all to the law developed by the Anglo-Norman institutions to protect and enforce the new feudal tenures. The use of brieves issued by the royal chapel developed the common understanding of normal practice concerning tenure and inheritance into a system of rules; fundamental in ensuring uniformity of practice was the rule, vouched for by 1270 but obviously older, that no one could be made to answer for his heritage except in an action commenced by royal brieve.[87]

(b) Canon law and ecclesiastical discipline

The period of the growth of the Scottish common law was also one of tremendous development in the canon law, as the revitalized Church reorganized and reformed itself in an attempt to impose a proper spiritual discipline on the laity and clergy. Scotland was not exempt from this movement, and a new parochial and diocesan structure was developed and funded.[88] Scotland had as yet no archbishop to exercise metropolitan powers over the Church, which led the Archbishops of York to claim such authority. This was resisted by Church and king in Scotland, and, in 1176, the papal bull *Cum Universi* recognized the *Ecclesia Scoticana* as the special daughter of the papal see.[89]

To cope with the lack of an archbishop, which caused problems, for example, in implementing the decrees of the Fourth Lateran Council, a Provincial Council of the Scottish Church was established in 1225, with authority both to legislate and to act as a court.[90] Within each diocese, the bishop was the ordinary judge; he presumably initially exercised such jurisdiction in an ad hoc manner in a meeting of clergy, but it became the practice for his legal responsibilities to be delegated to an Official, who was typically a specialist in the growing science of canon law. Officials are found in St Andrews by 1194, Aberdeen by 1199, Glasgow by 1189, Dunkeld by 1210, and Brechin by 1214.[91] In fact, the Scottish Church was fully integrated into the jurisdictional structure of Western Christendom in this period. Scottish cases could reach the papal *Curia*, and it was common for certain ecclesiastics to be invested with jurisdiction as papal judges-delegate.[92]

---

[87] MacQueen (n. 38), 105.

[88] Gordon Donaldson, 'Scottish Bishops' Sees before the Reign of David I', (1955) 87 *Proceedings of the Society of Antiquaries of Scotland* 106–17; idem, *Scottish Church History* (1985), 11–24; I. B. Cowan, *The Parishes of Medieval Scotland*, Scottish Record Society, Old Series, vol. 93 (1967).

[89] See A. D. M. Barrell, 'The Background to *Cum universi*: Scoto-Papal Relations, 1159–1192', (1995) 46 *Innes Review* 116–38.

[90] D. E. R. Watt, 'The Provincial Council of the Scottish Church, 1215–1472', in Grant/Stringer (n. 4), 140–55.

[91] See D. E. R. Watt, *Fasti Ecclesiae Scoticanae Medii Aevii ad Annum 1638*, Scottish Record Society, New Series, vol. 1 (1969), 23, 38, 56, 91–2, 124, 140, 187, 244, 288, and 323.

[92] See P. C. Ferguson, *Medieval Papal Representatives in Scotland: Legates, Nuncios, and Judges-Delegate, 1125–1286*, Stair Society, vol. 45 (1997), 118–90.

Ecclesiastical jurisdiction and competence within its own fields was fully accepted in Scotland and ecclesiastical courts dealt with matters such as faith, sacraments and sin, church lands, contracts made on oath, members of the clergy and monastic orders, issues of presentation to benefices, executries and moveable succession, bastardy, legitimacy, and marriage. In the 1240s, the Provincial Council enacted a series of statutes to ensure uniformity of practice in the various dioceses.[93] The papacy exerted pressure to ensure that, for example, the canonical norms for marriage were observed, so different from those of Gaelic Scotland.[94] In fact, Scotland became a loyal daughter of the Church, although there were occasional jurisdictional disputes, such as when the Church claimed that Scottish kings, using brieves of prohibition, were forcing cases involving church property to be heard before secular courts when the proper forum was ecclesiastical.[95] In general, the two systems existed side by side recognizing each other's proper sphere and, as MacQueen has put it, 'canonical norms were woven into the fabric of the secular law'.[96] Laymen can be found happy to litigate over land in ecclesiastical courts; a churchman and layman could agree to submit to the jurisdiction of the justiciar; an inquest before a sheriff could decide whether certain dues were payable to a religious house.[97]

(c) Canon lawyers

One result of the development of the canon law and the Church's courts was the appearance in Scotland of the university-educated canon lawyer.[98] Such individuals are difficult to trace with certainty at this time, but it is worth noting the contemporary description of Malveisin, who became Bishop of St Andrews in 1202, as '*utriusque juris peritus*', that is skilled in both the laws, canon and civil.[99] Malveisin had an active career under William I and Alexander II.[100] Churchmen are never found acting as sheriffs or justiciars, but they were often present in secular courts as suitors; furthermore, high churchmen attended the King's Council and the courts of the justiciar.[101] Men described as *jurisperiti* and *magistri* are often recorded as present in courts in thirteenth century Scotland; they may have assisted in reaching a decision on difficult legal issues, just as they are recorded as doing in a dispute before judges-delegate in 1233, where the advice was taken of men

---

[93] Watt (n. 90), 148–52.

[94] See Robert Somerville (ed.), *Scotia Pontificia: Papal Letters to Scotland before the Pontificate of Innocent III* (1982), 19–20 no. 2.

[95] See Barrow, *Kingdom* (n. 10), 90–4. For a brieve of prohibition, see Cooper, (n. 68), 46.

[96] H. L. MacQueen, 'Scots Law under Alexander III', in N. H. Reid, *Scotland in the Reign of Alexander III, 1249–1286* (1990), 74–102 at 81. [97] Ibid. 80–1 and 98 n. 38.

[98] Ferguson (n. 92), 176–7.

[99] D. E. R. Watt, *A Biographical Dictionary of Scottish Graduates to A.D. 1410* (1977), 374–9 at 375. [100] MacQueen (n. 84).

[101] MacQueen (n. 96), 81; Barrow, *Kingdom* (n. 10), 99–100.

skilled in both canon and civil law.[102] As well as advising courts, churchmen with an academic training in law assisted litigants. The moral tale of Adam Urry in the Chronicle of Lanercost is well known but worth repeating. On his deathbed, Urry, who was learned in secular laws, repented that he had been more concerned with the court of riches than the care of souls.[103] This intersection and interrelationship of Scottish common law and canon law may explain the ready secular acceptance of both canonical thinking in matters such as homicide and the Church's rejection of the ordeal as a mode of proof.[104] From an early date, aspects of the *jus commune* were being woven into practice and thinking in the secular courts.

(d) Common law and local practice

It must be stressed that the development of a common law in Scotland was not the result of a conscious policy of legal uniformity; rather, it derived from the institutions the kings of Scots adopted for the proper government of their realm. Certain differences were recognized and perpetuated, such as the special practices prevailing in Galloway and Carrick. The kings of Scots were content to allow the continued exercise of traditional local lordship through the right of 'kenkynnol' (from the Gaelic *cenn cenóil* or *ceann cineil*) of the head of a kindred. This institution started to become fused with feudal ideas, but older aspects of it remained: the lord continued to have a right to 'calps', a tribute in return for maintenance and protection; he continued to have the right to try his kindred and men by the process of '*surdit de sergeant*', whereby he maintained sergeants who had the right to investigate crimes and demand hospitality as they travelled the country.[105] Another special law

---

[102] *Register of Paisley Abbey: Registrum Monasterii de Passelet*, Maitland Club, vol. 17 (1832), 169–70; APS, I, 97.

[103] *Chronicon de Lanercost M.CC.I–M.CCC.XLVI. e Codice Cottoniano nunc Primum Typis Mandatum*, Maitland Club, vol. 46 (1839), 124. See W. M. Gordon, 'Roman Law in Scotland', in Robin Evans-Jones (ed.), *The Civil Law Tradition in Scotland* (1995), 13–40 at 15–16; P. G. Stein, 'Roman Law in Medieval Scotland', in idem, *Character and Influence of the Roman Civil Law: Historical Essays* (1988), 269–317 at 292–3 (= *Ius Romanum Medii Aevi*, Pars V, 13b (1968)). On canon lawyers taking fees, see J. A. Brundage, 'The Profits of the Law: Legal Fees of University-Trained Advocates', (1988) 32 *AJLH* 1–15.

[104] W. D. H. Sellar, 'Forethocht Felony, Malice Aforethought and the Classification of Homicide', in W. M Gordon and T. D. Fergus (eds.), *Legal History in the Making: Proceedings of the Ninth British Legal History Conference, Glasgow 1989* (1991), 43–59. See the case before the Bailies of Dumfries in the 13th century, where an inquest decided that Richard had slaughtered Adam the Miller in self-defence: this seems to recognize the distinctions that Sellar has shown for the later period: Cooper (n. 2), 58–9 no. 42.

[105] See H. L. MacQueen, 'The Kin of Kennedy, "Kenkynnol" and the Common Law', in Grant/Stringer (n. 4), 274–96; idem, 'The Laws of Galloway: A Preliminary Survey', in R. D. Orem and G. P. Stell (eds.), *Galloway: Land and Lordship* (1991), 131–43; W. Croft Dickinson, 'Surdit de Sergaunt', (1960) 39 *Scot Hist Rev* 170–5; George Neilson, ' "Surdit de Sergaunt": An Old Galloway Law', (1897) 11 *The Scottish Antiquary or Northern Notes and Queries* 155–7. In 1225, the Earl of Carrick agreed that the clergy in his Earldom need not be liable to give hospitality to his sergeants: *Glasgow Registrum Episcopatus Glasguensis: Munimenta Ecclesie*

that remained in force was that of Clan MacDuff. This constituted an obscure set of privileges that was associated with special rights of sanctuary, which probably, in some circumstances, gave the Earl of Fife the right to repledge his kindred within a certain degree to his own courts, even from royal courts.[106] The progress of the common law was closely linked with the progress of sheriffdom, justiciar, barony, and royal writ; in areas where such institutions did not penetrate fully, such as much of the Highlands, traditional legal practices held sway.[107]

Geoffrey Barrow has pointed out that it was possible to subsume Scots law under *lex Anglicana*.[108] F. W. Maitland's remark of the late thirteenth century that 'we may doubt whether a man who crossed the river [Tweed] felt that he had passed from the land of one law to the land of another' is well known. Thus, 'at the outbreak of the war of independence, the law of Scotland . . . was closely akin to English law'.[109] Indeed, there can be little doubt that great landowning families, such as the Bruces and Balliols, saw their holdings north and south of the border as subject to much the same rules and their rights as enforced by a similar mechanism—the brieve or writ. Yet, although Scots law had set off in a new direction by adopting the practices of Anglo-Norman and Angevin England, differences remained. Not only were the systems of brieves and writs north and south of the Tweed different, but, in Scotland, Celtic institutions had to some extent been blended into feudal land tenure, which was, after all, highly adaptable. Moving away from landholding, differences from England become greater. Though detailed evidence is lacking, MacQueen argues convincingly that, in the reign of Alexander III, 'the character of the law was much more archaic and complex than suggested by Maitland'.[110] Importation of the institutions and rules of the common law may have caused Scots law to set off in a new direction, but the route was also determined by the continuing influence of existing institutions and the openness of Scots legal practice to the personnel and thinking of the canon law.

Metropolitane Glasguensis a Sede Restaurata Seculo Ineunte XII ad Reformationem Religionem, Bannatyne Club, vol. 75 (1843), vol. I, 117 no. 139. The Earl of Lennox made a similar grant two years later: ibid. I, 119–20 no. 141.

[106] John Stuart, *The Sculptured Stones of Scotland* (1872), pp. lxvii–lxx.
[107] John Bannerman, 'The Scots Language and Kin-Based Society', in D. S. Thomson (ed.), *Gaelic and Scots in Harmony: Proceedings of the Second International Conference on the Languages of Scotland* (1990), 1–19.   [108] Barrow (n. 30), 119.
[109] Frederick Pollock and F. W. Maitland, *The History of English Law before the Time of Edward I* (2nd edn., reissued 1986), vol. 1, 222–3.   [110] MacQueen (n. 96), 85–93.

III. THE LATER MIDDLE AGES, 1286–1424

1. The Great Cause, the Edwardian occupation, and the succession of the Stewarts

(a) The succession of Margaret

On 19 March 1286, Alexander III died and with him ended the direct male line of King Malcolm's dynasty. His only surviving direct descendant was his granddaughter Margaret, daughter of the king of Norway. The situation was difficult: Margaret was not only female and a minor, but also in Norway. A Parliament met at Scone in April and appointed six *custodes* or Guardians: William Fraser, Bishop of St Andrews; Robert Wishart, Bishop of Glasgow; Duncan, Earl of Fife; Alexander Comyn, Earl of Buchan; James the Steward; and John Comyn, Lord of Badenoch. Notable exclusions from the guardianship were Robert Bruce, Lord of Annandale, and his son Robert Bruce, Earl of Carrick, and John Balliol. These men were descended from David I and had, after the infant Margaret, the best claims to the throne. The Guardians were, however, representative not only of Scotland north and south of the Forth but also of the factions of Bruce and Balliol. The magnates took an oath of loyalty to the rightful heir of Alexander.[111]

There had been peace with England for a substantial period during the last two reigns and issues on the border had been sufficiently settled that an inquest of Scottish and English knights had agreed a code of law to govern border issues in 1249.[112] The Scottish magnates accordingly sought the advice of Edward I in the summer of 1286. Edward had been the brother-in-law of Alexander III and his aunt had married Alexander II. Closely linked by blood to the Scottish royal house and the young heiress, he was the most experienced ruler in Europe, whose advice could have been invaluable. While the Guardians ruled Scotland in the name of the 'community of the realm', negotiations involving England and Norway resulted in the Treaty of Birgham of 18 July 1290, by which Margaret was to marry the English heir, Prince Edward, although the two kingdoms were to be kept distinct: no one accused of a crime in Scotland or sued at law would have to answer in a court outwith the country; no Parliament was to be held outwith the realm on any matter concerning it and its borders; only the Scottish royal chapel could issue valid writs; and Scottish tenants-in-chief would only have to offer

---

[111] Nicholson (n. 6), 27–9.
[112] See George Neilson, 'The March Laws', in *Miscellany I*, Stair Society, vol. 26 (1971), 11–77 at 12–24; W. W. Scott, 'The March Laws Reconsidered', in Grant/Stringer (n. 4), 114–30; Henry Summerson, 'The Early Development of the Laws of the Anglo-Scottish Marches, 1249–1448', in Gordon/Fergus (n. 104), 29–42; C. J. Neville, *Violence, Custom and Law: The Anglo-Scottish Border Lands in the Later Middle Ages* (1998), 1–14.

homage in Scotland.[113] Though it was envisaged there would be one king, the two kingdoms would remain separate with independent laws and legal systems.

(b) The Great Cause

Margaret died in the Orkney Islands (still part of Norway) on her way to her kingdom. It was feared that rumours of her death would cause civil war; the Bishop of St Andrews invoked the further aid of the English king.[114] Those with the strongest claim to the Scottish throne were Robert Bruce, Lord of Annandale, and John Balliol, both of whom were descended from Henry, son of David I, through his son, David, Earl of Huntingdon. Bruce was nearest in degree as the son of Earl David's second daughter; Balliol was descended from the senior line, as the grandson of the first daughter.[115] Edward astutely refused to assist the Scots in their dilemma unless he was able to adjudicate in the capacity of feudal overlord of Scotland. After difficult negotiations, the Guardians and magnates swore fealty to him as lord of the kingdom of Scotland; steps were taken to ensure that as many others as possible would also so swear. In return, Edward would hand over the kingdom to the successful competitor within two months of giving judgment.[116]

It had been agreed that Bruce and Balliol were each to nominate forty auditors and Edward twenty-four; these 104 were to report their findings to the king after hearing the cases of the claimants. This court was in essence Edward's own court; he was not an arbiter.[117] It first met at Berwick on 3 August 1291. There is no need to discuss its proceedings in detail, though it is worth noting that a *quaestio* was framed to gain the *consilia* of foreign lawyers, some of which have survived. Ultimately the court decided that Scotland as a kingdom was impartible and descended according to male primogeniture and Edward awarded the kingdom to Balliol on 19 November. Balliol swore fealty to Edward the next day and was inaugurated as king at

---

[113] See E. L. G. Stones and G. G. Simpson, *Edward I and the Throne of Scotland, 1290–1296: An Edition of the Record Sources for the Great Cause* (1978), vol. 1, 8–9; Nicholson (n. 6), 30–5; G. W. S. Barrow, *Robert Bruce and the Community of the Realm of Scotland* (3rd edn., 1988), 16–28.   [114] Stones/Simpson (n. 113), vol. 1, 5–6; vol. 2, 3–4.

[115] The two other most serious claimants were John Hastings of Abergavenny (who claimed entitlement to a third only) and Florence, Count of Holland. See Stones/Simpson (n. 113), vol. 1, 122–3, vol. 2, 311–25; G. G. Simpson, 'The Claim of Florence, Count of Holland, to the Scottish Throne in 1291–2', (1957) 36 *Scot Hist Rev* 111–24; J. A. Kossmann-Putto, 'Florence V, Count of Holland, Claimant to the Scottish Throne in 1291–2: His Personal and Political Background', in G. G. Simpson (ed.), *Scotland and the Low Countries, 1124–1994* (1996), 15–27.   [116] Stones/Simpson (n. 113), vol. 2, 16, 97–9, 102–6, 114, 121–6.

[117] Stones/Simpson (n. 113), vol. 1, 21–2; vol. 2, 70. Stones and Simpson dismiss the suggestion of George Neilson that the court was modelled on the Roman centumviral court (ibid., vol. 2, 371–2), although Barrow has recently defended it: Barrow (n. 113), 39 and 334 n. 2.

Scone ten days later, as King John offering homage to Edward at Newcastle on 26 December.[118]

(c) The Edwardian occupation

As overlord, Edward claimed the right to review the administration of justice in Scotland and argued that the provision of the Treaty of Birgham that Scottish lawsuits should not be heard outwith Scotland was no longer applicable.[119] In July 1292 he declared: 'Through the blessing of the All Highest, the realms of England and Scotland are joined together, and consequently royal writs originating in Scotland and presented or returned to the (English) justices of Common Pleas may be dealt with by them.'[120] He heard appeals from Scotland in his own court, although he is recorded as seeking advice on Scots law before giving judgment.[121] The issue of appeals was used to harass King John, who was periodically summoned to the King's Bench or the English Parliament to answer for his failure to do justice.[122] John's brief reign saw the dispensing of justice in regular Parliaments and an attempt to cope with some of the administrative problems of the kingdom by creating new sheriffdoms in the west.[123]

It was only a matter of time before King John fell out with Edward: it happened over war with the king of France in 1294, with whom John made an alliance of mutual defence in 1295. Edward, however, quickly managed to crush the Scots and symbolically humiliated King John. The Scottish *regalia*, the stone of Scone, and many sacred relics were removed to England to join the Scottish records, which had been inventoried for Edward in 1292. An English administration was established in Scotland.[124] In 1297, revolt began, led by William Wallace and Andrew Moray in the name of King John. A complex series of campaigns, where each side scored some notable successes, eventually resulted in Edward gaining the upper hand by 1304, although for some time the Scots had managed to set up their own administration under Guardians. Wallace was captured, tried for treason, and executed in London in 1305. Meanwhile, the Scots gained a diplomatic success, by gaining from Pope Boniface VIII a bull contesting Edward's claim to the overlordship of Scotland. Leading the embassy had been Baldred Bisset, Official of St Andrews, an ecclesiastical lawyer associated with Bologna, William Frere,

---

[118] See Stones/Simpson (n. 113), vol. 2, 240–73; Barrow (n. 113), 39–53; Nicholson (n. 6), 35–43. On the opinions of foreign lawyers, see Stones/Simpson (n. 113), vol. 2, 359–65; G. J. Hand, 'The Opinions of the Paris Lawyers upon the Scottish Succession *c*. 1292', (1970) 5 *Irish Jurist* 141–55. [119] Barrow (n. 113), 52–3.
[120] Ibid. 51. [121] MacQueen (n. 96), 83; Barrow (n. 113), 51–2.
[122] Barrow (n. 113), 57–60; Duncan, (1966) 45 *Scot Hist Rev* 39–48.
[123] Duncan, (1966) 45 *Scot Hist Rev* 36–47; Nicholson (n. 6), 44–5.
[124] Barrow (n. 113), 62–79. On the new administration, see Fiona Watson, *Under the Hammer: Edward I and Scotland, 1286–1307* (1998), 30–41.

Archdeacon of Lothian and Professor of Canon Law in Paris, and William of Eaglesham, doctor of canon law.[125]

(d) The Edwardian administration and the law

When the Scots surrendered in 1304, they requested that they 'should be protected in all their laws, usages, customs and liberties in every particular as they existed in the time of King Alexander III, unless there are laws to be amended, in which case it should be done with the advice of King Edward and the advice and assent of the responsible men of the land'.[126] This had not been granted; but Edward again does not seem to have had a strong desire to alter Scots law. Thus, when the burgesses of Berwick sought the extension to Scotland of the English 'statute of merchants' in 1305, he remitted it to a Scottish Parliament.[127] The same year, the 'community of Galloway' petitioned Edward for a remedy for their oppression by the outlandish law called 'Surdist des serjantes', which they claimed had not been used since the time of King Alexander, but which was now again being used by the barons and great lords. Edward ordered an inquiry; nothing is known of any result.[128] Also in 1305, he initiated an inquiry by a Scottish commission into 'the Laws of King David' and subsequent legislation with a view to their amendment where 'contrary to God and reason', although he straightaway abolished the 'usage of Scots and Brets'.[129] If this last referred to the system of compounding for homicides in the 'Leges inter Brettos et Scotos' found in some Scottish legal manuscripts, Edward in fact seems to have been following a policy of preserving those aspects of Scots law that were compatible with English law, but abolishing customs that seemed antithetical to it: this would have been comparable with his earlier practice in England and Wales. In September 1305, the Scottish government was organized, headed by a Lieutenant, Chancellor, and Chamberlain. Four pairs of justices were appointed to cover Galloway, Lothian, the country between the Forth and the Mounth, and the country north of the Mounth. Each pair was made up of an Englishman and a Scotsman.[130] Had Edward been able to hold on to Scotland, there can be little doubt but that Scots law would have been progressively assimilated to that of England, which had undergone tremendous development in the thirteenth century, especially in Edward's reign.[131]

---

[125] Barrow (n. 113), 79–144; Nicholson (n. 6), 52–68; Watson (n. 124), 41–196.
[126] Barrow (n. 113), 130.   [127] MacQueen (n. 96), 83–4.
[128] F. W. Maitland (ed.), *Memorando de Parliamenta* (Rolls Series, 1893), 171–2. See e.g. Neilson, (1897) 11 *The Scottish Antiquary or Northern Notes and Queries* 155.
[129] Barrow (n. 113), 135–6; MacQueen (n. 96), 92.
[130] Barrow (n. 113), 134–5; Watson (n. 124), 197–222.
[131] See e.g. T. F. T. Plucknett, *A Concise History of the Common Law* (5th edn., 1956), 22–31; P. A. Brand, 'Legal Change in the Later Thirteenth Century: Statutory and Judicial Remodelling of the Action of Replevin', (1978) 31 *AJLH* 43–55.

(e) Bruce, independence, and the Stewart succession

The story of the next half-century is of the successful bid for the throne of Robert Bruce (1306–29), grandson of the claimant in 1292, resulting in war with England for half a century or so and an enmity that lasted until the sixteenth century. Bruce was succeeded by his son, David II (1329–71), who had no heir.[132] Under entails of 1318 and 1326, Robert Stewart, son of Bruce's daughter Marjorie, succeeded to the throne as Robert II (1371–90), with his son, John, Earl of Carrick, recognized as his heir, despite some questions over his legitimacy. At a General Council at Holyrood in November 1384 Carrick was appointed guardian of the kingdom because of his father's age and infirmity, and specially given the duty of ensuring the execution of the common law throughout the kingdom. He was removed from the guardianship in December 1388, to be replaced by his brother Robert, Earl of Fife. On the death of Robert II, Carrick succeeded, taking the title Robert III (1390–1406). Adoption of this style avoided the thorny issue of the status of John Balliol and supported the title to the throne the Stewarts derived from Robert I. At his succession, Robert III had two living legitimate sons, David, now created Earl of Carrick, and Robert. A third son, James, was born in 1395. At first, Robert III's younger brother, Fife, continued as guardian, on the excuse of royal infirmity, but early in 1393, Fife lost the guardianship. In 1398, Carrick was created Duke of Rothesay and Fife that of Albany. In 1399, Rothesay was appointed Lieutenant of the Realm for three years and Robert III formally deprived of power on the excuse of his misgovernment of the realm caused by failure of keeping the common law. Late in 1401, Rothesay was arrested and given into the hands of Albany, in whose castle of Falkland he died in March 1402. The heir to the throne was now the 7-year-old Prince James. In 1406, there was an attempt to send him to France for safety and his education; the English captured his ship on 22 March 1406. On his father's death on 4 April of that year, he became the uncrowned king of Scots as James I (1406–37); he remained in English hands, however, until 1424, his uncle Albany governing until his death in 1420, to be succeeded in this role by his son Murdoch, the second Duke.[133]

---

[132] See A. A. M. Duncan, 'The War of the Scots, 1306–23', (1992) 2 *Transactions of the Royal Historical Society*, Sixth Series, 125–51; Colm McNamee, *The Wars of the Bruces: Scotland, England and Ireland: 1306–1328* (1997), 36–67; Barrow (n. 113), 145–324; Nicholson (n. 6), 69–183.

[133] Stephen Boardman, *The Early Stewart Kings: Robert II and Robert III, 1371–1406* (1996); Nicholson (n. 6), 184–280. On the rise of the great noble family of Douglas in this era, see Michael Brown, *The Black Douglases: War and Lordship in Late Medieval Scotland, 1300–1455* (1998).

2. Institutional continuities and changes

(a) *The new regime*

Robert I came to power as a result of *coup d'état*; perhaps as a result of this, the regime stressed its continuity with that of Alexander III. Not only did the diplomatic style of documents issued by King Robert's writing chapel take inspiration from that of Alexander III,[134] but over fifty of his *acta* refer to Alexander III, most describing him as 'our predecessor who last died'.[135] The reign of King John was ignored.[136] Bruce therefore governed through traditional mechanisms and institutions, though in some ways these started to be transformed.

(b) *Parliament and Council*

From the reign of Robert I onwards, there is increasing recourse to Parliament and a subtle shift in its business. While the frequent parliaments of Robert I were largely concerned with the great business of state, such as peace treaties, treason, legislation, and the tailzie of the Crown, the index to a lost roll of parliamentary documents from 1323 to 1331 demonstrates that the pleas and petitions of the king's subjects were also now dealt with in sessions of Parliament and of the King's Council within Parliament.[137] From at least 1341, judicial committees were appointed to hear appeals;[138] the business of 'falsed dooms' and petitions and complaints arising out of the operation of the common law became such that in 1399 a General Council provided that the king should hold a Parliament 'ilke yher ... swa that his subiectis be servit of the law'.[139]

As the role of Parliament developed in this way, so its composition started to change, as the great struggle for the freedom of the kingdom and the need to pay the ransom for David II (who was held a captive in England from 1346–57) led to the calling of representatives of the burghs; certainly present in 1326, 1328, and 1341, their attendance became regular after 1357 to participate in the raising of money.[140] The same necessity led to summonses to Parliament widening to include lesser landowners.[141] This change was signified by the developing use of the phrase 'the Three Estates' (first discovered used in 1357 as '*tres communitates*'), rather than the thirteenth century 'Community of the Realm' to encapsulate the governing class. This development is familiar in late medieval Europe: the Three Estates (clergy,

---

[134] RRS, V, 6–7.
[135] N. H. Reid, 'Crown and Community under Robert I', in Grant/Stringer (n. 4), 203–22 at 203.
[136] Ibid. 204.
[137] RMS, I, 556–8 (Appendix 2, nos. 692–726). See Duncan, (1966) 45 *Scot Hist Rev* 50.
[138] APS, I, 506 (1369), 547 (1372); Alexander Grant, *Independence and Nationhood: Scotland 1306–1469* (repr. 1991), 168.   [139] APS, I, 573.
[140] Duncan, (1966) 45 *Scot Hist Rev* 51–3.   [141] Ibid. 53–6.

nobility, and burgesses) and the monarch were seen as governing in a kind of partnership. A titled peerage developed in the fifteenth century; for the moment the title of 'lord' went with the land and the freeholders were simply the lesser lords of the second estate—as indeed they were always to be.[142] The significance of the burghs was well recognized and Bruce granted many new burgh charters and confirmed existing ones.[143]

(c) Justiciars

Bruce initially preserved Edward's innovations for the justiciarship, before reverting to a more traditional scheme and combining the justiciarship of Galloway with that of Lothian; henceforth there were only two justiciars— one north and one south of the Forth, a terminology standard from the end of the reign of David II.[144] Despite the political difficulties of the century there is enough evidence of continuity to show the continued vitality and activity of the justiciar in general administration and dispensing of justice.[145] The importance of the sheriffdom as a unit of government was recognized by the creation of a new sheriffdom of Argyll by 1325;[146] but though Bute became a sheriffdom later in the century, there was little further expansion until Renfrew separated as a sheriffdom from Lanark around 1414.[147]

(d) Baronies and regalities

In Robert I's time there were 200–300 baronies; within a hundred years there were at least 400.[148] Bruce also made strategic grants of regalities in an attempt to ensure control of difficult areas: thus he erected the Earldom of Moray, the Lordship of Man, and the Lordship of Annandale into regalities for his great captain and supporter Randolph.[149] More regalities were created through the fourteenth century both to reward individuals and to provide for royal relatives; some again were intended to aid government in a difficult or border area, so that Alexander Fleming was deprived of his regalian privileges when he failed to keep control of Western Galloway.[150]

(e) Conservatism and innovation

Robert I's emphasis on continuity from Alexander III meant that any innovations of King John and the Edwardian regime were rejected; Edward's abolition of the *Leges inter Brettos et Scotos* was now apparently undone. The conservatism of Bruce's reign and the long absence of David II might

---

[142] See generally Julian Goodare, 'The Estates in the Scottish Parliament, 1286–1707', in Clyve Jones (ed.), *The Scots and Parliament* (1996), 11–32 at 12–17; R. S. Rait, *The Parliaments of Scotland* (1924), 19–30. [143] RRS, V, 27–31; Barrow (n. 113), 300–2.
[144] H. L. MacQueen, 'Pleadable Brieves and Jurisdiction in Heritage in Later Medieval Scotland' (unpublished Ph.D. thesis, University of Edinburgh, 1985), 58–63.
[145] Ibid. 63–76. [146] Barrow (n. 113), 295. [147] McNeill/MacQueen (n. 4), 208.
[148] Ibid. 201. [149] RRS, V, 633–5 no. 389; Nicholson (n. 6), 112; Barrow (n. 113), 282–3.
[150] Grant (n. 138), 152–153; McNeill/MacQueen (n. 4), 207.

suggest there would be little innovation in Scots law and institutions; at one level this was so, but, on the other hand, there were changes reflecting the need to reconstruct the kingdom on its traditional lines. These came about because reconstruction required a clear reformulation of the institutions being reconstructed; such precision brought about change through a progressive legalization of Scottish feudal structures. The increasingly obvious presence of academically trained lawyers in Scottish society—such as John de Carrick, 'skilled in decrees' and John de Peblis, doctor of decreets, Chancellors under David II and Robert II[151]—must have facilitated this tendency to start to lay down precise rules about institutions. Thus, in 1321, an inquest into the nature of the tenure of Sprouston in Roxburghshire demonstrates the development of a general understanding of the nature and legal concept of regality.[152] Bruce's charters granting or confirming estates in land of any consequence started regularly to use the phrase *in liberam baroniam*.[153] The traditional lordship exercised by the king's tenants thus started to be given a new precision, with a more legalistic definition, and, although jurisdiction was not yet entirely identified with a grant in barony, but still regarded as an easement of the barony, a more defined idea of what the term 'barony' conveyed was developing.[154] There was a revival of military tenures, which thus predominate in grants, although, reflecting Scottish needs in contemporary warfare, archer service becomes common, while knight service is still found;[155] a number of charters from the Highlands and Islands specify the service of a ship.[156]

3. Law reform

(a) *Politics, problems, and law reform*

In 1318, a Parliament at Scone enacted a great code of law.[157] It started with an assertion of the liberties and privileges of the Church in the protection of the king and asserted that *communis lex* and *communis justicia* should be available to poor as well as to rich according to 'the old laws and liberties'; yet, though many of its provisions reflected earlier practice, much of it clearly was aimed at dealing with immediate problems. Thus, there was a considerable number of provisions relating to military matters and the conduct of the war.[158] The king's political problems ensured the enactment that conspirators

---

[151] Watt (n. 99), 89–91, 440–3.   [152] RRS, V, 447–8 no. 172.
[153] Barrow (n. 113), 292.   [154] RRS, V, 41–4.
[155] RRS, V, 48; Barrow (n. 113), 286–9.   [156] RRS, V, 54; Barrow (n. 113), 289–92.
[157] The most authoritative text is that established by Duncan in RRS, V, 405–15 no. 139. See also APS, I, 466–74.
[158] See RRS, V, 407–8 (the proper indictment of those travelling to the army; the supplies they should have; the defence before the justiciar of being on royal service), 413 (export of goods during war), 414 (the arms that men should possess).

and spreaders of malicious rumours creating discord between the king and his people were to be held at the king's will: in the 'Soules Conspiracy' Bruce was indeed soon to face a major challenge.[159] The whole thrust of the provisions was to impose order in disputes so that the realm would be peaceful, as one of the major problems Bruce faced was that of the dispossessed and the disinherited, as the confiscation and regranting of fiefs following the vicissitudes of war and changing allegiances had stored up a multitude of grievances and quarrels among the landed classes. One provision recounted the discords among the nobles that had arisen after the death of Alexander III and emphasized that complaints were to be pursued according to the laws of the land.[160] Since self-help was to be eschewed, an emphasis on proper procedure runs through the legislation: men condemned to death for certain crimes were not to be redeemed but to suffer justice; pleas as to why one should not appear before the justiciar were regulated; pleadings concerning debts, promises, and chattels were to be precise; the defender and his or her *prolocutor* were not to be made to reply until after the pursuer or his or her *prolocutor* had finished—a point developed specifically in connection with the brieve of right; frivolous defences were forbidden; there was control over poinding; the rule that no one could be ejected from a free tenement of which he claimed to be vested and saised in fee without a pleadable brieve was reaffirmed. There were two overt innovations: novel dissasine was reformed to favour the sitting tenant who had been infeft after the dissasine, while those who dissaised *vi et armis* were to be punished by imprisonment or at the king's will (these provisions showed an awareness of English practice); the scope of the brieve of mortancestry was extended to cover claims to succeed from grandparents.[161]

(b) The development of heritable rights

By reinforcing the existing feudal structures of Scots law, the legislation of 1318 secured its continued steady development through the rest of the century. There were, however, interesting results: the reform of novel dissasine showed a continuing royal willingness to intervene between lords and tenants (since the most common dissaisor envisaged is the tenant's lord) that in the long run would make heritable rights more secure. The rest of the century showed the continuing vitality of the traditional common law. The brieve of mortancestry—with its widened scope—was in regular use, as was novel dissasine, though it seemed largely to have been concerned with disputes between the king's tenants-in-chief and rights in land rather than recovery of possession. The brieve of right, though not well recorded, also remained in

---

[159] Barrow (n. 113), 309–10.   [160] RRS, V, 412.
[161] RRS, V, 407–14. See now MacQueen (n. 38), 146–53 on the significance of the changes in novel dissasine.

regular use. In fact, the picture given of these brieves in the fourteenth century registers appears generally accurate when tested against the surviving evidence.[162] The unsettled reigns of Robert II and Robert III also led to the enactment of a major code of practice regulating land tenure by a Parliament at Scone in 1401. The general thrust was again to protect tenants in their heritage under the common law: a procedure was established to ensure that no one could be unjustly deprived of their land and heritage by a prejudiced inquest and an improperly obtained precept of sasine following a retour; tenants were preserved against unjust recognition (a process of repossession) of their lands by their overlords (including the king); the rule that conquest ascended in the event of failure of heirs was reaffirmed; tenants currently holding of the king were to remain such and any purported royal grant of a superiority over their lands was null if without their consent; barons who held of the king in an earldom or lordship that had come into the king's hands were to continue to hold their lands of the king after he had infeft someone by charter in the earldom or lordship; the names of witnesses to the resignation of lands into the king's hands were to be properly preserved in the relevant deeds.[163] Robert III had himself declared in 1391 that 'it suld nocht be his wil . . . oucht to do or conferme that suld ryn ony man in preidiuce of thair heritage attour the commoune lauch'.[164] A more rigorous enforcement of traditional practices was creating greater legal rights in vassals.

4. Legal literature and the men of law

The legal literature that appeared for the first time demonstrates the strength and conservatism of the Scots common law. The earliest manuscript to contain Scots legal material is the Berne of *c*.1270;[165] the course of the fourteenth century, however, saw the appearance of two treatises of the first significance, respectively known from their opening words as *Regiam Majestatem* and *Quoniam Attachiamenta*.[166]

(*a*) Regiam Majestatem

Regiam is primarily based on the late twelfth-century English treatise known as Glanvill. As already noted, this work—*Tractatus de Legibus et Consuetu-*

---

[162] MacQueen (n. 38) 153–4, 177, 200–1. [163] APS, I, 575–6. [164] APS, I, 578–9.

[165] See n. 58 above. It is described in APS, I, 177–8. Lord Cooper has speculated on its authorship: Lord Cooper of Culross, *Selected Papers, 1922–1954* (1957), 161–71.

[166] For texts, see APS, I, 597–659; *Quoniam Attachiamenta* (n. 71). These are to be preferred to Lord Cooper (ed.), *Regiam Majestatem and Quoniam Attachiamenta*, Stair Society, vol. 11 (1947). For a discussion of the texts of *Regiam*, see John Buchanan, 'The MSS. of Regiam Majestatem: An Experiment', (1937) 49 *JR* 217–31; H. G. Richardson, 'Roman Law in the *Regiam Majestatem*', (1955) 67 *JR* 155–87; A. A. M. Duncan, 'Regiam Majestatem: A Reconsideration', [1961] *JR* 199–217; Peter Stein, 'The Source of the Romano-Canonical Part of Regiam Majestatem', (1969) 48 *Scot Hist Rev* 107–23.

dinibus Regni Angliae—was an account of English law based around the writs then in use. The first part of *Regiam* is Glanvill heavily edited; next there is a section taken from the *Summa in Titulos Decretalium* of the canonist Goffredus de Trano (dealing with pacts, arbitration, serfs, and gifts between spouses)—these passages have also been heavily edited for style and to suit Scottish conditions; more texts from Glanvill, only slightly revised, follow; finally, there is a collection of 'native' Scottish laws, some attributed to various early kings.[167] The work is generally divided into four books, though this is probably not original. Because of its importance, the book was regularly copied through the Middle Ages and early modern period, undergoing both unconscious and deliberate revision.[168]

The earliest manuscripts of *Regiam* date from the fifteenth century, but the work is evidently older.[169] Professor Duncan has demonstrated that *Regiam* must have been compiled after 1318 as material and words from the statutes of that year have been incorporated into the heavily edited part of the text in a way that shows they cannot be a later interpolation.[170] An Act of Parliament of 1426 refers to both *Regiam* and *Quoniam* in such a way as to suggest they were already of considerable antiquity.[171] While the opening words, 'Regiam majestatem', are a variation on Glanvill's 'Regiam potestatem' (and both look back to the opening of Justinian's *Institutes*), the phrase 'regia magestas' or 'regia maiestas' is relatively popular in the *acta* of Robert I in the context of the king's 'regia maiestas'.[172] The phrase originates in the canon law and Duncan has seen it as indicating a canonist drafter for at least one of Bruce's charters.[173] This hints that the date of *Regiam* is after 1318, but not long after, possibly in the reign of Robert I; moreover, the compiler may well have been trained in the canon law, as Stein has suggested.[174]

The use of a twelfth-century English text as the foundation for an early fourteenth-century Scots one emphasizes the conservative nature of Scots law. Glanvill suited the compiler's purpose better than the more modern English text of Bracton.[175] Nonetheless, the foundation of *Regiam* in Glanvill raises the difficult question of the extent to which it can be relied on as a statement of Scots law. There can be little doubt that the heavily edited portions are prima facie good evidence for its author's view of contemporary law.

[167] For more on this, see Duncan, [1961] *JR*; Stein, (1969) 48 *Scot Hist Rev*.
[168] See H. L. MacQueen, '*Regiam Majestatem*, Scots Law, and National Identity', (1995) 74 *Scot Hist Rev* 1–25.
[169] These are the Bute and the Cromertie MSS: National Library of Scotland (hereafter NLS), MS 21246 and Adv. MS 25.5.10. For a discussion of these MSS, see APS, I, 181–5.
[170] Duncan, [1961] *JR* 210–16.   [171] APS, II, 10 (c. 10).
[172] RRS, V, 76–7, 282, 299 no. 13, 350 no. 66, 415 no. 140, 661 no. 416, 692 no. 559, 696 no. 566; APS, I, 459; Cooper (n. 68), 47 no. lxvii.   [173] RRS, V, 76–7.
[174] Stein, (1969) 48 *Scot Hist Rev* 110.
[175] See *Bracton de Legibus et Consuetudinibus Angliae* (ed. G. E. Woodbine, tr. with revisions and notes S. E. Thorne, 1968–77). Some MSS of *Regiam* have indeed incorporated a section of Bracton: Duncan, [1961] *JR* 202–3 at 216.

It was also relied on extensively in Scottish legal practice, as its translation from Latin to Scots demonstrates.[176]

Alan Harding has argued that one should not view *Regiam* as an attempt to provide a statement of contemporary Scots law but as an attempt to mirror Scottish society in the manner of the famous *Sachsenspiegel* of Eike von Repgow; in other words, *Regiam* should be viewed as a highly ideological document, asserting the nature of the Scottish nation in the course of the long struggle with England.[177] This does not entirely convince, especially since the treatise very much smacks of a practical guide and was in fact used as one. Mysteries remain, but it does look as if *Regiam* was compiled by a canon lawyer, or someone with knowledge of canon law, who attributed his work to the command of King David (presumably David I, already considered as a great fount of legislation); rather than intending to deceive, this attribution may simply indicate that the law in *Regiam* was the traditional common law of the realm, although some editing did introduce a more legislative style into the texts used.[178]

(*b*) Quoniam Attachiamenta

If *Regiam* functioned as a guide to practice before the royal courts, *Quoniam* was 'a manual of instruction about feudal courts—their personnel, their procedures (in the widest sense of that term), and their competences'.[179] *Quoniam* cannot have been compiled before 1318, as its core text draws on the legislation of that year; its modern editor prefers an early date within the first half of the fourteenth century.[180] The text was intended for the use of those who ran the network of feudal courts that covered Scotland.

(*c*) *Tradition and reconstruction*

Both *Regiam* and *Quoniam* demonstrate the tenacity with which Scots law clung to its traditional forms and procedures. In contrast to England, where a legal profession, which had developed around central courts, had worked the basic ideas of English law into a sophisticated system of specialized learning, Scots law remained largely oral in its procedures and practice, with courts presided over by landowners, either as representatives of the king or as possessors of a franchise jurisdiction, where the decisions were made by an assize of the suitors. Events from 1296 onwards must have disrupted the continued oral transmission and acquisition of the necessary knowledge for the smooth running of the Scottish legal system. The real significance of the appearance of *Regiam* and *Quoniam* in, say, the second quarter of the fourteenth century, was the part they must have played in the reconstruction of

---

[176] MacQueen (n. 38), 89–98.
[177] Alan Harding, 'Regiam Majestatem amongst Medieval Law-Books' [1984] *JR* 97–111.
[178] Stein, (1969) 48 *Scot Hist Rev* 112.   [179] *Quoniam Attachiamenta* (n. 71), 61–2.
[180] Ibid. 99–100, 107.

Scots law after the tremendous dislocation caused by English occupation, the continuing wars with England (including invasion by Edward Balliol and Edward III of England), David II's sojourn in France and later imprisonment in England. These treatises were designed to help define jurisdiction and to explain the way to proceed in royal and baron courts; other medieval Scots treatises may fit this pattern and Professor Duncan has argued that the work known as 'The Laws of Malcolm MacKenneth' derived from the period of reconstruction under David II.[181]

5. Common law and *jus commune*

(a) Litigation and learned law

The absence of a secular legal profession was of tremendous significance; it made Scots common law more open to influence from the *jus commune*. The evidence is too slight for any definite conclusion, but, through the fourteenth century, the royal courts seem to have placed increasing reliance on the *jus commune* in dealing with land rights.[182] Thus, in a dispute over a claim for teind before the court of the justiciar north of the Forth, the court, 'de consilio jurisperitorum', ruled that the king could not grant lands more freely than he held them himself, 'quia nullus plus iuris transferre potest in alium quam possidet in seipso'.[183] In a dispute between David II and the Earl of Ross over land the king's advisers prepared for him a series of questions 'allegatis in eadem pluribus auctoritatibus iuris civilis'.[184] Two cases from around 1380 showed very considerable learning in the *jus commune*. The first arose out of a claim by the Earl of Douglas in his own court that the Abbot of Lindores owed him fealty; the Abbot rejected the claim to jurisdiction and appealed to the royal court, relying on the authority of the *Libri Feudorum*, the *Digest*, the *Code*, the *Decretum Gratiani*, the civilian Azo, and the canonists Petrus de Bellapertica, Hostiensis, and Durandus.[185] In 1382, the Bishop of Aberdeen brought an action for showing the holding in his baron court against John Crab (this was an action compelling a tenant to produce his charters in court); on losing, Crab falsed the doom in the sheriff court. The Bishop's pleadings cited civil law, canon law, and the *Libri Feudorum* and noted commentators such as the civilian Azo and the canonists Durandus and Innocentius.[186]

[181] A. A. M. Duncan, 'The "Laws of Malcolm MacKenneth"', in Grant/Stringer (n. 4), 239–73.
[182] MacQueen (n. 38), 78; Stein (n. 103), 297–306.
[183] W. Fraser, *History of the Carnegies Earls of Southesk, and of their Kindred* (1867), vol. 2, 486–7 (appendix, no. 36). The maxim is from Ulp. D. 50, 17, 54.
[184] A. Fraser, Lord Saltoun, *The Frasers of Philorth* (1879), vol. 2, 208–9 (appendix, no. 12).
[185] John Dowden (ed.), *Chartulary of the Abbey of Lindores, 1195–1479*, Scottish History Society, First Series, vol. 42, (1903), 202–12, 314–25 (app. V).
[186] *Registrum Episcopatus Aberdonensis*, Spalding Club, vol. 13 (1845), vol. 1, 143–55. See R. M. Maxtone Graham, 'Showing the Holding', [1957] *JR* 251–69 at 257–9; Stein (n. 103), 301–2.

(b) The influence of the Church's lawyers

That the Church was a litigant in a number of these cases is probably significant; already it had many personnel trained in the *jus commune*, especially in the canon law. It has been conjectured that William of Spynie, graduate of Paris, Doctor of Canon Law, drafted the learned pleadings in the last two cases.[187] If particularly distinguished, Spynie was not unique; it is possible to point to other contemporary members of the Aberdeen Cathedral Chapter who had studied civil and canon law.[188] Investigation of the careers of some 400 Scottish graduates between 1340 and 1410 reveals that, of the 230 whose faculties can be identified, 120 enrolled in law and 110 in arts; eighty of those who enrolled in arts subsequently pursued legal study. In other words, 200 out of the 230 acquired a legal training in a university.[189]

This cadre of academically qualified ecclesiastical lawyers did not restrict their legal work to the needs of the Church. Some served as notaries;[190] others feature as attorneys and *prelocutores* (or *prolocutores*) acting for secular litigants. The Aberdeen court roll of 1317 shows that representation by an attorney was already common; *prelocutores* feature and one party appoints 'his attorney and procurator'.[191] That litigants should turn to those with particular legal skills is understandable; process on brieves could raise complex issues, requiring a measure of familiarity with procedure and the general law.[192] It is no surprise to find that Harvey and John of Strathanery, both clerks, were appointed as attorneys to pursue a brieve of dissaine around 1319 on behalf of the heirs portioner of the barony of Fithkil in Fife.[193] More traditional *prelocutores*, such as a man's lord, can be found and those who were not clerics certainly also acted in this role, while great men still came to court with an impressive retinue.[194] It is worth noting, however, that, by the fifteenth century, the common term for one who acted on one's behalf in court was no longer 'attorney', a word borrowed from England, but 'procurator', a term of canon law, originating in Justinian's *Code*.[195]

(c) Jus commune *in Scotland*

This evidence supports the idea that the learning of the *jus commune* was to some extent starting to penetrate Scots common law. As the text of *Quoniam* developed through copying and revising some provisions of Roman law became embedded in it.[196] The Bute and Cromertie manuscripts of *Regiam*

---

[187] Stein (n. 103), 303–6.   [188] Ibid. 302–3.
[189] D. E. R. Watt, 'University Graduates in Scottish Benefices before 1410', (1964) 15 *Records of the Scottish Church History Society* 77–88 at 79.
[190] John Durkan, 'The Early Scottish Notary', in I. B. Cowan and Duncan Shaw (eds.), *The Renaissance and Reformation in Scotland: Essays in Honour of Gordon Donaldson* (1983), 22–40.
[191] Dickinson (n. 56), 3, 8, 10, 11–12, 14. See generally MacQueen (n. 38), 81.
[192] MacQueen (n. 38), 77.   [193] Ibid. 78.   [194] APS, I, 505.
[195] For some examples, see MacQueen (n. 38), 81.
[196] *Quoniam Attachiamenta* (n. 71), 102–4.

contained extensive glosses derived from the *utrumque jus*; they presumably accumulated as the manuscripts were copied and revised in an attempt to enhance their utility. This seems to denote a subtle move from a knowledge of Roman and canon law being displayed to an infiltration of some of the doctrines of the *jus commune* into Scots law. It is important not to exaggerate this; Scots law remained firmly rooted in its Anglo-Norman heritage. Likewise, it is important not to downplay this phenomenon; *Regiam* itself contained a good proportion of canon law. The reconstruction of Scots law in the fourteenth century involved academic lawyers who will have seen Scots law as a *jus proprium* within a framework provided by the *jus commune*. Men trained in the *jus commune* will have seen canon law, civil law, and the *Libri Feudorum* and their accumulated commentaries and glosses as providing material with which to understand, interpret, and expand the Scottish material.

6. Common law and social order

(a) Violence, order, and law

The insecurity of social and political life in fourteenth-century Scotland brought about the increasing security and clarity of tenurial rights and their definition in legal treatises such as *Regiam*. The need to restate the common law arose from the fact that tenants were at the mercy of great lords and great lords were likely to try to protect their followers from royal justice. Conflict over land was endemic in a violent society obsessed with honour and chivalry. Parliaments and councils regularly emphasized the need to hold justice ayres and execute the common law by punishing wrongdoers.[197] When illness prevented Robert III from properly governing the realm and restraining 'trespassours and rebellours', the Duke of Rothesay was appointed his Lieutenant 'generally throch al the kynrike' for three years 'to punys trespassours'.[198] One main aim was obviously to discourage self-help in the form of violent retaliation for alleged wrongs, as it could easily degenerate into the bloodfeud. While bloodfeud can be represented as a form of 'community justice' with its own mechanisms of resolution, there can be little doubt of its destabilizing potential.[199] This was why Parliaments and General Councils regularly legislated on homicide and remissions, for it was common for the king to grant a remission for homicide if the kin were compensated.[200]

Two important statutes in 1370 and 1372 on homicide distinguished different degrees of culpability in an attempt to regularize the granting of remissions and to control violence.[201] The first required that anyone seeking

---

[197] See e.g. APS, I, 491–2, 550, 552.   [198] APS, I, 572.
[199] See Wormald, (1980) 87 *Past and Present* 54–97.
[200] See e.g. APS, I, 492, 499, 570, 571.   [201] See Sellar (n. 104), 48–9.

remission for slaughter had to be put to the knowledge of an assize to determine whether the killing had been committed 'per murthyr vel per praecogitatem maliciam' (*vel* is conjunctive); the king would not grant remission for such a murder without the consent of a General Council.[202] In 1372, this was further elaborated by enacting that an assize was to decide whether slaughter had taken place 'ex certo et deliberato proposito vel per forthouchfelony sive murthir' (*vel* and *sive* are conjunctive) or 'ex calore iracundiae viz chaudemellee'. If the assize found the accused guilty of murder or forethocht felony, justice was to be executed immediately; if *chaudemellee* was found, the accused was to have 'the legal and appropriate defences hitherto granted by the laws and customs of the kingdom'. Fugitive killers could be banished and their goods and lands escheated to the king or baron. If officers of baronies and regalities did not enforce these provisions then the king's officers would. Those who fled to a girth (a sanctuary focused on a religious site) were to come out and be tried by an assize to determine whether the slaughter was by forethocht felony or not: if they would not, they were to be banished as guilty of murder; if they did and were tried and found guilty of slaughter by *chaudemellee*, they were to be restored to the sanctuary of the girth.[203] Sanctuary in the girth allowed the individual time to reach an agreement with the kin of the individual he had killed, although royal policy allowed this immunity to be withdrawn in certain circumstances.[204]

(b) Affirmation of the common law

Despite the difficulties of the fourteenth century, there was thus no turning away from the mechanisms of the common law to provide order in society and ordinances and statutes stressed the need for the regular functioning of the common law. There was concern to ensure that proper officials were appointed and were accountable.[205] Provisions show anxiety to ensure the proper working of the legal system through proper exercise of royal authority. Thus, so that *communis justicia* should be done to everyone with no one being shown any favour, letters issued by the royal chapel were not to be revoked by any other letters under any seal.[206] The correct form was established when the king sat on appeals in Parliament.[207] No judge should execute any mandate, no matter under what seal it had been issued, if it breached statute or the form of common law: instead he should endorse and return it.[208] The same concern with proper procedure is found in some actual pleas in the reign of David II. Thus, Parliament referred an action to the next Parliament because

---

[202] APS, I, 509 (see also 535).   [203] APS, I, 547–8.
[204] See now H. L. MacQueen, 'Girth: Society and the Law of Sanctuary in Scotland', in J. W. Cairns and O. F. Robinson (eds.), *Critical Studies in Roman Law, Comparative Law, and Legal History* (2000), 333–52.   [205] APS, I, 492 (1357), 572, 573–4 (1399).
[206] APS, I, 498 (1366).   [207] APS, I, 507 (6 Mar. 1369).
[208] APS, I, 547 (2 Mar. 1372); 509 (1370).

Historical Introduction 49

sufficient time had not been allowed, while the giving of a decision on the falsing of a doom was postponed because it was Lent and custom forbade the issuing of such sentences during that period.[209] The evidence demonstrates the regular and efficient operation of the writing chapel under succeeding chancellors that was necessary for the working of the common law.

This concern with proper procedure probably reflects the influence as royal functionaries or counsellors of men such as Walter Trail, *utriusque juris doctor*, former papal judge at Avignon, and ultimately Bishop of St Andrews, and Duncan Petit, *bacalaureus utriusque juris*, who was audit clerk before becoming Secretary (or Keeper of the Privy Seal).[210] Such men were clearly as valuable in royal service as they were in the running of the Church. Academic lawyers are also found in the service of great magnates: Gilbert Caven, a close associate of the Earls of Douglas (and tutor to the fifth earl) was a Bachelor of Decreets.[211] University graduates in law were thus coming to operate the institutions of the Scots common law in Parliament, Council, and the royal writing chapel and as the law agents of great lords exercising extensive franchise and royal jurisdiction.

The fifteenth century thus opened with legislation and practices that re-affirmed the traditional common law of Scotland. The growth of a more complex bureaucracy was symbolized by differentiation of seals and development of new offices;[212] the learning of academic lawyers played a significant role in all of this. This did not necessarily demonstrate centralizing tendencies at work in Scottish government; individual lordship remained vital to government of the realm.[213] Localities remained important, so that when, in 1384, provisions on the apprehension of criminals were explicitly stated to apply to regalities and ecclesiastical privileges, protests were entered by Archibald, Lord of Galloway, and the Earl of Fife, to protect the Laws of Galloway and the Law of Clan Macduff.[214] On the other hand, Robert Bruce, in 1324, had already extended to Galwegians the right to an assize when accused by a sergeant, so they no longer had to purge themselves 'according to the ancient laws of Galloway'.[215] In the following year, he freed the men of Glenswinton from *surdit de sergeaunt*.[216] Lordship in these localities was coming to conform more to the expectations of the common law. The centre was increasing its grip.

---

[209] APS, I, 504–5, 507.   [210] Watt (n. 99), 447–9, 539–42.
[211] Francis McGurk (ed.), *Papal Letters to Scotland of Benedict XIII of Avignon 1394–1419*, Scottish History Society, Fourth Series, vol. 12 (1976) 149–50. See Brown (n. 133), 162.
[212] See R. K. Hannay, 'The Early History of the Scottish Signet', in *The Society of Writers to His Majesty's Signet* (1936), 3–51 at 11–16 (= R. K. Hannay, *The College of Justice* (1990), 275–323 at 283–8).   [213] See Brown, (n. 133), 157–80.
[214] APS, 1, 550–1.   [215] RMS, I, 457 (appendix 1, no. 59).
[216] RRS, V, 535–7 (no. 275).

IV. FROM THE MIDDLE AGES TO THE RENAISSANCE

1. The Stewarts, politics, and government

(a) Royal authority

In 1469, Parliament noted that James III (1460–88) possessed 'ful Jurisdictioune and fre Impire within his Realme' and rejected the authority of imperial notaries in civil matters in Scotland.[217] Ten years later, a clergyman was accused before Parliament of 'tresonable usurpacioune' for his pretended legitimation of a child 'in the name and Autorite of the Emperoure, contrare to oure souverain lordis croune and maieste Riale'.[218] This assertion that *rex in regno suo est imperator* emphasized the independence of the kingdom from higher political authority. As James III entered his majority it may have seemed an opportune moment to assert the dignity of the Scottish Crown. Imperial imagery was enthusiastically adopted by the kings of Scots—the kings now wore the arched imperial crown, first on their coinage and then in reality.[219]

This, perhaps unexpected, stress on the imperial nature of the Scottish monarchy derived from Scots lawyers' encounter with the learning of the *jus commune*. Some medieval scholars had argued that *merum imperium*, full sovereignty, belonged to the Emperor alone. To defend the French Crown from the claims of the Emperor and Pope, scholars had developed the doctrine now expounded by Parliament.[220] The Scots king claimed full sovereignty: a way of emphasizing it was, in civilian terms, to argue he was an emperor in his own kingdom. Certainly, the vestiges of one of the claims of English authority over Scotland—that of the Archbishop of York to metropolitan status over the Scottish Church—were finally given their quietus, when, in 1472, St Andrews was raised to an archiepiscopal see with authority over the other Scottish dioceses (now including Orkney, Galloway, and the Isles).[221] The independence of the Scottish Kirk and Kingdom could be proudly emphasized.

---

[217] APS, II, 95 (c. 6).   [218] Nicholson (n. 6), 115.

[219] See I. H. Stewart, *The Scottish Coinage* (rev. edn., 1967), 65–7; R. A. Mason, *Kingship and the Commonweal: Political Thought in Renaissance and Reformation Scotland* (1998), 130–1, 137. On the imagery and iconography of power adopted by the Stewarts, see C. M. Burnett, 'Outward Signs of Majesty, 1535–1540', in Janet Hadley Williams (ed.), *Stewart Style, 1513–1542: Essays on the Court of James V* (1996), 289–302; H. M. Shire, 'The King in his House: Three Architectural Artefacts belonging to the Reign of James V', in Janet Hadley Williams (ed.), *Stewart Style, 1513–1542: Essays on the Court of James V* (1996), 62–96.

[220] L. J. Macfarlane, *William Elphinstone and the Kingdom of Scotland, 1431–1514: The Struggle for Order* (rev. edn., 1995), 40–4; Henry VIII made a similar declaration in 1533: Walter Ullmann, '"This Realm of England is an Empire"', (1979) 30 *Journal of Ecclesiastical History* 175–203. His target was the papacy.

[221] L. J. Macfarlane, 'The Primacy of the Scottish Church, 1472–1521', (1969) 22 *Innes Review* 111–29; J. A. F. Thomson, 'Some New Light on the Elevation of Patrick Graham', (1961) 40

(b) Consolidation of the dynasty

Despite repeated royal minorities and the continuing alternating warfare and truce with England, the era from the return of James I in 1424 to the death of James V (1513–42) was undoubtedly that of the ascent of the Stewarts. None of these kings died easily in his bed of old age: James I was murdered; James II (1437–60) was killed by an exploding canon at the siege of Roxburgh Castle; James III died in unexplained circumstances after defeat at the hands of an army headed by his son; James IV (1488–1513) died at Flodden in battle against the English; James V died shortly after the Scots defeat by the English at Solway Moss in 1542. This seemingly appalling record should be put in the perspective provided by the history of the English Crown, which, from 1399 until Henry Tudor defeated Richard III in 1485, was transferred by violence no less than six times. In fact, after the dynasty's shaky start, the Stewarts had become remarkably secure: they made distinguished foreign marriages; they created a cultured court in the settings of their palaces at Linlithgow, Falkland, Stirling, and Holyrood; they generally asserted their authority.[222] Two aspects of the last may be singled out as of particular significance. First, the kings of Scots progressively gained control over appointments to major benefices in the Church, until, for example, in 1504, James IV could appoint his 11-year-old illegitimate son as Archbishop of St Andrews.[223] Secondly, they carried out what amounted to an assault on the great territorial nobility: when James I returned from England there were eleven earls and one duke sharing seventeen earldoms—one month after his death there were only five earls left, each with only one earldom, and two of these were hostages in England;[224] in the reign of James II much of the power of the Douglas family was destroyed, with members executed, murdered, and forfeited;[225] under James IV the last great territorial lordship, that of the Isles, was forfeited, before being annexed inalienably to the Crown in 1540 under James V.[226] If all of this should not be viewed as part of a continuing struggle

---

Scot Hist Rev 83–8. Glasgow became an archiepiscopal see in 1492: L. J. Macfarlane, 'The Elevation of the Diocese of Glasgow into an Archbishopric in 1492', (1992) 43 *Innes Review* 99–118.

[222] Modern biographies, of variable and varying quality, now exist for all of them: Michael Brown, *James I* (1994); Christine McGladdery, *James II* (1990); Norman MacDougall, *James III: A Political Study* (1982); idem, *James IV* (1997); Jamie Cameron, *James V: The Personal Rule, 1528–1542* (1998). Still useful are E. W. Balfour-Melville, *James I King of Scots 1406–1437* (1936) and R. L. Mackie, *King James IV of Scotland: A Brief Survey of His Life and Times* (1958). See also J. M. Brown (now Wormald), 'The Exercise of Power', in Brown (now Wormald) (n. 11), 33–65; eadem, 'Taming the Magnates', in Gordon Menzies (ed.), *The Scottish Nation* (1972), 46–59. Grant (n. 138), 171–2 has a useful comparison of aspects of violence in Scotland and England in this era.   [223] See e.g. Nicholson (n. 6), 293–302, 385–6, 458–69, 556–62.

[224] Alexander Grant, 'The Development of the Scottish Peerage', (1978) 57 *Scot Hist Rev* 1–27 at 26; Brown (now Wormald), 'Exercise of Power' (n. 222), 49.

[225] Nicholson (n. 6), 353–74; Brown (n. 133), 283–308; Brown (now Wormald), 'Taming the Magnates' (n. 222), 53.   [226] Munro/Munro (n. 11), lxiv–lxxiv; APS, II, 360–1 (c. 19).

of the king to 'tame' the magnates, the effects of this assault on the older nobility of Scotland are important.[227] Nobility became less closely linked with *territorial* lordship; instead, a new parliamentary nobility came into existence. Moreover, the forfeitures served not only to enrich the king, but also removed a level of government between the king and many tenants, as Parliament in 1401 had provided that tenants-in-chief holding land in an earldom or lordship were to remain holding of the king, even after the king infeft someone by charter in the earldom or lordship, while the king could not create a superiority of lands held of him by his tenants without their consent.[228]

Between the reigns of James I and James V, the institutions of Scots common law underwent a profound transformation, resulting in a new pattern of development. The result was increasing centralization of both civil and criminal justice, together with the appearance of a recognizable legal profession. Yet, continuities remained. The new developments were built on what had gone before.

2. Continuity and development

(a) Kingship and justice

The Meroure of Wyssdome of John Ireland was the nearest anyone came to articulating a theory of politics in fifteenth-century Scotland;[229] Ireland saw the essence of kingship in the royal duty to dispense justice under God, wielding equity to dispense with the application of human laws that are repugnant to reason and justice.[230] This in many ways rather well described contemporary Scottish kingship, where the king remained central to the system of justice with his traditional duties of keeping the peace, punishing wrongdoers, and protecting the weak, such as widows, orphans, and strangers. He was also expected to ensure the proper conduct of his officers. The last was particularly important; many commands to his officers ended with the warning that he did not wish to hear of their failure to carry out their duties.[231] '[T]he execucioune of Justice ... concernis his hienes in sa gret nerenes baith his saul and liff and his trew liegis' as Parliament put it in the dramatic year of 1488.[232] Thus, while the king's lieges were generally expected to use the

---

[227] Brown (now Wormald), 'Taming the Magnates' (n. 222).   [228] APS, I, 575–6.
[229] Charles MacPherson, F. Quinn, and Craig McDonald (eds.), *The Meroure of Wyssdome Composed for the Use of James IV, King of Scots A.D. 1490 by Johannes de Irlandia Professor of Theology in the University of Paris*, Scottish Text Society, New Series, vol. 19, Fourth Series, vol. 2, vol. 19, (1926, 1965, 1990). On the relationship of this work to that of Jean Gerson, see Mason (n. 219), 13–14, 18–19, 23–5, 32–3; J. H. Burns, *The True Law of Kingship: Concepts of Monarchy in Early-Modern Scotland* (1996), 19–39.   [230] Ireland (n. 229), III, 105–14.
[231] APS, I, 576 (1401); II, 177 (c. 10) (1497); A. A. M. Duncan, 'The Central Courts before 1532', in Paton (n. 56), 321–40 at 329–30; MacQueen (n. 144), 253–60; Burns (n. 229), 93–121.
[232] APS, II, 207 (c. 6).

regular remedies provided by the common law, his duty to ensure that justice was done could lead to his subjects, in exceptional circumstances, taking complaints directly to him; these were dealt with in his Council, or in a Council General or in his Council in Parliament. It was also always open for the king to take any case before his own Council.[233]

The duty of punishing wrongdoers meant that the king was expected to hold regular justice ayres and, if possible, attend personally.[234] James IV, for one, certainly made a regular practice of attending justice ayres.[235] The king's attendance at justice ayres was thought to help strike terror into the hearts of wrongdoers. Though traditional justice ayres were reasonably frequent through the fifteenth century,[236] they became very infrequent in the next and the statutes of 1525, 1526, and 1535 to encourage the holding of ayres and make their process more expeditious were, according to Croft Dickinson, so much dead letter.[237] In fact, by the reign of James V the ancient division of the office of justiciar had disapppeared and the office of Justice General had become hereditary in the Argyll family. The Justice-Clerk and Deputes now dealt with most of the business in a now exclusively criminal court that had become settled in Edinburgh.[238]

Wrongdoers had put themselves outside the king's peace; it was always therefore possible and tempting for a king to grant respites (delays) from prosecution and remissions in return for payment.[239] As earlier, there were frequent statutes attempting to control the royal grant of respites and remissions. These tended to follow the established view that remissions should not be granted to those who committed slaughter on 'forethocht felony' (who also would not have the benefit of girth (sanctuary)) and also only after assythment (compensation) had been made to the kin.[240] The reality was that many were always able to negotiate with the king: the Privy Seal records reveal that James IV granted 182 remissions to those guilty of slaughter and no less than eighty-two to those guilty on 'forethocht felony'.[241]

---

[233] Duncan (n. 231), 324–8. [234] APS, II, 103 (c. 2), 104 (c. 7), 122, 208 (c. 8), 315 (c. 7).
[235] Nicholson (n. 6), 567–70. [236] MacQueen (n. 144), 63–93.
[237] W. Croft Dickinson, 'The High Court of Justiciary', in Paton (n. 56), 408–12 at 410.
[238] See R. K. Hannay, 'The Office of the Justice Clerk', (1935) 47 *JR* 311–29 (= Hannay, *College of Justice* (n. 212), 325–43). See APS, III, 41 (c. 50) (1567) where the court is described as one that sat in Edinburgh. [239] Nicholson (n. 6), 569–70.
[240] APS, II, 8 (c. 25) (1425); 9 (c. 7) (1426); 34 (cc. 2, 4) (1450); 95–6 (c. 11) (1469); 104 (c. 7) (1473); 118 (c. 2) (1478); 165 (c. 5) (1484); 170 (c. 4) (1485); 176 (c. 1) (1487); 250 (c. 7) (1504); 287 (c. 13) (1524); 332 (c. 3) (1529). Statutes such as APS, II, 20–1 (c. 1) (1432) and 225 (c. 9) (1491) emphasized that those guilty on 'forethocht felony' should suffer death. In 1535, it was again enacted that those who committed slaughter on 'forethocht felony' should not have the benefit of the girth and should be given up by masters of girths: APS, II, 348 (c. 30).
[241] Nicholson (n. 6), 569.

(b) *Parliaments and courts*

The role of Parliament as a court and a legislature was retained. Much important legislation was enacted, usually on the basis of 'articles' drafted for enactment by a committee *pro articulis advisandis*.[242] Judicial business before Parliament was of two types: first, there was a common law jurisdiction to false dooms, dealt with by a committee *ad decisionem judicii*; secondly, there was a jurisdiction over miscellaneous complaints, dealt with by a committee of Lords Auditors *ad causas et querelas* (of causes and complaints). These committees appear in the fuller parliamentary record preserved from 1466 onwards; there is evidence, however, of their existence as far back as the reign of David II.[243] Between 1424 and 1436, James I held at least ten Parliaments and three General Councils.[244] From the date of their majorities, James II and James III held virtually annual Parliaments; James IV departed from this practice; after near annual parliaments he did not hold one from 1496 until 1504, holding them again only in 1506 and 1509. Under James V, Parliaments were once again frequently held.[245] Despite James IV's preference for governing through his Privy Council, Parliaments and other meetings of the Estates thus held their importance in administration, although, after 1496, while the Lords Auditors *ad causas et querelas* continued to be appointed when Parliament met, up to 1544, they never again functioned.[246] Attempts to refine and define parliamentary attendance resulted in the recognition of a parliamentary peerage; furthermore in 1504 it was decided that barons, freeholders, and vassals whose lands were valued at less than 100 merks were excused attendance at Parliament unless specially summoned by the king.[247]

In the localities, the courts of sheriff, burgh, baron, and regality all maintained their significance, although developments at the centre were to affect them. An attempt, in 1504, to divide the sheriffdom of Inverness into more convenient units was unsuccessful, but Parliament in 1506 gave the king authority to divide, create, and annex sheriffdoms.[248]

---

[242] Nicholson (n. 6), 282, 424.

[243] See NAS, *A Guide to the National Archives of Scotland* (1996), 9; Duncan (n. 231), 328–9.

[244] On the distinction, see R. K. Hannay, 'On "Parliament" and "General Council"', (1921) 18 *Scot Hist Rev* 157–70; *idem*, 'General Council and Convention of Estates', (1923) 20 *Scot Hist Rev* 98–115; *idem*, 'General Council of Estates', (1923) 20 *Scot Hist Rev* 251–84 (= Hannay, *College of Justice* (n. 212), 217–72).

[245] For details of Parliaments, see the chronological table prefixed to APS, II. See generally, I. E. O'Brien, 'The Scottish Parliament in the Fifteenth and Sixteenth Centuries' (unpublished Ph.D. thesis, University of Glasgow, 1980). [246] Duncan (n. 231), 338–9.

[247] See APS, II, 9 (c. 8) (1426); 15 (c. 2) (1428); 50 (c. 21) (1458); 252 (c. 23) (1504).

[248] APS, II, 241–2 (cc. 3–5); 243 (cc. 18–19); 249 (cc. 3–5); 251 (c. 18) (1504); 267 (c. 5) (1506). The 1504 reforms were rescinded in 1509: APS, II, 268 (c. 2).

(c) *Burghs, free and unfree*

In this period, a great number of burghs of barony, both ecclesiastical and secular, were created, promoting the increasing clarity of distinction between 'royal' burghs, with their special privileges, and 'unfree' burghs.[249] Where once the only distinction was that royal burghs were held of the king and baronial from a subject superior, now only royal burghs sent representatives to Parliament, other than the great ecclesiastical burghs of St Andrews, Brechin, Glasgow, Arbroath, and Dunfermline, which all sent representatives by the late sixteenth century; these five also acquired the greater trading privileges of royal burghs.[250] The bailies in the burgh court continued to represent royal justice, subject to the supervision of the Chamberlain in his ayre through the process of falsing of dooms.[251] The last chamberlain ayre was, however, held in 1517 and the Court of the Four Burghs also ceased to operate in the early sixteenth century.[252] In general, the privileges of the burghs were respected, although growing tensions between the merchant guild and the craftsmen resulted in new modes of election of the officers that favoured the dominant merchants.[253]

(d) *Barons and tenants*

Baronies continued to be created in great numbers; James IV's reign saw the erection of more than eighty, still with the traditional purpose of establishing good rule and obedience to the laws.[254] By 1400, serfdom was obsolete in Scotland, so those who held land in the barony did so as rentallers (usually meaning they held a lease for life) or on a tack (lease) for a definite period, or as tenants-at-will. All of these groups could hold as 'kindly tenants': that is, they had a recognized customary right to take over tenancies previously held by members of their kin (hence 'kindly'). They thus possessed what was called the 'kindness', which, by the middle of the sixteenth century, was approaching a legal right that could be renounced, sold, bequeathed, and divided. All disputes over such tenancies were, of course, dealt with in the baron court, where the suitors would enforce the customary practices in this regard in the barony.[255] A series of statutes in the fifteenth century gave increased security to tenants holding land on tacks and protected them from being distrained for the debts of their lord.[256] It also became increasingly popular for landlords, instead of setting lands in tack, to feu them in feu-ferme

---

[249] McNeill/MacQueen (n. 4), 213–4; G. S. Pryde (ed.), *The Court Book of the Burgh of Kirkintilloch, 1658–1694*, Scottish History Society, Third Series, vol. 53 (1963), xxxviii–xxxix.
[250] Pryde, *Kirkintilloch Court Book* (n. 249), xii–xxxvii, lvii; McNeill/MacQueen (n. 4), 213.
[251] Dickinson (n. 56), xc–xcvii.
[252] Ibid. cxliv; Athol Murray, 'The Last Chamberlain Ayre', (1960) 39 *Scot Hist Rev* 85.
[253] APS, II, 95 (c. 5) (1469); 107 (c. 12) (1474); 178 (c. 14) (1487); 252 (c. 25) (1504).
[254] Ranald Nicholson, 'Feudal Developments in Late Medieval Scotland', [1973] *JR* 1–21.
[255] M. H. B. Sanderson, *Scottish Rural Life in the Sixteenth Century* (1982), 56–63.
[256] APS, II, 35–6 (c. 6) (1450); 96 (c. 12) (1469); 225 (c. 7) (1491).

tenure (*in feudifirma*). The advantage to the landlord was a substantial *grassum* (one-off lump sum) and a feu duty greater than the rent; the advantage to the tenant was the acquisition of a heritable title to the land. A number of statutes encouraged this practice, which, in the long run, had a tremendous importance in giving individuals an increasing independence through possession of a heritable real right in land.[257]

The phrase popular with fifteenth-century legislators, 'royalty and regality' neatly encapsulated the status of those holding regalian rights.[258] Legislation, such as that in 1455, that annexed to the royalty any regality that came into the king's hands and provided that no more regalities were to be created 'without deliverance of the parliament', betrayed a suspicion of the award of such great powers of jurisdiction;[259] other acts allowed royal interference in law enforcement in regalities.[260]

(e) New directions

If, in many ways, much of the traditional institutions of the common law thus remained active and effective, yet, around the beginning of the sixteenth century, changes and development started to have an impact. The Chamberlain's loss of authority over the burghs affected their legal institutions. Feuing of land became increasingly common. The institutions of central government betrayed an increasing suspicion of regalities. In Parliament, the Lords Auditors of Causes and Complaints ceased to operate. At the same time, the application of the common law was extended. In 1426, Parliament enacted that 'all and sindry the kingis liegis of the realme leif and be governyt undir the kingis lawis and statutis of this realme alanery and undir na particulare lawis na speciale privalegis na be the lawis of uther cuntreis nor realmis'.[261] This was probably aimed at the laws of Clan Macduff, as a number of individuals had recently claimed its privileges.[262] Indeed, James I's recent destruction of the Albany Stewarts (Earls of Fife) may have made this more pressing. Yet traditions linked with lordship died hard; in 1458, the Law of Clan MacDuff could still be claimed,[263] while it was not until the reign of James IV that the right to calps claimed by heads of kin in Galloway and Carrick was dealt with.[264] Finally, after the defeat of the Lord of the Isles, the Parliament in 1504 that tried to reorganize the system of justice in the Lordship, provided that 'all our soverane lordis liegis beand undir his obeyasance

---

[257] Sanderson (n. 255), 64–75; APS, II, 49 (c. 15) (1458); 253 (cc. 36–7) (1504); 376–7 (c. 35) (1540). [258] See e.g. APS, II, 20–1 (c. 1) (1432); 36 (c. 13) (1450); 347 (c. 28) (1535).
[259] APS, II, 43 (c. 4). [260] See e.g. APS, II, 344 (c. 14) (1535).
[261] APS, II, 9 (c. 3). I am unconvinced that this statute has anything to do with the laws on barratry or is in any way aimed at the papacy.
[262] Stuart (n. 106), lxix; Balfour-Melville (n. 222), 130.
[263] Balfour, *Practicks*, 511–12. The printed text states '1548'. I am indebted to Dr Michael Wasser for the information that this is an accidental transposition.
[264] APS, II, 214 (c. 5) (1489); 222 (cc. 19–20) (1490).

And in speciale the Ilis be Reulit be our soverane lordis aune lawis and the commone lawis of the Realme And be nain uthir lawis'.[265] The king had finally (at least in theory) applied his common law throughout the realm, other than Orkney and Shetland, which, though included in the original draft of this act, were not mentioned in the version enacted, presumably because of uncertainty about their status.[266]

3. Continuity and crisis

If it is an exaggeration to describe Scots common law as undergoing a crisis in the early Renaissance period, the stark term certainly helps focus attention on the linked developments that sent Scots law in a new direction. These were: a progressive loss of confidence in the common law courts; a turning away from traditional process on brieves; and a growing distrust of aspects of justice in the localities. The ultimate response, after some attempts to encourage use of the local 'ordinary' courts, was the erection of a central court, operated by a recognizable legal profession. Of course, there was considerable continuity—the central court was created from an expansion of the existing jurisdiction of the King's Council. Yet the fact of major change remains and must be accounted for.

(a) The Sessions

In 1425, Parliament referred to the 'billis of complayntis the qhilkis may not be determyt be the parliament for divers causis'; these were to be 'execut and determyt be the Jugis and officiaris of the courtis to quham thai pertene of law', that is, the 'Justice chawmerlane shereffis bailyies of burrowis baronis or spirituale Jugis'. If, however, a judge 'refusis to do the law evinly' (including, if necessary, appointing an advocate for a 'pure creatur'), then the party complaining would 'haf recourse to the king'.[267] This act was a first response to litigants' attempts to take cases before Parliament or the King's Council. The solution of encouraging use of the common law courts was clearly ineffective, as, the following year, Parliament appointed the Chamberlain with 'certane discret personis of the thre estatis' to sit at three specified times each year 'to knaw examyn conclude and finally determyn all and sindry complayntis causis and querellis that may be determynt befor the kingis counsal'.[268] The preservation, in 1425, of the right of recourse to the king, should his officers

---

[265] APS, II, 252 (c. 24).
[266] On the issue of Orkney and Shetland, see Donaldson (n. 6), 26. On the rich legal culture of the Isles, see Bannerman (n. 11), 227–8.   [267] APS, II, 8 (c. 24) (1425).
[268] APS, II, 11 (c. 19). The printed act mentions the Chancellor rather than the Chamberlain; Dr O'Brien's study shows that the act originally provided for the Chamberlain: O'Brien (n. 245), 26–8.

fail to do justice, may have encouraged individuals to seek a remedy from the king in his Council.

The history of this institution of what were called 'Sessions' is obscure and complex; suffice it to say that it can be traced through the records for some years, presumably with the jurisdiction the king generally exercised to look after the interests of the weak and deal with the failures of his officers to do justice. In 1458, however, a wider jurisdiction was granted, seemingly an authority to try all civil actions that did not concern fee and heritage (with which the Lords Auditors of Causes and Complaints in Parliament also could not deal, because of the rule that no one could be compelled to answer in court for heritage except on a pleadable royal brieve). This suggests that litigants were not satisfied with their 'ordinary' judges. The practice of holding such sessions died out sometime after 1468.[269]

(b) Council, Session, College of Justice

After the ending of the Sessions, Parliament once more exhorted litigants to go to their ordinary judge; Council was only to be approached if he failed to do justice.[270] The traditional rule was restated in 1487: 'all Civile accionis questionis and plewis movit betuix quhatsumevir partiis be determytt and decidit befor the Juge ordinaris . . . Sa that nane accions sal be deducit callit determyt nor decidit before the lordis of our soveran lordis . . . counsale', except those of churchmen, widows, orphans, pupils, and foreigners, and complaints against officers for default in the execution of justice.[271] This failed: in 1488, it was repealed because '[i]t wer deferring of Justice to mony partijs' who could not get law administered to them before the ordinary judges; they were once again to be allowed to pursue actions before the Council 'as thai wer wont in tymes bigane'.[272] From then on there was a progressive development of the jurisdiction of the Lords of Council through the reign of James IV, with the practice of appointing men specially to the Council to deal with judicial business, with the Lords Auditors of Causes and Complaints in Parliament often continuing business to the Lords of Council (until 1496). Various attempts were also made to improve the speed of business before the Council; by the death of James IV at Flodden, the judicial business of the Council was dealt with by a core of eight ecclesiastics and nine laymen as Lords of Session.[273] In the long minority of James V, the

---

[269] APS, II, 32 (c. 1) (1439); 34 (c. 5) (1450); 46 (c. 8) (1456); 47–8 (cc. 1–5) (1458); 92 (c. 4) (1468); Duncan (n. 231), 331–2. On the brieves rule, see MacQueen (n. 38), 233–4.

[270] APS, II, 94 (c. 2) (1469); 107 (c. 11) (1474).   [271] APS, II, 177–8 (c. 10).

[272] APS, II, 183 (c. 17). On the development of the Council's jurisdiction in this period, see A. R. Borthwick, 'The King, Council and Councillors in Scotland, c. 1430–1460' (unpublished Ph.D. thesis, University of Edinburgh, 1989), vol. 1, 242–315. On the Lords Auditors and Council, see T. M. Chalmers, 'The King's Council, Patronage and the Governance of Scotland, 1460–1513'. (unpublished Ph.D. thesis, University of Aberdeen, 1982), 170–83.

[273] APS, II, 220 (c. 11) (1490); 223 (c. 27) (1490); 226 (c. 16) (1491); 249 (c. 2) (1504). For *'domini sessionis communiter electi'*, see ADC, I, 143. See generally, Duncan (n. 231), 334–9;

Council seems to have stopped specially deputing men to be upon the Session; a serious backlog of business started to accumulate. From 1524 onwards, it became the practice to appoint a list of men to the Privy Council to sit upon the Session; from 1528, only this group was to attend to the judicial business. Eventually in 1531, Pope Clement VII issued a bull narrating that James intended to found a College of Justice and ordering the Scottish bishops to contribute towards its support.[274] The next year Parliament enacted:

Becaus our soverane Is maist desyrous to have ane permanent ordoure of Justice for the universale wele of all his liegis and therfor tendis to Institute ane college of cunning and wise men baith of spirituale and temporale Estate for the doing and administracioune of Justice In all civile actiounis and therfor thinkis to be chosin certane persounis maist convenient and qualifyit therfore to be nowmere of xiiij persounis half spirituale half temporall with ane president The quhilkis personis sall be auctorizate in this present parliament to sitt and decyde apone all actiouns civile and nane utheris to have voit with thaim onto the tyme that the said college may be Institute at mare lasare ... The thre estatis of this present parliament thinkis this artikle wele consavit And therfor the kingis grace with avise and consent of the saidis thre estaitis ordanis the samin to have effect ...

The act also provided that, should the Lord Chancellor be present, he should vote and preside, while the king could appoint three or four other Lords from his Council to sit.[275] The new College was derived from the Council, but it was quite distinct from it. A papal bull on 10 March 1535 erected the College and in 1541 Parliament ratified its erection.[276] From its inception, the College was intended to be a supreme civil court; matters of fee and heritage, which once the Lords of Council (and the Lords Auditors of Causes and Complaints) had declined because of the brieves rule, were competent before them and, indeed, the Lords of Council had already assumed such jurisdiction before 1532.[277]

(c) *The failure of the ordinary courts*

Though we lack sufficient records of the ordinary courts to form a definitive judgement, an obvious conclusion is that they were perceived as failing

---

R. K. Hannay, 'On the Antecedents of the College of Justice', (1922) 11 *The Book of the Old Edinburgh Club* 87–123 (= Hannay, *College of Justice* (n. 212), 179–215); Chalmers (n. 272), 183–296, 447–59; Macfarlane (n. 220), 420–4.

[274] See e.g. Hannay, (1922) 11 *Book of the Old Edinburgh Club* 109–21; R. K. Hannay, *The College of Justice: Essays on the Institution and Development of the Court of Session* (1933), 27–61 (= *The College of Justice: Essays by R. K. Hannay* (ed. by H. L. MacQueen, 1990)). For speculations as to why it was called a 'College' of Justice, see ibid. 48–50 and P. G. Stein, 'The College of Judges of Pavia', (1952) 64 *JR* 204–13.   [275] APS, II, 335–6 (c. 2).

[276] Hannay, *College of Justice* (n. 274), 63–78; APS, III, 71 (c. 10).

[277] See now on this, above all, A. M. Godfrey, 'The Lords of Council and Session and the Foundation of the College of Justice: A Study in Jurisdiction' (unpublished Ph.D. thesis, University of Edinburgh, 1998), 20–62, 268–307; MacQueen (n. 38), 216–42.

litigants in some way. The plain determination of so many litigants to bring their actions before the King's Council puts this beyond doubt. Statutory reforms point to some of the problems litigants may have found in approaching their local, ordinary judge for justice. In a society where men were armed, feud common, and bonds of manrent between lords and men often required various types of counsel and assistance, going to the local court could prove an intimidating experience.[278] To ameliorate this, statutes attempted to control the number of followers a man could bring to court and to require the sheriff to take security from the parties for the keeping of the peace, should feud be alleged.[279] Yet, such provisions could not always be relied on, as Robert, Lord Fleming, found when he refused to attend the justice ayre at Dumbarton because he had heard his opponent, Gilbert, Lord Kennedy, had come to the ayre with an army.[280] Close study of a feud in St Andrews shows the type of tensions that could arise and affect the operation of the courts in a burgh.[281] There was a traditional rule that the Chamberlain, in exercising his supervisory jurisdiction, should inquire whether anyone had purchased a lord dwelling landward to come to the burgh court to the harm of his neighbours.[282] In 1400, William Walker of Aberdeen had to secure acquittal by compurgation of the charge of procuring an outside lord to the prejudice of his neighbours.[283] The growing popularity of bonds of manrent and maintenance in the fifteenth century made this situation more complex. In 1491, Parliament repeated an earlier prohibition on the making of such bonds in burghs, with the significant addition that no burgess should procure a lord from outwith the burgh 'to Rout na Rid nor pley at bar'.[284] Another evident concern was to ensure that litigation was conducted fairly. A few examples will suffice. General provisions were made to deal with prejudiced assizes.[285] No man could be on the assize who was an officer of the court or who had indicted an accused.[286] Assizers also had to swear that they had not received gifts from any party and, if they had, this was to be declared in open court.[287] Legislation in 1504 attempted to deal with the issue of prejudiced sheriffs and other judges.[288] Neglectful judges were to suffer loss of office, perpetually if they held it for life, for a year and a day if they held it in fee and heritage.[289] It is worth noting that, at one stage, James I granted a general pardon to all his sheriffs and warned them to do justice and enforce the Acts of Parlia-

---

[278] Jenny Wormald, *Lords and Men in Scotland: Bonds of Manrent, 1442–1603* (1985), 68–9.
[279] APS, II, 16 (c. 10) (1428); 51 (c. 29) (1458); 177 (c. 9) (1487).
[280] MacQueen (n. 38), 75; idem, 'Kin of Kennedy' (n. 105), 275.
[281] See J. W. Cairns, 'Academic Feud, Bloodfeud, and William Welwood: Legal Education in St Andrews, 1560–1611', (1998) 2 *Edinburgh LR* 158–79, 255–87.
[282] APS, I, 702 (c. 28). [283] Dickinson (n. 56), 164. See also ibid. 148, 237.
[284] APS, II, 226–7 (c. 17) (1491); cf. APS, II, 50 (c. 24) (1458).
[285] APS, II, 111, (c. 4) (1475). [286] APS, II, 9 (c. 6) (1426).
[287] APS, II, 23 (c. 2) (1436). [288] APS, II, 250 (c. 11) (1504).
[289] APS, II, 50 (c. 23) (1458).

ment.[290] Moreover, it is easy to understand that one's neighbours, as suitors of the court, might give one either too little justice or too much. Such legislation does not indicate that a litigant inevitably faced such problems before the ordinary judges; it does suggest, however, that, from time to time, there were anxieties about the effective operation of the courts of common law.

(d) The decline of process on brieves

Hector McKechnie described the fifteenth century as 'the heyday of the brieve system'.[291] Yet, by the end of the century, judicial process on brieves was in decline. Thus, though, for example, brieves of right and mortancestry lasted through the century and appear in sixteenth-century formularies, the brieve of novel dissasine fell into disuse in the second half of the fifteenth century.[292] A growing suspicion of process on brieves is revealed by the act of 1491 providing that 'na brevez be gevin to na partij bot eftir the forme of the brevez of the chancellary usit in auld tymes'; moreover, the existing 'forme of chancellary' was to 'be observit and kepit without innovacioune'.[293] While certain 'retourable' brieves survived, by the end of the sixteenth century, all the 'pleadable' brieves had fallen into desuetude, and in 1543 the Lords of Council and Session rejected an argument that cases touching fee and heritage should be heard on a brieve, declaring that 'the breif of rycht is nor hes nocht yit bene mony yeiris usit in this realme'.[294]

The picture that emerges is of a decline in process on brieves as litigants used other means to pursue their claims. It is impossible to be certain which was the cause and which the effect; yet, there were some manifest disadvantages to process on brieves in comparison to a suit before the Council or the Session initiated by a simple signet summons. Not only was process on brieves slow, it also contained the possibility of deliberate delay by the defender. In general, after the pursuer had obtained the brieve from the Chapel, there could be a number of diets of the appropriate ordinary court before the diet became peremptory, that is, the defender had to compear. Moreover, the defender was often allowed a number of essonzies (legal excuses) for failing to compear.[295] The fifteenth century saw a number of

---

[290] APS, II, 22 (c. 3) (1434). [291] McKechnie (n. 69), 18–19.
[292] See MacQueen (n. 38), 161–2, 178–9, 180, 183, 209–10. On use of some of these brieves, see Alan Borthwick and H. L. MacQueen, 'Three Fifteenth-Century Cases', [1986] *JR* 123–51.
[293] APS, II, 224 (c. 5).
[294] See H. L. MacQueen, 'Jurisdiction in Heritage and the Lords of Council and Session after 1532', in Sellar (n. 6), 61–85 at 62–6. The following 'retourable' brieves survived: inquest or succession for service of heirs, idiotry or furiosity to determine the sanity of an individual, and tutory to decide who was entitled to be tutor to a minor; and the following 'non-retourable': perambulation and lining (both dealing with determining boundaries) and division and terce (both dealing with dividing land, the former between, for example, heirs-portioner, the latter to assign to a widow her liferent of a third of her deceased husband's lands).
[295] For a useful account of this procedure, see Dickinson (n. 11), 310–316; *Quoniam Attachiamenta* (n. 71), 209–251; Habakkuk Bisset, *Rolment of Courtis*, Scottish Text Society, New Series, vol. 10, 13, 18, (ed. by P. J. Hamilton-Grierson, 1920, 1922, 1926), vol. III, 53–62.

reforms intended to speed up procedure, notably in a series of rules enacted in 1430.[296] In 1471, an act tried to speed process when a pleadable brieve returned to an ayre after an earlier doom had been falsed, to try to bring the brieve to the cognition of an assize as soon as possible;[297] but in 1525 a statute could describe process before a justice ayre as 'sal lang and prolixt' as to deny parties justice.[298] While the evidence brought forward by MacQueen shows beyond doubt that justice ayres were much more frequent in the fifteenth century than had previously been thought, nonetheless, even if two ayres a year did occur (which seems unlikely), procedure on a brieve before an ayre could become lengthy.[299] For example, Andrew Bisset's action on a brieve of mortancestry involved falsing the doom of a justice ayre at Cupar before Parliament in 1471 and again in 1478.[300] Moreover, as the fifteenth century came to an end, the justiciar's jurisdiction seems to have become restricted almost exclusively to criminal matters; and in 1524 it was provided that the justiciar or his depute should remain permanently in Edinburgh to administer 'Justice in crimynale actiounis'.[301] It could no longer have been possible to sue on brieves that had to be taken before the justiciar. Thus, the ending of process on pleadable brieves is clearly linked to the move to sue before the Lords of Council and the Session.

(e) Rational procedure and learned law

It is also possible to identify an advantage that the Lords of Council were clearly perceived to have. In the anonymous *Thre Prestis of Peblis* of the reign of James III, the solution to complaints about the king's justices was for them to be accompanied by a 'Doctour in the Law'.[302] This does not reflect a desire to see canon law and civil law applied as such at the justice ayres; rather, it demonstrates the wish that proceedings be conducted according to the regularity and rationality represented by the learned laws. In 1496, the famous 'Education Act' required all barons and freeholders of substance to put their oldest sons and heirs 'to the sculis' so they could learn Latin, after which they were 'to remane thre yeris at the sculis of art and jure, sua that thai may haue knawlege and vnderstanding of the lawis'. The reason for this academic education in law was to enable those who would serve as 'shereffis or Jugeis Ordinaris vnder the kingis hienes may haue knawlege to do Justice', so that 'the pure pepill suld haue na neid to seik our soverane lordis principale auditoris for ilk small Iniure'.[303] A litigant in the Sheriff Court at Perth thus

---

[296] APS, II, 17–18 (cc. 3–4); 22 (c. 1) (the dating of this last in APS to 1434 is wrong: W. C. Dickinson, 'The Acts of the Parliament at Perth 6 March 1429–30', (1950) 29 *Scot Hist Rev* 1–12 at 9). [297] APS, II, 101.
[298] APS, II, 297 (c. 8) (1525); 350 (c. 39) (1535). [299] See MacQueen (n. 144), 76–87.
[300] ADA, 12, 66; APS, II, 101, 117. [301] APS, II, 286 (c. 8).
[302] T. D. Robb (ed.), *The Thre Prestis of Pebles how thai tald thar talis*, Scottish Text Society, New Series, vol. 8, (1920), 9, 22–3. [303] APS, II, 238 (c. 3).

protested against the sheriff and his deputes as judges in his 'greit and wechty' actions, because they were 'of our small knawledge and undirstanding'.[304] When the College of Justice was established under James V, it was described as 'ane college of litterate men'.[305] This meant more than that they could read and write; William Lauder in 1556 considered 'Iudges Illiturate' as those who lacked 'knawlage of boith the Iuris, Als weill the Canone as Civile law'.[306] Thus, part of what was valued by those suing before the Lords of Council and Session was that some of the Lords were educated in the canon and civil laws. Chalmers's study of the sederunts of the Lords of Council in the period to 1513 indicates the presence of a small, but important, number of academically trained lawyers, of whom William Elphinstone, graduate in canon law of Paris and student of civil law in Orléans, is only the most outstanding example; also found are such individuals as John Fresell and William Wawane, both Licentiates in Decreets, while Walter Drummond, Walter Lesley, and David Abercromby also possessed degrees in law.[307] What was generally important was that the churchmen and laity on the Council were usually individuals with highly developed administrative and financial skills, which, combined with the legal knowledge of some of their number, offered a more rational and educated approach than many of the ordinary common law courts.

(f) Romano-canonical procedure

Thus, by the middle years of the reign of James V, the College of Justice with its President and fourteen ordinary Senators (as they were described in the ratifying act of 1541) represented a major innovation in the Scottish legal system. Other than some retourable brieves, the system of process on brieves was dead; instead, the new court adopted a variation of the Romano-canonical procedure of the Church with its 'terminology of the libel, exception, probation and litiscontestation', though it developed its own forms and practices.[308] Initiated by a written document, procedure was oral, although the Lords would occasionally require parties to make submissions in writing.[309] The lack of a jury or inquest meant that testimony was presented before the Lords either in written form or by examination of witnesses in

---

[304] R. K. Hannay (ed.), *Acts of the Lords of Council in Public Affairs 1501–1554* (1932), 610. See ibid. 615 for a similar remark about Jedburgh, C. A. Malcolm, 'The Sheriff Court: Sixteenth Century and Later', in Paton (n. 56), 356–62 at 356–7.

[305] Hannay, *College of Justice* (n. 274), 59.

[306] F. Hall (ed.), *Ane Compendious and Breve Tractate Concernyng the Office and Dewtie of Kyngis, Spirituall Pastoris, and Temporall Iugis: Laitlie Compylit be William Lauder, for the Faithfull Instruction of Kyngis and Prencis*, rev. edn. (1869), 16 line 448–54; found quoted in Burns (n. 229), 120.   [307] Chalmers (n. 272), 264–80; Macfarlane (n. 220), 26–47, 94–118.

[308] John Finlay, 'Professional Men of Law Before the Lords of Council, c.1500–c.1550' (unpublished Ph.D. thesis, University of Edinburgh, 1997), vol. 1, 213. For two good, complementary accounts of procedure, with different focuses, see ibid., vol. 1, 153–213 and Godfrey (n. 277), 192–215.   [309] Godfrey (n. 277), 193.

front of them. In the latter case, a small committee of the Lords would examine the witnesses in private with neither the parties nor their lawyers present, although the parties could submit interrogatories. Their depositions would be reduced to writing and then sealed, to be opened later.[310] The process was similar to procedure before contemporary Scottish ecclesiastical courts.[311] The older procedure was also affected in civil matters in the lower courts, when, in a series of statutes reforming their operation in 1540, the judges were instructed to 'mak sic processis In all Things as Is usit befor the lordis of counsale and sessioune Notwithstanding any auld lawis or constitutionis maid therupoune of before'.[312] If it is inaccurate to describe as a crisis a sequence of events over nearly a hundred years that resulted in a variety of pragmatic responses, nonetheless, Scots law was now looking down a new route and was to set out on this different direction.

4. Common law, statute, and *jus commune*

(a) Statutes

In 1458, Parliament declared 'we haif bot a king and a law universale throu out the Realme';[313] in 1504, this 'law universale' was described as the king's laws and the common laws of the realm and no other laws.[314] The first component of this was the legislation of the Scottish Parliament, which had been very active in reforming the law. Access to the statutes was not always an easy matter in the period before printing and there were various attempts by Parliament to ensure copies were taken and publicized by sheriffs, barons, freeholders, and the commissioners for the burgh.[315] Copies of acts circulated in private manuscripts.[316] Printing offering the possibility of duplication of copies for distribution, the royal patent granted to Walter Chepman and Andrew Millar in 1507 mentioned the aim of 'imprinting within our realme of the bukis of our lawis [and] actis of parliament';[317] nothing resulted from this licence. In 1541, however, James V's Parliament authorized the Clerk of the Registry to make an authentic extract of the acts of the Parliament for printing.[318] As a result, Thomas Davidson printed versions of most of the acts of the Parliaments of 7 June 1535, 3 December 1540, and 14 March 1541, along with 'certane actis and constitutionis maid be our soverane lord

---

[310] Finlay (n. 308), vol. 1, 197–206; Godfrey (n. 277), 194, 204–7.

[311] See Simon Ollivant, *The Court of the Official in Pre-Reformation Scotland: Based on the Surviving Records of the Officials of St Andrews and Edinburgh*, Stair Society, vol. 34 (1982), 95–118. See also J. J. Robertson, 'The Development of the Law', in Brown (now Wormald) (n. 11), 136–52 at 151–2; *idem*, 'The Canon Law Vehicle of Civilian Influence with Particular Reference to Scotland', in Carey Miller/Zimmermann (n. 86), 117–33 at 121–5.

[312] APS, II, 358 (c. 7).   [313] APS, II, 50 (c. 18).   [314] APS, II, 252 (c. 24).

[315] APS, II, 52 (c. 39) (1458); 227 (c. 20) (1491).   [316] APS, I, 177–210.

[317] M. Livingsston et al. (ed.), *Registrum Secreti Sigilli Regum Scottorum* (1908–), vol. 1, 223–4 no 1546.   [318] APS, II, 379 (c. 47).

king James the fift ... in his les age' that the lords of the articles had 'sene over agane ... and fundin ... gude and reasonable';[319] though it was to be over twenty years before any more acts were printed.

The evident problem of access to an authoritative version of the texts of the statutes profoundly affected attitudes to them; it explains why provisions were often re-enacted and the wording of individual statutes reworked, in the way essentially the same provisions on slaughter by forethocht felony or by *chaudemellee* were repeatedly re-enacted.[320] The air of uncertainty and contingency surrounding the statutes resulted in the provision in 1450 for twelve men, four from each estate, to examine the acts of the Parliaments and General Councils of James I and James II and 'schaw thaim that are gude and accordande for the tym in the nixt parliament or general council'.[321] Despite an act of 1428 emphasizing that acts should be interpreted according to their literal meaning and the legislative intent, the accuracy and authenticity of acts cited to a court must frequently have been open to question;[322] it must always have been tempting for judges or assizes to follow their traditional understanding of the common law instead.

(b) The 'Auld Lawes'

Access to the common laws of the realm entailed its own problems. Much of the common law of Scotland was located in *Regiam Majestatem* and *Quoniam Attachiamenta* and other books of the 'auld lawes', although some of the legislation of the fifteenth century incorporated, updated, or reformed their provisions.[323] The importance and currency of these works is emphasized by the number of manuscripts that survive and the reliance placed on them in court.[324] In a manuscript tradition the text always undergoes a certain measure of change as it is copied, such change being either deliberate or accidental. This can indeed have its advantages, as the legal material may be updated to conform to current practice. The obvious disadvantage is that as texts develop they inevitably vary, so that individuals will have different versions of the same text. This was indeed a problem of which the scholars of the Middle Ages were well aware; they were always concerned to establish a *vera lectio*.

---

[319] *The New Actis and Constitutionis of Parliament Maid be the Rycht Excellent Prince Iames the Fift Kyng of Scottis. 1540* (1541). On Davidson, see Robert Dickson and J. P. Edmond, *Annals of Scottish Printing from the Introduction of the Art in 1507 to the Beginning of the Seventeenth Century* (1890), 104–35. The *New Actis* is discussed at 109–18.

[320] See Sellar (n. 104), 48–51.   [321] APS, II, 36 (c. 10).

[322] APS, II, 16 (c. 11). For examples of reference to Parliament of difficult issues of interpretation, see ADA, 12; APS, II, 101 (1471); 133 (1481); 349–50 (c. 38) (1535).

[323] See e.g. APS, II, 100 (c. 9) (1471); 111 (c. 4) (1475) (applying rules from *Regiam* to the punishment of false assizes); 176 (c. 3) (1487) (punishment of 'tresspassouris').

[324] On the MSS, see APS, I, 175–210; *Quoniam Attachiamenta* (n. 71), 5–6. On use in court, see MacQueen (n. 38), 94–8.

(c) *The law commissions*

For fifteenth-century Scots, the issue of moving texts and the uncertainty of the common law tradition may have seemed particularly acute, while some vital material, such as that in *Regiam*, was obviously obsolete and not in conformity with current practice.[325] This led to proposals to establish commissions to examine the laws in Scotland and propose remedies. The first came in James I's important Parliament of 1426, which also provided for the first Session and that only the king's laws should govern his lieges. Six men, who 'knawis the lawis best', were to be chosen from each of the three estates to 'se and examyn the bukis of law of this realme that is to say Regiam Maiestatem and Quoniam Attachiamenta and mend the lawis that nedis mendment'. That difficulties in practice underlay this statute is suggested by the additional enactment on exceptions in litigation, which exhorted that 'pleyis be not wrangfully prolongyt'.[326] Again, in 1469, another important reforming Parliament established a committee of the Three Estates to consider and advise on a variety of objects, including 'the Reductione of the kingis lawis Regiam maiestatem actis statutis and uthir bukis to be put in a volum and to be auctorizit and the laif to be distroyit'.[327] Finally, in 1473, a Parliament that exhorted James III to undertake his personal duty of ensuring the enforcement of justice also turned its attention to 'the mending of the lawis for the declaracione of diverse obscure materis that ar now in our lawis and that daily occuris'. The 'lordis baronis' were to request that the king would ensure two men from each estate were chosen 'for the cleirnes of the said matters to be had'. These men were first 'to fynd good Invencionis that sall accorde to law and conschience for to declare the daily materis that cumys befor the kingis hienes that as yit thare Is na law for the decisioune of thame'. Next, 'eftir thare gret wisdomes the thingis that thai hapin to avise tobe schewin at the next parliament to the kingis hienes and his thre estatis And gif thai be expedient tobe Ratifijt and approvit be auctorite of parliament.' Furthermore, there was then to 'be a buke maid contenand al the lawis of this Realme that sall Remain at a place quhare the lafe may have copy and nane uther bukis be usit'. This was because of 'the gret diversite now fundin in divers bukis put in be divers persons that ar callit men of law'. In future, however, 'thai that will use practik that thai use nane uther lawis as for the lawis of this Realme bot thai that ar fundin in that buke'.[328]

These proposals were without result, so that the problems identified remained: the law was in need of reform; there were *lacunae* in the law; the texts of the law were uncertain, varying from copy to copy. As the traditional institutions of Scots law started to be superseded by a central court, the older mechanisms of the inquest and the assize were no longer sufficient in dealing

---

[325] See the problems with the law on purpesture: APS, II, 133, 141; MacQueen (n. 38), 92.
[326] APS, II, 10 (c. 10).   [327] APS, II, 97 (c. 20).   [328] APS, II, 105 (c. 14).

Historical Introduction 67

with the law. The new system relied more on written texts and 'persons that ar callit men of law'; but the texts were difficult and out of date. Moreover, while the manuscripts compiled for those active in the law indicate what was thought important, there was not any kind of unified and rigorous body of knowledge learned for application as existed in contemporary England. It is little surprise that the Scots, like the French in 1498, but with less success, turned to codification of their customs.[329]

(*d*) *The attraction of the* jus commune

One obvious source for supplementing and interpreting the material in the manuscript collections made by and for the men of law was the universal *utrumque jus*; indeed, some of the collections have glosses taken from the civil and canon laws, while others incorporate extracts from its texts.[330] Embodied in *Regiam* in any case were texts of the canon law, while as the text of *Quoniam* developed it incorporated a provision, originally a marginal gloss, taken from Justinian's *Code*.[331] Much more study of these manuscripts and their glosses is necessary before any conclusions can be drawn, but such matter was obviously found useful, reflecting the use of the *utrumque jus* already noted for the fourteenth century. Indeed, the legislative and court records show that use of the sources of the *jus commune* in Scottish legal practice intensified in the period leading up to and beyond the foundation of the College of Justice.

The predominant influence from the *jus commune* on statutes was that of canon law. Thus, in 1425, the act requiring judges to appoint an advocate to deal with the cause of 'ony pure creature' derived from the practice of the church courts.[332] In 1430 a version of the canonist oath *de calumnia* was introduced for litigants and pleaders 'in temporalle courtis'.[333] In 1469, although the idea of prescription running to extinguish assertion of a right had already been received in Scots law, the canonist prescriptive period of forty years in obligations was adopted.[334] Parliament adopted the Roman rule that the tutor of a pupil child would be the nearest agnate who had turned 25 in 1474;[335] this provision marked the progressive Romanization of the Scots law on minority and guardianship that developed during the next century.[336] Acts of Parliament on fire-raising were drafted in the 1520s by someone familiar

---

[329] See e.g. René Filhol, 'The Codification of Customary Law in France in the Fifteenth and Sixteenth Centuries', in H. J. Cohn (ed.), *Government in Reformation Europe, 1520–1560* (1971), 265–83; J. P. Dawson, 'The Codification of the French Customs', (1940) 38 *Michigan LR* 765–800. [330] APS, I, 184, 198; Duncan, [1961] *JR* 216.
[331] *Quoniam Attachiamenta* (n. 71), 102–4, 154–5.
[332] APS, II, 8 (c. 24); Finlay (n. 308), vol. 1, 146–52; J. A. Brundage, 'Legal Aid for the Poor and the Professionalization of Law in the Middle Ages', (1988) 9 *JLH* 169–79.
[333] APS, II, 19 (c. 16); Helmholz (n. 26), 153–4.
[334] APS, II, 95 (c. 4). This was further clarified in APS, II, 107 (c. 9) (1474). APS, II, 37 (c. 18) (1450) shows prescription was already known. See MacQueen (n. 38), 79; Helmholz (n. 26), 174–99. [335] APS, II, 106–7 (c. 6).
[336] Balfour, *Practicks*, 114–15.

with the *Digest* texts on *incendium*.[337] The rule of the canon law on the legal presumption of marriage was enacted by Parliament in 1504; this was to ensure it was followed by the royal courts in deciding a widow's right to terce.[338] Further investigation would undoubtedly reveal more instances of such borrowing.

5. Lawyers and learning

(a) Men of law

The relatively complex procedure of the ecclesiastical courts adopted and adapted for the new College of Justice meant that 'it was increasingly important, especially for those unfamiliar with the courts, to obtain the services of a man of law'. Indeed, the 'vast majority of procedural points raised before the lords were made by a small number of men of law'.[339] It was these men, armed with their copies of the *Speculum Judiciale* of Guillaume Durand (Durandus) and other works on the procedure of the *jus commune*, who directed the actions before the Lords of Council and formed the nucleus of an emerging legal profession.[340]

While 'men of law' had existed for some time in Scotland, they were not in any sense members of a legal profession bound together with a shared educational and professional experience into a corporate body; to be an advocate, procurator, forespeaker, or notary was to have a particular role and the same individual might be described as a notary or an advocate or a procurator depending on the context. Moreover, 'advocate' and 'procurator' were synonyms and were to remain so for some time in Scotland, until the search for status of the advocates who practised before the Session led them to draw on the distinctions in this respect found in the *jus commune*.[341]

(b) Academic education

Men with an academic education in law were relatively common in Scotland, because it remained as popular as ever for Scots to study abroad, especially in higher faculties such as those of canon law and civil law.[342] Many who did

---

[337] Compare APS, II, 298 (c. 10) (1525) and 316 (c. 10) (1526) with D. 47, 9, 9 and 11 and D. 48, 19, 28, 12. This was discussed by Grant McLeod in an unpublished paper delivered to the Scottish Legal History Group on 18 Oct. 1986, abstracted in (1987) 8 *JLH* 370.

[338] APS, II, 252 (c. 22). See W. D. H. Sellar, 'Marriage by Cohabitation with Habit and Repute: Review and Requiem?', in D. L. Carey Miller and D. W. Meyers (eds.), *Comparative and Historical Essays in Scots Law: A Tribute to Professor Sir Thomas Smith, Q.C.* (1992), 117–36.

[339] Finlay (n. 308), vol. 1, 212.

[340] Ibid. 154; John Durkan and Anthony Ross, *Early Scottish Libraries* (1961), 5–167.

[341] See Finlay (n. 308), vol. 1, 12–30 on terminology. On the advocates' search for status, see e.g. J. W. Cairns, 'Advocates' Hats, Roman Law and Admission to the Bar, 1580–1812', (1999) 20, no. 2 *JLH* 24–61.

[342] See e.g. R. J. Lyall, 'Scottish Students and Masters at the Universities of Cologne and Louvain in the Fifteenth Century', (1985) 36 *Innes Review* 55–73; J. H. Baxter, 'Scottish Students

so would have been churchmen; but the number of secular men with a scholarly knowledge of the *utrumque jus* was expanding, although the phenomenon has been little studied. Indeed, the act of 1496, by which freeholders and barons were to put their sons to 'the sculis of art and Jure', suggests that the laird learned in academic law was a possibility.[343] Moreover, it became possible to get at least a basic education in the *utrumque jus* in Scotland, as three universities, each of which taught law, were founded in Scotland in the fifteenth century. The earliest was St Andrews, granted its charter of erection by Bishop Wardlaw in February 1412 and gaining papal confirmation of its privileges in 1413, with provision for faculties of theology, canon law, civil law, medicine, and liberal arts.[344] In 1451, Bishop Turnbull of Glasgow secured the creation of a university in his city and diocese.[345] In 1495, William Elphinstone, Bishop of Aberdeen, obtained a papal bull to establish a university with its traditional faculties, within which, over a number of years he erected a college, which came to be known as King's College, with extensive provision for legal education.[346] All three of these founders had a legal training. Bishop Wardlaw had studied civil and canon law in Orléans and Avignon.[347] Bishop Turnbull was educated in canon law in Leuven before matriculating at Pavia, where he gained his doctorate in canon law in 1439.[348] Bishop Elphinstone graduated in canon law in Paris and studied civil law in Orléans.[349] Legal education seems to have been relatively successful in St Andrews and Aberdeen, less so in Glasgow, where it does not seem to have continued for long.[350] While many of the men so trained would have served the administrative and legal needs of the Church, the courts of which remained very active with their staple business of matrimonial suits, disputes over legitimacy, contracts and debts, and succession, others were destined for

---

at Louvain University, 1425–1484', (1928) 25 *Scot Hist Rev* 327–34; R. J. Mitchell, 'Scottish Law Students in Italy in the Later Middle Ages', (1937) 49 *JR* 19–24; Robert Feenstra, 'Teaching the Civil Law at Louvain as Reported by Scottish Students in the 1430s (MSS. Aberdeen 195–197) with Addenda on Henricus de Piro (and Johannes Andreae)', (1997) 65 *TR* 245–80. Between 1408 and 1437, Paris was not an advisable place for Scots; this led them to explore other seats of learning. Later they resumed attendance there.

[343] APS, II, 238 (c. 3).

[344] McGurk (n. 211), 276–8; R. G. Cant, *The University of St Andrews: A Short History* (3rd edn., 1992), 3–7. In 1419, Martin V confirmed Benedict's foundation after the Scottish Church had returned to its Roman allegiance: A. I. Dunlop, *The Life and Times of James Kennedy Bishop of St Andrews* (1950), 261.

[345] John Durkan and John Kirk, *The University of Glasgow, 1451–1577* (1977), 3–20.

[346] Macfarlane (n. 220), 290–402; H. L. MacQueen, 'The Foundation of Law Teaching at the University of Aberdeen', in Carey Miller/Zimmermann (n. 86), 53–71 at 53–60.

[347] Watt (n. 99), 564–9.

[348] John Durkan, *William Turnbull, Bishop of Glasgow* (1951), 11, 15–16.

[349] Macfarlane (n. 220), 26–46.

[350] A. I. Dunlop (ed.), *Acta Facultatis Artium Universitatis Sancti Andree, 1413–1588*, 2 vols., Scottish History Society, Third Series, vol. 54, 55 (1964), vol. 1, xii, cxlix–clvii; MacQueen (n. 346), 60–3; Durkan/Kirk, (n. 345), 127–35.

secular administration and practice;[351] accordingly, the two papal bulls that granted Scottish clerics a dispensation to study civil law in St Andrews (1432) and in Aberdeen (1501) stressed the need to encourage pursuit of that discipline because there were 'few experts in civil law by whom justice can be ministered in civil business'.[352]

(c) The legal profession and the jus commune

On the establishment of the College of Justice in 1532, the Lords took advantage of their authority to create rules of practice to enact that ten advocates or procurators, 'of best name, knawledge and experience' would be admitted to procure in all actions; they would be called 'generale procuratouris of the counsall'. The requirements established were a novelty; in the past, most adult men—and sometimes even women—could act as procurators.[353] All of the men named had matriculated at a university, and six had studied abroad, four of them law at Orléans.[354] One of these, Henry Spittall, had also served as canonist at the University of Aberdeen.[355] Another of the new 'general procuratouris' was Robert Galbraith, who had taught logic at the College de Coqueret in Paris.[356] Galbraith was a member of the distinguished circle of philosophers and logicians associated with John Mair and author of the *Quadrupertitum* (1510), an important work on logic, which he dedicated to James Henryson, James IV's Advocate.[357] These eight were all already active as pleaders before the Lords of Council.[358] Given that the President and half of the Senators of the College of Justice had to be ecclesiastics, it is no surprise that many of the earliest Senators were academically trained in law. Examples include Robert Reid, sometime Official of Moray, who became the second President, Arthur Boece, canonist in the University of Aberdeen, John Sinclair, licentiate in civil and canon law, also canonist in Aberdeen, John Weddell, licentiate *in utroque jure*,

---

[351] Macfarlane (n. 220), 53–85 gives a good survey of the work of the church courts in this period. See also Ollivant (n. 311). Scottish cases continued to go to the papal *curia*: issues relating to benefices before the Rota; those concerning marriage and similar matters generally before the tribunal of the Penitentiary: J. J. Robertson, 'Scottish Legal Research in the Vatican Archives: A Preliminary Report', (1988) 2 *Renaissance Studies* 339–46.

[352] A. I. Dunlop and I. B. Cowan (ed.), *Calendar of Scottish Supplications to Rome [vol 3] 1428–1432* (1970), 210–11; *Fasti Aberdonenses: Selections from the Records of the University and King's College of Aberdeen*, Spalding Club, vol. 26 (1854), 36–9 nos. XX–XXI; Macfarlane, (n. 220), 321.   [353] Finlay (n. 308), vol. 1, 97–8.

[354] Ibid., vol. 1, 100.   [355] Ibid., vol. 1, 101.

[356] See John Finlay, 'Robert Galbraith and the Role of the Queen's Advocate', [1999] *JR* 277–90; *idem* (n. 308), vol. 1, 250–75.

[357] See Alexander Broadie, *The Circle of John Mair: Logic and Logicians in Pre-Reformation Scotland* (1985), 4–5; *idem, The Shadow of Scotus: Philosophy and Faith in Pre-Reformation Scotland* (1995), 6.

[358] It is worth noting that appearance before the Lords was not limited to these eight: Finlay (n. 308), vol. 1, 130.

sometime Official of Lothian, Adam Crichton, sometime Official of Lothian.[359]

The men chosen as general procurators in 1532 were part of the wider group of highly educated (generally lay) men who acted as procurators in Edinburgh before the Admiralty Court and the Court of the Official of Lothian.[360] It seems a fair assumption that, did earlier records survive, many of the men who appeared before the Lords of Council in the reign of James IV would also be found to be practising in these courts. It was from this group that a recognisable legal profession progressively developed through the sixteenth century; it was of particular importance that much of its background was in the traditions of practice before the ecclesiastical courts and the learning of the *jus commune*.

6. *Jus proprium* and *jus commune*

The education of many of the Senators and of many of those practising before the College of Justice will have led them to consider the learning of the *jus commune* as the appropriate source of inspiration for solutions to the problems presented by the statute and other laws. The richness of its sources and sophistication of its literature must have held many attractions for the educated procurator or judge. The already existing long Scottish tradition of looking to the canon and civil laws can only have reinforced such a tendency to turn to the *jus commune* for guidance.

(a) Litigation and the jus commune

The nature of the records kept of the work of the Lords of Council or the Lords Auditors did not normally allow for the preservation of legal argument and discussion; yet, where there is direct or interstitial evidence, it suggests that recourse to the *jus commune* was routine. Thus, in an action in 1479 before the Lords Auditors about a debt, the defender pleaded—without success—the *exceptio non numeratae pecuniae*.[361] In 1498, the Lords of Council decided an issue over anchorage below and above the floodmark in accordance with the rule of Roman law; although it is not possible to be certain, it

---

[359] For a listing of the early senators, see P. G. B. McNeill, 'Senators of the College of Justice, 1532–69', [1978] *JR*, 209–15. On Reid and his concerns to establish legal education, see James Kirk, 'Clement Little's Edinburgh', in J. R. Guild and Alexander Law (eds.), *Edinburgh University Library, 1580–1980: A Collection of Historical Essays* (1982), 1–42 at 7–11; on Boece see Macfarlane (n. 220), 321; on Sinclair, A. L. Murray, 'Sinclair's Practicks', in Alan Harding (ed.), *Law Making and Law Makers in British History* (1980), 90–104 at 94; on Weddell and Crichton, see Ollivant (n. 311), 173–4.

[360] Ollivant (n. 311), 57–62; Thomas Callander Wade (ed.), *Acta Curiae Admirallatus Scotiae, 6th Sept. 1557–11th March 1561-2*, Stair Society, vol. 2 (1937), xxvi.   [361] ADA,

is probable they based their ruling on Roman law.[362] A submission to arbitration referred to a style in Durand's *Speculum Judiciale*.[363] In 1503, James IV challenged the infeftment of the Earl of Buchan in the Barony of Kingedward before the Lords of Council. To support propositions in favour of the Earl, his forespeaker cited works of the canonists Nicholas de Tudeschis (Panormitanus) and Johannes Andreae and a work on Romano-canonical procedure by Johannes de Ferrarriis as well as texts from the *Institutes* and *Code*.[364] If the formal nature of the record of the Lords of Council and Lords Auditors generally omits any references to the sources of the *jus commune*, 'the knowledge of the learned laws by participants in the proceedings ... is clear to any reader of the *acta* who is familiar with these laws'.[365] It is no surprise that the lawyer Richard Lawson is to be found importing 'a lytill kist' holding 'viii volomys contenand the corss of bath the lawyss'.[366]

The mental world hinted at by these records is fully revealed by the collection of practicks (in the sense of custom and practice of the court) made by John Sinclair, senator from 1540 to 1566.[367] This is a personal rather than an official record, probably written up from notes. Since Sinclair rarely cites Scottish statutes, Scots law appears as an unwritten customary system, cited imprecisely as 'practick' or 'custom' or 'municipal law': thus '*practica Scotie*' is contrasted with '*jus scriptum*' and rules can be described as deriving '*de practica et municipali iure Scotie non scripto et consuetudinario*'.[368] There were evidently two problems: first access to reliable versions of statutes; secondly access to other sources of Scots law, since much custom was not recorded anywhere. Given the first of these, it is little surprise that once the *New Actis and Constitutionis ... maid be Iames the Fift* appeared, the collection immediately started to be cited in the Session as 'the new prentit actis' and made the basis of decision.[369] The second problem could lead the Lords to prefer a disposition of the common law (in the sense of *jus commune*) to an alleged

---

77.[362] ADC, II, 187, 245–246. W. M. Gordon, 'The Acts of the Lords of Council in the Late Fifteenth and Early Sixteenth Centuries: Records and Reports', in Chantal Stebbings (ed.), *Law Reporting in England* (1995), 55–71 at 62.
[363] ADC, II, 281–2. See Gordon (n. 362), 59 n. 15. [364] ADC, III, 309–10.
[365] Gordon (n. 362), 59.
[366] Cosmo Innes (ed.), *Ledger of Andrew Halyburton Conservator of the Privileges of the Scotch Nation in the Netherlands 1492–1503* (1867), 273.
[367] Murray (n. 359), 92–5; McNeill, [1978] *JR* 214. The best text of Sinclair's *Practicks* is Edinburgh University Library, MS La.III.388a. Dr Athol Murray is preparing the text for definitive publication. Professor Gero Dolezalek has worked on the identification of the *jus commune* references. I am much indebted to Mr Niall Whitty for giving me access to a copy of Professor Dolezalek's typescript (hereafter Dolezalek Typescript). The text is divided into different headings, which will be used here to cite it. The now lost mysterious 'Register' contained accounts of cases, though probably derived from the official record: Gordon (n. 362). On the term 'practick', see D. B. S[mith], 'Practicks', (1962) *SLT (News)* 147–8.
[368] Sinclair, *Practicks* (n. 367), c. 503.
[369] Sinclair, *Practicks* (n. 367), cc. 202 (12 May 1542), 295 (12 Dec. 1542). Please note that the number of the act cited in c. 202 is inaccurate.

'consuetude of this realme' demonstrated by an earlier decision, because 'thai culd nocht understand the consuetude allegit in the contrair to be trew in the selff, nor yit thair wes ony sic practik or consuetude'.[370] In the face of these difficulties the judges and lawyers turned to the *jus commune* and cited and relied on, as well as the texts of the *Corpus Juris Civilis* and *Corpus Juris Canonici*, a variety of civilian and canonist authors, classic works on the procedure of the *jus commune*, cases from the Roman Rota and the court of the Archbishop of Toulouse, and even a commentary on the Customs of Burgundy.[371] The general attitude may be summed up by a litigant in a case on restitution on the ground of minority: 'because the municipal law of the kingdom of Scotland did not decide this issue, so the civil law must be followed ... since a *casus omissus* remains at the disposition of the *jus commune*'.[372]

(b) *The blend of* jus commune *and* jus proprium

The usual position seems to have been that specific provisions of Scots law and practick were to be followed; in their absence the civil and canon laws could be turned to as the *jus commune* to the *jus proprium* of Scots law. Lawyers evidently shifted easily between *jus commune* and *jus proprium* and the two were not viewed as in simple opposition; the former had the advantage of being written and accessible. Use of the *jus commune* was sufficiently natural that it was called on to justify the revocations made by James IV and James V on reaching full age.[373] There is no need here to explore this blend of *jus commune* and *jus proprium* in the practice of the court; one example will suffice. Perhaps the most common action in fifteenth-century Scotland is that of spuilzie, which probably originated in the canon law's *actio spolii*.[374] Without going into its complex history, it seems that spuilzie absorbed the older actions for 'wrang and unlauch' and breach of the king's protection and it developed into a procedurally simple and expeditious action for the recovery of property. That this canon law action should have crossed over into Scots law to provide a category in which to deal with wrongs is in itself telling; Sinclair's *Practicks* show that once it had done so, the canon law and its interpreters could then readily be drawn on to develop the scope of the action and

---

[370] Sinclair, *Practicks* (n. 367), cc. 284–5.

[371] See Murray (n. 359), 103; Dolezalek Typescript (n. 367), 2–3.

[372] Sinclair, *Practicks* (n. 367), c. 444: 'quod ius municipale regni Scotie hunc passum non determinabat, ideo sequenda esse iura civilia ... quia casus omissus remanet in dispositione iuris communis'. I am here following Murray (n. 359), 101–2, though I have varied his translation. The litigant was unsuccessful in this case, but not because this proposition was rejected.

[373] APS, II, 236 (c. 22) (1491); 357 (c. 4) (1540). Note that where this last act in APS has 'canoune law actis and statutis of our realme', the *New Actis and Constitutionis ... Maid be Iames the Fift* (n. 319), fo. 11ʳ (there c. 34) has 'common law, actis and statutes of the Realme'.

[374] *Decretals Gregorii IX*, X, 2, 13, 1–19. For its popularity in Scotland, see the indexes to ADA and ADC and Godfrey (n. 277), 247–51.

explain its nature.[375] The Scottish action of spuilzie was placed in the wider context of the *jus commune*.

(c) *Continuity and change*

The legal system to which James I had returned in 1424 was still recognizably that of the time of the Great Cause; by the death of James V, it had been transformed. A rational emphasis on record keeping and an emphasis on writing started to pervade the operation of the law, symbolized not only by the increasing survival of formal records of proceedings in court and Parliament but also by the increasing popularity of notarial documents to record important procedures, such as the giving of sasine, and instruments of sasine indeed came into common use after 1430: deeds were becoming written rather than performed.[376]

While there were still strong elements of continuity in the land law and some of the institutions of the common law, a crisis in confidence in the old system and process on brieves had resulted in the once extraordinary jurisdiction of the King's Council developing into a central court and changing the direction of the development of Scots law. With that central court came the Romano-canonical procedure and lawyers trained in the *jus commune*; the lack of a 'common law' legal profession meant that the old institutions could not resist the impact of the jurists with their academic training and coherent body of legal knowledge in accessible and sophisticated sources. The stage was set for an increasing reception of the rules of the *jus commune* into Scots law, with a legal profession that looked to the models of the canonists and legists to understand its role.

V. FROM THE REFORMATION TO THE RESTORATION

1. Government, religion, and political thought, 1542–1651

(a) *Limited monarchy, absolute monarchy*

The Stewart dynasty survived a series of crises between the death of James V and the Restoration of his great-great-grandson, Charles II (1649–85) in 1660, demonstrating the power of the monarchical principle in Scottish

---

[375] Sinclair, *Practicks* (n. 367), cc. 95, 158–9, 310, 336, 373–5, 389–91, 406–407a.

[376] The earliest Protocol Book to be preserved is that of James Darow (1469), NAS, B66/1/1; the next is that of John Kerd (1471), NLS, Adv. MS 19.2.23, fos. 2–19ᵛ. See Durkan (n. 190), 23 n. 4. For printed examples, see e.g. Teresa Maley and Walter Elliot (ed.), *Selkirk Protocol Books 1511–1547*, Stair Society, vol. 40 (1993). In 1540, Parliament enacted a substantial code on notaries and their operation, with one statute on the giving of sasines: APS, II, 359–60 (cc. 11–16). Legislation now provided for authentication by signature rather than simply by seal: APS, II, 295 (c. 4) (1525). See also Robertson, 'Development of the Law' (n. 311), 148–9.

Historical Introduction

government; yet the nature of that monarchy was profoundly transformed in this period. The crises faced by the Scottish monarchy were significant, the product of new ways of thinking about politics. In the later Middle Ages, Scotland was some type of *Ständestaat*, where the Three Estates of Clergy, Nobility, and Burgesses and the monarchs had reciprocal and independent rights, duties, and privileges. Government involved the protection or voluntary diminution of these in gatherings such as Parliament or General Council, while the Church had its own bureaucratic structure as well as acting in the secular politics.[377]

In the sixteenth century, this vision of the Scottish polity—though aspects continued to affect political debate—gave way to competition over the location and nature of sovereignty (in the sense of the right to command) in the kingdom. This debate crystallized around the issue of the extent (if any) to which it was permissible to resist the monarch. John Craig, minister of Edinburgh, stated in 1564 that 'princes are not only bound to keep laws and promises to their subjects, but also in case they fail, they justly may be deposed; for the band betwixt the prince and the people is reciproce'.[378] In contrast, James VI (1567–1625), wrote in *The Trew Law of Free Monarchies* that 'the King is above the law, as both the author and giver of strength thereto; yet a good king will not onely delight to rule his subiects by the lawe, but even will conforme himselfe in his owne actions thereunto'. The people had no power to resist or displace him, even if he turned tyrant, as evil kings were to be regarded as a punishment sent from God.[379] George Buchanan in *De Iure Regni apud Scotos Dialogus*, first published in 1579, though written to justify the forced abdication of Mary (1542–67) in 1567, most elegantly put the claim that Scots monarchy was limited in its nature.[380] Strong apologists for the divine right of kings were, not least James VI himself, but also the lawyers Thomas Craig, in his treatise *De Iure Successionis*, and William Barclay, in his work *De Regno et Regali Potestate Libri Sex*.[381]

---

[377] On the idea of the *Ständestaat*, see Gianfranco Poggi, *The Development of the Modern State: A Sociological Introduction* (1978), 36–59.

[378] Found in John Knox, *On Rebellion* (ed. by R. A. Mason, 1994), 207.

[379] King James VI and I, *Political Writings* (ed. by J. P. Somerville, 1994), 75–6; 79–80.

[380] On Buchanan, see generally I. D. McFarlane, *Buchanan* (1981), esp. 392–415 on the *Dialogus*. Buchanan's political thinking is discussed in Mason (n. 219), 187–241; Burns (n. 229), 185–221; R. W. Bushnell, 'James VI and Neo-Classicism', in R. A. Mason (ed.), *Scots and Britons: Scottish Political Thought and the Union of 1603* (1994), 91–111; J. H. Burns, 'George Buchanan and the Anti-Monarchomachs', in R. A. Mason (ed.), *Scots and Britons: Scottish Political Thought and the Union of 1603* (1994), 138–58.

[381] On Craig there is a very out-of-date biography: P. Fraser Tytler, *An Account of the Life and Writings of Sir Thomas Craig of Riccarton* (1823). (Note that Craig was not in fact a knight.) On Barclay, see D. B. Smith, 'William Barclay', (1914) 11 *Scot Hist Rev* 136–63. Craig's treatise was later printed in a translation by James Gatherer as *The Right of Succession to the Kingdom of England* (1703). For some discussion of the MSS, see J. W. Cairns, 'The *Breve Testatum* and Craig's *Jus Feudale*' (1988) 56 *TR* 311–32 at 315 n. 23; William Barclay, *De Regno et Regali Potestate Adversus Buchananum, Brutum, Bocherum, et Reliquos Monarchomachos, Libri Sex* (1600).

The brief and disastrous personal reign of Mary, Queen of Scots, and the very much longer and successful one of her son started with lengthy minorities. The English invasion of the 1540s (the 'rough wooing') meant that Mary passed her childhood and adolescence in France; in Scotland, a pro-English faction competed for power with a pro-French one led by the Queen's mother, Mary of Guise, the Regent. The latter was successful until a Protestant group, known as the Lords of Congregation, deposed the Regent (who shortly thereafter died) and, in August 1560, held a Parliament that accepted a reformed Confession of Faith, abolished papal authority, and forbade the saying of mass. After the failure of Mary's rule and her flight to England, the early years of James's minority were marked by civil war between the 'Queen's Men' and the 'King's Men'.[382]

(b) Reformation of the Kirk

The Reformation Parliament of 1560 was just one important milepost on a long and difficult road. There had been earlier markers of reform.[383] Yet, after 1560, change was increasing and profound. Mary recognized the reformation of religion in 1567, but it was the act of a monarch losing power and it was only after her deposition that the acts of the Reformation Parliament were confirmed.[384] The Reformation was, however, thorough and largely bloodless and many of the older institutions were simply allowed to wither away until the Crown annexed the temporalities of church lands in 1587.[385] The major struggle that developed was over the government of the Kirk and its relations with secular authority. The complex and changing disputes were over whether the government of the Church was to be episcopal or Presbyterian and over whether the Crown had supremacy in church affairs or Church and State were separate according to the doctrine of 'the two kingdoms'. Furthermore, most of the radical Presbyterians, who supported the doctrine of the two kingdoms, also tended to view royal authority as limited; there was a corresponding likelihood that those supporting royal supremacy favoured an unlimited monarchy.

---

[382] APS, II, 525–35. See generally, Lynch (n. 4), 203–24; Gordon Donaldson, *Scotland: James V–James VII: The Edinburgh History of Scotland Volume 3* (1965; repr. 1987), 63–131; William Ferguson, *Scotland's Relations with England: A Survey to 1707* (1977; repr. 1994), 74–116. I have also found helpful: Jenny Wormald, *Mary Queen of Scots: A Study in Failure* (1988); Gordon Donaldson, *All the Queen's Men: Power and Politics in Mary Stewart's Scotland* (1983).

[383] APS, II, 415 (c. 12); Gordon Donaldson, *Scottish Historical Documents* (1970; repr. 1999), 114–15.

[384] APS, II, 548–9 (c. 2); III, 36 (cc. 1–3). This first Parliament of James VI also enacted a series of provisions on the structure and functioning of the reformed Kirk.

[385] APS, III, 431–7 (c. 8). See Gordon Donaldson, *The Scottish Reformation* (1960); James Kirk, *Patterns of Reform: Continuity and Change in the Reformation Kirk* (1989); Duncan Shaw, *The General Assemblies of the Church of Scotland, 1560–1600: Their Origins and Development* (1964), 75–88; D. G. Mullan, *Episcopacy in Scotland: The History of an Idea* (1986), 17–32. On the bishops, see e.g. Gordon Donaldson, *Reformed by Bishops* (1987).

James VI was ultimately successful in asserting his ideas of monarchy and his visions of an episcopal Kirk under royal supremacy. It was a slow progress. In 1578, the General Assembly of the Kirk accepted the Presbyterian programme set out in the *Second Book of Discipline* by Andrew Melville.[386] In 1584, the 'Black Acts' reasserted the Crown's supremacy over the Church and gave a full and general authority to bishops.[387] Sovereignty was firmly located in the Crown and the acts asserted 'the royall power and auctoritie over all statis alsweill spirituall as temporall' and stressed that 'his hienes his ... aris and successouris be thame selffis and thair counsellis ar and in tyme to cum salbe Juges competent to all personis his hienes subiectis of quhatsumevir estate degrie functioun or conditioun that ever they be of spirituall or temporall'.[388] These tensions continued through James's personal rule (from 1585). At first he had to compromise and a Presbyterian Kirk was recognized in 1592;[389] as he consolidated his authority, he increasingly gained his way, so that, by 1610, James, his Council, and his Parliament had erected a full diocesan episcopacy in the Kirk. The Estate of Bishops had been restored to Parliament and an act asserted the king's 'soverane authoritie princelie powere royall prerogative and privilege of his Crowne Over all estaittis persones and causis quhatsmevir within his ... kingdome [of Scotland]'.[390]

(c) The Jacobean state

The Jacobean state thus had great pretensions to royal authority and sometimes the power to make them effective.[391] While the traditional nobility continued to play an important role in government, James's reliance on new men of the 'middling' sort—lairds and lawyers—is evident. For the first time, representatives of the small barons and freeholders were called to Parliament in 1587;[392] no doubt the reasons were fiscal as James raised large taxes in the 1580s and 1590s. Feudal structures sat alongside new, more centralized, administrative methods. Absence from Scotland after James's succession to the English throne in 1603 may have created the illusion for the king that governing his northern kingdom was easier than it in fact was; James's success in gaining his way over the ecclesiastical establishment may have helped plant among the Scots the idea that their king was possibly no longer the best

---

[386] James Kirk (ed.), *The Second Book of Discipline: With Introduction and Commentary* (1980), 124–30; Kirk (n. 385), 334–67; Donaldson (n. 385), 183–202.
[387] APS, III, 292–303; Kirk (n. 386), 142–4; Donaldson (n. 385), 211–13.
[388] APS, III, 292–3 (c. 2).   [389] APS, III, 541–2, (c.8).
[390] APS, IV, 281 (c. 1). See Mullan (n. 385), 105–11; Kirk (n. 385), 429–30; W. R. Foster, *The Church before the Covenants: The Church of Scotland, 1596–1638* (1975), 6–31.
[391] See generally, Julian Goodare, *State and Society in Early Modern Scotland* (1999).
[392] APS, III, 509 (c. 120); Rait (n. 142), 205–10; Goodare (n. 142), 19–20.

guarantor of their traditional freedoms, independence, and laws.[393] If so, there was a bitter harvest for the Stewarts.

(d) Union projects

The Stewarts' great success was James's succession to the English throne in 1603, making the dynasty sovereigns of a major European power. From the first, union of the two kingdoms was a possibility.[394] James, who quickly adopted the style King of Great Britain, was an enthusiast for this project and its imperial implications, encompassing parliamentary and other governmental institutions, churches, laws, and economies. Commissions were appointed by the Parliaments of both nations in 1604 to discuss the possibilities.[395] The difficulties were formidable and a pamphlet debate developed.[396] There were considerable anxieties in both kingdoms, and the Scots commissioners were instructed to protect 'the fundamentall lawes, Ancient privilegeis, offices and liberteis of this kingdome'.[397] English common lawyers identified Scots law as civil law and considered it a threat to their system; Scots feared the imposition of English law. Some, however, argued that the laws were fundamentally the same. They overstated their case. It is important to note that Thomas Craig concluded that, to bring the laws of both countries into harmony, it would be necessary either to go back to Norman law, or the *jus feudale*; or, if common ground could not be found there, to the civil law, which, because it had so much natural equity (*naturalis aequitas*), shone forth among all peoples and was everywhere a common law (*jus commune*).[398] This was not an argument likely to compel the acceptance of the English common lawyers.[399] By 1608, James's full project for a more perfect union was essentially dead.

---

[393] Donaldson, *James V–James VII* (n. 382), 212–37; Lynch (n. 4), 225–44; Jenny Wormald, 'One King, Two Kingdoms', in Alexander Grant and K. J. Stringer (eds.), *Uniting the Kingdom? The Making of British History* (London, 1995), 123–32.

[394] See e.g. B. P. Levack, *The Formation of the British State: England, Scotland, and the Union 1603–1707* (1987); Bruce Galloway, *The Union of England and Scotland, 1603–1608* (1986); Burns (n. 229), 257–67.

[395] APS, IV, 263–4 (c. 1) (1604). On the imperial ideal and its meaning in the context of Union, see John Robertson, 'Empire and Union: Two Concepts of the Early Modern European Political Order', in John Robertson (ed.), *A Union for Empire: Political Thought and the British Union of 1707* (1995), 3–36.

[396] See B. R. Galloway and B. P. Levack (ed.), *The Jacobean Union: Six Tracts of 1604*, Scottish History Society, Fourth Series, vol. 21 (1985). [397] APS, IV, 263–4 (c. 1) (1604).

[398] Thomas Craig, *De Unione Regnorum Britanniae Tractatus* (ed. by C. Sanford Terry, Scottish History Society, First Series, vol. 60, 1909), 89–90, 328. See further, B. P. Levack, 'Law, Sovereignty and the Union', in Mason (n. 380), 213–37.

[399] See generally, Levack (n. 394), 76–85; *idem*, 'The Proposed Union of English Law and Scots Law in the Seventeenth Century', (1975) 20 *JR* 97–115; *idem*, 'English Law, Scots Law and the Union, 1603–1707', in Harding (n. 359), 105–19; E. J. Cowan, 'The Union of the Crowns and the Crisis of the Constitution in 17th Century Scotland', in Stale Dyrvik, Knut Mykland, and Jan Oldervoll (eds.), *The Satellite State in the 17th and 18th Centuries* (1979), 121–40 at 125–7.

(e) The problems of multiple monarchy

Scottish government had traditionally relied on the close contact of the political classes with the king; though an absentee monarch, James had managed to maintain a grip on Scottish affairs, not only through his Scottish Privy Council, but also through his personal experience of the Scottish nobility and Scottish matters.[400] He had a sense of the limits of the possibility of imposing his own will. Charles I (1625–49) appears to have had none. Multiple monarchies were frequently unstable; ruling more than one kingdom with its own institutions and practices was not an easy task. Yet Charles managed spectacularly badly.[401] His insensitivity to the Scottish scene was signalled at the start of his reign by the Act of Revocation. Such acts traditionally rescinded actions during the minority of a king. Charles, who succeeded as an adult, proposed cancellation of all grants of Crown property since 1540 and rescission of all dispositions of church property. This potentially threatened the temporal lordships erected for some individuals out of church lands; if this did not come to pass, a linked rearrangement of the collection of teinds for the support of the Kirk was clearly unsettling for landowners.[402] Charles continued with policies that alienated his Scottish subjects, such as heavy taxation and unpopular liturgical innovations. On the one visit to Scotland of his reign in 1633, he presided in Parliament to check on the voting on statutes, the bulk of which were considered 'hurtful to the liberty of the subjecte', while, in 1635, the trial of Lord Balmerino for treason caused further upset.[403] Faced with an indebted nobility and a clergy and laity suspicious of innovations in the Kirk, Charles's actions exacerbated any fears they might have had.[404] The new liturgy embodied in the prayer book introduced in 1637, in the face of general and particularly strong hostility, lit the fuse to

---

[400] See e.g. Conrad Russell, 'Composite Monarchies in Early Modern Europe: The British and Irish Example', in Grant/Stringer (n. 393), 133–46 at 138–40; John Morrill, 'Three Kingdoms and One Commonwealth? The Enigma of Mid-Seventeenth-Century Britain and Ireland', in Grant/Stringer (n. 393), 170–90 at 176–7.

[401] For a general account of Charles's actions, see Peter Donald, *An Uncounselled King: Charles I and the Scottish Troubles, 1637–1641* (1990). See also John Morrill, 'Historical Introduction and Overview: The Un-English Civil War', in J. R. Young (ed.), *Celtic Dimensions of the British Civil Wars: Proceedings of the Second Conference of the Research Centre in Scottish History, University of Strathclyde* (1997), 1–17 at 3.

[402] See A. I. Macinnes, *Charles I and the Making of the Covenanting Movement, 1625–1641* (1991), 49–101; Donaldson, *James V–James VII* (n. 382), 296–8; Lynch (n. 4), 266–7.

[403] Donaldson, *James V–James VII* (n. 382), 302–11; Lynch (n. 4), 267–8; Foster (n. 390), 32–65. The quotation is from Sir James Balfour, *The Annales of Scotland* in *The Historical Works of Sir James Balfour of Denmylne and Kinnaird, Knight and Baronet; Lord Lyon King at Arms to Charles the First, and Charles the Second. Published from the Original Manuscripts Preserved in the Library of the Faculty of Advocates* (1824–5), vol. 2, 200.

[404] The indebtedness of the nobility is a point well taken in K. M. Brown, 'Aristocratic Finances and the Origins of the Scottish Revolution', (1989) 104 *English Historical Review* 46–87; idem, 'Noble Indebtedness in Scotland between the Reformation and the Revolution', (1989) 62 *Historical Research* 260–75.

the powder keg formed out of the fiscal and high church policies of Charles I, which had united the political and intellectual classes of Scotland into a revolutionary movement.[405]

(f) The Covenanting Revolution

Opposition to Charles led to the drafting and signing of the National Covenant, initially at Greyfriars in Edinburgh early in 1638. The principal drafter of this document was an advocate, Archibald Johnston of Warriston.[406] A Covenant between God, the king, and the people, this clever, ambiguous, and legalistic document stressed the reciprocal duties of monarch and people, emphasizing that the king's subjects should live 'and be governed by the Kings lawes, the common lawes of this Realme allanerly', which not only upheld the king's authority but also served to preserve 'the peoples security of their Lands, livings, rights, offices, liberties, and dignities'. It also attacked 'novations' in the Kirk.[407] Breach of the Covenant by the king required action, as duty to God and true religion was paramount. The Covenanters' hope that Charles would back down was disappointed and a General Assembly at Glasgow in November 1638 abolished episcopacy, royal authority over the Kirk, and innovations in worship; Presbyterianism was established. The failure of Charles's planned invasion of Scotland (the first 'Bishops' War') led to the consolidation of Covenanter power. Another General Assembly and then Parliament approved and enacted the legislation of the General Assembly of 1638.[408]

Charles gained no support from the English Parliament he called and quickly dissolved in 1640. Meeting without royal permission on 2 June 1640, the Scottish Parliament embarked on major constitutional reform: the three estates were now to be the nobility, the barons, and the burgesses; Parliaments were to be triennial; the Committee of the Articles was abolished and

---

[405] See e.g. Maurice Lee, *The Road to Revolution: Scotland under Charles I: 1625–1637* (1985); David Stevenson, *The Scottish Revolution 1637–1644: The Triumph of the Covenanters* (1973), 15–55; Macinnes (n. 402), 128–54.

[406] D. M. Forrester, 'Archibald Johnston of Warriston, Especially as in his Diaries', (1947) 9 *Records of the Scottish Church History Society* 127–41. For recent consideration of the political thought of the Covenanters, see John Coffey, *Politics, Religion and the British Revolutions: The Mind of Samuel Rutherford* (1997); idem, 'Samuel Rutherford and the Political Thought of the Scottish Covenanters', in Young (n. 401), 75–95; J. D. Ford, '*Lex, rex iusto posita*: Samuel Rutherford on the Origins of Government', in Mason (n. 380), 262–90.

[407] Donaldson (n. 383), 194–201. For a discussion, see Macinnes (n. 402), 173–6; Donaldson, *James V–James VII* (n. 382), 313–16; Stevenson (n. 405), 56–87; J. D. Ford, 'The Lawful Bonds of Scottish Society: The Five Articles of Perth, the Negative Confession and the National Covenant', (1994) 37 *Historical Journal* 45–64; idem, 'Conformity in Conscience: The Structure of the Perth Articles Debate in Scotland', (1995) 46 *Journal of Ecclesiastical History* 256–77.

[408] M. C. Fissel, *The Bishops' Wars: Charles I's Campaigns against Scotland, 1638–1640* (1994), 3–39; Stevenson (n. 405), 88–161; Donaldson, *James V–James VII* (n. 382), 318–24. John Scally, 'Counsel in Crisis: James, Third Marquis of Hamilton and the Bishops' Wars, 1638–1640', in Young (n. 401), 18–34.

Parliament was to constitute such committees from time to time as it thought fit.[409] The Scots also invaded the north of England, occupying Newcastle (the second 'Bishops' War'); Charles was forced to make peace and, visiting Scotland in the autumn of 1641, conceded that appointments of Officers of State, Lords of the Privy Council, and Lords of Session were to be made with the consent of Parliament and that such offices were to be held *ad vitam aut culpam*.[410]

(g) Civil war and Cromwellian conquest

Civil war broke out between Charles and a hostile English Parliament he had been compelled to call in 1642. Both sides sought the support of the Scots, which the Parliament gained at the cost of the Solemn League and Covenant of 1643. This was intended to secure the Presbyterian establishment of the Kirk and to introduce it into England and Ireland.[411] Defeated at Naseby in 1645, Charles surrendered to the Scots the following year. After negotiations with the King broke down, the Scots handed him over to the English.[412] In 1647, the English army, which had been gaining power at the expense of the English Parliament, seized control of the King. Moderate Scots Covenanters (the 'Engagers'), with Parliamentary backing, invaded England on behalf of Charles, only to be defeated at Preston in August 1648 by Cromwell's New Model Army.[413] A coup by radical Covenanters (the 'Whiggamore Raid') destroyed the authority of the Engagers and a new regime, headed by the Marquis of Argyll, but dominated by the radicals in the Kirk, took power with Cromwell's support.[414]

To the horror of the Scots, Charles was now tried by the English and executed on 30 January.[415] On 5 February, the Scots Parliament proclaimed Charles II as King, not just of Scots, but also of his father's other dominions. After difficult negotiations, Charles signed the Covenants and landed in Scotland in June 1650. Cromwell invaded, however, and gained a major

---

[409] APS, V, 259–60 (c. 2), 268 (c. 12), 290–2 (c. 43). See Goodare (n. 142), 24–7; J. R. Young, 'The Scottish Parliament and the Covenanting Revolution: The Emergence of a Scottish Commons', in Young (n. 401), 164–84 at 164–9. For examples of the working of the committees of the Covenanters' Parliament, see David Stevenson (ed.), *The Government of Scotland under the Covenanters 1635–1651*, Scottish History Society, Fourth Series, vol. 18 (1982). See further J. J. Scally, 'Constitutional Revolution, Party and Faction in the Scottish Parliaments of Charles I', in Clyve Jones (ed.), *The Scots and Parliament* (1996), 54–73 at 59–61.

[410] APS, V, 354–5 (c. 21). See generally Fissell (n. 408), 39–61; Stevenson (n. 405), 162–213; Donaldson, *James V–James VII* (n. 382), 319–29; Scally (n. 409), 62–5.

[411] APS, VI, pt. i, 41–3; Stevenson (n. 405), 276–98; Donaldson, *James V–James VII* (n. 382), 328–33.

[412] Donaldson, *James V–James VII* (n. 382), 333–6. See also E. J. Cowan, *Monrose: For Covenant and King* (1977; repr. 1995).

[413] David Stevenson, *Revolution and Counter-Revolution in Scotland, 1644–1651* (1977), 82–122; K. M. Brown, *Kingdom or Province? Scotland and the Regal Union, 1603–1715* (1992), 131–4.   [414] Stevenson (n. 413), 123–45; Donaldson, *James V–James VII* (n. 382), 336–8.

[415] See C. V. Wedgwood, *The Trial of Charles I* (1964).

victory over the Scots at Dunbar on 3 September. Charles was nonetheless crowned king at Scone on 1 January 1651. Cromwell completed a military conquest of Scotland, while a Scottish invasion of England met defeat at Worcester.[416] Charles fled abroad and General Monck captured the remnant of the Estates. Without a government, Cromwell's solution for Scotland was incorporation into England. This was effective from 1652, though the statutory authority only came in April 1657.[417]

The Covenanting Revolution had led to loss of the monarchy, a central symbol of Scotland, and absorption into a Greater England. Its significance is profound, however, in the emphasis its political thinking put on theories of natural law as the foundation of civil government, even if some of the more extreme Covenanters, such as Samuel Rutherford, came to favour the rule of the Saints over natural law. Political discourse in Scotland had been permanently affected.[418]

2. Consolidation and innovation

(a) *The impact of the Session*

For James VI, the impartial and equitable administration of justice remained a central function of kingship. It is a prominent theme in the *Basilicon Doron* addressed to Prince Henry. The Prince was advised to 'studie well your owne Lawes' and to 'delite to haunt your Session, and spie carefully their proceedings'.[419] This remark testifies to the pre-eminence now achieved by the Session as the supreme civil court in Scotland. Yet that undoubted position had brought some problems. As a court, it lacked local knowledge; its situation in Edinburgh could be inconvenient to witnesses and litigants; a unitary court, proceedings before it could be slow. But such was the court's dominance that any attempt to provide a remedy for a problem in the administration of justice failed if it could be seen as diminishing its authority. Thus, a proposal that six lords and a president should hold sessions in Aberdeen or that pursuers should first take their cause to 'thair judge ordinar' were rejected.[420] The only measure dealing with such problems of locale and pressure of business came in 1585, when Parliament, following an Act of Sederunt of the Lords,

---

[416] Stevenson (n. 413), 129–210. On Cromwell's military conquest, see J. D. Grainger, *Cromwell against the Scots: The Last Anglo-Scottish War, 1650–1652* (1997); W. S. Douglas, *Cromwell's Scotch Campaigns: 1650–1651* (1898).

[417] Stevenson (n. 413), 208–10; J. R. Young, *The Scottish Parliament, 1639–1661: A Political and Constitutional Analysis* (1996), 297–301; F. D. Dow, *Cromwellian Scotland, 1651–1660* (1979), 35–51.

[418] See e.g. A. I. Macinnes, 'The Scottish Constitution, 1638–51: The Rise and Fall of Oligarchic Centralism', in John Morrill (ed.), *The Scottish National Covenant in its British Context* (1990), 106–33; John Coffey, 'Samuel Rutherford and the Political Thought of the Scottish Covenanters', (n. 406). [419] James VI and I (n. 379), 45.

[420] APS, III, 39 (c. 26); 44 (c. 81).

decided that lesser actions concerning 'molestatioun and trublance in the possession of properties', which formerly were dealt with by an inquest before sheriffs, bailies of regality and other ordinary judges, when they came before the Lords, should now be remitted by the Session to the appropriate ordinary judge for determination by an inquest.[421] The impact of the Session on the ordinary courts, which continued in theory as before, had therefore been profound. Thus, a lord of regality could not require his tenants to pursue their civil causes before him and exclude the Session's jurisdiction.[422] Individuals might well choose to sue before their ordinary judge for reasons of convenience and expense; they no longer had to, except in matters of trivial value.

(b) New consistorial courts

The old church courts remained effective until the Reformation, when the break with Rome caused a crisis. In 1560, an Act of Parliament (known only from its confirmation in 1581) provided that those who had actions depending before the old spiritual courts should now pursue them before the Lords of Session, the sheriff, the stewart, the bailies of regality or barony, the provost and bailies of burghs, or other temporal judges.[423] Thus, in December 1560 John Chalmer raised an action of adherence against his wife before the Session.[424] A number of such formerly 'spiritual' causes can be traced before the Lords in this period.[425] An important aspect of the work of the old spiritual courts had been jurisdiction over executries.[426] After the Reformation, litigation over these tended to go to burgh and sheriff courts as the local courts most able to deal with the business and the routine debt collecting involved.[427]

It was obvious, however, that a more organized system had to be established. Thus, Kirk Sessions in particular started to grant divorces *a vinculo matrimonii* on the grounds of adultery.[428] One case is known where the

---

[421] APS, III, 445–7 (c. 23).

[422] See e.g. the *Discours particulier d'Escosse, 1559/60*, ed. by P. G. B. McNeill, in Sellar (n. 6), 86–131 at 113.

[423] APS, III, 221–2 (c. 20). See further Julian Goodare, 'The Scottish Parliamentary Records 1560–1573', (1999) 72 *Historical Research* 244–67 at 251.

[424] See D. B. Smith, 'The Spiritual Jurisdiction 1560–64', (1993) 25 *Records of the Scottish Church History Society* 1–18 at 1. See also Balfour, *Practicks*, 269.

[425] Smith, (1993) (n. 424) 11–16.

[426] See A. E. Anton, 'Medieval Scottish Executors and the Courts Spiritual', (1955) 67 *JR* 129–54.

[427] Smith, (1993) (n. 424) 7–8.

[428] On the Kirk Sessions, see, *Register of the Minister Elders and Deacons of the Christian Congregation of St Andrews Comprising the Proceedings of the Kirk Session and of the Court of the Superintendent of Fife Fothrik and Strathearn, 1559–1600*, Scottish History Society, First Series, vol. 4, 7 (1889–90), vol. 1, 18–27. See also D. B. Smith, 'The Reformers and Divorce: A Study in Consistorial Jurisdiction', (1912) 9 *Scot Hist Rev* 10–36; C. J. Guthrie, 'The History of Divorce in Scotland', (1911) 8 *Scot Hist Rev* 39–52.

superintendent and elders of Glasgow dealt with an executry.[429] While some spiritual matters no doubt went appropriately to these new bodies, they did not necessarily provide a suitable forum for such business. In December 1563, the Privy Council accordingly established a new jurisdiction to deal with the causes that had gone to the former consistorial courts, appropriating the old term 'commissary' for the judge.[430] Making this establishment even more pressing was the need to provide for the collection of 'quots', the tax on the confirmation of testaments that was used to support the Session.[431] Four commissaries were appointed for Edinburgh, where the commissary court exercised a jurisdiction in divorce and consistorial matters over all Scotland and both a general and local executry jurisdiction. The Edinburgh commissaries, whose actions were subject to supervision by the Session, also exercised an appellate jurisdiction over the inferior commissaries appointed in the localities primarily to deal with executries, although they could exercise wider jurisdiction.[432] Of the first four commissaries of Edinburgh, three were graduates in law, while the fourth had been Dean of Aberdeen.[433]

There was in fact a considerable measure of continuity from the older consistoral courts. One of the commissaries of Edinburgh had previously been Official of Lothian.[434] Some of the local commissaries had exercised the same function before the Reformation.[435] They long continued to deal with cases involving oaths and for a while dealt with competing presentations to benefices.[436] The Chancellor, President, and Lords of the Session were given the right to present individuals to the Crown for nomination as commissaries and possessed a general regulatory function, although the establishment of the commissary jurisdiction was only given parliamentary ratification in 1592.[437] Despite the continuities, there was no denying that these were secular courts, until, in 1609, under James's religious policy, Parliament placed the commissaries under the authority of the bishops and archbishops.[438] This was reversed in 1640.[439]

---

[429] Smith, (1993) (n, 424) 7.   [430] RPC, I, 252.
[431] Smith, (1993) (n. 424) 17; Hannay, *College of Justice* (n. 274), 79–89.
[432] Smith, (1993) (n. 424) 17–18; Balfour, *Practicks*, 655–62. See generally, Gordon Donaldson, 'The Church Courts', in Paton (n. 56), 363–73 at 366–71.
[433] James Balfour, graduate of Wittenberg (Balfour, *Practicks*, xii); Edward Henryson, LL.D. (John Durkan, 'Henry Scrimgeour, Renaissance Bookman', (1978) 5 *Edinburgh Bibliographical Society Transactions* 1–31 at 2–4); Clement Little, graduate of Leuven (Kirk (n. 359), 14–15); Robert Maitland, Dean of Aberdeen (Kirk (n. 359), 19).
[434] Balfour: Balfour, *Practicks*, xii–xiii.   [435] Donaldson (n. 432), 369.
[436] See the Instruction to the Commissaries, 12 Mar. 1564: Balfour, *Practicks*, 655–62; Donaldson (n. 432), 370–1; APS, III, 33 (c. 36).
[437] Hannay, *College of Justice* (n. 274), 78, 82; APS, III, 105 (c. 17) (1578); 574 (c. 64) (1592); AS, I, 14–16 (29 Apr. 1587), 16–17 (7 June 1587).
[438] APS, IV, 430–1 (c. 8). The heritable right to the Commissariot in Argyll held by the Earl was preserved.   [439] APS, V, 277–8 (c. 20). See also, APS, V, 298 (c. 57).

(c) Improving the Session

The success of the College of Justice ensured that, rather than try to divert actions elsewhere, measures were taken to improve its operation.[440] Fairness in proceedings was emphasized in 1594 by two Acts of Sederunt. One prohibited a lord from sitting or voting in a case where one of the litigants was his father, brother, or son, while the other forbade the Senators, along with clerks, writers, advocates, and other members of the College of Justice, to purchase land or other property that was the subject of litigation before them.[441] The somewhat obscure development of the Outer House was of great importance in promoting the efficiency of the court. The Lords of Council and Session had always deputed one or some of their number to take evidence apart from the Session as a whole, and listings of Lords in groups of three to deal with bills and witnesses 'in the outtir tolbuyth' survive from 1555. From the 1560s onwards, however, a more systematic division of labour developed in the court, with the regular practice of three Lords sitting in the Outer House to deal respectively with bills and with witnesses, and as reporter of interlocutors. By 1600, the practice of the Lords going in turn to the Outer House for a week to deal with causes and then report them to the Inner House was definitively established.[442] More specific remedies were also adopted to promote the efficient running of the court, such as the organization of court rolls.[443] Of particular importance was the progressive development of written pleadings before the Lords. When the Lord Ordinary reported a matter to the Inner House for decision, the practice had developed of parties and their advocates soliciting the Lords to 'inform' them of their arguments on the case. In 1596, the Lords issued an Act of Sederunt stressing that the Lords should not be solicited outwith the court, because the report from the Outer House was sufficient information. It further provided, 'for better satisfactioun of pairteis quhais actionis being weichtie or intricate', that each Lord should appoint a time when he or a servant would receive 'the informatioun of the causis in wreitt'.[444] Importunate solicitations of the judges nonetheless remained a problem.[445] Orderliness in proceeding was also stressed. Interrupting procurators arguing before the Inner House was

---

[440] See the remarks of James in *Basilicon Doron* in James VI and I (n. 379), 45.
[441] APS, IV, 67 (c. 22); 68 (c. 26).
[442] Hannay, *College of Justice* (n. 274), 91–101. On the physical organization of the buildings for the court, see ibid. 95–6; Royal Commission on the Ancient and Historical Monuments of Scotland, *Tolbooths and Town-Houses: Civic Architecture in Scotland to 1833* (1996), 82–6; *Our Journall into Scotland Anno Domini 1629, 5th of November from Lowther* (1894), 26–30; C. A. Malcolm, 'The Parliament House and its Antecedents', in Paton (n. 56), 449–58.
[443] See e.g. AS, I, 62–3 (2 Jan. 1650). For a classic example of a provision to speed actions, see Bisset (n. 295), vol. 1, 170–1.
[444] AS, I, 26–7 (13 July 1596). See also AS, I, 45 (12 June 1632) ('informations' to be received by judges in their houses only between 2 and 7 in the afternoon).
[445] See Charles I's missive to the Estates in 1625: APS, V, 176, 184.

prohibited and there was an attempt to deal with the more serious issue of the need to control the number of friends and supporters who accompanied parties in court.[446]

(d) Appointment of Senators

For the Session to work well, it was necessary to have good judges. Appointed by the king, the Senators' tenure was sufficiently secure that they engaged in collusive resignations *in favorem*, although Charles I attempted to make the appointments *ad beneplacitum*.[447] From 1579, the President was to be chosen by the Ordinary Lords and need no longer be of the spiritual estate.[448] Under the Covenanters, appointments became *ad vitam aut culpam*, made by the king with the consent of Parliament, while from 1642, the President was elected each term of the Session, the anachronistic distinction between 'spiritual' and 'temporal' Lords having been abolished in 1640.[449]

A provision regulated the qualification of Senators in 1579. A man nominated by the king was to be God-fearing, 'of gude literature undirstanding of the lawes' and have a good reputation and have enough of his own resources to support himself. The Lords were also to try the nominee's suitability.[450] The trial, devised in 1590, required the nominated individual to sit in the Outer House with the Lord Ordinary and report to the Inner House on the interlocutors.[451] The emphasis on academic education—'gude literature' is notable; in 1605, when a new form of trial was proposed by the Lords, the nominated individual was to give a discourse in Latin on a text of the civil or canon law.[452]

3. The legal profession and legal education

(a) Advocates before the Session

By the time of the Cromwellian conquest, the men practising before the Session had come by stages to form a recognizable corporate profession headed by a Dean. In 1582, John Shairp, one of the leading practitioners before the Lords, is described as 'dene of the advocattis of the sessioun'.[453] This denotes

---

[446] AS, I, 53 (24 June, 1643). See also APS, V, 176, 183.
[447] Hannay, *College of Justice* (n. 274), 113–15; P. G. B. McNeill, 'The Independence of the Scottish Judiciary', [1958] *JR* 134–47 at 135–44; David Stevenson, 'The Covenanters and the Court of Session', [1972] *JR* 227–47 at 239.   [448] APS, III, 153 (c. 38).
[449] APS, V, 609; 297 (c. 53); 354–5 (c. 21); 389 (c. 72) (1641); Stevenson, [1972] *JR* 240.
[450] APS, III, 153 (c. 38).
[451] Hannay, *College of Justice* (n. 274), 100, 112–13, 117–18. These provisions were repeated in 1592.
[452] Hannay, *College of Justice* (n. 274), 121–3. Those appointed, according to James, were to be advocates, principal clerks of Session of at least ten years standing, and others if 'knawin and tryed to be sufficientlie qualifeit in learning, wisdome and good conversatioune'.
[453] RPC, III, 530. On Shairp, see M. H. B. Sanderson, *Mary Stewart's People: Life in Mary Stewart's Scotland* (1987), 22–33.

that Shairp in some way represented the interests of the advocates who practised before the Lords.[454] In 1610, the Lords requested the advocates to meet together and suggest remedies for problems in the operation of the court;[455] in 1619, an Act of Sederunt provided that each intrant advocate should present a book to be chosen by the 'dean of faculty'.[456] By 1633, the Dean could assist the Lords in exercising a disciplinary role and authority over the Faculty.[457]

The Lords continued to control admission to practice before the Session. Those petitioning the court for admission fell into two groups: those claiming an academic training and experience of 'practick'; and those claiming long experience of 'practick'. From around 1580, those claiming admission on the basis of academic training gave a 'proof' of their learning by reading a public lesson and giving 'specimen doctrine' before the Lords.[458] A regular pattern eventually emerges from the records: those founding on their academic learning give proof by academic exercises in the Outer House; those admitted on the basis of their long experience of 'practick' furnish a testimonial from the Lord Advocate and the other advocates as to their fitness. The proof given by the academic applicants was to resolve in Latin a *quaestio* of the civil or canon law.[459] There was a definite preference for the admission of men who had an academic training in the *utrumque jus*. Between 1575 and 1608, two-thirds of those admitted founded their petition on their academic learning.[460] A Visitation of the University of St Andrews in 1579 had required the Professor of Law, William Skene, probably a licentiate of Bourges in both the laws, to give four lessons each week. These were to be attended by all those who wished to act as procurators before the Lords and other courts, who also had to 'gif first specimen doctrine in the universitie of Sanctandrois'. An academic education in the laws was clearly thought the fittest training for all pleaders.[461]

---

[454] Consider his actions on their behalf in opposing the foundation of a chair of law in Edinburgh: Hannay, *College of Justice* (n. 274), 145; W. C. Dickinson, 'The Advocates' Protest against the Institution of a Chair of Law in the University of Edinburgh', (1926) 23 *Scot Hist Rev* 205–12.   [455] Bisset (n. 295), vol. 1, 157–8.
[456] NLS, Adv. MS 25.2.5, vol. 1, fo. 220 ʳ.
[457] *Practicks of the Laws of Scotland, Observed and Collected by Sir Robert Spotiswoode of Pentland, President of the College of Justice* (1706), v. See generally on the development of a corporate sense: J. W. Cairns, 'History of the Faculty of Advocates to 1900', in *The Laws of Scotland: Stair Memorial Encyclopaedia*, vol. 13 (1992), §§ 1239–85 at §§ 1240–5.
[458] See the discussion of this in Cairns, (1999) 20, no. 2 *JLH* 34–8.
[459] Cairns, (1999) 20, no. 2 *JLH* 34–8.   [460] Hannay, *College of Justice* (n. 274), 145.
[461] *Evidence, Oral and Documentary, Taken and Received by the Commissioners Appointed by His Majesty George IV., July 23d 1826; and Re-Appointed by His Majesty William IV., October 12th 1830; for Visiting the Universities of Scotland. Volume III. University of St Andrews*, Parliamentary Papers XXXVII (1837), 184–5; J. W. Cairns, 'The Law, the Advocates and the Universities in Late Sixteenth-Century Scotland', (1994) 73 *Scot Hist Rev* 171–90.

(b) Procurators, writers, and notaries

As well as the advocates, there was a large group of men acting as procurators before the other courts in Edinburgh.[462] There also were men acting as procurators before the sheriff and commissary courts elsewhere, about whom relatively little is known at this period, but later associations such as the Society of Advocates in Aberdeen and the Faculty of Procurators in Glasgow must have existed in an embryonic form by 1659.[463] Such associations generally developed requirements of apprenticeship for those who wished to be admitted to their numbers. One important group offering legal services consisted of the Writers or Clerks to the Signet in Edinburgh. Appointed by the Royal Secretary to carry out the secretarial duties linked to the use of the signet seals associated with the royal Council, the creation of the College of Justice had given them an important role because of the use of the signet summons and their association with the proceedings of the Council, while letters authorizing diligence also passed the signet. Like the advocates, they came to be considered as members of the College of Justice and identified themselves as an occupational group with particular interests and privileges. In 1594, they organized themselves as a Society to protect their privileges.[464] One of their concerns was to ensure the admission to their number only of properly qualified men. From 1594, they acquired the right normally to try individuals seeking admission;[465] a system of training through apprenticeship developed.[466] They frequently collaborated with the advocates to protect mutual interests in the College of Justice and the two groups occasionally considered amalgamating.[467]

Notaries were among the most important of the men who drafted the large numbers of deeds required by the Scottish legal system.[468] Their admission continued to be carefully regulated. From 1555, a series of statutes governing admission as a notary had brought the profession under the control of the Lords of Session, who took their oath and registered their sign. They had to

---

[462] APS, III, 41 lists as judicatures in Edinburgh: the Prince and the Privy Council; The College of Justice; the Justice (Criminal) Court; the Consistorial Court; the Constable's Court; the Admiral's Court; the Sheriff Court; and the Courts of the Burgh.

[463] See J. A. Henderson (ed.), *History of the Society of Advocates in Aberdeen*, New Spalding Club, vol. 40 (1912); J. S. Muirhead (ed.), *The Old Minute Book of the Faculty of Procurators in Glasgow, 1668–1758* (1948), 17–25.

[464] See Hannay, *College of Justice* (n. 212), 23–4, 27–31, 38–45, 48–51; See 'Abstract of Minutes', in *A History of the Society of Writers to Her Majesty's Signet, with a List of the Members of the Society from 1594 to 1890 and an Abstract of the Minutes* (1890), 229–454 at 229–32. See also, A. R. B. Haldane, 'The Society of Writers to Her Majesty's Signet', (1970) 15 *JLSS* 35–8. [465] *Signet Minutes* (n. 464), 230.

[466] Ibid. 245, 254.

[467] Hannay (n. 212), 44–5; *Signet Minutes* (n. 464), 234 (28 July 1599), 262–3 (1 Aug. 1633).

[468] A useful account of later notaries is in William Angus, 'Notarial Protocol Books, 1469–1700', in Hector McKechnie (ed.), *An Introductory Survey of the Sources and Literature of Scots Law*, Stair Society, vol. 1 (1936), 289–300.

have knowledge of Latin and to have served an apprenticeship.[469] One of the most important functions of a notary was to preserve records of transactions in his protocol book. Parliament twice passed acts requiring the protocol books of deceased notaries to be transmitted to the Lord Clerk Register;[470] but the increasing practice of registering important deeds in court books and the creation of special registers, such as that of sasines, started, however, to deprive protocol books of their earlier overwhelming significance.[471] Thus, while notaries retained some specific functions—such as the monopoly of the solemn recording of sasines—many important legal documents could be drafted by anyone who had sufficient knowledge.

It is important not to see the various groups of men of law as having clear and distinct spheres of practice. Those acting as procurators would also draft deeds and documents for clients; advocates practising before the Session also drafted documents for clients, who would approach them directly for such assistance and advice.[472] Lawyers formed an increasingly important group in Jacobean Scotland and legal practice was an important route to wealth and status.[473]

4. University study of law in Scotland

The sophisticated legal education desired for advocates had to be sought abroad, although, for a while, the Scottish universities continued to teach law after the Reformation. William Skene, licentiate *utriusque juris*, who had been the canonist in St Mary's College in St Andrews, became the civilist there until his death in 1582.[474] He was succeeded by his stepson, John Arthur (also a licentiate *utriusque juris*), who was a sinecurist; but he was replaced by William Welwood, educated in law at Wittenberg and holder of the degree of LL.D., who definitely taught.[475] A bloodfeud in St Andrews blighted Welwood's tenure of the chair; and shortly after 1600 legal education ceased in the university. Legal education had long failed in Glasgow while the civilist and canonist in King's College, Aberdeen had stopped teaching; moreover, the new charters given to both these universities and the foundation charter of Marischal College, Aberdeen, made no provision for legal education.[476]

There was nonetheless a continuing general commitment to academic

---

[469] APS, II, 496 (c. 18) (1555); 541–2 (cc. 16, 17) (1563); III, 448–9 (c. 29) (1587); AS, I, 24 (31 Dec. 1595).

[470] APS, III, 448 (c. 29) (1587); IV, 549 (c. 22) (1617). In 1567, it had been proposed that they should be lodged with sheriffs or the provost and bailies in the burghs: APS, III, 44 (c. 87) (1567).

[471] Angus (n. 468), 293.   [472] Sanderson (n. 453), 24–5.

[473] Sanderson (n. 453); Kirk (n. 359), 15–16; Cairns (n. 457), § 1243. See also C. P. Finlayson, *Clement Litill and His Library: The Origins of Edinburgh University Library* (1980), 3–9. On the wealth of lawyers, see Gordon Donaldson, 'The Legal Profession in Scottish Society in the Sixteenth and Seventeenth Centuries', [1976] *JR* 1–19 at 13–17.

[474] Cairns, (1998) 2 *Edinburgh LR* 168–70.   [475] Ibid. 170–1, 173–7.   [476] Ibid. 163–4.

instruction in law.[477] In 1556, the Regent Mary of Guise had appointed first Alexander Sym and then Edward Henryson, doctor of laws, as lecturers in law.[478] Henryson, who had taught at Bourges, was notable for his espousal of the new renaissance learning in law over the older medieval approach.[479] The Bishop of Orkney, Robert Reid, an enthusiast for Renaissance learning and second President of the College of Justice, in 1558, left a legacy, among other projects, to found a law school 'for the teching of the civile and canon lawis'. Nothing, however, was immediately done.[480] The Reformers also wished to promote academic study of Roman law.[481] The *First Book of Discipline* of 1561 provided for instruction in Roman and municipal law in the universities.[482] After Welwood's departure from the chair at St Andrews, the Archbishop informed King James that he had directed his son-in-law to teach canon law, though this was more aimed at counteracting Presbyterianism than anything else.[483] A royal letter of 1616 stated that those men who did not intend to train for the ministry after graduation should proceed to Edinburgh, where there would be at least one reader established 'to teache the lawis'. Students would thus be able to learn theory and practice.[484] This project bore no fruit. In 1619, the Lords issued another Act of Sederunt to found a professorship of laws, again with no obvious effect;[485] it is worth noting, however, that, in the same year, King's College returned to its old foundation and the innovations after the Reformation were swept away.[486] Once again a civilist and a canonist were elected.[487] The effectiveness of these appointments in promoting law classes may be doubted.[488] In the 1630s, there was again a

---

[477] Cairns, (1998) 2 *Edinburgh LR* 171–3.

[478] John Durkan, 'The Royal Lectureships under Mary of Lorraine', (1983) 62 *Scot Hist Rev* 73–8 at 73–4.

[479] See Durkan, (1978) 5 *Edinburgh Bibliographical Society Transactions* 3–4. His defence of Eguinaire Baron is particularly significant in this respect: *Pro Eg. Barone adversus A. Goveanum de Jurisdictione Libri II ad H. Fuggerum* (1555). For some further remarks on this see J. W. Cairns, T. D. Fergus, and H. L. MacQueen, 'Legal Humanism and the History of Scots Law: John Skene and Thomas Craig', in John MacQueen (ed.), *Humanism in Renaissance Scotland* (1990), 48–74 at 48–9.

[480] Kirk (n. 359), 8–10. He had also tried to provide for the teaching of canon law in his diocese by providing that the Chancellor was to be a doctor *utriusque juris* (or at least a bachelor of canon law) and not only to serve as the ecclesiastical judge but also to lecture weekly on canon law to the Cathedral Chapter. His legacy was later used in part to endow the University of Edinburgh. [481] Cairns, (1998) 2 *Edinburgh LR* 159–60.

[482] J. K. Cameron (ed.), *The First Book of Discipline with Introduction and Commentary* (1972), 140–1, 143–4.

[483] David Laing (ed.), *Original Letters Relating to the Ecclesiastical Affairs of Scotland, Chiefly Written by, or Addressed to, His Majesty King James the Sixth after his Accession to the English Throne*, Bannatyne Club, vol. 92 (1851), vol. 1, 269–70.

[484] St Andrews University Archives, Acta Rectorum, II, 176.

[485] Sir William Fraser, *Memorials of the Earls of Haddington* (1889), vol. 1, 76.

[486] David Stevenson, *King's College, Aberdeen, 1560–1641: From Protestant Reformation to Covenanting Revolution* (1990), 63–93. [487] Ibid. 67.

[488] Ibid. 68.

canonist, but the civilist was an absentee.[489] A Visitation in 1638 deprived the canonist of his office, because of the 'Popish' nature of his teaching.[490] The deprived canonist, James Sandilands, was given permission by the General Assembly in 1639 'to teiche the cannon lawis be limitatioun, viz, to teiche *de matrimonio, testamentis, and teyndis*, becaus all the rest of these lawis smellit of poperie, as thay alledgit'.[491] He was subsequently appointed civilist.[492] These classes can have had, at most, only a local impact.[493] The comment on Sandilands that it was 'Strange to sie ane man admittit to teiche lawis who wes never out of the countrie studdeing and lerning the lawis' reveals more than adequately the contemporary perceptions of what was necessary for proper academic study.[494]

5. Common law and social order

(a) *The problem of order*

In the *Basilicon Doron*, James VI advocated policies that reflected what he saw as the problems of order facing his realm. He stressed the role of the king in maintaining the welfare of his people through good laws, while tempering justice with mercy.[495] He advised Prince Henry to continue the pacification of the Highlands and the Borders. He identified the threats to order posed by each of the three estates. His opinions of the first estate reflected his experience of the Melvillians and their doctrine of the two kingdoms. The second estate misused bonds of manrent and maintenance to maintain servants and dependants as if they were not 'answerable to the lawes' and readily engaged in deadly feuds. The Prince was advised to 'teach your Nobilitie to keepe your lawes as precisely as the meanest'. The greatest hindrance to enforcement of the laws was, however, 'these heritable Shirefdomes and Regalities, which being in the hands of the great men, do wracke the whole countrie'. The Prince was advised not to dispone them heritably again should they fall into his hands. In the third estate the merchants wished to enrich themselves at the expense of the people, while craftsmen did not wish to have the quality of their work controlled.[496]

(b) *Extending royal authority*

These views reflect James's desire to intensify and centralize his government. They were not, of course, uniquely his. In 1567 a proposal had been prepared

---

[489] Ibid. 72–3, 75.   [490] Ibid. 114–6.
[491] John Spalding, *Memorialls of the Trubles in Scotland and in England, A.D. 1624–A.D. 1648*, Spalding Club, vol. 21, 23 (1850–1), vol. 1, 166.   [492] Stevenson (n. 486), 117.
[493] See MacQueen (n. 346), 60–3; J. W. Cairns, 'Lawyers, Law Professors and Localities: The Universities of Aberdeen, 1680–1750', (1995) 46 *Northern Ireland Legal Quarterly* 304–31 at 306, 309–15.   [494] Spalding (n. 491), vol. 1, 241.
[495] James VI and I (n. 379), 20–4, 43.   [496] Ibid., 24–30.

for Parliament that heritable jurisdictions should not be regranted heritably once they fell to the Crown, so that judgment should derive from 'experience and knowledge'.[497] In his Parliament of 1587, James saw the enactment of a series of measures to promote order and concord, including one requiring landowners in the Highlands and Borders to find caution for their good behaviour and take responsibility for the men who lived on their lands and whom they protected.[498] To take local justice out of the hands of great magnates, to whom special commissions had often been granted in the face of the ending of regular justice ayres, an act provided relatively elaborately for the twice-yearly holding of justice ayres in every shire.[499] The effectiveness of these measures may be questioned: feuds were not ended; the justice ayres did not take effect.[500] Yet, the intention was clear and further measures followed these examples of attempts to pacify the Borders, Highlands, and Islands.[501]

James's attempts to extend central power and authority into the Highlands met with limited success; it was otherwise with his attempts to stamp out the bloodfeud. Central to his policy was control of firearms through a series of statutes on guns and pistols.[502] An act of the Convention of Estates of 1598, confirmed in Parliament in 1600, enforced a system of arbitration between feuding parties; where, however, there had been a killing on one side, but not yet on the other, the Crown would intervene.[503] James undertook not to grant respites, remissions, and pardons 'albeit the pairties transact and agrie amang thameselfis'.[504] This was a significant royal concession. In 1587 James had already undertaken for five years not to grant any respites or remissions for a series of crimes of the type likely to be committed in the course of feuding.[505] From around 1600, violence among the landed classes declined, so that by the end of the reign of Charles I bloodfeud had all but vanished from Lowland Scotland.[506] Changes in manners and habits promoted through the new discipline imposed by the Kirk Sessions of the reformed Church facilitated this.[507] In 1649, the Parliament of the Covenanters denounced and forbade remissions and respites;[508] those who committed homicide were either to be

---

[497] APS, III, 39 (c. 23). [498] APS, III, 458 (c. 56); 461–7 (c. 59); 467–70 (c. 60).
[499] APS, III, 458–61 (c. 57).
[500] See e.g. Donaldson, *James V–James VII* (n. 382), 223; K. M. Brown, *Bloodfeud in Scotland, 1573–1625: Violence, Justice and Politics in an Early Modern Society* (1986), 240.
[501] APS, IV, 39–42 (1593); 71–3 (c. 37) (1594); 138–9 (c. 33) (1597); 139 (c. 34) (1597); 160–4 (c. 4) (1598); Donaldson, *James V–James VII* (n. 382), 227–8.
[502] APS, III, 29–30 (c. 23) (1567); 85; RPC, V, 204; APS, IV, 164 (c. 5) (1598). See Brown (n. 500), 246–9.
[503] APS, IV, 158–9 (c. 1) (1598), 233–5 (c. 31) (1600). See Brown (n. 500), 241–3.
[504] APS, IV, 159 (c. 31); 234 (c. 31) (1600).
[505] APS, III, 456–7 (c. 54). See also APS, III, 426 (1586); 575 (c. 67) (1592).
[506] See M. B. Wasser, 'Violence and the Central Criminal Courts in Scotland, 1603–1638' (unpublished Ph.D. thesis, Columbia University, 1995), 219–37.
[507] See the argument in Cairns, (1998) 2 *Edinburgh LR* 281–5.
[508] APS, VI, pt. ii, 173 (c. 95).

executed or fined as appropriate.[509] This provision reflects an undoubted turn away from self-help in criminal matters and a new emphasis on the central enforcement of criminal justice. It is the culmination of the policies originally pursued by James VI.

Two measures were aimed at the authority of the nobility. First, to provide a source of authority in the localities alternative to the nobility and responsible to the Crown, justices of the peace on the model of England were introduced in 1609.[510] In 1617, Parliament ratified further provisions already made on the justices of the peace and their constables.[511] How effective the office was in Scotland requires further study.[512] Secondly, in 1617, a commission was created to negotiate for the surrender of heritable offices of sheriff, stewart, and bailie.[513] The stated aim was to ensure that the men who enjoyed such offices were 'furnischit with giftis suittable to the dignitie and gravitie of the places'. The emphasis on suitable skills demonstrates a growing stress on a more professional administration of justice.

6. Common law, codification, reason, and justice

Despite James IV's legislation of 1504,[514] there were still uncertainties about the geographical reach of the common law. In 1567, the question whether Orkney and Shetland 'salbe subiect to the comone law of this realme or gif thai sall bruke thair aune lawis' was put to the commission considering articles to be presented to Parliament. The decision was that 'thai aucht to be subiect to thair aune Lawis'.[515] Much of the old law of Norse origin continued to be applied, although there was considerable influence from the common law and its institutions.[516] The fall of Patrick Stewart, Earl of Orkney, changed this.[517] In 1611, the Privy Council ruled that 'foreyne lawis' were 'to be no forder usit within the . . . cuntreyis of Orknay and Yetland at ony tyme heirefter'; in future, anyone exercising judicial office in the Northern Isles was only to decide according to 'the proper lawis of this kingdome'.[518] In 1612,

---

[509] APS, VI, pt. ii, 173–4 (c. 96).
[510] APS, IV, 434–5 (c. 14) (1609); see also, APS, III, 458–60 (c. 57) (1587). See C. A Malcolm (ed.), *The Minutes of the Justices of the Peace for Lanarkshire, 1707–1723*, Scottish History Society, Third Series, vol. 17 (1931), ix–xxviii. The office had already been envisaged by the act of 1587 on justice ayres. See generally, John Findlay, *All Manner of People: The History of the Justices of the Peace in Scotland* (2000).
[511] APS, IV, 535–40 (c. 8); Malcolm (n. 510), xix–xx.
[512] See J. I. Smith, 'The Transition to the Modern Law 1532–1600', in Paton (n. 56), xx–xxi.
[513] APS, IV, 549–50 (c. 24).   [514] APS, II, 252 (c. 24).
[515] APS, III, 41; see also Goodare, (1999) 72 *Historical Research* 257.
[516] See e.g Gordon Donaldson (ed.), *The Court Book of Shetland, 1602–1604*, Scottish Record Society, Old Series, vol. 84 (1954). For the complex politics underlying all this, see Donaldson (n. 6), 26–33.
[517] See generally Gordon Donaldson, *Shetland Life under Earl Patrick* (1958).
[518] Donaldson (n. 383), 177–8; RPC, IX, 181–2.

Orkney and Shetland were annexed by the Crown and erected as a Stewartry.[519] Court books reveal the progressive introduction of the laws and procedures of the common law until all that was left of the older system were some few small vestiges of 'udal' land tenure.[520]

(a) Reforming the common law

If, at least in theory, there was indeed a common law for all Scotland, its nature was changing as the position of the College of Justice was consolidated and academic learning in law gained ever more authority. Moreover, the common law was a contested field. Thus, when the radical Presbyterian William Welwood dedicated his *Sea-Law of Scotland* to King James on 30 June 1590 'in the common expectation and great hoip of all the peiple for a reformation of the Iustice within this land' he probably looked towards a Godly reformation of the law.[521] The Parliament of 1592, with the Presbyterians in the ascendant, enacted a certain amount of such legislation, as did the Covenanting Parliament of 1649, perhaps driven to avert God's apparent wrath as disasters befell Scotland.[522] Yet, reformation of justice concerned more than just a programme enacting some of the provisions of the Mosaic law. Justice and law were important in God's design. Thus, in the *Jus Feudale*, Thomas Craig argued that, in the beginnings of society, kings had dispensed justice according to 'the reason of natural equity that was inborn in the hearts of men'. Decay of *mores* necessitated written laws, however, as otherwise justice was no longer dispensed equitably.[523] This common view of the importance to justice of written laws lay behind projects for 'codification' of the laws of this period. Thus, in 1575, a Convention of Estates noted the harm 'quhilk this commoun weill sustenis throw want of a perfyte writtin law

---

[519] APS, IV, 481–2 (c. 15). On the subsequent arrangement with the Bishop of Orkney see RMS, VII, 411–12 no. 1119.

[520] See R. S. Barclay (ed.), *The Court Book of Orkney and Shetland, 1612–1613* (1962); R. S. Barclay (ed.), *The Court Books of Orkney and Shetland, 1614–1615*, Scottish History Society, Fourth Series, vol. 4 (1967); *Court Book of Shetland, 1615–1629* (1991). For a further discussion, see Donaldson (n. 6), 34–8.

[521] William Welwood, *The Sea-Law of Scotland, Shortly Gathered and Plainly Dressit for the Reddy Use of all Seafairing Men* (1590; facsimile reprint 1969).

[522] APS, III, 543–4 (c. 11); 548 (c. 17); APS, VI, pt. ii, 208 (c. 132); 220–1 (c. 161); 231 (c. 178); 231 (c. 179); 261–2 (c. 205); 475 (c. 210).

[523] Thomas Craig, *Jus Feudale Tribus Libris Comprehensum* (3rd edn., 1732), I, 1, 5; I, 1, 11–12. All passages quoted or referred to have been compared with the text of the 1st edition of 1655. There are no differences of substance. All translations are my own, though I have usually compared them with the translation by Lord Clyde in *The Jus Feudale by Sir Thomas Craig of Riccarton with an Appendix containing the Books of the Feus* (1934). On Craig's legal thinking, see J. W. Cairns, 'The Civil Law Tradition in Scottish Legal Thought', in Carey Miller/Zimmermann (n. 86), 191–223 at 200–3; J. G. A. Pocock, *The Ancient Constitution and the Feudal Law: A Study of English Historical Thought in the Seventeenth Century, A Reissue with a Retrospect* (1987), 79–90.

quhairupoun all iugeis may knaw how to proceid and decerne', before appointing a commission to 'visite the bukis of the law actis of parliament and decisionis befoir the sessioun And draw the forme of the body of our lawis alsweill of that quhilk is alreddy statute as thay thingis that were meit and convenient tobe statute'.[524] In 1649, Parliament noted the necessity of 'a constant certane and knowne modell and frame of Law according to equitie and Justice established be publict authoritie and published to all his Maiesties Leidges'. Such was necessary 'for the glorie of God the weill of his kirk and the Just and peaceable government of his Majesties Liedges'. So that 'alse farr as possible may be by the blessing of God ane perfyte rule for administratioune of Justice in all caussis befoir all Judicatories', the Estates appointed a commission to examine statutes, customs, and practicks in order to 'collect draw up and compyll ane formall modall and frame of a buik of Just and equitable lawis'.[525] After the Reformation a humanist reassessment of the secular and ecclesiastical polity brought a renewed emphasis on the need for all the law to be reduced to writing.[526]

(b) *The texts of the law*

As well as such grander ambitions, simply securing texts of statutes could be difficult. Thus, in 1566, a commission (including Sir James Balfour of Pittendreich and 'Maister Edward Henryson, doctour in the lawes') was appointed 'to visie, sycht, and correct the lawis of this Realme maid be [the Queen] and Her maist nobill progenitouris, by the avise of the Thre Estatis in Parliament haldin be thame, beginnand at the bukis of the law called *Regiam Majestatem* and *Quoniam Attachiamenta*'. The result was a volume limited to acts from James I (1424) to Mary (1564), because of the unreliability and problematic nature of earlier records and the difficulty found in texts such as *Regiam*.[527] More was hoped for, since an exclusive licence was also granted to Henryson to print 'the Bukis of Law callit *Regiam Majestatem*, and the remanent auld Lawis and Actis of Parliament'.[528] After 1566, however, selected Acts of Parliament were regularly printed.[529]

---

[524] APS, III, 89 (1575). See also the views of the Earl of Morton: APS, I, 30 note 2.
[525] APS, VI, pt. ii, 299–300 (c. 271).
[526] See a discussion of aspects of this in A. H. Williamson, *Scottish National Consciousness in the Age of James VI: The Apocalypse, the Union and the Shaping of Scotland's Public Culture* (1979), 64–6.
[527] APS, I, 29–30. *The Actis and Constituionis of the Realme of Scotland maid in Parliaments haldin be the rycht excellent, hie and mychtie Princeis kingis James the first, Secund, thrid, feird, fyft, and in tyme of Marie now Quene of Scottis, viseit, correctit, and extractit furth of the Registers be the Lordis depute be hir Maiesteis speciall commissioun thairto* (1566). There are two issues of this volume respectively dated 12 Oct. and 28 Nov. 1566. The later one excludes some of the legislation of James V and a single act of Mary concerning the Catholic Church.
[528] It is printed on the verso of the title-page; see also APS, I, 29 n. 1.
[529] See details, in APS, I, 31–2 n. 3. See also the special commission in APS, III, 520 (c. 132).

(c) *The law commissions*

The broader terms of the commission of 1575 have already been mentioned.[530] Though this commission sat and worked for some time, the only possible result of its labours is Balfour's *Practicks*, compiled, between 1574 and 1583, from the Acts of Parliament, the 'auld lawes', and the decisions of the Session, relying for the latter on the now lost 'Register'.[531] By 1578, the work of this commission had faltered and, in 1578, Parliament appointed another law commission, which included Thomas Craig, to consider and bring forward proposals for enactments.[532]

The most important commission to gather the Scottish statute law and print what was important was that granted in 1592.[533] The bulk of the work seems to have fallen to John Skene, who became Clerk Register, and, in 1597, *The Lawes and Actes of Parliament* duly appeared in a volume that also included a table of the kings of Scots and Skene's *De Verborum Significatione*, an account of the difficult and technical words found in the old laws.[534] This work again only covered from 1424 onwards. The further fruit of this commission was Skene's edition of *Regiam* and the 'auld lawes' in 1609 in a primary Latin edition with a translation 'out of Latine in Scottish language'.[535] The Latin edition has the more elaborate scholarly apparatus, while

---

[530] APS, III, 89; I, 30–1.

[531] There can now be little doubt but that Balfour's *Practicks* were in fact compiled by Balfour: Hector McKechnie, 'Balfour's Practicks', (1931) 43 *JR* 179–92; P. G. B. McNeill in Balfour, *Practicks*, xxxii. Cf. APS, I, 30–1. See Gordon (n. 362) on the 'Register'.

[532] APS, III, 105 (c. 18).   [533] APS, III, 564 (c. 45).

[534] *The Lawes and Actes of Parliament, Maid Be King Iames the First and his Successours Kings of Scotland: Visied, collected and extracted furth of the Register* (1597). With a separate title-page was *De verborum significatione. The Exposition of the Termes and Difficill Wordes, Conteined in the Foure Buikes of Regiam Majestatem, and uthers, in the Actes of Parliament, Infeftments, and used in Practique of this Realme, with Diverse rules, and commoun places, or principalles of the Lawes: Collected and expound be M. John Skene, Clerke of our Souveraine Lordis Register, Councell and Rolles* (1597). Facing the handsome title-page of the *Lawes and Actes* were lines by Thomas Craig on James VI, Queen Anne, Prince Henry, all James's predecessors from James I onwards, and on the lion of Scotland: see e.g. NLS, pressmark H.33.c.32(1). See also APS, IV, 165 (c. 9) on ensuring the purchase of the collection.

[535] *Regiam Majestatem Scotiae, Veteres Leges et Constitutiones, ex Archivis Publicis, et Antiquis Libris Manuscriptis Collectae, Recognitae, et Notis Juris Civilis, Canonici, Nortmannici Auctoritate Confirmatis, Illustratae, Opera et Studio Joannis Skenaei, Regiae Maiestati a Conciliis et Archivis Publicis. Annotantur in Margine, Concordantiae Juris Divini, Legum Angliae, et Iuris Novissimi Scotiae quod Acta Parliamenti, vulgo vocant. Catalogum Eorum Quae in his Libris Continetur Vicessima Pagina, Indicat. Cum Duplici Indice, Altero Rerum, Altero Verborum Locupletissimo* (1609). The purported London edition of 1613 is in fact another issue of the Edinburgh edition of 1609 with the title-page cancelled and a new title-page affixed. *Regiam Majestatem. The Auld Lawes and Constitutions of Scotland, Faithfullie Collected furth of the Register and other Auld authentick Bukes, fra the dayes of King Malcolme the second, untill the time of King James the first, of gude memorie: and trewlie corrected in Sindrie faults and errours, committed be ignorant writers. . . . Be Sir James Skene of Curriehill . . . Quhereunto are adjoined Twa Treatises, The ane, anent the order of proces observed before the lords of Counsell, and Session: The other of Crimes, and Judges in Criminall Causes* (1609). There was another edition of this version in Edinburgh, 1774. See APS, IV, 378–9 (c. 16) (1607) authorizing the printing.

the Scots includes treatises on process before the Lords and on crimes and criminal process; the prefatory material is quite different. In the volumes Skene gathered texts of *Regiam*, *Quoniam*, the Laws of the Burghs, and other statutory or purported statutory material. Skene's edition has been much criticized;[536] this is unfair and his work is typical of contemporary humanistic textual scholarship and editing.[537]

Study of the 'auld lawes' revealed for the first time the problems posed by the relationship between Glanvill and *Regiam*.[538] Attitudes differed. Craig argued that *Regiam* was copied from Glanvill and should be denied the status of a formal source of Scots law. He called for its 'correction' by 'learned men'—presumably to produce a text that reflected where its provisions had been adopted into Scots law through practice and where departed from.[539] Skene, on the other hand, argued that *Regiam* had been compiled by David I; since Glanvill was later, it must have been copied from *Regiam*. In his marginal notes, he provided citations that he believed demonstrated the authenticity and authority of *Regiam* and the other 'auld lawes'.[540] Thus, this attempt to make more certain the law, by editing *Regiam* and printing the text, led to a further uncertainty in the sources of Scots law, although, for practical purposes, the rules adopted into practice from *Regiam* were necessarily followed.

Skene's publications nonetheless meant that a considerable amount of legislative material was available in print for the first time and the regular printing of Acts of Parliament continued. The works of Welwood, if slight, gave guidance on mercantile matters;[541] Balfour's *Practicks* and Craig's *Jus Feudale* circulated in manuscript.[542] Attempts were made to secure the printing of Craig's treatise.[543] Rather more than hitherto of the 'godlie, and gude lawes' necessary to society could be 'knawin be the people; swa that they can pretend na ignorance thereof'.[544] The aims of justice were thereby better fulfilled.

---

[536] See e.g. APS, I, 33–4.

[537] See Cairns/Fergus/MacQueen (n. 479), 52–6. There is a good discussion of the issues here in D. J. Osler, 'Vestigia Doctorum Virorum: Tracking the Legal Humanists' Manuscripts', (1992) 5 *Subseciva Groningana: Studies in Roman and Byzantine Law* 77–94.

[538] H. L. MacQueen, '*Glanvill* Resarcinate: Sir John Skene and *Regiam Majestatem*', in A. A. MacDonald, Michael Lynch, and I. B. Cowan (eds.), *The Renaissance in Scotland: Studies in Literature, Religion, History and Culture Offered to John Durkan* (1994), 385–403.

[539] Craig (n. 523), I, 8, 11. Craig was sceptical of other parts of the 'auld lawes': see ibid., I, 8, 1–2; II, 8, 9–10; II, 20, 3–4; II, 20, 30; III, 5, 4.

[540] See also the epistle to the reader in the Scots text of Skene's *Regiam*.

[541] See Cairns, (1998) 2 *Edinburgh LR* 161–2.

[542] On the MSS of Balfour, *Practicks*, see the lists given by McNeill ibid., xxxiv–xxxviii. I am unaware of study of the MSS of Craig. There can be little doubt but that MS copies of Balfour and Craig circulated in the early 17th century: e.g. both were used by Hope in his *Practicks* and are cited in Spotiswoode's *Practicks* (n. 457), e.g. at 82 (among many).

[543] NLS, Adv. MS 33.1.1, vol. 2, fo. 116ʳ. (no. 59); RPC, IX, 572.

[544] Skene, *Regiam* (Scots version), epistle to the reader.

The aim of a comprehensive restatement of Scots law resurfaced in the reign of Charles I, who appointed a commission on 2 July 1628 to examine the statutes, customs, and 'consuetudes' of the realm. New commissions were granted in 1630 and 1633 giving a wide remit to examine all statutory and customary laws, practicks, and decreets of the Session and Justice General, and the old laws, with the aim that all could be clarified and ratified by Parliament in a public law.[545] It is no surprise that such a huge task was not fulfilled, especially as the country slipped towards war with the king. Substantially the same provisions were re-enacted in 1649, again with understandably little result.[546]

(*d*) Jus divinum, jus naturale, jus gentium

The law commissions of 1575 and 1649 emphasized the links between God, justice, and reducing the law to written and printed form. Skene and Welwood were also concerned with the relationship between *jus divinum* and the law.[547] Craig's *Jus Feudale* was inspired by the desire to reduce Scots law, which many considered to be vague and uncertain, to a structured science.[548] He placed contemporary Scots law in a framework provided by the law of nature and nations propounding an essentially Thomist view that human beings had an innate capacity to know the *aequum et bonum* through the use of their reason, so that the exercise of *recta ratio* allowed knowledge of natural law.[549] Thus, he explained that 'neither the legislation of a kingdom, nor prescription of even the longest time, nor custom has force against this law'.[550] The *jus gentium* had chiefly to be followed after natural law. It governed international affairs and 'everything all nations observed ought also to have force with us, no matter what the *jus Civile* or *Municipale*' so that in dealings with foreigners, the *jus gentium* had to be observed, even if contrary to a statute of the kingdom, while 'among citizens it would have authority unless some statute or specific law opposed it'.[551] Craig's was not an isolated view: the terms 'equity', 'reason', and 'bona fides' started to permeate the statute law and reference to the *jus divinum* and *jus gentium* could be used to justify reforming measures.[552]

[545] APS, V, 46–7 (c. 32) (1633); 225, 227 (1630). See also ibid., V, 57 (c. 47) on Craig's *De Feudis*.   [546] APS, VI, pt. ii, 299–300 (c. 271).
[547] See Cairns, (1998) 2 *Edinburgh LR* 161–2. Skene has cross-references to *jus divinum* in the margins of his Latin edition of *Regiam*.   [548] Craig (n. 523), viii.
[549] I have drawn this closely from Cairns (n. 523), 200–2. For a general outline of the development of ideas of *aequitas* in canon law, see Peter Landau, ' "Aequitas" in the "Corpus Iuris Canonici" ', (1994) 20 *Syracuse Journal of International Law and Commerce* 95–104.
[550] Craig (n. 523), I, 8, 7.   [551] Ibid. I, 8, 8.
[552] See APS, III, 223–4 (c. 24) (1581); 378 (c. 9) (1585); 379–80 (c. 14) (1585); 453–4 (c. 45) (1587); 571 (c. 56) (1592); IV, 544–5 (c. 13) (1617); 550 (c. 25) (1617); V, 269 (c. 14) (1640); VI, pt. ii, 133 (c. 17) (1649). See APS, III, 570 (c. 53) (1592): 'It is nocht onlie condempnit be the expres word of god Bot also be the lawes of all nationis'; APS, IV, 544–5 (c. 13) (1617): 'law of god and man'.

Historical Introduction 99

The language of the law of nature and nations now provided a vocabulary to discuss law and to justify its reform. Such language increasingly promoted departure from the norms and suppositions of the medieval law. It marked the penetration of essentially canonist ideas into the secular law, perhaps because of the disappearance of the separate ecclesiastical jurisdiction. The common law was taking on a different flavour and texture, although conflicts between the older medieval procedures as found in *Regiam* and the newer Romano-canonical procedures emphasizing equity could still cause problems.[553]

7. Common law and *jus commune*

(a) *Learned law and legal practice*

Descriptions of practice before the Session from the 1570s through to the reign of Charles I emphasized reliance on statutes and *Regiam Majestatem* in court. Failing any relevant act or 'auld lawe', or perhaps judgments, such accounts further stress that 'they have recourse and doe decide according to the ymperiall civill lawe', or cite 'out of the Romane lawis' whatever 'is thocht necessar to pacifie this controversie', or 'corroborate their cause with civil arguments and reasons'.[554] Such use of the civil and canon laws was authorized in practice before the Session. In the Act of Sederunt of 1596, requiring 'the informatioun of the causis' to be 'in wreitt', the Lords promised that they would 'try quhat is prescryveit or decidet thairanent, als weill be the common law as be the municipall law or practick of this realme'.[555] This in fact enjoins a wider reliance on the *jus commune* than merely as 'supplementary' law.

The education of the majority of the advocates made such use of Roman and canon law perfectly possible, while the relevant literature was readily available in Scotland and circulated among the learned classes.[556] The proposal in 1619 that each advocate should at his admission donate a book chosen from 'the works of any one of the doctors of Lawes as sould be enjoyned to him be the dean of faculty' demonstrates the lawyers' anxiety to ensure access to suitable literature.[557] The citations in Craig's *Jus Feudale*,

---

[553] See APS, III, 112 (c. 33).

[554] See J. D. Mackie and W. C. Dickinson (eds.), 'Relation of the Manner of Judicatores of Scotland', (1922) 19 *Scot Hist Rev* 254–72 at 268; E. G. Cody (ed.), *The Historie of Scotland Wrytten First in Latin by the Most Reverend and Worthy Jhone Leslie Bishop of Rosse and Translated in Scottish by Father James Dalrymple Religious in the Scottis Cloister of Regensburg, the Yeare of God, 1596*, Scottish Text Society, Old Series, vol. 5 (1888), vol. 1, 119–20; *Journall into Scotland* (n. 442), 31.

[555] AS, I, 26–7 (13 July 1596). While 'common law' can be used in a variety of senses, it is clear that here it is in contrast to *jus proprium*.

[556] See William Angus (ed.), *Protocol Book of Mr Gilbert Grote, 1552–1573*, Scottish Record Society, Old Series, vol. 43 (1914), 20–1 no. 107; Durkan/Ross (n. 340).

[557] NLS, Adv. MS 25.2.5, vol. 1, fo. 220ʳ.

Skene's works, and the manuscript practicks indicate the works relied on; these were a mixture of traditional standard authors of the *jus commune* and more modern authors such as Cujas, Duarenus, and Hotman, and the decisions of important continental courts.[558]

The strength and persuasive power of the literature of the *jus commune* lay in its accessibility and written character, while a justification for its use—necessary once Scots started to address issues such as sovereignty—could be found in natural law.[559] Craig explained that Scots used civil law because there was so little written law in Scotland (by which he primarily meant statutes) and stated that in Scotland 'we are bound by the Roman laws only in so far as they are congruent with the laws of nature and right reason'. If Roman law was only binding as *jus naturale* and the product of *recta ratio*, he emphasized that was indeed a major source of equity.[560] Furthermore, although Scotland had 'shaken off the papal yoke', where there was a conflict between the canon law and the civil law, the former was generally to be preferred.[561] This was a general view of the *jus commune*.

The received wisdom was that statutes and Scottish custom came first in a hierarchy of authority, with civil law only in a subsidiary and supplementary role.[562] Such hierarchies were less compelling than they might seem, however: Roman law may only have possessed authority insofar as it was compatible with natural law and right reason, but the *jus naturale* and, to some extent, the *jus gentium* had a higher authority than the *jus municipale*. Judges and pleaders had wide scope to open up arguments from the *jus commune*. Craig certainly saw the civil law as widely relied on in Scotland.[563] The relationship of the *jus proprium* to the *jus commune* was more complex than any simple hierarchy of sources would suggest. Study of the decisions of the courts in this respect is difficult.[564] Nonetheless, departure from the civil law in a deci-

---

[558] This is a topic in need of much further and systematic research. The general impression is that the works that loomed largest were the later medieval works of the *jus commune*, such as those of as Bartolus, Baldus, Jason de Mayno, Cinus de Pistoia, Paulus de Castro, and the like. On the other hand, more modern authors such as Cujas, Duarenus, and Hotman are also found. Older but very fundamental works such as those of Guillaume Durand and Panormitanus also remained important. Sir Robert Spotiswoode regularly cites the collection of decisions made by the French jurist Guy Papon as well as other such material. These very general remarks are based on my study of Craig and observations of the citations in Spotiswoode's *Practicks* (n. 457).
[559] Cairns/Fergus/MacQueen (n. 479), 60–6.   [560] Craig (n. 523), I, 2, 14.
[561] Ibid., I, 3, 24; I, 8, 17.
[562] Consider the remarks of Skene, *Regiam* (Latin) dedication to the king.
[563] See the list in Craig (n. 523), I, 2, 14.
[564] There are a variety of problems with such work, not least that frequently the practicks merely outline the argument of the court and lawyers without revealing the authorities relied on: see e.g. *The Decisions of the Lords of Council and Session, in Most Cases of Importance, Debated, and Brought before Them; From July 1621. to July 1642. . . . Observed by Sir Alexander Gibson of Dury* (1690); Nicholson's *Practicks*, Edinburgh University Library, MS Dc.4.13. Dury does occasionally cite some civil law texts: Dury, 570 (*Williamson v. Balgillo*).

sion or that Scots practick differed from civil law were things to be noted.[565] The Lords can be found considering the views of authors such as Cujas, Bartolus, Duarenus, Mynsinger, and even the English civilian Cowell.[566]

(b) The strength of the jus commune

The written sources of the *jus commune* were important because there was little written *Scottish* law, when having written law was in itself seen as just. Litigants had a lively expectation that the civil and canon laws would be applied to their causes.[567] The Lords were happy to adopt the provisions of the civil law to remedy fraudulent dispositions by bankrupts.[568] The Scottish advocates slipped as easily between Latin and Scots as between civil law and Scots law in their thinking.[569] English law was occasionally found as a source of Scottish legislation; but this was not the general trend.[570] In December 1567 it was proposed to the commission considering articles to be presented to Parliament that 'ane comissioun be gevin to sufficient personis to mak ane body of the civile and Municipale lawis devidit in heidis conforme to the fassone of the law Romane'.[571] When Mary's last Parliament passed an act concerning the Protestant religion it abrogated 'quhatsumevir lawis actis and constitutionis Canone civile or municipale' were contrary to the reformed religion and freed those who were under any penalties 'be vertew of the saidis actis lawis ordinances Canone Civile or Municipale'.[572] Variations on the formula 'as be the commoun law and lawis of this realme' were relied on to justify Acts of Parliament.[573] The theoretical foundation Craig had given for this justified the Scots in carrying on marrying the civil law with the Scots, as Robert Burnet said of Sir Alexander Gibson of Durie.[574]

8. Scotland under the Commonwealth and Protectorate, 1652–1659

(a) A new legal system

The Cromwellian settlement in Scotland was based on military occupation. Large forts—such as the citadel at Leith—were intended to control the

---

[565] See Spotiswoode, *Practicks* (n. 457), 160–1 (the Lords rejected an argument based on 'the comon and Civil Law' that a minor could not dispone his heritage '*sine decreto judicis*'— Spotiswoode notes that this 'was express against the Civil Law'); ibid. 195; see also Dury (n. 564), 308 (*Rowan v. Shaw*).
[566] For a small sample, see Spotiswoode, *Practicks* (n. 457), 14, 183–4 (Cujas), 81–3, 241, 275 (Mynsinger), 181 (Duarenus), 14, 182 (Bartolus), 309 (Cowell).
[567] Wormald (n. 278), 53 (concerning a bond of manrent).
[568] APS, IV, 615–6 (c. 18) (1621) enacting the earlier Act of Sederunt.
[569] See Edinburgh University Library, MS La.I.291.   [570] Sellar (n. 3), 92.
[571] APS, III, 40 (c. 42).   [572] APS, II, 548–9 (c. 2).
[573] APS, III, 349 (c. 6) (1584). See also APS, IV, 133 (c. 17) (1597) ('conform to the civill and cannoun law'); APS, IV, 543–4 (c. 12) (1617) ('by the Civill law and be the lawes of all natiounes ar declaired voyde and uneffectual').   [574] Preface to Craig (n. 523), xi.

populace.[575] The *Declaration of the Parliament of the Commonwealth of England, concerning the Settlement of Scotland* provided for an incorporating union and commissioners were sent to Scotland to settle the civil government, including the administration of justice; they had to ensure 'that the Lawes of England as to matter of government be put in Execution in Scotland'.[576] The creation of some kind of legal system was urgent as the Session had last sat in February 1650, after having sat irregularly during the Covenanting government.[577] For a while, an ad hoc court was held at Leith by English officers.[578] In January 1652, the commissioners announced that individuals would be appointed to dispense justice until permanent judicatories were established and abolished all jurisdictions not deriving authority from the English Parliament.[579] Commissioners for Administration of Justice were appointed in May 1652, first taking their seats in Parliament House on 18 May. Four were English, the other three Scots.[580] Two men were appointed for each shire, one an Englishman, the other a Scot, as sheriffs and commissaries.[581] A Court of Admiralty was also established.[582]

This settled a basic pattern for the administration of justice that was maintained until the Restoration.[583] In theory, the franchise jurisdictions had been abolished in 1652; in practice, however, it seems that they continued in operation, presumably because of local needs.[584] In 1654, the Ordinance 'for uniting Scotland into one Commonwealth with England' abolished all heritable jurisdictions along with military tenures and all feudal casualties; all that was preserved was the requirement to pay annual duties.[585] An ordinance of the

---

[575] Donaldson, *James V–James VII* (n. 382), 346–7.

[576] APS, VI, pt. ii, 771, 774; 809–10; C. H. Firth (ed.), *Scotland and the Protectorate: Letters and Papers Relating to the Military Government of Scotland from January 1654 to June 1659*, Scottish History Society, First Series, vol. 31(1899), 393–8; see Dow (n. 417), 30–4.

[577] Stevenson, [1972] *JR* 245–6; John Nicoll, *A Diary of Public Transactions and Other Occurrences, Chiefly in Scotland, from January 1650 to June 1667* (ed. by David Laing, Bannatyne Club, vol. 52, 1836), 69.

[578] C. H. Firth (eds.), *Scotland and the Commonwealth: Letters and Papers Relating to the Military Government of Scotland, from August 1651 to December 1653*, Scottish History Society, First Series, vol. 18 (1895), xxviii; Dow (n. 417), 25. See also L. M. Smith, 'Scotland and Cromwell: A Study in Early Modern Government' (unpublished D.Phil. thesis, University of Oxford, 1980), 44–6.   [579] Dow (n. 417), 36; Firth (n. 578), xxvii–xxviii; Nicoll (n. 577), 80.

[580] Firth (n. 578), 43; Nicoll (n. 577), 96.

[581] C. Sanford Terry (ed.), *The Cromwellian Union: Papers Relating to the Negotiations for an Incorporating Union between England and Scotland, 1651–1652*, Scottish History Society, First Series, vol. 40 (1902), 65–7, 164; Smith (n. 578), 69.

[582] Sanford Terry (n. 581), 67–8, 86–7. The commissions for these appointments were to be in force only until 1 Nov. 1652; but on 26 Oct. they were continued until 1653: C. H. Firth and R. S. Rait (eds.), *Acts and Ordinances of the Interregnum, 1642–1660* (1911; repr. 1982), vol. 2, 622–3.

[583] See generally, A. R. G. MacMillan, 'The Judicial System of the Commonwealth', (1937) 49 *JR* 232–55.

[584] See C. S. Romanes (ed.), *Selections from the Records of the Regality of Melrose, 1605–1661*, Scottish History Society, Second Series, vol. 6 (1914), 137–261; D. M. Hunter (ed.), *The Court Book of the Barony and Regality of Falkirk and Callendar. Volume 1. 1638–1656*, Stair Society, vol. 38 (1991), 256–67; Smith (n. 578), 192–218.   [585] Firth/Rait (n. 582), vol. 2, 873–5.

same date created 'Courts Baron' for every piece of land 'which really is, or hath commonly been called, known or reputed to be a Manor'. These courts had jurisdiction to deal with 'all contracts, debts, promises and trespasses whatsoever' not exceeding the value of 40 shillings sterling. Their structure was the traditional one, whereby suitors attended and dealt with the business and a jury was empanelled to decide any disputes and the 'Bayliff of the Manor' was authorized to enforce the court's orders.[586] The occupying forces felt the want of the familiar English justices of the peace to secure local order, since, from 1641, the system established under James VI had fallen into abeyance.[587] A system of justices of the peace was finally established in December 1655.[588]

The new Commissioners for the Administration of Justice ruled in 1652 that Latin should no longer be used in writs, which had to be in 'playne significant Englische language'. They had also imposed oaths of loyalty on the Writers to the Signet and managed eventually to get the initially unwilling advocates to take an oath of allegiance.[589] The old procedures in civil litigation seem basically to have continued and, for example, a regulation of 9 November had covered, *inter alia*, the delivery of written informations to the lodgings of the Commissioners.[590] The partial copy that survives of the Books of Sederunt for the Commonwealth or Protectorate period and the Minute Books and Registers of Acts and Decreets confirm that matters continued much as before, if carried out under a different authority.[591]

(b) The effectiveness of the new courts

The new regime was more concerned with the preservation of social order and stability through the criminal courts than with civil justice as such.[592] The Commissioners for the Administration of Justice also sat in criminal matters; for this, the English judges were much preferred.[593] There were attempts to hold regular circuit courts to deal with crime in the regions.[594] Local Kirk Sessions continued to police morals, acting alongside the secular courts in gathering evidence of wrongdoing.[595]

---

[586] Ibid. vol. 2, 883–4.   [587] See Sanford Terry (n. 581), 180–181; Malcolm (n. 510), xxi.
[588] Firth (n. 576), 308–16, 403–5; Dow (n. 417), 145–6, 178–81.
[589] Nicoll (n. 577), 94, 96. See Sanford Terry, (n. 581), 181.
[590] Nicoll (n. 577), 117.
[591] NLS, Adv. MS 25.2.5, vol. 1, fos. 303^r–324^r. contains 'The Sederunt Book of the Judges established by the Usurper Cromwell Called the Commissioners for administration of Justice To the People of Scotland', covering from 1 Nov. 1654 to 23 Feb. 1659. See NAS, CS7/557–607 (Registers of Acts and Decreets); CS 8/23–8/30; CS 12/1; CS 13/1; CS 14/1.
[592] They were concerned, however, about problems arising out of debt: see the letters of General Monck, 29 Apr. and 16 May 1654 in Firth (n. 576), 98, 106; Nicoll (n. 577), 129, 143, 180; Firth/Rait (n. 582), vol. 2, 898; Dow (n. 417), 182–5.
[593] See Smith (n. 578), 72.   [594] Dow (n. 417), 56–7, 145, 178–9, 221–2.
[595] See L. M. Smith, 'Sackcloth for the Sinner or Punishment for the Crime? Church and Secular Courts in Cromwellian Scotland', in John Dwyer, R. A. Mason, and Alexander Murdoch (eds.), *New Perspectives on the Politics and Culture of Early Modern Scotland* (1982), 116–32.

Union with England raised the issue of union of the laws and propaganda reports minimized the differences between the two systems.[596] When Cromwell appointed nine individuals to serve as a Council of State for Scotland in 1655, they were instructed to promote the assimilation of Scots law to that of England.[597] In fact, few steps seem to have been taken to promote this and, by 1658, there were generally more Scots than Englishmen sitting as judges; they seem to have generally been averse to any steps to promote assimilation.[598] The administration of justice during the English occupation has acquired a reputation for speed and impartiality.[599] The evidence is unconvincing.[600] By 1655, 50,000 cases were allegedly pending before the Commissioners. If some of this was due to a backlog inherited from the Session, much must have been due to the Commissioners themselves and Lord Broghill attributed it to a lack of judicial personnel.[601] In 1659 the criticism was made that 'in time of session by reason of the multitude of their imployments in civill afaires they keepe oley Courts one in the moneth'.[602] The removal of the public records to England (though it was decided to send some back) also hampered the running of the legal system.[603] Rather than praising, many contemporaries found much to criticize in the new system.[604]

(c) Continuities

Despite innovations and the aim of assimilation, continuity in the law is what is most obvious. The civil court continued to be called the Session; the Commissioners were referred to as 'the Judges of the Court of Session'.[605] The 'College of Justice'—named as such—would act collectively to assert its privileges.[606] Procedure before the court remained substantially unchanged. The court remained divided into Inner and Outer Houses.[607] Registration of deeds

---

[596] Sanford Terry (n. 581), 180.
[597] APS, VI, pt. ii, 826; see the discussion in Dow (n. 417), 166.
[598] See e.g. Macmillan, (1937) 49 *JR* 242–3; See Lord Broghill, 23 Oct. 1655, in John Thurloe, *A Collection of State Papers* (1742), vol. 7, 449–50. See Dow (n. 417), 221–2.
[599] See e.g. A. J. G. Mackay, *Memoir of Sir James Dalrymple, First Viscount Stair* (1873), 58.
[600] See Stevenson, (1972) 17 *JR* 244–5.
[601] Broghill to Thurloe, in Thurloe (n. 598), vol. 4, 268–9.
[602] Firth (n. 576), 386.
[603] David Stevenson, 'The English and the Public Records of Scotland, 1650–1660', in *Miscellany 1* (n. 112), 156–68.
[604] Firth (n. 576), 391–2. Robert Baillie to William Spang, *The Letters and Journals of Robert Baillie A.M., Principal of the University of Glasgow. M.DC.XXXVII.–M.DC.LXII* (ed. by David Laing, Bannatyne Club, vol. 73, 1841–2) vol. 3, 288.   [605] Nicoll (n. 577), 210.
[606] Ibid. 226, 229–33.
[607] William Forbes, *A Journal of the Session . . . from February 1705, till November 1713* (1714), xvii states that the Outer House was initially suppressed until revived in 1654. This view has been generally accepted. See e.g. Mackay (n. 599), 59; C. H. Firth, *The Last Years of the Protectorate, 1656–1658* (1964), vol. 2, 106; Dow (n. 417), 176–7; Smith (n. 578), 72; Cairns, (1999) 20, no. 2 *JLH* 38. It seems incorrect, however, as the 'Orders Issued by the Judges' on 23 Nov. 1653 presuppose a functioning Outer House: Firth (n. 578), 276–81.

remained of immense importance in practice.[608] Advocates continued to be admitted in two ways: they either gave proof of academic learning by reading a lesson on civil law before the judges, or had to produce a favourable report from the Protector's Advocate, the Dean of Faculty and other advocates if admitted on the ground of long experience. The preference remained for men with an academic training in civil law.[609]

There is nothing to suggest any major change in legal doctrine, even if one can point to the odd case where the judges departed from the civil law and prior decisions of the Session.[610] In 1655, the very year that Cromwell's Instructions to the Council of State urged assimilation of legal practice to that of England, Craig's *Jus Feudale* was printed for the first time in Edinburgh. In the preface, the advocate Robert Burnet noted that 'Civil law has no authority among us, but, in the absence of our own municipal law, the *ratio iuris civilis* is highly appreciated by us, and is greatly valued by the learned and the judges skilled in the laws who often follow this *ratio* in deciding cases'.[611] Moreover, the judges' commissions required them to administer justice according to Scots law and equity:[612] Craig strongly argued that equity was to be found in the civil law.[613]

The last recorded sederunt of the Protectorate's Session was on 23 February 1659.[614] Central civil justice was in abeyance until the restoration of the old Session in 1661.[615]

VI. FROM THE RESTORATION TO UNION AND THE END OF THE STEWART DYNASTY

1. Politics, religion, and government, 1660–1690

(a) The restored polity

On 14 May 1660, Charles II was proclaimed king of his three kingdoms in Edinburgh. The collapse of the Protectorate ended the Union with England.

---

[608] Firth (n. 578), 283–5. On return of the registers relating to private rights, see Stevenson (n. 603), 162–3.   [609] Cairns, (1999) 20, no. 2 *JLH* 38–40.

[610] See *The Decisions of the English Judges, During the Usurpation, from the Year 1655, to his Majesty's Restoration, and the Sitting Down of the Session in June 1661* (1762), 37. This was printed on the basis of NLS, Adv. MS 24.3.1.   [611] Craig (n. 523), xi.

[612] Broghill to Thurloe, 18 Dec. 1655, in Thurloe (n. 598), vol. 4, 323–4.

[613] Craig (n. 583), I, 2, 14.

[614] NLS, Adv. MS 25.2.5, vol. 1, fo. 324^r.; *Decisions of the English Judges* (n. 610), 232–3. The Registers and Minute Books of Acts and Decreets have their last entries on 26 Feb. 1659. The Commissioners sat in criminal matters until 5 July: NAS, JC 6/5.

[615] Dow (n. 417), 242–4, 261, 271. Some local courts did sit, however: Nicoll (n. 577), 266. It is worth noting that James Cockburne of Ryselaw chose his curators before the Bailies of Edinburgh in May 1660, 'ther being no other iudicatorie siting in Scotland for the tyme': APS, VII, 276–7 (c. 300). The Melrose Regality Court continued to function—no doubt other such courts did so too: Romanes (n. 584), 227–365.

Royalist legitimacy was restored by recall in August of the Committee of Estates that had met in 1651. The Earls of Middleton, Glencairn, and Lauderdale became respectively Commissioner to Parliament, Chancellor, and Secretary. There were a small number of show trials.[616] The Parliament that met on 1 January 1661 has the reputation of being notably submissive.[617] There were, however, clear differences of opinion within it and some contentious debates.[618] Its first enactment, however, enforced on the members an oath of allegiance that emphasized the king's authority and superiority in ecclesiastical and secular matters and jurisdictions.[619] A further series of acts quickly reasserted the royal prerogative, including creating, in time, the old committee of the Lords of the Articles, while removing any type of executive role from Parliament.[620]

A cleverly drafted and highly contentious act rescinded the actions of all parliaments after that of 1633; it stressed the illegalities that had resulted from ignoring the 'Sacred right inherent to the imperiall Croun (which his Maiestie holds imediately of God Almighty alone) and ... the antient and fundamentall lawes of the Kingdome'.[621] The wording emphasized the reversion of Scots civil government and legal institutions to their earlier forms and the *jure divino* indefeasible hereditary right of the monarchy.[622] In principle, despite the stress that the monarch should govern according to the law, the emphasis on the hereditary rights of the Stewarts was always in potential conflict with the developing theories of the *jus naturale* and *jus gentium*. The best-known exponent of *jure divino* kingship is Sir George Mackenzie of Rosehaugh, Lord Advocate to both Charles II and James VII (1685–8), whose work *Jus Regium: Or, the Just and Solid Foundations of Monarchy in General; and more especially of the Monarchy of Scotland* was the most sustained royalist tract of the period.[623] For Mackenzie, history, authority, and

---

[616] Lynch (n. 4), 286–7; Donaldson, *James V–James VII* (n. 382), 361; Coffey, *Politics, Religion and the British Revolutions* (n. 406), 60–1.

[617] George Mackenzie, *Memoirs of the Affairs of Scotland from the Restoration of King Charles II. A.D. M.DC. LX.* (1821), 19. See also Clare Jackson, 'Restoration to Revolution 1660–1690', in Glenn Burgess (ed.), *The New British History: Founding a Modern State, 1603–1715* (1999), 92–114 at 96; Ronnie Lee, 'Retreat from Revolution: The Scottish Parliament and the Restored Monarchy, 1661–1663', in Young (n. 401), 185–204 at 195–6; Lynch (n. 4), 291.

[618] A point well made in J. C. L. Jackson, 'Royalist Politics, Religion and Ideas in Restoration Scotland, 1660–1689' (unpublished Ph.D. thesis, University of Cambridge, 1998), 96.

[619] APS, VII, 7 (c. 1). [620] See the discussion in Lee (n. 617), 186–91.

[621] APS, VII, 86–7 (c. 126); the establishment of the Church was postponed: APS, VII, 87–8 (c. 127). [622] On royalist thought, see generally Jackson (n. 618), 49–124.

[623] George Mackenzie, *Jus Regium: Or, the Just and Solid Foundations of Monarchy in General; and More Especially of the Monarchy of Scotland: Maintain'd against Buchanan, Naphtali, Dolman, Milton, &c.* (Edinburgh, 1684; another edn., London, 1684) (I shall here cite the London edition). On Mackenzie, see Andrew Lang, *Sir George Mackenzie, King's Advocate, of Rosehaugh: His Life and Times 1636(?)–1691* (1909); J. W. Cairns, 'Sir George Mackenzie, The Faculty of Advocates, and the Advocates' Library', in George Mackenzie, *Oratio Inauguralis in Aperienda Jurisconsultorum Bibliotheca* (ed. by J. W. Cairns, and A. M. Cain, 1989), 18–35; Clare Jackson, 'The Paradoxical Virtue of the Historical Romance: Sir George Mackenzie's "Aretina"

reason all combined to prove the absolute nature of the Scottish monarchy.[624] A limited contrast can be provided by the work of Sir James Dalrymple of Stair, judge under the Protectorate, and subsequently Lord of Session and President of the College of Justice under Charles II. Stair emphasized the contractarian origin of human societies. This, however, did not imply any right to resist government: 'private opinion' had to 'give place to public authority' and it was sometimes necessary for human laws to depart from the *jus naturale*.[625] More radical thinkers, however, concluded from the contractual basis of society that there was an individual right to resist the prince or magistrate if he violated the *jus divinum* or *jus naturale*. Thus, James Steuart of Goodtrees put forward such an argument in his works *Naphtali, or the Wrestlings of the Church of Scotland for the Kingdom of Christ* (of which he was one of the authors) and *Jus Populi Vindicatum: Or the Peoples Right to Defend Themselves and their Covenanted Religion* (1669).[626]

Along with Parliament and Privy Council, the courts returned to their older forms. The king, who now also appointed a permanent President, appointed Lords of Session; the Session was to sit again on 4 June 1661.[627] The Earl of Cassilis became Justice-General, with courts being organized by the Justice-Clerk and held by deputes.[628] A transitional arrangement provided for the validity of the proceedings of the courts 'in name of the Usurpers', but individuals were allowed a year from the 'dounsitting of the Session' to challenge their decisions.[629]

By the end of 1661, a decision to restore episcopacy had been made and four Scottish bishops were consecrated at Westminster. Early the next year, the Privy Council prohibited meetings of Presbyteries and Synods without episcopal permission and Parliament duly re-erected an episcopalian establishment in the Kirk, restoring to the bishops the rights, privileges, properties, and jurisdictions they had possessed in 1637.[630] The Estate of Bishops was also restored to Parliament.[631] A whole series of acts attempted to impose uniformity and suppress dissent, while stressing the royal supremacy and the

---

(1660) and the Civil Wars', in Young (n. 401), 205–25. On the complex bibliography of Mackenzie's works, see F. S. Ferguson, 'A Bibliography of the Works of Sir George Mackenzie Lord Advocate Founder of the Advocates' Library', (1935–1938) 1 *Edinburgh Bibliographical Society Transactions* 1–60.

[624] Mackenzie, *Jus Regium* (n. 623), 13–49.

[625] Stair, I, 1, 16 (I shall refer to the edition by D. M. Walker for convenience; see further below on Stair and this work).

[626] See Jackson (n. 618), 77–89; Robert von Friedeburg, 'From Collective Representation to the Right of Individual Defence: James Steuart's *Ius Populi Vindicatum* and the Use of Johannes Althusius' *Politica* in Restoration Scotland', (1998) 24 *History of European Ideas* 19–42. On Steuart, see G. W. D. Omond, *The Lord Advocates of Scotland* (1883), vol. 1, 243–80.

[627] Hannay, *College of Justice* (n. 274), 110; APS, VII, 189 (c. 194).

[628] See Lynch (n. 4), 287.   [629] APS, VII, 62–3 (c. 87).

[630] APS, VII, 372–4 (c. 3); Lynch (n. 4), 289–90; Ferguson (n. 382), 147–8.

[631] APS, VII, 370–1 (c. 1).

illegality of the Covenants.[632] Those holding offices of public trust—including Lords of Session, Commissioners in Exchequer, members of the College of Justice, sheriffs, stewarts, commissaries, their deputes and clerks, magistrates and councillors in burghs, justices of the peace and their clerks—had to swear an oath rejecting the legality of the National Covenant and the Solemn League and Covenant.[633] Those who absented themselves from worship at their parish church were to be fined.[634]

(b) Struggles in Kirk and State

Alternating policies of repression and toleration followed. Just over a quarter of ministers were deprived of their charges. Opposition led to a rebellion that was suppressed in 1666. An 'Indulgence' in 1669 allowed some Presbyterian ministers to return to their parishes; a subsequent Indulgence of 1672 permitted nearly 100 more to preach.[635] In 1669, Parliament passed the Act of Supremacy asserting that the king had 'the Supream Authority and Supremacie over all persons and in all causes ecclesiastical'. This meant that 'the ordering and disposall of the Externall Government and policie of the Church Doth propperlie belong to his Maiestie and his Successours'.[636] This act removed any claims that episcopacy was imposed *jure divino* and emphasized that it had no greater legitimacy than the will of the king. The bishops were manifestly creatures of the court.[637] Outside the indulgences, conformity had to be imposed by repression, the policy adopted once more in 1673, although there were already strong measures taken against field conventicles.[638] Fining and quartering troops on the disaffected resulted in another rising, defeated by the Duke of Monmouth at Bothwell Brig on 22 June 1679; tensions had also risen after the murder of the Archbishop of St Andrews in May of that year.[639]

Further repression followed in the 1680s, largely due to the policy of James, Duke of York, whose dislike of the third Indulgence of 1679 led to its withdrawal the next year.[640] Sent north to Edinburgh in 1679, in the aftermath of the 'Popish Plot', to escape the tensions in England over the issue of his potential succession to the throne, the Roman Catholic York returned from 1680 to the end of 1681. He had an immediate impact as the King's Commissioner to Parliament and used his presence to build up a clientele and following, especially in the Highlands.[641] York's most notable achievements

---

[632] APS, VII, 376 (c. 7); 376–7 (c. 8); 377–9 (c. 12); 379 (c. 13).
[633] APS, VII, 405–6 (c. 54).   [634] APS, VII, 455–6 (c. 9).
[635] Donaldson, *James V–James VII* (n. 382), 365–9.   [636] APS, VII, 554 (c. 2).
[637] See Jackson (n. 618), 225–35.   [638] Donaldson, *James V–James VII* (n. 382), 369–70.
[639] Ibid. 370–1.   [640] Lynch (n. 4), 296.
[641] Ferguson (n. 382), 159–61; Donaldson, *James V–James VII* (n. 382), 379–80; Rosalind Mitchison, *Lordship to Patronage: Scotland 1603–1745* (1983), 113–14; Hugh Ouston, 'York in Edinburgh: James VII and the Patronage of Learning in Scotland, 1679–1688', in Dwyer/Mason/Murdoch (n. 595), 133–55.

were in the Parliament of 1681, where an act was passed declaring the principle of indefeasible hereditary succession to the Crown, unaffected by difference of religion and unalterable by Parliament.[642] Most important, however, was the Test Act, imposing on office-holders an oath accepting the Confession of Faith of 1560 and the royal supremacy in spiritual as well as temporal affairs.[643] This oath had a number of notable casualties: the Earl of Argyll, who was tried for leasing-making and condemned to death, but who escaped; James Dalrymple of Stair, the President of the Session, who fled to Holland; and Andrew Fletcher of Saltoun, who also joined the growing band of exiles.[644]

(c) The succession of James VII

York succeeded as James VII (1685–8) in 1685. The two rebellions that broke out, led by Argyll in Scotland and Monmouth in England, were defeated and their leaders executed, although there was a considerable number of people opposed to James's mode of government and religious policies.[645] In 1685, James's supporter Louis XIV revoked the edict of Nantes and commenced persecution of the Huguenots. This was the alarming backdrop to James's use of his dispensing powers to promote Roman Catholics to office in England and his attempts to persuade the Scottish Parliament to remove the civil disabilities of Catholics in Spring 1686, which provoked rioting in Edinburgh.[646] In 1687, the Privy Council issued two indulgences, the second giving a wide degree of toleration of religious opinion and practice, including that of the Presbyterians.[647] Although there had already been riots in Edinburgh when mass was celebrated at the home of the Chancellor, the Earl of Perth, who with his brother, the Earl of Melfort, had converted to Catholicism, James proceeded to appoint Catholics to office and placed a Catholic earl at the head of the army.[648]

James's policies destabilized Scottish political society, raising the spectre of 'popery'. General toleration was disastrous for the established Church, removing any authority that the bishops may have had. James had undermined his own support. William of Orange, married to James's Protestant daughter, Mary, invited by an alliance of English Tories and Whigs, landed in England on 5 November 1688, pleased to preserve his and his wife's claims to the British thrones. On 23 December, James fled in panic to France. There

---

[642] APS, VIII, 238–9 (c. 2). [643] APS, VIII, 243–4 (c. 6).
[644] Lynch (n. 4), 296; Donaldson, *James V–James VII* (n. 382), 379–80; Mitchison (n. 641), 113.
[645] Lynch (n. 4), 296–7; Donaldson, *James V–James VII* (n. 382), 380; Mitchison (n. 641), 114.
[646] Lynch (n. 4), 297; Mitchison (n. 641), 115; Donaldson, *James V–James VII* (n. 382), 381.
[647] RPC, 3rd ser., XIII, 123–4, 156–8.
[648] Mitchison (n. 641), 115–16; Donaldson, *James V–James VII* (n. 382), 383.

was no significant military opposition to William and Mary in England or Scotland, other than Claverhouse's doomed campaign in the Highlands. The defeat of James at the Battle of the Boyne in Ireland secured the new settlement.[649]

(d) The Claim of Right

A Convention of Estates met in Edinburgh on 14 March 1689.[650] William and Mary had already jointly accepted the English throne. On 4 April, the Convention resolved that James had 'forefaulted' the throne.[651] On 11 April the Convention adopted a Claim of Right declaring that, by his illegal actions, subverting the constitution and the Protestant religion, James VII had 'forefaulted the right to the Croune, and the throne is become vacant'.[652] The throne was accordingly offered to William and Mary jointly, who duly accepted it as William II (1689–1702) and Mary II (1689–95) of Scotland. The Claim of Right was a more radical document than the English Declaration of Rights and it is difficult to construe it as founded on anything other than a contractual view of the Scottish monarchy.[653] From the work of Buchanan onwards, there had been a wealth of radical theorizing on politics on which the Scots could draw to explain and justify what had happened, some of which was based on the doctrines of the *jus gentium*.[654]

The Claim of Right set out a series of principles in response to the wrongs attributed to James VII, describing them as 'undoubted rights and liberties'. Among the more notable of these was the denial to the monarch of a right to assert 'an absolute power to Cass, annull, and Dissable laws'. It was also declared that a 'Papist' could be neither king nor queen, nor 'bear any Office whatsomever'. Fair and due process in criminal trials was emphasized by asserting the illegality of 'forceing the leidges to Depone against themselves in capitall Crymes' and of the use of torture 'without evidence, or in ordinary Crymes'. The process of lawburrows was not to be abused, nor were advocates to be penalized for failing to cooperate in such abuse. Furthermore, it

---

[649] Brown (n. 413), 168. For the narrative of events leading to James's flight, see, e.g., Donaldson, *James V–James VII* (n. 382), 383–4; Ferguson (n. 382), 163–5; Mitchison (n. 641), 116–17. On the Jacobite threat from 1690–1716, see Daniel Szechi, *The Jacobites: Britain and Europe, 1688–1788* (1994), 41–84.

[650] See generally, E. W. M. Balfour-Melville (ed.), *An Account of the Proceedings of the Estates in Scotland, 1689–1690*, Scottish History Society, Third Series, vol. 46, 47 (1954–5).

[651] APS, IX, 33–4.   [652] APS, IX, 37–40.

[653] There is a question of how 'radical' was the term 'forefaulted': see B. P. Lenman, 'The Poverty of Political Theory in the Scottish Revolution of 1688–1690', in L. G. Schwoerer (ed.), *The Revolution of 1688–1689: Changing Perspectives* (1992), 244–59 at 255. To most contemporary Scots the term seemed distinctly radical: see Tim Harris, 'The People, the Law, and the Constitution in Scotland and England: A Comparative Approach to the Glorious Revolution', (1999) 38 *Journal of British Studies* 28–58 at 47.

[654] See now Jackson (n. 618), 165–206. For a contrasting view, see I. B. Cowan, 'The Reluctant Revolutionaries: Scotland in 1688', in Eveline Cruickshanks (ed.), *By Force or by Default? The Revolution of 1688–1689* (1989), 65–81; Lenman (n. 653), *passim*.

was declared that 'it is the right and priviledge of the subjects to protest for remeed of law to the King and Parliament, against Sentences pronounced by the lords of Sessione, Provydeing the samen Do not stop Execution of these sentences'. 'Prelacy and the superiority of any office in the Church, above Presbyters' was claimed as 'a great and insupportable greivance and trouble to this Nation, and contrary to the Inclinationes of the generality of the people ever since the reformatione'.[655] On 13 April, the Estates passed a number of 'Articles of Grievances', which included a provision condemning the Committee of the Lords of the Articles.[656]

(e) The new regime

The first Parliament of William and Mary met on 5 June 1689 and abolished prelacy without providing a new settlement.[657] This came in the spring of 1690 and was based on the Presbyterian settlement of 1592, rather than that of the Covenanting period, while the Westminster Confession of Faith was adopted as the basis of doctrine.[658] Patronage was abolished, with the right to appoint ministers transferred to the elders and heritors of the parish.[659] The effects of this settlement were complex.[660] Eventually 664 ministers were ejected; many episcopalians would not take the oaths of allegiance to William and Mary and episcopalianism became strongly identified with Jacobitism.[661]

The necessary transition in civil institutions was also difficult to achieve. Appointment of a new bench for the Session proved difficult, as the Parliament of 1689, mindful of the settlement agreed with Charles I, argued against simple nomination under the royal prerogative.[662] Much of this opposition was directed at the unpopular Sir James Dalrymple of Stair, who was to be President, just as some other measures were directed at his son, Sir John Dalrymple, who had briefly been Lord Advocate to James VII.[663] Later in 1689, William proclaimed the reopening of the Signet and nominated Lords of Session. The nominated Lords duly started to sit and commenced regular business.[664]

The Convention Parliament has often been viewed as a chaotic and difficult forum, where, without the Committee of the Articles (abolished in 1690) to impose discipline and order, the Scottish magnates competed selfishly and

---

[655] APS, IX, 37–40.   [656] APS, IX, 45.
[657] APS, IX, 104 (c. 4); see William Ferguson, *Scotland: 1689 to the Present. The Edinburgh History of Scotland*, vol. 4 (1968), 8–9.
[658] APS, IX, 133–4 (c. 7). See also APS, IX, 111 (cc. 1, 2).   [659] APS, IX, 196–7 (c. 53).
[660] L. K. Glassey, 'William II and the Settlement of Religion in Scotland, 1688–1690', (1989) 23 *Records of the Scottish Church History Society* 317–29.
[661] Brown (n. 413), 178–9; Ferguson (n. 657), 14–15.
[662] Balfour-Melville (n. 650), vol. 1, 176–8, 181.
[663] See e.g. Ferguson (n. 657), 7; P. W. J. Riley, *King William and the Scottish Politicians* (1979), 23–4.   [664] Balfour-Melville (n. 650), vol. 2, 36–7, 45–6, 48, 60, 116, 187–8.

ruthlessly for their own advantage.[665] This is unconvincing.[666] The Restoration Parliaments were not exactly docile and, when Parliament had proved difficult to manage in 1673, it was not called again until 1681.[667] The Convention Parliament not only had a reasonably effective committee structure, but also managed to enact a great deal of important legislation.

2. Relations with England and proposals for Union, 1660–1715

(a) Political tensions and Union proposals

The Restoration of 1660 revived the Stewart multiple monarchy and various expedients had to be used to cope with Scottish government by a king based in London.[668] Moreover, the tensions between England and Scotland re-emerged and, if anything, the two nations grew further apart in the Restoration period.[669] The two countries' Navigation Acts and English measures against trade with the Dutch, traditional trading partners of the Scots, contributed to a climate of distrust as Scots sought new markets and opportunities.[670] In 1668, there was a failed attempt to create a commercial union to resolve these problems over trade.[671]

The king's letter of 15 September 1669 to the Scottish Parliament enjoined the project of 'as close and strict an Union as is possible' between the two kingdoms.[672] There was little will for such an incorporating Union and the negotiations foundered—perhaps deliberately.[673] The topic of 'The preserving to either Kingdome their Laws Civil and Ecclesiasticall entire' caused the Scots Commissioners to propose a complete separation and preservation of the laws and legal systems of each kingdom with no Scottish actions to be heard in England either at first instance or on appeal. The English Commissioners' understandable question of how the law would be changed after the Union was shelved.[674] The evident aim was to ensure the preservation of Scots law. The Scottish Commissioners were also of the view that, after the Union, there would be no appeals from the Court of Session to the new

---

[665] APS, IX, 113 (c. 3). See Rait (n. 142), 386–91. Riley (n. 663), argues this strongly. The view had a long pedigree: see Mackay (n. 599), 221–5; Rait (n. 142), 101–6.

[666] See e.g. B. P. Lenman, 'The Scottish Nobility and the Revolution of 1688–1690', in Robert Beddard (ed.), *The Revolutions of 1688* (1991), 137–62; James Halliday, 'The Club and the Revolution in Scotland, 1689–90', (1966) 45 *Scot Hist Rev* 143–59.

[667] Donaldson, *James V–James VII* (n. 382), 377–8.

[668] Donaldson, *James V–James VII* (n. 382), 283–4, 373, 375–7; Jackson (n. 618), 98.

[669] Levack (n. 394), 10; Ferguson (n. 382), 142–65.

[670] For contrasting views, see T. C. Smout, *Scottish Trade on the Eve of Union, 1660–1707* (1963), 240; Ferguson (n. 382), 153–4. For general surveys see Mitchison (n. 641), 103–8; Donaldson, *James V–James VII* (n. 382), 387–90.

[671] Edward Hughes, 'Negotiations for a Commercial Union between England and Scotland', (1927) 24 *Scot Hist Rev* 30–47.   [672] APS, VII, 551.

[673] See Ferguson (n. 382), 154–7; Reports of the debates among the Commissioners are collected in Sanford Terry (n. 581), 188–222.   [674] Sanford Terry (n. 581), 197–203.

Parliament; this the English Commissioners found objectionable.[675] The issue of appeals and protestations for remeid of law from the Session to Parliament had not yet emerged as the controversial issue that led to the provision noted in the Claim of Right.[676] The issue of a union with England arose once again at the time of the Revolution but came to nothing.[677]

William's accession involved his British kingdoms in unpopular wars with France, again disrupting Scottish trade, while the English Navigation Acts continued to prohibit Scottish trade with the English colonies.[678] A solution to these problems was sought in the foundation of the 'Company of Scotland Trading to Africa and the Indies' established by Parliament in 1695. The powerful English East India Company successfully opposed initial English interest in investing in the adventure and Scottish attempts to raise capital were deliberately hampered. The foolish attempt to found a colony at Darien on the Isthmus of Panama failed, leaving a legacy of bitterness towards William and the English.[679]

Other events increased tensions between the two kingdoms in the 1690s, as crop failures in Scotland resulted in famine with considerable distress and loss of life.[680] Pacification of the Highlands after the suppression of Claverhouse's rebellion led to the decision to make an example of the Macdonalds of Glencoe for failing to take an oath of allegiance timeously. One of the main movers in this was the Master of Stair, now one of William's Secretaries of State. The resulting massacre caused a scandal.[681]

(b) The problem of the succession

William and Mary had no children; the surviving son of James VII's other daughter, Princess Anne, died in 1700. In 1701, Louis XIV recognized James VII's son, the Old Pretender, as King James VIII and III. A succession crisis loomed. In 1701, the English Parliament passed the Act of Settlement, whereby the crown was to pass to Sophia, Electress of Hanover, and her heirs, on the death of Anne without heirs. Though having no authority in Scotland, the act mentioned Scotland in certain of the limitations it put on Hanoverian successors and, as well as causing general offence in Scotland, it stirred up the old debate over whether the Crown of Scotland was imperial

---

[675] Mackenzie (n. 617), 204.
[676] See J. M. Simpson, 'The Advocates as Trade Union Pioneers', in G. W. S. Barrow (ed.), *The Scottish Tradition: Essays in Honour of Ronald Gordon Cant* (1974), 164–77 at 171–6; Rait (n. 142), 474–8.   [677] APS, IX, 60 (c. 60); see the discussion in Ferguson (n. 382), 170–2.
[678] Ferguson (n. 382), 176.
[679] APS, IX, 377–81 (c. 10). For some of the intellectual background, see David Armitage, 'The Scottish Vision of Empire: Intellectual Origins of the Darien Venture', in Robertson (n. 395), 97–118. G. P. Insh, *The Company of Scotland Trading to Africa and the Indies* (1932); Lynch (n. 4), 307–9; Ferguson (n. 657), 26–33.   [680] Mitchison (n. 641), 108–10.
[681] See e.g. Ferguson (n. 657), 19–25; Lynch (n. 4), 305–7.

and whether the Scottish kings had offered homage to the English kings for their kingdom.[682]

When the Scottish Parliament met after William's death in 1702, the Duke of Queensberry pushed through Parliament an act for the nomination of commissioners to treat for a Union with England.[683] While these negotiations ultimately came to nothing, they revealed what were considered the most pressing problems between the two countries: free trade, debts, taxes, the Scottish Company of the Indies, and the succession (the last being the easiest agreed).[684] The following issues, however, were left unsettled: 'the Constitution of the Parliament, the Affairs of the Church, and the Municipall Lawes and Judicatures of Scotland for security of the Properties of the Subjects of that Kingdom'.[685]

The elections of 1703 produced a Parliament that refused the Crown supply until various acts were passed.[686] An English book reflecting on the independence and sovereignty of the Scottish Crown was ordered to be burned by the hangman and a clause inserted in the draft Act of Security excluding English holders of Scottish peerages from voting in the Estates unless they held extensive lands in Scotland.[687] The Act of Security was eventually passed by a large majority on 13 August 1703. This had developed into a radical measure that did not decide the issue of the succession; instead, it provided that on the death of Anne the Estates would meet and nominate her successor, who was to be of the Scots royal line and Protestant faith, but different from the person already nominated to succeed to the English throne, unless the sovereignty of the kingdom was secured and guaranteed.[688] The High Commissioner withheld the royal assent. The debates reveal Scottish anxieties about trade, about being drawn into English wars, and about being manipulated in the interests of an English administration. Parliament also voted to extinguish the Commission treating for Union with England.[689] To draw proceedings to an end, the High Commissioner granted royal assent to a number of popular, patriotic measures.[690] At the next session, to secure supply, the Marquess of Tweeddale, as High Commissioner, eventually granted the royal assent to a version of the Act of Security.[691]

(c) Negotiating Union

In 1705, the English Parliament passed the Aliens Act. Under this, the Queen was to appoint commissioners to treat for a Union; further, unless the Scots,

---

[682] See Ferguson (n. 382), 197–8; *idem*, 'Imperial Crowns: A Neglected Facet of the Background to the Treaty of Union of 1707', (1974) 53 *Scot Hist Rev* 22–44.
[683] APS, XI, 26 (c. 7); Ferguson (n. 382), 199.   [684] APS, XI, appendix, 145–61.
[685] APS, XI, appendix, 161.   [686] APS, XI, 45.
[687] APS, XI, 66, 67; Ferguson, (1974) 53 *Scot Hist Rev* 34–5.
[688] APS, XI, 67, 69–70, 72, 74.   [689] APS, XI, 101.   [690] APS, XI, 104–12 (cc. 2–13).
[691] APS, XI, 136–8 (cc. 3, 4).

by 25 December, were either treating for Union or had accepted the Hanoverian succession, they were to be treated as aliens in England and its possessions and the importation of Scotland's main exports to England was to cease.[692] The Scottish Parliament met on 28 June 1705 with this gun at its head. The Duke of Argyll, as Lord High Commissioner, through adroit dispensing of patronage and clever manœuvring, carried the Union project for the Crown.[693] A difficult issue was nomination of the Commissioners; on 1 September 1705, in a thinly attended house, the Duke of Hamilton successfully moved that the nomination be left to the Queen.[694]

The Scottish Commissioners were nominated on 27 February 1706.[695] The Scots quickly conceded the basic idea of an incorporating Union.[696] Financial and economic matters took much longer and there was hard bargaining over the level of Scottish representation in the new Parliament of Great Britain. On 23 July, the twenty-five articles of Union were presented to the Queen. Most concerned fiscal measures, such as free trade, a unified system of weights and measures, and a single coinage. There were to be forty-five elected members in the House of Commons and sixteen elected peers in the Lords. Because of the new liability for the English National Debt, an Equivalent of nearly £400,000 was to be paid to cover the debts of the Scottish government and to compensate the stockholders of the Company of Scotland. There was no mention of the national Church of either kingdom.[697]

Given that the model of Union chosen was essentially to incorporate Scotland into existing English legislative structures, a number of articles clarified the position of the Scottish courts and Scots law, maintaining the existing administrative and legal framework. The 18th article provided for the application in Scotland of the same laws on trade, customs, and excise as in England; but 'all other Laws in use within the Kingdom of Scotland doe after the Union and notwithstanding thereof remain in the same force as before ... but alterable, by the Parliament of Great Britain'. A difference was drawn, however, between those 'concerning Publick Right, Pollicy and Civil Government', which could be made the same throughout the United Kingdom, while, on the other hand, 'no alteration may be made in Laws which concern Privat Right Except for the evident utility of the Subjects

---

[692] 3 and 4 Anne (c. 6).
[693] See e.g. Ferguson (n. 382), 226–31; *idem* (n. 657), 45–7; P. H. Scott, *Andrew Fletcher and the Treaty of Union* (1992), 121–45; J. R. Young, 'The Parliamentary Incorporating Union of 1707: Political Management, Anti-Unionism and Foreign Policy', in T. M. Devine and J. R. Young (eds.), *Eighteenth Century Scotland: New Perspectives* (1999), 24–52.
[694] APS, XI, 236–7. I have deliberately chosen not to venture into the important issue of underlying 'causes' of the Union; the topic is too vast. But see C. A. Whately, *'Bought and Sold for English Gold'? Explaining the Union of 1707* (1994); *idem*, 'Economic Causes and Consequences of the Union of 1707: A Survey', (1989) 68 *Scot Hist Rev* 150–81.
[695] APS, XI, appendix, 162–3.   [696] APS, XI, appendix, 166.
[697] APS, XI, appendix, 190–1, 203–5. See further Ferguson (n. 382), 235–7; Scott (n. 693), 146–70.

within Scotland'.[698] The 19th article preserved the Court of Session and Court of Justiciary 'in all time coming within Scotland', though subject to such 'Regulations for the better administration of Justice' as the Parliament of Great Britain might make. The existing Admiralty Jurisdiction was preserved, though now under the Lord High Admiral or Commissioners of Admiralty of Great Britain; the Parliament of Great Britain was empowered to alter this court, though an admiralty court was always to be preserved in Scotland to deal with 'Maritim Cases, relating to Private Rights'. Heritable rights of admiralty were preserved as rights of property to their proprietors. All inferior courts were preserved, though alterable by Parliament, while 'no Causes in Scotland be Cognoscable, by the Courts of Chancery, Queens Bench, Common Pleas or other Court in Westminster Hall'; moreover, these courts were not after the Union to have 'Power to Cognosce, Review, or Alter the Acts, or Sentences of the Judicatures within Scotland, or Stop the Execution of the same'. A new Court of Exchequer was to be erected in Scotland, 'for deciding Questions Concerning the Revenues of Customs and Excises . . . having the same Power and Authority in such Cases, as the Court of Exchequer has in England'. The new court was to continue to exercise the Scottish Exchequer's traditional jurisdiction over the 'power of passing Signatures, Gifts, Tutories, and in other things' and was not to have the type of extensive jurisdiction at common law potentially possessed by the English court. The Privy Council was retained 'for preserving of Publick Peace and Order' until the Parliament thought fit to alter it. The 20th article preserved the Scottish heritable jurisdictions 'as Rights of Property in the same manner as they are now enjoy'd by the Laws of Scotland'.[699]

(d) The aftermath of Union

Although the parliamentary session, with Queensberry once more as High Commissioner, that opened on 3 October 1706 proved difficult to manage, the treaty was finally ratified by Act of Parliament on 16 January 1707.[700] The only significant alteration to the provisions on the courts and Scots law made by the Parliament was a regulation on the qualifications of a Lord of Session.[701] A number of measures consequent on the Union were also passed. The 'Act for Securing the Protestant Religion and Presbyterian Church Government' had already been enacted to protect the position of the Church of Scotland.[702] The mode of electing the Scottish representatives to the Houses of Commons and Lords was settled.[703] The Lords of Council and

---

[698] APS, XI, appendix, 203.   [699] APS, XI, appendix, 203–4.
[700] APS, XI, 404–6. For discussion, see e.g. Ferguson (n. 382), 238–72.
[701] APS, XI, 411; see the discussion in Parliament at ibid. 380–1.
[702] APS, XI, 402–3 (c. 6).   [703] APS, XI, 425–7 (c. 8).

Session were given jurisdiction over the valuation of teinds and plantation of kirks that had hitherto been exercised by a committee of the Parliament.[704]

The first few years of the Union were sufficiently unhappy that, in 1713, the Earl of Findlater and Seafield, listing the Scottish grievances, moved its dissolution in the House of Lords; this nearly passed.[705] A number of events had triggered Scottish anger and fear. A Jacobite scare in 1708 had led to the replacement of the Scots law of treason with that of England. The system of Commissions of Oyer and Terminer thus introduced limited the jurisdiction of the Court of Justiciary.[706] The Scottish Privy Council had been abolished in 1708, largely due to the Scottish party, the Squadrone Volante, who had developed into a Whig interest.[707] To fill the administrative and power vacuum thus created, justices of the peace were now granted the authority that belonged to 'the office and trust of a justice of peace by virtue of the laws and Acts of Parliament made in England before the union in relation to or for the preservation of the publick peace'.[708] Those holding heritable jurisdictions could see this as an attack on their rights.[709] In 1711, the House of Lords decided that the Duke of Hamilton, as holder of a *Scottish* peerage was not automatically entitled to sit in the upper chamber by virtue of his *British* peerage as Duke of Brandon and that he could no longer vote for the Scottish representative peers.[710] Finally, as a result of the case of an episcopalian minister, Greenshields, whose prosecution for using the Anglican prayer book and liturgy was reversed by the House of Lords, the Toleration Act of 1712 was passed 'to prevent the disturbing those of the Episcopal Communion in . . . Scotland in the Exercise of their Religious Worship and in the Use of the Liturgy of the Church of England'.[711] This attacked the position of the Kirk as the established Church, reducing the authority of its courts, while emphasizing the authority of Westminster, where bishops of the Anglican communion sat in the Lords.[712] This was underscored the very next month, when Parliament, dominated by high Tory Anglicans, passed the Patronage Act, restoring to lay patrons the right to appoint ministers that had been given to the elders and heritors in 1690.[713] This act was to prove the source of considerable division and dispute in the Kirk, culminating in the Disruption in the 1840s.[714]

---

[704] APS, XI, 433 (c. 10).   [705] Ferguson (n. 657), 61–2.

[706] Treason Act 1709, 7 Anne (c. 21). See Bruce Lenman, *The Jacobite Risings in Britain 1689–1746* (1980), 88–91, 107–8; Ferguson (n. 657), 57–8.

[707] See e.g. Ferguson (n. 657), 54–5; P. W. J. Riley, *The English Ministers and Scotland* (1964), 90–3.   [708] Union with Scotland (Amendment) Act, 6 Anne (c. 40), s. 2.

[709] Lenman (n. 706), 94–6.

[710] See G. S. Holmes, 'The Hamilton Affair of 1711–1712: A Crisis in Anglo-Scottish Relations', (1962) 77 *English Historical Review* 257–82; Lenman (n. 706), 97.

[711] 10 Anne (c.10); R. S. Tompson, 'James Greenshields and the House of Lords: A Reappraisal', in Gordon/Fergus (n. 104), 109–24.   [712] See e.g. Lenman (n. 706), 103.

[713] 10 Anne (c. 21), repealing the relevant provisions of APS, IX, 196 (c. 53).

[714] C. G. Brown, *Religion and Society in Scotland since 1707* (1997), 22–8.

George I (1714–27) succeeded smoothly on the death of Anne on 1 August 1714. Snubbed by King George, the Earl of Mar, who had been one of Anne's Secretaries for Scotland, in his pique discovered his true allegiance to James Stewart and raised the Jacobite standard on 6 September 1715. Despite the widespread sympathy in Scotland for the cause, compounded of loyalty to the Stewarts and anxiety about the Union, the failure of the rebellion secured the political settlement of 1689–90 as modified by the Union.[715] Ideas of *jure divino* kingship by hereditary right died in Scotland on the militarily inconclusive field of Sheriffmuir on 13 November 1715. Henceforth political debates were to revolve around different issues.

3. The institutions of the common law

(a) Heritable jurisdictions

With the Restoration came the return of the traditional institutions and offices of the common law.[716] The centre's desire to exercise greater authority over the localities also returned. Reflecting policies dating from the time of James VI, heritable jurisdictions were threatened by the Crown's wish to enforce its ecclesiastical policies. There were two crucial acts in 1681. The first, aimed at field conventicles, empowered 'his Majestie to nominat sherif-deputs';[717] the second stressed that, although the king and his predecessors had 'bestowed Offices and Jurisdictions upon several of his weill deserving subjects', such grants were 'not privative of his Jurisdiction', so that the king could exert jurisdiction over any cause he pleased.[718] These provisions were seen as a direct attack on the heritable jurisdictions.[719] It does seem that in 1683 revocation of heritable sheriffships was being considered.[720] Since the acts of 1681 were seen as an attack on property rights, the Claim of Right stated that one of the violations of the laws and liberties of the kingdom had been to employ army officers as judges, imposing them where there were heritable offices, while the king's cumulative jurisdiction was listed as a grievance.[721]

---

[715] See Lenman (n. 706), 126–54.

[716] For a discussion of aspects of the courts in this period, see S. J. Davies, 'The Courts and the Scottish Legal System 1600–1747: The Case of Stirlingshire', in V. A. C. Gatrell, Bruce Lenman, and Geoffrey Parker (eds.), *Crime and the Law: The Social History of Crime in Western Europe since 1500* (1980), 120–54. [717] APS, VIII, 242 (c. 4).

[718] APS, VIII, 352 (c. 84).

[719] Sir John Lauder of Fountainhall, *Historical Notices of Scotish Affairs, Selected from the Manuscripts of Sir John Lauder of Fountainhall, Bart., One of the Senators of the College of Justice*, Bannatyne Club, vol. 87 (1848), vol. 1, 374. For an example of such a conflict, see Mackay (n. 599), 177–86; A. G. Stevenson, 'Claverhouse and the Dalrymples', [1995] *JR* 227–35.

[720] Historical Manuscripts Commission, *Report on the Buccleuch and Queensberry Manuscripts (Fifteenth Report, Appendix Part VIII)* (1897), 192.

[721] APS, IX, 45; Balfour-Melville (n. 650), vol. 1, 38.

Both acts were quickly repealed.[722] The 20th article of the Union preserved such heritable judicial offices 'as Rights of Property'.[723]

Two-thirds of the sheriffdoms were held heritably and the sheriff court retained its pivotal role as the most important local court with a criminal and civil jurisdiction, restricted only by that of regalities. It dealt with a regular diet of debt, spuilzie, riot, lawburrows, and lesser crimes.[724] The activity and effectiveness of the franchise jurisdictions of the lords of regality and the barons is unclear for this period, though general consensus that they were of decreasing significance is not necessarily well founded. Further examination of their records is needed.[725]

(b) Justices of the peace

The Cromwellian justices had been abolished by the rescissory act, but in 1661 the justices of the peace were restored as agents of the Privy Council.[726] Their authority grew during the Restoration as the Crown attempted to enforce the unpopular ecclesiastical regime in some of the localities, notably through an act in 1685 empowering them to enforce the laws against 'irregular' marriages and baptisms and conventicles.[727] The difficulty of getting men to act as justices led to threats to punish those who refused to accept office.[728] The act of 1685 was presumably one of the 'impious and intolerable Grievances' repealed in 1690.[729]

In 1701, Parliament considered a draft act ratifying that of 1661; but the justices were to be appointed by the king, rather than the Privy Council.[730] When, in 1707, they acquired the same rights as justices of the peace enjoyed in England, the act provided that 'the methods of tryal and judgments' would continue to be 'according to the law and customs of Scotland'.[731] In practice, this limited their authority considerably because of the manner in which serious prosecutions were conducted in Scotland, while the importance of the sheriff largely restricted their functions to administrative matters and minor issues of public order.[732]

---

[722] APS, IX, 198–9 (c. 58).   [723] APS, XI, 383, 204.

[724] A. E. Whetstone, *Scottish County Government in the Eighteenth and Nineteenth Centuries* (1981), 3; Davies (n. 716), 134–8.

[725] See e.g. Davies (n. 716), 141–6; Whetstone (n. 724), 1–3. Both of these accounts are influenced by the remarks by Croft Dickinson in the introduction to *Carnwath Court Book* (n. 60), xlvi–xlvii. For printed examples, see C. B. Gunn (ed.), *Records of the Baron Court of Stitchill, 1655–1807*, Scottish History Society, First Series, vol. 50 (1905); D. G. Baron (ed.), *The Court Book of the Barony of Urie in Kincardineshire 1604–1747*, Scottish History Society, First Series, vol. 12 (1892).   [726] APS, VII, 306–13 (c. 338).

[727] APS, VIII, 472 (c. 16). See generally Malcolm (n. 510), xxiii–xxv.

[728] RPC, 3rd Ser, VIII, 170.

[729] Balfour-Melville (n. 650), vol. I, 38; APS, IX, 198–9 (c. 58).

[730] APS, X, 294, appendix, 102; Malcolm (n. 510), xxv–xxvi.

[731] Union with Scotland (Amendment) Act, s. 2 (6 Anne (c. 40)).

[732] See Whetstone (n. 724), 27–8; Malcolm (n. 510), xxvi; 8 Anne (c. 16).

(c) The operation of the courts

Through the Restoration and Revolution periods, there were several attempts to improve the operation of the courts. In 1669, 1685, 1686, and again in 1693, a variety of commissions were appointed to examine the operation of the commissary, sheriff, burgh, and other inferior courts, with the aim of clarifying their jurisdictions and devising means whereby individuals could avoid having to appear before different courts for the same case.[733] The local commissaries were considered as presenting particular problems. Regulated by provisions issued under the royal prerogative in 1666, they had a potentially very wide jurisdiction if parties wished to submit to it.[734] In 1693, they were accused of taking 'cognition of all causes of whatsoever nature', including pronouncing 'decreets of poynding of the ground'.[735] The current constitution of the commissary courts was a grievance in 1689, largely because of the appointment of the commissaries by the bishops; but during the early 1690s, dissatisfaction led to an attempt to abolish them and award their jurisdiction to the Session and local courts.[736] This failed and the local and Edinburgh commissary courts continued to confirm testaments, control executries, and carry out their other work; the Edinburgh court also continued to deal with consistorial issues such as adherence, divorce, nullity of marriage, legitimacy, as well as matters of 'scandal'.[737]

On 21 September 1669, Charles II appointed a Commission to examine the functioning of the Privy Council, Justice Courts, and Session.[738] Insofar as it concerned the Session, the Commission's report of 1670, subject to some minor amendments, was enacted in 1672. The aims were to make the Session fairer and more expeditious by setting up a system of orderly enrolling of causes, while denying jurisdiction in trivial actions.[739] Fairness and expedition were the general motives behind a number of other reforms in the procedure of the Session during the Restoration, covering issues from the enrolling and calling of actions to the examination of witnesses in the presence of the

---

[733] APS, VII, 661 (c. 127) (this commission was already examining the superior courts); VIII, 494 (c. 57); 599–600 (c. 31); IX, 330–1 (c. 72). [734] AS, I, 95–101.

[735] APS, IX, appendix, 88.

[736] Balfour-Melville (n. 650), vol. 1, 38; APS, IX, 45; 133 (c. 7); 185–6; 198 (c. 56); appendix, 87–8.

[737] For a glimpse of the operation of the Edinburgh Commissary Court in consistorial matters, see F. P. Walton (ed.), *Lord Hermand's Consistorial Decisions, 1684–1777*, Stair Society, vol. 6 (1940). On its divorce work see Leah Leneman, *Alienated Affections: The Scottish Experience of Divorce and Separation, 1684–1830* (1998). On the lower commissary courts, see M. C. Meston and M. G. A. Christie, 'The Jurisdiction of Local Commissary Courts in the Eighteenth Century: An Interim Report', [1995] *JR* 377–84. [738] APS, VII, 661 (c. 127).

[739] *Articles for Regulating of the Judicatories, &c. Set down by the Commissioners Thereunto Authorized by His Majesty, Under the Great Seal: With His Majesties Approbation thereof prefixed thereunto* (1670), 7–17; The Courts Act 1672, APS, VIII, 80–8 (c. 40) at 80–7. There is a brief discussion in Mackay (n. 599), 95–8.

parties and their advocates.[740] This trend continued after the Revolution when a commission to improve the functioning of the courts was appointed in 1693.[741] Its recommendations were approved and embodied in an Act of Sederunt.[742] In 1693, Parliament also enacted a sequence of statutes regulating the procedure of the Outer House and the preparation of concluded causes after proof before report to the Inner House. Moreover, it was decided that in future the Lords would advise causes 'with open doors' with the parties and their lawyers permitted to be present. These various statutes and Acts of Sederunt established a procedure by 1700 that was to last substantially unchanged until the nineteenth century.[743]

(d) The development of written pleadings

One prominent feature of procedure before the Session was the continuing growth of written pleading. In 1677, Acts of Sederunt endorsed the system of written informations, which 'were become ordinary', further organizing their delivery to the Lords and using their prevalence to regulate the record made by the clerks for the report of causes to the Inner House.[744] In 1690, it was decided that each judge should have a box in Parliament House into which all informations and bills should be put, while the procedures for reporting and preparation of informations were tightened.[745] These written pleadings tended to verbosity and, in 1692, the Lords tried to control the nature of bills by ensuring they were clear and supported by documents or offers to prove allegations of fact, while informations were to follow the order of the allegations and contain nothing extraneous to the minutes of the dispute.[746] In 1710 an Act of Sederunt endorsed the existing rules but provided that petitions, informations, and answers were now to be printed only with the warrant of an advocate whose name was to appear at the bottom.[747] Through the eighteenth century, printing the pleadings and other documents in the process became a marked feature of practice before the Court of Session. It should always be remembered that witness evidence was reduced to writing, concluded causes after proof were reduced to writing, and advocates were often asked to prepare memorials, not only for the Inner House, but also for the Ordinary in the Outer. The practice of printing the documents for

---

[740] See AS, I, 85–7 (28 Feb. 1662); APS, VIII, 64–5 (c. 6) (The Summary Execution Act 1672); AS, I, 108–9 (11 July 1672); APS, VIII, 350 (c. 79) (The Declinature Act 1681); 585–6 (c. 4) (Interlocutors Act 1686); 599 (c. 30) (1686).

[741] APS, IX, 330–1 (c. 72). This was in virtually identical terms to one of 1686: APS, VIII, 599–600 (c. 31).

[742] AS, I, 209–16 (2 Nov. 1695); see also additional provisions, ibid. 216–8.

[743] APS, IX, 282–3 (cc. 30–4); AS, I, 205–6 (1 Nov. 1693); APS, IX, 305 (c. 42) (Court of Session Act 1693). [744] AS, I, 135 (3 Nov. 1677), 135–6 (6 Nov. 1677).

[745] AS, I, 188–9 (29 Nov. 1690). See also ibid. 190 (2 June 1691).

[746] AS, I, 196 (6 Feb. 1692). See also ibid. 209–16 at 214 (2 Nov. 1695) on the length of bills.

[747] AS, I, 241–2 (19 Dec. 1710).

convenience in a court, in which written process had become central, led to the collection of the sets of Session Papers that survive.[748]

(e) The new Justiciary Court

The report of Charles II's Commission of 1669 recommended a reconstruction of the Justiciary Court.[749] Instead of Justice Deputes, five Lords of Session were appointed as Commissioners of Justiciary, who, along with the Lord Justice-General and Lord Justice-Clerk, were to be 'all of them invested with the same and equall power and jurisdiction in Criminall Causes', with a quorum of four 'except at the Circuit Courts'. The latter were to sit in the spring at various towns. The defender or his advocates were to speak last (except in treason cases) and to have copies of the indictment and lists of the witnesses and those called to sit on the assize, to allow preparation of the defence, objection to witnesses and assizers, and calling of defence witnesses.[750]

The new court first sat in Edinburgh on 6 February 1671, with the Justice-Clerk presiding, although circuit courts remained irregular until revived after the Union. These were increased to twice yearly, until, in 1711, again reduced to a single circuit in the spring.[751] Among a variety of further reforms were provisions on advising with open doors and examining witnesses in the presence of the parties and their advocates.[752] Trials commonly started with a debate on the relevancy of the libel exploring the legal issues at stake. Until an act of 1695, advocates dictated to the clerk their arguments in the form of 'Defences, Duplyes, Triplyes, Quadruplyes, and so furth'; thereafter debate was *viva voce* with the arguments subsequently reduced to a written 'Information' given in by the prosecuting counsel and answered in writing by the defence.[753] Much of such procedural reform was aimed at protection of the accused and in 1701 came the 'Act for preventing wrongous Imprisonments and against undue delays in Tryals', covering issues of bail and imprisonment and setting time limits for trials if the accused were incarcerated.[754]

The Justiciary Court's jurisdiction was limited in a number of ways. First, the regalities, depending on the level of justice granted to them, could exclude it, but regular circuit courts after 1708 seem to have taken at least some of the business of the lords of regality, since they or their bailies had to turn up in

---

[748] On procedure in ordinary actions, see John Spottiswoode, *The Form of Process, before the Lords of Council and Session* (1711), 34–121.

[749] *Articles for Regulating of the Judicatories* (n. 739), 17–19; APS, VIII, 87–8 (c. 40) (Courts Act 1672). [750] APS, VIII, 87–8.

[751] Hannay (n. 238), 327; Croft Dickinson (n. 237), 411 (there were in fact some ayres between 1671 and 1707); 8 Anne (c. 16); 10 Anne (c. 40). (A second ayre could be held in the autumn if it was specially decided to do so.)

[752] APS, VIII, 599 (c. 30) (Evidence Act 1686); APS, IX, 305 (c. 43) (Criminal Procedure Act 1693). See also APS, VIII, 354 (c. 8) (1681) (quorum in time of vacation); 480 (c. 32) (1685) (citations before circuit courts). [753] APS, IX, 365–6 (c. 6).

[754] APS, X, 272–5 (c. 6) (Criminal Procedure Act 1701).

person to repledge the accused.[755] Secondly, when Lord Lorne surrendered the hereditary office of Justice-General in 1628, he had retained the hereditary position of Justice-General of Argyll and the Isles, which remained effective.[756] Thirdly, special commissions of justiciary were still occasionally granted before 1707, such as those for the Highlands in the 1690s.[757]

(f) *Protestations and appeals*

Protestations for remeid of law—the means of obtaining Parliament's review of the actions of the Lords of Session—were highly contentious in Restoration Scotland, but the matter is as much obscured as illuminated by the famous dispute between members of the Faculty and the Lords of Session over appeals or protestations from the Session to Parliament.[758] This dispute was ultimately resolved by the King simply pronouncing that such appeals were not allowed.[759] This simple exercise of royal authority undoubtedly explains why the Claim of Right asserted the legality of such protestations in 1689. The evidence about Protestations is inconclusive; but it does seem that Parliament could only review the decisions of the Session on the ground of positive wrongdoing by the Lords.[760] The Claim of Right stated that it was 'the right and priviledge of the subjects to protest for remeed of law to the King and Parliament against Sentences pronounced by the lords of Sessione', provided that 'the samen Do not stop Execution of these sentences'.[761] How well and clearly established this remedy was by 1707 is questionable, although a number of such protestations were taken from 1689 to 1707.[762]

In 1707, it was simply assumed that appeal lay from the Court of Session to the House of Lords. While the matter is obscure, MacLean has argued that such appeals were always intended and that they were not mentioned in the Articles of Union because of recent debates in England over the respective jurisdictions of the Commons and the Lords.[763] He has also demonstrated that the Lords occasionally exercised jurisdiction over the Court of Justiciary.[764] However this may be, the remedy after 1707 was clearly by way of appeal and the House of Lords decided that when there was an appeal from

---

[755] Davies (n. 716), 145, 150.

[756] See John Cameron (ed.), *Justiciary Records of Argyll and the Isles, 1664–1705*, Stair Society, vol. 12 (1949); John Imrie (ed.), *Justiciary Records of Argyll and the Isles, 1664–1742*, Stair Society, vol. 25 (1969).

[757] See, APS, IX, 324–5 (c. 62), 461–2 (c. 68); APS, X, 79 (c. 43).

[758] See Simpson (n. 676), 171–5; Mackenzie (n. 617), 267–310; Rait (n. 142), 475–7; Mackay (n. 599), 113–20.   [759] See e.g. Mackenzie (n. 617), 269–72.

[760] For the legal arguments, see ibid. 280–93 (also RPC, 3rd Ser., IV, 623–8; RPC, 3rd Ser., IV, 631–45; APS, VII, 500.   [761] APS, IX, 40.

[762] There is a brief account of the procedure in Spottiswoode (n. 748), 151–3.

[763] See A. J. MacLean, 'The 1707 Union: Scots Law and the House of Lords', in Kiralfy/MacQueen (n. 69), 50–75 (= (1983) 4 *JLH* 50–75), at 50–1.

[764] A. J. MacLean, 'The House of Lords and Appeals from the High Court of Justiciary', [1985] *JR* 192–226.

Scotland, the decree appealed against could not be executed.[765] As contemporaries recognized, a system was thus established that encouraged disgruntled litigants to take appeals to the House of Lords.[766] The numbers grew swiftly.

Appeals to the House of Lords were to have far-reaching consequences for Scots law as a potential route of English influence. The new Court of Exchequer, established by British statute in 1707 was also a potential source of English legal influence.[767] With a judicial complement of a Chief Baron and four barons (at least one of whom was always an English barrister) it introduced into Scots law a considerable body of English law and procedure in treasury matters. In the exercise of jurisdiction on matters of private right, however, Scots law was to be followed. It is likely that this court had little impact on Scots law given its special jurisdiction and low level of business.[768]

4. The development of the legal profession

(a) The Lords of Session

In 1661, the bench of the Session was filled under the royal prerogative. The normal arrangements for admission and trial were inapplicable, because of the total vacancy. The bench included men who had served as Senators under Charles I and as commissioners under the Cromwellian regime.[769] Subsequent admissions purported to be made for life, but in 1683 a new commission was issued for the Session omitting three of the Senators (including Stair, the President), while three judges were dismissed summarily for opposing James VII's policies: in all, nine judges were removed from the bench between the Restoration and the Revolution.[770] In 1674, on the request of Charles II a new regulation was made for the trial of Senators.[771] The bench nonetheless had a poor reputation for learning in law and a number of men 'not . . . bred as lawyers were appointed'.[772] Judges, including Stair, were also accused of corruption and favouritism.[773] These circumstances led to the pro-

---

[765] Tompson (n. 711), 109–10.

[766] See, John Lauder of Fountainhall, *The Decisions of the Lords of Council and Session, From June 6th 1678, to July 30th, 1712* (1759–61), vol. 2, 643.

[767] Exchequer Court (Scotland) Act 1707, 6 Anne (c. 53).

[768] The best account is MacLean (n. 763), 53–7. It is worth noting the publication of the following pamphlet to aid in dealings with the new court: *An Explanation of the Several Writs Issued (in Exchequer Hand) from His Majesty's Court of Exchequer, with the Reasons for Issuing such Writs, and their Relation to and Dependence with Each Other* (1731).

[769] McNeill, [1958] *JR* 145.   [770] Ibid. 145–6.

[771] AS, I, 115 (31 July, 1674); NAS, Books of Sederunt of the Lords of Council and Session (hereafter BS), CS 1/6/1, 448–9, 468 (10 June and 31 July 1674); Hannay, *College of Justice* (n. 274), 127–8.   [772] Mackenzie (n. 617), 240.

[773] Ibid. 239–40; Fountainhall (n. 719), vol. 1, 13, 16–17, 34–9. On attempts to influence judges, see H. M. Paton (ed.), 'Letters from John, Earl of Lauderdale, and Others, to Sir John

visions in the Claim of Right condemning royal attempts to interfere with the administration of justice and the granting of appointments to the bench *ad bene placitum*, thus denying judicial independence.[774] To ensure the appointment of qualified men to the Session, a provision was added to the Act of Union, restricting appointment to advocates or Principal Clerks of Session of five years' standing or Writers to the Signet of ten years' standing, who, two years before admission as a Senator, had undergone private and public examination in civil law by the Faculty of Advocates.[775]

(b) The independence of the advocates

During the Restoration, the status of the advocates changed and the Faculty came to be dominated by men from the landed classes who saw themselves as independent with an important role in protecting the liberty and property of the subject.[776] This sense of themselves explains the two episodes in which the Faculty defied the Lords and the government in the 1670s, even if initially the advocates lost the struggles. The first dispute was caused by the recommendations on fees of the Commission, appointed in 1669, for the better 'Regulating of the Judicatories'. Fees were set according to the status of the client, while advocates who usually pleaded in the Inner House could charge more than those who did not.[777] Charles II approved the report on 4 June 1670 and required the advocates to swear to observe the new rules.[778] The Faculty voted to refuse to do so on 8 November 1670.[779] The advocates withdrew from the court for two months, eventually returning after the Lord Advocate took the new oath.[780] The second defiance of the Senators and the Crown was that over appeals and protestations for remeid of law in 1674.[781] The opposition of the judges and the King led to the disbarring of the advocates who refused to disown the process, with a large number of other advocates following them out.[782] On royal instruction the 'outed' advocates were banished from Edinburgh on 29 September 1674.[783] Pressure from the government and

Gilmour, President of Session', in *Miscellany of the Scottish History Society (Fifth Volume)*, Scottish History Society, Third Series, vol. 21 (1933), 109–94.

[774] APS, IX, 37.   [775] APS, XI, 411.

[776] T. I. Rae, 'The Origins of the Advocates' Library', in Patrick Cadell and Ann Matheson (eds.), *For the Encouragement of Learning: Scotland's National Library 1689–1989* (1989), 1–22, esp. at 3–7.   [777] Articles for Regulating of the Judicatories (n. 739), 15.

[778] Ibid. 3–4.

[779] J. M. Pinkerton (ed.), *The Minute Book of the Faculty of Advocates. Volume 1, 1661–1712*, Stair Society (1976), 20–1.

[780] Mackenzie (n. 617), 213–6; Donald Crawford (ed.), *Journals of Sir John Lauder Lord Fountainhall with his Observations on Public Affairs and other Memoranda, 1665–1676*, Scottish History Society, First Series, vol. 36 (1900), 214. When the regulations were ratified by Parliament in 1672 in a modified form, the distinction in fees between those pleading in the Inner and those in the Outer House had gone: APS, VIII, 80–8 (c. 40) (Courts Act 1672) at 85.

[781] Mackenzie (n. 617), 267–9; Simpson (n. 676), 171–2; Mackay (n. 599), 113–14.

[782] Mackenzie (n. 617), 269–72, 276–7; AS, I, 113–14 (17 June 1674).

[783] RPC, 3rd Ser., IV, 283–5.

distrust among the main players in these events eventually led to a return, so that by January 1676 the secession was over.[784]

These two secessions were defining moments for the Faculty, indicating the advocates' corporate sense of themselves as an independent liberal profession. Sir George Mackenzie published two seminal works expressing this self-image. The first was *Pleadings, in some Remarkable Cases* of 1672;[785] the second, *Idea Eloquentiae Forensis Hodiernae* of 1681.[786] These two works contained essays on the art of oral pleading followed by examples of forensic speeches conceived in a highly Ciceronian fashion. Drawing on imagery of the Roman jurists and orators, Mackenzie put forward a vision of the advocate as skilled in both oratory and law, as, unlike the ancient orator, the contemporary advocate had to be skilled in law, 'since nowadays the body of law has grown so great'. The advocate now had to follow study of the *literae humaniores* with that of the civil law; from the former he would learn the history of law and the *mores* of the Romans, while the *Corpus Juris Civilis* was 'the pure fountain of true eloquence and justice'.[787] In the midst of the bar's struggle for greater independence from the Senators, this articulation of what it was to be an advocate—stressing the models of the orators and jurists of the Roman world and the authority *Corpus Juris Civilis*—was an important new expression of the traditional reliance on Roman law.[788]

(c) *The admission of advocates*

Securing the admission as advocates only of men who had the necessary knowledge of the *literae humaniores* and the *jus civile* was another struggle with the Lords that the advocates ultimately won. At the Restoration admissions were still founded on the traditional two avenues of admission—long experience of practick, typically as servitor to an advocate, or proof of academic learning.[789] An Act of Sederunt of 1664 provided that, when a man petitioned for admission, the Lords would refer him to the Dean and Faculty of Advocates for private and public examination on civil law. The Dean would then assign him a title of the civil law for a public lesson before the

---

[784] Mackenzie (n. 617), 308–310; AS, I, 120–4 (25 Jan. 1676).

[785] George Mackenzie, *Pleadings, in some Remarkable Cases, before the Supreme Courts of Scotland, Since the Year, 1661* (1672).

[786] George Mackenzie, *Idea Eloquentiae Forensis Hodiernae: una cum Actione Forensi ex Unaquaque Juris Parte* (1681). There is an English translation by Robert Hepburn entitled: *An Idea of the Modern Eloquence of the Bar. Together with a Pleading out of Every Part of Law* (1711).

[787] Mackenzie, *Eloquentiae* (n. 786), 11–13. See the general discussion in Cairns (n. 623), 22–3, 25–8.

[788] See Cairns (n. 623), 27–8. Note the account of Scots lawyers in George Mackenzie, *Characteres quorundam apud Scotos Advocatorum*, in *The Works of that Eminent and Learned Lawyer, Sir George Mackenzie of Rosehaugh, Advocate to King Charles II. and King James VII. With Many Learned Treatises of His, Never before Printed* (1716–22), vol. 1, 6–7 at 7 (Law Treatises). The same account is found in NLS, Adv. MS 33.3.19, fos. 64^v–65^v.

[789] Cairns, (1999) 20, no. 2 *JLH* 40–2.

Lords. For the public trial, the intrant had to prepare theses for disputation based on one of the titles of the *Corpus Juris Civilis*, while the Dean would assign him the topic of the public lesson from the title on which the theses had been prepared. The Lords, however, retained a power to dispense with these provisions.[790]

In the 1680s, the Lords became increasingly willing to admit men without referring them for trial by the Dean and Faculty.[791] To discourage this, the advocates set double entry dues of 1,000 merks for those admitted who 'did not undergoe the three ordinarie poynts of tryall'.[792] For a number of years the Lords refused to ratify the Faculty's regulation, largely to enable them to admit men whom they favoured without the usual trials or a financial penalty.[793] As the regime of James VII moved towards its close, the Faculty seized the opportunity to obtain from the Lords an Act of Sederunt approving the ordinary manner of admission by trial on civil law and providing that those admitted without such a trial would be 'examined by the Lords *in praesentia*, concerneing their knowledge of the styles, the forme of process, and of the principles of our law'. The Lords moreover would 'be well informed of their integrity and honest deportment, before they shall be admitted'.[794]

After the Revolution, an Act of Sederunt prohibited the 'extraordinary' admission of the close relatives of ordinary and extraordinary Lords, while another provided that an intrant seeking extraordinary admission would now be referred to the Dean and Faculty for examination on 'his knowledge of the practique of our law, the styles and form of process'.[795] At first, the Faculty decided that this should be a public examination, but in 1696, the decision was made that those admitted by trial on Scots law would now undergo both a private and public examination; thereafter no one was ever again admitted extraordinarily by trial on Scots law. The advocates had secured their aim of having all intrants undergo the ordinary trials on civil law.[796]

(d) *Status, 'breeding', and civil law*

Doubled entry dues may have contributed to this success; but, given the expense of obtaining an education in civil law, this is not a full explanation. In fact, the Faculty had managed to condemn extraordinary admission on a bill, ultimately leading to trial on Scots law, as less 'honourable'.[797] The 'breeding' of an intrant educated in civil law was 'oft more liberall and

---

[790] Ibid. 42–3.   [791] Ibid. 43. See Pinkerton (n. 779), 55 (5 Feb. 1681).
[792] Pinkerton (n. 779), 37 (1 Jan. 1678).
[793] AS, I, 141–2, 158–9 (7 Feb. 1679; 18 Jan. 1684); Fountainhall (n. 719), vol. 2, 461, 799; Cairns, (1999) 20, no. 2 *JLH* 44.   [794] AS, I, 181 (6 July 1688); Pinkerton (n. 779), 85 (30 June 1688).
[795] AS, I, 195 (24 Nov. 1691), 200 (25 June 1692).
[796] Pinkerton (n. 779), 117, 164–5 (8 July 1692, 15 Jan. 1696); Cairns, (1999) 20, no. 2 *JLH* 47–8.   [797] See Spottiswoode (n. 748), xxxix; Forbes (n. 607), viii.

worthy'.[798] It was necessary to be 'well informed of the ... integrity, good-breeding, honest deportment and fitness for exerceing the office of ane advocate' of those admitted extraordinarily.[799] To a society based on rank and status these distinctions were crucial in promoting admission by trial on civil law. The elaborate ceremonies and rituals for admission by trial on civil law, consciously modelled on those for a doctoral degree, reinforced status and emphasized the intrant was joining a learned, honourable, and liberal body. These rituals stressed that advocates had a 'scientific' rather than a 'mechanical' training; unlike writers, they did not serve an apprenticeship. Finally, in 1693, the Faculty decided that intrants should print the theses with *annexa* and *corollaria* for disputation, because it would 'both add to the honor of the society and regulation of the candidat if the said publict tryall shall proceid in the same way and method as is practised abroad'.[800] The advocates were to be an elite group, set apart by learning and social status, their profession modelled on that of the advocates of the *jus commune*.[801]

Reinforcing this understanding of themselves, from around 1680 the Faculty started to collect a substantial library, primarily of the learning of the *jus commune*.[802] Sir George Mackenzie, in a speech prepared for the inauguration of the Library, explained its focus as on law, especially the civil law. He allowed a place for the 'servants of jurisprudence', history, criticism, rhetoric, as necessary adjuncts and aids to legal scholarship. [803] The collection quickly grew into a remarkable scholarly library.[804]

(e) *The education of the advocates*

Until the Revocation of the Edict of Nantes, it remained common for Scots to study law in the French universities. There, if they pursued their studies to

[798] Fountainhall (n. 719), II, 464.
[799] AS, I, 200 (25 June 1692); see also ibid. 181 (6 July 1688).
[800] Pinkerton (n. 779), 121 (3 Jan. 1693).
[801] J. W. Cairns, 'Importing our Lawyers from Holland: Netherlands' Influences on Scots Law and Lawyers in the Eighteenth Century', in Simpson (n. 115), 136–53 at 140–3; *idem*, (1999) 20, no. 2 *JLH* 49–52.
[802] See generally Rae (n. 776), 1–22; Brian Hillyard, 'The Formation of the Library, 1682–1728', in Cadell/Matheson (n. 776), 23–66.
[803] *Oratio Inauguralis habita Edenburgi Id. Mar. 1689. a Dom. Georgio Mackenzeo, de Structura Bibliothecae Pure Juridicae, et hinc de Vario in Jure Scribendi Genere* (1689), 8–9, 24–5. J. H. Loudon translated as 'Sir George Mackenzie's Speech at the Formal Opening of the Advocates' Library Edinburgh 15 March 1689', (1946) 2 *Edinburgh Bibliographical Society Transactions* 273–84 the Latin text found in Mackenzie, *Works* (n. 788), vol. 1 , 1–6 (Law Treatises) at 6, which contains an additional paragraph at the end. The Latin text of 1689 and Loudon's translation (with notes by J. W. Cairns) are reprinted with other matter in Sir George Mackenzie, *Oratio Inauguralis Aperienda Jurisconsultorum Bibliotheca* (1989).
[804] See e.g. M. Townley, *The Best and Fynest Lawers and other Raire Bookes: A Facsimile of the Earliest List of Books in the Advocates' Library, Edinburgh with an Introduction and Modern Catalogue* (1990); *Catalogus Librorum Bibliothecae Juris Utriusque, Civilis quam Canonici, Publici quam Privati, Feudalis quam Municipalis Variorum Regnorum, cum Historicis Graecis et Latinis, Literatis et Philosophis Plerisque Celebrioribus; a Facultate Advocatorum in Supremo Senatu Judicum in Scotia, in usum Cupidae Legum Juventutis, Constructae* (1692).

the licentiate *utriusque juris*, they would have followed a three-year programme primarily devoted to civil law, with some courses in canon law, the only innovation in this traditional curriculum being, from 1679, classes in French law.[805] A number of factors, however, made the universities of the northern Netherlands increasingly popular for Scots, especially between 1675 and 1725.[806] Those who studied there rarely took a degree.[807] Presented with a system, with a modern curriculum, in which it was possible for students to make up their own course of study, Scots generally started with courses on the *Institutes* and natural law, after six months adding to them classes on the *Digest*. They also commonly studied feudal law, criminal law, sometimes canon law, and a whole variety of auxiliary disciplines such as Greek and Roman antiquities, history, rhetoric, and philology.[808]

(*f*) *The development of Scottish law faculties*

The cost of obtaining such education created pressure to establish legal education on the Dutch model in the Scottish universities, particularly Edinburgh.[809] The failure of this campaign caused private enterprise to fill an obvious gap. From 1699 to 1710, three men—Alexander Drummond, John Spotswood (or Spottiswoode), and John Cunninghame—can be traced offering a variety of classes on Scots law and civil law, the most successful being Cunninghame.[810] They followed the *methodus compendiaria*, which had revolutionized law teaching in the Netherlands.[811] The success of these private teachers resulted in the erection of chairs in law in the Universities of Edinburgh and Glasgow. The first chair was that of Public Law and the Law of Nature and Nations in Edinburgh in 1707, to encourage teaching on the model of the *collegia Grotiana* in the Netherlands, Charles Areskine being the first professor. The second was that of Civil Law, again in Edinburgh, to which James Craig was appointed in 1710. In 1713, the University of

---

[805] See L. W. B. Brockliss, *French Higher Education in the Seventeenth and Eighteenth Centuries: A Cultural History* (1987), 277–330.

[806] Cairns (n. 801), 143–6; Robert Feenstra, 'Scottish-Dutch Legal Relations in the Seventeenth and Eighteenth Centuries', in *idem, Legal Scholarship and Doctrines of Private Law, 13th–18th Centuries* (1996), XVI at 36 (= Hilde de Ridder-Symoens and J. M. Fletcher (eds.) *Academic Relations between the Low Countries and the British Isles, 1450–1700. Proceedings of the First Conference of Belgian, British and Dutch Historians of Universities held in Ghent, September 30–October 2, 1987* (1987), 25–45); Kees van Strien and Margreet Ahsmann, 'Scottish Law Students in Leiden at the End of the Seventeenth Century. The Correspondence of John Clerk, 1694–1697', (1992) 19 *Lias* 271–330 and (1993) 20 *Lias* 1–65.

[807] Paul Nève, 'Disputations of Scots Students Attending Universities in the Northern Netherlands', in Gordon/Fergus (n. 104), 95–108.

[808] Cairns (n. 801), 136–9; van Strien/Ahsmann, (1992) 19 *Lias* 287–98.

[809] See Cairns (n. 801), 146–7; *idem* (n. 623), 23; *idem*, 'John Spotswood, Professor of Law: A Preliminary Sketch', in W. M. Gordon (ed.), *Miscellany Three*, Stair Society, vol. 39 (1992), 131–59 at 131–3. Cairns, (1995) 46 *Northern Ireland Legal Quarterly* 304–31 indicates the unimportance of the teaching of the law professor at Aberdeen, even when it occurred.

[810] Cairns (n. 809), 131–3. [811] Cairns (n.809), 143–7.

Glasgow, in emulation of developments in Edinburgh, secured the establishment of a chair in Civil Law in Glasgow, the first professor, William Forbes, initially teaching Scots law as well as civil law. In 1719, Charles Mackie was appointed Professor of Universal History in Edinburgh; he later started to teach Roman antiquities, a course of great significance for law students. Finally, in 1722, Alexander Bayne was appointed to a new chair of Municipal Law in Edinburgh. By the 1720s, therefore, the Faculty of Advocates had secured its aim of legal education in the Scottish universities, largely modelled on the Dutch *collegia privata*, where feasible using the textbooks used in the Netherlands, which offered the type of curriculum—especially in civil law—that they desired.[812]

(g) *Advocates, writers, and procurators*

By 1715, the Faculty had thus successfully asserted its status and independence as a body of men learned in civil law and emphasized its difference from the other groups of procurators and writers in Scotland. Nonetheless, it is worth noting, although the evidence is slight, that it was in the Restoration period that later prominent bodies of procurators, such as the Society of Advocates in Aberdeen and the Faculty of Procurators in Glasgow, came to acquire a greater organized corporate identity, while the Writers to the Signet were already well established, all groups relying on apprenticeships to train their future members.[813]

5. Liberty and property: codification, legislation, and the common law

(a) *Procedure and substantive law*

Rights of liberty and property were increasingly the philosophical commonplaces of the age and Stair stressed that the aims of positive law were to secure 'society, property and commerce'.[814] The general influence of such thinking in Scotland can readily be identified. Liberty of the subject influenced the act of 1701 on bail and many of the procedural reforms in the criminal courts. One factor leading to the end of the witch-hunt in Scotland (after the horrors of the major witch-hunt of 1661–2) was lawyers' anxieties over the adequacy of the evidence (especially if torture was used) and the fairness

---

[812] Cairns (n. 801), 148–50; *idem*, 'The Origins of the Glasgow Law School: The Professors of Civil Law, 1714–61', in Peter Birks (ed.), *The Life of the Law: Proceedings of the Tenth British Legal History Conference, Oxford 1991* (1993), 151–94 at 152–83; *idem*, 'Three Unnoticed Scottish Editions of Pieter Burman's *Antiquitatum Romanarum Brevis Descriptio*', (1997) 22 *The Bibliothek* 20–33; Sir Alexander Grant, *The Story of the University of Edinburgh during its First Three Hundred Years* (1884), vol. 1, 232–3, 284–5; vol. 2, 364.

[813] See J. H. Begg, *A Treatise on the Law of Scotland Relating to Law Agents* (1873), 14–17.

[814] Stair, I, 1, 18.

Historical Introduction 131

of the procedure against the accused.[815] One should not assume, however, an easy rise of procedural protection of the accused.[816] Reforms in the civil courts were also geared to fair, expeditious, and open proceedings.

Major reforms in substantive laws also reflected such concerns. Most prominent here were the statutes and Acts of Sederunt dealing with credit, in which there can be traced a general desire to make credit easier by improving the procedures by which creditors could realize the assets of their debtors in case of bankruptcy or failure to pay.[817] There was much legislation and many Acts of Sederunt dealing with arrestment, adjudication, apprising, bankruptcy, procedures such as *cessio bonorum*, vitious intromission, defraud of creditors by heirs and executors, and sale of bankrupts' lands.[818] Of crucial importance was a statutory clarification of the difference between heritable and moveable bonds in 1661.[819] Attempts were made to control the protections against diligence the Crown would grant to favoured individuals; ultimately these were listed in the Claim of Right as one of the ways in which James VII acted in an arbitrary and despotic manner.[820] Two Acts of Parliament created summary procedures for dealing with bills of exchange.[821] Individuals were generally to be held to their contracts in good faith with effective process if something went wrong.

While minors and incompetents were protected, property rights were also made more certain.[822] Prescription was reformed, with extension of the practice of registration the manner favoured to secure rights.[823] Individuals could

---

[815] On the witch-hunt, see B. P. Levack, 'The Great Scottish Witch Hunt of 1661–1662', (1980) 20 *Journal of British Studies* 90–108; Christina Larner, *Enemies of God: The Witch-hunt in Scotland* (1981). On lawyers' anxieties over these prosecutions, see Sir George Mackenzie, *Pleadings, in some Remarkable Cases, before the Supreme Courts of Scotland, Since the Year, 1661. To which the Decisions are Subjoyn'd* (2nd edn., 1704), 229–46 (Larner, loc. cit., 186–90 analyses Mackenzie's strategies in this defence of a witchcraft prosecution).

[816] As prosecutions for witchcraft declined, anxieties over child-murder grew and a statute of 1690 provided that if a mother concealed her pregnancy and could not produce a child then she was to be held and repute the murder of her child: APS, IX, 195 (c. 50). On the anxieties over child-murder and the call for a statute modelled on that of England, see Fountainhall (n. 719), vol. 1, 224, 289–90. [817] See e.g. the wording of Diligence Act 1661: APS, VII, 317–20 (c. 344).

[818] APS, VII, 63 (c. 88) (1661), 229–30 (c. 243) (1661), 262–3 (c. 283) (Arrestments Act 1661), 476–7 (c. 36) (1663), 576 (c. 39) (1669), 577 (c. 40) (1669); VIII, 69–70 (c. 17) (1672), 351–2 (c. 83) (Judicial Sale Act 1681), 598 (c. 27) (1686); IX, 369–70 (c. 8) (Judicial Sale Act 1695), 427–8 (c. 39) (1695); X, 33–4 (c. 5) (Bankruptcy Act 1696), 57–8 (c. 11) (1696), 61 (c. 20) (Vitious Intromittors Act 1696). AS, I, 82–3 (28 Feb. 1662), 132 (1 Feb. 1677), 143 (14 Nov. 1679), 159–60 (26 Feb. 1684), 167 (31 Mar. 1685), 169–70 (1 Dec. 1685), 179–80 (8 Feb. 1688), 181–2 (18 July 1688), 197–8 (24 Feb. 1692), 249–52 (23 Nov. 1711).

[819] APS, VII, 230 (c. 244) (Bonds Act 1661).

[820] APS, VII, 451 (c. 2) (1663); VIII, 247 (c. 11) (1681); AS, I, 124 (1 Feb. 1676); APS, IX, 39.

[821] APS, VIII, 352–3 (c. 86) (Bills of Exchange Act 1681); X, 77 (c. 38) (Inland Bills Act 1696).

[822] See e.g. APS, VII, 452 (c. 4) (The Minority Act 1663); VIII, 59–60 (c. 2) (The Tutors and Curators Act 1672), 372 (c. 85) (The Oaths of Minors Act 1681); X, 34–5 (c. 8) (The Tutors and Curators Act 1696); 35 (c. 9) (The Prescription Act 1696); 79 (c. 44) (1696); 149 (c. 5) (1698). [823] APS, VII, 561 (c. 14) (Prescription Act 1669).

rely on the faith of the registers in their transactions.[824] The most important measures were both passed in 1693. The Real Rights Act provided that all infeftments were to be preferred in competitions according to their date and priority in the Register of Sasines.[825] The Register of Sasines Act established that the minute books kept for the registers were to record exactly when deeds were presented for registration and the writs were to be registered exactly in accordance with the minute books, so that 'Purchasers and Creditors might know with whom they might safely contract'.[826] In a system relying ever more on written documents, the subscription of deeds to ensure their probative value was also regulated.[827] The rights of property protected were those of individual proprietors, even if within the structures of the feudal system. Economic measures also promoted the rights of individuals.[828] Feudal survivals came under attack in the Clan Act of 1715, which abolished various personal military services as not only oppressive but also inhibiting of the development of trade and manufactures.[829]

(b) *Improving the sources of the law*

If there was important substantive reform of the laws, there were still evident problems with the main sources of the law—statutes and court decisions. At the Restoration the most recent collected edition of the statutes was still that of Skene, while decisions of the court still circulated only in manuscript. The continuing desire to reduce the law of Scotland entirely to a written form was now linked with a perception that the certainty this produced would protect liberty and property.[830] In 1681, a commission was granted in Parliament 'for revising the Laws'. Those appointed were to peruse and consider 'the whole Laws Statuts and Acts of Parliament of this his ancient Kingdom as weel printed as not printed, Together with the Customs Consuetuds and Judiciall Practicks Either in the Supream or Subalterne Courts whether Civil or Criminal, which are or have been observed as Laws or Rules of Judgement'. They were then to collect and digest them, resolving any difficulties or contradictions and omitting all obsolete matter. Finally these collections were to be digested and reduced 'into such convenient order As they shall judge fitt' and,

---

[824] APS, VII, 556 (c. 4) (1669); VIII, 477–8 (c. 26) (Entail Act 1685); X, 60 (c. 18) (1696), 60–1 (c. 19) (Interruptions Act 1696). For a contemporary view of the significance of the registers, see George Mackenzie, *An Answer to Some Reasons Printed in England, against the Overture of Bringing into that Kingdom, such Registers as are Used in Scotland*, in *idem, Pleadings* (n. 785), 279–95.   [825] APS, IX, 271 (c. 22).
[826] APS, IX, 271 (c. 23). See also APS, IX, 271–2 (c. 24).
[827] See, eg. APS, VIII, 242–3 (c. 5) (Subscription of Deeds Act 1681), 599 (c. 29) (1686); X, 59 (c. 15) (Deeds Act 1696).
[828] APS, VII, 263–4 (c. 284) (The March Dykes Act 1661); IX, 421 (c. 36) (The Runrig Lands Act 1695); 462 (c. 69) (Division of Commonties Act 1695). See also e.g. APS, VII, 476 (c. 35) (1663); VIII, 595 (c. 21) (The Winter Herding Act 1686).   [829] 1 Geo. I (c. 54).
[830] See Jackson (n. 618), 103–4.

omitting all obsolete or abrogated acts, delivered to be enacted in the form of laws.[831] Lord Fountainhall, for one, welcomed this proposal.[832] Nothing resulted from this project and, in 1695, another commission was granted in Parliament, emphasizing the importance of certain and known laws 'for the Security ... of [the] lives and fortunes' of the king's subjects. The terms of the instructions were broadly similar to those of 1681, covering statutes, decisions and practicks, and Acts of Sederunt.[833] This proposal for some sort of codification of Scots law or at least a sorting out of its sources, again produced no result. The task—a general code or statement of all of Scots law—was probably too great to be accomplished with the resources available.

(c) The statute book

These proposals were the product of the general view that expressing the laws in writing was inherently just. Moreover, many Scots adhered to the opinion of Sir George Mackenzie that 'our Statutes ... be the chief Pillars of our Law'.[834] For Mackenzie, the publicity involved in statutes inevitably favoured the liberty of the subject.[835] Concern with the statute book had also led to the grant to Sir Thomas Murray of Glendook, Clerk Register, of an exclusive nineteen-year licence to print an edition of the statutes.[836] He duly produced two editions of the statutes from 1424 onwards. The first was a fine folio edition, the other a less luxurious working edition in duodecimo.[837] Glendook did go some way to providing a working collected edition, the utility of which was greatly enhanced by the publication in 1686 of Sir George Mackenzie's *Observations on the Acts of Parliament*. In many ways, this substituted for the work of the Commissioners of 1681, not only by indicating which statutes

---

[831] APS, VIII, 356 (c. 94).   [832] Fountainhall (n. 719), vol. 1, 322.
[833] APS, IX, 455 (c. 57).
[834] George Mackenzie, *Observations on the Acts of Parliament, Made by King James the First, King James the Second, King James the Third, King James the Fourth, King James the Fifth, Queen Mary, King James the Sixth, King Charles the First, King Charles the Second. Wherein 1. It is Observ'd, if they be in Desuetude, Abrogated, Limited, or Enlarged. 2. The Decisions relating to these Acts are mention'd. 3. Some new Doubts not yet decided, are hinted at. 4. Parallel Citations from the Civil, Canon, Feudal and Municipal Laws, and the Laws of other Nations, are adduc'd for clearing these Statutes* (1686), sig. A4^r.
[835] George Mackenzie, *The Laws and Customes of Scotland, in Matters Criminal. Wherein is to be seen how the Civil Law, and the Laws and Customs of other Nations do agree with, and supply ours* (1678). For convenience of reference, all citations from this book will be taken from the version in Mackenzie, *Works* (n. 788), vol. 2, 49–275 at 53 and 60–1.
[836] APS, VIII, 388–9 (c. 133). The 1681 Commission was not to infringe his patent.
[837] *The Laws and Acts of Parliament made by King James the First, Second, Third, Fourth, Fifth, Queen Mary, King James the Sixth, King Charles the First, King Charles the Second Who now presently Reigns, Kings and Queen of Scotland. Collected, and extracted, from the Publick Records of the said Kingdom, by Sir Thomas Murray of Glendook Knight, and Baronet, Clerk to His Majestie's Council, Register, and Rols, by his Majestie's special warrand* (1681); *The Laws and Acts of Parliament Made by King James the First, and his Royal Successors, Kings and Queen of Scotland In Two Parts ... Collected, and Extracted, from the Publick Records of the said Kingdom, by Sir Thomas Murray of Glendook* (1682–3).

were in desuetude or abrogated, but also by providing a general legal commentary on their operation and interpretation.[838]

(d) The decisions of the Lords

The first printed collection of decisions of the Lords came in 1683 and 1687, published by Lord Stair.[839] This initiated erratic publication of further volumes of decisions or practick.[840] Much remained in manuscript, however, encouraging the advocates in 1684 to try to copy or purchase 'all the Scotts practiques ... for the Bibliothecq'.[841] From 1692, they also tried to collect decisions in a relatively systematic way.[842] Decisions, if of great authority, did not, in theory, make the law, but constituted evidence of what it might be.[843] Mackenzie set out a series of rules for weighing the authority of decisions: 'A constant Series of Decisions ... ought to be in great veneration'; 'Where the Lords declare they will decide soe in all tyme comeing great respect ought to be had to them'; 'Respect is to be had to solemn Decisions in praesentia', but the 'Remarker of the Decision should observe whither the Cause was decided upon a Debate in praesentia or upon a Report from the Utter House', because 'there is great difference amongst Reporters both as to Learning and Integrity'; a single decision could 'cast the Ballance' if, in the case being considered, 'the Reasons of both Sides seem to be equally in the Scale of Justice'; furthermore, those relying on a decision must consider whether 'the cause was well debated' and 'the prevailer neither related to great Men, nor Judges'.[844]

Indeed, Mackenzie was distinctly sceptical about the value of decisions because the judges might be either corrupt or ignorant or both.[845] Moreover, until 1693, judges advised in secret, so the reasons behind their decisions were unknown, as they were never incorporated into the formal sentence of the court.[846] Furthermore, decisions being made by voting, there could well be no single reason behind a finding for one party or another.[847] In such a system, it was always safer to rely on a tract of decisions as establishing practice, focusing on the pleadings to determine what had been at issue. Liberty and property might require certainty in the law, but in the face of the failure to

---

[838] Mackenzie (n. 834).

[839] *The Decisions of the Lords of Council and Session, In the Most Important Cases Debate before them, with the Acts of Sederunt ... Observed by Sir James Dalrymple of Stair, Knight and Baronet* (1683–7).

[840] See the appendix to J. S. Leadbetter, 'The Printed Law Reports 1540–1935', in McKechnie (n. 468), 42–58 at 47–9. [841] Pinkerton (n. 779), 68 (9 Feb. 1684).

[842] Pinkerton (n. 779), 109 (16 Jan. 1692), 117–18 (2 Aug. 1692), 138 (24 Nov. 1694), 182 (8 Jan. 1698). [843] Stair, I, 1, 16.

[844] British Library, MS Add. 18236, fos. 60^v–61^r. [845] Ibid., fo. 57.

[846] APS, IX, 305 (c. 42) (Court of Session Act 1693).

[847] See J. A. Inglis, 'Eighteenth Century Pleading', (1907–8) 19 *JR* 42–57 at 52.

reduce all the law to writing and the problems with the statute book, the sources of the municipal law were proving insufficient.

6. Pleading, common law, and *jus commune*

(*a*) Jus commune, jus proprium, *and interpretation*

Rather than rely on judicial decisions, Mackenzie's solution to this problem was 'to have our Law directed by the Writings of Learned Lawyers who give their Judgment in abstract Cases wherein none are concern'd ... and who have great Leisure to meditate upon what they transmit to Posterity as Law'. He went to assess the authority to be given to *consilia* and the opinions of universities, which 'resemble much the Responsa Prudentium which were in great Reputation among the Romans'. Thus, the writings of jurists of the *jus commune* were to be used to supplement and interpret Scots law.[848] This mode of dealing with the deficiencies of Scots law reflects Mackenzie's view that '[t]he Old Customs of Scotland are originally derived from the Roman Law in what Concerns moveables; From the Feudall in what Concerns heritage; and the Cannon, in what Concerns Ecclesiasticall Matters'.[849] Of Roman law in particular he commented:

God Almighty did inspire the Romans to digest the principles of Reason into a Body of their positive Law, to the End Nations might have common principles wherein they might agree, and it is therefore called by the French and us and by most of all other Nations, the Common Law.[850]

Mackenzie stated that civil law was followed 'in judging Crimes, as is clear by several Acts of Parliament, wherein the Civil Law is called the Common Law'.[851] Civil law was 'the great Foundation of our Laws and Forms', so that the Roman laws, 'in undecided Cases, are of universal Use'.[852] The civil law was 'the Generall Supplement of our Law'.[853]

Mackenzie's emphasis on the civil law as the proper resource for arguments and doctrine to supplement and interpret the municipal law was common. John Cunninghame told his classes in Scots law in Edinburgh that 'the Civill Law and the Cannon Law' made up 'a part of our Laws'. He argued that the civil law, because of its 'equity and exactness' was in 'our acts of Parliament frequently called the Common Law' and it was commonly received, not only in Scotland, 'but likewise in many other places of Europe as in Holland, Germany, France and Spain'.[854] Thus, the divinely inspired Roman law was

---

[848] British Library, MS Add. 18236, fos. 57^v–58^r. [849] Ibid. fo. 16^v. [850] Ibid. fo. 18^r.
[851] Mackenzie, *Laws and Customes of Scotland, in Matters Criminal*, in idem, *Works* (n. 788), vol. 2, 54.
[852] George Mackenzie, *Observations upon the 18th Act of the 23d Parliament of King James the Sixth against Dispositions Made in Defraud of Creditors* (1675; 2nd edn., 1698), in idem, *Works* (n. 788), vol. 2, 1 at 7. [853] British Library, MS Add. 18236, fo. 33^v.
[854] Edinburgh University Library, MS Gen. 1735, 5. He added, cautiously, 'and even in England though many are of the contrair opinion'.

not simply *ratio scripta*, but a valid part of the armoury of every Scots lawyer in presenting arguments about the law applicable in Scotland. It is possible to find in Mackenzie's various accounts of Roman law the germs of the idea that its authority derived from the *jus naturale*, but his accounts of natural law are generally slight and incomplete.[855] His uneasiness with natural law probably derived from his appreciation that it was easy to develop republican arguments from the work of Grotius. He generally preferred to legitimate use of civil law in Scotland by historical argument: 'And that the Civil Law is our Rule, where our own Statutes and Customs are silent or deficient, is clear from our own Lawyers . . . [a]s also from our Historians . . . And the same is recorded of us by the Historians and Lawyers of other Nations.'[856]

Mackenzie's own publications manifest this blending of the civil with the Scots law, demonstrating the need to use both the *jus commune* and the *jus proprium* to give a full account of the law. Thus he relies on the civil law and its commentaries to explain Scots criminal law.[857] He also relies extensively on interpretation from civilian sources and commentaries in his treatise on the act of James VI against defraud of creditors, his *Observations on the Acts of Parliament*, and indeed other works such as those on precedency and heraldry.[858] William Forbes's treatise on bills of exchange draws on civilian literature.[859] Sir Alexander Seton of Pitmedden's *Treatise of Mutilation and Demembration and their Punishments* relies heavily on canon and civil laws to develop the Scots, though noting where the last differed from the *jus commune*.[860] In the *Tutor's Guide* of 1714, Alexander Bruce, following to some extent the structure found in Justinian's *Institutes*, in each of the titles into which the work is divided, first gave an account of the Roman or civil law, followed by a section headed 'Laws and Customs of Scotland relating to this

---

[855] British Library, MS Add. 18236, fo. 8ᵛ.; George Mackenzie, *The Institutions of the Law of Scotland* (2nd edn., 1688), 1–9. See Alan Watson, 'Some Notes on Mackenzie's *Institutions* and the European Legal Tradition', (1989) 16 *Ius Commune* 303–13; Cairns (n. 523), 207–8; H. L. MacQueen, 'Mackenzie's Institutions in Scottish Legal History', (1984) *JLSS* 498–501.

[856] Mackenzie (n. 852), in *idem*, *Works* (n. 788), vol. 2, 7.

[857] The full title of his work (see n. 835) is instructive.

[858] Mackenzie (n. 852), in *idem*, *Works* (n. 788), vol. 2, 1–47; Mackenzie (n. 834); George Mackenzie, *Observations upon the Laws and Customs of Nations, as to Precedency* (1680); *idem*, *The Science of Herauldry, Treated as Part of the Civil Law, and Law of Nations* (1680). In reality, these form one book: Ferguson, (1935–8) 1 *Edinburgh Bibliographical Society Transactions* 26–8.

[859] William Forbes, *A Methodical Treatise Concerning Bills of Exchange. Wherein Is an account of the Rise and Progress of Exchange; The Nature and Kinds of it explained; The prevailing Custom of Merchants, Illustrated and confirm'd from Civil Law, the Authority of Lawyers and Writers, Ancient and Modern, Forein Statutes, and Sentences of Courts, Acts of Parliament, and Decisions of the Lords of Session; And all curious and useful Cases, Questions and Controversies touching Bills fairly stated and discuss'd, according to the Analogy of the Scots Law* (1703).

[860] George Mackenzie, *The Laws and Customs of Scotland, in Matters Criminal Wherein is to be seen how the Civil Law, and the Laws and Customs of other Nations doth agree with, and supply Ours . . . To this Second Edition is now added (by way of Appendix) A Treatise of Mutiliation and Demembration and their Punishments, by Sir Alexander Seton of Pitmedden Knight Baronet* (1699).

Title'. Bruce explained that 'the *Roman* or *Civil Law* is generally lookt upon as the *Standard* of *all* Municipal Statutes and Customs thro'out the *Christian World*'. Moreover, 'this elaborate Collection of the *Roman* Laws is with us considered as the *Rule*, and our own Statutes and Customs as the *Exception*'.[861] The relationship of the *jus commune* to the *jus proprium* is thus clarified.

Aspects of the *jus commune* other than the *jus civile* were understood in the same way. Forbes's account of church property and teinds paid appropriate attention to canon law.[862] In each of two studies of feudal law published shortly after the Union, the *jus feudale* was treated as the primary system and the Scots law, the *jus proprium*, as a variant. Thus, John Dundas set out the feudal law at length before setting out in a single chapter the points on which Scots law departed from it.[863] Alexander Bruce set out a hierarchy of sources to which one turned in Scotland in disputes about feudal matters. The first *locus* (in the sense of a source of an argument on a topic) was Scottish legislation, the second a continuous tract of decisions, the third the *jus feudale scriptum*, and the fourth the *jus civile*. Yet, the structure of the book contradicts this hierarchy. Each title gives a full account of the *jus feudale commune*, drawing extensively on authoritative writers, before concluding with a section, starting '*moribus*', setting out the manner in which Scots law departs from the feudal, obviously considered as the normal rule.[864]

(*b*) Jus naturale, jus gentium, *and interpretation*

The growing popularity in Scotland of the *jus naturale* and *jus gentium* offered an alternative manner of dealing with insufficiencies in the Scottish sources and a more critical approach to the use of Roman law.[865] Stair's *Institutions*, first published in 1681, gave the most important account of Scots law within a framework drawn from natural law.[866] Stair wrote that '[w]here our

---

[861] Alexander Bruce, *The Tutor's Guide: Or, The Principles of the Civil and Municipal Laws and Customs, Relating to Pupils and Minors, and their Tutors and Curators* (1714), iv–vi.

[862] William Forbes, *A Treatise of Church-lands and Tithes: In Two Parts: Containing an Historical Account of Ecclesiastical Revenues, Churches, Church-yards, Church-offices, Benefices, Glebes, Manses, Patronage, Monachism, Religious, and Military-orders, with a Particular History of Tithes: And a clear and full Discussion of Points of Right and Controversy, relating to these Matters; and shewing how far the Scots and Canon Laws do agree, and differ* (1705).

[863] John Dundas, *A Summary View of the Feudal Law, with the Differences of the Scots Law from it; Together with a Dictionary of the Select Terms of the Scots and English Law, by way of Appendix* (1710). The feudal law is on pp. 1–87, the Scots departures from it on pp. 88–109.

[864] Alexander Bruce, *Principia Juris Feudalis, Institutionum Imperialum Methodo (Quantum Feudalis Ratio Patitur) Disposita. Accedunt Notae et Observationes Practicae, ad Mores Patrios tam Antiquos quam Hodiernos, Singulis Titulis Annexae* (1713), 8.

[865] Libraries were building up collections of works on the *jus naturale*: J. W. Cairns, 'Scottish Law, Scottish Lawyers and the Status of the Union', in Robertson (n. 395), 243–68 at 258.

[866] Though the best-known work on Scots law, little of value has been published on the crucial issue of the development of the text of Stair's *Institutions*. There is a complex manuscript history and a complex relationship between the first edition of 1681 (including the separate *Modus Litigandi, or Forms of Process delivered before the Lords of Council and Session* sometimes bound with copies of the first edition) and the second of 1693.

ancient law, statutes, and our recent customs and practiques are defective, recourse is had to equity, as the first and universal law, and to expediency, whereby laws are drawn in consequence *ad similes casus*'.[867] Natural law— 'equity'—was obligatory, although municipal laws could depart from it for good reason.[868] Stair wrote that the law of Scotland had an 'affinity' with the civil law and that 'though it be not acknowledged as a law binding for its authority, yet [it was], as a rule, followed for its equity'.[869] Stair thus considered civil law to have no special authority in itself; any authority it might have only derived from its embodiment of a rule of natural law. Professor Gordon has shown that Stair did not simply use civil law to fill 'gaps' he found in Scots law; rather, he 'did use it to suggest questions and possible solutions to problems on which there was no native authority, as on the law of risk in sale' and 'even where he might appear at first sight to be relying on Roman law he is in fact testing it against natural law'.[870] The influence of Roman law in the *Institutions* is, however, sufficiently obvious that it was perfectly plausible, if inaccurate, for a contemporary to say of the work that it was 'a system of the civil law, intermixt with the law of Scotland'.[871]

(c) Jus commune *in practice*

Perhaps more important than the differences in theoretical accounts of the use of civil law in Scotland is the simple and obvious fact of its wide use in

---

[867] Stair, I, 1, 16.

[868] Stair, I, 1, 15. On Stair's views of natural law, see e.g. A. H. Campbell, *The Structure of Stair's Institutions: Being the Twenty-First Lecture on the David Murray Foundation in the University of Glasgow Delivered on 24th February, 1954* (1954); Neil MacCormick, 'Law, Obligation and Consent: Reflections on Stair and Locke', (1979) 65 *Archiv für Rechts und Sozial Philosophie* 387–411; idem, 'Stair's General Concepts. 2. Stair as Analytical Jurist', in D. M. Walker (ed.), *Stair Tercentenary Studies*, Stair Society, vol. 33 (1981), 187–99; idem, 'The Rational Discipline of Law', [1981] *JR* 146–60; P. G. Stein, 'Stair's General Concepts. I. The Theory of Law', in D. M. Walker (ed.), *Stair Tercentenary Studies*, Stair Society, vol. 33 (1981), 181–7; J. D. Ford, 'Stair's Title "Of Liberty and Servitude"', in A. D. E. Lewis and D. J. Ibbetson (eds.), *The Roman Law Tradition* (1994), 135–58.

[869] Stair, I, 1, 12. Note that 'as a rule' has the sense of 'as a code of regulation': see Alan Watson, 'The Rise of Modern Scots Law' in *La formazione storica del diritto moderno in Europa, Atti del Terzo Congresso Internzionale della Società Italiana di Storia del Diritto* (1977), III, 1167–76 at 1175; Cairns (n. 523), 212–13.

[870] Gordon (n. 103), 28–9. This summarizes the work in idem, 'Stair's Use of Roman Law', in Harding (n. 359), 120–6; idem, 'Roman Law as a Source [of Stair's *Institutions*]', in Walker (n. 868), 107–12; and idem, 'Stair, Grotius and the Sources of Stair's Institutions', in J. A. Ankum, J. E. Spruit, and F. B. J. Ankum (eds.), *Satura Roberto Feenstra Sexagesimum Quintum Annum Aetatis Complenti ab Alumnis Collegis Amicis Oblata* (1985), 571–83. Consider the full title: *The Institutions of the Law of Scotland: Deduced from its Originals, and Collated with the Civil, Canon and Feudal Laws, and with the Customs of Neighbouring Nations*.

[871] Walter Scott (ed.), *A Collection of Scarce and Valuable Tracts, on the Most Interesting and Entertaining Subjects: But Chiefly Such as Relate to the History and Constitution of these Kingdoms. Selected from an Infinite Number in Print and Manuscript, in the Royal, Cotton, Sion, and other Public, as well as Private, Libraries, particularly that of the late Lord Somers* (2nd edn., 1809–15), vol. 11, 550.

Historical Introduction

legal argument and the reliance put on it by courts and writers, even in areas not derived from Roman law. For example, though entails in Scotland did not originate in the civil law, their similarity to substitution and *fideicommissa* meant that 'Topicks from these may be urged in debate'.[872] This explains Cunninghame's remark that, in pleading, 'all our reasoning and Topicks are taken' from the civil law.[873] In 1681 Mackenzie published one of his pleadings on municipal law, intending in part to show the utility of '*Juris Civilis & Feudalis Scientia*' in pleading causes where Scots law was *not* founded on the civil.[874] He supported his argument by showing that to decide against him would be contrary to the rules of the civil and feudal laws, and, relying on a Scottish case, argued that on this point the Scottish customs (*mores nostri*) imitated the civil law.[875] Similar attitudes to use of Roman law are found in the arguments preserved in reports. For example, in the case of *Burnet v. Burnet* (1701), which also concerned entails, as well as the *Corpus Juris Civilis*, Bartolus, Gothofredus, Cujas, and Zoesius were cited to the court. One litigant also relied on a recent opinion of Van Eck, Professor at Utrecht, which the other party dismissed, by pointing out that Van Eck would have been paid for his opinion, while it was also directly contradicted by a decision of the Supreme Court of Savoy as reported by Antonius Faber.[876] Cases can also be found where issues of succession were decided according to the civil law.[877]

Such reliance on the *jus commune* explains the anxiety to have a learned bench. Fountainhall once noted despairingly that a 'debate ran on a gross ignorance of the civil law'.[878] Mackenzie gave his opinion that 'it were fit the Lords of Session understood exactly the Civil Law'.[879] This was achieved by the provision in the Act of Union on the appointment of Senators. While no doubt some of the Senators would have only the slightest of knowledge, in a bench of fifteen, it was always likely that there would always be some Senators, under such a system, who had a profound grasp of the civil law and the more modern civilian literature.

---

[872] George Mackenzie, *A Treatise of Tailies*, in *idem*, *Works* (n. 788), vol. 2, 484–91 at 484. The term 'Topics' is being used in its technical sense from rhetoric.

[873] Cunninghame, Edinburgh University Library, MS Gen. 1735, 6; NLS, MS 3413, 3: 'It is usefull in regard we borrow all our Topicks from it, in pleading'.

[874] Mackenzie, *Eloquentiae* (n. 786), *Elenchus Contentorum*. [875] Ibid. 150–82.

[876] Fountainhall (n. 766), vol. 2, 127–8.

[877] *Couts v. Straiton* (1683) 2 Brown's Supp 30. Sometimes reporters have preserved the differing opinions given by the judges when they were advising: *Ross's Creditors* 5 Brown's Supp 95–7. [878] Fountainhall, reporting a case *Anent Fidejussion* in 2 Brown's Supp 565.

[879] Mackenzie (n. 852), 7.

7. The development of a Scottish law library

(a) Sources, general works, and treatises

Such attempts to blend Scots law with the *jus commune* allowed the emergence of a much more extensive and varied printed Scottish legal literature. The most important of these works were undoubtedly Stair's *Institutions*, which gave a reasonably comprehensive account of private law, and Mackenzie's *Law of Scotland, in Matters Criminal*, which did the same for criminal law. Both these works took account of the custom and decisions of the courts and the statutes and attempted to accommodate and rationalize the traditional habit of drawing on the *jus commune* in Scottish legal reasoning and practice. Both works revealed the further development of an approach that attempted, following Craig, to see Scots law as an integrated whole, in which the relevant learning of the *jus commune* was coming to be ever more incorporated into a law seen as a national law. In sum, these works reveal the way in which the law was now viewed as a coherent and logical whole integrated as a hierarchical series of norms, justified and made obligatory by a higher authority. In this sense, Stair and Mackenzie's general works were typical of the institutional writings that marked an important stage in the development of the *usus modernus Pandectarum*, which led to the creation of national laws in Europe.[880]

Glendook's edition provided a working text of the statutes, while Mackenzie's *Observations* gave the necessary extensive annotation on them. Some reports had been printed. Stair's *Institutions* and Mackenzie's *Matters Criminal* provided wide-ranging general texts analysing the law. The latter's *Institutions* served as a basic textbook for students, and went through a number of editions.[881] The first printed collection of styles was published, setting a standard for the crucial documents on which the legal system depended.[882] A far-ranging series of difficult issues was discussed in John Nisbet, Lord Dirleton's work entitled *Some Doubts and Questions, in the Law; Especially of Scotland*, posthumously published in 1698.[883]

---

[880] See Klaus Luig, 'The Institutes of National Law in the Seventeenth and Eighteenth Centuries', [1972] *JR* 193–226; J. W. Cairns, 'Institutional Writings in Scotland Reconsidered', in Kiralfy/MacQueen (n. 69) (= (1983) 4 *JLH*), 76–117.

[881] On the editions, see Ferguson, (1935–8) 1 *Edinburgh Bibliographical Society Transactions* 30–4. See also J. W. Cairns, 'Andrew Bell, Jonas Luntley and the London Edition of Mackenzie's *Institutions*', (1996) 21 *The Bibliothek* 7–11; idem, 'The Moveable Text of Mackenzie: Bibliographical Problems for the Scottish Concept of Institutional Writing', in Cairns/Robinson (n. 204) 235–48.

[882] George Dallas, *System of Stiles, as now Practicable within the Kingdom of Scotland: and Reduced to a Clear Method* (1697).

[883] *Some Doubts and Questions, in the Law; Especially of Scotland. As also, Some Decisions of the Lords of Council and Session: Collected and Observ'd by Sir John Nisbet of Dirleton* (1698). Answered by Sir James Steuart of Goodtrees in another posthumous publication, *Dirleton's Doubts and Questions in the Law of Scotland, Resolved and Answered by Sir James Steuart of Goodtrees* (1715).

More specialized treatises were also published, such as William Forbes's *Treatise of Church-lands and Tithes*, published in 1705. Current problems and interest often produced such works: thus, Mackenzie's publication of his *Observations upon the 18. Act.23. Parl. K. James VI. Against Dispositions Made in Defraud of Creditors* was a response to the intense concern over debt and diligence in this period, while Forbes's work on *Bills of Exchange* is a reflection of the current interest in the proper development of commercial instruments. Other examples (more could be given) are Bruce's *Tutor's Guide* of 1714, probably prompted by the relatively extensive legislation on tutory, pupillage, and minority, while the general election in 1710 caused John Spottiswoode to publish a treatise on elections, which engendered a rival work by William Forbes.[884] Academic legal instruction promoted the publication of textbooks, such as Spottiswoode's works on writs and form of process and new editions of Mackenzie's *Institutions*.[885]

(b) Jus commune, libraries, and English law

The appearance of an expanded Scottish law library and statements of Scots law as a whole in a framework of the law of nature and nations still did not replace the older reliance on the learning of the *jus commune* for specific legal argument in a system in which individual court decisions did not lay down clear and specific rules of law. The enormous and growing collection of the Advocates' Library gave the bar and bench access to a storehouse of the *jus commune*. Private collections mirrored this in a lesser way, as the catalogues of lawyers' libraries reveal.[886] Fountainhall's direct comparison of the Scottish Commissions to the work carried out for Justinian by Tribonian is symptomatic of how the minds of the lawyers worked, as is Mackenzie's

---

[884] John Spottiswoode, *The Law Concerning Election of Members for Scotland, To Sit and Vote in the Parliament of Great-Britain* (1710); *A Letter from William Forbes Advocate, to his Friend in England a Member of the House of Commons, Concerning the Law of Election of Members of Parliament; Collected out of the Acts and Records of the Parliament of Scotland, and the Statutes of England and Great Britain* (1710). On the rivalry, see Cairns (n. 812), 173.

[885] John Spottiswoode, *An Introduction to the Knowldege of the Stile of Writs, Simple and Compound, Made Use of in Scotland; . . . Written for Use of Students in Spotiswood's Colledge of Law, and now Publish'd for the Common Good* (1708); idem, *The Form of Process, before the Lords of Council and Session . . . Written for the Use of the Students in Spotswood's College of Law* (1711); *The Institutions of the Law of Scotland. By Sir George Mackenzie of Rosehaugh, Advocate to K. Cha. II. and to K. Ja. VII. The Sixth Edition, Revised, Corrected and Augmented* (1723). See Cairns (n. 809), 143–4.

[886] See e.g. Fountainhall (n. 780), 153–63, 283–99; *A Catalogue of Valuable Books in Several languages and faculties, . . . being the library which belong'd to Sir Alexander Seaton of Pitmedden* (1719), copy in NLS, MS 3802; NLS, MS 3283 (Library of Charles Areskine); *A Catalogue of Curious and Valuable Books, being the Library of Mr John Spotiswood of that Ilk Advocate, lately deceas'd* (1728); *A Catalogue of Curious and Valuable Books; Being chiefly the Library of the Right Hon. Duncan Forbes of Culloden, Esq; late Lord President of the Session* (1748); *A Catalogue of Curious and Valuable Books, Being Chiefly the Library of the late Mr Alexander Bane Professor of Scots Law in the University of Edinburgh* (1749).

claim that the calling of advocate was based on Roman law.[887] The education of the bar facilitated and the increasing development of written pleadings encouraged the statement of Scots law with an extensive civilian interpretative gloss.

On the other hand, Scots lawyers' concern with English law inevitably intensified after 1707: the second edition of Forbes's *Bills of Exchange* added in references to English law and statutes; his unpublished 'Great Body' of the Scots law included an account of the relevant English law after his discussion of a subject area of the Scots.[888] The Advocates' Library initially had very few English law books (four in 1683; thirty-four in 1692); after the Copyright Act of 1709, the right to demand copies of works printed in England facilitated collection of materials on English law.[889] Acceptability of arguments from the law of nations opened the possibility of reliance on arguments from English law alongside more traditional sources.

VII. UNION, INTEGRATION, AND REFORM, 1716–1832

1. From patronage to party, 1707 to 1832

(a) New administrative structures

Events immediately after the Union left Scotland with a lack of central administration. The only permanent government officers of any significance were the Lord Advocate and the Solicitor-General. Scottish administration had to be fitted into the essentially English structures of the Lords of the Treasury and the Secretaries of State for the Northern and Southern Departments. Thus, from 1724 to 1754, Scottish business was formally under the authority of the Duke of Newcastle, Secretary for the Southern Department until 1748, thereafter for the Northern Department. Scottish affairs then remained under the authority of the Secretary of State for the Northern Department until the formation of the Home Office in 1782. For most of the years from 1708 to 1725 there had been a third Secretary, to deal with Scottish matters. This office was briefly revived between 1742 and 1746, but thereafter was allowed to lapse.[890]

---

[887] Fountainhall (n. 719), vol. 1, 322; Mackenzie, *Oratio Inauguralis* (1989 edn.) (n. 803), 65.
[888] William Forbes, *A Methodical Treatise Concerning Bills of Exchange . . . According to the Analogy of the Law of Scotland: With Incident Comparative Views* (1718); Glasgow University Library, MSS Gen. 1246–52. [889] See Cairns (n. 865), 243–5; 8 Anne (c. 21).
[890] For a most useful account of the structures of Hanoverian government in Scotland, see Alexander Murdoch, *'The People Above': Politics and Administration in Mid-Eighteenth-Century Scotland* (1980), 1–27.

(b) The politics of patronage

The Jacobite Rebellion of 1715 profoundly affected Scottish politics and essentially destroyed Toryism as an effective force.[891] Jacobitism, often linked to episcopalianism, remained, however, important in parts of Scotland.[892] After 1716, however, Scottish politics was driven by the intensification of an existing struggle between the ducal houses of Montrose and Argyll, whose heads were essentially Whig magnates. Montrose (with the Duke of Roxburghe) was the head of the Squadrone Volante, which, after the Union, tended to turn into an alliance of related families, linked by their opposition to the rise and advancement of John, second Duke of Argyll, and his brother Archibald, Earl of Ilay (who succeeded to his brother's dukedom in 1743). The Squadrone and the Argathelians (as the faction led by Argyll and Ilay was known) competed for control over patronage in Scotland, which English ministers, especially when there was no Scottish Secretary, were unable to exercise effectively. After 1725, Ilay, in alliance with Sir Robert Walpole, became the most important Scottish politician. His close associate, Andrew Fletcher of Saltoun, Lord of Session as Lord Milton and Lord Justice-Clerk, operated as his main agent in Edinburgh, feeding him information and responding to his concerns. Broadly put, Ilay's aim was to ensure the return of as many as possible Scottish elected peers and Members of Parliament loyal to the administration. In return for this and, indeed, as a necessary means to achieve it, he was given a large measure of control over Scottish patronage. Patronage created a complex system of interdependency, in which it was in the interests of patrons to keep their clients happy and vice versa. Furthermore, given the smallness of the electorate, politics was an intimate matter, in which Members of Parliament had to be responsive to those they represented.[893] Indeed, Ilay was a skilful and sensitive dispenser of patronage who had an eye for quality; his influence on university patronage shows this clearly.[894]

Ilay's dominance wobbled slightly in the early 1740s because of the fall of Walpole, which allowed, for a short time, the appointment of a Squadrone

---

[891] See David Hayton, 'Traces of Party Politics in Early Eighteenth-Century Scottish Elections', in Jones (n. 142), 74–99.

[892] On Jacobitism, see e.g. Lenman (n. 706), 155–230; *idem*, 'The Scottish Episcopal Clergy and the Ideology of Jacobitism', in Eveline Cruickshanks (ed.), *Ideology and Conspiracy: Aspects of Jacobitism, 1689–1759* (1982), 36–48; A. I. Macinnes, 'Scottish Jacobitism: In Search of a Movement', in Devine/Young (n. 693), 70–89; *idem*, *Clanship, Commerce, and the House of Stewart, 1603–1788* (1996).

[893] See J. S. Shaw, *The Political History of Eighteenth-Century Scotland* (1999), 53–71; *idem*, *The Management of Scottish Society, 1707–1764: Power, Nobles, Lawyers, Edinburgh Agents and English Influences* (1983), 86–117. A classic on this now is J. M. Simpson, 'Who Steered the Gravy Train, 1707–1766?', in N. T. Phillipson and Rosalind Mitchison (eds.), *Scotland in the Age of Improvement: Essays in Scottish History in the Eighteenth Century* (1970), 47–72.

[894] A point made convincingly by R. L. Emerson, *Professors, Patronage and Politics: The Aberdeen Universities in the Eighteenth Century* (1992), 1–9.

Secretary for Scotland.[895] Nonetheless, his careful exercise of power brought a basic stability to what remained a distinctively Scottish politics, as the exercise of patronage by a great magnate prevented Scotland's absorption into a more general British system and preserved the management of Scottish affairs by the Scottish political classes, other than when events, such as the Rebellion of 1745, menaced the British state as a whole. It is a mistake to consider Ilay as a London-based politician, out-of-touch with Scottish concerns. His education at the University of Glasgow and legal studies in the Netherlands meant he shared the intellectual background of the lesser landowning class who operated the Scottish legal system.[896] He took seriously his duties as a representative peer in Scottish appeals to the Lords; he also ensured his nephews, Lord Bute and James Stuart Mackenzie, studied law in the Netherlands to equip them to carry out this important role.[897] Ilay had been appointed Lord Justice-General in 1710 and, when in Edinburgh, he presided on the Justiciary Court Bench.[898] He was also one of the last Extraordinary Lords of Session and can be traced sitting on the Court of Session bench in the 1750s.[899]

Ilay died in 1761. George III (1760–1820) attempted to play a more active role in politics than either George I or George II (1727–60) had chosen to do. He appointed his favourite, Lord Bute, as Secretary of State in 1761 and First Lord of the Treasury in 1762. It looked as if Bute might take over his uncle, Ilay's, Scottish political machine and he employed his brother, James Stuart Mackenzie, to deal with Scottish affairs.[900] Unpopular as the king's friend and attacked by the egregious John Wilkes, Bute resigned in 1763. His departure from power created once more a political problem in Scotland, with no one in secure management of Scottish business.[901] In fact, the English ministers were largely able to ignore Scotland as most Scots politicians supported the ministry. The Secretary for the Northern Department continued to have formal authority, but none ever got to grips with Scottish business. Legal appointments tended to be made on the advice of Lord Mansfield, the Scottish Chief Justice of England; other patronage was dealt with in a variety of shifting ways.[902]

---

[895] Murdoch (n. 890), 31–2, 34–51; Ferguson (n. 657), 144–6.
[896] J. W. Cairns, 'William Crosse, Regius Professor of Civil Law in the University of Glasgow, 1746–1749: A Failure of Enlightened Patronage', (1993) 12 *History of Universities* 159–96 at 161.
[897] Shaw, *Political History* (n. 893), 95–6; Cairns, (1993) 12 *History of Universities* 161.
[898] NAS, JC 3/29, 145 (20 Nov. 1752).
[899] NAS, CS 1/13, fos. 142ʳ., 143ᵛ., and 185 (20 July, 24 July, Aug. 1753).
[900] See Alexander Murdoch, 'Lord Bute, James Stuart Mackenzie and the Government of Scotland', in K. W. Schweizer (ed.), *Lord Bute: Essays in Re-interpretation* (1988), 117–46. On one aspect of Bute and patronage, see R. L. Emerson, 'Lord Bute and the Scottish Universities, 1760–1792', in K. W. Schweizer (ed.), *Lord Bute: Essays in Re-interpretation* (1988), 147–79.
[901] Shaw, *Management* (n. 893), 180–6; Murdoch, (n. 890), 104–23.
[902] See Murdoch (n. 890), 124–8; Michael Fry, *The Dundas Despotism* (1992), 31–5.

(c) The 'Dundas Despotism'

This presented an opportunity for Henry Dundas, the younger son of Lord President Dundas. Solicitor-General, then Lord Advocate, and finally MP from 1774 to 1802 when he was ennobled as Viscount Melville, Dundas made himself the most powerful politician in Scotland, filling the void left by the collapse of the system of Ilay and Milton. By the 1780s, he was political manager for Scotland, a role consolidated by his long alliance with William Pitt the younger. Dundas used the authority he acquired to carve out a *British* political career: Treasurer of the Navy, Lord of Trade, Commissioner and President of the Board of Control, Home Secretary, and First Lord of the Admiralty.[903]

Dundas's long period of power—the 'Dundas Despotism'—raised the ire of individuals, such as Henry Cockburn, when a form of party politics revived in Scotland towards the end of the eighteenth century. Dundas was associated with the suppression of radical agitation that developed in the 1790s, while managing the long hard war with Revolutionary France. In 1802, his grip on the Scottish constituencies loosened, though in 1804 he became First Lord of the Admiralty in Pitt's new administration. His enemies thereafter found the opportunity to bring him down over the financial irregularities of the Navy's Paymaster General. Dundas was impeached; though acquitted in 1806, his long dominance was ended. His son Robert inherited his role as political manager, but never acquired his father's power and authority. Pitt died in 1806 and the misleadingly named 'Ministry of all the Talents' took over with a reforming agenda, which included Scottish legal institutions. Change was coming; the long period of leaving Scotland to be self-regulating was over.[904]

(d) The Whigs and reform

In 1802, the *Edinburgh Review* had been established by a group of disgruntled young Whigs—Francis Jeffrey, Francis Horner, Henry Brougham, and Sidney Smith. Its phenomenal success helped promote the cause of moderate reform, while translating some of the ideas of the late Enlightenment in Scotland into a form suitable for the modern age.[905] The peace with France that finally came in 1815 brought with it a depressed economy; once more hardship provoked protest and desire for reform. Scotland was no longer a

---

[903] Fry (n. 902), *passim*; John Dwyer and Alexander Murdoch, 'Paradigms and Politics: Manners, Morals and the Rise of Henry Dundas, 1770–1784', in Dwyer/Mason/Murdoch (n. 595), 210–48; D. J. Brown, '"Nothing but Strugalls and Corruption": The Commons' Elections for Scotland in 1774', in Jones (n. 409), 100–19.

[904] Ferguson (n. 657), 248–70; Fry (n. 902), 155–239; Alan Wharum, *The Treason Trials, 1794* (1992), 47–67, 137–42.

[905] See e.g. Biancamaria Fontana, *Rethinking the Politics of Commercial Society: The Edinburgh Review, 1802–1832* (1985).

near-exclusively agricultural country. Textiles, coal, and iron had brought a measure of urbanization and industrialization, stimulated by the economic growth and technological innovation of the later eighteenth century. A large urban working population had developed to be as badly affected by the sharp economic downturn as that still on the land. Fears of disorder brought trials for sedition in 1817 and for treason in 1820.[906]

The younger Whigs—originally associated with the *Edinburgh Review*—were gaining more authority in Scotland and a liberal press in favour of reform (notably *The Scotsman* founded in 1817) was exercising an increasing influence. Heightened political sensibilities were motivating recognition of the need and also the desire for change in political and other structures.[907] A new breed of Tory politicians such as George Canning and Robert Peel exercised influence within the party. Scottish politics were increasingly—if never completely—integrated in this more clearly emerging two-party system. By 1830 and the coming of the Whigs to power, with Francis Jeffrey as Lord Advocate and Cockburn as Solicitor-General, the *ancien régime* of management was over in Scotland.[908]

The Reform Act of 1832 greatly extended the franchise. After the Union of 1707, most of the burghs had been organized into groupings to return their members. The electorate had remained the Town Councils. The electorate in the counties continued tiny.[909] After 1832, the number of constituencies was increased with a more rational organization, especially of the burghs; there was a direct franchise in the towns for property-holders of a yearly value of £10; county electors were proprietors of heritable subjects, liferenters, and tenants of the annual value of £10.[910] The total electorate jumped from around 4,500 to 65,000; before 1832 only one in 125 adult males could vote, after the act, one in eight had the franchise.[911] Scottish politics still continued distinctive. The Reform Act for England and Wales had increased representation there from one in eight to one in five.[912] The lack of secret ballots meant that tenants in country districts were under pressure to vote as their landlords wished, while poor drafting of the bill still left considerable scope for electoral manipulation.[913] Brash has nonetheless emphasized the significance of the widening of the franchise and concluded that after 1832 'the county electors ... formed a not altogether unrepresentative and varied cross-section of adult male occupations in Scotland'.[914]

---

[906] Ferguson (n. 657), 266–84.
[907] See e.g. Joanne Shattock, *Politics and Reviewers: The Edinburgh and the Quarterly in the Early Victorian Age* (1989).   [908] Ferguson (n. 657), 284–90; Fry (n. 902), 345–84.
[909] William Ferguson, 'The Electoral System in the Scottish Counties before 1832', in Sellar (n. 6), 261–94.   [910] Scottish Reform Act, 2 and 3 Will IV (c. 65).
[911] For the figures, see Ferguson (n. 657), 290; Lynch (n. 4), 391.
[912] Lynch (n. 4), 391; 2 and 3 Will IV (c. 45).   [913] Ferguson (n. 909), 293–4.
[914] See Ferguson (n. 657), 289–90; J. I Brash, 'The New Scottish County Electors in 1832: An Occupational Analysis', in Jones (n. 409), 120–39 at 136.

2. Reform and continuity in the institutions of the common law

(a) Legislative neglect and pressures for reform

The most obvious feature of much of the eighteenth century was relative legislative neglect of Scottish affairs, so that most of the first half-century of the Union was marked by continuity in Scottish legal institutions. Some minor changes can be noted. The Lords of Session regularly tried to streamline litigation before them by issuing Acts of Sederunt to promote greater efficiency in the operation of the existing, increasingly written, process.[915] The crisis over the nomination of Patrick Haldane as a senator led to a minor reform of the mode of appointment and the abolition of the Extraordinary Lords.[916] The authority of justices of the peace was increased, but the legislation they and their constables were expected to enforce was primarily regulatory and administrative.[917] Anxieties about Jacobitism led to the act 'for more effectual disarming the Highlands', which, as well as the specific provisions indicated by its title, increased the sums that could be set for bail under the act of 1701. To make criminal prosecution more effective, the freeholders at the head courts of the shire or stewartry were empowered to make an assessment of the area to provide sums for apprehending, detaining, and prosecuting criminals.[918] These were all relatively superficial changes; the basic architecture of Scottish legal institutions continued intact.

The most important exception to this picture of little change came in 1747 with the abolition of heritable jurisdictions and ward holding, which were seen as reflecting an archaic society that had facilitated the Jacobite rebellion of 1745.[919] Their abolition was part of a more general programme of legislation relating to Highland Dress, disarming the Highlands, and treason.[920] Pressure for the change came from London rather than Edinburgh, with the Lord Chancellor, Lord Hardwicke, as main mover.[921] There was some resistance to this reform in Scotland, partly because of the abolition of useful local courts, and partly because of anxiety over whether the change breached the Treaty of Union.[922]

---

[915] See e.g. the Act of Sederunt 'to restrain reclaiming bills', AS, I, 273 (26 Nov. 1718), that 'anent inrolling Bills and Answers, Reports and Hearings, in Presence', AS, I, 325–7 (13 July 1739). See also, AS, I, 316 (29 June 1738) relating to the 'boxing' of informations when cases were taken to report.

[916] Court of Session Act, 10 Geo I (c. 19). See J. M. Pinkerton (ed.), *The Minute Book of the Faculty of Advocates. Volume 2, 1713–1750*, Stair Society, vol. 32 (1980), 41 (23 Dec. 1721); 42–3 (26 Dec. 1721). See e.g. Lord Cooper of Culross, 'The Central Courts after 1532', in Paton (n. 56), 341–9 at 342. Political rivalry seems to have been at the bottom of this affair. In 1734, Lords of Session and Barons of Exchequer became ineligible for election to the House of Commons: 7 Geo II (c. 16), s. 4.

[917] See e.g. 5 Geo I (c. 30) (1719); 12 Geo I (c. 34) (1725); 13 Geo I (c. 26).

[918] 11 Geo I (c. 26) s. 12.   [919] See Lenman (n. 706), 277–80; Kidd (n. 8), 150–60.

[920] See e.g. 19 Geo II (cc. 9), 25, 39; 20 Geo II (cc. 30), 46, 51; 21 Geo II (cc. 19), 34.

[921] Lenman (n. 706), 278–9.

[922] There was an extensive pamphlet debate, especially on the abolition of ward holding.

With reform in mind, towards the end of 1746, the House of Lords ordered the Lords of Session to draft a bill for the abolition of heritable jurisdictions and to provide a list of the regalities. The Lords of Session declined to draft a bill and explained that it was not possible to furnish a definitive list of regalities. They appear, however, to have seized the parliamentary interest in Scotland as an opportunity to reform aspects of criminal procedure, suggesting that circuits be held twice a year and commenting that the practice of reducing all parole evidence to writing in criminal trials was a waste of time. They also stressed that local courts were useful, since circuits only dealt with crime, while also arguing that, though barons should probably lose their higher criminal jurisdiction, it would be useful if they retained their civil and a minor criminal jurisdiction.[923]

(b) Heritable jurisdictions and the criminal courts

The Heritable Jurisdictions (Scotland) Act was a complex statute. Its main provisions abolished all heritable sheriffships, stewartries, baillieries, and constabularies, vesting their jurisdictions in the Session, Justiciary Court, circuits, and sheriff and stewartry courts that would have possessed them. Barons lost their franchise jurisdiction to try serious crimes, but could deal with their tenants, minor crimes, and civil suits to the value of 40 shillings. Henceforth, the Crown would nominate sheriffs depute and stewarts depute for the counties; they had to be advocates of at least three years' standing, reside for at least four months in their sheriffdom or stewartry, and could appoint substitutes. There was a transitional provision on their tenure.[924]

Following the recommendations of the Lords, the act also overhauled the criminal courts. There were to be two circuits each year, with the western one covering Argyll, since the hereditary justiciarship of Argyll was abolished. The circuits were granted jurisdiction to hear appeals from sheriff courts, burgh courts, and baron courts in matters not inferring loss of life or demembration and civil matters below £12. The king was granted the authority in his Privy Council to alter the circuits. The requirement in the act of 1695 that the advocates give in written informations after the debate on the relevancy of the libel was repealed; instead, the accused was to give advance notice of his objections and defences, while the court would pronounce on the relevancy immediately after debate *viva voce*, though the judges could still ask for written informations on points of difficulty. The Lords' request that evidence no longer be reduced to writing was dealt with in an act the follow-

---

[923] AS, I, 390–1 (16 Dec. 1746), 392–7 (9 Jan. 1747).

[924] The Heritable Jurisdictions (Scotland) Act 1747, 20 Geo II (c. 43). On the tenure of the sheriffs depute, see 28 Geo II (c. 7). The residence rules were later varied in some instances: 21 Geo II (c. 19), s. 12; 3 Geo IV (c. 49) (1822). For an insightful account of the 1747 act with a different focus, see Lindsay Farmer, *Criminal Law, Tradition and Legal Order: Crime and the Genius of Scots Law, 1747 to the Present* (1997), 60–6.

Historical Introduction 149

ing year, but limited only to crimes 'not inferring the punishment of death or demembration'. Such parole evidence was to be presented *viva voce* to the jury and witnesses could be questioned by the advocates and the panel, while the judges were to sum up the evidence before the jury was enclosed.[925] The provision was not extended to all crimes until 1783.[926]

The impact of these reforms was profound. Heritable jurisdictions were property rights and compensation had to be paid. Assessment of the existence of these jurisdictions was a legal problem, which, along with their valuation, was dealt with by the Court of Session in an expedited process.[927] Secondly, direct Crown patronage over the legal system greatly increased, while that of the landowners diminished. Thirdly, revitalization of the office of sheriff kept justices of the peace as minor figures in the Scottish legal system, as the sheriffs depute and their substitutes became key figures, central to the functioning of the Scottish legal system.

(c) *Criticism of the Session*

The abolition of heritable jurisdictions and military tenures promoted a considerable pamphlet literature, which engaged with the history of jurisdiction and tenures. Old topics such as the authority of *Regiam* and the 'auld lawes' fed into other discussions such as on the introduction of feudalism. Here a seminal text was Henry Home, Lord Kames's *Essays upon Several Subjects Concerning British Antiquities* of 1747.[928] In the year that the Court of Session decided the claims over heritable jurisdictions, Adam Smith, under Kames's patronage, commenced a series of well-attended private lectures in Edinburgh on rhetoric, the history of philosophy, and law, the content of which is unknown, but must have included an early version of his historical account of the development of law and government.[929] Prominent among those attending were law students and young lawyers.[930] Smith argued that justice was best served through the development of law by the courts: this put

---

[925] 21 Geo II (c. 19), s. 7.

[926] 23 Geo III (c. 45), ss. 3–5. This still preserved the option of reduction of testimony to writing, in crimes inferring 'the punishment of death or demembration ... according to the present practice'; even so, counsel and the panel or prisoner were to have the right to 'interrogate the witnesses' and the judge was to sum up the evidence before the jury was enclosed.

[927] See AS, I, 401–3 (15 Dec. 1747). Ibid. 418–31 contains the valuation of the heritable jurisdictions. See also Lenman (n. 706), 279–80.

[928] [Henry Home, Lord Kames], *Essays upon Several Subjects Concerning British Antiquities ... Composed anno M.DCC.XLV.* (1747); David Dalrymple, Lord Hailes, *An Examination of Some of the Arguments for the High Antiquity of Regiam Majestatem and an Inquiry into the Authenticity of Leges Malcolmi* (1769). See Kidd (n. 8), 148–50; MacQueen, (1995) 74 *Scot Hist Rev* 20–3. On Kames, see I. S. Ross, *Lord Kames and the Scotland of his Day* (1972); W. C. Lehmann, *Lord Kames and the Scottish Enlightenment: A Study in National Character and in the History of Ideas* (1971). [929] I. S. Ross, *The Life of Adam Smith* (1995), 84–7, 97–108.

[930] See the remarks of Lord President Dundas, well calculated to encourage intending advocates to attend: Pinkerton (n. 916), 225 (3 Nov. 1748).

a premium on well-structured courts.[931] Other Scots expressed similar ideas.[932]

The circulation of such views fed into debates later in the century over reform of the Court of Session, after the Lords started to accumulate a significant backlog of business, which critics attributed to the form of process and structure of the court.[933] Critics argued that litigants were never compelled to focus carefully on the real issues, so that cases were often amended, with their nature changing as they progressed. Moreover, there was tremendous scope for review of interlocutors and there could be two reclaiming motions on each interlocutor. The development of written process meant that complex cases could develop into a vast bulk of paper. In the Inner House cases were decided on the plurality of the votes of the judges; the Lords would vote one way or another for a variety of reasons, so that the value of decisions as precedents was not always clear.[934] The Lords responded to criticisms;[935] they appear, however, to have been unwilling to allow litigants to be penalized by the failure of their agents or advocates to conform to tighter requirements.[936]

In 1785, Henry Dundas proposed reducing the number of judges. The aims were twofold. Reduction of the number of judges in the Inner House was thought likely to improve judicial quality and promote better discussion of the law and greater speed; it would also release funds to increase judicial salaries. Attacked on a variety of grounds, including breach of the Treaty of Union, this proposal was dropped.[937] In 1787, the Lords themselves made another attempt to streamline process in 1787.[938] Further proposals for reform emerged. John Swinton, an experienced advocate and recently appointed Senator, proposed in 1787 the splitting of the Inner House into two chambers and the introduction of civil jury trial—he was not alone in seeing advantages both practical and ideological in the latter. Historical researches had demonstrated the earlier presence of civil 'juries' in Scotland;

---

[931] For a full discussion of this aspect of Smith's legal theory, see J. W. Cairns, 'Adam Smith and the Role of the Courts in Securing Justice and liberty', in R. P. Malloy and Jerry Evensky (eds.), *Adam Smith and the Philosophy of Law and Economics* (1994), 31–61.

[932] See David Lieberman, *The Province of Legislation Determined: Legal Theory in Eighteenth-Century Britain* (1989), 144–75.

[933] See N. T. Phillipson, *The Scottish Whigs and the Reform of the Court of Session, 1785–1830*, Stair Society, vol. 37 (1990), 46–7.

[934] See Cairns (n. 865), 260–2; Phillipson (n. 933), 42–61.

[935] See AS, I, 624–7 (11 Aug. 1787); AS, II, 59–62 (11 Mar. 1800).

[936] See Phillipson (n. 933), 78–9.

[937] Ibid. 62–77. The judges' salaries were increased the next year: 26 Geo III (c. 46).

[938] AS, I, 624–7 (11 Aug. 1787); see generally, James Watson, *New Form of Process before the Court of Session and Commission of Teinds with a General Account of the College of Justice* (1791), which takes into account the reform.

adopting trial by jury could thus be presented as a return to earlier Scottish practice as a means of perfecting the Union.[939]

Feeding these desires to improve the functioning of the Session was the popularity of appeals to the House of Lords.[940] Ilay Campbell, Lord President, 1787–1808, thought these were prompted by litigants' uncertainty as to how decisions were reached in the Session, while the unclear nature of Scottish process could lead to a reversal by the Lords.[941] There can be little doubt, however, that the fact that an appeal still stopped execution of the sentence of the Session encouraged appeals, since the House of Lords was scarcely a model of expeditious procedure. Some also saw the large number of appeals as being encouraged by that delay and the hope of having a decision 'by the principles of the law of England'.[942]

3. The creation of the modern court system

(a) The division of the Session

In 1805, reform once more was proposed. Featuring the division of the court into two, civil jury trial, and an intermediate appeal court, it reveals the ideas with which all further proposals tended to play.[943] While the death of Pitt ended this proposal, the new self-consciously reforming ministry brought forward its own proposals in 1807. The Session was to be split into three chambers with concurrent jurisdictions, while litigants were to be able in most cases to opt for a jury trial modelled on English procedure. There was also to be a permanent Court of Appeal. A Whiggish belief in the superiority of the English court system and civil jury trial informed the whole scheme. The ministry fell before the bill was enacted.[944]

The new Tory ministry was also persuaded of the need for reform. It came in two stages. In 1808, the Court was split into two divisions, each with the full powers of the Court. There were to be no appeals to the House of Lords on interlocutory judgments, except with the leave of the Division or in the case of a difference among the judges. The interlocutors or decrees of Lords Ordinary could only be appealed to the House of Lords if the judges of the Division had already reviewed them, while the Divisions could make interim

---

[939] John Swinton, *Considerations Concerning a Proposal for Dividing the Court of Session into Two Classes or Chambers; and for limiting Litigation in Small Causes; and for the Revival of Jury Trial in Certain Civil Actions* (1789). See Phillipson (n. 933), 79–84. See Kidd (n. 8), 120–8.

[940] Between 1794 and 1807, 419 of the 501 appeals to the Lords came from Scotland: Phillipson (n. 933), 85.   [941] See Phillipson (n. 933), 86.

[942] See Walter Scott, 'View of the Changes Proposed and Adopted in the Administration of Justice in Scotland', (1810) 1, pt. 2 *The Edinburgh Annual Register for 1808*, 342–71, repr. in *Sir Walter Scott's Annual Register* (ed. by Kenneth Curry, 1977), 170–211 at 199.

[943] Phillipson (n. 933), 86–8.

[944] Ibid. 88–95. See also A. J. MacLean, 'Jeremy Bentham and the Scottish Legal System', [1979] *JR* 21–44.

orders of possession or execution, thus removing one of the incentives of an appeal. The Lord Justice-Clerk became president of the Second Division.[945]

The Court of Session Act also granted power to appoint a Commission to 'inquire into the Forms of Process in the Court of Session'. Its particular tasks included investigation of introduction of jury trial, of the possibility of more pleading *viva voce*, of creation of permanent Lords Ordinary, and of limitation of the powers of the Ordinaries to review their own interlocutors.[946] Such conclusions as the Commissioners came to resulted in an Act of Sederunt 'anent the Form of Process in the Inner and Outer House' and an Act of Parliament abridging and reforming the mode of extracting the decrees of the Court of Session and, most importantly, creating the permanent Outer House, given its final form in 1813.[947]

(b) The Jury Court

In December 1814, a bill was introduced in Parliament to establish jury trial. It finally provided for the Court of Session to send issues for decision by a jury. A separate Jury Court was to be established for seven years, headed by a Lord Chief Commissioner with two Commissioners.[948] The first Chief Commissioner was William Adam, a Scots member of the English bar. Adam's talents undoubtedly helped this innovation to success. By 1819, the Jury Court was judged to have been successful and was made permanent by a statute that also required the Lord Ordinary to send to the Jury Court any case raised in the Outer House concerning 'injuries to the person, whether real or verbal, as assault or battery, libel or defamation, or on account of any injury to moveables, or to lands, where the title is not in question, or on account of breach of promise of marriage, seduction, or adultery, or any action founded on delinquency or quasi delinquency of any kind, where the conclusion shall be for damages and expences only'.[949]

(c) Outer House, Inner House, and reformed procedure

The number of Scottish appeals to the Lords remained such that another Commission was established in 1823 to investigate procedure before the

---

[945] Court of Session Act 1808, 48 Geo III (c. 151); AS, III, 33–6 (9 July, 20 Oct., 11 Nov. 1808); Phillipson (n. 933), 113.

[946] Court of Session Act 1808, 48 Geo III (c. 151), s. 22; Phillipson (n. 933), 113–26.

[947] AS, III, 49–50 (7 Feb. 1810); Court of Session Act 1810, 50 Geo III (c. 112); Court of Session Act 1813, 53 Geo III (c. 64); AS, IV, 45–8 (8 June 1813), 49 (10 June 1813), 55–8 (15 Jan. 1814). The 1813 statute dealt with the fact that the junior existing Lords Ordinary in 1810 could only permanently sit in the Outer House if they consented to do so; by 1813, there were enough new Lords appointed to sit as permanent Ordinaries in the Outer House, whose consent was not required.

[948] Jury Trials (Scotland) Act 1815, 55 Geo III (c. 42). On the background to the act, see William Adam, *A Practical Treatise and Observations on Trial by Jury in Civil Causes, As now Incorporated with the Jurisdiction of the Court of Session* (1836), appendix, 92–104; Phillipson (n. 933), 127–36.

[949] Jury Trials (Scotland) Act 1819, 59 Geo III (c. 35). See Phillipson (n. 933), 140.

Session.[950] The Commission agreed that the permanent Outer House had been a success and considered there should be more permanent Lords Ordinary. What was necessary therefore was to ensure the more efficient conduct of business. The legislation that emerged from these debates provided in ordinary actions for a summons and defences that set out clearly what was at issue between the parties in matters of both fact and law. There was to be no judgement on the merits of the case until a record with its condescendences and pleas in law had been made up, adjusted, and closed. The Ordinary could then decide the cause on its merits or report it to the Inner House. Procedures were to be expeditious, disciplined, and simple. Neither the Ordinaries nor the Inner House could be asked to reconsider their decisions. The list of causes that had to be sent to the Jury Court from the Court of Session or the Admiralty Court was very greatly expanded to cover the main areas of commercial law. In adopting the relevant Acts of Sederunt, the Lords recognized the significance of the changes and evinced a determination not only to enforce strictly the new forms of process but also to ensure that pleading became primarily oral.[951]

(d) *Rationalization and amalgamation of jurisdictions*

The 1820s saw important and regular reform of the Scottish court system so that, by 1830, the basic architecture and much of the detail of the modern system existed. Central to this was the progressive amalgamation of the various jurisdictions. In 1823, the jurisdiction of the inferior commissaries was amalgamated into that of the local sheriffdom, although the Commissaries of Edinburgh retained their traditional jurisdiction over the sheriffdoms of Edinburgh, Haddington, and Linlithgow, while losing their power of review of the lower commissaries and coming under the supervision of the Session.[952] By a major reforming act in 1830, the jurisdiction of the Commissaries of Edinburgh was restricted to that possessed by 'sheriffs being commissaries in other sheriffdoms'. This meant that consistorial actions had to be brought before the Court of Session, although actions of aliment could be taken before any sheriff. Moreover, Linlithgow and Haddington were now to form their own commissariat, with the sheriff depute as commissary.[953] The same act abolished the separate Jury Court and merged its jurisdiction

---

[950] 4 Geo IV (c. 85) (1823); W. M. Gordon, 'George Joseph Bell—Law Commissioner', in A. J. Gamble (ed.), *Obligations in Context: Essays on Honour of Professor D. M. Walker* (Edinburgh, 1990), 79–99; Phillipson (n. 933), 142.

[951] Court of Session Act 1825, 6 Geo IV (c. 120); AS, V, 97–103.

[952] Commissary Courts (Scotland) Act 1823, 4 Geo IV (c. 97). See also Confirmation of Executors (Scotland) Act 1823, 4 Geo IV (c. 98).

[953] Court of Session Act 1830, 11 Geo IV and 1 Will IV (c. 69), ss. 30–40.

with that of the Session.[954] The admiralty jurisdictions were merged with the local sheriff court and the Court of Session.[955]

A similar process of rationalization and reform affected the criminal courts. In 1814, it became unnecessary for jury verdicts to be in writing.[956] The selection of those eligible for jury service was changed in 1825, by the introduction of a 'General Jury Book', listing those who met certain formal criteria.[957] In 1828 came major reform. The system of circuit courts was extended. The High Court of Justiciary was now to have a cumulative criminal jurisdiction with that of the Admiralty Court. The Admiralty Court and the sheriff courts could conduct jury trials *viva voce*, without reducing the evidence to writing: the same practice was to be observed in trials without juries, the sheriff keeping a note of the evidence. There was a simple summary process for minor offences.[958] In 1830, further fine-tuning attempted to speed procedure.[959]

(e) *The sheriff court*

The effect of the reforms in the civil and criminal courts was to raise the significance of the sheriff courts and the sheriffs substitute who normally presided in them. From 1811, after a substantial rise in the salaries of the substitutes (payment of which had been taken over by the Crown), appointment of substitutes by the sheriffs depute had to be approved by two out of the Lord President, Lord Justice-Clerk, and Chief Baron, the aim being to ensure only men with legal qualifications should be chosen.[960] In 1825, statute provided that no one could be a sheriff substitute unless he were 'an advocate of three years standing at the least, or a clerk to his Majesty's Signet or a solicitor before the supreme courts in Scotland or a procurator before a sheriff court ... who shall have been admitted ... for at least three years'. The commission appointing him had to have an attached certificate signed by the Lord President and the Lord Justice-Clerk.[961]

(f) *Local courts and central courts*

The profound transformation in the structure and procedure of the Scottish courts in the third decade of the nineteenth century gave a new articulation

---

[954] Court of Session Act 1830, 11 Geo IV and 1 Will IV (c. 69), ss. 1–16 See the discussion in Phillipson (n. 933), 158–64.
[955] Court of Session Act 1830, 11 Geo IV and 1 Will IV (c. 69), ss. 21–9. In 1825, the prize jurisdiction had been transferred to the English Court of Admiralty: Court of Session Act, 6 Geo IV (c. 120), s. 57.   [956] Justiciary Courts (Scotland) Act, 54 Geo III (c. 67).
[957] Jurors (Scotland) Act 1825, 6 Geo IV (c. 22).
[958] Circuit Courts (Scotland) Act 1828, 9 Geo IV (c. 29).
[959] Criminal Law (Scotland) Act, 11 Geo IV and 1 Will IV (c. 37).
[960] Whetstone (n. 724), 9–11.
[961] Sheriff Courts (Scotland) Act 1825, 6 Geo IV (c. 23), s. 9. Circuit Courts (Scotland) Act 1828, 9 Geo IV (c. 29), s. 22 made this apply only to those paid from the civil list.

to the links between local and central courts. Much of this was driven by a desire to reduce costs through speedier and more effective process. One aim—that of reducing the number of Scottish appeals to the House of Lords—was not easily achieved: they still constituted around 60 per cent of the House's judicial work.[962] The increasing emphasis on legal professionals in the system is reflected not only in the new provisions on the appointment of sheriffs substitute, but also in the enactment in 1830 that, on the death of the current Lord Justice-General, the office should devolve on the Lord President of the Court of Session.[963]

4. The legal profession and legal education

(a) The growth of the legal profession

In 1714, there were around 200 advocates, of whom some 170 were in practice.[964] Until the mid-1790s, this remained fairly constant. Following three decades of rapid growth, there were around 450 advocates in 1832. In 1731, there were slightly over 100 Writers to the Signet; in 1795 there were 223, while, by 1830, there were over 650.[965] There was a similarly explosive growth among other groups of lawyers, reflecting population growth and expansion of business opportunities, following the start of industrialization.[966]

(b) Tensions in the Faculty of Advocates

Such expansion created a much less homogeneous legal profession. In the first quarter of the eighteenth century, the advocates continued to be largely drawn from the lesser landed classes of Scotland; in the first quarter of the nineteenth, the great increase in numbers had come from the admission of men from non-landed backgrounds.[967] The Faculty responded to this change by trying to develop mechanisms to ensure the suitability of intrants, as the broader social basis from which the Faculty was increasingly drawn led to anxieties over ethics and behaviour.[968] These strains were particularly acute from the 1790s onwards as the Faculty became a much more divided and disputatious body. In part this was due to political differences; moreover, the continuing reforms of the courts from 1808 onwards must have been

---

[962] See Phillipson (n. 933), 168.
[963] Court of Session Act 1830, 11 Geo IV and 1 Will IV (c. 69), s. 18.
[964] Forbes (n. 607), vii.   [965] Phillipson (n. 933), 9–10.
[966] See e.g. Olive and Sydney Checkland, *Industry and Ethos: Scotland 1832–1914* (1984), 12–13.
[967] See Shaw, *Management* (n. 893), 18–40; N. T. Phillipson, 'The Social Structure of the Faculty of Advocates in Scotland 1661–1840', in Harding (n. 359), 146–56.
[968] See Cairns (n. 457), §§ 1263–4. See also J. W. Cairns, 'The Formation of the Scottish Legal Mind: Themes of Humanism and Enlightenment in the Admission of Advocates', in Neil MacCormick and Peter Birks (eds.), *The Legal Mind: Essays for Tony Honoré* (1986), 253–77 at 267–72.

disorienting. Particularly telling is that in 1807 one side in a dispute over reform in the courts employed a shorthand writer to record its speeches in Faculty. Trust was low. At the same time, maintenance of the Faculty's by now enormous Library was a tremendous strain on the Faculty's limited resources.[969]

(c) The Faculty's examinations

The only important and lasting reform in the Faculty's examinations came in 1750 when a compulsory examination in Scots law was introduced. The opening up to the advocates of the office of sheriff depute under the Heritable Jurisdictions Act was the spur to action. The examination was added into the existing sequence of examinations after the private examination on civil law but before the public one.[970] This marked a reorientation of the Faculty's educational aspirations and growth of emphasis on a proper 'enlightened' education for lawyers, while learning in Roman law was progressively less valued.[971] Until around 1750, it remained common for men intending to go to the bar to study law in the Netherlands, although the numbers were declining from around 1725 onwards.[972] Instead, the law courses offered in Scotland were favoured. This cut Scots lawyers off from the continuing continental tradition of study of Roman law. This was especially significant, since none of the Professors of Civil Law in Scotland until the Victorian period was of any distinction as a Romanist. Despite the primacy given to civil law in the Faculty's examinations, legal study reorientated around Scots law and a Smithian version of natural jurisprudence.[973] Scots advocates were increasingly likely to see the model for their profession as the English barrister rather than the continental advocate academically trained in Roman law.

(d) Agents before the Court of Session

The history of the development of agents for causes before the Session and their relationship with the advocates is obscure, but obviously relates to the progressive emergence of the view that advocates should not take instructions directly from clients. By the early eighteenth century, it was a normal part of Court of Session practice, undertaken by the advocates' own clerks or servitors and the Writers to the Signet; thus, in 1754, an Act of Sederunt 'concerning the Admission of Agents and Solicitors' recognized these two groups

---

[969] Cairns (n. 457), § 1264.

[970] Ibid., § 1261; *idem* (n. 968), 264–5; *idem*, (1999) 20, no. 2 *JLH* 28–33.

[971] Cairns (n. 457), § 1261; *idem* (n. 968), 264–5, 274–7; *idem*, 'The Influence of Smith's Jurisprudence on Legal Education in Scotland', in Peter Jones and A. S. Skinner (eds.), *Adam Smith Reviewed* (1992), 168–89. [972] Feenstra (n. 806), 30.

[973] J. W. Cairns, '"Famous as a School for Law, as Edinburgh ... for medicine": Legal Education in Glasgow, 1761–1801', in Andrew Hook and R. B. Sher (eds.), *The Glasgow Enlightenment* (1994), 133–59; *idem*, 'Rhetoric, Language, and Roman Law: Legal Education and Improvement in Eighteenth-Century Scotland', (1991) 9 *Law and History Review* 31–58.

as agents, but noted the Lords' ability to admit others as agents on examination. An Act of Sederunt confirmed this in 1772, requiring the solicitors to choose eight examiners of intrant agents.[974] This third group developed into another corporation of lawyers, who, in 1784, formally constituted themselves as the Society of Solicitors of the Court of Session and other Supreme Courts of Scotland. In 1797, they acquired a royal charter.[975] By 1830, in which year the advocates' first clerks themselves formed themselves into a society, there were three groups acting as agents before the Court of Session.[976]

(e) The rise of local faculties and societies

Those admitted to practice before particular courts commonly formed themselves into local faculties of procurators and the earliest recognizable groups of lawyers outside Edinburgh were those acting as procurators before major local courts, such as the Faculty of Procurators in Glasgow or the Society of Advocates in Aberdeen.[977] Both these societies developed out of practitioners before the commissary court, as did the Society of Solicitors at Law, the Edinburgh equivalent.[978] The desire to protect group interests and provide for widows, orphans, and indigent procurators also motivated such organization.[979] Such groups also practised in their local sheriff and burgh courts, the Edinburgh Solicitors at Law, for example, acquiring a monopoly right in pleading before these courts in 1765.[980]

All these procurators drafted legal documents, acted as conveyancers, and carried out a general legal practice as well. Many of the more important faculties of procurators sought incorporation by royal charter both to mark their growing status and to enforce a monopoly of audience or agenting before particular courts. The Society of Advocates in Aberdeen did so in 1774, the Solicitors at Law of Edinburgh in 1780, the Faculty of Procurators of Glasgow in 1796, and the Society of Solicitors to the Supreme Courts in 1797.[981] These groups all had roughly similar educational and training requirements for admission: a certain number of years of study of Latin followed by a period of apprenticeship of five years (though it could be for less).

---

[974] AS, I, 480–1 (10 Aug. 1754), 575–7 (11 Mar. 1772). See also ibid. 619–20 (13 Feb. 1787). See generally Begg (n. 813), 8–13.

[975] J. B. Barclay, *The S.S.C. Story, 1784–1984: Two Hundred Years of Service in the College of Justice* (1984), 1–30.   [976] Ibid. 54.

[977] See Muirhead (n. 463), 17–35; 'Local Law Societies. I. The Royal Faculty of Procurators in Glasgow', (1969) 14 *Journal of the Law Society of Scotland* 295–7; Henderson (n. 463); 'Local Law Societies. II. The Advocates in Aberdeen', (1969) 14 *Journal of the Law Society of Scotland* 325–6.   [978] Begg (n. 813), 17.

[979] See e.g. Muirhead (n. 463), 9; Henderson (n. 463), xiii; Begg (n. 813), 17.

[980] Begg (n. 813), 17–18; J. S. Muirhead, 'Notes on the History of the Solicitors' Profession in Scotland', (1952) 68 *Scottish Law Review* 25–36, 59–70 at 34.

[981] Muirhead, (1952) 68 *Scottish Law Review* 36.

As noted, there was usually an examination on Scots law and the form of process for those seeking to join.[982]

The history of the large numbers of individuals, described as writers, found in all Scottish towns of any size, remains obscure.[983] The training of country procurators and writers caused concern to their contemporaries.[984] Yet, in a major town with important courts, they seem to have served regular apprenticeships and there was a practice of the sheriff referring applicants for admission to a group of local procurators for trial.[985] Moreover, many such men attended university lectures on law during their training.[986] An Act of Sederunt of 1825 required those practising as procurators before the sheriff court to have 'served three years as an apprentice to a writer to the signet, solicitor before the Supreme Courts, or to a procurator before any Sheriff-court in Scotland, or court of a royal burgh, or Sheriff-clerk, [to] be twenty-one years of age, and [to] be regularly admitted by the Sheriff'.[987]

(f) *The education of writers and procurators*

By 1832 all the major incorporated societies required apprentices to attend university law classes.[988] They were generally interested in attendance at classes in Scots law and the newly developing subject specialism of conveyancing (initially taught outwith the universities). In 1819, the Society of Advocates in Aberdeen managed the foundation of a lectureship in law in Marischall College, while, in 1825, the Writers to the Signet eventually secured the appointment of a Professor of Conveyancing in Edinburgh University.[989] By 1832, the classes in Scots law and conveyancing in

---

[982] Muirhead (n. 463), 35–39; Cairns, (1995) 46 *Northern Ireland Legal Quarterly* 314–15; 'Abstract of Minutes', in *A History of the Society of Writers to Her Majesty's Signet, With a List of the Members of the Society from 1594 to 1890 and an Abstract of the Minutes* (1890), 392.

[983] The best general account is to be found in Muirhead, (1952) 68 *Scottish Law Review* 25–36, 59–70.

[984] See e.g. 'Law—Country Writers, &c', (1823) 1 *Edinburgh University Journal, and Critical Review* 246–52.

[985] Hector McKechnie, 'An Eighteenth-Century Dumfries Procurators' Examination', (1931) 43 *JR* 337–48.

[986] Ibid. 341; T. St. J. N. Bates, 'Mr. M'Connachie's Notes and Mr. Fraser's Confessional', [1980] *JR* 166–84.

[987] Act of Sederunt relative to the Form of Process in Civil Causes before the Sheriff-Courts (12 Nov. 1825), in AS, V, 133–50 at 149–50. A similar provision was made for burgh courts: Act of Sederunt relative to the Form of Process in Civil Causes in the Courts of the Royal Burghs, and of Burghs of Barony, ibid. 150–69 at 167–8. This also took into account the role of the town clerk.

[988] *History of the Society of Writers to Her Majesty's Signet* (n. 982), cxi, 424; Library of the Royal Faculty of Procurators, MS Sederunt Book 1761–96, 4 Mar. 1796, MS Sederunt Book of the Faculty of Procurators 1796–1832, 1, 8, and 15 (15 July 1796), 40–9 at 47; Barclay (n. 975), 29; Henderson, *Advocates in Aberdeen* (n. 463), 62–3.

[989] *History of the Society of Writers to Her Majesty's Signet* (n. 982), cvii–cxxvi; A. A. Maclaren, 'Privilege, Patronage and the Professions: Aberdeen and its Universities, 1760–1860', in J. J. Carter and D. J. Withrington (eds.), *Scottish Universities: Distinctiveness and Diversity* (1992), 96–104 at 100–1.

Edinburgh and Glasgow were dominated by the apprentices of procurators and writers.[990]

The rise of the procurators and law agents is a marked feature of the half-century before 1832. Acquisition of royal charters, emphasis on the importance of law as a university discipline, and foundation of scholarly libraries are signs of their drive for status and position. Given the increasing importance of the sheriff court before which they acted as procurators, it is interesting to reflect that most of them probably did not study civil law, while the teaching of Scots law and conveyancing followed a style pioneered by David Hume as Professor of Scots Law in Edinburgh—an exhaustive account of the law founded on the decisions of the court.[991]

5. The development of a law for a commercial society

(a) The importance of natural jurisprudence

In the second half of the eighteenth century, the well-established Scottish tradition in natural jurisprudence had developed into a mode of thinking and analysis concerned with the progress of society and the means of achieving it.[992] For lawyers, the work of Adam Smith's pupil John Millar was of particular importance in propagating these ideas.[993] Through the eighteenth century the linked topics of property, commerce, and liberty became ever more prominent in reforms in the substantive law. Some of the early reforms reflected the general concerns of the early European Enlightenment.[994] There was a more rational and humane approach to evidence and proof.[995] The creation of the Jury Court, where issues of admissibility now had to be determined by a judge in open court on the basis of argument from counsel, helped develop a new law on evidence.[996]

---

[990] See J. W. Cairns, 'From "Speculative" to "Practical" Legal Education: The Decline of the Glasgow Law School, 1801–1830', (1994) 62 *TR* 331–56 at 342–3.   [991] Ibid. 341–3.

[992] Knud Haakonssen, *The Science of a Legislator: The Natural Jurisprudence of David Hume and Adam Smith* (1981); idem, *Natural Law and Moral Philosophy: From Grotius to the Scottish Enlightenment* (1996), 154–81, 226–93; Donald Winch, *Adam Smith's Politics: An Essay in Historiographic Revision* (1978); idem, 'Science and the Legislator: Adam Smith and After', (1983) 93 *Economic Journal* 501–20.

[993] See e.g. Cairns, (1991) 9 *Law and History Review* 41–3; idem, 'Legal Education in Glasgow' (n. 973), *passim*.

[994] See 9 Geo II (c. 5) (prohibition of witchcraft prosecutions); 15 Geo III (c. 28); 39 Geo III (c. 56) (on colliers and salters: see C. A. Whatley, 'The Dark Side of the Enlightenment? Sorting out Serfdom', in Devine/Young (n. 693), 259–74); *Knight* v. *Wedderburn* (1778) Mor 14545 (no slaves).   [995] Concealment of Birth (Scotland) Act 1809, 49 Geo III (c. 14).

[996] See 'Speech of the Lord Chief Commissioner, at Opening the Jury Court, On 22nd January 1816', in *Reports of Cases Tried in the Jury Court, from the Institution of the Court in 1815, to the Sittings at Edinburgh in July 1818* (1818), xv–xxviii at xxi.

(b) Statutory reform of property and commercial law

Refashioning the law into a form more suitable for a commercial society was a major concern. Feudal land law came in for particular attack from Adam Smith and Lord Kames as inhibiting the development of a property law suited to a commercial society.[997] The crisis of the Jacobite Rebellion of 1745 brought significant change.[998] Thus, an act abolished ward holdings (military tenures), converting them into blench tenure if held of the Crown and into feu-ferme if held of a subject superior. The casualty of non-entry was regulated while that of marriage and prohibitions of alienation of feus without the consent of the superior were both abolished, as were the casualties of single and liferent escheats for horning and denunciation in civil causes. A more expeditious process was provided for heirs to gain entry from subject superiors. Suit and presence at head courts were abolished.[999] The spread of feu-ferme tenure and the abolition of these casualties increased the security of ownership of land in a way beneficial to a commercial society.

The act also created a trivial breach in strict entails, regarded by the Enlightened *literati* as a curious malformation of feudalism. Entails were recognized as a major barrier to commerce and agricultural improvement because of the limitations on the heir of entail's ability to grant long leases or raise capital on the security of the land.[1000] Attempts to reform entails were unsuccessful until, in 1770, heirs of entail were empowered to grant longer tacks or leases and raise money for improvements by making it recoverable from subsequent heirs of entail.[1001] It was not until 1836, however, that it became possible to apply to the Court of Session for sale of part of an entailed estate to settle the debts of an heir of entail, although heirs of entail were empowered in 1824 to make provision for spouses and children out of an entailed estate.[1002]

There was also pressure to improve the laws on commercial dealings and the middle years of the eighteenth century once again proved a watershed. The area of law that caused most problems was bankruptcy, since it was vital to a commercial society to have a suitable means of dealing with insolvent debtors that, while fair to creditors, did not inhibit enterprise and trade. The first steps in improvement were taken by the Court of Session in temporary Acts of Sederunt of 1735 and 1754, aimed at making creditors more secure and providing a fairer means of dealing with the estates of bankrupts and of

---

[997] See e.g. Lieberman (n. 932), 156–75.   [998] Kidd (n. 8), 156–8.
[999] Tenures Abolition Act 1746, 20 Geo II (c. 50).
[1000] See e.g. Henry Home, *Historical Law Tracts* (4th edn., 1792), 135–56.
[1001] 10 Geo III (c. 51). On earlier attempts at reform, see Lehmann (n. 928), 327–45; N. T. Phillipson, 'Lawyers, Landowners, and the Civic Leadership of Post-Union Scotland: An Essay on the Social Role of the Faculty of Advocates 1661–1830 in 18th Century Scottish Society', [1976] *JR* 97–120 at 112–18.
[1002] Entail Powers Act 1836, 6 and 7 Will IV (c. 42); Entail Provisions Act 1825, 5 Geo IV (c. 87).

ranking creditors.[1003] Agitation for reform finally led to the passing of the Bankruptcy Act in 1772, the value of which was to be tested by the famous collapse of Douglas, Heron & Co. (the Ayr Bank) a few months later. As well as providing for a fair ranking of creditors, this act provided further regulation of diligence on promissory notes and bills of exchange.[1004] The importance of a proper law of bankruptcy in an early and developing capitalist economy is demonstrated by George Joseph Bell's publication of his two-volume *Treatise on the Law of Bankruptcy in Scotland* in 1800–4.[1005]

(c) *The courts and English law*

These statutory reforms were relatively few and occasional, so the task of promoting commerce through appropriate development of the law fell to the courts.[1006] Lack of research on the actual records and the printed Session Papers means that it is not easy to trace the courts' development of the law in particular detail. It is instructive here to consider the topic of insurance. Efficient mechanisms of sharing risk were vital for trade and enterprise. Marine insurance had been little used in Scotland in the seventeenth century; after 1700, however, Scots' experience of the Dutch trade encouraged their use of insurance to distribute risk of loss, frequently insuring in the Netherlands at Amsterdam. From around 1750, however, as Scotland increasingly participated in trade with the North American Empire, insurance practice reoriented southwards, while the law on insurance developed rapidly only from around 1775.[1007] The Scottish judges and legal profession consciously developed this law on the basis of the recent developments in English commercial law, influenced by the prestige of the work of, above all, Lord Mansfield. It was even common to secure the opinion of English counsel on points of insurance law.[1008] When continental authority was cited in court, the references can frequently be traced to the treatise published by John Millar, junior, in 1787 and other, English, works

---

[1003] AS, I, 303–8 (29 July 1735), 490–3 (17 Jan. 1756).

[1004] Bills of Exchange (Scotland) Act 1772, 12 Geo III (c. 72); see Fry (n. 902), 44–5. (Bank notes or bills were not covered, as an act of 1765 had already made them generally payable on demand with summary diligence: Bank Notes (Scotland) Act 1765, 5 Geo III (c. 49)).

[1005] On the editions, see the introduction by Robert Black to George Joseph Bell, *Commentaries on the Law of Scotland and on the Principles of Mercantile Jurisprudence* (7th edn., repr. 1990).

[1006] N. T. Phillipson, 'Scottish Public Opinion and the Union in the Age of the Association', in Phillipson/Mitchison (n. 893), 125–47 at 141: such statutory reforms generally originated in Scotland and were drafted by the Scottish law officers and involved consultation with the judges, the legal profession, and the freeholders before enactment.

[1007] See A. D. M. Forte, 'Marine Insurance and Risk Distribution in Scotland before 1800', (1987) 5 *Law and History Review* 393–412.

[1008] Ibid. 395–8; A. D. M. Forte, 'Opinions by "Eminent English Counsel": Their Use in Insurance Cases before the Court of Session in the Late Eighteenth and Early Nineteenth Centuries', [1995] *JR* 345–64.

on insurance.[1009] English law was followed because, as Lord Hailes put it in 1774, '[w]e in Scotland are in the helpless infancy of commerce'. This meant that '[o]n a mercantile question, especially concerning insurance, I would rather have the opinion of English merchants, than of all the theorists and all the foreign ordinances in Europe'.[1010]

England was not in the infancy of commerce; thus its law was arguably the best source from which to develop Scots commercial law. This contrasts with fifty or so years before. Forbes's work on bills of exchange is replete with the learning of the *jus commune*; now English law was the important source for development of that of Scotland. Representing *jus gentium* (in the traditional sense of the law of other nations), English law could be seen as a suitable source for the development of Scots law.[1011] Yet, reference to other legal systems was becoming limited to that of England. Instead of being an example of the *jus gentium*, it was tending to become an exclusive source of authority, especially when the assimilation of Scots and English mercantile law was considered desirable.

6 History, common law, and *jus commune*

(a) Jus commune *and Scots law*

In the first half of the eighteenth century, the traditional Scottish use of the sources of the *jus commune* continued to prevail. The practice of the courts also continued to reflect a broad approach to the sources of law. Thus, in *Arbuthnot v. Morison* (1716), counsel cited Voet, Groenewegen, Perezius, and a decision of the Parlement de Paris to support his argument.[1012] William Forbes, the first Professor of Civil Law in Glasgow, declared that '[t]he Civil Law ... is effectually naturaliz'd in Scotland'.[1013] His contemporary, Alexander Bayne, the first Professor of Scots law in Edinburgh, followed Craig in arguing that because there was a 'great Penury of any written Law with us ... we have the more naturally had Recourse to the Civil Law'. He explicitly claimed 'the Civil Law, as having become for some Time our proper written Law'. This meant that Scotland had been 'plentifully supplied from

---

[1009] Forte, (1987) 5 *Law and History Review* 397; John Millar, *Elements of the Law Relating to Insurances* (1787): see A. D. M. Forte, 'John Millar Junior—A Biographical Sketch of a Minor Jurist of the Eighteenth Century', in Gamble (n. 950), 67–78.

[1010] David Dalrymple, Lord Hailes, *Decisions of the Lords of Council and Session from 1766 to 1791* (ed. by M. P. Brown, 1826), II, 622. (16 Dec. 1774). See Forte, [1995] *JR* 351–2.

[1011] Cairns (n. 16), 170–1, 173–9.

[1012] See [Henry Home, Lord Kames], *Remarkable Decisions of the Court of Session, from 1716, to 1728* (1728), 1–4 at 2.

[1013] William Forbes, *The Institutes of the Law of Scotland. Volume First. Comprehending the Private Law* (1722), 8–9.

Historical Introduction 163

the Pandects and Code with Laws touching private Right', so that 'the Civil Law has all along been considered as our Law, and is justly made the rule of Judgment in all Cases wherein our Law is silent'.[1014] James Innes commented more generally in 1732 of the Scots that, 'the Civil Law is truly theirs by Adoption' so that it was not possible to 'be altogether Master of the Scotch, without acquiring a tolerable clear Idea of the Civil Law'.[1015] Bayne and Forbes (who had both studied law at Leiden) were among the last to consider the Court of Session as developing a *jurisprudentia Romano-Scotica forensis* to eke out the meagre native sources.[1016] Such views meant that works of Scots law were to be interpreted using the *jus commune*. Thus James Baillie provided his new edition of Craig's *Jus Feudale* of 1732 with an extensive apparatus of citations and references to the *jus commune*, locating it firmly within that body of learning.[1017]

Neither Bayne nor Forbes paid much attention to natural law. In works published in the 1750s, Andrew McDouall, Lord Bankton, and John Erskine, Bayne's successor as Professor of Scots Law, placed Scots law within a framework of the *jus naturale* and the *jus gentium*. Their somewhat unoriginal systematic approach to natural law emphasized the origins of law in the command of a sovereign.[1018] Despite this emphasis on rationalism and the willed nature of law, both still tended to emphasize the role of the *jus commune* in Scotland, recognizing its authority from statutory endorsement and the historical fact of use.[1019]

(b) Moral sense, history, and English law

When Erskine's *Institute of the Law of Scotland* was published posthumously in 1773, its rationalist and voluntarist account of natural law must have already seemed outdated. Under the influence of thinkers such as Francis Hutcheson, Professor of Moral Philosophy in Glasgow from 1728, such views had been progressively superseded by versions of moral sense theory.[1020] The most radical version of such thinking was that of David Hume, who, in his *Treatise of Human Nature* (1740), emphasized that justice was an 'artificial', rather than natural, virtue and purported to destroy the

---

[1014] Alexander Bayne, *A Discourse on the Rise and Progress of the Law of Scotland, and the Method of Studying it. For the Use of the Students of the Municipal Law*, in Thomas Hope, *Minor Practicks* (ed. by Alexander Bayne, 1726), 162–8.

[1015] James Innes, *Idea Iuris Scotici: Or, A Summary View of the Laws of Scotland* (1733), i–ii. See also Patrick Turnbull, *Analogia Legum: Or, A View of the Institutes of the Laws of England and Scotland, Set One against the Other; To shew wherein those Two Laws agree and differ* (1745), viii. Only the introduction was ever published. On Turnbull, see Cairns (n. 865), 245–6.

[1016] See Cairns (n. 523), 214–17.   [1017] See n. 523 above.

[1018] Bankton, I, 1, 3; John Erskine, *Principles of the Law of Scotland* (1754), I, 1, 1.

[1019] Bankton, I, 1, 16; I, 1, 24; I, 1, 38; I, 1, 42; Erskine (n. 1018), I, 1, 15. See especially the discussion in John Erskine, *An Institute of the Law of Scotland* (1773), I, 1, 41.

[1020] See e.g. Haakonssen, *Natural Law* (n. 992), 63–99; P. B. Wood, *The Aberdeen Enlightenment: The Arts Curriculum in the Eighteenth Century* (1993), 40–9.

philosophical foundations of current theories of natural law.[1021] To put it bluntly, Hume argued that justice, founded in utility, arose historically from the social nature of human beings.[1022]

The publication of *L'Esprit des lois* by the Baron de Montesquieu in 1748 aroused tremendous interest in Scotland.[1023] In this large and somewhat diffuse work, he pointed out links between the laws and whether a nation lives by trade and navigation, or by cultivation of the soil, or by keeping flocks and herds, or by hunting.[1024] In the 1750s, this insight was developed, in both France and Scotland, into a theory that society developed through various stages of differing modes of subsistence.[1025] Thus, having already published the essays on *British Antiquities* in 1747, Lord Kames now went on to publish the *Historical Law-Tracts* in 1758, in which he blended his version of the theory of the moral sense (partly developed in opposition to Hume's utilitarian views) with a theory of legal development derived and adapted from the work of Montesquieu.[1026] The message of the work was the need to reform Scots law to make it a law suitable for a commercial nation.

This type of concern chimed with the debates over feudalism promoted by the reforms in 1747, in which the Scots could be represented as having not yet reached the happy state of the English.[1027] Moreover, discussions of feudal law necessarily emphasized the historical links between the Scots and English laws. This theme can be traced to Craig. Thus, Kames's essay on the introduction of the feudal law into Scotland in his *Essays Concerning British Antiquities* argued that feudal law came to Scotland from England.[1028] By stressing the historical links between the laws of England and Scotland, such histories inevitably raised the problematic issue of a 'reunification' of Scots law with English. For Lord Kames this was a desirable possibility, since 'the whole island originally was governed by the same law; and even at present, the difference consists more in terms of art than in substance'.[1029] If such discussion raised once again the vexed debates of the authenticity and authority of *Regiam* and the 'auld lawes' and the origin of feudalism in

---

[1021] David Hume, *A Treatise of Human Nature: Being an Attempt to Introduce the Experimental Method of Reasoning into Moral Subjects* (ed. by D. F. Norton and M. J. Norton, 2000).

[1022] See e.g. Haakonssen, *Natural Law* (n. 992), 100–28; idem, *Science of a Legislator* (n. 992), 4–44.

[1023] See e.g. Charles de Secondat de Montesquieu, *The Spirit of the Laws* (tr. A. M. Cohler, B. C. Miller, and H. S. Stone, 1989). [1024] Ibid., XVIII.8.

[1025] R. L. Meek, *Social Science and the Ignoble Savage* (1976), 68–130; Peter Stein, 'The Four Stage Theory of the Development of Societies', in idem, *The Character and Influence of the Roman Civil Law: Historical Essays* (1988), 395–409.

[1026] Kames first set out his moral—and legal—philosophy in *Essays on the Principles of Morality and Natural Religion* (1751). See also his *Sketches of the History of Man* (1774), especially the 4th edition, 1788. [1027] See Kidd (n. 8), 150–60.

[1028] Kames (n. 928), 5–7.

[1029] Kames (n. 1000), x–xi. See also John Dalrymple, *An Essay towards a General History of Feudal Property in Great Britain* (1757), vi, 22–6.

Scotland,[1030] it allowed Kames and others to stress the extent to which Scots law had borrowed from English. He often returned to this theme, for example, commenting in the *Essays on British Antiquities* that 'When one dives into the antiquities of *Scotland* and *England*, it will appear that we borrowed all our Laws and Customs from the *English*. No sooner is a Statute enacted in *England*, but, upon the first opportunity, it is introduced into *Scotland*; so that our oldest Statutes are mere Copies of theirs.'[1031] In another work he noted of the brieve of mortancestor that 'it must be observed here, as almost upon every other branch of our law, that this action was copied from the law of England'.[1032] Kames's historical observations on medieval Scots law were perceptive. There was a definite ideological programme, however, behind his emphasis on its English origins. Such a history permitted the development of an argument in favour of the possibility of the rapprochement of Scots and English law that inevitably devalued the history of the reception of Roman law in Scotland. Scotland's links with the *jus commune* became an irrelevant interlude, easily ignored. Commerce and politics required *English* law to be copied where appropriate.

(c) Roman law in the Scottish Enlightenment

As civil law was seen as less significant and connections with English law emphasized, the tradition of legal study abroad ended, so that Scots lawyers lost their links with the *jus commune*. Many still studied civil law in the Scottish universities. Robert Dick, who held the chair of Civil Law in Edinburgh in the crucial period from 1755 to 1792, however, was a man of no distinction, with diminishing classes.[1033] In Glasgow, on the other hand, John Millar was highly successful and taught two courses on Justinian's *Institutes* and one on his *Digest*. In these courses he used the popular compendiary textbooks of Heineccius.[1034] Millar was not concerned, however, to use his courses to explore civilian learning and doctrines in general. Rather, he advised his students in his second course on the *Institutes* to read 'some good author on general Jurisprudence'. For this, Millar recommended Grotius, with the commentary of the Enlightenment jurist and Prussian law reformer, Samuel von Cocceji, probably attracted by its emphasis on *rights* rather than contractual natural law.[1035] This was because Millar valued civil law as

---

[1030] See e.g. Bankton, I, 13–19, 29–32; Hailes (n. 928); Bayne (n. 1014), 155–60. See also Kidd (n. 8), 101–7, 148–50; MacQueen, (1995) 74 *Scot Hist Rev* 20–3. [1031] Kames (n. 928), 4.
[1032] [Henry Home, Lord Kames], *Statute Law of Scotland Abridged. With Historical Notes* (1757), 411. [1033] See Cairns, 'Legal Education in Glasgow' (n. 973), 149.
[1034] Ibid. 140–2; J. G. Heineccius, *Elementa Juris Civilis Secundum Ordinem Institutionum* (1725; and many subsequent edns.); *idem, Elementa Juris Civilis Secundum Ordinem Pandectarum* (1727; and many subsequent editions).
[1035] Cairns, 'Legal Education in Glasgow' (n. 973), 147–8. The work Millar had in mind was probably *Samuelis de Cocceii Introductio ad Henrici de Coceii Grotium Illustratum* (1748); it could also have been his *Novum Systema Jurisprudentiae Naturalis et Romanae* (1740). See

providing illustrations of his Smithian natural jurisprudence; indeed the second course on the *Institutes* was described as on jurisprudence. In it students were 'to enquire into the principles of the Roman Law', that is, the history and philosophy underlying its rules. There he explained the value he saw in the study of Roman law 'as the system of Lawiers and Judges of great experience, and of a country which subsisted for such a long tract of time, and where we may consequently expect to find the rules of Jurisprudence of the most perfect kind'. To study it 'was a very usefull exercise, as it enlarges our experience'. Knowing 'what was the Roman System ... would be of little consequence of itself'.[1036]

Thus, the most influential teacher of Roman law in Scotland stressed Roman law as an experimental example of natural jurisprudence, as an exercise in the Smithian science of legislation.[1037] This followed the views of Kames, who criticized teachers of Roman law who limited their teaching to the rules of Roman law, dismissing a pupil 'without a single idea, but what is strictly Roman', so that 'such ideas [were] ignorantly applied by him to the law of his own country, as chance or conceit directs'. For Kames, Roman law ought to be taught emphasizing its underlying rationality and its links with manners and politics.[1038]

(d) Roman law, English law, and completing the Union

Millar and Kames exemplify an approach that no longer considered civil law as of great significance in itself as a source of Scots law. Given the emphasis on the historical links of Scots with English law and the advantages of 'completing' the Union by amalgamating the laws, the Smithian project of creating institutions for a commercial country led to the view that the need for a modern commercial law could be met by adopting that of England. Better than the civil law, English law could perfect Scots law because it corresponded to 'the manners of the people, their circumstances, their government'.[1039] Millar's pupil, David Hume, in his account of criminal law, while claiming not to possess that 'superstitious admiration of the English Law, which prevails among some persons, and especially, like other superstitions,

---

generally Haakonssen, *Natural Law* (n. 992), 136–9, 140–8. Students in the second course on the *Institutes*, who had the time to spare, were advised to read Vinnius' commentary on the *Institutes*: Arnoldus Vinnius, *In Quattuor Libros Institutionum Imperialium Commentarius Academicus et Forensis* (1642; many subsequent edns).

[1036] NLS, Adv. MS 20.4.7, fos. 1–2^r.; see Cairns, 'Legal Education in Glasgow' (n. 973), 141; Cairns, (1991) 9 *Law and History Review* 41–3.

[1037] John Craig, 'Account of the Life and Writings of John Millar, Esq.', prefixed to John Millar, *The Origin of the Distinction of Ranks: Or, an Inquiry into the Circumstances which give rise to Influence and Authority, in the different Members of Society* (4th edn., 1806), xx, xl–xli.

[1038] See Henry Home, Lord Kames, *Elucidations Respecting the Common and Statute Law of Scotland* (1777), viii–x.

[1039] [Henry Home, Lord Kames], *Select Decisions of the Court of Session, From the Year 1752 to the Year 1768. Collected by a Member of the Court* (1780), iii.

Historical Introduction

among the ignorant', also stressed the advantages of drawing on English law as the law of 'a free and an enlightened people', especially since 'the form of our Government, and the general spirit of our jurisprudence are the same as that of England'.[1040] In other words, the 'manners', 'circumstances', and 'government' of Scotland were so close to those of England as to encourage borrowing from its law.

This shift from reliance on the *jus commune* to borrowing from England took place in the third quarter of the eighteenth century. In 1754, reliance on the authority of Roman law was still strong.[1041] In 1780, however, Boswell and Lord Kames could note that civil law was no longer much cited or studied.[1042] Civil law was still cited, but as Robert Bell put it in 1794, 'civil law . . . is now reduced to that place which it always ought to have held; it serves only to enrich the pleading of the lawyer, or by its wisdom to aid the decision of the judge'.[1043] David Hume told his class in Scots law that in many areas civil law had become 'naturalised' by being 'incorporated into our practice, by a long and uniform train of decisions', and also had commonly had respect paid to it in analogous areas. Yet he refused 'allegiance to the Civil Law, as having dominion over us', although it was an excellent introduction to legal study.[1044] For Hume, Roman law was only a historical not a living source of Scots law. The Professor of Civil Law in the University of Edinburgh in 1826 told the Commission visiting the Scottish Universities that once the doctrines of civil law 'have entered into the works of our Institutional writers, and are confirmed by judgments and decisions of the courts, become part of the Scotch Law, and are studied in the Class of Scotch Law, so the student has less occasion to resort to the Civil law than originally'.[1045] His successor in the Edinburgh chair, Douglas Cheape, agreed.[1046] Civil law teaching was indeed at a low ebb in Scotland after 1800.[1047] The revivifying of Roman law by the German Historical School under Hugo and Savigny was largely ignored.[1048]

[1040] David Hume, *Commentaries on the Law of Scotland, Respecting the Description and Punishment of Crimes* (1797), vol. 1, liv.

[1041] See e.g. *Strachan v. Creditors of Strachan* (1754) 5 Brown's Supp 814–15.

[1042] G. Scott and F. A. Pottle (ed.), *Private Papers of James Boswell from Malahide Castle* (1928–34), vol. 15, 290–1.

[1043] *Cases Decided in the Court of Session, from November 1790 to July 1792. Collected by Robert Bell, Clerk to the Signet* (1794), vi.   [1044] Hume, *Lectures*, I, 13–14.

[1045] *Evidence, Oral and Documentary, Taken and Received by the Commissioners Appointed by His Majesty George IV. July 23d, 1826; and Re-appointed by his Majesty William IV., October 12th 1830; For Visiting the Universities of Scotland. Volume I. University of Edinburgh*, 1837 Parliamentary Papers XXXV, 183. See also his remarks to his students in NLS, MS 24612, fo. 104^r.

[1046] Douglas Cheape, *An Introductory Lecture on the Civil Law, Delivered in the University of Edinburgh, on Tuesday, 13th November 1827* (1827), 30–1.

[1047] Cairns, (1994) 62 *TR* 333, 343–5.

[1048] J. W. Cairns, 'The Influence of the German Historical School in Early Nineteenth Century Edinburgh', (1994) 20 *Syracuse Journal of International Law and Commerce* 191–203.

The age of the *jus Romano-Scoticum* and creative reception of Roman law was over.

7. Courts, legislation, and common law

George Joseph Bell felt no need to place Scots law in a theoretical framework of the law of nature and nations in either his *Commentaries* or his *Principles of the Law of Scotland*.[1049] He almost presented it as a system complete in itself. The formal sources he relied on were statute and precedent. He later published three volumes of *Illustrations from Adjudged Cases of the Principles of the Law of Scotland* to accompany his textbook, leaving his students in no doubt as to what was most important in Scots law.[1050] This reflects the revolution in thinking about Scots law that had occurred after 1750. David Hume's lectures to the Scots law class in Edinburgh explain this approach. After setting out an analytical jurisprudence derived from the thinking on rights of John Millar, he described Scots law as consisting of '*Lex non scripta*' and '*Lex scripta*'.[1051] Tacit consent from the people gave authority to the first, while the second was identified with statute. Unwritten law had been founded in 'feelings of natural justice' and the 'sense of what was suitable and convenient', and was improved from 'imitation of the policy of other neighbouring realms', particularly England, 'our more civilised neighbour'. Roman law had also served 'not a little to purify our Jurisprudence'. Scots common law was found in 'collections of reports' and in 'the writings of ... learned and eminent persons, skilled in the law'.[1052]

Having assimilated the thinking of the Scottish Enlightenment, Hume limited Scots law to statutes and common law, the latter being found in case reports, although there was some scope for writers to provide evidence of the common law where they were found to agree on a point.[1053] In his work on criminal law, Hume admitted that it was possible to draw on 'the sentiments, and sometimes even the words of the English writers on law', but he added that 'their works cannot properly be quoted as authorities in a book of Scots law'.[1054] The writers that could be cited as authoritative were accordingly only Scottish authors. This contrasts with the views of Sir George Mackenzie, for whom reliance on authors had meant reliance on the commentaries and treatises of the *jus commune*.[1055] Hume emphasized the essentially *national* nature of sources of law.

[1049] G. J. Bell, *Principles of the Law of Scotland, for the Use of Students in the University of Edinburgh* (1829). For the *Commentaries*, see n. 1005 above.

[1050] G. J. Bell, *Illustrations from Adjudged Cases, of the Principles of the Law of Scotland* (1836–8).

[1051] Hume, *Lectures*, I, 9–11; see J. W. Cairns, 'John Millar's Lectures on Scots Criminal Law', (1988) 8 *OJLS* 364–400 at 396–7; *idem*, (1994) 62 *TR* 341–2, 352–5.

[1052] Hume, *Lectures*, I, 11–14.   [1053] Ibid. 14.
[1054] Hume, *Lectures*, I, liv.   [1055] Above at pp. 135–7.

(a) The authority of statutes

Statutes were first in any hierarchy of authority. The acts of the Westminster Parliament were published regularly and a number of collections were printed; help in isolating from the messy Georgian statute book the material relevant to Scotland after the Union could be obtained from Swinton's *Abridgement* of 1755 with supplementary volumes (1788 and 1827).[1056] The text used of the older Scots statutes was that established by Glendook, until, from 1814 onwards, the Record Commission started to publish *The Acts of the Parliaments of Scotland*.[1057] That this edition was primarily antiquarian in aim indicates the extent to which this material was considered superseded. A commentator could remark that the 'statutory law' was 'confined within a very narrow compass'. Moreover, 'those statutes to which we principally have recourse are the enactments of a military age, and can therefore afford small assistance in deciding the questions which arise in a Commercial state'.[1058] The perennial issue of desuetude remained. Mackenzie's *Observations* remained the best guide on this, until the publication of Lord Kames's *Statute Law of Scotland Abridged* in 1757. Organized under headings, it drew together the provisions of the 'auld lawes', Scottish statutes, and post-1707 legislation affecting Scotland.[1059] A similar alphabetical guide was published by James Watson in 1828.[1060]

There was no definitive collection of the Acts of Sederunt of the court, which were also considered *lex scripta*, until, in 1790, a volume was printed covering 1553–1790. Four volumes (1800, 1810, 1821, 1832) continued this collection 'by Authority of the Court' to 1831, while, in 1811, earlier acts were printed, mainly from 1532 to 1553, but including some to 1628.[1061] This mass of undigested material contained many acts in desuetude, while the reforms of the 1820s rendered much of the older procedure obsolete. It was only in 1838, however, that an abridgement remedied these problems, providing a working collection of acts in force.[1062]

[1056] John (Lord) Swinton, *An Abridgement of the Public Statutes in Force and Use Relative to Scotland from the Union . . . to the Twenty-Seventh Year of his Present Majesty King George II* (1755). Swinton published the Supplement in 1788–9. The continuation from 1789 to 1826 was by William Forsyth, who also published a supplement in 1829. For a survey of the development of the Georgian statute book, see Lieberman (n. 932), 13–28.

[1057] Volumes 2–11 were printed between 1814 and 1824, though volumes 5 and 6 were superseded in 1870. Volume 1 appeared in 1844 and 12 in 1875.

[1058] *Cases Decided in the Court of Session, from November 1790 to July 1792* (n. 1043), vi–vii.

[1059] Kames (n. 1032).

[1060] *Practical View of the Statute Law of Scotland from 1424–1827* (1828).

[1061] The 1790 volume has been cited here as AS, I; subsequent volumes as AS, II, III, and so on.

[1062] William Alexander, *Abridgement of the Acts of Sederunt of the Lords of Council and Session* (1838), xiv–xv (on the problems).

(b) Common law: authoritative and other writings

Hume singled out Craig's *Jus Feudale* and Stair's *Institutions* as authoritative works.[1063] If Hume did not rate Bankton's and Erskine's works so highly, certainly the latter's *Institutes* was accorded considerable respect, while new editions of Stair and Erskine continued to be published.[1064] Kames asked rhetorically: 'What greater service to his country can a Lawyer in high estimation perform, than to bring their substance [that is, of collections of decisions] into a new institute, leaving nothing to the student but to consult the originals when not satisfied with his author?'[1065] The value of such institutes was their synthesis of the decisions of the court. Hume's own *Commentaries*, in which he brought together the cases of the Court of Justiciary, was typical of what was thought useful. The new editions of Stair's *Institutions* and Erskine's *Institute* updated the law through inserting new references to cases and statutes. Reinforcing the high regard paid to Stair was the fact that he purported to base his account of Scots law on Scottish cases and emphasized the significance of custom—now interpreted as case law—as a source. The background of these older works in the *jus commune* was forgotten; annotations such as those provided by Baillie for Craig's *Jus Feudale* were not attempted. Such works were increasingly coming to be seen as works *exclusively* of Scots law;[1066] they were not considered as statements of *jus proprium* within the context of *jus commune*.

Contemporaries emphasized the importance of accounts of the common law contained in 'institutes', by which they usually meant systematic works covering Scots law as a whole.[1067] Their authority was not taken for granted; much emphasis was placed on their accuracy.[1068] Nonetheless, around the beginning of the nineteenth century, increasing authority was being given to the statements of law found in, especially, Stair.[1069] Citations to the riches of the *jus commune* were disappearing. Instead, Stair's *Institutions* started to

---

[1063] Hume, *Lectures*, I, 14–15.

[1064] The following subsequent editions of Stair's *Institutions* were published: the third, edited John Gordon and William Johnstone, Edinburgh, 1759; the fourth, by George Brodie, Edinburgh, 1826–31; the new [fifth] by J. S. More, Edinburgh, 1832. The following editions of Erskine's *Institutes* appeared: the second, edited by Alexander Tytler, Edinburgh, 1785; the third, Edinburgh, 1793; the fourth by Joseph Gillon, Edinburgh, 1805; the fifth by W. M. Morison, Edinburgh, 1812; the sixth by James Ivory, Edinburgh, 1824–8; the seventh by Alexander Macallan, Edinburgh, 1838; the eighth, by J. Badenach Nicholson, Edinburgh, 1871). There also were numerous editions of his *Principles*. [1065] Kames (n. 1039), iv.

[1066] More could still write in his edition of Stair (1832), I, xi that the work was 'a Treatise of General Jurisprudence, illustrated by reference to the Law of Scotland, than as a mere Digest of Municipal Law'. But, he wished to emphasize its significance.

[1067] See Kames (n. 1000), xii–xiii.

[1068] [Robert Hannay], *Address to the Right Honourable Lord President Hope, and to the Members of the College of Justice, on the Method of Collecting and Reporting Decisions* (1821), 32–3.

[1069] See on this J. W. G. Blackie, 'Stair's Later Reputation as a Jurist', in Walker (n. 868), 207–27 at 219–20.

appear to be a definitive statement of the older Scots law complete in itself, beyond which it was not necessary to go. This focus on Stair is pointed up by the manner in which the older work of Craig, though much relied on by Stair, was, in contrast, increasingly condemned as not expressing Scots law. Thus, Walter Ross remarked of Craig that '[e]very thing, it seems, was regulated by the civil and canon codes, but more especially by the feudal law'.[1070] Scottish links with the *jus commune* were forgotten; Scots law was now seen as starting with Stair, whose *Institutions*, divorced from context and updated by an increasing apparatus of case citations, took on the guise of the foundational statement of Scots law. The foundations are being laid for the later Scottish idea of an 'institutional writing' as a work of special authority.[1071]

Until the end of the eighteenth century, relatively few specialized treatises on specific areas of Scots law had been published.[1072] After 1800, as 'institutional' works rose in authority, the number of more specialized works grew, often justified by their authors as dealing with a subject not dealt with in sufficient detail or at all in the 'institutional' works.[1073] Some such publications developed out of specific problems and developments, notably the works on procedure published because of the reforms in the courts.[1074] Others were on standard and important areas of practice, such as land law, conveyancing, and elections.[1075]

[1070] Walter Ross, *Lectures on the History and Practice of the Law of Scotland Relative to Conveyancing and Legal Diligence* (2nd edn., 1822), vol. 2, 7. For a critique of this, see Cairns, (1988) 56 *TR* 312–13.   [1071] See Cairns (n. 880), *passim* for a critique.

[1072] An example would be John Millar's treatise on insurance, above.

[1073] See e.g. the remarks in Robert Bell, *A Treatise on the Conveyance of Land to a Purchaser and on the Manner of Completing his Title* (1815; there were two subsequent editions), vii; James Fergusson, *Reports of Some Recent Decisions by the Consistorial Court of Scotland, in Actions of Divorce, Concluding for Dissolution of Marriages Celebrated under the English Law* (1817), 3–4.

[1074] James Watson, *New Form of Process before the Court of Session and Commission of Teinds with a General Account of the College of Justice* (1791); James Glassford, *Remarks on the Constitution and Procedure of the Scottish Courts of Law* (1812); James Ivory, *Form of Process before the Court of Session* (1815–18); Thomas Beveridge, *A Practical Treatise on the Forms of Process: Containing the New Regulations before the Court of Session, Inner-House, Outer-House and Bill-Chamber, the Court of Teinds, and the Jury Court. With a Historical Introduction; a Detailed Account of the Public Registers and Public Offices: And a Copious Appendix of Original Documents, Statutes, Acts of Sederunt etc* (1826); J. J. Darling, *The Practice of the Court of Session* (1833). See also James Fergusson, *A Treatise on the Present State of the Consistorial Law in Scotland, With Reports of Decided Cases* (1829). For a discussion of the problems behind this work, see Leah Leneman, 'English Marriages and Scottish Divorces in the Early Nineteenth Century', (1996) 17 *JLH* 225–43; Cairns, (1994) 20 *Syracuse Journal of International Law and Commerce* 201.

[1075] Alexander Wight, *A Treatise on the Laws Concerning the Election of the Different Representatives sent from Scotland to the Parliament of Great Britain. With a Preliminary View of the Constitution of the Parliaments of England and Scotland, before the Union of the Two Kingdoms* (1773); idem, *An Inquiry into the Rise and Progress of Parliament, Chiefly in Scotland, and a Complete System of the Law Concerning the Elections of the Representatives from Scotland to the Parliament of Great Britain* (1784; new edn., 1806); Robert Bell, *A Treatise on Election Laws, as they Relate to the Representation of Scotland, in the Parliament of the United Kingdom of Great Britain and Ireland* (1812); Arthur Connell, *Treatise on the Election Law of Scotland* (1827);

Discussion and citation of case law was clearly considered of the greatest value in either general institutes or specialized treatises. Thus, the publication of Burnett's work on criminal law and the various editions of Hume's treatise reflect the lack of systematic reporting of criminal cases.[1076] Even after such had started, Archibald Alison still advertised his study of criminal law with the claim that, 'besides embodying every decision in HUME and BURNETT on the subjects on which it treats of practical application at this time, this Volume contains above a thousand unreported cases'.[1077]

(c) Common law: case reports

Robert Bell remarked in 1794 that 'the law of this country consists principally of the decisions of the Court of Session'.[1078] Contemporary Scots believed that case decisions were the best means of developing the law.[1079] Partly this was because of the scarcity of written law;[1080] generally, however, incremental growth of the law through case decisions was simply thought to create better law.[1081] Forming the law through case decisions meant that it possessed 'that flexibility, which enables it to follow the manners and customs of a nation through all the changes to which they are subject'. Legislation, on the other hand, meant that the law is 'in a great measure stationary' and would even-

---

E. D. Sandford, *A Treatise on the History and Law of Entails in Scotland* (1822); idem, *A Treatise on the Law of Heritable Succession in Scotland* (1830); Bell (n. 1073); idem, *A Treatise on Leases: Explaining the Nature and Effect of the Contract of Lease, and Pointing out the Legal Rights enjoyed by the Parties* (1803; 2nd edn., 1805; 3rd edn., 1820).

[1076] John Burnett, *A Treatise on Various Branches of the Criminal Law of Scotland* (1811). As well as the *Commentaries on the Law of Scotland, Respecting the Description and Punishment of Crimes* (1797), Hume published *Commentaries on the Law of Scotland, Respecting Trial for Crimes* (1800). Next came *Supplemental Notes to Mr Hume's Commentaries on the Law of Scotland Respecting Crimes* (1814). The separate works of 1797 and 1800 were combined and updated as *Commentaries on the Law of Scotland, Respecting Crimes* (2nd edn., 1819; 3rd edn., 1829). In 1844 was published B. R. Bell, *A Supplement to Hume's Commentaries on the Law of Scotland Respecting Crimes* (1844); which, as well as separately, is found bound with the *Commentaries* (1844). This last is not a new edition.

[1077] Archibald Alison, *Principles of the Criminal Law of Scotland* (1832), vol. 1, vi. See also his *Practice of the Criminal Law of Scotland* (1833). There is a good biography of Alison: Michael Michie, *An Enlightenment Tory in Victorian Scotland: The Career of Sir Archibald Alison* (1997).

[1078] *Cases Decided in the Court of Session, from November 1790 to July 1792* (n. 1043), vii.

[1079] For a discussion, see J. W. Cairns, 'Ethics and the Science of Legislation: Legislators, Philosophers, and Courts in Eighteenth-Century Scotland', (2000) 8 *Jahrbuch für Recht und Ethik* (forthcoming).

[1080] [Henry Home, Lord Kames], *The Decisions of the Court of Session: From Its First Institution to the Present Time. Abridged, and Digested under Proper Heads, In Form of a Dictionary. Collected from a Great Number of Manuscripts, never before Published, as well as from the Printed Decisions* (1741), vol. 1, i.

[1081] [Henry Home, Lord Kames], *Remarkable Decisions of the Court of Session, From the year 1730 to the Year 1752* (1766), preface; [Alexander Tytler], *The Decisions of the Court of Session, From its first Institution to the Present Time. Abridged, and Digested under proper Heads, In Form of a Dictionary. Collected from the Printed Decisions, Session-Papers, and Manuscripts. Vol. III. Containing the Decisions from 1738 to 1770* (1778), iii.

Historical Introduction 173

tually turn 'the statute-book' into 'a contradictory, unwieldy, and oppressive mass'.[1082]

With such focus on decisions as the building blocks of the law, reporting them became of great importance.[1083] Through the first half of the eighteenth century, the Faculty of Advocates appointed various collectors of decisions. The results were unimpressive. After William Forbes published his *Journal of the Session* in 1714, covering 1705–13, Alexander Bruce was appointed collector of decisions. All he produced was a single volume covering 1714–15.[1084] John Edgar succeeded Bruce. He was similarly unsuccessful, printing only a volume covering 1724–5.[1085] On Edgar's death in 1744, David Falconer became collector of decisions. He published two volumes, covering 1744–51.[1086] On Falconer's resignation as collector, a new system was instituted, producing the series of reports known as the *Faculty Collection*, covering 1752–1825.[1087]

The Faculty's problems in regular publishing of reports encouraged private enterprise. To fill the gaps in the period to 1750, Lord Kames printed his two collections of *Remarkable Decisions*.[1088] Alexander Home, a Clerk of Session, likewise published in 1757 a volume of reports dealing with the years 1735–44.[1089] Earlier gaps were also filled. The *Decisions of the English Judges* were printed in 1762. In 1757 the collection of Lord Harcarse, covering 1681–91, was published, to be followed in 1758 by that made by Sir Hew Dalrymple of North Berwick, dealing with 1698–1718, while two volumes, covering 1678–1712, were produced from the papers of Lord Fountainhall in 1759 and 1761.[1090] Given earlier publications, this meant there was a relatively substantial selection of decisions of the Session accessible in print. Much remained in manuscript, however, while the scattered nature of the volumes was inconvenient. In 1741, Lord Kames, founding on some initial work by Alexander Bruce, published in the form of a dictionary a collection of

---

[1082] *Cases Decided in the Court of Session, From November 1790 to July 1792* (n. 1043), vii–x.

[1083] The best general account of the various collections of reports is: *Index to the Decisions of the Court of Session, Contained in all the Original Collections, and in Mr. Morisons's Dictionary of Decisions* (1823; hereafter *Tait's Index*), 499–532.

[1084] *The Decisions of the Lords of Council and Session, in Most Cases of Importance, for the Months of November and December 1714, and January, February, June and July 1715. With an Alphabetical Abridgement, and the Acts of Sederunt Made in that Time. Observed by Mr A. Bruce Advocate* (1720). See Pinkerton (n. 916), 9 (3 Feb. 1716).

[1085] *The Decisions of the Court of Session, from the Month of January 1724, Collected by Appointment of the Faculty of Advocates, by John Edgar Advocate* (1742). See Pinkerton (n. 916), 72 (18 Jan. 1724).

[1086] *The Decisions of the Court of Session. From the Month of November 1744. By David Falconer Advocate* (1746–53). See Pinkerton (n. 916), 199–200 (24 Nov. 1744).

[1087] Angus Stewart (ed.), *The Minute Book of the Faculty of Advocates. Volume 3, 1751–1783*, Stair Society, vol. 46 (1999), 12 (28 Jan. 1752).

[1088] Kames (n. 1012); Kames (n. 1081).

[1089] *Decisions of the Court of Session, from the Month of November M,DCC,XXV* (1757), 1.

[1090] On all of these, see e.g. Leadbetter (n. 840), 47.

decisions from the institution of the College of Justice, drawing on manuscript as well as printed volumes.[1091] Alexander Tytler published subsequent volumes in 1778 and 1797.[1092] The same desire to provide a comprehensive collection of decisions in an organized form led to the publication of Morison's *Dictionary of Decisions*, which gathered decisions from the foundation of the College of Justice to the division of the Session in 1808.[1093]

The mode of reporting the decisions of the Session was increasingly found flawed. Reports generally consisted of a summary of the arguments of counsel and the formal sentence of the Lords. Their quality very much depended on the ability of the reporter; yet, given the mass of paper produced by Scottish litigation it could be difficult to isolate the significant arguments, while, moreover, hearings *in praesentia* tended to produce a debate among the judges rather than a clear decision on the law. The difficulty in securing satisfactory reports because 'the mode in which the pleadings are conducted' created problems in 'ascertaining precisely the grounds on which the decision is placed by the Court' was solved when the introduction of the system of the open and closed record in 1825 helped clarify what was at issue before the court.[1094] The greatest problem, however, was the way reporters ignored 'the reasoning upon the Bench', which could 'justly be esteemed the surest road to come at the true principles upon which each particular question was decided'.[1095] The first printed reports that systematically reported the opinions of the judges were those of Robert Bell. In the preface to his reports for 1790–2 he asserted that 'it is what passes on the Bench; it is the opinion of the judges, which ought to be preserved in our reports'. This was because it was 'not what is to be found in printed papers that can give a just notice of the principle of a decision'.[1096] On 17 December 1808, in the year the court was split into two divisions, the Faculty resolved '[t]hat a report of the opinions of the Judges ought to accompany the decisions', as otherwise, 'the reports of decisions must always remain imperfect and unsatisfactory'.[1097] Recording judicial opinions thereafter became the norm, although there was no initial consistency in how this was done: sometimes in a précis, sometimes a direct report. Indeed, complex speeches were occasionally omitted because of their very difficulty.[1098] Yet, it was well established that the most important

---

[1091] Kames (n. 1080). [1092] Tytler (n. 1081). In 1804 another supplement was published.
[1093] See *Tait's Index* (n. 1083), 515–26.
[1094] Robert Hannay, *Letter to the Dean of the Faculty of Advocates, Relative to a Plan which has been proposed for Reporting the Decisions of the Court of Session* (1823), 15.
[1095] *Decisions of the Court of Session, from the Year 1738 to the year 1752. Collected and Digested into the Form of a Dictionary. By Sir James Fergusson of Kilkerran, Baronet, One of the Senators of the College of Justice. Published by his Son* (1775), iv.
[1096] *Cases Decided in the Court of Session, from November 1790 to July 1792* (n. 1043), v; see also *Cases Decided in the Court of Session, Summer Session 1794,—Winter Session 1794–5,—and Summer Session 1795* (1796), advertisement. [1097] Hannay (n. 1068), 6–7.
[1098] Ibid. 7–8.

part of a report was now the judicial opinion, so that the publication in 1826 of reports made by Lord Hailes from 1766 to 1791 of cases, many of which appeared in the *Faculty Collection*, was justified because of 'the notes preserved by Lord Hailes of the opinions delivered by the Judges', since in 'estimating the authority of a decision upon a question of law, it is frequently of the utmost importance to have an accurate report of the opinions delivered upon the Bench'.[1099] From the start of the new series of *Faculty Decisions* in 1825 and the first series of annual reports of decisions in the Court of Session, edited by Patrick Shaw, in 1821, it was taken for granted that judicial opinions would now be the most important part of the report.[1100]

The focus on the significance of the judicial opinion reflected a new role for decisions with a new understanding of the law. Kames argued that what was important was a decision's congruence with reason: '[i]f the deduction upon which the decision is founded be fair, the decision is just; but then the reason is the authority, not the decision. If the decision be founded upon wrong principles, it can signify nothing'.[1101] A decision, if correct, turned an equitable principle, identified by the moral sense, into law.[1102] A few years later, Alexander Tytler stressed the limitations of individual precedents, but argued that decisions helped establish the law over time, so that it 'gradually matured into a system'. Thereby was created 'a rule of practice, founded on the most perfect scrutiny of its reason and consequences, and adhered to only from the conviction of its wisdom and expediency'.[1103]

(d) Scots law as an autonomous national law

Kames, and to a lesser extent Tytler, still viewed the courts as turning precepts of ethics into legal norms. Scots lawyers, however, progressively disassociated the decision-making of courts from ethics and started to see law as a more autonomous discipline, sufficient in itself to generate answers to problems. Thus, in 1821, Robert Hannay argued that '[r]eports furnish not only the evidence of established rules, but materials for the invention of new'. This was because, when an issue covered neither by a statute nor former decision came before a court, it could be decided by drawing on 'that artificial reason obtained by long study, observation, and experience, exercised upon analogies of existing laws, which are gathered from the comparison of statutes, rules, and cases, that is to say, by the comparison of facts, arguments, and decisions, a part of the Law itself'.[1104] Hannay is clearly alluding to Coke's famous defence of 'the artificial reason' of English common law against the exercise of 'natural reason'.[1105] The claim is that the Scottish common law

---

[1099] Hailes (n. 1010), vi.   [1100] See Leadbetter (n. 840), 45, 49, 51.
[1101] Kames, *Dictionary* (n. 1080), vol. 1, ii.
[1102] [Henry Home, Lord Kames], *Principles of Equity* (1760).   [1103] Tytler (n. 1081), iv–v.
[1104] Hannay (n. 1068), 27.
[1105] 12 Coke's Reports 63 at 65; see G. J. Postema, *Bentham and the Common Law Tradition* (1986), 30–8.

contains an immanent reason from which answers to new problems may be derived. This means that trained lawyers can extend the rules and develop them into new areas by a process of deduction and analogy. Thus, when an unforeseen case came for decision, there was in fact broad agreement among 'the best Lawyers' as to its solution, because of their 'like trains of thought, like affections, like habits and wants'.[1106] Decisions became, not exemplars of an authoritative rationality lying outside themselves, but building blocks of law's own inherent rationality.

The more Scots lawyers thought this way, the more important it was to have good reports and a court process that produced clear precedents. From 1825, this was achieved. The emphasis on court decisions was reflected in the publication for the first time of decisions of the House of Lords in Scottish appeals, because there were 'sundry instances . . . where the Judgments of the Court of Session have been reversed in Parliament, [but] the original decisions remain as precedents . . . in the Collections of decided Cases, in the Dictionary of Decisions, and in the works of Law Writers of authority'.[1107] Now that decisions were seen as *embodying* the common law, this was a major problem. After 1820, reporting of decisions of other courts likewise became more common.[1108]

Scots common law was now viewed as a complete, autonomous, and national system, sufficient in itself to provide answers to novel legal problems. The Scots legal *illuminati* had considered that historical investigation and the progressive development of ethics in new historical contexts would reveal new legal needs, which would then need to be inscribed in law, preferably through the decisions of a court. The new view saw Scots law as containing its own inner logic of development and its own progressive morality. If Scots lawyers continued to pay attention to English law in the development of their own, Bell emphasized the need to exercise caution in relying on English judgments, 'lest the purity of this part of our jurisprudence, and the integrity of our own system of law, should be impaired by too indiscriminate a use of English authorities'.[1109] Scots law was a complete system with its own inner logic.

By 1832, much of continental Europe had adopted civil codes. Although to some extent the *jus commune* continued in Germany, the internationalism of law had ended.[1110] Legal scholarship now focused on national laws derived

---

[1106] Hannay (n. 1068), 27

[1107] David Robertson in *Cases on Appeal from Scotland Decided in the House of Peers, from 1707 to 1727* (1807), xvi–xvii.

[1108] *Reports of Cases Tried in the Jury Court, . . . by Joseph Murray, Esq. Advocate* (1818–31); *Cases Decided in the Court of Teinds from May 1821, to June 1831* (1831). Reporting of criminal cases started to become regular at this time. [1109] Bell (n. 1005), XIII.

[1110] See Bellomo (n. 19), 9–21.

from national sources, in states conceived as sovereign. The Scottish emphasis on the superiority of common law over statute law—in dramatic contrast to seventeenth-century views (other than that of Stair)—undoubtedly reflects the experience of a legal system without a legislature. Indeed, as the British Parliament, after the benign neglect of the eighteenth century, became much more active in Scots law, Scots could find arguments for the preservation of their law from an active legislature in the ideas of Friedrich Carl von Savigny.[1111]

VIII. EPILOGUE—AFTER 1832

1. General themes

The natural conclusion for this historical introduction is at the end of the third decade of the nineteenth century. Complex and interesting though developments in Scots law may have been since then, the basic features of the institutions of the modern Scottish legal system were already in place. The route Scots law was to take was already mapped out. The most important developments after 1832 were to be in the doctrines of Scots law, with which this introduction has not been primarily concerned, but which are dealt with elsewhere in these volumes. The new court structure, the reformed procedure, the new attitude to sources of law, and the increasing orientation—both intellectual and political—towards England meant that the influence of English law, with its plentiful and dynamic case law, was inevitably powerful. The route was away from the *jus commune*. In this respect, Lord Cockburn was for once correct in weary old age to characterize the era to 1832 as 'the last purely Scotch age'.[1112] Empire, turning away from a (now in any case irrevocably changed) continental Europe, and, perhaps above all, the development of the railways meant that this was so.

In surveying the history of Scots law, this introduction has focused on the political context, the development of courts and procedure, trends in the law, the legal profession, and legal education. Special attention has also been paid to intellectual issues, particularly the changing influence of the *jus commune*. This brief epilogue will conclude with an outline of some of the developments in these areas after 1832. This will give a general overview of some of the major issues of the period.

[1111] Cairns, (1994) 20 *Syracuse Journal of International Law and Commerce* 199–201.
[1112] Henry Cockburn, *Life of Lord Jeffrey with a Selection from his Correspondence* (1852), vol. 1, 157.

2. The Scottish Office and the Parliament

The Union of 1707 has continued to be renegotiated with the ebb and flow of politics. Major change started as the greater activity and intervention of the Victorian Parliament created strains in the Union. Although formal responsibility for Scotland lay with the Home Secretary, the end of the politics of management with the Reform Act of 1832 turned the Lord Advocate into a de facto minister for Scotland; yet, since his was not a cabinet post, Scottish interests were increasingly considered to be inadequately represented. Agitation for formal recognition of a specifically Scottish dimension to British politics led to the creation of a Scottish Education Department in 1872, while the office of Secretary for Scotland was created in 1885. Based in Dover House in Whitehall the Secretary was, from 1892, always a member of the Cabinet. The Local Government Act of 1894 made the Scottish Secretary head of a Scottish administration, while a Scottish Grand Committee was to deal with Scottish bills.[1113]

In 1926, the Scottish Secretary became a Secretary of State, while, in the 1930s, the Scottish administration was reorganized and concentrated in St Andrews House in Edinburgh, creating administrative devolution. Many of these reforms were a response to the growth of nationalist sentiment.

In 1977, as the Scottish National Party achieved a 36 per cent share of the votes, the then Labour government introduced a devolution measure, which passed into law in 1978. On its basis a referendum was held, where 52 per cent voted in favour of devolution, but less than the 40 per cent of the total electorate required by the legislation. From 1979, a powerful Conservative administration progressively lost seats and political legitimacy in Scotland, provoking further moves for devolution, culminating in the Scotland Act, endorsed by a referendum, establishing the new Parliament.[1114]

3. Courts and procedure

Though the basic architecture of the Scottish legal system was in place by the accession of Victoria (1837–1901), existing trends continued, such as that of amalgamation of separate jurisdictions. Thus, in 1836, the separate Commissary Court for Edinburgh was finally abolished, its remaining jurisdiction incorporated into that of the sheriff.[1115] The separate Exchequer Court was merged into the Session in 1856.[1116] Thus emerged the existing simple and

---

[1113] Lynch (n. 4), 414–16; Ian Levitt, 'The State', in Anthony Cooke, Ian Donnachie, Ann MacSween, and C. A. Whatley, *Modern Scottish History, 1707 to the Present. Volume 2: The Modernisation of Scotland, 1850 to the Present* (1998), 1–24 at 2–12.

[1114] Levitt (n. 1113), 12–22; Lynch (n. 4), 441–9; T. M. Devine, *The Scottish Nation 1700–2000* (1999), 574–617.   [1115] 6 and 7 Will IV (c. 41).

[1116] Exchequer Court (Scotland) Act, 19 and 20 Vict (c. 56).

clearly defined structure of sheriff court, Court of Session, and High Court of Justiciary.

If tinkering was continual, there was a major reform of criminal process by the Criminal Procedure (Scotland) 1887;[1117] while criminal procedure has continued to evolve, the basic system established under that act has lasted. The new model of civil procedure created by the Court of Session Act in 1825 and consequent Acts of Sederunt was developed and consolidated in the Court of Session Act 1868, which established what is substantially still modern procedure.[1118] The 1825 act had left open the possibility for written memorials and informations; in 1850, however, Parliament prohibited the court from ordering 'written argument'. Pleading was only to be oral. The old system was completely dead.[1119]

4. Trends in the law

There is little point in attempting other than the briefest sketch of the history of substantive law since 1832, which has hitherto largely followed the route prepared for it by the first quarter of the nineteenth century. Moreover, the development of thinking about law in the period is too complex to distil in a few words. Thus, competition between regulation and freedom of action has been continuous, with principles of one or the other dominant at differing times because of particular circumstances. Nonetheless, some events and features of legal development do stand out as worthy of mention.

Through the nineteenth century, commercial law was progressively developed and reformed following established patterns. There was also considerable agitation for its codification, with many in favour of a general British code.[1120] Ultimately, a series of important statutes was enacted, transforming and updating this field of law.[1121] Underlying such reforms were the aims of promoting enterprise and development, while trying to protect against excessive risk. The development of the incorporated company with limited liability has proved to be a major means of promoting such ends; it has engendered a large body of law.

[1117] Criminal Procedure (Scotland) Act, 50 and 51 Vict (c. 35).

[1118] Court of Session Act 1868, 31 and 32 Vict (c. 100). See the discussion in J. C. Watt, *John Inglis, Lord Justice-General of Scotland: A Memoir* (1893), 239–47.

[1119] Court of Session Act 1850, 13 and 14 Vict (c. 36), s. 14. Under SI 1994/2310, the Court of Session once again assumed power to order 'notes of argument' and to direct the determination of actions 'on the basis of written submissions without any oral hearing': see Angus Stewart, Review, (1999) 3 *Edinburgh LR* 265–7 at 266.

[1120] Alan Rodger, 'The Codification of Commercial Law in Victorian Britain', (1992) 109 *LQR* 570–90.

[1121] Consider e.g. Mercantile Law Amendment (Scotland) Act 1856, 19 and 20 Vict (c. 60); Bills of Exchange Act 1882, 45 and 46 Vict (c. 61); Bankruptcy (Scotland) Act 1856, 19 and 20 Vict (c. 79); Bankruptcy (Scotland) Act 1913, 3 and 4 Geo 5 (c. 20); Merchant Shipping Act 1894, 57 and 58 Vict (c. 60): Sale of Goods Act 1893, 56 and 57 Vict (c. 71).

Land law and conveyancing have been and continue to be steadily developed to confirm the powers of individual owners and to ease transfers and registration, although property owners have been the subject of increasingly strict planning and other regulation. Many aspects of the feudal system of tenure have already been amended and the remains of this once central and defining area of the common law will shortly be abolished, while the Register of Sasines is being progressively replaced by a Land Register.[1122] Male primogeniture in succession to heritage finally disappeared in 1964 (other than for noble titles).[1123] Through the nineteenth century, the power of entails was dismantled.[1124] There have been countervailing trends to the emphasis on individual property. The clearances in the Highlands and other social problems led to the 'Crofters' Wars' of the 1880s and ultimately to various Crofters Acts.[1125]

The laws of contract and delict have, putting it broadly, continued to stress individual rights and responsibilities. Legislation to protect consumers has developed significantly, however, while a welfare system has complemented, if far from replaced, the rules on delictual liability for personal injury.

Recent reforms of family law have cut across traditional ideals of individual responsibility and ownership, instead emphasizing welfare principles and dealing with certain assets as belonging to married couples.[1126] In a similar way, there has been a move away from 'fault' as the ground of divorce.[1127] Much of this reflects the development of the Welfare State after 1945 and mirrors changes in other European countries. The resolution of these conflicting trends of individual rights and general welfare will be for the new Parliament, though in some areas subject to the European Convention on Human Rights, Westminster, and the European Union; at the moment, they create an interesting and creative dynamic tension in the law.

[1122] Titles to Land (Scotland) Act 1858, 21 and 22 Vict (c. 76); Titles to Land Consolidation (Scotland) Act 1868, 31 and 32 Vict (c. 101); Conveyancing (Scotland) Act 1874, 37 and 38 Vict (c. 94); Conveyancing (Scotland) Act 1924, 14 and 15 Geo V (c. 27); Conveyancing Amendment (Scotland) Act 1938, 1 and 2 Geo VI (c. 24); Conveyancing and Feudal Reform (Scotland) Act 1970 (c. 35); Land Tenure Reform (Scotland) Act 1974 (c. 38); Land Registration (Scotland) Act 1979 (c. 33); Abolition of Feudal Tenure etc. (Scotland) Act 200 (asp 5).

[1123] Succession (Scotland) Act 1964 (c. 41).

[1124] Entail Amendment Act 1848, 11 and 12 Vict (c. 36); Entail Amendment (Scotland) Act 1875, 38 and 39 Vict (c. 61); Entail (Scotland) Act 1882, 45 and 46 Vict (c. 53); Entail (Scotland) Act 1914, 4 and 5 Geo V (c. 43).

[1125] Crofters Holdings (Scotland) Act, 1886, 49 and 50 Vict (c. 29); Small Landholders (Scotland) Act 1911, 1 and 2 Geo V (c. 49); E. A. Cameron, *Land for the People? The British Government and the Scottish Highlands, c.1880–1925* (1996).

[1126] See e.g. The Matrimonial Homes (Family Protection) (Scotland) Act 1981 (c. 59); Family Law (Scotland) Act 1985 (c. 37); Children (Scotland) Act 1995 (c. 36). For a general discussion, see Lilian Edwards and Anne Griffiths, *Family Law* (1997).

[1127] The Divorce (Scotland) Act 1976 (c. 39).

5. The legal profession

The past 170 years have also seen strong conflicting tendencies of continuity and change in the legal profession. In many respects, it is recognizably similar to the legal profession of 1830: the division between membership of the Faculty of Advocates and other groups of lawyers still stands, though eroded slightly by the new status of solicitor-advocate.[1128] On the other hand, reflecting wider social changes, there are now, especially since 1970, substantial numbers of women lawyers.[1129]

A notable development among the advocates was the creation of a role of Queen's Counsel on the English model in 1897 to resolve problems of precedency both within the Scots bar and in members' dealings with English barristers.[1130] More recently, the position of the advocates' clerks was reformed with the establishment of Faculty Services, while the older, nineteenth century tradition of advocates having chambers in the New Town of Edinburgh has been supplanted by practice out of the Advocates' Library in Parliament House.[1131]

In itself, this last development hints at a change in the nature of the Advocates' Library. By the end of the nineteenth century, it had grown into a vast general collection rather beyond the ability of a relatively small bar to maintain and make accessible. A solution came in 1925 with the establishment of the National Library of Scotland, to which the non-legal books of the Faculty were transferred.[1132] The Advocates' Library is now restricted to law books, though it remains much more than a mere professional library.

The Procurators Act of 1865 finally laid down a complete educational programme for admission as a procurator and provided a mechanism for the incorporation of local groups of procurators.[1133] The Law Agents Act of 1873 restructured the profession of law agent and procurator, providing for a uniform general examination for admission, and giving uniform rights of appearance.[1134] While individual societies and faculties could have further requirements for admission, this act provided a common base.[1135] The tendency towards centralization and unification of the profession of procurator and law agent was furthered by the Solicitors (Scotland) Act of 1933 and culminated in the Legal Aid and Solicitors (Scotland) Act of 1949.[1136] This second act created the Law Society of Scotland as the general

---

[1128] Law Reform (Miscellaneous Provisions) (Scotland) Act 1990 (c. 40), s. 24.
[1129] See the Sex Disqualification (Removal) Act 1919 (c. 71).
[1130] Cairns (n. 457), §§ 1271–4.
[1131] J. R. Doherty, 'History of the Faculty of Advocates from 1900', in *The Laws of Scotland: Stair Memorial Encyclopaedia*, vol. 13 (1992), §§ 1286–301 at §§ 1292–4.
[1132] See I. F. Maciver, 'The Making of a National Library', in Cadell/Matheson (n. 776), 215–65. [1133] 28 and 29 Vict (c. 85).
[1134] 36 and 37 Vict (c. 63). [1135] See Begg (n. 813), 19–22.
[1136] See also the Solicitors (Scotland) Act 1980 (c. 46).

professional body of solicitors (as such lawyers were now generally called) and provided for legal aid and advice to facilitate the exercise of legal rights by people of modest means.

At the start of the twenty-first century, though it is possible to qualify without studying law at a university, virtually all members of both branches of the Scottish legal profession possess a university degree in law. While there has long been a belief in the importance and advantage of university studies in law for intending advocates and procurators, crucial in this were the reforms inaugurated by the Universities (Scotland) Act of 1858, under which a degree of LL.B. had been created in 1862. Around the same period, the Faculty of Advocates reorganized their admission regulations, requiring both a general education and a greater breadth of legal study. Ultimately the Faculty recognized the degree of LL.B., which could only be taken after that of MA, as exempting from their examinations.[1137] In this century, the Law Society of Scotland has also recognized possession of the degree of LL.B., providing it includes necessary professional subjects, as exempting from its examinations.[1138] In this context, the expansion of the Faculties of Law, the introduction of the undergraduate degree of LL.B., and financial assistance for university study have generally promoted an entirely graduate profession. At the same time, there has been a corresponding, powerful development in academic and practical literature in law, as law faculties have expanded and modernized.[1139]

6. Scots law, civil law, and the future

The late Victorian period saw an interesting intellectual revival in Scots law, signified by publication, not only of journals such as the *Juridical Review* and the *Journal of Jurisprudence*, but also of major works such as McLaren on *Succession*, Rankine on *Landownership*, and Goudy on *Bankruptcy*.[1140] While Roman law was cited in these treatises, they are not founded in the learning of the *jus commune*. This perhaps reflects the training in law in Germany of some of these men, who often also looked to codification as the way for-

---

[1137] Cairns (n. 457), §§ 1278–9.

[1138] 'Solicitors', in *The Laws of Scotland: Stair Memorial Encyclopaedia*, vol. 13 (1992), §§ 1126–223 at §§ 1160–5.

[1139] K. G. C. Reid, 'The Third Branch of the Legal Profession: The Academic Lawyer in Scotland', in H. L. MacQueen (ed.), *Scots Law into the 21st Century: Essays in Honour of W. A. Wilson* (1996), 39–49.

[1140] Lord McLaren, *The Law of Wills and Succession as Administered in Scotland, Including Trusts, Entails, Powers and Executry* (3rd edn., 1894); John Rankine, *The Law of Landownership in Scotland: A Treatise on the Rights and Burdens Incident to the Ownership of Lands and other Heritages in Scotland* (1879); Henry Goudy, *A Treatise on the Law of Bankruptcy in Scotland* (1886).

ward.[1141] Scots law was founded mainly in Scottish sources, above all in decisions, even though some of these might well have doctrine ultimately founded in civil law.[1142]

Henry Goudy, Professor of Civil Law in Edinburgh, and then Regius Professor of Civil Law in the University of Oxford, remarked in his inaugural lecture in Oxford that 'in the Scotch Reports of the present century citations of Justinian's texts and the civilians will be found to be comparatively rare'. He explained that this was because 'a wealth of decided cases has accumulated', while, 'in matters of commercial law, the well-furnished storehouses of the English Reports have been largely resorted to'.[1143] It is difficult to quarrel with this assessment and the hundred years since have not altered the position.

All of this reflects the general nineteenth-century vision of law as essentially national, which, for Scots law, has meant that it should be understood as a complete system derived from decisions and statutes. This has presented particular problems, however, as Scotland had a national legal system without a legislature. Given the dominance of England within the United Kingdom, the models for reform and development adopted in Scotland—as Goudy has pointed out—tended to be those of English practice and law. Through the nineteenth century and beyond, the influence of English law on Scots law has accordingly been profound, both through legislation and the decisions of the courts, in which the role of the House of Lords has been particularly controversial. Again this has followed a trend evident by the end of the first quarter of the nineteenth century.

Perhaps the last tangible vestige of the former centrality of the *jus commune* to Scottish legal practice is the requirement of the Faculty of Advocates that its intrants have a pass in the Roman law of property and obligations. Indeed, the entry in the Books of Sederunt for the admission of an advocate still bears that he or she was found qualified after 'a public and private examination . . . upon the Civil and Scots Law' (though the public examination was abolished in 1966).[1144] In the degree of LL.B. as established in 1862, civil law was just one subject, if compulsory. Since then, civil law has become a very minor component of legal study and primarily of historic interest.[1145]

Despite the assimilation of much English practice and doctrine, Scots law

---

[1141] See Alan Rodger, 'Scottish Advocates in the Nineteenth Century: The German Connection', (1994) 110 *LQR* 563–91.

[1142] The essays in Robin Evans-Jones (ed.), *The Civil Law Tradition in Scotland* (1995) contain much of interest on use of Roman law by the Scottish courts over the past 200 years.

[1143] Henry Goudy, *An Inaugural Lecture on the Fate of Roman Law North and South of the Tweed* (1894), 27.

[1144] Lord Davidson and Lord Rodger, 'The Modern Faculty of Advocates', in *The Laws of Scotland: Stair Memorial Encyclopaedia*, vol. 13 (1992), §§ 1302–91 at §§ 1304–14.

[1145] See J. W. Cairns, *James Muirhead, Teacher, Scholar, Book-Collector* (Part One of *The Muirhead Collection Catalogue*) (= *Bibliographica Belgica* 146) (1999), 1–32 at 9–11, 16.

nonetheless has remained different from English law because of its civilian heritage derived from the *jus commune*. The European Union and the incorporation of the European Convention on Human Rights have reopened older and wider links for Scots law, raising again the possibility of participation in a more international legal culture for its scholars, practitioners, and new legislature. The effects of this are uncertain. Much of the regulation emanating from the European Union is concerned with commercial and company law, areas in which Scots law is hardly civilian. Moreover, the institutions and forms of law of the Union are derived from continental, particularly French, administrative practice and institutions, which have little in common either with Scottish institutions or, for that matter, with those of the old *jus commune*. Whether the end of the twentieth century marks another turning point in Scots law awaits to be seen. The road ahead is as yet uncertain.

3

Property Law: Sources and Doctrine

KENNETH REID

This chapter introduces the remainder of volume 1, which is concerned with the law of property. Necessarily, the chapter is both general and selective, although some of the themes mentioned here are taken up again in the chapters which follow.

The fact that a legal system is 'mixed' does not imply consistency in the mixture, whether measured by subject or by time. Not only may the proportions differ from subject to subject, but the ingredients themselves may not be the same. In this respect, the law of property is as different from the law of contract as that law, in turn, is different from the law of delict. Part I of this chapter seeks to examine, through historical eyes, the mixture of sources and influences which make up the law of property. Part II considers the literature of the law, and the attempts to bind the disparate sources into some kind of a unified theory. In the final part there is a brief consideration of two doctrines which, in different ways, typify the law of property in Scotland. These doctrines are possession and the law of the tenement.

I. SOURCES AND INFLUENCES

1. Feudal law

For much of its written history, property law was feudal law and little more. The treatment of property law in the digest practicks of the sixteenth and seventeenth centuries[1] is dominated by feudal law; and the first systematic exposition of legal doctrine in Scotland is a work on feudalism, the *Jus Feudale* of Thomas Craig, completed around 1600 and first published,

---

[1] For practicks generally, see Hector McKechnie's account in *idem* (ed.), *Sources and Literature of Scots Law*, Stair Society, vol. 1 (1936), 25 sqq. McKechnie divides practicks into decision practicks and digest practicks. The latter contain materials collected together from a variety of sources and amount to rudimentary textbooks but with an emphasis firmly on practice. McKechnie lists twelve digest practicks, of which the following have been published (in all cases long after they were written): Balfour (1754, reproduced in 1962–3 as vols. 21 and 22 of the Stair Society series); Spotiswoode (1706); Hope's *Minor Practicks* (1726 and 1734); and Hope's *Major Practicks* (Stair Society, vols. 3 and 4, 1937–8). The most substantial is the practicks of Balfour, described by the editor of the modern reprint (Peter G. B. McNeill, at xxxix) as 'the pre-eminent written record of Scots Law until the publication of Stair's *Institutions*'.

posthumously, in 1655.[2] The leading position given to feudalism continued throughout the institutional period and into the nineteenth century.

Nor was its influence confined to property law. Among the other fields of law affected were succession, and the law of actions. The name usually given to immoveable property in Scotland—'heritable property', meaning the property that is inherited by the deceased's heir—is a product of the feudal rule of primogeniture.[3]

(a) Chronology

According to Craig[4] 'the Feudal Law was established in Scotland before the Norman conquest, and therefore before its introduction into England', but this view is not supported by modern scholarship, which has shown that feudalism arrived in England with William the Conqueror and spread to Scotland shortly thereafter.[5] The oldest feudal charter by a Scottish king to survive dates from 1094.[6]

It is often emphasized that, in its origins, feudal law in Scotland was Anglo-Norman law. But just as important was the manner in which the law in the two countries began to diverge.[7] England was the first to move away, with fundamental legislative change during the reign of Edward I (1272–1307). Of particular importance was the statute *Quia Emptores* which, by prohibiting subinfeudation, cut off the future growth of the feudal system. Whether because of the wars of independence, or for other reasons, this legislation was not copied in Scotland. There subinfeudation remained competent, and continues to be employed even today, usually by volume builders seeking to impose uniform conditions on housing or commercial developments.[8] The result is two quite different systems. Whereas in England land is held directly from the Crown, in Scotland the vassal in possession is separated from the Crown by a, sometimes lengthy, chain of feudal estates in land.

Later, Scotland was also to move in a different direction. The reception of

---

[2] It was republished, first in Leipzig in 1716, and then in Edinburgh in 1732. It is written in Latin, but a translation in two volumes, by Lord Clyde, was published in 1934.

[3] At one time a further distinction in immoveable property was made between heritage and conquest. See G. L. Gretton, 'The Feudal System', in K. G. C. Reid (ed.), *The Law of Property in Scotland* (1996), § 56.   [4] Craig, I, 8, 3.

[5] See e.g. A. A. M. Duncan, *Scotland: The Making of a Kingdom* (1975), 133 sqq.; M. Lynch, *Scotland: A New History* (1991), 55 sqq. An essential guide to the medieval period is Hector L. MacQueen, *Common Law and Feudal Society in Medieval Scotland* (1993).

[6] It is reproduced in P. Gouldesbrough, *Formulary of Old Scots Legal Documents*, Stair Society, vol. 36 (1985), 158–9. It is a charter of Duncan II in favour of the monks of Durham.

[7] Although superseded to some extent by later scholarship, C. D. Farran's *The Principles of Scots and English Land Law* (1958) remains a stimulating account of the separate development of feudal law in the two countries. C. F. Kolbert and N. A. M. Mackay, *History of Scots and English Land Law* (1977) is based on Farran's work.

[8] This is true even on the eve of feudal abolition. The writer has given up conveyancing, but in 1999 he acted for a relative in a purchase which proceeded by subinfeudation.

feudalism was followed by the beginnings of a reception of Roman law; and, while not easily susceptible, feudalism was Romanized to some degree. A civil law analysis raised as a central question the location of *dominium* (ownership). The feudal relationship involved two or more parties. Which was owner? In his *Jus Feudale*, Craig adopted the view of Bartolus and others that in feudal law, exceptionally, there was *duplex dominium*.[9] Land was owned *both* by the vassal and also by the Crown or other superior. But each had *dominium* of a different kind. The vassal had *dominium directum* and the superior *dominium utile*. Craig attacked strongly the views of Cujacius 'and other moderns' that the vassal had merely a right of usufruct.[10] Craig's work is both evidence for, and also an independent cause of, a shift in orientation from Anglo-Norman to continental feudalism. While England is not neglected, Craig makes extensive use of the *Libri Feudorum*, the twelfth-century compilation of Lombardic law which had come to be included as an appendix to the *Corpus Juris Civilis*,[11] and his text contains many references to the *Corpus Juris* itself and to writers of the *jus commune*. This approach was not universally admired. Much later, Walter Ross condemned Craig's 'refusal to know or acknowledge any jurisprudence but the Roman, and the Books of the Fiefs',[12] while George Joseph Bell warned his students at Edinburgh University that Craig's work 'is more imbued with Continental law than the feudal law of Scotland'.[13] But many of Craig's views were accepted by Stair,[14] and, through Stair, by later writers.

Already in 1600 Craig was complaining of the senility of feudalism ('feudorum senium').[15] By 1820 Bell was able to tell his students that 'the feudal system is now abolished except as to the system of conveyancing formed upon it'.[16] A century later even the system of conveyancing had become too much for at least some lawyers.[17] For the most part these

---

[9] Craig, I, 9, 9. For a review of the issues, see A. J. van der Walt and D. G. Kleyn, '*Duplex Dominium*: The History and Significance of the Concept of Divided Ownership', in D. P. Visser (ed.), *Essays on the History of Law* (1989), 213–60.

[10] Craig, I, 9, 10. See further J. W. Cairns, 'Craig, Cujas, and the Definition of *feudum*: Is a Feu a Usufruct?', in Peter Birks (ed.), *New Perspectives in the Roman Law of Property* (1989), 75–84.

[11] A translation is given at the end of the second volume of Lord Clyde's translation of the *Jus Feudale*.

[12] W. Ross, *Lectures on the History and Practice of the Law of Scotland Relative to Conveyancing and Legal Diligence* (2nd edn., 1822), 62.

[13] G. J. Bell, *Lectures on the Law of Scotland*, 164. This is a set of detailed notes, taken by a student, of lectures delivered by Professor Bell between 26 Oct. 1825 and 7 Apr. 1826. The notes are in the possession of the writer. Bell's lectures were the basis of his *Principles* but the notes show some interesting variations including, in this case, candour as to the value of particular texts.

[14] J. M. Halliday, 'Feudal Law as a Source', in D. M. Walker (ed.), *Stair Tercentenary Studies*, Stair Society, vol. 33 (1981), 136–40.   [15] Craig, I, 9, 19.

[16] Bell (n. 13), 164.

[17] Though not for Lord Dunedin: see *Hay* v. *Corporation of Aberdeen* 1909 SC 554, 558.

comments merely indicate adaptability and vitality. They testify to the fact that feudalism was forever changing.[18] Without change it could hardly have survived.

The last vestiges of feudalism as a social and political system disappeared with the abolition, in the aftermath of the 1745 Rebellion, of the military tenure of wardholding, and of the right of heritable jurisdiction.[19] The main surviving tenure, feu farm, was little more than an arrangement for the purchase of land on credit: instead of paying the price at once, the acquirer paid a twice-yearly sum, known as feuduty, in perpetuity.[20] Feu farm tenure was often characterized as a form of *emphyteusis*.[21]

To this convenient solution to a problem of capital formation there was added, in the nineteenth century, a solution to a problem of urbanization. By means of conditions in feudal grants it was possible to provide a detailed regulatory framework for urban land use which anticipated the regulatory public law of a later age.[22] Known, eventually, as real burdens, these conditions have become a prominent feature of conveyancing in the last 200 years.

The inventiveness of feudalism continued into modern times. In owner-occupied sheltered housing for the elderly, introduced to Scotland in the 1980s, the relationship of superior and vassal is recast as a relationship of manager and householder. All sheltered housing developments are feued and, as the law currently stands, could not easily take place in the absence of the feudal system. Similarly, local authorities have discovered the value of subinfeudation as a means of control over council houses which are sold under the right-to-buy legislation.[23] That the tenant should thus become a feudal vassal seems an ironic commentary on the social purposes of the legislation.

The feudal system was abolished in France in 1789, and throughout most of the rest of Europe by about 1850. Its survival, uniquely, in Scotland was due mainly to its adaptability. Feudalism could not be abolished for as long as it was useful. By the closing years of the twentieth century that usefulness had declined. Banks and building societies were available to finance land purchase, and no new feuduties were allowed after 1974.[24] Existing feuduties were to be bought out under a statutory scheme,[25] their value for the most part eroded by inflation. Planning and other regulatory law was carrying out some, although not all of,[26] the work of real burdens; but in any event real

---

[18] For the changes, see Gretton (n. 3), §§ 41–113. This article is an outstanding historical account of the legal aspects of feudalism.
[19] Tenures Abolition Act 1746; Heritable Jurisdictions (Scotland) Act 1746.
[20] Sometimes, though, part of the price had to be paid at once by way of a *grassum*.
[21] Craig, I, 9, 19; Stair, II, 3, 34; Erskine, II, 4, 6.
[22] Kenneth G. C. Reid, 'Real Burdens', in *idem* (n. 3), § 382.
[23] Now contained in part III of the Housing (Scotland) Act 1987.
[24] Land Tenure Reform (Scotland) Act 1974, s. 1.
[25] Land Tenure Reform (Scotland) Act 1974, ss. 4–6.
[26] K. Gray and S. F. Gray, 'The Future of Real Burdens in Scots Law', (1999) 2 *Edinburgh LR* 229.

burdens could be created non-feudally. Although feudalism had been radically simplified over the centuries, the complexity inherent in a system of multiple ownership could no longer be justified. An Act to abolish the feudal system[27] was passed in 2000 but, at the time of writing, was not yet in force. After a transitional period of several years, the long history of feudalism will have come to a close.

(b) Influence

Feudalism was of the first importance, both for the law and for legal practice. Something was said earlier about legal literature. The pattern of litigation was much the same. Innumerable decisions on feudalism are reported in Morison's *Dictionary of Decisions* under headings such as 'feu', 'feu-duties', 'infeftment', and 'superior and vassal'. Even as late as the eighteenth century, feudalism remained a central part of the practice of most lawyers. Looking back on that period, George Joseph Bell,[28] probably a hostile witness,[29] noted that

[t]he Union [i.e. with England] was soon followed by two rebellions, which not only disturbed the tranquillity, and interrupted the natural advancement of industry, wealth, and commerce, but produced a similar effect on the progress of the law. The numerous forfeitures which followed the rebellions of 1715 and 1745 gave rise to a multitude of difficult questions of high interest relative to the connection of superior and vassal, the nature and efficacy of destinations in deeds of entail, and the force of real securities over land. All the learning of the feudal law came more immediately to be called into use, and the professional success, as well as the character of a lawyer, was estimated chiefly according to his skill in the law of heritable property.

If, during the nineteenth century, the dominance of feudal law began to wane, the process was surprisingly slow. The *Scots Digest*, which covers decisions of the Court of Session from 1800 to 1873, digests 250 cases under the heading 'Superior and Vassal' and 57 more under 'Sasine', as compared with 492 cases under 'Property' (covering many of the non-feudal aspects of land law). By way of comparison, 324 cases were digested under 'Contract'. Supplementary volumes show only a gradual falling back, as the table demonstrates, and the last two volumes appear to show a revival in the inter-war period, although the numbers are too small for any definite conclusions

---

[27] The Abolition of Feudal Tenure etc. (Scotland) Act 2000 was in almost identical terms to the draft bill appended to the Scottish Law Commission Report No. 168 on *Abolition of the Feudal System* (1999). The continuing usefulness of the feudal system is shown by the elaborate savings, particularly in relation to real burdens.   [28] *Commentaries*, I, viii–ix.

[29] As we will see later, Bell saw the 'progress of the law' as resting in the development of a modern commercial law. Feudal law held little interest.

Table of cases digested in the *Scots Digest* (%)[b]

Period	Superior & Vassal[a]	Property	Contract
1800–1873	27 (307)	44 (492)	29 (324)
1873–1904	27 (157)	41 (236)	32 (184)
1904–1914	19 (27)	34 (48)	47 (65)
1914–1923	19 (17)	13 (12)	68 (61)
1923–1930	12 (4)	26 (9)	62 (21)
1930–1937	29 (7)	33 (8)	38 (9)
1937–1940	25 (5)	35 (7)	40 (8)

[a] 'Sasine', a separate title in the first volume, is included in the total.
[b] Actual number of cases is given in parentheses.

to be drawn. The table also reveals the inexorable rise of contract law. It shows the ratio of cases in the three categories, expressed as a percentage.[30]

(c) Effects

Much could be written about the effect, both on the law of property and on the wider law, of so prolonged a period of dominance by feudal law. Here only three points will be mentioned.

First, the existence of feudalism inhibited the development of a general theory of the law of property. This is because there was not one law of property but two. Bell put it this way:[31]

> A double system of jurisprudence, in relation to the subjects of property, has thus arisen in Scotland, as in most European nations;—the one regulating Land and its accessories according to the spirit and arrangements of the feudal system; the other regulating the rights to Moveables according to the principles of Roman jurisprudence which prevailed before the establishment of feus.

For as long as feudal law remained a dominant force, attempts to identify common principles which might apply across the moveable/immoveable divide were half-hearted and unconvincing. In other countries the abolition of feudalism was sometimes followed by codification. Unsurprisingly, codification did not usually come first.[32] The position should not, however, be exaggerated for, as we will see later, other obstacles also existed to the development of a general theory.

Secondly, the law of immoveable property was itself divided by feudalism. Some real rights were feudal (ownership, liferent,[33] and security) while others

---

[30] These figures are necessarily crude. In particular, other titles could have been used to supplement both 'Property' (e.g. 'Building Restrictions', 'Servitudes', or 'Water' and 'Contract'). But the table gives an accurate account of the decline of feudalism as a subject of litigation.
[31] Bell, *Principles*, § 636.
[32] A well-known exception is the *Allgemeines Landrecht für die Preussichen Staaten* of 1794.
[33] Liferent is usufruct.

(servitude and lease[34]) were not. Curiously, the difference was rarely remarked on, and never fully explained. In principle, such an arrangement was unstable, for the feudal rights could not but interact with the non-feudal. In practice the difficulties were often brushed aside. A typical issue was the creation of a servitude. Who must sign the deed? The logic of *duplex dominium* was to require the signature of both superior and vassal, for both were owners of the putative servient tenement. That appears to have been the position taken by Craig.[35] But this rule was not accepted by later writers, presumably for practical reasons. Stair's view was:[36]

> As to these who can impose servitudes, when they are constitute by express consent; yet they cannot be constitute without consent of the proprietor; and if the superior consent not, they will not be effectual against him, if the fee be open and return to him by right of superiority, for a time, or for ever.

This was a compromise. For as long as the estate of *dominium utile* remained intact, the servitude was good, but it was lost if the feu reverted to the superior. But what was the *res* in respect of which such a servitude was held? *Dominium* (whether *utile* or *directum*) was, of course, a right in the land itself. The same was true of the other feudal real rights (security and liferent). With servitude, however, the right seemed to lie, not in the land itself, but in the *dominium utile* of the land. The position of lease seemed to be the same, for if the feu returned to the superior, any right of lease was lost.[37] The result was paradoxical. A feudal real right could be expressed, in the simple language of the civil law, as a right in a (corporeal) thing; but a non-feudal real right was merely a right in a right which itself was a right in a thing. In the event, these differences seem to have gone unobserved, or at least undiscussed.

The silence is not untypical. Feudal questions attracted much recondite learning, but except where the issue was one between superior and vassal there was an increasing tendency to ignore the feudal system altogether and to treat the vassal as outright owner. That may be the underlying explanation of the rule just described, where the right attributed to the superior seems to fall short of proper ownership.[38]

The same tendency can be seen in the law of accession. If I build a wall on land which is not mine, the wall (if I have built it properly) accedes to the land and becomes the property of the owner of the land. But at this point Roman law meets feudal law. In feudal law the land has more than one owner. As well as the vassal there might, in a typical case, be two or three superiors and also

---

[34] Following the Leases Act 1449 (c. 6), which provided that leases bound successive owners of the land, lease came to be treated in Scotland as a real right. [35] Craig, II, 8, 43.
[36] Stair, II, 7, 3. [37] J. Rankine, *The Law of Leases in Scotland* (3rd edn., 1916), 133.
[38] Thus the position of the superior is not notably different from that of a heritable creditor, for which see *Edinburgh Entertainments Ltd* v. *Stevenson* 1926 SC 363, and *Trade Development Bank* v. *Warriner & Mason (Scotland) Ltd* 1980 SC 74.

the Crown, as holder of the paramount superiority. Do they all own the bricks? For as long as the wall remains standing, the question can be evaded by saying that a superior holds *dominium directum*. But if the wall is demolished and the bricks resume their status as moveable property, this explanation falls away. In practice the issue has been ignored, and the vassal treated as the only owner of the bricks. Other examples of the marginalization of feudalism can also be found.[39]

This leads on to the final point. Marginalization was accompanied by assimilation. As the non-feudal parts of property law began, slowly, to gain the upper hand, so the feudal parts began to resemble them. But the most important episode of assimilation had happened much earlier, with the Romanization of feudal concepts in the late medieval period. It is easy to make fun of the result. The theory of *duplex dominium* is both ungainly and, in the modern period, a serious misrepresentation of the relative positions of superior and vassal. But in the long run it was better than the alternative, which was, as in England, to interpose a legal estate between the person and the land. *Dominium utile* has at least the merit of being a type of *dominium*, and its adoption was to ease the path of feudal abolition some 600 years later. Section 2(1) of the Abolition of Feudal Tenure etc. (Scotland) Act 2000 simply provides that '[a]n estate of *dominium utile* of land shall, on the appointed day, cease to exist as a feudal estate but shall forthwith become the ownership of the land and, in so far as is consistent with the provisions of this Act, the land shall be subject to the same subordinate real rights and other encumbrances as was the estate of *dominium utile*.' The effect of this provision is that rights will be held in land in precisely the same way as, at present, they are held in moveable property. There are no interposed estates. The assimilation of the two branches of the law of property is complete. The final legacy of feudalism is the ease of its passing; and for all its historical dominance, its enduring influence seems likely to be small.

2. Roman law

There was, of course, no adoption of Roman law *as a system* in the manner of feudal law. But in property law the influence of Roman law is everywhere. It is true that on points of detail the rules developed in Scotland are often different from Roman law, and sometimes strikingly so; and it is also true that many doctrines of Roman law were not received at all. But the underlying concepts of the law are typically Roman, or at least civilian in origin—for

---

[39] For example, if A (a non-owner) grants a feu disposition to B which is registered in the Register of Sasines and followed by possession for ten years, the effect of positive prescription is that B is owner. See *Lockhart* v. *Duke of Hamilton* 1890, OH (unreported), but summarized in J. H. Millar, *A Handbook of Prescription* (1893), 11. But does B then hold from A?

example, real rights, *dominium, traditio*, possession, *accessio, specificatio*—and often the Roman name has been retained.

The position is so well known, and well documented, that it is not necessary to say much more here. Roman influence on moveable property was greater than on immoveable, and even today there are rules in moveable property—in *occupatio*, for example, or *accessio*—which seem barely to have shifted from their Roman base. But the Roman legacy has also been substantial in immoveable property. The, admittedly superficial, Romanization of feudal law has already been mentioned. The law of servitudes is substantially Roman, in Scotland as in other countries, and there has been some Roman influence on other subordinate real rights in land such as liferent (usufruct) and security.

A question which has been barely examined is *which* Roman law. Grant McLeod's chapter later in this volume examines citations of the *Corpus Juris Civilis*. But there were also frequent citations of contemporary civilian writing, both in the pleadings of cases and in the legal literature, and such writing could also be used without acknowledgement. The same writers, or pleaders, often cited from both the *Corpus Juris Civilis* and from the *jus commune*, but the relative influence of these sources remains to be assessed. No doubt then, as now, some of the citation was done merely for effect.

At the beginning of the twenty-first century there is no sign of Roman influence abating. On the contrary, Roman ideas are poised to fill the conceptual void left in immoveable property by the abolition of the feudal system. In post-feudal Scotland the law of property is likely to be resolutely civilian.

3. Canon law

Canon law had little influence on mainstream property law even before the Reformation, which in Scotland occurred in 1560. After the Reformation, its direct influence was confined to the law of teinds (tithes) and benefices.[40] However, the important doctrine of spuilzie, discussed later,[41] seems founded on the *exceptio spolii* of the canon law.

4. English law

(a) Receptions

So far as English law is concerned, the most substantial direct reception was of Anglo-Norman feudal law although, as mentioned earlier, the paths of the

---

[40] 'It could be argued that here is the only area in post-Reformation Scots law where canon law was still an active source': J. J. Robertson, 'Canon Law as a Source', in Walker (n. 14), 118.
[41] In part III.1.

two countries soon diverged. English influence, however, continued for a considerable time. David Sellar has shown that the bulk of the references to English law in Stair's *Institutions* concern matters of property and succession, although these usually derive from Craig's *Jus Feudale* and may be a throwback to an earlier age.[42] By the time of Stair the law of property had been too thoroughly Romanized to make English law attractive as a source of new rules.

Other direct receptions came only much later, and then by statute. In 1893 a Sale of Goods Act, passed for the whole United Kingdom, was in substance a codification of the English law of sale. One result was to replace the Romanist requirement of delivery with a rule that ownership in goods passes by intention of the parties. An act of 1961 introduced floating charges to Scotland, while the new system of land registration adopted in 1979 was closely modelled on the English Land Registration Act of 1925. The statutory receptions have caused difficulties. The floating charge is said to be 'genetically incompatible' with Scots law,[43] and has certainly troubled the courts. The new land registration system has serious deficiencies and is to be re-examined by the Scottish Law Commission, although the problems are not all due to the use of an inappropriate model. The Sale of Goods Act, although attacked by legal nationalists, has been reasonably successful in practice; and so far as doctrine is concerned there does not seem much difference between a rule that ownership passes by intention and without delivery, and a rule that insists on delivery but allows the seller to keep possession by the fiction of *constitutum possessorium*.[44]

(b) Borrowings

In other respects the influence of English law has usually been confined to the few areas of property law where the rules are similar in both jurisdictions—most notably trusts, servitudes, and fixtures (accession by building). While, as George Gretton shows later in this volume, trust law in Scotland had an independent origin, it has borrowed widely, and usually wisely, from England. Servitudes and fixtures have Roman roots in both jurisdictions and there has been some sharing of case law.

It is another matter where the rules are fundamentally dissimilar. In English law ownership can be split into separate legal and equitable titles. The identity of the owner then depends on the circumstances in which the ques-

---

[42] W. D. H. Sellar, 'English Law as a Source', in Walker (n. 14), 142.

[43] G. L. Gretton, 'What went wrong with floating charges?', 1984 *SLT (News)* 172, 173.

[44] See e.g. the position in German law, which, in § 930 of the BGB, recognizes the systematic use of *Bezitzkonstitut*. For *constitutum possessorium* in Scottish common law, see D. L. Carey Miller, *Corporeal Moveables in Scots Law* (1991), 129–33; W. M. Gordon, 'Transfer of Ownership', in Reid (n. 3), § 623.

tion arises. For some purposes it is the equitable (or beneficial) owner while for others it is the legal owner. This sophisticated, but complex, idea has no place in the civil law world. If feudal law is discounted, as it usually is, then in Scotland there can only be one right of ownership, although that right can of course be shared, as in the case of common property. So if A is owner, then B is not. It is not possible that A should be owner for some purposes, and B owner for some other purposes.

Nonetheless the flexibility of the English model won some converts, and from time to time attempts were made in Scotland to distinguish formal title from beneficial interest. These took two forms in particular. One was to deny that the person holding the formal title was owner at all. Such was the doctrine of radical right which held that, in certain circumstances, a conveyance of property by A to B left A as owner. While B had the appearance of owner, A had the 'radical right'. This was never mainstream property law, however. The doctrine of radical right was used mainly in reference to the small class of trusts for administration, to trust deeds for creditors, and to heritable securities constituted by *ex facie* absolute disposition.[45]

In a famous speech in a famous case, *Heritable Reversionary Co. Ltd* v. *Millar*,[46] Lord Watson applied a similar analysis to explain the relationship of trustee and beneficiary in an ordinary trust:[47] 'As between them [i.e. trustee and beneficiary] there can, in my opinion, be no doubt that according to the law of Scotland the one, though possessed of the legal title, and being the apparent owner, is in reality a bare trustee; and that the other, to whom the whole beneficial interest belongs, is the true owner.' But this was only 'as between them'. It was beyond challenge that a third party could acquire ownership from the trustee. Why? According to Lord Watson, this was not because the trustee was owner. Instead there was a different explanation:[48]

[T]he validity of a right acquired in such circumstances by a *bona fide* disponee for value does not rest upon the recognition of any power in the trustee which he can lawfully exercise, because breach of trust duty and wilful fraud can never be in themselves lawful, but upon the well-known principle that a true owner [i.e. the beneficiary] who chooses to conceal his right from the public, and to clothe his trustee with all the *indicia* of ownership, is thereby barred from challenging rights acquired by innocent third parties for onerous considerations under contracts with his fraudulent trustee.

The alternative approach was more English still. Rather than the 'wrong' party being owner, both were owners, but for different purposes. Again this was used to explain the relationship between trustee and beneficiary. Thus in one case decided in 1898 Lord McLaren referred to 'the owners of the legal

---

[45] An important historical study of this curious doctrine is G. L. Gretton, 'Radical Rights and Radical Wrongs: A Study in the Law of Trusts, Securities and Insolvency', [1986] *JR* 51 and 192.
[46] (1892) 19 R (HL) 43.   [47] Ibid. at 46–7. See further ch. 12, 506–8.   [48] Ibid. at 47.

estate and the owners of the beneficial estate', while making clear that he regarded the latter as 'the true owner'.[49]

These were mainly ideas of the nineteenth century, and in particular of the final years of that century, when English influence on Scots law as a whole was particularly strong. After the First World War they subsided. Thus in the landmark case of *Inland Revenue* v. *Clark*,[50] decided in 1939, both views of trusts described above were rejected and it was finally determined by the First Division that ownership lay where it appeared to lie, that is, with the trustee, and that the beneficiary had no more than a personal right.

Yet in the closing years of the twentieth century there was an unexpected revival, although not in the field of trusts. Two important litigations concerned broadly similar facts.[51] A person bought a house, paid for it, and moved in, but, before his title could be registered, the seller became insolvent. Under Scottish conveyancing practice the price is handed over in exchange for delivery of the deed of transfer; but since ownership does not pass until the deed is registered, there is a brief period in which the purchaser is vulnerable to the insolvency of the seller. In both litigations the court developed the idea that, once the price is paid and the disposition delivered, the purchaser is, in a certain sense, the owner. For a time, therefore, there are two owners or quasi-owners—the seller, who has legal title, and the buyer, who has beneficial interest. This doctrine appeared most clearly from the speech of Lord Jauncey in the later case, *Sharp* v. *Thomson*; but Lord Jauncey's views were not identical to those of Lord Clyde, the other judge to give an opinion in the House of Lords, and they were sharply at variance with the view of the First Division, which had held to the traditional civilian line. The decision of the House of Lords was not well received,[52] but whether it marks a dead end or a new beginning is too early to say.

5. Native invention

It should not be supposed that the law of property in Scotland was simply an amalgam of the laws of other countries. On the contrary, there was much that was home-made, and even foreign importations had a tendency to acquire native features.

---

[49] *Govan New Bowling-Green Club* v. *Geddes* (1898) 25 R 485 at 492.   [50] 1939 SC 11.

[51] *Gibson* v. *Hunter Home Designs Ltd* 1976 SC 23; *Sharp* v. *Thomson* 1995 SC 455, revised 1997 SC (HL) 66.

[52] The case has been much discussed. For a list of articles, see K. G. C. Reid, 'Equity Triumphant: Sharp v. Thomson', (1997) 1 *Edinburgh LR* 464 and G. L. Gretton and K. G. C. Reid, *Conveyancing* (2nd edn., 1999), para. 11.31 n. 6. For a continental perspective, see Anja Fenge, 'Englishes Kreditsicherungsrecht versus schottisches Sachenrecht: Sharp v. Thomson', (1999) 98 *Zeitschrift für Vergleichende Rechtswissenschaft* 410. See also ch. 6 of this volume. A full analysis will be found in the Scottish Law Commission's Discussion Paper No. 107 on *Diligence against Land* (1998), 28 sqq. A broad view of *Sharp* was taken in *Burnett's Tr* v. *Grainger*, 2000 GWD 28-1093.

Partly this was a product of legislation. The Acts of the pre-Union Scottish Parliament contain many references to property law. An act of 1449[53] had the effect of transforming the contract of lease into a real right—a logical step, if one which many other legal systems have yet to take.[54] Reversions were also made a real right, by an act of 1469.[55] A public land register, the Register of Sasines, was established in 1617.[56] The fact that registration then became mandatory for most real rights in land had a profound and lasting effect on the development of the law. Another act of the same year provided for acquisitive prescription in the case of land, without the need for good faith.[57] Except for the last case,[58] these acts remain in force today.

The practice of the law was also an important influence on the development of doctrine. Dissatisfaction with the limitations of praedial servitudes led to the development of an entirely new real right, known as the real burden.[59] Fifty years after they were first used by conveyancers their existence was finally accepted by the courts.[60] Similarly, conveyancers avoided the inconvenience and uncertainty, in the transmission of land, of resignation to the feudal superior by developing the idea of the alternative manner of holding. The idea was that the transferee would hold initially as vassal of the transferor. Only later, and sometimes much later, was feudal entry taken with the superior, who adopted the sasine of the transferor by issuing a charter of confirmation. At that point the transferor vanished from the feudal chain, and the transferee held directly from the superior. This inventive response to a practical difficulty became standard conveyancing practice until legislative reform in 1874[61] made the whole subterfuge unnecessary. It too was sanctioned by the courts.[62] A third example of practitioner law, the law of the tenement, will be considered in Part III.

---

[53] Leases Act 1449 (c. 6).
[54] T. J. R. Stadnik, 'The Doctrinal Origins of the Juridical Nature of Leases in the Civil Law', (1980) 54 *Tul LR* 1094. [55] Reversion Act 1469 (c. 3).
[56] Registration Act 1617 (c. 16). For a history of registration, see L. Ockrent, *Land Rights: An Enquiry into the History of Registration for Publication in Scotland* (1942).
[57] Prescription Act 1617 (c. 12).
[58] The 1617 Prescription Act was repealed and replaced by the Prescription and Limitation (Scotland) Act 1973. [59] The history is traced in Reid (n. 22), §§ 376-85.
[60] *Tailors of Aberdeen* v. *Coutts* (1840) 1 Rob 296.
[61] By s. 4 of the Conveyancing (Scotland) Act 1874 the transferee was automatically entered with the superior on registration of the disposition (i.e. the deed of transfer).
[62] Thus Robert Bell, *A System of Forms of Deed Used in Scotland* (2nd edn., 1802), vol. 1, 189: 'Such is the change introduced by expediency, sanctioned by the decisions of the Court in the end of the last century, and now firmly established in modern practice.'

II. TEXTS AND THEORIES

1. Reading the texts

A historical account of legal theory must rest largely on the works of the leading jurists. But the texts are not always what they seem.

For example, in book II of his *Institute*,[63] Erskine defines ownership as 'the right of using and disposing of a subject as our own, except in so far as we are restrained by law or paction'. This well-known definition has launched a thousand undergraduate lectures. Its pedagogical value lies in paying attention not merely to the powers which ownership confers (use and disposal) but also to the restraints on the exercise of those powers (general law or contract). The definition seems balanced and sophisticated, a characteristic product of the age of reason. And it is also forward-looking, anticipating the famous definition which was to appear as article 544 of the *Code Napoléon*: 'La propriété est le droit de jouir et disposer d'une chose de la manière la plus absolue, pourvu qu'on n'en fasse un usage prohibé par les lois ou par les règlements.'[64] But this analysis is misleading. As quite often happens, Erskine's text can be traced back to Mackenzie's *Institutions*, a hundred years earlier:[65] '*Dominium* or Property is the power of Using and Disponing what is ours, except in so far as we are restricted by Law or Paction.' And, on further examination, the text turns out to be a stock definition of the *jus commune*, originating with Bartolus in the fourteenth century and repeated, with some variation, by successive generations of jurists up to and including Pothier.[66] Bartolus' definition is: 'ius in re corporali perfecti dispondendi, nisi lege prohibeatur'.[67] Mackenzie's source is unclear, but may have been Craig's *Jus Feudale*, where Bartolus' definition is quoted.[68]

There is nothing suprising in any of this. Even as late as the eighteenth century the unattributed borrowing of ideas seems to have been regarded as an acceptable practice. Copyright law was in its infancy.[69] So it was natural for Erskine to turn to earlier writers, and to draw, directly or indirectly, on the jurists of the *jus commune*. And this was more likely to occur in the parts concerned with general theory than in the parts devoted to some arcane doctrine of the municipal law. For the legal historian, however, this poses a serious dif-

---

[63] Erskine, II, 1, 1.

[64] Ownership is the right of enjoying and disposing of things in the most absolute manner, provided no use is made of them which is prohibited by laws or by regulations.

[65] Mackenzie, *Institutions*, II, 1.

[66] See e.g. E. J. H. Schrage, 'Property from Bartolus to the New Dutch Civil Code', in G. E. van Maanen and A. J. van der Walt (eds.), *Property Law on the Threshold of the 21st Century* (1996), 43–6.

[67] The right in a corporeal thing to have it perfectly at one's disposal, unless it is forbidden by law (translation by Schrage). [68] Craig, I, 9, 9.

[69] H. L. MacQueen, *Copyright, Competition and Industrial Design* (2nd edn., 1995), 1–8.

ficulty. It is clear that, while some parts of the institutional works are the original product of the jurist's intellect, or at least of his time, others are not. But until textual scholarship is much further advanced, it will not always be possible to tell which are which. The example given above is an easy one. Others are harder to detect. As evidence of the state of contemporary legal thought, therefore, the institutional works must be treated with caution. The analysis which follows is therefore provisional, and vulnerable to further textual scholarship.

2. Which texts?

(a) Before Stair

In Scotland the literature on property law begins only with the publication in the 1680s of the *Institutions* of Stair and Mackenzie. From an earlier period, Craig's *Jus Feudale*, though a work of the first importance, is concerned mainly with the feudal law. The digest practicks of the sixteenth and seventeenth centuries[70] offer wider coverage but little analysis. Their terse statements of the law, and of the results of cases, make them more source books than literature.

The absence of literature is itself an important historical fact. The practicks seem almost to presuppose the existence of a literature somewhere else, but, if that is so, it was not a literature which was written in Scotland. Whether *jus commune* texts were routinely used by ordinary lawyers of the sixteenth and seventeenth centuries is a matter of speculation. Certainly their ready availability, and in a language that all educated men could read, must be a partial explanation for the absence of discursive writing in Scotland in this period. Significantly, the first truly discursive work, Craig's *Jus Feudale*, is as much a contribution to the *jus commune* as an exposition of the law of Scotland.[71]

The 1680s mark the slow beginnings of a native legal literature, and by the end of the following century the position had been transformed. The implications for the *jus commune* seem obvious. With books readily available in the vernacular, recourse to foreign authors may have become a luxury, attractive only to those of a speculative and enquiring turn of mind.

(b) From Stair to Erskine

Stair's *Institutions of the Law of Scotland* was published in 1681, to be followed in 1684 by the much shorter work of the same name by Sir George Mackenzie. Bankton published his *Institute of the Laws of Scotland* between 1751 and 1753, and Erskine's *Institute* was published posthumously in 1773. In the course of less than a century, therefore, there were no fewer than four

---

[70] For which see n. 1.   [71] It too, of course, was written in Latin.

published restatements of the law of Scotland. By the standards of a previous age, these were inconceivable riches.

As their titles suggest, the works were modelled on, or at least inspired by, the example of the *Institutes* of Justinian. But the detailed division of topics was necessarily different. Each work was divided into four parts or books. Stair dealt with property law in book II and the first part of book III. The 'titles' (i.e. chapters) of book II were:[72]

 I. Rights Real or Dominion; Where, of Community, Possession, and Property
 II. Reprisals, Where, of Prizes, &c.
 III. Infeftments of Property, Where, of Charters, Seasins, Resignations, Confirmations, &c.
 IV. Superiority and its Casualties; Where, of Non-entry, Relief, Compositions for Entries, Ward, Marriage, Liferent-Escheat, &c.
 V. Infeftments of Annualrent, Where, of Poinding of the Ground, and of Pensions
 VI. Liferent-Infeftments, Where, of Conjunct-fees, Terces, and Liferents, by the Courtesy of Scotland
 VII. Servitudes Real, Where, of *Actus, iter, et via*, Pasturage, and Thirlage, &c.
 VIII. Teinds, Where, of Benefices, Stipends, Presentation, Collation, Institution, Tacks, Annats, and Patronage
 IX. Tacks, Where, of Rentals, Tacit Relocation and Removing
 X. Wadsets, Where, of Reversion, Regress, and Redemption
 XI. Extinction of Infeftments, Where, of Resignation *ad remanentiam*, Recognition, Disclamation, Purpresture, and other Feudal Delinquencies
 XII. Prescription, Where, of Usucapion, Long & Short Prescriptions, &c.

Title 2 (reprisals and prizes) was concerned with the confiscation of the ships and goods of enemies of the state. Annualrents (title 5) and wadsets (title 10) were types of rights in security over land, the ancestors of modern forms. Liferent (title 6) is usufruct, and tack (title 9) is lease. Three titles (3, 4, and 11) were directly concerned with feudal law, while four others (titles 5, 6, 8, and 10) were concerned with feudalized real rights. Only the first title offered much in the way of general analysis.

The opening titles of book III were:

 1. Assignations, where of Arrestments, and actions for making Forthcoming
 2. Dispositions, where of Resignations *in Favorem*, Apprisings and Adjudications of Real Rights, &c

The first title dealt with the transfer of personal rights, and their attachment for debt, while the second title covered the same ground in relation to real rights.

Book II of Mackenzie's *Institutions* was also devoted to property law and covered much the same ground as Stair, although the division of topics was

---

[72] The spelling adopted here is from the tercentenary edition of Stair's *Institutions* edited by David Walker (1981).

different.[73] Book III was largely concerned with obligations, which in Stair had been dealt with in book I, and the assignation of personal rights was dealt with in that context rather than, as in Stair, in the context of property law. The organization of Bankton's *Institute* was based closely on Stair, while Erskine followed Mackenzie. Bankton's one deviation was to include a short introductory title on property law (title 3: 'Division and Quality of Things') which was modelled, self-consciously, on book 1, 8 ('de divisione rerum et qualitate')[74] of Justinian's *Digest*.[75] There the choice of subjects seems slightly random but includes core concepts such as the distinction between real rights and personal rights, heritable and moveable property, feudal and allodial property, and so on.

The importance of these works is self-evident. They presented, for the first time, a systematic account of the law of Scotland. At times they seemed to be written almost on two levels. First, there was a presentation of general principles, drawn, often, from Roman law or the *jus commune*, and this was followed by a discussion and development of these principles by reference to indigenous law, including case law. Sometimes the principles became lost altogether in the thickets of native doctrine.

So far as property law is concerned, many of the leading rules were articulated, and for the first time. As early as the first title of the first book, Stair explained the distinction between real and personal rights:[76]

> Obligation is that which is correspondent to a personal right . . . and it is nothing else but a legal tie, whereby the debtor may be compelled to pay or perform something, to which he is bound by obedience to God, or by his own consent and engagement . . . and this is called a personal right, as looking directly to the person obliged, but to things indirectly, as they belong to that person. So dominion is called a real right, because it respecteth things directly, but persons, as they have meddled with those things.

Later, in title 1 of book II, Stair set about making a list of the real rights: possession, property, servitude, and pledge.[77] Servitude was intended as a broad term encompassing both praedial servitudes and also personal servitudes such as liferent.[78] Such multiplication of real rights, however, was found only in immoveable property:[79] 'In immoveables the constitution or transmission of property, is expressed in writ, and is parted in many interests; but in moveables, property is simple and full without servitude, and there is no other interest in them, unless they be impledged.'

Another preoccupation was the methods by which property can be

---

[73] For example Mackenzie introduced separate titles on 'the difference betwixt Heritable, and Moveable Rights' (title 2) and on 'the several kinds of Holdings' (title 4), while annualrent and wadset were combined in a single title (title 8: 'Of Redeemable Rights').
[74] Rendered in the Watson translation as: 'Things subdivided and qualitatively analysed'.
[75] Bankton, vii (preface).   [76] Stair, I, 1, 22.   [77] Stair, II, 1, 2.
[78] Stair, II, 7, pr.   [79] Stair, II, 1, 42.

acquired. Erskine expressed the rules succinctly:[80] 'The ways of obtaining the property of such things as fall under commerce flow either from natural or positive law. By the law of nature, property is acquired either by occupation or accession; and it is transferred from one to another by tradition.' Transfer—by tradition (delivery)—was then considered with reference to the different types of property. Book III of Bankton was headed 'Transmission of Rights Personal and Real', a structural device borrowed from Stair and which allowed for a general discussion of the principles of transfer.[81] Bankton began with an overview of the topic:[82]

> Transmission of rights among the living is accomplished by Assignations and Dispositions. In the general sense, Assignation or Assignment is applicable to real as well as personal rights, but more particularly to personal; and the term Disposition (of which I am to discourse in the next title) is proper to real rights, either of moveable or heritable subjects, but more especially is applied to heritage.

Later Bankton considered dispositions:[83] 'Dispositions vary according to the subjects disponed. Dispositions to liferent infeftments, tacks and servitudes, become effectual by real possession, which completes the rights ... Dispositions of moveables are completed, by delivery of the subjects disponed.'

These accounts of property law prompt a number of comments. First, there was a preoccupation, almost an obsession, with classification. Invariably there were two types of this and three types of that. In the end, everything could be reduced to neat rules, and each rule could be shown to relate to other rules. What was being offered was no less than a theory of property law; and so powerful was the theory that it was capable of taming even the most unruly native case law.

Secondly, the theory was overwhelmingly Roman—or at least civilian—in character. And it was a universal theory rather than one dictated by local peculiarities, although no doubt capable of local adaptation. There is little in the first title of book II in any of these works which would have surprised a jurist from a continental jurisdiction.

Thirdly, while there were many differences of detail, which would repay closer study, there was also a broad similarity of treatment. Take, for example, the accounts of transfer of ownership. Mackenzie wrote:[84]

> The last, and most ordinary way of acquiring of Property, is by *Tradition*, which is defined *a delivery of possession by the true owner, with a design to transfer the Property to the Receiver*, and this *translation*, is made either by the real delivery of the thing itself, as of a *horse*, a *Cup, &c.* or by a *Symbolick delivery*. As, is the *delivery of a little*

---

[80] Erskine, II, 1, 9.
[81] By contrast, Mackenzie and Erskine deal with assignation in the context of obligations, in book III, rather than in the context of property, in book II. This means that the transmission of personal rights is separated from the transmission of real rights, although Erskine is careful to insert cross-references: see Erskine, II, 7 and III, 5, 1.   [82] Bankton, III, 1, 1.
[83] Bankton, III, 2, 1 and 2.   [84] Mackenzie, II, 1 (84 of the 2nd edn. of 1688).

Earth and Stone in place of the Land it self; For where the thing cannot be truly delivered the Law allows some *Symbols*, or *marks of tradition*, and so far is *tradition* necessary to the acquiring of the Property in such Cases, that he who gets the last Right, with the *first tradition* is still preferr'd by our Law.

Bankton was in similar vein:[85]

The last and most important manner of acquiring real rights, by the law of nations, is Tradition or Delivery. This must be done by the owner, who has the free administration, or one having his warrant; and is founded on the will of the disposer, which is not understood to be perfected till, in evidence thereof, delivery follows ... Delivery is either Real, Symbolical or Feigned: true and real delivery is most properly of moveables, when they are given by hand to another. In lands or tenements, the putting the acquirer in possession is in place of delivery: this was the proper way of perfecting feudal rights, and, in the books of the feudal law, is termed *Investiture*.

Erskine wrote:[86]

The property of such subjects as have already had an owner, is chiefly acquired, or transferred from the owner to another, by tradition; which may be defined, the delivery of possession of a subject by the proprietor of it to the receiver ... [H]e who gets the last conveyance with the first tradition, is preferred to the property, according to the rule, *Traditionibus et usucapionibus, non nudis pactis, transferuntur rerum dominia*[87] ... Tradition is made either by the actual or real delivery of the subject itself, as in moveables, the *ipsa corpora* of which are put by tradition under the power of the acquirer; or *2ndly*, by a symbolical delivery, which must of necessity be made use of where real delivery is impracticable.

Stair alone was different, as so often. In place of a standard statement of the standard rule, he offered an analysis which was both detailed and profound. Some idea of the quality and originality of Stair's treatment is given by the following brief passage in which he considered the nature of the transferor's act of will:[88]

There may be three acts of the will about the disposal of rights; a resolution to dispone, a paction, contract or obligation to dispone, and a present will or consent that that which is the disponer's be the acquirer's. Resolution terminates within the resolver, and may be dissolved by a contrary resolution, and so transmits no right: paction does only constitute or transmit a personal right or obligation, whereby the person obliged may be compelled to transmit the real right. It must needs then be the present dispositive will of the owner, which conveyeth the right to any other ...[89]

---

[85] Bankton, II, 1, 20.   [86] Erskine, II, 1, 18 and 19.

[87] ('Ownership of a thing is transferred by delivery or usucapio and not by mere contract'). The same maxim is quoted in Bankton, III, 2, 2. It comes from C. 2, 3, 20.

[88] Stair, III, 2, 3.

[89] David Carey Miller has written of this passage: 'The treatment reflects what is generally true of Stair—his success in producing an original account, both systematic and rationally strong but, at the same time, reflecting the law of the day. In doing this Stair is distinguishable from the seventeenth century Roman-Dutch writers and, indeed, by the criteria of originality

A fourth point is the confidence of the accounts. If Stair and Mackenzie, in particular, were introducing ideas which were novel to Scotland, the deception was well disguised. The rules were presented as well settled and even as self-evident. And often there was little in the way of explanation, so that the reader was assumed to be familiar with concepts such as real rights, or tradition, or possession. The works give the impression of emerging, not only from European legal culture, but from Scottish legal culture also. In setting out a general theory of property, Stair and Mackenzie seemed to be dealing with ideas which were already current in Scotland. This suggests that the importance of these works lies partly in making existing ideas available in the vernacular, and partly in showing how they could be applied to the law as it had developed in Scotland.

The final point follows from the others. To a considerable extent, the writers must have shared common sources. This is true not only of primary sources—decisions of the court and statutes—but of secondary sources also. The debt to the *Corpus Juris Civilis* is obvious, and is quantified in Grant McLeod's chapter later in this volume. For example, in the passage on tradition, quoted above, Erskine expressly relied on texts from the *Institutes*[90] and from the *Codex*.[91] The debt to writings of the *jus commune* is equally obvious but harder to trace. In addition, of course, Bankton and Erskine made extensive use of the earlier works by Stair and Mackenzie.

(c) *Hume and Bell*

David Hume held the chair of Scots law in the University of Edinburgh from 1786 to 1822. George Joseph Bell was his successor in the chair, which he held until 1832.[92] Bell published a handbook based on his lectures in 1829. Known as the *Principles of the Law of Scotland* this work went through four editions during Bell's life, and there were a number of subsequent editions.[93] Hume's lectures were not published during his life, although manuscript copies of notes taken by students were in circulation,[94] but they were eventually published by the Stair Society, in six volumes, between 1939 and 1958.[95]

Both sets of lectures are held in high regard, and Bell's have been accorded 'institutional' status.[96] So far as property law is concerned they make an

---

and philosophical strength his work is probably superior.' See D. L. Carey Miller, 'Systems of Property: Grotius and Stair', in D. L. Carey Miller and D. W. Meyers (eds.), *Comparative and Historical Essays in Scots Law* (1992), 19.

[90] Inst. 2, 1, 40. The text begins: 'per traditionem quoque iure naturali res nobis adquiruntur' ('Tradition is another method of acquiring things according to natural law').

[91] C. 2, 3, 20.   [92] Erskine had also previously held this chair, from 1737 to 1765.

[93] The last edition in Bell's life was the fourth, of 1839. The final edition was the tenth (edited by Sheriff William Guthrie) of 1899.

[94] See the discussion by G. C. H. Paton, in Hume, *Lectures*, VI, 394–7.

[95] Hume, however, had forbidden their publication in his Settlement dated 31 July 1832.

[96] The same would surely have been true of Hume's lectures if they had been published during his lifetime. In many ways they are superior to Bell's.

instructive contrast. Hume built on the foundations laid by Stair and later writers to present an authoritative account of the law, strong both on principle and on detail. The discursive nature of a lecture allowed Hume to engage in argument and speculation, and to give many examples of how the principles might apply in practice. Hume's treatment was in two parts, for '[i]t seems to be desirable to bestow on the doctrine of Real Rights a twofold discussion—one according to common and natural principles, so far as our practice has received these, and the other according to our feudal notions . . .'.[97] The first part—part III of his lecture course—dealt with property law in general, including the rights of owners and the methods of transfer. There were separate chapters on the subordinate real rights: servitude, pledge and hypothec, exclusive privilege and tacks.[98] The second part (part IV of the course) comprised chapters on the following topics: the feudal investiture; the superior's estate; the vassal's estate; transmission of feudal rights; infeftments in conjunct fee; liferent; wadset; heritable bonds; real liens; adjudication; judicial sale; prescription; and heritable and moveable.[99] Both parts were substantial, but the second part was almost twice as long as the first, running to 400 printed pages of the Stair Society edition.

Bell's treatment was also divided into two parts, but in a different way. For Bell, the differences between moveable and immoveable property were so fundamental that there seemed little advantage in treating them together.[100] Each, accordingly, was given its own separate part.[101] Some discussion of principle survived, mainly in the account of moveable property,[102] but a general theory of property law was wholly absent. Even the description of ownership—separated by some 150 pages—was different as between the two types of property.[103]

This was a sign of things to come. No new work published after Bell's *Principles* dealt with property law in the round. It is true that Erskine's student text, the *Principles of the Law of Scotland*, continued to be published in successive editions throughout the nineteenth century[104] and continued to find some space for a general account of property law. But its twentieth-century successor did not. Gloag and Henderson's *Introduction to the Law of Scotland*, first published in 1927, was, and remains even today,[105] remarkably

[97] Hume, *Lectures*, I, 11.
[98] This part forms consecutive chapters, beginning on p. 201 of vol. III and continuing until p. 126 of vol. IV.   [99] Hume, *Lectures*, IV, 127–577.
[100] Bell, *Principles*, § 636.
[101] Part 1 of book II (§§ 636–1282) is entitled 'Real Rights in Heritable Property' and part 2 of book II (§§ 1283–1505) 'Real Rights of Property and Possession in Moveables'.
[102] 'Moveable property is left to the undisturbed guidance of rules and principles of more universal application': Bell, *Principles*, § 636.
[103] Bell, *Principles*, §§ 939 (immoveable) and 1284 (moveable).
[104] The twenty-first and last edition, edited by Sir John Rankine, was published in 1911. The book was first published in 1754.
[105] The current edition is the tenth of 1995. The title is now *The Law of Scotland*.

free from property law in the sense that would have been understood by Stair or Hume—or by a lawyer from a modern civil law jurisdiction.

As the nineteenth century wore on, property law began to disappear as a recognizable intellectual unit. This happened in two different ways. First, following Bell, immoveable property began to be treated separately from moveable property. And secondly, the study of immoveable property itself tended to collapse into a study of conveyancing. Practice thus replaced theory, a change which in the end was advantageous to neither. The rise of conveyancing is the subject of the next section.

(d) Breaking through the Roman wall

The publishing boom of the Victorian age encompassed books on conveyancing rather than on property law. And then, as now, publication was closely linked to teaching. In the years 1783 and 1784 Walter Ross WS[106] taught a private class in conveyancing in Edinburgh 'to a numerous body of the Gentlemen of the law'.[107] The results were published, posthumously, in 1792 as *Lectures on the History and Practice of the Law of Scotland Relative to Conveyancing and Legal Diligence*.[108] Although Ross's work had a strong historical foundation, its primary aim was to instruct the working conveyancer:[109]

I wish to accompany the young Writer, during the time of his apprenticeship, to analyse the Deeds he sees passing under his eye; and to give an account of their origin, their progress, their principles, and their effects; to explain the different terms he meets with; and to trace actual business in all its steps, from the beginning to the end of every branch.

For this task, the approach of Stair and his successors was felt to have little relevance:[110]

I will hazard the assertion, that, however the Institutional Order[111] may best comprehend the *Theory* of the Law, it is by no means suited to the *Practice*, or the purposes of Practitioners; and it is the chief part of my proposal to break through this Roman wall, and to range at large in the direction of our own customs, rules, and business.

Soon, breaking through the Roman wall had become a fashionable enterprise. Ross's lectures were followed by other courses of lectures in Edinburgh,

---

[106] 'WS' is an abbreviation for Writer to His (or Her) Majesty's Signet. The present author is a WS. For a history of the Society, see the introduction to the *Register of the Society of Writers to Her Majesty's Signet* (1983).

[107] Advertisement to the first edition of Ross's *Lectures* (1792). Thereafter, as the Advertisement explains, the lectures were discontinued because of 'a new line of business, in which Mr Ross found himself unexpectedly engaged, and which required almost constant attendance in another country'. [108] A second edition followed in 1822.

[109] Ross (n. 107), xviii.

[110] Ross (n. 107), xix. This passage can be read as a protest against excessive Romanization by the institutional writers. [111] i.e. of persons, things and actions (as the context makes clear).

usually under the auspices of the Society of Writers to His Majesty's Signet.[112] Robert Bell WS,[113] the most distinguished of those lecturers, published a part of his lectures in 1815 under the title of *A Treatise on the Conveyance of Land to a Purchaser*.[114] In 1824 the Society endowed a chair of conveyancing at Edinburgh University. The first professor was Macvey Napier, better known as the editor of the *Encyclopaedia Britannica*.[115] In Glasgow, lectures on conveyancing were instituted by the Faculty of Procurators in 1817, and a chair of conveyancing was created at Glasgow University in 1861. In due course the professors began to publish their notes. Professor Allan Menzies of Edinburgh was first into the field in 1856,[116] to be followed by two successors in the Edinburgh chair, Professor Montgomerie Bell in 1867,[117] and Professor Philip Wood in 1903. After some interruption the tradition was continued into the modern period by Professor J. M. Halliday of Glasgow University[118] and Professor A. J. McDonald of the University of Dundee.[119] Sir John Rankine's *Treatise on the Rights and Burdens Incident to the Ownership of Lands and Other Heritages in Scotland* (1879)[120] was a pioneering account of the rights and duties of an owner of land, with extensive references both to Roman law and to Anglo-American case law.

There was, however, no professorial monopoly. The numerous texts written by practitioners in the nineteenth century and beyond included some reputable works as well as others of more modest ambition. Notable among the former were a *Treatise on Deeds and Forms used in the Constitution, Transmission and Extinction of Feudal Rights* (1838) by Alexander Duff, John Craigie's *Heritable Rights* (1887)[121] and *Moveable Rights* (1888),[122] and John Burns's *Conveyancing Practice* (1894).[123]

That there should be a desire to break though the Roman wall was understandable enough. Walter Ross was both a practical conveyancer and also a

---

[112] *Register* (n. 106), xviii.   [113] Later advocate.
[114] There were two further editions, the last in 1830. On the title-page Bell is described as 'Lecturer on Conveyancing appointed by the Society of Writers to His Majesty's Signet'. Bell also published other works on conveyancing, including a book on execution of deeds (*Lectures on the Solemnities used in Scotland in the Testing of Deeds* (1795)), and a multi-volume book of styles, with commentary (*A System of the Forms of Deeds used in Scotland* (1st edn., 1797; 3rd edn., 1811–17)).
[115] This may have been a consolation prize for Napier's failure to be appointed to the chair of moral philosophy several years earlier. See H. Cockburn, *Memorials of His Time* (1909 edn.), 348–9. Not many of his successors could have professed both moral philosophy and conveyancing.
[116] There were four editions in all, the last in 1900.
[117] The third and final edition was published in 1882.
[118] *Conveyancing Law and Practice* (1985–90; 2nd edn., by Iain J. S. Talman, 1996–7).
[119] *Conveyancing Manual* (1982; the latest edition is the sixth of 1997).
[120] The last edition, still quite often cited by the courts, is the fourth of 1909.
[121] The third and last edition was in 1899.
[122] Second edn., 1894. Books on conveyancing usually included the conveyancing of moveable property, particularly incorporeal moveables.
[123] The fourth and final edition, by F. MacRitchie, was published as recently as 1957.

distinguished historian of land law. Neither preoccupation was much touched by Roman law. And Ross may have felt impatience both with the classical veneer (as it may have seemed) imposed on native doctrine, and with the sophistry of its exponents, who nonetheless could hardly be trusted to draft an instrument of sasine. Ross, however, was no anti-intellectual. On the contrary, his *Lectures* are a work of considerable scholarship which illumine a subject on which little had previously been written.

Not all Ross's successors were so talented. The professors in particular were prone to copying from one another, and the template established by the early writers was one much used by those who came later. As the nineteenth century wore on, there was a tendency for the coverage to narrow and to become more uncompromisingly practical. In a sense this was a reversion to the digest practicks of the period before Stair. Typical of this trend was Burns's *Conveyancing Practice*, which was the standard conveyancing textbook from its first appearance in 1894 until the publication of Halliday's book in 1985. Although learned in its field, Burns's work had no truck with theory, and was written in a terse and forbidding style unlikely to stimulate the reader.[124] With Burns and similar works we are as far away from the brilliant paradoxes of Walter Ross as it is possible to be. And the Roman wall is not only breached but dismantled.

3. The strange death of property law

Property law flourished as a subject of intellectual inquiry only for the brief 150 years of the institutional period. By 1830 it was beginning to fade slowly away. As often with gradual change, no one seems to have noticed. It was to be another 150 years before, in the closing years of the twentieth century, the old books were taken up once more and the subject was revived.[125]

For this strange death a number of causes may be suggested. In the first place, there was the continuing presence of feudalism. Although superficially Romanized, feudal law remained, as Hume admitted, 'very remote from any likeness of the Civil Law, or of what may seem to be the general principles of the Law of Nature'.[126] Feudalism persistently obstructed attempts to develop a general theory of property law. This, of course, was an old difficulty and not a new one. But the fact that feudalism survived in Scotland for 200 years

---

[124] David Walker, who presumably learned his conveyancing from Burns, described *Conveyancing Practice* as 'a valuable but badly-written book of practical guidance'. See D. M. Walker, *Scottish Jurists* (1985), 399.

[125] The revival of property law can be seen both from books and from periodical literature. For the former, see in particular: Carey Miller (n. 44); D. J. Cusine and R. R. M. Paisley, *Servitudes and Rights of Way* (1998); W. M. Gordon, *Scottish Land Law* (2nd edn., 1999); Reid (n. 3).

[126] Hume, *Lectures*, I, 11.

after it had been abolished in most other countries gives the topic a special significance in the modern period.

Secondly, there was the rise of the conveyancer, and hence of conveyancing. The Industrial Revolution led to the sale and purchase of land on a scale hitherto unknown. The conveyancer serviced this demand.[127] One result was the proliferation of conveyancing texts already described, and the emphasis on the practical at the expense of the theoretical.

Thirdly, there was the increased importance of moveable property, both corporeal and also incorporeal. This too was a product of the Industrial Revolution. Bell made this point well in his *Principles*:[128]

In modern times, moveable property is frequently of much greater value than property in land. It is the part of the wealth of the people most generally diffused, and the most frequent subject of transaction and of transference ... Besides money, jewels, and goods in immediate possession, one may have shares in Government or bank stock; ships; commodities and money in distant countries; or in the hands of manufacturers, factors, bankers, debtors.

But if moveable property was as important—or even more important—than land, then there were strong arguments for treating it as a separate subject. No doubt this is the explanation for the structure adopted by Bell in his *Principles*. A difficulty was that the increased importance of moveable property was not balanced by a diminution in the importance of feudal law,[129] and without such a diminution, property law was in danger of becoming unmanageably large. If a unified account of the law was more necessary than ever, it was also more difficult to achieve. It is noteworthy that the revival in modern times of a general theory of property law was preceded by the virtual extinction of feudalism as a living doctrine.

Finally, there was the introduction by statute, on 1 January 1894, of what was in substance the English law of sale of goods.[130] In Scotland ownership of property, whether moveable or immoveable, had been transferred only by *traditio* (delivery or equivalent). But now this long-settled and uniform rule was replaced by a rule that, in the sale of goods, ownership could be transferred merely by intention.[131] In effect, ownership passed with the contract,[132] so that the proprietary effects of sale were fused with the contractual effects. The change was designed to achieve the commercial advantage of a single law of sale which would apply throughout the United Kingdom, but it made more difficult still the development of a general theory of property law.

---

[127] For example, the number of Writers to the Signet increased more than threefold in the first forty years of the 19th century. By 1840 there were 685 members, although the total fell again in the later years of the century. See *Register* (n. 106), xv. Of course not all Writers to the Signet were conveyancers.   [128] Bell, *Principles*, § 1283.
[129] The continuing hold of feudal law in the 19th century was discussed in section I.1 above.
[130] Sale of Goods Act 1893, now replaced by the Sale of Goods Act 1979.
[131] 1893 Act, s. 17.   [132] See in particular s. 18 rule 1.

Whatever the causes, however, the results were unwelcome. By the closing years of the nineteenth century, property law had largely disappeared as a discrete discipline. In its place was a jumble of smaller topics: feudal law, conveyancing, landlord and tenant,[133] sale of goods, intellectual property, and so on. So far had the subject fallen that issues of property law were quite often overlooked in the courts;[134] and where they were not overlooked, there could be no assurance that the rules would be correctly applied. That this has caused lasting damage is shown by the reliance, in the celebrated modern case of *Sharp* v. *Thomson*,[135] on *Heritable Reversionary Co. Ltd* v. *Millar*,[136] a decision from 1892 which stands as a monument to the fall of property law. Cases from this period have to be approached with greater circumspection than the system of *stare decisis* might seem to allow.

III. TWO DOCTRINES

In this final section mention will be made of two doctrines which, in different ways, are representative of the history of property law in Scotland. The doctrines are possession and the law of the tenement. For reasons of space only the briefest of accounts will be possible.

1. Possession

As might be expected, the approach to possession in Scots law was, and remains today, resolutely civilian. A clear distinction was maintained between possession and ownership,[137] and between possessory actions and petitory actions;[138] and, particularly in the early period, possessory actions seem to have been much more common than petitory actions.

---

[133] Robert Hunter's *Law of Landord and Tenant* (1833) was the first book to be devoted to this subject. There are later books by John Rankine (1887; 3rd edn., 1916), and by G. C. H. Paton and J. G. S. Cameron (1967).

[134] Thus *Morrisson* v. *Robertson* 1908 SC 322, a case of disputed ownership of cows, was treated as involving only issues of contract law. See K. G. C. Reid, 'Obligations and Property: Exploring the Border', 1997 *Acta Juridica* 225 at 233–5. Another example is *International Banking Corporation* v. *Ferguson, Shaw & Sons* 1910 SC 182 where the property law solution (*specificatio*) occurred to the (ultimately successful) pursuers only when the case went on appeal, and then only 'at the eleventh hour' (at 190). It had been overlooked altogether in an earlier case, *Oliver & Boyd* v. *Marr Typefounding Co.* 1901 9 SLT 170.

[135] 1997 SC (HL) 66, discussed in part I.4 above.

[136] (1892) 19 R (HL) 43. There is some discussion of this case in section I.4 above.

[137] Traditionally, common law countries are said not to maintain such a distinction, although this view has been challenged: see James Gordley and Ugo Mattei, 'Protecting Possession', (1996) 44 *AJCL* 293.

[138] Stair, IV, 3, 47; IV, 21, 1; IV, 26, 1–3; Bankton, IV, 24, 49; Erskine, IV, 1, 47.

(a) Meaning of possession

There is no definition of possession before Stair. Although the digest practicks of Balfour and Hope contain separate titles on possession, these are concerned with the minutiae of law and practice and no general definition is attempted.[139] Stair's definition[140] was, avowedly, based on Roman law:[141]

> Possession is the holding or detaining of any thing by ourselves, or others for our use ... To possession there must be an act of the body, which is detention and holding: and an act of the mind, which is the inclination or affection to make use of the thing detained; which being of the mind, is not so easily perceivable as that of the body; but it is presumed whensoever the profit of the detainer may be to make use of the thing; but where it may be wrong, or hurtful, it is not presumed.

Stair then considered how possession was acquired, maintained, and lost. Possession began when there was coincidence of an act of the body with an act of the mind.[142] It was continued for so long as there was an act of the mind, and no contrary acts of the body by others.[143] And it was lost when another came to possess.[144] Broadly similar accounts are found in the other institutional writers.[145]

There were two points of uncertainty, one of terminology and the other of substance. The uncertainty of terminology concerned the nature of the distinction between civil and natural possession. In a passage which can be traced back to Voet,[146] Bankton offered two possible versions of this distinction.[147] On one view, natural possession was possession by the person with actual detention of the property while civil possession was possession through the detention of another, such as a tenant or custodier. The alternative version depended on whether the possessor was owner. A possessor who owned, or at least believed himself to be owner, had civil possession. Conversely, a person who possessed for his own use, knowing that he was not owner, had natural possession. These versions are not reconcilable, but Bankton expressed no preference. Stair, however, had seemed to support the first version,[148] and, later, Erskine and Bell were to the same effect.[149] That usage is firmly established in the modern law.[150]

The uncertainty of substance concerned the category of persons who might

---

[139] Balfour, *Practicks*, 148–9; Hope, *Major Practicks*, III, 21. [140] Stair, II, 1, 17.
[141] Among the *Digest* titles cited were D. 41, 2, 3, 1 and 8; 41, 2, 6, pr and 1; and 50, 17, 153.
[142] Stair, II, 1, 18.   [143] Stair, II, 1, 19.   [144] Stair, II, 1, 20.
[145] See in particular Bankton, II, 1, 26–9; Erskine, II, 1, 20 and 21.
[146] Johannes Voet, *Commentarius ad Pandectas*, XLI, 2, 3.
[147] Bankton, II, 1, 26.
[148] Stair, II, 1, 10 and 14. Stair's meaning, however, is not always clear.
[149] Erskine, II, 1, 22; Bell, *Principles*, § 1312.
[150] K. G. C. Reid, 'Possession', in *idem* (n. 3), § 121.

212   *Kenneth Reid*

qualify as possessors.[151] In Roman law possession had been confined to a relatively narrow category, and usually *animus domini* (the intention as owner) was required. The Roman rule was followed by Erskine,[152] but not by Stair who required only detention 'for our use'.[153] Stair's formulation was adopted by Bankton, but without comment.[154] Stair's view has prevailed.[155] In the modern law possession is extended to tenants, those holding by agreement (whether revocable or not), and even to thieves and squatters. The fact that a person holds for someone else does not of itself prevent him from holding on his own account. Thus a tenant holds partly for his landlord, who has civil possession, and partly for himself.

(b) Spuilzie

It was recognized early in Scots law that a person who was dispossessed against his will, and without judicial warrant, had a right to be reinstated forthwith in his possession. The civil wrong committed by the act of dispossession was known as 'spuilzie',[156] a term which dates from the mid-fifteenth century, although the doctrine is older.[157] The action for reinstatement of possession was known as an action of 'spuilzie' in the case of moveable property, and an action of 'ejection'[158] in the case of land.

It seems reasonable to infer that in Scotland, as in some other European countries, spuilzie derived ultimately from the *exceptio spolii* of the canon law.[159] The very name suggests as much. Yet, in the present state of research, direct evidence is lacking. Thus canon law is not mentioned in this connection by the institutional writers, who emphasize instead the similarities between spuilzie and the possessory interdicts of Roman law.[160] According to Bankton,[161] spuilzie comes 'in place of' the Roman interdicts. Further, it is clear that spuilzie had native antecedents, in particular claims of 'wrang and unlauch'.[162] In his *Practicks*, Balfour tended to bracket spuilzie with novel dissasine.[163] Bankton, however, quoted the rule 'spoliatus ante omnia est

---

[151] The same difficulty is traced, for South African law, by Duard Kleyn, 'Possession', in Reinhard Zimmermann and Daniel Visser (eds.), *Southern Cross: Civil Law and Common Law in South Africa* (1996), 824–5.

[152] Erskine, II, 1, 20: possession is 'detention of a subject, with an *animus* or design in the detainer of holding it as his own property'. See also Bell, *Principles*, § 1311.

[153] Stair, II, 1, 17.   [154] Bankton, II, 1, 26.

[155] Reid (n. 150), § 125; Gordon (n.125), paras. 14-03 to 14-06.

[156] Pronounced spool-ee. The 'z' is silent.   [157] MacQueen (n. 5), 129.

[158] If the land had been vacant when it was spuilzied, the action was one of intrusion rather than ejection.

[159] The same is true in South African law: see Kleyn (n. 151), 835–46. Kleyn points out that while spoliation was originally an *exceptio* only (in practice a defence for someone who had been despoiled against subsequent criminal or civil proceedings), it gradually came to be transformed into an *actio*.   [160] Stair, II, 1, 20; Bankton, II, 1 30.

[161] Bankton, II, 1, 31.   [162] MacQueen (n. 5), 129.

[163] Balfour, *Practicks*, 465–76. For novel dissasine, see MacQueen (n. 5), ch. 5.

restituendus',[164] a maxim of canon law,[165] and the same maxim can be found in a number of cases, the earliest traced dating from 1541.[166]

A persistent controversy was whether spuilzie was a true possessory remedy, or whether the pursuer required to show at least some semblance of a title. But while the case law was divided,[167] the institutional writers stood firm in the view that no title was required. Bankton is characteristically clear:[168]

> The pursuer's title, in an action of spuilie, is possession of the goods ... and if the possession was peaceable, even the true owner, seizing the goods from the possessor, will be liable in a spuilie ... The party that is violently deprived of the possession must be first restored, and then the question of property considered ...

Earlier in this volume, John Cairns characterized spuilzie as 'perhaps the most common action in fifteenth-century Scotland'. Its popularity continued into the next century and beyond. Sinclair's *Practicks*, which collected cases from the 1540s, contains a number of decisions concerned with spuilzie, while the earliest cases in Morison's *Dictionary* date from the same period and continue right up to the end of the eighteenth century.[169] Thereafter spuilzie disappears, suddenly but conclusively, from the law reports. Apart from a brief flurry of cases towards the end of the twentieth century, most of which were not true examples of the doctrine,[170] spuilzie ceased to be pled in the courts. The reasons are unclear.

One was presumably a decline in lawlessness. Spuilzie thrives in a society where dispossession is routine. Bankton explained that:[171] 'There was of old a kind of spuiliers, very frequent and troublesome in this country, called Katharines or Sorners; they were masterful sturdy beggars, that went in companies, oppressing the people, by consuming victuals, and taking away goods without consent of the owners, and some such are at this day.' As times became more orderly, so spuilzie declined in importance; and in modern times a person whose goods were stolen was more likely to contact the police or an insurer than to seek restitution from the thief by private litigation.

---

[164] Bankton, I, 10, 126.
[165] See e.g. Decretum Gratiani, Secunda Pars, causa 3, quaestio 1, canon 3–4.
[166] e.g. *Haliburton v. Rutherford* (1541) Mor 14739; *Lady Renton v. Her Son* (1629) Mor 14733; *Yeoman v. Moncreif* (1669) Mor 14740; *A v. B* (1677) Mor 14751.
[167] Cases requiring a title included: *Wishart v. Arbuthnot* (1573) Mor 3605; *Gib v. Hamilton* (1583) Mor 16080; *Mudiall v. Frissal* (1628) Mor 14749; and *Strachan v. Gordons* (1671) Mor 1819. Cases recognizing spuilzie as a possessory action included: *Montgomery v. Hamilton* (1548) Mor 14731; *Lady Renton v. Her Son* (1629) Mor 14733; and *Gadzeard v. Sheriff of Ayr* (1781) Mor 14732.
[168] Bankton, I, 10, 126. And see also Stair, I, 9, 17; IV, 28, 2; Erskine, IV, 1, 15.
[169] The cases are digested in Morison mainly under 'Ejection' and 'Spuilzie'.
[170] *FC Finance Ltd v. Brown & Son* 1969 SLT (Sh Ct) 41; *Mercantile Credit Co. Ltd v. Townsley* 1971 SLT (Sh Ct) 37; *Mackinnon v. Avonside Homes Ltd* 1993 SCLR 976; *Harris v. Abbey National plc* 1997 SCLR 359; *Gemmell v. Bank of Scotland* 1998 SCLR 144.
[171] Bankton, I, 10, 125.

Another reason, which applied to land only, was the setting up of a land register, the Register of Sasines, in 1617. For ease of registration there was a series of local ('particular' or 'burgh') registers, as well as a central ('general') register held in Edinburgh.[172] Registration was mandatory in the sense that it was the only means of acquiring ownership and certain other real rights.[173] As a result, disputes as to ownership became less common and more easily resolved, and proof of title was greatly simplified. In those circumstances the attraction of a possessory remedy was apt to diminish. If a possessory dispute was in substance a dispute about title, there was little to be gained from seeking a remedy which could confer no more than interim possession; and even in disputes which were purely possessory in character, it was often a simple matter for the owner to prove his title.

These are partial explanations only, however, and the decline of spuilzie remains one of the unsolved mysteries of doctrinal history.[174]

(c) The decline of possession

The decline of spuilzie was accompanied, though much more slowly, by a decline in the importance of possession as a whole. Once again, the Register of Sasines played a part. A characteristic feature of possession was the rights given to the bona fide possessor. As usual, the source was the civil law:

[S]eeing the possessor is . . . bound to restore to the true owner the subject itself, there is the same reason, in the nature of things, why he should restore also the whole fruits which it produced during his possession as an accessory: Yet positive law has, from equity, conferred on the *bona fide* possessor the right to a certain part of the intermediate fruits that the subject yielded while he had reason to think his own title good. It has been disputed by doctors[175] whether the *bona fide* possessor was, by the Roman law, entitled to such of those fruits as he had gathered during that period, if he did not also consume them, *perceptos sed non consumptos*; but however this point might have stood by the Roman law, it is universally agreed that, by our customs, perception of the fruits is by itself sufficient for acquiring their property.[176]

In addition, the bona fide possessor was entitled to compensation for improvements. This was a positive claim, founded in unjustified enrichment,

---

[172] Today there is only a general register, but some of the local registers continued in existence into the 20th century. The last to close was the burgh register for Dingwall, in 1963. As is explained below, the Register of Sasines is itself in the process of being replaced by a new register known as the Land Register of Scotland.

[173] *Young* v. *Leith* (1847) 9 D 932, 2 Ross LC 81.

[174] To some extent, spuilzie may have been a victim of misclassification. In the case of moveable property, at least, it may often be difficult to distinguish spuilzie from vindication. Since possession presumes ownership, the pursuer in a vindicatory action will usually seek to demonstrate (*a*) that he had possession, and (*b*) that he was then dispossessed by the defender. See Reid (n. 150), § 150. This is barely distinguishable from spuilzie.

[175] i.e. by jurists of the *jus commune*.

[176] Erskine, II, 1, 25. And see also Stair, II, 1, 23; Bankton, I, 8, 12.

and not merely, as in Roman law, a right of retention.[177] For all the elaboration of treatment by the institutional writers, however, this law has faded away in the modern period. Once deeds relating to land came to be registered, a person was unlikely to be mistaken as to his ownership; and if, for some reason, he failed to check the register, he forfeited his claim to be in good faith. The doctrine of bona fide possession survives, of course, but mainly[178] in the less important area of moveable property.

Something of the same pattern can be seen in positive (acquisitive) prescription, another traditionally key area for possession. It seems doubtful whether Scots law has ever recognized positive prescription for moveable property,[179] but in relation to land prescription was always of the first importance. That is now changing. In a process which began in 1981 the Register of Sasines is gradually being replaced by a new register, known as the Land Register of Scotland.[180] The new register introduces a 'positive' system of land registration,[181] under which the person registered as owner is, as a matter of law, conclusively the owner.[182] But a positive system leaves little scope for prescription, and prescription is generally excluded for Land Register titles.[183] As a result, positive prescription will virtually disappear once all land has been entered in the new register.

Delivery, once required for the transfer of ownership of moveables, is now excused in the most common case, transfer on sale. Under the Sale of Goods Act 1893 (now 1979), ownership is transferred by intention and without a change in possession.[184] In the transfer of land, delivery (sasine), by delivery of a symbol, ceased to be required in 1845.[185]

Something remains, of course. In moveable property, possession raises a presumption of ownership.[186] In immoveable property, a proprietor in possession is protected against rectification of errors in the Land Register.[187] Possession is a means of acquiring ownerless moveables, under the doctrine

---

[177] Stair, I, 8, 6; Bankton, I, 8, 15; Erskine, III, 1, 11; Bell, *Principles*, § 538.

[178] In marginal cases, it might still apply to land. For example, the Register of Sasines often fails to disclose precise boundaries, so that a person might possess land which he believed to be his but which actually belonged to his neighbour. Precise boundaries are indicated in the new Land Register.

[179] Carey Miller (n. 44), paras. 7.01-7.04; D. Johnston, *Prescription and Limitation* (1999), ch. 18.

[180] The legislative framework is contained in the Land Registration (Scotland) Act 1979.

[181] Also known as 'registration of title'. The Register of Sasines operated a 'negative' system, being no more than a register of deeds.

[182] Land Registration (Scotland) Act 1979, s. 3(1)(*a*).

[183] Prescription can apply only in the unusual case where the Keeper of the Register withholds the state indemnity. See Prescription and Limitation (Scotland) Act 1973, s. 1(1)(*b*). This approach can be criticized as taking too optimistic a view of the accuracy of the Register.

[184] Sale of Goods Act 1979, s. 17.   [185] Infeftment Act 1845, s. 1.

[186] Stair, IV, 45, 17 (VIII); Bankton, II, 1, 34; Erskine, II, 1, 24.

[187] Land Registration (Scotland) Act 1979, s. 9(3). The meaning of possession in this context has been the subject of dispute, and litigation: see *Kaur* v. *Singh* 1999 SLT 412.

of *occupatio*.[188] Some subordinate real rights are constituted by possession, most notably pledge of moveables and lease of immoveables.[189] Other examples of the use of possession can also be found.[190] But compared with its active past, possession today is much diminished.

2. Law of the tenement

By contrast with possession, the law of the tenement is largely home-grown. A 'tenement' in the sense used here is a building where ownership is divided horizontally. So for example, a building comprising four storeys might be divided into four separate flats or apartments, one on each floor. The *law* of the tenement comprises the rules developed by the common law for regulating the rights and obligations of the owners within the building.

Tenements were a particularly suitable form of housing for the narrow ridge, running eastwards from the castle, which constituted medieval Edinburgh. It seems doubtful, however, that the inhabitants of tenements were much exercised by the legal niceties of their domestic arrangements, and the competency of vertical (or sectional) ownership seems to have been assumed rather than discussed. In the end the legal model which emerged was a simple one. A tenement was viewed as a series of separate houses, one built on top of the other. Each house was treated autonomously. Its owner owned the four walls, and the floor and ceiling. The owner of the highest flat owned the roof of the building, while the owner of the lowest flat owned the land on which the building was constructed. None of the building was common property, apart from the shared entrance way and stairs. This rather primitive model was close to the *Stockwerkseigentum* of Germanic law,[191] although no direct influence has been traced. In theory it survives to the present day, although modern practice is for the title deeds to make various parts of the building into common property.[192]

There is no discussion of the law of the tenement before Stair's *Institutions*, several hundred years after tenements first came to be used. Stair's concern was the crucial issue of maintenance:[193]

[W]hen divers owners have parts of the same tenement, it cannot be said to be a perfect division, because the roof remaineth roof to both, and the ground supporteth

---

[188] Stair, II, 1, 33; Bankton, II, 1, 7; Erskine, II, 1, 10.
[189] This is confined to leases of 20 years or less by s. 3(3) of the Land Registration (Scotland) Act 1979. Longer leases require registration.
[190] For example, the protection for purchasers from possessors contained in ss. 24 and 25 of the Sale of Goods Act 1979.
[191] C. G. van der Merwe, *Apartment Ownership* (1994) (being vol. 6, ch. 5 of the *International Encyclopaedia of Comparative Law*), 4.
[192] K. G. C. Reid, 'Landownership', in *idem* (n. 3), § 241.
[193] Stair, II, 7, 6. Stair's treatment is largely copied by Bankton, II, 7, 9 and Erskine, II, 9, 11. There is a more extended discussion, founded on case law, in Hume, *Lectures*, III, 225-8.

both; and therefore by the nature of communion, there are mutual obligations upon both, viz. that the owner of the lower tenement must uphold his tenement as a foundation to the upper, and the owner of the upper tenement must uphold his tenement as a roof and cover to the lower.

Thus, in rather a crude way, was the physical integrity of the building secured. The owner of the highest flat must maintain the roof, while those further down must maintain their walls so as to support those above them. In a tenement, therefore, owners were bound together by a reciprocal network of right and obligation. It may be assumed that these rules were not invented by Stair. Stair himself refers to 'positive statute or custom',[194] and the attribution is later repeated by Bankton.[195]

But if customary law was to be reduced to writing, and analysis, there remained the difficulty of showing how it related to existing concepts of the learned law. Although Stair dealt with the maintenance of tenements in his title on praedial servitudes (as later writers did also), he was firm in his view that the obligations identified were not, in the strict sense, servitudes.[196] The conclusion was hardly surprising. A servitude required positive steps for its creation and, even once created, could not impose an affirmative obligation such as an obligation to maintain. This would hardly do to explain a set of affirmative obligations which arose by operation of law. But no alternative classification was offered. Instead Stair made do with a factual explanation: the obligations came into being because of the 'nature of the communion' between the different flats in the building.[197] It was left to case law a hundred years hence to develop the idea of 'common interest' as a reciprocal network of rights and obligation implied by law in circumstances where a single thing, such as a tenement or a river,[198] came to be owned in sections by different people.[199]

The essence of common interest was reciprocity of right and obligation. But, in tenements at least, the bargain did not seem entirely fair, for the owner of the uppermost flat was left with sole liability for the roof—in a country whose climate ensured that roof maintenance was of frequent occurrence. Conveyancers tried to find a way round the difficulty. The litigation in

---

[194] Stair, II, 7, 6.   [195] Bankton, II, 7, 9 ('custom of borow').

[196] Stair, II, 7, 6: 'though they have the resemblance of servitudes, and pass with the thing to singular successors; yet they are rather personal obligations, such as pass in communion even to the singular successors of either party'. Contemporary case law did not accept this view: see *Luke* v. *Dundass* (1695) 4 Brown's Supp 258 ('natural servitude'), and *Hall* v. *Corbet* (1698) Mor 12775 ('servitude *oneris ferendi*').

[197] Stair, II, 7, 6. And see also Bankton, II, 7, 9 ('this regulation takes place from the nature of the thing'), and Erskine, II, 9, 11 ('by the nature and condition of his property').

[198] For common interest in rivers, see ch. 11 in this volume, iv. 2.

[199] The first use of the term in this context may be Kames, *Principles of Equity* (3rd edn., 1778), I, 50 (but not earlier editions). For the history of common interest, see K. G. C. Reid, 'Real Conditions', in *idem* (n. 3), § 354–7.

Nicolson v. *Melvill*[200] concerned a renovated tenement in the High Street in Edinburgh. The developers 'considering, that if the uppermost stories were burdened with maintenance and upholding of the roof alone, none would buy them; and it being the interest of the whole land [i.e. tenement] from top to bottom, to have the roof kept tight, otherwise the rain will fall down upon them; and therefore, in selling the several tenements and stories of that land, they take the sundry purchasers, in their dispositions, bound and obliged by their acceptation thereof, to repair, uphold, and maintain the roof . . .'. Subsequently, the owner of a lower flat refused to pay her share of a roof repair. Since she was not the original purchaser, but a successor, the maintenance obligation would bind only if it was a real right—which, as the law then stood, meant a servitude. By a majority of six to five, the court declined to acknowledge such an 'exotic and extraneous obligation'[201] as a servitude.[202] That decision was handed down in 1708. By the beginning of the following century conveyancers had circumvented the limitations of servitudes by inventing an entirely new type of obligation, known as a 'real burden', which allowed affirmative obligations to be imposed in perpetuity.[203] From that point onwards the common law of the tenement was routinely supplemented by real burdens which redistributed liability for maintenance of the roof and other shared items. Indeed without real burdens, legislation on tenements, as in other countries, would probably have been unavoidable.

Even from this brief sketch a number of themes emerge which are of general significance in the history of property law. First, there is the importance of custom. The law evolved from the practical experience of tenement living and, until the time of Stair, was an unwritten law. If there was litigation, as presumably there was, the records have not been traced in the printed reports. Custom continued to be important into the modern period. As recently as 1902 a case was decided partly on the basis of the accepted custom in Edinburgh.[204]

Secondly, there is a shortage of case law. Frequently, Scotland does not produce enough case law of its own, and in property law it is rarely possible to borrow from other jurisdictions. For uncodified countries do not usually

---

[200] (1708) Mor 14516.   [201] The expression is Bankton's: see II, 7, 9.
[202] One might have expected the main objection to be that the obligation was affirmative in nature. But the report in Morison's *Dictionary* mentions only a floodgates argument: 'that if this servitude were once allowed, then other unheard of servitudes might be introduced, such as that you shall bear a share of the expenses of the floors, and glass windows of your neighbouring tenements, seeing you are benefited thereby'.
[203] For the history of real burdens, see Reid (n. 22) §§ 376–85.
[204] *Whitmore* v. *Stuart and Stuart* (1902) 10 SLT 290. The case concerned liability for the maintenance of chimney stacks, and evidence was led to the effect that the universal practice in Edinburgh (in the absence of anything to the contrary in the titles) was to charge according to the number of vents belonging to each proprietor.

have a civilian system of property law.[205] In the absence of case law, the development of the law of the tenement has been the work of jurists, beginning with Rankine in 1879.[206] The jurists, however, have not always agreed with one another, and a number of important questions remain unresolved. In 1998 the Scottish Law Commission recommended that the common law be replaced by a comprehensive statutory restatement,[207] and legislation is expected in the next few years.

Finally, civilian principle is tempered by common law pragmatism. Sectional ownership is a breach of the Roman law doctrine of accession,[208] but in Scotland, as in some other countries,[209] the difficulty was ignored.[210] The rule, nowhere expressed but universally followed, became that accession operated *within* a flat but not *between* different flats. Why this should be so was never explained. Pragmatism was also evident in the shift from servitudes to real burdens. Roman law was the foundation of property law, no doubt; but if Roman law failed, native law could provide.

---

[205] The most notable exception is South Africa. Insufficient use has been made of case law from this source, although there are indications that this may change. For a recent example from the law of servitudes, see *Axis West Developments Ltd* v. *Chartwell* 1999 SLT 1416.

[206] J. Rankine, *The Law of Land-Ownership in Scotland*. The last edition was the fourth, of 1909.

[207] Report No. 162 on the *Law of the Tenement* (1998).

[208] Even in Roman law, however, accession was qualified by the doctrine of *superficies*. There is no evidence that *superficies* influenced the law of Scotland.

[209] For example, France. See J. Leyser, 'The Ownership of Flats: A Comparative Study', (1958) 7 *ICLQ* 31, 33–4.

[210] One reason for this is that the use of tenements pre-dated the full reception of Roman law principles.

4

The Romanization of Property Law

GRANT McLEOD

I. INTRODUCTION

> The subject of quotation being introduced, Mr. Wilkes censured it as pedantry. JOHNSON. 'No, Sir, it is a good thing; there is a community of mind in it. Classical quotation is the *parole* of literary men all over the world.'[1]

The Scottish institutional writers often refer to, and sometimes quote from, Roman law texts. Whether this went beyond mere pedantry is an important and a difficult question. Any attempt at an answer must begin by investigating the number of references, the subjects referred to, the place in the law in which they occur, and the reasons given for their use. No detailed figures can be found in the literature on the institutional writers.[2] Yet some kind of quantitative analysis, however crude, seems part of the groundwork required in order to measure the impact of Roman law on the institutional writers, and through them on modern Scots law. Further it is necessary to look not merely at what is said about Roman law in theory but at how it is used in practice. We must not confine ourselves to a writer's general position on Roman law as set out at the beginning of his book, but go on to examine how he uses it in his detailed treatment of the rules of Scots law.

Having seen what references to Roman law are made by each institutional writer in turn, we would then be in a position to compare their approaches. This investigation might entitle us to say something about how far the writers

---

[1] J. Boswell, *The Life of Samuel Johnson, LL.D.* (1791)
[2] See for example K. Luig, 'The Institutes of the National Law in the 17th and 18th Centuries', [1972] *JR* 193 sqq.; W. M. Gordon, 'Roman Law as a Source', in D. M. Walker (ed.), *Stair Tercentenary Studies*, Stair Society, vol. 33 (1981), 107 sqq.; J. W. Cairns, 'Institutional Writings in Scotland Reconsidered', (1983) 4 *JLH* 76 sqq.; D. M. Walker, *The Scottish Jurists* (1985); A. Watson, 'Some Notes on Mackenzie's *Institutions* and the European Legal Tradition', (1989) 16 *Ius Commune* 303 sqq.; W. M. Gordon, 'Roman Law in Scotland', in R. Evans-Jones (ed.), *The Civil Law Tradition in Scotland* (1995), 13 sqq., esp. 26–35: see also *idem*, 'Roman Law and Scots Law— a Bibliography', *ibid.* 310 sqq., including pre-1970 literature; J. W. Cairns, 'The Civil Law Tradition in Scottish Legal Thought', in D. L. Carey Miller and R. Zimmermann (eds.), *The Civil Law Tradition in Scots Law* (1997), 191 sqq. These works deal in a general way with Roman law influence on the institutional writers: for recent literature on their treatment of property, see n. 131 below. Gordon, 'Roman Law as a Source' (n. 2), 111 says of Stair's references that 'it may not be out of place to begin by giving some statistics', though he does not do so in any detail.

allowed themselves to be influenced by Roman law, how far they *wanted* Scots law to look Roman. It is only in this limited sense that this chapter considers the Romanization of Scots law. By its very nature, this survey will tell us nothing about any unconscious, or at least unacknowledged, borrowings. As we shall see, however, this is rarely a problem: only Hume is coy about saying when he thinks Roman and Scots law are the same.

It is beyond the scope of this chapter to consider why the writers came to refer to Roman law as they did, that is, how their legal education and reading (other than reading of earlier institutional writers) affected their views on Scots law and Roman law. Nor does it ask whether they were right about the influence of Roman law on Scots law, past or present. For present purposes, it does not matter whether there is historical evidence for any claim made about Scots law having adopted a given rule from Roman law. In fact many such claims look flimsy. For even if they were wrong, it is views of the institutional writers on Roman law which have influenced modern Scots law.

The law of property provides a promising area for exploration. The law of immoveable (or 'heritable') property was heavily influenced by feudalism from the early twelfth century onwards, so that many of its basic rules and institutions are clearly not of Roman origin.[3] It will therefore be interesting to see whether feudalism acted as a barrier to Romanization. In comparison, the law of moveable property is quite Roman in appearance, although appearances may sometimes deceive. Another interesting question is whether the institutional writers thought that a unitary treatment of moveable and immoveable property on the Roman model was either possible or desirable.[4]

As is explained below, the survey is not quite complete. It has been necessary to leave out some of the topics in the law of property which the institutional writers discuss, either because they are not really part of private law or because some institutional writers do not consider them as part of the law of property.

The method adopted here is to find, count, and classify the references to Roman law by institutional writers in their treatment of the Scots law of property. These references are of two kinds. Some cite actual texts from the *Corpus Juris Civilis*. Each text has been counted separately, even though they sometimes appear in clusters. Citations of consecutive sections of a text on the same point (e.g. D. 41, 1, 5, 2–4) have been counted as a single reference. But where sections of the same text are not consecutive and make different points (e.g. D. 41, 2, 3, 5 and 9) they are counted as two references. If the same *Corpus Juris* text is cited in different contexts in the same work it is counted separately each time.

---

[3] See the short account of feudalism in Scots law given by G. L. Gretton, 'The Feudal System', in K. G. C. Reid (ed.), *The Law of Property in Scotland* (1996), §§ 41–113.
[4] See K. G. C. Reid, 'Right and Things', in Reid (n. 3), § 1.

The second kind of reference is where the writer does not cite a text from the *Corpus Juris*. To be included in this category, it has to be obvious that the writer means to refer to Roman law: he must be explicit. So the text has to have clear words showing this, such as Erskine's favourite 'by the Roman law', or Bankton's 'by the civil law'. Latin words and phrases are not included unless they are part of an explicit reference to Roman law, nor are Latin maxims which are not from the *Corpus Juris*. Excluded also are references to civilian writers which do not contain references to Roman law itself.

The treatment of the references follows the same pattern for each writer. First comes a short account of the writer's view on the relationship between Scots law and Roman law in general. Secondly, there is an account of the number of references made to Roman law. All percentages are given to the nearest whole per cent. Where a Roman text is cited, there is a cross-check to see whether it can be found in the *Corpus Juris Civilis* at the place cited and whether it says something like it is represented as saying. Thirdly, Roman references on property are extracted which are unimportant, either because they simply give the Roman equivalents of Scots law terms, or because they are purely historical, in the sense that they make no comparison between particular Roman and Scots law rules. The latter are not, of course, unimportant when considering the separate issue of the writer's general approach to Roman law and his view on the relationship between it and feudalism: indeed, I have quoted from some of these at length. But although there are borderline cases, it seems useful to distinguish between a writer saying, in a vague and general way, that Roman law influenced Scots law in the past, and the writer stating that this *particular* rule or institution of Scots law is *still* the same as the Roman one. Fourthly, there is an examination of references where either Scots law is explicitly said to have adopted a Roman rule, or where the Roman rules are given without any Scots authority. This is followed by a survey of the occasions where Roman law and Scots law are contrasted. Finally, there is a consideration of where the references appear, to see if any pattern can be established. The way each writer reacts to feudalism will be seen to be important here and affects the question of whether any unitary treatment of moveable and immoveable property was possible.

Some references are difficult to classify under this scheme and other schemes could no doubt be suggested. One could, for example, count the cluster of Roman texts often found at the end of a paragraph as a single reference. This would reduce the total number of references. The trouble with this approach is that, on examination, each text usually deals with different aspects of the rules found in the paragraph. Besides, the writer has chosen to make multiple references to Roman law in such cases: would it be scientific to ignore his choice? It must be conceded, though, that there is an unavoidable element of subjectivity both in setting up this scheme of classification and in applying it.

The term 'institutional writers' requires some explanation. Modern Scots law considers some writers of the seventeenth, eighteenth and nineteenth centuries to be authoritative sources of the law. What this means, and exactly which writers, and which writings, are to be included in the canon, is disputed.[5] But for our purposes all that matters is that the writers considered below are, with one exception (Hume), generally considered institutional writers and have been extremely influential in the development of Scots law. The survey is confined to Stair's *Institutions of the Law of Scotland*,[6] Bankton's *Institute of the Laws of Scotland*,[7] Erskine's *Institute of the Law of Scotland*,[8] and Hume's *Lectures*.[9] These works are comparable in the length of their treatment of property.

Some explanation is due for not beginning with Craig's *Jus Feudale*, first published in 1655.[10] There is no doubt that Craig refers to Roman law on numerous occasions. He also provides the first sophisticated example of its use in Scots law. It would be wrong to 'play down the general importance of Craig',[11] as some modern scholars have done, so as to make Scots law appear to start with Stair. As we shall see, later writers were in Craig's debt for many of their comparisons between Roman law and Scots law. But there are good reasons for not beginning this study with Craig. Craig does not deal with moveable property to any extent.[12] More importantly, it is difficult to ascertain which of the references to Roman law in the published version of *Jus Feudale* are actually Craig's, a complicated issue beyond the scope of this chapter.[13]

Although Mackenzie's *Institutions*[14] was closely modelled on Justinian's

---

[5] See Cairns, (1983) 4 *JLH* 98 sqq.

[6] J. Dalrymple, Viscount Stair, *The Institutions of the Law of Scotland, Deduced from its Originals, and Collated with the Civil, Canon and Feudal Laws, and with the Customs of Neighbouring Nations* (ed. D. M. Walker, 1981). This is a tercentenary commemorative version of Stair's second edition of 1693.

[7] A. McDouall, Lord Bankton, *An Institute of the Laws of Scotland in Civil Rights: With Observations on the Agreement and Diversity between them and the Laws of England* (1751–53, repr. in Stair Society, vols. 41–3, 1993–5).

[8] J. Erskine, *An Institute of the Law of Scotland* (1773). I have used, for convenience, the sixth edition (1824) by James (later Lord) Ivory. The same references to Roman law are made in both editions.

[9] *Baron David Hume's Lectures 1786–1822*, Stair Society, vols. 5, 13, 15, 17, 18, 19 (1939–58).

[10] T. Craig, *Jus Feudale* (1665). The work was written much earlier; Craig died in 1608.

[11] See Cairns (n. 2), (194–5).

[12] Bankton, Preface, v, criticizes *Jus Feudale* because it 'only concerns feudal subjects' and 'was never intended for a complete system of our law'.

[13] See the comments of Lord Clyde in his translation of T. Craig's *Jus Feudale* (1934), Translator's Note, xvi, xix. John Cairns has suggested to me that the additional references to Roman law found in footnotes to J. Baillie's third edition (1732) provide another example of what I have called the Romanization of the law of property.

[14] G. Mackenzie, *The Institutions of the Law of Scotland* (1684). I have used the author's second and final edition (1688). In the Epistle Dedicatory, Mackenzie says he has expressed 'every thing in Terms of the Civil Law, or in the Stile of Ours respectively'. At I, 2, 9 he says this is so that 'there may be as little difference found betwixt the Civil Law and ours, as is possible'. In his

and contains some references to Roman law, it is a short, elementary work in comparison with the others. I have also left out of consideration Kames's *Principles of Equity*[15] and Bell's *Commentaries*,[16] since they are different kinds of work from the others and do not contain extensive discussions of the whole of the law of property. Hume's *Lectures*, although unpublished, were so influential and give such a reasoned account of the property law of his time that they must be included in any survey of institutional writings.

II. STAIR: ROMAN LAW RISES AS EQUITY

James Dalrymple, Viscount Stair, was born in 1619 and died in 1695. He was an important political figure as well as an outstanding lawyer, serving as Lord President of the Court of Session twice, in 1671–81 and again in 1688 until his death. His *Institutions* was written around 1660, with the first edition published in 1681. The enlarged and more influential second edition appeared in 1693.[17] Although drawing on many sources, including Roman law, Stair had an independent mind and certainly did not follow these sources slavishly. Although calling his work *Institutions*, he rejects much of the order found in Justinian's Institutes. While he clearly respects Roman law, he is reserved in his handling of it. His general approach is shown in the following text:

> The law of each society . . . is called civil law . . . though that now be appropriate to the civil law of the Roman commonwealth or empire, as the most excellent. And because of that affinity that the law of Scotland hath with it, (as have also the laws . . . of the chief nations, to which the victorious arms of the Romans did propagate it, and its own worth, even after the ruin of the Roman empire which hath so commended it,) that though it be not acknowledged as a law binding for its authority, yet being, as a rule, followed for its equity, it shall not be amiss here to say something of it.[18]

---

treatment of the law of property in book II he makes only seven explicit references to Roman law: II, 1, 81 (*alluvio*); II, 1, 85 (*pro derelicto habere*); II, 1, 85 (prescription); II, 4, 110 (*emphyteusis*); II, 7, 154 (possession); II, 9, 180 (servitudes); II, 9, 183 (usufruct). Mackenzie never cites actual texts from the *Corpus Juris Civilis*. Erskine followed the order of Mackenzie's *Institutions*, but obviously could not get his 156 references to the Roman law of property from it.

[15] H. Home, Lord Kames, *Principles of Equity* (1760). See Cairns, (1983) 4 *JLH* 101.

[16] G. J. Bell, *Commentaries on the Laws of Scotland and on the Principles of Mercantile Jurisprudence, Considered in Relation to Bankruptcy; Competitions of Creditors; and Imprisonment for Debt* (2nd edn., 1810). As Cairns, (1983) 4 *JLH* 101 points out, this work is primarily on commercial law. His *Principles of the Law of Scotland* (4th edn., 1839) has only eighteen Roman references on property, five of which cite an actual Roman text.

[17] Gordon, 'Roman Law as a Source' (n. 2), 111 n. 11 says that the number of texts cited in this second edition is 'significantly higher' than in the first edition, and that 'in general at least, the citations are merely added to vouch a statement on Roman law which is already in the text, they are not additional references to Roman law'. I have not attempted to compare the first and second editions, nor have I looked beyond the version of the second edition cited above at n. 6.

[18] Stair, I, 1, 12. This passage is partly based on Justinian: see Inst. 1, 2, 2.

Stair praises Roman law as the 'most excellent' civil law system, *the* civil law of civil laws, as it were. Scots law has an 'affinity' with it, not simply because of the historical importance of the Roman Empire, but because of Roman law's 'own worth', its intrinsic value. Although not automatically binding, Roman law *may* be followed in Scotland, but only where the Roman law in question is equitable. To be taken into account, Roman law must provide an equitable code of conduct ('as a rule, followed for its equity').[19] Equity, or natural law, was for Stair the original, God-given law of all mankind. Human law was later introduced by each nation, including Scotland, 'for utility's sake', first by custom and then by statute.[20] So there is a further hurdle before we can refer to Roman law: there must be no Scots custom or statute available:

Our customs, as they have arisen mainly from equity, so they are also from the civil, canon, and feudal laws, from which the terms, tenors, and forms of them are much borrowed; and therefore, these (especially the civil law,) have great weight with us, namely, in cases where a custom is not yet formed. But none of these have with us the authority of law; and therefore are only received according to their equity and expediency.[21]

This theory on the use of Roman law, whatever Stair's sources for it were,[22] is prominent in his detailed account of the rules of Scots law. It limits the number of references made to Roman law and affects the way in which it is referred to. Where clear Scots 'custom' has 'formed', as in the case of feudal land law, Stair sees little room for Roman law. Even where there is not much Scots material, as in the case of moveable property, Stair may not refer to Roman law if equitable rules can be derived from first principles. When he does choose to refer to Roman law, his purpose seems to be to set out in specific rules what he already considers as the equitable position.

When we turn to Stair's treatment of property in books II and III we find out how he applies this theory in practice. Here some of Stair's titles (i.e. chapters) have been left out of account. Capturing property in war is not what we would now consider a private law matter.[23] The law on 'teinds', burdens on land for paying clergy stipends, has ecclesiastical aspects which make it unsuitable for present purposes.[24] Stair's treatment of prescription is also omitted because it covers 'the common extinction and abolition of all

---

[19] See A. Watson, 'The Rise of Modern Scots Law', in *La formazione storica del diritto moderno in Europa: Atti del III Congresso Internazionale della Societa Italiana di Storia del Diritto* (1977), vol. 3, 1167 sqq., 1175. Stair sees equity, utility, natural law, and the law of nations as related concepts: see I, 1, 6; I, 1,10; I, 1, 11.   [20] Stair, I, 1, 1–7; I, 1, 10; I, 1, 16.
[21] Stair, I, 1, 16.   [22] See Cairns, 'The Civil Law Tradition' (n. 2), 204–6.
[23] Stair, II, 2. In any case, I can find no references to Roman law in this title.
[24] Stair, II, 8. Again, I can find no references to Roman in this title.

rights',[25] including personal ones.[26] Stair's title on assignation is excluded because it concerns personal, not real rights.[27] Finally, there is excluded the title on the confiscation of property by the state.[28]

In the remainder of Stair's treatment of property there are only sixty-seven references to Roman law.[29] Of these, fifteen (22 per cent) do not cite a Roman text,[30] but use words like 'the Roman law', 'the Romans', or 'the civil law'.[31] The remaining fifty-two references (77 per cent) which do cite a Roman text[32] all seem to do so accurately.[33] Stair's account of the texts is reasonably reliable. There are three references (4 per cent) which can be classified as unimportant. The first two do no more than point out vague similarities between certain Roman and Scots procedures: both examples can be found in Craig.[34] The third is purely historical and will be discussed below.[35] There are only five occasions (7 per cent) when Stair says with any degree of explicitness that Scots law has adopted or should adopt the Roman rule given.[36] But there are thirty-three more instances where, although Stair is obviously

---

[25] Stair, II, 12, 1. I count fifteen references to Roman law in Stair's treatment of prescription.

[26] Following Mackenzie (n. 14), III, 7, Erskine (n. 8), III, 7 deals with prescription as part of the law of obligations, which would make comparison difficult. [27] Stair, III, 1.

[28] Stair, III, 3. [29] Stair, II, 1; II, 3–7; II, 9–11; III, 2. Stair, III, 4–9 is on succession.

[30] Stair, II, 1, 38 (2 refs.); II, 1, 40 (2 refs.); II, 1, 41; II, 3, 1; II, 4, 61; II, 7, 2; II, 7, 6; II, 7, 7 (2 refs., although the first has the words *auctore Marciano* which suggest D. 8, 2, 14 is meant); II, 7, 10; II, 10, 6; II, 11, 19; III, 2, 5.

[31] Stair, II, 1, 41 does not use any of these but mentions Proculus, Sabinus, and Tribonian.

[32] Stair, II, 1, 5 (4 refs.: D. 43, 7, 1–2; D. 43, 11, 2; Inst. 2, 1, 5; Inst. 2, 1, 3); II, 1, 18 (3 refs.: D. 41, 2, 3, 1; D. 41, 2, 3, 8; D. 50, 17, 153); II, 1, 19 (D. 41, 2, 6 pr.–1); II, 1, 20 (2 refs.: D. 43, 16, 1, 27; D. 43, 16, 3, 9); II, 1, 23 (3 refs.: C. 3, 32, 22; D. 50, 17, 136; D. 5, 3, 25, 11); II, 1, 24 (D. 50, 16, 109); II, 1, 33 (8 refs.: D. 8, 3, 16; Inst. 2, 1, 12 (cited twice on diff. points); D. 47, 10, 13, 7; Inst. 2, 1, 12–18; Inst. 2, 1, 22; D. 41, 2, 3, 14; D. 10, 2, 8, 1–2); II, 1, 34 (D. 46, 3, 78); II, 1, 39 (6 refs.: Inst. 2, 1, 26; D. 6, 1, 23, 3; D. 41, 1, 9, 2; Inst. 2, 1, 34; Inst. 2, 1, 33; D. 10, 4, 3, 14); II, 3, 19 (C. 8, 17, 11); II, 3, 34 (3 refs.: Inst. 3, 24, 3; D. 6, 3; C. 4, 66); II, 3, 46 (D. 18, 4, 4); II, 3, 51 (C. 66, 2); II, 3, 60 (2 refs.: C. 10, 15, 1; D. 41, 1, 31, 1); II, 4, 26 (Nov. Leo., c. 13); II, 6, 1 (6 refs.: D. 7, 8, 12; Inst. 2, 5, 1; D. 7, 8, 15, 1; D. 7, 8, 11; Inst. 2, 5, 5; D. 7, 8)); II, 19 (C. 6, 60, 1); II, 7, 1 (3 refs.: D. 19, 1, 3, 2; D. 8, 1, 20; D. 8, 3, 1, 2); II, 7, 2 (D. 8, 4, 11); II, 7, 10 (2 refs.: D. 8, 3, 7; D. 8, 3, 11); II, 7, 11 (D. 8, 3, 3, 3).

[33] The edition used (n. 6) gives Stair's original old-style citations as well as translations of these into modern references to the Berlin Stereotype. The editor (Introduction, 52) says that some of Stair's citations are inaccurate, so that the original and modern references will not correspond. In the texts on property this only seems to happen at II, 6, 1 where Stair's '*et. l.*110 *eod*' must be a mistake for D. 7, 8, 11.

[34] Stair, II, 10, 6 (irritant clauses in reversions are called *pacta legis commissoriae in pignoribus* in the civil law). See Craig (n. 10), II, 6, 1); II, 11, 19 (suspensive clauses depending on the superior's consent resemble *addictiones in diem* in the civil law, citing Craig (n. 10), III, 2, 26, although the comparison with Roman law is not found there).

[35] See text cited below at n. 49.

[36] Stair, II, 2, 38–9 (on accession by conjuncture and contexture, 'we would proceed upon the like grounds of equity and utility'); II, 1, 40 (on accession of houses to land 'a rule in Roman law, which we follow'); II, 6, 19 ('the original of this liferent by courtesy ... is from the rescript of the Emperor Constantine'); II, 7, 10 ('another distinction ... amongst the Romans, and with us, in public and private ways'); III, 2, 5 ('for utility's sake, not only the Romans, but almost all nations require some kind of possession, to accomplish real rights ... with which our custom accordeth').

describing Scots law, the Roman references given provide the only authority for the rules laid down in his text.[37] The implication would seem to be that, in these areas, the Scots law rules are basically the same as the Roman ones. Although Stair would say that these rules should be followed in Scotland not because they are Roman, but because they are equitable, the source of the rules is clear.[38] However, there are some instances where the Roman rule is given but the Scots law position is contrasted with it: I count only seven of these (10 per cent).[39] Usually, then, when Stair does mention Roman law, he is favourably disposed towards it.

As to where these references mostly appear, a clear pattern can be found. Four are on things common to everyone, 10 are on possession, 8 are on occupation, 12 are on accession and 19 are on servitudes, making 53 in total (79 per cent). Leaving all these topics aside, Stair has only 14 references (21 per cent) scattered amongst the other areas of property law. Three of these have already been classed as unimportant: two of them can be found in Craig.[40] Two more concern the definition of treasure, which can also be found in Craig.[41] Another quotes the rule that contract alone does not transfer property, which Stair applies to moveable as well as heritable property.[42] Of the remainder, four concern a comparison between feu farm tenure and *emphyteusis*, which can be found in Craig.[43] The last four are miscellaneous in nature, two of which again are in Craig.[44] So what the vast majority of Stair's Roman references have in common is something obvious but negative: they are in areas of Scots law which were not feudal. In the parts of book II concerned with feudal law, whole titles go past with few or no references to Roman law.[45] We might say that Stair could not Romanize Scots law where it had already been feudalized.

---

[37] Stair, II, 1, 5 (4 refs.); II, 1, 18 (3 refs.); II, 1, 19; II, 1, 20 (2 refs.); II, 1, 23 (3 refs.); II, 1, 33 (8 refs.); II, 1, 34; II, 1, 39 (3 refs. on *accessio* in painting); II, 3, 60 (2 refs.); II, 7, 1 (3 refs.); II, 7, 6; II, 7, 7 (2 refs.); II, 7, 11. There are equally obvious instances, e.g. II, 6, 1 where Stair is describing Roman, not Scots law.

[38] Stair specifically mentions equity, utility, natural law, the law of nations or a similar expression in connection with a Roman reference eight times: at II, 1, 5; II, 1, 33; II, 1, 38 (common benefit); II, 1, 39 (3 times); II, 7, 7; III, 2, 5. The connection between Roman law and these concepts must, however, be taken as implicit in all he says about property.

[39] Stair, II, 1, 39 (2 refs. on *accessio* in writing); II, 1, 40 (*accessio* of one's own materials to another's ground); II, 3, 19; II, 7, 2; II, 7,10 (2 refs. on the servitude of *via*).

[40] See above n. 34 and below n. 49.   [41] Stair, II, 3, 60 (2 refs.; see Craig (n. 10), I, 16, 40).

[42] Stair, III, 2, 5.

[43] Stair, II, 3, 34 (3 refs. See Craig (n. 10), II, 3, 34; see also Craig (n. 10), I, 9, 12); II, 3, 51. (See Craig (n. 10), II, 3, 34.)

[44] Stair, II, 3, 19 (use of notaries and witnesses, citing Craig (n. 10), II, 7, 9, though II, 7, 7 has Roman rules); II, 3, 46 (absolute warrandice in assignations); II, 4, 26 (relief on entry by the vassal. See Craig (n. 10), II, 20, 30); II, 4, 61 (effect of rebellion on fee like *capitis deminutio*).

[45] Stair, II, 4 'Superiority and its Casualties etc.' (2 refs.); II, 5 'Infeftments of Annualrent etc.'(no refs.); II, 10 'Wadsets etc.'(one ref.); II, 11 'Extinction of Infeftments etc.' (one ref.); III, 2 'Dispositions etc' (one ref.).

Stair himself does not quite see it in this way. His approach to property is intended to be historical as well as philosophical.[46] He thinks that the law on the topics discussed in title II, 1 (things common to everyone, possession, occupation, accession and specification, as well as the law on servitudes) 'necessarily followeth, ... by the law of nature'. Since natural law was the original property law of mankind, these rules were there long before feudalism. Logically they are dealt with first, but Romanized to a certain extent. They are 'generally as they were of old, common to both things moveable and immoveable'. Stair might, then, be said in book II, 1 to be treating the law of property in a 'unitary' way, pointing out any differences between how the rules apply to moveable and immoveable property as they occur. However, he goes on to say that he will afterwards discuss the law 'specially in relation to things immoveable, and to the heritable ground-rights of the earth, ... which now by the feudal customs is much changed from what it was, and yet is in moveables'.[47]

This is exactly what he does, beginning at title II, 3, for the remainder of his treatment of the law of property (apart from servitudes and prescription). Here the attempt at a unitary treatment breaks down. Stair is presenting a completely separate regime for heritable property, not just 'local variations in particular cases'.[48] It is a historical event which has made this necessary: the fall of the Roman Empire, the subsequent barbarian invasions and the coming of feudalism.

> By this irruption, which happened in the sixth century, the Roman civil law was sopite [put to sleep] for five hundred years, ... and did take in with it the feudal customs, which have been propagated through the most civil nations of the world.[49]

Stair recognizes that feudalism had an enormous impact: he says of feudal jurisdiction that 'no nation is more exact in this than Scotland'. Feudalism strengthens the bond between sovereign and subject.[50] Nor does Stair consider it unnatural or inferior to Roman law, as Bankton and Hume were later to do. It is simply that, now that land law has been feudalized by custom and statute, the original natural law is largely abrogated. So whereas Stair can describe non-feudal areas of property in Roman terms, because they are still so close to nature, the new feudal law does not lend itself to the same degree of Romanization. Interestingly, Stair sees much less scope for referring to Roman law in this context than Craig, his acknowledged guide to feudal law. Stair says of him:

---

[46] Stair, II, 1 talks of 'unfolding this right, and the progress thereof, both according to the order of time and nature'.

[47] Stair, II, 1, 1. He immediately follows these remarks with a long and detailed analysis of the difference between heritable and moveable property at II, 1, 2–4.   [48] Reid (n. 4), § 1.

[49] Stair, II, 3, 1.   [50] Ibid.

The Romanization of Property Law 229

Our learned countryman, Craig ... hath learnedly handled the feudal rights of this and other nations ... and therefore we shall only follow closely what since his time by statute or custom hath been cleared or altered in our feudal rights, which is very much ... these things which Craig could but conjecture from the nature of the feudal rights ... are now commonly known, and come to a fixed custom.[51]

As we have seen, when Stair *does* refer to Roman law in a feudal context, he nearly always takes his comparisons straight from Craig, usually without acknowledgement. But Stair chooses not to refer to Roman law as often as Craig had done. Part of the explanation for this must be that Stair thought that, since Craig's time, Scots feudal law was 'now commonly known, and come to a fixed custom' and would no longer have the gaps which Craig so often filled with Roman law.

III. BANKTON: THE HIGH NOON OF ROMAN LAW

Andrew McDouall, Lord Bankton, was born in 1685 and died in 1760. After practising at the bar he became a judge in 1755. His *Institute of the Laws of Scotland* appeared in three volumes between 1751 and 1753, exactly sixty years after the second edition of Stair's *Institutions* was published. Much had changed over this period, not least the Union of Scotland and England in 1707. Both Roman law and Scots law were now being taught in Scotland, privately and also at the universities of Edinburgh and Glasgow. Natural law ideas, especially those of Pufendorf, had become highly influential in intellectual circles. Bankton's work reflects some of these changes. Its full title includes the words 'with Observations upon the Agreement and Diversity between them [the laws of Scotland] and the Laws of England'. He places these, fairly extensive, comparative remarks at the end of most his titles. But in his treatment of Scots law it is Roman law, not English law, to which he turns for inspiration. Although he models the general plan of his work on Stair's *Institutions* (rather than Mackenzie's as Erskine was later to do) there is no doubt that he was more heavily influenced by Roman law than any other institutional writer.

Bankton sets out in his preface the various ways in which he has departed from Stair's order. In the three main cases where he does so—adding titles on 'The State and Distinction of Persons',[52] 'The Division and Quality of Things'[53] and 'Rules of the Civil Law, illustrated and adapted to the Law of Scotland'[54]—he is avowedly following Justinian in the *Digest*. Of the last of these titles he says it 'tends to the perfection of the work: since, as shall appear in the progress, we regard the civil law very much, where our own

---

[51] Stair, II, 3, 3.   [52] Bankton, I, 2.   [53] Bankton, I, 3.
[54] Bankton, IV, 45.

statutes and customs fail'.[55] Bankton's work contains many other statements about the importance Roman law had for Scots law. He says for example:

> The civil law ... was compiled for the most part from the laws of nature and nations. Even after the destruction of the Roman Empire it remained, for its native excellency, the standard of laws to most nations, and is emphatically called THE CIVIL LAW. This in a proper sense denotes the law of any particular nation; but, because the law of no nation is comparable to that of the Romans, and the laws of most nations in Europe are very much founded upon it, therefore it hath justly deserved that appellation.[56]

Roman law is highly commended because it is largely the same as the law of nature and nations, high praise indeed in the eighteenth century. Comparing this passage with the one from Stair quoted above[57] (which must have influenced Bankton) one detects a noticeably warmer feeling towards Roman law. The lyrical note Bankton attaches to this passage describing the work of Justinian bears this impression out: 'These are the codes or body of the civil law ... which, next to the sacred writings, is the greatest and most valuable magazine of knowledge that ever the world was favoured with; those laws, for their excellency, being in effect a transcript of the law of nature for the most part.'[58] However, Bankton sets some limits to the authority of Roman law. 'Only a superior can give laws', he says.[59] Although Roman, canon, and feudal law are all 'in some measure sources of our law', they are 'only to be regarded as law with us, so far as they are received by our statutory or consuetudinary law, that is, either by the express or tacite consent of the legislature'.[60] Many Scots statutes show, says Bankton, that our legislators *have* followed Roman and canon law 'for their reasonableness and expediency' in the past. Judges ought to continue to do so in the future where there is no Scots authority on the point:

> [O]ur judges ought to direct themselves by the civil and canon laws, as a rule, where our own statutes and customs fail, or where the question, tho' concerning a feudal subject, is not decided by our feudal customs. In such case the civil law most commonly takes place, unless we have entirely rejected it in matters of that kind. Thus, for example, it were absurd to argue from the civil law, in favour of adoption, of slavery, and other matters, which are entirely abolished by universal custom of nations.[61]

This limitation still leaves plenty of scope for reference to Roman law. Indeed, where there are gaps in Scots law, Bankton presumes that Roman law will apply, unless there are very strong reasons for it not to do so. This goes further than the passages quoted above from Stair on which Bankton seems to

---

[55] Bankton, Preface, ix.   [56] Bankton, I, 1, 38.   [57] See text cited above at n. 18.
[58] Bankton, note to I, 1, 38.   [59] Bankton, I, 1, 3, citing D. 1, 3, 1.
[60] Bankton, I, 1, 16.
[61] Bankton, I, 1, 42. He takes his list of old statutes in which Roman law was applied from Stair, I, 1, 16.

The Romanization of Property Law 231

rely.[62] And certainly Bankton's treatment of the law of property demonstrates much more enthusiasm for Roman law than was shown by Stair. Bankton says in his preface that he has 'referred on the margin to the authorities whereon I found my positions, which was very troublesome, but worth all the pains'.[63] He certainly spares himself no troublesome pains when referring to the Roman law of property.

Bankton covers property in books II and III of his *Institute*. For the purposes of counting citations there is also included the references to Roman law in book I, title 3 mentioned above;[64] there is only a slight overlap here with the rest of his treatment. So as to make Bankton's references comparable with both Stair's and Erskine's, some titles have been disregarded. Since Bankton follows Stair's order title by title, the titles omitted for Stair are omitted here also.[65] There are twenty references to Roman law in book II, title 3, and 150 in the titles considered in the rest of books II and III, making 170 in total. This excludes the references to Roman law made in the sections on English law. Bankton rarely refers to Roman law without citing a text from the *Corpus Juris*. Only eleven such occasions have been traced (6 per cent of references).[66] Unlike Stair and Erskine, a number of Bankton's citations are inaccurate: I have detected fourteen (8 per cent) and suggested which texts he may have intended to cite.[67] They look like the result of inadequate proofreading and might have been corrected if there had been further editions of the work. The remaining 145 Roman texts cited all seem to contain, more or less, the rules that Bankton claims.[68] Of these six (4 per cent) seem unimportant.

---

[62] See texts cited above at nn. 18 and 21. [63] Bankton, Preface, x.

[64] See text above at n. 53.

[65] See above at nn. 23–5. Thus I have omitted Bankton, II, 2; II, 8; II, 12; III, 1; III, 3. As with Stair, there seem to be a significant number of references to Roman law in Bankton on prescription, though not many in the other titles omitted.

[66] Bankton, I, 3, 19; I, 3, 20; II, 1, 13; II, 3, 1; II, 3, 4; II, 3, 5 (in note attached); II, 3, 167; II, 6, 26; II, 7, 16; II, 7, 19; II, 7, 31.

[67] Bankton, I, 3, 2 (D. 41, 1, 19 [14?]); I, 3, 4 (D. 41, 1, 40,1 [41?]); I, 3, 13 (2 refs.: D. 1, 8, 3 [1?] pr.; D. 1, 8, 5 [9?] 3); II, 1, 8 (Inst. 2, 1, 29 [39?]); II, 1, 10 (2 refs.: Inst. 2, 1, 3 [32?]; D. 39, 2, 19 [9?], 2); II, 1, 17 (Inst. 2, 1, 29 [26?]); II, 1, 18 (Inst. 2, 1, 37 [34?]); II, 7, 12 (D. 8, 2, 21 [14?]); II, 7, 14 (D. 8, 2, 8 [6?]); II, 7, 33 (D. 50. 17, 79 [74?]); II, 7, 37 (D. 8, 2, 28 [30?]); II, 9, 17 (D. 50, 17, 73 [74?]).

[68] Bankton, I, 3, 2 (3 refs.: D. 1, 8, 2, 1; D. 1, 8, 4 pr.; D. 41, 1, 19 [14?]); I, 3, 4 (5 refs.: D. 41, 1, 40, 1 [41?]; Inst. 2, 1, 23; D. 41, 1, 7, 5; Inst. 2, 1, 24; D. 41, 1, 7, 6); I, 3, 7 (D. 1, 8, 6, 1); I, 3, 9 (D. 1, 8, 6, 1); I, 3, 11 (D. 1, 8, 9, 1); I, 3, 12 (3 refs.: D. 1, 8, 6, 4; D. 47, 12; D. 18, 1, 22 sqq.); I, 3, 13 (2 refs.: D. 1, 8, 3 [1?] pr.; D. 1, 8, 5, [9?] 3); I, 3, 14 (Inst. 2, 1, 12); I, 3, 17 (D. 46, 3, 94, 1); II, 1, 5 (Inst. 2, 1, 5); II, 1, 6 (Inst. 1, 8, 2); II, 1, 7 (4 refs.: D. 41, 1, 3 pr. sqq.; D. 47, 10, 13, 7; D. 41, 1, 5, 1; Inst. 2, 1, 15–16); II, 1, 8 (4 refs.: Inst. 2, 1, 29 [39?]; C. 10, 15; D. 41, 1, 5, 7; D. 49, 15, 20, 1) II, 1, 10 (10 refs.: Inst. 2, 1, 29–33; Inst. 2, 1, 3 [32?]; D. 41, 1, 7, 1; D. 41, 1, 16; D. 41, 1, 7, 2; D. 39, 2, 19 [9?] 2; D. 41, 1, 7, 3; D. 41, 1, 29; D. 41, 1, 7, 5; D. 41, 1, 65, 20); II, 1, 11 (D. 5, 1, 9); II, 1, 13 (D. 41, 1, 7, 7); II, 1, 14 (Inst. 2, 1, 25–7); II, 1, 15 (Inst. 2, 1, 28); II, 1, 16 (D. 46, 3, 78); II, 1, 17 (2 refs.: Inst. 2, 1, 29 [26?]; D. 47, 3); II, 1, 18 (2 refs.: D. 41, 1, 7, 12; Inst. 2, 1, 37 [34?]); II, 1, 20 (Inst. 2, 1, 40); II, 1, 22 (2 refs.: Inst. 2, 1, 45; D. 18, 1, 74) II, 1, 23 (2 refs.: Inst. 2, 1, 43; D. 23, 3, 43, 1); II, I, 24 (Inst. 2, 3, 4); II, 1, 26 (7 refs.: D. 41, 2, 18 pr.; D. 41, 2, 3, 1; D. 41, 2, 8 sqq.; D. 41, 2, 3, 13; D. 41, 2, 18; D. 41, 2, 44, 1 sqq.; D. 41, 2, 6 pr.–1); II, 1, 27

Two simply give the Roman terminology for Scots law institutions;[69] and four are purely historical with no comparisons made between specific rules.[70] Bankton quotes Roman rules as general maxims only sixteen times (9 per cent) in his treatment of property.[71] Like Stair, Bankton does not often state explicitly that Scots law has adopted or should adopt a Roman rule. There are only seven possible examples (4 per cent).[72] But this figure gives a misleading impression, for there are 101 other occasions where Roman law is the only authority given for rules of Scots law (59 per cent),[73] and it is directly on Roman law that he founds his positions.

(2 refs.: D. 41, 2, 6; D. 43, 17, 3 pr.); II, 1, 28 (D. 8, 1, 20); II, 1, 29 (2 refs.: D. 41, 2, 3, 8; D. 41, 2, 6); II, I, 30 (5 refs.: Inst. 4, 15 pr.; D. 5, 2, 62; Inst. 4, 15, 8; C. 8, 1, 4; D. 5, 1, 62); II, 1, 33 (D. 6, 2); II, 1, 38 (C. 4, 65, 25); II, 3, 2 (2 refs.: C. 11, 62, 12; C. 4, 66); II, 3, 5 (2 refs.: D. 6, 3; C. 4, 66, 3); II, 3, 11 (D. 2, 14, 38); II, 3, 12 (2 refs.: Inst. 2, 14, 10; Inst. 3, 19, 11); II, 3, 53 (C. 4, 66); II, 3, 119 (D. 2, 14, 38); II, 3, 122 (D. 50, 17, 149); II, 3, 134 (D. 50, 17, 27); II, 3, 135 (4 refs.: D. 30, 1, 114, 14; D. 32, 4, 38, 4; D. 33, 4, 38 pr.; C. 4, 51); II, 3, 137 (D. 35, 1, 102); II, 3, 144 (D. 50, 17, 56); II, 3, 146 (D. 2, 14, 38); II, 3, 147 (Nov. 159, 2); II, 3, 160 (D. 50, 17, 35); II, 3, 165 (D. 7, 9, 1 pr.); II, 4, 6 (C. 3, 36); II, 6, 3 (2 refs.: Inst. 2, 4; Inst. 2, 5); II, 6, 5 (D. 7, 5); II, 6, 21 (C. 6, 60, 1); II, 6, 24 (D. 33, 1); II, 6, 27 (2 refs.: D. 7, 1, 13 pr.; C. 3, 33, 4); II, 6, 28 (3 refs.: D. 7, 1, 7, 2; C. 3, 33, 7; D. 7, 1, 27, 3); II, 6, 31 (D. 7, 1, 56); II, 7, 1 (Inst. 2, 3, 4); II, 7, 2 (C. 7, 22); II, 7, 5 (D. 50, 16, 198); II, 7, 6 (D. 8, 2, 33); II, 7, 7 (5 refs.: D. 8, 2, 33; D. 8, 5, 6, 2; D. 8, 5, 8 pr.–2; D. 8, 2, 20, 2; D. 8, 2, 33); II, 7, 8 (D. 9, 2, 29, 1); II, 7, 11 (3 refs.: D. 8, 2, 26; D. 8, 2, 27, 1; D. 8, 2, 28); II, 7, 12 (4 refs.: D. 43, 19, 3, 15; D. 10, 3, 12; D. 39, 2, 35–7; D. 8, 2, 21 [14?]); II, 7, 13 (D. 8, 2, 20, 5–6); II, 7, 14 (5 refs.: D. 8, 2, 2; D. 8, 2, 8 [6?]; D. 8, 2, 9; D. 8, 2, 12; D. 8, 2, 170); II, 7, 15 (D. 8, 2, 15–17); II, 7, 18 (4 refs.: D. 8, 3, 21–2; D. 8, 1, 9; D. 8, 1, 6; D. 8, 3, 13, 1); II, 7, 19 (2 refs.: D. 8, 3, 1; D. 8, 3, 7); II, 7, 20 (D. 8, 3, 8); II, 7, 28 (D. 8, 3, 3); II, 7, 29 (D. 39, 3, 21); II, 7, 30 (4 refs.: D. 39, 3, 1; D. 8, 3, 3, 2; D. 8, 5, 8, 5; D. 8, 3, 9); II, 7, 33 (D. 50, 17, 79 [74?]); II, 7, 37 (D. 8, 2, 28 [30?]); II, 7, 61 (2 refs.: D. 8, 2, 6; D. 8, 2, 1); II, 9, 6 (D. 19, 2, 46); II, 9, 17 (2 refs.: D. 50, 17, 73 [74?]; D. 19, 2, 24, 1); II, 9, 24 (C. 4, 65, 8); II, 9, 40 (2 refs.: D. 50, 17, 168; D. 50, 17, 41, 1); II, 9, 68 (D. 50, 17, 206); II, 10, 9 (C. 8, 34, 3); II, 11, 30 (C. 3, 39); II, 11, 49 (C. 4, 66, 3); III, 2, 2 (C. 2, 3, 20); III, 2, 26 (D. 42, 1, 15, 2–3); III, 2, 68 (C. 1, 14, 25).

[69] Bankton, I, 3, 19 (expression *nomina debitorum* used 'with us, as in the civil law'); II, 6, 26 (liferent called *ususfructus* in the civil law).

[70] Bankton, II, 3, 1 (where private interests yield to the public good, owners are entitled to compensation, as where goods are jettisoned under the *Lex Rhodia*); II, 3, 1 (origin of feudalism wrongly attributed to the Romans); II, 3, 5 (in note attached on 'The Progress and Declining of the Feudal Law'); II, 3, 133 (only absolute fiar can entail since the Twelve Tables says '*uti quisque legasset rei suae, ita ius esto*').

[71] Bankton, II, 1, 6; II, 1, 35; II, 3, 11; II, 3, 119; II, 3, 122; II, 3, 134; II, 3, 144; II, 3, 146; II, 3, 160; II, 6, 24; II, 7, 33; II, 9, 40 (2 refs.); II, 9, 68; III, 2, 2; III, 2, 68. In each case the maxim is quoted in Latin and a citation is given. The word 'maxim' or something like it is used in all but the last two cases.

[72] Bankton, I, 3, 16 ('we follow the foresaid rule' on *occupatio* of wild creatures); II, 1, 13 ('the rule of the civil law, followed by us' on *specificatio*); II, 1, 35 (of *nemo potest mutare causam possessionis suae*, 'this rule is derived to us from the civil law'); II, 3, 53 (feu farm holdings resemble *emphyteusis*, 'from whence they have been derived to us'); II, 3, 135 ('our tallies, even those with strict irritant clauses, are founded in the civil law: their *Fidei-commisses* [sic] resembled them greatly'); II, 6, 21 ('the conjecture' that courtesy 'has its rife from the constitution of the civil law . . . is not groundless'); III, 2, 26 ('this method of execution . . . hath been derived to us from the civil law').

[73] Bankton, I, 3, 4 (4 refs. on river-banks); I, 3, 7; I, 3, 12 (3 refs. on burial-places); I, 3, 13 (2 refs.); I, 3, 17; II, 1, 7 (3 refs.); II, 1, 8 (3 of 4 refs. on occupation); II, 1, 10 (one ref. on accession in general, 4 refs. on alluvion and avulsion); II, 1, 13; II, 1, 14; II, 1, 15; II, 1, 16; II, 1, 17 (one of

In contrast with Stair, Bankton rarely attempts to relate Roman law to natural law or equity in other than a very general way. For example, although he subtitles the second section of book II, title 1 'Property, and the Means of acquiring it, by the Law of Nature and Nations', he refers explicitly to the law of nature or law of nations only four times.[74] In the same section there are thirty-five references to Roman law, all but one of which cites a Roman text. As with Stair, there are relatively few cases where Roman law is referred to in order to contrast it with Scots law.[75]

The pattern of Bankton's references is in many respects similar to that already encountered in Stair. There are 18 on things common to everyone and public property, 8 on occupation, 20 on accession and specification, 6 on delivery, 19 on possession, and 56 on servitudes, 44 of these being on praedial servitudes, a total of 127 references (75 per cent). In those areas the percentage is slightly lower than Stair but higher than Erskine. Bankton has two references which relate to the Roman divisions of fungibles and non-fungibles and corporeal and incorporeal property. He also has seven references to Roman law in his title on 'tacks' or leases, though three of these simply apply general maxims and most are on the contractual aspects of leases.

A feature unique to Bankton's treatment of property is his theory that the Scots law on entails is similar to and perhaps even derived from the Roman law on *fideicommissa*. This comparison leads him to make eleven references to Roman law, though one, citing the Twelve Tables,[76] is clearly historical and four are general maxims. It is interesting to note that Bankton applies general maxims much more often in connection with feudal topics than with non-feudal ones. Of the sixteen times Roman rules are quoted as maxims, only five are on moveable property, servitudes and leases: the rest are on feudal topics. Leaving maxims and unimportant references aside, there are only fourteen occasions where Bankton refers to Roman law in a feudal context. Of these, six deal with the comparison which can be found in Craig and Stair between feu farm tenure and *emphyteusis*.[77] Another applies the rules on occupation

---

2 refs. on contexture); II, 1, 20; II, 1, 22 (2 refs.); II, 1, 23 (2 refs.); II, 1, 24; II, 1, 25 (7 refs.); II, 1, 27 (2 refs.); II, 1, 28; II, 1, 29 (2 refs.); II, 1, 30 (5 refs.); II, 3, 135 (4 refs.); II, 6, 28 (3 refs.); II, 7, 1; II, 7, 2; II, 7, 5; II, 7, 6; II, 7, 7 (5 refs.); II, 7, 8; II, 7, 11 (6 refs.); II, 7, 13; II, 7, 14 (5 refs.); II, 7, 15 (3 refs.); II, 7, 18 (4 refs.); II, 7, 19 (2 refs.); II, 7, 28; II, 7, 29; II, 7, 30 (5 refs.); II, 7, 37; II, 7, 61; II, 9, 17 (2 refs.); II, 9, 24; II, 9, 40 (2 refs.); II, 9, 68.

[74] Bankton, II, 1, 6 (2 refs. to 'the law of nature and nations'); II, 1, 10 ('the law of nations'); II, 1, 20 ('the law of nations'). II, 1, 20 also has a reference to 'natural reason'.

[75] Only 30 have been found (18%): Bankton, I, 3, 2 (3 refs.); I, 3, 11; I, 3, 14 (treasure and abandoned property); I, 3, 20; II, 1, 5; II, 1, 8 (2 refs. on treasure); II, 1, 10 (one ref. on industrial fruits, 4 refs. on islands); II, 1, 17; II, 1, 18 (2 refs.); II, 3, 5 (2 refs.); II, 6, 3 (2 refs.); II, 6, 5; II, 7, 16; II, 7, 19 (3 refs.); II, 7, 20; II, 7, 31; II, 9, 6; II, 11, 49.

[76] See text quoted above in n. 72.

[77] Bankton, II, 3, 2 (2 refs.); II, 3, 5 (2 refs.); II, 3, 53; II, 11, 49. See above n. 43 for Stair and Craig on this.

to animals like deer killed outside their enclosures.[78] Another two are on whether unlawful or impossible conditions in feudal holdings resemble those in Roman contracts or wills.[79] Two more are on a liferenter's right to quarry and adjudications between heirs-portioners.[80] Another is on conditions in reversions,[81] another on encroachments,[82] a third on the execution of debts.[83] None of these is a central area of feudal law. Beyond them, Bankton includes a few Roman maxims as if to keep up appearances: one senses a whiff of desperation. But however keen he was to Romanize Scots law, the feudalization of the core areas of land law was as effective a barrier against Bankton as it was against Stair.

Bankton deals in a long note with the introduction of feudalism to Scotland, which he thinks happened at an early period and independently of English influence. He disagrees with Grotius 'in preferring the feudal law of the Goths to the civil law of the Romans'. Even though feudal law 'produced security to the public quiet, and the rights and liberties of the subjects', Bankton considers Roman law vastly superior:

[T]he civil law was the wisdom of ages, the quintessence of the learning of old Rome, in questions concerning right or wrong, and there is no comparison betwixt it and the feudal law . . . In some respects the feudal law that obtains with us, e.g. our customary law or usages touching hereditary rights, as being part of our municipal law, is preferable with us to the civil law; but in default of these, we respect the civil law.[84]

As in the text quoted above, Bankton is forced to concede that Scots law is sometimes based on feudal rather than Roman law, though it is the latter he would apply by default. In title I, 3 'The Division and Quality of Things', based as we have seen on its namesake in the *Digest*, Bankton is able to refer extensively to Roman law for as long as he is dealing with moveable property; but whenever he mentions land law it becomes necessary to explain divisions which are not Roman but feudal, for example ones between allodial and feudal rights, and moveable and heritable rights: here there are no significant references to Roman law.[85] Bankton's approach in book II is identical. At the start of title II, 3 ('Fees, the Constitution of Feudal Holdings'), where the treatment of feudal land law begins, he says: 'The acquiring of property by the law of nature and nations, and by our law in moveables, is already discust; but in land-rights it comes under several considerations, and requires divers solemnities, by our law and custom.'[86] Here begins the long dark feudal night for Roman references, even for Bankton, until at II, 6 and 7 they see the light

---

[78] Bankton, II, 3, 167.   [79] Bankton, II, 3, 12 (2 refs.). See Craig (n. 10), II, 5, 11.
[80] Bankton, II, 3, 165; II, 4, 6.   [81] Bankton, II, 10, 9 (see Stair, II, 10, 6).
[82] Bankton, II, 11, 30.   [83] Bankton, III, 2, 26.
[84] Bankton, I, 1, 41 note attached, section 24.
[85] Bankton, I, 3, 10; I, 3, 18, which mentions written debts are sometimes called *nomina debitorum* as in Roman law.   [86] Bankton, II, 3, 1.

again in the law of servitudes. But apart from a few Roman references on leases, it is back to feudal law again for the rest of his treatment of property.

IV. ERSKINE: THE LONG AFTERNOON OF ROMAN LAW

John Erskine, who was born in 1695 and died in 1768, was a younger contemporary of Bankton and the second Professor of Scots Law at the University of Edinburgh, from 1737 until 1765. In 1754 he published his short introductory textbook *Principles of the Law of Scotland*, a very successful work with numerous subsequent editions. But his *Institute of the Law of Scotland*, posthumously published in 1773, is his *magnum opus* and gives a more detailed account of his views. Its full title says it is 'in the order of Sir George Mackenzie's Institutions of that Law', which are themselves modelled as far as possible on Justinian's *Institutes*.[87] Like Bankton, Erskine stresses that '*law* may be defined [as] the command of a sovereign',[88] who is God as far as natural law and the law of nations are concerned and each state as regards its own civil law.[89] Not all civil law, including some Roman civil law and most feudal law, is seen by Erskine as 'plainly founded' on natural law: 'That is barely civil, which derives its whole force from the arbitrary will of the lawgiver, without any obvious foundation in nature; as the Roman laws of adoption, and most of those which have been calculated for the forming and perfecting of the feudal system.'[90] Although not always based on nature, Roman law is highly regarded:

Among all the systems of human law which now exist, the Roman so well deserves the first place, on account of the equity of its precepts, and the justness of its reasonings, that wherever the civil law is mentioned, without the addition of any other particular state, the Roman law is always understood by way of excellency . . . great weight therefore is given to it, not only in Scotland . . . but in most of the nations of Europe.[91]

This passage resembles those quoted above from Stair and Bankton, though it also owes something to Mackenzie.[92] It is rather surprising, then, that Erskine says later that, while Mackenzie 'considers the Roman law as the written law of Scotland', Stair 'rejects its authority'.[93] In a rather opaque passage Erskine suggests tentatively that certain sixteenth century statutes show that 'the powers exercised, both by our sovereigns and judges, have been justified

---

[87] See above n. 14.   [88] Erskine (n. 8), I, 1, 2.
[89] Erskine (n. 8), I, 1, 7; I, 1, 14; I, 1, 18.   [90] Erskine (n. 8), I, 1, 25.
[91] Erskine (n. 8), I, 1, 27.
[92] See texts quoted above at nn. 17 and 55 and Mackenzie (n. 14), I, 1, 3, who talks about Roman law's 'excellency' and 'great influence'.
[93] Cairns, 'The Civil Law Tradition' (n. 2), 219 points out at n. 169 that the reference to Craig sharing Stair's view does not appear in the original 1773 edition.

by parliament, on this single ground, that they were conformable to the Roman law'. He concludes:

> These observations prove at least, that great weight is to be laid on the Roman law in all cases not fixed by statute or custom, and in which the genius of our law will suffer us to apply it ... Yet where any rule of the Roman law appears to have been founded on a subtilty peculiar to their system, it were absurd to pay the smallest regard to it.[94]

Whatever his precise theory, Erskine, like Stair and Bankton before him, thinks that Roman law should only be applied where there is no relevant Scots law. Although in a general way he thinks, like Stair, that Roman law is usually based on equity, he plays down even more than Bankton the relationship between Roman and natural law. For Erskine, Roman law seems to be given 'great weight' primarily for the 'justness of its reasonings', provided these are not too subtle or too Roman for Scottish consumption. Erskine is slightly keener than Bankton to point out Roman rules which are incompatible with the 'genius' of Scots law.

Erskine deals with property in book II of his *Institute*. For present purposes the title on teinds is omitted, as with Stair and Bankton.[95] Prescription, discussed only in book III under obligations, is also omitted.[96] In the remaining titles on property there are 156 references to Roman law, a large number though fewer than Bankton. Erskine refers to Roman law without citing a text from the *Corpus Juris* slightly more often than Stair and much more often than Bankton: there are forty-four examples altogether (28 per cent of references).[97] The remaining 112 texts all seem to be cited accurately and contain in some sense the rules Erskine says they do.[98] Of these, nine (6 per cent)

---

[94] Erskine (n. 8), I, 1, 41, citing Mackenzie (n. 14), I, 7, 3–4; Stair, I, 1, 12, 16.

[95] Erskine (n. 8), II, 10.   [96] See above nn. 25 and 26.

[97] Erskine (n. 8), II, 1, 1; II, 1, 4; II, 1, 5 (2 refs.); II, 1, 6 (2 refs.); II, 1, 7; II, 1, 8 (2 refs.); II, 1, 9; II, 1, 19; II, 1, 25; II, 2, 1; II, 2, 2 (2 refs.); II, 2, 3; II, 2, 4 (2 refs.); II, 2, 9; II, 2, 10; II, 2, 12; II, 3, 2; II, 3, 5; II, 3, 8; II, 3, 34; II, 4, 6 (2 refs.); II, 5, 28; II, 6, 17 (2 refs.); II, 6, 56; II, 6, 61; II, 7, 18; II, 8, 2; II, 9, 6; II, 9, 8; II, 9, 9; II, 9, 10; II, 9, 12 (2 refs.); II, 9, 17; II, 9, 39 (2 refs.); II, 11, 2.

[98] Erskine (n. 8), II, 1, 5 (3 refs.: Inst. 2, 1, 4; Inst. 2, 1, 23; D. 43, 15); II, 1, 6 (2 refs.: Inst. 2, 1, 1; D. 43, 8, 3 pr.); II, 1, 10 (4 refs.: D. 41, 1, 3, 2; D. 41, 1, 5, 2–4; D. 41, 1, 4; D. 41, 1, 5, 6); II, 1, 12 (Inst. 2, 1, 39); II, 1, 14 (3 refs.: Inst. 2, 1, 19; Inst. 2, 1, 20; Inst. 2, 1, 21); II, 1, 15 (Inst. 2, 1, 34); II, 1, 16 (Inst. 2, 1, 25); II, 1, 17 (2 refs.: D. 6, 1, 5, 1; Inst. 2, 1, 28); II, 1, 18 (2 refs.: Inst. 2, 1, 40; C. 2, 3, 20); II, 3, 19 (2 refs.: Inst. 2, 1, 45; Inst. 2, 1, 44); II, 1, 20 (D. 41, 2, 3, 1); II, 1, 21 (6 refs.: D. 41, 2, 3, 7; D. 41, 2, 3, 11; D. 41, 2, 3, 9; D. 41, 2, 3, 5; D. 41, 2, 3, 9; D. 41, 2, 15); II, 1, 22 (D. 41, 2, 9); II, I, 23 (2 refs.: D. 41, 2, 6; D. 43, 16, 3, 9); II, I, 24 (5 refs.: D. 22, 3, 2; D. 22, 3, 21); D. 50, 17, 218 pr.; D. 5, 1, 62; (Inst. 4, 15, 6); II, 1, 25 (D. 15, 16, 109); II, 1, 26 (6 refs.: D. 6, 1, 44; D. 41, 1, 48; D. 41, 1, 48; D. 22, 1, 34; D. 5, 2, 25, 2; C. 3, 32, 20); II, 1, 28 (2 refs.: D. 41, 1, 23, 1; D. 5, 3, 20, 11); II, 1, 29 (C. 3, 32, 22); II, 1, 30 (D. 41, 2, 3, 19); II, 2, 12 (D. 50, 17, 194); II, 2, 14 (D. 19, 1, 18); II, 3, 10 (C. 3, 33, 14); II, 3, 25 (2 refs.: D. 50, 17, 149; D. 18, 4, 4); II, 5, 26 (2 refs.: C. 4, 66, 2; Nov. 128, 8); II, 5, 47 (C. 4, 66, 3); II, 6, 17 (2 refs.: D. 43, 12, 1, 4; D. 39, 3, 21); II, 6, 23 (C. 4, 65, 9); II, 6, 33 (2 refs.: D. 19, 2, 24, 1; C. 4, 65, 6); II, 6, 35 (D. 19, 2, 14); II, 6, 38 (C. 3, 33, 14); II, 6, 39 (D. 19, 2, 25, 3); II, 6, 41 (5 refs.: D. 19, 2, 15, 1–2; D. 19, 2, 25, 6; D. 19, 2, 15, 2; D. 19, 2, 15, 4; D. 19, 2, 25, 6); II, 6, 43 (5 refs.: D. 19, 2, 27 pr.; D. 19, 2, 30 pr.; D. 19, 2, 38; D. 19, 2, 27, 1; D. 20, 2, 2); II, 6, 44 (2 refs.: D. 19, 2, 54, 1; D. 19, 2, 56); II,

seem unimportant: seven merely give the Roman equivalent of some Scots law expressions[99] and two are purely historical.[100] Erskine almost never quotes Roman law rules as maxims after the manner of Bankton.[101] As with Stair and Bankton, Erskine does not often explicitly state that Scots law has or should adopt a rule of Roman law.[102] However, to the same extent as Stair but slightly less often than Bankton, Erskine gives Roman references as the only authority for rules of Scots law. This accounts for seventy-six references (49 per cent).[103] Again, in contrast to Stair but like Bankton, Erskine rarely refers to natural law or equity in connection with Roman law. In comparison with the equivalent section in Bankton's title quoted above,[104] Erskine's subtitle in the margin at II, 1, 9 does not mention natural law: it is called simply 'Method of obtaining and transferring property'. The text here says that there are natural law as well as positive law ways of transferring property, but this is almost the last mention of natural law between II, 1, 9 and II, 1, 19.[105] Meanwhile, Erskine has made eighteen references to Roman law. Erskine contrasts Roman law with Scots law much more than Stair and slightly more than Bankton: thirty-four references can be classified under this head (22 per cent).[106]

6, 57 (3 refs.: D. 20, 2, 7 pr.; D. 47, 2, 62, 8; D. 20, 2, 4 pr.); II, 6, 64 (D. 20, 2, 6); II, 8, 14 (C. 8, 34, 3); II, 9, 3 (D. 8, 5, 10 pr.); II, 9, 6 (D. 50, 16, 198); II, 9, 7 (4 refs.: D. 8, 2, 33; D. 8, 5, 6, 2: D. 8, 2, 33; D. 8, 2, 6, 2); II, 9, 9 (D. 8, 2, 14); II, 9, 10 (4 refs.: D. 8, 2, 4; D. 8, 2, 12; D. 8, 2, 21; D. 2, 14, 38); II, 9, 14 (D. 8, 3, 4); II, 9, 33 (3 refs.: D. 8, 3, 5, 1; D. 8, 2, 38–9; D. 8, 5, 5–6 pr.); II, 9, 34 (2 refs.: D. 8, 3, 13, 1; D. 8, 1, 9); II, 9, 36 (D. 8, 2, 26); II, 9, 37 (3 refs.: D. 8, 2, 30 pr.; D. 8, 2, 6; D. 50, 17, 35); II, 9, 40 (2 refs.: D. 7, 5, 7; D. 7, 5, 1); II, 9, 53 (C. 6, 60, 1); II, 9, 56 (2 refs.: D. 7, 1, 9 pr.; D, 7, 1, 12, 1–2); II, 9, 57 (D, 24, 3, 7, 13); II, 9, 59 (D. 7, 1, 13 pr.); II, 9, 60 (D. 7, 1, 7, 2); II, 12, 2 (D. 42, 1, 15, 2); II, 12, 56 (2 refs.: D. 2, 8, 7; C. 7, 19, 7).

[99] Erskine (n. 8), II, 1, 1; II, 2, 9; II, 2, 10; II, 3, 34; II, 6, 56; II, 6, 64; II, 9, 9.
[100] Erskine (n. 8), II, 3, 2; II, 3, 5.
[101] Erskine (n. 8), II, 1, 24 quotes the rules *actore non probante, absolvitur reus* and *in pari causa, potior est conditio possidentis* backed up by three Roman law citations.
[102] There are only seven examples (4%): Erskine (n. 8), II, 1, 10 ('the doctrine of occupancy [of ownerless moveables] is also agreeable to the law of Scotland'); II, 1, 28 (rule on good faith and possession 'is universally held to be also the law of Scotland'); II, 5, 26 (1597 Act, APS, IV, 133 (c. 17), c. 246 'refers to the Roman law'); II, 6, 35 ('this doctrine we have adopted into our law, and given it the name of *tacit relocation*); II, 6, 41 (on abatement of rent for sterility, 'these rules have been adopted into the law of Scotland'); II, 9, 6 ('praedial servitudes may be divided by the law of Scotland, after the example of the Romans, into *rusticae* and *urbanae*'); II, 9, 39 ('the only one of these servitudes which has been received into our law, is usufruct').
[103] Erskine (n. 8), II, 1, 5 (5 refs.); II, 1, 7; II, 1, 10 (4 refs.); II, 1, 14 (3 refs.); II, 1, 15; II, 1, 16; II, 1, 17 (first ref.); II, 1, 18; II, 1, 19 (3 refs.); II, 1, 20; II, 1, 21 (6 refs.); II, 1, 22; II, 1, 23 (2 refs.); II, 1, 24 (5 refs.); II, 1, 25 (first ref.); II, 1, 26 (5 refs.); II, 1, 28 (first ref.); II, 2, 14; II, 3, 25 (first ref.); II, 6, 17 (2 refs.); II, 6, 43 (5 refs.); II, 6, 44 (2 refs.); II, 6, 57 (first 2 refs.); II, 9, 3; II, 9, 6; II, 9, 7 (4 refs.); II, 9, 10 (3 refs.); II, 9, 14; II, 9, 33 (3 refs.); II, 9, 34 (2 refs.); II, 9, 36; II, 9, 37 (3 refs.); II, 9, 56 (2 refs.).   [104] See above at n. 74.
[105] Erskine (n. 8), II, 1, 18 mentions 'natural equity'. The odd reference to 'nature', 'reason' and 'equity' can be found in conjunction with a reference to Roman law in the remainder of the work: e.g. at II, 1, 5; II, 1, 28; II, 9, 60.
[106] Erskine (n. 8), II, 1, (3 refs.); II, 1, 8 (first 2 refs.); II, 1, 12; II, 1, 17 (second ref.); II, 1, 25 (last ref.); II, 1, 26 (first ref.); II, 1, 29 (2 refs.); II, 1, 30; II, 2, 3; II, 2, 4 (2 refs.); II, 2, 12 (second

There are few surprises where the references to Roman law occur. There are 12 on things common to everyone and public property, 6 on occupation, 7 on accession and specification, 5 on delivery, 27 on possession, and 37 on servitudes, 28 of these being on praedial servitudes: a total of 94 references (60 per cent). Erskine has therefore a smaller proportion of references devoted to these topics than either Stair or Bankton. Other differences include a large number of references to Roman law in Erskine's treatment of leases: there are 24 of these (15 per cent), mainly on contractual aspects of leases. By contrast, while Stair also has a title on leases ('tacks'), it does not contain a single reference to Roman law.[107] Bankton's treatment of leases was, as we have seen, in a midway position between the two, with seven references to Roman law.

Erskine shares with Stair and Bankton a lack of significant references to Roman law in connection with feudal land law. He deals with this topic in the remaining titles of book II, from title II, 2 ('Of Heritable and Moveable Rights') onwards, interrupted only by the bursts of Romanization in leases and servitudes already noticed. If one also leaves aside the nine references already classed as unimportant, there are only twenty-nine (19 per cent) on feudal topics. Of these, four concern the now seemingly obligatory comparison between feu farm tenure and *emphyteusis*, which was in Craig, Stair, and Bankton.[108] Two more involve similar comparisons between Roman and Scots institutions which Erskine takes straight from Craig.[109] Four are on the extent to which rivers and the seashore form part of the king's *regalia*, again citing Craig.[110] Erskine appears to have found some of the references for himself: at any rate some are different from Craig's.[111] Eight more involve trite comparisons between Roman and Scots classifications of property.[112] The remaining eleven references are a mixed bunch, some of which can be found in Craig or Stair.[113]

ref.); II, 3, 8; II, 3, 10; II, 3, 34; II, 4, 6 (second ref.); II, 5, 28; II, 6, 17 (first and last refs.); II, 6, 57 (last ref.); II, 6, 61; II, 8, 2; II, 8, 14; II, 9, 10 (last ref.); II, 9, 12 (second ref.); II, 9, 17; II, 9, 40 (2 refs.); II, 9, 57; II, 11, 2.

[107] Stair, II, 9. Stair seems to regard the law as based entirely on Scots statute and case law.

[108] Erskine (n. 8), II, 4, 6 (2 refs.); II, 5, 26 (2 refs.); II, 5, 28. Craig is cited in II, 4, 6. Mackenzie (n. 14), II, 4 also mentions this comparison.

[109] Erskine (n. 8), II, 3, 10 (citing Craig on the comparison between feudal tenure and *ususfructus*); II, 5, 47 (citing but disagreeing with Craig on the origin of the casualty of relief).

[110] Erskine (n. 8), II, 6, 17 (4 refs.).

[111] Although see above at n. 13 for the problem with Craig's references to Roman law.

[112] Erskine (n. 8), II, 2, 1; II, 2, 2 (2 refs.); II, 2, 3; II, 2, 4 (2 refs.); II, 2, 12 (second ref.); II, 3, 8.

[113] Erskine (n. 8), II, 2, 12 (application of Roman rule that heir of my heir is my heir); II, 2, 14 (materials from demolished house remain heritable); II, 3, 25 (2 refs. on clauses of warrandice: see on second Stair, II, 3, 46); II, 7, 18 (use of symbols of delivery in Roman and feudal law); II, 8, 2 (cf. reversion and *pactum de retrovendendo*: see Stair, II, 10, 1 though no explicit ref. to Roman law); II, 8, 14 (comparison between condition in reversion and *pactum legis commissoriae in pignoribus*: see Stair, II, 10, 6); II, 11, 2 (comparison between inhibition and *actio Pauliana*: see Stair, I, 9, 15); II, 12, 2 (execution on moveable estate first); II, 12, 56 (2 refs. on security to prevent sequestration).

Erskine deals with the feudalization of land law in exactly the same way as Stair and Bankton, though his acknowledged model is not Stair but Mackenzie. His title-headings are virtually identical to Mackenzie's, as is his order of topics within each title. In book II, title 1 ('Of the Division of Rights, and the several Ways by which a Right may be acquired') he discusses both moveable and heritable property, distinguishing the Romanized rules of the former from the feudalized rules of the latter. Then at book II, title 2 ('Of Heritable and Moveable Rights') he contrasts the relatively unimportant distinction in Roman law between moveable and immoveable property with the enormously important one in Scots law between moveable and heritable property 'since the introduction of the feudal plan'. At the very beginning of book II, title 3 ('Of the Constitution of Heritable rights by Charter and Seisin') he says that heritable and moveable rights 'fall now to be handled separately, beginning with the first, as the most eminent branch of the division'. And as Mackenzie says bluntly in the original of this passage, 'Our *Heritable Rights* are *Regulated* by the *Feudal Law*'.[114] Erskine then, like his predecessors, plunges into his account of feudal land law, with Romanized intermissions only for leases and servitudes.

V. HUME: THE TWILIGHT OF THE IDOLS

With Hume we reach the end of the story. David, later Baron, Hume, the nephew of the famous philosopher, was born in 1757 and died in 1838. He was Professor of Scots Law at the University of Edinburgh from 1786 to 1822. His most famous published work was his *Commentaries on the Law of Scotland Respecting Crimes* of 1797. His brilliant *Lectures*, given their final form in 1822, he consistently refused to publish during his lifetime. They were eventually published by the Stair Society between 1939 and 1958. It is his *Lectures* which are examined here.

Although he rejects all previous 'orders of arrangement' including Justinian's, Hume's general view of the historical importance of Roman law seems at first sight similar to that of the other institutional writers. So he says 'our Municipal Law is in many respects founded on that of the Romans, which is our highest authority where our own statutes or customs are silent'.[115] Again, he says of Roman law that 'so eminent, indeed, is the equity of that system, and so suitable had it been found to our condition of society and affairs, that in many kinds of business it was long ago adopted by our Judges as their model and rule of decision'.[116] But it is the words 'long ago adopted' which are significant. Hume is only interested in Roman law insofar as it has

---

[114] Mackenzie (n. 14), II, 3, 95. [115] Hume, *Lectures*, I, 2.
[116] Hume, *Lectures*, I, 13.

been 'incorporated into our practice' or 'become a proper integral part of our common or customary law' or 'been naturalised' by Scots law. He goes on: '[T]he obeisance we pay to the Civil [sic] is now, and always has been, a voluntary obeisance, and a matter of courtesy,—such as depends, in the main, on its agreement with equity and reason, its analogy to the rest of our practice, and its suitableness to our state of things and kinds of business.'[117] This sets a new tone of independence for Scots law and suggests that Hume doubted whether Roman law was still an active source of Scots law.

Hume deals with property law in parts III and IV of his *Lectures*. There are only twenty-four references to Roman law.[118] None cites a text from the *Corpus Juris*, though it is possible that he might have added these if he had prepared the *Lectures* for publication.[119] Three seem unimportant: two are purely historical remarks and the third a matter of terminology.[120] Another, although mentioning 'the Roman law', is actually from later civilian commentators.[121] Hume states that Scots law follows, or has adopted, Roman law more often than any of his predecessors. There are fourteen examples.[122] He contrasts Roman law and Scots law on nine occasions.[123] For Hume the position about Roman rules is clear-cut: either they have been adopted or they have been rejected. Unlike the other writers, Hume never simply gives references to Roman law as the only authority for his propositions on Scots law, without further comment. The small number of references to the Roman law of property, and the way in which they are made, is consistent with his general approach to Roman law.

Hume also differs from the other writers in where his references to Roman law occur. True, there is one on delivery, two on possession in good faith, and three on servitudes. There is also one on tacit relocation in leases, which Erskine at least thought of as Roman. But three are on damage to another's property while exercising one's own rights, a topic not covered under the law of property by the other writers. Nor do they have anything which corresponds to Hume's six references to Roman law on pledge and hypothec. As with the earlier writers there is a dearth of Roman references on feudal topics, there being only five altogether. Two of these, discussed below, con-

---

[117] Hume, *Lectures*, I, 13. He did not deny the educational value of studying Roman law and indeed assumes that some of his students have already done so: see pp. 3 and 14.

[118] Hume, *Lectures*, III, 209; III, 213; III, 221; III, 240; III, 241; III, 243; III, 248; III, 264; III, 269; III, 271; III, 1; III, 4; III, 8; III, 29; III, 32; III, 36; III, 38; III, 101; IV, 127; IV, 211; IV, 238; IV, 260; IV, 557; IV, 565.

[119] Hume, *Lectures*, III, 213 has a reference to Voet's commentary on the *Digest*.

[120] Hume, *Lectures*, III, 243 (ancient Roman restrictions on selling land); IV, 1, 127 (many principles of Scots and civil law similar); IV, 13, 565 (*dies nec cedit nec venit* applies to annuities).

[121] Hume, *Lectures*, III, 38.

[122] Hume, *Lectures*, III, 209; III, 213; III, 221; III, 264; III, 271; III, 1; III, 29; III, 36; III, 101; IV, 211; IV, 238. The three texts cited above in n. 111 although unimportant must also be included under this head.

[123] Hume *Lectures*, III, 240; III, 241; III, 248; III, 269; III, 4; III, 8; III, 32; IV, 260; IV, 557.

trast Roman law with feudal law in general terms.[124] The remaining three can be found in Stair or Craig.[125]

Hume's views on the relationship between Roman law and feudalism are very similar to those of his predecessors. Thus he continues the passage quoted above[126] with the words:

[Y]et the instances in which those customs and statutes differ from [Roman law] are so numerous, and the alterations they make so very considerable, that it is frequently far less difficult to understand the original doctrines of Justinian, than to perceive their application to our own practice. This is in particular the case with that branch of our Law which is derived from the Feudal system; and which relates to some of the most important parts of the business of life. Even there, indeed, a knowledge of the Civil Law is necessary: since ... the general principles of Right and Wrong must still be concerned in it; and these we find illustrated [in an unrivalled way] by the Roman writers.

As we have seen, though, Hume does not actually apply to feudal Scots law many 'general principles of Right and Wrong' from Roman law. The reason he cannot do this appears in his explanation of how he will treat property law:

I have thought it desirable thus to subdivide into two portions on account of the different, and indeed in some instances opposite, rules and principles which our practice has received ... As applied to subjects of a movable nature, the real rights of property ... are regulated in the main by common and natural principles, analogous in some measure to those which seem to have been established in the Law of Rome ... On the other hand, with respect to the Property of all immovable tenements ... which are among the most important articles of our law, have been modelled after the peculiar standard of the system of Feudal Tenures, which involves a great map of new and artificial doctrine, very remote from any likeness of the Civil Law, or of what may seem to be the general principles of the Law of Nature.[127]

Hume resembles Bankton rather more than Stair and Erskine in his slightly critical assessment of the feudal system. But like all three, he recognizes that its coming transformed huge areas of land law, so that Hume's order of treatment *has* to be similar to theirs. After a short introductory chapter on the right of property in general, covering both moveables and immoveables, he is forced to deal with feudal land law separately and at great length. It is difficult to see much of a 'unitary' treatment of property law in Hume any more

---

[124] See below n. 127.
[125] Hume *Lectures*, IV, 211 (tinsel of the feu for non-payment for two years: see Stair, II, 3, 51); IV, 238 (*res publicae* and *regalia*: Craig cited); IV, 260 (right to prevent others taking game depends on ownership of the land: Stair, II, 3, 76 cited, but see also Stair, II, 1, 33).
[126] See passage quoted above at n. 115.
[127] Hume *Lectures*, I, 10–11. He goes on to call feudalism 'artificial' here, as he does at IV, 127. At IV, 557 he again says feudalism is un-Roman and unnatural.

than in the other institutional writers.[128] The big difference is that nearly all the references to Roman law have gone, even in areas which have already been heavily Romanized by the earlier institutional writers. But it is only the references which diminish in Hume, not the influence of Roman law itself. That can still be found in many places in his *Lectures*, though it has gone underground, as it were. Roman law has, to use Hume's own expression, been 'naturalised' into Scots law. From Hume's time onwards, academic writing and judicial decisions will often present a highly Romanized version of property law, based on Craig, Mackenzie, Stair, Bankton and Erskine, but one which does not often make direct reference to Roman law. Counting such references in the nineteenth century would not tell as much about the influence of Roman law as it does with these earlier writers, who are usually happy to say when they are following Roman law.

VI. CONCLUSIONS

As any Scots lawyer knows, there are lots of references to Roman law in the institutional writers. Now we know what 'lots' means as far as property is concerned, and what it means for each of them. Again, it is not news that Stair has a certain number of such references, that there are many more in Bankton and Erskine, but fewer in Hume. Now we can put a figure on these differences. And now we also see the differences between how Roman law is used in practice, whatever they may say about it in theory. Stair refers to Roman law to some extent, and does so because it is usually the same as natural law, which he takes seriously. Bankton and Erskine refer to Roman law much more, and do so because it is Roman law, which they apply directly, paying only lip-service to its relationship with natural law, unless the Scots rules are different. Hume hardly refers to Roman law at all, and does so only when he thinks he should clarify whether or not Scots law has or has not adopted it in one or two situations.

What comes as a surprise is some of the features which the references to Roman law (other than by Hume) have in common. The writers mostly cite texts from the *Corpus Juris Civilis* rather than simply referring to 'the Roman law'. These texts are not just from the *Institutes*: the *Digest* and even the *Code* and *Novels* are drawn on. All these careful citations must have been intended as invitations to any interested reader to look up the texts and check whether they say what the writer claims they do. There were, no doubt, more readers

---

[128] Reid (n. 3), 5 says that Hume's is 'the most extended attempt to present a unified treatment of the law' amongst the institutional writers. Hume's ch. 1 is in fact no longer than and similar in many respects to the sections on non-feudal property law found in Stair, Bankton, and Erskine. According to Campbell Paton (n. 9), vol. 3, 201 n. 1, earlier versions of Hume's *Lectures* dealt with the original modes of acquisition here, making the resemblance even greater.

in the seventeenth and eighteenth centuries sufficiently interested in Roman law to do this than there are now. If they did examine the texts, as we have seen, they would generally find some apposite Roman law: the references are tools which do work if anyone chooses to use them. Even where a Roman text is not cited, the references are usually clear as to the rules involved, so that it would not take our imaginary reader long to find appropriate Roman texts. The large number of careful references make it unlikely that they are all purely ornamental. Nor are many unimportant, in the sense that they merely make historical remarks about Roman law in general or simply give Latin equivalents of Scots terms. Nor are there as many quotations of general maxims drawn from Roman law as one might have expected, even in Bankton. By not counting merely any Latin word or phrase as a reference to Roman law, and by not including Latin maxims from outside the *Corpus Juris*, I have tried to take account of the observation that 'the use of Roman terminology alone does not necessarily indicate the adoption of a Roman institution'.[129] In all the references used in this chapter the writer makes it clear that it is Roman law he is referring to, either by citing a Roman text or using explicit words such as 'in the Roman law'.

Most of the references to Roman law in Stair, Bankton, and Erskine are in some sense favourable towards it. They do not often refer to Roman law in order to contrast it with Scots law. Where Roman law is very different from Scots law, as in the feudal parts of its land law, they simply do not refer much to it. When Roman references are made, they sometimes say that Scots law has adopted a Roman rule, but more commonly they just sit there as the only authority given for a proposition on Scots law. In practice, irrespective of what is said about the authority of Roman law in theory, it is treated by implication as authoritative again and again. This is Romanization at its strongest and occurs a great deal in the treatment of moveable property, possession, and servitudes. In these areas there was probably little native law, allowing the writers to make up the rules as they went along, with constant reference to Roman law.

Feudal land law though, as we have seen, presented an effective barrier to Romanization. The maxim of the institutional writers might be stated as 'what has been feudalized, cannot be Romanized'. Craig had been enthusiastic about the Romanization even of feudal law, and most of the small number of references to Roman law in later writers are taken from Craig. But even Bankton, ardent Romanizer though he was, did not penetrate the wastes of feudal land law much beyond Craig's pioneering efforts. The feudalization of Scots land law also prevented the institutional writers from attempting much

---

[129] T. D. Fergus, 'Sources of Law (General and Historical): The Historical Sources of Scots law (1) Roman Law', in *The Laws of Scotland: Stair Memorial Encyclopedia*, vol. 22, (1987), § 556.

in the way of a unitary treatment of moveables and immoveables on the Roman model. Romanization was, therefore, largely confined to the law on moveable property, possession, and servitudes. Obviously, even in these areas, it is not the case that Roman law was 'received complete and unaltered in Scotland'.[130] There were Scots rules and institutions which were different from the Roman ones and the institutional writers recognized this. Nor did they follow Roman law slavishly in their own approach to these topics.[131] The institutional writers found and left Scots property law only partially Romanized. It is not my purpose to deny what has been called the 'resilience of the Scottish common law' in the face of Roman law.[132] But the common law was Romanized. This chapter has sought to examine the process by offering, for Stair, Bankton, Erskine, and Hume, what a recent writer suggested we lack, namely 'a scientific measure of the extent of the influence of Roman law', however crude it may be.[133] That it confirms some of the things we always thought we knew might be said to be in its favour.[134]

---

[130] D. L. Carey Miller, 'Derivative Acquisition of Moveables', in R. Evans-Jones (ed.), *The Civil Law Tradition in Scotland* (1995), 128 sqq., 128.

[131] For examples of such divergences in the law of moveable property, see D. L. Carey Miller, 'Systems of Property: Grotius and Stair', in D. L. Carey Miller and D. W. Meyers (eds.), *Comparative and Historical Essays in Scots Law* (1992), 14 sqq.; idem, 'Stair's Property: A Romanist System?', [1995] *JR* 70 sqq.; idem, (n. 130), 128.

[132] W. D. H. Sellar, 'The Resilience of the Scottish Common Law', in D. L. Carey Miller and R. Zimmermann (eds.), *The Civilian Tradition and Scots Law* (1997), 149 sqq.

[133] Carey Miller (n. 130), 154. He is discussing only moveable property, and goes on to say of it that 'it is difficult to see that there could be any plausible challenge to the proposition that the influence was considerable'. The same must be true of possession and servitudes.

[134] I would like to thank my friend and colleague John Cairns for his many helpful comments during my research for this article.

5

Accession by Building

C. G. VAN DER MERWE

[T]hose not trained to the practice of a foreign system can never be sure that they understand either its principles or its terms. I venture to speak of the Scots cases therefore, with the utmost respect, and the utmost diffidence.[1]

I. INTRODUCTION

The Scottish law of accession by building (*inaedificatio*) has a chequered history mainly because of the various competitive interests involved in issues of this kind. In this chapter it will be shown that the development of the modern law has been shaped by legal policy considerations favouring first one group and then another. As a result of this, not only the requirements for accession, but also their application present difficulties in modern Scots law.[2] The factors for determining whether accession has taken place are for instance interpreted in various ways. Whereas Gloag catalogues seven individual factors, Gordon and Carey Miller arrange similar factors under three main headings which do not correspond. Finally Reid abstracts from the cases three completely new 'conditions' for accession.[3] All these writers are in broad agreement as to the nature and relative importance of these factors. Nevertheless, a statement of the Scots law remains problematic and its application somewhat obscure.

---

[1] This passage is adapted from a dictum of Lord Cockburn in *Dixon* v. *Fisher* (1843) 5 D 775 at 799.
[2] See e.g. Lord Scarman in *Berkley* v. *Poulett* [1977] EGD 754 at 761: 'The difficulty is not the formulation but the application of the law.' See further Kenneth Reid, 'The Lord Chancellor's Fixtures', (1983) 28 *JLSS* 49.
[3] See W. M. Gloag, *Green's Encyclopaedia of the Laws of Scotland*, 3rd edn., vol. 7 (1929), § 363; W. M. Gordon, *Scottish Land Law* (2nd edn.,1999), paras. 5.06-5.15; D. L. Carey Miller, *Corporeal Moveables in Scots Law* (1991), para. 3-12 and Kenneth Reid, 'Accession', in *idem* (ed.), *The Law of Property in Scotland* (1996), § 579. The headings used by Gordon and Carey Miller are fact of annexation, purpose of annexation and custom of district, and physical circumstances, role factors, and annexor's intention respectively. The 'conditions' laid down by Reid are physical attachment, functional subordination, and permanence.

II. ROMAN LAW

The Scots concept of accession by building has its roots in Roman law. Unfortunately, the sources on *inaedificatio* as an original mode of acquisition of property deal primarily with remedies and contain no clear guidelines on what constitutes accession. In principle, beams and other materials used in the erection of houses became, for the time being, the property of the owner of the house. The owner of the materials retained the *dominium dormiens* in the materials which revived if the building was pulled down. The rationale was that a completed building should not be demolished but should remain intact.[4]

Inaedificatio is, however, also discussed in the context of what was included in a sale or legacy of land. Articles physically attached to the land or a building like beams,[5] roof-tiles,[6] doors and windows,[7] book-cases,[8] frescoes and mosaics painted on walls,[9] mirrors fixed into walls,[10] marble facings,[11] pipes and water-cocks soldered thereto, cisterns and bath-houses[12] were definitely included. In addition, Ulpian states that articles which serve the permanent utility and enjoyment of the land or building[13] like locks, keys, bolts, and the covers of wells are also included.[14]

Two *Digest* texts, one from Iavolenus and another from Ulpian, have a similar effect. Iavolenus quotes Labeo:[15] 'Straturam loci alicuius ex tabulis factis, quae aestate tollerentur et hieme ponerentur, aedium esse ait Labeo, quoniam perpetui usus paratae essent: neque ad rem pertinere, quod interim tollerentur.' A passage from Ulpian states the following:[16] 'Ea, quae ex aedificio detracta sunt ut reponantur, aedificii sunt: at quae parata sunt ut imponantur, non sunt aedificii. Pali, quae vineae causa parati sunt antequam collocentur, fundi non sunt, sed qui exempti sunt hac mente ut collocentur, fundi sunt.' By contrast, so-called *instrumenta fundi* like ploughs, vehicles, baskets, wine-vats, pitchers, pack animals, stock-in-trade (in the case of the

---

[4] See Paul. D. 6, 1, 23, 6, 7; Ulp. D. 9, 2, 50; Gai. D. 41, 1, 7, 10–12; Gai. 2, 73. See further W. W. Buckland, *A Textbook of Roman Law* (3rd edn., 1963), 212–15; J. A. C. Thomas, *Textbook of Roman Law* (1976), 173–4; Van Oven, *Leerboek van Romeinsch Privaatrecht* (3rd edn., 1948), 93–4. [5] Ulp. D. 47, 3, 1, 1.
[6] Iav. D. 19, 1, 18, 1.   [7] Iul. D. 6, 1, 59; Ulp. D. 33, 7, 12, 25.   [8] Ulp. D. 32, 52, 7.
[9] Ulp. D. 19, 1, 17, 3.   [10] Ulp. D. 33, 7, 12, 25.   [11] Ulp. D. 19, 1, 17, 3.
[12] Ulp. D. 19, 1, 17, 7–8; Pap. D. 32, 91, 4.
[13] Ulp. D 19, 1, 17, 7: 'quae perpetui usus causa in aedificiis sunt, aedificii esse' ('things inside buildings for permament use are part of the building'—author's trans.).
[14] Ulp. D. 19, 1, 17, 7–8.
[15] Iav. D. 50, 16, 242, 4 ('Labeo says that the covering of some place made from planks which are removed in summer and put back in winter does form part of the house because they are intended for permanent use; nor does it make any difference that they are taken off at intervals').
[16] Ulp. D. 19, 1, 17, 10–11 ('Things removed from structures for eventual return are part of the structure, but things collected for installation, are not part of the structure. Props collected for a vineyard are not part of a farm before they are set up; but those removed with the intention that they be set up again are part of the farm').

sale of business venture) are not considered to be included in a sale or legacy of land, unless there is an express stipulation to that effect.[17]

From the above it may be concluded that *inaedificatio* in the strict sense found application only in cases of physical attachment, whereas in the context of sale and succession a wider range of articles was considered accessories or at least pertinents of the land.

III. INSTITUTIONAL WRITERS

The institutional writers discuss *inaedificatio* either under the original modes of acquisition of property or in passages dealing with the distinction between immoveable ('heritable') and moveable property. A stronger physical connection between accessory and heritable property seems required for the former than for the latter. Thus Stair insists that a 'beam or other material' must be 'built into' a house.[18] However, when dealing with the distinction between heritable and moveable property he describes immoveables *inter alia* as things 'fixed to the earth, not to be removed therefrom as trees, houses etc. which *though they may be possibly moved, yet it is not their use to be so*'.[19] Bankton, likewise, states that 'when one builds or plants on another's ground the house and planting is carried as pertinents to the ground, *inaedificatum solo cedit solo* ...'.[20] By contrast, he defines immoveables as 'the earth and what adheres to its surface naturally as growing trees ... or artificially, as houses, and everything fixed to them *for their perpetual use*'.[21] Erskine is to the same effect. When dealing with *inaedificatio* as a mode of acquisition of property he writes the following:[22] 'By the same rule, if one shall, even with his own materials, build a house on my ground, the house is mine, because the ground is mine on which it is built, and the builder cannot so much as sue upon an action to have the materials separated from the ground, that they may be restored to himself; for public policy will not suffer buildings once finished to be pulled down.' Later on, when discussing the difference between heritable and moveable property, Erskine combines the factor of physical attachment with the notion of permanent utility:[23] 'Things by their own nature moveable might become immoveable by their being fixed or united to an immoveable subject *for its perpetual use*, as stone, marble, wood, used either in building an edifice, or for additional ornaments to it after it is built.' Bell combines the same two factors in the context of heritable securities.[24] In a different passage[25] he distinguishes heritable and moveable property, first, by their own nature and description, secondly, by their connection with other things and,

---

[17] Call. D. 33, 10, 14.   [18] Stair, II, 1, 38.   [19] Stair, II, 1, 2 (my emphasis).
[20] Bankton, II, 1, 18.   [21] Bankton, I, 3, 17 (my emphasis).   [22] Erskine, II, 1, 14.
[23] Erskine, II, 2, 2 (my emphasis).   [24] Bell, *Commentaries*, I, 787 (my emphasis).
[25] Bell, *Commentaries*, V, 1 and 2.

thirdly, by their destination towards such connection. An article which is by its nature immoveable or though capable of being moved is not accustomed to be moved, is immoveable. Again, articles connected with land, like houses, buildings, and machinery intended for the permanent use of the land are in principle considered immoveable. In addition articles may become heritable by express or implied destination.[26]

The institutional writers thus merged the notion of physical attachment with that of functional utility and laid down two requirements for *inaedificatio*. First, the moveable article must to some extent be physically fixed to or united with heritable property. Secondly, this attachment must be for the perpetual utility of the heritage: the article must be functionally subordinated to the heritage and the attachment must be permanent. These requirements are phrased quite generally, without an indication of their relative importance.

IV. BEFORE 1820: THE DOMINANCE OF SUCCESSION LAW

In this period, and for a long time thereafter,[27] the disposal of property on death depended on whether the property was moveable or immoveable (heritable). Land and other heritable property was subject to primogeniture and passed to the heir. Moveable property was administered by an executor and distributed to a wider class of descendants. The early law of accession was primarily concerned with the question of which articles could properly be considered as heritable; and since the aim of succession law was to transmit a well-stocked estate to the heir, articles which would today be regarded as moveable were sometimes classified as fixtures.[28] Stewart, answering Dirleton's *Doubts*, took the view that a horse and other moveable objects required for the proper functioning of a horse-mill, and the buckets and chains used in a coal-mine, were (for the purpose of succession) heritable.[29] A century later, in *Johnstone* v. *Dobie*,[30] the court found that window-frames, doors, and other building materials which were not yet fixed to their proper places were heritable, since the articles were completely formed, fitted, and adjusted for specific places in a particular tenement. Since the *animus destinandi* of the owner was carried into execution by overt acts the court felt that these articles should fall to the heir and not to the executor. The concept of

---

[26] See also Bell, *Principles*, §§ 743 and 1471–5. On articles heritable by destination, see further Hume, *Lectures*, IV, 565–9.

[27] Primogeniture was not abolished until the Succession (Scotland) Act 1964. But in practice it could be avoided by a number of devices, including, in the later law, the making of a will.

[28] By 'fixture' is meant an article which has become heritable by accession to land or to a heritable structure on land.

[29] Lord Dirleton, *Doubts and Questions, in the Law; Especially of Scotland* (1698) and James Steuart, *Dirleton's Doubts and Questions in the Law of Scotland, Resolved and Answered* (1715), s.v. Executry, Mill.   [30] (1783) Mor 5443.

Accession by Building

implied destination was taken even further in *Malloch* v. *McLean*[31] where a child claimed *legitim*[32] when the father died in the course of erecting a house. Lord Ormidale held that that portion of the father's moveable funds which was required to complete the house according to plans, specifications, and contracts adopted by the deceased was heritable by destination. In similar vein heirship moveables like books, jewellery, and the best furniture of a house were deemed to become heritable property in questions of succession.[33]

Besides the fact that the law of succession favoured the preservation of the family estate[34] this situation was also justified by the notion that moveable property was in earlier times of little value and was readily regarded as subordinate to and therefore an accessory to land.[35]

In questions not concerned with succession, moveable articles were either not included under heritable property, or were included on grounds other than destination. In *McKnight* v. *Irving*,[36] for example, the court found that a large counter, dressers, shelves, and grates fastened to the floor of a house by the owner's daughter merely by means of bolts and wooden wedges were moveable and therefore not included in the sale of the house. The reason for the decision was that these articles could be removed without material injury to the building beyond some bits of broken plaster or superficial damage.[37]

In *Arkwright* v. *Billinge*[38] the Court of Session had to decide whether the machinery of a cotton mill was included in a heritable security of the land to which the mill was attached. The majority of the court concluded from the terms of the disposition and the surrounding circumstances that it was the intention of the parties that the machinery should be included under the heritable security.[39] Lords Robertson and Bannatyne, however, adopted a novel approach. According to Lord Robertson the moveable parts of the mill (e.g. the strap which communicated motion to the jennies) formed part of a *unum quid* and were thus also heritable. Similarly, Lord Bannatyne found that the machinery was so intimately connected with the mill itself that the heritable security necessarily covered the machinery.[40] Intention was not thought

---

[31] (1867) 5 M 335.
[32] i.e. the share in the moveable estate of a deceased which falls to a child.
[33] See in general on things heritable by destination and heirship moveables: Stair, III, 5, 9; Erskine, II, 2, 12; III, 8, 37; Bell, *Principles*, § 1475; idem, *Commentaries*, V, 3. In *Hyslop* v. *Hyslop* 18 Jan. 1811 FC it was held that the machinery of a threshing-mill was moveable and thus belonged to the executor. This decision is criticized by Hume, *Lectures*, IV, 566.
[34] See Erskine, II, 2, 3. Bell, *Commentaries*, II, 3 gives the policy of the law as being that the heir 'may not succeed in his mansion and estate totally dismantled'. Hume, *Lectures*, IV, 566 states that heirs are favoured in order that 'they might reap ... the produce of that immoveable estate'.
[35] See Reid, (1983) 28 *JLSS* 49.
[36] (1805) Hume 412.   [37] Ibid. at 412.   [38] 3 Dec. 1819 FC.
[39] See also *Niven* v. *Pitcairn* (1823) 2 S 204 at 207 *per* Lord Glenlee.
[40] 3 Dec. 1819 FC 59.

to be relevant in *Niven* v. *Pitcairn*,[41] decided four years later, and reaching the same result on broadly similar facts.[42]

The position at the end of this period is well summarized in the submissions put forward by the heritable creditor in *Arkwright* v. *Billinge*:[43]

> In the law of Scotland, questions whether subjects be moveable or immoveable occur among three descriptions of persons; between the heir and the executor of the proprietor,—between the proprietor and a tenant, or other occupant, upon a title of temporary possession,—and between a person having a real right to a subject, whether the proprietor, his heir, or a real creditor, and the personal creditors of the proprietor. It is chiefly with reference to the first class that our authorities have considered the question. But, with certain modifications, the great distinctions are the same, and may be relied on in all the cases. And the authorities consider all things as immoveable which are attached to an immoveable subject for its perpetual use; or of which, although they may possibly be moved, it is not the proper use to be so; ... In the first class of cases, the general rule is in favour of the heir, to give him the subject which is to descend to him, as ample as possible. In the second, it is in favour of the tenant, to have as much as possible considered moveable, so as to remain still the property of the tenant. In the third, it is in favour of creditor, having right in the immoveable subject. And where it is doubtful, in such a case, what subjects fall under the real security, the intention of the parties ought to have weight.[44]

V. 1820-1876: TRADE AND ITS FIXTURES

1. The industrial revolution

The industrial revolution brought about new technology and an expanding economy. In order to open up factories, entrepreneurs invested in expensive and often cumbersome machinery. The result was that succession cases lost their former pre-eminence and that the problems relating to fixtures emerged as a matter of course in ordinary commercial life. This is aptly illustrated by the cases of *Arkwright* v. *Billinge*[45] and *Niven* v. *Pitcairn*,[46] mentioned earlier,

---

[41] (1823) 2 S 204, 3 Mar. 1823 FC.

[42] The case concerned large vessels used in a factory for the manufacture of oil of vitriol. The vessels were not fixed to the ground. The case is notable for the weight given by one judge (Lord Robertson at 208) to the fact that the buildings were expressly designed and adapted to contain these particular vessels.   [43] 3 Dec. 1819 FC 56–7.

[44] The rest of the argument seems to equate the doctrine of immoveable by destination with the requirement of perpetual use: 'There are many illustrations of the doctrine that moveables become part of an immovable subject by destination, whether attached to it or not, if they be necessary to make it answer its purpose, and intended for its perpetual use, e.g. an inclosure of loose stones, such as a Galloway dike, a gate made so as to be easily removed from its hinges, props for hops or fruit trees, sheep flakes, the glass frames of a hot-house, the keys of a house, the shutters of a shop, the moveable cover on the mouth of a well, etc.'

[45] 3 Dec. 1819 FC.   [46] 3 Mar. 1823 FC.

which concerned a competition between heritable and ordinary creditors on the insolvency of the proprietor of a cotton mill and a mill for the production of oil of vitriol respectively, and by the case of *Syme* v. *Harvey*[47] which involved a competition between a landlord and his tenant with regard to improvements effected on the land during the currency of the lease. The enormous economic interests involved baulked at persisting with the approach that valuable machinery acceded to land in all circumstances. In *Dixon* v. *Fisher*[48] Lord Justice-Clerk Hope went so far as to declare that old maxims were inadequate to determine important questions concerning industrial machinery and an expanding economy, and that a fresh approach was required.[49]

Such radical ideas did not, however, find much support. Instead the existing law was gradually transformed so as to modify the favour bestowed on heirs. The first requirement of Bankton and Erskine, namely that the article be fixed or connected with land, was more strictly interpreted. Whatever the position may have been in the seventeenth century, it was impossible to regard the buckets and chain of a water mill as heritable in the nineteenth. Furthermore it became more difficult to satisfy the second requirement, namely that the article be attached for the permanent use of the land.

Three factors played an important role in this regard. First, the land was no longer considered as necessarily more valuable than expensive moveable machinery attached thereto: in commercial life, engines and machinery came to be regarded more as accessories to the trade in which they were employed than as accessories to land. Secondly, the idea that moveable articles of value were functionally subordinate to the land came under attack. The machinery of a steam engine or a cotton mill is undoubtedly moveable before it is installed on land. For its efficient exploitation, however, it must to some extent be stabilized by being annexed to a building or sunk into the ground. But such machinery was not erected for the purpose of exploiting the (agricultural) potential of the land. The ground was no more than a temporary location for machinery to be exploited for a specific industry. Thirdly, with the growth of commercial leasing, moveable machinery was often attached for merely temporary exploitation. In such cases the ordinary rules applicable to physical annexation of machinery to land appeared to be superseded by the lessee's economic interest to remove the machinery at the end of the lease or to make his machinery the subject of a security interest.[50]

---

[47] (1861) 24 D 202.
[48] (1843) 5 D 775 at 827: 'There can be no question that the older maxims are acknowledged to be insufficient to rule such a question, and that it will not do to attempt to decide such large and important question as must now arise respecting machinery, by brocards or *dicta* which never really formed any part of the law, and were repeated from the civilians without much consideration.'   [49] See also Reid, (1983) 28 *JLSS* 49–50.
[50] See Bell, *Commentaries*, I, 787. See further Reid, (1983) 28 *JLSS* 49, 50.

2. *Fisher v. Dixon* (1835–1845)

The task of reconciling the virtually settled law with regard to *inaedificatio* with commercial demands to treat trade fixtures as a special case fell on the judges in *Fisher v. Dixon*.[51] Dixon had an extensive interest in coal and iron mines situated for the most part on his own land but also on a few parcels of land leased by him. His trade consisted in the manufacture of iron and lime and the production of coal to be used in his factories or for sale. On his death the machinery which worked these mines was claimed as part of the *legitim*. The argument was that all instruments, engines, and utensils whether fixed or loose which were necessary or subservient to his trade should be treated as moveables: they were moveable before being placed in that particular spot and did not lose their moveable character through being affixed to a heritable subject unless they were affixed *perpetui usu gratia* as in the case of the windows of a mansion.

The Lord Ordinary remitted the cause to an engineer to give a scientific report on the exact nature of each part of the machinery involved. He found that all the machinery in question was capable of being moved and replaced albeit in certain instances at considerable cost; that the value of the machinery would to a greater or lesser extent decrease as a result of such removal; that certain machinery under consideration, such as steam-engines for pumping mines, had to be replaced instantly if removed to prevent serious damage to the mine; that though the engines were essential for the exploitation of the factories, they were readily replaceable by similar articles; and that it was customary practice for the tenant to remove all machinery brought onto the land.[52]

On account of the intricacy of the point raised, the Lord Ordinary referred the case to the Second Division, which in turn decided to consult the First Division and the permanent Lords Ordinary. The great majority of their Lordships ultimately found that all the machinery fixed to the soil for the profitable exploitation of the land was heritable. By contrast, they held that certain parts of the machinery which were not necessarily affixed thereto and which were capable of being employed elsewhere in the same manner, as well as certain parts which were prepared for fixing but not actually affixed, were moveable. With regard to the machinery erected on land which had been leased, the court followed the established trend and held that, since the machinery was erected for the purposes of trade, it remained the moveable property of the tenant.[53] This interlocutor was confirmed by the House of Lords with little discussion. Both Lord Brougham[54] and Lord Cottenham,[55] however, concluded that the exception in favour of trade fixtures (relating to

---

[51] (1843) 5 D 775.   [52] Ibid. at 781–90.   [53] See the interlocutor ibid. at 839–40.
[54] (1854) 4 Bell App 286 at 360.   [55] Ibid. at 355.

the land leased by *Dixon*), had no application in the present case. Lord Campbell went further and stated unequivocally:[56] 'A distinction was attempted to be made between leasehold and freehold, but when we bear in mind that by the law of Scotland the leasehold is realty and that it goes to the heir, the distinction entirely fails.'

3. From *Fisher* to *Brand's Trs*

The leading authority on trade fixtures between *Fisher* and the decision of the House of Lords in *Brand's Trs*[57] is *Syme* v. *Harvey*.[58] In this case it was decided that greenhouses, forcing pits, and hotbed frames erected by nursery gardeners on land leased for their trade, could, insofar as they did not consist of brickwork, be removed by the tenants on the expiry of the lease. The reasons advanced for this decision were characteristic: the occupation of the land by the tenants was only temporary; the erections were for the purpose of trade; and such a great outlay would not have been incurred if the tenants had thought that removal would not have been allowed or compensation would not have been offered.[59] Two of their Lordships were of opinion that the exception with regard to trade fixtures was authoritatively settled by *Dixon* v. *Fisher*.[60] Lord President McNeill[61] went so far as to say that the tenant would also have been entitled to remove the brickwork of the greenhouses, although Lord Curriehill[62] and Lord Deas[63] expressed their doubt on this point.

The exceptional position of trade fixtures was again confirmed in *Duke of Buccleuch* v. *Tod's Trustees*.[64] The court held that the wire fencing, wooden palings, and wooden folds erected by the tenant of a sheep farm at his own expense for the purpose of experimenting in the rearing of sheep and not in substitution of previously existing fences or necessary for the proper management of the farm, remained moveable and could be removed by the tenant. Their Lordships found that the fences were erected for the benefit of the tenant to serve his experimentation of the sheep flock and not for the permanent improvement of the farm.[65] Lord Benholme concluded[66] that the tenant's intention in erecting those structures was for his own benefit. The fencing, palings, and folds therefore remained moveable and did not become part of the farm.

Dowall v. *Miln*,[67] the leading case of this whole period, was not concerned

---

[56] Ibid. at 360.   [57] *Brand's Trs* v. *Brand's Trs* (1876) 3 R (HL) 16, discussed below.
[58] (1861) 24 D 202.
[59] See Lord President McNeill (1861) 24 D 202 at 210, Lord Curriehill at 212, Lord Deas at 212–13.   [60] See Lord Ivory (1861) 24 D 202 at 211, Lord Curriehill at 212.
[61] Ibid. at 211.   [62] Ibid. at 212.   [63] Ibid. at 214.
[64] (1871) 9 M 1014.
[65] See the Lord Justice-Clerk (1871) 9 M 1014 at 1016 and Lord Cowan at 1018.
[66] Ibid. at 1019.   [67] (1874) 1 R 1180.

with tenants.[68] Nonetheless Lord Justice-Clerk Moncreiff, in a wide-ranging review of the law, offered the following account of trade fixtures:[69]

> [T]here are now well established principles on which trade fixtures are held not to become heritable by accession in questions between landlord and tenant. It is not accurate to say that these questions are exceptions to the general rule, proceeding on favour to trade. On the contrary, these decisions rest on a very clear legal principle, which runs throughout the whole category. That principle is nothing but this, that in such cases the manifest object and intention with which the articles were placed in their relation to the real estate were not the advantage or benefit of the owner of the property, or of the property itself, but solely the convenience of the tenant's trade.

From the above it is clear that in the period before *Brand's Trs* a distinction was drawn between ordinary fixtures and so-called trade fixtures. In the case of ordinary fixtures the traditional rules with regard to *inaedificatio* based on Bankton's and Erskine's two requirements were confirmed and refined.[70] First, there had to be some form of physical attachment. However, unless separation was impossible without material injury to either the principal or accessory,[71] attachment in itself was not sufficient. Then the second requirement, namely whether the article was intended for the permanent use of the land, had to be considered. Although evidence could be led as to the annexer's actual intention,[72] this requirement was usually established by objective factors such as the function of the accessory in relation to the principal, the mutual physical adaptation of both the accessory and the principal, and the probable duration of the attachment.

The law with regard to trade fixtures was different. These articles remained moveable since they were placed on the land not with the object of benefiting the landowner, but solely for the convenience of the tenant's trade.[73] In principle this difference should not be explained by the relationship between the parties in dispute, which is a matter of chance, but by the relationship of the annexer to the ground. Thus if an article attached by a tenant was held to be moveable (as in *Syme* v. *Harvey*) it was to be considered moveable for all purposes.

It is true that in a question between heir and executor certain articles were regarded as heritable for the limited purposes of succession.[74] But this was attributable to destination rather than to accession.

---

[68] For other cases of this period not concerned with articles annexed by tenants, see *McGregor* v. *Tolmie* (1860) 22 D 1183, and *Tod's Trs* v. *Finlay* (1872) 10 M 422.
[69] (1874) 1 R 1180 at 1183.   [70] Reid, (1983) 28 *JLSS* 49 at 50.
[71] Bell, *Commentaries*, I, 786–7; *Dowall* v. *Miln* (1874) 1 R 1180 at 1182 *per* Lord Moncreiff.
[72] See *Dowall* v. *Miln* (1874) 1 R 1180 at 1182 *per* Lord Moncreiff.
[73] See especially *Dowall* v. *Miln* (1874) 1 R 1180 at 1183 *per* Lord Moncreiff.
[74] The doctrine of articles heritable by destination has in modern law lost its former significance. See J. McLaren, *The Law of Wills and Succession* (3rd edn., 1894), para. 378.

It is interesting to note that trade fixtures were treated, not as exceptions to the ordinary rules of accession, but as cases which failed to satisfy Erskine's second requirement. Rather than being intended for the permanent benefit or advantage of the owner or his land, the articles were placed on the soil solely for the convenience of the tenants' trade. Because they could readily be removed to another location, they were considered accessories to the trade rather than accessories to the land. To obtain this result, certain non-objective factors crept into the equation.

Although the rules in England at this time closely resembled those of Scotland, a very important distinction existed in the case of articles erected by a tenant on land leased for the purposes of trade. Although English law established as early as 1703[75] that a tenant was entitled to remove trade fixtures erected by him, it was not until the 1870s that it was accepted that the article became a fixture, and therefore the property of the landlord at the moment of attachment, leaving only a right to sever on the part of the tenant. In *Holland* v. *Hodgson*[76] Blackburn J. accepted that the reason why trade fixtures were considered to have become part of the land was that the tenant indicated by the mode in which he installed the fixtures that he regarded them as attached to the property during the period of his interest.[77] This is in sharp contrast with the position in Scots law where the fact that the annexer was a tenant would by itself prevent an article used in his trade from becoming a fixture. Accordingly, Scots law did not need a separate right of severance.

4. Outside influences

In *Syme* v. *Harvey*,[78] argued in 1860, the sheriff substitute concluded his judgment with the following remarks:

The cases and authorities founded on, and by which the Sheriff-substitute has been mainly guided, are English,—and to these the pursuer took some exception at the debate, but, as is remarked by Lord Cockburn in *Fisher v. Dixon,* 'we are not so rich in cases on the subject of fixtures as our Southern neighbours';—and Mr. Hunter, on commenting on this branch of the law, observes that 'attention to the law of England is peculiarly requisite, by reason of the number of cases which it contains embodying rules which have been deemed of practical application in this country'. Finally, Lord Brougham, in *Fisher v. Dixon*,[79] says, '[t]he Scotch law appears to me only to differ from the English law in carrying its principles as laid down in the cases a little farther rather than falling short of them'.

In fact the use of English authority goes back at least to the beginning of the nineteenth century, and probably earlier. The attraction is not hard to

---

[75] *Poole's* Case (1703) 1 Salk 368.   [76] (1872) LR 7 CP 328 at 336 *per* Blackburn J.
[77] See also Wood VC in *Boyd* v. *Shorrock* (1867) LR 5 Eq 72 at 78.
[78] (1861) 24 D 202 at 207.   [79] (1845) 4 Bell App 286 at 353.

explain. Litigation in Scotland had been slow, and it was not until later in the century that a sufficient body of case law had been established. In the meantime English cases were an obvious source for borrowing. They were decided against a common social and economic background; and in this area of property law, almost uniquely, common law and civil law were close together. The former indeed owed much to the latter. The use of English material was encouraged by the publication, in 1827, of Amos's *Law of Fixtures*,[80] the first textbook in England to be devoted to the subject. The high point of English influence came with the decision of the House of Lords in *Brand's Trs* v. *Brand's Trs*, described in the next section. Thereafter it fell away, but has continued as a significant presence.

Civil law sources were also cited, although less frequently. These included references both to the *Digest* and also to the literature of the *jus commune*. The most extensive citations appear in *Arkwright* v. *Billinge*,[81] where counsel referred to Heineccius, Paulus and Johannes Voet, and Pothier. Heineccius was also referred to in the argument presented to the Court of Session in *Fisher* v. *Dixon*,[82] although the reference was not persevered with before the House of Lords. Thereafter civilian sources disappear.

A citation count may underestimate the extent of civilian influence, particularly in the period before 1800. Certainly there is much common ground between the institutional writers[83] and the jurists cited in *Arkwright* v. *Billinge*. For example, Paulus Voet, writing shortly before Stair, states that moveables accede by being attached to immoveables in such a way that they are destined to serve the immoveable.[84] His examples include pigeon-houses and winepresses attached to the soil or a building for their perpetual use, and kitchen-gardens which are joined to a house and serve its convenience and amenity.[85] Voet compares huge wine barrels structurally integrated to a winepress and serving its purpose (immoveable) with wine bottles buried in the soil for a merely temporary purpose (moveable).

The idea of 'perpetual use', which plays a central role in the analyses of Bankton[86] and Erskine,[87] can be found in all of the writers cited in *Arkwright*. According to Johannes Voet, for example, the attachment must be 'non temporarii sed perpetui usus causa'.[88] Similarly, Heineccius' definition of immoveables is of articles which cannot be moved without being damaged or those which are joined to immoveables and destined for their perpetual use.[89]

---

[80] The third edition of 1883 added Ferard as an author.   [81] 3 Dec. 1819 FC 52.
[82] (1843) 5 D 775 at 791.   [83] For the institutional writers, see above III.
[84] *Mobilium et Immobilium Natura* (Utrecht, 1714), cap. IV, 2. Voet's dates are 1619–67.
[85] Cap. IV, 3.   [86] Bankton, I, 3, 17.   [87] Erskine, II, 2, 2.
[88] *Commentarius ad Pandectas* (1698–1704), VIII, 1: 'non temporarii sed perpetui usus causa' ('not for temporary but for permanent use').
[89] *Elementa Iuris Civilis Secundum Ordinem Pandectarum* (4th edn., 1740), ad D. 1, 8 sec., CLXXXXIIII: 'vel usus perpetui causa iunguntur immobilibus; aut horum usui destinantur' ('they are attached to immoveables for the sake of perpetual use; or destined to serve them

In this matter, however, *Digest* texts provided a common source,[90] and there is no evidence of cross-influence.

Pothier is rich in examples. Vine props, even though fixed only slightly to the soil and removed in winter, should nevertheless be considered immoveable since they are joined to the soil for perpetual use, are intended to complete the vineyard, and are destined to serve its purpose until entirely used up.[91] Articles in a house are to be divided into those placed for permanent utility and which are necessary to complete the house (*ad integrandam domum*) and those placed merely as decoration (*ad instruendam domum*). Only the former are immoveable. Pothier illustrates the distinction by the case of a mirror inserted as part of a fireplace. If the place where it is inserted has been finished off in the same way as the rest of the fireplace, the mirror is nothing more than a large ornament inserted *ad instruendam domum* and not *ad integrandam domum*. Even without the mirror the fireplace would form a structural whole. By contrast, if the place where it is inserted is raw and unplastered, the mirror is an integral part of the house.[92]

VI. THE LAW TURNS: *BRAND'S TRS V. BRAND'S TRS* (1874–1876)

In *Brand's Trs* v. *Brand's Trs*[93] the court was called upon to adjudicate on the nature of machinery erected and used by a tenant under a nineteen-year mining lease. The tenant died halfway through the lease, having testated in relation to his moveable property only.[94] A dispute arose in relation to machinery used for mining. If the machinery was heritable (immoveable), it passed to the heir along with the lease, but if it was moveable it passed to the deceased's testamentary trustees and fell to be distributed in terms of his trust disposition and settlement.

At first instance, the Lord Ordinary (Shand) decided in favour of the heir. He found that the machinery was directly or indirectly fixed to the ground for the purpose of working the colliery. Though removable without injury to the land, it was constructed and fixed to form part of the structure of the colliery.

---

permanently'). See also Paulus Voet (n. 84), cap. XV, 10: 'Quae aedibus vel fundo non sunt affixa, vel non inhaerent, vel non deposita perpetua usus gratia' ('which are not physically attached to buildings or the land, nor imbedded, nor placed for the sake of perpetual use').

[90] Ulp. D. 19, 1, 17, 7; Iav. D. 50, 16, 242, 4.

[91] *Traités de droit civil* (3rd edn., 1781), vol. 3, part I, ch. II, sect. 1, art. 1, § 1 (at 509): 'parce qu'ils y sont placés pour perpétuelle demeure et destinés à cet usage jusqu'à ce qu'ils soient entièrement usés, et qu'ils ne puissent plus servir' ('because they are placed there permanently and destined for such use until they are entirely worn off and are no longer capable of rendering a service'). This example comes from Ulp. D. 19, 1, 17, 10–11.

[92] Ibid. 641. This final example anticipates the facts of *Cochrane* v. *Stevenson* (1891) 18 R 1208.   [93] (1874) 2 R 258, reversed (1876) 3 R (HL) 16.

[94] Being under the age of 21 at his death, he could not, under the law then in force, testate in relation to his heritable property.

The machinery was accessory to the lease, and, since the lease was heritable, the machinery was heritable also.[95]

On appeal the Second Division reversed the decision of the Lord Ordinary and held that the tenant's trade fixtures at the colliery were moveable not only in a question between landlord and tenant, but also in a question between heir and executor in the tenant's succession. Lord Gifford relied strongly on *Fisher* v. *Dixon* and found that the majority of the court in that case was of the opinion that the tenant's trade fixtures were moveable.[96] In a direct application of the rules pertaining to trade fixtures, he decided that accession had not taken place, that the machinery remained moveable, and that accordingly it was moveable for the purposes of succession. He cogently summarized the law of trade fixtures:[97]

> I take it to be perfectly fixed law ... that in leases of ordinary duration, where the tenant erects fixtures solely for the purposes of his trade, these trade fixtures remain his property, and cannot be claimed by the landlord as *partes soli*, as it is said that they are moveable in a question between landlord and tenant. *Syme v. Harvey* ... and other cases are illustrations of the application of this principle.
>
> Now, it humbly appears to me that if trade fixtures do not go to the landlord, they must of necessity remain the moveable property of the tenant and must remain moveable *quoad omnia*. The only thing that can make them heritable is their fixture,—their annexation to the soil; but that would carry them to the landlord to whom alone the soil belongs. If the fixture have not this effect, and this is conceded, it is difficult to see how it can make them heritable to any effect at all. The tenant could remove the fixtures at pleasure. He could convey them by assignation ... The tenant could bequeath them by will or testament, separate from the mineral lease ... [T]hey could be sequestrated under the landlord's hypothec or poinded by the tenant's creditors.

Lord Gifford then dealt with the argument that the fixtures, though moveable, should be considered heritable in succession because, though not fixed to the soil, they were fixed to the *lease* so as to go with the lease to the tenant's heir. His answer was that[98] 'a lease is an incorporeal right, and it is difficult to follow what is meant by fixture to a lease. Fixture to the subject of a lease is not the same as fixture to or incorporation with the lease itself. The fixture may be for the most temporary purpose, and without the least reference to the duration of the lease or to its destination ...' Finally, he rejected the principle that the proprietor of moveable subjects may, in a question of his own succession, make these subjects heritable *destinatione*, especially since it was the clear intention of the deceased that moveables should go to his trustee and not to his heir.[99]

---

[95] See (1874) 2 R 258 at 261 and 265 of the Court of Session report. The Lord Ordinary's decision seems to be based on the rules relating to trade fixtures rather than on the doctrine of implied destination as accepted by Reid, (1983) 28 *JLSS* 49 at 51.
[96] (1874) 2 R 258 at 268–9.   [97] Ibid. at 269–70.   [98] Ibid. at 270.
[99] Ibid. at 271.

Accession by Building

The heir appealed and in the House of Lords three English judges and an Irish judge decided in his favour. The Lord Chancellor, Lord Cairns, took the view that the issue had not been authoritatively settled by the decision of the House of Lords in *Fisher* v. *Dixon*. In *Fisher* the question concerning the legal position of the machinery on the *leased* land was comparatively insignificant, there was a considerable difference of opinion amongst their Lordships, and a concession of counsel resulted in the point not being fully argued. Lord Cairns therefore concluded that he was not bound by *Fisher* to decide that machinery erected on land which had been leased went to the executor of the tenant and not to his heir.[100]

In a passage which was later to become famous, Lord Cairns stated the general principles applicable to cases involving fixtures: [101]

[T]here are with regard to matters of [fixtures] two general rules, a correct appreciation of which will, as it seems to me, go far to solve the whole difficulty in this case. My Lords, one of those rules is the general well-known rule that whatever is fixed to the freehold [*sic*] of land becomes part of the freehold or the inheritance. The other is a quite different and separate rule. Whatever once becomes part of the inheritance cannot be severed by a limited owner, whether he be an owner for life or for years ... Those, my Lords, are two rules—not one by way of exception to the other, but two rules standing consistently together. My Lords, an exception indeed, and a very important exception, has been made not to the first of these rules, but to the second ... namely the irremoveability of things fixed to the inheritance ... That exception has been established in favour of the fixtures which have been attached to the inheritance for the purpose of trade ... Under that exception a tenant who has fixed to the inheritance things for the purpose of trade has a certain power of severance and removal during his tenancy.

As Professor Reid[102] has demonstrated, this was no more than a restatement of English law. Trade fixtures attached by a tenant acceded to the land and thus became the property of the landlord at the moment of annexure. The tenant, however, retained the right to remove the fixtures at any time until the lease expired. On the facts, the Lord Chancellor found that the mining machinery became the property of the landlord when attached, but that the tenant retained the right of removal. Upon the death of the tenant, the right of removal passed with the lease (as an accessory to heritable property) to the heir.[103]

Professor Reid has criticized the decision of the House of Lords as departing from a tract of previous authority, as proceeding on a misunderstanding of the nature of a lease in Scots law, and as an example of unconsidered Anglicization.[104] For many years thereafter its legacy was to be uncertain, and disputed.

---

[100] Ibid. at 19. See also Lord Chelmsford at 23. [101] Ibid. at 20.
[102] Ibid. at 51.
[103] The cumbersome reasoning ibid. at 21 to explain this finding is not so easy to understand.
[104] Reid, (1983) 28 *JLSS* 49 at 51–2.

VII. THE LEGACY OF *BRAND'S TRS*

1. The two rules in *Brand's Trs*

Brand's Trs changed the law of Scotland by assimilating it to the law of England. The Lord Chancellor laid down two rules.[105] The first rule sets the criterion for an article to become a fixture: 'whatever is fixed to the freehold of land, becomes part of the freehold'. The second rule states that once an article has become a fixture, it cannot be removed by a limited 'owner', such as a tenant, unless it is a trade fixture.

By the time of *Brand's Trs* the criteria for answering the first question (whether the article was a fixture) was already well established. These criteria were roughly similar to Bankton's and Erskine's two requirements for fixtures, namely (*a*) physical attachment to the soil accompanied by (*b*) an intention of permanent use on the land.

The changes made by *Brand's Trs* did not concern the criteria themselves, but the considerations which may be taken into account in order to satisfy them. Prior to *Brand's Trs* the fact that the annexer was a tenant or liferenter, with only a limited interest in the land, barred compliance with the second requirement—the Second Division in *Brand's Trustees* therefore held that the machinery was moveable. The House of Lords changed this: henceforth the annexer's relationship with the land was to be irrelevant for all purposes connected with the *first* rule. A distinction was no longer drawn between an article affixed by a landowner and the same article fixed by a tenant. This meant that the second requirement of Bankton and Erskine was framed more objectively in the sense that it was abstracted from the annexer's subjective intention by concentrating on the objective factors of the attachment.

The annexer's relationship with the land, however, still remained relevant when the *second* rule was applied. Contrary to the position before *Brand's Trs*, when trade fixtures of tenants retained their moveable character throughout, the second rule in *Brand's Trustees* allowed annexers with a limited interest in the land to remove fixtures attached for the purpose of their trade. The House of Lords accordingly found in *Brand's Trs* that the machinery, though heritable under the first rule, was removable under the second.

This remains the position in Scots law today. The only subsequent change was an adaptation of Bankton's and Erskine's second requirement (intention of the annexer).[106] After the English decision in *Hobson* v. *Gorringe*[107] was adopted as part of Scots law by the Court of Session in *Christie* v. *Smith's Exrs*,[108] it was no longer competent to lead evidence of an annexer's actual

---

[105] Analysed in Reid, (1983) 28 *JLSS* 49 at 52. [106] Reid, (1983) 28 *JLSS* 49 at 52.
[107] [1892] 1 Ch 182.   [108] 1949 SC 572.

intention. Only evidence featuring objective circumstances 'patent for all to see' was admissible to prove an intention of permanency.

The new law introduced by *Brand's Trs* creates certain difficulties.[109] First, it is not clear whether a tenant or other limited possessor is entitled under the second rule to remove only trade fixtures or also (as under English law) fixtures erected for ornament or domestic convenience. Secondly, even if brought under this exception, the fixtures remain the property of the landlord until severance. This means that the landlord could pass a good title to a bona fide third party, that the fixtures would be included in a heritable security granted by the landlord, and that on the latter's sequestration the fixtures would form part of his insolvent estate, presumably leaving the tenant to rank as an ordinary creditor by virtue of his right of removal.[110]

2. *Brand's Trs* ignored

At first *Brand's Trs* created considerable confusion. One response was to ignore it.[111] In *Marshall v. Tannoch Chemical Co. Ltd*,[112] for example, the Court of Session decided, without any reference to *Brand's Trs* (although the case was pled in argument), that in assessing fixtures for the purposes of feudal casualties, the applicable rules were those which applied between landlord and tenant rather than heir and executor. On this basis machinery in a chemical work was held to be moveable. Similarly, in *Hewett v. Bishop of Glasgow's Fund Committee*,[113] the court found that the nature of the tenancy in question, the extent to which the building would be affected by removal, the character of the articles under consideration and the probable intention of the parties regarding them, were relevant in deciding whether articles attached by the Mission Board to a hall leased by it were removable. In its interlocutor, the court allowed the Mission Board to remove a rood screen, altar steps, altar rails, oak standards with brass rods, and gas coronae. This was decided without any reference to the rules set out in *Brand's Trs*, and with strong reliance on the temporary nature of the tenant's occupation.

In more recent times strong dicta, especially in valuation cases, failed to observe the change and created further confusion. These dicta can be traced to remarks by Lord Kyllachy that the test of heritability in valuation cases closely resembles the tests applied in cases between heir and executor rather

---

[109] See the Lord Ordinary (Stewart) in *Cliffplant Ltd v. Kinnaird* 1982 SLT 2 at 5.
[110] See also Reid, (1983) 28 *JLSS* 49 at 52. It is not altogether clear whether the right of removal will be converted into a pecuniary amount and treated as an ordinary debt.
[111] See *Marshall v. Tannoch Chemical Co. Ltd* (1886) 13 R 1042; *Schooler v. Lawson* (1890) 6 Sh Ct Rep 110; *Hewett v. Bishop of Glasgow's Fund Committee* (1898) 4 Sh Ct Rep 95; *Malcolm v. High* (1909) 25 Sh Ct Rep 264.   [112] (1886) 13 R 1042.
[113] (1898) 4 Sh Ct Rep 95.

than those as between landlord and tenant.[114] For example, in *Assessor of Fife* v. *Hodgson*[115] Lord Kilbrandon stated that:[116] 'Whether things of their own nature moveable have become heritable by accession is a question which according to long-established practice ... falls to be settled by reference to the law as between heir and executor.' Even outside valuation cases, the confusion has continued into modern times. In *Christie* v. *Smith's Exrs*[117] Lord Justice-Clerk Thompson again ignored the changes introduced by *Brand's Trs* and bluntly stated:[118] 'It is difficult to extract from the authorities and text writers any very satisfactory general statements of the law, but this is probably due to the fact that the character of the problem varies so much according to the legal relationship in which the parties stand. What may be suitably stated in a case of a heir and executor, may be almost misleading in a case of landlord and tenant.' In that case the court had to decide whether a summerhouse was included in a sale of land including 'houses, biggings, etc' but which made no reference to the summer-house. The summer-house weighed about two tons, rested on stones placed on a previously levelled site by its own weight and without mechanical attachment, formed the boundary between a field and the garden of a farm house and had remained in this position for more than ten years. Relying on the relationship between the parties, the court decided that the applicable test was the same as applied between heir and executor. On account of its substantial construction, its permanent or quasi-permanent location, and the fact that it performed a useful function on the farm, the summer-house was found to be a heritable subject and therefore included in the sale despite the fact it was not definitely attached to the soil and had indeed been removed without damage to itself or to the site.

3. *Brand's Trs* misunderstood

In at least three cases, the Court of Session allowed itself to be persuaded that the change brought about by *Brand's Trustees* was even greater than it really was. The most prominent is also the most recent. In *Cliffplant Ltd* v. *Kinnaird*,[119] decided in 1980, the appellants had hired out two bulky structures, namely a Bailey footbridge spanning 90 feet and a five-unit prefabricated building measuring 40 feet by 20 feet, to the operators of a racing circuit for motor-racing and motor-cycle events. The lower floor of the two-storeyed building was used as a store and the upper floor as a race-control

---

[114] *Gilchrist* v. *Assessor for Lanarkshire* (1898) 25 R 589, 591; *Assessor for Dundee* v. *Carmichael & Co. Ltd* (1902) 4 F 525 at 532. See also Reid, (1983) 28 *JLSS* 49 at 53, and J. A. Copeland, 'Fixtures in and out of valuation', (1967) 12 *JLSS* 54 at 57.   [115] 1966 SC 30.
[116] Ibid. at 35.   [117] 1949 SC 572.   [118] Ibid. at 578.
[119] 1981 SC 9, 1982 SLT 2. The other cases are *Reid's Exrs* v. *Reid* (1890) 17 R 519 and *Chalmer's Tr* v. *Dick* 1909 SC 761.

centre. These structures were erected on land leased by the operators from the respondents under a twelve-year lease. Two years after the lease was concluded, the respondents went into receivership and the lease was terminated. When the respondents claimed the structures as their property, the appellants approached the court for a declarator that they were the owners of the structures. They not only claimed delivery of the structures but also for damages for wrongful withholding of property. An Extra Division of the Court of Session followed the Lord Ordinary and held that the structures had become fixtures. Since the appellants were neither parties to nor assignees of the lease, the court further held that they were not entitled to remove the structures. Proof, except on the separate question of recompense, was refused.

The court's initial finding that the structures were immoveable was based on the first rule in *Brand's Trs* (that whatever is fixed or united to land, becomes part of the land). This was taken to mean that physical attachment was conclusive, so that in cases where this was present, structures automatically became part of the land. Lord Dunpark developed this argument as follows:[120]

Counsel for the company submitted that we should apply the principles stated in *Howie's Trs* v. *McLay*[121] ... which should lead us to find that this bridge was not heritable property, or at least to allow a proof before answer on the question ... He submitted that a Bailey bridge was *prima facie* moveable, that this bridge had not become heritable by mere attachment to the soil, but that, in order to classify it as heritable or moveable, it was necessary to consider all the factors referred to in ... *Howie's Trs* namely, the character and degree of its attachment to the soil, the permanency or quasi-permanency of its erection, the intention of the person who attached it, how far the soil and the bridge would be affected by its removal, and, as Lord McLaren said at p 219 'the species of property which is in question' ... *However sympathetic I may be towards this submission in the circumstances of this case, I cannot read Brand's Trs as deciding other than that whatever becomes fixed to the soil immediately becomes, as the Lord Chancellor put it, 'part of the inheritance'.*[122]

This obvious misreading of *Brand's Trs* attracted adverse comment.[123] Within five years the decision had been overruled, in the case of *Scottish Discount Co.* v. *Blin*,[124] by a court of seven judges assembled expressly for that purpose.

4. Brand's Trs applied

For the most part, however, *Brand's Trs* was accepted and applied. In *Ferguson* v. *Paul*,[125] for example, where an amateur gardener attempted to

---

[120] 1981 SC 9 at 35.   [121] (1902) 5 F 214.   [122] My emphasis.
[123] Notably by Reid, (1983) 28 *JLSS* 49.   [124] 1985 SC 216, 1986 SLT 123.
[125] (1885) 12 R 1222.

remove a greenhouse set up on leased property, Lord Rutherfurd Clark stated that:

> I see nothing in the nature of the tenure from which a right to remove buildings erected on the ground can be implied. Such a right may be inferred in a lease for the purposes of trade, so as to give a tenant a right to remove what are called trade fixtures. I know of no other lease from which such an inference can be drawn.

In *Cochrane v. Stevenson*[126] Lord Kinnear again confirmed the rules in *Brand's Trs*, but concluded that considerations of removal were inapplicable in a case between seller and purchaser.

The clearest exposition of the law in *Brand's Trs* is found in another judgment of Lord Rutherfurd Clark, in *Miller v. Muirhead*:[127] 'The law with regard to trade fixtures was very authoritatively settled by the House of Lords in the case of *Brand*. Though the case was between heir and executor only, the noble Lords ... were at pains to state the general law.' After quoting relevant passages from the speeches of the Lord Chancellor and Lord Chelmsford, Lord Rutherfurd Clark continued:

> No language could be clearer. The trade fixture, by being attached to the ground, becomes 'a part of the inheritance', 'a part of the freehold'. So long as it is so attached, it must belong to the owner of the soil, for he is necessarily owner of everything which is part of it. The tenant possesses it as part of the subject of the lease, but in no other character. He has a right to make it his own by severing it from the soil, but until the right is exercised, he can have no right of property.[128]

In *Howie's Trs v. McLay*,[129] in a dispute whether lace looms installed in a factory were included in a heritable security of the land, the Lord President and Lord McLaren gave a full exposition of the law laid down in *Brand's Trs* and concluded that the issue before the court was concerned with the two rules and not with the exception to the second rule.

Finally, the authority of *Brand's Trs* was fully accepted in the leading modern case, the seven-judge decision in *Scottish Discount Co. Ltd v. Blin*.[130]

VIII. CODA: THE EFFECT OF HIRE-PURCHASE

The two most recent cases have been concerned with the effect of hire-purchase. In *Scottish Discount Co. v. Blin*[131] a scrap metal dealer had acquired two very bulky scrap shears on hire-purchase from a finance company. In terms of the hire-purchase agreement, the suppliers retained ownership and hence the right to reclaim the shears in default of instalments being paid. The

---

[126] (1891) 18 R 1208.   [127] (1894) 21 R 658 at 660.
[128] The only right that remained with the tenant was his right to remove the trade fixtures until the expiry of his lease. It seems uncertain whether such a right is assignable.
[129] (1902) 5 F 214.   [130] 1985 SC 216, 1986 SLT 123.   [131] 1985 SC 216.

shears were delivered in a dismantled condition and installed on specially designed foundations in a specially designed shed on the premises in such a way that they became physically attached to the scrapyard and were used as part of the operations of a scrapyard business. The dealer later granted a heritable security over the scrapyard to a second finance company. When insolvency followed, the court was required to determine whether the shears remained the (moveable) property of the supplier, or whether they had acceded to the ground and so fell under the heritable security.

The most interesting aspect of the case was the effect of the hire-purchase agreement, and in particular whether it prevented the dealer from having the objective intention that the shears should serve the scrapyard in a permanent or quasi-permanent way. At first instance Lord Murray[132] took the view that the intended result of the hire-purchase agreement was that the dealer would in due course become the absolute owner of the shears. Both parties knew that the shears had to be physically attached to the land in order to function properly. The purpose of the machinery was to serve the function of the land used as a scrapyard. There was therefore implied authority for the dealer to convert these articles into heritable fixtures. The key question then became whether an exception could be allowed to the otherwise inevitable accession of the shears to the heritage; but while attracted by the idea that accession might be defeated if the articles were not the property of the annexer, Lord Murray considered that he was bound by the decision in *Cliffplant*[133] (where the articles had been hired). Accordingly he concluded that accession had occurred.

This view was affirmed on appeal. Having reflected upon English authority (most notably *Hobson* v. *Gorringe*[134]) on the relevance of the terms of a hire-purchase agreement for ascertaining the intention of the annexer who installed the machinery on the land, the Lord President (Emslie) declared:[135] 'In my opinion all that is to be taken from *Hobson* v. *Gorringe* is that where upon the evidence it is clear that an article has become a fixture no declaration of intent in any hire-purchase agreement or other agreement of a private nature that it should not become a fixture can influence the court's decision.'[136] Lord Emslie, however, considered that where the matter is otherwise in a fine balance, the fact that the fixture was acquired in terms of a hire-purchase agreement, could be of some relevance in deciding whether the installation was or was not intended to be a permanent or quasi-permanent addition to the land. In this regard the suppliers argued[137] that the shears

---

[132] Ibid. at 224. [133] *Cliffplant Ltd* v. *Kinnaird* 1981 SC 9, discussed earlier.
[134] [1897] 1 Ch 182. [135] 1985 SC 216 at 234.
[136] As authority he referred to a statement by Lord Cockburn in *Dixon* v. *Fisher* (1843) 5 D 775 at 793 in which his Lordship disregarded the view formed by the deceased himself ('no man can make his property real or personal by merely thinking it so'). See also the more recent case of *Shetland Island Council* v. *BP Petroleum Development Ltd* 1990 SLT 82, 94H-J.
[137] See the summary of Lord Emslie 1985 SC 216 at 236.

were installed, not to enlarge the scrap dealer's heritable estate, but merely to convenience the trade he was carrying on. They warned of the dire consequences which might flow from the rejection of this contention: suppliers of shears who carried on business in the belief that they retain their right of ownership until the charges have been paid would have lost their rights.

Lord Emslie found himself unable to accept this submission. Both the scrap dealer and the suppliers had contemplated that the dealer would install the shears to further his business, and their intention and indeed expectation was that the dealer would purchase them at the expiry of the short three-year period of hire. In these circumstances no doubt was cast on the clear inference from the mass of other material that these shears, when installed, were intended to be a permanent or quasi-permanent feature of the land to which they were attached for the enhancement of the value of the scrapyard itself.

Commenting on the intention of the owner as a factor in ascertaining whether an article attached to land has become a fixture, Lord Cameron[138] remarked that parties by private agreement cannot change the legal character of what the law regards as heritable so as to affect third parties who are strangers to and ignorant of such an agreement. Like Lord Emslie, however, he conceded that the nature of the contract between the parties, which was the legal instrument by which the piece of machinery was moved and installed in a factory or yard, may have to be taken into account as itself an item of evidence relevant to the objective determination of the matter of intention. Despite the English authority referred to above, Lord Cameron concluded that such a contract may at least be taken into account as one of the facts which may bear upon the ultimate decision of the court.[139]

Lord Grieve pointed out that the scrap dealer could not afford to purchase either of the shears outright. In order to acquire them for his business, he bought them on hire-purchase. However, his intention in installing the shears was exactly the same as if he had bought them outright. The intention of the dealer, coupled with the method of installation and attachment and the other facts referred to above, therefore pointed to a clear intention to attach the shears permanently or at least quasi-permanently.[140]

Scottish Discount Co. v. *Blin* was followed in the Outer House, on similar facts, in *TSB Scotland plc* v. *James Mills (Montrose) Ltd (in receivership)*.[141] Both decisions provide strong authority for the view that the intention of permanency required on the part of the annexer must be deduced from purely objective facts. They further indicate that, although the provisions of a hire-purchase contract may be a factor in ascertaining the intention of permanency, it is not the provisions themselves but rather the impression created

---

[138] See the summary of Lord Emslie 1985 SC 216 at 240. [139] Ibid. at 241.
[140] See ibid. at 245.   [141] 1991 GWD 39-2406.

by these provisions that are taken into account. It is also clear that the only relevant intention is that of the annexer (hire-purchaser) and not that of the supplier. Far from being conclusive as to the moveable character of the article attached, the fact that the supplier did not intend ownership to pass until the last instalment has been paid does not enter the equation at all.[142]

IX. CONCLUSION

While the Scottish law of fixtures finds its origins in the Roman law of *inaedificatio*, the often cryptic nature of that law led the institutional writers to the Roman texts on sale and legacies in order to develop an approach which was wider than mere physical attachment. This in turn produced the requirement of perpetual or quasi-perpetual utility.

The preoccupation of the early law with questions of succession is signalled by the use of 'heritable' in place of 'immoveable'. And that early law stretched permanent utility to its limits through the concept of property heritable by destination, so as to provide the heir with a well-stocked estate. With the Industrial Revolution came the exception accorded to trade fixtures, an unashamed device to allow the tenant-trader the fullest possible exploitation of machinery fixed to land leased by him. Because the machinery was not deemed to enhance the exploitation of (agricultural) land, but rather the tenant's trade, the industrial implements and machinery were considered the moveable property of the tenant and out of reach of heritable creditors and subsequent purchasers of the land on which they were erected.

This changed with the decision of the House of Lords in *Brand's Trs*.[143] The House of Lords took the view that, once industrial machinery was erected on land, the character of the land changed, and that the aim of erecting machinery was to enhance the utility of the land as industrial premises. Hence the machinery acceded and fell to the owner of the land and his heritable creditors. To accommodate the needs of the tenant-trader, the law accorded the tenant a right of severance during the currency of his lease, corresponding to the *jus tollendi* of a tenant in Roman-Dutch and modern South African law.[144] Despite the criticism levelled against *Brand's Trs* as an unwarranted foreign intruder, the rules enunciated in that case were, in the

---

[142] Cf. the South African cases of *MacDonald Ltd* v. *Radin NO & The Potchefstroom Dairies & Industries Co. Ltd* 1915 AD 454 and *Konstanz Properties (Pty) Ltd* v. *WM Spilhaus (WP) Bpk* 1996 (3) SA 273 (A), where the court decided that if the nature and purpose of the article and the manner of attachment are equivocal the intention of the *owner* of the moveable would be decisive. See also Bugalo Maripe, 'Intention and the Original Acquisition of Ownership: Whither Inaedificatio?', (1998) 115 *SALJ* 544; C.G. van der Merwe, 'Die Impak van die Bedoeling van die Eienaar van die Roerende Saak by *Inaedificatio*', [2000] *TSAR* 155.
[143] *Brand's Trs* v. *Brand's Trs* (1876) 3 R (HL) 16.
[144] For authorities see C. G. Van der Merwe, *Sakereg* (2nd edn., 1989), 165.

course of time, accepted as the leading principles which govern the law of *inaedificatio*.

In *Scottish Discount Co. Ltd* v. *Blin*[145] an attempt was made to extend to hire-purchase sellers the favourable status accorded to tenants who had annexed trade fixtures to land for the furtherance of their trade. But by the time this case came to court, the use of objective factors had gained such an unassailable foothold that the Court of Session found it impossible to consider the subjective intention of the annexer, let alone that of the hire-purchase supplier who did not intend to part with his valuable property until the last instalment had been paid. This more objective approach to accession is in harmony with one of the fundamental principles of the law of property, namely the principle of publicity which strives to accord primacy to factual situations as they appear to the outside world.[146] A fixture should be a fixture if it is patent for all the world to see.

[145] 1985 SC 216.   [146] See van der Merwe (n. 144), 12–15.

6
Transfer of Ownership

D. L. CAREY MILLER*

I. INTRODUCTION

Unlike English law, in which property rights are essentially thought of in terms of degrees of possession,[1] Scots law, at an early stage in its development, recognized the fundamental importance of a distinction between ownership and possession. It would not be inaccurate to say that the distinction between possession as a factual condition and ownership as a legally recognized status was a matter of fundamental dogmatics in the development of Scots law.[2] The early recognition of the distinction between real and personal rights was, of course, only possible on the basis of a clear understanding of the distinction between ownership and possession. One might go further and note that the former distinction, which must necessarily be a product of the latter one, is inherent in a structural aspect of Scots law, found in all civilian systems: i.e. the division between the law of obligations, concerned with personal rights, and the law of property, in which the benchmark concept is the notion of title—a real right which trumps all other rights.

Balfour's *Practicks* has been identified by Sheriff Peter G. B. McNeill[3] as the 'first exhaustive legal work of Scots law' in which '[t]he strength of native institutions extends to the use of the vernacular, and the absence of Roman nomenclature'. The following is one of a number of passages which demonstrate Balfour's clear understanding of the fundamental distinction between contract and conveyance.

Gif ony man puttis his sone, or ony uther persoun in the fie of his landis, haldin of himself, and thairefter sellis the saidis landis, *titulo oneroso*, to ony uther man, and

---

* While I am solely responsible for any errors and imperfections in this chapter I wish to acknowledge the valuable contribution of Andrew Pringle LL.B. (Hons.) (Aberd.) who worked as a part-time research assistant in the preparation of my final text. I would also acknowledge the contribution of the Centre for the Study of the Civil Law Tradition, University of Aberdeen, in funding the research assistantship.

[1] 'So far is the common law from the sharp distinction of the Roman law between ownership and possession that we learn that there is a hierarchy of actions, a sort of descending scale from the purely proprietary to the purely possessory.' W. W. Buckland and Arnold D. McNair, *Roman Law and Common Law* (2nd edn., 1952), 67.

[2] In the early 17th century *Hope's Major Practicks* (a work which predated Stair by some fifty years) the title 'of possessioun' indicates how well established the distinction was in the formative stages of the law. See Hope, *Practicks*, I, 3, 21.   [3] Balfour, *Practicks*, xxxix, xli.

puttis him in possessioun thairof be vertue of his infeftment; his sone, or the uther persoun to quhome the landis wer first disponit, may not, be vertue of his first infeftment, remove the secund buyer of the saidis landis or tenementis; because the first infeftment was private, clandestine, and unknawin to the secund buyar, and thairfoir sould not be hurtfull nor prejudiciall to him quha bocht the saidis landis *bona fide, titulo onerofo*, and is in possessioun be vertue of the samin . . .[4]

For a large part of the development of Scots law there has been a tendency to think in terms of a distinction between moveable and immoveable property as a matter of doctrine rather than a mere distinction between the two major categories of property within a unitary law of property.[5] A possible explanation for this at a general level is the scope for ambivalence in a system in which the very roots are to some extent mixed.[6] Although the civilian distinction between real and personal rights came to be dominant it did so in a context which included legal concepts which were not civilian.

The transfer of ownership in moveable property has been analysed in a number of recent works.[7] The present chapter will accordingly concentrate entirely on immoveable property. In a quest to identify the doctrinal features

---

[4] Balfour, *Practicks*, 166.

[5] Even the great modern champion of Scots law Professor Sir Thomas Smith in his classic general textbook draws a line between the derivative acquisition of heritable property and that applying to moveables; see T. B. Smith, *A Short Commentary on the Law of Scotland* (1962), 525: '[d]iscussion of the methods of Scottish conveyancing is beyond the scope of this book' while the acquisition of corporeal moveables is seen to be subject to basic civilian principles (at 538). But this should not be seen as a distinction concerned with dogmatics for as Professor Kenneth Reid has shown modern law has tended to apply an unsystematic distinction based on subsuming land law into the separate subject of conveyancing; see Kenneth Reid, 'Rights and Things', in *The Laws of Scotland: Stair Memorial Encyclopaedia*, vol. 18 (1993), § 1 (repr. and updated as K. G. C. Reid, *The Law of Property in Scotland* (1996)).

[6] See generally W. D. H. Sellar, 'A Historical Perspective', in M. C. Meston, W. D. H. Sellar, and Lord Cooper (eds.), *The Scottish Legal Tradition* (new edn., 1991), 29. The identification of Scots law as belonging to a family of 'mixed' legal sytems is principally attributable to Professor Sir Thomas Smith QC; see, generally, the introduction and various essays in his collection *Studies Critical and Comparative* (1962). Recent relevant contributions include R. Evans-Jones, 'Civil Law in the Scottish Legal Tradition', in *idem* (ed.), *The Civil Law Tradition in Scotland* (1995), 3; Reinhard Zimmermann and Johann A. Dieckmann, 'Das schottische Privatrecht im Spiegel seiner Literatur', 1995 *ZEuP* 898; Elspeth Attwooll, 'Scotland: A Multi-dimensional Jigsaw', in Esin Örücü, Elspeth Attwooll, and Sean Coyle (eds.), *Studies in Legal Systems: Mixed and Mixing* (1996), 17; Alan Rodger, 'Thinking about Scots Law', (1996) 1 *Edinburgh LR* 3; Niall R. Whitty, 'The Civilian Tradition and Debates on Scots Law', 1996 *TSAR* 227; D. P. Visser, 'Placing the Civilian Influence in Scotland', in D. L. Carey Miller and Reinhard Zimmermann (eds.), *The Civilian Tradition and Scots Law: Aberdeen Quincentenary Essays* (1997), 239; H. L. MacQueen, 'Mixture or Muddle?—Teaching and Research in Scottish Legal History', 1997 *ZEuP* 369; R. Evans-Jones, 'Receptions of Law, Mixed Legal Systems and the Genius of Scots Private Law' (1998) 114 *LQR* 228; H. L. MacQueen, 'Scots Law and the Road to the New *Ius Commune*', M. Hesselink *et al* (eds.), *Ius Commune Lectures on European Private Law* (2000) and W. D. H. Sellar, 'Scots Law: Mixed from the Very Beginning? A Tale of Two Receptions', (2000) 4 Edinburgh LR. 3.

[7] See D. L. Carey Miller, 'Stair's Property: A Romanist System?', [1995] *JR* 70 and *idem*, 'Derivative Acquisition of Moveables', in R. Evans-Jones (ed.), *The Civil Law Tradition in Scotland* (1995), 128.

of the transfer of ownership of heritable (immoveable) property the various matters central to the actual process of transfer and the manner in which the consequences of transfer are dealt with will be considered under the following headings: II. A unitary system?; III. The feudal context; IV. Conveyancing in the feudal context; V. Sasine; VI. Prescription; VII. The modern system; VIII. Consequences of transfer; IX. Conclusion.

II. A UNITARY SYSTEM?

Looking initially at the present position one may note that Professor Kenneth Reid, in the property volume of the *Stair Memorial Encyclopaedia*, presents the view that a bifurcation of Scottish property law commenced in the nineteenth century with the classic Edinburgh lectures of Professor David Hume as the point of departure.[8] Hume, who held the Chair of Scots law from 1786 to 1822, maintained the integrity of the law of property but, recognizing the distinctive and specialized nature of land law, divided the treatment of the subject between general principles and land law. Hume's immediate successor as Professor of Scots law, George Joseph Bell, commenced the departure from a unified law of property by treating moveable and heritable property separately without concession to any notion of underlying general principles.[9] As Reid notes the bifurcation of the subject was entrenched by the creation of a chair of conveyancing at Edinburgh in 1825—soon after the commencement of Bell's tenure of the Chair of Scots Law. The moveable/heritable dichotomy which came to overshadow any notion of underlying general principles of property was probably seen to be justified because, in important respects, land law was a product of the development of feudal law whereas the law in respect of moveable property was traditionally seen to be more or less civilian.

That Hume saw the process of transferring ownership as something common to all forms of property is clear from the concise statement opening his treatment of derivative acquisition.

The natural way of transferring property, whether moveable or immoveable, is by an agreement to convey as in property, followed with delivery, real or symbolical, of the thing. These two circumstances (I have said) must concur in any case towards transference of the real right.[10]

---

[8] Reid (n. 5), § 1.
[9] Reid, ibid., refers to this treatment being noticeable in Bell's *Lectures* and followed in his *Principles* which first appeared in 1829 based on the lectures. The section on property begins with an introduction in which the difference between heritable and moveable subjects and the importance of feudal law for the former is noted. It concludes as follows: 'These different systems it may be proper to consider separately; taking first into view the jurisprudence of Land rights, and proceeding afterwards to the doctrines of property in Moveables.' (Bell, *Principles*, § 636.)
[10] Hume, *Lectures*, III, 245.

The natural logic of an agreement to transfer necessarily preceding an identifiable act of handing over was presented by Hume on the basis of the premise of a 'power of disposal'.[11] The analysis of derivative acquisition—from both a philosophical and a practical perspective—in terms of a transferor's empowering right of disposal, with transfer given effect to by an appropriate dispositive act, independently agreed to by the parties, was, of course, well understood in Scots law having been clearly explained by Stair.[12]

It is significant that Hume notes reservations, on two fronts, in respect of the application to land of the natural philosophical analysis of the transfer of ownership. He first draws attention to the historic factor of the interests of the family at least de facto inhibiting the free exercise of a power of disposal of land. While conceding that the relevance of this consideration has diminished he also observes that 'there remained to be got the better of, in all the Countries which received the plan of Feudal Property, another and equally troublesome restraint, from the interest and privileges of the superior'.[13] Hume goes on to note that because the feudal factor has 'entered deeply into the structure of the law of Land Rights' feudal property has to be dealt with separately.[14]

III. THE FEUDAL CONTEXT

Accepting that the primary impact of the feudal system is in regulating the basis upon which land is held—the system of tenure—in what way did this affect the process of transfer of property? This question can only be answered by examining the difference between what was involved in the Romanist system of 'absolute' or, perhaps more accurately, 'outright' ownership ('allodial' tenure in the Germanic terminology of feudalism[15]), and the subsequently developed system of holding subject to the ultimate right of a superior. In the Roman system the justification for the label of 'absolute ownership' is that in respect of any particular item of owned property, at any given point in time, the owner has an absolute right of disposal. The central importance of this, as the hallmark of ownership (*dominium*), is demonstrated by the basic notion of ownership in which the right of disposal (designated *abusus*) is the core or residual right which must remain available for the right to subsist as one of ownership—although, it should be noted, not all aspects of civilian development remain fully consistent with this model. This fundamental requirement leads to a relatively simple notion of ownership in which lesser rights may be hived off by the owner provided the ulti-

---

[11] Hume, *Lectures*, III, 243.
[12] Stair, III, 2, 3. On Stair's analysis of derivative acquisition see, generally, my 'Systems of Property: Grotius and Stair', in D. L. Carey Miller and D. W. Meyers (eds.), *Comparative and Historical Essays in Scots Law* (1992), 13. [13] Hume, *Lectures*, III, 245.
[14] Ibid. [15] Craig, I, 9, 24. Further discussion of this point appears in Stair, II, 3, 4.

mate right of disposal is retained. On this basis ownership is taken to be constituted by the simple generalized breakdown into rights of *usus, fructus,* and *abusus*; it being open to the owner to part with the rights to use and to fruits and remain owner provided the right of disposal is retained. In respect that the right of disposal is the core feature of ownership, and insofar as the civilian system did not allow for any possible form of breakdown of this right, ownership was said to be indivisible. By contrast, the feudal system's defining characteristic of an ultimate superior necessarily implies a limitation of the concept of ownership. Professor J. M. Halliday referred to this fundamental difficulty of fit with reference to the development of Scots law in his contribution to the Stair Society's volume published to mark the tercentenary of the publication of Stair's *Institutions of the Law of Scotland*.

To the medieval jurists there were formidable theoretical difficulties in accommodating within a predominantly civilian system the concepts of feudalism which had not existed in the classical period of Roman law. In particular the traditional civilian view of *dominium* was that it was indivisible: there could be derivative rights *utendi* or *fruendi*, but the *res* remained with the *dominus*.[16]

The ingenuity of the medieval Glossatorial school of jurists produced the solution to the problem of locating ownership in the feudal dispensation by the recognition of the concept of *dominium utile*.[17] It may be noted, however, that the true origin and reason for the medieval emergence of the concept of *dominium utile* is a matter of academic debate,[18] with, apparently, only one school of thought accepting that the Glossators were concerned with providing an explanation for the system of feudal landholding.[19] What is significant for present purposes is that the Glossatorial solution was accepted in subsequent legal thinking as the appropriate analysis of the feudal division of rights.[20] Professor G. L. Gretton has summarized the relevant development in this regard in his contribution on the feudal system in the property volume of the *Stair Memorial Encyclopaedia*.

---

[16] J. M. Halliday, 'Feudal Law as a Source', in D. M. Walker (ed.), *Stair Tercentenary Studies* (1981), 136.

[17] See G. L. Gretton, 'Feudal System', in *The Laws of Scotland: Stair Memorial Encyclopaedia*, vol. 18 (1993), § 49 in which Gretton notes that the terms *dominium directum* and *dominium utile* are traditionally attributed to Accursius but were, in fact, used earlier by Pillius (Pilius) a 12th-century Bologna professor. The leading study on this is R. Feenstra, 'Les Origines du Dominium Utile chez les Glosateurs', in *idem, Fata Iuris Romani* (1974), 215–59.

[18] See the valuable survey of A. J. van der Walt and D. G. Kleyn, 'Duplex Dominium: The History and Significance of the Concept of Divided Ownership', in D. P. Visser (ed.), *Essays on the History of Law* (1989), 213 at 235–43.

[19] See Van der Walt/Kleyn (n. 18), 236–40. What would appear to be the more plausible view is the one presented by Dutch scholars to the effect that the Glossators were simply addressing a contemporary problem in what was a direct analysis of the nature of feudal rights. See M. Meijers, 'Les Glossateurs et le droit feodal', (1934) 2 *TR* 129; R. Feenstra (n. 17). See also regarding the Glossators and feudal law the lucid survey of W. M. Gordon, *Studies in the Transfer of Property by Tradition* (1970), 194–202.

[20] See the observations of Lord Balgray in *Hamilton v. Bogle* (1819) 1 Ross LC 22 at 26–7.

A compromise was adopted, at some violence both to feudal and to civilian principles, by saying that feudal land was in multiple ownership, the superior having ownership of one sort, to which the name *dominium directum* was given, and the vassal ownership of another sort, *dominium utile*. These terms were the inventions of the Glossators, and were adopted throughout Europe, including, of course, Scotland.[21]

But, as Professor Gretton notes,[22] there was not universal agreement in post-medieval legal thought concerning the nature of the vassal's right. The sixteenth-century jurist Cujacius (Cujas) in his *Libri Feudorum* (1566) interpreted it as a usufruct with undivided *dominium* vesting in the superior, an analysis which, of course, fitted the Roman concept of ownership.[23] Again, what is decisive for present purposes is that Scotland's seventeenth-century institutional writer on feudal law Craig adopted the notion of ownership divided on the *dominium directum, dominium utile* basis.[24] Professor Halliday[25] notes appositely that the most compelling reason for Craig's conclusion 'is that the notion of a vassal's right, transmissible to his heirs, being a mere usufruct was unacceptable to Scottish landowners who regarded themselves as proprietors of their estates'.

That the labelling of the vassal's right as *dominium utile* did not signify any affinity to the notion of usufruct—on the basis of the simple tripartite Roman breakdown *usus, fructus, abusus*—is confirmed by what is accepted concerning the derivation of the term. This is simply that the right accorded the vassal to recover the property from a third party was not an outright *vindicatio* but a derivative extension of that action designated *actio utilis*—thus '*dominium utile*'.[26]

IV. CONVEYANCING IN THE FEUDAL CONTEXT

1. The conveyancing template

It is important to note that the system of conveyancing, as it developed in Scots law, was essentially a framework, or template, giving scope for variation in the balance between superior and vassal as regards the critical issue of

---

[21] Gretton (n. 17), § 49. [22] Ibid., § 50.
[23] See John W. Cairns, 'Craig, Cujas, and the Definition of *feudum*', in Peter Birks (ed.), *New Perspectives in the Roman Law of Property* (1989), 75 at 81 where the author translates the relevant passage of Cujacius, *De Feudis* (Cologne edn. of 1588), 10, as follows: '[A] right in perpetuity of using and taking the fruits from another's land, which the owner gives as a benefice by this law so that he who receives it offers fealty, and military duty or another service to the owner.' Craig, I, 9, 10 and 11 discusses Cujacius' opinion in detail but rejects it.
[24] Craig, I, 9, 11. See also Stair, II, 3, 7. [25] Halliday (n. 16), 136–7.
[26] See Craig, I, 9, 11; Stair, II, 3, 7. See also W. M. Gordon, *Scottish Land Law* (2nd edn., 1999), para. 2-03; Gretton (n. 17), § 49.

control. Professor W. M. Gordon[27] has explained this in his definitive work on modern land law:

> How extensive the respective estates of superiors and vassals are depends, of course, on the terms of the grant. A superior who makes a grant on blench tenure, making no reservations to himself, say, of minerals, and imposing no conditions on his vassal, will have very little more than the name of superior. For all practical purposes the vassal will be an unfettered owner of the land and, as the holder of the *dominium utile*, might well be regarded as 'the owner'.

As this quotation implies, the matter of the terms of a particular grant was something distinguishable from the form of feudal tenure on the basis of which the grant was made. While the terms of the grant controlled the balance of *dominium* between superior and vassal the various forms of tenure[28] 'were distinguished according to the services fixed as consideration for the feudal grant'.[29] The latter are of limited relevance in the context of the present chapter but it may be noted that the blench form referred to by Professor Gordon in the passage quoted was the general form of tenure involving a minimal, possibly nominal, service factor.[30]

Accepting the feudal division of the right of ownership, what is involved in the constitution of the right and what is the position concerning transmission of the *dominium utile*? In respect of both these matters Scots feudal conveyancing, throughout its development, proceeded on a basis which could readily be recognized from a civilian perspective. But, of course, the fact that the system caused the right of ownership to be rent and apportioned between superior and vassal made it inevitable that there would be differences from the straightforward case of an absolute owner transferring the full right to one receiving the same. What the constitution of feudal title was seeking to do—and what its transmission was seeking to perpetuate—was, of course, in principle, foreign to the notion of property of Roman law. That it came, over a period of some centuries, to be analysed and enunciated in civilian terms— as Stair notes 'the Roman civil law ... did take in with it the feudal customs'[31]—is a statement about the *jus commune* and, so it would seem with the benefit of hindsight, rather more than what may have been the original Glossatorial aim of explaining Germanic custom in Roman terminology.[32]

The starting point of the coming into being of a feudal right in land is described by Stair following Craig.[33]

---

[27] Gordon (n. 26), para. 2-30. See also, generally, Gordon (n. 19), 190–209.
[28] Described by Stair, II, 3, 15. [29] Gordon (n. 26), para. 2-08.
[30] See Craig, I, 9, 22. [31] Stair, II, 3, 1. [32] See Van der Walt/Kleyn (n. 18), 236.
[33] See Craig, II, 1, 5. Halliday (n. 16), 137 comments: 'As to the constitution of feudal infeftment of property, Stair again follows the principles enunciated by Craig, but states them more succinctly and with greater clarity. To Craig a feudal grant was in origin a donation which in remuneratory grants contained an element of bargain since the feu was contracted for on consideration of performance of some duty or service.'

To come now to the constitution of the property of lands, in fee and heritage, the feudal contract is of itself alienative, as loan, sale, exchange, and the contracts in law, called, *do ut des*, and *do ut facias*: of which last two, the feudal contract is a kind, seeing thereby land or other immoveable is given, for giving or doing something . . .[34]

In the same passage Stair proceeds to identify the actual conveyance of property in terms of the requirements of the civil law.

[T]herefore, as in others, so in it, the will of the owner must constitute the right in the vassal; and seeing by the custom of nations, some kind of possession is necessary to constitute or transfer property, the superior's delivery of possession to the vassal, or acknowledgement and approbation thereof in the vassal, to be holden by him in fee, were sufficient to constitute and perfect the fee.[35]

2. Infeftment

The constitution of a feudal right in favour of a vassal came to be designated 'infeftment';[36] as Stair[37] noted '[i]nfeftment or infeudatio, signifieth the right constitutive of a fee'.[38] A vassal became 'infeft' upon receiving 'sasine' of the land. The development of this central aspect of the process of delivery is summarized by Professor Gordon.[39]

This originally meant that he had been formally inducted into possession of the land, with symbolical delivery of the land to him on the land itself. The ceremony was recorded in an instrument of sasine drawn up by a notary—an instrument also referred to as 'a sasine'. From the fifteenth century the instrument of sasine became the only admissible evidence of the ceremony of giving sasine. When a system of registration of deeds was set up, as it was on a permanent basis in the seventeenth century, the main deeds registered were instruments of sasine and the registers were called Registers of Sasines.[40]

In the case of the initial constitution of the vassal's tenure, the entirely familiar act of conveyance transferring possession is applied and the only material difference is that the nature of the right created is feudal rather than

---

[34] Stair, II, 3, 10. As Halliday (n. 16), 137 notes Stair follows Craig in labelling the constituting contract of feu as *do ut facias*, a contract 'created by the will of the superior with [the contemplation of] delivery of possession and acceptance thereof by the vassal to be held in fee'.

[35] Ibid.

[36] H. H. Monteath, 'Heritable Rights: From Early Times to the Twentieth Century', in G. Campbell H. Paton (ed.), *An Introduction to Scottish Legal History*, Stair Society, vol. 20 (1958), 156 notes the literal meaning as, 'clothing with the fief'; this being 'the step, in conveying heritable property under feudal tenure, by which a real right is constituted'.

[37] See Stair, II, 3, 12.

[38] As an example of this see also *Purves v. Strachan* (1677) 2 Ross LC 140: It was held that a vassal resigning is not divested until infeftment is expede on the charter following on the resignation.

[39] Gordon (n. 26), para. 2-05.

[40] See also John Craigie, *Scottish Law of Conveyancing, Heritable Rights* (3rd edn., 1899), 30–64; J. M. Halliday, *Conveyancing Law and Practice in Scotland*, vol. 2 (2nd ed., 1997), paras. 31.18–22.

allodial. It is significant, as Erskine notes, that the constitution of '[t]he udal right of the stewartry of Orkney and Shetland is of the same nature'.[41] When, however, the transmission of a vassal's *dominium utile* to a subsequent vassal comes into contemplation the question of the role of the superior arises.

3. Role of superior

Given the superior's position in the division of *dominium* between superior and vassal it was necessary that the superior be involved in any act of disposition by the vassal. Stair's passage, quoted above,[42] makes this point in the economical statement that 'the will of the owner must constitute the right in the vassal'. Professor Gretton explains the position in the *Stair Memorial Encyclopaedia*.[43]

> The feudal problem was that the consent of the superior was requisite. This was a matter of first principles, for a superior cannot, by the feudal law, acquire a new vassal without giving entry to that vassal, in other words investing him, which involved among other things the rigmarole of sasine.

Even in subinfeudation—in which the original superior remained superior to the original vassal, with the right/duty relationship prevailing, while the latter became a 'midsuperior' to the new holder of the property—although modern experts say that the position is somewhat obscure, the superior's consent was probably required,[44] while, apparently, in continental Europe this was not the case.[45] In any event, in the case of an outright disposition of the fee,[46] in which the grantee was substituted as vassal, the common law requirement of consent by the superior is clearly stated by Stair.[47] H. H. Monteath, former Edinburgh Professor of Conveyancing (1935–55), has commented on the requirement of consent in amplification of the observation that '[u]ntil 1874[48] the superior was an active participant'.[49]

According to ancient feudal ideas the vassal had no power to alienate his feu. The grant was personal to him, originally entailing fealty and service, the superior thus

---

[41] Erskine, II, 3, 18.
[42] See Stair, II, 3, 10, quoted above, text at n. 35; see also Craig, III, 1, 13.
[43] Gretton (n. 17), § 99.
[44] Stair, II, 3, 32 states that land held on wardholding could not be subinfeudated without the Lord's consent; Erskine, II, 3, 13 indicates that the vassal is free to subfeu. The position is discussed by Gretton (n. 17), § 58.
[45] Ibid. The authority which Gretton cites for the view that consent was not required is F. L. Ganshof, *Qu'est-ce que la Féodalité?* (1944, in English *Feudalism*), 3, 2, XV. However, he points out that it may be doubted whether this is strictly true and cites *Libri Feudorum*, I, 13. See also Gordon (n. 26), para. 2-04.
[46] As in 'property' signifying the right concerned as well as the subject to which it applied. See Stair, II, 3, 5.
[47] Stair, II, 3, 5.
[48] Conveyancing (Scotland) Act 1874, s. 4.
[49] Monteath (n. 36), 160.

having a *delectus personae*. By the time the feudal system was introduced into Scotland in the 11th century, feus had for long been inheritable, but transmission to a singular successor was an entirely different thing, being viewed as an invasion of the superior's prerogative, and only to be contemplated with his consent, which in fact was often given, and alienation appears to have been recognised in towns, if sale was the only means by which a vassal could keep above the starvation level.

As regards the strict legal position Professor Gretton[50] has shown that the power of disposition *a me*, aiming to substitute the grantee for the granter as vassal, was subject to a gradual and protracted development from legislation in 1469[51] which allowed a creditor of the vassal to obtain the property. Case law authority of some two centuries later recognizes the superior as being obliged to enter the vassal.[52] In a subsequent passage Professor Gretton sums up the development.

We have seen that after 1469 this consent could be compelled if necessary by a collusive litigation between disponer and disponee, and that after the Tenures Abolition Act 1746 it could be compelled by a non-collusive action, but until the Conveyancing (Scotland) Act 1874 it was still necessary as a conveyancing formality.[53]

Accepting the justification in principle for the consent to disposition requirement it necessarily followed that the vassal could not act in any manner effectively to give a better title than he had. Various rules were recognized in early Scottish legal development to protect the continuation of the status quo in the event of any attempt to contrary effect by the vassal.[54] Thus Hope[55] notes: 'Lands may not be disponed to be haulden of the disponer, bot of his immediat superior in the same manner as he held them himself.' That this gives effect to a civilian principle is less significant than that it is the only rational position open to the law.

4. Alternative forms in development of conveyancing

Different as well as alternative forms of disposition applied through the centuries of development leading up to the modern system of conveyancing. In attempting to identify the main aspects of the developments I rely on and largely follow the account of Professor G. L. Gretton in the *Stair Memorial Encyclopaedia*.[56]

In the simple form of conveyance *a me de superiore meo* the disponer dropped out of the feudal chain on the basis of an act of substitution of the

---

[50] Gretton (n. 17), § 59.   [51] Diligence Act 1469, APS, II, 96 (c. 23).
[52] See *Black* v. *Pitmedden* (1632) Mor 201; *Scot* v. *Elliot of Stobs* (1636) Mor 201; *Cowan* v. *Lord Elphingstoun* (1636) Mor 202; *Elizabeth Ramsay* v. *Ker of Westnisbet* (1667) Mor 203. See also Craig, III, 1, 13.   [53] Gretton (n. 17), § 99.
[54] Ibid., § 59.   [55] Hope, *Practicks*, III, 3, 1.   [56] Gretton (n. 17), § 99 sq.

disponee.[57] In this form entry as vassal could be obtained by the disponee in two ways. The first method was for the disponer to resign his interest in favour of the superior, the later practice being to appoint an agent to effect the resignation whereupon the superior would grant a fresh charter to the disponee. This 'charter of resignation' included a 'precept of sasine'[58]—i.e. an authorization for the disponee to take sasine; when he had done so an instrument of sasine would be granted which, after 1617, would be recorded to perfect the title. An alternative to disposition following resignation by the grantor was entry by confirmation. In this, somewhat more streamlined form, the clause providing for the grantor's resignation was followed by a precept of sasine on the basis of which the disponee would take sasine and (from 1617) record the instrument of sasine.[59] The merely '*de facto*' sasine which the grantee had obtained only became '*de jure*' when the superior ratified and adopted it in a 'charter of confirmation'.[60] Professor Gretton notes[61] that the confirmation form is probably later than the more pedantic resignation form and that it came to be more widely used.

Professor Gretton[62] goes on to observe that both the resignation and confirmation modes of disposition were deficient from the disponee's perspective in that a real right was only acquired on the basis of the cooperation of the superior[63]—in the confirmation form only on the basis of the very last act in the process. As Professor Monteath[64] noted '[a] sasine *a me*, unconfirmed, was of course no better than a personal title'.[65] The weakness has not only been recognized by modern writers. Bell[66] drew attention to the unsatisfactory nature of disposition by confirmation in that it was 'null and ineffectual, in so far as respects the superior and the feudal right, until confirmed by the superior's charter' and, in consequence, open to attachment at the instance of the undivested disponer's creditors. Bell[67] shows the vulnerability of the process to intervening acquisition by a bona fide party who obtains sasine.

Another early development in conveyancing practice—described by Monteath[68] as an 'extraordinary device' avoided the problem of a hiatus in which the right sought was vulnerable to events outwith the control of the grantee. Disposition *a me vel de me*,[69] which could be based on either the

---

[57] Erskine, II, 3, 20 gives a concise account of this form of conveyance.
[58] On the use of this see Stair, II, 3, 16; Erskine, II, 3, 33.
[59] For a discussion of this see Craig, II, 2, 17–18; Stair, II, 3, 16–17; Erskine, II, 3, 34–5.
[60] On the effect of a charter of confirmation see the cases listed in Morison's *Dictionary*, 6459 sqq.   [61] Gretton (n. 17), § 99.
[62] Ibid., § 100.   [63] See *Purves* v. *Strachan* (1677) 2 Ross LC 140.
[64] Monteath (n. 36), 162–3.
[65] This is confirmed by the cases of *The Queen* v. *George Cranston of Corsbie* (1566) Mor 3007 and *Balmernock* v. *Coutfield* (1620) Mor 3007.
[66] G. J. Bell, *Principles of the Law of Scotland* (4th edn., 1839), § 807.   [67] Ibid., § 813.
[68] Monteath (n. 36), 162.
[69] Craigie (n. 40), 319–22 gives an account of the history of this device.

resignation or the confirmation form,[70] achieved this by a process involving two separate acts of acquisition on different bases. The initial act, involving a *de me* disposition, made the disponee a sub-vassal of the disponer pending the displacement of this state by the adoption of a form under which the disponee became the outright vassal, under an *a me* disposition. The effect of the first stage was to give the disponee the *dominium utile* while the disponer was left with a 'commercially barren midsuperiority'.[71] On this basis a proprietary right was acquired by the disponee. Hume[72] shows the utility of this for the disponee.

Now, if this plan was followed, then, according to a convenient construction, which came to be received in practice, the infeftment was in the meantime, held to be a base one; and this for the benefit of the disponee, who thus secured the property, or *dominium utile*, against the granting of double rights by his own author, and also against the diligence of his author's creditors, adjudging.

Regularization was obtained by what, in the circumstances, amounted to a formal act of confirmation by the superior. Philosophical rationality was subsumed under form and the desired effect was achieved by something amounting to legal sleight of hand. In Monteath's[73] description of the final stage there is reference by implication to the stratagem he has already expressly alluded to.

When the disponee found it expedient or imperative to enter with the true superior, he produced his *a me* charter and the ambiguous instrument of sasine, which fitted the *a me* charter equally well, and he had these confirmed.

Professor Gretton's[74] overall assessment puts the emphasis upon a tension between the particular utility factor and the objective priority of rationality.

There is no escaping the verdict that the disposition *a me vel de me* was a convoluted conception, which reflects well on the ingenuity of its unknown inventor, but poorly on the coherence of conveyancing as a logical system. For it involved a sort of doublethink, namely thinking of one and the same disposition as a disposition *de me* at one time but as a disposition *a me* at another time.

Disposition *a me vel de me* may be seen as an instance of what was probably inevitable in the move away from the controlling feudal feature of the superior's consent, a development which was a central feature in the coming into being of a system of conveyancing in Scotland appropriate to changing patterns of landholding. The particular device was plainly a response to the problem of vulnerability of title to land; a problem which, it will be shown below, has emerged as a serious difficulty in present-day Scots law as a consequence of a particular instance of legal borrowing.

---

[70] See Gretton (n. 17), § 100.
[71] Monteath (n. 36), 163.
[72] Hume, *Lectures*, IV, 304.
[73] Monteath (n. 36), 163.
[74] Gretton (n. 17), § 100.

Transfer of Ownership

The same tension is evident in respect of a simplified form of conveyancing applying in royal burghs, giving 'burgage' tenure,[75] which provided an exception to the requirement of consent by the superior.[76] This is shown by Hume who gives an account of divergent views on the effect of a form in which 'seisin is given instantly by the magistrate of the burgh, to the purchaser, or his attorney, *unico contextu* with the act of resignation'.[77] Craig[78] canvasses Roman law authority[79] in some detail in making the point that if the disponor is not divested in favour of a first party it must necessarily remain open for property to be passed to a subsequent party. On the basis of what he sees as a departure from principle Craig comments that 'this innovation upon ancient doctrine and practice wholly fails to commend itself'.

Hume,[80] some two centuries later, explains the development which, in the case of burgage tenure, gave a real right on the basis of a fiction of consent by the superior as a gradual recognition of the de facto primacy of the vassal's position.

> The truth is,—it was quite natural that such a change of doctrine should in the course of time take place. Very long ago, in the times of the pure feudal law,—while the history of things was fresh,—the superior's title was the main and fundamental matter: he was the author of the right,—the donor of the lands;—and the resignation just replaced them in his hands, to be given away again, as if by a new gift, like the former, and a gift, you observe, which he could not then be constrained to make. But this notion etc. grew gradually weaker, owing to the long devolution of the lands in the family of the vassal; and the superior came to be viewed, more and more, as a person ministerially engaged in this business, and resorted to by the parties, in the way of form, to accomplish the transmission.

Hume, however, makes it clear that the evolution of what was required in terms of the superior's consent did not lead to any general departure from the prerequisite of participation by the superior. From a doctrinal point of view one might go further and identify the fictitious act of resignation of burgage tenure as an underlining of the formal necessity of retaining an at least token role of the superior. That the development was more concerned with simplification of process than departure from principle is evident from what Hume[81] says, immediately following the above quotation, regarding the general position in respect of the transmission of rights in the case of resignation *ad favorem*.

> Thus it was naturally inferred, that until this purpose was fully gained, by charter and seisin, in the person of the disponee, the resigner himself was still in the feudal right;

---

[75] See Craig, I, 10, 31; Gordon (n. 26), 2–11. *Town of Peebles* v. *The Lady Halton* (1628) Mor 6885.
[76] Gretton (n. 17), § 59.   [77] Hume, *Lectures*, IV, 281.   [78] Craig, III, 1, 17.
[79] Referring to C. 6, 35, 11; Pap. D. 4, 6, 20; Inst. 2, 9; Paul. D. 41, 2, 1, 5; Inst. 2, 1, 47; Ulp. D. 41, 7, 1; Pomp. D. 41, 7, 5, 1; Gai. D. 35, 2, 76, 1; Ulp. D. 41, 2, 34.
[80] Hume, *Lectures*, IV, 282.   [81] Ibid. 282–3.

and that, of course, he may make a second resignation in favour of another disponee; which other, if he gets the first charter and seisin, shall prevail over the former disponee, in a competition for the lands. In so doing, the resigner does indeed contravene his warrandice, and is liable in damages; and so may the superior also be liable, who receives a second resignation in prejudice of his obligation, contracted by his acceptance of a former one. But those consequences are personal to the individuals concerned: they nowise affect the second purchaser, unless he knows of the former right, and is thus participant of their wrong.

This quotation is but another example of a reference to the theme of the distinction between real and personal rights and the critical issue of when a real right comes into being—all a matter of fundamental doctrine in Scots law.

V. SASINE

1. The actuating event

The act of sasine involved the formal delivery of 'the proper symbols'[82] appropriate to the subject being conveyed.[83] Thus the handing over of earth and stone was required for the common case of a conveyance of land; clap and happer for a mill; net and coble for fishing rights; hasp and staple for a burgage tenement and so on.[84] That the giving of sasine was the actuating event which effected a transfer of ownership is universally accepted.[85] Hume,[86] in his authoritative Edinburgh lectures, notes that its importance lies in the fact that '[i]t settles and proclaims, the state of ownership of the whole lands of the kingdom'. As Stair[87] observes the charters which authorized the taking of sasine demonstrated the dispositive will of the superior but their place in the process of conveyance was anticipatory of the act itself:

[Y]et they never become a real right till they be completed by seasin, which imports the taking of possession; for seasin and seizure are from the same original, signifying laying hold of, or taking possession: and disseasing is dispossession; and therefore, it is a needless question, whether seasin or possession are distinct, and which are most effectual; for till the solemnity of instruments of seasin was introduced to accomplish the real right of fees, possession was necessary to be joined in the disposition, which possession might either be natural by actual inhabitation, manuring or stocking of the ground, *positione sedium*; or might be civil, by uplifting the fruits and duties: or it

---

[82] Erskine, II, 3, 34.
[83] A failure to use the correct symbols rendered the sasine null: *Ker* v. *Scot's Creditors* (1702) Mor 14310; *Carnegy* v. *Creditors of Cruikshanks* (1729) Mor 14316; *Brechin Town Council* v. *Arbuthnot* (1840) 3 D 216.
[84] See Craig, II, 7, 6; Erskine, II, 3, 36. See also Gretton (n. 17), § 90.
[85] See Craig, II, 7, 1; Erskine, II, 3, 17. See also above, text to nn. 36–8.
[86] Hume, *Lectures*, IV, 169.   [87] Stair, II, 3, 16.

might be symbolical, *positione pedum*, by entering upon the land as vassal upon the superior's warrant.

In a passage which has been influential in a landmark modern case[88] Erskine[89] notes the significance of the requirement that the feudal right only vests in the transferee upon the taking of seisin.

> A charter or disposition which is not followed by seisin, creates in the disponee a right barely personal. It lays the granter and his heirs under an obligation to divest themselves agreeably to the tenor of the grant. But it has not the effect of transferring to the acquirer the feudal right of the lands; and consequently, the subject may be affected and carried off from the disponee, before his taking infeftment, by any debt or diligence which is capable of divesting the disponer, in whom the feudal right of the lands still continues vested. A creditor or purchaser, therefore, contracting with one who has a bare personal right to the subject, rests not on the security of the records, but contracts at his peril, and must accept of the right as it stands, with all its burdens, and be affected with every declaration or deed, however latent, which could affect his author. But from the moment that the author perfects his right by seisin, the grantee, if he purchases from the true proprietor, acquires a complete real right in the subject; which therefore secures him, as soon as his own right is protected by seisin, against the consequence of all deeds, even seisins themselves, the registration of which is posterior, though the charters that they proceed upon should be prior in date to his.

Hume's *Lectures* have recently been identified by Lord Coulsfield as 'one of the clearest and most authoritative' descriptions of the development of the Scottish system of property law.[90] The following passage is quoted by the learned judge to show the limited nature of a merely personal right not made real by sasine. The passage also illustrates the extent to which the feudal conveyancing of Scotland reflects civilian dogma.

> Let us now return one step further back on the investiture, and suppose, that charter only has been given, or disposition executed, but that no seisin has followed. You will here anticipate the consequence, which is, that there is no real investiture, but the constitution only of an ordinary personal right or *jus ad rem* to the lands—such a right as is good, indeed, against the granter and his heirs, or others who come into his place, and are liable to the like personal obligation as he,—but which shall not stand the test of trial with any perfect investiture acquired by a third party, who has no concern with and is not reached by that objection. The deed of conveyance, not followed with seisin, which is the feudal delivery of the lands, (and as necessary as the real delivery is in the case of moveable *corpora*) is a mere expression of consent; neither divests the disponer nor really qualifies, nor intrinsically limits his previous feudal right to the lands. Being still vested with that feudal right he can, therefore, effectually make it over to another, who can defend himself therein, and maintain his right.[91]

---

[88] *Sharp v. Thomson* 1995 SLT 837.
[89] Erskine, II, 3, 48.
[90] *Sharp v. Thomson* 1995 SLT 859.
[91] Hume, *Lectures*, IV, 182–3.

2. Real/personal rights dichotomy

From the earliest reported case law one finds disputes relating to ownership of land dealt with on the basis of the fundamental civilian dichotomy of personal and real rights. In the seventeenth-century case of *Warnock* v. *Anderson*[92] an arrester was preferred in a competition with a wadsetter because the act of sasine—the only basis of a complete real right to the land—was subsequent to the arrestment. Similarly, in the eighteenth-century case of *Mitchell* v. *Ferguson*[93] the Lords found in favour of a creditor, whose right of security, obtained through the process of adjudication, had been completed by infeftment, in a competition with a prior party in possession of the heritable subjects who had a disposition in his favour but had not actually become infeft by act of sasine. The argument of the adjudging creditors proceeded from the proposition that it is 'in the nature of feudal rights, that they cannot be affected, qualified, or burdened by any personal deed' and '[n]otwithstanding even a conveyance, if only personal, the feudal right still remains in the disponer'.[94] The Lords found in favour of this approach. Implicit in their cryptic statement that 'the adjudication, and infeftment following upon it' was preferable 'to the personal disposition'[95] is the notion of a distinct and determinate right of property created by a prescribed formal legal act.

Case law in the 1840s clarified the role of the instruments of sasine in relation to the critical act itself. In *Town Council of Brechin* v. *Arbuthnot*[96] Lord Fullerton described instruments of sasine as follows: 'They are not obligations, but attestations of a fact, the delivery of the lands, which delivery is necessarily so dependant on that attestation, that the attestation may be held to be part of the fact itself.'

In *Young* v. *Leith*[97] the First Division held that an unrecorded sasine did not give title. The decision was appealed to the House of Lords but the Lords remitted the matter to be determined by the Full Court. Lord Fullerton wrote the opinion representing the majority position.[98] In another description of the import of instruments of sasine the opinion states: '[T]hey are attestations of a fact—the delivery of possession; but then they are attestations so indissolubly embodied by law with the fact itself, that the one cannot be separated from the other.'[99] In consequence, the opinion notes: 'In the case of

---

[92] (1633) Mor 2787.   [93] (1781) Mor 10296. See also 3 Ross LC 120.
[94] (1781) Mor 10298.   [95] (1781) Mor 10299.   [96] (1840) 3 D 216 at 229
[97] (1844) 6 D 370.   [98] (1847) 9 D 932.
[99] (1847) 9 D 935. The opinion refers to Stair, II, 3, 16: 'After instruments of seasin became in use, they were not only sustained as the means of probation, that possession or seasin was given or taken, but they were the necessary solemnities to accomplish the right, which could not be supplied by any other means of probation . . . in which sense the vulgar maxim is to be understood, *Nulla sasina nulla terra* . . .'

an original conveyance, the seisin of the disponee, if unregistered, does not divest the granter; for it leaves to him the heritable right, which may be validly acquired from him by a second disponee completing his title by a registered seisin.'[100] The opinion continues on this theme in an important passage which underlines the extent to which the civilian delivery requirement is entrenched.

But if an unregistered seisin does not, and can not prevent third parties from completing a perfect title to the lands, which will in competition be preferable to all rights founded on the unregistered seisin itself, the practical consequence is, that the unregistered seisin, as designative of the act completing a real right, is null. It is not good for the only important purpose which a valid seisin is intended to answer, viz., the prevention of any title which can enter into competition with that seisin.[101]

3. Respective roles of natural and symbolic possession

Walter Ross, in his late eighteenth-century lectures on conveyancing, makes a fundamental point which is relevant to the pervading importance of sasine in Scots law. The point is simply that natural and symbolical possession are not in competition in the sense that the presence of the former makes the latter superfluous. Rather, Ross suggests, the two are complementary. Moreover, the requirement of a symbolic act of the transfer of possession entrenches the critical factor of the transferor's dispositive intent. Ross[102] urges these matters in an important passage:

The distinction we have endeavoured to explain is a capital one in the history of our law, and the understanding of our forms. From thence we shall afterwards find the differences arise between the English and the Scottish system of securities. We therefore repeat it, that the transmission of land property by symbols was not introduced with a design of superseding the actual or natural possession; on the contrary, it was brought in to aid and support that possession. It was brought in, to show that the natural possession had been obtained by the free will of the former possessor, which, in many cases, could only be done by symbol.

Subsequently Ross gives a concise statement of the function of sasine in its context, as a precursor to a detailed analysis of the role of the device.

A charter, then, gives only the right; the precept carries the will, or consent, of the seller to give the possession. The execution of that precept, or the delivery of the

---

[100] (1847) 9 D 937.
[101] (1847) 9 D 938. In the Inner House decision of *Sharp* v. *Thomson* 1995 SLT 837, considered below, Lord Sutherland (at 856) noted that the distinction between property and obligations was 'made quite clear' in *Young* v. *Leith* and that '[t]he opinion of the majority makes it clear that an unregistered sasine may be left operative as a personal obligation but cannot constitute a real right'.
[102] W. Ross, *Lectures on the History and Practice of the Law of Scotland Relative to Conveyancing and Legal Diligence* (2nd edn., 1822), vol. 2, 92.

sasine, completes the right; and the instrument containing the ceremony is, with us, the only legal evidence of its being performed.[103]

This statement follows a somewhat cryptic comment that it must always be borne in mind that 'the delivery, and not the possession, completes the sale'; according to Ross this is in accordance with what is very well understood in Roman law.[104] The point Ross would appear to be making here is that, other things being equal, the act of delivery transmits the right of ownership, i.e. gives title which, of course, may or may not be accompanied by actual possession but necessarily involved an act which represented the 'giving and taking of possession'.[105] Ross[106] goes on to describe in some detail the ceremony of sasine.[107]

The first movement is made by the party, or his attorney, possessor of the charter containing the precept. He requires the attendance of a notary public to certify the act: They next, in virtue of the blank left in the precept for the bailie, choose a person to fill that office, and witnesses to attend the whole fact. Then all of them repair to the ground of the lands described in the charter: When there, the vassal or attorney produces the charter, and desires the notary public, as clerk to the act, to read it. The notary, accordingly, reads it verbatim; and the vassal or attorney desires the bailie to obey the precept, by giving him sasine in terms thereof. The bailie obeys; takes up a parcel of earth and stone of the lands, and delivers them into the hands of the vassal or his attorney, declaring that he thereby gives him real, actual, and corporeal possession of the subject. Upon this the vassal or attorney gives the notary public a piece of money, and desires him to extend an instrument upon the *res gesta*, in the usual form.

As Professor Gretton[108] explains the parties involved could personally carry out the ceremony 'but in the post-medieval period it was done by agents, the agent for the grantor being called the "bailie" or "ballie" and that of the grantee being the "procurator and attorney"'.

4. Scots and English sasine distinguished

The prominence of sasine in Scots law might be taken, on a superficial view, to suggest a close affinity to the means of transmission of rights in land in English law where, of course, the counterpart of 'seisin' was also a central feature. But the better view is that doctrinal features identified, or came to identify, critical differences between the two systems. From a doctrinal point

---

[103] Ross (n. 102), 178. Erskine, II, 3, 48 states that it is by sasine alone that the feudal right is perfected. See also Balfour, *Practicks*, 187; Craig, II, 7, 1; Stair, II, 3, 16.
[104] Ross (n. 102). [105] Gretton (n. 17), § 89. [106] Ross (n. 102), 178–9.
[107] See also Stair, II, 3, 17; Erskine, II, 3, 35; Craigie (n. 40), 42; A. M. Bell, *Lecture on Conveyancing* (3rd edn., 1882), vol. 1, 650–1; A. M. Menzies, *Conveyancing According to the Law of Scotland* (new edn. by J. S. Sturrock, 1900), 544. [108] Gretton (n. 17), § 89.

of view one might venture that the Scots sasine was closer in actual character to the Roman *mancipatio* ceremony than to its English relation, seisin. At a superficial level these are similar—and predictably similar—means of transmission of the 'best right' in land. But what is achieved by the act of transmission depends upon how the best right is defined and, crucially, how the system of hierarchy of rights works. In the case of the Scottish development, at least by the time the foundation sources of the law began to be written, the received civilian doctrinal basis was very much apparent albeit within a form not itself civilian.

A modern history of Scots and English land law identifies the important doctrinal differences between the two systems. Noting the importance of occupation in the development of concepts of title to land the authors observe the critical doctrinal difference between the two systems.

This view has had effects of considerable importance in the development of land law in England and Scotland, especially in the former, if theory be looked at; especially in the latter, if practice is considered. Respect for occupation as such has been a characteristic of English law throughout the centuries. Scotland also well knew the strength of possession as a hard fact and by the strength of a man's right arm, but when order was established and law followed, Scots were too imbued with the sense of legal principle to recognise occupation as such, although an extremely important survival of the older view was that which required a symbolical delivery of possession (sasine) to complete a real right to lands.[109]

While it is beyond the scope of this chapter to consider the English common law it may be worth quoting from the classic modern work of Buckland and McNair[110] comparing English and Roman law.

When, in our ancient courts, two persons were disputing about land, both might have some sort of seisin and the question was, which had the better seisin. The question was never simply which of these two is owner, but which has the better right of the two, which has *maius ius*. 'No one is ever called on to demonstrate an ownership good against all men; he does enough even in a proprietary action if he proves an older right than that of the person whom he attacks.'[111] It is a relative ownership: 'I own it more than you do.' This is very different from the Roman way of thinking.

In contrast it is apparent that from an early stage in the development of the modern system of Scots law the affinity was very much with Roman law in respect of the actual ordering of rights in land. Sasine may have meant possession but what is significant is that obtaining sasine in principle meant acquiring the right of ownership. This, of course, was ownership in the feudal context but that it was recognized, from an early stage, as an ultimate

---

[109] C. F. Kolbert and N. A. M. Mackay, *History of Scots and English Land Law* (1977), 227.
[110] Buckland/McNair (n. 1), 67.
[111] Quoting F. Pollock and F. W. Maitland, *History of English Law* (2nd edn., 1898), vol. 2, 77.

right is clear. Thus Craig,[112] as translated by Lord Clyde, is to the effect that '[t]he vassal has even the right to vindicate the property of the feu—a kind of action which, according to the principles of general law, is never competent to any but the true owner'.[113]

On the basis of this fundamental difference which emerged in the development of the two systems the possible early affinity between English and Scots law becomes irrelevant. It may be noted here that the *Regiam Majestatem*[114] is taken to support the proposition of early affinity.[115] That the *Regiam* provided a possible link between English and Scots law was probably not irrelevant to Craig's emphatic denial of its authority in Scotland;[116] a denial consistent with the strongly civilian agenda which Craig manifests.[117] In any event, what is significant is the very material difference which emerged in the respective development of English and Scots law. After referring to a claimed position of early affinity Kolbert and Mackay[118] go on to note this bifurcation.

> The close affinity between Scots and English land law at the time of the *Regiam Majestatem* suggests that the English law as just set forth then applied also in Scotland. However it was here Scots law which struck out on a new course by requiring formalities and eventually registration to attend the giving of sasine, thereby largely preventing those illegal sasines, which were recognised to such a surprising extent in England. One who occupied land without sasine in the developed law of Scotland was accounted a mere trespasser or tenant at will who could be ejected by the true owners.

It may be observed that the civilian doctrine of a distinctive ultimate right of ownership, arrived at on the basis of a prescribed identifiable legal act, was fundamental to the wholly different route taken by Scots law. The civil law thinking, clearly present in Craig and Stair, is consistent with the *raison d'être* of a distinct right of ownership. On this basis the emphasis on form in Scottish conveyancing may be seen as the building blocks of a system constructed around the essential act of delivery set in a feudal context. English law, in contrast, did not develop any doctrine of an ultimate right of ownership and the circumstances of a system based on relativities of possession did not support the need for a formal act of delivery.[119] As Kolbert and Mackay[120] indicate the result of this doctrinal divergence is to be seen in the

---

[112] Craig, II, 8, 1.   [113] Craig cites Paul. D. 6, 1, 23.   [114] *Regiam Majestatem*, 3, 36.
[115] See Kolbert/Mackay (n. 109), 235; see also 170–3.
[116] Craig, I, 8, 11. On the question of the authority of the work see also Erskine, I, 1, 32–3 and the following modern literature: A. A. M. Duncan, 'Regiam Majestatem, a Reconsideration', [1961] *JR* 199; A. Harding, 'Regiam Majestatem amongst Mediaeval Law Books', [1984] *JR* 97; H. L. MacQueen, 'Regiam Majestatem, Scots Law and National Identity', (1995) 74 *Scot Hist Rev* 1 and *idem, Common Law and Feudal Society in Medieval Scotland* (1993), 89–98.
[117] See Craig, I, 2, 14: 'we in this kingdom are bound by the laws of the Romans insofar as they are in harmony with the laws of nature and right reason.'
[118] Kolbert/Mackay (n. 109), 235.   [119] See above, text to n. 110.
[120] Kolbert/Mackay (n. 109), 235.

difference, in the two systems, between the weak distinction between possession and title in English law and the strong distinction in Scots law.

5. Inherent civilian factor

None of this should be taken to suggest any detraction from the role and significance of sasine but simply to draw attention to the importance of distinguishing, on the one hand, what the law required by way of formality and, on the other hand, the legal consequences which followed from compliance—on non-compliance—with the necessary form. The development of the law concerning the formalities of the giving of sasine and the associated notarial act[121] was marked by relative rigidity and a pervasiveness of the notion *nulla sasina, nulla terra*.[122] This probably shows an increasing concern for the certainty and security, but it does not tell anything about the nature of the right which sasine gave. Although the feudal factor was a dominating feature in the development of the law, its implications were for form. While what was acquired, for very long, had a feudal shape, its fundamental substance was civilian. Moreover, taking an overall view, it is open to argument that the development of the law reflects a shift in what was seen as significant. The emphasis moved from an initial domination of the feudal form to the modern recognition of the overriding importance of the civilian substance, as exemplified by *Sharp* v. *Thomson*, considered below. Indeed the civilian factor was present from an early stage; in this respect it is worth noting that the very brocard of the feudal law—*nulla sasina, nulla terra*—reflects the civilian notion of a real right coming into being on the basis of an act of delivery.

VI. PRESCRIPTION

The civilian tradition of acquisition of property as a process giving primacy to the abstract notion of title allows this badge of ownership to come into being in certain circumstances and subject to certain conditions where it would not otherwise be possible. *Usucapio* provided for the recognition of a title of ownership on the basis of possession for a set period and subject to certain conditions in a process of 'positive' or 'acquisitive' prescription. It may be noted that these labels suffer from fundamental inaccuracy because

---

[121] Gordon (n. 19), 222–36, gives a survey of great clarity and insight.

[122] As Gordon (n. 19), 228 shows, following Craig, II, 7, 8 this maxim came to be interpreted to signify the evidential requirement of a notarial instrument but it was 'also used to express the necessity for infeftment as the basis of any feudal right in land'. Gordon goes on to show that Stair uses the maxim in the former technical (II, 3, 16) as well as the latter abstract (II, 4, 18 and IV, 8, 1) sense and that Erskine also does (II, 1, 11 and II, 3, 34) while Bankton (II, 1, 21) appears to achieve an omnibus definition in taking the maxim to signify symbolical delivery and 'instrument of seisin taken thereupon in the hands of a notary'.

they tend to blur the distinct processes of the acquisition of title by a period of possession and prescription proper—the prescribing of a claimant's right through non-exercise. Scots law, in its development, well understood the position of the civil law in respect of *usucapio* and prescription and Stair gives a detailed survey of it before coming to 'our law concerning prescription'.[123]

The significance of prescription in the present context is that the way in which it has worked in the different stages of its development in Scots law has been consistent with the system's emphasis upon a distinct notion of title. The starting point in demonstrating this is the initial Scottish prescription legislation—acts of 1469[124] and 1474.[125] These acts were concerned with the prescription of obligations—as Stair[126] notes 'personal rights'—rather than rights in property. The identification of the scope of the early legislation as extending to moveable rather than heritable property is unexceptionable insofar as the label 'moveable' is taken in the sense of indicating non-proprietary rights. Whether the legislation was interpreted as applying to moveable property in the sense of a right of property applying to a moveable subject remains a matter of some debate;[127] the better view, consistent with principle involved in the distinction between obligation and property, is that it should not have been interpreted in this way.[128] This said, it is entirely clear that the early legislation was not taken to apply to rights classified as heritable. Thus J. H. Millar, an advocate, in a late nineteenth-century monograph on prescription, writes concerning the scope of the acts of 1469 and 1474 that 'their application was rigorously excluded from anything in the nature of an heritable right'.[129] The author refers to two late sixteenth-century cases[130] which do support the exclusion of heritable rights from the ambit of the legislation.[131]

The nineteenth-century writers on prescription justify the position of the earliest law on the view that, given the feudal factor, it would have been inconceivable to contemplate prescription extending to heritable rights on the basis of mere possession and without a requirement of title in some form. Napier notes that the traditional civilian arguments in justification of pre-

---

[123] Stair, II, 12, 11. Stair's treatment of the civil law is found in the preceding passages: II, 12 1–10. For a history of and justification for prescription from a Scottish perspective, see David Johnston, *Prescription and Limitation* (1999), ch. 1.

[124] Prescription Act 1469, APS, II, 95 (c. 4).

[125] Prescription Act 1474, APS II, 107 (c. 9). [126] Stair, II, 12, 12.

[127] M. Napier, *Commentaries on the Law of Prescription* (2nd edn., 1854), 37 takes it to be clear that it did: 'The term Obligations indicated an application of this prescriptive rule generally to *all moveable rights and actions*, both real and personal . . .'

[128] Even though the effect may have been the same because of the presumption that the possessor of a moveable is its owner; see Stair, II, 12, 13.

[129] *A Handbook of Prescription* (1893), 2.

[130] *Lord Cathcart v. Laird of Gadzat* (1585) Mor 10716; *A v. B* (1589) Mor 10717.

[131] These two cases are also cited by Napier (n. 127), 44, who also refers to a decision of 1575 from Wallace's Collections (Manuscript in the Advocates' Library, Edinburgh) in which the Lords stated: 'quod in regno Scotiae non currit Praescriptio nisi in obligationibus.'

scription 'are apt to be vaguely and confusedly pleaded upon, and without sufficiently close attention to the modifications which that philosophy has undergone in its application to *feudal* rights'.[132] Miller, accepting that there could be no question of the prescription of heritable rights on the basis of mere possession, notes that this puts the untitled feudal proprietor at the mercy of a forger 'or of any one who could produce a perfect series of infeftments with their warrants reaching back to the original grant from the sovereign'.[133] It is interesting to note that Craig, writing when the late fifteenth-century legislation was current, takes an entirely different perspective and is critical of Scots law for failing adequately to recognize the possible application of prescription to the acquisition of feudal title and for failing 'to follow in this respect the principles of the Civil and the Feudal Laws'.[134]

The next stage in the development of the law was legislation which provided for the acquisition of real rights in heritable property by prescription but, significantly, on the basis of a title as a condition precedent to the running of the prescriptive clock.[135] The operative part of the act of 1617[136] required possession 'for the space of forty years, continually and together, following and ensuing the date of their said infeftments'. In truth the legislation was concerned with the remedying of defective titles rather than any concept of acquisitive prescription in the pure sense.[137] Thus Hume[138] states that the essence of the act was to allow the 'favorable circumstance' of possession 'to confirm and validate, his otherwise imperfect, and exceptionable, or at least questionable titles'. But, of course, insofar as the legislation provided for an unimpeachable title following forty years' possession where there was an *ex facie* valid infeftment it was available as a vehicle for acquisition which would not otherwise be possible on a derivative basis.

That this development reflected a general civilian influence in recognizing the primacy of an ultimate right of ownership manifested, in the case of heritable property in Scots law, in a written title seems arguable.[139] Napier,[140] however, saw the development as one which deviated from civil law and reflected feudal influence.

But the right to possess landed property in Scotland is, for the most part, founded on very different principles. By the feudal constitutions a mere possessor of the soil is nothing in a competition for the *right* to possess, while the holder of a written feudal

---

[132] Napier (n. 127), 40.   [133] Millar (n. 129), 3.   [134] Craig, II, 1, 8.
[135] An unrecorded sasine is not sufficient title for prescription: see *Fraser* v. *Hogg* (1679) Mor 10784; *Crawford* v. *McMichen* (1729) 2 Ross LC 112.
[136] Prescription Act 1617, APS IV, 543 (c. 12). Johnson (n. 123), 5 notes the reference to the civil law in the preamble to this statute.
[137] See the dictum of Lord President Hope in *Duke of Buccleuch* v. *Cunynghame* (1826) 3 Ross LC 338 at 342.   [138] Hume, *Lectures*, IV, 510.
[139] Mancipation was never, of course, a prerequisite for prescription in Roman law and the protected bonitary owner was one who had received from the true owner without the formality of mancipation. See Buckland/McNair (n. 1), 64.   [140] Napier (n. 127), 45.

title is every thing. The principle expressed in the brocard *proprietas a possessione separari non potest*, enabled the Romans to protect even the possessor of immoveable property by their negative rule. For possession being their great criterion of property, a certain continuity of its endurance could be taken as absolutely presumptive of property. But while we could take the benefit of such a rule in our doctrine of moveable rights and actions, the principle failed in its application to our heritable possessions, where the controlling brocard is, *nulla sasina nulla terra*. By the feudal constitutions, mere possession, supposing it held *animo dominantis* for any period, is absolutely nothing in estimating the right of property.

That possession was the 'great criterion of property' is, of course, an inaccurate statement applied to the civil law. The statement is only tenable in the context of an acknowledgement that the civilian system of property is founded upon the recognition of an ultimate right of ownership which is a concept quite distinct from that of possession. As Hume[141] observed, the position of Scots law in relation to heritable property is that 'there is no presumption in favor of the possessor' and that 'any person who can shew, that he was once owner of certain lands,—can produce a sufficient title to them,— may recover them from the person possessor, unless he can produce a better and a preferable title'. The resort to the requirement of an *ex facie* valid title in the late sixteenth- and early seventeenth-century reforms of Scots law which introduced the possibility of obtaining a title to land by prescription arguably reflect a 'more civilian than the civilians' approach. While one would not deny that the requirement has its foundation in the entrenchment of the principle *nulla sasina, nulla terra* the better view is that this itself reflected civilian thinking, albeit applied in a feudal context.

In the next part of this chapter it will be suggested that the abandoning of the requirement of the actual act of sasine in the modern system of conveyancing was not of any significance from the point of view of the civilian character of the system.

VII. THE MODERN SYSTEM

The requirement of a formal ceremony of delivery, taking place on the land itself, survived as a prerequisite until the Infeftment Act of 1845. As Professor W. M. Gordon[142] puts it the prescribed symbols of the old law were replaced in this legislation 'by the pen of a notary, in the first step towards total abolition of the symbolical delivery'.

But it is not the case, nor does Professor Gordon suggest that it is, that what was initially an informal act of registration came 'out of the blue' to replace sasine as the critical factor in the transfer of a real right. Rather, it was a matter of a change of emphasis in the context of a development

---

[141] Hume, *Lectures*, IV, 510.   [142] Gordon (n. 26), para. 2-33.

marked by continuity of the notion that a real right could only come into being on the basis of a distinct legal act; a development which, from an early stage, worked hand-in-hand with the recording of changes relating to rights in land. Professor Gordon's survey of the main developments shows both these things.[143] Thus, by the sixteenth century, the legal act of delivery of sasine which gave the transferee a real right required notarization[144] which, from 1617, was itself subject to the additional requirement of recording in a public register.[145] Failure to record a sasine rendered it null.[146] It was not until the mid-nineteenth-century Infeftment Act that the system of creation of real rights on the basis of an actual act of delivery of sasine was rendered de facto obsolete by relegation to optional status. But it must be borne in mind that to establish a real right on the basis of a claim of sasine depended, from a much earlier date, upon requirements of recording and registration. As Professor Gordon[147] notes, priority of right was in 1693[148] made to depend upon the date of competing instruments of sasine by legislation which simplified problems of priorities previously dealt with by interpretation of a statute of 1540.

A more subtle manifestation of the civilian character of Scots law as a system based upon the recognition of an ultimate right of ownership is the emphasis on the aspect of a dispositive act on the basis of which ownership is transferred by an existing owner to a party acquiring the right. On Stair's analysis of the transfer of ownership the 'dispositive will of the owner'[149] is fundamental. Acquisition of owned property *inter vivos* can, in principle, only be on the basis of a derivative act involving the owner. Proof of ownership therefore involves proof of acquisition by the requisite process from the existing owner. In Scots conveyancing the centrality of the derivative act is demonstrated by the prerequisite, which prevailed until 1874,[150] that the word

---

[143] Ibid., paras. 2-32 sqq.
[144] Craig, II, 7, 7 refers to 16th-century legislation providing for the established practice of the notarial attestation of sasines. See also Ross (n. 102), 187 sqq.
[145] Registration Act 1617, APS, IV, 545 (c. 16). In *Logan* v. *Hunter* (1628) Mor 13542 a disponee whose sasine was registered was preferred to an appriser first infeft whose sasine was not registered within 60 days. Prior to 1617 there were several statutes relating to recording: see *Young* v. *Leith* (1847) 9 D 932 *per* Lord Fullerton at 933; see also Erskine, II, 3, 39; Bell (n. 107), 662; Craigie (n. 40), 56; Menzies (n. 107), 556. Generally on the history of recording of real rights in land see L. Ockrent, *Land Rights: An Enquiry into the History of Registration for Publication in Scotland* (1942).
[146] *Paterson* v. *Douglas* (1705) 2 Ross LC 78; see also *Young* v. *Leith* (1847) 9 D 932.
[147] Gordon (n. 26), para. 2-35.
[148] Real Rights Act 1693, APS, IX, 271 (c. 22). On this Act see Erskine, II, 3, 42; Bell (n. 107), I, 664; Menzies (n. 107), 558.
[149] Stair, III, 2, 4. See also Hume, *Lectures*, IV, 128 sqq. Hume cites the cases of *Duke of Hamilton* v. *Douglas* (1762) Mor 4358 and *Ogilvie* v. *Mercer* (1793) Mor 3336. On Stair's basis of derivative acquisition see Carey Miller (n. 12), 14–16.
[150] Conveyancing (Scotland) Act 1874, s. 27.

'dispone' be used in any conveyance of heritable property.[151] Kolbert and Mackay[152] describe this as a 'rigid technicality' but it is a feature consistent with the system reflecting an emphasis which continues to be present in modern law.

The strength of the traditional emphasis of Scots law on registration is very much in contrast to the long-standing position in English law; Kolbert and Mackay[153] observe this.

England has never attempted to compete with Scotland in this regard: indeed it might be fair to say that it is not the early establishment of registration in Scotland which is remarkable, but rather its continued absence as a general institution in England.

Arguably this difference is in a large part to do with the strength of the civilian factor in Scots law. Recording and registration has an obvious place in the context of a system organized on the basis of an ultimate right of ownership which comes into being through a particular prescribed legal act. Where the abstract notion of 'title' prevails there must necessarily be a means of establishing the act upon which title is contingent. In contrast, where property rights are determined by reference to relative rights to possession the circumstances under which possession was obtained takes precedence over any requirement of a formal act of transfer. The strength of the notion of the protection of the bona fide purchaser—'equity's darling'—in English property law and its relative absence from the Scottish scene derives from the difference between an emphasis on the right to possession and the notion of title.

The modern system introduced by the legislative reforms of the nineteenth century[154] involves two stages in the legal process of the transfer of property: the delivery from transferor to transferee of a written deed of conveyance—the 'disposition'—and its registration in a register which, significantly, continued to be called 'the Register of Sasines'. In the usual case of derivative acquisition on the basis of the *causa* of sale these two stages are preceded by a contractual stage know as the 'conclusion of missives' which, of course, does no more than create a personal right between the parties.

Reference to 'the modern system' should not be taken to indicate a break in the continuity of the system of transfer of ownership in land. On the

---

[151] In notes to the first section ('Forms of Conveyance') of 1 Ross's Leading Cases, n. 20, 21–2 the cases of *Henderson* v. *Selkrig* (1795), *Stewart* v. *Stewart* (1803) and *Hamilton* v. *Macdowal* 3 Mar. 1815 FC 302 are referred to in support of the proposition (at 21) that '[A] conveyance of land would not be deemed valid, in which the word "dispone" was omitted.' See also *Kirkpatrick's Trustees* v. *Kirkpatrick* (1874) 1 R (HL) 37.   [152] Kolbert/Mackay (n. 109), 221.
[153] Ibid. 280. Referring to the position before the Land Registration Act 1925.
[154] Infeftment Act 1845; Lands Transference Act 1847; Titles to Land Act 1858; Titles to Land Consolidation Act 1868; Titles to Land Consolidation Amendment Act 1869; Conveyancing (Scotland) Act 1874. See Craigie (n. 40), 64–78 for a discussion of these reforms.

contrary, the modern system has its roots firmly fixed in the conveyancing of the past. Thus Professor Kenneth Reid has observed as follows.

[T]he current method of transfer is defined entirely by reference to the old law, so that registration of the disposition is the equivalent both of feudal entry with the superior by charter of confirmation and of registration of an instrument of sasine, and the deemed registration of the instrument of sasine is itself the equivalent of the giving of sasine by symbolical delivery.[155]

In an important recent decision the then Lord President identified the changes which have occurred, over the course of the development of the law, in the requirements for the creation of a real right in the case of the derivative acquisition of heritable property.

Originally there were three steps: (1) the execution of a charter containing a de praesenti dispositive act of the disponer; (2) delivery of that charter to the disponee; and (3) seisin, which was the formal public ceremony, enacted on the land in question, by which the land was delivered to the disponee by handing over to him the symbols of earth and stone. In the 15th century a further solemnity was added to this list: (4) the execution of an instrument of sasine prepared by a notary who was present to record the ceremony in a notarial instrument, as the only competent evidence of the fact that seisin had been taken:[156] Then, by the Registration Act 1617, c 16, registration of the instrument of sasine in the public register within 60 days was made compulsory.[157]

Lord President Hope went on to note how the nineteenth-century legislation had simplified the process of conveyancing without departure from the fundamental principle of the requirement of a formal act of transfer to create a real right in the transferee.

Reforms introduced during the 19th century, by the Infeftment Act 1845 and the Titles to Land Act 1858, made it possible to dispense with steps (3) and (4). So the ceremony of sasine and the execution and registration of an instrument of sasine might be, and in practice are now always, omitted. But it was not sufficient for the transfer of property to carry out only steps (1) and (2). Step (5) was the statutory equivalent of sasine, the fundamental importance of which is recognised in the maxim nulla sasina nulla terra: Stair, II, 3, 16.[158]

For present purposes it is particularly important to note that the Lord President preceded his remarks with comments which endorse the accepted view of the civilian character of the process of conveyancing in Scots law.

I think it is sufficient for present purposes to note that Scots law has always required a public act of some kind to transfer property in land. This step is the equivalent of traditio in the case of moveables. It is an essential step in the process of transferring

---

[155] Kenneth Reid, 'Transfer of Ownership', in *The Laws of Scotland: Stair Memorial Encyclopedia*, vol. 18 (1993), § 640.
[156] Hume, *Lectures*, IV, 167 cited.
[157] *Sharp v. Thomson* 1995 SLT 837, 846.
[158] Ibid.

ownership, according to the maxim *traditionibus non nudis pactis transferuntur rerum dominia*.[159]

The case in which Lord President Hope identified the basis and critical stages in the development of the conveyancing process of Scots law was concerned with the question of when the real right of ownership came into being in the context of the three-stage system of missives (contract), delivery of disposition and registration of modern law. At the time of the decision the existing leading case law was not completely clear on this issue. The question was central in the circumstances of the case in which the purchasers of a flat had obtained delivery of the disposition, paid, and taken possession of the property but had not yet obtained registration in their names when a creditor of their now insolvent seller company obtained a real right of security against the flat on the basis of a floating charge. This device, imported into Scotland from English law through the Companies Acts, gives a creditor a real right of security—an effective priority over otherwise unencumbered assets held by the company—on the appointment of a receiver. The circumstances meant that the purchasers' only hope was a decision which departed from conventional wisdom and held that a real right, or something amounting to a real right, passed on delivery of the disposition. There was seen to be possible support for a decision to that effect in an analysis of the three stages of transfer given by Lord President Emslie, the immediate predecessor of Lord President Hope.

In the law of Scotland no right of property vests in a purchaser until there has been delivered to him the relevant disposition. On delivery of the disposition the purchaser becomes vested in a personal right to the subjects in question and his acquisition of a real right to the subjects is dependent upon recording the disposition in the appropriate Register of Sasines. Putting the matter in another way, the seller of subjects under missives is not, in a question with the purchaser, divested of any part of his right of property in the subjects of sale until in implementation of his contractual obligation to do so, he delivers to the purchaser the appropriate disposition.[160]

In *Sharp* v. *Thomson*[161] Lord Sutherland observes that in the initial reference to the delivery of the disposition Lord President Emslie states that the purchaser obtains a personal right with the acquisition of a real right dependent on recording. Lord Sutherland notes that the mention of the divesting of the seller is in the context of 'a question between the seller and the purchaser and not a question between the seller or purchaser and third parties'.[162] Accordingly, Lord Sutherland observes:

---

[159] *Sharp* v. *Thomson* 1995 SLT 837, 846.
[160] *Gibson* v. *Hunter Home Designs Ltd* 1976 SC 23 at 27.   [161] 1995 SLT 837 at 857.
[162] Ibid.

In my opinion while the Lord President negatives any suggestion that there is any transfer of property prior to delivery of the disposition he does not necessarily imply that any real right of any kind is transferred after delivery of the disposition.[163]

The affirmation in *Sharp* v. *Thomson* of certain general features of Scots property law as civilian was hardly surprising in the circumstances of the clarity of the institutional writing on the issues concerned. As Professor Kenneth Reid showed in an article[164] following the decision of the Lord Ordinary[165] the features of an ultimate real right of ownership[166] and its indivisibility[167] are matters of first principle in the law of Scotland. In the reclaiming motion already referred to Lord President Hope emphasized the significance of the unititular aspect of ownership in a dictum in which the ultimate character of the concept is clearly accepted.

As Professor K. G. C. Reid has pointed out in Vol 18, *Stair Memorial Encyclopaedia*, para 603, Scots law, following Roman law, is unititular, which means that only one title of ownership is recognised in any one thing at any one time. Although this title can be shared, as in the case of common property, only one person can be the owner in competition with others about ownership. There is no opportunity for fragmentation of the concept of ownership, as the transfer of ownership one to the other occurs in a single moment which, in the case of heritable property, is that of recording the disposition in the appropriate register.[168]

VIII. CONSEQUENCES OF TRANSFER

The consequences which follow from the conclusion of the act of transfer are consistent with its identification as a separate legal act on the basis of which the transferee (or grantee) obtains a real right—the civilian process of the transfer of property. The reasoning here is not circular in the sense of a positive contention that the consequences play a part in establishing the civilian character. Rather, it is merely sought to point out that, in a negative sense, the consequences which are recognized and established are not inconsistent with what is presented as the appropriate model.

The first consequence is that an owner's power to transfer his right is absolute provided his real right of ownership is absolute. This is axiomatic and a necessary consequence of the notion of a real right of ownership which is properly defined in terms of the power of disposal. The acquisition of title to property necessarily implies the acquisition of a power of disposal.[169] Where the right is feudal the relevance of that factor is in the context in which

---

[163] Ibid. [164] '*Sharp* v. *Thomson*: a civilian perspective', 1995 *SLT (News)* 75.
[165] 1994 SLT 1068. [166] Stair, II, 1, 28. [167] Erskine, II, 1, 1.
[168] 1995 SLT 837 at 847. [169] See Stair, II, 1, 28. See *McDonald's Trustee* v. *Aberdeen City Council* 2000 SLT 185 at 192 (*per* Lord Gill) as to the implication arising from an act terminating the power to deal with property as owner.

the right subsists. Hume[170] makes the position clear in a passage in his section on the transmission of feudal rights.

> According to our system, in all questions concerning heritage, the investiture of written titles,—the charter and seisin,—are equivalent to what real possession is—what actual power and command are,—according to the law of nature. They represent,—supersede,—stand, and are received for and instead of the other. Now it is obvious enough, that the powers and privileges of alienation, disposal, incumbrance and so forth, which arise out of this condition of things,—which wait upon the state of natural possession and real command,—must endure, and apply, (must operate and be effectual) as long as the state itself endures,—and that these cannot be extinguished by any transaction, or covenant, of what form soever, which leaves that condition of real connection subsisting, undissolved as before. Tis true the owner, in possession, may have come under engagements as to the disposal of his property, and he is blameable, and shall be liable in damages, if he infringe or forget them. But still, though under promise, he is owner and possessor, undivested of his real power and natural command of the thing; and if he shall use and apply that power, by sale and delivery to another, the ordinary effect of a transference of the property must ensue.

As Hume shows in this passage, the transcending nature of a real right of ownership is such that the transferee is not affected by a personal obligation which binds his or her transferor (or granter) in respect of the thing.[171] Accordingly, in the case of a double sale, the first transferee, in principle, obtains an unassailable right. By way of exception, this principle is departed from on grounds of policy where the transferee's personal right was subsequent to that of the third party and the transferee was aware of the prior competing claim. Stair[172] sees the acquirer as being in bad faith—a 'partaker of the fraud of his author'—where the 'prior disposition or assignation made to another party is certainly known'. The 'arresting metaphor'[173] of 'offside goals', applied by Lord Justice-Clerk Thomson in a modern case,[174] is an apposite one because it encapsulates the point that what would otherwise be effective must fail in the circumstances on policy grounds driven by considerations of justice.

The second consequence is that a valid act of delivery must be reduced (set aside) for its effect in transferring the real right to be rescinded. The first relevant point in this regard is something already explained, i.e. that Scots law follows the civil law in operating on the basis of a clear distinction between the underlying basis for the transfer of property and the actual act of transfer. The act of transfer, as a distinct and self-standing legal act, derives

---

[170] Hume, *Lectures*, IV, 313.
[171] See also Erskine, I, 2, 23 and Hume in his commentary to *Calder* v. *Stewart* (1806) 3 Ross LC, 250-2.　　　　　　　　　　　　　　　　　　　　[172] Stair, I, 14, 5 *in fine*.
[173] Reid (n. 155), § 690; see also §§ 695 sqq.
[174] *Rodger (Builders) Ltd* v. *Fawdry* 1950 SC 483 at 501. See D. L. Carey Miller, 'Good Faith in Scots Property Law in Angelo D. M. Forte (ed.), *Good Faith in Contract and Property Law* (1999), 103 at 107-10.

its force from the intentions of the parties to the act, in principle, without regard to anterior circumstances. In particular the owner/transferor's active motivating intention to dispone drives the act. Thus Stair[175] comments in respect of feudal conveyancing:

> [A]lbeit no cause or title be expressed or implied, but only that the superior dispones: or though the cause or title insinuated be not true, yet it was sufficient with possession, until the solemnity of instruments of seasin was introduced, and is still sufficient when seasin is rightly adhibited; for we follow not that subtilty of annulling deeds, because they are *sine causa*, but do esteem them as gratuitous donations; and therefore narratives expressing the cause of the disposition, are never inquired into, because, though there was no cause, the disposition is good.

Stair's passage could hardly represent a more manifest adherence to the 'abstract theory' of the passing of ownership.[176] The essence of this theory is that the agreement of the parties that ownership should pass must exist as an integral part of the act of conveyance rather than as a motivation derived from an external anterior cause—an approach labelled the 'causal theory'.[177] In the context of the clear civilian distinction between, on the one hand, the underlying act or cause which only gives rise to a personal right, and, on the other hand, the actual act of conveyance, the abstract theory is a more appropriate model than the causal one.[178] This is because the latter tends to reduce the act of conveyance to a consequence of the operative contractual or other basis but, of course, if the act of conveyance is a completely separate legal act it is not appropriate to conceive of it as driven by an anterior legal act. Accepting that it is appropriate to apply the abstract model it follows that a valid act of conveyance must be reduced for its consequences as a transfer of real rights to be rescinded. But, of course, this means that until the act of conveyance is reduced the transferee (grantee) will, in principle, be able to give a good title to a subsequent party.

As long as a potentially valid act of transfer has taken place, in the required manner, the transferee is owner until the act which invested him or her is set aside—if, indeed, it is open to reduction. In the case of a conveyance of heritable property in the requisite form, provided the transferor was himself or herself owner, title will pass to the transferee. Obviously, in the

---

[175] Stair, II, 3, 14.

[176] Reid (n. 155), § 611, founding upon this passage, comments: 'In view of the fact that the conveyance of land requires a written deed and hence a new act of consent manifestly separate from the *causa*, this rejection is not perhaps surprising, and it has never been suggested that a registered disposition might fail on account of infirmities affecting the missives of sale. Indeed the acceptance of the abstract theory seems clearly acknowledged in the prior communings rule, by which a delivered disposition supersedes the missives, and in the statutory rule that registration in the Land Register passes ownership.'

[177] See, generally, D. L. Carey Miller, *The Acquisition and Protection of Ownership* (1986), para. 9.2.2.3.

[178] See Reid (n. 155), §§ 608–12 and D. L. Carey Miller, *Corporeal Moveables in Scots Law* (1991), paras. 8.06–8.10.

circumstances of derivative acquisition, title cannot pass unless the owner motivates, or is taken by the law to motivate, the act of transfer. Where the owner can show that he or she did not and cannot be taken to have motivated the transfer it is a void act from which a party in the position of a transferee, immediate or subsequent, cannot derive any right.

Professor Kenneth Reid has demonstrated the importance of the distinction between void and voidable titles as a matter of fundamental principle in Scots property law.

A person either owns a thing or he does not own a thing; from which proposition it follows that a person holding an ostensible title to a thing either has a good, 'subsistent' title to that thing or he has no title at all. There is no intermediate category of title which is subsistent in some respects but not in others. A 'void' title is, quite simply, no title at all. So if A dispones to B land which he does not own, and if B registers the disposition in the Register of Sasines, B has an ostensible title to the land but one which is void. The land does not belong to B. But if the land had in fact belonged to A, ownership would have passed to B on registration and B would have acquired a title which was absolutely good, in other words, a subsistent title.[179]

Following this basic distinction between the situation in which title passes and that in which it does not pass, Professor Reid goes on point out that a subsistent title may be open to challenge or 'voidable'—the illustrative model still being the transfer of land.

So if A dispones land which he owns to B, but the disposition is subject to challenge, for example as a gratuitous alienation in defraud of A's creditors, the existence of the right to challenge does not prevent B from becoming owner on registration, for the land belonged to A and the transfer process has been properly carried out. But while B's title is subsistent it is also voidable, which is to say that it is capable of being reduced: the real right of ownership is unqualified but the party who holds it, B, incurs personal liability in a question with the party holding the right to reduce. It frequently happens in practice that voidable titles are not reduced at all, and for as long as there is no reduction B remains owner in precisely the same sense as one whose title is absolutely good. Thus if B dispones to C, C will acquire a valid title in turn.[180]

In the present context the significance of this distinction between a void and a voidable title is that it is consistent with the civilian basis upon which the property law of Scotland is founded. In particular, it is consistent with derivative acquisition in which the controlling factors are the extent of the transferor's right and the essential intention to convey given effect to through the requisite mode of delivery. The extent of the entrenchment of the civilian principles which underpin the void/voidable distinction explained in Professor Reid's analysis is reflected in Lord Clyde's translation of Craig.

[179] Reid (n. 155), § 601. [180] Ibid.

The effect of sasine is to make the vassal, when infeft, the beneficial owner of the lands, provided always they were the property of the grantor who can only transfer such rights as he himself had, and provided also the sasine was given with the intention of making such a transfer. For it is always possible that the purpose behind the sasine was only to create an usufruct or a location for a long period of years.[181]

IX. CONCLUSION

Lord Coulsfield, in his opinion in *Sharp* v. *Thomson*,[182] observed that 'although weight should be given to the arguments that the purity of Scots law, as a system based on the civil law, should be maintained and the unitary conception of ownership preserved, these arguments should not be over-emphasised or treated as in themselves decisive'.[183] This dictum raises the question as to whether there are, or should be, matters which are so much seen as fundamental first principles as to be infrangible. The better view would appear to be that the structural dogmatics of the system of property—which happen, in Scots law, to be civilian—should remain controlling. Considerations of policy should be given effect to in a manner which allow the foundation principles of the law to remain paramount. The lesson of the need to be vigilant, in the development of the law, concerning possible interference with basic principles is demonstrated in *Sharp* v. *Thomson*.[184] The salutary warning of Professor W. A. Wilson concerning the incompatibility of the floating charge with the Scottish system of conveyancing[185] has only been paid serious attention to since the difficulty emerged.[186] The approach of Lord Justice-Clerk Ross in seeing certain reservation of title clauses—those which afforded protection to the seller beyond his claim for the purchase price—as contrary to the principle against non-possessory security[187] was criticized[188] and eventually overturned.[189] The better view is that in this instance the development, supported by compelling policy reasons, was in fact in accordance with principle but, possibly, at odds with an entrenched policy position in Scots property law—that there should be no non-possessory security of corporeal moveable property. The *Romalpa* problem has been solved in Scots law without apparent detriment to the integrity of

---

[181] Craig, II, 7, 27.   [182] 1995 SLT 837.   [183] 1995 SLT 869.
[184] 1995 SLT 837.
[185] W. A. Wilson, 'Floating Charges', 1962 *SLT (News)* 53 at 55.
[186] See H. L. MacQueen (ed.), *Scots Law in the 21st Century: Essays in Honour of W. A. Wilson* (1996), 1.
[187] See *Emerald Stainless Steel Ltd* v. *South Side Distribution Ltd* 1982 SC 61 at 64; *Deutz Engines Ltd* v. *Terex Ltd* 1984 SLT 273 at 274–5; *Armour* v. *Thyssen Edelstahlwerke AG* 1989 SLT 182 at 186–7.
[188] K. G. C. Reid and G. L. Gretton, 'Retention of Title in Romalpa Clauses', 1983 *SLT (News)* 77 and idem, 'Retention of Title for all Sums: A Reply', 1983 *SLT (News)* 165.
[189] *Armour* v. *Thyssen Edelstahlwerke AG* (HL) 1990 SLT 891.

the system of property but, of course, this does not mean that Lord Justice-Clerk Ross was wrong to approach the apparent departure from a matter of principle in a circumspect manner. On one view, the healthy debate which occurred in relation to the *Romalpa* development acted to protect the structural integrity of the system.

Whereas the decision of the First Division in *Sharp* v. *Thomson*[190] provided a clear and valuable reassertion of the fundamental principles of the transfer of ownership in Scots law, the decision of the House of Lords[191] has created uncertainty and confusion.[192] The issue in *Sharp* was whether the 'property' in a flat remained with the seller—and so subject to the crystallization of a floating charge—in a situation in which the price had been paid, entry had been given, and the disposition had been delivered but remained unrecorded at the date of crystallization.

A significant part of the problem in *Sharp* arose from the fact that the statutory innovation of a floating charge is incompatible with basic principles of Scots law. This is because upon crystallization the charge has the effect of a recorded heritable security but without any act of prior recording in a public register. When faced with the question of how to construe the 'property and undertaking' of the seller, in terms of the floating charge, the House of Lords was influenced by the argument that an analysis of the floating charge according to the general law of property tended to produce an unjust result. The speeches of Lords Clyde and Jauncey, with whom the rest of the House agreed, reveal the desire to remedy the perceived injustice of the matter, i.e. that the receiver would finish with both the purchase price and the property. Of relevance to the present context, their Lordships held that 'property' is not a technical legal expression, but its meaning depends on the context and there is no general requirement to equiparate 'property' with a real right or feudal title. This surprising and controversial position has been justly questioned by Professor Kenneth Reid,[193] who comments that it is rather like saying that contract is not a technical legal expression. Professor Reid goes on to observe that it is difficult to believe that 'property' used in mainstream insolvency legislation was intended to apply in anything other than a technical sense.

Having decided that they were unfettered by the principles of property law their Lordships chose to interpret 'property' in a pragmatic and commonsense manner consistent with the ordinary use of language. Against this

[190] 1995 SLT 837. [191] 1997 SLT 636.
[192] See K. G. C. Reid, 'Equity Triumphant: *Sharp* v. *Thomson*', (1997) 1 *Edinburgh LR* 464–9; idem, 'Jam Today: Sharp in the House of Lords', 1997 *SLT (News)* 79–84; D. J. Cusine, '*Sharp* v. *Thomson*: The House of Lords Strikes Back', (1997) 26 *Green's Property Law Bulletin* 5–7; J. G. Birrell, '*Sharp* v. *Thomson*: The Impact on Banking and Insolvency Law', 1997 *SLT (News)* 151–5; R. Rennie, '*Sharp* v. *Thomson*: The Final Act', (1997) 42 *JLSS* 130–4; D. P. Sellar, 'Commercial Law Update', (1997) 42 *JLSS* 181–4; D. Guild, '*Sharp* v. *Thomson*: A Practitioner's View', (1997) 42 *JLSS* 274–6. [193] Reid, 1997 *SLT (News)* 79 at 80.

background their Lordships accepted the argument of the appellant that 'property and undertaking' in terms of a floating charge related to property in which the company had a beneficial interest, and which it was in law entitled to dispone or make subject to a heritable security. It was held that upon delivery of the disposition, the flat ceased to be within the 'property and undertaking' of the company and so the floating charge did not attach.[194]

One difficulty with the decision of the House of Lords is that, although Lords Clyde and Jauncey agreed as to the proper result, their decisions diverged on the question of the scope of the decision and its effect on property law. Lord Clyde was at pains to emphasize that he did not intend the principles of property law to be affected by a decision directed to the particular facts in hand.[195] This position produces the problematical result of 'property' in mainstream legislation being interpreted differently from 'property' in the general law. However, as Professor Kenneth Reid points out, Lord Clyde's approach does appear to create a compromise in which a fair result is achieved without the erosion of fundamental principles.[196] Lord Jauncey's speech, on the other hand, pays considerable attention to the existence of a form of beneficial ownership—apparently falling somewhere between a real right and a personal right—passing when the disposition is delivered.[197] Any development of this approach would be contrary to basic principles of Scots property law. At best the dichotomy between the two speeches on this point leaves the law in a state of confusion.

It is trite that the principles of the civil law have been a primary source of influence over the development of the common law of Scotland in respect of the transfer of corporeal moveable property.[198] The survey carried out in this chapter supports the conclusion that this is also true in respect of fundamental aspects of the transfer of land. This conclusion does not in the least gainsay the position of conveyancing as a distinctive branch of property law and a significant specialism. However, that said, there can hardly be any hesitation concerning the importance of a correct identification of matters of fundamental structure. Comparing the decisions of the Court of Session and the House of Lords in *Sharp* v. *Thomson* illustrates this in graphic manner. The case also shows the paradox of a mixed system in which civilian principles live in not always safe coexistence with a form of legal rule controlled by case law, the development of which is potentially open to variation on the basis of what may be perceived to be the requirements of justice in a given case. That centuries of essentially consistent development may be open to being subverted in a single decision illustrates the vulnerability of civilian

---

[194] 1997 SLT 636 at 643.
[195] 1997 SLT 636 at 645. The decision has, however, been applied, in the sheriff court, in a case concerned with bankruptcy; see *Burnett's Tr* v. *Grainger*, 2000 GWD 28–1093.
[196] Reid, (1997) 1 Edinburgh LR 464 at 467.　　　　[197] 1997 SLT 636 at 643.
[198] See Ch. 4 above.

principles in a case law as against a codified system. The fact that the divergence may be rectified—at some stage—is also redolent of an attitude to the functioning and development of the law which has more in common with the ethos of the English common law than with the great systems of Europe which have their roots in Roman law.

7

Servitudes

M. J. DE WAAL

I. INTRODUCTION

A first step is to isolate servitudes within the broader context of the law of property. In a comparable civilian system this would be a relatively easy task. In the constellation of real rights (with ownership as the 'mother right' in the nucleus) servitudes would be classified as belonging to the so-called limited real rights. In this subcategory they lead a distinct existence with no danger of being confused with any of the other limited real rights. In Scots law the task requires more care. Here, at least on one view, servitudes fall to be classified together with real burdens, rights of common interest, and certain other rights. The name suggested for this family of rights is 'real conditions'.[1] In this chapter the focus falls exclusively on servitudes, and the other members of the real condition family will, as far as possible, be left out of the discussion.

In many civilian systems, servitudes include both praedial and personal servitudes. In Scotland the position is different. Although older authorities maintain the distinction,[2] Bell[3] had already stated that 'the only servitudes in Scotland are praedial'. It admits of no doubt that this is also the modern view,[4] and the traditional personal servitude of liferent will not be considered in this chapter. Therefore, further use of the term 'servitude' in this chapter denotes praedial servitude, and the adjective 'praedial' will not be used unless the context so requires.

Only the so-called 'conventional' servitudes will be considered. This classification is used by Bell[5] and Erskine,[6] and also some modern authors,[7] in

---

[1] See Kenneth G. C. Reid, *The Law of Property in Scotland* (1996), § 344 (being an updated version of *The Laws of Scotland: Stair Memorial Encyclopaedia*, vol. 18, 1993).
[2] e.g. George Mackenzie, *Institutions of the Law of Scotland* (2nd edn., 1688), II, 9 at 183; Erskine, II, 9, 5. [3] Bell, *Principles*, § 981.
[4] A. G. M. Duncan, 'Servitudes', in *The Laws of Scotland: Stair Memorial Encyclopedia*, vol. 18, (1993), § 439; W. M. Gordon, *Scottish Land Law* (2nd edn, 1999), 723; David M. Walker, *Principles of Scottish Private Law* (4th edn., 1989), vol. 3, 193; D. J. Cusine and R. R. M. Paisley, *Servitudes and Rights of Way* (1998), 41. [5] Bell, *Principles*, § 980.
[6] Erskine, II, 9, 2. [7] e.g. Cusine/Paisley (n. 4), 11–12.

order to explain that 'natural'[8] or 'legal'[9] servitudes do not properly fall under the rubric servitudes. Also excluded from consideration are the 'public' servitudes such as public rights of way or other rights maintained by or on behalf of the public.[10] One guise in which these servitudes come, however, will be incorporated in the discussion. This is where 'proper servitude rights [are] claimed on behalf of members of a community, who, individually as feuars, or collectively as members of a corporate community with its own territory, such as a royal burgh, qualify as dominant proprietors'.[11] As will be indicated at various stages, cases on this category of right occasionally contain principles which are significant for the law of servitudes in general.

The final stage of demarcation is perhaps the most difficult. It is obvious that not all aspects of the law of servitudes, as outlined above, can be subjected to a historical analysis within the confines of a single chapter. Perhaps less suitable for such an exercise are those aspects of the law which can be described as more or less formal or even technical: examples are the different methods of constitution and extinction of servitudes as well as matters relating to exercise and enforcement. Some of these matters will feature in the discussion which follows, but only incidentally. Instead the main focus will fall on certain core elements, namely the definition and concept of a servitude, the classification of servitudes, the fundamental difference between an 'open' and a 'closed' structure of servitudes, the requirements for the establishment of servitudes and, finally, the application and development of servitudes in practice. An analysis of these issues provides an insight into the historical growth of the institution as a whole because they represent, so to speak, the jurisprudential essence of this branch of the law. That was also the broad approach of the present author in the contributions on servitudes to two other books of which this one forms, in a sense, a logical sequence.[12] By following the same approach here, these other contributions may serve as comparative points of reference to enrich the evaluation of the same elements in Scots law.

Comparative analysis in this chapter will be confined, as far as historical legal comparison is concerned, to Roman, Roman-Dutch and German

---

[8] An example would be where an inferior tenement is obliged to receive water draining naturally from a higher tenement. Duncan (n. 4), § 442 explains why these rights are not considered to be servitudes: 'But servitudes, in their strict and proper sense, confer rights not implied by law and accordingly have to be constituted with the consent or agreement of the servient owner or by some means which the law recognises as an acceptable equivalent to such consent or agreement.'

[9] Walker (n. 4), 193 explains: 'A legal servitude may be created by statute, or by long-standing custom for reasons of public necessity or utility.'

[10] Cusine/Paisley (n. 4), 18 sqq. [11] Gordon (n. 4), 724.

[12] These other contributions are M. J. de Waal, 'Servitudes', in Robert Feenstra and Reinhard Zimmermann (eds.), *Das römisch-holländische Recht: Fortschritte des Zivilrechts im 17. und 18. Jahrhundert* (1992), 567 sqq.; idem, 'Servitudes', in Reinhard Zimmermann and Daniel Visser (eds.), *Southern Cross: Civil Law and Common Law in South Africa* (1996), 785 sqq.

Pandectist law and, as far as modern law is concerned, to German and South African law.

II. NATURE AND DEFINITION

1. The Roman law basis

The word 'servitude' can be traced back to the Latin term *servitus*. *Servitus* is derived from the verb *servire*, which means 'to be of service'.[13] This, very literally, was the meaning attached to the legal concept of a servitude in the Roman law of antiquity. The lawyers of this early age did not feel the need, nor indeed did they possess the ability, to define the concept in formal jurisprudential terms. For them a servitude was merely another expression of ownership or *dominium*.[14] For example, a servitude of way (*iter, actus*, or *via*) indicated that the holder of the right of way was in fact owner of the strip of land constituting the way. In the case of a servitude of leading water (*servitus aquaeductus*) the holder of the right was treated as being the owner of the canals and pipes used to lead the water over the servient tenement. This view may go some way towards explaining why these original servitudes were treated as *res mancipi* and therefore had to be transferred by way of *mancipatio*.[15]

Most probably the Roman jurists had already abandoned this primitive view during the classical period. But it is unlikely that even the jurists of the classical and later eras would have been able to give a definition of the concept of servitude which a modern jurist would find satisfying. Notions such as real right (*jus in re*) and restricted real right (*jus in re aliena*) which feature prominently in most modern definitions did not crystallize fully in the Roman legal mind. The efforts of modern Romanists in this regard must therefore be viewed with circumspection. The essential nature of a servitude right in Roman law can nevertheless be deduced from the definitions of a

---

[13] The term *Dienstbarkeit* in German law can be traced back to the same root: Bernhard Windscheid, *Lehrbuch des Pandektenrechts* (8th edn., 1900), 907 n. 1. See also W. W. Buckland, *A Text-Book of Roman Law from Augustus to Justinian* (1950), 259 n. 1. In this regard the roots of the Afrikaans terms *serwituut* and *diensbaarheid* are obvious.

[14] Max Kaser, 'Geteiltes Eigentum im älteren römischen Recht', in *Festschrift für Paul Koschaker* (1950), vol. 1, 446; Moritz Voigt, *Das Civil- und Criminalrecht der XII Tafeln* (1883), 345 sqq. See also in general De Waal, *Das römisch-holländische Recht* (n. 12), 568.

[15] Gai. 2, 17, 29; Buckland (n. 13), 263; Max Kaser, *Das römische Privatrecht*, vol. 1 (2nd edn., 1971), 441; Fritz Schulz, *Classical Roman Law* (1951), 395; Fritz Schwind, *Römisches Recht*, vol. 1 (1950), 232; J. C. van Oven, *Leerboek van Romeinsch Privaatrecht* (3rd edn., 1948), 141. The view that servitudes were originally treated as merely another expression of ownership or *dominium* is criticized by György Diósdi, *Ownership in Ancient and Preclassical Roman Law* (1978), 109 sqq.

servitude offered by various Romanists.[16] Kaser's definition,[17] for example, reads as follows:

> Ihnen ist gemeinsam, dass der jeweilige Eigentümer des 'herrschenden' Grundstücks ein Recht am 'dienenden' Grundstück erhält, auf Grund dessen der jeweilige Eigentümer dieses dienenden Grundstücks eine bestimmte Einwirkung des Berechtigten zu dulden oder eine bestimmte eigene Einwirkung zu unterlassen hat.[18]

According to this definition (and the other definitions referred to) a servitude in Roman law was a real right with respect to the land of somebody else (a *jus in re aliena*) in terms of which the holder of the right (the owner of the dominant tenement) acquired direct, but circumscribed and limited, powers relating to the land of the other person (the servient tenement). Of course, these powers could also be acquired in terms of a contract between the two persons involved. Such a contract differed from a servitude, however, in the sense that a servitude placed a burden on the servient tenement.[19] This meant that the successive owners of the servient tenement also had to bear the particular burden and, conversely, that the successive owners of the dominant tenement could also benefit from the right.[20] This attachment to the two tenements encapsulated the 'real character' of a servitude in Roman law.

It should be noted that most of the definitions referred to[21] cover praedial servitudes only and not personal servitudes.[22] The latter category was not treated as a type of servitude until post-classical law.

2. Reception into Scots law

An analysis of the definitions of servitude provided by the institutional writers leaves no doubt that the Roman institution was received into Scots law. Stair[23] identified the fundamental element of servitude when he wrote that 'one tenement is subservient to another tenement'. Bankton[24] used almost exactly the same words. On a more abstract level this implied, of course, that a servitude right constituted a real right—a right 'running with the land'.[25] Both

---

[16] See, for instance, the definitions by the following Romanists: Buckland (n. 13), 261; Kaser (n. 15), 440; Ernst Rabel, *Grundzüge des römischen Privatrechts* (2nd edn., 1955), 81; Schulz (n. 15), 382; Schwind (n. 15), 229; Rudolf Sohm, *Institutionen (Geschichte und System des römischen Privatrechts)* (17th edn., 1949), 324; Van Oven (n. 15), 141; Leopold Wenger, *Die Quellen des römischen Rechts* (1953), 767.   [17] Kaser (n. 15), 440.
[18] ('These rights have in common the fact that the owner for the time being of the "dominant" tenement acquires a right in respect of the "servient" tenement in terms of which the owner for the time being of the servient tenement must allow the holder of the right to exercise a specified act on the servient tenement or must himself refrain from exercising a specified act on the servient tenement.')   [19] Buckland (n. 13), 259; Schulz (n. 15), 381.
[20] Buckland (n.13), 259; Schulz (n.15), 381. See also Van Oven (n. 15), 140–1.
[21] Above, n. 16.   [22] As to this distinction, see above I.   [23] Stair, II, 7, 1.
[24] Bankton, II, 7, 1.
[25] Duncan (n. 4), § 446: 'Servitudes run with the land representing the respective tenements, affecting all successors in ownership and not requiring any form of transmission.'

Stair and Hume stated this explicitly,[26] but without elaborating in any way. The definitions of both Erskine[27] and, especially, Bell[28] are quite comprehensive and descriptive, reminiscent of the one Kaser gave for Roman law.[29]

The general profile of servitudes that can be gleaned from these definitions is very much in evidence from the earliest cases onwards. The fact that a servitude connected two tenements with each other, thereby making it possible for the owner of the one tenement to exercise a right with regard to the other tenement, was stressed in quite a number of cases. For example in *Patrick* v. *Napier*[30] Lord Ardmillan declared that:

In every case of praedial servitude there must be a *praedium serviens praedio*, a dominant and servient tenement, and the burden to which the servient tenement is subjected must be of a proper praedial character, for the benefit of the dominant tenement.[31]

This idea was also sometimes expressed in the general maxim *praedium servit praedio*.[32]

In *Turnbull* v. *Blanerne*,[33] a decision dating from 1622 and one of the oldest reported under the rubric 'Servitude' in Morison's *Dictionary*, the court stressed that the right in question in that case, being a servitude, 'affected the ground thereof, in whose hands soever the right of the land came . . .'. This statement is, of course, a clear confirmation of the other essential element stressed above, namely the real character of a servitude right.[34] In the much later case of *Drummond* v. *Milligan*[35] this element was formulated in very much the same vein:

---

[26] Stair, II, 7, 1; Hume, *Lectures*, III, 271.

[27] Erskine, II, 9, 1: 'A servitude may therefore be defined a burden affecting lands or other heritable subjects, by which the proprietor is either restrained from the full use of his property, or is obliged to suffer another to do certain acts upon it, which, were it not for that burden, would be competent solely to the owner.'

[28] Bell, *Principles*, § 979: 'Servitude is a burden on land or houses, imposed by agreement—express or implied—in favour of the owners of other tenements; whereby the owner of the burdened or "servient" tenement, and his heirs and singular successors in the subject, must submit to certain uses to be exercised by the owner of the other or "dominant" tenement; or must suffer restraint in his own use and occupation of the property.'   [29] Above II.1.

[30] (1867) 5 M 683 at 709.

[31] See also the statement by the Lord President in the same case (699): 'I think a predial servitude must be something which constitutes a burden upon one tenement or predium, for the purpose of creating an advantage or benefit to another predium.' Both these statements are also important in the context of the so-called *utilitas* requirement for praedial servitudes: see below V.2. (*c*).

[32] See e.g. *Metcalfe* v. *Purdon* (1902) 4 F 507, at 511; Hume, *Lectures*, III, 269. See also in general *Crichton* v. *Turnbull* 1945 SC 52 at 64.   [33] (1622) Mor 14499.

[34] See also *Town of Edinburgh* v. *Town of Leith* (1630) Mor 14500; *Peter* v. *Eccles* (1686) Mor 14515.   [35] (1890) 17 R 316 at 317 *per* the Lord President.

Such a servitude [a praedial servitude] depends on the obligation of the servient tenement to the dominant tenement, and is quite apart from the question of who the possessor of either tenement may be.[36]

It is only in more recent cases, however, that servitudes came to be defined in what may be termed modern rights terminology. A good example is the following somewhat cryptic statement by Lord Maxwell in *Safeway Food Stores Limited* v. *Wellington Motor Company (Ayr) Ltd*:[37] 'Servitudes are not mere personal obligations but are real rights of a special nature . . .'

A right will only be constituted as a servitude if there was a clear intention that the right should 'run with the land' (in other words, that a real right and not merely a personal right should be created). Gordon[38] formulates this as one of the formal requirements[39] for a servitude: 'Before a burden on land such as a servitude can become a real burden, it must be shown that it was intended to affect the land in the hands of anyone holding it.'

However, as this is such a fundamental issue, it is probably better to state it at a more general level. If such an intention is absent or cannot be proven, the whole question as to the establishment of a servitude becomes irrelevant.

III. CLASSIFICATION

1. Rural and urban

The classification into rural and urban servitudes can be traced back to classical Roman law,[40] and the practice of dividing servitudes into these two categories has been firmly established ever since.[41] Unfortunately there is not complete consensus regarding the true basis for this classification, an uncertainty which can probably be ascribed to a number of confusing *Digest* texts.[42] Generally speaking, the following views have crystallized in this regard:[43]

---

[36] See also *Johnston* v. *MacRitchie* (1893) 20 R 539 at 547; *Proprietors of Royal Exchange Buildings, Glasgow, Limited* v. *Cotton* 1912 SC 1151 at 1157; *Harper* v. *Flaws* 1940 SLT 150 at 152; *Ferguson* v. *Tennant* 1978 SC (HL) 19 at 50.   [37] 1976 SLT 53 at 55.
[38] Gordon (n. 4), 730; Cusine/Paisley (n.4) 120 sqq.
[39] As to the formal requirements for the establishment of servitudes, see below V.
[40] Gai. 2, 14; Kaser (n. 15), 441; Schulz (n. 15), 392.
[41] De Waal, *Das römisch-holländische Recht* (n. 12), 572.
[42] e.g. in Gai. D. 8, 2, 2 and Ulp. D. 8, 3, 1 lists of rural and urban servitudes are given. This creates the impression that servitudes were always either rural or urban. Ner. D. 8, 3, 2 illustrates, however, that this was not the case. In this text there is no sign of such a stark division. All these texts and a text such as Ulp. D. 50, 16, 198 also contradict each other regarding the true basis of any division. See also Buckland (n. 13), 262 n. 1.
[43] De Waal, *Das römisch-holländische Recht* (n. 12), 572–3 and the authorities cited there.

(a) The determining factor is the location of the property. In urban property a servitude is urban. Otherwise a servitude is rural. This view is not generally accepted. Not only was there already authority against such an approach in Roman law,[44] but it does not provide a reliable yardstick. It is obvious that it will not always be easy to distinguish clearly between rural and urban property.[45]

(b) The determining factor is whether the dominant tenement has any buildings upon it. A servitude in favour of a built-up tenement is an urban servitude and one in favour of a tenement with no buildings upon it a rural servitude (regardless of the location of the respective tenements). This simplistic view is not acceptable. Carried through to its logical conclusion, it would mean that virtually no rural servitudes will exist, for most tenements have buildings upon them in order to facilitate their exploitation.

(c) The nature and exploitation of the dominant tenement are decisive. Rural servitudes are established in tenements exploited for agricultural purposes. Urban servitudes are established in tenements used for residential, commercial, or industrial purposes. Again, location plays no role whatsoever. The fact that this view is perhaps logically the most satisfying may explain why it received strong support in both Roman-Dutch and German Pandectist law.[46] It is also the view adhered to in modern South African law.[47]

The classification of servitudes into rural and urban (or 'city' or 'borow')[48] is found in the institutional writers and, according to Erskine, was done 'after the example of the Romans'.[49] The majority of writers who commented on the subject gave as the basis of the classification the nature and exploitation of the dominant tenement (that is, the third view mentioned above). Erskine[50] was clearest:

City servitudes, or of house, are those which are constituted in favour of a tenement of houses, though such tenement should not be within the gates of any city. Rural servitudes, or of land, are acquired for the use of a rural or country tenement—as a farm, field, inclosure, garden, though they should be situated within the liberties of a city; for it is not the place, but the matter and use of the tenement, which makes this distinction . . .[51]

---

[44] Ner. D. 8. 3, 2 pr.
[45] Cf. the South African case of *Redelinghuis* v. *Bazzoni* 1976 (1) SA 110 (T) where the court tried, somewhat unconvincingly, to distinguish between rural and urban tenements for purposes of the *actio aquae pluviae arcendae*.
[46] De Waal, *Das römisch-holländische Recht* (n. 12), 573 and the authorities cited there.
[47] *Badenhorst* v. *Joubert and Others* 1920 TPD 100 at 108; H. J. Delport and N. J. J. Olivier, *Sakereg Vonnisbundel* (2nd edn., 1985), 546; C. G. Hall and E. A. Kellaway, *Servitudes* (3rd edn., 1973), 8; C. G. van der Merwe, *Sakereg* (2nd edn., 1989), 479.
[48] Bankton, II, 7, 2; Erskine II, 9, 6.   [49] Erskine, II, 9, 6.   [50] Ibid.
[51] See also Bankton, II, 7, 2; Stair, II, 7, 5.

However, one comment by Bell[52] can be read as supporting the view that the determining factor is whether the dominant tenement has any buildings upon it (that is, the second view mentioned above).

It is not clear that this classification retains practical value. It was important in classical Roman law, as rural servitudes were treated as *res mancipi* and urban servitudes as *res nec mancipi*.[53] This meant, *inter alia*, that different methods of establishment were required for servitudes in the respective categories. In post-classical law the importance of the distinction between *res mancipi* and *res nec mancipi* had already disappeared and it is safe to assume that the classification of servitudes into rural and urban categories had also lost its significance.[54] It seems as if authors nevertheless continued in a mechanical fashion to draw this distinction, although it had ceased to fulfil any useful function.

In Scotland modern authors continue to distinguish between rural and urban servitudes. As to the basis for this distinction, they, too, generally support the view that the exploitation of the dominant tenement is the decisive factor.[55] However, Rankine[56] had already admitted that this distinction is adopted for the sake of convenience only and that it is of no practical value. This opinion is shared by other authors.[57] Duncan goes even further and calls it 'misleading rather than informative'.[58] It is obvious, therefore, that this classification plays no significant role in the modern law.[59] The same is true for South African law[60] and the codified continental systems.[61] The continuing use of this classification in all these systems can therefore be questioned.

2. Positive and negative

A positive servitude (*servitus faciendi*) entitles the owner of the dominant tenement to perform a specific act on the servient tenement (such as walking over the tenement). A negative servitude (*servitus prohibendi*) entitles the

---

[52] Bell, *Principles*, § 1002; but compare § 983.

[53] Buckland (n. 13), 263; Van Oven (n. 15), 146.

[54] Anton Friedrich Justus Thibaut, *System des Pandekten-Rechts* (1809), 46 n. (f); Otto Wendt, *Lehrbuch der Pandekten* (1888), 383.

[55] See e.g. Duncan (n. 4), § 483. Cusine/Paisley (n. 4), 33 support the second view.

[56] J. Rankine, *A Treatise on the Rights and Burdens Incident to the Ownership of Lands and Other Heritages in Scotland* (4th edn., 1909), 446.

[57] Gordon (n. 4), 733; Cusine/Paisley (n. 4), 33.

[58] Duncan (n. 4), § 483.

[59] It strikes one that this distinction is hardly ever referred to in the case law. An early example is found in *Cochran v. Fairholm* (1759) Mor 14518.

[60] M. J. de Waal, 'Die Vereistes vir die Vestiging van Grondserwitute in die Suid-Afrikaanse Reg' (unpublished LL.D. thesis, University of Stellenbosch, 1989), 12.

[61] See e.g. C. Asser and J. H. Beekhuis, *Handleiding tot de Beoefening van het Nederlands Burgerlijk Recht: Zakenrecht* (11th edn., 1983), vol. 2, 201 (The Netherlands); Wolfgang Ring, in *J. von Staudingers Kommentar zum Bürgerlichen Gesetzbuch* (12th edn., 1981), preliminary notes to §§ 1018 sqq. n. 1 (Germany).

owner of the dominant tenement to prohibit the owner of the servient tenement from performing a specific act on the servient tenement (such as building higher than a specified height). All the rural servitudes are positive servitudes and most of the urban servitudes are negative servitudes.

This distinction is of later origin than that between rural and urban servitudes, although there are indications that it was already in use in Roman law.[62] It was certainly one of the standard classifications in Roman-Dutch law[63] and Pandectist law,[64] and it is hardly surprising that both the institutional writers[65] and modern authors[66] should also employ this classification. In fact it is of considerable significance in Scots law,[67] for while positive servitudes can be constituted by express or implied grant or by prescription, negative servitudes require an express grant.[68]

3. Other classifications

Bell[69] mentioned another possible classification of servitudes: 'Another distinction has been made between servitudes of *Continuous* and *Interrupted* use; and again between servitudes *Manifest* and *Not manifest.*'

Both distinctions were found in French law,[70] and the first was also mentioned by Van Leeuwen.[71]

---

[62] A text such as Pomp. D. 8, 1, 15, 1 suggests a distinction of this nature. See also Buckland (n. 13), 259; W. Modderman, *Handboek voor het Romeinsch Recht* (1892), 169.

[63] Simon van Leeuwen, *Het Rooms-Hollands-Regt* (Amsterdam, 1708), II, 19, 7; idem, *Censura Forensis* (Leiden, 1741), II, II, 14, 3.

[64] Alois Brinz, *Lehrbuch der Pandekten* (1884), 765; Heinrich Dernburg, *Pandekten*, vol. 1 (1892), 570; Bernhard Windscheid, *Lehrbuch des Pandektenrechts* (1900), 910.

[65] Stair, II, 7, 5; Bankton, II, 7, 3; Erskine, II, 9, 1; Hume, *Lectures*, III, 262 n. 2; Bell, *Principles*, §§ 981 sq.; idem, *Commentaries*, IV, 793.

[66] Rankine (n. 56), 415, 417, 419, and 425; Duncan (n. 4), § 441; W. M. Gloag and R. C. Henderson, *The Law of Scotland* (10th edn., 1995), 660; Gordon (n. 4), 730; Cusine/Paisley (n. 4), 34.

[67] Rankine (n. 56), 415 calls it 'the leading division'. Compare here South African law where negative servitudes can be created by prescription. See in general *Ellis v. Laubscher* 1956 (4) SA 692 (A); D. G. Kleyn and A. Boraine, *Silberberg and Schoeman's: The Law of Property* (3rd edn., 1992), 374 sq. and 383 sq.; Van der Merwe (n. 47), 530 sqq. and 539 sq. The Scottish Law Commission has recommended that negative servitudes should be assimilated to negative real burdens, and that it should no longer be possible to create negative servitudes. See *Report on Real Burdens* (Scot. Law Com. No. 181, 2000), paras 12.2 to 12.14.

[68] See e.g. *Dundas v. Blair* (1886) 13 R 759 at 762; *Johnston v. MacRitchie* (1893) 20 R 539 at 547; *Inglis v. Clark* (1901) 4 F 288 at 294; *Metcalfe v. Purdon* (1902) 4 F 507 at 512. For other cases where this classification is referred to, see *Gray v. Ferguson* (1792) Mor 14513; *Sivright v. Borthwick* (1828) 7 S 210 at 213; *Gould v. McCorquodale* (1869) 8 M 165 at 175; *McGibbon v. Rankin* (1871) 9 M 423 at 433; *Cowan v. Stewart* (1872) 10 M 735 at 742, 743; *Banks and Co. v. Walker* (1874) 1 R 981 at 986; *Anderson v. Robertson* 1958 SC 367 at 372; *Hunter v. Fox* 1964 SC (HL) 95 at 99.

[69] Bell, *Principles*, § 980.

[70] Articles 688 and 689 CC.

[71] Van Leeuwen, *Het Rooms-Hollands-Regt* (n. 63), II, 19, 7; idem, *Censura Forensis* (n. 63), II, II, 14, 13. However, it hardly features in modern South African law. See De Waal (n. 60), 13 n. 73 for a number of cases in which casual references to this distinction will be found.

Continuous servitudes are exercised without interruption, as in the case of a *servitus oneris ferendi*. Interrupted servitudes are exercised only at intervals, as in the case of a servitude of way. The exercise of a manifest servitude will be obvious to an observer, as (again) in the case of a servitude of way. The exercise of a non-manifest servitude will not be obvious to an observer, as in the case of a servitude of view. Broadly speaking, interrupted and manifest servitudes will also be positive servitudes, while continuous and non-manifest servitudes will be negative servitudes. The importance of these classifications really lies in this last observation: the rules pertaining to the constitution and extinction of, respectively, positive and negative servitudes are also applicable to the relevant classes mentioned here. This explains the statement by Bell following directly after the one quoted above:[72] 'And both those distinguishing features may be of importance in the question of the constitution or extinction of servitude.'

The important distinction, therefore, remains the one between positive and negative servitudes. This may explain why references to other classifications are far less frequent in Scots sources.[73]

IV. AN OPEN OR CLOSED STRUCTURE?

1. The function of requirements in an open structure of servitudes

Although one would not find an unequivocal pronouncement in any of the relevant texts, it is safe to state that there was no *numerus clausus*[74] of servitudes in classical and post-classical Roman law.[75] The standard examples of praedial servitudes found in the *praetor's* edict[76] did not imply that further examples could not be created. Voet[77] stated this categorically for Roman-Dutch law: 'Porro non dubium, quin hisce iam enumeratis servitutibus novae aliae ex voto contrahentium addi possint, si modo servitutum praedialium aut personalium natura in iis inveniatur.'[78]

As is clear from Voet's statement, the only precondition for the creation of new servitudes was 'that the nature of praedial or personal servitudes [should be] discovered' in these new examples. In other words, certain basic requirements had to be satisfied before a servitude could be added to the list already in existence. Neither in Roman nor in Roman-Dutch law was there a system-

---

[72] Bell, *Principles*, § 980.   [73] For an example, see Rankine (n. 56), 446.
[74] i.e. fixed list.
[75] Rudolf Elvers, *Die römische Servitutenlehre* (1856), 134 sqq.; Schulz (n. 15), 383; J. A. C. Thomas, *Textbook of Roman Law* (1976), 197.   [76] Schulz (n. 15), 383.
[77] Johannes Voet, *Commentarius ad Pandectas* (1698), VIII, 3, 12.
[78] ('There is furthermore no doubt that other fresh servitudes may be added at the desire of contracting parties to those already enumerated, if only the nature of praedial or personal servitudes is discovered in them.'—tr. Percival Gane, *The Selective Voet* (1955)).

atic treatment of these requirements. It was left to the German Pandectists to enumerate a list of formal requirements and to present them in an organized fashion.[79]

The importance of such an open structure cannot be overemphasized. Any legal system of which the starting point is that only a closed list of servitudes is acknowledged will hardly allow room for the natural development of this branch of the law. For it is the ability of a legal institution to grow and to adapt itself to new challenges and needs which ensures its continuing relevance. An open structure of servitudes is characteristic of systems where the Roman law has been received.[80] Examples include the law of the Netherlands, Germany, and South Africa.

In all such systems the requirements just mentioned operate as measures of internal control over the creation of new servitudes. The reason why control is necessary is obvious. Servitudes constitute a burden upon ownership and new kinds of burdens should not, for policy reasons, be allowed to develop unchecked.[81] At the same time, however, the requirements should remain sufficiently flexible to allow for the creation of new servitudes when the needs of a developing society so dictate.

2. The position in Scots law

The question as to the development of the Scots law of servitudes is therefore intimately linked with a more basic question, namely whether Scots law has an open or a closed structure of servitudes. Bell[82] answered this question as follows:

What shall be deemed a servitude of a regular and definite kind is a secondary question, as to which the only description that can be given generally seems to be, that it shall be such a use or restraint as by law or custom is known to be likely and incident to the property in question, and to which the attention of a prudent purchaser will, in the circumstances, naturally be called.

Although by no means unequivocal, this proposition is indicative of support for an open structure of servitudes. The determining consideration seemed to be that the new servitude should be 'known' by law or custom. Passages from Stair,[83] Hume,[84] and Erskine[85] can also be read as implying an open

---

[79] Justus Wilhelm Hedemann, *Sachenrecht des Bürgerlichen Gesetzbuches* (3rd edn., 1960), 247. See also De Waal, *Das römisch-holländische Recht* (n. 12), 573 sq.

[80] M. J. de Waal, 'Die Vereistes vir die Vestiging van Grondserwitute: 'n Herformulering', (1990) 2 *Stellenbosch LR* 171 sqq.

[81] De Waal (n. 60), 15 sqq.; idem, (1990) 2 *Stellenbosch LR* 172–5.

[82] Bell, *Principles*, § 979.

[83] Stair, II, 7, 5. See also Stair II, 7, 9: 'The predial or country servitudes ... may be as manifold as the free use of the one may be restrained or impaired, for the profit or pleasure of the other ...' [84] Hume, *Lectures*, III, 269–70.

[85] Erskine, II, 9, 33.

structure, although only Erskine linked this with standard requirements for the establishment of servitudes.[86]

An analysis of the case law shows that the courts also took for granted that there was no *numerus clausus*. In *Sinclair v. The Magistrates and Town Council of Dysart*,[87] a case of 1779, the question to be decided was whether the inhabitants of Dysart had acquired through immemorial use the right 'of bleaching their linen on a spot of ground', owned by Sinclair. Although this case concerned a so-called public servitude,[88] it was decided on the basis of the normal law of servitudes. It was argued for the Town Council of Dysart that 'Though law-books take notice of particular servitudes which occur most frequently under known names, they do not say that no other servitudes can be legally constituted. Servitudes are as various as there are lawful uses which one man may make of another's property'. As authority for this view the court was referred to Stair[89] and also to the text from Voet quoted above.[90] The court decided that the servitude contended for was indeed established.[91]

A somewhat similar issue arose in *Dyce v. Hay*,[92] where it was contended that the inhabitants of a number of neighbouring burghs had acquired, through prescription, the right to use the land of the defender 'for the purpose of recreation, and taking air and exercise, by walking over and through the same, and resting thereon, as they saw proper'. While refusing to recognize such a servitude, the court made clear that the class of servitudes was not closed:[93]

Every party who has ever resisted the introduction of a new servitude, has invariably argued that the whole possible class of them was already known and named; and that the introduction of a new one was proved to be illegal by the mere fact of its novelty. I am not aware of any authority for this principle, and it has been conspicuously refuted by the past history of the law. If it had been sound, we would never have got

---

[86] The requirements of *utilitas* (utility) and *vicinitas* (vicinity): see below V.2.b and c.
[87] (1779) Mor 14519.
[88] As indicated by Duncan (n. 4), § 443 one is required to draw a distinction 'between, on the one hand, cases in which a category of persons such as householders within a town are claiming rights of the nature of servitudes over private property and, on the other hand, cases where the inhabitants of a town or burgh are claiming rights over ground held by the town or burgh for public use. Certain privileges such as golfing facilities not within the category of recognised servitudes and not governed by the rules applicable to servitudes have been successfully claimed on the latter basis.' [89] Stair, II, 7, 5.
[90] Above IV.1. More or less the same argument, again with specific reference to the same text from Voet, was relied upon only a few years earlier in *Yeaman v. Crawford* (1770) Mor 14537. As to the interaction between the Roman-Dutch and Scots systems of property law, see D. L. Carey Miller, 'Systems of Property: Grotius and Stair', in D. L. Carey Miller and D. W. Meyers (eds.), *Comparative and Historical Essays in Scots Law: A Tribute to Professor Sir Thomas Smith QC* (1992), 13 sqq.; and more generally, Daniel Visser, 'Placing the Civilian Influence in Scotland: A Roman-Dutch Perspective', in David L. Carey Miller and Reinhard Zimmermann (eds.), *The Civilian Tradition and Scots Law: Aberdeen Quincentenary Essays* (1997), 239 sqq.
[91] See further below VI.1. [92] (1849) 11 D 1266.
[93] (1849) 11 D 1266 at 1283 *per* Lord Cockburn.

Servitudes   317

beyond the days in which land was only required for its simplest primary uses; and the admissible servitudes would all have been fixed and catalogued ages ago. But, in place of this, it is certain, that new circumstances have been constantly changing and multiplying them . . . The law nowhere pretends to specify all possible servitudes prospectively. It only supplies the root from which they are to spring.

Similar views were expressed in the House of Lords, although the appeal was unsuccessful;[94] and this flexible approach towards servitudes is discernible as a basic theme throughout the cases.[95]

V. THE REQUIREMENTS FOR THE ESTABLISHMENT OF SERVITUDES

1. Introduction

While the institutional writers made no attempt to systematize the requirements for servitudes, it is at least clear that the function of such requirements was to control the creation of new servitudes.[96] The requirements discussed below have been identified *ex post facto* from an analysis of the institutional writers and from other sources.[97]

2. Specific requirements

(a) *Two tenements separately held*

In both Roman and Roman-Dutch law the first and fundamental requirement for the establishment of a praedial servitude was the existence of a dominant tenement (*praedium dominans*) and a servient tenement (*praedium serviens*), belonging to different owners.[98] In the absence of a dominant tenement a personal servitude could be established, but not a praedial servitude.

---

[94] *Dyce* v. *Hay* (1852) 15 D (HL) 14.
[95] See e.g. *Harvey* v. *Lindsay* (1853) 15 D 768 at 775 *per* Lord Robertson: 'I go quite along with the observations which have been made in recent cases, that we are not to limit servitudes to those already known and recognised in law, as in the progress of society alterations may take place, and new servitudes may arise. The best recognised servitudes must at some time have been new.' See also *Patrick* v. *Napier* (1867) 5 M 683 at 706; *Ferguson* v. *Tennant* 1978 SC (HL) 15. Textbook writers concur: Rankine (n. 56), 419; David M. Walker, *A Legal History of Scotland*, vol. 1 (1988), 358; Gordon (n. 4), 726; Duncan (n. 4), § 447; Cusine/Paisley (n. 4), 36 sqq.
[96] See e.g. *Patrick* v. *Napier* (1867) 5 M 683 at 706; *McGibbon* v. *Rankin* (1871) 9 M 423 at 433.
[97] e.g. De Waal, (1990) 2 *Stellenbosch LR* 171 sqq.; idem (n. 60), 23 sqq.; Gordon (n. 4), 727 sqq; Cusine/Paisley (n. 4), ch. 2.
[98] As to Roman law see e.g.: Ulp. D. 8, 4, 1, 1; Kaser (n. 15), 440; Modderman (n. 62), 164; Thomas (n. 75), 195; Van Oven (n. 15), 140; Egon Weiss, *Institutionen des römischen Privatrechts* (1949), 220. As to Roman-Dutch law see e.g.: Hugo de Groot (Grotius), *Inleydinge tot de Hollandsche Rechtsgeleertheyd* (1910 edn. by S. J Fockema Andrea), II, 33, 3; Voet (n. 77), VIII, 1, 2 and VIII, 4, 8; Johannes van der Linden, *Regtsgeleerd, Practicaal, en Koopmans Handboek* (1806), I, 11, 1; Ulrich Huber, *Heedensdaegse Rechts-Geleertheyt* (1768), II, 42, 3 and II, 43, 15.

This fundamental requirement is still regarded as fundamental in modern civilian systems.[99]

The position in Scots law is the same, although—no doubt because this requirement is naturally encapsulated in the concept and definition of a servitude—the institutional writers did not find it necessary to articulate it as a formal requirement. An exception was Erskine:[100] 'In predial servitudes, therefore, there must be two tenements; a dominant, to which the servitude is due, and a servient, which owes the servitude, or is charged with it.'

This requirement was also reflected in the fundamental Roman law rule *nulli res sua servit*[101]—nobody can have a servitude over his own land. This rule was mentioned in case law as early as 1542[102] and was confirmed in later cases.[103]

It follows from this requirement that servitude rights could not be created by, or in favour of, persons who held only tenancy rights or between tenants of the same landlord (even where both hold in terms of a long lease).[104] This did not mean that a tenant (or other occupiers, such as family members) of the dominant tenement could not *exercise* the servitude: it meant only that the tenant could not *create* the servitude in favour of the tenement.

Unlike the position in many other legal systems, the dominant tenement was not always a corporeal piece of land. Salmon fishings could constitute a dominant tenement with regard to such rights of access as were required over adjacent land for the proper exercise of the fishing rights.[105] Furthermore, in the case of thirlage (another apparently unique servitude) the mill was treated as the dominant tenement and the lands astricted as the servient.[106]

(*b*) Vicinitas *(vicinity or locality)*

Roman texts provide ample evidence for the requirement of *vicinitas* (vicinity or locality) for the establishment of praedial servitudes. What is not immediately obvious, however, is how this requirement is to be interpreted in the context of the establishment of servitudes. *Vicinitas* is an elastic concept with

---

[99] e.g. South African law: see De Waal (n. 60), 27 sqq. [100] Erskine, II, 9, 5.
[101] Paul. D. 8, 2, 26.
[102] *Innes* v. *Stewart* (1542) Mor 3081. See Gordon (n. 4), 752.
[103] e.g. *Mackenzie* v. *Carrick* (1869) 7 M 419 at 420; *Walton Brothers* v. *Magistrates of Glasgow* (1876) 3 R 1130 at 1133; *Grierson* v. *School Board of Sandsting and Aithsting* (1882) 9 R 437 at 441. See also generally as to the requirement of two tenements *Patrick* v. *Napier* (1867) 5 M 683 at 699; *Harvie* v. *Stewart* (1870) 9 M 129 at 154; *North British Railway Co.* v. *Park Yard Co. Ltd* (1898) 25 R (HL) 47 at 48; *Metcalfe* v. *Purdon* (1902) 4 F 507 at 511; *Braid Hills Hotel Co. Ltd* v. *Manuels* 1908 SC 120 at 126; *Proprietors of Royal Exchange Buildings, Glasgow, Ltd* v. *Cotton* 1912 SC 1151 at 1160-1; *Crichton* v. *Turnbull* 1945 SC 52 at 61; *Safeway Food Stores Ltd* v. *Wellington Motor Co. (Ayr) Ltd* 1976 SLT 53 at 56; *Irvine Knitters Ltd* v. *North Ayrshire Co-operative Society Ltd* 1978 SLT 105 at 107.
[104] Duncan (n. 4), § 449; Cusine/Paisley (n. 4), 89 sqq. See, however, Gordon (n. 4), 729.
[105] Rankine (n. 56), 421 sq; Duncan (n. 4), § 443; Gordon (n. 4), 729; Cusine/Paisley (n. 4), 53.
[106] Erskine, II, 9, 19; *Harris* v. *Magistrates of Dundee* (1863) 1 M 833 at 846.

many possible nuances.[107] On the one hand, it can mean that the dominant and servient tenements must have a common border. On the other hand, it can merely imply that the respective tenements must be situated in such a way in relation to each other that the servitude can be effectively exercised for the benefit of the dominant tenement.

There is a view that the strict interpretation of the *vicinitas* requirement was adhered to in Roman law and thus constituted an extraordinarily strong restriction on the establishment of servitudes.[108] But an analysis of relevant texts shows that this is an oversimplification.[109] There are indeed indications that this might have been the early interpretation in the case of rural servitudes (or at least some of them);[110] but this approach was gradually tempered as far as rural servitudes were concerned[111] and it was in any event never evident in the context of urban servitudes.[112] Already in classical Roman law *vicinitas* was such a vague conception that it could hardly have been a special requirement.[113] It merely became one of the criteria on the basis of which it could be determined whether or not the more fundamental requirement of *utilitas* (utility)[114] was satisfied.[115]

The *vicinitas* requirement did not receive much attention from the Roman-Dutch jurists.[116] Leading authors such as De Groot, Van der Keessel, and Groenewegen said nothing on the subject. Among the authors who dealt with this requirement, traces of both the narrow and the more flexible interpretations can be found. However, the liberal view clearly enjoyed more support. Voet, for example, followed the Roman law approach by treating *vicinitas*, not as an independent requirement for the establishment of servitudes, but rather as a factor which had to be taken into consideration in the application of the *utilitas* requirement.[117]

In Scotland the sources on *vicinitas* are meagre, although Erskine wrote in support of the liberal interpretation evident in Roman and Roman-Dutch law:[118]

---

[107] De Waal, *Das römisch-holländische Recht* (n. 12), 574.

[108] Josef Kohler, 'Beitrage zum Servitutenrecht', (1897) 87 *AcP* 157 at 183 sqq. See also the statement by Lord Deas in *McGibbon* v. *Rankin* (1871) 9 M 423 at 433.

[109] For a more comprehensive discussion of these texts, see De Waal (n. 60), 31 sqq.; *idem*, 'Vicinitas of Nabuurskap as Vestigingsvereiste vir Grondserwitute', 1990 *TSAR* 186 sqq.

[110] Ulp. D. 8, 3, 5, 1.

[111] See e.g. Paul. D. 8, 2, 1 pr.; Paul. D. 8, 3, 7, 1; Paul. D. 8, 3, 38; Paul. D. 8, 4, 7, 1.

[112] See e.g. Ulp. D. 8, 4, 6; Paul. D. 8, 4, 7, 1; Ulp. D. 8, 5, 4, 8; Paul. D. 8, 5, 5. Of course, in the case of some urban servitudes, such as the *servitus oneris ferendi* and the *servitus tigni immittendi*, the tenements had to be contiguous: Paul. D. 8, 2, 1 pr.   [113] Schulz (n. 15), 394.

[114] Below V.2.c.

[115] Buckland (n. 13), 262; Elvers (n. 75), 166; Kaser (n. 15), 442; Sohm (n. 16), 329; G. L. J. van der Ploeg, *Het Romeinsche Regt, naar Aanleiding der Instituten* (1851), 158.

[116] For an analysis of this requirement in Roman-Dutch law, see De Waal (n. 60), 42 sqq.; *idem*, *Das römisch-holländische Recht* (n. 12), 574 sqq.; *idem*, 1990 *TSAR* 191 sqq.

[117] Voet (n. 77), VIII, 4, 19. See also Huber (n. 98), II, 43, 17; Arnoldus Vinnius, *Institutionum Imperialium Commentarius* (2nd edn., 1655), II, 3.   [118] Erskine, II, 9, 33.

Upon this ground, the Roman law required, towards the constitution of a servitude, vicinity in the dominant and servient tenements ... Yet this is not always precisely necessary; for though the two tenements be not contiguous to one another, a servitude may be constituted if the distance between the two be not so great as to obstruct all benefit from the servitude.

Erskine illustrated this by explaining that the owner of land may acquire a servitude of pasturing his cattle upon another's land, although the dominant and servient tenements are not contiguous. The only qualification is that there must also exist a servitude of passage over the intermediate tenement or tenements.[119] This example is not unlike those found in the Roman[120] sources as illustration of the more liberal approach.

Case law provides few direct pointers regarding the application of the *vicinitas* requirement. However, it was recognized as early as 1632 that the dominant and servient tenements need not be directly contiguous.[121] This was stated explicitly in 1871 by Lord Deas in *McGibbon* v. *Rankin*:[122]

The Roman law carried this last principle [the requirement of *utilitas* (utility)] so far as to require vicinity, even in the case of a servitude of pasturage, which we do not require, provided there is access between the dominant and servient subject.

Although this is not an accurate statement as to the position in Roman law, it is a clear enough indication of the flexible approach towards the *vicinitas* requirement in Scots law. Furthermore, the facts of numerous cases, especially those dealing with urban servitudes such as the *servitus altius non tollendi*, bear testimony to the acceptance that direct contiguity cannot be a general requirement for the establishment of servitudes.[123] It is suggested that certain dicta in *Patrick* v. *Napier*,[124] which may seem to imply the opposite, are in fact completely reconcilable with this conclusion.[125] In that case the court refused to acknowledge a right of angling as a servitude, *inter alia* because the dominant tenement was not adjacent to the stream in question. The court confirmed that a positive servitude (normally a rural servitude) can only be established if the dominant and servient tenements are either contiguous or if there is another form of access to the servient tenement. This, of course, is only an endorsement of the view already held in Roman law and a confirmation of what Erskine (to whom the court referred with approval)[126] had previously stated for Scots law.[127]

It is therefore clear that *vicinitas* is not, and has never been, an independent

---

[119] Erskine, II, 9, 33.   [120] Paul. D. 8, 3, 7, 1 read with Ulp. D. 8, 3, 5, 1.
[121] *Laird of Penniemuir* (1632) Mor 14502; Gordon (n. 4), 754.
[122] (1871) 9 M 423 at 433.
[123] See e.g. *Cockburn* v. *Wallace and Governors of Heriot's Hospital* (1825) 4 S 128; *McGibbon* v. *Rankin* (1871) 9 M 423.   [124] (1867) 5 M 683 at 699 and 701.
[125] See also Gordon (n. 4), 729; Cusine/Paisley (n. 4), 118 sqq.
[126] (1867) 5 M 683 at 701 *per* Lord Curriehill.
[127] See above for the quotation from Erskine, II, 9, 33.

requirement for the establishment of servitudes in Scots law. It is, at most, treated as a factor which has to be taken into consideration when the more fundamental requirement of *utilitas* (utility) is at issue. In other words, the distance between the dominant and servient tenements is merely one of the factors to be examined when the question is asked whether a particular servitude can be of benefit to the dominant tenement.[128] Practically speaking this would mean, in some instances, that the dominant and servient tenements must indeed be contiguous (such as in the case of the servitudes *oneris ferendi* or *tigni immittendi*);[129] in other instances, that there must at least be a form of access (for example, a servitude of way over the intermediate land) to the servient tenement if the tenements are not contiguous (such as in the case of a servitude of pasturage or a servitude *aquaehaustus*);[130] and finally, in still other cases, that there need not be any physical connection between the tenements at all, provided that the servitude can still be beneficially exercised (such as in the case of *servitus altius non tollendi*).[131] This flexible approach towards the *vicinitas* requirement is in complete consonance with the prevailing view in both South African[132] and German law.[133]

(c) Utilitas *(utility)*

By now it will be clear that *utilitas* (utility) operates as a core requirement for the establishment of servitudes. Perhaps for that reason, it is a complex and nuanced requirement, a detailed discussion of which falls outside the scope of this contribution.[134]

Paul. D. 8, 1, 8 pr. is rightly seen as the *fons et origo* of this requirement for the establishment of servitudes: 'Ut pomum decerpere liceat et ut spatiari et ut cenare in alieno possimus, servitus imponi non potest.'[135] This text, and other texts dealing with the right to take raw materials (such as chalk, clay, sand, or stone) from the servient tenement,[136] seem indicative of a narrow interpretation of *utilitas*.[137] They suggest that the requirement is satisfied only if the particular servitude is of direct utility to the dominant tenement in accordance with the tenement's natural character and condition. This interpretation, which must be understood in the context of the inception of the oldest (rural) servitudes in an ancient agricultural age, will only allow for the

---

[128] Rankine (n. 56), 414; Gordon (n. 4), 729; Cusine/Paisley (n. 4), 115 sqq.
[129] See further below V.2.e.   [130] Erskine II, 9, 33.   [131] Ibid.
[132] De Waal, *Southern Cross* (n. 12), 785, 790 sqq.; *idem* (n. 60), 52 sqq; *idem*, 1990 *TSAR* 197 sqq.   [133] De Waal (n. 60), 47 sq.; *idem*, 1990 *TSAR* 194 sq.
[134] For a more comprehensive historical and comparative analysis of this requirement, see De Waal (n. 60), 99 sq. See also Jan L. Neels, 'Erfdiensbaarhede: Nut vir die Heersende Erf', 1988 *TSAR* 154 sqq.; C. G. van der Merwe, 'Die Nutvereiste by Erfdiensbaarhede', in D. J. Joubert (ed.), *Petere Fontes: L. C. Steyn-Gedenkbundel*, (n.d.), 164 sqq.
[135] ('A servitude cannot be created to the effect that a man shall be at liberty to pluck apples, or to walk about, or to dine on another man's ground.'—tr. C. H. Monro, *Translation of the Digest of Justinian* (1909), vol. 2).   [136] e.g. Ulp. D. 8, 3, 5, 1; Paul. D. 8, 3, 6, 1 pr.
[137] See the authorities quoted above in n. 121.

establishment of servitudes which enhance the exploitation of the dominant tenement as an agricultural unit.

In time the Romans outgrew this intimate relationship with agriculture and progressive urbanization became the norm, and with this change the urban servitudes[138] developed. These servitudes could no longer be explained by reference to a narrow interpretation of the *utilitas* requirement, and their development is itself proof of a widening of the interpretation of the requirement. In terms of this new interpretation a servitude must increase the utility, or usefulness, of the dominant tenement in accordance with the tenement's economic, industrial, or professional purpose. In other words, the tenement's economic exploitation is of importance and not only its natural character and condition.

As is the case with the other requirements, there is not much evidence of a theoretical discourse among the institutional writers. Rather reference to *utilitas* was made in the discussion of specific servitudes.[139] However, Erskine[140] was again an exception:

As all servitudes are restraints upon property, they are *stricti iuris*, and so not to be inferred by implication. Neither does the law give them countenance unless they have some tendency to promote the advantage of the dominant tenement.

This is not a very precise formulation, but it conveys the essence of the *utilitas* requirement: the servitude should enhance the usefulness and enjoyment of the dominant tenement as such and it should not merely be aimed at the pleasure or caprice of the person who happens to be its owner at a particular time. This was the guiding criterion in Roman and Roman-Dutch law and it is still regarded as such in German and South African law.[141] The criterion is, of course, easier to formulate than to apply, as the case law shows.

The first (and perhaps most problematic) group of cases dealt with attempts to create servitudes aimed solely at the pleasure or entertainment of the owner of the dominant tenement. An early example was *Cochran* v. *Fairholm*,[142] where Cochran and others alleged that they had acquired a servitude *spatiandi* over the land of Fairholm in terms of which they enjoyed the right to 'amuse themselves by playing at golf, and in walking' on the land. This case, as well as *Dyce* v. *Hay* discussed next, dealt with public rights and not, strictly speaking, with servitude rights. However, these cases are analysed here both because the rights claimed were referred to as 'servitudes' and

---

[138] For examples, see Ulp. D. 8, 2, 1, 5; Ulp. D. 8, 2, 1, 7; Gai. D. 8, 2, 2; Ulp. D. 8, 2, 3; Ulp. D. 8, 5, 8, 1. See also above III.1.

[139] e.g. Bell, *Principles*, § 986 (the taking of fuel or slate) and § 1013 (pasturage); Hume, *Lectures* III, 268 sq. (bleaching and the *jus spatiandi*).

[140] Erskine, II, 9, 33. See, however, also Stair, II, 7, 9: 'The predial or country servitudes, whereby one ground or field is subservient to another, may be as manifold as the free use of the one may be restrained or impaired, *for the profit or pleasure of the other* . . .' (my emphasis).

[141] See n. 134.   [142] (1759) Mor 14518.

because they contain pronouncements which seem important for the law of servitudes in general. The court in the *Cochran* case refused to acknowledge the servitude claimed. No reason was given, but it was argued on behalf of Fairholm that there was no dominant tenement in favour of which the servitude could be constituted.[143] It is possible that the court was swayed by this argument. But it is in any event clear that, falling squarely within the prohibition of Paul. D. 8, 1, 8 pr., this was exactly the kind of servitude the Romans would not have allowed. The non-compliance with the *utilitas* requirement can therefore also be advanced as a ground for the court's decision.

In *Dyce* v. *Hay*[144] the pursuer argued that a servitude, enabling him to use the land of the defender for recreation, walking, 'taking air' and exercise, was established through prescription over the land of the defender. Again the court refused to give recognition to a servitude of this kind. Contrasting the servitude claimed with a servitude of 'foot-road', one of the 'well-known and recognized servitudes in the Law of Scotland',[145] the court proclaimed that it was not recognized in Scots law.[146] This decision was confirmed by the House of Lords[147] on the ground that '[a]ll the servitudes hitherto recognized sanctioned no principle which would entitle a party not merely to walk and recreate over public grounds, but over the enclosed domain of a private gentleman—a right inconsistent with property'.[148]

It is significant that in neither case was the court's decision explicitly based on the non-compliance with the *utilitas* requirement. The same is true of *Harvey* v. *Lindsay*[149] where the court, only one year after the decision of the House of Lords in *Dyce* v. *Hay*, concluded that a 'right of curling and skating' on a lake in winter could not be acquired as a servitude by the feuars and inhabitants of a neighbouring village.

Patrick v. *Napier*[150] was more forthcoming. The case concerned a 'right of angling or rod-fishing', and in the course of the judgment the following was said concerning the *utilitas* requirement:[151] 'I think a predial servitude must be something which constitutes a burden upon one tenement or predium, for the purpose of creating an advantage or benefit to another predium.'

And again:[152] 'I think that none of the servitudes known to the law of Scotland as predial servitudes are of such a nature that it cannot be fairly and properly said that the dominant tenement, as a predium, receives a benefit from the servient.'

But how was this interpreted by the court? For the Lord President the criterion seemed to be whether the servitude in question would be one that is

---

[143] See above V.2.a.   [144] (1849) 11 D 1266. See also above IV.2.
[145] At 1278 *per* Lord Medwyn.
[146] See also *Sanderson* v. *Lees* (1859) 22 D 24 at 29; *Magistrates of Edinburgh* v. *Magistrates of Leith* (1877) 4 R 997 at 1000.   [147] *Dyce* v. *Hay* (1852) 15 D (HL) 14.
[148] (1852) 15 D (HL) 14 at 15–16 *per* the Lord Chancellor.
[149] (1853) 15 D 768. See also above IV.2.   [150] (1867) 5 M 683.
[151] (1867) 5 M 683 at 699 *per* the Lord President.   [152] Ibid.

peculiarly suitable or convenient for the particular dominant tenement—more so than for any other tenement from which access to the stream could be obtained.[153] This interpretation was endorsed by Lord Deas, who stressed the importance of a 'peculiar advantage of the dominant tenement' in contrast with the 'general and slighter advantage' which would equally accrue to any other tenement on which the privilege might be conferred.[154] In the event the court ruled that this 'peculiar advantage' was absent because the dominant tenement was not adjacent to the stream.[155] This decision was approved more than seventy years later in *Harper* v. *Flaws*.[156]

The interpretation advanced in *Patrick* v. *Napier* is a sophisticated one which seeks to explain why a servitude cannot confer a right to walk (for recreation), skate, play golf, or fish on the servient tenement. However, it does more than that. It also goes a long way towards explaining the establishment of those servitudes which are not aimed at the better economic exploitation of the dominant tenement (as in the traditional rural servitudes),[157] but rather at the enhancement of the enjoyment or pleasure which successive owners derive from the tenement (mainly the traditional urban servitudes).[158] The point is that the advantage or benefit generated by the servitude must be the result of the utilization of the dominant tenement. It cannot exist independently of the dominant tenement. This approach, already noticeable in Hume[159] and among the Roman-Dutch authors,[160] also explains how modern versions of urban servitudes[161] can be established within the regulatory confines of the *utilitas* requirement.

Mention may also be made of some other servitudes. In the servitude of pasturage, special difficulties arose if the number of sheep or cattle was not stipulated in the original grant. In such instances the number allowed to graze was then limited by reference to the requirements of the dominant tenement. In this respect the proper utilization of the dominant tenement seemed to be decisive, rather than its size, nature, or other physical charac-

---

[153] (1867) 5 M 683 at 699 *per* the Lord President.   [154] (1867) 5 M 683 at 706.

[155] See above V.2.b. And see also *Marquis of Huntly* v. *Nicol* (1896) 23 R 610 at 616 *per* Lord McLaren as to the right of shooting: 'I cannot see how it can be represented as an advantage to the estate of Ballogie that its proprietor should have the right of shooting in the forest of Birse.'

[156] 1940 SLT 150 at 151.

[157] e.g. the servitudes of way, pasturage and drawing or leading water (*aquaehaustus* or *aquaeductus*).   [158] e.g. the servitudes of view and light.

[159] Hume, *Lectures*, III, 269: 'It seems rather to be of the nature of a personal privilege (which our law does not recognise) and for the gratification of an individual—than a matter of substantial benefit to a tenement, so as to bring it under the maxim of *praedium servit praedio*.'

[160] e.g. Voet (n. 77), VIII, 4, 15; Huber (n. 98), II, 43, 11; Dionysius Godefridus van der Keessel, *Dictata ad Justiniani Institutionum* (1965 edn. by B. Beinart, B. L. Hijmans, and P. van Warmelo), II, 3, 8. See also De Waal (n. 60), 118 sqq.

[161] e.g. the so-called *Annehmlichkeitsdienstbarkeiten* in German law and restrictive conditions in South African law: De Waal (n. 60), 139 sqq. and 196 sqq.; *idem*, 1995 *TSAR* 197 sqq. and 205 sqq. See further below VI.1.

teristics,[162] an approach indicative of the more flexible interpretation of the *utilitas* requirement.[163]

In the servitude permitting the taking of raw materials from the servient tenement, the limit set by the *utilitas* requirement was that the material must be used for the benefit of the dominant tenement as such and not for the incidental personal benefit of a particular owner. A servitude could therefore be established allowing seaware to be taken as manure for the dominant tenement, but not for the manufacture of kelp.[164] A servitude of taking slate entitled the owner of the dominant tenement to use the slate on the dominant tenement, but not to sell it.[165] Likewise, a servitude of taking material (for example, peat) for fuel did not entitle the owner of the dominant tenement to supply fuel to a limework opened on his land.[166] These examples illustrate a reluctance in the older authorities to recognize servitudes for commercial purposes, an issue discussed again below.[167]

(*d*) Perpetua causa *(permanent cause)*

Paul. D. 8, 2, 28 is sometimes referred to as Roman law authority for another requirement for the establishment of servitudes, namely that of permanent basis or cause (*perpetua causa*). This requirement implies that the servient tenement must be continuously capable of fulfilling the needs of the dominant.[168] If applied literally, this formulation would, of course, severely restrict the establishment of praedial servitudes, but the practice has been more flexible. The Pandectists saw *perpetua causa* as no more than an aspect of *utilitas*: the nature and qualities of the servient tenement, from which the

---

[162] *Ferguson v. Tennant* 1978 SC (HL) 19 at 50 *per* Lord Robertson: 'I agree with the argument presented on behalf of the petitioner to the effect that it is the *utilitas* or potential of the dominant tenement that has to be considered, and that this concept includes the use of the pasture available on the servient tenement, with its limitations.' See also *Beaumont v. Lord Glenlyon* (1843) 5 D 1337 at 1343; *Fraser v. Secretary of State for Scotland and Others* 1959 SLT 36. By and large, this also seems to be the approach both of the institutional writers (see e.g. Bell, *Principles*, § 1013; Erskine, II, 9, 14) and of modern authors (see e.g. Duncan (n. 4), § 488; Rankine (n. 56), 455).

[163] And is in line with developments in e.g. South African law. See De Waal (n. 60), 176 sqq.; *idem, Southern Cross* (n. 12), 796.

[164] *McTaggart v. McDouall* (1867) 5 M 534 at 547 *per* Lord Benholme: 'But in regard to the right of cutting ware for making kelp, that is a mere means of mercantile advantage. It is not a means of enriching the dominant tenement at all; it has none of the characters of a predial servitude; and therefore, so far as that is concerned, I do not see that the idea of servitude could ever be entertained.' See also *Baird v. Fortune* (1861) 23 D (HL) 5; *Agnew v. Lord Advocate* (1873) 11 M 309.   [165] Bell, *Principles*, § 986.

[166] *Leslie v. Cumming* (1793) Mor 14542 at 14544; Bell, *Principles*, § 986. As to the taking of material for fuel, see also in general *Grierson v. School Board of Sandsting and Aithsting* (1882) 9 R 437. One imagines that in instances like these the owner of the dominant tenement should not be allowed to sell the material; however, see the facts of the following cases: *Murdoch v. Carstairs* (1823) 2 S 159; *Carstairs v. Brown* (1829) 7 S 607. A servitude of this nature can apparently not be constituted for the extraction of a mineral such as coal: *Harvie v. Stewart* (1870) 9 M 129; Duncan (n. 4), § 489. See, however, *Harrowar's Trustees v. Erskine* (1827) 5 S 284.

[167] See further below VI.1.   [168] De Waal, *Southern Cross* (n. 12), 793.

benefit for the dominant tenement is to be derived, cannot be merely transient or incidental.[169]

There is no indication that *perpetua causa* was ever considered as an independent requirement in Scots law. For example, adherence to the literal interpretation of Paul. D. 8, 2, 28 would have made the establishment of some of the urban servitudes (such as the *servitus oneris ferendi* or the *servitus tigni immittendi*) impossible: *neque enim perpetuam causam habet quod manu fit*.[170] Rankine[171] writes:

> The rule of Roman law that a servitude must have a *causa perpetua*,—i.e., that the state of things on which it rests for its existence must be permanent, though its exercise may be subject to terms and conditions—will apply in Scotland so far as to exclude from the category of servitudes such rights as depend on the continued or recurrent activity of the servient owner, or on the transient, easily exhaustible character of the servient tenement, such as a *stagnum*.

(e) Servitus in faciendo consistere nequit *(passivity)*

The requirement of passivity begins with Pomp. D. 8, 1, 15, 1: 'Servitutium non ea natura est, ut aliquid faciat quis, veluti viridia tollat aut amoeniorem prospectum praestet, aut in hoc ut in suo pingat, sed ut aliquid patiatur aut non faciat.'[172]

According to this text the owner of the servient tenement could be obliged to endure some act being performed on his tenement or to refrain from performing an act himself. But, subject to one exception,[173] he could not be compelled to perform a positive act. This rule is reflected in the (post-Roman[174]) maxim *servitus in faciendo consistere nequit*. It is apparent that passivity is a corollary to the real character of servitudes. But it also serves to keep the content of servitudes within certain limits. By contrast with *utilitas*, it does not prescribe what the content of a servitude can be, but rather what it cannot be.

The institutional writers treated passivity as a fundamental requirement, although without much inquiry as to the underlying principle.[175]

---

[169] For a historical and comparative discussion of this requirement, see De Waal (n. 60), 66 sqq.; idem, '*Perpetua Causa* (Permanente Grondslag) as Vestigingsvereiste vir Grondserwitute', (1991) 54 *THRHR* 717 sqq.

[170] ('[A]s what is effected by human hands has no perpetual cause'—tr. Monro (n. 135)).

[171] Rankine (n. 56), 425.

[172] ('It is not of the nature of servitudes that a man should do anything; for instance, remove shrubs so as to afford a more pleasing view, or, with the same object, paint something on his own ground; but only that he should submit to something being done or abstain from doing something.'—tr. Monro (n. 135)). See also Paul. D. 33, 1, 12.

[173] The *servitus oneris ferendi*: see below.

[174] Probably attributable to the Glossators and Post-glossators.

[175] Stair, II, 7, 5 and 6; Bankton, II, 7, 2; Erskine, II 9, 1; Bell, *Principles*, § 984. The Pandectists used passivity as a mechanism to free the German law of servitudes from the *Reallasten*, under which positive duties could be imposed on owners of land (e.g. payment of rent, the

Hume,[176] however, saw passivity as 'a proper and a natural consequence of the notion of servitude as a real right, which is exerted over an inert and passive subject.' As well as stating the requirement, the institutional writers provided abundant evidence of its application in practice. Their examples included the following: in the case of a servitude of drainage, the dominant owner must clean and repair the drain;[177] in the case of a servitude of way, the dominant owner must keep the road in a state of good repair;[178] and in the case of a *servitus aquaeductus*, the dominant owner must 'preserve the aqueducts and damheads in such condition that the adjacent grounds may suffer no prejudice by the breaking out of the water'.[179]

The only exception to passivity acknowledged in Roman law was the servitude of support (*servitus oneris ferendi*).[180] Here the servient owner could be compelled to perform a positive duty, namely the maintenance of the building providing the support,[181] and the duty ran with the land.[182] It was, furthermore, part and parcel of the servitude as such, and an agreement between the parties was not necessary in order to create the obligation.

There was disagreement among the institutional writers as to whether the *servitus oneris ferendi* constituted an exception to passivity.[183] There was support both for the view that it did[184] and also for the opposite view.[185] Then there also appeared to be a *via media*, namely 'that the owner of the servient tenement is not bound to repair it for the use of the dominant, unless an obligation to repair be inserted in the right . . .'[186]—a view which can also be found in Heineccius.[187] There was, however, agreement that the owner of an

supply of wood, foodstuffs and other products, and the performance of maintenance duties). See De Waal (n. 60), 210 sqq.; *idem*, 'Die Passiwiteitsvereiste by Grondserwitute en die Skepping van Positiewe Serwituutverpligtinge', 1991 *TSAR* 233 sqq.

[176] Hume, *Lectures*, III, 271.   [177] Bell, *Principles*, § 984.   [178] Ibid.
[179] Erskine, II, 9, 13.
[180] The position was the same in Roman-Dutch law and has been taken over into South African law. See De Waal (n. 60), 224 and 257 sqq.; *idem, Das römisch-holländische Recht* (n. 12), 584 and 799 sqq.; *idem*, 1991 *TSAR* 237 sqq.
[181] Ulp. D. 8, 5, 6, 2. Several other texts confirm that the *servitus oneris ferendi* constituted an exception to the requirement of passivity: see Paul. D. 8, 2, 1, 1; Paul. D. 8, 2, 33; Ulp. D. 8, 5, 6, 5–7; Paul. D. 8, 5, 7; Ulp. D. 8, 5, 8. See also in general Buckland (n. 13), 259; Elvers (n. 75), 55; Kaser (n. 15), 443; Schulz (n. 15), 384 (who doubts the exception for classical Roman law); Schwind (n. 15), 229; Van der Ploeg (n. 115), 155; Van Oven (n 15), 143; Weiss (n. 98), 222.
[182] Ulp. D. 8, 5, 6, 3.
[183] It should be pointed out that there has never been any suggestion, from Roman law onwards, that the *servitus tigni immittendi* (although akin to the *servitus oneris ferendi*) also constitutes an exception to the requirement of passivity. Both these servitudes are classified as positive servitudes, which is important regarding the ways they may be constituted: see in general Duncan (n. 4), § 484; Cusine/Paisley (n. 4), 194 sqq; and also the English case of *Dalton v. Angus* (1881) 6 AC (HL) 740 (referred to with approval in *Troup v. Aberdeen Heritable Securities Co.* 1916 SC 918 at 928).   [184] Bankton, II, 7, 2; Mackenzie (n. 2), II, 9 at 179.
[185] Bell, *Principles*, § 984 and § 1003.   [186] Erskine, II, 9, 8. See also Stair, II, 7, 9.
[187] Johann Gotlieb Heineccius, *Recitationes in Elementa Iuris Civilis secundum Ordinem Institutionem* (1773), II, 3, 399–401. A number of Pandectists also interpreted the servitude in this way: see e.g. Thibaut (n. 54), 48; Windscheid (n. 64), 955 n. 3.

apartment in a block consisting of more than one storey had a duty to provide support for the storey above.[188] Furthermore it was not doubted that, in this case, the duty also entailed that the property be kept in such a state of repair as to be capable of providing the necessary support. But this was characterized, not as servitude but as common interest. According to Hume[189] it 'may resemble a servitude' but actually 'arises naturally and immediately from that joint and common interest, which all heritors have in the whole building'.[190] This left thirlage[191] as the only true exception to the requirement of passivity.

When case law considered passivity, the issue tended to arise in the practical context of whether a duty of repair could be devolved on a servient owner.[192] According to the cryptic report in *Parson of Dundee* v. *Inglish*,[193] a case from 1687, 'when one hath the servitude of an aqueduct to a mill, through a neighbour's ground, the person who hath the benefit of the aqueduct (and not the party servient) is liable to maintain the same . . .'.[194]

In *Nicolson* v. *Mellvill*,[195] decided thirty years later, it was held that an obligation on the owner of a lower flat in a tenement building to contribute towards the maintenance of the roof of the building could not be constituted as a servitude. And regarding a servitude of way, it was confirmed in *Allan* v. *MacLachlan*[196] that repairs required to keep the road in a serviceable condition must be executed by the dominant owner.[197]

It was generally accepted that thirlage could not be reconciled with the requirement of passivity.[198] Rankine considered passivity as of such overriding importance that he preferred to exclude thirlage from the category of servitudes.[199] But in *Harris* v. *Magistrates of Dundee*[200] Lord Ardmillan

[188] Bankton, II, 7, 2; Erskine, II, 9, 11; Hume, *Lectures*, III, 272; Stair, II, 7, 6.
[189] Hume, *Lectures*, III, 272.
[190] See also Bankton, II, 7, 2; Erskine, II, 9, 11; Stair, II, 7, 6.
[191] Thirlage was the obligation, long since obsolete, to bring grain from particular land (the servient tenement) to a particular mill (the dominant tenement) to be ground. See Gordon (n. 4), 306–10. It is abolished by the Abolition of Feudal Tenure etc (Scotland) Act 2000.
[192] Abstract statements concerning the requirement in general (or the principle underlying it) seem to be quite rare. See, however, *Mackenzie* v. *Carrick* (1869) 7 M 419 at 420.
[193] (1687) Mor 14521.
[194] As far as a *servitus aquaeductus* is concerned, the court reached exactly the same conclusion nearly 200 years later in *Scottish Highland Distillery Co.* v. *Reid* (1877) 4 R 1118 at 1122. See also *Central Regional Council* v. *Ferns* 1979 SC 136.
[195] (1708) Mor 14516. According to the report (14517) the Lords expressed the view that if a servitude such as this were allowed, 'then other unheard of servitudes might be introduced, such as that you shall bear a share of the expenses of the floors, and glass windows of your neighbouring tenements, seeing you are benefited thereby'.
[196] (1900) 2 F 699.
[197] For further case law on this point, see *Robertson* v. *Scottish Union and National Insurance Co.* 1943 SC 427; *Rogano Ltd* v. *British Railways Board* 1979 SC 297.
[198] Gordon (n. 4), 756. See also in general *Harris* v. *Magistrates of Dundee* (1863) 1 M 833; *Forbes' Trustees* v. *Davidson* (1892) 19 R 1022.
[199] Rankine (n. 56), 416. Cusine/Paisley (n. 4), 196 are of the same view.
[200] (1863) 1 M 833 at 846. However, in the same case (at 844) Lord Deas states his opinion that thirlage is not 'properly speaking' a servitude. See further below VI.1.

was not prepared, in the light of the 'predominance of authority' to the contrary, to deny thirlage its status as a servitude.

(f) Known to the law

According to Bell,[201] a servitude 'shall be such a use or restraint as by law or custom is known to be likely and incident to the property in question, and to which the attention of a prudent purchaser will, in the circumstances, naturally be called'.

This would seem intended to limit the dangers which may flow from the fact that servitudes do not require registration. Gordon[202] lists being 'known to the law' as a formal requirement, emphasizing as it does 'that the final test of the existence of a servitude is its recognition as such by the courts'. And no doubt there are many cases in which a formulation of this nature can be found.[203] Other modern authors also refer to this element.[204]

This is, perhaps, a surprising approach. The function of the traditional requirements, already discussed, is to ensure that the creation of new servitudes should only take place along certain clear guidelines—in other words, to enable a court to put its seal of approval on a new servitude right. Furthermore, it seems paradoxical to set 'known to the law' as an independent requirement in a structure of servitudes which has been characterized as 'open'. This, it is suggested, is really what Lord Robertson tried to convey in *Harvey* v. *Lindsay*[205] where he said: 'I go quite along with the observations which have been made in recent cases, that we are not to limit servitudes to those already known and recognised in law, as in the progress of society alterations may take place, and new servitudes may arise.'

It will be argued below that the formulation and acceptance of this element as a formal requirement might have been an inhibiting factor in the development of the law.

VI. DEVELOPMENT AND CHANGE

1. Creation of new servitude types

The thrust of what has been said thus far is that nothing in the structure of the law of servitudes would have prevented a process of natural growth and development. First, the system has remained an open one in that it was

---

[201] Bell, *Principles*, § 979.   [202] Gordon (n. 4), 732 sq.

[203] e.g. *McGibbon* v. *Rankin* (1871) 9 M 423 at 433; *Alexander* v. *Butchart* (1875) 3 R 156 at 160; *Braid Hills Hotel Co. Ltd* v. *Manuels* 1908 SC 120 at 126; *Anderson* v. *Dickie* 1914 SC 706 at 717; *McLean* v. *Marwhirn Developments Ltd* 1976 SLT (Notes) 47.

[204] Rankine (n. 56), 418; Duncan (n. 4), § 451; Cusine/Paisley (n. 4), 144 sqq. The position may be about to change. The Scottish Law Commission has recommended the abandonment of the 'known to the law' test in the case of servitudes constituted by registration. See *Report on Real Burdens* (Scot. Law Com. No. 181, 2000), Paras 12.22 to 12.25.

[205] (1853) 15 D 768 at 775.

always accepted that there is no *numerus clausus* of servitudes.[206] Secondly, the interpretation and application of the core requirement of *utilitas* has always remained flexible.[207] Did these fundamentals translate into practical development and growth?

Regarding the creation of new types of servitudes, the overall picture is one of initial development and later stagnation. Already in Hume[208] one finds a list of servitudes recognized in practice in the eighteenth and early nineteenth centuries 'besides those which were known in the Roman Law'. These included the following:[209]

(a) the servitude of cutting timber in another's woods for use on the dominant tenement;

(b) the servitude of spreading and watering lint on the servient tenement;

(c) the servitude of washing and drying linen by a stream or pool on the servient tenement;

(d) the servitude of winning stone slate in a pit or quarry on the servient tenement for use on the dominant tenement; and

(e) a servitude of bleaching linen on the servient tenement.

To these modern authors can add only three further examples,[210] the most recent being from the early twentieth century:

(a) the servitude of taking seaware or seaweed from the shore adjacent to the servient tenement for use on the dominant tenement;

(b) the servitude of taking sand and gravel from the servient tenement for use on the dominant tenement; and

(c) the servitude of discharging waste water from the dominant onto the servient tenement.

An independent survey of the case law did not yield any further examples.

What is immediately striking is the absence from this list of the more 'modern' negative servitudes found in other legal systems. There are no conditions aimed at protecting aesthetic, hygienic, or social standards within residential areas; and there are no conditions to protect a trade or business on the dominant tenement against a competitor activity on the servient.[211] There has also been a reluctance to recognize new positive servitudes, such as the right to lead electricity.[212]

---

[206] Above IV.2. [207] Above V.2.c. [208] Hume, *Lectures*, III, 269 sq.
[209] See Hume, *Lectures*, III, 270 for references to case law.
[210] Rankine (n. 56), 418 sqq.; Gordon (n. 4), 734 sq.; Duncan (n. 4), § 491; Cusine/Paisley (n. 4), 36 sqq.
[211] For an analysis of these types of servitudes and references to relevant sources, see De Waal (n. 60), 139 sqq. and 180 sqq.; *idem*, 1995 *TSAR* 197 sqq. and 205 sqq.; *idem*, *Southern Cross* (n. 12), 796 sq.
[212] *Neill* v. *Scobbie* 1993 GWD 13-887. See also *Mendelsohn* v. *The Wee Pub Co. Ltd* 1991 GWD 26-1518 (hanging of signs).

Servitudes

Various factors may explain this lack of development.

First, there is the 'known to the law' requirement mentioned earlier.[213] It may not have been sufficiently appreciated that the more traditional requirements already served to control the creation of new servitudes. An additional 'known to the law' requirement could easily come to be the sole criterion, thereby undermining the principle of an open structure of servitudes.

Secondly, while the *utilitas* requirement was interpreted flexibly,[214] there were signs almost from the beginning that servitudes would not be extended to commercial matters.[215] This was evident in the decisions that fuel could not be taken for a limework on the dominant tenement,[216] and that seaware could not be taken for the manufacture of kelp.[217] In this last instance the court felt that 'a mere means of mercantile advantage' could not be 'a means of enriching the dominant tenement at all'.[218] This was presumably a matter of policy, for as the experience of other systems shows, there is nothing in the *utilitas* requirement which would have prevented such a development. A notable exception was thirlage, which protected the capital outlay in the construction of a mill by ensuring that servient owners brought their corn there to be ground. Its aim and the effect was quite blatantly 'to restrain the right of selection, and to create a monopoly'.[219]

Thirdly, the emergence of real burdens, in the last years of the eighteenth century,[220] had a negative impact on the vitality of the law of servitudes. Real burdens provided an alternative, and perhaps an easier, way to accomplish many of the objectives for which servitudes might otherwise have been used; and, unlike servitudes, they were capable of imposing a positive obligation. In the nineteenth century amenity and commercial restrictions were created, not as servitudes, but as real burdens.

Finally, the fact that servitudes (unlike real burdens) did not require to be registered was an inhibiting factor, particularly in the later period when the value of a public register of real rights was frequently acknowledged.

2. Flexibility within the traditional types

A trend noticeable in the development of servitudes in other countries is the inherent ability of traditional servitudes to adapt themselves to changing circumstances. Common and obvious examples include the following: a servitude of way constituted for use by horses and horse carts is later used to apply to transport by modern motor vehicles; a *servitus aquaeductus* in terms

---

[213] Above V.2.f. [214] Above V.2.c.
[215] e.g. *Town of Edinburgh* v. *Town of Leith* (1630) Mor 14500.
[216] *Leslie* v. *Cumming* (1793) Mor 14542 at 14544; Bell, *Principles*, § 986.
[217] *McTaggart* v. *McDouall* (1867) 5 M 534 at 547.   [218] Ibid. *per* Lord Benholme.
[219] *Harris* v. *Magistrates of Dundee* (1863) 1 M 833 at 846 *per* Lord Ardmillan.
[220] Reid (n. 1), § 375 sqq.

of which water was initially conveyed via rough canals is later exercised by using stainless steel pipes; and in terms of a *servitus aquaehaustus* water is initially extracted by means of a windmill and later by means of an electric pump. [221]

A survey of the case law shows that this natural process of development took place in Scots law also. Indeed the adaptability of traditional servitudes to changing conditions may be a further reason for the lack of development in the creation of new servitude types.[222]

VII. CONCLUSION AND EVALUATION

Like other civilian systems, Scots law drew deeply from Roman law in the development of a law of servitudes. And, like South African law, there may have been some resistance to receiving English law in this area. As far as South African law is concerned, the following explanation has been ventured:[223]

> With a clearly worked out system of rules and principles received from the Romans, the Roman-Dutch lawyers did not find it necessary to make much use of the works of other continental authors writing on servitudes. This probably explains the limited reliance on English law by the South African courts in their endeavour to develop this branch of the law. A sophisticated system was available to the courts and there was therefore little need to fall back on outside sources.

This explanation may likewise be valid for Scotland. But it has been suggested that there is, in any event, a close correspondence between the English law of easements and the Scots law of servitudes in that both were formulated with constant assistance from the Roman law.[224]

If there has been less development of the law of servitudes than might have been expected, this does not mean that servitudes have become unimportant. Many of the reasons why servitudes were constituted in ancient times remain relevant today. Nonetheless the fact that relatively few cases have been reported in the course of the twentieth century suggests a law where the essentials are well understood and which is disinclined to move into new areas.

---

[221] De Waal, *Das römisch-holländische Recht* (n. 12), 586 sqq.; *idem*, *Southern Cross* (n. 12), 804 sqq.   [222] Duncan (n. 4), § 447.
[223] De Waal, *Southern Cross* (n. 12), 816.
[224] Duncan (n. 4), § 440 who refers to the view of J. Mackintosh, *Roman Law in Modern Practice* (1934), 141. See also Cusine/Paisley (n. 4), 3.

8

Rights in Security over Moveables

ANDREW J. M. STEVEN

I. INTRODUCTION

The law on the subject of security-rights over corporeal moveables is beset with difficulties; and is not, perhaps, in a very satisfactory state, as the result of its rules is often to deprive the owner of such property of the power to make use of it as a security for his debts.[1]

More than 100 years after this statement was made by Gloag and Irvine, little has changed, apart from some statutory intervention.[2] In Scotland the law of rights in security over moveables remains underdeveloped. One of the greatest problems, and the one alluded to by the writers, is the rigid rule that in general there can be no real right in security unless the creditor has possession of the property. In the words of Lord Trayner: 'Now it is quite certain that an effectual security over moveables can only be effected by delivery of the subject of the security.'[3] One of the aims of this chapter will be to investigate how Scots law developed in order to reach this position.

Constraints of space make it impossible to provide an all-embracing account of the evolution of the law of moveable security. Rather, what will be attempted is an examination of the development of the three main types of real security over corporeal moveables: pledge, hypothec and lien. Their history will be explored to see to what extent they are based on Roman concepts and to what extent they have been influenced by other sources, in particular English law. It is not proposed to examine security over incorporeal moveables, security by transfer of ownership, or the various forms of functional securities such as retention of title clauses and trusts. The story of their development must be left for another day.

---

[1] W. M. Gloag and J. M. Irvine, *Law of Rights in Security* (1897), 187.
[2] In particular, the introduction of agricultural credits by the Agricultural Credits (Scotland) Act 1929 and floating charges by the Companies (Floating Charges) (Scotland) Act 1961. The present legislation governing floating charges is found in the Companies Act 1985 and the Insolvency Act 1986.   [3] *Pattison's Trs* v. *Liston* (1893) 20 R 806 at 813.

II. PLEDGE

1. Systems prior to Scots law

The concept of handing an item over in order to secure the performance of an obligation is of great antiquity.[4] It may be traced back to Genesis in the Old Testament.[5] In ancient Egypt, the practice grew up of individuals pledging their father's mummy. Such a pledge was particularly effective, for a debtor who failed in his obligation would be denied burial after his death.[6] Evidence of the existence of pledge can also be found in the early Greek, Indian, and Turkish civilizations.[7] The most important early system of law in terms of influencing the Scots law of pledge was however, undoubtedly the law of ancient Rome.[8]

Pledge (or *pignus*) was not the earliest type of security in Roman law. The original form was *fiducia cum creditore*, which involved the debtor transferring ownership of the property to the creditor by *mancipatio* or *in jure cessio*, subject to a covenant, *fiducia* or *pactum fiduciae*, that the creditor would reconvey upon the debtor fulfilling his obligation.[9] The essence of *fiducia cum creditore* was the transfer of ownership. The debtor lost his real right. This meant that the creditor could alienate the property to a third party, in breach of his *fiducia*, leaving the debtor with only his personal *actio fiduciae* against the creditor. It was this unsatisfactory characteristic of *fiducia* which most probably led to the development of *pignus*, which was in widespread use before the time of the Empire.

With *pignus*, the debtor transferred merely the possession of the property.[10] Ownership was retained, thus preventing the creditor from making a wrongful sale. However, *pignus* too was not entirely satisfactory in that the debtor was denied the use of the property because he had to hand it over to the creditor. This led to the development of *hypotheca*, the non-possessory pledge.[11]

---

[4] See generally, J. H. Wigmore, 'The Pledge-Idea: A Study in Comparative Legal Ideas', (1897) 10 *Harv LR* 321 sqq., (1897) 10 *Harv LR* 389 sqq., and (1898) 11 *Harv LR* 18 sqq.

[5] Genesis 38: 18.

[6] See S. Pufendorf, *De Iure Naturae et Gentium* (1672), V, 10, 13 and V. S. Meiners, 'Formal Requirements of Pledge under Louisiana Civil Code Article 3158 and Related Articles', (1987) 48 *La LR* 12 sqq.

[7] For Greece, see Meiners, (1987) 48 *La LR* 129. For India, see Wigmore, (1897) 10 *Harv LR* 389 at 416–17. For Turkey, see Sir William Jones, *An Essay on the Law of Bailments* (1781), 84–5.

[8] On the Roman law of pledge in general, see M. Kaser, *Roman Private Law* (2nd edn., 1968, trs. R. Dannenbring), 129–34; R. Sohm, *Institutes of Roman Law* (3rd edn., 1907, tr. J. C. Ledlie), 351–7; J. A. C. Thomas, *Textbook of Roman Law* (1976), 329–34; W. W. Buckland, *A Textbook of Roman Law* (3rd edn., 1966), 470–8; F. Schulz, *Classical Roman Law* (1951), 400–27 and R. J. Goebel, 'Reconstructing the Roman Law of Real Security', (1961–2) 36 *Tul LR* 29 sqq.

[9] Buckland (n. 8), 471; Goebel, (1961–2) 36 *Tul LR* 29 at 33–4.

[10] Buckland (n. 8), 472; Reinhard Zimmermann, *The Law of Obligations: Roman Foundations of the Civilian Tradition* (1990), 220.

[11] Thomas (n. 8), 332; Buckland (n. 8), 472–3; Goebel, (1961–2) 36 *Tul LR* 29 at 37–44.

2. Early Scots law

(a) The Regiam Majestatem

The first reference to pledge in the context of moveable property in Scots law appears in the *Regiam Majestatem*. The accuracy of *Regiam* as a statement of medieval Scots law has attracted much controversy,[12] and its treatment of pledge must be approached with care. That treatment is to be found in chapters 2–6 of book III of the work. The first thing to note is the terminology. The word used for pledge is *vadium*.[13] *Pignus* does get a passing reference in the title to chapter 2, in the form *pignoris*. It reads: 'De rebus creditis et mutuo dato sub vadii vel pignoris positione.'[14] The word *vadium* is the Latin term which has been used by English law since the Middle Ages to mean pledge.[15] The English influence, however, is more strikingly demonstrated by the fact that chapters 2–6 of book III of *Regiam* are based closely upon parallel passages in the English work, the *De Legibus et Consuetudinibus Angliae* of Glanvill.[16]

Regiam, following Glanvill, states that both moveable and immoveable property may be pledged.[17] There may be Roman influence here, for the civil law allowed the pledge of moveables and immoveables.[18] Indeed, the approach in *Regiam* makes the point that the law of real security, like the law of property in general, has a unitary foundation. Erskine clearly regarded it as an accurate statement of the law, as he used it to justify the following statement of the early Scots law of heritable security: 'Originally the property of the lands ... remained with the debtor, agreeably to the genuine nature of impignoration: it was the possession only which was transferred to the creditor for his security.'[19] Although the basic law of pledge applied to both moveables and immoveables, *Regiam* sets out some specific rules with respect to the latter much in line with the English law of the time.[20]

As regards constituting the security, *Regiam* states that in pledge the subject matter of the security is either immediately delivered by the debtor to the creditor on receipt of the loan, or it is not so delivered.[21] Whilst a parallel

---

[12] See e.g. A. A. M. Duncan, '*Regiam Majestatem*: A Reconsideration', [1961] *JR* 199 sqq. A. Harding, '*Regiam Majestatem* among Medieval Law-Books', [1984] *JR* 97 sqq., ch. 2 of this volume, 42–4.

[13] See e.g. *Regiam Majestatem*, III, 2, 1.

[14] Translated by Lord Cooper as 'Loans made subject to a pledge'. The use of *vel* i.e. 'or' suggests that *vadium* and *pignus* were alternatives. However, in the body of the text it is *vadium* which is used.

[15] For the Middle Ages, see F. Pollock and F. W. Maitland, *The History of English Law before Edward I* (2nd edn., 1896), vol. 2, 117. For today, see N. E. Palmer, *Bailment* (2nd edn., 1991), ch. 22.

[16] See G. D. G. Hall (ed.), *Tractabus de Legibus et Consuetudinibus Regni Anglie qui Glanvilla Voccator* (1965), X, 6–10.   [17] *Regiam Majestatem*, III, 2, 1; Glanvill (n. 16), X, 6.

[18] Thomas (n. 8), 332–3; Buckland (n. 8), 475–6.   [19] Erskine, II, 8, 4.

[20] *Regiam Majestatem*, III, 2, 5 and III, 5, 4.   [21] Ibid., III, 2.

passage is to be found in Glanvill,[22] the origin of this rule may well be Roman. For, in civil law the property was either delivered (*pignus*) or not delivered (*hypotheca*).[23] In fact, however, the flexibility available to the Roman debtor was in practice unavailable in early Scots law, for a later passage in *Regiam* states:

> When a bargain has been made between debtor and creditor regarding the pledging of some thing, if the debtor after having received the loan fails to deliver the pledge, what action is open to the creditor in such circumstances, especially in view of the risk that the same thing may have previously been pledged and may again be pledged, to other creditors? Upon this point it must be noted that the King's court is not in use to take cognisance of or warrant such private bargains about the giving or receiving of pledges.[24]

Thus an agreement resembling *hypotheca* was unenforceable. Lord Cooper is sceptical as to the accuracy of this passage.[25] Skene opined that the sheriff and barony courts would enforce such agreements, but there is no clear evidence to justify such a proposition.[26] The same may be said with regard to Professor Gordon's suggestion that action could be taken in the ecclesiastical courts.[27] The English authorities are clear that delivery was a necessity.[28] Glanvill requires it, because otherwise the property might be pledged to successive creditors, resulting in a situation much too complex for royal justice to resolve.[29] That delivery was a necessity in early Scots law is a proposition which finds support in later works.[30]

With respect to the contract of pledge, *Regiam* divides pledges into those for a limited period and those for an unlimited period.[31] Notwithstanding the division, a number of rules are set out which apply to both types. The duty of care of every pledgee is to keep the property in safe custody and not to make use of it in any way which will cause it to deteriorate.[32] Where the property requires expense, it is a matter for the parties to decide who is liable for the cost.[33]

Under the English law of Glanvill the pledgee's right did not amount to a real right. If a stranger dispossessed the pledgee, he had no remedy and had to rely on the pledger to take action.[34] Worse still, the pledgee had no remedy if the pledger himself repossessed the property. This rule was justified on the

---

[22] Glanvill (n. 16), X, 6.   [23] See generally, Goebel, (1961–2) 36 *Tul LR* 29 sqq.
[24] *Regiam Majestatem*, III, 4, 4–6.
[25] Lord Cooper, 'Notes', in *idem* (ed.), *Regiam Majestatem and Quoniam Attachiamenta*, Stair Society, vol. 11, (1947), 196.   [26] Ibid.
[27] W. M. Gordon, 'Roman Influence on the Scots Law of Real Security', in Robin Evans-Jones (ed.), *The Civil Law Tradition in Scotland* (1995), 157 at 161.
[28] Pollock/Maitland (n. 15), 120; T. F. T. Plucknett, *A Concise History of the Common Law* (5th edn., 1956), 603–4.   [29] Glanvill (n. 16), X, 8.
[30] In particular, Balfour, *Practicks*. See below II.4.c.
[31] *Regiam Majestatem*, III, 2, 1; III, 3, and III, 4.   [32] Ibid., III, 3–4.
[33] Ibid., III, 3, 3.   [34] Glanvill (n. 16), X, 11.

ground that the pledgee was entitled to the debt rather than the property and the court could award the pledgee his money rather than possession.[35] It is unsurprising that pledge in this form fell into disuse.

As regards Scotland, the passage in Glanvill denying the pledgee a possessory remedy was not transplanted into *Regiam*.[36] Additionally, Lord Cooper states that there is 'no evidence in Scottish records' that the pledger could reduce the pledgee from being a secured creditor to being an unsecured creditor merely by ejecting him from the property.[37] This may suggest that the medieval Scots pledgee had the real right which his English counterpart did not, but no definite conclusion seems possible.

With respect to enforcing the security, where property was pledged for a set period of time the parties could agree that it became the pledgee's if the pledger defaulted.[38] Where there was no such agreement, the pledgee could bring the pledger to court. The court would set a fixed period for the debt to be discharged. If this was not done within that period, the property became the pledgee's.[39] Thus with both types of pledge, the remedy was forfeiture. Pledge was not viewed as a collateral security. There is no Roman influence here: in the fourth century AD Constantine ruled out forfeiture as a remedy available to the pledgee.[40]

It may be useful in conclusion to summarize the key aspects of *Regiam*'s treatment of pledge. First, the term used for pledge is *vadium*. Secondly, pledge is a security which applies equally to moveable and immoveable properly. Thirdly, delivery of the property from pledger to pledgee is a necessity. Fourthly, the Scots pledgee has something more akin to a real right than his English counterpart. Fifthly, the remedy of the pledgee is forfeiture. In general, these rules can be said to be relatively primitive, particularly in regard to their unitary application and in regard to the pledgee's remedy.

(*b*) Leges Quatuor Burgorum

There are not actually any rules in this collection of laws directly applicable to the pledge of moveables. However, one title deals with the pledge of land.[41] As has been seen, pledge in terms of *Regiam* was a unitary concept, so the relevant title here is worthy of study. As regards terminology, the Latin *vadimonium* is used for pledge, a word which probably has the same root as *vadium*.[42] In the old Scots version of the text, the terms *wed* and *wedset* are used. *Wed* was the term used for pledge in Anglo-Saxon England.[43]

---

[35] Pollock/Maitland (n. 15), 120–1. [36] That is Glanvill (n. 16), X, 11.
[37] Lord Cooper (n. 25), 195. [38] *Regiam Majestatem*, III, 3, 4–11. [39] Ibid.
[40] Thomas (n. 8), 331; Zimmermann (n. 10), 223.
[41] *Leges Quatuor Burgorum*, title 79, in T. Thomson and C. Innes (eds.), *The Acts of the Parliaments of Scotland* (1814), vol. 1.
[42] In Roman law *vadimonium* meant bail: see Gai. 4, 184. In English law, *vadium* (pledge) is a type of bailment: see Palmer (n. 15). [43] Pollock/Maitland (n. 15), 117.

Consequently, more English influence can be seen. In terms of content, the title is a brief one. For present purposes, the point of note is the remedy of the creditor, which is to sell the land, recover his debt and return any excess to the debtor. This contrasts sharply with *Regiam* where the remedy was forfeiture.

3. The fifteenth century

As far as can be traced, the earliest cases on the pledge of moveables are to be found in the fifteenth century, in the collection of the Acts of the Lord Auditors of Causes and Complaints between the years of 1466 and 1494.[44] The term used for pledge here is *wed*, as in the *Leges Quatuor Burgorum*. The cases involve items made from precious metal. In two decisions, the Lord Auditors require property to be returned to the pledger upon his discharge of the debt.[45] Another case, *Elspeth of Douglas* v. *Wach of Dawik*[46] appears to apply the rule *nemo plus juris ad alienum transferre potest, quam ipse haberet*. The Lord Auditors order Wach to deliver to Elspeth a gold chain which a David Redehuch had pledged to him. A day is set down for Elspeth to prove that she owns the chain. The case shows that the Lord Auditors were prepared to prevent proprietorial rights from being infringed by unauthorized pledges.

4. The sixteenth century

(a) Wad-wives

Evidence of pledge in sixteenth-century Scotland can be found from records of the activities of wad-wives.[47] A wad-wife was a lady merchant and money lender. She took pledges of items such as jewellery and may be seen as the forerunner of the pawnbroker, although she does not appear to have been subject to any specific form of regulation. It seems that the pledges made to wad-wives were forfeiture pledges.[48] This view is consistent with that of contemporary legal writing.[49]

---

[44] T. Thomson (ed.), *Acta Dominorum Auditorum: The Acts of the Lord Auditors of Causes and Complaints 1466–1494* (1839).

[45] *Cokburn* v. *Twedy of Drumelior* (1478) ADA 65 and *Fleming* v. *Lord Crechton* (1479) ADA 87. See D. M. Walker, *A Legal History of Scotland*, vol. 2 (1990), 602.

[46] (1484) ADA 149*.

[47] Scottish Burgh Records Society, *Extracts from the Burgh Records of Edinburgh 1403–1528* (1869), 106 (3 Oct. 1505); Scottish Burgh Records Society, *Extracts from the Burgh Records of Edinburgh 1573–1589* (1882), 28 (26 Oct. 1574); M. H. B. Sanderson, *Mary Stewart's People* (1987), 91–101.

[48] There is no evidence in the records of wad-wives exposing pledged property to public sale on default upon the loan secured and thereafter paying any excess money raised to the debtor.

[49] See Balfour, *Practicks*, discussed below II.3.c.

(b) The Burgh Records

The Records of the Scottish Burghs in the sixteenth century show further examples of pledge in practice.[50] In these records the word *wed*, or a derivative, is used to mean pledge, just as in the *Leges Quatuor Burgorum* of four centuries before. Some interesting references to pledge concern the plague. When it affected Edinburgh, on several occasions, the council banned the pledging of clothes. For example, on 25 May 1530 the city fathers pronounced: 'Item that na maner of parsonis man nor woman tak ony claith in wedd fra utheris, or by ony auld clads, wou or lynnyn, under the pane of burning of thar chekis and banasing of the toune for all the dayes of thar lyffis.'[51] On a separate occasion it was provided that anyone caught breaching the rule for the second time would face death.[52]

(c) *Balfour's* Practicks

Unlike *Regiam* and the *Leges Quatuor Burgorum*, Balfour's account of Scots law up to 1579 was written in the vernacular. Balfour uses 'pledge' to mean caution, that is personal security.[53] Norman England used the word in the same manner, its term for security over a thing being 'gage'.[54] The apparent English influence upon medieval Scots law is demonstrated again.

Balfour discusses what we recognize now as pledge in the title immediately after that on caution.[55] The heading is 'Anent thingis laid in wad'. This is clearly an evolution from the 'wed' of the *Leges Quatuor Burgorum*. The chief source of Balfour's account is *Regiam*.[56] Like that work, Balfour states that both moveables and immoveables may be pledged.[57] For a statement of the law of the late sixteenth century, this is not entirely accurate. By that time, the pledge of immoveables had evolved into the wadset, where the creditor was not only given possession of the property, but also ownership.[58] For his part, Balfour uses the term wadset more or less interchangeably with wad.[59]

Balfour goes on to discuss the role of delivery in the following terms: 'Item, Efter that it is accordit and agreit betwix the debtour and the creditour, anent the laying of ony thing in wadset, quhat kind of thing that ever it be, movabill or immovabill, the debtour incontinent, efter he hes ressavit the

---

[50] See e.g. Scottish Burgh Records Society, *Extracts from the Burgh Records of Lanark 1150–1722* (1893), 53 (15 Feb. 1570–71); Scottish Burgh Records Society, *Extracts from the Burgh Records of Stirling 1519–1666* (1887), 78 (10 Apr. 1561).

[51] Scottish Burgh Records Society, *Extracts from the Burgh Records of Edinburgh 1528–1557* (1871), 28.

[52] Scottish Burgh Records Society, *Extracts from the Burgh Records of Edinburgh 1573–1589* (1882), 28 (26 Oct. 1574).   [53] Balfour, *Practicks*, 191–4.

[54] Pollock/Maitland (n. 15), 185, n. 2; Plucknett (n. 28), 628.   [55] Balfour, *Practicks*, 194.

[56] See the references at the end of c. 1, c. 2, c. 3, c. 4, c. 5, c. 8, and c. 9 (ibid., 194–6).

[57] Balfour, *Practicks*, 194, c. 1: 'Of divers kindis of waddis.'

[58] See Walker (n. 45), 683–8 and Gordon (n. 27), 160–4.

[59] For example, in Balfour, *Practicks*, 194, c. 2.

thing borrowit be him, sould put the creditour in possessioun or sasine of the wad.'[60] The passage gives *Regiam* as its source. Nevertheless, the wording here is rather different. Gone is the statement that either the property is delivered to the creditor or it is not. Instead, we are told that the property *should* be delivered to him. There is no express statement that the courts will not uphold agreements where there is no delivery. However, the implication is very clear. The property must be delivered to the creditor. There is no security without possession.

Like *Regiam*, Balfour's work divides pledges into those which are for a fixed period and those which are not.[61] The remedy for default on the debtor's part remains forfeiture of the property to the creditor. Balfour also sets out some distinct rules for pledges of moveables and immoveables. As regards moveables, his emphasis is on the contractual duties of the parties, such as the pledgee's duty of care in respect of the property.[62] He cites the case of *Foulis* v. *Cognerlie*,[63] which expresses the rule that if the pledged property is stolen or lost without the creditor being negligent, the debtor is still liable upon the debt. A second case, *Douglas* v. *Menzeis*,[64] holds that the debtor has no right to repossess his property until he has discharged the debt.

The main features of Balfour's work are the continuing influence of English law, the demand for delivery from pledger to pledger, and the fact that forfeiture remains the remedy in the event of default. Further, by the time he wrote, the law of real security is beginning to lose its unitary nature.

5. The seventeenth century

(a) Hope's Major Practicks

Hope's *Major Practicks* contains a short section on pledge entitled 'De Pignore'.[65] The terms *vadium*, *wed*, and *wad* have been put to one side. For the first time, the Roman *pignus* is used as the principal term for pledge in Scots law. It must be noted, however that the term *wed* is to be found within the title and that in a subsequent title *pledge* is used to mean caution.[66] There would appear to be a terminological struggle going on, between the Anglo-Norman law and Roman law. Hope's emphasis is on the duties of the pledger and pledgee. The pledgee is required to return the property on the debt being discharged.[67] If the property is destroyed without the pledgee being negligent, the pledger retains the duty to discharge the debt.[68] Hope, like Balfour, draws on *Regiam* as an authority.[69]

---

[60] For example, in Balfour, *Practicks*, 194, c. 2. 'The wad sould be deliverit to the creditour.'
[61] Ibid. 194 sq., c. 3: 'Of thingis wadset to a certane day'; 195, c. 4: 'Of thingis laid in wad without a certane day'. [62] Ibid. 195, c.5: 'Of movabill gudis laid in wad'.
[63] 6 Apr. 1566, reported in Balfour, *Practicks*, 195 sq., c. 6.
[64] 1 Mar. 1569, reported in Balfour, *Practicks*, 196, c. 7.   [65] Hope, *Practicks*, II, 9.
[66] Ibid.; and II, 11.   [67] Hope, *Practicks*, II, 9, 1.   [68] Hope, *Practicks*, II, 9, 2.
[69] Hope, *Practicks*, II, 9, 1.

(b) Stair's Institutions

The modern law of pledge began in 1681 with the publication of Stair's *Institutions of the Law of Scotland*. Indeed, it might be said that the law has hardly changed since 1681 in this area. Stair's main treatment of pledge appears in book I of his work in the section on real contracts, which has a clear Roman basis. Stair writes:

> Pledge either simplifies the thing impignorated or the contract of impignoration, in the same way as *pignus* in the law is taken; and it is a kind of mandate whereby the debtor for his creditor's security gives him the pawn, or thing impignorated, to detain or keep it for his own security.[70]

Here we have *pledge* being used for the first time in its modern sense. No longer does it mean caution. The term, however, is confined to security over moveable property. The term for heritable security is *wadset* and Stair treats it elsewhere in his work.[71] Nevertheless, he is aware of the common roots of the two securities, describing a wadset as 'the giving of a wad or pledge in security'.[72]

Stair states that a pledge is a real right,[73] the first writer to do so. Another development can be seen in Stair's statement that the creditor may sell the pledge to recover the debt, but must restore any excess to the debtor. No longer is forfeiture the remedy. Even where an express forfeiture clause is provided for, the courts will go out of their way to stop it being enforced.[74] The reason for this development must surely be the Roman influence, where forfeiture had been rejected.[75] Nevertheless, the move away from the Anglo-Norman law is not complete. Stair writes: 'Our custom allows not the creditor to sell the pledge, but he may poind it, or assign his debt, and cause arrest it in his hand, and pursue to make furthcoming.'[76] Thus the creditor's remedy was diligence. As in previous centuries he had to go to court to enforce his security. It was, however, competent even before Stair's time to give the creditor an express power of sale.[77]

6. The eighteenth century

(a) Institutional writings

An examination of the law of pledge in this period, although showing considerable Roman influence, also finds principles which have been retained from the Anglo-Norman period. The institutional writers Bankton and Erskine both treat pledge in the sections of their works upon real contracts

---

[70] Stair, I, 13, 11. [71] Stair, II, 10. [72] Stair, II, 10, pr.
[73] Stair, I, 13, 11. [74] Stair, I, 13, 14.
[75] Thomas (n. 8), 331; Zimmermann (n. 10), 224. [76] Stair, I, 13, 11.
[77] *Murray of Philiphauch* v. *Cuninghame* (1668) 1 Brown's Supp 575.

and both state that the right of the creditor is a real right.[78] The terminology is Roman; indeed Erskine introduces his subject as '*Pignus*, or pledge'.[79] The Anglo-Norman law, however, persists with the demand that the subject matter of the pledge be delivered from debtor to creditor. As Bankton states: 'no conventional pledge in moveables [is] competent by our law, without delivery of the same to the creditor'.[80] Equally the maintenance of the security is dependent on the creditor keeping hold of the property. In the words of Erskine, 'the creditor who quits the possession of the subject loses the real right he had upon it'.[81]

The requirement of Anglo-Norman law of judicial authority to enforce a security remains unchanged. Bankton writes: 'The creditor cannot, at his own hand, with us, dispose of the pledge for his payment, upon the debtor's default, as was the law with the Romans, but he must follow the course of legal diligence.'[82] Erskine states similarly that 'by the usage of Scotland, moveables pledged cannot be sold without the order of a judge'.[83] Whilst diligence certainly was still used in Bankton and Erskine's day, it was becoming less popular. Erskine points out that if the creditor chose to assign the debt to a trustee, who then arrested the property in his hands, there was a risk that another creditor had executed a prior arrestment.[84] Such an arrestment would prevail, as the pledge was extinguished by the property no longer being in the possession of the holder of the debt. To avoid problems such as this, creditors would instead apply to the judge ordinary (in other words the sheriff) for permission to have the property sold at a public sale, to which the debtor had to be made a party.

There is also evidence in Bankton and Erskine's works of the original unitary nature of pledge. Both writers see the heritable security of wadset as essentially a type of pledge.[85]

(b) Case law

There are very few reported cases on pledge from the eighteenth century and none contains any serious discussion.[86] This contrasts with England where Chief Justice Holt gave a detailed exposition of the law in the landmark decision of *Coggs* v. *Bernard*.[87]

---

[78] Bankton, I, 17; Erskine, III, 1, 33.   [79] Erskine, III, 1, 33.   [80] Bankton, I, 17, 1.
[81] Erskine, III, 1, 33.   [82] Bankton, I, 17, 4.   [83] Erskine, III, 1, 33.
[84] Ibid.   [85] Erskine, III, 1, 33; Bankton, I, 17, 2.
[86] See *Pringle* v. *Gribton* (1710) Mor 9123; *Mitchell* v. *Burnet and Mouat* (1746) Mor 4468 and *Hariot* v. *Cuninghame* (1791) Mor 12405.   [87] (1703) 2 Raym 909, 92 ER 107.

7. The nineteenth century

(a) Institutional writings

The beginning of the nineteenth century saw pledge being written about both by Bell and by Hume. In his *Commentaries on the Law of Scotland*, Bell analyses the subject as part of his treatment of real security.[88] In his *Principles of the Law of Scotland*, he treats it in two separate sections. The first deals with pledge as a real contract, in a manner similar to Stair and Erskine, and the second deals with pledge as a real security.[89] Hume treats the subject in a chapter entitled 'Pledge and Hypotheck'.[90] The law remains much the same as before. Delivery from debtor to creditor is required.[91] The creditor must go to court to enforce his security. It is clear, however, that by the nineteenth century the remedy was always to ask the sheriff for permission to sell and that diligence was no longer used.[92]

The accounts given by Bell and Hume are more detailed than those of previous writers and they fill some gaps in the law. Thus we are told that the creditor generally has no right to use the property.[93] This rule is a Roman one, where the creditor was liable for theft if he used the subject matter.[94] By contrast, in the Anglo-Norman period the property could be used provided the use did not cause it to deteriorate.[95]

Bell and Hume also state what sort of property may be pledged. As well as corporeal moveables, negotiable instruments can be the subject matter of the security.[96] The two writers disagree on title deeds to heritable property. Bell believed that they could be pledged as corporeal moveables.[97] Hume, however, thought that they were too closely associated to the land to which they refer to be pledged in their own right.[98] Hume's reasoning was preferred by the Court of Session in 1862 in *Christie v. Ruxton*.[99]

(b) Case law

The period contains a significant number of decisions on pledge. The most important concern the way in which the property can be delivered from debtor to creditor. In *Hamilton v. Western Bank of Scotland* in 1856 the Inner House of the Court of Session ruled that pledge could only be constituted by actual delivery.[100] Constructive delivery was not possible; neither was symbolical delivery. Lord President McNeill stated that he knew of no authority which took a contrary position.[101] Such authority, however, exists. The case

---

[88] Bell, *Commentaries*, II, 19–24.   [89] Bell, *Principles*, §§ 203–9 and §§ 1362–7.
[90] Hume, *Lectures*, IV, 1.
[91] Bell, *Commentaries*, II, 19; Bell, *Principles*, § 1364; Hume, *Lectures*, IV, 1.
[92] Hume, *Lectures*, IV, 5; Bell, *Principles*, §§ 203, 207, and 1364.
[93] Bell, *Principles*, § 206; Hume, *Lectures*, IV, 2.   [94] Gai. D. 47, 2, 55 pr.
[95] Balfour, *Practicks*, 195.   [96] Bell, *Principles*, § 205; Hume, *Lectures*, IV, 7.
[97] Bell, *Principles*, § 205.   [98] Hume, *Lectures*, IV, 7–8.   [99] (1862) 24 D 1182.
[100] (1856) 19 D 152.   [101] (1856) 19 D 152 at 159.

of *Auld* v. *Hall and Co.* decided in 1811, concerned the transfer of moveable property by constructive delivery.[102] In the course of his judgment, Lord President Hope stated: 'Moveables cannot be effectually transferred or pledged without delivery, if in the possession of the party transferring or pledging, or if in the possession of a third party, without intimation to the custodier.'[103] Although the comments are *obiter* they are unequivocal. Further, Lord Deas, who agreed with Lord President McNeill in *Hamilton*, expressly approved Lord President Hope's statement in a later judgment.[104]

Hamilton has been the subject of vigorous academic criticism,[105] but never overruled. Two later decisions, however, represent a move away from it. In *Robertson* v. *Baxter and Inglis*,[106] a case which concerned the provisions of the Factors Acts, a number of judges in the Whole Court expressed the view that the common law sanctioned pledge by constructive delivery.[107] Symbolical delivery in the form of the pledge of bills of lading seems to have been accepted by both the Court of Session and the House of Lords in *North Western Bank* v. *Poynter, Sons and Macdonald*.[108] This case is also significant in allowing the creditor to return the pledged bills to the debtor so that the goods they represented could be sold, but without losing his right of pledge.[109] In this limited situation, Scots law will tolerate security without possession.

(c) The development of pawnbroking

The wad-wife of the sixteenth century was more of a general businesswoman than a specialized pledge-taker.[110] Pawnbroking in the form it is known today began in the early part of the nineteenth century. It had started some decades earlier in England upon the relaxation of the Usury Acts.[111] Bell described pawnbroking as 'one species of pledge, affording a resource to poverty'.[112] The experience south of the border, however, was that the poor were being exploited by the pawnbrokers. This caused Adam Smith to attack the licensing of pawnbrokers as 'one of the great nuisances in the English constitution,

---

[102] 12 June 1811 FC.   [103] Ibid.
[104] *Wyper* v. *Harveys* (1861) 23 D 606 at 629–30.
[105] See Bell, *Commentaries*, II, 21 n. 1 (Lord McLaren); Gloag/Irvine (n. 1), 256–7; J. Graham Stewart, *The Law of Diligence* (1898), 155 n. 3; Lord Rodger of Earlsferry, 'Pledge of Bills of Lading in Scots Law', [1971] *JR* 193 sqq.; G. L. Gretton, 'Pledge, Bills of Lading, Trusts and Property Law', [1990] *JR* 23 sqq.
[106] (1897) 24 R 758. See also the appeal to the House of Lords: *Inglis* v. *Robertson and Baxter* (1898) 25 R (HL) 70.
[107] See in particular Lord Moncreiff at (1897) 24 R 758, 817. See also Lord McLaren at 777 (Lord President and Lord Adam concurring), Lord Kinnear at 780, Lord Stormonth Darling at 789.   [108] (1894) 22 R (HL) 1.
[109] On the basis of a 'trust receipt'. See the articles by Rodger and Gretton referred to in n. 105.   [110] Above II.4.a.
[111] J. K. Macleod, 'Pawnbroking: A Regulatory Issue', 1995 *JBL* 155 at 159.
[112] Bell, *Principles*, § 209.

especially in great cities'.[113] The Pawnbrokers Act 1800 consolidated and updated the previous legislation in this area and helped protect the pawners. It was at first not clear that this act applied to Scotland, where local acts also regulated pawnbroking.[114] Attempts to evade the legislation in later years of the nineteenth century eventually caused a new consolidation statute, the Pawnbrokers Act 1872, to be enacted.

8. The modern period

There has been little development in the law of pledge in modern times. The first two decades of the twentieth century saw a number of sheriff court cases concerning pawnbroking.[115] There appears to be only one later case dealing with a substantive question on the law of pledge and the point which it decides—that a pledgee has no right to use the pledged property—was clear more than a century and a half earlier from the writings of Bell and Hume.[116] In terms of legislation, the main development has been the replacement of the Pawnbrokers Act 1872 by provisions of the Consumer Credit Act 1974.[117]

Presumably the main reason for the lack of development is that pledge is of limited commercial utility. There are some familiar uses, such as pawnbroking, the creation of security over documents of title, and the depositing of alcohol in bonded warehouses. Otherwise pledge is little used. Businesses generally require possession of their assets and so cannot deliver them to creditors. The restrictive nature of pledge is one of the reasons why floating charges were introduced to Scotland for companies in 1961 and why further reform of the law of moveable security is proposed.[118]

III. HYPOTHEC

1. The civilian background

The non-possessory pledge of Roman law, *hypotheca*, developed first in agricultural areas, where any valuable property owned by the debtor was needed

---

[113] Adam Smith, *Lectures on Jurisprudence* (edn. by R. L. Meek, D. D. Raphael, and P. G. Stein, 1978), 80. [114] Macleod, 1995 *JBL* 155.
[115] For example, *McMillan v. Conrad* (1914) 30 Sh Ct Rep 275; *Elliot v. Conway* (1915) 31 Sh Ct Rep 79 and *Hislop v. Anderson* (1919) 35 Sh Ct Rep 116.
[116] *Wolifson v. Harrison* 1977 SC 384. On Bell and Hume, see above II.7.a.
[117] Consumer Credit Act 1974, ss. 116–21.
[118] See the Department of Trade and Industry Consultation Paper, *Security over Moveable Property in Scotland*, Nov. 1994, discussed in D. O'Donnell and D. L. Carey Miller, 'Security over Moveables: A Longstanding Reform Agenda in Scots Law', (1997) 5 *ZEuP* 807. And see also G. L. Gretton, 'The Reform of Moveable Security Law', 1999 *SLT (News)* 301.

to work the ground.[119] A practice developed of tenants 'pledging' to their landlord in security of their rent the property they had brought on to the land (*invecta et illata*). However, this form of pledge amounted merely to an agreement that if the rent was not duly paid, the landlord would be entitled to take possession of the property. Probably around the end of the Republic, this arrangement was given force of law by the Praetor Salvius who granted the landlord the *interdictum Salvianum* to seize the property. Sometime later the landlord was given an *actio in rem*, the *actio Serviana*.[120] The whole area of law then grew at an explosive rate. The conventional *hypotheca* became generally available. A large number of cases of tacit *hypotheca* were also recognized; indeed the *hypotheca* of the landlord became recognized as tacit.[121]

Doctrinally, the Romans viewed pledge as a *genus* with *pignus* as the possessory, and *hypotheca* the non-possessory, species. In the words of Ulpian: 'Proprie pignus dicimus, quod ad creditorem transit, hypothecam, cum non transit nec possessio ad creditorem.'[122] As Nicholas stresses, the conclusion should not be drawn 'that there were two distinct institutions'.[123] The problem with *hypotheca*, however, was that it permitted creditors to have a real right without publicity. Creditors could not be sure what conventional hypothecs already subsisted, nor which tacit hypothecs were enforceable in respect of the property. Additionally, the law regarded certain hypothecs as privileged in the sense that they were given a higher ranking. The precise rules of ranking were, however, unclear. The entire later law was unsatisfactory in its recognition of so many tacit and privileged hypothecs, and in its failure to deal adequately with ranking.[124]

2. The Anglo-Norman period

Early Scots law had a simple solution to the problems that the *hypotheca* created in the later Roman law. It refused to enforce conventional hypothecs. As has already been seen, the *Regiam Majestatem* declared that in pledge the subject matter of the security was either immediately delivered to the creditor or it was not so delivered.[125] If there was no delivery the security would not be capable of judicial enforcement. The court was not prepared to resolve situations where a piece of property had been pledged a number of times to successive creditors. To create an enforceable security, the debtor, in

---

[119] Thomas (n. 8), 332.   [120] Ibid.; Schulz (n. 8), 408; Buckland (n. 8), 472–3.
[121] Ulp. D. 20, 2, 3; Pomp. D. 20, 2, 7; Afr. D. 47, 2, 62, 8.
[122] Ulp. D. 13, 7, 9, 2. 'Strictly speaking, we use *pignus* for the pledge which is handed over to the creditor and *hypothec* for the case in which he does not even get possession.'
[123] B. Nicholas, *An Introduction to Roman Law* (1962), 152. See also Goebel, (1961–2) 36 *Tul LR* 29 at 37–44.   [124] Nicholas (n. 123), 152–3; Goebel, (1961–2) 36 *Tul LR* 29 at 63.
[125] Above II.2.*a*.

Balfour's words, 'sould put the creditor in possessioun'.[126] The position was very clear. As George Joseph Bell stated: 'In this country the common law verly [sic] early declared itself against conventional hypothecs. This repugnance may be traced back to the days of Sir James Balfour (p. 194) and even to the Regiam Majestatem (lib. 3, c.3).'[127]

Tacit hypothecs seem to have been in much the same position. In the case of landlords, however, a remedy known as the brieve of distress was available against tenants.[128] This amounted to a type of diligence and was obviously based on the English law of distress. Balfour refers to some cases involving distress in Scotland. In *Wauchop* v. *Borthwik*, decided in 1537, it was held that the proprietor 'of ony landis, may poind and distreinzie his tenentis, occuparis thairof, thair gudis and geir . . . for the last three termis maillis bypass auchtand to him of the saidis landis'.[129] There is no reference to a right of hypothec.

The position began to change at the start of the seventeenth century, evidently under Roman influence. In 1611 there was reference in a decision to the 'privilege' of the landlord.[130] The term 'hypothecated' appeared for the first time in the case of *Hay* v. *Keith*,[131] decided in 1623. A decision a year later used the term '*tacite* hypothecated'.[132] As the years of the seventeenth century went on, the landlord's right of hypothec became firmly established and references to distress were no longer to be found. What then is the relationship between the hypothec and the right of distress? Walter Ross regarded the hypothec as having developed out of the law of distress.[133] This is probably not accurate because distress was in essence a diligence whereas the hypothec is a real right in security. A more plausible analysis is that there was no difficulty in embracing the Roman hypothec because Scots law already recognized a distinct, though similar, remedy.[134] Further, the new remedy of hypothec was to be enforced by a type of diligence: sequestration for rent.

3. The institutional period

The reception in this period of Roman ideas might have been expected to have included a general acceptance of the hypothec. This in fact was not the case. Stair writes: '[O]ur custom hath taken away express hypothecations, of all or part of the debtor's goods, without delivery, and of the tacit legal

---

[126] Balfour, *Practicks*, 194. [127] Bell, *Commentaries*, II, 25.
[128] R. Hunter, *Landlord and Tenant* (4th edn. by W. Guthrie, 1876), vol. 2, 358–9.
[129] 13 Dec. 1537, reported in Balfour, *Practicks*, 398, c. 9.
[130] *Wardlaw* v. *Mitchell* (1611) Mor 6187. [131] (1623) Mor 6188.
[132] *Lady Dun* v. *Lord Dun* (1624) Mor 6217.
[133] W. Ross, *Lectures on Conveyancing* (2nd edn., 1822), vol. 2, 406–7.
[134] Hunter (n. 128), 360.

hypothecations hath only allowed a few, allowing ordinarily parties to be preferred according to the priority of their legal diligence, that commerce may be the more sure.'[135] Erskine expressed similar sentiments: 'The Romans admitted a variety of tacit or legal hypothecs upon moveables, most of which we have rejected, because the impignoration of moveable goods without their delivery to the creditor cannot but put a heavy weight on the free currency of trade.'[136] Thus there is a continuity in Scots law in terms of the repudiation of hypothecs. The reason for this is probably twofold. In the first place, as already mentioned, the later Roman law which admitted the conventional hypothec and a wide range of tacit hypothecs was acknowledged as unsatisfactory. And in the second place, a number of other European countries, such as France, had eschewed this form of security to a greater or lesser extent.[137]

The institutional writers set out the limited circumstances in which the hypothec is to be admitted. A number appear in the context of maritime law, accepted because 'they are generally received by commercial states'.[138] For example, foreign repairers have a tacit hypothec over a ship in respect of the cost of the repair.[139] It is in the context of maritime law too that the only conventional hypothecs recognized by Scots law are found. These are the bonds of bottomry and *respondentia*.[140] The former may be granted over a ship; the latter over its cargo. Their purpose was to allow shipmasters in foreign ports to acquire advances of money, so as they could proceed on their journey.

The most important example of hypothec is that conferred on a landlord. Stair gives a reasonably detailed treatment of this right.[141] He points out that the landlord's hypothec is available to secure the payment of rent in both agricultural and urban leases. He also states that it extends only to the rent of the current year. Bankton's account contains further detail.[142] Of particular interest is his discussion of what property is subject to the hypothec: 'It is only the tenant's own goods, as *invecta et illata* into the house, that are hypothecated, or such of other mens as are used for furniture to the same; for, by consenting to their being applied to that use, they are understood to agree to their being subjected to the rent.'[143] Therefore, in such circumstances the landlord's hypothec covers property which is not owned by the tenant. Bankton also deals with the process of enforcing the security: the diligence of sequestration for rent.[144] Erskine and Bell confirm the rules set out in

[135] Stair, I, 13, 14. [136] Erskine, III, 1, 34.
[137] Bell, *Commentaries*, II, 25; T. B. Smith, A *Short Commentary on the Law of Scotland* (1962), 472–4. [38] Erskine, III, 1, 34.
[139] Bell, *Principles*, § 1398. There is no hypothec for repairs effected in a home port: *Hamilton v. Wood* (1788) Mor 6269.
[140] Bell, *Commentaries*, I, 578; Bell, *Principles*, §§ 452–6 and 1386. [141] Stair, I, 13, 15.
[142] Bankton, I, 17, 8–12. More generally, Bankton's account is interesting for the way in which he defines 'hypothec', a matter discussed below IV.3.a.
[143] Bankton, I, 17, 10. A similar rule applies in South African law: see T. J. Scott and S. Scott, *Wille's Law of Mortgage and Pledge in South Africa* (3rd edn., 1987), 101–4.
[144] Bankton, I, 17, 11.

Bankton,[145] and there is little substantive development in the law from Stair to Bell. It is simply a case of the Roman principles becoming more and more established over time.

The final tacit hypothec to be established in the institutional period is the hypothec of the superior in respect of feu duty. Mackenzie is the first writer to mention it.[146] However, its exact origins are unclear and it is a curious mix of the Roman and the feudal. Erskine states that the superior's hypothec prevails over that of the landlord, 'for where a vassal lets his land to a tenant, it is to be understood with the burden of all feu-duties payable to the superior, whose right cannot be impaired by any act of the vassal'.[147] Bell agrees with this.[148] As far as can be seen, however, there has only been the one reported decision on the superior's hypothec, a case of 1823 which held that the right applies in urban as well as agricultural subjects.[149]

4. The modern period

Over the last hundred years, the general aversion to hypothecs has been subsumed under a wider doctrine that there can be no security over moveables without the creditor having possession.[150] While this rationalization has a certain practical value, more questionable is its justification by reference to the brocard *traditionibus, non nudis pactis, dominia rerum transferuntur* (ownership of things is transferred by delivery, not by bare agreements).[151] The use of a Roman rule to justify rejection of the hypothec seems surprising when it is recalled that the hypothec was embraced by Roman law.[152]

As regards actual developments, modern communications have seen the bonds of bottomry and *respondentia* fall into disuse. There have been some statutory developments. The misleadingly named Hypothec Abolition Act 1880 abolished the landlord's hypothec in respect of agricultural leases.[153] The law governing the creation of ship mortgages has been developed by statute.[154] The twentieth century saw the introduction of agricultural credits and aircraft mortgages.[155] Such hypothecs have proved acceptable, because the creditor's right in security is dependent on registration. Finally, the superior's hypothec will be abolished, with the feudal system itself, by the Abolition of Feudal Tenure etc. (Scotland) Act 2000, s. 13(3).

---

[145] Erskine, II, 6, 56–64; Bell, *Commentaries*, II, 27–34; Bell, *Principles*, §§ 1275–1277.
[146] Sir G. Mackenzie, *Institutions of the Law of Scotland* (2nd edn., 1688), II, 6.
[147] Erskine, II, 6, 63.   [148] Bell, *Commentaries*, II, 26–7.
[149] *Yuille v. Laurie* (1823) 2 S 155.
[150] See e.g. Gloag/Irvine (n. 1), 187–91; D. L. Carey Miller, *Corporeal Moveables in Scots Law* (1991), para. 11-03.   [151] C. 2, 3, 20 (Diocletian, 293). See Gloag/Irvine (n. 1), 188.
[152] Gordon (n. 27), 170.   [153] Hypothec Abolition Act 1880, s. 1.
[154] By the Merchant Shipping Acts 1854, 1894, and 1995. See the 1995 Act, s. 16 and Sch. 1.
[155] See the Agricultural Credits (Scotland) Act 1929, ss. 5–9 and the Civil Aviation Act 1982, s. 86.

Undoubtedly, the most controversial statutory development has been the importation of the floating charge, and its enforcement procedure of receivership, from England.[156] Only companies and a few other bodies may grant this security. They may grant over all their 'property and undertaking'.[157] The floating charge cannot be viewed in strict terms as a hypothec, because the creditor does not obtain a real right unless or until the charge attaches to the property.[158] No entry needs to be made in the Companies Register to effect the attachment, something which has caused much trouble with respect to immoveable property.[159] This feature of floating charges confirms Stair's reasoned rejection of hypothecs, so 'that commerce may be the more sure'.[160] It is an area of law much in need of reform.

IV. LIEN

1. The civilian and English background

It is not possible to understand the basis of the Scottish law of lien without an understanding of the two systems which have influenced it most: the civil law and English law.

(a) Civil law

The Romans appeared to recognize the lien—the *jus retentionis*—in two main areas. The first was in the context of accession (*accessio*), i.e. the doctrine that held in certain circumstances where two pieces of corporeal property became joined together, one (the accessory) was deemed to have become subsumed in the other (the principal).[161] The effect was that the owner of the principal became owner of the accessory too. Where an individual caused his property to accede to the property of another he suffered a loss of ownership; but where he acted in the bona fide belief that the principal was his own, he was entitled to compensation. If he remained in possession of the whole property, the civil law gave him a *jus retentionis* until he was compensated by the owner of the principal.[162] In practice this involved him meeting the owner of the

---

[156] Floating charges were introduced by the Companies (Floating Charges) (Scotland) Act 1961. Receivership was introduced by the Companies (Floating Charges and Receivers) (Scotland) Act 1972. The present legislation is largely contained in the Companies Act 1985, ss. 410–24 and ss. 462–6 and the Insolvency Act 1986, ss. 50–71. See, generally, R. B. Jack, 'The Coming of the Floating Charge to Scotland', in D. J. Cusine (ed.), *A Scots Conveyancing Miscellany* (1987), 33 sqq. For a more critical view, see G. L. Gretton, 'What went Wrong with Floating Charges?', 1986 *SLT (News)* 325 sqq.   [157] Companies Act 1985, s. 462.
[158] *National Commercial Bank of Scotland* v. *Liquidators of Telford Grier Mackay & Co. Ltd* 1969 SC 181.   [159] See e.g. *Sharp* v. *Thomson* 1997 SC (HL) 66.
[160] Stair, I, 13, 14.   [161] Buckland (n. 8), 208–15; Thomas (n. 8), 169–74.
[162] Kaser (n. 8), 112; D. H. van Zyl, *History and Principles of Roman Private Law* (1983), 160–2.

principal's *rei vindicatio* with the *exceptio doli*, a defence in the civil law which ameliorated the severity of a pursuer's claim.[163]

Secondly, lien developed in the context of contract. At first, it seems to have been confined to the gratuitous contracts of *depositum* and *commodatum* and allowed the depositary or borrower to hold on to the property until its owner refunded any expenses laid out on it.[164] As time went on, however, it seems to have developed into a more general contractual doctrine. Kaser writes: 'Instead of bringing a counter-action, the debtor who had a due counter-claim arising from the same obligation, could exercise a right of retention (*retentio*), that is, he could refuse to make his performance until the counter-performance was tendered to him. This he did by means of the *exceptio doli.*'[165] In the specific case of a contract of sale, Sohm notes that the right of the seller to defend an action for delivery by the buyer, on the ground that the price has not been paid, is termed the *exceptio non adimpleti contractus.*[166] This *exceptio* seems to have become viewed as the basis of the contractual lien in the later civil law.[167]

Both with regard to accession and with regard to contract, lien arose in the context of reciprocal obligations. For example, the obligation of the bona fide possessor to deliver the property to its owner was reciprocal to the owner's obligation to compensate him for the improvement made to the property. Civilian writers such as Pufendorf and Voet also treated lien, or perhaps more correctly, retention in this way.[168] It was not seen as a right limited to certain specific circumstances but, more generally, as a doctrine of the law of obligations.

(b) English law

The lien became recognized in English law in the Middle Ages in respect of particular professions.[169] A common tie among these professions was public duty. Thus innkeepers were given a lien over their guests' luggage because they had a duty to receive any traveller who wished to stay at their establishment.[170] Common carriers had a duty to carry and were also awarded a

---

[163] Gai. 2, 76; Inst. 2, 1, 30; Inst. 2, 1, 32–3; Buckland (n. 8), 210; Schulz (n. 8), 365. On the *exceptio doli* in general, see Zimmermann (n. 10), 667–8 and the judgment of Joubert JA in *Bank of Lisbon and South Africa Ltd* v. *De Ornalas* 1988 (3) SA 580 A at 592–601.

[164] Iul. D. 47, 2, 60; Gai. D. 13, 6, 18, 4; Buckland (n. 8), 468 and 473; Kaser (n. 8), 166; Thomas (n. 8), 276. Both liens were apparently later abolished: see C. 4, 34, 11; Buckland (n. 8), 468 and J. Voet, *Commentarius ad Pandectas* (1829), XIII, 6, 10.   [165] Kaser (n. 8), 166.

[166] Sohm (n. 8), 397.

[167] Van Zyl (n. 162), 254. See also G. H. Treitel, *Remedies for Breach of Contract* (1988), 299 sqq.   [168] Pufendorf (n. 6), V, 11, 6; Voet (n. 164), XVI, 6, 20.

[169] See, generally, Sir William Holdsworth, *History of English Law* (1937), vol. 7, 511–12; A. P. Bell, *The Modern Law of Personal Property in England and Ireland* (1989), 138–9.

[170] Holdsworth (n. 169), vol. 7, 511–12; Bell (n. 169), 138–9; Y.BB. 5 Ed. IV. Pasch. pl. 20; 22 Ed. IV. Hill pl. 5 *per* Brian CJ.

lien.[171] In the fifteenth century English law conferred a lien on a new category of individuals: those who carried out work on a chattel under a contract could retain it until paid.[172] Around the same time, the lien of the unpaid seller was first recognized.[173] The essential point, however, was that, apart from specific cases, a lien could not be asserted. The English doctrine of lien was a limited one. Further, in the Middle Ages the right was known as the right to 'reteign', not as 'lien'.[174]

It was in the first half of the eighteenth century that the term 'lien' first became used in English law to mean retention.[175] Why this was the case is not very clear, but the reason probably was the natural meaning of 'lien' in French as a bond or tie. The idea of somebody having a lien in English law is that he has a nexus on a particular thing. This point is demonstrated by the fact that retention is not always required, for in addition to possessory liens the law also admits equitable liens and maritime liens.[176]

The other important change in the eighteenth century was the development of the general lien.[177] The liens which had existed since the Middle Ages were all particular liens, involving a person detaining a particular item for a service performed in connection with it. The recognition of a general lien, however, allowed the relevant item to be retained for a general balance of accounts between the debtor and creditor in respect of like dealings between them. General liens proved advantageous to the parties involved. For, in a series of contracts the knowledge that he had a general lien would make the lien-holder feel safe to return property held under earlier contracts, knowing that the property which he held under later contracts could serve as security for the total debt outstanding.

General liens arose initially from express contractual provision. But it soon became clear that certain professions, such as bankers, factors and solicitors, were entitled to general liens as a matter of usage.[178] In the latter half of the eighteenth century, the courts extended the list of professions entitled to general liens at every opportunity. 'The convenience of commerce and natural justice are on the side of liens', declared Lord Mansfield.[179] However,

---

[171] Holdsworth (n. 169). See also *Skinner* v. *Upshaw* (1702) 2 Raym 752, 92 ER 3.

[172] Y.B. 5 Ed. IV. Pasch. pl. 20, referred to by Lord Ellenborough CJ in *Chase* v. *Westmore* (1816) 5 M & S 180 at 187, 105 ER 1016 at 1019 and by Gloag/Irvine (n. 1), 351.

[173] Y.B. 5 Ed. IV. Pasch. pl. 20.

[174] Ibid. See, generally, the authorities cited by Holdsworth (n. 169).

[175] See *Ex parte Bush* (1734) 2 Eq Cas Ab 109 pl 4, 22 ER 93; *Ex parte Shank* (1745) 1 Atk 234, 26 ER 151 and *Turwin* v. *Gibson* (1749) 3 Atk 720, 26 ER 1212. The term apparently did not make an instant impression upon everyday English law, for Dr Johnson in his famous dictionary of 1755 only lists it as the past participle of the verb 'to lie': Samuel Johnson, *Dictionary of the English Language* (1755), s.v. 'lien'. He cites Genesis 26: 10 (King James Version).

[176] For equitable liens, see Halsbury, *Laws of England* (4th edn., 1979), vol. 28, §§ 551–82. For maritime liens, see D. R. Thomas, *Maritime Liens* (vol. 14 of the series *British Shipping Laws* ed. by R. Colinvaux, 1980), ch. 1.

[177] See, generally, Bell (n. 169), 142.

[178] Bell (n. 169), 142; Halsbury (n. 176), § 525.

[179] *Green* v. *Farmer* (1768) 4 Burr 2214 at 2221, 98 ER 154 at 158.

in the opening years of the nineteenth century the courts realized the damage the general lien was causing to the interests of other creditors of the debtor. In the words of Le Blanc J.: 'All these general liens infringe upon the system of the bankrupt laws, the object of which is to distribute the debtor's estate proportionally amongst all the creditors and they ought not to be encouraged.'[180] The result of this is that the list of general liens recognized in English law effectively remains the same as it was at the beginning of the nineteenth century. In other respects too, the English law of lien crystallized into the state which has existed ever since. In summary, two types of possessory lien are recognized: the particular lien and the general lien. Particular liens are conferred upon certain individuals who have duties to the public, upon unpaid sellers, and upon individuals who perform work on a particular thing. General liens are conferred upon certain professions.

2. The seventeenth century

It is difficult to locate any writing or cases on what we now recognize as lien in the Anglo-Norman period of Scots law.[181] The first treatment of the matter is apparently that of Stair. Stair discusses 'retention' in a very civilian manner. In his sections on *commodatum* and *depositum* he states that the borrower and depositary have a right to retain the relevant property until compensated for necessary or profitable expenses laid out upon it.[182] His discussion of retention in the context of deposit is particularly interesting for the following sentence: 'And in all cases in the law where action is competent, exception is also competent, and so with us, if instantly verified.'[183] Thus for Stair, exception is a remedy available in any situation in which it is clear that there is a right of action. As a form of exception, retention too is subject to this rule. Retention is not limited to particular types of contract, as under English law.

Stair's main treatment of retention comes after his discussion of compensation, in his title on liberation from obligations. He writes:

Retention is not an absolute extinction of the obligation of repayment or restitution, but rather a suspension thereof, till satisfaction be made to the retainer ... Such is the right of mandators, impledgers and the like, who have interest to retain the things possessed by them, until the necessary and profitable expenses wared out by them thereupon be satisfied.[184]

---

[180] *Rushforth* v. *Hadfield* (1805) 6 East 519 at 528, 102 ER 1386 at 1390. See also Rooke J. in *Richardson* v. *Goss* (1802) 3 Bos & P 119 at 126, 127 ER 65 at 69. See, generally, Bell (n. 169), 142–3.

[181] For example, the *Regiam Majestatem* and Balfour, *Practicks*, appear to be silent on the matter.

[182] Stair, I, 11, 12 and I, 13, 9. The latter passage contains an interesting discussion on why Scots law allows a right of retention, when the later Roman law abolished it.

[183] Stair, I, 13, 9.   [184] Stair, I, 18, 7.

It seems clear from this passage and its context that Stair sees retention as an exception or defence which is generally available within the law of obligations. Further, the main example is where expenses have been laid out upon a piece of property. It is interesting that Stair does not mention one of the main rights of retention of the civil law, that of bona fide possessors to retain for improvements. Yet the case of *Binning* v. *Brotherstones*,[185] decided in 1676, recognized the right in Scots law. Nevertheless, this omission does not detract from the profoundly civilian nature of Stair's treatment.

There are a small number of other seventeenth-century cases concerning retention. In one, it was held that seamen have a '*ius insistendi* and *retinendi*'[186] for their wages, while in possession of a ship. In another, the solicitor's lien was recognized for the first time, being referred to as a '*ius retentionis et hypothecae*'.[187] The terminology being used shows again the civilian influence in the area.

3. The eighteenth century

(a) Institutional writings

Like Stair, Bankton's treatment of retention is very civilian. Unlike Stair, however, he makes express reference to the bona fide possessor's right to retain for improvements. His most detailed discussion appears within his title on recompense.[188] This is an important piece of evidence that retention is not confined to contract but may arise in the context of other obligations. In his main treatment of retention, in his section on liberation from obligations, Bankton states his understanding of the doctrine: 'It is granted for one's security till he is paid or relieved, in respect to counter claims he has against the party whose effects are retained.'[189] Once again, then, retention is seen as a remedy available generally within the law of obligations. What is also interesting is that Bankton views retention as a form of security.

Bankton develops his theme of retention as a security elsewhere in his work. In his section on loan for use, he states that the borrower 'has an hypothec or right of retention'[190] for expenses. Such a statement seems to confuse a possessory security (retention) with a non-possessory security (hypothec). The explanation, however, is that Bankton regarded hypothec as any security arising by operation of law.[191] Thus, in his title on pledge, he expressly mentions the 'tacit hypothec or right of retention'[192] of the lawful possessor and gives two examples: the right of the law agent to retain his

---

[185] (1676) Mor 13401.   [186] *Seamen of 'Golden Star'* v. *Miln* (1682) Mor 6259.
[187] *Cuthberts* v. *Ross* (1697) 4 Brown's Supp 374.
[188] Bankton, I, 9, 42. See also the same work at I, 8, 15 and II, 9, 68.
[189] Bankton, I, 24, 34.   [190] Bankton, I, 14, 6.
[191] See Bankton, I, 17, 2: 'But, with us, in the proper sense, Hypothec is applied to the creditor's security, introduced by the provision of law.'   [192] Bankton, I, 17, 15.

client's papers and the right of a tradesman to detain the subject he has worked upon. The emphasis placed on retention as a security is perhaps the most important thing to take out of Bankton's work, cohering as it does with the way in which lien is mainly viewed today.

Erskine's examination of retention is closer to Stair than Bankton. Once again the subject is discussed in the context of liberation from obligations.[193] Erskine points out that the main example of retention is where work has been bestowed upon a particular piece of property. He also mentions the right of a law agent to retain his client's papers 'till his bill of accounts be paid',[194] and the right of retention of a factor. Erskine does not discuss retention as a security. Further, he does not view it as a hypothec, which, for him, is a non-possessory security.[195] For writers who lived in the same era, it is striking that their definitions of hypothec are so different. It was Erskine's (and Stair's) that was to prevail.

(b) Case law

Most eighteenth-century decisions concern the right of retention of the law agent.[196] This right seems to have developed at the same time in Scotland as in England and in the view of one Scottish judge 'if not originally borrowed from English practice, is in many respects the same'.[197] The right became increasingly more powerful as the century went on. It became clear that it was a real right enforceable against third parties.[198] Further, in 1781 in the case of *Provenhall's Creditors*,[199] it was held that the agent could retain title deeds even in a question with a creditor with a prior constituted heritable security— a decision reported to have made Lord Justice-Clerk Macqueen's hair stand on end.[200]

Elsewhere, the case of *Stephens* v. *Creditors of the York Building Company*,[201] decided in 1735, recognized the right of retention of a factor. The most important decision from the period, however, is *Harper's Creditors* v. *Faulds*,[202] decided in 1791. The issue was relatively simple. Harper regularly sent linen to Faulds for bleaching. The account between the two was settled annually. Harper became bankrupt. Faulds sought to retain the linen which he presently held for the entire balance of the account. Harper's trustee in sequestration argued that he could retain it only for the amount due for bleaching that particular linen itself. The Whole Court by a majority preferred the trustee, holding that other than in exceptional cases retention is restricted to securing only debts due in respect of the actual property being detained. In the words of

---

[193] Erskine, III, 4, 21.   [194] Ibid.   [195] Erskine, III, 1, 34.
[196] See e.g. *Ayton* v. *Colville* (1705) Mor 6247; *Earl of Sutherland* v. *Coupar* (1738) Mor 6247; and *Lidderdale's Creditors* v. *Nasmyth* (1749) Mor 6248.
[197] *Kemp* v. *Youngs* (1838) 16 S 500 at 503 *per* Lord Cuninghame.
[198] See *Lidderdale's Creditors* v. *Nasmyth* (1749) Mor 6248 at 6249.   [199] (1781) Mor 6253.
[200] Bell, *Commentaries*, II, 109.   [201] (1735) Mor 9140.   [202] (1791) Bell Oct Cas 440.

the Lord President, Sir Ilay Campbell, retention is 'a right of refusing delivery of a subject, till the counter-obligation under which the subject was lodged, be performed'.[203] The decision of the majority may be supported by reference to the development of retention in the civil law, where the right has always operated in the context of reciprocal obligations.[204]

(c) Terminology

The right of a law agent to retain his client's papers is referred to throughout the eighteenth century as a right of hypothec,[205] thus supporting Bankton's statement that Scots law regards 'hypothec' as meaning any tacit security.[206] The second half of the century, however, saw an addition to the Scottish legal vocabulary which was subsequently to have a profound effect on this whole area.

Bankton appears to have been the first Scottish writer to use the word 'lien'. He uses it during his discussion of a type of heritable security, the pecuniary real burden, stating that the creditor, to use an English term, has 'a real Lien' upon the land.[207] Therefore, it would appear that 'lien' came to Scotland from south of the border. Erskine refers to the origin of the word, writing that the pecuniary real burden constitutes 'as it is called of late, a *lien*, a vocable borrowed from the French, signifying a tie or bond'.[208]

It will be remembered that 'lien' became used in English law from the early eighteenth century as a general term for nexus.[209] In fact the majority of Scottish authority in the late 1700s uses it in this way also. Kames expressly does so.[210] In *Provenhall's Creditors*,[211] the competition is stated to be between the 'lien' of a law agent by 'virtue of his right of hypothec' and the 'real lien' of a heritable creditor in respect of certain title deeds. In *Hamilton* v. *Wood*,[212] reference is made to 'the *lien* created by bonds of bottomry'.[213] As a general point, it appears from these cases and others that the nexus which a lien confers is a real right upon the property in question, either a real right in security or a real right by diligence.[214] It cannot be said that in the later years of the eighteenth century that lien was specifically being used to mean a right to retain.

---

[203] (1791) Bell Oct Cas 440 at 471. [204] Above IV.1.a and 2.
[205] See e.g. the cases cited in n. 196. [206] Above IV.3.a. [207] Bankton, II, 5, 18.
[208] Erskine, II, 3, 49. [209] Above IV.1.b.
[210] Kames, *Historical Law Tracts* (4th edn., 1817), 101. [211] (1781) Mor 6253.
[212] (1788) Mor 6269. [213] (1788) Mor 6269 at 6271.
[214] For a case involving diligence, see *Tait v. Cockburn* (1780) Mor 14110. The earliest case in which 'lien' is used in the sense of nexus appears to be *McDowal and Gray* v. *Annand and Colhoun's Assignees* (1776) 2 Pat App 387.

4. The nineteenth century

(a) Bell

A pivotal role in the development of the Scottish law of lien was played by George Joseph Bell. In the second volume of his *A Treatise on the Law of Bankruptcy in Scotland*, published in 1804,[215] he lays what amounts to the foundation stone of the modern law. Under the heading 'Of securities of the nature of real right resulting from possession' he writes: 'The securities includable under this class correspond with the set-off and equitable liens of the English law; the terms used in this country are compensation and retention.'[216] Like previous institutional writers, Bell deals with compensation and retention in the same part of his work. He, however, treats retention first and places the emphasis on security rather than liberation from obligations. Only Bankton had come close to such an approach. Bell also directly equates our doctrines with those of English law. Under the subheading 'Of the doctrine of retention or lien',[217] Bell states that liens or rights of retention are either special or general. A special lien secures only the debt due under a particular contract whereas a general lien secures the whole balance of debts due by the proprietor to the possessor of goods.

Bell uses 'lien' as a synonym for retention; and this was the principal use of the word in English law at the time, within the general context of nexus.[218] Bell's usage, however, is narrower, referring purely to retention. His approach goes against the grain of contemporary Scots usage, where 'lien' meant a general term for nexus.[219] If there was a more specialized use of the word, it came in the shape of 'real lien', a term used to mean pecuniary real burden.[220] Bell, however, unlike Bankton and Erskine, does not refer to 'real liens' when discussing real burdens.[221] For Bell, then, 'lien' is only to be used to mean retention.[222] In fact he uses 'retention' as often as 'lien', but over the coming decades the latter term was to gain ascendancy.

Bell's distinction between 'special liens' and 'general liens' had not previously been made by a Scottish writer. The way in which he discusses the subject leaves little doubt that he has been studying English law and its comparable 'particular liens' and 'general liens'.[223] Nevertheless, there were grounds for applying the distinction in Scots law. For whilst special retention was the normal rule, the law recognized general retention in certain cases,

---

[215] The first volume was published in 1800.
[216] G. J. Bell, *A Treatise on the Law of Bankruptcy in Scotland* (1804), vol. 2, 362. Bell's reference to 'equitable liens' is rather misleading as the term denotes a class of non-possessory rights in English law. See Halsbury (n. 176).
[217] Ibid.
[218] Above IV.1.b.
[219] Above IV.3.c.
[220] Ibid.
[221] See Bell, *Commentaries*, I, 726–32.
[222] He does, however, use it once to mean nexus in his section on diligence, when he states 'Arrestment in execution was a lien created by attachment': Bell, *Commentaries*, I, 6.
[223] Above IV.1.b.

such as that of the factor and law agent.[224] Bell's discussion of special liens is very civilian. Special retention is seen as a right which is not confined to specific contracts, but as something founded on the doctrine of mutuality of obligations.

As regards general retention, Bell makes much reference to English law. Nevertheless, he is also able to point to Scottish authority to show that the law north of the border recognizes general liens in favour of law agents, factors, brokers, trustees, and cautioners. There are, however, clear conceptual difficulties with the last two cases. Trustees own trust property and therefore their right of retention is based on ownership and not possession, which Bell saw as the foundation of lien.[225] A difficulty with cautioners is that the case law involves the retention of debts which, being incorporeal, cannot be possessed.

In summary, Bell can be absolved from a wholesale introduction of an alien concept (lien) into Scots law. Rather, he took the comparable English law and used it to embellish the Scots law of retention already existing. His realization that Scots law recognizes general retention in certain places, like English law, is perceptive. His emphasis on retention or lien as a form of security is important, as this view is now generally accepted. Finally, his work is valuable for its recognition that lien is a real right.

Bell's *Treatise on Bankruptcy*, in the revised form of his *Commentaries on the Law of Scotland*, went to seven editions.[226] In the second edition Bell introduces the banker's lien to Scotland and states it to be a general lien.[227] No Scottish authority is cited, but it is stated that 'bankers are in the nature of money-factors'.[228] Thus because factors have a general lien in Scotland, and bankers are money factors, bankers must have a general lien in Scotland too. In the third edition of his *Commentaries*, Bell recognizes the innkeeper's lien as a type of special lien.[229] His methodology is to set out the relevant English law and then state that the lien would be recognized in Scotland in terms of civilian principles. A difficulty is that the English innkeeper's lien has certain idiosyncrasies. In particular, it can attach to property not belonging to the guest.[230] There is, however, now judicial authority that the same rule applies in Scotland.[231]

In his *Principles of the Law of Scotland*, Bell treats retention or lien in its

---

[224] See Erskine, III, 4, 21 and *Harper's Creditors* v. *Faulds* (1791) Bell Oct Cas 440.

[225] Although there is confusion liable to arise here as trust was formerly seen in terms of deposit. See W. A. Wilson and A. G. M. Duncan, *Trusts, Trustees and Executors* (2nd edn., 1995), 13–17.   [226] The last edition was published in 1870.

[227] George J. Bell, *Commentaries on the Law of Scotland and the Principles of Mercantile Jurisprudence* (2nd edn., 1810), 488.   [228] Ibid.

[229] Bell, *Commentaries* (3rd edn., 1819), II, 147.

[230] See the leading case of *Robins & Co.* v. *Gray* [1895] 2 QB 501 and the authorities referred to therein.   [231] *Bermans and Nathans Ltd* v. *Weibye* 1983 SLT 299.

own chapter, following upon a chapter on pledge and hypothec.[232] Compensation is treated in a completely different part of the work,[233] lien being seen squarely as a form of security. His detailed treatment of lien follows the same pattern in the *Commentaries*, with his pioneering distinction between special and general liens featuring prominently.[234]

(b) *Other nineteenth-century developments*

The century saw Bell's work becoming gradually accepted as the orthodox treatment of the subject. With regard to terminology, the word 'lien' as used by Bell slowly but surely embedded itself into Scots law.[235] This may be seen particularly in the context of bankruptcy legislation, where lien had formerly been used as a synonym for security in general.[236] In the specific area of the law agent's right of retention the word 'hypothec' continued to be used.[237] Further, 'real lien' was still used to mean pecuniary real burden.[238]

The distinction between special and general liens was also admitted in the case law.[239] There were cases too in areas where Bell recognized a lien but where there had previously been little or no judicial authority. Examples include cases on the banker's and innkeeper's lien.[240] English law was regarded as persuasive on the question of whether a general lien was recognized in Scotland.[241] In one case, in a mistaken dalliance with English principle, the court held that a special lien could only be asserted over a piece of property which had actually been worked upon.[242] This decision has not been followed. Later cases upheld the civilian principle that a special lien requires only mutual obligations combined with possession[243] or, it may be, custody.[244]

Other cases underlined Bell's view that lien was real security.[245] Thus a lien-holder was not generally obliged to give up his lien in return for

---

[232] Bell, *Principles*, §§ 1410–54.
[233] Bell, *Principles*, §§ 572–5. At § 1410, he does, however, distinguish retention from it.
[234] He discusses special lien at §§ 1419–30 and general lien at §§ 1431–54.
[235] See e.g. *Skinner v. Paterson* (1823) 2 S 554; *Laurie v. Black* (1831) 10 S 1 and *Paton v. Wyllie* (1833) 11 S 703.
[236] Compare the Payment of Creditors (Scotland) Act 1793, ss. 33 and 39 and the Payment of Creditors (Scotland) Act 1814, ss. 42 and 50 with the Bankruptcy (Scotland) Act 1839, s. 3 and the Bankruptcy (Scotland) Act 1856, s. 4.
[237] Even late in the century: see, for example, *Morrison v. Watson* (1883) 2 Guth Sh Cas 502.
[238] For example, *Brown v. Miller* (1820) 3 Ross LC 29; *Wilson v. Fraser* (1824) 3 Ross LC 23; *Tailors of Aberdeen v. Coutts* (1840) 1 Rob 296.
[239] See e.g. *Anderson's Tr v. Fleming* (1871) 9 M 718. This case actually established a general lien in favour of bleachers created by usage of trade. Bleachers had been previously denied general retention in *Harper's Creditors v. Faulds* (1791) Bell Oct Cas 440, discussed above IV.3.b.
[240] *Robertson's Tr v. Royal Bank of Scotland* (1890) 18 R 12 (banker's lien) and *McKichen v. Muir* (1849) J Shaw 223 (innkeeper's lien).
[241] *Strong v. Phillips & Co.* (1878) 5 R 770.   [242] *Brown v. Sommerville* (1844) 6 D 1267.
[243] *Meikle and Wilson v. Pollard* (1880) 8 R 69; *Robertson v. Ross* (1887) 15 R 67.
[244] For example, storekeepers, who are clearly mere custodiers, have a special lien: *Laurie v. Denny's Tr* (1853) 15 D 404. The point is admitted by Gloag/Irvine (n. 1), 342.
[245] See e.g. *Wyper v. Harveys* (1861) 23 D 606 at 620 per Lord President McNeill.

caution.[246] However, lien was said to be an equitable right, in the sense that it could not be exercised 'unfairly and oppressively'.[247] For example, in the case of a dispute as to the cost of repairing a ship, the court would not regard it as desirable for the vessel to be retained under a lien for an unlimited period.[248]

Bell's reformulation of the law of retention was not universally welcomed. A particular critic was More, who in 1832 wrote: 'The right of *retention*, as originally understood and established in our law, seems to have been much obscured and perverted by the modern attempts which have been made to assimilate it to the English doctrine of *lien*.'[249] He also attacked the decision of the majority in *Harper's Creditors* v. *Faulds*,[250] being of the view that Scots law allowed general retention in all cases. The criticism seems misplaced, More failing to take account of retention based on ownership and retention based on custody or possession. This is an area on which Bell himself might have been clearer.[251] Nonetheless, nineteenth-century case law firmly established that, while retention based on ownership could secure all sums owed to the retainer, retention based on a lesser title was restricted to sums due in respect of the particular property being held.[252]

5. The modern period

In the modern period the developments of the nineteenth century have been consolidated, with Bell remaining influential. The dichotomy of special liens and general liens has become universally accepted.[253] 'Retention' and 'lien' are rarely used interchangeably. The former is generally used for retention based upon ownership and the latter for when the retainer does not have ownership but rather a subordinate real right.[254] However, the term 'real lien' has made a consistent struggle for survival. It remains used as an alternative expression for the pecuniary real burden, even in an Act of Parliament.[255]

In terms of statutory developments, there has been a weakening of the

---

[246] *Wilmot* v. *Wilson* (1841) 3 D 815.
[247] *Ferguson and Stuart* v. *Grant* (1856) 18 D 536 at 539 *per* Lord Deas.
[248] See the 20th-century case, *Garscadden* v. *Ardrossan Dry Dock Co Ltd* 1910 SC 178.
[249] J. S. More, *Notes to Stair's Institutions* (1832), cxxxi.
[250] (1791) Bell Oct Cas 440, discussed above IV.3.b.
[251] See, however, Bell, *Principles*, § 1431 and Bell, *Commentaries*, II, 117–8.
[252] *Brown* v. *Sommerville* (1844) 6 D 1267; *Melrose and Co.* v. *Hastie* (1851) 13 D 880; *Laurie* v. *Denny's Tr* (1853) 15 D 404 and *Wyper* v. *Harveys* (1861) 23 D 606.
[253] See e.g. A. J. Sim, 'Rights in Security', in *The Laws of Scotland: Stair Memorial Encyclopaedia*, vol. 20, (1992), § 75; W. A. Wilson, *The Scottish Law of Debt* (2nd edn., 1991), 95–7; and *National Homecare Ltd* v. *Belling & Co.* 1994 SLT 50.
[254] See G. L. Gretton, 'The Concept of Security', in Cusine (n. 156), 130–1 and 144–5.
[255] See the Glasgow Streets, Sewers and Buildings Consolidation Order Confirmation Act 1937, s. 236(1), discussed in *Pickard* v. *Glasgow Corporation* 1970 SLT (Sh Ct) 63 and *Sowman* v. *City of Glasgow DC* 1985 SLT 65.

power of the lien of the law agent (or solicitor). The decision in *Provenhall's Creditors*[256] was reversed by the Conveyancing (Scotland) Act 1924.[257] A later statute provided that a sasine extract is equivalent in law to a recorded deed,[258] thus allowing the exercise of a lien over title deeds to be circumvented by the client—or any other party wishing the deeds—going to Register House and obtaining extracts.

There has been a steady flow of case law, a sign that lien is of greater commercial importance than pledge. Many of the cases involve the operation of lien on insolvency, with the lien-holder asserting his real security.[259] With the partial exception of Gloag and Irvine,[260] there has been little juristic analysis of the law since Bell.

As an area of law, lien remains underdeveloped. This is borne out by a decision from 1676, to which reference has already been made. *Binning* v. *Brotherstones*[261] held that a bona fide possessor of land could remain in possession until recompensed for improvements. This shows, first, that Scots law is capable of recognizing a lien in the context of unjustified enrichment, and secondly, that it is capable of recognizing a lien over land. Other jurisdictions recognize similar liens.[262] Whether it is still prepared to do so in the twenty-first century remains to be seen. In any event, it can be assumed that the long and complicated evolution of the Scottish law of lien is not yet complete.

V. CONCLUSION

Pledge, hypothec, and lien have been influenced both by civil law and by English law. With respect to pledge, there existed a distinct set of rules in Anglo-Norman times which were to a large extent replaced by a reception of Roman law. In particular, forfeiture was discarded as the creditor's remedy, pledge being regarded as a collateral security. Certain Anglo-Norman rules persisted, however, such as the need for the creditor to go to court to enforce his right, in the absence of special agreement with the debtor.

The most important survival of Anglo-Norman law was the requirement of delivery. One consequence was a broad refusal to recognize the conventional hypothec.[263] Tacit hypothecs, however, were accepted in limited cases. It is interesting to note that the main example—the landlord's hypothec—

---

[256] (1781) Mor 6253. See above IV.3.b.   [257] Conveyancing (Scotland) Act 1924, s. 27.
[258] Conveyancing and Feudal Reform (Scotland) Act 1970, s. 45.
[259] For example, *Liquidator of Grand Empire Theatres* v. *Snodgrass* 1932 SC (HL) 73 and *Garden Haig-Scott & Wallace* v. *White* 1962 SLT 78.   [260] Gloag/Irvine (n. 1), ch. 10 and 11.
[261] (1676) Mor 13401.
[262] In particular, South African law. See D. G. Kleyn and A. Boraine, *Silberberg and Schoeman's The Law of Property* (3rd edn., 1992), 464–7.
[263] To this the bonds of bottomry and *respondentia* form minor exceptions. See above III.3.

bears some resemblance to the landlord's right of distress from the Anglo–Norman period.

As for lien, once again the modern law is an amalgam of civil and English law. Its main architect was Bell who developed a civilian doctrine, retention, by making free use of English authority. In particular, Bell introduced the dichotomy of special and general liens, based on a similar distinction south of the border.

The further development of the law of moveable security is of great interest. A consultation paper by the Department of Trade and Industry on the reform of the law was published in 1994[264] but has not been acted upon. It proposed the creation of a new fixed security over moveables, created by registration. Further research has now been commissioned by the Scottish Executive and an expert committee formed. As regards existing securities, the floating charge, much criticized by some, may be the subject of amendment. The law of lien has much scope for wider application. All this, however, lies in the future. The story of the evolution of moveable security so far may be summed up by the statement that it represents a classic case of Scots law as a mixed system.

[264] Above n. 118.

9

Leases: Four Historical Portraits

MARTIN HOGG*

I. INTRODUCTION

The tenure of land by lease in Scotland has an ancient pedigree. While other forms of land tenure, such as the rental and kindly tenancy, thrived alongside lease only to wither, the lease seems certain to outlive them all. The pattern of decline applies equally to feu farm, a form of tenure which did not appear on these shores until well into the history of the lease, and which will, with the forthcoming abolition of the feudal system, pass into the history books. To borrow the language of horticulture, the lease is one of Scotland's hardiest perennials.

The longevity of the lease, or 'tack' to use its Scots name, must be attributable in large part to its adaptability to meet changing social and political needs.[1] From obscure origins as a form of unilateral grant in use mostly by nobles and prelates, it has undergone many metamorphoses, until today it is in use by all degrees and types of landowner, utilized as much for the needs of private individuals in search of short-term accommodation, as for complex mercantile arrangements.

In what follows, I will address several issues. First, I will ask whether it is possible to discover the origins of leasehold tenure in Scotland. Second, I will set the phenomenon of the lease against other forms of land tenure and in so doing explain some of the terms which might puzzle the reader of historical leases. And third, I will examine a lease from each of four different points in

---

* The author wishes to express his thanks to the following persons: in particular, to Dr John Finlay of the University of Glasgow, for his invaluable help in tracking down numerous historical documents and his advice regarding terminology; to Mr David Sellar, Honorary Fellow of the Faculty of Law, University of Edinburgh, and Professor Hector MacQueen of the Faculty of Law, University of Edinburgh, for much helpful advice and comments on a draft of the text; and to Almira Delibegovic and to Murray Earle of the University of Glasgow who undertook initial research on the author's behalf. Any failings and errors in what follows are the fault of the author alone.

[1] H. M. Conacher offered this simple explanation for the popularity of the lease in Scotland: 'The universality of the practice of letting lands on lease in Scotland seems due to the history of the country. There never was a Norman Conquest in Scotland, so the feudal system was not imposed on an earlier rural economy of a subject people': 'Feudal Tenures in Scotland in the Fifteenth and Sixteenth Centuries', (1936) 48 *JR* 189, 226. However, this observation is not sufficient to explain the continuing popularity of the lease after the encouragement of feu farm by the legislature.

the history of Scots law, considering its form and content, and setting it in its socio-political and legal context.

II. TERMINOLOGY

It is necessary to begin with a few words on terminology, both in order to describe the phenomenon of the lease, and to distinguish other forms of land tenure which are similar but not identical.

1. Main terms

The language of 'location' (from the civil law) is seldom used. The main terms which will be encountered are (*a*) 'tack', (*b*) 'assedation', (*c*) 'maills', and (*d*) 'lease' itself.

(*a*) *Tack*

The native Scots term for the lease, seldom encountered today, is the 'tack' (or 'tak', or even 'take'). The term is the principal one used by the institutional writers and by all commentators up to the early nineteenth century. From 'tack' derive the terms 'tacksman', meaning a tenant, and 'tack-duty',[2] meaning rent.

(*b*) *Assedation*

Assedation (or in earlier times, 'assedatioun') was often used in conjunction with tack. Thus Balfour, in his title 'Of assedatioun' began: 'Gif ony persoun gevis to ane uther ane tak and assedatioun of ony landis, rentis, fisching . . .'.[3] Assedation is thus synonymous with tack.[4]

Craig's view of the etymological origins of assedation was that '"Assedatio" (tack) is a Norman word—some attribute to it a Lombardic origin—and signifies a settling of lands to a tenant for a fixed term . . .'.[5] Hence, Craig renders the alternative to tacksman as 'assedatarius'.[6]

Worth noting is Erskine's comment that the term was 'given in some old statutes to grants holden in feu farm'.[7] He refers to the statute encouraging feu farm in 1457.[8]

(*c*) *Maills*

The final principal term which may be encountered in leases is 'maills',[9] often conjoined with 'duties' in the phrase 'maills and duties'. This term refers to

[2] Stair, II, 9, 1: '. . . for a hire, which is called the tack-duty'. [3] Balfour, *Practicks*, 200.
[4] Stair, II, 9, 2 uses it as a synonym for tack: 'tacks are also called assedations'.
[5] Craig, II, 9, 22. [6] Ibid. [7] Erskine, II, 6, 20
[8] The Feuing Act 1457, APS II, 49 (c. 15). See main text accompanying n. 61 below.
[9] The *Concise Scots Dictionary* (1985), ed. Mairi Robinson, suggests an etymology deriving from old Norse 'mál' (speech) and 'máli' contract, via late Old English 'mal' (payment).

the rent. From maills, derives the term 'mailler', another term for the tenant.[10]

(d) *Lease*[11]

Lease, the modern term, was not used until the nineteenth century. Stair,[12] writing in 1681, said of tacks: 'the English call them leases, as letting the tenement to the tenant'.[13]

A further word which may be encountered, as a verb meaning to lease, or hire out, is 'set'.[14] Hence in the first lease we shall consider, the landlord declares that he 'has set' the subjects of the lease.[15]

2. Civilian terminology: *Locatio conductio*

If the view that the Scottish lease derived from Roman law is correct,[16] then the Roman phenomenon of most relevance is that of *locatio conductio*, literally 'lease and hire'. This term is rarely encountered in Scots law, save in tracts explaining the origins of leases, where one may also encounter the more specific term *locatio conductio rei*,[17] the lease and hire of a thing, as opposed to *locatio conductio operarum* (the letting and hire of services) or *locatio conductio operis* (the letting and hire of work).[18]

Stair devotes a title[19] in his *Institutions of the Law of Scotland* to 'Location and conduction' where he discusses the 'contract whereby hire is given for the fruits, use or work of persons or things',[20] and a further title to the contract of 'Tack', which he defines as a 'personal contract of location'[21] for the hire of land, though he discusses aspects of the tack in the first title also.

---

[10] Balfour, *Practicks*, 208 uses the term mailler and seems to use it as a synonym for tenant: 'ane tenant being in possessioun, as tenent or mailler of any landis, . . .'.

[11] The origins of the term seem to lie in the Latin, *laxare*, to loosen, and thence via old French (lais) and Anglo-French, into old English.   [12] Stair, II, 9, 2.

[13] Walter Ross, *Lectures on the History and Practice of the Law of Scotland* (2nd edn., 1822), vol. 2, 456, referred to the giving of land 'in lease, or as we may say, in tack, to tenants for a term of years'.

[14] Although it is also used of feu. Thus, Margaret Sanderson, *Scottish Rural Society in the Sixteenth Century* (1982), 248 talks of 'a setting of land, by tack or feu'.

[15] See the grant by John Melville to Sir William Douglas discussed below IV. The term is also referred to by Balfour, *Practicks*, 201: 'Tak and assedatioun set to ane man . . .', and Stair, II, 9, 1: 'land . . . is set to the tacksman'.

[16] As to the competing theories on the origins of the lease in Scots law, see below III.

[17] This term was that used by the pandectists: see Reinhard Zimmermann, *The Law of Obligations: Roman Foundations of the Civilian Tradition* (paperback edn., 1996), 338 sq.

[18] The medieval jurists also distinguished the *locatio ad modicum tempus* (which gave no security to tenants against singular successors) and the *locatio ad longum tempus* (which gave the tenant a *jus in re*): E. J. H. Schrage, 'Emptio (Nondum) Tollit Locatum', 1978 *Acta Juridica* 1, 6.

[19] Stair, I, 15.   [20] Stair, I, 15, 1.   [21] Stair, II, 9, 1.

3. Other types of tenure with similarities to the lease

Apart from the traditional lease, there were other related types of tenure of which space does not permit a detailed study, but which are worth mentioning in passing. In particular, brief mention should be made of: (*a*) *emphyteusis*, (*b*) rentals, (*c*) kindly tenancy, and (*d*) tenancies-at-will. Leasehold tenure is also connected to various heritable tenures, especially that of feu farm. Of this important relationship, more will be said later.

4. *Emphyteusis*

The debate over the influence of Roman law on Scots law encompasses questions concerning the Roman institution of *emphyteusis*.[22] Was it assimilated into Scots law? While *emphyteusis* resembles feu farm tenure,[23] the two are not to be equated. As George Gretton says: 'Early Scottish writers often called feufarm "emphyteusis" after the Roman institution of that name, with which it had much in common, though they were probably not historically connected'.[24] Stair said that the relationship was merely one of resemblance: 'Infeftments feu are like to the emphyteusis in the civil law'.[25] Other authors were less scrupulous in distinguishing between feu farm, lease, and *emphyteusis*. Robert Bell, for instance, discussing leases, cited continental medieval charters of *emphyteusis*. However, if Scots land tenure was influenced both by the canon law and by the feudal system, it is possible that the origins of feu farm may be found both in *emphyteusis* and the feudal system.[26]

Later Roman law recognized *emphyteusis* as an institution distinct from *locatio conductio*. This divergence continued into the *jus commune*, which also recognized both *locatio conductio* (whether for fixed periods of time or in perpetuity) and *emphyteusis*.[27] In the medieval civil tradition, a *jus in re* could be acquired both by the *emphyteote*[28] and the *conductor ad longum tempus*.[29]

5. Rentals

The term 'rental' is most frequently used in Scots law to refer to a perpetual grant of land, extending for the life of the grantee and thereafter transmitting

---

[22] Zimmermann (n. 17), 358–9; also, Barry Nicholas, *An Introduction to Roman Law* (repr. 1969), 148–9. Nicholas comments at 149 that '[b]ecause [*emphyteusis*] drains almost all content from ownership, particularly where it is granted in perpetuity, [it] therefore conflicts with the Roman and Romanistic conception of the unity of ownership'. This conceptual problem has also affected Scots law's treatment of feu farm, which fits uneasily into a system which purports to model its property law on the civil law.   [23] As to which form of land tenure, see below.
[24] George Gretton, 'Feudal System', in Kenneth Reid (ed.), *The Law of Property in Scotland* (1996), § 68.   [25] Stair, II, 3, 34.
[26] The investigation of such a hypothesis is beyond the scope of this chapter.
[27] Zimmermann (n. 17), 359.   [28] Or '*emphyteuta*'.   [29] Schrage (n. 18), 6 sq.

to his heirs in perpetuity.[30] In many cases, the tenant's right derived from nothing more than an entry in a landlord's 'rental book'.[31] Thus, the rentaller frequently had no written copy of his title, save in some cases a copy of the entry in the rental book.[32] It is thought that no rentals have been granted in recent times.

There is, however, some divergence of usage among Scottish commentators. It seems that Balfour uses the term in the sense described above.[33] Stair, however, sees the phenomenon as a synonym for kindly tenancy (discussed below): 'A rental is a tack set to kindly tenants...'.[34] He also remarks that 'some tacks are also called rentals, as being the constitution of a fixed rent, and they are of longer endurance than ordinary tacks, being of one or more liferents, and have somewhat special in them, of which hereafter'.[35] Bankton also seems to equate the two, saying: 'Rentals are special kinds of tacks: by those the ancient possessors, or others, are received as Kindly tenants and Rentallers'.[36] Craig, whilst mentioning rentals, is obscure as to their nature.[37]

Margaret Sanderson[38] has undertaken the most detailed modern investigation of rentallers, commenting that this form of tenure was most popular in the South West of Scotland. Sanderson says of the rental that 'at first sight [it] appears to have been more secure than the tack'.[39] Rentals were usually renewed to a rentaller's nearest heir: 'Rentalling was, in fact, a system of inheritance subject to a renewal which preserved continuity of possession in a family.'[40] Sanderson notes that, provided a rentaller kept his conditions, his rights were incontrovertible.[41]

---

[30] However, Bankton says that rentals are either effectual (in the normal case) 'during the lives of the receiver' or *may* be granted to 'one and his heirs': II, 9, 41. Even where the latter is the case, Bankton says that only the first heir has a right against singular successors, although, in his opinion, a rental granted to a tenant and his heirs 'would bind the granter and his heirs to receive heirs of the rentallers as kindly tenants in all time coming, without limitation': II, 9, 41.

[31] Ross says that rentallers were people who had immemorially occupied land but without charter, leases, or other rights. They had their names entered in rental lists of the owner of the land. Ross says that the origins of these kindly tenants was the same as that of *copyholders* in English law: see Ross (n. 13), 479. George Joseph Bell says similarly (*Principles*, § 1279) that the rental-right may be equated with kindly tenancy. Rentallers were enrolled in a rental book, and this, or a copy of their entry, was their sole title. 'They came to be admitted to a sort of hereditary right; their widows being permitted to continue their possession, and their sons to succeed. Rental-rights had no ish, or term of expiration; and so the alternative was, either to regard them ... as perpetual tenants (which they could not effectually be against singular successors without sasine) or as liferenters.'

[32] Although Bankton, II, 9, 41 says: 'A rental must be perfected by writing duly signed and delivered to the tenant, nor will an enrolment of tenants, as rentallers, in the heritors court-book be good against his singular successors, tho' it is effectual against him and his heirs.'

[33] Balfour, *Practicks*, 205 has a passage beginning: 'Ane man beand rentallit in the King's rentall of any landis...'.   [34] Stair, II, 9, 15.

[35] Stair, II, 9, 2.   [36] Bankton, II, 9, 41. See also II, 9, 44.   [37] Craig, II, 9, 24.

[38] Sanderson (n. 14), 50 sqq.   [39] Ibid. 51.   [40] Ibid.

[41] Sanderson (n. 14) cites the following two examples from the pleadings of cases. In 1558, an advocate defending a rentaller from removing argued he could not be removed 'becaus of the consuetude of the barony ... ane tenand being anis rentallit ... be vertew of his rentale hes tytle

As to the origins of rentals, Sanderson says: 'The fact that the position of tenants who held by tack and by rental was so similar in practice makes it arguable that tack and rental were simply variations on a basic type of customary tenure which in England came to be known as copyhold.'[42] However as Sanderson has not been discussing tacks in general, but merely tacksmen for life and their heirs, this conclusion is not without its difficulties.

As rentals were granted for the life of the tenant, they bear a resemblance to the liferent lease, that is, a lease granted for the life of the tenant. It is questionable whether the rental and the liferent lease are synonymous. Bankton stated that the rental was a species of liferent tack, though with the difference that a tenant under an ordinary liferent tack could assign the lease, but a rentaller could not.[43]

6. Kindly tenants

As we have seen, Stair and Bankton equated rentals with the phenomenon of kindly tenancy. Sanderson explains the terminology of 'kindliness' as a derivation from the word *kin*, expressing rightness in possession by inheritance.[44] However, Sanderson does not agree with the view of rental as a synonym for kindly tenancy.[45] She argues that kindly tenancy was not how the tenant held, but *why*. One could be a kindly tack-holder, a kindly rentaller, or a kindly tenant-at-will. Kindly tenancy was the claim to customary inheritance, however the tenant held.[46] The kindly tenant is now all but extinct.[47]

The Report of the Scottish Leases Committee[48] expressed the opinion that

---

and ryt to the landis quhilkis he is rentallit in . . . ay and quhill the same be forfaltit in ane court' (Acts and decreets, XVIII, fo. 273ʳ). In a similar defence from 1534: 'quhat tennentis havand takkis of thar landis be rentalling in thar rentale and pais thar males and dewties with ane gratitude to everie abbot at that interes, thia sall bruke thar malingis for lyftymes, quhilkis unbrokin as yit' (Acts of the Lords of Council in Public Affairs (1501–54), 413, 421).

[42] Sanderson (n. 14), 54. In particular, Sanderson equates Scottish rentallers and English copyholders of inheritance (at 56).　　　　　　　　　　　　　　[43] Bankton, II, 9, 42, 45, 46.

[44] Sanderson (n. 14), 58. Gretton (n. 24), § 72 says '"Kindly" here means hereditary', but argues that 'what was special about the kindly tenancy was that it was perpetual and alienable, rather than that it was inheritable'.

[45] Gretton (n. 24), § 72 n. 2 is more open about the issue, saying: 'Whether these two terms were absolutely synonymous is not clear.'

[46] Sanderson (n. 14) adds that there were some kindly tenants who occupied without written rights. But the kindly tenant of the sixteenth century, she points out, did have a written, although customary, right to his holding, in form of a tack or rental. His claim was called his kindness.

[47] See John Carmont's discussion of those he calls the 'last kindly tenants' in 'The King's Kindlie Tenants of Lochmaben', (1909) 21 *JR* 323. See also Bankton, II, 9, 43. Gretton (n. 24), § 72 agrees with Carmont but points out that now 'virtually all the rents have been redeemed'— i.e. under the Land Tenure Reform (Scotland) Act 1974, s. 4(7), which would give the tenants, in effect, an absolute right of ownership in the land. That conversion is formally effected by the Abolition of Feudal Tenure etc. (Scotland) Act 2000, s. 64.

[48] *Report of the Scottish Leases Committee* (Cmnd. 8656, 1952).

one species of kindly tenancy appeared to be the 'tenancy-at-will', of which they identified extant examples at the time of their report.[49] Tenancies-at-will have been described as 'a perpetual lease which exists by virtue of ancient custom'.[50]

7. Leases and feudal tenure

The most interesting question concerning lease and other forms of landholding is the connection between lease and the various types of feudal tenure, in particular feu farm. In the early period the similarities between the two tenures are remarkable, though a full study of the relationship has yet to be made.

(a) Origins of tenure at ferme

A 'ferme' was a money rent, and it appears that feu farm is the result of a grafting on to existing tenures for money rent of feudal and heritable features.[51] As noted below, many tacks were converted into feus.

(b) Comparison of lease and feu farm

Various commentators have drawn comparisons between leases and feu farm. Stair said of grants at feu that 'where they have a considerable rent, they are far from being purely gratuitous, and are rather perpetual locations'.[52] The use of the word 'rent' is telling. Robert Bell, comparing the two phenomena, said: 'The feu duty and the rent corresponded; both of them consisted either of victual or cattle, or of agricultural services; and it is only in the endurance of the right that any difference is to be discovered.'[53] An early statute seems to consider the two types of tenure as interchangeable.[54]

Heritable grants of land 'at ferme' and leases both have a long pedigree. A. A. M. Duncan notes that David I set land in tack in the village of Ednam to St Cuthbert in the twelfth century for an annual rent of 2 shillings, but also that in 1211 the Earl of Fife succeeded heritably to land, paying a specified rent both in money and kind.[55] The first recorded case of a feu farm occurred in the mid-twelfth century.[56]

---

[49] Ibid. 34–8.   [50] Gretton (n. 24), § 72.

[51] Isabel A. Milne, 'Heritable Rights: The Early Feudal Tenures', in G. C. H. Paton (ed.), *An Introduction to Scottish Legal History*, Stair Society, vol. 20 (1958), 147 at 154.

[52] Stair, II, 11, 31.   [53] Robert Bell, *A Treatise on Leases* (3rd edn., 1820), 18.

[54] The Feuing Act 1457, APS, II, 49 (c. 15), provided: 'Quhat prelate, baronne or free-holder, that can accord with his tennent, upon setting of few-ferme of his awin land in all or in part, our soveraine lord sall ratifie and appreive the said assedatioun', thus interchanging 'few-ferme' and 'assedatioun'.

[55] A. A. M. Duncan, *Scotland: The Making of the Kingdom* (1975), vol. 1, 394–5.

[56] In a grant by Kelso Abbey: *Liber de Calchou*, Bannantyne Club, 1846, I, no. 102 (see further Milne (n. 51), 154). The phrase in the grant is '*liberum firmum feudum*'.

Recent research by Duncan and Sanderson has contributed to a greater understanding of the relationship between lease and feu farm. In particular it has demonstrated that the success of feu farm as an institution occurred on the whole as a result of the conversion of finite leases into heritable feu farm tenure. However, it is interesting to note that even with some leases, the grant was in favour of the grantee and his heirs and assignees, providing in effect a type of heritable tenure. Whilst the Church for one was conscious of the need to restrict the dealing in lands granted heritably by them,[57] Duncan notes that as early as 1210 a grant included the beneficiary, his heirs and assignees.[58]

Sanderson, like Bell, draws comparisons between tack-holders (in particular customary tenants) and feudal vassals,[59] noting similarities such as the formal basis of possession, the upholding of titles in the royal courts, the same descent of title for a customary tenant as for a vassal, and the payments due from each, for vassals their feu duty and services, for tenants their maill and ferme (that is, money and rent in kind), as well as *grassum*, entry silver and herezeld.[60]

Since at least 1457,[61] when statute provided: 'Quhat prelate, baronne or free-holder, that can accord with his tennent, upon setting of few-ferme of his awin land in all or in part, our soveraine lord sall ratifie and appreive the said assedatioun'[62] and the king was advised[63] to 'begyne and gif exempill to the laif'[64] by feuing the Crown lands, feu farm had begun its inexorable rise. However, it was not until the sixteenth century that the greatest number of conversions from lease to feu farm occurred. Several reasons for the conversion of leases to feu charters have been identified: the pressure of financial and economic conditions;[65] conflict with England and resultant financial losses; the desire to shift the burden of estate management; and many personal and local circumstances.[66] James IV, conscious that by an act of 1504[67] he was allowed to grant feus of Crown land so long as the rental, grassum, and other duties were not diminished, often granted feus with a much higher feu duty than the level of rent in the leases they replaced.[68]

There is some debate as to the classes of tenant whose leases were converted to a feu. Sanderson's research indicates that 'in the business of feuing, the small man did reasonably well for himself, better in some places, certainly,

---

[57] Duncan (n. 55), 397.   [58] Ibid. 398.
[59] She also draws comparisons between rentallers and feudal vassals.
[60] Sanderson (n. 14), 57.
[61] Though as Sanderson points out, churchmen had been setting lands in feu farm since the late 13th century: Sanderson (n. 14), 64.   [62] Feuing Act 1457, APS, II, 49 (c. 15).
[63] APS, II, 49 (c. 15).   [64] the laif = the others.
[65] Such pressures could be alleviated by the granting of land at feu for, as Sanderson notes, the grant of a feu would be purchased, sometimes for a vast sum, even from ecclesiastical landowners (for whom such grants were meant to be prohibited by canon law, save exceptionally).
[66] Sanderson (n. 14), ch. 6 *passim*.   [67] APS, II, 244 (c.30); 253 (c. 36).
[68] On this point, see Ranald Nicholson, 'Feudal Developments in Late Medieval Scotland', [1973] *JR* 1

than in others'.[69] However, Ranald Nicholson has concluded '[t]he relative security which in England devolved upon a large and lowly section of rural society was in Scotland, thanks to feuing, reserved for a minority composed, in the main, of substantial landholders'.[70] He also says, however, of the Crown lands in Fife, that '[i]n the rental of March 1510 nearly all the lands were granted in feu',[71] which suggests that small landholders benefited here also. It may be that Nicholson's comments are reconcilable with Sanderson's geographical *caveat*.

It would be wrong to think that, with the coming of feu farm, the lease went into terminal decline. In fact, there were very good reasons why lease remained a preferred medium of land tenure in many cases. Restrictions upon the ability to feu were a factor in this. Feu restrictions might come from prohibitions within the grant itself, such as a prohibition against sub-feuing,[72] or via entail restrictions.[73] The loosening of entail restrictions in the Entail Improvement Act 1770, permitting building leases[74] of up to ninety-nine years, was to be one reason for the continuing popularity of the lease.

8. Conclusion on terminology

The above discussion is an indication that the history of lease in Scotland is intermixed with other similar but distinct types of land tenure. Comparison of the tenures is made more difficult by different usage of the terms by different authors, something of which the researcher must be continually aware.

III. THE EARLY ORIGINS OF LEASES

The origins of such tenure in, or at, ferme are probably remote. It was an indirect form of land management, an entrusting of parts of an estate to middlemen standing between the lord and the peasantry; these middlemen paid to the lord a fixed annual rent in kind, later in cash or both, for the term of their lease which might be a number of years or life.[75]

The legal origins of the lease are unclear, and competing theories exist as

---

[69] Sanderson (n. 14), 80.   [70] Nicholson (n. 68), 8.   [71] Ibid. 5.
[72] Future restrictions of this nature were prohibited by the Conveyancing (Scotland) Act 1874, and in the Conveyancing Amendment (Scotland) Act 1938 such prohibitions of any date were declared null and void.
[73] The Scottish Leases Report (n. 48) identified title restrictions, deeds of entail, and the type of tenure, e.g. burgage tenure, as amongst the factors which favoured the frequent granting of ground leases between 1770 and 1860 (and in some cases to 1900) in some parts of the country: see at 15.
[74] A 'building lease' (also sometimes referred to as a 'ground lease') is not a term of art in Scots law, but is used to refer to leases where land was let for the purposes of erecting buildings thereon.   [75] Duncan (n. 55), 392.

to whether they truly lie in the *jus civile*, in feudal law, in native law, or in a mixture of some or all of these. The controversy was taken up by different writers in the nineteenth century, but was never properly resolved. Its solution is still tantalizingly out of reach. All that is possible here is to raise some interesting questions. Further investigation of the issue would necessitate examination of early legal sources, including the various Abbey Chartularies and diocesan records.

1. Comparison of Roman and Scots leases

There are many sources to which one may turn in discussing both the Roman lease[76] and the Scots lease, but no extensive comparison between the rules of the two systems governing the lease appears to have been made.

There are both similarities and differences. The Roman contract of lease was bilateral, and imposed obligations upon both parties. As we shall see, the Scottish legal style was first a bilateral contract, then a unilateral grant, and finally a return to a bilateral contract once more. In the civil law, as in Scots law, there were cardinal elements to be settled. In the civil law these were the subjects and the rent. In Rome, the lease could be finite (in which case neither party could terminate prior to the agreed term), or indefinite (in which case either party could terminate at any time). In Scots law, indefinite leases were not permitted in the early period, though this rule was later modified. Roman law recognized the rule of tacit relocation, as did Scots law.

A comparison of the more detailed rules of the two systems is possible.[77] For example, the Roman rule, that a lease was forfeit by non-payment of rent for two years,[78] was mirrored in certain circumstances in early Scots law,[79] and came into use later as a general rule in irritancy. In Roman law, a tenant deprived of the use and enjoyment of the property was entitled to rescind the lease;[80] the same rule was adopted in Scots law. A corollary was the Roman rule that a tenant who was evicted was excused the obligation to pay rent.[81] This too was adopted in Scotland.[82] In Roman law, a tenant was not permitted to change the character of the *res* let or to deal with it in an unauthorized way;[83] in Scots law, the principle of inversion of possession states a similar

---

[76] See, most recently, Zimmermann (n. 17), ch. 11.

[77] In the following examples, the corresponding rule in Scots law may have been adopted at an early stage in the development of our law, or at a later stage.

[78] Paul. D. 19, 2, 54, 1; C. 4, 65, 3.

[79] *Regiam Majestatem*, III, 14. The two-year irritancy applied to feus also: statute 1597, APS, IV, 133 (c. 17). The history of the feudal right of irritancy is discussed by Lord Watson in *Sandeman v. The Scottish Property Investment Co.* (1884) 12 R 67 (HL), 71 sq.

[80] Paul. D. 19, 2, 24, 4; Lab. D. 19, 2, 60 pr.   [81] Ulp. D. 19, 2, 19, 6.

[82] Robert Hunter, *A Treatise on the Law of Landlord and Tenant* (4th edn., 1876), vol. 2, 461; Bell (n. 53), 175.   [83] Inst. 3, 24, 5; Gai. D. 19, 2, 25, 3.

rule. The Roman rule that a tenant must keep agricultural land in proper cultivation[84] was mirrored by various provisions in Scots law.[85] The rule that the landlord was bound to repair the property, unless otherwise agreed, applied in both systems.[86]

However, the pattern is not all one of similarity. Whereas the Roman rule was that a landlord had to compensate the tenant for improvements,[87] Scots law did not provide a remedy until the modern period.[88] In Roman law, the tenant might sublet;[89] in Scotland, subletting was not permitted, unless power to do so was conferred in the deed: 'sub-tack . . . is competent to tacksmen, where lands are set to them or their sub-tenants, or that they have power to out-put and in-put tenants'.[90]

This comparison points to a large number of similarities between the two systems. However, many of the Scots rules might be the result of mere good sense, and indeed the provisions regarding the maintenance of agricultural land come from statute. Whether the other rules were drawn directly from the civil law is open to conjecture. Certainly, Balfour, writing in 1579, cites no civilian authority in his statement of the law of tacks,[91] nor does Stair, writing at the end of the following century. This is not to say that the prelates who were granting leases at a much earlier date were not utilizing a form and institution which was civilian in origin. This was, as we shall see, the view of Robert Bell, writing in 1820. Moreover, Scots lawyers were clearly aware of Roman law in this area even by the medieval period: *Regiam Majestatem* draws a comparison at one point between the Scots and Roman meaning of a particular term.[92] It may be that with leases there was Roman influence (via canon law) in the general form and origin of the institution, but that a large part of the substance was native in origin, even if there were striking similarities between particular rules of the two systems.

In the following paragraphs something is said of the views of some

---

[84] Gai. D. 19, 2, 25, 3; Iav. D. 19, 2, 51; Paul. D. 19, 2, 55, 2; PS 2, 18, 2.

[85] See, for instance, Bell (n. 53), 251–61.

[86] Ulp. D. 19, 2, 15, 1; Gai. D. 19, 2, 25, 2; PS 2, 18, 2; Inst. 3, 24, 5; see on the Scots position, Bell (n. 53), 186–95. [87] Pap. D. 43, 10, 1, 3; Paul. D. 19, 2, 55, 1.

[88] At the time of Hunter's 4th edn. in 1876 (n. 82), 222 it was still stated that '[t]he lessee of urban subjects is not entitled to recompense for monies expended for ornaments, or even greater conveniency, unless the landlord has previously consented'. The modern right to compensation for improvements extends to agricultural tenants: see the Agricultural Holdings (Scotland) Act 1991. [89] Paul. D. 19, 2, 7, 30.

[90] Stair, II, 9, 22.

[91] The explanation may lie (in the view of one author) in the fact that Balfour was writing 'on the basis of the traditional sources of Scottish customary law and statutes, largely ignoring the civil law' because 'he was still part of a tradition that considered Scots law, civil law, and Canon law as separate valid sources of rules for deciding legal disputes': J. Cairns, 'The Civil Law Tradition in Scottish Legal Thought', in D. L. Carey Miller and R. Zimmermann (ed.), *The Civilian Tradition and Scots Law* (1997), 191–223, 199.

[92] The term at issue is 'dos': quoted in O. F. Robinson, T. D. Fergus, and W. M. Gordon, *European Legal History* (2nd edn., 1994), para. 9.6.4.

historical authors writing on lease. However, it must be recalled that the state of legal knowledge and analysis at the various times of their writing was much poorer than in the present century. It is therefore also instructive to refer to more recent commentators who have researched the influence of the civilian tradition on Scots legal thought and practice. In particular, two collections of essays have made important contributions to a better understanding of the influence of Roman law on Scots law.[93] This has produced various insights into the early reception of Roman law, including that: (*a*) Roman law was known during the early medieval period (prior to the fourteenth century), principally via canon law and through contact with the Roman law taught in continental universities;[94] (*b*) in the early medieval period, its use was as a subsidiary authority in the ecclesiastical courts, and as both a source of ideas and a 'badge of learning' in the civil courts;[95] (*c*) by the fourteenth century, there was greater use of civil law in the secular courts;[96] and (*d*) it was with the establishment of the Scottish universities that the teaching of civil law began to flourish in Scotland.[97]

The importance of civil law is underlined by the injunction in the Education Act 1496[98] that substantial barons and freeholders were to send their eldest sons to the grammar schools to learn Latin and thereafter for three years at 'the sculis of art and Jure sua that thai may haue knawlege and vnderstanding of the lawis. Throw the quhilkis Justice may reigne vniversalie throw all the realme. Sua thai that ar schereffis or Jugeis Ordinaris vnder the kingis hienes may haue knawledge to do Justice'.

The better understanding of the civil law tradition has produced a more accurate view of the role of Roman law in Scots legal history. However, it has yet to throw much light on the details of the origins of the law of lease in Scotland. Whilst we await further research in this area, a reminder of the views of earlier writers is instructive, at least for shedding light on the view of Roman law held in a previous age.

2. Views of jurists

Amongst the Scottish legal pantheon, few say much about the origin of the lease.[99] Stair briefly discusses the form of the lease, commenting that prior to the Leases Act 1449, a tack was 'no more than a personal contract of location'.[100] However, in apparent contradiction to this, he says elsewhere of the old form of tack that 'it was ordinarily granted by the setter to the tacksman

---

[93] Carey Miller/Zimmermann (n. 91) and Robin Evans-Jones (ed.), *The Civil Law Tradition in Scotland* (1995). [94] W. M. Gordon, 'Roman Law in Scotland', in Evans-Jones (n. 93), 15.
[95] Ibid. 17. [96] Ibid. [97] Ibid. 19.
[98] APS II, 238 (c. 3), discussed both in Gordon (n. 94), and Cairns (n. 91).
[99] For instance, Stair says very little, and Balfour, in his *Practicks*, says nothing at all.
[100] Stair, II, 9, 1.

for such a duty, without any mutual obligement upon his part, like unto a charter; but because the tenant, not being bound, might at the end of any year before Whitsunday, renounce such a tack and be free, as being in his favour; therefore they are now ordinarily by way of contract . . .'.[101] Stair makes no direct citation of any Roman law texts in his discussion on tacks.

The three authors who have most to say on the origins of the lease wrote in the late eighteenth or nineteenth centuries: the advocates Robert Bell[102] and Robert Hunter,[103] and the writer to the signet Walter Ross.[104] Lord Kames also made passing reference to the origins of the lease in his *Historical Legal Tracts*.[105]

(a) *Robert Bell*

Robert Bell saw the origins of leases as Roman, the device having been retained in the provinces after the break-up of the Western Empire:

The lease, we have found, was introduced by the Romans, and was in use, during the times of the Empire, and has continued, with no very essential alterations, until the present time. Its form was preserved by the Churchmen, whose notaries, having succeeded to those of the Empire, transmitted the Roman forms of deeds to the conveyancers of modern Europe.[106]

Bell's view was that in the former Roman provinces 'the lease must have been common among the ancient inhabitants';[107] however, he gives very scant authority for this statement. He points to a statute of Robert I, saying that such enactments 'prove that the forms of conveyancing were the same in all the countries of Europe'.[108] Bell says that ecclesiastical leases 'appear in the form of a charter; and they are granted by the proprietor to the person who is to possess',[109] and suggests that such tenure existed in Scotland, arguing that 'it is obvious, that the forms of the Church were, in all its establishments,

---

[101] Ibid., II, 9, 5. More will be said later on the actual form of the lease.
[102] The first edition of whose *Treatise on Leases* was published in 1803, with a second edition in 1805, and a third in 1820.
[103] The first edition of whose *Treatise on the Law of Landlord and Tenant* was published in 1833, with the second in 1845, third in 1860, and fourth 1876.
[104] The first edition of whose *Lectures on the History and Practice of the Law of Scotland* was published in 1792, with the second in 1822.
[105] Lord Kames, *Historical Law Tracts* (4th edn., 1792). [106] Bell (n. 53), 21.
[107] Ibid. 5.
[108] Ibid. 7. One may say in support of Bell here, that the act he cites includes reference to the phenomenon of a donation of land to ecclesiastical houses followed by a lease to the donor, a phenomenon which seems to have occurred in other parts of Europe: see, for instance, Susan Reynolds, *Fiefs and Vassals* (1994), 329.
[109] Bell (n. 53), 8. Interestingly, in his footnote Bell quotes from a charter referred to by Muratori, and the quotation of the charter begins: 'Non dissimiles fuerunt interdum census *Emphyteusibus* . . .' The reference to *emphyteusis* is interesting, for Bell is using this reference to support a point about leases.

the same'.[110] He saw little difference between lease and feu farm, even at the time of James VI.

Bell's view is that the earliest non-ecclesiastical leases were oral rather than written, and that writing only appeared later: 'The lease was ... reduced into writing, and took the form of the charter, with this difference, that its endurance was limited'.[111]

Bell's argument suffers from a lack of supporting authority (save reference to Acts of the Scottish Parliament and some continental ecclesiastical charters), and his conclusions must therefore be viewed with caution. Bell himself admits that he has provided his history using 'the very imperfect state of the records, and the slender materials we possess for such a history'.[112]

(b) Walter Ross

Walter Ross, writing before Bell, takes a contrasting view, rejecting Roman law as the origin of the Scots lease: '[T]hough the Roman contract bears a near resemblance to our modern tack, we must seek the origins and principle of that deed in another quarter.'[113] Ross views the origins of the lease in the land management of Germanic tribes, propagated through the feudal law to other parts of Europe. The feudal law was introduced into Scotland, and the lease grew out of the performance rendered by bondsmen (slaves) for possession of the land.

While Ross rejects a Roman origin for lease law, he admits some connections with Roman law. Thus, the Scots rule[114] that a completed lease is not good against the granter's heirs and all coming in to his right, is, says Ross, 'taken from the Roman law, [and] seems to have been adapted in a very early period by our ecclesiastical Judges'.[115]

Ross further argues that '[l]eases or tacks were also introduced from the practice of neighbouring countries', but he gives neither authority nor examples, nor does he consider whether such neighbouring countries had been influenced by the *jus commune*.

Having rejected the Roman origins of lease, Ross continues, however, by saying of the Leases Act 1449: 'This statute proves that tacks had long been in use, though considered under the Roman idea of personal contracts, binding only the granter and falling with his right.'

Of Ross's explanation, we must be very sceptical. Not only is his authority scant, but his argument for a non-Roman origin of the lease takes no account of the influence of the *jus commune* on canon or native law.[116]

---

[110] Bell (n. 53), 9–10. [111] Ibid. 18. [112] Ibid. 20.
[113] Ross (n. 13), 456–7. [114] As stated by Ross. [115] Ross (n. 13), 474.
[116] The recent scholarship on which has been referred to above III.1.

(c) Robert Hunter

Only Robert Hunter makes a serious historical analysis of the origins of the lease. Hunter, like Bell, sees the origin as lying in Roman law:

> [Ross] has erred in deeming that the Roman contract was not the origin of the Scottish lease. Not only was the contract the same in principle and conception, but the style and clauses alike ... The form and tenor of the contract were transmitted from the jurists of the Upper Empire through those of the Lower Empire to the churchmen who, during the Middle Ages, were the only conveyancers. By them the form of the contract was preserved, nearly in a state of uniformity throughout Europe. The deed, as practically known upon the Continent, is substantially the same as that adopted in England and Scotland, in which countries precisely the same style existed for many centuries.[117]

Hunter makes extensive reference to the various Abbey Chartularies as the best source of leases from the early period, drawing comparison with collections of similar deeds on the Continent. He refers to what he says is one of the oldest leases upon record, a lease from 1190 granted by Robert de Kent and others to the Abbacy of Kelso.[118]

3. Evidence of finite leases for short terms

Much of the difficulty in assessing the origins of leases, and their use in the early period, is due to a scarcity of documentation. As Duncan notes, discussing the thirteenth century, 'there are few examples of what must have been the commonest kind, a lease of limited duration' since the recipient had no long title to secure in writing.[119] The most extensive documentation is that preserved in monastic Chartularies, by some of the historical clubs in the nineteenth century, and in a few private collections. For the four leases selected for the following historical portraits, the grants are all secular, and the deed is to be found either in one of the published collections or in Register House in Edinburgh.

IV. PORTRAIT ONE: A LEASE FROM THE LATE FOURTEENTH CENTURY

In this first period, that just prior to the passing of the groundbreaking 1449 act,[120] leases were usually drawn up in Latin, but by the late fourteenth century Scots was also beginning to be used. In a lease granted by John

---

[117] Hunter (n. 82), 49. [118] Cited ibid.: Chart. Kelso No. 252.

[119] Duncan (n. 55), 395. Duncan, noting the problem the Church had at this time in enforcing finite terms against magnates, comments that '[a]lmost every example of a finite lease, therefore, suggests that they were recorded when there was a fear or expectation that they would be extended into perpetuity': at 396. [120] See below IV.2.

Melville to William Douglas in 1386 Latin was the chosen language, but in 1399, in a further lease between the same parties, the language used was Scots.[121] Latin predominates amongst the extant lease documentation, especially where the grant is by a prelate.

The lease selected as our example is a grant, in Scots, by John Melville to Sir William Douglas, of the lands of Hawthornden, dated 10 July 1399. Like most leases until the end of the seventeenth century, it is in the form of a unilateral charter rather than a bilateral contract: [122]

Be it made kende til[123] al that thir[124] letteris heris and seis[125] that I, John of Malvile, lorde of that ilke, has set[126] and to ferme[127] has latyn, and throw[128] thir presentis letteris settis and ferme lattis, al my landis the qwhilkis[129] I hafe[130] and ar myne in Hawthorndene, lyande within the schirrafdome of Edynburgh, and al my landis that I hafe and ar myne in the Grevistoune, lyande within the schirrafdome of Peblis, with the apportenance,[131] to my cosyne Schir Williame of Douglas of Straboke, knycht, for the term of ten zere[132] next eftir folowande the oyse[133] of his take made of tha landys as his euidente proportis and contenys of befor betwix hym and me, the qwilkis ar selit[134] wyth myne awyn propir seale, fullily and pessably to be passit[135] and fulfillit, the terme of his entre begynnande at the next Qwhyssonday[136] folowande of his saide take[137] that he has of me befor this present take for twenty punde[138] of vsuale mone of Scotlande, the qwilkis twenty punde I graunt me hafe ressavit[139] and of it fullily paide and assithit,[140] and in to myne oyse conuertit, of the qwhilkis soume alsua the forsaide Schir Williame, his ayris[141] and his assignes,[142] for me and myne ayris and myne executouris and assignes, I euer mare qwytcleme;[143] the forsaide landis to halde and to hafe with al profitis of courtis and oyscheis of courtis,[144] commodites, and esementis,[145] als wele vnnemmyt as nemmyt,[146] lelily,[147] trewly, and pesably, and frely but ony entermettyng[148] of me or of myne ayris or ony of thair name, outhir in the lauch[149] or by the lauche, durande thir forsaide termys of ten zere, to the forsaide Schir Williame and to his ayris and assignes of me and myne ayris and myne assignes, but ony gaine callyng[150] or in the contrare of this take, the qwilkis take alsua to the oysche of his terme

---

[121] W. Fraser, *The Melvilles Earls of Melville and the Leslies Earls of Leven* (1890), 14 no. 19 and no. 20; W. Fraser, *The Red Book of Menteith* (1880), 16 sq. no. 22.
[122] As to the form of leases, see below III.1. [123] Til = to. [124] thir = these.
[125] seis = see. [126] set = let.
[127] The *Concise Scots Dictionary* (n. 10) defines ferm as a farm, or a fixed yearly amount frequently paid in kind as a rent for land; Margaret Sanderson (n. 14), agreeing, defines ferme as 'land let at a fixed rent; the rent itself . . .' (Glossary). The Latin *firma* means rent, and is the derivation of the *firmarius*. [128] throw = through.
[129] qwhilkis = which. [130] hafe = have. [131] apportenance = appertenances.
[132] zere = years. [133] oyse or oysche = ish. [134] selit = sealed.
[135] to be passit = to be given effect to. [136] Qwhyssonday = Whitsunday.
[137] take = tack (lease). [138] punde = pounds. [139] ressavit = received.
[140] assithit = satisfied. [141] ayris = heirs. [142] assignes = assignees.
[143] qwytcleme = renounce the claim.
[144] profitis of courtis and oyscheis of courtis = revenues of court.
[145] esementis = easements, i.e. servitudes.
[146] vnnemmyt as nemmyt = unnamed as named. [147] lelily = lawfully.
[148] entermettyng = intromitting. [149] lauch = law.
[150] ony gaine callyng = without any calling against.

of ten zere as is forspokyne[151] til the forsaide Schir Williame, his ayris and his assignes, I and myne ayris warandis[152] and sal warande: And I graunt gif[153] the forsaide landis in somme or alle hapnys or beis in the mene tyme of his take throuche commone were[154] distroyit that the forsaide Schir Williame, his ayris or his assignes sal als lange joyse[155] thaim eftir the oysche of his terme as he or thai ar skathit[156] within the forsaide ten zere: And til al thir thingis forwretyne to be kepit and haldyn to the forsaide Schir Williame, his ayris or his assignes, in al poyntis as is fornemmyt, durande the take forsaid I oblyce me and myne ayris, executouris, and assignes, but[157] fraude and gile, lely and trewly in gude fayth. In witnes of the qwhilkis thing I hafe put to my seale at Dalketh the ten day of Julii, the zere of our Lorde a thowsande thre hundreth nynty and nyne; thir witnes, Nicole of Douglas, lorde of Wakmanfeld, Williame of Ross, chapellane, Adam of Corry, notare, and Johne of Lukvpe, with othir syndry.

Several preliminary points may be noted about this lease. First, it is a lease to a relative of the granter. This is a common feature of many grants at this time. The lease narrates that the lease is of land which has already been let to the grantee under a previous lease.[158] The term of the lease is ten years, but with provision that if the lessee is deprived of possession through war, he is entitled to possess the subjects beyond the term of the lease for so long as he was deprived of possession during the lease. Such a clause may be found in other leases of the period, and its appearance in a lease of lands in a border county such as Peebleshire is not surprising given the political instability of the time.

The grant is to the grantee and his heirs and assignees, thus making clear that both transmission to an heir in the event of the death of the granter, and alienation to a third party, are possible, things which would not otherwise have been permitted by law at this time.[159]

An interesting feature of this lease is that the only consideration is a single sum of £20, of which the granter acknowledges receipt. This is surprising, for the lease thus appears to lack what would now be considered an essential of a lease, namely a periodic payment (rent). In modern lease law, a one-off payment, or *grassum*, is not considered a sufficient substitute for rent. When, earlier in the same year, on 12 March, the same parties entered into another lease of lands in Peebleshire, a rent was specified of 'twa merkis and a half of vsuall money of Scotland', payable 'at twa termes in the yeare customable, that is to say, Whytsonday and Mertimes'.[160] The reason for the omission of a periodic rent in the July lease is unclear.

---

[151] forspokyne = spoken (i.e. as set out above). [152] warandis = warrant.
[153] gif = if. [154] were = war. [155] joyse = enjoy or have possession of.
[156] skathit = harmed. [157] but = free from.
[158] The previous lease being for ten years also. The earlier lease is drawn up in Latin: Fraser, *Melvilles* (n. 121), 14 no. 19. It is not apparent why a gap of three years exists between the first and second leases. [159] Craig, II, 10, 5 and Bankton, II, 9, 11,15.
[160] Lease by John of Melville, lord of that ilk, to Sir William Douglas of Strabrock, of the lands of Hallmyre, 12 Mar. 1399: Fraser, *Red Book* (n. 121), 16 sq. no 22.

The term of ten years is one of a variety of durations specified in leases of the period. Three years is also a popular term; the longer leases tend to be of nineteen years' duration.

Because leases entered into before the passing of the 1449 act would have given the tenant no security of tenure against singular successors of the landlord, there is evidence that sasine was taken on some leases of the period in order to obtain security of tenure. Ross, commenting on this practice, says 'frequent attempts were made to render [leases] real by Sasine'.[161] Ross cites Mackenzie, who says 'the reason why they used Sasines then, being to make the tack real, and to defend against singular successors, this was no more used after the act of Parliament which makes a tack a real right'.[162] However, there is no reference to any sasine being taken on the July 1399 lease. Extant instruments of sasine of any kind are rare prior to the end of the fourteenth century.[163]

1. Form of the lease: unilateral grant

All of the leases prior to the beginning of the seventeenth century examined by the author are (with one exception[164]) in the form of a unilateral grant. There is some disagreement between the commentators on the form of lease adopted at various times and the reasons for this. Ross was of the opinion that the Leases Act 1449 is proof that tacks had long been in use 'though considered under the Roman idea of contracts, binding only the granter'.[165] Ross cites Stair who says of the tack: '[I]t was ordinarily granted by the setter to the tacksman for such a duty, without any mutual obligement upon his part, like unto a charter; but because the tenant not being bound, might at the end of any year before Whitsunday, renounce such a tack and be free, as being in his favour; therefore they are now ordinarily by way of contract, whereby the tacksman, as well as the setter, is obliged to stand thereto.'[166] This description of the history of the lease suggests a two-stage progression of form: from unilateral grant to bilateral contract.[167] However, Robert Hunter thought that before 1342 leases were mainly bilateral: '[L]eases were unquestionably bilateral deeds, for the term *conventio* is used, and the contract bears expressly to have been executed by the two parties appending their seals before witnesses.'[168]

---

[161] Ross (n. 13), 475.
[162] Mackenzie, *Institutions of the Laws of Scotland* (2nd edn., 1688), 189.
[163] See on this point, Gordon Donaldson, 'Aspects of Early Scottish Conveyancing', in Peter Gouldesbrough (ed.), *Formulary of Old Scots Legal Documents* (1985), Stair Society, vol. 36, 153 sqq. Donaldson's view is that sasine may often have preceded the charter itself.
[164] Namely, a lease of 18 years' duration.
[165] Ross (n. 13), 475. Ross's view of Roman contracts as unilateral cannot be upheld.
[166] Stair, II, 9, 5.   [167] Bankton, II, 9, 20 takes a similar view, as does Erskine, II, 6, 20.
[168] Hunter (n. 82), vol. 1, 60. Hunter notes however that in this early period there were some unilateral grants also.

Hunter does not explain the significance of the date 1342, and indeed its significance is not readily apparent.[169] However, his narrative points to a three-stage progression of the form of the lease: bilateral contract to unilateral charter to bilateral contract once more. Hunter had the benefit of consulting the various monastic Chartularies, of which Ross makes no mention, and his view of a three-stage progression may be the result of more extensive research. However, prior to 1342 there were a large number of the poorest tenants who held land without any written title at all, often for short periods of time, so any characterization, whether it is of a two- or three-stage development of the form of the lease, will not be the whole picture.[170]

2. Security of tenure

After the granting of the above 1399 lease, but prior to the lease examined in the following section, the Leases Act of 1449 came into force. This was the most important statutory change of the period, and its continuing importance is testified to by its place as one of the oldest acts of the pre-Union Scottish Parliament still in force. It is a model of brevity:

Item It is ordanit for the sauftie and fauour of the pure pepil that labouris the grunde that thai and al vthiris that has takyn or sal tak landis in tym to cum fra lordis and has termes and yeris thereof that suppose the lordis sel or analy thai landis that the takaris sall remayn with thare takis on to the ische of thare termes quhais handis at euir thai landes cum to for sic lik male as thai tuk thaim of befoir.[171]

This statute, enacted to alleviate evident hardship caused by the expulsion of sitting tenants by new landlords, gave such tenants automatic security of tenure, removing the necessity for sasine to be taken.[172] The early period at

---

[169] Is the significance found in the rise of the feudal system? In other words, did the relationship of superior and vassal lend itself more easily to a form of unilateral charter? This may be the explanation, but a difficulty with this theory is that if the unilateral form did not appear until after 1342, this coincides with a period when '[T]he decline of feudalism was already in progress': Gretton (n. 24), § 45. Hunter (n. 82), 61 notes this difficulty also and also notes that the reason for the change from bilateral to unilateral form is 'now difficult to determine': (n. 82), 61.

[170] As Duncan (n. 55), 394 notes, there are few extant examples of what must have been the 'commonest kind of tenure', a lease of limited duration, since the recipient had no long title to secure in writing.

[171] APS, II, 35 (c. 6). In approximate transliteration to modern English the act reads: 'It is ordained for the safety and favour of the poor people that labour the ground, that they and all others that have taken or shall take lands in time to come from [land]lords, and have terms and years thereof [i.e. have a fixed lease term], that if the [land]lord sells or alienates the land or lands, the tenants shall remain with their tacks to the ish, no matter who the landlord is, for the same rent as originally agreed.'

[172] Though, interestingly, the authority given by Stair for this statement is from the 17th century, suggesting that some doubt remained about this point for a number of years: Stair, II, 9, 7. Moreover, it seems to have been the case that the practice of taking sasine on leases did not die out overnight; on the contrary, Craig, I, 10, 7, comments that '[i]n Scotland sasine is not only necessary to complete title to feudal property, but is in common use in leases for a fixed term of

which this statute was passed prompts comparison with other European countries. In France, the position of the ordinary lessee remained precarious until the passing of the Civil Code, and a tenant could be evicted by a new owner. However, there also existed in France the emphyteutic lease, which gave the tenant (the emphyteote) a real right of occupancy. This emphyteutic lease had existed since Roman times.[173] In the territories which were later to form Germany, *per contra*, tenants had already fared better even before 1449: 'On the whole, the development down to about the 1300's was characterized by a growing betterment in the legal status of the tenant . . . For all leaseholds conferred upon the tenant a real right in the land, a leasehold seisin.'[174]

3. Other statutory development

It is clear that some statutes of the time were passed, not to establish legal rights, but to redress the neglect of rights already established. Into this category falls the statute of 1457[175] concerning 'spoliacioune' of land. The 1449 act had been in place for eight years, but the provision in the act enjoining the courts to 'knowe apone all spoliacioune of takis and malingis' suggests that not all landlords were upholding the provisions of the 1449 act. Following the 1449 act, further statutory improvements to tenants' rights were made, some establishing new rights, some reinforcing existing provisions. By an act of 1469 the right of a landlord's debtors to seize tenants' property was restricted.[176] In a statute of 1491 protection was given to tenants affected by the transfer of land on the death of a woman holding under conjunct-fee, on reversion, and in other circumstances.[177] In a statute of 1555 tenants were granted forty days warning of a requirement to remove.[178] If the tenant so warned failed to remove on the due date, the landlord was obliged to petition the court for an order requiring the tenant to appear before the court within six days. By a statute of 1585,[179] tenants who had paid rent directly to those having securities over land were freed from the obligation to pay the rent a second time to any other party.

Other statutes of the time referring to landlord and tenant do not relate so much to the tenure of the land as to the relationship between the parties in

---

years. This practice is still followed especially in the northern parts of the country.' Hunter (n. 82) also refers to a case where sasine appears to have been taken on a lease in 1670: *HMA* v. *Fraser of Belladrum* (1758) Mor 15196.

[173] Marcel Planiol, *Treatise on the Civil Law* (12th edn., 1939), vol. 1, part 2, para. 2991: 'Emphyteusis was recognised under the old French law as being what it was at Roman law.' As Planiol notes, *emphyteusis* in France is now restricted to a maximum term of 99 years (para. 2994).

[174] Rudolf Huebner, *A History of Germanic Private Law* (1918, repr. 1968, tr. Francis Philbrick), 326. [175] APS, II, 47 (c. 2).
[176] APS, II, 96 (c. 12).   [177] APS, II, 225 (c. 7).   [178] APS, II, 494 (c. 12).
[179] APS, III, 379 (c. 14).

society at large, and the prevention of criminal or undesirable conduct by tenants. The relationship of landlord and tenant was utilized by Parliament as an effective means of controlling the conduct of tenants by holding landlords responsible for their good behaviour. Thus, a statute of 1524,[180] enacted 'anent the stanching of thift' (to stem the flow of theft), bound landlords to ensure the 'gud reule' of their tenants. This was followed by a similar provision in 1531.[181]

V. PORTRAIT TWO: A LEASE FROM THE SIXTEENTH CENTURY

By the time of the late sixteenth century much had changed in Scotland. The Reformation was under way,[182] church lands were forfeit to the Crown,[183] and Parliament was taking a much greater interest in the tenure of land.

The lease selected as the portrait for this period is from relatively late in the century, a tack granted by Marie Ruthven, Countess of Athole, with the consent of her husband John, Earl of Athole, to John Grant of Fruchie, dated 3 September 1597: [184]

Be it kend till all men be thir present letteris, ws,[185] Dame Marie Ruthuen, countes of Atholl, lyfrenter and coniunctfear of the landis and lordschip of Balveny, with expres consent and assent of ane nobill and potent lord, John erle of Atholl, lord Inuermey and Balvany, now my spous, for his entres,[186] to haue sett, and in tak and assedatioune lattin, and be thir presentis settis, and in tak and assedatioune lattis to our weilbelouit[187] friend, Johne Grant of Frewquhy, his airis, assignayis and subtennentis of na[188] hier degre nor[189] himself, all and haill[190] ... the towne and landis of Kynnermonie with fischeingis, scheillingis, pairtis, pendiclis and pertinentis thairof, lyand within the lordschip of Balvany and schirrefdome of Banf, for all the space, zeiris and termis of fyve zeiris, beginnand the first terme at the feist of Witsonday nixtocum,[191] in the zeir of God j^{m}v^c[192] fourscoir auchtein[193] zeiris, and fra thynefurthe[194] to endure during the said space, but ony intervall or brek of termis: Payand thairfoir zeirly the said Johne Grant and his foirsaidis to ws, our factouris,

---

[180] APS, II, 286 (c. 9).   [181] APS, II, 332 (c. 2).

[182] The Reformation in Scotland occurred in phases: an Act of Parliament in 1560 abolished the papal jurisdiction in Scotland, and left Scotland with a reformed episcopacy. This was replaced by Presbyterian Church government in 1592, until a reformed episcopacy was restored in 1610. The struggle continued in the 17th century until in 1689 Presbyterianism finally reasserted itself as the established form of church government.

[183] Crown interference with church lands took place over several years via various Acts of Parliament, until in 1587 (see the statute of 1587, APS, III, 431 (c. 8)) all church lands were vested in the Crown, saving those already feued out: see Conacher, (1936) 48 *JR* 189.

[184] W. Fraser, *The Chiefs of Grant* (1868), 192–3 no. 168. Transliteration of words already explained in section IV is not repeated here.   [185] ws = we.

[186] entres = interest.   [187] weilbelouit = well-beloved.   [188] na = no.

[189] nor = than.   [190] all and haill = all and whole.   [191] nixtocum = following.

[192] j^{m}v^c is shorthand for 1500.   [193] auchtein = eighteen.

[194] thynefurthe = thenceforth.

doaris[195] and chalmerlaneis[196] in our nameis, all maillis, customeis and dewteis quhatsumeuer, vsit and wont; togidder with seruice, vsit and wont, allenerly;[197] And we forsuthe, the said Dame Marie and my said spous for his enteres, faithfullie bindis and obleisssis ws, coniunctly and seuerallie, our airis, executoris and assignayis, to warrand, acquiet and defend this present tak and assedatioune to the said Johne and his foirsaidis, in all and be all thingis abonewrittin, frome our awin deid allenerly;[198] and that we haue done nor sall do nothing preiudiciall thairto: In witnes of the quhilk we haue subscryveit[199] thir presentis, quhilkis ar wrettin be Walter Dog, notar, with our hand, at Dunkeld, the third day of September $j^m v^c$ fourscoir sevintein[200] zeiris, befor thir witnesses, Schir James Stewart of Auchmadeis, Mr James Grant of Arnely, Patrik Muray sone to the lord Tullibardin, and Walter Dog, writer herof.

The lease is subscribed by the Earl and Countess before the four witnesses mentioned. As will be seen, the lease is a grant by a liferenter with the consent of her spouse. Also of interest is the clause designed to control the persons to whom the grantee could assign or sublet. They are to be 'of na hier degre nor himself'. The Countess is clearly concerned not to have a tenant or subtenant that may be her equal or superior, as this would offend against the social order.[201] Not all landlords of the time were prepared to allow assignation or subletting, at least without their permission.[202]

This period marks the introduction of phrases that, with modification of spelling, would remain in conveyancing documents to the present day. The grant is of 'all and haill' the subjects let (the modern 'all and whole') and the land is let together with the 'pairtis, pendiclis and pertinentis' (the modern 'parts, pendicles and pertinents').

Unlike the first, this lease contains a clause of warrandice, undertaken jointly and severally by the Countess and her spouse. The fact that the degree of warrandice given is 'frome our awin deid allenerly' ('from our own deed only'), indicates that there was already by this period a distinction between types of warrandice.[203]

It is again interesting to note that no specific rent is stipulated, but merely 'all maillis, customeis and dewteis quhatsumeuer, vsit and wont; togidder with seruice, vsit and wont, allenerly'. It is unclear how the precise amount of rent would be calculated.[204] The reference to 'seruice, vsit and wont' indicates

---

[195] doaris = doer (i.e. agent).   [196] chalmerlaneis = steward.   [197] allenerly = only.
[198] our awin deid allenerly = our own deed only.   [199] subscryveit = subscribed.
[200] sevintein = seventeen.   [201] Similar clauses are found in feudal grants.
[202] e.g. a tack by James Hammiltoun to Mongo Anderson of the lands of Leclyok, parish of Blantyre, dated 8 Jan. 1593: W. Fraser, *Inventories of the Muniments of the Families of Maxwell* (1865), 321–2. The provision was: 'it sall nocht be leissum to the said Mongo to sett the saidis landis, nor no part thairof, to ony persoun or persones, but my liciance askit and obteanit thairto'.
[203] For a discussion of the different degrees of warrandice, see Kenneth G. C. Reid, 'Transfer of Ownership', in Reid (n. 24), §§ 702–9.
[204] This tack does not appear to be unique, however, in the failure to specify an exact rent. Duncan (n. 55), 395 refers to a rental of land at Airlie in 1212 for twenty years, at a rent described as 'traditional'.

the performance of feudal tasks, not specified here. Such a stipulation was later prohibited by statute.[205]

The rent of agricultural leases of the period was frequently stated in terms of produce, or a mixture of money and produce. Examples include 'twentie bollis ferme meill, ten bollis ferme beir, zearlie, betwixt Zuill and Candilmess; . . . And fourscoir staneis kane cheis zeirlie'[206] and 'tua hennis, and tua sufficient caponis, at Fasting-even zeirlie, and ane boll beir at Beltane zeirlie'.[207]

1. Legal literature

In this period, we encounter the first serious examination of the tack in Scots law. Among the important writers of the period, or in the period just following, are Balfour (*Practicks*, 1579), Craig (*Jus Feudale*, 1600[208]), and Hope (*Major Practicks*, 1608–33).

Balfour devotes a section of his work to 'assedatioun',[209] as well as referring *en passant* to tacks in other sections of the work. Many of the rules mentioned concern church lettings, and there is also discussion of liferent and rental. As usual with Balfour, there is no systematic account of the law, and even the 1449 act is not mentioned.[210]

Craig discusses leases at several points in the *Jus Feudale*. His view of the civil law as authoritative insofar as it identified with the *jus naturale* has been noted elsewhere.[211] Craig refers to the *Digest* at several points when discussing tacks.[212] At one point (I, 11) he provides an interesting comparison of English and Scottish tenancies for a fixed term of years and highlights the absence of tacit location in England. At the same time he emphasizes similarities between Scots and English law. Later an entire title (II, 10) is devoted to tacks. Craig notes that tenants may not generally assign leases, but elsewhere points out that a feudal vassal may 'let it [his estate] for a moderate period provided that the let is not prejudicial to the interests of the superior, as would be the case if the lessee was a person of higher position than the superior, from whom it might be difficult for the latter to exact due service'.[213] This may partly explain the popularity of feu farm, and also the reason for

---

[205] Tenures Abolition Act 1746.

[206] Stipulation in Tack of part of Knockewart, Ardrossan Parish, by the Laird of Caldwell to Henry Boyd, dated 6 Apr. 1598: *Selections from the Family Papers preserved at Caldwell* (1854), XCVI, 274–6. [207] Stipulation in Tack by James Hammiltoun referred to at n. 202 above.

[208] The *Jus Feudale* was first published, posthumously, in 1655. Lord Clyde's translation (not always reliable) is of the third edition of 1732.

[209] Balfour, *Practicks*, 200 sq.

[210] Cairns (n. 91), 199 notes that 'it was still possible for Sir James Balfour to write his "Practicks" on the basis of traditional sources of Scottish customary law and statutes, largely ignoring the civil law.' [211] Ibid. 203.

[212] Craig, I, 11, 4; I, 11, 5. See also Gordon (n. 94), 26–7. [213] Craig, II, 8, 40.

the inclusion in some leases, such as that extracted above, of clauses permitting assignation to persons of no higher degree than the landlord.

Hope devotes a title of his work to 'Tacks and Tennents' but, as in Balfour, the treatment is patchy, and consists of fifty-six short paragraphs which refer to sections of the *Quoniam Attachiamenta*, Craig, and Balfour. There are, however, seven further paragraphs referring specifically to Acts of Parliament, which add a dimension lacking in Balfour, and twenty further paragraphs referring to case decisions. A systematic approach would, however, have to wait for Stair in 1681.

2. Statutes

Statutes just prior to the period of the 1597 lease were discussed above. Others around the same time continued the pattern of using leasehold tenure as a means of controlling the general behaviour of the tenantry. These included a statute of 1594[214] requiring landlords to find surety to relieve the king's baillies in the apprehension of criminal tenants. Following the Reformation, a statute of 1593[215] declared that 'maisteris and landislordis be haldin to ansuer for thair men tennentis and servandis suspectit and dilaitit of papistrie as for personis indytit for crymes . . .'.

In addition to the statutory concern for the conditions of the tenantry, there is evidence of the concern of the king for the improvement of conditions on his own lands. From a record in the Exchequer Rolls, it may be seen that in 1541 the King's Comptroller for Fife devised a standard form of clause to be inserted in every royal grant of lands in Fife and Strathearn.[216] The conditions included a requirement that every tenant should have 'ane gud, large yard, weil dykit and heggit with hawthorne, sawch,[217] allir[218] or esp',[219] and, for some tenants, the specification that they have an 'honest mansioun, with hall, chalmer, pantry, kiching, and uthir office houssis substantiously biggit,[220] efferand[221] to the quantitie of thair maling'.[222] These requirements appear somewhat idealistic, and it has not been possible to discover whether they were ever enforced.

3. Duration of leases

In this period, once again, there is a wide range of terms discoverable from extant leases and records. Of the leases examined by the author in the period

---

[214] APS, IV, 71–3 (c. 37).   [215] APS, IV, 46 (Appendix).
[216] Conditions of Tenure on Royal Lands, 1541, in Gordon Donaldson (ed.), *Scottish Historical Documents* (1970), 108–9. Why Fife and Strathearn were singled out is not clear.
[217] sawch = willow.   [218] allir = alder.   [219] esp = aspen.
[220] biggit = built.   [221] efferand = corresponding.   [222] maling = holding.

1550 to 1599, a variety of terms were found: three years,[223] seven years,[224] and a greater number of leases for nineteen years[225] than in the earlier period. There are also numerous examples of tacks granted for the life of the granter or of the grantee. Occasionally, parties might agree a lease to run from year to year until terminated by proper notice.[226] Ecclesiastical rental books provide a continuing valuable source of information for this period. The Coupar Angus rental books offer a particularly useful comparison of the two periods they cover, that is 1464 to 1516 and 1539 to 1560,[227] and indicate the growing trend towards granting longer leases, of nineteen years' duration. Some of the grants recorded in the Coupar Angus Rental do not seem in accordance with the legal position at the time.[228] Other grants were made to persons whose title would have been susceptible to annulment. Thus Balfour notes in his *Practicks* that:

Gif ony Bischop, or ecclesiastical person, settis in tak and assedatioun ony landis, fischings, rentis, possessiounis, pertening to him as part and pertinent of his bischoprik or benefice, to ony persoun or persounis, for all the dayis of thair lifetimes, his successouris may call him or thame to quhom the said assedatioun was maid, to heir and se the samin decernit null and of nane avail ... quhilk kind of tak and assedatioun is alienatioun, and contrare the lawis of this realme, except the samin be dewlie confirmit.[229]

The Coupar Angus Rental discloses several liferent grants. Those receiving such liferent leases from the Abbot took a gamble that they would be upheld by his successors.[230]

The Coupar Angus books indicate two further interesting features. First,

---

[223] For instance, lease of the vicarage teinds of the Mains of Leslie dated 27 Jan. 1579: *Illustrations of the Topography and Antiquities of the Shires of Aberdeen and Banff* (1847–69), 399–400.

[224] For instance, tack by the Archbishop of St Andrews of the teind sheaves of the lands of Ormesheucht, dated 3 Mar. 1549: W. Fraser, *Memorials of the Montgomeries of Eglinton* (1859), vol. 2, 147 no. 150.

[225] For instance, lease by James Crichton of the lands of Cranstoun Riddall, dated 20 Aug. 1550: W. Fraser, *The Scotts of Bucleuch* (1878), 199 no. 178.

[226] Such as the lease granted by John Maxwell to Walter Anderson of land in Meikle Govan, dated 12 Jan. 1562. The original term is stated to run from 12 Jan. to Martinmas (that is, 11 Nov.) the same year, but if the granter does not warn the grantee to quit before Martinmas 'in that cais the saidis Walter sall brwik the saidis sex schilling thre penny land quhill Mertimes nixt thaireftir; and swafurth fra Mertimes to Mertimes, ay and quhill he be lauchfullie warnit befoir ane Mertimes to remufe ...': Fraser (n. 202), 297.

[227] These rental books have been carefully examined both by Margaret Sanderson (n. 14), ch. 4, and also recently in the valuable *Atlas of Scottish History to 1707* (1996), edited by P. G. B. McNeill and H. L. MacQueen, 292.

[228] Hunter (n. 168) has a useful chapter (ch. 10) on the various provisions governing ecclesiastical leases. Discussing a canon of the Councils of Perth restrictive of certain grants of lease, Hunter notes '[a] strong doubt has been expressed whether that canon was ever strictly observed; and the chartularies shew that it was not': at 70.   [229] Balfour, *Practicks*, 200, c. 17.

[230] Sanderson (n. 14) notes that during the first period of the Rental Book, 11 leases were granted for life, while in the second period, 32.

the Abbot was granting these longer leases in the 1550s when he was also feuing much of the abbey land.[231] The motivation for choosing a long lease in one case and a feu in another is not clear. Secondly, a strong policy by a major landlord could be an important factor in landholding patterns. This is true of Abbot Donald Campbell in Coupar Angus, and also of Cardinal David Beaton, who granted important leases[232] and feu charters in the 1540s.

Useful work has recently been done on the comparative figures for feu grants to sitting tenants compared to grants to non-occupants.[233]

VI. PORTRAIT THREE: A LEASE FROM THE MID-EIGHTEENTH CENTURY

By the mid-eighteenth century, the change in lease styles and content is quite dramatic. We have moved abruptly to the era of the lease as bilateral contract.[234] The currency of rent payments had just altered from Scots money to sterling.[235] Leases began to contain a greater number of stipulations and conditions, though the lease below is relatively short compared to some of the time. There had been a marked increase in the number of tacks granted for a long period.[236] George Dallas's *Styles* included styles for tacks, and had been available for almost a hundred years,[237] providing an impetus to greater uniformity of style and content. Indeed, Dallas's collection may have acted as the impetus for styles used by individual landowners for their leasings.[238] The last major Jacobite uprising had been recently suppressed.

The lease chosen as the portrait for this period is one between George Gillanders (a commissioner for the Earl of Seaforth) and George Greig,

---

[231] Ibid. 46.

[232] See for instance the leases by Cardinal Beaton to David Bonthron of land at Letham, dated 5 Jan. 1540, and to Henry Balnavis of Petcunte and Murefield dated 7 Mar. 1540: Fraser, *Melvilles* (n. 121), 19–84 nos. 78 and 79. These leases are interesting for the greater length and detail than in many of the secular leases of the time.

[233] Sanderson (n. 14), 80 sq., especially her table 3 at 81.

[234] From the leases examined, this change appears to have occurred at the beginning of the 17th century. The last lease examined in the form of a unilateral grant dates from 1603, and the first (save an exceptional case from 1564) in the bilateral form dates from 1617.

[235] The last lease examined where rent is specified in Scots money dates from 1742, and the first in sterling from 1765.

[236] Leases examined from this period include the commonly occurring term of 19 years, as well as others with terms of 12, 18, 20, and 38 years.

[237] George Dallas, *A System of Styles as now Practised within the Kingdom of Scotland* (1666–88).

[238] For instance, the style adopted by the Earl of Findlater for his leasings. The record of this lodged with the Registers of Scotland is headed: 'Scroll of a Tack or Lease by the Earl of Findlater and Seafield; Being the form fixed upon for all Leases to be granted by his Lordship for Nineteen Years, or any shorter space, Except in so far as this may be departed from, or added to by Particular agreement . . .': SRO, GD 23/9/24.

dated 3 and 12 September 1774.[239] Due to its length, what follows are extracts only:

It is Contracted and Agreed betwixt the Parties following, Towitt George Gillanders Esquire Chamberlain of the Lewis Sole Commissioners appointed by the Right Honourable Kenneth Earl of Seaforth Viscount Fortrose Lord Mackenzie and Kintail Baron of Ardelve heretable Proprietor of the Gardens and Crofts of Land aftermentioned, for Setting the said lands and others conform to Commission in his favour to that effect dated the twelfth day of October last On the One Part and George Greig Town Clerk of Fortrose On the Other part in manner aftermentioned That is to say the said George Gillanders Commissioner forsaid hath Sett and by these presents Setts and in Tack and Assedation for payment of the yearly Tack Duty and with and under the Conditions Provision and Declaration Letts to the said George Greig and to his heirs secluding[240] his Assignees and Sub Tenants without the Special Advice and Consent of the said Noble Lord or of his factor for the time being first had and Obtained thereto by a writing under ether of their hands All and Whole the Castle Gardens of Fortrose . . . With the several Crofts of Land . . . with all and sundry parts pendicles privileges Commonities and universal pertinents belonging to the haill pertinents All lying within the Town of Fortrose Parish of Rosemarkie and County of Ross And that for the Space of Eighteen full and compleat years and Crops next and immediately following the said George Greig his Entry thereto which is hereby Declared to have been and begun at the term of Whitsunday last notwithstanding the date hereof and from thence forth to be peaceably possessed acquired and enjoyed by the said George Greig and his above written during the foresaid Space of Eighteen years Which Tack the said George Gillanders Commissioner foresaid (with and under the Condition Provisions and Declaration aftermentioned) hereby binds and obliges his said Constituent his heirs and successors to warrand at all hands and against all Deadly as Law will For the Which Causes and on the Other part the said George Greig as principal and Baillie Alexander Falconer Merchant in Fortrose as Cautioner Surety and full Debtor with and for the said George Greig and his successors whatsoever Conjunctly and severally To Consent and pay to the said Kenneth Earl of Seaforth his heirs or assignees or to his Factor and Chamberlain for the time being yearly in the name of Tack Duty for the forsaid Lands the Sum of Twelve pounds twelve Shillings Sterling money Beginning the first years payment thereof at the term of Martinmas One thousand seven hundred and seventy five for the Crop and year $j^{m}v^{iic}$ and seventy five and so on at the term of Martinmas yearly thereafter during the currency of this Lease And it is hereby expressly Conditioned Provided and Declared that notwithstanding the present Lease is entered into for the term of Eighteen years from Whitsunday last It shall be lawful for the said George Greig and his forsaids to give up the Subjects hereby Sett either at the term of Whitsunday One thousand seven hundred and Eighty or at the term of Whitsunday $j^{m}v^{iic}$ and eighty four upon their giving three Months promonition to the said Noble Lord or to his factor for the time being of such their Intention previous to either of the said terms . . . And on the other hand it shall be lawful for the said Kenneth Earl of Seaforth and his forsaids to Remove the said George Greig and his above written from the Subjects

---

[239] SRO, GD 46/1/212 at 124–5. [240] secluding = excluding.

hereby Sett at either of the terms of Whitsunday last above mentioned upon his Lordship or his factors giving the said George Greig three months previous Notice to that effect . . . And under which express Condition Provision and Declaration this Tack is entered into and not otherways And both the saids Parties hereby bind and oblige them and their forsaids to Implement fulfill and perform their respective parts of the promises to each other under the penalty of Ten pounds Sterling to be paid by the Party failing to the Party Observing or willing to observe his part of the Promises by and allows performance And for the more Security They Consent to the Registration hereof in the Books of Council and Session of others competent that Letters of Horning on ten days Charge and all other Execution needful may pass hereon in form as effiers and to that effect they Constitute[241] Their Procurators [and] In Witness whereof . . .

As will be noted, whereas the language of the first two leases of 1399 and 1597 was relatively similar, this lease contains almost no Scots and is almost wholly understandable to the modern reader. This reflects the change in linguistic usage between the beginning of the seventeenth century and the point now reached, the late eighteenth century.[242] However, in legal documents the change occurred only gradually. Some leases of the period mix older Scots words with modern English.[243]

Also immediately noticeable is the form of this lease: that of the bilateral contract, a development which has already been noted. One of the rights granted to both parties is a break right at one of two specified dates. This is a feature of leasing which will be immediately recognizable to any drafter of current commercial leases.

In general the content of the lease follows very closely that of Dallas's basic style of tack between a heritor and his tenant. Dallas's style progresses thus: (*a*) a general statement that the land is set in tack and assedation; (*b*) designation of the property; (*c*) statement of the term; (*d*) statement of warranty against all hands and deadly; (*e*) an obligation on the tenant to pay the tack duty, and statement of the dates for payment; (*f*) a penalty clause;[244] and (*g*) a clause of registration.[245] As can be seen, this is almost precisely the content of the lease above, save for the addition of the break clause.[246]

---

[241] The presence of a blank line here reflects the same feature in the original lease.

[242] See further on this interesting linguistic development, the Introduction to *The Concise Scots Dictionary* (n. 9).

[243] In a lease between The Hon. Kenneth Mackenzie and George Gillanders dated 19 Feb. 1765 (SRO, GD 46/1/212). English terminology mixes with Scots phrases such as 'All and Haill' and 'sicklike'.

[244] It is made clear neither in our lease nor in Dallas (n. 237) whether failure to pay the annual tack duty (in our lease, £12) would result in the mere payment of the penalty (in our lease, £10), or the penalty plus the unpaid rent.   [245] Dallas (n. 237), vol. 1, 509–10.

[246] This is not the earliest lease examined with a break clause: in a lease dated 30 Oct. 1568 between Sir George Gordon of Haddo and John Reith, the term of the let is 'the space of sevine or nyne yeiris, in the optione of the said Sir George': SRO, GD 33/36/73/2 (Haddo House Charters).

Other leases of the time are more detailed in the obligations imposed on the parties. For instance, in the style drawn up for the Earl of Findlater's leases,[247] the obligations imposed include a specific obligation of residency by the tenant and his family, obligations concerning upkeep and crop rotation, restrictions on the sale of alcohol, and the maximum number of servants' dwellings permitted. The style also contains a clause reserving the mineral rights to the Earl.

1. Background to leases of the period

Not only had Dallas's *Styles* been published by the date of the above lease, but Craig and Stair had been in print for many years. There was thus a much greater legal literature for drafters to draw upon when considering the content of leases. Published shortly prior to the above lease were the three volumes of Bankton's *Institute*, and shortly after, the first edition of Robert Bell's *Treatise on Leases*.[248]

(a) Stair

The first systematic discussion of the lease is by James Dalrymple, Viscount of Stair, in his *Institutions of the Law of Scotland*.[249] Stair was well acquainted with the civil law,[250] and with continental jurists, such as Grotius, although in his title on tacks he limits himself to native authority. Stair devotes a title in book II to tacks.[251] He progresses through his discussion of leases by considering their constitution, their extent and effect, varieties of lease, restrictions and defects, and finally avoidance and removal.[252] Already by the time of Stair, certain rules were settled which would be recognized today: oral tacks were permitted for leases of one year or less;[253] tacks could be set by husband and wife, with rent payable to the longest liver;[254] rentals were clearly distinguished as a special kind of lease;[255] tacit relocation was recognized as extending leases where the requisite warning was not given;[256] the tenant was required to take possession of the subjects.[257] Many of the other rules stated by Stair, however, have not surprisingly been superseded by later statutory or common law alteration.

A feature of leasing which had become popular by Stair's day was the wadset tack. This exemplifies the emerging trend in the sixteenth and seventeenth centuries of utilizing legal tools for mercantile purposes, in this case the leasing of lands conveyed in security of a debt.[258] A wadsetter (the creditor)

---

[247] See n. 238 above.   [248] The first edition was published in 1803.
[249] First edition 1681; second edition 1693.
[250] See Cairns (n. 91), 204–6, and Gordon (n. 94), 28–9.   [251] Stair, II, 9.
[252] His plan is set out in Stair, II, 9, 2.   [253] Stair, II, 9, 4.
[254] Stair, II, 9, 13.   [255] Stair writes extensively on rentals: II, 9, 15–21.
[256] Stair, II, 9, 23.   [257] Stair, II, 9, 31.
[258] Wadset was a contract by which a debtor conveyed lands to his creditor and his creditor undertook to reconvey the lands to the debtor when the debt had been cleared. The conveyance

might either grant a tack to a third party, or else a back-tack to the reverser (the debtor), who would therefore remain in possession of the subjects.[259]

(b) *Bankton*

Bankton deals with leases at some length in title IX of volume 2 of his *Institute*. In addition, he makes passing reference to leases in his discussion of 'location conduction'.[260] Bankton refers frequently to case decisions and occasionally to the civil law. Of note is his inclusion of a section on 'Observations on the Law of England'.[261]

(c) *Erskine*

Erskine's *Institute of the Law of Scotland* was published posthumously in 1773. Interestingly, Erskine deals with lease in book II, as part of his discussion of superiority and vassalage, rather than in his discussion of contract in book III. There is frequent citation of case authority and of other Scottish writers. There is only occasional reference to Roman law (for instance, in a passage dealing with the 'fruits of the farm'[262]), and it is often used as a contrast for the Scots law.

(d) *Robert Bell*

Late in the eighteenth century, the first edition of Robert Bell's *Treatise on Leases* was published. His treatment of the historical origins of the lease has already been commented on. Bell's work is useful not only in its commentary on the law of the period, but for its inclusion of several appendices containing, amongst other things, a draft lease style by Kames, and styles of, and extracts from, leases and related documents of the time. Bell also includes a summary list of typical clauses. In addition to some of the clauses we have already encountered, Bell cites the following (which seem to relate to an agricultural lease): reservation of mines and minerals; reservation of privilege of hunting and shooting; meliorations or deteriorations of the houses and buildings on the farm; the party who is to rebuild in the event of fire; rotation of crops and plan of management; obligation on the tenant to perform certain services 'such as furnishing horses and carts at certain times to the landlord or his factors';[263] power of subsetting or assigning; and provisions for the bankruptcy of the tenant. Many of these suggested clauses are reflected in the terms of the lease in the following section of this chapter.

Also influential in legal thought during this period was Baron David

---

was thus in security. The normal means of fulfilment of the debt was for the creditor to lease the subjects, under a wadset tack.

[259] For an example of a back-tack of this type from 1658, see Gouldesbrough (n. 163), ch. 18, 140–1.   [260] Bankton, I, 20.
[261] Bankton, II, 9, 1–24 (Observations on the Law of England).   [262] Erskine, II, 6, 57.
[263] Bell (n. 53), 538.

Hume, Professor of Scots Law at the University of Edinburgh, whose published *Lectures* contained a chapter on location.[264]

2. Statute

Statutory reform continued in this period. The most important statute, though not directly concerned with landlord and tenant, was the Tenures Abolition Act 1746, abolishing wardholding and making other far reaching changes to the feudal system. Another important statute followed in the Entail Improvement Act 1770, which removed restrictions imposed in the Entail Act 1685 in respect of the lease of lands held under entail.[265] The act of 1770 allowed heirs in entail to lease lands held under entail for up to thirty-one years.[266]

3. Duration of leases

By this period, there has been a marked increase in the number of tacks granted for a long term. Leases examined include the commonly occurring term of 19 years, as well as others with terms of 12, 18, 20, and 38 years. Research has shown that in the late eighteenth and early nineteenth centuries some leases were granted for even longer periods, ranging from 99 to 992 years, and in one case for a term of 5,000 years.[267] Indeed, the Scottish Leases Committee, reporting in 1951, were prompted to comment: 'a large proportion of all recorded leases with more than 100 years still to run in 1951 (8,744) were originally granted in the late 18th century or in the 19th century for terms of about 1,000 years'.[268]

However, the granting of leases for long periods is not a uniform pattern, and a letter written by Lord Grange to the Earl of Ilay on 24 December 1724[269] gives an interesting insight into more temporary letting conditions in some parts of the country:

I believe it could not yet be done to oblige all leases to be in write and for any number of years; for in some countries[270] the Tennants will not have it so. It is thus in the

---

[264] Hume, *Lectures*, II, ch. 2.
[265] In an article in the *Edinburgh Review*, 1826, it was estimated that 'one half of the soil of Scotland' was entailed (quoted in the *Scottish Leases Report* (n. 48), 16). All remaining entails are extinguished by the Abolition of Feudal Tenure etc. (Scotland) Act 2000, as p. 5.
[266] Entail Improvement Act 1770, s. 1. As well as the grant of leases for 31 years, the heir in entail was also permitted to let the lands for other combinations of time, including for 14 years and the life of the lessee (whichever was longer), and to grant building leases for up to 99 years.
[267] *Scottish Leases Report* (n. 48), 14.   [268] Ibid. 15.
[269] SRO, GD 124/15/1262/3 (Mar and Kellie Muniments).
[270] 'Countries' in this context means 'counties'.

Southern border countries, where all being pafluse[271] they are afraid of a lease, because a very hard winter destroys so many of their cattle that next year they must take a smaller possession. And therefor every spring their lands are set of new. An ill custom I am persuaded, but not to be helped all at once nor by an Act of Parliament but by custom, which is wearing it out gradually and even in the Highlands. I see tacks or leases in write, and for a good many years, are not unusual in Argyle; and in Breamar [sic] the Tennants are fond of them.

This letter indicates that the popularity of longer leases was a process which occurred over a period of time and one which happened more frequently in some parts of the country than in others.

Indeed, the Scottish Leases Committee, which reviewed much historical material, noted that of the 13,151 leases recorded in the Register of Sasines which still had terms left to run, '4,153 were found in Lanarkshire and 1,988 in Ayrshire, while the next highest figure was Dumfries with 793 unexpired leases. The thirteen thousand odd unexpired leases included nearly nine thousand with more than 100 years still to run'.[272] The information collected by the Committee not only counters the commonly stated myth that long leases are unknown in Scotland, but sheds light on the fact that the counties of the north-east of Scotland exhibit both the lowest number of leases recorded, and, on the whole, a lower number of leases with terms exceeding one hundred years. By contrast

In north Ayrshire . . . we were told that some landowners held doubts as to the competency or propriety of sub-feuing even in the absence of any express or implied prohibition, and on other estates in that district the excellent relationship existing between the landowner and the community led to the use of the simple and inexpensive tack . . . In some places the use of ground leases may have been a practice continued from pre-Reformation times.[273]

This provides a reminder that patterns of land tenure often have as much to do with social phenomena and relationships as with the law.

VII. PORTRAIT FOUR: A LEASE FROM THE LATE NINETEENTH CENTURY

By the time of our last snapshot, leases have become even more detailed and lengthy, and what follows is a much reduced extract of the essential clauses from a lease between Ralph Dundas, Clerk to the Signet, acting as commissioner for James Graham, and Andrew James Knox, dated 10 and 18 May 1889: [274]

---

[271] The adjective 'pafluse' appears to derive from the noun, 'paffle', defined by the *Concise Scots Dictionary* (n. 9) as 'a person who farms a paffle, a small tenant-farmer'.
[272] *Scottish Leases Report* (n. 48), 14.   [273] Ibid. 16.   [274] SRO, GD 155/730/3.

It is Contracted and Agreed upon between Ralph Dundas Clerk to the Signet Edinburgh Commissioner for James Maxtone Graham of Cultoquhey and Redgorton Esquire conform to Commission by the said James Maxtone Graham in favor of the said Ralph Dundas ... On the one part and Andrew James Knox residing at Balgeroho House Coupar Angus On the other part in manner following namely The said Ralph Dundas as Commissioner foresaid hereby Lets to the said Andrew James Knox and his heirs the eldest female always succeeding without division, but expressly excluding Subtenants and assignees legal and voluntary and all persons acting for behoof of Creditors All and Whole the Sheep Farm of Bracketriggs ... situate in the Parish of Fowlis Wester and County of Perth and that for the space of Fifteen years from and after the term of Whitsunday Eighteen hundred and eighty nine; But with breaks in favor of either party at the expiry of five and ten years from the commencement of the Lease on condition of the party desiring to take advantage of either of these breaks giving one years notice to the other party of his intention to do so. Reserving to the said James Maxtone Graham and his heirs and successors the use of all roads, paths, water lades, watering places, mosses and underground substances and power to straighten marches without any claim of damages being competent to the said Andrew James Knox or his forsaids on account thereof. And also reserving powers to use said roads and others dig search for and take all or any part of the said mosses and underground substances to make roads and erect works for any or all of those purposes on condition of allowing surface damages to the tenant as the same shall be ascertained by arbitration. Reserving also to the said James Maxtone Graham and his forsaids or any tenants under him the whole game of any description on the Lands ... the Tenant binds himself and his Shepherds to preserve the birds and their nests during the breeding season so far as lies in their powers ... For which causes and on the other part the said Andrew James Knox binds and obliges himself his heirs Executors and representatives whomsoever to pay to the said James Maxtone Graham and his foresaids or to his or their Factor the sum of Fifty pounds Sterling of yearly rent beginning the first payment of the said money Rent at Candlemas Eighteen hundred and ninety and so on yearly thereafter during the endurance of this Tack with the interest at the rate of five per centum per annum on said Rent after said term of payment until paid and one fifth part more of said rent of penalty in case of failure ...

The lease continues with a multitude of conditions to be performed by the tenant, including conditions prohibiting the keeping of goats, the cutting of peat (except for his family's use), and the burning of heather (except with permission). The tenant also declares that he accepts the houses, fences, and drains as in good condition and obliges himself to maintain them and at the termination of the lease to leave them in the same 'sufficient and tenantable condition'.

Interestingly, this is the only lease from our four portraits where the term 'lease' appears in the body of the deed, though it does so alongside the term tack. This reflects the Anglicization of Scots law in the nineteenth century.

This is the first of the leases from our portraits to contain an insurance clause: '[T]he said Tenant binds and obliges himself and his foresaids to pay to the Proprietor or his foresaids over and above the rent . . . the half of the premium on a Policy of Insurance against Fire in name of the said [landlord] over the Buildings on said Farm.' This clause, together with the provisions on the upkeep of the farm, are the forebears of the full repairing and insurance lease found in many of today's leases.

The lease contains another clause found in many commercial lettings of the present day, that is, one stipulating for irritancy if the tenant becomes bankrupt. The lease continues with yet another current standard clause, obliging the tenant to quit at the end of the lease 'without any warning or process of removing'. The lease ends with a penalty clause for failure to adhere to the terms of the lease, similar to the clause in the 1774 lease in part VI.

1. Statutes

The majority of statutes in the nineteenth century affecting landlord and tenant concerned the law of entail. The list of entail amendment acts includes the statutes: 1836, 1838, 1840, the Entail Amendment (Scotland) Act 1848, 1853, the Entail Amendment (Scotland) Act 1868, the Entail (Scotland) Act 1882. The other acts affecting leases were principally the Registration of Leases (Scotland) Act 1857,[275] the Hypothec Abolition (Scotland) Act 1880, the Removal Terms (Scotland) Act 1886, and the Crofters Holdings (Scotland) Act 1886.

The Registration of Leases (Scotland) Act 1857 permitted the recording of long leases[276] in the General or Particular Registers of Sasines. The effect of so doing was to render such leases effectual against singular successors without the necessity of reliance upon the 1449 Act and its various conditions. Long leases continued to be popular in this period, both for commercial and domestic lets.[277] The Removal Terms (Scotland) Act 1886[278] made various stipulations about the timing of removals from property, and provided that a notice of removal from a house could be given by registered letter.

2. Legal literature

The most important work on leases from this period is Hunter's two-volume *Treatise on Landlord and Tenant*, with editions in 1833, 1845, 1860, and 1876. This work formed the basis for the later treatise of Rankine,[279] the other prin-

---

[275] Amended by the Registration of Long Leases (Scotland) Amendment Act 1877.
[276] Defined in s. 1 of the act as those 'for a Period of Thirty-one Years, and for any greater Number of Years'.
[277] It was not until the Land Tenure Reform (Scotland) Act 1974 that leases of dwellinghouses for periods of greater than 20 years were prohibited. [278] The act is still in force.
[279] John Rankine, *A Treatise on the Law of Leases in Scotland* (1st edn., 1887; 2nd edn., 1893; 3rd edn., 1916). Rankine had studied for a period in Heidelberg, and must therefore have had

cipal commentator of the modern era. Hunter devotes a large chapter to leases by heirs in entail, a subject which was still of great importance even as late as 1876. Hunter also notes in the preface to his third edition (1860) that many of the alterations to his text since the previous edition deal with the growing importance of mineral leases (the result of the industrial revolution), and the flurry of statutes in the field of landlord and tenant: 'During the last fifteen years there have been more statutory changes . . . than there had been during the previous half century'.[280] These statutes have already been noted.

While Hunter's work influenced conveyancers of the period, it was not their only source of guidance. Hunter himself makes frequent references to various editions of a collection of styles entitled *Juridical Styles*,[281] commonly used in the nineteenth century. This collection was followed in 1902 by the publication of the first volume of Green's *Scots Style Book*. The volume containing lease styles was published in 1904. It contains model leases of many varieties: for a shop, a public house, a farm, fishings, coal, a deer forest, and shootings, amongst others. Many of the leases employ schedules to contain more detailed information. The clauses contained in the styles include clauses on repairing obligations, insurance, public burdens, and arbitration. With such collections, we have reached the time of the modern lease.

VIII. CONCLUSIONS

If one were merely to scan the leases examined above, one might think there was little in common between them. Yet the difficulties of language should not obscure the important similarities. Between the two leases of 1399 and 1597 there are few differences in content: the parties are designed, the property described, the right of assignation addressed, and the rent specified. With the lease of 1774 there is still a large degree of similarity, the difference coming in the imposition of additional obligations upon the parties, mostly the tenant. The feature of such additions is even more evident with the lease of 1889, where there is an explosion in the detail of the obligations of the parties. The story of the Scots lease in the periods examined is thus one of continuity and growth. The explanation for the growing specification must be sought in various factors: in the growth of legal study and literature; in the industrialization of society; in the increasing wealth of the middle classes; in

---

direct connection with the continental civilian tradition. However, references to civilian or continental sources in his work are sparse.

[280] Hunter (n. 82), preface to third edition.
[281] Juridical Society of Edinburgh (ed.), *Collection of Styles or Complete System of Conveyancing* (1787–94 and later editions in the 19th century), 3 vols.

the mobility of workers; in changing land uses; and in the creation of a mercantile society.

Leasehold tenure is a feature of all European societies. Its origins in Scotland appear to be a mixture of feudal, customary, and Romano-canonical law. Its longevity is due to its ability to adapt to changing social and political circumstances and to meet the vastly divergent intentions of landlords from the various centuries examined. It continues to thrive in modern Scotland.[282] The present-day commercial law firm attaches great importance to the lease as a vehicle for institutional income and economic development, while the continuing statutory interest in domestic leases indicates its necessity in the provision of affordable housing.

---

[282] However, the Abolition of Feudal Tenure etc. (Scotland) Act 2000, s. 67 restricts the duration of all new leases to a maximum period of 175 years. The purpose is to prevent leases from being used as a substitute for the feudal system, which the Act abolishes.

10

Assignation

KLAUS LUIG

I. THE BEGINNINGS

1. Uses of assignation

Viscount Stair in his *Institutions* of 1681 held that originally in Scots law all obligations were intransmissible.[1] Yet Stair's text merely reflects contemporary textbooks on Roman law. In practice assignations existed from early times in Scotland. The oldest instrument containing the term 'assignation' was drafted before 1212. This was a charter by which the grantor gave land to the grantee 'et haeredibus suis et assignatis'. The use of 'assignati' can be regarded as licence for further alienation of the lands by the grantee.[2]

As to obligations, the *Regiam Majestatem* contains at least one allusion to assignation when it is said that homage has to be done for services and returns assigned in money.[3] The first specific mention of assignation of a personal right is to be found in an instrument of the Abbey of Coupar Angus dating back to 1257.[4] Through this instrument the cedent granted an annual rent to his creditor in security for a loan. The rent was due by Coupar Angus Abbey from a tenement which the monks held in perpetual alms from the cedent and his heirs. One should notice that the first documented assignation in Scots law was in the sophisticated form of an assignation for purposes of security, something not found so often in later times. Another instrument of nearly the same time, surviving in the *Fragmenta Collecta*, states that a tenant can give or sell his lease (*firma*) to whomever he wishes before the term but not after.[5] From these two examples we can draw the conclusion that already in the thirteenth century both sides of obligations concerning land were assignable, the right of the tenant to use the land and the right of the landlord to the rent.

In 1372 King Robert II granted to his son James the reversion of an annual return of £6 due to him from the barony of Abernethy and in the hands of

---

[1] Stair, III, 1, 2.
[2] Hector L. MacQueen, 'Title to Sue', in *The Laws of Scotland: Stair Memorial Encyclopaedia*, vol. 15 (1996), § 854, n. 1 and 2.
[3] D. M. Walker, *A Legal History of Scotland*, vol. 1 (1988), 381, referring to *Regiam Majestatem*, III, 60 (recte 'II 60').   [4] Walker (n. 3), 381.
[5] Walker (n. 3), 382 n. 403, referring to APS, I, 733 c. 24.

Margaret.[6] The assignation of rights of annualrent was relatively widespread.[7] But in old instruments, even those drafted by a notary, it is not always easy to distinguish between the creation of an annualrent and its assignation (as security).

Some rights created by contract were considered as having a proprietary character and thus assignable.[8] By the end of the fifteenth century assignations were quite normal as part of a well-elaborated law of obligations.[9] A case of 1482 concerned an assignation of an obligation to deliver sheep, wool, lambs, and other goods.[10] But there were also assignations of simple claims to money. Thus in 1493 the Bishop of Aberdeen conferred on a lady 200 merks owed to him by William Earl of Errol for two years' fruits of the kirk of Cruden.[11]

Assignation of corporeal subjects,[12] and of immoveable[13] rights generally, lie outside the scope of this chapter. But some objects of a mixed nature, e.g. the 'bygone interests of an heritable bond',[14] cannot be completely excluded from a history of assignation.

Assignations of reversions were common in the early period. 'Reversion' was the right of a seller/debtor to buy back, or to redeem on repayment of the money received as the price/loan, property such as land or rents which had been sold in order to secure a debt.[15] The reversion could be constituted in favour, not only of the seller/debtor and his heirs, but also of his assignees, provided this was mentioned in the instrument. Presumably a reason for assigning reversions was as security for further loans. In his *De Verborum Significatione*[16] of 1597 Skene quotes from an instrument of 1395 which pledged a barony as security for a loan of 200 merks sterling. This was made 'ipsi comiti et haeredibus suis' until the debtor 'aut haeredes sui' repaid the loan. The debtor 'pro se et haeredibus suis' granted to the creditor 'et haeredibus suis' all 'firmas, reditus, commoditates . . . de dicta Baronie'. In other deeds this might be in the vernacular, as for example 'to ony man, and his airis, or to him and his bairnis'.[17] In such cases the creditor's right was not transferable, because only his heirs or his children were mentioned. This becomes

---

[6] D. M. Walker, *A Legal History of Scotland*, vol. 2 (1990), 682.   [7] Ibid.
[8] Walker (n. 6), 710.
[9] Ibid. Further 15th-century cases are mentioned in MacQueen (n. 2), § 854, text at n. 4.
[10] Walker (n. 6), 710 n. 886 referring to (1482) ADA 98.
[11] Walker (n. 6), 710 n. 887 referring to ADC I, 313.
[12] The deed transferring land is known as a 'disposition' rather than an 'assignation'. For transfer of land, see Ch. 6.
[13] 'Heritable property' is the usual term for immoveable property.
[14] *Turnbull* v. *Stewart* (1751) Mor 868, 870.
[15] Usually this involved a 'wadset', which was a type of heritable security.
[16] John Skene, *De Verborum Significatione* (1826, 1st edn. 1597), 133. The heading is 'Sterlingus'.   [17] Balfour, *Practicks*, 455, c. VI. Bairnis = children.

clear from the fact that the right ended with the creditor's death unless heirs were expressly mentioned.[18]

Later on heirs tended to be accompanied by *assignati*. For example, in an instrument from 1419 quoted by Skene,[19] the debtor declares that all his lands are granted to the creditor 'haeredibus suis et assignatis, a me, haeredibus meis et assignatis'. This demonstrates that the creditor too was entitled to dispose of his rights. In Balfour we find quoted the clause 'his airis and assignayis, he may mak assignay thairto ony quhom he pleisis . . .'[20]

The underlying law is unclear. It may be that rights were normally intransmissible, but could be made transmissible by the clause 'haeredibus et assignatis'. Or it may be that rights were normally transmissible unless the contrary was provided, so that the clause merely made clear that the normal rule applied. In addition, it seems that a right which, lacking the clause 'et assignati', was not transmissible could nonetheless be transferred to a procurator *in rem suam*.[21] But at a later stage the procurator *in rem suam* was merely the technical term for the assignee, who, according to a Romanistic doctrine, could act either as the procurator of the cedent or in his own name.[22] The result was that, with reversions, the creditor generally was entitled to dispose of his right, while the debtor's right to redeem was constituted in favour of the debtor 'et haeredibus suis et assignatis'.

There was a risk that the creditor might sell on the lands, thus destroying the reversioner's rights or those of his assignee. In order to prevent this the Reversion Act 1469[23] (still in force[24]) enacted

that the sellare [i.e. the debtor] sall have Recourse to the samyn landis sauld be him vnder lettre of Reuersione to quhatsumeuir handis the said lettre cummys payand the mone and schawand the Reversione and have sic privelege and fredome aganis the personis that haldis the said landis as he suld have again the principale byare [i.e. the creditor] . . .

For our purpose the decisive words are 'to quhatsumeuir handis the said lettre cummys', implying that the reversion was alienable. One almost gets the impression that assignations of reversions were a particularly common type of assignation. While a reversion was classified as an 'immovabill gud',[25] its assignation seems to have avoided the forms of the feudal law—leading to a difficulty about intimation to the creditor, discussed below. The act of 1469

---

[18] Balfour, *Practicks*, 455, cc. VI & VIII.
[19] Skene (n. 16), 106. The heading is 'Reversion'.   [20] Balfour, *Practicks*, 455, c. IX.
[21] Erskine, III, 5, 2.
[22] *Grier* v. *Maxwell* (1621) Mor 828; *Westraw* v. *Williamson & Carmichael* (1626) Mor 859.
[23] Act 1469, c. 3 (APS II, 94). Cf. D. M. Walker, *A Legal History of Scotland*, vol. 3 (1995), 785.
[24] Its repeal, however, has been recommended. See Scottish Law Commission, *Report on Real Burdens* (Scot Law Com No. 181, 2000), paras. 10.17 and 10.18.
[25] Balfour, *Practicks*, 456, c. XIII.

had far-reaching consequences and was applied to analogous cases. Thus Balfour reports two decisions of the Court of Session according to which the 'redemptor' was not bound to a liferent[26] or a tack[27] created by the buyer. After the setting up of a land register, known as the Register of Sasines, in 1617, it became necessary to register both reversions and also assignations of reversions.[28]

The assignation of a reversion required intimation to the buyer/creditor.[29] Consequently the rule was, as in all cases of assignation, that in the event of more than one assignation of the same right the assignee 'who makes first intimation and warning has just titill[30] to redeme ... and sould be preferrit'.[31]

The social situations in which those transactions took place were sometimes rather intricate. Balfour quotes a case of assignation of a reversion with intimation, followed by retrocession for which a new intimation was held necessary.[32] In a further case of 1577 the judges found that the assignee was not bound by a suspension of reversion agreed upon between the seller/debtor and the buyer/creditor because the right of the assignee was based exclusively on the terms of the original reversion.[33]

To summarize, one can say that almost all rights were regarded as being transferable by assignation. These included loans, security rights, rights to rents,[34] liferents,[35] duties of victual,[36] and bonds.[37] Thus in a bond of 1615 the debtor undertook that he 'faithfully bind and obleiss me, my airis executouris, assignais' to make payment to the creditor and 'his airis, executouris or assignais'.[38] Also transferable were claims for reparation of any type, including assythment and rights in respect of the slaughter, burning, and mutilation of horses and cattle.[39]

2. *Causa*

An assignation without 'onerous or lucrative' cause was null.[40] The cause might be purchase, or the intention to give help in suing the debtor,[41] or donation.[42] Presumably in the normal case the agreement of cause and the act of

---

[26] Balfour, *Practicks*, 445, c. VI. Liferent is *ususfructus*.
[27] Balfour, *Practicks*, 446, c. VII; but compare 449 c. XVIII.
[28] Registration Act 1617 c. 16 (APS IV, 545). See D. M. Walker, *A Legal History of Scotland*, vol. 5 (1998), 754 n. 146.   [29] Balfour, *Practicks*, 449, c. XIV, citing a decision from 1564.
[30] 'Titill' (= titulus) here is not the contract but the act of assigning itself.
[31] Balfour, *Practicks*, 449, c. XV.   [32] Balfour, *Practicks*, 448, c. XIII.
[33] Balfour, *Practicks*, 449, c. XVII. Cf. the discussion of *assignatus utitur jure auctoris* in K. G. C. Reid, *The Law of Property in Scotland* (1996) § 660.
[34] *Kinloch* v. *Finlayson* (1629) Mor 847.   [35] *Lord Elphingston* v. *Ord* (1624) Mor 858.
[36] *Hume* v. *Hume* (1632) Mor 848.   [37] *Faculty of Advocates* v. *Dickson* (1718) Mor 864.
[38] Peter Gouldesbrough, *Formulary of Old Scots Legal Documents* (Stair Society vol. 36, 1985), 1.   [39] Walker (n. 23), 737.
[40] Balfour, *Practicks*, 169, c. 1.   [41] Walker (n. 23), 737.
[42] Including a donation which operated *mortis causa*: see Walker (n. 23), 818.

transfer would be combined in a single document which would name the cause.[43]

3. Intimation

(a) Payment to the cedent

The first mention of intimation seems to be in a case of 1492 dealing with a claim for reparation,[44] where it was said that 'the assignay aucht and sould make lauchful intimation of the said assignation to the debtour'.[45] This reasoning reveals two underlying principles: first, that in a question between cedent and assignee, the assignation itself was sufficient to give a valid right;[46] and secondly, that in order to make the assignation effective against the debtor, an intimation was necessary. Before intimation took place the debtor entitled to pay the cedent or persons named by him.[47] Hence the reason given in the decision of 1492 for intimation was that 'utherways gif the said debtour happinis to pay the creditour, or ony utheris in his name, havand his richt and power before ony intimatioun maid to him, he onnawayis sould be compellit to mak ony payment to the said assignay be ressoun of his assignation'. This principle was confirmed in later decisions. For example, in *McGill* v. *Laureston*, decided in 1558,[48] it was said that before the intimation of an 'actioun, assedatioun, or reversioun', the debtor can 'compone, transact, or agrie with the maker thairof, touching the contentis of the samin, and obtene his discharge, richt or titil thairanent'.

The rule was that intimation was made by the assignee.[49] But in *A* v. *B*, decided in 1540,[50] intimation by the cedent was held sufficient to the extent of removing from the cedent 'all actioun that he had, or may have, agains the said debtour'. At first glance this seems to be a step in the direction of a rule that mere knowledge by the debtor, regardless of source, was decisive for the effect of the assignation or, in other words, that in the relationship between assignee and debtor knowledge by the debtor was equivalent to intimation. But in a later case, decided in 1586,[51] a debtor who witnessed the instrument of intimation 'was found thereby not to be put in *mala fide*, but only by a formal intimation'. The rule as set out in *Stevinson* v. *Craigmiller*[52] was that

---

[43] An example is given by Gouldesbrough (n. 38), 2.
[44] *Drummond* v. *Muschet* (1492) Mor 843.
[45] For an example of intimation from 1642, see Gouldesbrough (n. 38), 32.
[46] *Thome* v. *Thome* (1683), cited by Gloag and Henderson, *The Law of Scotland* (10th edn. (1998), ed. W. A. Wilson and Angelo Forte), para. 38.4, n. 13, with reference to Stair III, 1, 15.
[47] *Drummond* v. *Muschet* (1492) Mor 843; Balfour, *Practicks*, 169; Walker (n. 23), 737, nn. 471 and 472; MacQueen (n. 2), § 854 n. 5, with further references to intimation.
[48] (1558) Mor 843; Balfour, *Practicks*, 169.   [49] *Drummond* v. *Muschet* (1492) Mor 843.
[50] (1540) Mor 843; Balfour, *Practicks*, 170.
[51] *Mackalzean* v. *Mackalzean* (1586) Mor 854.
[52] (1624) Mor 858; Fol Dic, I, 64; Durie, 102.

intimation 'ought to be legally made by a notary, before witnesses, which, as it was most solemn and requisite so to be done, so these were the most probable means to eschew falset . . .' On this ground a 'privy ratification' of the assignation made by the debtor was held insufficient. *Murray* v. *Durham and the Lady Winton*[53] was to like effect.

Yet the impression caused by *A* v. *B* of 1540[54] was confirmed by *Dunipace* v. *Sandis* (1624)[55] where the Lords sustained as equivalent to a formal intimation the fact that the debtor had treated 'sundry times with the assignee anent the payment to him . . . and had offered to him some satisfaction therefor . . .'. In this way the debtor had 'acknowledged the assignation, as if it had been intimate'. In another decision of the same year, however, the Lords demanded an intimation 'legally and solemnly made' and declared that knowledge was not equivalent to an intimation albeit that it was confessed by the debtor.[56]

Two years later, in *Westraw* v. *Williamson & Carmichael*,[57] it was confirmed that payment to the cedent liberated the debtor notwithstanding that the debtor not only knew that the debt was assigned but had offered to transact with the assignee thereanent. In *Hume* v. *Hume* (1632)[58] the debtor was again successful in claiming exoneration though the cedent's discharge came after assignation and intimation of the debt. This was because the intimation, which took place at the market-cross of the head burgh of the sheriffdom, was found to be defective. The case established the rule that intimation could not be made at the market-cross or even at the debtor's dwelling-house, but must be put personally into his hands. The broad field of application of assignations is illustrated by the fact that the object of the debt was 'to pay to his mother yearly, a yearly duty of victual'. If another decision of the same year, *Livingston* v. *Lindsay*,[59] suggests that payment to the assignee is the equivalent of intimation, the case is perhaps special on its facts.

(b) Competitions

The second aspect of intimation was as a necessary means to complete the assignation in order to give a valid right against all other parties and in particular, in a case of double assignation of the same debt, against other assignees or claimants. The principle was that of two competing assignations the first intimated had priority even if later assigned.[60] Similarly, in a competition with an arrester[61] an assignation without intimation was regarded as

---

[53] (1622) Mor 855.   [54] (1540) Mor 843.   [55] (1624) Mor 859.
[56] *Adamson* v. *McMitchell* (1624) Mor 859.
[57] (1626) Mor 859; Fol Dic, I, 64; Durie, 128. Gloag/Henderson (n. 46), para. 38.6 n. 20.
[58] (1632) Mor 848. See also *Kinloch* v. *Finlayson* (1629) Mor 847.
[59] (1626) Mor 860.   [60] *Lawrie* v. *Hay* (1696) Mor 849.
[61] Arrestment is a form of execution for debt ('diligence') which may be used against, among other things, debts owed to the debtor. A creditor who carries out an arrestment is known as an

null. The principle was clearly stated in *Lord Elphingston v. Ord* (1624) where 'An assignee to a woman's liferent . . . was found preferable to prior assignees, whose assignations were not intimated.'[62]

But while the principle itself was simple, its application often involved a consideration of difficult issues concerning the validity of intimations. For example, in a competition between an arrester and an assignee, the intimation was found null on the ground that it was made by a procurator who was also acting as notary. The Lords found 'the same person could not be both procurator to intimate in the assignee's name, and also notary to take instruments on the doing thereof'.[63] It is worth underlining that this was not only a question between the cedent and the debtor, but a case of competition between an assignee and a third person (the arrester) who claimed the debt. It was obvious that in such a case *bona* or *mala fides* of the debtor as to the assignation could not be relevant.

This was clear also from *Kinloch v. Finlayson* (1629).[64] An assignee of the rent of a house was met by a defence of payment to an arrester. Prior to the arrestment the assignation had been intimated at the tenant's house, and a copy delivered to his wife (the tenant being out of the country). While he knew of the intimation, the tenant argued that intimation during his absence should have been made at the market-cross and at the pier of Leith. Though the case was not decided, it suggests that knowledge was irrelevant in cases of competition.

More flexibility was shown in *McGill v. Hutchison* (1630),[65] a competition between an assignation and a subsequent arrestment. While there was no formal intimation, the assignee had written to the debtor and the debtor had written back promising to make payment. Both letters preceded the arrestment. This was regarded as sufficient intimation. A similar view would have prevailed in *Home and Elphingstone v. Muray of Stenhope* (1674)[66] if the debtor's undertaking to pay had been made in writing.[67] A mere letter by the *assignee*, however, was not sufficient.[68]

Lawrie v. Hay (1696)[69] brought out the importance of distinguishing between the debtor's position (i) in a competition between cedent and assignee and (ii) in a competition between two assignees or an arrester and assignee. Greater formality of intimation was required in the second case than in the first. Another decision of about the same time, which was treated as a case of competition without belonging exactly to this group of cases,

---

'arrester'. A competition with assignation would come about if the debtor was in the process of assigning the debt owed to him.

[62] (1624) Mor 858.   [63] *Scot v. Drumlanrig* (1628) Mor 846.   [64] (1629) Mor 847.
[65] (1630) Mor 860. For a different type of informal intimation see *Ogilvie v. Ogilvie* (1681) Mor 863.   [66] (1674) Mor 863.
[67] Cf. *Dunipace v. Sandis* (1624) Mor 859.
[68] *Bain v. Cunningham McMillan* (1679) Mor 863.   [69] (1696) Mor 849; Fount, I, 721.

took the view that a partial discharge granted by the cedent to the debtor and referring to the assignation could not be regarded as a sufficient intimation.[70] The distinction suggested in *Lawrie* v. *Hay* was confirmed by *Leith* v. *Garden* (1703).[71] Whereas most of the earlier cases rest on isolated reasoning, *Leith* v. *Garden* sought to identify a series of decisions which might form the basis for an affirmed custom with 'full consistence'[72] and which would be followed in future cases.[73] In this case the assignee of a credit of '197 merks by ticket' wrote a letter to the debtor and afterwards showed him the assignation, but there was no formal intimation. When the debtor made payment to the cedent, the assignee sued the debtor on the ground that the payment was made in *mala fide*. The debtor disputed the relevance of private knowledge, on the basis of decisions such as *Durham* v. *Lady Winton*,[74] *Adamson* v. *McMitchell*,[75] and *Westraw* v. *Williamson & Carmichael*.[76] The assignee argued that the solemnities of intimation were essential only in a competition between two assignees or arrester and assignee, and that bad faith was relevant in a question between assignee and debtor. The court found for the assignee.

The case law, however, remained inconsistent. Some later decisions returned to the older doctrine[77] that only formal intimation could create *mala fides*.[78] But in another case it was held as sufficient intimation that the debtor had subscribed a notice on the back of the bond which had been assigned.[79] *Turnbull* v. *Stewart* (1751)[80] illustrates the intricate social and economic background of some of the litigations, especially those involving immoveable rights. The particular decision was that an assignation was sufficiently intimated when contained in a deed to which the debtor was a party. Much later, *Leith* v. *Garden*[81] was cited by Bell in his *Principles*[82] and became a leading decision. Curiously Gloag and Henderson[83] were to use it as authority for the directly opposite rule (i.e. that private knowledge is never relevant).

(c) *Conclusion*

What conclusion can be drawn from these decisions? Intimation was, of course, essential. Yet within the triangle of cedent, assignee, and debtor there was no absolute necessity to comply with all formalities in perfect form. Under certain circumstances the *bona* or *mala fides* of the debtor were decisive. On the other hand, in cases of competition between more than one

---

[70] *Johnstone* v. *Spevin* (1682) Mor 864.
[71] (1703) Mor 865; Fol Dic, I, 64; Fount, II, 180.   [72] Stair, I, 1, 15.
[73] Cf. below n. 203.   [74] (1622) Mor 855; see above, text accompanying n. 53.
[75] (1624) Mor 859; see above, text accompanying n. 56.
[76] (1626) Mor 859; see above, text accompanying n. 57.   [77] See above nn. 74, 75, 76.
[78] *Faculty of Advocates* v. *Dickson* (1718) Mor 866; *Dicksons* v. *Trotter* (1776) Mor 873.
[79] *Creditors of Lord Ballenden* (1707) Mor 865.   [80] (1751) Mor 868.
[81] (1703) Mor 865.   [82] See below n. 226.
[83] Gloag/Henderson (n. 46), para 38.7, n. 30.

assignee or between an assignee and an arrester, intimation had to be performed in the strict form and there was only limited scope for leniency—as for example in the case where the debtor was party to the deed or gave his acknowledgement on the back of the bond or where, in his absence, the intimation was made to his 'confidential man of business'.[84]

II. LEGAL LITERATURE BEFORE STAIR

1. Balfour's *Practicks* (*c*.1583)

The first full account of decisions on assignation was given by Balfour in his *Practicks*, collected between 1574 and 1583. Balfour lists eight decisions, although as many as four deal with assignations of immoveable property. According to Balfour an assignation must contain 'ane titll onerous or lucrative',[85] i.e. it is void without an onerous or lucrative cause. In any event, an assignee could not acquire greater rights than the cedent.[86] Here Balfour's rule was the Romanist version of a principle drawn from a decision of 1533,[87] that a person who holds a debt 'conjunctly and severally' with another cannot assign more than his own share.

Balfour relies on a decision of 1492[88] for the proposition that assignations must be intimated.[89] The intimation might be made by the cedent, but a 'verbal intimatioun maid *nuda voce* is not sufficient.'[90] In the absence of intimation the debtor could pay the original creditor and so become free, and the same applied if the debtor could 'compone, transact or agrie' with the cedent.[91] Balfour shows no interest in cases of competition.

2. Skene's *De Verborum Significatione* (1597)

In his *De Verborum Significatione* of 1597 Skene quotes without comment from a charter of 1395, which was mentioned above.[92]

3. Craig's *Jus Feudale* (*c*.1600)

Craig treated assignations mainly in the context of reversions. Craig's work marked the beginning of the influence of Romanist theory. The legal basis for

---

[84] *Dougal* v. *Gordon* (1795) Mor 851.
[85] Balfour, *Practicks*, 169, c. I . Cf. Reid (n. 33) § 612. [86] Balfour, *Practicks*, 169, c. II.
[87] *Cairnis* v. *Leyis* (1533) Mor 827. [88] *Drummond* v. *Muschet* (1492) Mor 843.
[89] Balfour, *Practicks*, 169, c. III.
[90] Balfour, *Practicks*, 169–70, cc. V & VI. The authority for the first proposition is *A* v. *B* (1540) Mor 843, mentioned earlier.
[91] Balfour, *Practicks*, 169, cc. III & IV. The authority quoted is *McGill* v. *Laurestoun* (1558) Mor 843. [92] Skene (n. 16).

reversions Craig found in C. 4.54.2 ('If your ancestors have sold an estate ...'). As to assignations of reversions, these were both possible[93] and, apparently, frequent. Competitions were resolved in this way:[94]

if the right has been given or assigned to two persons separately, preference is given to that one of the two who first makes intimation to the possessor of the lands of his intention to redeem, because the intimation adds to his naked right to redeem a sort of civil possession; and he is preferred as quasi-possessor.

It followed that it was the assignee who had to make the intimation. Intimation was also necessary for a retrocession. Of two successive assignees the one to intimate first was preferred. The intimation was almost identical with the 'premonition' required as preliminary notice for the exercise of a reversion.[95]

Craig also considers the assignability of the buyer/creditor's right to the sum due for repurchase. As a future debt, it could not be assigned:[96] '[A]n assignation of this sort is a nullity, and the assignee gets nothing by it. One reason is that, at the date of the assignation, there is nothing to assign ... It depends entirely on the reverser whether redemption ever takes place.'

4. Hope's *Major Practicks*

Hope's digest covering the period from 1608 to 1633[97] exhibits a rich variety of assignations. Hope offers an almost complete view of all essential rules concerning assignation. Although the author sometimes uses 'assignation' in a broad sense, 'dispone' is the normal term for transmission of land, and 'assign' is reserved for incorporeal rights.

According to Hope, almost all rights were assignable. Among the numerous examples given were reversions,[98] claims to the price of a thing sold,[99] other monetary claims,[100] rights to ejection and removing ('who wes made assigney to the ejection be his father'),[101] and 'pensione cum potestate'.[102] Like Craig, Hope considered a sum in reversion (i.e. the sum the seller pays on redemption) to be intransmissible.[103] In Hope's view tacks (i.e. leases) were not assignable: 'Assedatio in assignatos transferri non potest nisi aut vitalis

---

[93] Craig, II, 6, 18.   [94] Craig, II, 6, 7 (Clyde's translation).
[95] Craig, II, 6, 9. The form of premonition is described at II, 6, 14.
[96] Craig, II, 6, 16 (Clyde's translation).
[97] D. M. Walker, *A Legal History of Scotland*, vol. 4 (1996), 374.
[98] Hope, *Major Practicks*, II, 12, 4 and 6.   [99] Ibid., II, 12, 11.
[100] Ibid., II, 12, 13, 14, 16, 18, 19, 20, 21, 22, 24, 25, 26, 29.
[101] Ibid., II,12, 12. Hope cites *Crichton* v. *Bandoun* (1613) Mor 13443.
[102] Ibid., II, 12, 23. This was 'fund null because it wes made 2 yeirs befoir the pensioner's decease and naither intimat nor cled with possessione'. The decision in question was *Bishop of Aberdeen* v. *Lord Dunlagery* (1622) Mor 828.
[103] Ibid., II, 12, 4; III, 11, 2. Cf. Craig, *Jus Feudale*, II, 6, 16.

sit, aut id specialiter sit permissum.'[104] The reason was that 'ane tack *est stricti juris*, and will not mor exceed the persones contained therein.'[105] The main question was the permission of the superior. The question of a tack being 'vitalis' remained unanswered.

Issues of intimation covered a wide field. Among the questions to be solved were conflicts between more than one assignation, between assignations and donations (the latter normally being regarded as a special form of assignation),[106] and, very often, between assignations and arrestments,[107] comprisings,[108] or summons.[109] With Hope the rule was confirmed as: 'Si duo sint cessionarii qui primus intimationem fecerit praefertur.'[110] It was the duty of the assignee to make intimation. Prior to the intimation the cedent could dispose of the right, either by receiving payment or by renouncing the debt.[111] But if the cedent accepted payment he was bound to pay the assignee. To that extent at least the (unintimated) assignation denuded the cedent; but it was also a consequence of the fact that the cedent guaranteed the assignation.[112]

Hope's justification for intimation reveals a theoretical structure borrowed from Roman law. The first to intimate was given priority in spite of the principle 'licet tempore posterior, prior est iure.'[113] Referring to Bartolus (ad D. 30.1.82) Hope says: 'Lyke as *in incorporalibus* the first assignatione should have place, siclyke as the first possession and traditione hes place in rebus corporalibus'.[114] Further, intimation put the debtor in bad faith. Yet in spite of this, 'knowledge of ane assignation mad supplies not the neccessar solemnitie of intimation'.[115] Apparently the courts had difficulties with concurrent assignations; and perhaps for that reason an Act of Parliament of 1540, quoted by Hope, threatened with punishment 'they that make double assignations'.[116]

The intimation was based on 'solemnitie'.[117] Yet some judicial measures taken by the assignee had the same effect, for example a declarator of reversion[118] or a comprising.[119] In one decision it was 'Found that wer ther is double assignations mad of ane reversione, he that useth the first order and getts the first declarator of redemptione is preferred, and that albeit it wes alleadgeat for ane of the assigneys that he wes superior of the wodsett lands and had the first assignation to the reversione, be virtue quherof he mad wairneing and consignit the mony, and therby the property wes consolidat

---

[104] Ibid., III, 19, 3. See also III, 19, 12; III, 19, 30; III, 30, 4; III, 30, 6 (noting *Hamilton* v. *Boyd* (1610) Mor 7188); III, 30, 9, 10, and 11.   [105] Ibid., III, 19, 12.
[106] Ibid., II, 12, 26. Cf. II, 12, 31 and 32.   [107] Ibid., II, 12, 20.   [108] Ibid., II, 12, 29.
[109] Ibid., II, 12, 21.   [110] Ibid., II, 12, 1.   [111] Ibid.
[112] Ibid., II, 12, 7.   [113] Ibid., II, 12, 1.   [114] Ibid., II, 12, 6.
[115] Ibid., II, 12, 7–9.
[116] Ibid., II, 12, 10. See also Sylvia Sella-Geusen, *Doppelverkauf: Zur Rechtsstellung des ersten Käufers im gelehrten Recht des Mittelalters* (1999).   [117] Ibid., II, 12, 9.
[118] Ibid., II, 12, 6.
[119] Ibid., II, 12, 36, reporting *Bruce* v. *Buckie* (1619) Mor 207 and 10415.

with the superiority'.[120] Sometimes the rigid form of intimation was not insisted on. In a case of 1630 the Lords found that an intimation was proven 'be ane letter written be the assigney to the debitor, and be his anser craveing dayes of peyment'.[121]

Rights connected with the object of assignation passed to the assignee, so that 'ane inhibition perteins to the assigney, albeit it be not assignit per expressum'.[122] However, the assignee was 'in no better cas nor the cedent', and a renunciation by the cedent bound the assignee.[123]

The unrest of the time left its mark on the law. With assignations by persons who were or became 'rebells'[124] the assignation was considered null if not intimated before the rebellion or the horning of the rebel.[125]

III. DECISIONS OF THE COURT OF SESSION 1633–1681

For the period between Hope and Stair, and for questions not dealt with by Balfour and Hope, the decisions collected in Morison's *Dictionary* offer rich material drawn from several collections and practicks.[126] Many decisions of this time disclose an intricate relationship between incorporeal rights and immoveables. Another aspect of importance is the influence of Roman law theory. Many cases concern concurrent assignations, or the concurrence of assignations with other rights.

In a case of 1626 the creditor, having charter and sasine for his claim, made an assignation. Intimation followed. Later the debt was comprised[127] by a third party. This was effective 'seeing the assignation was not *habilis modus* to denude the cedent of his real right'.[128] Debts secured by real rights, it appeared, had to be transferred by the rules concerning immoveables. Another case established the right of the debtor to insist, in a question with the assignee, that the cedent 'fulfil his part first, or at least *per simul & semel*'. But this applied only to an obligation due under the same contract.[129] The source of the rule was Roman law.

Roman law was also evident in the rules of compensation (set-off). Once again intimation was decisive. The debtor was entitled to compensation only for credits acquired before intimation.[130] In one decision *Digest* texts[131] were

---

[120] Hope, *Major Practicks*, II, 12, 6.
[121] Ibid., II, 12, 33. The case is *McGill* v. *Hutchison* (1630) Mor 861. Cf. below n. 136.
[122] Ibid., II, 12, 34, reporting *Hay* v. *Ker* (1622) Mor 828.
[123] Ibid., II, 12, 25, reporting *Schaw* (1622) Mor 829. See also II, 12, 16.
[124] Ibid., II, 12, 2, 13, 14, 15, 17, 18, 26.   [125] *Clerk* v. *Napier* (1614) Mor 835.
[126] For the 17th century, see Walker (n. 97), 803.
[127] Sometimes in cases of this type there is poinding or other diligence.
[128] *Anstruther* v. *Black* (1626) Mor 829.   [129] *Hamilton* v. *Hamilton* (1629) Mor 830.
[130] *Wallace* v. *Edgar* (1662) Mor 837.   [131] D. 18. 4. 4 & 5.

cited for the rule that the cedent warrants that the debt is truly owing but not that the debtor is solvent.[132]

The issue most frequently litigated was intimation. Was intimation needed and, if so, had it been properly effected? Some examples serve to illustrate the wide range of possible situations. An unintimated retrocession, it was held, discharged an unintimated assignation.[133] The case concerned a bond assigned from wife to husband, retrocessed, and later assigned to a second husband. An assignation by the creditor to the debtor—of feuduties—did not require intimation and discharged the debt.[134]

If the debtor began payment to the assignee, this was treated as the equivalent of intimation,[135] and the result was the same if the debtor 'had treated sundry times with the assignee anent the payment . . . and had offered to him some satisfaction therefor'.[136] But in another case the Lords insisted on an intimation 'legally and solemnly made' and stated that 'knowledge, albeit it were confessed by the party, could not put him in *mala fide*'.[137] That was confirmed by a decision of 1626 where the court held as necessary an intimation 'after a legal manner' and said that an inhibition 'not being *specifice* execute, and intimate to the suspenders, could not be repute an intimation'.[138] By contrast, the beginning of a lawsuit against the debtor was sufficient intimation.[139]

The overall impression given by these cases is that, while the court insisted on full intimation if the protection of the debtor was involved, it showed greater flexibility where this was to the debtor's advantage. It was for this reason that payment was considered equivalent to intimation. The impression is confirmed by a case of 1630 where the assignee was given priority over an arrester on account of a letter to which the debtor replied, before the arrestment, promising payment.[140] Writing, however, was essential,[141] and must be by the debtor.[142]

In a competition of assignations, priority of intimation might be defeated by bad faith on the part of the assignee.[143] This indeed had been settled as early as a case of 1582, though only 'after long reasoning' on the part of the court.[144]

---

[132] *Macklonaquhen v. Carsan* (1632) Mor 830.   [133] *Craig v. Edgar* (1674) Mor 838.
[134] *Earl of Argyle v. Lord McDonald* (1676) Mor 842.
[135] *Livingston v. Lindsay* (1626) Mor 860.
[136] *Dunipace v. Sandis* (1624) Mor 859. Cf. Hope, *Major Practicks*, II, 12, 23.
[137] *Adamson v. McMitchell* (1624) Mor 859.
[138] *Westraw v. Williamson & Carmichael* (1626) Mor 859.
[139] *Ogilvie v. Ogilvie* (1681) Mor 863.   [140] *McGill v. Hutchison* (1630) Mor 860.
[141] *Home & Elphingston v. Murray* (1674) Mor 863.
[142] *Bain v. Cunningham McMillan* (1679) Mor 863.
[143] *Lawder v. Goodwife of Whitekirk* (1637) Mor 1692.
[144] *Stirling v. White & Drummond* (1582) Mor 7127.

IV. STAIR

Stair's *Institutions*, published in 1681, was the first systematic analysis of the law of Scotland. In the case of assignation, however, Stair was able to rely on the framework provided by the decisions reported by writers such as Balfour and Hope, and there is little in his account which is new. What Stair provided instead were some Romanist theories, not all beyond reproach.

After discussing the constitution of rights, i.e. personal freedom and obligation (book I) and property (book II), Stair turns to 'the conveyance and transmission of these rights'.[145] For Stair, obligations were often not capable of transmission without the consent of the other party.[146] But in order to make obligations more useful and effectual, custom had introduced an indirect manner of transmission, without the debtor's consent, whereby the assignee was viewed as the procurator both of the cedent and of himself.[147] Stair believed that the invention of the procurator meant that assignations, little mentioned in the civil law, were more frequent in Scotland than elsewhere. But this view seems due rather to the influence of Romanist doctrine than to the practice of Scots law as reflected in the decisions of the Court of Session and in the *Practicks* of Balfour and Hope. That practice demonstrates that the figure of a mandator was not necessary to explain what happens with an assignation of rights; and even the formularies show that the cedent 'makis, constitutes and ordaines' the assignee and his heirs and assignees 'cessioneris, assignais, donatouris and procuratouris *in rem suam*'.[148] In fact the idea of a *procurator in rem suam*, which was borrowed from Roman law, had no apparent consequences for the rest of Stair's exposition.[149]

With or without the theory of a procurator, Stair's views can be summarized in this way. Like all other rights[150] personal rights were generally transmissible, the proper method being assignation.[151] Real rights could also be assigned—Stair mentions liferents, tacks, reversions, mails, duties, teinds, and annualrents—but only before infeftment.[152] For a reader brought up in a civil law system it is startling to learn that even marriage was regarded as being a legal assignation, of the moveable rights of the wife.[153] Some rights were not transferable, in particular where there was a 'singular consideration of the person'. This was the case with most conjugal and parental obligations[154] and with commissions and trusts.[155]

An assignation must name the cedent, the assignee, and the thing assigned.

---

[145] Stair, III, 1, 1; D. M. Walker, 'The Content of the Institutions', in D. M. Walker (ed.), *Stair Tercentenary Studies* (Stair Society vol. 33, 1981), 169.
[146] Stair, III, 1, 2. But see also III, 1, 16.   [147] Stair, III, 1, 3.
[148] Gouldesbrough (n. 38), 2. This was in correspondence with what the notaries did in civil law, cf. K. Luig, *Zur Geschichte der Zessionslehre* (1968), 14.   [149] Stair, III, 1, 4.
[150] Stair, I, 1, 15 at 'Thirdly'.   [151] Walker (n. 97), 803; Stair, III, 1, 1.
[152] Stair, III, 1, 16.   [153] Stair, III, 1, 14.   [154] Walker (n. 97), 803.
[155] Stair, III, 1, 2.

Assignation

While there were customary styles, any terms expressive of transmission were sufficient, 'as if the cedent assign, transfer and dispone, make over, set over, gift, or grant the thing assigned to the assignee, or nominate or constitute him his cessioner, assignee, donatar, or procurator to his own behoof . . .'[156]

Donation, for Stair and his predecessors, was not only a possible cause for an assignation but also a special form of it. Further, Stair mentions that, for the benefit of creditors, law had introduced the judicial assignations of arrestment, apprising and adjudication.[157] Stair deals thoroughly with the transfer of bonds, in particular blank bonds which were of great importance for daily practice.[158]

As before, however, the dominant theme is intimation.[159] By the time of Stair the doctrine of intimation was acknowledged by legislation and fully elaborated by the case law. According to Stair intimation had first been used to put the debtor in *mala fide* to pay to the cedent. Later it became a solemnity of assignation, without which the right did not pass. Stair is clear that intimation could not be supplied by the debtor's knowledge of the assignation.[160] Stair regarded intimation as part of Scots law ('our proper custom')[161] and not as a Roman institution.[162] For that reason intimation was not essential among merchants, 'who act as oft with strangers especially, *qui utuntur communi jure gentium*'. As earlier with procurator *in rem suam*, it is surprising to find a typical Roman institution like intimation being regarded as an invention of the customary law of Scotland.

The main consequence of the necessity of intimation 'as full accomplishment of the assignation' was that 'if there be diverse assignations, the first intimation is preferable, though of the last assignation'.[163] This simple and clear principle was confirmed and, to some extent, qualified by a number of decisions discussed by Stair. Here it is possible to give only a brief impression of decisions which, quite apart from their legal interest, often shed light on the economic and social situations in which assignation took place.

In a case where both assignations were gratuitous, the last assignation, though intimated first, was not preferred because the cedent was bound to the first assignee by the implied warrandice against future facts and deeds. Thus the last assignation, being gratuitous, was reducible on the warrandice.[164] This shows a certain weakness in the position of gratuitous assignations.

Intimation, while usually effected by instrument, could also be made by legal diligence such as arrestment or a charge or process on the assignation.[165]

---

[156] Stair, III, 1, 4. [157] Stair, III, 1, 24 and 3. [158] Stair, III, 1, 5.
[159] Stair, III, 1, 6. Cf. Walker (n. 145), 169.
[160] Stair, II, 1, 7, citing *Adamson* v. *McMitchell* (1624) Mor 859 and *Westraw* v. *Williamson & Carmichael* (1626) Mor 859. [161] Stair, III,1,12.
[162] See also Walker (n. 97), 630. [163] Stair, III, 1, 6.
[164] Ibid., discussing *Alexander* v. *Lundies* (1675) Mor 940. [165] Stair, III, 1, 45.

Though knowledge did not of itself amount to intimation, any writ under the debtor's hand acknowledging the assignation was sufficient intimation.[166]

In some cases intimation was not necessary, for example 'assignations to annual prestations, as to mails and duties, teinds, or annualrents or assignations to rights, requiring possession to complete them, as tacks'.[167] Such assignations were perfected by payment or, as the case may be, by possession.[168]

The establishment of the Register of Sasines in 1617 meant that some assignations—for example, of reversions—required to be registered. Registration made intimation unnecessary.[169] Nor was intimation necessary for judicial assignations by apprising or adjudication. But since in such a case the debtor did not know what had occurred, he was liberated by payment *bona fide*.[170]

All exceptions competent to the debtor against the cedent before the assignation or intimation remained competent against the assignee, including payment and compensation.[171] In the assignation of a mutual contract, performance could not be required of the debtor unless performance had already been made by the cedent.[172]

An intimated assignation was 'a full and complete transmission of the right assigned... and thereby the right of the cedent ceaseth, and the assignee becomes creditor'.[173] In a competition with an arrestment, therefore, the assignation would prevail if it was intimated first.[174] The timing could sometimes be close. In one case 'an arrestment was preferred to an assignation intimate the same day, but two hours thereafter'.[175] In a competition of arrestments, the first, 'not failing in diligence', was preferred.[176]

V. JURISTS OF THE EIGHTEENTH CENTURY

1. Bankton

In his *Institute of the Laws of Scotland* (1751–3), Bankton follows the 'general method of the Viscount of Stair's Institutions'[177] to present, in a systematized form, material mainly drawn from the decisions of the Court of Session. If he is often clearer than Stair, however, this is because of his use of the civil law.

Bankton distinguishes between dispositions of real rights and assignations

---

[166] Stair, III, 1, 7, 9 and 45.   [167] Stair, III, 1, 8. As to tacks see III, 1, 16.
[168] *Halkerton* v. *Falconer* (1628) Mor 765. Cf. above n. 28.
[169] Stair, III, 1, 11. And see *Begg* v. *Begg* (1665) Mor 6304.   [170] Stair, III, 1, 13 and 40.
[171] Stair, III, 1, 20.   [172] Stair, I, 10, 16; III, 1, 23. Cf. above n. 129.
[173] Stair, III, 1, 43. It will be noted that there is no mention of the theory of procurator *in rem suam*.   [174] Stair, III, 1, 44.
[175] *Davidson* v. *Balcanqual* (1629) Mor 2773, discussed at III, 1, 44.   [176] Stair, III, 1, 46.
[177] The subtitle of the book.

of personal rights.[178] Assignations were either by the deeds of the parties or by the decree of the judge; and the former could be voluntary or necessary.[179] All persons were able to grant or receive voluntary assignations.[180] An assignation must be intimated to the debtor 'which regularly ought to be done, by causing read it to him, and thereon protesting, that the debtor may not pay the debt to any other, upon which he must take instruments, in the hands of a notary, before two witnesses, who must sign the instrument when extended by the notary'.[181] Other methods were also recognized. It was sufficient intimation to raise an action against the debtor or do diligence by horning. The debtor's written acknowledgement was also sufficient, as was his consent to the assignation, and a promise to pay or the beginning of payment. But the debtor's private knowledge did not suffice.[182]

Sometimes intimation was not required at all: in registered assignations of reversions, judicial assignations, and in the legal assignation effected by marriage. The assignation of a tack was completed by possession, not intimation. But intimation was always needed to prevent *bona fide* payment to the cedent, for intimation not only completed assignation (in the usual case) but put the debtor in *mala fide*.[183]

In a competition, a second assignation was preferred if it was for valuable consideration and intimated first. The same was true for an arrestment or, in case of the cedent's death, if another person confirmed to the debt as executor-creditor of the deceased. Such acts, being authoritative or judicial, needed no intimation.[184] But if the second assignation was gratuitous, the first was preferred even if that was also gratuitous.[185]

Collateral securities passed with the assignation.[186] And all exceptions against the cedent were available also against the assignee, '*qui utitur iure auctoris*'.[187] Under reference to D. 50.17.175(4).1, Bankton adds: 'and in this respect the rule in the civil law, *Non debeo melioris conditionis esse quam autor meus* . . . takes place'.

So far as land was concerned, only personal rights (i.e. rights not yet made real by infeftment) could be transferred by assignation. Yet assignations of this sort were not perfected by intimation, for the assignee's right required infeftment according to the feudal law.[188] But if there were two assignations and no infeftment had followed, the first was preferable, the rule being *prior tempore potior jure* and the second assignation being 'stellionate' in terms of the civil law.[189]

Reversions were in principle unassignable, unless with the clause 'to assignees'. Bankton, however, seeks to avoid this result by saying that

---

[178] Bankton, III, 1, 1. [179] Bankton, III, 1, 3. [180] Bankton, III, 1, 4 and 5.
[181] Bankton, III, 1, 6. [182] Bankton, III, 1, 12–14. [183] Bankton, III, 1, 16.
[184] Bankton, III, 1, 6. [185] Bankton, III, 1, 8. [186] Bankton, III, 1, 7.
[187] Bankton, III, 1, 8. [188] Bankton, III, 1, 9.
[189] Bankton, III, 1, 9, with reference to the act of 1540 c. 23 (APS, II, 375) Cf. D. 47.20.

reversions were nonetheless assignable unless it appeared from the tenor of the deed that they were intended to be personal.[190] Sometimes all assignations were excluded, expressly or implicitly, by the terms of the original contract.[191] In rights constituted by infeftment, the mails, duties, or rents were assignable for as long as the right to the lands remained with the cedent.[192] For liferents only the power to receive profits could be assigned.[193]

2. Erskine[194]

As we have seen, the doctrine of assignation was based primarily on the decisions of the Court of Session, guided, to some extent, by the civil law. By the middle of the eighteenth century the doctrine had attained a new maturity,[195] and Erskine's *Institute of the Law of Scotland* (1773) may be taken as representative of the refinement and systematization of the law.

By assignation, Erskine writes, was to be understood a written deed of conveyance by the proprietor to another of any subject not properly feudal. Even heritable rights, when they were not perfected by sasine or did not require sasine, could be assigned.[196] An assignation could be in trust,[197] a point not mentioned by earlier writers.

Erskine's account of the history of assignation[198] departs from the story told by some other writers. According to Erskine, all rights were originally intransmissible unless they contained the express clause 'to assignees'. The procurator *in rem suam* device was an attempt to circumvent this difficulty, but was used even in cases where assignation was permissible. It seems, therefore, that the clause 'to assignees' did not affect the basis of transmissibility, and that an assignee was always a procurator *in rem suam* and not a true creditor. Later, as Erskine notes, all rights came to be viewed as fully transmissible, by proper conveyance, with the exception of conjugal rights, parental rights, liferents (only the profits being transmissible[199]), alimentary rights, and rights involving *delectus personae*.

Intimation or some equivalent was necessary both to prevent the debtor from making payment to the cedent and in order to complete the assignation in a competition between two assignees.[200] A formal intimation was attested by a notary, but less would do. Less formal methods of intimation included: an action, a charge on letters of horning, a citation upon a diligence, and the debtor's promise to pay or his payment of interest.[201] While the debtor's private knowledge did not amount to intimation, Erskine's view was that it put him in *mala fide* to pay the cedent.[202] Erskine's authority is *Leith* v.

---

[190] Bankton, III, 1, 19.
[191] Bankton, III, 1, 20; MacQueen (n. 2), § 860.
[192] Bankton, III, 1, 23.
[193] Bankton, III, 1, 24. Cf. above n. 152.
[194] Walker (n. 28), 352.
[195] See Walker (n. 28), 771.
[196] Erskine, III, 5, 1.
[197] Erskine, III, 5, 8.
[198] Erskine, III, 5, 2.
[199] Cf. above nn. 152, 193.
[200] Erskine, III, 5, 3.
[201] Erskine, III, 5, 4 and 5.
[202] Erskine, III, 5, 5.

Garden (1703).[203] But, as Erskine's editor was later to point out, earlier cases had been less inclined to give effect to private knowledge,[204] and this tendency was confirmed by *Dickson* v. *Trotter*,[205] decided shortly after the publication of Erskine's work.

An assignation of rents was not valid in a competition with creditors, if the cedent remained in possession, but was rather considered to be collusive, for the cedent's own benefit.[206]

Some assignations did not require intimation: bills of exchange, banknotes, reversions (which must however be recorded in the register of reversions), and rights to land, which followed the rules of feudal law.[207] Similarly, intimation was not required for legal or judicial assignation.[208]

Since the cedent continued as creditor until the assignation was intimated, all exceptions competent to the debtor against the cedent (e.g. compensation or payment) affected the assignee also.[209] No creditor could put his debtor in a worse position than before[210] or—to put the matter the other way round— no assignee could be in a better position than his cedent: *assignatus utitur jure auctoris*. Even the bona fide purchaser was not protected. That a justification for this rule was the principle that the assignee was only procurator *in rem suam*[211] serves to emphasize once again the endurance of a doctrine taken originally by Stair from Roman law. This is all the more surprising in view of the fact that Stair himself conceded that assignation was acknowledged by custom;[212] and indeed there seem no rules accepted into Scots law which depend on the idea of the assignee as procurator, as was shown above with Stair.

3. Kames

Kames devotes the second article of his *Elucidations Respecting the Common and Statute Law of Scotland* (1777) to the subject of 'What obligations are effectually conveyed by assignment'. Like Stair, Kames records the theory of the intransmissibility of rights and the invention of the procurator *in rem suam*. But Kames confines this idea to money obligations. An obligation *ad factum praestandum* involved *delectus personae*[213] and could not usually be transmitted. Tacks and reversions, for example, were *stricti juris* and could not be assigned unless the assignee were named in the deed. Kames disputes Stair's view[214] that liferent-tacks can be assigned even without assignees being

---

[203] *Leith* v. *Garden* (1703) Mor 865.
[204] See the eighth and final edition, edited by James Badenach Nicolson (1871). The cases were *Drummond* v. *Muschet* (1492) Mor 843 (see above, text accompanying n. 44) and *Westraw* v. *Williamson & Carmichael* (1626) Mor 859 (see above, text accompanying n. 57).
[205] (1776) Mor 873. [206] Erskine, III, 5, 5. [207] Erskine, III, 5, 6.
[208] Erskine, III, 5, 7. [209] Erskine, III, 5, 9. [210] Erskine, III, 5, 10.
[211] Erskine, III, 5, 8 and 10. [212] Stair, III, 1, 3. [213] Cf. MacQueen (n. 2), § 859.
[214] Stair, II, 9, 26.

named in the deed. In particular Kames sees no reason to deduce from the Leases Act 1449, which secured tacks against the purchaser of the land, that tacks were other than personal rights. They could not, therefore, be transferred in the same manner as real rights.

VI. THE NINETEENTH CENTURY: GEORGE JOSEPH BELL

George Joseph Bell published his *Commentaries on the Law of Scotland* in 1800–4,[215] and his *Principles of the Law of Scotland* in 1829. Both ran to a number of editions.[216] Bell's approach to assignation is similar to that adopted by Stair and his successors. But it comes as no surprise to find that the older decisions of the Court of Session begin to give way, in successive editions of Bell's work, to decisions of the late eighteenth or nineteenth centuries.[217] The growing importance of legislation is also to be observed, though the important Transmission of Moveable Property (Scotland) Act was not passed until 1862, almost twenty years after Bell's death.

The historical origins of assignation lay, for Bell, in bonds in blank and mandates *in rem suam*.[218] But in modern times the assignation substituted the assignee in the cedent's place.[219] *Delectus personae* limited the creditor's power to assign in the case of leases and partnerships. A future debt could not be assigned. With reference to Erskine[220] Bell explains that 'Assignation, as a sale of the debt, implies warrandice . . . that the debt is due; and the title to assign good. The cedent is not, without special stipulation, held to warrant the solvency of the debtor.'[221] Bell underlines that intimation had two distinct aims, namely the interruption of *bona fides* on the part of the debtor, and the completion of the transference giving preference in a competition.[222] It was for the assignee[223] to intimate, usually in the presence of a notary and witnesses.[224] But there were alternatives to formal intimation, for example judicial notice, an action of mails and duties, having the debtor as party to the assignation, written acknowledgement by the debtor (but not a letter *to* the debtor), the debtor's written promise to pay, partial payment or payment of interest.[225] Mere private knowledge did not count as intimation in a com-

---

[215] The first edition was called *Treatise on the Law of Bankruptcy in Scotland*. By the second edition of 1810 this had become *Commentaries on the Law of Scotland in Relation to Mercantile and Maritime Law, Moveable and Heritable Rights and Bankruptcy*.

[216] Bell died in 1843. The last (7th) edition of the *Commentaries* (edited by Lord McLaren) was published in 1870, and the last (10th) edition of the *Principles* in 1899 (edited by Sheriff William Guthrie). [217] e.g. Bell, *Commentaries*, II, 15, n. 7.

[218] Bell, *Principles*, § 1459; *Commentaries*, II, 15. [219] Bell, *Principles*, § 1467.

[220] Erskine, II, 3, 25. [221] Bell, *Principles*, § 1469. [222] Bell, *Principles*, § 1462.

[223] Bell here takes no account of *A* v. *B* (1540) Mor 843, where intimation by the cedent was held to be sufficient. [224] Bell, *Principles*, § 1463.

[225] Bell, *Principles*, § 1465; *Commentaries*, II, 16.

petition between assignees, though such knowledge was a sufficient bar to paying the cedent.[226] Some assignations required no intimation: the conveyance to a trustee in sequestration, judicial assignations, and marriage as an assignation to the husband of rights falling under the *jus mariti*.[227] Though the general rule was *assignatus utitur jure auctoris*, exceptions grounded on latent trusts in favour of third parties, though pleadable against the cedent and his creditors, were not effectual against onerous and bona fide assignees.[228]

Much of this was, of course, standard fare. But there were always new situations which required to be decided. An example, noted by Bell in his *Commentaries*,[229] was *Bedwells & Yates* v. *Tod*,[230] where it was held that a legacy was not capable of assignation during the testator's life.

VII. SOME FINAL REMARKS

The tenacity of the theory of mandate and procurator *in rem suam* is a matter of surprise, and undoubtedly caused some confusion in the development of the law.[231] Theoretical uncertainty also affected moveables, at least from time to time. Erskine, for example, did not distinguish properly between the disposition of corporeal moveables and the assignation of rights to moveables under a contract. Yet the property in corporeal moveables passed only on delivery.[232]

Lawyers were sometimes slow to acknowledge the difference between an agreement to transfer and the transfer itself.[233] Before transfer the (future) assignee has an enforceable contract with the cedent but no claim against the debtor. Another question left open was whether a debtor can question the validity of an assignation.[234] If the act of assignation is itself void, the assignee has no claim; and the same is true if the underlying contract, containing the promise to assign, is void also.[235]

The law of assignation was already well settled by the time of Stair, and little of a fundamental nature has changed since then. But in modern times there has been both development and clarification.[236]

---

[226] Bell, *Principles*, § 1465, founding on *Leith* v. *Garden* (1703) Mor 865.
[227] Bell, *Principles*, § 1466.
[228] Bell, *Principles*, § 1468. This was the result of the decision of the House of Lords in the celebrated case of *Redfearn* v. *Somervail* 22 Nov. 1805 FC rev. (1813) 1 Dow 50, 5 Pat App. 707.
[229] Bell, *Commentaries*, II, 16, n. 4.   [230] 2 Dec. 1819 FC.
[231] W. W. McBryde, *The Law of Contract in Scotland* (1987), paras. 17-71, 17-94.
[232] McBryde (n. 231), para. 17-14.   [233] McBryde (n. 231), para. 17-56.
[234] McBryde (n. 231), para. 17-96.   [235] Balfour, *Practicks*, 169. Cf. above n. 85.
[236] Gloag/Henderson (n. 46), ch. 38.

11

Water Law Regimes

NIALL WHITTY

> Whisky is for drinking, but water is for fighting over.
> Mark Twain

I. INTRODUCTION

The water resources of a nation are too important to be regulated solely by the rights of individual citizens under private law. Each legal system must therefore strike its own balance between public and private water rights. In Roman law, reflecting the relative aridity of Mediterranean countries, almost all rivers were public and the public interest in the use of rivers was protected by public law interdicts. Under the common law of Scotland, 'a land of liberal rainfall, of mosses rich in springs, and of perennial rivers',[1] private rivers and private riparian and littoral rights are more extensive than in Roman law.[2]

The development of the Scots law of water rights broadly follows the familiar three-stage pattern found in areas throughout Scots law: a first medieval reception of English (Glanvillian) law, followed by a reception of Roman law as developed in the European *jus commune*, followed by a second reception of English law beginning in the late eighteenth century. In the domain of water rights, doctrinal history can explain the taxonomic and semantic difficulties of the modern Scots law, a factor adding spice to the more truly historical task of understanding the universal and local factors[3] which have influenced its development.

---

[1] J. Ferguson, *The Law of Water and Water Rights in Scotland* (1907), 1 (the only Scottish monograph).

[2] The public interest in water resources is now protected by statutory codes more than by common law categories: see VIII below.

[3] e.g. important developments in economic history (such as the industrial revolution with its impact on water-power; and the improvement of drainage in the agricultural revolution) and social history (the pressure for urban improvement and the rise of the public health movement focusing on clean water supply and adequate sewerage); together with relatively constant elements like climate and topography.

1. Water rights and the influence of medieval English law

The evolution of the English law on water rights is largely subsumed within the history of nuisance which is mainly the story of two distinct, albeit intersecting, lines of development—one leading from the feudal wrong of purpresture to the modern crime and tort of public nuisance and the other (concerning interference with private rights) linking the forms of action for nuisance (including the writ of novel disseisin and the assize of nuisance) with the modern tort of private nuisance.[4] In medieval Scots law, purpresture (or purprision) was accepted as a remedy protecting water rights, but it is less clear that the brieve of novel dissasine played that role. If not, the reason would be one of those accidents of timing which have been so influential in the history of European legal science.[5] The use of purpresture to prevent diversion of a river is treated in Glanvill, who influenced Scots law.[6] The use of the English writ of novel disseisin (parent of the Scottish brieve) for that purpose, though contemporaneous with Glanvill, is only hinted at in Glanvill and did not receive detailed treatment in England till later in Bracton, Britton, and Fleta,[7] who did not influence medieval Scots law.

2. Glanvill, *Regiam Majestatem*, and purpresture

In the 1180s, Glanvill said that in English law the wrong of purpresture is committed 'quando aliquid super dominum regem iniuste occupatur, ut in dominicis regiis, vel in viis publicis astopatis, vel aquis publicis trestornatis a recto cursu'.[8] This text was adopted by *Regiam Majestatem*, with the

---

[4] C. H. S. Fifoot, *History and Sources of the Common Law* (1949), chs. 1 and 5; J. H. Baker, *An Introduction to English Legal History* (3rd edn., 1990), ch. 20; P. H. Winfield, 'Nuisance as a Tort', (1931) 4 *CLJ* 189; idem, *Select Legal Essays* (1952), 113; F. H. Newark, 'The Boundaries of Nuisance', (1949) 65 *LQR* 480; J. Loengard, 'The Assize of Nuisance: Origins of an Action at Common Law', (1978) 37 *CLJ* 144. Specifically on the early history of English water law, see E. F. Murphy, 'English Water Law Doctrines before 1400', (1957) 1 *AJLH* 103; T. E. Lauer, 'The Common Law Background of the Riparian Doctrine', (1963) 28 *Miss LR* 60. In addition to public and private nuisance, English law for long recognized a third category, viz. 'common nuisance'. See Coke, *Institutes*, vol. 2, 406: 'Public is that which is a nuisance to the whole realm; common is that which is to the common nuisance of all passing by; private is that which is to a house or mill ...'. The distinction between 'public' and 'common' nuisances disappeared in the late 19th century: see E. W. Garrett, *The Law of Nuisances* (3rd edn., 1908), 1.

[5] The role of chance and chronological accident is a main theme in R. C. van Caenegem, *The Birth of the English Common Law* (2nd edn., 1988). [6] See next paragraph.

[7] Lauer, (1963) 28 *Miss LR* 60.

[8] G. D. G. Hall (ed.), *Tractatus de Legibus et Consuetudinibus Regni Anglie qui Glanvilla Vocatur* (1965), IX, 11: 'when there is unjustifiable encroachment on the property of the lord king: for example, in the royal demesnes, or by obstructing public ways or diverting public watercourses ...' (tr. G. D. G. Hall).

modification that the words after 'dominicis regis' became: 'in viis publicis astopatis, vel in aliquibus passagiis sicut in aquis distornatis a recto cursu'[9] subsequently (about 1579) translated by Balfour as: 'in stopping of the common gaittis, or of ony passages, or in turning water fra the richt course'.[10]

In Scots law, purpresture was the feudal delict committed by a person encroaching on the land or other heritable rights of his feudal superior, whether the king or subject superior, or on public places under the protection of the king.[11] Purpresture was part of Scots law from the thirteenth century.[12] There was a retourable brieve requiring an inquest on whether a purpresture had been committed against the king's patrimony,[13] but subject superiors of baronial rank could competently raise an action for forfeiture in their own court without a brieve.[14] It is understood that an actual case of purpresture by diversion of water has not, or not yet, been traced.[15]

After the reception of the *jus commune*, which characterized navigable rivers as *inter regalia*[16] and therefore not only subject to the control and protection of the Crown but also, as Craig pointed out,[17] within the patrimony of the Crown, the need arose to reconcile this theory with the role of purpresture. Could a purpresture against the king be committed by a stranger as well as a royal vassal and thus differ from a purpresture against a subject feudal superior? Craig said there was really only one kind of purpresture, namely, a vassal's appropriation of lands or rights belonging to his superior.[18] It followed that an invasion of Crown rights in navigable rivers was not strictly speaking a purpresture unless committed by a vassal of the king. Moreover, since navigable rivers as *inter regalia* were part of the Crown patrimony, they were in Craig's view subject to the same rules as any other part of that patrimony.[19] So he and later institutional writers considered them in that light.[20]

Until the late sixteenth century, purpresture could also denote a delict between neighbours.[21] This usage was disapproved by Stair and Bankton who

---

[9] *Regiam Majestatem*, II, 74 (now generally reckoned to date from the early 14th century). The Scottish version does not qualify 'water' with the adjective 'public' ('*publicis*'), and changes '*trestornatis*' to '*distornatis*' both of which refer to diversion of water from its proper course (*a recto cursu*).   [10] Balfour, *Practicks*, 442.

[11] On the medieval history of purpresture in Scotland, the controlling study is H. L. MacQueen, *Common Law & Feudal Society in Medieval Scotland* (1993), 83, 118–20. Also useful is I. D. Willock, *The Origins and Development of the Jury in Scotland* (1966), 131 sq. The later history can be traced through Balfour, *Practicks*, 442; Skene, *De Verborum Significatione* (1597), s.v. 'purpresture'; Hope, *Practicks*, III, 7, 14; V, 3, 1 and 7; Craig, I, 16, 10; III, 5, 6–10; Stair, II, 11, 30; Bankton, II, 11, 26; Kames, *Statute Law of Scotland Abridged* (1769), s.v. 'purprision'; Erskine, II, 5, 52; Bell, *Principles*, § 730.   [12] MacQueen (n. 11), 118–20.

[13] MacQueen (n. 11), 118; H. McKechnie, *Judicial Process upon Brieves, 1219–1532* (23rd David Murray Lecture) (1956), 22.   [14] MacQueen (n. 11), 119.

[15] McKechnie (n. 13), 14 remarked that he had not found a single brieve of purpresture at any date. Most purprestures related to encroachments on the king's highway.

[16] See II and IV.1.c below.   [17] Craig, III, 5, 8.   [18] Ibid.

[19] Ibid.   [20] See text accompanying nn. 61–3 below.

[21] MacQueen (n. 11), 119 sq.; *Regiam Majestatem*, II, 74; Balfour, *Practicks*, 443.

followed Craig in describing purpresture restrictively as a purely feudal delict which could only be committed by a vassal against a superior, and characterized a delict between neighbours as molestation.[22] In this way, the development of purpresture, as the Anglo-Norman root of a remedy of public nuisance protecting the public use of public rivers, was stultified by its characterization as a feudal delict and what took its place was not a remedy or actional package on the medieval pattern but a rule of law derived from the *jus commune* that navigable rivers are *inter regalia*. In 1686, Mackenzie remarked that '*purpresture* is much in desuetude'[23] and Erskine said it had 'long fallen into disuse'.[24] In its role as an action between neighbours, it had been superseded[25] by the brieve of perambulation, or by the action of molestation or of declarator of property.[26] One judge sought to resurrect the concept of purpresture in the 1920s,[27] but unsuccessfully.

3. The possessory brieves of novel dissasine and *de aqueductu*

There is some doubt whether in Scots law the brieve of novel dissasine operated as a remedy against the diversion of mill lades and other watercourses.[28] From soon after its introduction in 1166, the English assize of novel disseisin was used for that purpose,[29] though the reference to this in Glanvill is oblique. Following Glanvill, *Regiam Majestatem*, II, 74 provided that purpresture was available after the time limit for novel dissasine had expired thereby obliquely implying that, like purpresture, novel dissasine lay in respect of diversion of watercourses. Willock states that there is no evidence of the imposition of such time limits in Scotland and suggests that novel dissasine and purpresture 'were in Scotland straight alternatives, as far as superiors were

---

[22] Craig, III, 5, 7; Stair, II, 11, 30: purpresture 'is thought to be incurred by encroachment upon the highways, and public rivers, as belonging to the King; but it could be inferred against no other than his vassal . . .'; Bankton, II, 11, 30; also II, 7, 27. Erskine, II, 6, 17, after stating that the Roman *res publica* became *inter regalia* after the introduction of the feus, continues: 'From hence, the narrowing of a highway, or altering the course of a river, is said by our most ancient law to infer the crime of purpresture', citing *Regiam Majestatem*, II, 74, 1. But at II, 5, 52 Erskine describes purpresture, as a feudal delinquency.

[23] Sir George Mackenzie, *Observations on the Acts of Parliament* (1686), 85 commenting on an act of the Lords Auditors recorded as APS, II, 141 (23 Mar. 1481); 6 Aug. 1477, 12mo, c. 80. Mackenzie (ibid.) remarked that purpresture was 'not absolutely in desuetude' because of the 'Act anent purprision in the King's commonties',—1600, APS, IV, 228 (c. 13); 12mo, c. 5.

[24] Erskine, II, 5, 52.   [25] Cf. Bell, *Principles*, § 730 ('purpresture . . . now superseded').

[26] Cf. Mackenzie (n. 23); Stair, II, 11, 30: purpresture 'now belongs only to the jurisdiction of the Lords of Session'; cf. Bankton, II, 11, 30 conceding jurisdiction in perambulation and molestation to the sheriff.

[27] To denote the law prohibiting the appropriation of public rights for private use. See dicta of Lord President Clyde in *Glasgow Corporation v. Barclay, Curle & Co. Ltd* 1922 SC 413 at 427; *Slater v. McLellan* 1924 SC 854 at 858. These cases did not involve watercourses.

[28] The issue is treated with ability in MacQueen (n. 11), 158–61.

[29] D. W. Sutherland, *The Assize of Novel Disseisin* (1973), 63, 216 sq.; Loengard, (1978) 37 CLJ 144, both cited by MacQueen (n. 11), 160 at n. 117.

concerned'.[30] Consistently with this view, MacQueen suggests that it would be surprising if the Scottish brieve of novel dissasine was of lesser scope than the English writ.[31]

By a statute of 1434 a new possessory, pleadable brieve of *de aqueductu* or watergang was introduced[32] which, after narrating the pursuer's complaint that he had been molested unlawfully in possession of his mill lade, directed the court (sheriff or justiciar) to restore the pursuer to his possession if the complaint were found proven. The purpose of the 1434 act, MacQueen suggests, may have been to make the procedures of novel dissasine more readily available in watergang cases by allowing the process in the sheriff court as well as the justice ayre.[33] This is possible though it does not explain why the act proceeded by introducing a new brieve rather than by merely amending the rules on novel dissasine.

The new brieve *de aqueductu*, like novel dissasine, was possessory in the sense that it restored the *status quo ante* and regulated use *ad interim* without prejudice to the final resolution in an appropriate forum of the rights of the parties under the common law.[34] On the basis of several cases in the late fifteenth century involving the use of the brieve *de aqueductu*,[35] MacQueen suggests 'that the typical scenario was a struggle between neighbouring lords where an upstream proprietor had made adjustments to the watercourse in order to increase the power of his mill, and had thereby adversely affected the power downstream at his neighbour's mill; or it was a battle over the profits of the mill'.[36]

Although the statutory brieve *de aqueductu* may have outlived novel dissasine,[37] it was not one of the seven classical styles of brieve which lasted into the institutional period.[38] It seems to have fallen into disuse along with the other contentious brieves which were superseded by the signeted summons in the sixteenth century.[39]

---

[30] Willock (n. 11), 132.   [31] MacQueen (n. 11), 160.

[32] APS (1434), II, 22 (c. 2); on which see McKechnie (n. 13), 19 sq.; and MacQueen (n. 11), 158–61.   [33] MacQueen (n. 11), 160.

[34] The brieve expressly saved the defender's title to pursue his rights (if any) 'in forma juris communis vel per brevia de capella nostra, vel alias prout secundum leges regni' ('in the form of the common law, or by brieve of our chapel, or in other ways in accordance with the laws of the kingdom'): McKechnie (n. 13), 20; MacQueen (n. 11), 158. There is a style of brieve *de aqueductu* in G. Donaldson (ed.), *St. Andrews Formulare 1514–1546*, vol. 1, Stair Society, vol. 7 (1942), 254, style (j).   [35] MacQueen (n. 11), 159–61.

[36] Ibid. 161.

[37] MacQueen (n. 11), 162 points out that there is a style of brieve *de aqueductu* in the *St. Andrews Formulare 1514–1546* (n. 34) but not a style of novel dissasine.

[38] McKechnie (n. 13), 8. The seven classical brieves are described in Stair, IV, 3, 5–18.

[39] Though referred to by Balfour, the brieve *de aqueductu* was not mentioned by Craig or the later institutional writers.

4. The end of medieval English influence

The desuetude of the brieve of novel dissasine, together with the waning of purpresture, in the sixteenth century marked the end of the medieval English influence on Scots law generally, and the law on water rights in particular, until the second reception of English law beginning in the eighteenth century. The brieve system was borrowed from the Anglo-Norman law as it existed up to and including Henry II's reign, but influence from any later period of English law seems to have been slight. The brieve *de aqueductu* for example was not borrowed from England but was invented by statute, indigenous and apparently short-lived. Moreover from the thirteenth century, English law grew away from Glanvill's simple forms of action, and became 'an island in the Romanist sea ... an anomaly, a freak in the history of western civilisation'.[40] In Scotland, the brieve system was both a form of process or procedure and a remedy-based system of private law though not comprehensive. As a contentious procedure, it was replaced in the sixteenth century by a Romano-canonical replication procedure, originated by a form of summons which was readily adaptable to an infinite variety of different claims.[41] This form of process no doubt had its defects but it was an effective vehicle for developing Scots law, as a rights-based rather than a remedy-based system, on the foundation of the Romanist *jus commune* which became the most formative external influence on Scottish water law.

It seems that it was not till 1793, in the second reception of English law, that Bracton on novel disseisin, in its application to rivers, was first cited in a Scottish case.[42] In the case of water law regimes,—notably the seabed and the foreshore; lochs and stanks; and casual waters[43]—this study has not found any trace of Southron influence before the second reception of English law.[44] The seabed and foreshore regimes were not mentioned in Glanvill or *Regiam Majestatem*[45] and the treatment in subsequent English authorities such as Britton[46] came too late to influence the Scots law.

---

[40] Van Caenegem (n. 5), 105.

[41] There is no adequate modern history of Scottish civil procedure, but see D. Maxwell, 'Civil Procedure', in G. C. H. Paton (ed.), *An Introduction to Scottish Legal History*, Stair Society, vol. 20 (1958), ch. 32, 413 sqq. The first vernacular treatises are: Sir John Skene, *Ane Short Form of Proces* (1609, published with Skene's edition of *Regiam Majestatem*); P. J. Hamilton-Grierson (ed.), *Habakkuk Bisset's Rolment of Courtis* (3 vols., 1920–6), compiled about 1622.

[42] See *Hamilton v. Edington* (1793) Mor 12824 at 12825: see n. 349 below.

[43] See III, V, and VI below respectively.   [44] See IX below.

[45] See the speech of Mr Serjeant Merewether of 1849, in R. L. Loveland (ed.), *Hall's Essay on the Rights of the Crown and the Privileges of the Subject in the Sea Shores of the Realm* (2nd edn., 1875), lxix at lxxv.   [46] Ibid., lxxvii–lxxix.

5. The influence of the *jus commune*: the *regalia* and the classification of real rights

In Roman law, things which could not be the object of private rights (*res extra commercium*; *res extra nostrum patrimonium*) and were *humani juris*[47] were (*a*) things open for use by all people—*res communes omnium*—such as the air (*aer*), flowing water (*aqua profluens*), the sea (*mare*), and the seashore (*litus maris*);[48] and (*b*) *res publicae* which were things belonging to the Roman people. These included rivers (*flumina*) and river-banks (*ripae*), though apparently not lakes.[49] Justinian's *Institutes* did not distinguish very clearly between *res communes omnium* and *res publicae*.[50] Things capable of private ownership (*res in commercio*) might in fact be owned by nobody (*res nullius*). The rights exercisable by the public in *res publicae* and *res communes omnium* included (in Van der Vyver's description[51]) 'the entitlement to fish or cast a net in the sea[52] and to fish in ports and rivers;[53] the entitlement to navigate a stream, to bring a boat to land on the river bank, to fasten ropes to trees growing thereon, to dry nets and for that purpose to draw them up from the sea and to place cargo on the river-banks;[54] the entitlement to erect huts on the sea-shore in which the person concerned might take shelter[55] and to haul his nets from the sea on to the sea-shore and to dry them there'.[56]

After the Reception, '[a]t least as far as immovable property was concerned, the idea of things being without an owner did not find favour in Germanic law'.[57] Things which were in Roman law *res publicae*, and those elements of the *res communes omnium* which were physically capable of ownership such as rivers and the seashore (i.e. excluding the open seas and running water), were treated as *inter regalia*, a concept which denoted imperial rights and prerogatives within the Holy Roman Empire. A list of the *regalia* was enacted in the imperial *Constitutio de Regalibus* of 1158[58] and copied in the *Libri Feudorum* of the late twelfth century,[59] whence

---

[47] As distinct from *res divini iuris* viz. *res sacrae*; *res religiosae*; and *res sanctae*. These form a category of *res extra commercium*.

[48] Inst. 2, 1, 1; Marc. D. 1, 8, 2, 1; Ulp. D. 47, 10, 13, 7.

[49] At any rate lakes (*lacus*) are not mentioned in the texts on *res publicae*.

[50] See e.g. Inst. 2, 1, 2: describing rivers and ports as *res publica* and the right of fishing therein as common to all—*omnibus commune*.

[51] J. D. van der Vyver, 'The Étatisation of Public Property', in D. P. Visser (ed.), *Essays on the History of Law* (1989), 261, 265 sq. Footnotes in original and renumbered.

[52] Ulp. D. 47, 10, 13, 7.   [53] Inst. 2, 1, 2.   [54] Inst. 2, 1, 4; Gai. D. 1, 8, 5 pr.

[55] Inst. 2, 1, 5; Gai. D. 1, 8, 5, 1.

[56] Inst. 2, 1, 5.   [57] Van der Vyver (n. 51), 266.

[58] Promulgated by the Emperor Frederick I (Barbarossa) at the Imperial Diet of Roncaglia of that year. The text was sometimes printed as a *decima collatio Novellarum* in older editions of the *Corpus Juris Civilis* (Van der Vyver (n. 51), 267 at n. 53). For the background, see H. J. Berman, *Law and Revolution: The Formation of the Western Legal Tradition* (1983), 490.

[59] The list is set out in *Libri Feudorum*, 2, 56, from which it was copied by Craig, I, 16, 8. Craig (ibid.) was uncertain as to its ultimate derivation but thought it 'not unlikely' that it was copied

the doctrine of the *regalia* entered Scots law at some point as yet unchronicled.[60]

Stair, Bankton, and Erskine treated of the *regalia* in two different places, one inspired mainly by Roman law, and the other mainly by feudal law. The first was their discussion of the classification of property rights influenced by Inst. 2, 1 and D. 1, 8 (*de rerum divisione et qualitate*).[61] The second was their treatment (possibly following Craig's example[62]) of the parts and pertinents carried by, or excluded from, a feudal conveyance.[63] Stair and Erskine accept implicitly a fourfold classification of property (things) stated expressly by Bankton: 'things ... are either common, publick, belonging to particular persons, or to no person'.[64] A similar fourfold classification of *res humani juris* is found in Grotius.[65]

The first category of *res communes omnium* (or 'commonty') consisted of 'things by nature itself incapable of appropriation, so that they cannot be brought under the power of any one'.[66] These were defined as '[t]hings, the property of which belongs to no person, but the use to all'.[67] It was use (*usus*), not ownership (*dominium*), that was common.[68] The historical interaction of this concept with the development of water law is traced in section III below.

In defining the second category, 'public property', there were minor variations but all writers included the *regalia*. As in the *jus commune*, the *regalia* derived in part from the Roman concepts of *res publica* and (insofar as susceptible to human control) *res communes omnium*.[69] The distinction made by the *jus commune* between the *regalia majora* and *minora* was accepted. The former, being inalienable, were said to 'inhere in the bones of the king',[70] and

from a constitution of Frederick I. While the *regalia* usually were given out in a feudal grant, they exist separately from the feudal system both in Europe (Van der Vyver (n. 51), 270) and Scotland, where they exist on the Udal territory of Orkney and Shetland and are likely to survive the forthcoming statutory abolition of feudal tenure.

[60] Craig, I, 16, 7–47; Stair, II, 1, 5; II, 3, 60; Bankton, I, 3, 4; II, 3, 107–11; Erskine, II, 1, 6; II, 6, 13; Hume, *Lectures*, IV, 237 sqq.; Bell, *Principles*, § 748; J. S. More, *Notes to Stair's Institutions* (1832), cci. For an authoritative treatment of the modern law, see W. M. Gordon, *Scottish Land Law* (2nd edn., 1999), paras. 27-06, 27-07.
[61] Stair, II, 1, 5; Bankton, I, 3, 1; Erskine, II, 1, 5–12.   [62] Craig, I, 16, 43 sq.
[63] Stair, II, 3, 60 sqq.; Bankton, II, 3, 20; II, 3, 86; II, 3, 106–11; Erskine, II, 6, 13–18.
[64] Bankton, I, 3, 1.
[65] Grotius, *Inleydinge tot de Hollandsche Rechtsgeleertheyd*, II, 1, 16; Van der Vyver (n. 51), at 272 sqq.   [66] Erskine, II, 1, 5.
[67] Ibid. See also Stair, II, 1, 5: 'The right of commonty ... which all men have of things which cannot be appropriated'; Bankton, I, 3, 2.   [68] Erskine, II, 1, 5–8.
[69] Bankton, I, 3, 4–9; Erskine, II, 1, 5: 'Other things, though they be of their own nature capable of property, are exempted from commerce in respect of the uses to which they are destined. Of this last kind are, first, *res publicae* of the Romans ... [II, 1, 7] second ... *res universitatis* ... [II, 1, 8] subjects set apart for the service of God' i.e. '*iuris divini*'. Sir John Nisbet of Dirleton, *Doubts and Questions in the Law* (1698), s.v. '*regalia*' 151 quotes Heringius, *De Molendinis* for the view that the *regalia* are not things (*res*) but rights of the king in virtue of his supreme power.
[70] Dirleton (n. 69), 150: 'Majora regalia cohaerere dicuntur Imperatoris ossibus, ut ab eo avelli nequeant' (citing 'Bes. Thes. In Litera K. 3 verbo Kayserliche, P. 450'. This is a reference to

were held by him as *tutor populi* or *parens patriae*,[71] or in 'trust for behoof of his people'.[72] They came to include rights in the sea and seabed, the foreshore,[73] and in the water, bed, and banks of navigable rivers,[74] but not lochs.[75] Whether the alienable *regalia minora* included the foreshore and seabed was disputed and the answer changed over time.

The third category—things capable of appropriation and in private ownership—is the norm and unremarkable.[76]

The fourth category—*res nullius*—is more interesting. Scottish feudal law disapproved of the notion of ownerless land.[77] Bankton explained that things are *res nullius* in a double sense.[78] First, some things are incapable of ownership and not 'the subject of commerce' such as sacred or religious things.[79] Second, 'in an other sense, things are *nullius*, or belong to none, that are not in the property of any, tho' they are capable of being appropriated', such as *inter alia* 'fishes in the sea'.

There was a tendency to confuse or merge *res communis omnium*, and *res publica*.[80] Bankton and to some extent Erskine associated *res communes omnium* and *res nullius* with the original state of nature which they believed existed before the establishment of civil society and the recognition of property rights and which 'obtains still as to parts of the world not yet inhabited, whereof the first occupancy gives a property therein: but, even where property has already taken place, divers things still remain common, as the air, running water, the ocean, and the shore on which it ebbs and flows by the civil law'.[81] Ownership of *res nullius* is acquired by occupation 'according to the state of nature, and rules of civil law of the Romans; the maxim with them being *quod nullius est cedit occupanti*, What is in the property of none belongs to the first seizer or occupant'.[82] However 'by the law of most nations, and particularly with us, this natural liberty is brought under divers regulations', especially as to salmon fishing which is *inter regalia minora*.[83]

Christophorus Besoldus, *Thesaurus Practicus* (1629; 1666 eds.). For the distinction, see Craig, I, 16, 43 sq.; Bankton, II, 3, 20; II, 3, 107; Erskine, II, 6, 13.

[71] Craig, I, 16, 11.   [72] Erskine, II, 6, 17.   [73] See III below.
[74] See IV below.   [75] See V. below.   [76] Cf. Bankton, I, 3, 10.
[77] The maxim *quod nullius est fit domini regis* was applied to immoveable property and to derelinquished or lost moveables presumed to have had a proprietor now unknown: Erskine, II, 1, 11 sq. Further until the early 18th century the maxim '*dominium non potest in pendente*' was thought to apply to heritable property: Stair, III, 5, 50; G. Mackenzie, *Institutions of the Law of Scotland*, II, 1, 3; Bell, *Principles*, §§ 1710 sq., 1951; but cf. Erskine, II, 1, 4; Dirleton (n. 69), s.v. 'Fiar' nos. 9, 10.   [78] Bankton, I, 3, 11.
[79] Ibid.
[80] e.g. Hume, *Lectures*, IV, 238 sq. says that *res publicae* were considered as property of the State *inter alia* 'by reason of their natural condition as refusing complete occupancy'.
[81] Bankton, II, 1, 5; see also Erskine, II, 1, 9.   [82] Bankton, I, 3, 14.
[83] Bankton, I, 3, 15; see also Stair, II, 1, 5 (Fourthly), refers to 'herring-fishings' as well as salmon but this is an unresolved puzzle.

This pre-Enlightenment historical view was consistent with the 'natural jurisprudence' and conjectural history of Adam Smith[84] who observed that running water and the sea, the water of rivers and the navigation of them 'are by nature common to all' because 'they cannot be lessend (*sic*) or impaired by use, nor can anyone be injured by the use of them'.[85] The philosopher, David Hume, remarked that 'whenever any benefit is bestowed by nature in unlimited abundance, we leave it always in common among the whole human race, and make no subdivisions of right and property'.[86]

III. THE SEA, THE SEABED, AND THE FORESHORE

1. The concept of *res communes omnium* in Roman law

In Roman law the category of *res communes omnium* was created by the academic writer Marcian, and not referred to by any other Roman jurist of the classical period.[87] In Monier's view, to classify flowing water (*aqua profluens*) among *res communes* was inaccurate because the water which flows in rivers has the same nature as the rivers themselves i.e. either *res publicae* or *res privatae* as the case may be.[88] It is said that the category was not very useful[89] and did not represent the true position in Roman law.

2. The *res communes* doctrine and the freedom of the seas

After the Reception, however, the concept of *res communes omnium* assumed a new importance. When the Romans characterized the sea, seabed, and seashore (called in legal terminology the foreshore) as *res communes*, they

---

[84] Adam Smith, *Lectures on Jurisprudence* (edn. by R. L. Meek, D. D. Raphael, and P. G. Stein, 1978), 24 sq.

[85] Ibid. 25. He added (ibid. 26) that the sea coast was 'common to the whole community ... but the king had usurped it to himself'. See also ibid. 459 sq. Smith also thought that 'the tyranny of feudal government' had encroached on the rights and liberty of the lower ranks of people to take wild animals and the fish of the sea by reserving the larger or 'royal' fish to the Crown: ibid.

[86] David Hume, *Enquiries Concerning the Human Understanding and Concerning the Principles of Morals* (edn. by L. A. Selby-Bigge, 1777, repr. 1902). In his *Treatise of Human Nature* (1740), book III (Fontana edn. by P. S. Ardal, 1972), 239 sq., Hume referred to 'the general opinion of philosophers and civilians, that the sea is incapable of becoming the property of any nation; and that because it is impossible to take possession of it, or form any distinct relation with it, as may be the foundation of property. Where this reason ceases property immediately takes place.'

[87] See P. Bonfante, *Corso di Diritto Romano* (1926, repr. 1966), vol. 2, 51 sqq.

[88] R. Monier, *Manuel élémentaire de droit romain* (6th edn., 1947), vol. 1, 346.

[89] W. W. Buckland, 'Marcian', in *Studi in onore di Salvatore Riccobono* (1936), vol. 1, 275–83 at 279: 'It overlaps the class of "*res publicae*" and, so far as it covers the same field, it can, without much difficulty, be understood as using the word "*res*" in what may be called its legal sense of asset, or potential asset. But when it deals with such a thing as the air, unsusceptible of appropriation, it seems to use the word "*res*" in the sense of physical thing.'

had in mind immunity from appropriation by private persons, a question of private law. Nevertheless in the *jus commune*, at the dawn of modern public international law, their concept influenced the great juridical debates between European maritime states on freedom of the seas, for it could be seen as providing that states could not appropriate part of the sea so as to exclude other states.[90] Craig characterized the sea as common for navigation purposes but thought that it belonged to the states of the nearest mainland.[91] In Scotland, where the herring fisheries were of great economic importance and herring shoals susceptible to overfishing, there was a tradition from medieval times of excluding foreigners from the fisheries in 'reserved waters' i.e. the firths and bays and an area within sight of the coast known as a 'land kenning'[92] fixed at 14 miles, a unit of distance reflecting the notional range of vision.[93] English fisheries policy had been more liberal and James VI and I extended the restrictive Scottish policy to his new kingdom. In 1609, he issued a proclamation excluding Dutch fishermen from fishing in 'British' waters.[94] Coincidentally, about the same time, Grotius in his *Mare Liberum*[95] affirmed his famous doctrine of freedom of navigation of the seas. Though aimed at the Portuguese, this was thought to endanger King James's fisheries policy and was challenged first by the Scottish professor of civil law William Welwood in two works[96] (which provoked a reply from Grotius[97]) and later by English authors including Selden.[98]

---

[90] See T. W. Fulton, *The Sovereignty of the Seas: An Historical Account of the Claims of England to the Dominion of the British Seas* (1911), 338–77; R. R. Churchill and A. V. Lowe, *The Law of the Sea* (2nd edn., 1988), ch. 4 on the territorial sea.

[91] Craig, I, 15, 13.: 'the princes of the world make a kind of division of the whole ocean among them'. (The translations of Craig in this chapter are Lord Clyde's.)

[92] On the meaning of 'kenning' as a unit of distance, see A. D. M. Forte, '"Kenning be Kenning and Course be Course": Maritime Jurimetrics in Scotland and Northern Europe 1400–1600', (1998) 2 *Edinburgh LR* 56.

[93] Fulton (n. 90), 77, 545. The extent of the land-kenning at 14 miles was the distance expressed in the abortive draft treaty of Union of 1604 (ibid. at 545). It was also 'claimed against other nations by the Privy Council, the Parliament and the King': Fulton, ibid. at 545. The range of vision test was accepted by Stair, II, 1, 5: 'within the views of such shores . . .'. At one time it was adopted as a boundary by other states (Fulton, ibid. at 544 sq.) and by H. Grotius, *Mare Liberum sive de Iure quod Batavis Competit ad Indicana Commercia, Dissertatio* (1608), ch. 5—*The Freedom of the Seas or the Right which Belongs to the Dutch to Take Part in the East Indian Trade* (edn. by J. B. Scott, tr. R. v. D. Magoffin, 1916), 36 sq.—observing that the controversy did not concern 'eo quod e litore conspici potest' (all the expanse of sea which is visible from the shore).

[94] See Fulton (n. 90), Appendix F.   [95] Grotius (n. 93).

[96] W. Welwood, *Abridgement of all Sea-Lawes* (1613), title xxvii, dealing with community of the seas; *idem, De Dominio Maris Ivribusque ad Dominium Praecipve Spectantibus Assertio Brevis et Methodica* (1615). As to the background see J. D. Alsop, 'William Welwood, Anne of Denmark and the Sovereignty of the Sea', (1980) 59 *Scot Hist Rev* 171; J. Cairns, 'Academic Feud, Bloodfeud, and William Welwood: Legal Education in St. Andrews, 1560–1611', (1998) 2 *Edinburgh LR* 255, 279 sq.

[97] H. Grotius, *Defensio Capitis Quinti Maris Liberi Oppugnati a Guillielmo Welwodo*. Grotius conceded that states had sovereignty or jurisdiction and control (*imperium*) without property rights (*dominium*) in coastal waters.

[98] J. Selden, *Mare Clausum: seu De Dominio Maris Libro Duo* (1635).

Water Law Regimes

During the seventeenth century the idea developed in the *jus commune* that while the high seas are free and open to all, coastal waters (nowadays called 'the territorial sea') could be appropriated by the adjacent state which then has sovereignty over them: this dichotomy formed the basis of Bynkershoek's influential treatise, *De Dominio Maris Dissertatio* (1702), and is reflected in Stair's distinction between the ocean (which is *res communis omnium*) and the 'reserved' waters (which may be appropriated).[99] Likewise Bankton and Erskine qualified the Roman *res communes* doctrine expressly by citing the 'British' theory of Selden, *Mare Clausum*.[100]

The width of the territorial sea was long disputed. The vague criteria based on visibility were superseded in the eighteenth century by the 'cannon shot rule' (covering the waters controlled by shore-based cannon) which then developed into the 'three-mile rule'[101] which was accepted in Scotland, England, and elsewhere in the nineteenth century.[102] The idea of *res communes omnium* is kept alive in international conventions on extra-territorial waters.[103]

3. The withering of the concept of *res communes omnium*

Outside the great juridical debates on freedom of the seas, the history of the concept of *res communes omnium* in Scots law is undistinguished.[104] Though adopted with modifications by Craig, Stair, Bankton, and Erskine[105] and

---

[99] Stair, II, 1, 5.

[100] Namely, that 'however incapable the ocean may be of property, yet the seas which wash the coasts of any state are subjects which may be as fitly appropriated to private uses as rivers bays, creeks etc; and that, in fact, our sovereigns are Lords or *domini* of the British seas which surround this island; . . .'; see Bankton, I, 3, 2; Erskine, II, 1, 6. This fails to distinguish clearly between the distinct concepts of sovereignty, ownership, and use.

[101] H. S. K. Kent, 'Historical Origins of the Three Mile Limit', (1954) 48 *AJIL* 537.

[102] e.g. Bell, *Principles*, § 639 ('the sovereign . . . is proprietor of the narrow seas within cannon-shot of the land, and the firths, gulfs and bays around the Kingdom') approved in *Mortensen* v. *Peters* (1906) 8 F (J) 93 at 102 *per* Lord Justice-General Dunedin; cf. § 646 ('the three mile limit'); *Duchess of Sutherland* v. *Watson* (1868) 6 M 199; *Lord Advocate* v. *Clyde Navigation Trs* (1891) 19 R 174 at 177 *per* Lord Kyllachy; *Lord Advocate* v. *Wemyss* (1899) 2 F (HL) 1 at 8 *per* Lord Watson. General international agreement on 12 miles was reached by the Third United Nations Conference on the Law of the Sea of 1973–82 and is embodied in the United Nations Convention on the Law of the Sea (1982), art. 3 and the Territorial Sea Act 1987, s. 1(1).

[103] See e.g. Declaration of Principles governing the Sea-Bed and the Ocean Floor, and the Subsoil thereof beyond the Limits of National Jurisdictions (1970), GA Res. 2749 (XXV); United Nations Convention on the Law of the Sea (1982), art. 1(1) proclaiming the sea-bed and ocean floor to be the 'common heritage of mankind'; Van der Vyver (n. 51), 284–6; Churchill/Lowe (n. 90), 182.

[104] For an example of its stultifying effect in the application of the *immissio* principle in Ulp. D. 8, 5, 8, 5 and 6 to pollution of air by smoke, see *Dewar* v. *Fraser* (1767) Mor 12803, Hailes 177 at 178 *per* Lord Auchinleck: 'If the principle *non licet immittere in alienum* is to apply to air, *which is common to every body*, there can be no drawkiln in Scotland . . .' (emphasis added).

[105] Craig, I, 15, 13–15; Stair, II, 1, 5; II, 3, 69; Bankton, I, 3, 2; II, 1, 5; Erskine, II, 1, 5.

relied on in case law,[106] it was ignored by Kames, Hume, and Bell. It was occasionally founded on by defenders, always unsuccessfully, to support the appropriation theory of riparian rights.[107] While referred to in some textbooks,[108] it has scarcely (if at all) influenced the development of Scottish private law.

4. The foreshore

In Scots law, the foreshore was defined as the shore between the high- and low-water mark of ordinary spring tides[109] and this differed from both Roman law[110] and English law.[111]

In Roman law, since the seabed was *res communes omnium*[112] nobody could be prohibited from going on to it.[113] But the law was confused. Two texts stated that a person could become owner of part of the seashore by building thereon,[114] and another text suggested that the shore was owned by the Roman people i.e. *res publica*[115] as distinct from *res communis*. It is not clear why the seashore was said to be incapable of ownership. In the *jus commune*, the seashore was *inter regalia*[116] though not mentioned in the *Constitutio de Regalibus*.

The first problem confronting Scots law was to resolve the doubt, inherited from Roman law, as to the legal status of the foreshore. It was treated some-

---

[106] e.g. *Town of Craill* v. *Gresill Meldrum* 24 May 1549, reported in Balfour, *Practicks*, 626.
[107] On this theory, see IV.2.c below.
[108] e.g. J. Rankine, *The Law of Land-Ownership in Scotland* (4th edn., 1909), 512 sq.: K. G. C. Reid, 'Public Rights over Waters and Adjacent Dry Land', in K. G. C. Reid (ed.), *The Law of Property in Scotland* (1996), § 514 and K. G. C. Reid, 'Water', ibid. § 274.
[109] See e.g. Erskine, II, 6, 17; Bell, *Principles*, § 641; *Bowie* v. *Marquis of Ailsa* (1887) 14 R 649; dicta cited in *Fisherrow Harbour Commissioners* v. *Musselburgh Real Estate Co. Ltd* (1903) 5 F 387 at 393 sq. *per* Lord Low. There are three categories of tides: '1st. The high spring tides, which are the fluxes of the sea at those tides which happen at the two equinoctials. 2nd. The spring tides, which happen twice every month at the full and change of the moon. 3rd. The neap, or ordinary tides, which happen between the full and change of the moon, twice in the twenty-four hours.' See Loveland (n. 45), 10.
[110] Inst. 2, 1, 3. 'Est autem litus maris, quatenus hibernus fluctus maximus excurrit', translated by Stair, II, 1, 5 as meaning 'so far as the greatest winter tides do run' adding 'which must be understood of ordinary tides, and not of extraordinary spring tides'. Hume, *Lectures*, IV, 255 said that whereas in Roman law 'all was sea shore and *respublica* which the tide at any time covered', in Scots law 'as an heritor on the shore is liable to lose his property, or have it impaired and worn away by the tide, so he is entitled to the benefit, on the other hand of gaining by alluvion or embankment'.
[111] In English law the foreshore is the shore covered by the sea at the average of the medium high tides between the spring and the neap. As to the debate on whether Scots law should copy the English definition of the foreshore, see IX below, text accompanying nn. 524–31.
[112] Inst. 2, 1, 1 and 5.   [113] Ibid.   [114] Marc. D. 1, 8, 6 pr.; Ner. D. 41, 1, 14.
[115] Cels. D. 43, 8, 3 pr.
[116] Van der Vyver (n. 51), 287; J. Voet, *Commentarius ad Pandectas*, I, 8, 9.

times as *res communis*[117] and sometimes as *res publica*[118] though always as *inter regalia*. In the sixteenth century, it was accepted that the Crown could by charter grant a right to gather 'wair of the sea' and seafoods within (or outwith) the floodmark and that any littoral proprietor not 'speciallie infeft within the said flude mark, als weill as without the samin' could not prevent the king or the lieges from gathering them.[119] Stair failed to resolve the ambiguity: he said that certain 'common uses' of the foreshore were common to all nations[120] but then qualified that proposition by affirming that houses and works thereon and minerals and coals therein 'doth remain proper'.[121] In *Magistrates of Culross* v. *Earl of Dundonald*[122] the pursuers argued that the foreshore was as in Roman law 'among things common which belong in property to none'. Lord Monboddo, however, observed: 'By the Roman law, the shore was *res nullius* but this is not modern law.[123] We follow the constitution of the Emperor Frederic I',[124] though the *Constitutio de Regalibus* does not mention the seashore. It was Erskine who was principally responsible for disapplying the notion of *res communes omnium* from the foreshore. Conceding that '[t]he sea shore was also reckoned common by the Roman law',[125] Erskine[126] said that 'it is obvious that by the *jus gentium* the sea shore is not entitled to the appellation of common because it is in its nature as capable of appropriation as any part of the grounds to which it is contiguous; wherefore it is with greater propriety accounted, in other texts of that law, a *res publica*.'[127] On that basis, he included the 'narrow seas' and the seashore among the *regalia maiora* and *minora*.[128] In modern Scots law, the seabed and foreshore 'are not *res communes* as they were by Roman law'.[129]

---

[117] In *Town of Craill* v. *Gresill Meldrum* 24 May 1549, reported in Balfour, *Practicks*, 626, the Court of Session held: 'It is leasum to all our soverane lord's lieges to use and exerce ony industrie within the flude mark of the sea; *quia usus littoris est communis omnium*'.

[118] Craig, I, 15, 15 described the shore as a public place, yet classified among things belonging to all men.

[119] *The King* v. *Laird of Seafield* 29 July 1500, reported in Balfour, *Practicks*, 626; *Town of Craill* v. *Gresill Meldrum* 24 May 1549, reported in Balfour, *Practicks*, 626; Sir John Skene, *De Verborum Significatione* (1597), s.v. 'Wair of the Sea, *alga maris*'.

[120] Stair, II, 1, 5 (Thirdly); see also ibid. (Fifthly).

[121] Stair, II, 1, 5 (Fifthly). He seems to contradict himself somewhat by stating (ibid.) that 'the use of the banks of the sea, or rivers, to cast anchors or lay goods thereon ... are not common to all men, but public to their own people'.

[122] (1769) Mor 12810, Hailes 291 (concerning the interpretation of two competing bounding charters).

[123] Hailes 292. The defenders had argued that though a subject may in some respects be understood as *inter res communes*, yet it may be capable of property, citing Stair, II, 1, 5. The pursuers were successful on another ground.

[124] A reference to the *Constitutio de Regalibus* of 1158 (n. 58).   [125] Citing Inst. 2, 1, 1.

[126] Erskine, II, 1, 6.   [127] Citing Cels. D. 43, 8, 3.

[128] Erskine, II, 1, 6 as read with II, 6, 17.

[129] *Crown Estates Commissioners* v. *Fairlie Yacht Slip Ltd* 1979 SC 156 at 160 *per* Lord Dunpark (Ordinary).

Erskine[130] and Hume[131] treated the foreshore and its products as *inter regalia minora* and therefore as requiring a special or express Crown grant.[132] Hume said that the foreshore 'is not only under a servitude to the public, like the bank of a [navigable] river, but is properly *inter regalia*, and at the disposal of the King, under the provision always that the public service is not interfered with'.[133] In the early nineteenth century, however, the rule developed that the foreshore was not *inter regalia minora* but passed under a Crown grant by implication to a littoral proprietor as part or pertinent of the contiguous lands.[134] Then the Crown, through the Commissioners of Woods and Forests,[135] began to vindicate public rights in the foreshore in 1846[136] and the Crown's own private patrimonial rights against individual littoral proprietors in the 1860s.[137] These included some of the leading landed nobility and lairds who organized themselves into a Foreshore Association and feelings ran high.[138] Erskine's editor said in 1871 that, while the Crown's fiduciary right was established, it was impossible to say whether the weight of authority affirms or negatives the Crown's claim to patrimonial rights to the foreshore.[139]

Finally in a test case in 1873, *Agnew* v. *Lord Advocate*,[140] it was held that on the one hand the foreshore was originally vested in the Crown in the same way as all other land and not as *inter regalia minora*,[141] but that on the other hand the foreshore does not pass by implication: there must be an express Crown grant or prescriptive possession. The Crown's limited victory was

---

[130] Erskine, II, 6, 17.   [131] Hume, *Lectures*, IV, 256–8.

[132] Cf. *Bruce* v. *Rashiehill* (1711) Mor 9342 (pursuer's argument: seagreens being part of foreshore are *inter regalia* and can only be alienated by Crown by special grant; held, seagreens not part of foreshore).

[133] Hume, *Lectures*, IV, 256 sq. See also at 258: 'a trust in His Majesty for the public uses, and not exclusive of a power of disposal in His Majesty'. Reid (n. 108), § 514 cites a different passage from Hume, *Lectures*, IV, namely 238 and 239.

[134] The earlier cases were *Innes* v. *Downie* (1807) Hume 552; *Campbell* v. *Brown* 18 Nov. 1813 FC; *Boucher* v. *Crawford* 30 Nov. 1814 FC; *Macalister* v. *Campbell* (1837) 15 S 490; see also Bell, *Principles*, § 642 (4th edn., 1839): the shore 'is not, as in England held to be the property reserved to the Crown, but presumed to be granted'.

[135] The Crown Lands (Scotland) Act 1833 transferred responsibility for the foreshore from the Scottish Court of Exchequer to the Commissioners.

[136] *Officers of State* v. *Smith* (1846) 8 D 711, affirmed *sub. nom. Smith* v. *Earl of Stair* (1849) 6 Bell App 487.   [137] *Lord Advocate* v. *Maclean of Ardgour* (1866) 2 SLR 25.

[138] See e.g. Anon., 'The Right of the Crown to the Foreshores', (1866) 5 *SLM* 82. In a dispute with the Commissioners of Woods and Forests about the foreshore abutting his estate of Roseneath, the Duke of Argyll 'protested against the practice of attempting to establish by force of accumulated precedents, claims up to that date new in Scotland, which, when resisted, are immediately dropped, lest one conspicuous failure should seriously affect the success of the whole scheme'.

[139] Erskine, II, 6, 17 (8th edn. by J. Badenach Nicholson, 1871), vol. 1, 409 n. (b).

[140] (1873) 11 M 309 approved in *Lord Advocate* v. *Lord Blantyre* (1879) 6 R (HL) 72. For the background see Rankine (n. 108), 274.

[141] Following *Innes* v. *Downie* (1807) Hume 552 *per* Lord President Campbell: 'Property of the land adjacent to an heritor's shore is not a *regale*'.

Pyrrhic: such titles or possession 'could be produced for almost every yard of foreshore in Scotland'.[142] In the modern law, the public rights in the foreshore include 'tacit' rights in connection with navigation and fishing for white fish and certain other 'acquired' rights e.g. for recreation.[143]

Reid presents a different account influenced by insistence on strict usage of the trust concept in Scots law.[144] He postulates two historical phases. Before the mid-nineteenth century, to 'satisfy feudal theory, ownership [of the foreshore] was technically in the Crown, but that ownership was in trust only, for the satisfaction of various public rights'.[145] The second phase occurred in the late nineteenth century, when: [146]

this doctrine was discarded, and the Crown was said to own sea and foreshore, not merely in trust but beneficially, in full *dominium*. The property was *inter regalia minora*[147] and not,[148] as it had been before, *inter regalia majora*. It could be alienated by the Crown to private individuals. The public rights, of course, remained, and the simplest course might have been to treat them as a public limitation on Crown or, as the case may be, on private ownership of the sea and foreshore, on the model of public rights of way. Instead, however, the idea of trust, discarded now from ownership itself, came to be attached to the limitation on ownership.

A simpler and (it is thought) more accurate explanation is that the theory of foreshore as *inter regalia maiora* did not change materially. The doctrinal changes which did occur related to *dominium* or ownership of the foreshore[149] and culminated in the compromise in the *Lochnaw* case in 1873.[150] It is thought that the concept of the king as trustee was invoked not, or not primarily, to satisfy feudal theory (that a fee cannot be vacant) but rather to describe the king's role in protecting public rights. The concept was only a loose analogy and an alternative to guardianship[151] (which did not imply ownership) or 'sovereign power of the nation'[152] and other concepts[153] all of which were also used. Since it was and is only an analogy, the concept of the Crown as trustee cannot be followed exactly in all contexts, for example in relation to title to sue. But the Crown's power to vindicate public rights in the foreshore[154] may provide a useful alternative to an *actio popularis*.

---

[142] Rankine (n. 108), 276.
[143] On this terminology see Reid (n. 108), § 516. On the controversy in modern law as to the nature and extent of the public rights, see ibid., § 526.   [144] Reid (n. 108), § 514.
[145] Ibid.   [146] Ibid.
[147] This proposition must be qualified by the authorities at n. 134 above.
[148] i.e. 'not merely'.   [149] See nn. 132–40 above.
[150] *Agnew* v. *Lord Advocate* (1873) 11 M 309; see n. 136 above.
[151] Craig, I, 16, 11; n. 65 above.   [152] Bankton, I, 3, 4.
[153] Such as 'protectorate' (*Lord Advocate* v. *Clyde Navigation Trs* (1891) 19 R 174 at 177 *per* Lord Kyllachy) or 'conservator' (n. 199).
[154] *Officers of State* v. *Smith* (1846) 8 D 711; *Crown Estate Commissioners* v. *Fairlie Yacht Slip Ltd* 1979 SC 156 at 178.

5. The seabed (*fundus* or *solum maris*)

For long there was doubt about ownership of the bed and subsoil of the territorial sea below low-water mark (i.e. in charter-Latin, *infra fluxum maris*). The sovereignty (*imperium*) of the State did not necessarily imply ownership (*dominium*) by the Crown. Was the seabed *res communis omnium*, or subject to appropriation by *occupatio*, or did it belong to the Crown? If the last, was the Crown's right patrimonial and proprietary like its original right to the foreshore? Or was it only a trust for public uses such as navigation and fishing?

These questions were not merely theoretical. Littoral proprietors built important harbours[155] with piers on the seabed. Then there were issues relating to oyster-beds, mussel-beds, and *maritima incrementa*. Further the coasts were rich in coal seams. Undersea coalmines in Scotland date from the late sixteenth century, the most famous being Sir George Bruce's mine at Culross which extended for more than a mile under the tidal waters of the Forth.[156] Craig, in considering coal under the sea, stated: 'Now as the sea is of common right (*juris communis*), whatever is above to the sky, and whatever is below down to the lower world (*ad manes*), ought to be of the same legal character (*ejusdem juris*), and therefore as it is in the ownership of nobody, should be enumerated as *inter regalia*.'[157] His solution was that 'for the encouragement of industry, and as the reward of meritorious enterprise, under-sea coals are allowed to belong to those who undertake the working of them'.[158]

But the question whether the *regale* (if it was such) was *maior* or *minor* was left unanswered by the institutional writers.[159] Could there be a part of Scotland not given out to anyone, yet not belonging to the Crown? The status of the territorial seabed in national and international law was largely ignored until it became a live issue in Britain for a period from the 1870s.[160]

---

[155] See e.g. T. C. Smout, *Scottish Trade on the Eve of the Union 1660–1707* (1963), 73 sq.

[156] S. G. E. Lythe, *The Economy of Scotland 1550–1625* (1960), 47 sq.; P. Hume Brown, *Early Travellers in Scotland* (1891, repr. 1973), 115–18. In the 17th century coal was an important export and was also used to make salt. [157] Craig, II, 8, 20.

[158] Ibid.

[159] Stair, II, 1, 5; Bankton, I, 3, 2; Bell, *Principles*, § 639; Erskine, II, 1, 6: 'however incapable the ocean may be of property, yet the seas which wash the coast of any state may be appropriated to private uses . . . '. However the king's right of sovereignty 'must differ much in its effect from private property, for the king holds both the sea and the shore as trustee for the public. Both therefore are to be ranked in the same class with several other subjects which by the Roman law were public, but are by our feudal plan deemed *regalia*, or rights belonging to the Crown.'

[160] e.g. during negotiations in the 1870s to construct a Channel tunnel. In *Regina* v. *Keyn (The Franconia)* (1876) LR 2 Ex D 63, the English Court of Crown Cases Reserved held that while Great Britain might be entitled to claim a territorial sea, until it did so by statute, the English court did not possess criminal jurisdiction in respect of offences by foreigners and foreign ships beyond the shore. Surprisingly, under the English common law, British territorial waters lie outside 'the realm'. Quoad criminal jurisdiction, this omission was repaired by the Territorial

In 1891 in *Lord Advocate* v. *Clyde Navigation Trustees*,[161] where the Crown sought interdict against the dumping of dredging waste on the bed of Loch Long, it was held that the Crown owned the bed of a tidal loch *intra fauces terrae* (within the jaws of the land).[162] Then in 1899 in a case concerning the coast at Methil, *Lord Advocate* v. *Wemyss*,[163] Lord Watson affirmed Crown ownership of the solum and minerals under the open sea and the Crown's right to convey minerals but expressed doubt (*obiter*) about the Crown's right to convey the solum to a subject.[164] It was not till cases in 1979 and 1990 that the Crown's patrimonial right was held to be one of ownership (subject to public rights of navigation and fishing) and as such transmissible *inter vivos*.[165] The basis of the Crown's patrimonial right was held to be not its paramount feudal superiority (which could not apply in the udal law territories of Orkney and Shetland) but one or other of two aspects of the prerogative of the Crown, namely, either the Crown's right to claim national territory which has not been appropriated to private use,[166] or the maxim '*quod nullius est fit domini regis*'.[167]

The distinction drawn was slender. Rankine had pointed out that when Scots law rejected the Roman theory that the seas and shores were *res communes omnium* and not subject to ownership, the gap was filled by feudal law: 'The feudal law which demanded an owner for everything within the realm and for a certain distance beyond its shores, found an owner for these subjects in the sovereign, leaving the right of user untouched.'[168] A different view

Waters Jurisdiction Act 1878. In the *Franconia* case, Cockburn CJ held (ibid. at 116) that below low-water mark, the bed of the sea might be unappropriated and if capable of appropriation become the property of the first occupier. See Marston, 'The Evolution of the Concept of Sovereignty over the Bed and Subsoil of the Territorial Sea', (1976–7) 48 *British Yearbook of International Law* 321 at 322, 323. It was not till the Hague Conference of 1930 that the doctrine of coastal sovereignty over the territorial sea won general acceptance. The Geneva Convention on the Territorial Sea and the Contiguous Zone 1958, art. 1, provides: 'The sovereignty of a State extends, beyond its land territory and its internal waters, to a belt of sea adjacent to its coast, described as the territorial sea.'

[161] (1891) 19 R 174.

[162] See also the rating cases *Forth Bridge Railway* v. *Assessor of Railways* (1890) 1 PLM (NS) 147 (Forth Bridge entered in valuation roll though part is on piers below low-water mark); *Cuninghame* v. *Assessor for Ayrshire* (1895) 22 R 596 (submarine minerals below low-water mark rateable). [163] (1899) 2 F (HL) 1, reversing (1896) 24 R 216.

[164] (1899) 2 F (HL) 1 at 8, 9; similar doubts were expressed by Lord Justice-Clerk Moncreiff in *Agnew* v. *Lord Advocate* (1873) 11 M 309.

[165] *Crown Estate Commissioners* v. *Fairlie Yacht Slip Ltd* 1979 SC 156, affirming 1976 SC 161(OH); *Shetland Salmon Farmers' Association* v. *Crown Estate Commissioners* 1991 SLT 166.

[166] Which was supported *inter alia* by *Secretary of State for India* v. *Chelikani Rama Rao* (1916) 32 TLR 652 (PC) *per* Lord Shaw of Dunfermline approving Lord Watson's view in *Lord Advocate* v. *Wemyss* (1899) 2 F (HL) 1 at 8, 9. The principal reference to the prerogative as such was a dictum of Lord Chancellor Campbell in *Smith* v. *Earl of Stair* (1849) 6 Bell App 487 stating (at 500) a rule common to England and Scotland.

[167] *Shetland Salmon Farmers' Association* v. *Crown Estate Commissioners* 1991 SLT 166.

[168] Rankine (n. 108), 251; see also at 253: 'The ownership of the Crown is further supported by the theory of feudal law, which appropriates to some one every immoveable subject that is capable of appropriation; . . .'. Both passages are cited in 1991 SLT 166 at 172.

was upheld by the court namely that 'one looks inside the feudal system to determine the character and style of all rights held from the king but one has to look outside it in order to ascertain the source and character of the king's original right. The king's right is allodial, although by grant he can and does create a feudal tenure in which he is the superior.'[169]

IV. RIVERS

1. The criteria for classifying 'public' and 'private' rivers

(a) Overview

In Scottish legal history, three different criteria—perennial flow (*perennitas*), navigability, and tidality—have been accepted at different times as the legal criterion for characterizing a river as public. The effects of such a characterization have changed over time but are principally relevant to determine whether ownership of the river bed (*alveus*) is vested in the State or the riparian owners, and whether rights of passage[170] and of fishing are vested in the public or exclusively in the riparian owners. In Roman law the test for whether a river was public was perennial flow. In the *jus commune*, however, navigability became the mark of a public river and this was accepted in Scotland at least by the institutional period. For this reason, the Roman test of *perennitas* never became established as the criterion of the public character of a river in Scots law. It did however become the test for determining whether under Scots law a river was subject to the regime of common interest and riparian rights.

Again, the Roman rule that perennial rivers are *res publica* (owned by the Roman people) was replaced in the *jus commune* by a rule that navigable rivers are *inter regalia* (owned by the *princeps* or, eventually, the state) subject to certain public rights of use especially fishing and passage.[171] In these respects, in the early nineteenth century, Scots law resembled the Roman-Dutch law and the French law. Later in that century, however, the English law criterion of tidality ousted the *jus commune* test of navigability with the effect that, in the modern law, only tidal rivers—or, some would say, tidal and navigable rivers—are classified as public.

(b) The Roman classification of watercourses and rivers

Running water (*aqua profluens*) may either flow in a watercourse with a definite channel or percolate as casual water in or over the ground. The initial

---

[169] *Shetland Salmon Farmers' Association* v. *Crown Estate Commissioners* 1991 SLT 166 at 185 *per* Lord McCluskey. [170] i.e. navigation of ships or boats, and flotation of rafts or logs.
[171] Van der Vyver (n. 51), 298.

classification of watercourses in Roman law was between streams or rivulets (*rivi*) and rivers (*flumina*). This distinction depended on size (*magnitudo*) or on the opinion of the neighbourhood (*existimatio circumcolentium*).[172]

Rivers were divided into perennial rivers in which the water generally flowed all the year round (ignoring occasional summers when it dried up) and torrents (which flowed only in winter).[173] This formed the basis of the important distinction between public rivers (*flumina publica*), which were defined as being perennial, and private rivers (*flumina privata*).[174] The praetor granted interdicts to protect public rights of navigation[175] but a public river did not have to be navigable.[176] Since almost all rivers were perennial, it followed that almost all rivers were public.[177] The bed (*alveus*) of a public river was in public ownership.[178] The public right to use the water included the right of fishing.[179] The state (the praetor or later the Emperor) had power to grant licences to use the water in a public river.[180]

There has been much debate about the meaning and effect in Roman law of classifying perennial rivers as *res publicae*.[181] Buckland refers to three possible theories.[182] The first is that the bed (*alveus*) of public rivers as well as the water was public. This view however is inconsistent with the rules on *alluvio* and *insula nata*, which assume that the bed is owned by the riparian proprietors.[183] Second, there is the view of Pernice[184] that what was public was the river as such, not the water, which was common, nor the soil of the bed which he argued belonged to the riparians.[185] Third, others held that the river was public only *quoad usum*.[186] Buckland concluded: [187] 'The more probable view seems to be that the earlier lawyers merely held that a river was public, without refinements. As early as Cicero[188] rules arose giving riparian owners rights, and there was a tendency among classical lawyers to regard them as owners of the soil, the public rights being merely of use.'[189]

---

[172] Ulp. D. 43, 12, 1, 1. [173] Ulp. D. 43, 12, 1, 2; Paul. D. 43, 12, 3 pr.
[174] Ulp. D. 43, 12, 1, 3. [175] D. 43, 12–15. [176] Ulp. D. 43, 13, 1, 2.
[177] Marc. D. 1, 8, 4: 'Sed flumina paene omnia et portus publica sunt.' ('But almost all rivers and harbours are public property.') Most translations from the *Digest* in this chapter are taken from the Pennsylvania edition edited by Alan Watson. Contrast Inst. 2, 1, 2 (omitting 'paene'): 'Flumina autem omnia et portus publica sunt: ideoque ius piscandi omnibus commune est in portubus fluminibusque.' ('All rivers and harbours are public; accordingly the right of fishing in harbours and rivers is common to all.')
[178] Ulp. D. 43, 12, 1, 7. [179] Inst. 2, 1, 2.
[180] Papirius Iustus D. 8, 3, 17; Ulp. D. 39, 3, 10, 2; Ulp. D. 43, 20, 1, 41–3.
[181] As to the meaning of *res publica*, see F. Schulz, *Classical Roman Law* (1951), 89, 340.
[182] W. W. Buckland, *Textbook of Roman Law* (3rd edn., rev. P. Stein, 1963), 185. (See also 1st edn., at 186). [183] See ibid.
[184] Alfred Pernice, *Labeo*, (1873; repr. 1963), 1, 273. [185] Buckland (n. 182), 185.
[186] Ibid. [187] Ibid. 186 sq. [188] Cicero, *De Oratore*, 1, 38, 173.
[189] Citing D. 41, 1, 65, 2: 'If an island should arise in a public river nearer to your land, it is yours.'

(c) The institutional period: navigability as the test of public rivers

The Roman criterion of *perennitas* reflected the comparatively arid climate of Mediterranean countries. After the Reception, certain northern European countries (including the Netherlands and Scotland), and France with its large rivers, adopted navigability as the criterion of the public character of rivers.[190] Extremely influential were the *Constitutio de Regalibus* and the *Libri Feudorum* which in the twelfth century had included 'navigable rivers and works for improving their navigability' in a list of the *regalia*.[191] Following this pattern, the Scottish institutional writers included navigable rivers among the *regalia maiora*.[192] Erskine remarked: [193]

All the subjects which were by Roman law accounted *res publicae* are, since the introduction of feus, held to be *inter regalia* or *in patrimonio principis* as rivers, free ports, and highways. ... It is public rivers only which are *inter regalia*; by which writers generally understand navigable rivers, or those on which floats may be carried to navigable rivers. Smaller rivulets or brooks are, according to the general opinion, *juris privati*; [citing Ulp. D. 43, 12, 1, 4] ...

Hume defined 'public rivers' as 'those streams to which not only the adjacent heritors, but the people at large, have free right of access, and to take the use of for fishery and navigation, and other common uses'.[194] He and Bell made it clear that navigability was the test of a proper public river.[195] Likewise, in case law until the late nineteenth century, the mark of a public river was generally held to be navigability so that the non-tidal reaches of rivers, if navigable, were characterized as public.[196]

While it was recognized that a navigable river was *inter regalia maiora* (subject to an inalienable trust for the public) there was scant authority on whether the *alveus* of a navigable river was also *inter regalia minora* (an alienable patrimonial right of the Crown). In a case in 1849,[197] the question was

---

[190] Bonfante (n. 87), vol. 2, at 88. As to the Roman-Dutch law, see e.g. J. C. de Wet, 'Hundred Years of Water Law', 1959 *Acta Juridica* 31 at 31 sq.; K. D. Nunes, 'Sources of Public Streams in Modern South African Law', 1975 *Acta Juridica* 298 at 303 sq.; Van der Vyver (n. 51), *passim*; Grotius (n. 65), II, 1, 25–7; Vinnius, *Institutionum Imperialium Commentarius*, II, 1, 2; Voet (n. 116), I, 8, 8 (9); 41, 1, 17, 18.

[191] *Libri Feudorum* (n. 59), 2, 56 cited in Craig, I, 16, 8; Bankton, I, 3, 4. See nn. 58 and 59.

[192] Craig, I, 16, 11; Stair, II, 1, 5; Bankton, I, 3, 4; II, 7, 25; Erskine, II, 1, 5; II, 6, 17; Hume, *Lectures*, IV, 238, 239; Bell, *Principles*, §§ 638 and 648–50.   [193] Erskine, II, 6, 17.

[194] Hume, *Lectures*, IV, 243.

[195] Bell, *Principles*, § 648: 'Navigable rivers are, like the sea, public: and are for similar purposes vested in the Crown. They are held as highways or common passages. It is not tide rivers only which are held public but rivers above tide water, where fit for the transportation of the country products, though that should only be down the stream on a public river.'

[196] *Grant v. Duke of Gordon* (1781) Mor 12820, affirmed (1782) 2 Pat App 582 (HL); *Carron & Co. v. Ogilvie* (1806) 5 Pat App 61; *Baillie v. Lady Saltoun* (1821) Hume 523, 1 S 227; *Macdonnell v. Caledonian Canal Commissioners* (1830) 8 S 881 per Lord Cringletie and Lord Glenlee; *Lord Advocate v. Clyde Trs and Hamilton* (1852) 1 Macq 46, (1849) 11 D 391; *Duke of Buccleuch v. Cowan* (1866) 5 M 214 at 215, 216 per Lord Justice-Clerk Inglis.

[197] *Lord Advocate v. Clyde Navigation Trs* (1849) 11 D 391.

raised but not decided 'as to the original nature of the Crown's right to the *alveus* of a navigable river;—whether it is merely a right of trust for behoof of the lieges, or an absolute right of property.... It is a *questio vexata*.'[198] In the First Division, conflicting views were expressed *obiter*[199] but in the House of Lords, Lord St Leonards remarked: '[B]eyond all doubt the soil and bed of a river (we are speaking now of navigable rivers only) belongs to the Crown.'[200] The *alveus* has been classified as *inter regalia minora*[201] which implies alienability. In the *Midlothian Esk pollution* case, Lord Justice-Clerk Inglis defined a public river as 'a river which is fit for navigation ... whether it be fresh water or salt, whether it be a tidal river or a river in which the tide does not ebb and flow' and affirmed that such a river was public property vested in the Crown and not in the proprietors of the banks.[202]

(d) Reception of the English concept of tidality as the test of public rivers

In the *Wills' Trs* case, Lord Hailsham remarked that one of the 'ways ... in which the law of Scotland has moved away from the law of Rome' is that 'Roman law never came to terms with tidality which was known only on the confines of the Western Empire, and the distinction between tidal and non-tidal stretches of river, which bulks large in English and Scottish law, was unknown to them'.[203]

(aa) Tidality and ownership of the *alveus* of rivers

The *jus commune* concept of navigability was accepted as the mark of a public river and therefore of Crown ownership of the *alveus*[204] up to 1877 when, in the landmark case of *Colquhoun's Trs v. Orr Ewing and Co.*,[205] the House of Lords changed the law by holding that the Crown's right to ownership of the *alveus* extends only to tidal stretches (and then perhaps only as a presumption) and that, in freshwater stretches, ownership of the *alveus* is vested in the riparian proprietors. This was not a case in which the House of Lords imposed English law over the protests of a reluctant Court of Session. Rather

---

[198] (1849) 11 D 391 at 403 *per* Lord Jeffrey.

[199] Ibid. *per* Lord President Boyle at 396: 'While the right of the Crown to the alveus of all navigable rivers is acknowledged by the law of Scotland, I see nothing in our institutional writers which says that that right is not in the Crown as proprietor.' Contrast Lord Fullerton at 401: 'Now the right of the Crown in the solum ... stands on a very different footing from that of property in the normal sense of the term. The right is no doubt in the Crown but it is a right like that of the solum still forming alveus, held for the benefit of the public by the Crown, as the conservator of the navigable river' and Lord Jeffrey at 403.

[200] *Lord Advocate v. Clyde Trs and Hamilton* (1852) 1 Macq 46, (1849) 11 D 391.

[201] Reid (n. 108), § 275.   [202] *Duke of Buccleuch v. Cowan* (1866) 5 M 214 at 215 sq.

[203] *Wills' Trs v. Cairngorm Canoeing and Sailing School Ltd* 1976 SC (HL) 30.

[204] See the reference in *Wills' Trs v. Cairngorm Canoeing and Sailing School Ltd* 1976 SC (HL) 30 at 142 to the opinion in 1875 of Mr J. B. Balfour QC (later Lord President Kinross) to the effect that the bed of the non-tidal navigable Spey was vested in the Crown.

[205] (1877) 4 R (HL) 116, reversing (1877) 4 R 344 (1st Div.).

it was the First Division which introduced English law despite the pursuer's protests and their decision was affirmed on appeal. The issue was whether the proprietor of lands on both banks of the freshwater River Leven in Dunbartonshire (which had long been navigable by small craft plying between Loch Lomond and the Firth of Clyde) could be prohibited from building a bridge over the river with two piers erected on the *alveus*.[206] Both the First Division and the House of Lords held that though the *alveus* in the tidal part of a navigable river is public and belongs to the Crown, the *alveus* in the non-tidal part is private and belongs to the riparian proprietors. This latter proposition represented a major change in Scots law which was inconsistent with its natural development. To reach that result, for example, Lord President Inglis had to eat his own words and expressly to disapprove as 'rather loosely made' his own orthodox and unexceptionable statement of the navigability doctrine in the *Esk pollution* case.[207] None of the judges explained their policy reasons for this surreptitious Anglicization (for such it was), nor even admitted that it was a change. A frank acknowledgement that Scots law was being changed would have raised questions as to the propriety of depriving the public of historic rights in navigable, non-tidal waters and fuelled the controversy on public rights of fishing.[208] Before the First Division, the defenders relied primarily on English[209] and American[210] authority for the proposition that above the flow of the tide, the *alveus* (like the rest of the soil of Scotland) belonged to the proprietors who prima facie could erect anything on their own property. The Scottish authorities cited by the defenders[211] did not support the proposition. The judges simply ignored the pursuers' argument that while that proposition 'might be the law of England', it 'was not the law of Scotland'.[212]

The reason is a puzzle. In the previous year, the House of Lords decided a leading case on the English law on tidal rivers[213] which came to be 'understood as laying down a permanent rule for all parts of the British Empire where the law of water rights is based on the same principles as are recognized in England and Scotland'.[214] There may have been an assimilationist

---

[206] The First Division held that any member of the public could require the removal of buildings constructed on the *alveus* of a public navigable river. This decision was reversed by the House of Lords on the ground that where the public have the right of navigation in a non-tidal river, the riparian owners, as owners of the *alveus,* may erect a building on it provided the building does not materially interfere with or obstruct navigation. Here any interference was *de minimis*. [207] *Duke of Buccleuch* v. *Cowan* (1866) 5 M 214 at 215 sq. quoted above.
[208] As to this controversy see below, especially the text at nn. 234 and 235.
[209] Hale, '*De Jure Maris*', in Loveland (n. 45), App., 5,. The defenders' counsel included Mr J. B. Balfour QC, who in 1875 had given advice to the opposite effect.
[210] Angel (*sic*), *Watercourses*, 552, 560. (As to this work, see below n. 348.)
[211] Craig, I, 16, 11; Stair, II, 1, 5.   [212] (1877) 4 R 344 at 348.
[213] *Lyon* v. *Fishmongers Co.* (1876) LR 1 AC 662 (HL).   [214] Ferguson (n. 1), 120.

climate of opinion in which it was thought that the civilian criterion of navigability stood little chance of being upheld by the House of Lords.[215]

The basis of the English criterion of tidality is that the bed of tidal rivers is in the same position as the seashore and that 'it is vested in the Crown on the presumption that it is waste of the kingdom which has not been granted'.[216] The notion of residual property not yet conveyed out of the Crown's patrimony is consonant with the Scots feudal theory of the original ownership by the Crown of the *dominium utile* of the whole feudal land of Scotland.[217]

(bb) Public rivers and the conflict between public and private rights of fishing

In Roman law there was a public right of fishing (*jus piscandi*) in public (perennial) rivers.[218] In the *jus commune*, while there was authority that the right of fishing in navigable rivers was *inter regalia*,[219] there was (according to Craig[220]) 'much controversy among the learned[221] as to why fishings and their profits should be included among the rights of the Crown, seeing that by the *jus gentium* the right to fish both in the sea and in rivers is free to all i.e. "*res communis omnium*"'.[222] At all events the rights of the public to fish for trout and white fish in public (i.e. navigable) rivers was fully established in the institutional period.[223]

In that period, on the other hand, the Scots law on the right of trout fishing in private rivers was still unclear. Arguably, since fish in a private river were *res nullius*, they might be lawfully captured by anyone having access to the water. It was also arguable that even if access does not imply a right to fish, such a right may be acquired by possession for the period of the positive prescription. Stair thought that there were 'common freedoms of every nation' to fish in tidal and non-tidal waters for 'common fishes' (e.g. trout, cod, and perch) without any feudal grant from king or superior and was therefore puzzled by feudal grants *cum piscationibus*.[224] With great lucidity, Erskine pointed out that Stair's 'common freedoms' theory was inconsistent with another view of Stair to the effect that a proprietor infeft *cum*

---

[215] On the growth in use of English authorities about this time, see A. Rodger, 'Thinking about Scots Law', (1996–7) 1 *Edinburgh LR* 3 at 16.
[216] *Halsbury's Laws of England* (4th edn.), vol. 49, para. 379.   [217] See n. 168 above.
[218] Justinian, Inst. 2, 1, 2.
[219] Vinnius (n. 190), II, 1, 2 citing the *Constitutio de Regalibus* (n. 58); Voet (n. 116), I, 8, 8; Ulrich Huber, *Heedendaagse Rechtsgeleertheyt*, II, 1, 16, 17 ; cf. *Transvaal Canoe Union* v. *Butgeriet* 1986 4 SA (TPD) 207.   [220] Craig, I, 16, 38.
[221] Craig cites Hotman and Cujacius.
[222] Ibid. (Lord Clyde's translation) citing Gai. D. 41, 1, 1.
[223] Hume, *Lectures*, IV, 245 said: 'As far as relates to the inferior sorts of fish—trouts and the like, which are sought for sport rather than profit; it is not disputed, that the lieges at large have right to resort to a public river, and there, to take them in the ordinary and accustomed ways of fishing.'   [224] Stair, II, 3, 69.

piscationibus may acquire by positive prescription an exclusive right to fishing 'for no right common to mankind can be taken away from one, and acquired by another, by interrupting particular persons in the use of it for the longest course of time'.[225] Nevertheless in 1787 the Court of Session is reported as holding that 'trouts were *res nullius* in this sense only, that any person standing on a high road or any public ground contiguous to the stream, might lawfully catch them'.[226]

These authorities raised the inference that a right of access to a river implies the right to fish for trout in it. Fishing for trout by members of the public in private (i.e. non-navigable) as well as public rivers was very common for much of the nineteenth century.[227] Yet the theory that the right of trout fishing is an exclusive pertinent of ownership of the banks of private rivers (rather than a public right) was affirmed first in 1844 in a non-navigable, non-tidal river ('private' both in the *jus commune* and English senses of the term) and then in 1894 (after the Anglicizing revolution of 1877) in a navigable, non-tidal river ('private' only in the English sense).

So in 1844 in *Fergusson* v. *Shirreff*[228] the Second Division, after much hesitation and apparent angst, held that a right of access to a private, non-tidal and non-navigable river (the Tyne running through the lands of Hailes near East Linton) did not confer a right of fishing for trout in it; that the exclusive right of trout fishing was vested in riparian proprietors of private rivers; and that proof of fishing for trout in the stream by the inhabitants of East Linton and the public generally, not based on any title, would not found a prescriptive public right to fish for trout.[229] The court, showing 'all deference to followers of the gentle science',[230] acknowledged that the 'very common'[231] practice of trout fishing by the public in Scottish private rivers suggested 'a common belief of right' on the part of the public, including 'schoolboys, old men, . . . and wandering lawyers, whom it would be thought alike hard and uncivil to interrupt'. The court also emphasized its 'reluctance to come to a result which may interfere so much with an amusement, in many parts of the country enjoyed without molestation, only because understood to be a right'.[232] Nevertheless, although by the civil law and Scots law fish are *res nullius*, and like all animals *ferae naturae* become by *occupatio* the

---

[225] Erskine, II, 6, 6.
[226] *Carmichael* v. *Colquhoun* (1787) Mor 9645. See however the diversity of opinions in the report in Hailes 1033. [227] See nn. 228–39 below.
[228] (1844) 6 D 1363 applied to lochs; see *Montgomery* v. *Watson* (1861) 23 D 635, at n. 286 below.
[229] (1844) 6 D 1363 at 1370 *per* Lord Medwyn: 'I do not see it laid down in any of our authorities, that by usage a right will be acquired abridging the right of property without a title. I think we acknowledge prescription only according to the principles of the civil law in such a case, and that must be founded on a dominant title.'
[230] Ibid. at 1372 *per* Lord Moncreiff; 'the gentle art': ibid. at 1370 *per* Lord Medwyn.
[231] Ibid. at 1370 *per* Lord Medwyn. [232] Ibid. at 1366 sq. *per* Lord Justice-Clerk Hope.

property of the occupant, it was a non sequitur to deduce from that a public right of fishing in a private river.[233] Then in 1875 a member of the public was interdicted from trout fishing in a non-tidal and non-navigable stretch of the River Ayr. It was again held that immemorial public usage could not found a defence of positive prescription but must be attributed to the tolerance of the riparian owners.[234] It appears that in parliamentary election meetings in the 1880s, hecklers were wont to ask candidates whether they were in favour of *restoring* to the public the right of open fishing in rivers being 'under the impression that the public at some previous time possessed such right, and that it had been surreptitiously filched away from them by the rapacity of landowners'.[235]

Then in 1894, soon after tidality was accepted as the mark of public river in the *Colquhoun's Trs* case of 1877,[236] the right of fishing for trout and coarse fish in navigable rivers, 'long cherished as a supposed right by the common people of Scotland',[237] was held in *Grant* v. *Henry*[238] to be confined to tidal stretches. Lord Kinnear observed:[239]

We know that there are rivers which are practically open, where not only the inhabitants of the neighbourhood but persons coming from a distance, have been accustomed to fish for trout without let or hindrance from time immemorial; and one would have expected to find that a use and enjoyment so extensive and so continuous rested rather on public right than on the goodwill and good sense of private landowners.

The reason for the change is unclear. In 1869 a monograph on fishing rights by an advocate, Charles Stewart,[240] contended that while the public right of navigation may extend to freshwater, 'the public right of fishing probably extends no further than the ebb and flow of the tide, or to those waters where the influence of the salt water is perceptible'. The grounds for this view were, first, that the navigability test was too vague and indefinite as a criterion deciding the public or private character of the right to fish[241] whereas the tidality test was 'definite and unambiguous'. Secondly, English and Irish common law authorities supported tidality.[242] Thirdly, 'that part of a river where the sea ebbs and flows, is of the same nature as the sea itself; and the

---

[233] Ibid. at 1368 *per* Lord Medwyn.
[234] *Campbell* v. *Arkison & Clark* (unreported) noted in *The Edinburgh Courant* on 7 Sept. 1875; see also W. S. C., 'The Law of Trout-Fishing', (1879) 23 *J Juris* 420 at 420 n. 1.
[235] R. P. L., 'Some Subjects of Heckling', (1886) 2 *SL Rev* 69 at 73 sq.
[236] (1877) 4 R (HL) 116, affirming (1877) 4 R 344.
[237] *Wills' Trs* v. *Cairngorm Canoeing and Sailing School Ltd* 1976 SC (HL) 30 at 142 sq.
[238] (1894) 21 R 358—a case concerning trout fishing on the non-tidal stretch of the Spey. Cf. *Bowie* v. *Marquis of Ailsa* (1887) 14 R 649. [239] (1894) 21 R 358 at 365.
[240] C. Stewart, *A Treatise on the Law of Scotland Relating to Rights of Fishing* (1869), 26–31.
[241] Ibid. 27 sq.
[242] Ibid. 28 citing Sir John Davies' Report on the Banne Fishery case 149; Paterson, *Fishery Laws*, 32; Hale (n. 209), c. 2, 8; Comyn, *Digest* s.v. 'Prerogative' 50, vol. 7, 70. In Ireland *Murphy* v. *Ryan* (1867) Ir Rep 2 CL 143.

white fish of the sea, the only kind to which the public privilege of fishing extends, are to be found only in those waters where the influence of the tide is perceptible'.[243] It may be that these arguments influenced the court in the *Colquhoun's Trs* case and its sequels.

(e) Perennitas *as the test of riparian common interest*

Although Scots law, differing from Roman law, came to define 'public rivers' by reference to the tests of navigability or tidality, it applied the Roman test of *perennitas* or perennial flow to determine what watercourses were protected by the doctrine of common interest of riparian owners or its seventeenth- and eighteenth-century precursors.[244] The Roman distinction between *publica flumina* and *aqua privata* was applied in 1768 in *Magistrates of Linlithgow* v. *Elphinstone*[245] in which the issue was whether the owner of a loch whose water fed a river was entitled to divert the water into another river. It was held by a majority that the riparian owners were not entitled to object to the diversion, the main ground of decision being that the water did not flow perennially. Lord Monboddo said:[246] 'The distinction in the Roman law between *flumen publicum* and *aqua privata* determines this case. *Publicum flumen* is not as we commonly suppose, a navigable river, but *flumen quod perenniter fluit*.' This case was decided while the doctrine of riparian common interest was still evolving but it concerned the most basic of the riparian rights conferred by that doctrine and is still authoritative.[247]

---

[243] Stewart (n. 240), 28.

[244] The doctrine of common interest only reached maturity in the late 18th century. Its precursor was the innominate interdict against diversion, or other alteration of the natural flow, based on the praetorian interdicts especially the interdict *uti priori aestate*: see Stair, II, 7, 12; Bankton, II, 7, 29; Erskine, II, 9, 13. See further below.

[245] (1768) Mor 12805, 5 Brown's Supp 936, Hailes 203. The diversion of the water was designed to serve the famous Carron Iron Works, the greatest user of water-power within the iron industry, whose use of water-power to drive the blast furnaces, mills for boring cannon (e.g. Nelson's carronades) etc. is well described in J. Shaw, *Water Power in Scotland 1550–1870* (1984), 431–6.

[246] (1768) Hailes 204. Hailes's report shows that the majority included Lord Justice-Clerk Glenlee, and Lords Kames, Monboddo, Kennet, Pitfour, Alemore, and Auchinleck. Lord President Dundas and Lords Gardenston, Coalston, and Elliock dissented. Lord Kames said: 'I distinguish between water *publici juris* and *privati juris*. Perennis aqua is *publici juris*; but here I see no proof of *perennis aqua*.' Lord Justice-Clerk Glenlee: 'I do not think that this course can be diverted, for there is a perpetual cause TE DUNAMEI, as Cujacius expresses it.' Lord Pitfour: 'As to *aqua perennis*, it is laid down in the civil law. I do not say it is a subtlety; but still it ought not to be extended.' Lord Alemore: 'This is not a perennial water. Cujacius's authority not in point: he speaks of a lake with a perpetual outlet.' Lord Auchinleck: 'When a person claims water, he must show that he has either a servitude or a right to it. If he has a perennial burn running through his ground he has a right to it . . . Here there is no perennial run . . .' Of the dissenting judges, Lord Gardenston held a servitude right to the water to be established and Lord Coalston held the civil law test satisfied since in his view the water had 'a perpetual cause'.

[247] It was followed by the First Division in *Magistrates of Ardrossan* v. *Dickie* (1906) 14 SLT 349. See below n. 255.

Again in 1768, in *Kelso* v. *Boyds*[248] it was held that the owner of higher ground was not entitled to divert a rivulet, which passed through his own grounds, from reaching a lower property. The successful pursuer correctly pointed out that the defender's Roman law authorities to the effect that the owner of higher ground can intercept water so as to prevent it from flowing on to lower ground, if not done *in aemulationem*,[249] related not to perennial runs of water or rivulets but collections of rainwater (*aqua pluvia*) or springs in the higher ground. Lord Auchinleck[250] observed that: 'A perennial burn cannot be diverted by the superior heritor so as to be prevented from descending to the inferior.' Lord Monboddo remarked:

The Roman law furnishes us with principles for determining this case. The doctrine of *aqua pluvia* is not to the purpose; for the question here is concerning a *flumen*, not a torrent, but perennial by the Roman law. *Flumen publicum* is not a navigable river, but any streams *usus publici*, whereof a navigable river is composed. To such the Praetor's edict applies, *uti priore aestate*, etc.[251]

As noted below,[252] the praetor's edict *uti priore aestate*, though introducing a public law interdict, formed the starting point of the development of the Scottish private law doctrine of riparian common interest.

In 1791 in *Marquis of Abercorn* v. *Jamieson*,[253] there occurs what seems to be the first reference by name in Scots case reports to the expression 'common interest' in the context of riparian rights. The case involved cross-actions between higher and lower riparian proprietors. The action by the upper proprietor, the Marquis, was settled, leaving the cross-action by Jamieson, the lower proprietor, for declarator that the upper proprietor could not abstract water from the river by a side-cut, and could not erect a dam to discharge water irregularly. The court held:[254]

The Figgate burn, as *aqua perennis*, is a matter of common interest to the several adjoining heritors. As such, it is subject to the natural uses of each heritor in his turn; and it is not at the disposal of any of them by turning it, or any portion of it, aside, or otherwise to the prejudice of the others.

---

[248] (1768) Mor 12807, Hailes 224.
[249] Ulp. D. 39, 3, 1, 21; also cited were D. 39, 3, 2, 9; D. 39, 3, 21, 23; C. 3, 34, 10.
[250] (1768) Hailes 224.
[251] Ibid. He continued: 'The right of the inferior tenement is not a servitude, but it is a right owing to the nature of the subject. The superior heritor may use the water even for fructifying his ground, but he must use it so that the water returns to its channel.'
[252] See text at nn. 293–300 below.   [253] (1791) Hume 510.
[254] Ibid. at 511. This reasoning is reflected in the Court's interlocutor: 'Find, that the burn or water of Figgate, being a *flumen publicum*, the course thereof cannot be diverted or altered by the Marquis of Abercorn . . .' except to the extent that it had been taken for the prescriptive period.

Finally in *Magistrates of Ardrossan* v. *Dickie*,[255] the First Division, applying the *Linlithgow Magistrates* case,[256] held[257] that it was essential that the water would have run in a perennial flow in a definite channel into the stream to which the complainers had alleged a right.[258] For the purposes of common interest, therefore, a 'stream' implies a perennial flow in a definite channel.[259]

(f) Common interest and tidal rivers

There is a school of thought which holds that, subject to the public rights of navigation and fishing and apart from ownership of the bed, the rights of riparian owners on tidal rivers are (as in English law)[260] similar to those of riparian owners on non-tidal rivers.[261] As the word 'riparian' implies, it is not ownership of the bed (*alveus*) which matters but ownership of a river-bank (*ripa*).[262] But the opposite view has been expressed.[263] Since our doctrine of riparian common interest developed out of Roman public law interdicts, the civilian tradition in our law—as well as the English tradition—supports the first view.

(g) Public rights of passage

The Anglicizing tidality revolution meant that from 1877 public ownership of the river bed,[264] and from 1894 public rights of fishing,[265] were confined by the courts to tidal stretches. To complete the tidality revolution, one might have expected that the third mark of a public river,—the public right of passage— would also have been so confined. That step was never taken presumably partly because of its effect on vested rights and partly because English law distinguished navigability and tidality.[266] Though in 1877 that right was detached from ownership of the bed, its nature was not altered.[267] Some

---

[255] *Magistrates of Ardrossan* v. *Dickie* (1906) 14 SLT 349.

[256] Ibid. at 354 *per* Lord President Kinross; see also at 351 *per* Lord Kincairney (Ordinary).

[257] Despite some disagreement as to the precise formulation of the test of whether an upper proprietor could, by drainage operations, divert water in a loch or *stagnum* from flowing into a stream. [258] Ibid. at 354 sq. *per* Lord President Kinross, at 357 *per* Lord Kinnear.

[259] Gordon (n. 60), para. 7-25, correcting the first edition of 1989.

[260] See *Lyon* v. *Fishmongers Co.* (1876) LR 1 AC 662 (HL) at 682 *per* the Earl of Selborne: 'private riparian rights may and do exist in a tidal navigable river'.

[261] Lord Murray, J. Keith, and J. F. G. Thomson, 'Water and Water Rights', in *Encyclopaedia of the Laws of Scotland,* vol. 13 (1933), § 1134; Gordon (n. 60), para. 7-28; *Ross* v. *Powrie and Pitcaithley* (1891) 19 R 314; *Gay* v. *Malloch* 1959 SC 110 especially at 116, 123.

[262] Cf. Reid (n. 108), § 278. The proposition that a ' "riparian proprietor" is one who owns the *alveus*, or part of the *alveus*, of a river or stream' is *per incuriam*.

[263] Ferguson (n. 1), 119 sq.; Burn-Murdoch, *Interdict in the Law of Scotland* (1933), 41; *Macbraire* v. *Mather* (1871) 9 M 913; *Moncreiffe* v. *Perth Police Commissioners* (1886) 13 R 921; Reid (n. 108), § 312. [264] *Colquhoun's Trs* v. *Orr Ewing & Co.* (1877) 4 R (HL) 116.

[265] *Grant* v. *Henry* (1894) 21 R 358.

[266] See e.g. Hale, *De Jure Maris et Brachiorum Ejusdem*, I, cap. II, in Loveland (n. 45), Appendix, 4, 5.

[267] *Wills' Trs* v. *Cairngorm Canoeing and Sailing School Ltd* 1976 SC (HL) 30 at 142 *per* Lord Hailsham.

rivers like the Leven in Dunbarton are navigable by boats both upstream and downstream[268] while others, like stretches of the Spey, have a tradition of flotation of rafts or logs downstream only. Following the first Spey case,[269] Hume laid down a simple, elegant, and practical test for the existence of a public (navigable) river: 'Is the river of such depth and capacity as makes it fit to serve, and has made it in the use of serving, as a channel of transportation, upwards or downwards, for the commodities or produce of the adjacent country?'[270] Hume's test was approved and applied by the House of Lords in the great case of *Will's Trs*[271] as the criterion of public rights of passage whether by navigation or flotation[272] and public use for forty years is capable of proof by evidence and the opinion of the neighbourhood (*existimatio circumcolentium*).[273]

(h) The modern law

With such a history[274] it is not surprising that the modern law is afflicted by a certain amount of taxonomic and semantic confusion. Such is the disagreement on the meanings to be ascribed to the terms 'public' and 'private' as criteria for classifying waters[275] that some authorities avoid the classification altogether.[276] In summary, three criteria are used which have entered Scots law at different times. First, the Roman test of *perennitas* or perennial flow determines the category of rivers in which the riparian owners have rights under the doctrine of common interest. Second, navigability or 'floatability' (the modern civil law tests of a public river), coupled with use for forty years, determines the category of rivers which are subject to public

---

[268] *Colquhoun's Trs* v. *Orr Ewing & Co.* (1877) 4 R (HL) 116.
[269] *Grant* v. *Duke of Gordon* (1781) Mor 12820, (1782) 2 Pat App 582.
[270] Hume, *Lectures*, IV, 243.
[271] See *Wills' Trs* v. *Cairngorm Canoeing and Sailing School Ltd* 1976 SC (HL) 30 at 124 and 126 *per* Lord Wilberforce, at 145 *per* Lord Hailsham, at 164 *per* Lord Fraser. A. Watson, 'Aspects of Reception of Law', (1996) 44 *AJCL* 335, at 348 dismisses the 'old authority such as *Regiam Majestatem*, Stair, Erskine, Bankton, and Baron Hume' as 'extremely vague as to what made a river navigable'. But surely Baron Hume's test was very clear, and indeed not easy to improve upon. This however does not detract from the validity of Watson's general point (*idem*) that 'in systems that develop by scholarly opinion and judicial precedent, whole areas may remain unclear for centuries'.
[272] On the Roman acceptance of a public right of flotation, see Ulp. D. 43, 12, 1, 14 quoted in the *Will's Trs* case (n. 271) at 123 *per* Lord Wilberforce, at 141 *per* Lord Hailsham, at 156 *per* Lord Fraser. [273] Ibid. at 126.
[274] See IV.1.a–g.
[275] Rankine (n. 108), 533 first suggested that the phrases 'public river' and 'private river' 'ought be confined' to their original Roman signification 'though the private rivers in this country would thereby be reduced to a very small number' but later suggested that it would be well to discard that usage 'as of no practical importance and to adhere to the more useful modern terminology' i.e. navigable and non-navigable. Ferguson (n. 1), 99 states: 'Public rivers are of two kinds—(1) Those which are navigable and tidal, and (2) those which are navigable but non-tidal.'
[276] Reid (n. 108), § 277 expressly rejects the public/private dichotomy as too confusing. It is not used as a criterion of classification by Gordon (n. 60) nor by W. M. Gloag, and R. C. Henderson, *The Law of Scotland* (10th edn., 1995), paras. 40.22 and 40.23.

rights of passage. Third, tidality (borrowed with slight modifications from English law) determines whether ownership of the *alveus* and rights of fishing for white fish are public rights vested in the Crown as *inter regalia majora* on behalf of the public or private rights vested in the riparian proprietors to the exclusion of the public.

2. The development of the Scottish doctrine of riparian common interest

(*a*) *The Scottish regime of riparian common interest*

(aa) Overview

The leading idea of the Scottish doctrine of common interest is that the natural flow of a river is a matter of common interest to riparian proprietors.[277] The doctrine rests on three main rules. First, and most importantly: 'Every riparian proprietor is ... entitled to the water of his stream in its natural flow without sensible diminution or increase, and without sensible alteration in its character or quality.'[278] Second, a riparian proprietor can take and use water from the stream for 'primary' purposes. In English law there is high, albeit *obiter*, authority that this right is virtually absolute so that the riparian proprietor can consume the whole stream for those purposes.[279] The Scots authorities are less explicit,[280] and this rule has been criticized by Scots commentators.[281] Third, water from rivers may be taken and used for 'secondary' purposes provided that three conditions were satisfied, viz. that the use is (i) connected with riparian land;[282] (ii) reasonable;[283] and (iii) such that the water will be returned without delay substantially undiminished in volume and unaltered in character.[284]

---

[277] *Morris v. Bicket* (1864) 2 M 1082 at 1091.

[278] *Young & Co. v. Bankier Distillery Co.* (1893) 20 R (HL) 76 at 78.

[279] *Miner v. Gilmour* (1858) 12 Moo PCC 131 at 156 (obiter); *McCartney v. Londonderry & Lough Swilly Railway Co. Ltd* [1904] AC 301 HL at 307 *per* Lord Macnaghten: 'In the ordinary or primary use of flowing water a person dwelling on the banks of a stream is under no restriction. In the exercise of his ordinary rights he may exhaust the water altogether.'

[280] *Ogilvy v. Kincaid* (1791) Hume 508, note at 509; *Hood v. Williamsons* (1861) 23 D 496 *per* Lord Kinloch.

[281] Murray/Keith/Thomson (n. 261), § 1158 at 543 sq.: see also Rankine (n. 108), 555 suggesting that if primary uses exhaust a stream while other sources are available, the court may intervene to regulate user.

[282] *Lord Melville v. Denniston* (1842) 4 D 1231; *Bonthrone v. Downie* (1878) 6 R 324; *Marquis of Breadalbane v. West Highland Railway* (1895) 22 R 307.

[283] *Young & Co. v. Bankier Distillery Co.* (1893) 20 R (HL) 76 at 78 *per* Lord Macnaghten stating that riparian owners are entitled to the natural flow 'subject to the ordinary use of the flowing water by upper proprietors, and subject to such further use, if any, on their part in connection with their property as may be reasonable under the circumstances'.

[284] *Young & Co. v. Bankier Distillery Co.* (1893) 20 R (HL) 76 at 77 *per* Lord Watson (*obiter*): 'I am not satisfied that a riparian owner is entitled to use water for secondary purposes except upon condition that he return it to the stream practically undiminished in volume, and with its natural qualities unimpaired'; at 79 *per* Lord Macnaghten (*obiter*): 'if the appellants had abstracted the natural water of the burn, and returned it to the stream so altered in quality or

In the Scottish system, a riparian owner's right of common interest is proprietary rather than delictual in character. An act materially affecting the natural flow is treated as an infringement of the pursuer's proprietary rights in the river even though the water is not necessary for his use and the act does not inflict any patrimonial loss or injury on him at all.[285] Moreover, while the doctrine of common interest developed originally, and is usually presented, as if it merely regulated the relations of riparian owners between themselves, the nineteenth-century fishing cases[286] and other cases show that riparian rights are available also against members of the public. In terms of the fundamental principles of Scottish property law, riparian rights are real rights.[287]

In terms of comparative law, the Scottish doctrine is very similar if not identical to the English doctrine of riparian rights and it thus differs from the 'reasonable use' doctrines of riparian rights found in some states of the USA.[288] The history of the Scottish doctrine of common interest however is very different from the history of the English doctrine of riparian rights. The latter emerged only in the second quarter of the nineteenth century when it replaced the previous orthodoxy, often called the doctrine of prior appropriation.[289] By contrast Scots law developed directly from the *jus commune* beginning in the early seventeenth century at latest and at no time received the English doctrine of prior appropriation.

(bb) Roman influence: the interdict *uti priori aestate*

Though Rankine observed[290] that the original Roman distinction between *flumina publica* and *aqua privata* is no longer important in our law, nevertheless it was applied in the series of cases from 1768[291] to 1906[292] described above, and still applies, to define the scope of riparian common interest.

The most important Roman root of the common interest doctrine was the praetorian interdict *uti priori aestate* forbidding anything to be done (*facere*) or introduced (*immittere*) in a public river or on its banks which might cause the water to flow otherwise than it did last summer. The remedy is discussed

---

character as to be materially less serviceable for the reasonable use of the respondents, though still fit for primary or ordinary uses, they would have been equally liable to an interdict . . .'

[285] See *Lord Blantyre* v. *Dunn* (1848) 10 D 509 at 542 *per* Lord Moncreiff quoted in text at n. 344.

[286] e.g. *Fergusson* v. *Shirreff* (1844) 6 D 1363; *Montgomery* v. *Watson* (1861) 23 D 635; *Grant* v. *Henry* (1894) 21 R 358.   [287] See Reid (n. 108), § 290.

[288] American Law Institute, *First Restatement of the Law of Torts* (1939), 344, s. 849; S. V. Kinyon, 'What can a riparian proprietor do?', (1937) 21 *Minn LR* 512 at 522.

[289] Under which anyone may abstract as much water as he wishes from rivers and the first person to abstract water may continue to do so thereafter: 'first come, first served'.

[290] Rankine (n. 108), 533, in a passage cited with approval in *Wills' Trs* v. *Cairngorm Canoeing and Sailing School Ltd* 1976 SC (HL) 30 at 141 *per* Lord Hailsham.

[291] *Magistrates of Linlithgow* v. *Elphinstone* (1768) Mor 12805, 5 Brown's Supp 935, Hailes 203.   [292] *Magistrates of Ardrossan* v. *Dickie* (1906) 14 SLT 349.

in the *Digest* title, D. 43, 13. It applied to *flumina publica*, whether navigable or not.[293] Describing the interdict, Ulpian states:[294]

> The praetor says: 'I forbid anything to be done in a public river or on its bank, or anything to be introduced into that river or on its bank, which might cause the water to flow otherwise than it did last summer.'

The interdict protected interests of the public, other than interests in navigation or flotation,[295] in public rivers. Thus the praetor could prevent a river from drying up as a result of unauthorized tapping of watercourses or from injuring neighbours by changing its *alveus*.[296] The interdict was a public law remedy since it enforced the rights of the public in public rivers. Any member of the public had a title to sue: 'Hoc interdictum cuius ex populo competit . . .'[297] Roman public law remedies could be influential in the development of rules of Scots private law: [298] riparian common interest is an example. In 1624, in one of the two foundation cases *Bannatyne* v. *Cranston*[299] where a riparian owner obtained an order against the diversion of a march burn by the opposite riparian proprietor, the only authority cited in the report is Ulp. D. 43, 13, 1.[300]

(cc) *The evolution of doctrine of riparian common interest: the main developments*

The treatment by Stair, Bankton, and Erskine of riparian common interest was short and fragmentary. Rivers were very briefly discussed by them (first) in connection with the classification of real rights or property, including *res publicae*,[301] and (second) in connection with the *regalia*.[302] Third, the cases

---

[293] Ulp. D. 43, 13, 1, 2: 'Pertinet autem ad flumina publica, sive navigabilia sunt sive non sunt.' ('It applies to public rivers, navigable and unnavigable.')

[294] Ulp. D. 43, 13, 1 pr.: 'Ait praetor: "In flumine publico inve ripa eius facere aut in id flumen ripamve eius immittere, quo aliter aqua fluat, quam priore aestate fluxit, veto".' The Pennsylvania edition's translation of the heading of D. 43, 13 and of D. 43, 13, 1 pr., contains mistaken references to a private river.

[295] Which were protected by another public law interdict which influenced Scots law: see D. 43, 14 (*ut in flumine publico navigare liceat*). [296] Ulp. D. 43, 13, 1, 1.

[297] Ulp. D. 43, 13, 1, 9. In addition to an *interdictum prohibitorium*, there was an *interdictum restituendum* by which the praetor required the defender to undo or restore what he had done in a public river or on its bank, if it caused the river to flow otherwise than it had flowed last summer: Ulp. D. 43, 13, 1, 11–13.

[298] Cf. the role of Macer D. 50, 10, 3 pr. in the development of the Scottish doctrine of *aemulatio vicini*: N. R. Whitty, 'Nuisance', in *The Laws of Scotland: Stair Memorial Encyclopaedia*, vol. 14 (1988), § 2008.

[299] (1624) Mor 12769. The other case is *Bairdie* v. *Scartsonse* (1624) Mor 14529; Hope, *Practicks*, VI, 40, 6.

[300] The report gives the citation '*L unica. Ne quis aquam de flumine publico*'.

[301] Stair, II, 1, 5; Bankton, I, 3, 2; Erskine, II, 1, 5.

[302] Stair, II, 1, 5; Bankton, I, 3, 4; II, 7, 27; Erskine, II, 1, 5; II, 6, 17. See also Craig, I, 16, 11; Hume, *Lectures*, IV, 238 sq.; Bell, *Principles*, §§ 638 and 648–50.

invoking the *interdictum uti priore aestate* in 1624[303] were referred to by Stair, Bankton, and Erskine in a very brief discussion tagged incongruously on to their discussion of the servitude of watergang or aqueduct.[304]

This reflected the rudimentary organization of Scots neighbourhood law at that period.[305] Throughout the eighteenth century, however, the Court of Session entertained many actions relating to competing riparian rights,[306] thereby creating the raw materials for an institutional synthesis. This was achieved by Hume's original and seminal statement of neighbourhood law,[307] subsuming both riparian rights and the law of the tenement under common interest.[308]

In the gradual development of riparian common interest, several strands of development were interwoven. First, many of the rights *publici juris* available to all members of the public under Roman law to use and enjoy the river, and to prevent interference with it,[309] were transformed into rights *privati juris* exercisable only by riparian owners as an incident of their right of property in the river-banks. This transformation occurred gradually. From 1624 onwards, reported cases involving actions to prevent or undo interference with the flow of rivers—whether stemming from diversion or abstraction,[310] or retardation[311] of the water, erections *in alveo*,[312] fortification of the

---

[303] *Bannatyne v. Cranston* (1624) Mor 12769; *Bairdie v. Scartsonse* (1624) Mor 14529.

[304] Stair, II, 7, 12; Bankton, II, 7, 29; Erskine, II, 9, 13.

[305] In the same way, Stair's famous description of the law of the tenement in II, 7, 6—another subcategory of common interest in modern Scots law—was tagged on to his discussion of the servitude of support.

[306] Of 50 case reports in Morison's *Dictionary*, s.v. 'Property' and Appendix, the majority (about 29) concerned disputes between riparian proprietors.

[307] Hume, *Lectures*, III, 207–28 (part III, chapter 1, 'The Right of Property').

[308] Hume, *Lectures*, III, 216–25 (riparian rights); 225–8 (law of the tenement).

[309] D. 43, 12 (interdict to prevent anything from being done in a river, or on its bank, to hamper navigation); D. 43, 13 (interdict to prevent acts in private river causing the water to flow otherwise than it did last summer); D. 43, 14 (interdict to allow navigation in public river); D. 43, 15 (interdict preventing interference with works in a public river or its banks for protecting the bank from flooding).

[310] *Hay v. Feuars* (1677) Mor 1818; *Cuningham v. Kennedy* (1713) Mor 12778; *Aberdeen Magistrates v. Menzies* (1748) Mor 12787; *Magistrates of Linlithgow v. Elphinstone* (1768) Mor 12805, 5 Brown's Supp 935, Hailes 203; *Kelso v. Boyds* (1768) Mor 12807, Hailes 224; *Cruikshanks v. Henderson* (1791) Hume 506; *Ogilvy v. Kincaid* (1791) Mor 12824, Hume 508; *Hamilton v. Edington & Co.* (1793) Mor 12824; *Braid v. Douglas* (1800) Mor Appendix, 'Property', no. 2; *Aytoun v. Douglas* (1800) Mor Appendix, 'Property', no. 5; *Edmonstone v. Lanark Twist Co.* (1810) Hume 520; *Duke of Roxburghe v. Waldie* (1821) Hume 524; *Johnstone v. Ritchie* (1822) 1 S 327.

[311] *Marquis of Abercorn v. Jamieson* (1791) Mor 14285, Hume 510 (forming fishponds in stream; regulation by court of times of opening sluices of ponds); *Lord Glenlee v. Gordon* (1804) Mor 12834 (reservoir at cotton mill which in dry weather absorbed stream for several hours daily).

[312] *Farqhuarson v. Farqhuarson* (1741) Mor 12779, 5 Brown's Supp 688, Elchies, 'Property', no. 5; *Earl of Kinnoull v. Keir* 18 Jan. 1814 FC.

banks,[313] regurgitation[314] or the like,—were brought by riparian owners. The *Linlithgow Magistrates* case[315] shows that the principle underlying the right to prevent interference with the flow of perennial rivers was still uncertain in 1768. By 1800 however, the right to prevent such interference had crystallized into a private law right incidental to riparian ownership.

A second essential step was to distinguish the actual running water (*aqua profluens*), which has a transient presence in a river, (and while still flowing could be regarded as *res communis omnium* or the property of no one)[316] from the concept of the river (*flumen*) itself as a geographical entity with a continuing existence which can be, and is, the object of rights of use and enjoyment that are permanent and proprietary in character. The law has to draw this distinction in order to avoid the non sequitur that since the water in a river may to some extent be appropriated, the river itself may likewise be appropriated. The distinction is essential to the modern doctrine of common interest in rivers because that doctrine predicates the concept of private proprietary rights attaching to the river itself, and its natural or accustomed flow, rather than to the particles of running water of which it is composed at any given time. The distinction between the transient *aqua profluens* and the permanent *flumen* developed by the *jus commune*[317] came to be explicitly recognized in Scots law. The idea of a proprietary right in the flow of a river was touched on in *Fairly* v. *Eglinton*,[318] which held that the defender lower riparian owner could not insist on the pursuer upper owner raising his millwheel (at the defender's expense) as a protective measure against regurgitation. The successful pursuer argued that if he 'were to agree to the elevation of his wheel, he would thereby lose a considerable force of water which he possessed formerly, and must be considered his property'.[319] If any one case

---

[313] *Duke of Gordon* v. *Duff* (1735) Mor 12778; *Nairn Magistrates* v. *Brodie* (1738) Mor 12779; *Aberdeen Magistrates* v. *Menzies* (1748) Mor 12787; *Menzies* v. *Earl of Breadalbane* (1828) 3 W & S 235.

[314] *Fairly* v. *Eglinton* (1744) Mor 12780, Kilk 452, Elchies, 'Property', no. 7, Hume 506; *Burgess* v. *Brown* (1790) Hume 504; *Baillie* v. *Lady Saltoun* (1821) Hume 523, 1 S 227.

[315] *Magistrates of Linlithgow* v. *Elphinstone* (1768) Mor 12805, 5 Brown's Supp 935, Hailes 203. At Mor 12806 Kames's report states: 'Water drawn from a river into vessels or into ponds becomes private property; but to admit of such property with respect to the river itself, considered as a complex body, would be inconsistent with the public interest . . .'

[316] Cf. *Lord Blantyre* v. *Dunn* (1848) 10 D 509 at 538 *per* Lord Moncreiff: 'as . . . a stream passes from one territory to another, and the water as it passes is replaced by other water from above,—and so it cannot be said that, in strictness, there is property in the particles of water which run past . . .'; *Morris* v. *Bicket* (1864) 2 M 1082 at 1092 *per* Lord Neaves: '*aqua profluens* is not the subject of property as long as it is running. When you get it into your pitcher or pipe it becomes your property . . .; but while it is flowing . . . [i]t is as much the property of no one as the air that we breathe or the sunlight that shines upon us.'

[317] e.g. Vinnius (n. 190), II, 1, 2, quoted in part in n. 323.

[318] *Fairly* v. *Eglinton* (1744) Mor 12780, Kilk 452, Elchies, 'Property', no. 7, Hume 506 (defender lower riparian owner held not entitled to build a dam-dike causing restagnation harming the operation of an upper riparian proprietor's mill).   [319] Ibid. at 12786.

may be said to mark the final establishment of the doctrine of common interest (though not yet *eo nomine*), it would be Hamilton v. Edington & Co. in 1793,[320] regarded as the leading case before *Morris* v. *Bicket*.[321] The successful pursuer argued:[322]

> If from the nature of running water, it cannot in a strict sense, be the object of property, every heritor through whose lands it runs, has, at least, the exclusive use and enjoyment of it, which is the most essential mark of that right. But whatever may be said of the water or *aqua profluens*, the stream or *flumen* continues the same from one age to another, and is therefore the object of permanent rights; Vinn p 127.

In support, he cited Vinnius who remarked:[323]

> *Notandum autem est discrimen fluminis et aquae fluentis, unde usus utriusque nascitur diversitas. Flumen est totum quid, unumque et idem corpus, quod mille abiunc annis fuit, arg. l. proponebatur 76. de. judic.* [Alfenus D. 5, 1, 76] *denique sub imperio eorum est, quorum finibus continetur.*

He also argued that 'a common property arises where a stream forms a march between two tenements'.[324] In a very important passage, the majority of the Court held:[325]

> that in the case of a private river, of whatever extent, running between the lands of opposite proprietors, the mere possibility of damage, (and as some expressed themselves) even in point of amenity, gave either a title to object to any material alteration upon its course. Whatever may be said (it was observed) of the water of which it is composed, the stream itself is the object of property, or at least of a right equally entitled to protection. The water may be used for all ordinary purposes, but the stream cannot be diverted. It is acknowledged the chargers[326] cannot divert the whole river, and where is the line to be drawn? Manufactures will not be injured by this doctrine, because there is little danger that consent will be refused where an adequate consideration is offered: at all events, the right of private property is sacred.

Third, the development of the idea of common interest and its application to riparian rights began from Roman law and culminated in a largely indigenous concept. As we have seen, in *Bannatyne* v. *Cranston*,[327] the authority relied on to strike at diversion was Ulp. D. 43, 13, 1, 1, a text on the public law *interdictum uti priore aestate*.[328] Bankton derived from the case a rule of private

---

[320] *Hamilton* v. *Edington & Co.* (1793) Mor 12824.
[321] *Morris* v. *Bicket* (1864) 2 M 1082, (1866) 4 M (HL) 44.
[322] *Hamilton* v. *Edington & Co.* (1793) Mor 12824 at 12825.
[323] Vinnius (n. 190), II, 1, 2, quoted in modified form in *Lord Blantyre* v. *Dunn* (1848) 10 D 509 at 543 *per* Lord Moncreiff. ('It should be noted, however, that there is a distinction between a river and flowing water, whence from the use of each a difference emerges. The river is the whole entity, one and the same body, which has existed for a thousand years. Finally it is under the control of those within whose boundaries it is confined.')
[324] *Hamilton* v. *Edington & Co.* (1793) Mor 12824 at 12825.   [325] Ibid at 12826–7.
[326] i.e. 'defenders' or 'respondents'. See n. 490 below.
[327] *Bannatyne* v. *Cranston* (1624) Mor 12769.   [328] See n. 294 above.

law against diversion of a common march watercourse and based the rule on a brocard drawn from the Roman private law regime of common (*pro indiviso*) property: *in re communi melior est conditio prohibentis*.[329] Other concepts were relied on, notably the notion that a lower riparian owner is 'under a natural servitude of receiving water',[330] a rule relating not to a *flumen* but to *aqua pluvia*.[331] In 1791 in *Marquis of Abercorn* v. *Jamieson*[332] occurs the first reference in our case reports to 'common interest' in the context of riparian rights. In 1793 in the leading *Edington* case,[333] the pursuer used the concept of 'common property in a stream' and the Court spoke of the stream being 'the object of property, or at least of a right equally entitled to protection'. In 1800 in *Braid* v. *Douglas*[334] the court referred to 'the common interest which the parties have in the river opposite to their respective lands ...'. In 1804 in *Lord Glenlee* v. *Gordon*[335] the successful pursuer argued that the riparian owners had a 'joint usufructuary right to the stream in its natural condition'. In 1810 in *Lanark Twist Co.* v. *Edmonstone*[336] the pursuer argued that the defender's works on a stream would prejudice her in various ways but pleaded *separatim* 'on the principle of her joint and equal interest in this march stream, which gave her a negative on any work which would withdraw a portion of the stream, whether the works were or were not attended with any immediate prejudicial effect'.[337] Lord President Blair observed that 'the general point of law was settled in *Edington's* case and carried still further in Lord Glenlee's case ..., and is not now to be touched'.[338] On the basis of these cases, Hume[339] and Bell[340] subsumed riparian rights under a doctrine of common interest a label also applied to the law of the tenement. Yet as late as 1828 in *Menzies* v. *Earl of Breadalbane*[341] the House of Lords was citing Roman texts on *aqua pluvia* in order to vouch riparian rights.[342] In 1848 in *Lord Blantyre* v. *Dunn*[343] Lord Moncreiff observed of the *Edington*, *Lord Glenlee*, and *Lanark Twist Co.* cases:[344]

---

[329] Bankton, II, 7, 29. See Pap. D. 10, 3, 28: 'Sabinus ait in re communi neminem dominorum iure facere quicquam invito altero posse. unde manifestum est prohibendi ius esse: in re enim pari potiorem causam esse prohibentis constat.' ('Sabinus says that none of the owners of common property can build anything on it against the wishes of the other owner. From which it is clear that a right of veto exists; for where people have equal rights, it is an established principle that a veto overrides any proposal.') The brocard was relied on by the successful pursuer in *Hamilton* v. *Edington & Co.* (1793) Mor 12824 at 12825. In *Morris* v. *Bicket* (1864) 2 M 1082, (1866) 4 M (HL) 44, a difference of opinion arose as to whether the brocard was applicable to riparian common interest. Lord Benholme (2 M at 1090) and Lord Westbury (4 M at 52) thought the brocard applicable while Lord Justice-Clerk Inglis (2 M at 1087) thought it only applicable to common property. [330] See *Burgess* v. *Brown* (1790) Hume 504.
[331] See e.g. Ulp. D. 39, 3, 1, 23; Bankton, II, 7, 30; Erskine, II, 9, 2. [332] (1791) Hume 510.
[333] *Hamilton* v. *Edington & Co.* (1793) Mor 12824.
[334] (1800) Mor Appendix, 'Property', 2. [335] (1804) Mor 12834.
[336] (1810) Hume 520. [337] Ibid. at 521. [338] Ibid.
[339] Hume, *Lectures*, III, 216–25. [340] Bell, *Principles*, §§ 1100–11.
[341] (1828) 3 W & S 235, reversing (1826) 4 S 783.
[342] Ibid. at 244 *per* Lord Chancellor citing Ulp. D. 39, 3, 1, 2 and D. 39, 3, 1, 1.
[343] (1848) 10 D 509. [344] Ibid. at 542.

These cases settle general principles; and in particular as I read the case of Edington, which was simply followed in the case of the Lanark Twist Company, they settled the rights of adjoining or inferior heritors on a river, either as rights of property, or by some equivalent title or charter; to give effect to which, especially where there has been prescriptive possession, it is not necessary for the party complaining of a violation of his right, to prove that the water is necessary for his use, or that he will suffer patrimonial injury by the alleged diversion or interference with it.

The modern doctrine of riparian common interest was expounded in 1864 in classic judgments in *Morris* v. *Bicket*[345] largely without reference to the Roman law. The term 'riparian', first used in Scots law in the 1860s,[346] seems to have been borrowed from English law,[347] into which it had apparently been introduced from French law through the medium of American sources.[348]

Fourth, the development of common interest necessarily meant rejection of any doctrine of prior appropriation. English cases were cited in Scottish cases on common interest in rivers only in the late nineteenth century.[349] Defenders vainly relied on the Roman law texts to the effect that *aqua profluens* is *res communis*[350] as if those texts supported a rule that water in a *flumen* or the *flumen* itself could be appropriated.[351] They also unsuccessfully relied on

---

[345] *Morris* v. *Bicket* (1864) 2 M 1082, (1866) 4 M (HL) 44.

[346] In *Morris* v. *Bicket* (n. 345), the expression 'riparian proprietors' was used in all three speeches in the House of Lords (Lords Chelmsford LC, Cranworth, and Westbury) and in none of the opinions of the Second Division judges.

[347] According to S. C. Wiel, 'Waters: American Law and French Authority', (1919–20) 33 *Harv LR* 133 at 146, the term 'riparian' in reference to this subject occurs for the first time in English law in *Wood* v. *Waud* (1849) 3 Exch 748, 154 ER 1047.

[348] Weil (n. 347) points out (at 136 sq.) that the term 'riparian' was used by Story J in the landmark American case of *Tyler* v. *Wilkinson* (1827) 4 Mason 397, Fed Cas No. 14, 312. It then appeared in the second edition (1833) of an influential American textbook, Joseph K. Angell, *A Treatise on the Law of Watercourses*, which stated: 'Those who own the land bounding upon a watercourse are denominated by the civilians riparian proprietors, and the same convenient term was adopted by Mr J. Story in giving his opinion in the case of *Tyler* v. *Wilkinson*.' The 4th edn. (1850), 8 states, 'and the use of the same significant and convenient term is now fully introduced into the Common Law'. The *Tyler* case, and Angell on *The Law of Watercourses* were cited in English cases such as *Wood* v. *Waud* (1849) 3 Exch 748, 154 ER 1047 and *Embrey* v. *Owen* (1851) 6 Exch 353, 155 ER 579. J. K. Angell, *The Law of Watercourses* (4th edn., 1850) is in the Advocates' Library and was eventually cited in Scots cases: see e.g. *Morris* v. *Bicket* (1864) 2 M 1082 at 1086 (defender's authorities) as well as by Rankine (n. 108) and Ferguson (n. 1). See further text at nn. 390–404 below.

[349] In *Hamilton* v. *Edington and Co.* (1793) Mor 12824, the pursuer relied (at 12825) on English authority, namely, Bracton, fo. 234, 1 4 c 45; *De assisa novae dississinae* (sic); s. 9 *De aquadiversa*; and *Brown* v. *Best* (1747) 1 Wilson KB 174, 95 ER 557. According to Lauer, (1963) 28 *Miss LR* 60 at 96, *Brown* v. *Best* was the only English case on water rights in the 18th century before its closing decades. It was decided on principles of ancient use. The first reference to English authority in water rights cases in Morison's *Dictionary*, s.v. 'Property', is a case on the ownership of the beds of lochs: *Dick* v. *Earl of Abercorn* (1769) Mor 12813 in which the defender (at 12814) relied on Blackstone's *Commentaries* b, 2, c, 2; and Brownlaw's Reports, part 1, 142. Blackstone's *Commentaries* were first published in 1765. See p. 466 below.

[350] Inst. II, 1, 1; Marc. D. 1, 8, 2, 1.

[351] e.g. *Magistrates of Linlithgow* v. *Elphinstone* (1768) Mor 12805, 5 Brown's Supp 935, Hailes 203.

Roman texts allowing an owner of higher rural land to appropriate casual rainwater (*aqua pluvia*).[352] These arguments were rejected by the court, which in 1791 remarked that 'if any of the foreign doctors have expressed themselves more largely, or have opinions to the contrary, it is not sound law, and has not been acknowledged in our practice, or in that of other countries'.[353] There were virtually no Scots decisions supporting the 'prior appropriation' doctrine of the English law.[354] So it is not surprising that not one of the authorities relied on by the unsuccessful defender in the leading modern case of *Morris* v. *Bicket*[355] were Scottish.[356]

(dd) The idea of 'natural flow'

The origin of the natural flow theory of riparian common interest in Scots law lies mainly in the prohibition in the interdict *uti priore aestate*[357] against anything being done which might cause the water to flow otherwise than it did last summer.[358] Also relevant were texts showing that the *actio aquae pluviae arcendae* did not lie to prevent harm caused by the 'natural' flow of casual water and texts on the *actio* speaking of a 'natural servitude' binding the owner of lower ground to receive that 'natural' flow.[359] Somewhat incongruously, (for the *actio* applied to casual rainwater not rivers),[360] these texts were sometimes applied, or misapplied, in Scots law to riparian rights.[361]

While Hume nowhere uses the expression 'natural flow', in his analysis of riparian common interest, the concept of maintaining 'the natural order of things' plays a central role.[362] In Bell's *Principles*[363] the reference to 'natural flow'[364] was introduced only in the sixth edition (1872) under reference to *Morris* v. *Bicket* in 1864/1866.[365] In his classic statement, Lord Neaves said

---

[352] Ulp. D. 39, 3, 1, 21; Paul. D. 39, 3, 2, 9; C. 3, 34, 11, 10.

[353] *Cruikshanks* v. *Henderson* (1791) Hume 506 at 507 which also states: 'The Judges seem to be agreed on these matters at advising . . . [t]hat the texts of the Roman law are not to be understood of a wilful and prejudicial alteration of the superficial course of a rivulet, but of veins of water only under ground, which the owner of the upper lands happens casually to cut in the course of his lawful operations of casting drains, sinking for coal, or the like, *in sua*.' To a like effect see also *Magistrates of Linlithgow* v. *Elphinstone* (1768) Mor 12805, 5 Brown's Supp 935, Hailes 203; *Kelso* v. *Boyds* (1768) Mor 12807, Hailes 224. [354] See IV.2.c below.

[355] *Morris* v. *Bicket* (1864) 2 M 1082 at 1086.

[356] These authorities were Ulp. D. 39, 3 (*De aqua et aquae pluv arc*), 1 and 3; Pothier, Comm *in hoc loco*; *Wright* v. *Howard* (1823) 1 Sim & St 190, 57 ER 76; *Williams* v. *Morland* (1824) 2 B & C 910, 107 ER 620; Angell on *Watercourses*, 118 (edn. not cited; probably 4th edn. (1850), which is in point). [357] D. 43, 13.

[358] Ulp. D. 43, 13, 1, 1.

[359] Ulp. D. 39, 3, 1, 1; D. 39, 3, 1, 14; D. 39, 3, 1, 23; D. 39, 3, 3, 4. [360] See VI below.

[361] See *Kelso* v. *Boyds* (1768) Hailes 224, Mor 12807 (defender's argument): 'Nature has imposed a servitude on the inferior ground'; *Menzies* v. *Earl of Breadalbane* (1828) 3 W & S 235 at 244 *per* Lord Eldon LC citing *inter alia* Ulp. D. 39, 3, 1, 1; 'a superior heritor cannot direct any part of a stream to the prejudice of an inferior heritor' and that 'the ordinary course of the river in the different seasons of the year must . . . be subject to the same principle'.

[362] Hume, *Lectures*, III, 217. [363] Bell, *Principles*, §§ 1100–8.

[364] Ibid. (6th and 10th edns.), § 1107.

[365] *Morris* v. *Bicket* (1864) 2 M 1082, affirmed (1866) 4 M (HL) 44.

that a lower heritor had an interest that the stream 'shall be transmitted to him undiminished in quantity, unpolluted in quality, and unaffected in force and natural direction and current, except in so far as the primary uses of it may legitimately operate upon it within the lands of the upper heritor'.[366]

(ee) Primary and secondary purposes

In Roman law perennial rivers were *res in usu populi* and as such open to all free of charge provided that they did not impede the exercise of the same right by other citizens.[367] Bonfante identified various uses, including the most elementary, i.e. the right to drink or to water animals;[368] the right to bathe or wash[369] also elementary; the right to fish;[370] and to navigate.[371] The State could sell licences for some uses. There does not seem to have been a fixed order of priority between competing uses.

In Scots law, the view of what uses of a river are acceptable have changed dramatically over time. In a pollution case in 1661,[372] the Lords considered that 'it was the proper use of rivers to carry away the corruption and filth of the earth, which should not be hindered by any right of fishing, which is but a casualty given and taken with the common use of the river'.[373] The idea of primary and secondary purposes developed late. Kames[374] stated that if the water in a river is insufficient for all riparian owners, 'there ought to be [a] rule for using it with discretion; though, hitherto, no rule has been laid down', and made some suggestions for rules on the order of priority of competing uses 'which practice may in time ripen to a precise rule'.[375] The distinction between primary and secondary uses entered Scots law in 1791 in *Russell* v. *Haig*,[376] which together with *Miller* v. *Stein*,[377] marks also the beginning of

---

[366] Ibid., (1864) 2 M 1082 at 1092. See also at 1093: 'Now the common interest ... amounts to a right of preventing anything which shall palpably affect the water ...' On appeal, Lord Chelmsford LC said that opposite proprietors 'have a common interest in the stream' and that 'neither is entitled to use the *alveus* in such a manner as to interfere with the natural flow of the water'.   [367] Bonfante (n. 87), 93 sqq.
[368] Ibid. See Cicero, *De Officiis*, 1, 16.   [369] Bonfante (n. 87), 95.
[370] Ibid. citing Inst. 2, 1, 2.   [371] Bonfante (n. 87), 95.
[372] *Mayor of Berwick* v. *Lord Hayning* (1661) Mor 12772, 2 Brown's Supp 292; George Mackenzie, *The Works of that Eminent and Learned Lawyer, Sir George Mackenzie of Rosehaugh* (1716), vol. 1, 320, 364; George Mackenzie, *Pleadings in some Remarkable Cases before the Supreme Courts of Scotland* (1672), 24 at 25: public rivers 'have been very wisely by Providence spread up and down the world to be easy and natural vehicles for conveying away to the sea (that great receptacle of all things that are unnecessary) excrements and other noxious things which would otherwise have very much prejudged mankind'.   [373] (1661) Mor 12772 at 12773 sq.
[374] Kames, *Principles of Equity* (5th edn., 1825), 33.
[375] Ibid. In his view, 'if there be not a sufficiency of water for every purpose, those purposes ought to be preferred that are most essential to the well-being of the adjacent proprietors'. His suggested order of priorities was (1) drink for man and beast; (2) washing; (3) corn-mill; (4) irrigation; (5) bleachfield; and (6) machinery.
[376] *Russell* v. *Haig* (1791) Mor 12823, Bell Oct Cas 338, 3 Pat App 403 (refuse from distillery polluting small stream of clear water fit for family uses) at 345 *per* Lord Monboddo and at 346 *per* Lord Justice-Clerk Braxfield.
[377] *Miller* v. *Stein* (1791) Mor 12823, Bell Oct Cas 334 (refuse from distillery at Lochrin polluting rivulet formerly used for domestic purposes and by cattle).

the modern common law on river pollution.[378] Thereafter the primary/secondary dichotomy was applied to determine liability for pollution of water, especially in rivers, as well as infringement of common interest.

(b) River pollution, common interest, and nuisance

Roman law said little about pollution of rivers. In Scotland, though occasional early river pollution cases invoked the *immissio* principle,[379] the modern law begins with two cases in 1791[380] concerning pollution by effluent from distilleries. The court relied on the analogy of the Roman rules against diversion of a *flumen publicum*,[381] narrowing its channel[382] or intercepting a spring[383] and the Scots authorities introducing those rules.[384] The other authorities related to the new doctrine of nuisance which was becoming established by a tract of 'public police' cases and blending with English sources on nuisance.[385] One reason why Hume categorized river pollution as an infringement of a right of common interest was that he thought that nuisance was applicable only within burgh.[386]

So we can see that whereas in English law violations of riparian rights were and still are subsumed under the tort of nuisance, in Scots law water law regimes developed from civilian sources long before the emergence of nuisance and are not generally treated as part of nuisance law, despite a few solecisms in the House of Lords.[387] Several commentators treat pollution of

---

[378] For subsequent case law, see J. C. C. Broun, *The Law of Nuisance in Scotland* (1891), part 1, ch. 2 on 'Pollution of Water'.

[379] Paul. D. 8, 5, 8, 5 and 6: see *Mayor of Berwick* v. *Lord Hayning* (1661) Mor 12772, 2 Brown's Supp 292; Mackenzie, *Works* (n. 372), 24; *Brodie* v. *Cadel* (1707) 4 Brown's Supp 660.

[380] *Miller* v. *Stein* (1791) Mor 12823, Bell Oct Cas 334, 3 Pat App 403; *Russell* v. *Haig* (1791) Mor 12823, Bell Oct Cas 338.

[381] *Russell* v. *Haig* (1791) Mor 12823, Bell Oct Cas 338 pursuer's argument (at 343) citing Pomp. D. 43, 20, 3 pr.: 'if the superior heritor cannot deprive the inferior one of the use of his stream by diverting its course, neither can he do it by corrupting it so as to render it unfit for the primary uses of water': *Miller* v. *Stein* (1791) Mor 12823. See also Hume, *Lectures*, III, 220.

[382] *Russell* v. *Haig* (1791) Mor 12823, 3 Pat App 338, Bell Oct Cas 338 at 345 *per* Lord Dreghorn: 'Amongst the Romans, it was unlawful to narrow a channel, so as to impede the velocity of the current. I do not see the difference betwixt diverting the course of a stream and altogether destroying the use of it to the inferior proprietor.'

[383] *Miller* v. *Stein* (1791) Mor 12823, Bell Oct Cas 334 at 337 *per* Lord Justice-Clerk Braxfield: 'We have after the Roman law, found, that an inferior tenement cannot be deprived of a spring; the heritor is bound to transmit it to the inferior tenement, *multo magis*, he cannot send it down in such a state as to be of no use.'

[384] *Bairdie* v. *Scartsonse* (1624) Mor 14529; *Kelso* v. *Boyds* (1768) Mor 12807, Hailes 224.

[385] See e.g. *Miller* v. *Stein* (1791) Bell Oct Cas 334 at 335 referring to English authorities on the defence of coming to the nuisance; *Russell* v. *Haig* (1791) Bell Oct Cas 338 *per* Lord President Campbell: 'Blackstone's authority is to be respected'. On the emergence of nuisance in Scots law, see Whitty (n. 298), § 2012.   [386] Hume, *Lectures*, III, 220; Bell, *Principles*, § 1106.

[387] See e.g. *Viscount Arbuthnot* v. *Scott* (1802) 4 Pat App 337 at 343 *per* Lord Alvanley, criticized by A. D. Gibb, *Law from over the Border* (1950), 19, 58. Things not treated as nuisance in the Court of Session could become such in the House of Lords: see e.g. *Colquhoun's Trs* v. *Orr Ewing & Co.* (1877) 4 R (HL) 116 at 133 *per* Lord Blackburn.

streams as part of nuisance,[388] so that alteration of flow infringes common interest whereas deterioration of quality is nuisance. These distinctions await exploration.[389]

(c) The comparative law context

(aa) 'Prior appropriation' and 'riparian rights' theories of rights in watercourses

In common law systems, two theories of rights in natural watercourses have competed for dominance, namely, the 'prior appropriation' and the 'riparian rights' theories.[390] The former was dominant in English law at the beginning of the nineteenth century[391] but was supplanted by the riparian rights theory as a result of a line of cases commencing with *Wright* v. *Howard* in 1823,[392] followed by *Mason* v. *Hill* in 1833[393] (the turning point) and *Wood* v. *Waud* in 1849,[394] and culminating in the leading modern case of *Embrey* v. *Owen* in 1851.[395] The source of the riparian rights theory in English law is problematic.

---

[388] See e.g. Broun (n. 378), ch. 2 (Pollution of water); Gordon (n. 60), paras. 7-34; Whitty (n. 298), § 2079; Reid (n. 108), § 298. The American Law Institute, *First Restatement of the Law of Torts* (1939) and *Second* (1979) both treat nuisance (ch. 40) separately from infringements of riparian rights (ch. 41).

[389] It is thought that under Scots law, in principle, common interest and nuisance relate as overlapping rather than mutually exclusive categories; that only riparian property is protected by common interest whereas nuisance protects all property; that (subject to one exception) the doctrine of primary and secondary uses is a branch only of the law of riparian common interest; and cannot be invoked in a nuisance action by the pursuer who may be a non-riparian. The exception is that 'primary use' should in principle give a riparian owner a defence to a nuisance action because a non-riparian suing in nuisance should not in principle have a higher right than a riparian suing under common interest. In common interest, the test of infringement is interference with natural flow otherwise than for legally protected 'primary' purposes. In nuisance the '*plus quam tolerabile*' test of liability depends much more on a balancing of interests and is more elastic and uncertain.

[390] See S. C. Wiel, 'Theories of Water Law', (1913-14) 27 *Harv LR* 530 at 531 sq.; ALI (n. 288), vol. 4, 342 sq., ch. 41, topic 3, Scope Note; vol. 4, 341 sq.; Lauer, (1963) 28 *Miss LR* 60 at 96 sqq.; J. P. S. McLaren, 'Nuisance Law and the Industrial Revolution—Some Lessons from Social History', (1983) 5 *OJLS* 155, 170 sqq.

[391] See Blackstone, *Commentaries on the Laws of England* (14th edn., 1803), 403: 'If a stream be unoccupied, I may erect a mill thereon, and detain the water; yet not so as to injure my neighbour's prior mill, or his meadow; for he hath by the first occupancy acquired a property in the current.' See also *Robinson* v. *Lord Byron* (1785) 1 Brown Ch 588, 28 ER 1315; *Bealey* v. *Shaw* (1805) 6 East 208, 102 ER 1266; *Williams* v. *Morland* (1824) 2 B & C 910, 107 ER 620; *Liggins* v. *Inge* (1831) 7 Bing 682 at 693, 131 ER 263 at 268 *per* Tindal CJ: 'by the law of England, the person who first appropriates any part of the water flowing through his own land to his own use has the right to the use of so much as he thus appropriates against any other'; Lauer, (1963) 28 *Miss LR* 60 at 96-104.   [392] *Wright* v. *Howard* (1823) 1 Sim & St 190, 57 ER 76.

[393] *Mason* v. *Hill* (1833) 5 B & Ad 1, 110 ER 692, where Denman CJ (at 23 sq.) expressly relied on the same distinction drawn by Vinnius between a river and its water as the Court of Session had invoked in 1793 (see n. 323). Cf. J. Mackintosh, *Roman Law in Modern Practice* (1934), 132-4.   [394] *Wood* v. *Waud* (1849) 3 Exch 748; 154 ER 1047.

[395] *Embrey* v. *Owen* (1851) 6 Exch 353; 155 ER 579.

About seventy years ago, Professor Wiel[396] argued that the sources were civilian (especially the *Digest*, French authors, and the Code Napoleon[397]) which were mediated to English law via American law[398] by the citation in English cases of such American sources as Judge Story's judgment in *Tyler* v. *Wilkinson*,[399] Kent's *Commentaries*,[400] and Angell on *Watercourses*.[401] Reacting against Wiel's conclusions in 1963, T. E. Lauer argued that, while Story and Kent drew heavily on the Code Napoleon and Roman law in constructing the American riparian rights doctrine, the 'gestation of that doctrine occurred within the matrix of the common law, over centuries of judicial experience and growth'.[402] More recently, Alan Watson has argued that even less credit is due to Roman law and the Code Napoleon than Lauer conceded and that Kent's citations of civilian sources on water law were not only sloppy but also superfluous—mere window dressing—because Kent could have relied on English or native American common law authority, and that more easily.[403] However that may be, by the time when the second reception of English law into Scots law occurred, English law had rejected the 'prior appropriation' theory in favour of the 'riparian rights' theory which closely resembled the Scottish rules on riparian common interest developed directly from the *jus commune*.[404]

(bb) Forms of riparian rights theories: 'natural flow' or 'reasonable use'

Since gaining dominance over the appropriation theory in Anglo-American law, the riparian rights theory has subdivided into two distinct doctrines.[405] One is the 'natural flow' doctrine which applies in English law and some states of the USA.[406] The other is the 'reasonable use' doctrine which is

[396] Wiel, (1919–1920) 32 *Harv LR* 133; *idem*, 'Origin and Comparative Development of the Law of Watercourses in the Common Law and in the Civil Law', (1918) 6 *California LR* 245, 342.

[397] Wiel, (1919–20) 32 *Harv LR* 133 at 137 n. 15 referring to J. Kent, *Commentaries on American Law* (12th edn., 1896), vol. 3, 439 note c: the French authors include Pothier, Toullier, and Merlin.; and the Code Civil, arts. 641, 643 sq.

[398] Especially the work of Judge Story and Chancellor Kent who had a strong interest in Roman law and French law: cf. M. H. Hoeflich, *Roman and Civil Law and the Development of Anglo-American Jurisprudence in the Nineteenth Century* (1997), 26 sqq.; A. Watson, 'Chancellor Kent's Use of Foreign Law', in M. Reimann (ed.), *The Reception of Continental Ideas in the Common Law World 1820–1920* (1993), 45, at 52–7.

[399] *Tyler* v. *Wilkinson* (1827) 4 Mason 397, 24 Fed Cas 472.

[400] See Kent (n. 397), 439: 'Every proprietor of lands on the banks of a river has naturally an equal right to the use of the water. . . . He has no property in the water itself, but a simple usufruct as it passes along': cited in *Wood* v. *Waud* (1849) 3 Exch 748 at 775, 154 ER 1047; *Embrey* v. *Owen* (1851) 6 Exch 353 at 369, 155 ER 579; *Rugby Joint Water Board* v. *Walters* [1967] 1 Ch 397 at 418 sq. [401] Angell (n. 348), 1st edn., 1820.

[402] Lauer, (1963) 28 *Miss LR* 60 at 170. [403] Watson (n. 398), 52–7.

[404] This was expressly recognized in *Colquhoun's Trs* v. *Orr Ewing & Co.* (1877) 4 R (HL) 116 at 127 *per* Lord Blackburn quoted in text accompanying n. 539 below.

[405] See ALI (n. 288), s. 849, Introductory Note on Riparian Rights; this follows closely S. V. Kinyon, 'What can a riparian proprietor do?', (1937) 21 *Minn LR* 512.

[406] Kinyon, (1937) 21 *Minn LR* 512.

dominant in the USA.[407] From the beginning Scots law adopted the natural flow theory.

(d) The role of economic and social factors

The prominent place of nuisance including water pollution in the literature on 'law and economics'[408] lies beyond the scope of this article but something must be said about the impact of economic and social factors in effecting doctrinal change. In the Anglo-American common law tradition, the change from the prior appropriation theory to the riparian rights theory is sometimes regarded as a response to the industrial revolution.[409] On this view, before the industrial revolution, a riparian owner's use of a stream 'seldom had any material effect on others. There was water enough for all because there was no such thing as public water works, sewage disposal systems, large factories and power plants.' After the industrial revolution (it is said) '[t]here arose many new uses for water which either consumed large quantities of it or polluted it to such an extent that it was of little use to others. The resulting conflict of interests in the user of water demanded a more equitable rule than "first come, first served".'[410] Alan Watson by contrast has argued that whether the economy is agricultural or industrial, riparian owners and the wider public will have the same concerns: too much water, or too little, resulting from another landowner's activity.[411]

It would not be true to say of Scotland that before the industrial revolution a riparian owner's use of a stream 'seldom had any material effect on others' or that 'there was water enough for all'. In Scots law, the main elements of the doctrine of riparian common interest were established long before the industrial revolution.[412] Many early cases related to watermills,[413] apart from horses and humans the most important source of motive power in the Scottish economy until overtaken by steam power in the 1830s.[414] Other uses such as fishing and navigation, which required protection from dams or

---

[407] Ibid.
[408] e.g. R. Coase, 'The Problem of Social Cost', (1960) 3 *J L & Econ* 1; R. Posner, *Economic Analysis of the Law* (1972).
[409] The prior appropriation theory is said also to have been developed in late 18th-century England as the initial response of the English courts to the industrial revolution: McLaren, (1983) 5 *OJLS* 155, 170 sqq.   [410] ALI (n. 288), vol. 4, 341 sq.
[411] A. Watson, 'The Transformation of American Property Law: A Comparative Law Approach', (1990) 24 *Georgia LR* 163, at 216. He continues (ibid.): 'It is not the case with water rights that the most effective law will vary according to whether the use is for agricultural or industrial purposes.'
[412] *Bannatyne* v. *Cranston* (1624) Mor 12769; *Bairdie* v. *Scartsonse* (1624) Mor 14529.
[413] Of the 20 or so cases on water rights before 1770 reported in Morison's *Dictionary*'s title on 'Property', eight related to watermills, viz. Nos. 3, 10, 11, 15, 17, 20, 24, and 28.
[414] See Shaw (n. 245); cf. Alexander Fenton, *Scottish Country Life* (1977), 87.

cruives, were also important. These cases provide an economic reason for the development of common interest.[415]

As Shaw's fine monograph shows,[416] in Scotland use of water power reached its apogee between 1730 and 1830 and the amount of water power continued to grow in the age of steam until the 1850s. The first phase of the industrial revolution (led by textiles, especially cotton) may be taken as beginning with the establishment of the first cotton mill at Penicuik in 1778.[417] By 1795 about thirty-nine cotton mills had been established, and 110 by 1810, mostly water-powered.[418] Many other trades and industries used water-power.[419] The pressure on water resources triggered much litigation and cooperative water management schemes designed to avoid litigation.[420] It is no accident that the doctrine of riparian common interest reached maturity in this period.[421]

After 1830, the iron industry, by then largely steam-powered, overtook textiles as the most important economic sector but water-power, though declining relative to steam-power, remained important till the late nineteenth century and continued to generate litigation.[422] Although the courts were conscious of the importance of manufacturing industry, their approach (consolidated during the debates on property triggered by the French Revolution)[423] was that riparian rights as a form of property were sacred; that manufacturers would not be harmed because they could always buy riparian rights;[424] that expropriation was not legally possible or desirable at common law;[425] and that if the public wanted expropriation, they must pay for it.[426] In the action raised by Lord Justice-Clerk Glenlee against the Catrine Cotton Co. to prevent it from constructing a new reservoir upstream on the River

---

[415] But from the beginning, amenity and fishing trout for sport rather than for profit, have been treated as a legally protected riparian interest: *Bannatyne* v. *Cranston* (1624) Mor 12769.

[416] See n. 245.   [417] C. A. Whatley, *The Industrial Revolution in Scotland* (1997), 24.

[418] Ibid. at 25; Shaw (n. 245), ch. 20, 317–40. In 1835, 43.6% of horse power in the Scottish cotton industry still came from water-power while in the north of England it was only 18.6%: S. D. Chapman, *The Cotton Industry and the Industrial Revolution* (1987), 19.

[419] Shaw (n. 245) identifies *inter alia* grain, corn, and barley mills; paper mills; coal-mining; mining and manufacture of non-ferrous metals; sawmills; breweries and distilleries; iron industry; farm mills; many different types of textile mills (e.g. wool, lint, flax and cotton); and bleachfields.   [420] See Shaw (n. 245), 481.

[421] For example the three leading cases cited at nn. 333, 335, and 336 above concerned the taking of water to use for an ironworks (*Edington* (1793)) or cotton mills (*Lord Glenlee* (1804) and *Lanark Twist* (1810)) .

[422] Shaw (n. 245), 494 sqq.; cases on mills in the 20th century included *McCrone* v. *Ramsay* (1901) 9 SLT 118(OH); *J White & Sons* v. *J & M White* (1905) 8 F (HL) 41; *Earl of Kintore* v. *Pirie & Sons* (1906) 8 F (HL) 16.

[423] See e.g. A. Cobban (ed.), *The Debate on the French Revolution 1789–1800* (2nd edn., 1960), 383–418.

[424] e.g. *Hamilton* v. *Edington & Co.* (1793) Mor 12824 at 12825 (last sentence of quotation accompanying n. 325).

[425] Ibid; cf. *Fraser's Trs* v. *Cran* (1879) 6 R 451, 453; Whitty (n. 298), § 2073.

[426] *Duke of Buccleuch* v. *Cowan* (1866) 5 M 214 at 238 *per* Lord Neaves: 'If the public want it, let them acquire the right to the water altogether.'

Ayr to serve its cotton factory, the defenders attacked the natural flow doctrine as tending 'to restrain the exertion of industry, and prevent the extension of useful manufactures' and argued that 'the Romans were so little acquainted with manufactures, that the authority of their law is of less weight in such cases'.[427] The defence failed. To a great extent, therefore, the Scottish experience is consistent with Watson's view (namely that whether the economy is agricultural or industrial, riparian owners have the same concerns) which focuses on the *amount* of water available.

But what of the *quality* of the water? The intrusion of nuisance into the domain of water rights in Scotland begins with the two distillery cases of 1791[428] and the idea of primary and secondary purposes emerges not long before.[429] A contributory factor no doubt was the influx of English authority on nuisance beginning in the late eighteenth century.[430] The court however relied heavily on the analogy of the Roman rules on interference with the flow of a river[431] as well as English sources on nuisance, so that it would have reached the same result in the absence of the English influence. The dominant influence was not doctrinal fashion, still less a legal transplant from England, but the enormous environmental impact of the industrial revolution, the new aspirations towards higher living standards of 'polite' society, and generally the same deep social changes as initiated the public health movement and urban improvement.[432] The prevention of river pollution, together with the introduction of piped supplies of clean water, became one of the principal objects of the public health movement in and after the nineteenth century.[433]

V. LOCHS AND STANKS

1. **Introductory**

Roman law distinguished[434] between a lake (*lacus*) which has water perpetually and a pool (*stagnum*) which contains standing water for the time being. The difference between the corresponding Scottish concepts of a loch and a stank (*stagnum*) is sometimes said to be that a loch, unlike a stank, has a

---

[427] *Lord Glenlee* v. *Gordon* (1804) Mor 12834 at 12837. The pursuer's Roman law authorities were Ulp. D. 39, 3, 1, 1; Ulp. D. 43, 13, 1, 1; and Ulp. D. 43, 12, 1, 12.
[428] *Miller* v. *Stein* (1791) Mor 12823, Bell Oct Cas 334; *Russell* v. *Haig* (1791) Mor 12823, Bell Oct Cas 338, 3 Pat App 403. There was a wave of construction of whisky distilleries in Lowland Scotland in the 1780s: M. Moss and J. R. Hume, *A History of the Scottish Whisky Industry* (1981), 48–72. [429] See nn. 310–13 above.
[430] See Whitty (n. 298), § 2015 sq. [431] See nn. 381–3 above.
[432] See e.g. Whitty (n. 298), § 2011 n. 4, citing Glasgow Dean of Guild's clerk in 1808 who in his explanation of the law of nuisance to the Dean, attributed it to 'the progress of society' from a 'comparatively rude and uncultivated state' to 'a high degree of civilisation': *Charity* v. *Riddell* (1808) Mor Appendix, 'Public Police', no. 6, Signet Library, Old Session Papers, vol. 480, 4, App 2.
[433] See n. 495. [434] Ulp. D. 43, 14, 1, 3 and 4.

perennial outflow (in a definite channel) to a river[435] but the definitions are fluid and can cause confusion.[436] In the institutional period, the rules were mainly an amalgam of feudal and Roman law. Stair and Bankton discussed ownership of lochs and *stagna* in their description of the pertinents which pass with heritable property in a conveyance.[437] In the nineteenth century recourse to Roman law virtually ceased. As in rivers, the English concept of tidality replaced navigability as the test of the public character of a loch[438] and a tidal loch is now treated as a branch of the sea.

2. Ownership of the *alveus*

The first problem was whether ownership of an inland loch implied ownership of the *alveus*. This was debated in *Dick* v. *Earl of Abercorn*[439] which concerned whether the feudal grant of a loch[440] conveyed not only the water but the *alveus* to the grantee (the pursuer's author). The defender argued that although the pursuer had by charter right to the loch considered as a body of water, yet he had no right to the *alveus*. On the analogy of ownership of the bed of rivers, as governed by Justinian's *Institutes* 2, 1, 23, if the loch dried up, the *alveus derelictus* belonged to the coterminous heritors. He contended 'the ground may be the property of one person when covered with water, and of another when dry. In the one case it was a pertinent of the water, in the other it became a pertinent of the adjacent lands . . .,' citing the Roman law on *alluvio* and *insula in flumine nata* together with Huber, Sande, and Blackstone.[441] The pursuer argued that the *Institutes* text did not apply; that in feudal law *alveus derelictus* and *insula in flumine nata* belonged to the Crown; that the authority quoted referred to a public river, but a loch was *privati iuris*; and that the right of coterminous heritors was presumptive and excluded by an express right; and cited Blackstone as well as Bankton.[442] Further, lands on the banks of a loch were *agri limitati* (lands enclosed within boundaries) and so the Roman doctrine of *alluvio* did not support the

---

[435] Reid (n. 108), § 303.
[436] See *Magistrates of Ardrossan* v. *Dickie* (1906) 14 SLT 349 at 356 sq. *per* Lord Kinnear.
[437] Stair, II, 3, 73; Bankton, II, 3, 165.
[438] e.g. *Lord Advocate* v. *Clyde Navigation Trustees* (1891) 19 R 174 (Loch Long).
[439] (1769) Mor 12813.   [440] Duddingston Loch in Edinburgh.
[441] Editions not cited. See however, U. Huber, *Praelectiones juris civilis* (1690), vol. 3, *ad* D. 41, 1, 10; J. van den Sande, *Decisiones Frisicae* (4th edn. 1664), book V, title 2 (*De Flumine publico, ejusque exsiccatione*), *Definitio* 2 (*Ad lacum publicum exsiccandum omnes ejus accolas esse admittendos*). English authority (Blackstone, *Commentaries*, book 2, ch. 2 and Brownlaw's Reports, part 1, 142) was cited for the proposition that a conveyance of a lake did not include the *alveus* unless specially mentioned. On the basic Roman texts as applied to a *lacus* see, A. Lewis, 'Alluvio: The Meaning of Institutes II, 1, 20', in P. G. Stein and A. D. E. Lewis (eds.), *Studies in Justinian's Institutes in Memory of J. A. C. Thomas* (1983), 87 at 90–2.
[442] Mor 28151: 'Blackstone B. 2, c. 2, s. 5 says an action for a piece of water would be inept, unless laid as a claim for land covered by water'; Bankton, II, 3, 165.

defender's claim to ground which the loch might desert opposite his land.[443] The court found that the pursuer had exclusive ownership of the loch and its *alveus*.

3. The change from common ownership to several ownership.

It was early established that if a loch was wholly within the land of one proprietor, its *alveus* and its waters belonged to him, but a loch touching the lands of two or more riparian owners was presumed to belong to them rateably and, like rivers, was subject to rules of common interest.[444] At first it was thought that the ownership was *pro indiviso* or common property shares proportionate to the riparian frontages.[445] In 1878, however, in *Mackenzie v. Bankes*[446] the House of Lords stated the law in terms of 'the *ex adverso* rule' of several ownership whereby each riparian owner owns a section of the *alveus* within lines from his boundaries to the *medium filum* as in a river. It has been doubted whether the House of Lords was 'aware of the significance of its own adopted stance'.[447]

4. Common interest

The *ex adverso* rule did not extend to rights (such as boating, fishing, and fowling) exercised on the surface of the water: '[T]hese are to be enjoyed over the whole water's face by all the riparian owners in common, subject (if need be) to judicial regulation'[448] and are sometimes described as based on common interest.[449]

A loch within one proprietor's land could also be subject to common interest if it feeds a perennial river by a definite channel,[450] depending on the degree of constancy of the discharge.[451] So a loch which is the constant and

---

[443] Flor. D. 41, 1, 16 ('In agris limitatis ius alluvionis locum non habere constat.'—'In the case of lands measured out, it is generally agreed that the right of alluvion has no place.') cited at Mor 12826 by defender who also cites Call. D. 41, 1, 12 (although a *lacus* or *stagnum* may sometimes increase, sometimes dry up, it still retains its bounds and so the *ius alluvionis* is not acknowledged); and Vinnius (n. 190), ad D. 39, 3, 24, 3.
[444] Stair, II, 3, 73; Bankton, II, 3, 12; Hume, *Lectures*, III, 225; Bell, *Principles*, §§ 651, 1110 sq.
[445] Bell, *Principles*, § 1111; *Menzies v. Macdonald* (1854) 16 D 827 (Loch Rannoch); *Montgomery v. Watson* (1861) 23 D 635 (Lochleven, Fife); *Stewart's Trs v. Robertson* (1874) 1 R 334 (Loch Derculich). [446] (1878) 5 R (HL) 192, affirming (1877) 5 R 278.
[447] Reid (n. 108), § 305.
[448] *Mackenzie v. Bankes* (1878) 5 R (HL) 192 at 202 *per* Lord Selborne.
[449] *Kilsyth Fish Protection Association v. McFarlane* 1937 SC 757 *per* Lord Moncrieff.
[450] *Magistrates of Linlithgow v. Elphinstone* (1768) Mor 12805, 5 Brown's Supp 935, Hailes 203 approved in *Magistrates of Ardrossan v. Dickie* (1906) 14 SLT 349.
[451] *Magistrates of Linlithgow v. Elphinstone* (1768) Hailes 203 at 204 *per* Lord Gardenston: 'There are two sorts of lochs in Scotland: one a stagnating loch, not the source of running water; the other a loch, the source of running water. That one which is stagnating is the property of the person in whose lands it lies, though arising from springs as well as from rain or artificial

perennial feeder of a river owned by others, becomes subject to the common interest of the riparian owners and cannot be diverted.

5. Public rights of navigation and fishing in lochs

Navigable lochs, unlike navigable rivers, were originally not *inter regalia*. Nevertheless Bell remarked that if 'lakes' owned by several riparians 'form great channels of communication in a district of country, there seems to be some reason to regard them as *res publicae*' and subject to the same rules as public rivers.[452] After tidality replaced navigability as the test of the public character of a loch,[453] it was no longer believed that the Crown owned the *alveus* of a navigable but non-tidal loch. Lord President Inglis in 1877 thought Loch Lomond must be regarded as a continuation inland of the navigable River Leven.[454] In 1931 a public right of navigation on Loch Lomond was conceded by counsel though Lord President Clyde reserved his opinion on that matter and on whether the public right of navigability on a private (i.e. non-tidal) loch depends on prescriptive use by the public or the fact of navigability.[455]

In 1861, rejecting an argument that *Fergusson* v. *Shirreff*[456] was 'a solitary decision ... contrary to all principle', the Court of Session extended to private lochs the rules that a public right of fishing for trout is neither implied from a public right of access to the water nor capable of being acquired by prescriptive usage.[457]

VI. CASUAL WATERS

Compared with the Roman law heartlands of Italy and Byzantium, the need to restrain the interception of casual waters by a neighbour arises but rarely in Scotland, which tends to suffer from too much water rather than too little. In Scots law an owner of land has a right to appropriate and use casual water such as rainwater (*aqua pluvia*) which has fallen on his land or percolated

---

runners. That which is not stagnating, but affording running water, is not the property of the person in whose land it lies.' The last sentence goes too far. The loch may be in that person's ownership but subject to the common interest of the riparian owners on the perennial stream fed by the loch.

[452] Bell, *Principles*, § 651 citing *McDonnell* v. *Caledonian Canal Commissioners* (1830) 8 S 881.
[453] e.g. *Lord Advocate* v. *Clyde Navigation Trustees* (1891) 19 R 174 (Loch Long), discussed above.   [454] *Colquhoun's Trs* v. *Orr Ewing & Co.* (1877) 4 R 344 at 350.
[455] *Leith-Buchanan* v. *Hogg* 1931 SC 204 at 211 *per* Lord President Clyde, at 214 *per* Lord Blackburn.   [456] (1844) 6 D 1363; nn. 228–33 above.
[457] *Montgomery* v. *Watson* (1861) 23 D 635 (concerning Lochleven, by Kinross) applying *Fergusson* v. *Shirreff* (1844) 6 D 1363.

there from neighbouring land.[458] Probably the only restraint is the civilian doctrine prohibiting acts done *in aemulationem vicini*.[459]

The owner of higher ground has also a right—which has been called a right of free drainage[460]—correlative to the obligation of the owner of lower ground to receive casual water running naturally off the higher. This right stems historically from texts on the Roman action for fending off rainwater (*actio aquae pluviae arcendae*)[461] and the *actio negatoria*.[462] By the *actio aquae pluviae arcendae*, someone harmed by an increase in the flow of rainwater on his land resulting from works or alterations on neighbouring land could obtain a specific remedy stopping the increased flow and damages. The action lay if the damage caused by rainwater did not occur naturally but as a result of operations, unless the operations were agricultural: 'non naturaliter, sed opere facto, nisi si agri colendi causa'.[463] Bankton treated the right of drainage in his title on ordinary rural servitudes[464] and Erskine characterized the right as a natural servitude according to civilian classification.[465]

Prior to the eighteenth century drainage was undertaken on a small scale[466] and arable land was drained by the ridge and furrow method. An important aspect of the agricultural revolution was the 'drainage revolution' which transformed the landscape of rural Scotland.[467] This began with the drainage of bogs, stanks, and lochs in the eighteenth century to extend usable acreage,[468] and continued in its second phase with the introduction of systematic underground tile drainage in the nineteenth century.[469] '[T]his great surge

---

[458] See e.g. Bankton, II, 7, 29 citing D. 39, 3, 21 sqq.

[459] Bankton I, 10, 40; IV, 45, 112; Lord Kames, *Principles of Equity* (5th edn., 1825), 36 sq.; *Irving v. Leadhills Mining Co.* (1856) 18 D 833 at 837; *Blair v. Hunter Finlay and Co.* (1870) 9 M 204 at 208; *Milton v. Glen-Moray Glenlivet Distillery Co. Ltd* (1898) 1 F 135; Whitty (n. 298), §§ 2008, 2033–35.

[460] Reid (n. 108), §§ 337 and 339. D. P. Derham, 'Interference with Surface Waters by Lower Landholders', (1958) 74 *LQR* 361 contends (at 364) that in English law the upper riparian owner has, in terms of the Hohfeld analysis, a liberty, rather than a right, to discharge casual waters on his neighbour's lower contiguous land, and accordingly there is no distinct secondary rule that the lower owner is under a duty to receive such waters. Ibid. at 373 he argues that 'the civil law rule which would prevent a lower landholder from defending himself from the consequences of his higher neighbour's activities is very defective and ought not to be accepted in any common law jurisdiction these days'.

[461] D. 39, 3. See A. Rodger, *Owners and Neighbours in Roman Law* (1972), ch. 5.

[462] Ulp. D. 8, 5, 8, 5, a famous text from which the *immissio* principle developed, in which Ulpian quotes Aristo as stating that it is not permissible to discharge water from upper on to lower property.

[463] Ulp. D. 39, 3, 1, 15, cited by both parties in *Campbell v. Bryson* (1864) 3 M 254.

[464] Bankton, II, 7, 30 citing Ulp. D. 39, 3, 1, 23; Ulp. D. 8, 5, 8, 5. Bankton's reference to Ulp. D. 8, 3, 3, 2 is not in point.   [465] Erskine, II, 9, 2.

[466] See e.g. the Pow of Inchaffray Act 1696, APS, X, 67b.

[467] See A. Fenton, *Scottish Country Life* (1977), 18 sqq.

[468] e.g. the drainage and reclamation of the 1,130 acres of Blairdrummond Moss between the 1760s and 1817, an enterprise initiated by Lord Kames and described by the *First Statistical Account* as 'the most singular and considerable improvement in Scotland': see I. S. Ross, *Lord Kames and the Scotland of his Day* (1972), 362 sq.

[469] Financed partly by loans under the Private Money Drainage Acts 1846 and 1849.

of activity, in the middle span of the nineteenth century, ... effectively created the face of farming Scotland as we know it at the present day—with level fields free from ridge and furrow.'[470]

Despite this transformation, there were remarkably few reported cases. The law rested, and still rests, largely on Erskine, Bell, and the comments thereon in *Campbell* v. *Bryson*.[471] In a classic statement, Erskine said that 'if the water which would otherwise fall from the higher grounds insensibly, without hurting the inferior tenement, should be collected into one body by the owner of the superior in the natural use of his property, for draining his lands or otherwise improving them, the owner of the inferior tenement is ... bound to receive that body of water on his property though it should be endamaged by it'.[472] On the other hand, he also said that the right may be 'overstreched in the use of it' and therefore 'the question, How far it may be extended in particular circumstances? must be arbitrary'.[473] In 1853 Erskine's statement of the natural burdens of an inferior heritor was said to be overstated[474] but was approved in 1864 in *Campbell* v. *Bryson*[475] in which the Second Division refused interdict against the formation of tiled furrow drains of the usual modern pattern in higher ground which would not have increased the volume of the outfall.[476] The parties relied only on Scottish and civilian authorities,[477] but the court did not look beyond Erskine's statement quoted above which was construed as meaning that the court has power, if 'the superior heritor is unduly pressing his right' to regulate the matter on equitable terms.[478] The decision was based on policy. Lord Cowan[479] seemed to allow little more than a slight increase in the natural outfall of water. Lord Neaves however argued that it would be 'lamentable' and 'anti-social' to confine the natural servitude to cases where the upper tenement was in a state of nature and that once it is accepted that cultivation must be permitted, though tending to send down more water, the upper heritor must not be required 'to lag behind in the improvements of the day'.[480]

This natural servitude doctrine contrasts with the 'common enemy rule'

---

[470] Fenton (n. 467), 23.   [471] (1864) 3 M 254.

[472] Erskine, II, 9, 2. At II, 1, 2 Erskine illustrates freedom of ownership by stating that a proprietor 'may lawfully drain his swampy or marshy grounds, though the water thrown off from them by that improvement should happen to hurt the inferior tenement'. Bell, *Principles*, § 968 said that '[T]he inferior ground [using the Hohfeld analysis] must receive the natural drainage of the upper ground; but is not bound to submit to what is produced by artificial changes in the condition of the water. So the inferior must receive the superfluous water, even under the operations of draining, in all the variations of agricultural improvement.'   [473] Erskine, II, 9, 2.

[474] *Montgomerie* v. *Buchanan's Trs* (1853) 15 D 853 at 859 *per* Lord Ivory.

[475] (1864) 3 M 254. Lord Benholme said (at 262): '[T]his is a very important case, and one deeply interesting to the agricultural part of the community.'   [476] Ibid. at 255.

[477] Including Pothier's and Voet's commentaries on operations '*agri colendi causa*' in D. 39, 3, 1, 15.   [478] Ibid. at 260 *per* Lord Justice-Clerk Inglis.

[479] Ibid. at 261, 262.   [480] Ibid. at 263.

found in English law.[481] Both are also found in the USA, as is a doctrine of reasonable use.[482] The natural servitude doctrine has flexibility and reaches reasonable results only because of the requirement that the upper landowner must not unduly press his rights. This flexibility would be lost if it were held necessary to prove *aemulatio vicini* before this requirement could be established.[483]

VII. REMEDIES

Water rights were enforced by ordinary common law remedies which were and are general throughout our unitary law. Because of the medieval break with English law, the idiosyncratic common law/equity dualism was avoided together with its unsustainable corollary that, since 'Equity comes to the aid of the Common Law', no injunction in equity lies if damages at common law would be an adequate remedy.[484] The Roman law remedies were not directly received[485] but there are hints at partial recognition of some of them.[486] Declarators were always available at common law.[487] The early judicial

---

[481] See Derham, (1958) 74 *LQR* 361 at 376 sqq. Under the common enemy rule, the water is a sort of common enemy against which each man must defend himself: *Smith* v. *Kenrick* (1849) 7 CB 515 at 566.

[482] See S. V. Kinyon and R. C. McClure, 'Interferences with Surface Waters', (1940) 24 *Minn LR* 891.

[483] A suggestion to that effect was made in *Logan* v. *Wang (UK) Ltd* 1991 SLT 580 (OH) at 584D *per* Lord Prosser.

[484] This rule has atrophied in English law because it is counter-balanced by the rule that the court must not compel a sale of the plaintiff's rights: *Shelfer* v. *City of London Lighting Co.* [1895] 1 Ch 287 (CA); *Halsey* v. *Esso Petroleum Co. Ltd* [1961] 1 WLR 683 at 783.

[485] e.g. the *actio negatoria*, the *interdictum uti possidetis*, *operis novi nuntiatio*, *cautio damni infecti*, *actio aquae pluviae arcendae*; and the public law interdicts on rivers D. 43, titles 12–15. The link with Romano-canonical remedies is unexplored.

[486] In *Magistrates of Dumfries* v. *Water of Nith Heritors* (1705) Mor 12776, Fountainhall's report states (at 12777) 'the Heritors above the said dike, *novi operis nuntiatione* interrupt the work and give in a bill of suspension'. In *Duke of Gordon* v. *Duff* (1735) Mor 12778, it was conceded that 'a proprietor may *munire ripam*, face up and defend his banks from the encroachment of the waters' (cf. D. 43, 15 *de ripa munienda*) provided he furnished caution, described as a *cautio damni infecti* in *Magistrates of Aberdeen* v. *Menzies* (1748) Mor 12787 at 12789. In *Auchindryne* v. *Invercauld* (1740) 5 Brown's Supp 688, a summary application, by way of petition and complaint without the formality of a declarator, was held competent which (according to Lord Monboddo) 'was in effect introducing into our law an *interdictum restitutorium*, since the intent of the action was to have the work demolished and things restored to their former state'.

[487] Stair, IV, 3, 47; IV, 4. Declarators were an invention of Roman law, the *actio negatoria* being used in the case of *immissiones* of water (Ulp. D. 8, 5, 8, 5, 6). They probably entered Scots law through Romano-canonical procedure. The nearest English equivalent was an action of nominal damages until (on the model of the Scots declarator) the declaration was introduced by the Court of Chancery, England, Act (Special Case Act) 1850; the Court of Chancery Procedure Act 1852, s. 50; and the Supreme Court of Judicature (Consolidation) Act 1875, s. 17. For the background see *Earl of Mansfield* v. *Walker's Trs* (1835) 1 S & McL 203; *Trotter* v. *Farnie* (1831) 5 W & S 649.

remedies were normally decrees or orders 'prohibiting and discharging'[488] the defender (or respondent in the bill chamber) from conducting operations infringing water rights.[489] Such cases were steps in the historical process by which the remedy of suspension, or suspension and interdict, spread beyond the review of diligence to become the paradigm prohibitory remedy, now known simply as interdict.[490] Characteristically, Roman law texts were cited to support indigenous remedies such as declarator,[491] suspension[492] or decree *ad factum praestandum*.[493]

VIII. THE STATUTORY PUBLIC LAW ON WATER

'The well-being of the people depends on an adequate and constant supply of wholesome water for domestic, sanitary, fire-fighting, commercial, industrial and agricultural purposes.'[494] In 1842, Edwin Chadwick's famous *Sanitary Report*, together with its *travaux préparatoires*,[495] showed that the private law rules and remedies on water rights were a wholly inadequate mechanism for improving the quality of the water supply, and in getting rid

---

[488] Early interlocutors used the verb 'to discharge' (commonly with the preposition 'from') which in the 18th century had the now obsolete meaning (largely then confined to Scotland and English dialect) of 'to forbid' or 'to prohibit' (*Scottish National Dictionary* (1952), vol. 3, s. v. 'discharge') and thus logically enough meaning the opposite of 'to charge' which is still used in the law and practice of diligence in the sense of 'to require'.

[489] e.g. *Magistrates of Dumfries* v. *Water of Nith Heritors* (1705) Mor 12776; *Magistrates of Aberdeen* v. *Menzies* (1748) 12787; *Trotter* v. *Hume* (1757) Mor 12798 (interim order).

[490] This practice is recognized by Erskine, IV, 3, 20 (citing the Digest title 39, 1 *De operis novi nuntiatione*); and Hume, *Lectures*, VI, 54; see also H. Burn-Murdoch, Interdict in the Law of Scotland (1933), 6. This is the reason why the respondent in the Bill Chamber was for long called 'the charger' even in property law and other cases where no charge had been served: see e.g. *Hamilton* v. *Edington & Co.* (1793) Mor 12824; *Menzies* v. *Earl of Breadalbane* (1828) 3 W & S 235.

[491] e.g. *Brodie* v. *Cadel* (1707) 4 Brown's Supp 660; *Magistrates of Aberdeen* v. *Menzies* (1748) Mor 12787; *Magistrates of Linlithgow* v. *Elphinstone* (1768) Mor 12805, 5 Brown's Supp 936, Hailes 203. [492] See n. 489.

[493] e.g. *Bannatyne* v. *Cranston* (1624) Mor 12769; *Fairly* v. *Earl of Eglinton* (1744) Mor 12780; *Trotter* v. *Hume* (1757) Mor 12798. As to the remedy of regulation see Ferguson (n. 1), 237 at n. 1; *McCrone* v. *Ramsay* (1901) 9 SLT 118(OH).

[494] A. A. Templeton, 'Water', in M. R. McLarty (ed.), *A Source Book and History of Administrative Law in Scotland* (1956), 220.

[495] E. Chadwick, *Report of the Sanitary Condition of the Labouring Population of Great Britain* (1842; new edn. M. W. Flinn, 1965). The *travaux préparatoires* included J. Hill Burton, *On the State of the Law as regards the Abatement of Nuisances and the Protection of the Public Health, in Scotland, with Suggestions for Amendment* (1840); and local *Reports on the Sanitary Condition of the Labouring Population of Scotland* (1842). J. H. F. Brotherston, *Observations on the Early Public Health Movement in Scotland* (1952) is useful but there is as yet no adequate history of the relation between Scottish private law and the public health movement in Scotland. See from the standpoint of English law, J. F. Brenner, 'Nuisance Law and the Industrial Revolution', (1973) 3 JLS 403; McLaren, (1983) 5 *OJLS* 155 both of whom deal with *inter alia* river pollution.

of river pollution, so as to comply with the minimal standards required for the public health.

Though the history of the piped water supply from upland catchment areas to cities began in Edinburgh as early as 1674, its modern history begins with local waterworks acts responding to the urban crisis precipitated by the industrial revolution.[496] Perhaps its greatest triumph was the statutory scheme for pumping water 35 miles from Loch Katrine to Glasgow opened in 1859.[497]

Increasingly since the mid-nineteenth century, the improvement of water supply, the prevention of water pollution, and other functions connected with water,[498] have been regulated by public law enactments,[499] kept under review by many official advisory bodies, usually with United Kingdom (rather than purely Scottish) terms of reference, whose complex history lies outside the scope of this chapter. The legislation, now supplemented by European Community legislation and international conventions, coexists with the private law and makes good its deficiencies in the public interest.[500]

IX. THE SECOND RECEPTION OF ENGLISH LAW

Scottish water law reflects trends found throughout our law, namely a reception from the *jus commune* unevenly overlaid by a second reception of

---

[496] In 1674, water was led from Comiston in a three-inch pipe to the Edinburgh's reservoir on the Castlehill and from there distributed to the public wells: Templeton (n. 494), 220. The Waterworks Clauses Acts 1847 and 1863 consolidated the provisions usually contained in private acts authorizing the making of waterworks for supplying towns with water.

[497] Glasgow Corporation Waterworks Act 1855: see T. C. Smout, *A Century of the Scottish People 1830–1950* (1986), 43 sq.

[498] Including agricultural drainage, coastal protection, control of fisheries, flood control, sewers and drains, and spray irrigation. See e.g. 'Fisheries', in *The Laws of Scotland: Stair Memorial Encyclopaedia*, vol. 11 (1990); F. Lyall, 'Water and Water Rights', ibid., vol. 25 (1989), §§ 301 sqq.; E. Bain, 'Water Supply', ibid., vol. 25 (1989), §§ 501 sqq. C. T. Reid (ed.), *Environmental Law in Scotland* (2nd edn., 1997), especially chs. 1 (C. T. Reid), 3 on water pollution (F. Lyall), and 5 on integrated pollution control (J. M. G. Blair).

[499] For a lonely precursor, see the act anent the laying of lint in lochs 1606, APS, IV, 287b (c. 12), 12mo, c. 13. Before the 19th century perhaps the only. The Report of the River Commissioners from 1866 onwards (e.g. Parl. Papers, HC (1872), XXXIV) led to the Rivers Pollution Act 1876, a United Kingdom Act: see Brenner, (1973) 3 *JLS* 403, 429–31. The 1876 act was replaced by the Rivers (Prevention of Pollution) (Scotland) Acts 1951 which in turn was replaced by the Control of Pollution Act 1974, Part II (as amended). The Scottish Environment Protection Agency (established under the Environment Act 1995), the three water authorities, and local authorities have statutory functions. The Protection of the Environment Bill 1973 would have taken away the court's power to interdict pollution of rivers at common law by discharges made in accordance with statutory consents, but the clause was dropped after criticism in the House of Lords: Parl. Debs., HL (1973–4), vol. 349, cols. 206–25.

[500] Under the private law doctrine of common interest, for example, a water authority seeking to increase its abstraction of water from a river for water supply purposes would require to obtain the consent of all riparian owners downstream from the point of abstraction to the sea. Under the Water (Scotland) Act 1980, however, the Secretary of State may make a water order by statutory instrument authorizing the increase.

English law in the nineteenth century, heralded by the citation of English sources in the late eighteenth century. The first reference to English sources in the 'Property' title of Morison's *Dictionary* occurs in a water rights case in 1769.[501] By then English law was ceasing to be 'an isolated island in a Romanist sea',[502] because it had already begun to procreate the Anglo-American, common law family of legal systems and thereby to create its own rival *jus commune* in which, by a reversal of roles, it was the turn of Scots law to become an isolated island. At the same time, civilian systems had some influence on areas of the American and English common law systems, and water law was one of those areas, though the nature and extent of the influence is controversial.[503] Lord Rodger has pointed out that in the late nineteenth and early twentieth centuries, many Scots lawyers saw themselves as part of a larger English-speaking family of lawyers scattered throughout the British Empire and the United States of America and some (like Lord Shaw) believed that in this scheme a non-English system like Scots law had a special place since the law which bound the British Empire was not imposed uniformly from above but sprang upwards from the diverse component systems.[504] How far did that ideal correspond with reality in the domain of water rights?

The answer is not simple. When the issue of cross-border assimilation arose, the non-English elements of the Scots law were sometimes expunged and sometimes tolerated. In the nineteenth century, English influence grows, with tidality ousting the well-established civilian concept of navigability as the mark of a public river in 1877.[505] When what were thought to be public rights of fishing were replaced by private riparian rights, the change was justified *inter alia* on cross-border assimilationist grounds.[506] At the end of the century, Rankine said that the principles of the Roman jurisprudence on water rights 'have been recognised as a safe guide during the whole history of Scots law, have been appealed to in the Courts of England and America, and have been taken over as authoritative in France and Germany'. In his chapter on 'water', he cited Romanist,[507] Roman-Dutch,[508] French,[509] and German[510] authors as well as English,[511] and

---

[501] *Dick* v. *Earl of Abercorn* (1769) Mor 12813, citing Blackstone, *Commentaries*, book. 2, ch. 2.
[502] See n. 5 above. [503] See on riparian rights nn. 396–403 above.
[504] Rodger (n. 215), 20–2.
[505] *Colquhoun's Trs* v. *Orr Ewing* (1877) 4 R 344, 4 R (HL) 116. [506] See n. 242.
[507] Molitor, *La Possession et les servitudes en droit romain* (2nd edn, 1868).
[508] Vinnius, *In Quatuor Libros Institutionum Imperialium Commentarius* (1761 edn.); J. Voet, *Commentarius ad Pandectas* (1827 edn.).
[509] Code Napoleon, art. 644; Championnière, *La Propriété des eaux courantes* (1846); Pardessus, *Traité des servitudes* (6th edn., 1823).
[510] Ernst Pagenstecher, *Römische Lehre vom Eigenthum* (1857–9); Karl A. Vangerow, *Lehrbuch der Pandekten* (7th edn., 1863–9).
[511] Callis, *Reading on the Statute of Sewers* (4th edn., 1824); Coulson and Forbes, *Law of Waters* (2nd edn., 1902); Wood, *Law of Nuisances* (2nd edn., 1883).

American[512] authors, and English, Irish, and American cases (reflecting the closer British–American links in legal culture than exist today). Nevertheless he made it fairly plain that if the past had been civilian, the future lay with Anglo-American common law for he expressly stated that, apart from specialties in the English law of prescription, the rules of the Scots and English systems of water law seem to be identical.[513] Among foreign sources, it was the Anglo-American common law cases and textbooks which were generally cited in the courts and Sheriff Ferguson's monograph.[514]

Sometimes however Anglicizing pressure was resisted. In *Lord Blantyre* v. *Dunn*[515] for example Lord Cockburn (reputedly an Anglicizing Whig) observed: 'Of the English authorities I say nothing, except that, in all human probability, we do not understand them.'[516] In *Agnew* v. *Lord Advocate*,[517] Lord Justice-Clerk Moncreiff affirmed: 'We have little or nothing which is new to learn in this department of jurisprudence. English analogies may mislead us. . . . The safest guides we have are to be found in the decisions of the great feudalists of the two last generations, and they leave nothing which is material undetermined.'[518] On the other hand, Lord Cowan could not resist commending Hale's *De Jure Maris* for its description of the kind and extent of possession which would support a littoral owner's claim to the foreshore.[519] Sometimes, the greater volume and detail of English authority exerted a gravitational pull[520] and the two laws were then described as 'not different'.[521] Cross-border assimilation in one area of water law may become a reason for assimilation in a related area.[522]

As mentioned above,[523] the foreshore was defined as the shore between the high- and low-water marks of ordinary spring tides. In a Scottish appeal in 1849, *Smith* v. *Earl of Stair*, argued by English counsel, Lord Brougham

---

[512] Angell (n. 348); Washburn, *American Law of Easements and Servitudes* (3rd edn., 1873); Woolrych, *Law of Waters* (2nd edn., 1851). [513] Rankine (n. 108), 511.

[514] (N. 1). Citation by the judge of English cases was frequent. Of American authority it was unusual, but did occur; see e.g. *Lady Willoughby de Eresby* v. *Wood* (1884) 22 SL Rep 471 (OH) at 475. [515] (1848) 10 D 509.

[516] Ibid. at 549. See also at 544 *per* Lord Moncreiff: 'Neither do I think it at all necessary or useful to resort to cases in the law of England. The case here seems to me to depend on the Scotch law of prescription . . . on which the law of England cannot be expected to throw any satisfactory light.' See also *Menzies* v. *Breadalbane* (1828) 3 W & S 235 at 243 *per* Lord Chancellor Eldon: 'Many circumstances were referred to at the Bar, with respect to the law of England upon this subject . . . the law of England . . . can be referred to only by way of illustration. This case must be decided by the law of Scotland.' [517] (1873) 11 M 309.

[518] Ibid. at 322.   [519] Ibid. at 328.

[520] e.g. as regards the definition of the incidents of the right of navigation or passage over tidal and non-tidal waters: *Crown Estate Commissioners* v. *Fairlie Yacht Slip Ltd* 1979 SC 156.

[521] Ibid. at 175 per Lord President Emslie.

[522] Ibid. at 186 per Lord Cameron stating that the English authority on passage is valuable because the Crown's right to the seabed is the same in England and Scotland.

[523] See n. 109.

spoke as if the matter was governed by Hale, *De Jure Maris*.[524] In a later case[525] Lord Jerviswoode, gently observing that the course which *Smith* v. *Earl of Stair* took 'was such as to create doubt as to the law applicable' to the question of ownership of the foreshore, confessed to hesitation in applying English sources 'lest he should mistake their import and effect'. In 1854, the House of Lords approved a different definition of the foreshore for English law,[526] which Rankine subsequently contended should be received in Scots law.[527] This contention, however, was rejected in 1903 when Lord Young[528] observed: [529]

> I quite see the desirableness of uniformity in the law of England and the law of Scotland in defining the boundaries of the seashore. But such uniformity should be obtained by choosing the best definition. I regard the definition arrived at by our own law as the best, and I therefore consider that uniformity should be attained not by the Scottish authorities adopting the rule on this subject which has been determined in the law of England, but by the English authorities adopting the rule laid down in our own law.

So too Scots law rejected Lord Watson's *obiter dicta* disapproving *aemulatio vicini*.[530]

Different branches of the Scots water law matured at different times; for instance ownership of the seabed below the foreshore came late.[531] After 1800, direct citation of *jus commune* sources was not unknown[532] but very rare. By the mid-nineteenth century probably most branches of water law had become sufficiently mature to be able to rely wholly or mainly on Scottish authorities. In *Gammell* v. *Commissioners of Woods and Forests*,[533] for example, the leading case in the cognate area of Crown rights to salmon fish-

---

[524] *Smith* v. *Earl of Stair* (1849) 6 Bell App 487 at 494. In similar solecistic vein, Lord Campbell (at 498, 499) said that 'there ought to be judgment *quod prosternetur*' a reference to one of the ancient English forms of action.

[525] *Lord Advocate* v. *Maclean of Ardgour* (1866) 2 SLR 25 (OH).

[526] *Attorney-General* v. *Chambers* (1854) 4 De G M & G 206 (the average of the medium high tides between the spring and the neap).

[527] Rankine, *Land-Ownership* (3rd edn., 1891), 230; cf. ibid. (4th edn., 1909), 255, 256.

[528] When Lord Advocate, Lord Young 'was believed to favour changes which would merge the law of Scotland with that of England, and diminish the authority of the national judges': G. W. T. Omond, *The Lord Advocates of Scotland, Second Series, 1834–1880* (1914), 269, 270.

[529] *Fisherrow Harbour Commissioners* v. *Musselburgh Real Estate Co. Ltd* (1903) 5 F 387 at 393, 394 (delivering the opinion of the Second Division).

[530] *Mayor of Bradford* v. *Pickles* [1895] AC 587 (HL) at 597 per Lord Watson; and cf. *Campbell* v. *Muir* 1908 SC 387. See Whitty (n. 298), para. 2035; E. Reid, 'Abuse of Rights in Scots Law', (1998) 2 *Edinburgh LR* 129, 153–5.

[531] See *Lord Advocate* v. *Clyde Navigation Trs* (1891) 19 R 174; *Lord Advocate* v. *Wemyss* (1899) 2 F (HL) 1.

[532] See e.g. nn. 271, 356, 477. Hume's *Lectures* of 1822 cite very few *jus commune* sources on water rights. One (at *Lectures*, IV, 245) is a quotation from Fritschius, *Jus Fluviaticum* (1672), 28, no. 362, copied from Dirleton (n. 69), 177.

[533] (1859) 6 Macq 419, affirming (1851) 13 D 854.

ings in the sea, there was very extensive citation of Scots, English, and *jus commune* sources including commentaries on the *Constitutio de Regalibus*.[534] The non-Scottish sources were given short shrift. All the judges adopted the approach of Lord Murray[535] who considered 'this entirely a question of Scotch law. He does not think it necessary therefore to discuss the different authorities quoted by the defenders, from Reygerus, Vulteius, Menochius, Peregrinus, or the English reports or authorities down to Jagoe on Fishery, and Schultes on Aquatic Right.'[536] By then however the *jus commune* had worked its magic and indigenous law could take over without reference to English law.

In the domain of riparian rights, English law has moved towards the Scots law of common interest but in this development, the Scots law was largely (though not completely)[537] ignored. So in *Colquhoun's Trs v. Orr Ewing & Co.*, Lord Blackburn observed (referring to *Bannatyne v. Cranston*[538]) that:

Precisely the same law has been now established in America (*Blanchard* v. *Miller*, 8 Greenleaf American Reports, 268) and in England (*Mason* v. *Hill*, 5 B and Ad 1) without, I think, either the American or English Judges being aware that the Scottish Judges had so long before anticipated their reasoning.[539]

This suggests that the 'special place' of Scots law within the British Empire was rather different from the idealized picture painted by Lord Shaw.[540]

Times change. Whereas Rankine borrowed freely from the English law,[541] nowadays the best Scottish textbooks on water law rarely find it necessary to rely on English authority.[542]

---

[534] (1859) 6 Macq 419 especially at 433 sqq.; (1854) 13 D 854 at 857, 858;

[535] (1854) 13 D 854 at 856, approved at 860 by the consulted judges; at 866 per Lord Justice-Clerk Hope; at 871 per Lord Medwyn; (1859) 6 Macq 419 at 455 per Lord Chelmsford LC: 'The question must be determined entirely by reference to the law of Scotland. The right of the Crown is rested solely upon that law, and it cannot be met by arguments derived from the works of foreign jurists or from the municipal laws of other countries.'

[536] (The citation was to Jagoe on Fishery, 6, 8 [not traced: possibly? J. Jagoe, *Practice of the County Courts* (6th edn., 1850)], H. Schultes, *Essay on Aquatic Rights Illustrative of the Law Relating to Fishing etc.* (1811)

[537] In *Embrey* v. *Owen* (1851) 6 Exch 353 at 360, 361, 155 ER 579 at 582, 583, passages from Lord Kames's report of *Magistrates of Linlithgow* v. *Elphinstone* (1768) Mor 12805 (also reported 5 Brown's Supp 936, Hailes 203) (discussed above) were cited to the court as well as the little known Scots authors Hutcheson, *Justice of the Peace*, book 4, ch. 2 (vol. 2, p. 391), and McCallem's *Lawyer*. The latter is presumably A. Macallan, *Pocket Lawyer; or Digest of the Law of Scotland, Mercantile Law of Great Britain, and Forms Regulating the Law of Scotland* (edns. in 1830, 1834, and 1840). [538] (1624) Mor 12769.

[539] (1877) 4 R(HL) 116 at 127.

[540] It is nothing to the point that a few decisions of the House of Lords on riparian rights in Scots cases (e.g. *Morris* v. *Bicket* (1866) 4 M (HL) 44; *Colquhoun's Trs* v. *Orr Ewing & Co.* (1877) 4 R (HL) 116; *Young and Co.* v. *Bankier Distillery Co.* (1893) 20 R (HL) 76) are cited in English textbooks. [541] (n. 103) 511.

[542] e.g. Gordon (n. 60), ch. 7; Reid (n. 108), paras. 273–343.

X. CONCLUSION

The history of water law regimes in Scotland is a relatively self-contained subject which provides a convenient test-bed on which to assess some of the more interesting generalizations about Scottish legal history. A few of these are easily dismissed, for example, the view that land law is one of the 'areas of Scots common law which were largely unaffected by civilian concepts',[543] and the peculiar idea that modern Scots law is a common law system rather than a mixed system.[544]

Then there is the controversy over the late Lord Cooper's historical theory of 'false starts and rejected experiments'.[545] Lord Cooper emphasized the discontinuity of Scottish legal history. Writing in 1951, he divided the history of Scots law before 1820 into 'three chapters—the first recording the false start of the Scoto-Norman law; the second devoted to a prolonged retrogression and decline; and the third containing the story of a fresh start and the fashioning of a new system in the construction of which the old law was only one, and by no means the most important, of the ingredients'.[546] Cooper saw two great changes of direction, one in the late Middle Ages away from English law as an external source towards the *jus commune* and the other beginning in the early nineteenth century away from the *jus commune* back towards English law. By basing the protection of water rights on the brieves of purpresture, novel dissasine derived from English law and its statutory offshoot *de aqueductu*, Scottish water law did indeed make, in the relevant senses, 'a false start' and 'rejected experiment', for these were replaced in the sixteenth century by *jus commune* sources brought before the Court of Session by an action commenced by signeted summons and debated in Romano-canonical replication procedure.[547] On the other hand, the introduction in 1434 of the brieve *de aqueductu* was an element in McKechnie's argument that, far from being (as Cooper had said) 'a dark age', the fifteenth century was 'the heyday of the brieve system'.[548] The study also shows that by the institutional period, there was little trace of the Scoto-Norman feudal system in our law on water rights which instead had become part of a system of land law on the cosmopolitan, European pattern, combining continental feudalism with the developed Roman law of the *jus commune*.

Then beginning in the late eighteenth century there was a trend away from

---

[543] See J. Thomson, 'When Homer Nodded?', in H. L. MacQueen (ed.), *Scots Law into the 21st Century* (1996), 18, 20.

[544] D. A. O. Edward, 'The Scottish Reactions—an Epilogue', in B. S. Markesinis (ed.), *The Gradual Convergence* (1994), 263 at 264.

[545] See generally Lord Cooper of Culross, *Selected Papers 1922–1954* (1957).

[546] T. M. Cooper, 'The Dark Age of Scottish Legal History 1350–1650', in *Selected Papers 1922–1954* (1957), 219 at 236; being the 19th David Murray Lecture in the University of Glasgow also published by Glasgow University Publications (1952).   [547] See II above.

[548] McKechnie (n. 13), 19.

the *jus commune* and back towards English law as the main external source. In the second quarter of the nineteenth century, English law, influenced at least in part by *jus commune* sources mediated by American jurists, rejected the appropriation theory, and accepted the natural flow theory, of riparian rights[549] and thereby drew closer to the Scottish doctrine of riparian common interest which had developed independently from civilian roots.[550] In the nineteenth century there was Anglicizing pressure in some regimes, (including the main regimes on riparian and littoral rights)[551] but not others (e.g. the right to drain casual waters).[552] Where it existed, the pressure was sometimes resisted and sometimes accepted.[553] The replacement in 1877 of navigability by tidality as the criterion of the public character of a river was the most important volte-face[554] and in its time was controversial.[555] It could not be openly justified for reasons given above. Whatever one's view of the merits, it is difficult to deny that the volte-face represented another 'rejected experiment' which bears eloquent witness to the discontinuity in legal change of which Cooper wrote.[556]

[549] See IV.2.c above. [550] See IV.2.a above. [551] See III, IV, and VII above.
[552] See VI above. [553] See IX above. [554] See nn. 205–17. [555] See nn. 218–43.
[556] The author wishes to thank Mr Angus Stewart QC, Keeper of the Advocates' Library, for permission to consult the Library's holdings.

12

Trusts

GEORGE GRETTON[*]

I. INTRODUCTION

1. Defining the trust

To write the history of a legal institution, of a *Rechtsinstitut*, is to presuppose an institution for which a history can be written. Thus the present controls and rewrites the past, by reconceptualising it. That is a truism, but it bears repeating. In the case of the trust, the problem is acute. Modern categories are projected into the past, and reorganize the past. To look for the trust, to look for its history, is already to think in a certain way. To identify what are commonly called 'trust-like devices' is already to accept the trust as a discrete legal institution, along with 'person' or 'obligation' or 'action' or 'right' or 'delict' or 'succession'. Perhaps that is the right approach, but that it is right should not be presupposed.

If a foreign friend asked me to tell him in one word whether the right of the English *Destinär* (the person for whom property is held in trust) is *dinglich* or *obligatorisch*, I should be inclined to say: 'No, I cannot do that. If I said *dinglich*, that would be untrue. If I said *obligatorisch*, I should suggest what is false. In the ultimate analysis the right may be *obligatorisch*, but for many practical purposes of great importance it has been treated as though it were *dinglich*, and indeed people habitually speak and think of it as a kind of *Eigenthum*.'

Thus Maitland,[1] on the ambiguous nature of the trust. English law does not readily fit into civilian pigeon-holes. That is legitimate.[2] But one must beware of the converse. It does not follow that a system which has the trust

---

[*] I would like to thank Almira Delibegovic, Ruth Dukes, Murray Earle, John Finlay, Ross D. McClelland, and Emma Williamson for research assistance. An earlier version of this chapter appeared in Richard Helmholz and Reinhard Zimmermann, *Itinera Fiduciae: Trust and Treuhand in Historical Perspective* (1998), 507.

[1] H. A. L. Fisher (ed.), *Collected Papers of Frederic William Maitland* (1911), vol. 3, 326 ('Trust and Corporation'). *Dinglich* means real and *Eigent[h]um* means ownership.

[2] Though this sort of thing can be overstated. Already in Maitland's time the *Treuhand* seems to have had something of the ambiguity of the English trust, while the modern German *Anwartschaftsrecht* looks like equitable ownership. Something similar is true of the position of the creditor in *Sicherungsübereignung*.

must have an English pigeon-hole for it.[3] Thus Professor Fratcher's formulation in the *International Encyclopaedia of Comparative Law*[4] is unacceptable:

The interest of a beneficiary is . . . a property interest in the subject matter; it is not a mere personal or contract claim against the trustee. Neither trustee nor beneficiary has a mere *jus in re aliena*. In other words, the interests of both the trustee and the beneficiary in the subject matter are interests *in rem*.

This, true only of the Anglo-American systems, seeks to impose a certain conception as a matter of universal definitional validity.[5] Indeed, one may ask whether it is even true of those systems: the European Court of Justice has held that the right of a beneficiary in *English* law is *not* a real right.[6] In Québec law, not only does the beneficiary not have a real right, but the trustee does not have one either.[7] In South African law a *bewind* is classified as a kind of trust, though the trustee has no real right.[8]

This chapter is a historical one, but the conceptual issue cannot be dodged. Thus if one describes trust as an arrangement under which one person manages assets for another, then all developed legal systems have the trust, and Scots law has had it from the earliest times. If it is defined more narrowly as such an arrangement, but with the added feature that the assets are vested in the administrator, then again one encounters such 'trusts' almost universally, and again Scots law has had them from the earliest times. If one defines trust as involving a division of ownership into legal and equitable, then Scots law does not have the trust at all. These conceptual issues are particularly vital in delving into the origins of the trust. If you are looking for something, it makes sense to know what it is you are looking for. One needs not only to

---

[3] Cf. H. R. Hahlo, 'The Trust in South African Law', (1961) 78 *SALJ* 195.

[4] Vol. 6, ch. 11.

[5] Thus again Fratcher (ibid.): 'The trust is a legal device developed in England whereby ownership of property is split between a person known as a trustee, who has the rights and powers of an owner, and a beneficiary, for whose exclusive benefit the trustee is bound to use those rights and powers.'

[6] *Webb* v. *Webb* [1994] ECR 1–1717, interpreting art. 16 of the Brussels Convention. The expression *droit réel* in the English text becomes 'right *in rem*'. (That is unsatisfactory for Scots law, where the correct translation of *droit réel* is 'real right'.) While the *Webb* case is in line with Scots law, the Scots lawyer may be permitted to regret that Advocate-General Darmon seemed unaware that English law does not extend to the whole of the United Kingdom.

[7] 'Le patrimoine fiduciaire, formé des biens transférés en fiducie, constitue un patrimoine d'affectation autonome et distinct de celui du constituant, du fiduciaire, ou du bénéficiare, sur lequel aucun d'entre eux n'a de droit réél.' ('The trust property, consisting of the property transferred, constitutes a patrimony by appropriation, autonomous and distinct from that of the settlor, trustee or beneficiary, and in which none of them has any real right.': Official translation)—art. 1261 Code Civil of Québec. This formulation can be traced to the work of Pierre Lepaulle. It comes close to making a trust a juristic person, an idea for which much could be said.

[8] Trust Property Control Act 1988. On the history of the South African trust, see Tony Honoré, 'Trust', in Reinhard Zimmermann and Daniel Visser (eds.), *Southern Cross: Civil Law and Common Law in South Africa* (1996), 850 sqq.

be clear about concepts, but also to treat names with circumspection. For instance, the fact that the term 'trust' first appears in the seventeenth century does not mean that trusts first appeared in the seventeenth century. They might have existed earlier, without the name. But equally, they might not have evolved until later, for the word 'trust' can be used where there is no trust. In fact, in my view the trust—in something roughly like the sense which I am about to explain—did indeed develop in that century. But that fact cannot be inferred solely from the introduction of a particular word. Nothing is more familiar than the fact that the term 'trustee' is often applied, even in legal usage, to those who are not, in the accepted sense, trustees at all, such as company directors. Indeed, curators, tutors, and judicial factors are expressly included under the definition of 'trustees' in the Trusts (Scotland) Act 1921.[9]

The problem of defining what is meant by trust is a difficult one both for Scots law[10] and indeed at an international level.[11] I give here what is I think the modern Scots concept.[12] Our law knows no division between law and equity, and so the Anglo-American approach is of no relevance. Trust involves the administration of assets by one person (or more, jointly) for another person or group of persons. That relation is a fiduciary one: every trustee is a *fiduciarius*, i.e. must act in the interests of the beneficiary to the exclusion of his own. But there must be more than that: the assets must be vested (in some sense) in the trustee: it is for this reason that company directors, commercial agents, judicial factors, and so on are not strictly trustees.[13] Vesting in what sense? This too is a difficult area. Lord Stair in a passage which has had a powerful formative influence on the development of the concept, writes that 'the property of the thing intrusted, be it land or moveables, is in the person of the intrusted, else it is not proper trust'.[14] The trustee is owner, albeit a *nudus dominus*. What sort of right do the beneficiaries have? A personal right against the trustee.[15] Just as the trustee's ownership is an odd sort of ownership, but ownership nonetheless, so the beneficiary's personal right is an odd sort of personal right, but personal nonetheless. If the bene-

---

[9] S. 2. Charles Forsyth, *Principles and Practice of the Law of Trusts and Trustees in Scotland* (1844), of which more later, divided trusts into 'proprietary' and 'accessory', the latter being 'trusts' where the trustee did not acquire *dominium*. It is an interesting approach, but did not establish itself, the latter category being regarded as cases of fiduciary obligation but not trust. Forsyth subverted his own idea by placing some trusts which were in fact proprietary under the accessory category.

[10] For a valuable outline of the Scottish conception of the trust see K. G. C. Reid, 'National Report for Scotland', in D. J. Hayton, S. C. K. K. Kortmann, and H. L. E. Verhagen, *Principles of European Trust Law* (1999), 67 sqq.

[11] See the Hague Trusts Convention, adopted into UK law by the Recognition of Trusts Act 1987.

[12] As seen by the writer. Others might not analyse the trust in quite the same way, and they might accordingly see its history differently.

[13] In certain exceptional cases, however, assets may become vested in such persons, at which point they may become trustees in the full sense.   [14] Stair, I, 13, 7.

[15] This formulation works better for private than for public trusts.

ficiary has a right to particular assets, his right is still personal not real. A right *ad rem* is not real but personal. This way of looking at the trust is probably made necessary by the fact that whilst Scots private law is 'mixed' in the sense that it derives both from the *jus commune* and from the English traditions,[16] the degree of mixture varies from area to area, and Scots property law, both moveable and immoveable, is for the most part unmixed, and belongs to the *jus commune*.[17] As such, it takes the civilian framework of personal and real rights as its starting point, the latter being divided into *dominium* on the one hand and *jus in re aliena* (*jus in re minus quam dominium*) on the other, this being itself subdivided into particular nominate kinds—a *numerus clausus* of real rights. Trusts have to be located in this framework. The rights of the parties must be either personal or real. That it is perfectly possible to locate trusts in a civilian system of property law—albeit with certain stresses—is not always fully appreciated at an international level. It is sometimes imagined, both by those from the Anglo-American tradition and by others, that trusts of necessity bring in equity, and therefore cannot be understood in *jus commune* terms. That is not true,[18] as the Scottish example shows. Indeed, Scots law is of comparative interest in that it adopted a more or less full system of trusts into a civilian system of property law at an early stage. Some other countries with similar systems have done the same, but Scotland was the first.

But we have still not finished sketching the concept. All that has so far been said could be achieved without any special *Rechtsinstitut*, by means of the law of contract. X can transfer property to the ownership of Y and contract with Y that Y will administer it in such-and-such a way. That is simple contract. If X asks Y to administer for Z, then Z can be given title to sue by the *stipulatio in favorem tertii*. Is this trust? It could be so called, but it can be built up solely from the bricks of the law of voluntary obligations.[19] As late as 1866 a judge could say that 'the law of trusts has always been treated as part of the general principles of contracts, and the obligations upon the trustee, and the rights of the truster and the beneficiaries as against him, have been given effect to on the ground of contracts'.[20] But this is doubtful as a historical proposition, for trust has been considered a distinct institution from the

---

[16] Not to mention a good deal of home-grown law.

[17] The *jus commune* comprises not only the medieval and modern transformed Roman law, but also other elements, such as feudal law. Scotland is the last country in the world which retains feudalism in any real sense: see K. G. C. Reid (ed.), *The Law of Property in Scotland* (1996). (Soon, however, to be abolished under the Abolition of Feudal Tenure etc. (Scotland) Act 2000.) But as the feudal element has declined, the civilian element has increased in importance.

[18] Unless one makes it true definitionally, but that seems unhelpful. See further, G. L. Gretton, 'Trusts without Equity', (2000) 49 *ICLQ* 599.

[19] More or less. Modern trust law, with its ability to confer, extinguish, and transfer rights without the consent or even knowledge of the beneficiary, who may even be unborn, probably goes beyond even the maximum that could be achieved by the *stipulatio in favorem tertii*.

[20] Lord Barcaple in *Gordon v. Gordon's Tr* (1866) 4 M 501 at 535.

time of Stair. It is also doubtful conceptually. For a distinctive institution, something more than contract is needed. That something more is the separation of Y's estate into an ordinary patrimony and a trust patrimony. (The word 'patrimony'[21] is better than 'estate',[22] but nonetheless 'estate' is the word commonly used.) The effect of this is wonderful: because of the separation ordinary assets are (in general) immune to creditors of the trustee as trustee, while, even more important, trusts assets are (in general) immune to the creditor of the trustee as an individual. Those immunities could not be achieved merely by contract.[23] Moreover, since the trust property forms a distinct patrimony, real subrogation takes place, so that if a thing is sold, the price forms parts of the patrimony, and vice versa for purchases with trust money. The net effect is to make a trust into something very like a separate juristic person, and some theorists[24] have argued that it should be so conceptualized. Be that as it may, Scots law has never quite taken this step, though, as will be seen later, it has come close to it for public trusts.

The fact that a trust can function as a virtual juristic person has led to its use in some countries as a trading enterprise, the 'directors' being the trustees and the 'shareholders' being the beneficiaries. This has never happened in Scotland to any substantial degree.

2. The influence of English law

One of the central questions in any attempt to study the history of the trust must be the extent of English influence. It is a question of considerable difficulty, which will be discussed below, but it may be as well to summarize here the conclusions which will be reached. The origins of the trust remain uncertain, and while it must be presumed that English law had some influence—the adoption of the English name is suggestive—the evidence does not support the theory of anything like a reception of English trust law, and, indeed, it is hard to prove *any* substantial degree of English influence before about the middle of the nineteenth century, by which time the institution had long been established. There is a certain tendency to assume that the trust *must* have come from England. One remembers Maitland's remark that the trust was 'the greatest and most distinctive achievement performed by Englishmen in the field of jurisprudence'.[25] To trace the trust from any-

[21] The discussions of the concept of patrimony which took place on the Continent in the nineteenth century were largely ignored in Scotland. In my opinion this has caused difficulties in the development of the concept of trust, and, indeed, difficulties in other areas.

[22] 'Estate' is cluttered by other senses, such as landed estates and the English doctrine of 'estates in land'.

[23] Particular creditors might, of course, agree to restrict their rights of enforcement, but the nature of the trust is that the immunities arise *ex lege*, and are (in general) good against all creditors, consenting or not.

[24] Such as Pierre Lepaulle. See e.g. his *Traité théorique et pratique des trusts* (1932).

[25] F. W. Maitland, 'The Unincorporate Body', in *idem, Selected Historical Essays* (1957), 129.

where else than England seems as implausible as to suggest that golf originated in Italy. But the close association of the trust with English law is misleading. Trust-like devices have developed in other systems.[26] (Indeed the expression 'trust-like' is a loaded one, suggesting that the 'real' institution is the English trust.) There would be nothing particularly surprising if Scots law had developed the trust wholly independently. As a matter of fact there was some English influence, but in the earlier period its degree seems to be rather slight. More substantial English influence starts about the middle of the nineteenth century, by which time the trust was already old.

II. ORIGINS

1. Nineteenth- and twentieth-century ideas as to origins

'In Scotland, the origin of trusts is co-eval with the law of the land. For being a part and parcel of the civil law, on which the law of Scotland is based, they were necessarily introduced . . .' Thus writes Forsyth in the first book devoted to the law of trusts, published in 1844.[27] Earlier he writes that the trust derives from the *fideicommissum* of the Roman law.[28] Forsyth also says that the English law of trusts has the same origins, a convenient view if one wishes, as Forsyth did, to cast the Scots law of trusts in an English mould. The question of whether the origins were the same became something of a point of dispute. In 1868 Lord Westbury, an English judge sitting in a Scottish case, stated that 'the doctrine of trusts has the same origin and rests on the same principles both in Scots and English law, and it is desirable that it should be developed to the same extent in both systems'.[29] Westbury's agenda seems clear. One should, however, not necessarily bracket Westbury with Forsyth. Westbury might not have agreed that the trust originated in *fideicommissum*.[30] It became important for those concerned with the autonomy of Scots law to

---

[26] Most obviously the *fiducia* and *fideicommissum* of Roman law and the *Treuhand* of German law; on which see David Johnston, 'Trust and Trust-like Devices in Roman Law', and Karl Otto Scherner, 'Formen der Treuhand im alten deutschen Recht', both in Richard Helmholz and Reinhard Zimmermann, *Itinera Fiduciae: Trust and Treuhand in Historical Perspective* (1998), 45 sqq. and 237 sqq. [27] Forsyth (n. 9), 9.
[28] Forsyth (n. 9), 3.
[29] *Fleeming* v. *Howden* (1868) 6 M (HL) 113 at 121. Nothing was more common in 19th-century House of Lords appeals coming from Scotland than for the judges to discover, to their convenience, that the Scots law on a certain point was the same as the English law. However, one must sympathize: their position was an impossible one. For a study of great value (despite its populist title) see Andrew Dewar Gibb, *Law from over the Border* (1950).
[30] However, some English authors of the 17th and 18th centuries traced the trust to *fideicommissum*. William Blackstone, *Commentaries on the Laws of England* (1765–9), vol. 2, 327–8, compares the trust to *fideicommissum* and hints that there might be a connection. And see Michael Macnair, 'The Conceptual Basis of English Trusts in the later 17th and early 18th Centuries', in Helmholz/Zimmermann (n. 26), 207 sqq.

assert the independence of the Scottish law of trusts from the English law. That meant accepting Forsyth's thesis as to the antiquity of trusts and their civil origin, but rejecting the English connection. 'The history of the origin and development of the law of trusts in Scotland is not at all the same as the history of the origin and development of the law of trusts in England,' asserted Lord Normand in 1955.[31] 'The origin of trusts is very different from its origin in England,' said Lord Reid in 1971.[32] T. B. Smith in 1962 was prepared to follow Forsyth and Normand.[33] Smith's essay, interesting and valuable though it is, is not precisely a historical one. Indeed, only one serious attempt has ever been made to look at the origins of the trust, by Burgess in 1974.[34]

2. The seventeenth century and before

The term 'trust' came into use in the course of the seventeenth century. That fact takes us only so far: the trust might have existed without the name already in 1600, or might by 1700 have not yet been born, despite the use of the name. As to the latter doubt, it can be laid to rest at once. The discussion of trust in Stair's *Institutions* is admittedly (to modern eyes) brief, fragmentary, and unsatisfactory, but it would be difficult to deny that this is, in a rudimentary and unevolved form, the trust. Nor does the trust vanish after Stair: the texts writers keep it in view, and the courts decide cases. The modern broad river can be traced back, without interruption, to the narrow stream of Stair, and on the way certain tributaries are to be found. But if we move back before Stair the stream ends. But there is no sudden source or fountain. Rather there are wetlands which, in the course of the seventeenth century, form into a flow. To anticipate conclusions, the trust, in something like the modern sense, emerged in the course of the seventeenth century. Before looking to see what actually happened in the seventeenth century, let us look back before its start.

3. Pre-seventeenth century private arrangements

Examples of trust-like arrangements where X and Y agree that Y should hold property, corporeal or incorporeal, for X, go back a long way. All the examples

---

[31] *Camille & Henry Dreyfus Foundation* v. *IRC* [1956] AC 39 at 47.
[32] *Allan's Trs* v. *Lord Advocate* 1971 SC (HL) 45 at 53.
[33] T. B. Smith, 'Trusts and Fiduciary Relationships in the Law of Scotland', in *idem*, *Studies Critical and Comparative* (1962), 200.
[34] Robert Burgess, 'Thoughts on the Origins of the Trust in Scots Law', [1974] *JR* 196. I am indebted to this pioneering essay, even though there are things in it with which I disagree. The standard texts on trust law, notably that of W. A. Wilson and A. G. M. Duncan, *Trusts Trustees & Executors* (1st edn., 1975; 2nd edn., 1995; henceforth references are only made to the 2nd edn.), also have some incidental historical material.

given in this section may be categorized as trusts or not according to taste. They could be categorized as purely contractual arrangements.

In his *Legal History of Scotland*[35] D. M. Walker writes that 'the practice developed among landowners in the 15th century of conveyancing estates to patrons' relatives or friends in trust'.[36] He cites no authority or examples, but such conveyances may have been common. Whether they should be classified as trusts depends on what is meant by trust. Certainly in the fifteenth and sixteenth centuries it was common to have 'trusts' of moveables, X holding for Y. Irritatingly, the sources often fail to disclose why such arrangements were entered into. Here are some examples.[37]

(*a*) In 1492 Lord Johnne Kennedy makes over to Sir Johnne Kennedy 'twa hundreth merkis to the utilitie and profit of Jane Kennedy his dochter'[38] to be paid to her upon her marriage.[39] The expression 'utility and profit' is one which seems to have been something of a standard one.

(*b*) In 1498 Janet Innes sues Patrick Gordon for 100 merks, being the value of unspecified goods which her father 'deliverit til Georg of Gordoun, bruther to the sade Patrik, quilk ressavit the sadis gudis fra hir sade fadir to hir utilitie and profitts'.[40] It is noteworthy that the action is not against the 'trustee' but against a party who was the successor of the 'trustee' and who is described as an 'intromettour'. This is, curiously, a feature to be found in some other early cases of trust or quasi-trust, such as *Lady Stanipath* v. *Her Son's Relict and Bairns*.[41] According to later concepts, one would wish to know whether the defender was *in bona fide* and what had been the *causa* whereby he acquired the property, but the early reports are tantalizingly brief.

(*c*) In 1521 James Lokhart is owed money by John Crauford, but agrees that this money shall be received by John Lokhart, to be used to buy land for James Lokhart, though John Lokhart at the same time agrees that he shall

---

[35] (1990), vol. 2, 687.
[36] Walter Ross says much the same in his valuable *Lectures on the Law of Scotland* (1st edn., 1792; 2nd edn., 1822; henceforth references are only made to the 2nd edn.), vol. 2, 334.
[37] These examples have been gathered rather at random. A survey of the sources, such as protocol books, suggests that such examples were not particularly common.
[38] It is unclear which John Kennedy she is the daughter of.
[39] Gordon Donaldson (ed.), *Protocol Book of James Young 1485–1518* (1952), 121.
[40] *Acta Dominorum Concilii*, vol. 2, 131. D. M. Walker, 'Equity in Scots Law', (1954) 66 *JR* 103 sqq. at 141, cites this case as being perhaps one of trust. Professor Walker also there cites as a trust case *Rollock* v. *Hamilton* (1560) discussed in Balfour, *Practicks*, 198. This, however, seems to be a simple case of deposit, though it is striking that the term 'utilitie and proffeit' is used. Of course, the trust/deposit borderline is problematic, and trust was from Stair onwards often characterized as a threefold combination of deposit, transfer, and mandate. For a case of 1440 in which there was a deposit and mandate but no transfer see Annie I. Dunlop and David Maclauchlan, *Calendar of Scottish Supplications to Rome 1443–1477* (1983), 158. Annie I. Cameron, 'Vatican Archives 1073–1560', in Hector McKechnie (ed.), *Introductory Survey of the Sources and Literature of Scots Law*, Stair Society, vol. 1 (1936), 274 sqq. at 278 calls this a case of 'charitable trust'. I am grateful to W. David H. Sellar for drawing this reference to my attention.
[41] (1624) Durie 141.

pay the money to James Lokhart as and when required to do so.[42] Apparently James Lokhart was a minor and John Lokhart his curator.

(d) In *Spittell* v. *Urquhart*, a case of 1532, as reported by Balfour,[43] it was held that 'gif ony man ressave in keiping ony infeftment of landis ... to be deliverit to him to quhom the samin was maid and gevin, and beand requirit be him to deliver the samin, refusis, postponis and delayis to mak deliverance to him thairof, he may be callit and convenit to refound, content and pay to him the haill proffeits of girs, pasturage of cattell, or of ony uther gudis quhatsumever quhilkis he micht have had of the saidis landis ...'.

(e) In 1540 Alexander Forester wishes to repay £100, seemingly secured on land. He 'warns' his creditor, David Forester, to appear at the altar of St. Giles Church at a certain day to receive the money. The latter does not appear, so Alexander Forester pays the money to Thomas Marjoribanks 'to the utilitie and proffit' of David Forester.[44]

(f) In 1540 David Bruis assigns to his son Ninian Bruis a debt owed by Alexander Hwyme. Ninian is to hold the money until his sister, Jonet Bruis, is of marriageable age, and thereupon is to pay the money to her.[45]

(g) In 1542 Alexander Mortoun is going off to fight the invading English. He conveys his land to his son, Alexander the younger. If he returns alive, his son is to reconvey. Otherwise, his son is to hold for the heirs and assignees of his father,[46] though the lands are to burdened by provisions for the daughters (i.e. sisters of Alexander the younger), Isabella, Janet, Margaret, and Elizabeth.[47]

(h) In 1551 Eduard Maxwell, a minor, is due an annuity from Robert Maxwell of £40 per annum. Sir John Maxwell, seemingly Eduard's curator, arranges that Robert should pay the money to John Glendonyn 'to the utilitie and profett' of Edward.[48]

(i) In 1554 Robert Forman is going to Flanders. He conveys all his

---

[42] John Anderson and Francis J. Grant (eds.), *The Protocol Book of Gavin Ros 1512–1532* (1908), 77.

[43] Balfour, *Practicks*, 198. As noted by Burgess, [1974] *JR* 196 Balfour's report is possibly not accurate, but for present purposes what a distinguished lawyer thought in 1579 is as important as what the court decided in 1532. Dr Mark Godfrey has pointed out to me that the record in the National Archives of Scotland 26 July 1532 (NAS/SRO CS 6/1 fo. 84^v–85^r) suggests that this may in fact have been simply an enrichment action.

[44] NAS/SRO MS no. CS 6/14 fo. 46^v. Thomas Marjoribanks was one of the leading lawyers of the day. Many similar examples could be cited: see for instance John Anderson (ed.), *The Protocol Book of Sir Alex Gaw 1540–1558* (1910), 8; William Angus (ed.), *Protocol Book of Gilbert Grote 1552–1573* (1914), 32; R. H. Lindsay (ed.), *Protocol Book of Sir John Cristisone 1518–1551* (1931), 13 and 192; James Beveridge and James Russell (eds.), *Protocol Books of Dominus Thomas Johnsoun 1528–1578* (1920), 74. In this latter volume there is an interesting example at 140 suggesting that in such cases the consignee had to be a person of a certain status.

[45] Lindsay (n. 44), 69. [46] Presumably the son himself will be the heir.

[47] Anderson (n. 44), 3.

[48] R. C. Reid (ed.), *Protocol Book of Mark Carruther 1531–1561* (1956), 47 sq.

property to his wife Elizabeth, for her benefit and for the benefit of their children, the conveyance to be void if he returns alive, while at the same time she conveys all her property to him for his benefit and that of their children in the event that he returns alive but she is dead.[49] The reference to the children is interesting.[50]

(j) In 1580 James Mosman pays Andro Lamby £1200 which the latter is to pay to Alaxander King for the benefit of Barbara Troupe. Lamby fails to do this and Troupe sues.[51]

The term 'trust' had not yet come into use. These examples are all trust-like, but one should hesitate before calling them 'true' trusts. It is to be noted that the chapter in Balfour's *Practicks* from which *Spittell* v. *Urquhart* is taken deals with the contract *de deposito*, and the very next case reported is of deposit of moveables. There can be no doubt that one of the roots of trust law was the contract of *depositum* which was varied in such a way as to involve not only the transfer of possession but also the transfer of ownership. If the depositee was contractually authorized not merely to hold but also to deal with the asset in relation to third parties (which would often be convenient) then a further contractual element entered, namely that of *mandatum*. The institutional writers tend to characterize trust as a combination of deposit and mandate.[52] This has often caused puzzlement, because no one now would adopt such a conceptualization, since deposit and mandate are not conveyances. But if one approaches the matter from the standpoint of early practice, in which property was transferred subject to contractual conditions, the characterization is an appropriate one, and indeed the only real hurdle is to realize that the deposit is an irregular one, in that ownership passes.[53] The significance of the characterization, in Stair and other writers, of trust as being a combination of mandate and deposit is that it lends support to the view that trust cannot be regarded simply as a seventeenth-century import from England. There is a continuity going back before 1600.

Of course, the pre-1600 examples might themselves reflect English influence, and to some extent they probably do. For instance, one sometimes comes across the very English word 'use', as in a case of 1523/4, where the defender, Johne Mure, is averred to have owed money to Margret Ruderford

---

[49] Angus (n. 44), 3 paras. 12 and 13.
[50] In addition, we seem to have here an early example of the device of evading the rule that a proprietor cannot test on heritage by means of a conditional conveyance *de praesenti*.
[51] *Register of the Privy Council*, vol. 3, 271. The report does not give the original wording. D. M. Walker, *Legal History of Scotland*, vol. 3 (1995), 207 calls this a case of trust.
[52] See below III.6. One might suppose that the trust/deposit relationship was especially Scottish, but it can be found in English law too. Blackstone (n. 30), 451 calls bailment a trust.
[53] Burgess, [1974] *JR* 196 at 202 questions the role of mandate in the history of trust, saying that prior to Stair mandate was unknown. But with respect that is simply not the case.

'to the use and profit' of her daughter Kathryne Wallace.[54] To what extent English influence before 1600 can be identified is unclear. My impression is that that influence was slight. The word 'use' may indicate linguistic more than doctrinal influence, and there was no reception of the English doctrine of uses in any developed sense.

Burgess[55] sees as a possible precursor the *resignatio in favorem* which was one of two methods[56] by which land could be transferred from X to Y. What happened is that X surrendered the land to his superior, with the latter regranting it to Y. In a sense one could see X as the truster, Y as the beneficiary, and the superior as trustee.[57]

Finally, it should be noted that in some situations where 'trust' might have been used, one does not find it. In 1557 Oswald Porteus intends to go abroad for a considerable time. He will leave behind in Scotland 'twa zoung barnis callit Marion Porteous and Margaret Porteous, his dochtaris, being pupillis in thair minoritie and les age and thair moder decessit'. Oswald conveys certain tacks (leases) to them, to be retrocessed to him if he returns alive, while at the same time he makes his friends Patrik Nicolsoune and William Porteus 'actouris factouris rewalris and gidaris' in respect of the tacks.[58] To a modern eye it might have been simpler to assign the tacks to Nicolsoune and Porteus direct, in trust. That was not done.

4. *Fideicommissum* and Roman law

In Roman law *fideicommissum* was an institution where X, by testament, conveyed assets to Y under obligation to convey to Z. Y was the *fiduciarius*[59] and Z the *fideicommissarius*.[60] Stair repeatedly compares the trust to *fideicom-*

---

[54] NAS/SRO MS no. CS 5/34 fo. 86ᵛ (11 Feb. 1523/24). Interestingly, the action against Mure is by the daughter, i.e. the 'beneficiary'. [55] See above n. 34.
[56] The other was the charter of confirmation.
[57] Compare Scherner (n. 26), 263. Scherner remarks that such *resignatio* should be 'regarded as a consequence of feudal law and not as a case of *Treuhand*' (my translation). But one may wonder whether this is not too sharp an antithesis. [58] Angus (n. 44), 26.
[59] This term was also used to describe the 'trustee' in the institution of *fiducia*, but that was a two-party arrangement (either *cum amico* or *cum creditore*) and seems to have disappeared by the time of Justinian.
[60] See David Johnston, *Roman Law of Trusts* (1988). One form of this institution was fideicommissary substitution, which became a common European institution, under varying names. In Scots law it was called the tailzie. R. Burgess, *Perpetuities in Scots Law* (1979), 62 sqq. denies the role of fideicommissary substitution in the formation of the tailzie, just as he denies (see next section of the text) the role of *fideicommissum* in the formation of the trust. But this is a mistake. Even if the medieval tailzie were purely English in origin, and even if the continental links of the English entail were to be disregarded, the post-medieval civilian influence on the tailzie is apparent. The same pattern is observable on the Continent, especially as a result of the work of Philipp Knipschildt. See further Klaus Luig, 'Philipp Knipschildt und das Familienfideikomiss im Zeitalter des Usus Modernus', in Helmholz/Zimmermann (n. 26), 361. See generally William Lewis, *Das Recht des Familienfideikommisses* (1868). Some account of the medieval tailzie can be found in D. M. Walker, *Legal History of Scotland*, vol. 2 (1990), 634–6.

missum,⁶¹ and the word has been used in other countries to mean trust.⁶² As has already been seen, the origin of the Scots law of trust has frequently been attributed to *fideicommissum*. Burgess controverts that view. He argues⁶³ that 'what Stair is doing is attempting to fit the trust into the framework of Roman ideas and principles and that he is finding that it does not fit precisely into either mandate or deposit or *fideicommissum*. This, in other words, is an acknowledgement, if any were needed, that the trust in Scotland had an origin and development independent of Roman ideas and institutions'. Burgess sees the reception of Roman law as having taken place in the late seventeenth century, by which time, he argued, the trust was already established. But the reception cannot be pinned down to any particular period. It has been pervasive over the centuries. It began much earlier than the late seventeenth century and indeed continues to the present day.⁶⁴ *Fideicommissum* was a concept which lawyers had always been familiar with. Stair, in comparing trust with *fideicommissum*, was articulating an established idea. Already before Stair an executry was called *fideicommissum*,⁶⁵ though it was not until later that executry and trust came together.

There is one case, in 1717, when a *fideicommissum* was held to exist as a distinct institution.⁶⁶ A marriage contract provided that on the eventual death of the bride's father she would take certain sums from his estate to pay over to her own future children, but to keep the money if she had none. One of her sons eventually sued her for his share. He was successful, and the case was called 'fidei-commiss'. The de-Latinized form suggests long linguistic usage. But this seems to be the only reported case of the kind. It may be that *fideicommissum* had an extensive life as a half-accepted institution, not quite distinct from, nor quite merged with, trust. At all events, the time when the traditional trust-like arrangements were emerging into the trust was precisely the time when lawyers were using *fideicommissum* as a way of modelling the emerging institution. *Fideicommissum* was one of the sources of the trust. Whether its role was marginal or something more substantial would be hard to say.

5. The seventeenth century

Williamson v. *Law*, decided in 1623,⁶⁷ is sometimes said to be the first reported case on trusts. It is indeed the earliest case in which one finds the

---

⁶¹ For example Stair, IV, 6, 2 and IV, 45, 21, but elsewhere also.
⁶² For example, Mexico, where trust is called *fideicomiso*.
⁶³ See Burgess, [1974] *JR* 196 at 202, with particular reference to Stair, IV, 6, 2 and 3.
⁶⁴ Especially if we speak of the partial reception of 'Civil' rather than 'Roman' law.
⁶⁵ Thus in *Southall* v. *Cunninghamhead* (1657) Eng Judg 49 we read that 'all the *dominium* he [the executor] has is *fideicommissum*'. (Incidentally, Stair was not counsel in this case.) I would imagine that earlier examples of this idea could be found. For executry, see later.
⁶⁶ *Seton* v. *Pitmeddon* (1717) Mor 4425.   ⁶⁷ (1623) Durie 54.

terminology of trust in the report. But *Williamson* v. *Law* is less important than it seems. The report does speak of 'trust'. However, Durie's *Reports* were not published until 1690. The dates of Alexander Gibson of Durie's birth and death seem to be unknown, but he became a Court of Session judge in 1621 and it was his grandson who edited and published his reports in 1690. By that time the trust was already established. Might the editor have succumbed to conceptual anachronism? The original papers in this case[68] suggest that this might be so. A bond was payable to Dickson.[69] Williamson paid Dickson to assign it to him, and she did so, but for reasons which do not appear he arranged for the assignee to be named not as himself but as his nephew, Law. Law later denied that he held the bond for Williamson. Hence the action,[70] which was by Williamson's executor. The word 'trust' is not used.[71] The expression used is that the assignation was 'to the behuif utilitie and proffeit' of Williamson. The case seems to be simply another example of the traditional private arrangements described above. It may be classified as a trust, but so may earlier cases. Even if one is interested in terminology rather than doctrine, the case is of limited significance since it seems not to have used the word 'trust'.[72] One might equally—and equally inconclusively—argue that it must have been a trust case because it uses the word 'behoof', and 'for behoof of' is (at least since the late seventeenth century) a synonym for 'in trust for'.

It would not have been surprising if *Williamson* v. *Law* had in fact been a case of trust in the fullest sense. In 1603 Elizabeth of England died, and her successor was the Scottish King, James VI. He left Edinburgh for London, and never returned. The Union of the Crowns had begun, to be followed in 1707 by the Union of the Parliaments. The effect of the Union of the Crowns was substantial. We know that intercourse between the two kingdoms increased. We know that many prominent Scots spent much time in London. To some extent they doubtless picked up the idea of the trust. But the evidence suggests that English influence at this stage was slight. Indeed, for the period before the Civil Wars I have come across only one example which can be so categorized,[73] namely the creation of George Heriot's Trust, one of the largest, possibly the longest-running, of Scottish trusts, for it was founded in

---

[68] NAS/SRO MS no. CS 7/371 fos. 46ʳ–49ᵛ.

[69] The original papers show that this 'Dickson' was Janet, sister of the celebrated George Heriot. [70] Proof of trust was a major theme in the 17th century, as later.

[71] Except at fo. 48ᵛ of the MS where Williamson is said to have been 'trusting'. It should be added, that the fact that 'trust' is not used in the original papers does not necessarily mean that it was added by the editor in 1690. It is possible that Durie used it in his own manuscript report, which has not survived.

[72] I have not been able to locate the original papers in what is sometimes said to be the second reported trust case, decided the year after Williamson, namely *Lady Stanipath* v. *Her Creditors* (1624) Durie 141. [73] Of course, this may reflect the inadequacies of my researches.

1623 and still flourishes today.[74] Heriot was an extraordinarily successful businessman. Though he settled in London, he never forgot his native city, and shortly before he died he established the educational trust which bears his name. The trust was established by two deeds, the first being an *inter vivos* conveyance of 3 September 1623 and the second his testament of 10 December 1623.[75] Both make over assets to Edinburgh City Council, to establish a school 'in imitatione of the publict pios and religious work foundat within the Citie of London callit Chrystis Hospitall'. The deed is generally in Scottish style. Of course, even in London Heriot would have had access to Scots lawyers. But there are some intriguing Anglicisms. In the testament we read: 'I give and devyse unto the said Provest baillies[76] . . . quho are namit and appointit as feoffeis in trust in this behalf.' 'Devise' is an English term, but what follows is more dramatic. 'Feoffees', to give the word its more usual spelling, is purely English, and Heriot's testament is probably the only Scottish deed in which the word has ever been employed. Linguistically, all we have here is a dead-end, but the word, appearing in a Scottish deed, is evidence of contact and influence. 'Feoffeis *in trust*', as a phrase, is truly striking. Heriot and his advisers, who evidently included Scots lawyers, must have been confident that this expression would be understood in Edinburgh. But the two deeds are also full of Scots terminology too, and the word 'mortification' is repeatedly used.[77]

It is possible that there was English influence during the Cromwellian occupation in the 1650s. During this period Scotland was in part governed by English officials and some judges were English. Scots lawyers had to handle legislation based on the trust concept. Thus on 12 April 1654 an act was passed dealing with certain lands which had been confiscated by the government for political reasons. The title is '[a]n Ordinance for settling the Estates of Severall Excepted Persons in Scotland in Trustees to the Uses herein expressed',[78] and the act itself is drafted very much in the terms of English law. We know that the word 'trust' begins to be used in cases increasingly often after the Restoration, and we know that Lord Stair, who was appointed to the bench in 1657 and thus sat with English judges, was the first jurist to deal with trusts as such. But attractive though this theory is, evidence is sparse. One might expect to see the trust emerging in the decisions of the Cromwellian court which was in fact though not in name the Court of Session.[79] But these show no trace of trusts. It is a striking silence.

---

[74] I am grateful to the George Heriot Trust Office in Edinburgh for permission to examine their records.
[75] See William Steven, *Memoir of George Heriot with the History of the Hospital Founded by him in Edinburgh* (1845). [76] That is to say, the Council.
[77] For mortification, see III.7 below.
[78] APS, VI, 821 (c. 21); C. H. Firth and R. S. Tait, *Acts and Ordinances of the Interregnum* (1911), vol. 2, 884. [79] The reports (cited as 'Eng Judg') were eventually published in 1762.

That there was some degree of formative influence coming from England in the seventeenth century seems probable, perhaps associated with the accession of James VI to the English throne in 1603 and with the Cromwellian occupation of Scotland in the 1650s. But all this does not amount to a 'reception' of English trust law. It would, indeed, be a defensible position, on the evidence which we have, to say that nothing was borrowed except the name.[80]

As the reign of Charles II continued, the trust established itself as an institution. Two significant cases are *Livingston* v. *Forrester*[81] in 1664 and *Mackenzie* v. *Watson*[82] in 1678, both of them holding that where property is held in trust it is immune to the diligence (execution) of the ordinary creditors of the trustee.[83] If this immunity is the single most important distinguishing feature of the trust as a separate legal institution, one might say that with these cases the trust had emerged from gestation into the light of day. However, doctrinal history has an irritating habit of refusing to be neat. It is far from certain that in these cases the beneficiary succeeded because of the trust. At that time it was still arguable that diligence (forced execution) was subject to *any* third party *jus in personam ad rem acquirendam*. It was also arguable that it was subject to *no* third party personal right. Long after these cases the question of immunity remained to some extent in doubt. The modern law is that diligence is in general not subject to third party personal rights, but there are some exceptions, notably rights arising out of trusts and certain other personal rights.[84] (Exactly which is arguable.) But this was unclear in the seventeenth century. Moreover, Stair, who reported both cases, does not in his *Institutions* cite *Mackenzie* v. *Watson*, and though he cites *Livingston* v. *Forrester* he does so only in connection with another point of law.[85] Though to the modern eye these cases seem of the first importance, contemporary observers perhaps saw differently.

As well as bearing an affinity to deposit and mandate, trust also has an affinity with the contract creating third party rights.[86] It is a puzzle, to which I cannot offer any solution, that the two doctrines have been streams flowing in separate courses. For instance, one of the key problems in third party rights is that of the means by which the third party can be vested in his right. A plausible attempt to short-circuit that difficulty would be to argue that the

---

[80] Another example of the gradual introduction of the term: the act 1633, APS, V, 22 (c. 6) which deals with mortifications refers to those 'entrusted' with the administration of the mortifications. As will be seen later, mortifications were public trusts. This act is of interest, in that it narrates that mortifications for the benefit of 'colledges schooles and hospitalls' are sometimes being 'inverted' by those 'entrusted' and provides a mechanism for enforcement, either by the beneficiary (which seems to presuppose that the beneficiary already exists to the extent of being able to raise an action) or by the bishop. (In 1633 the Church of Scotland was episcopalian.)
[81] (1664) Mor 191 and 10200, 1 Stair Rep 232.   [82] (1678) Mor 10188, 2 Stair Rep 607.
[83] I would guess that Stair sat on both cases, but this is to speculate.
[84] Niall Whitty has suggested the term 'protected personal rights'.   [85] Stair, III, 2, 47.
[86] See vol. 2, ch. 9, to which I am indebted.

arrangement should be regarded as a trust. Yet that step has, it seems, never been taken. The affinity of the two institutions has only occasionally been glimpsed.[87]

Stair is the first jurist to deal with trust. But one should not overlook the place of trust in Dirleton's *Doubts*.[88] For instance he observes that 'a backbond declaring a trust, with an obligement to denude, hath been found to be binding even against an assigny and arrester. And so it seems to be better than an assignation, which requires intimation to complete it'.[89] It is an acute remark, showing that the nature of trust was being looked at carefully.[90] Again, he asks: 'A right being granted to one, his heirs and assigneys, for the use and behoof of another person and his heirs, whether the casualties of ward, marriage etc. do fall by his decease, and with respect to the person infeft, or to the person to whose behoof the right is granted'.[91] This again is an acute question. The fact that the question was an open one suggests that trusts of land held ward were uncommon (the casualties of ward and marriage related only to wardholding) since otherwise it would presumably have become settled. The question also suggests that the parallel question for other tenures, such as the casualty of relief in feu farm, must already have had a settled answer, though if so I have not found it. (The nineteenth-century practice seems to have been that casualties were a matter for agreement between the superior and the vassal-trustees. The trustees could hardly avoid reaching such agreement if they wished to obtain public infeftment, since that would require a charter by progress from the superior.[92])

One final observation is that in the seventeenth century there developed a conveyancing device called entry by adjudication on a trust bond. This was a means by which an heir could obtain entry with the superior in a manner different from the ordinary methods, which were *clare constat* and service. The heir granted a fictitious bond to a friend, who held it in trust,[93] but who acted as if he were creditor to the heir. By this means the heir obtained what was called a tentative title. The device is said to have been invented by Thomas

---

[87] One person to glimpse it was James Condie Sandeman: see vol 2, ch. 9.

[88] Sir John Nisbet of Dirleton, *Doubts and Questions in the Law* (1698). Presumably it was composed between his retirement in 1677 and his death in 1687. Walker writes of Dirleton that '[a]t a time when bad men were common, he was one of the worst' (D. M. Walker, *The Oxford Companion to Law* (1980), 882). [89] Dirleton (n. 88), 215.

[90] It is in general true for modern law, except that a transferee from a trustee will normally be protected.

[91] Dirleton (n. 88), 215. Sir James Steuart of Goodtrees, *Dirleton's Doubts and Questions in the Law of Scotland Resolved and Answered* (1715), 317 sq., says that if the fact of the trust enters the infeftment then the casualties attach to the beneficiary, or, to use Dirleton's word, the *usuarius*.

[92] See A. M. Bell, *Lectures of Conveyancing* (3rd edn., 1882), 1146.

[93] i.e. the creditor held the bond in trust for the debtor.

Hope about 1630.[94] But the subject has not been researched and details are obscure.[95]

6. Proof of trust

Many of the cases of the seventeenth century concerning trusts or arrangements similar to trusts turn on the question of proof.[96] The alleged trustee denies the fact of trust and claims that he holds the assets absolutely. No written acknowledgement of the fact of trust exists. One issue which faced the courts was whether there should be any restrictions as to mode of proof. The cases culminated in *Higgins* v. *Callander*[97] in 1696, in which it was held that no restrictions existed, but that such restrictions ought to exist.

> The Lords thought the evidences and presumptions of trust very strong; yet, on the other hand, such exorbitant and implicit trusts were not so favourable as to deserve encouragement, being oftentimes used as blinds to intrap and defraud; and, therefore, wished there were an Act for the future, that no trust should be otherwise proveable but by writ or the intrusted party's oath.

That wish was promptly granted by the passing of the Blank Bonds and Trusts Act 1696,[98] the first enactment on trust law.[99] It is an interesting question whether this act was influenced by the English Statute of Frauds of 1677[100] which restricted proof of trust of land, requiring writing. However, there seems to be no evidence bearing on the question, either one way or the other.

III. HISTORY SINCE THE SEVENTEENTH CENTURY[101]

1. Some uses of the trust

The trust is an institution of remarkable flexibility, which can be made use of in many different ways. In the seventeenth and eighteenth centuries, however, its uses were very limited. Perhaps the only two common ones were both connected with insolvency. The first was the practice whereby creditors would

---

[94] Hope, who was Lord Advocate, seems to have been an ingenious conveyancer, for he is also credited with the invention of the unbreakable tailzie (entail).
[95] See e.g. Alexander Duff, *Treatise on the Deeds and Forms used in the Constitution Transmission and Extinction of Feudal Rights* (commonly called 'Duff's Feudal Conveyancing') (1838), 489 sqq.   [96] *Williamson* v. *Law* (1623) Durie 54 is an example.
[97] (1696) Mor 16182. Stair was not involved in this case, having died the year before.
[98] APS, X, 63 (c. 25).
[99] C. R. A. Howden, *Trusts Trustees and the Trusts Acts in Scotland* (1893), 6, calls the act 1617, APS, IV, 544 (c. 14) 'the first legislative recognition of trusts in our statute book'. But this requires the eye of faith.   [100] 29 Car II (c. 3).
[101] Inevitably this part must be highly selective.

assign their claims to one of their number who would then enforce on behalf of everyone.[102] This had the advantages of speed and convenience. The assigned debts were held in trust by the assignee. The device can also be found in Roman law. (The *missio in bona* in favour of a *magister.*) It seems to have been rare by the end of the eighteenth century. The second was the trust deed for behoof of creditors. This was initiated by the debtor himself. He chose someone to act as his trustee, and conveyed to him most or all of his assets, in trust for his creditors, the trust purposes being realization and distribution. This arrangement continues to flourish today, and indeed in 1985 received a measure of statutory encouragement.[103] In 1772 came the first of a long line of Bankruptcy (Scotland) Acts providing for the judicial sequestration of the estate of a bankrupt and its vesting in a trustee for realization and distribution.[104] The vast history of bankruptcy law cannot be explored here, but the device of making the administrator a trustee was continued through successive statutes, notably the Bankruptcy (Scotland) Acts of 1856,[105] 1913, and 1985.

There were other miscellaneous uses. In *Workman* v. *Crawford*[106] land was disponed to secure a debt. (This was an example of what was later to be called the *ex facie* absolute disposition.[107]) The disponee was regarded as a trustee.[108] In many cases one comes across assignation of debt to a trustee to do diligence against the debtor. These may be examples of the device mentioned earlier (creditors assigning to a *magister*), but some of them look as if the assignee is acting only for that cedent and not for others. If so, it is puzzling.[109]

Antenuptial marriage contracts are, of course, of considerable antiquity,

---

[102] John Russell, *Theory of Conveyancing* (1788)—admittedly not a work of the first rank—observes (at 337) that 'hitherto, trust rights in Scotland have been chiefly confined to the security of creditors, and the expediting of the affairs of bankrupts'. The meaning of the first category is uncertain, but probably refers to the *ex facie* absolute disposition.

[103] Bankruptcy (Scotland) Act 1985, s. 59.

[104] 12 Geo 3 (c. 72). Later this statute was, rather curiously, given the official short title of the Bills of Exchange Act 1772.   [105] 19 & 20 Vict (c. 19).

[106] (1672) Mor 10208, 2 Stair Rep 121.

[107] That is to say, ownership was vested in the creditor as a security, the debtor having a personal right to a reconveyance on payment of the debt. This was not a true right in security—neither *pignus* nor *hypotheca*—because in a true security there are two real rights in one thing: the debtor has *dominium* and the creditor a *jus in re minus quam dominium*. In an *ex facie* absolute disposition there is only one real right, *dominium*, and it is the creditor who has it. However, if an owner purported to convey ownership to a creditor, but the deed revealed that it was intended as security, it took effect as *hypotheca*. This device is effectively the same as *fiducia cum creditore*.

[108] This established itself as the law. For a later example, involving an *ex facie* absolute assignation, see *Purnell* v. *Shannon* (1894) 22 R 74. Much the same result has been arrived at in German law, where the debtor in a *fiducia cum creditore* (*Sicherungsübereignung*) is protected in the event of the creditor's insolvency.

[109] For example see *Craig* v. *Carbiston* (1677) Mor 16174, 2 Stair Rep 571; *Ogilvie* v. *Lyon* (1729) Mor 16200, 2 K & W Dic 477. In *Mackenzie* v. *Watson* (1678) Mor 10188, 2 Stair Rep 607, we are told that the creditor assigned the claim in trust because he was 'unwilling to distress Elphinston [the debtor] his own name' (i.e. in the name of the creditor/cedent).

but originally made no use of trusts. In the course of the eighteenth century it began to be the practice to appoint 'trustees' who had the right to enforce the provisions.[110] But nothing was vested in them, and so they were (to modern eyes) not trustees at all. There was evidently a problem as to whether such persons had title to sue: in *Hill* v. *Hunter* in 1766[111] it was held that they had. Later in the century there was a further development: the idea that the marriage contract should convey to trustees.[112] This idea was, one suspects, borrowed from England. It made rapid progress and during the nineteenth century the trust arising out of marriage contracts became one of the main uses of the trust. The old idea of unvested 'trustees' continued side-by-side with the new system long into the nineteenth century.[113] It seems that the modern division of trusts into *inter vivos* and *mortis causa* only came into existence in the nineteenth century, since before that time there were no *mortis causa* trusts. Trusts were either purely *inter vivos* or, if intended to operate after death, nevertheless established *inter vivos*.

In the nineteenth century liferents (usufructs) increasingly became organized as trusts, so that instead of ownership being vested in the fiar and a subordinate real right being vested in the liferenter (usufructuary), a three-handed arrangement was devised, with ownership being vested in trustees, and the rights of fiar and beneficiary being personal rights against the trustees. This proved much more convenient, if also more expensive, and 'proper' liferents of the old sort are today rare, though by no means unknown. Since lawyers are general employed to draft the documents, and since lawyers are commonly appointed trustees with the right to charge for their services, there was a natural motivation on the part of the legal profession to recommend trust liferents. The same motivation had doubtless operated to widen the use of trusts in other fields.[114]

2. Proof of trust[115]

The issue of proof of trust, which was such a dominant one in the seventeenth century, was not laid to rest by the 1696 act. The act became one of the main topics of trust law. That trust can be proved only by writing was

---

[110] The subject would merit investigation. There is a curious similarity with the continental institution of the *conservator fideicommissi*.   [111] (1766) Mor 16207.

[112] See Russell (n. 102), 337, where it is said that trusts were seldom used except for creditors but that its use of trust in marriage contracts was a very new invention.

[113] See e.g. *Complete System of Conveyancing* (commonly called *Juridical Styles*) (3rd edn., 1826), vol. 1, 179, and Duff (n. 95), 426 sq.

[114] This sort of thing tends never to become public, but in my own experience I can confirm that lawyers are not unaware of their own interest. Nevertheless, this aspect should not be exaggerated.

[115] A valuable account of the law, prior to the repeal of the 1696 act in 1995, is given in c. 4 of the first edition of Wilson/Duncan (n. 34).

regarded as being no less than a 'sacred principle of the law of Scotland' by a judge in 1832.[116] The act naturally generated a great deal of case law. The act was brief and left plenty of scope for dispute. It naturally exposed itself to ceaseless assaults by disgruntled litigants, and many subtle exceptions to it gradually grew up through case law, giving rise to a maze of decisions full of artificial distinctions. The act seems never to have commanded universal approval, because it enabled fraudulent trustees in certain cases to embezzle with impunity. When it was repealed in 1995[117] there were no mourners.

The act dealt with *proof* of trust rather than with *constitution* of trust, which was perhaps not a happy plan.[118] Since the courts eventually held that the restrictions on proof applied only to some litigants and not others,[119] it could lead to 'limping' trusts, i.e. trusts which existed for some purposes but not others. The question as to whether the act applied as between husband and wife gave rise to much dispute and was never finally settled.[120] Similar issues arose as between partners. The act also generated much case law about whether it applied to all trusts or only some. The act spoke of trusts which arise out of a 'deed of trust', and so those asserting the existence of a trust had an incentive to argue that their particular trust did not arise out of a 'deed'. Much subtle learning evolved on this point. For instance, registered company shares were held to fall under the act,[121] but not registered Treasury Bonds.[122] Again, the view came to be accepted that the act applied only where the truster had consented to the taking of the title in the name of the trustee. That principle, reasonable in itself, generated much case law, in which the courts had to decide what amounted to true 'consent' in a multitude of different contexts.

3. Immunity to creditors

The doctrine that trust assets are immune to creditors began to emerge in the 1660s and 1670s: see *Livingston* v. *Forrester*[123] and *Mackenzie* v. *Watson*.[124] But as has already been observed, the doctrine was by no means fully established at that time, or for long after, though in retrospect the trend was clear.

---

[116] *Scott* v. *Miller* (1832) 11 S 21 at 29 *per* Lord Gillies. For a style action of declarator of trust immediately after the 1696 act see George Dallas of St Martins, *System of Styles* (1697), 263.

[117] Requirement of Writings (Scotland) Act 1995.

[118] Though the repeal of the act left no mourners, there are those who would like to see restrictive rules on the creation (as opposed to proof) of trusts.

[119] The first case seems to be *Elibank* v. *Hamilton* (1827) 6 S 69. It may be added that it is doubtful whether this approach is consistent with the wording of the act.

[120] *Anderson* v. *Anderson's Tr* (1898) 6 SLT 204 held that the act did not apply but this was later doubted, e.g. in *Adam* v. *Adam* 1962 SLT 332.   [121] *Anderson* v. *Yorston* (1906) 14 SLT 54.

[122] *Beveridge* v. *Beveridge* 1925 SLT 234.   [123] (1664) Mor 10200, 1 Stair Rep 232.

[124] (1678) Mor 10188, 2 Stair Rep 607.

In 1717 we find another case, *Bannerman*, in favour of immunity.[125] Bankton, writing in 1752, says that immunity exists if the trust is constituted in writing but not otherwise.[126] He cites, not *Livingston* and *Mackenzie* or *Bannerman*, but *Street* v. *Hume*[127] and *Boylstoun* v. *Robertson*,[128] cases whose status as trust cases is marginal.[129] Erskine does not discuss the question of immunity at all. There was a school of thought that merely personal rights of third parties, even by way of trust, should never prevail against diligence.[130] Matters were still in dispute in 1803 when *Wylie* v. *Duncan*[131] was decided. That case held, or seemed to hold, that heritable property was not immune unless the fact of trust appeared in the title itself. Bell[132] adopted that view, and in the nineteenth century the law finally became settled: beneficiaries always won against creditors of the trustee, with one important exception. The exception was that if (a) the property in question was heritable (immoveable), and if (b) the trust was latent, meaning that the publicly recorded title did not reveal the trust, then creditors prevailed over beneficiaries. A final attempt was made to deny the immunity doctrine in *Gordon* v. *Cheyne* in 1824.[133] Here it was argued that the position of the trustee in sequestration was like that of a bona fide purchaser: the attempt failed. In 1891, in *Heritable Reversionary Co.* v. *Millar*,[134] an attempt was made to deny the exception mentioned above, i.e. the rule that a latent trust of land is not good against creditors of the trustee. The Court of Session reaffirmed the now settled view. But the House of Lords reversed.[135] Although it is evident that the Court of Session was right and the House of Lords wrong,[136] the decision established itself, and has even been enshrined in statute, at least for sequestration.[137] (In diligence and liquidation the rule remains non-statutory.)

---

[125] *Bannerman* v. *Masters of Queen's College* (1710) Mor 16187, Forbes 420. It should be noted that though this case is classified in Morison's *Dictionary* under the head of 'Trust' that word itself does not appear in the report. [126] Bankton, I, 18, 15.
[127] (1669) Mor 15122, 1 Stair Rep 616.   [128] (1672) Mor 15125, 2 Stair Rep 54.
[129] Stair, I, 12, 17 calls *Boylstoun* (which he cites as *Roiston*) a trust case.
[130] For a valuable insight into the way one distinguised jurist viewed the issues in the mid-18th century, see Patrick Grant, Lord Elchies, *Annotations on Lord Stair's Institutions* (1824), 69 sqq. (The publication was posthumous, Elchies having died in 1754.) For Elchies 'it may be doubted in whose person the property of the thing trusted is', though in fact he is ready to accept Stair's view. An unregistered trust of heritable property is ineffective against the creditors of the trustees. (I am grateful to Niall Whitty for this reference.)
[131] (1803) Mor 10269, 3 Ross LC 134. This was a case of sequestration rather than diligence.
[132] G. J. Bell, *Commentaries on the Law of Scotland and on the Principles of Mercantile Jurisprudence* (2nd edn., 1810; 7th edn., 1870; henceforth references will be made to the 7th edn.), I, 301.   [133] 5 Feb. 1824 FC.
[134] (1891) 18 R 1166.   [135] (1892) 19 R (HL) 43.
[136] It is apparent that the House of Lords was much under the influence of English law. The Scottish judge, Watson, was Anglicized to a high degree.
[137] Bankruptcy (Scotland) Act 1985, s. 33(1)(b).

4. Powers

What can trustees do? Can they buy? Sell? Lease? Originally such questions were regarded as being primarily a matter for the deed of trust to regulate, though courts were ready to imply powers in appropriate cases.[138] Both cases cited below were public trusts, for at first the issue seemed to crop up much more with public than with private trusts. One reason for this is probably that whereas public trusts are usually permanent, and thus liable to throw up such problems eventually, private trusts tended to be short-lived, since the long-term family trusts were almost unknown before the nineteenth century. Although the court was prepared to find implied powers, it was more reluctant to grant, under the *nobile officium*, powers which were neither express nor implied.[139] It was not until 1861 that the first statute was passed to confer powers on trustees. This act[140] gave power to resign and to assume new trustees. Like its successors it was suppletive rather than imperative, so that the power was merely presumed, and could be excluded by the terms of the trust itself. Then appeared the Trusts (Scotland) Act 1867, which, with amendments and supplementary legislation, was to last until replaced by the Trusts (Scotland) Act 1921, which, however, was largely a consolidating measure. The 1921 act, with amendments and supplementary legislation, remains in force today. The 1867 and 1921 acts gave presumed powers of sundry sorts, such as power to sell both moveable and immoveable property, to grant leases, to appoint factors and law agents, to invest (but subject to restrictions), and so forth.[141]

The word 'powers' has always been used in connection with trustees, as with companies. But whereas acts *ultra vires* of a company are at common law void,[142] acts *ultra vires* of trustees have, it seems, never been so conceived. Such acts have been regarded as acts in breach of the obligations of the trustees to the beneficiaries, and thus potentially voidable at their instance,[143]

---

[138] e.g., *Magistrates of Edinburgh v. Binny* (1694) 1 Fount 635, Mor 9107, where trustees were held entitled to grant leases, and *Merchant Co. of Edinburgh v. Governors of Heriot's Hospital* 9 Aug. 1765 FC, Mor 5750,—a decision which was to have an impact on the local history of Edinburgh—where it was held that trustees had an implied power to feu.

[139] Forsyth (n. 9), 168 states that the court in his time would not grant powers. This was confirmed in *Kinloch Petitioner* (1859) 22 D 175, where the court refused to confer power to borrow.

[140] 24 & 25 Vict (c. 84).

[141] These acts also deal with matters other than powers of trustees. For instance, they provide for the court supervision of trusts by the court. It must be stressed, however, that these statutes do not form a code of trust law. To a large extent the law of trusts remains unenacted.

[142] This may be an oversimplification, but the law of persons is remarkably undeveloped.

[143] But since the Trusts (Scotland) Act 1961 even voidability is usually excluded. The history of the question of whether, and if so when, successors of the trustee may be bound is one not covered in this chapter, except for successors by way of diligence. I am not sure that the law is or ever has been clear. I will, however, quote a remarkable passage from the early 18th century. 'As to a singular successor, who, being ignorant of the trust, acquires honestly for an onerous cause from the trustee, he is secure, unless the trust be instructed [= proved] by writ of the trustee. . . .

but not void. The expressions 'powers' and 'vires' are thus arguably misleading, but have generally been used.

5. English influence after 1700

As has already been indicated, evidence of English influence before 1700 is slight, and is also slight until well into the nineteenth century. There are occasional hints. In *Drummond v. McKenzie*[144] we find a reference to 'equitable title' and 'legal title' which suggests that by 1758 English trust law was not unknown. But English authorities on trust law are almost never cited before the 1840s. Even Bell, who was not averse to citing English cases, does not cite English authorities on trust,[145] though he does use the term 'beneficial interest', which is presumably of English origin.

In 1844 appeared *The Principles and Practice of the Law of Trusts and Trustees in Scotland* by Charles Forsyth, 'advocate and barrister-at-law'. This was the first work to be devoted to trusts, and in many ways is admirable.[146] Whether its introduction of English law is to be admired is a matter on which opinions may differ. Whereas before 1844 English authorities were not cited by authors, of the 1600 or so decisions cited by Forsyth, about 890 are English. Forsyth says[147] that he does not regard English cases as being, strictly speaking, of true authority, but rather as being 'notes or illustrations'. But this qualification had no influence. The book was a tidal wave from a calm sea. One may even speak of a partial nineteenth-century reception of English trust law. In A. J. P. Menzies, *Law of Scotland Affecting Trustees*, published in 1913,[148] about 44 per cent of cases cited are English. In A. MacKenzie Stuart, *The Law of Trusts*, published in 1932, 40 per cent of cases are English. But the flood gradually lessened. In the standard modern text, published in 1995[149] the proportion of English cases falls to 14 per cent.[150]

But trusts don't affect or burden real rights whereon seisin has followed, so as to oblige singular successors to take notice of them': William Forbes, *Institutes of the Law of Scotland* (1722), III, 1, 4.

[144] (1758) Mor 16206, Kames Sel Dec 203.

[145] *Principles of the Law of Scotland* (4th edn., 1839), the last by Bell himself. It is striking that by the time this classic work reached its tenth and last edition in 1899 (ed. W. Guthrie) about 98% of the trust cases cited are still Scottish. English authority on trusts is equally absent from the *Commentaries*.

[146] His statement (n. 9), 12 that 'the right of the beneficiary has never in Scotland been acknowledged as a positive, vested, equitable and co-existent right, as distinguished from the legal right of the trustee, as in England' has often been quoted with approval, and whether one likes or dislikes the particular formulation, the underlying thought was as true then as it is true now.   [147] Ibid. at ix.

[148] Second edition. The first edition appeared in 1893.   [149] Wilson/Duncan (n. 34).

[150] John (Lord) McLaren, *The Law of Wills and Succession* (3rd edn., 1894), deals with trusts at some length, but citation figures would be problematic since the work deals to a large extent with succession, as to which the citations would be almost purely Scottish. Oddly, a minor work, Howden (n. 99) has only about 11% of its citations English, even though this was the time of

It would be natural to conclude that there was a sort of nineteenth-century reception of English trust law and that it began with Forsyth. But doctrinal history maddeningly refuses to do what you expect it to do. The strange fact is that *in the courts* English authorities have played a surprisingly small role: a much smaller role than they have played in the Scottish textbooks. One would naturally suppose that the case law of the 1830s would have contained few English citations and the case law of the 1850s many. But that is not what one finds. Certainly, in the 200 or so trust cases reported in the 1830s I have not seen a single English citation.[151] In two or three cases there is a reference to an English textbook, for instance *Earl of Strathmore* v. *Earl of Strathmore's Trs*[152] which cites 'Randall on Trusts, Accumulations Etc.'. But in the 1850s the picture is only slightly different.[153] It is difficult, for various reasons, to compile reliable statistics, but perhaps 95 per cent of the trust cases in that decade cite no English authority. The picture does change in subsequent decades, but less so than one might expect, especially since the late nineteenth and early twentieth centuries are generally thought of as the high-water mark of English influence. I am puzzled: the impression one gets from the books and the impression one gets from the case law going through the courts are not easy to reconcile.[154] But the difficulty should not be overstated: the second half of the nineteenth century is clearly a period in which English authority is influencing the Scottish courts in trust cases, and that influence continued well into the twentieth century. The influence of English law has been extensive.

Forsyth made great use of Thomas Lewin, *A Practical Treatise on the Law of Trusts*, the second edition of which appeared in 1842. This was a standard English text, which survived in successive editions until 1964.[155] His liking for Lewin's book is reflected to some extent in the cases.[156] Indeed, in the Scottish cases, what one finds is that where English authority is cited, what is cited is a textbook rather than a case. One can understand why: the text writers turned the bewildering riot of English trust law into something that could be understood, or half-understood, by those who did not practise before the Court of Chancery. Lewin was always the first choice.[157] Snell on Equity

maximum English influence, in trusts as in other areas of law. In K. McK. Norrie and E. M. Scobbie, *Trusts* (1991), a student text, 22% of citations are English.

[151] Except cases dealing with other matters. Thus in a case involving shipping law and trust, English cases are likely to be cited on shipping law. [152] (1830) 8 S 530.
[153] There are some striking cases. Thus *Cochrane* v. *Black* (1855) 17 D 321 and *Laird* v. *Laird* (1858) 20 D 984, both involving a trustee's failure to invest as directed, bristle with English authority.
[154] One possible solution is that English influence is to be found more in the landmark decisions. But this is speculative.
[155] Sixteenth edition, ed. by W. J. Mowbray. The first edition appeared in 1837.
[156] e.g. *Ross* v. *Allan's Trs* (1850) 13 D 44.
[157] The final edition of *Lewin* even makes it to the list of 'Authorities Cited' at xciii of Wilson/Duncan (n. 34). A search on the SLT database 1893–1997 revealed 21 cases in which

never made an impression north of the border,[158] perhaps understandably, because it covers equity in general, and not just trusts. Lewin was canonized by Forsyth.[159] No other English text ever had anything like the same role. If the inference is drawn that, since new editions of Lewin's work have ceased, English texts on trusts are not much cited, that conclusion would be correct. Since the English cases cited to the courts tend to be the cases in the texts, the result is the influence of English trust jurisprudence is ebbing.[160] The English cases which are cited today look increasingly antique. One example would be *Soar* v. *Ashwell*.[161]

To some extent English influence was confined to particular topics. Thus it was natural that cases turning on the Thelluson Act,[162] which dealt with accumulations and applied both sides of the border, should cite English authority.[163] Another example, and a more interesting one, concerns the question of whether a trustee can, as an individual (other than as a beneficiary), have relations with the trust, for instance by buying from it or by charging it for his professional services. The basic idea of fiduciary duties is already in the civil law: 'Tutor rem pupilli emere non potest: idemque porrigendum est ad simila; id est ad curatores procuratores et qui negotia aliena gerunt.'[164] Cases of conflict of interest can be found at least as early as 1712.[165] But the English rules proved tighter than the native ones,[166] and were imposed by the House of Lords in two cases in particular, *York Buildings Co.* v. *Mackenzie*[167] in 1795 and *Home* v. *Pringle* in 1841.[168] The latter decision was regarded as so demonstrably a case of judicial legislation that the Court of Session treated

---

Lewin was cited. The most recent citation is in an unreported case of 1 Mar. 1996, *Lutea Trustees Ltd* v. *Orbis Trustees Guernsey Ltd.* As a comparison, the number is lower than that for citations of *Chitty on Contracts* (33 cases) but many of the latter are recent, and whereas Lewin went out of print more than 30 years ago *Chitty* continues in successive editions. Moreover, in the pre-1893 period, which at present is not computer-searchable, it is evident that there were many citations of Lewin and probably none of *Chitty*.

[158] A combined LEXIS and SLT search reveals since 1893 only three citations of *Snell* namely, *Southern Cross Commodities Property Ltd* v. *Martin* 1991 SLT 83 and *Kennedy* v. *Begg Kennedy & Elder Ltd* 1954 SLT (Sh Ct) 103, *Roger (Builders) Ltd* v. *Fawdry* 1950 SC 483.

[159] The Signet Library bought twelve of the sixteen editions, the missing ones being the 2nd, 4th, 5th and 6th. Edinburgh University Library, curiously, acquired only the 2nd (1842) and the 5th (1867). (Of course the Advocates' Library, as a library of deposit, took all editions.)

[160] But I have no statistics on this point. [161] [1893] 2 QB 390.

[162] 39 & 40 Geo III (c. 98).

[163] For instance *Muir's Trs* v. *Jameson* (1903) 10 SLT 70. Eventually the Thelluson Act was replaced by separate legislation in both jurisdictions. For Scotland see the Trusts (Scotland) Act 1961, s. 5.

[164] Paul. D. 18, 1, 34, 7 ('a tutor cannot buy a thing belonging to his ward; this rule extends to other persons with similar responsibilities, that is curators, procurators and those who conduct another's affairs'—tr. Mommsen/Krüger/Watson edn.).

[165] *Wright* v. *Wright* 1712 Mor 16193.

[166] For an interesting and valuable account of the Scottish rules, see Lord Neaves in *Aitken* v. *Hunter* (1871) 9 M 756. [167] (1795) 3 Pat App 378.

[168] (1841) 2 Rob 384.

it as exactly that, and declined to give it retrospective effect.[169] I am unaware of any other instance in which the Court of Session has responded in this manner to legislation from the House of Lords. But the Court of Session was, in other respects, only too willing to accept the English rules.[170] The House of Lords naturally tended to turn to English law unless wholly inappropriate. A quotation from Lord Lindley in 1902[171] illustrates the attitude:

> It is so well settled that there is no conversion of land into money, or of money into land, if the trust for conversion is not imperative, that it is quite unnecessary to cite authorities on the point. They will be found collected in Lewin on Trusts, 10th ed, pp. 1158 and 1163.

But it would not be true to say that the House of Lords imposed English law in a blanket way. Very likely it would have done so if it had had the opportunity, but the number of trust cases going to it was limited. Moreover, a good deal of English influence was through counsel pleading before the Court of Session, and snatching at what authority they could find that favoured their position. For instance in a case in 1905[172] we read: 'Argued for the respondent:—The reclaimers had no direct claim against the trust estate: Lewin on Trusts 11th ed. p. 779; McLaren on Wills 3rd ed. sect. 2296; *Worral* [1802] 8 Vesey 4; *Hall* [1842] 1 Hare, 571; *Staniar* [1886] 34 Ch. D. 470. ... The reclaimers could have no higher right than their principal: *Pelly* [1851], 1 De Gex, M. & G. 16.' Although it was often the case that English authorities were more often cited to than by the court, this was not always so. For instance in a case in 1907 we find English authority much cited from the bench. It is noteworthy in this case that even the 'Scottish' cases cited are often House of Lords decisions based on English law.[173]

One last example will suffice to illustrate the sort of thing that sometimes (but not particularly often) happened: in a case in 1908[174] we read this submission by counsel:

---

[169] See notably *Miller's Trs* v. *Miller* (1848) 10 D 765.

[170] See for instance *Gray Petitioner* (1856) 19 D 1, where the fees of the celebrated law firm of Dundas & Wilson were disallowed because a partner was a trustee of the trust. I cannot refrain from quoting the opening words of the report: 'Lord Justice Clerk: It is better at once to fix the principle applicable to this case. In *New* v. *Jones* (1 Hall & Twells 632) . . .'.

[171] *Lord Advocate* v. *Sprot's Tr* (1901) 4 F (HL) 11 at 19.

[172] *Ferme, Ferme & Williamson* v. *Stephenson's Trs* (1905) 13 SLT 236.

[173] *Hay's Trs* v. *Baillie* 1908 SC 1224, (1907) 15 SLT 494. The authorities cited are: *Crichton* (1828) 3 W & S 329; *Cobb's Trs* (1894) 21 R 638; *Williams* v. *Kershaw* (1835) 5 Cl & Fin 111; *Pemsel's Case* [1891] AC 531; *Morice* v. *Bishop of Durham* (1804) 9 Ves Jun 399; *James* v. *Allen* (1817) 3 Mer 17; *Lewin on Trusts* (11th edn., 1904), 763; *Hagan* v. *Duff* (1889) 23 LR Ir 516; *Hill* v. *Burns* (1826) 2 W & S 80; *Millar* v. *Black's Trs* (1837) 2 S & M 866; *In re Best* [1904] Ch 354; *In re Sutton* (1885) 28 Ch D 464; *In re Jarman's Estate* (1878) 8 Ch D 584; *In re Rilands* (1881) WN 173; *Ellis* v. *Selby* (1836) 1 M & Cr 286; *Duncan* v. *Blair* (1900) 3 F 274 and (1901) 4 F (HL) 1; *Grimond's Trs* (1904) 6 F 285 and (1905) 7 F (HL) 90; *Cocks* [1871] LR 12 Eq 574; *Hill* v. *Burns* (1826) 2 W & S 80; *Baird's Trustees* (1888) 15 R 682.

[174] *Buchanan and Another* v. *Buchanan's Trustees* (1908) 16 SLT 421. The version at 1909 SC 47 is slightly different.

The lenders had a duty to enquire as to the application of the money when it appeared from the terms of the will that the trustees' power to borrow was limited, and there was a real burden (*In re Rebbech*, 1894, 63 L.J. Ch. 596; *Horn v. Horn*, 1825; 2 Simon and Stuart, 448; Lewin on Trusts, p. 530). Whether or not that duty was upon him in the above circumstances, it certainly was upon him when he knew that the money was not to be applied to trust purposes (*Corser v. Cartwright*, 1875, L.R. 7, E. and I. App. 781; *Howard v. Chaffer*, 1863, 32 L.J. Ch. 686, at p. 695). It must be assumed that the appellants knew of the burden on the heritage, if their solicitor knew, that was sufficient to affect them with knowledge (*Watkins v. Cheek*, 1825, 2 Simon and Stuart, 199).

It is not possible to pursue these matters further. It remains only to add that as the present century has advanced, English influence has tended to decline. No particular landmark can be identified, though *Inland Revenue* v. *Clark's Trs* in 1939,[175] holding a beneficial right to be simply a type of personal right, stands out. It is striking that a leading English House of Lords case such as *Barclays Bank* v. *Quistclose Investments*,[176] decided in 1970, has in thirty years only once been cited in a Scottish court.[177] One suspects that had it been decided in 1870, it would, by 1900, have been cited many times.[178]

I have left to the last what is perhaps the most important question: did English influence bring about an English understanding of the trust? Did equity arrive? One reason for the importance of the question is that the legal/equitable division is difficult or impossible to integrate with a civilian system of property law. The answer is, in general, negative, as can be seen from the case just cited, *Inland Revenue* v. *Clark's Trs*.

6. Conceptualizations

In the seventeenth, eighteenth, and nineteenth-centuries one often encounters the statement that trust is a form of the contract of deposit, or mandate, or a combination thereof. Stair takes this approach[179] as do Bankton[180] and Erskine.[181] In 1879 Lord Inglis asserted that 'the position of trustees . . . is . . . that they are depositaries of the trust estate and mandataries for its administration'.[182] This is an interesting attempt to reconcile the trust with civilian categories, and is not without merit. 'Deposit' was not meant literally, for in ordinary deposit ownership does not pass, whereas it does pass in the case of trust, as Stair himself emphasized: '[T]he property of the thing intrusted, be

---

[175] 1939 SC 11.　　[176] [1970] AC 567.
[177] *Mercedes-Benz Finance Ltd* v. *Clydesdale Bank plc* 1997 SLT 905, 1996 SCLR 1005, where it is mentioned only briefly and dismissively.
[178] It is cited in both the first edition of 1975 and the second of 1995 of Wilson/Duncan (n. 34), an example of how an English case may reach Scottish texts without reaching the Scottish courts.　　[179] Erskine, I, 13, 7 and IV, 6, 3.
[180] Bankton, I, 18, 12: a trustee is a mandatary who is invested in ownership.
[181] Erskine, III, 1, 32.　　[182] *Cuningham* v. *Montgomerie* (1879) 6 R 1333 at 1337.

it land or moveables, is in the person of the intrusted, else it is not proper trust'.[183]

Difficulty was long experienced as to the nature of the right of the beneficiary. The subject is indeed intrinsically problematic. The modern view is that beneficial rights are personal, but this was conclusively settled only during the twentieth century. The earliest source I have found in which the question is expressly addressed is a case of 1813, in which a judge mused that 'I doubt if trusts[184] ... are to be held as real. I rather think that they are in their own nature personal.'[185]

In what seems to have been the first serious attempt by a jurist to state the nature of trust, George Joseph Bell in his seminal *Principles of the Law of Scotland*[186] wrote:

> The whole doctrine ... depends on these principles. (1) That a full legal estate is created in the person of the trustee, to be held by him against all adverse parties and interests, for the accomplishment of certain ends and purposes. (2) That the uses and purposes of the trust operate as qualifications on the estate in the trustee, and as burdens on it preferable to all who may lay claim through him. (3) That those purposes and uses are effectually declared by directions in the deed, or by a reservation of power to declare in future, and a declaration made accordingly. (4) And that the reversionary right, so far as the estate is not exhausted by the uses and purposes, remains with the truster, available to him, his heirs and creditors.

Of this much might be said. The most interesting proposition is the second. It is curious that Bell avoids the words 'real' and 'personal'. With respect to the great jurist, this looks evasive.[187]

After Bell matters continued to be unclear. John (Lord) McLaren, in one of his less valuable contributions to legal thought, said that trust was an example of 'quasi-contract'.[188] A more remarkable theory was that of Lord Watson in *Heritable Reversionary Co. v. Millar.*[189] Here he said that 'an apparent title to land or personal estate[190] carrying *no real right*[191] of property with it, does not, in the ordinary or in any true legal sense, make such land or personal estate the property of the person who holds the title'. Whilst this is not the Scots law either of the nineteenth century or of any other century, it is not English law either. For if English law accepted the concept of a real right,[192] it would presumably say that the trustee had such a right, for in

---

[183] Stair, I, 13, 7.   [184] Meaning the rights of the trust beneficiary.
[185] *Redfearn v. Sommervail* (1813) Pat App 707 per Lord Meadowbank.
[186] Fourth edition, 1839.
[187] I think that I am not being anachronistic: cf. the words of Lord Meadowbank, just quoted. Bell was no doubt conscious of the difficulties of committing himself either way.
[188] Lord McLaren, *Wills and Succession* (3rd edn., 1894), 825.   [189] (1892) 19 R (HL) 43.
[190] Meaning moveables. Watson's choice of the English term is significant.
[191] Emphasis added.
[192] It has a concept of rights *in rem*—presumably the Latin term is used to distinguish the concept from that of *real* property, by which is meant immoveable property—but this is not the same

English law the trustee has 'ownership in law'. For English law, there is a *duplex dominium*. By contrast, for Lord Watson, ownership was undivided, and was solely in the beneficiary. If, for Lord Watson, the trustee had no real right at all,[193] what did he have? A personal right of some sort. An obvious difficulty for this curious theory is that if the trustee is not owner, how can he transfer ownership? *Nemo plus ad alium transferre potest quam ipse habet.* Lord Watson gets round this by saying that 'a true owner who chooses to conceal his right from the public and to clothe his trustee with all the *indicia* of ownership is thereby barred from challenging rights acquired by innocent third parties'. The law reports contain few odder theories. Finally, A. Mackenzie Stuart in his standard text of 1932[194] states in his first paragraph that in a trust the 'estate is owned by two persons at the same time' and that a trust is something which is enforceable 'in a court of equity'. One suspects that even in the Anglicizing 1930s many readers must have rubbed their eyes. Since *Inland Revenue* v. *Clark's Trs* in 1939,[195] the status of the beneficiary's right as personal has not been seriously questioned.[196]

7. Mortification, charities, public trusts, and foundations

Thus far this chapter is concerned chiefly with private trusts. But what of public trusts? Their history is, if anything, even older than that of private trusts, under the name of mortification. This word is liable to confuse, for it has meant both a public trust and a form of tenure. Parallel to the military tenure of wardholding (*feudum militare*) and the commercial tenure of feu farm and the urban tenure of burgage there was the ecclesiastical tenure of mortification. Land was infeudated to the Church to hold for *preces et lachrymae*. In other words, masses were to be said for the soul of the founder and (sometimes) other souls too. This was a form of tenure but it was also an incipient trust. With the Reformation in 1560, saying masses for the dead came to be regarded as popish superstition, and mortification as a tenure came to an end. But already before the Reformation mortification had come also to mean any transfer of property (regardless of tenure) for ongoing public good, such as education or the relief of poverty, and such mortifi-

---

as the civilian concept of a real right. For example an English trust beneficiary often has a right *in rem*.

[193] One possibility is that by 'real' right he meant not *real* right but right of an *immoveable* nature. The basis for this argument is that in the same sentence he uses *personal* to mean *moveable*, so that one might expect him to use *real* to mean *immoveable*. But this interpretation makes no sense.   [194] A. Mackenzie Stuart, *Law of Trusts* (1932).

[195] 1939 SC 11.

[196] But trusts continue to give rise to conceptual confusion. Thus D. M. Walker in his *Principles of Scottish Private Law*, vol. 4 (4th edn., 1989), writes at 4 that the 'full legal right of property' is in the trustee, while at 218 he writes that 'full legal right of property' is in the beneficiary.

Trusts 509

cations, if not popish in their tendency,[197] survived the Reformation,[198] and new ones were created. The usual practice was to grant land, or (perhaps more commonly) a perpetual income from certain land, to a church or to a burgh council,[199] or at all events to trustees *ex officio*[200] which thus became a trustee of the fund, and obliged to use it appropriately.[201] Mortifications for universities were sometimes given direct to the university, but sometimes to independent trustees.[202] The word 'mortification' is no longer in general use, but many older public trusts still have the word as part of their name.[203]

Over the centuries mortifications gave rise to a trickle of case law, but jurists had little interest in them. The institutional writers say little. It may even be asked as to whether the category of public trust existed at all until the nineteenth century. In other words, the question is whether lawyers conceptualized public and private trusts as being two branches of the same tree. If one looks at the institutional writers one might be inclined to a negative answer. They deal with trusts as private trusts only, and public trusts are either not dealt with or classified as mortifications without reference to trust. Nevertheless, the answer is affirmative. For instance, a case in 1752[204] involved a benefaction for education in a parish. Five trustees were nominated. This is evidently a public trust. Or again, in 1686 Viscount Tarbet establishes a trust for the poor of Tarbet: 'We . . . Dispone, Give, Grant, Annailzie,[205] Dot[206] and Mortifie . . . to . . . the very Reverend Mr Andrew Ross, now Minister at Tarbet, and the present elders of the Kirk at Tarbet, and their Successors in

---

[197] Some originally popish ones also survived. In 1477 land in St Monans was burdened by a form of annualrent in favour of 'friars predicators'. Presumably this was for masses for the dead, but at some stage the benefit was transferred to the University of St Andrews, and it was still in existence when litigated in 1762, though its existence caused surprise. See *University of St Andrews* v. *Creditors of Newark* (1762) Mor 10171.

[198] Thus *Magistrates of Edinburgh* v. *Binny* (1694) 1 Fount 635, Mor 9107, involves a 15th-century mortification made by the Bishop of Aberdeen to Edinburgh City Council for the education, discipline, and training of delinquent youths in Edinburgh.

[199] For example Heriot's Hospital, discussed above.

[200] e.g., *Leslie and Black Petitioners* 8 June 1819 FC where a 'foundation and mortification' was established in 1659 in favour of the Earl of Wemyss, and the minister and members of the kirk session as 'patrons'. Other examples abound, e.g. *Anderson, Petitioner* (1857) 19 D 329.

[201] Such earmarked funds, when vested direct in a public body, are sometimes held on public trust, and sometimes are merely part of the general assets to be employed for public purposes. The distinction tends to be unimportant, and in many cases it would be hard to say into which category a particular mortification belongs.

[202] For instance, *Magistrates of Aberdeen* v. *University of Aberdeen* (1877) 4 R 48 (HL) involved a mortification in which a benefactor wished to found a chair in the University of Aberdeen, and to that end transferred assets to Aberdeen City Council for behoof of the university (early 17th century).

[203] The term 'mortification' is used in a trust set up in 1873: see *McCrie's Trs, Petitioners* 1927 SC 556. Probably later examples could be found.

[204] *Campbell* v. *Campbell* (1752) Kames Sel Dec 35, Mor 16203.   [205] Alienate.
[206] Endow.

the said Ministry and Eldership (in Being for the Time) as Trustees and Fide-Commissaries for the Use and behove of the Poor . . .'.[207] The draftsman evidently had no doubt that here mortification, public trust, and *fideicommissum* coincided. And as we have already seen, the language of trust was used by Heriot, or his lawyers, in 1623.

Continental lawyers often ask where, in English (or Scots) law, the 'foundation' is to be found—the *fondation* of French law or the *Stiftung* of German law. Whereupon the English (or Scots) lawyer looks rather blank. It is a problem typical of what motivates the study of comparative law. Though the question is too large and too complex to be considered here, a few remarks may be made. Continental foundations are earmarked funds, and are normally for public purposes, though certain private foundations have also existed. Some are separate juristic persons,[208] while others are simply public trusts (the German *unselbständige Stiftung*). The foundation is thus much the same as the mortification.[209] Indeed, the mortification more or less developed, in certain particular cases, into separate juristic personality. Thus in 1765 the Court of Session seems to have accepted that Heriot's Trust—originally established as an *unselbständige Stiftung* with the City Council as trustee—had evolved into a 'community', a term which, in context, means a juristic person.[210] Again, in 1637 John Cowan established a mortification to establish an almshouse for the poor.[211] The burgh council were to be the 'patrons', which is to say a governing body, but the immediate management was to be in a 'preceptor or master'. How was the property vested? Not, curiously, in the burgh council, but in the preceptor. Moreover, it seems to have been vested in him not personally but in his capacity as preceptor, so that as preceptors came and went no change to the title was needed. This looks very like a juristic person.[212] In 1868 and 1874 statutory provisions were introduced to bring about the same result for most public trusts, so that a conveyance to the first trustees was deemed a conveyance to all future trustees.[213] That turned many public trusts into virtual juristic persons. Some public trusts converted

---

[207] See George Dallas of St Martins, *System of Styles* (1697), 833. Unlike a modern styles book, this contained chiefly actual deeds.   [208] Having no members.

[209] Indeed, the two words were sometimes used as synonyms, as where a 'foundation and mortification' were established in 1659 for the poor of the parish of Largo. See *Leslie & Black, Petitioners* 8 June 1816 FC.

[210] *Merchant Company of Edinburgh v. Governors of Heriot's Hospital* 9 Aug. 1765 FC. 'Community' suggests a *universitas personarum* rather than a *universitas bonorum*, but this theoretical distinction has never been one of which Scots lawyers have been conscious.

[211] *Christie v. Magistrates of Edinburgh* (1774) Mor 5755.

[212] And very like the English 'corporation sole'. No doubt many other examples of this general sort could be found. For one from 1528 see James Beveridge and James Russel (eds.), *Protocol Books of Dominus Thomas Johnsoun* (1920), 15.

[213] Titles to Land Consolidation (Scotland) Act 1868, s. 26 and Conveyancing (Scotland) Act 1874, s. 45 (both still in force).

into actual juristic persons.[214] Indeed, many entities having the status of juristic persons are (confusingly but revealingly) called 'trusts'. Many are incorporated under the Companies Acts, a practice that is doubly strange, since such 'companies' are not only not trusts but not companies either.[215] (Most other countries have legislation allowing the grant of personality without the absurdity of creating a pseudo-company.) Some are incorporated by other means: a well-known example is the National Trust for Scotland.[216] Of course, there are also many foundations which are juristic persons without the word 'trust' in their title.

In much of the Continent, foundations developed into juristic persons distinct from corporations. The theoretical basis for this was provided only in the first half of the nineteenth century, by Heise and Savigny.[217] Scotland could have gone down the same road: it was poised to do so. But the new continental thinking happened when the influence of continental thinking in Scotland was in decline. Moreover, the nineteenth century was precisely the same when trust law became more evolved and thus more available for public purposes. Accordingly, the foundation as such[218] has never properly established itself as part of Scots law, though of course at a functional level the picture is quite different.

'Charity' as a legal term seems to be of English origin, and yet another aspect of English influence in the nineteenth century. I have not noticed its use before Forsyth in 1844, and even he merely has an index entry reading: 'Charitable trusts: see Mortifications'.[219] But by the end of the nineteenth century 'mortification' was fading and 'charity' had become dominant. Nowadays charity and public trust are concepts which largely overlap, but do not coincide. There are charities which are not public trusts, because they are not in the form of a trust, and there are public trusts which are not charities, because, although for public benefit, they do not promote charitable purposes. Whether an entity (trust or not) is a 'charity' matters mainly for tax purposes, though there are other consequences also.[220] Whether 'mortifications' were limited to what we now call charity is, perhaps, to ask an anachronistic question.

---

[214] See e.g. *Scott's Hospital Trs Petitioners* 1913 SC 289. The same happened to the Heriot Trust itself: 6 & 7 Guilelmi (c. 25). For some background see *Incorporated Trades of Edinburgh v. Governors of Heriot's Hospital* (1836) 14 S 873.

[215] Except in the purely technical sense that they are companies for the purposes of the Companies Acts.

[216] 26 Geo V. & 1 Edw VIII (c. 2) (local and private statutes). Incidentally, it had previously been incorporated (with its 'trust' title) under the Companies Act 1929.

[217] See further Robert Feenstra, 'Foundations in Continental law since the 12th century' and Andreas Richter, 'German and American Law of Charity in the Early 19th century', both in Helmholz/Zimmermann (n. 26), 305 and 427.

[218] That is, in the Savigny conceptualization.   [219] Forsyth (n. 9), 508.

[220] The Law Reform (Miscellaneous Provisions) (Scotland) Act 1990 contains provisions about both 'charities' and 'public trusts'.

One final remark. The law of mortifications or foundations—which is to say the law of public trusts and of juristic persons dedicated to the promotion of a public good—has not attracted much academic attention in Scotland. The institutional writers say little. Later writers mention public trusts, but as an addendum to private trusts. The category of foundation, straddling the division between trust and juristic person, has been recognized with little more than a nod. Our legal system has been impoverished thereby. Much needs to be done.[221]

8. Constructive trusts

Constructive trusts are those arising by implication of law (*ex lege*) rather than by the intention, expressed or implied, of the parties (*ex voluntate*). To what extent Scots law has the constructive trust is uncertain: the answer seems to be that it has them but only to a very limited degree, and that most of the categories of constructive trust in English law are not recognized in Scotland. To a great extent, cases which in England are constructive trusts are in Scotland handled under the concepts of contract, delict, express trusts, and, perhaps especially, unjustified enrichment.[222] The term 'constructive trust' began to arrive in the late nineteenth century. Forsyth, writing in 1844, has a section devoted to 'Trusts by Operation of Law'[223] but the term 'constructive trust' is not mentioned. I have not located its arrival with accuracy, but by the late nineteenth century it was common.[224] That is to say, the term was common. As already indicated, the term was on the whole being used to describe situations which were not in fact constructive trusts. Mention must be made of *Jopp* v. *Johnston's Tr* in 1904[225] in which English authority was accepted—one might say received—on a large scale.[226] Curiously, this case, though often enough cited, has had less influence than one might have expected. Likewise, when Lord Westbury made his famous remark in 1868[227] that 'an obligation to do an act with respect to property creates a trust' the consequences might have been dramatic, for this proposition—broadly true in English law—would turn much of Scots law upside down. But the remark was, for the most part, politely ignored. The soil of Scots law is constantly sown with English seeds, but some do not germinate, while some germinate but do not thrive.[228]

[221] The Law Reform (Miscellaneous Provisions) (Scotland) Act 1990, and the publication of C. R. Barker (ed.), *Charity Law in Scotland* (1996) may indicate a change in the wind.
[222] For an extended study see my own, 'Constructive Trusts', (1997) 1 *Edinburgh LR* 281 and 408. This however is only partially historical. [223] Forsyth (n. 9), 382 sqq.
[224] Thus it is used both in Howden (n. 99) and in A. J. P. Menzies, *Law of Scotland Affecting Trustees* (1st edn., 1893). [225] (1904) 6 F 1028.
[226] In particular this case performed the remarkable feat of accepting *Re Hallett's Estate* (1880) 13 Ch D 696. [227] *Fleeming* v. *Howden* (1868) 6 M 113 (HL) at 121.
[228] One possible analysis of *Sharp* v. *Thomson* 1997 SC (HL) 66, is that the House of Lords decided that upon delivery of the disposition the sellers held in constructive trust for the buyers.

9. *Frog's Creditors v. His Children*[229]

Curiously, one situation which perhaps should be classified as constructive trust has always been treated as a special doctrine. This is the doctrine in *Frog's Creditors v. His Children*[230] in 1735 and *Newlands v. Newlands' Creditors*[231] in 1794. Some background is needed, and a curious background it is. In the eighteenth century—and perhaps before—it was often desired to convey property to X for his lifetime and then to his children. How could this be done? To convey to X with a destination (i.e. a *substitutio*[232] to the children) was possible but capable of being defeated by 'evacuation'. A tailzie (entail) was possible but cumbersome, expensive, and inflexible. The obvious solution, to a modern conveyancer, would be to dispone to trustees to hold for X in liferent (usufruct) and to the children in fee. What is curious and instructive is that this solution seems simply not to have occurred to eighteenth-century conveyancers. They attempted a direct conveyance to X in liferent and his children in fee. But that obviously could not work, since the owners were at the time of the conveyance indeterminate. When I write 'obviously' I hope I am not being anachronistic, but surely even at that period the impossibility was clear enough. What happened if the attempt was made? In the leading case of *Frog's Creditors v. His Children*[233] it was held that the effect was to give ownership to X. Undeterred, and rather like lemmings, conveyancers continued, but now added the word 'allenarly'[234] to the liferent. The courts decided that the word had to be given effect to. But it was still obvious that 'a fee cannot be *in pendente*' to use the traditional maxim. So in *Newlands* it was held that the effect would be to give *dominium* to X (and to that extent following *Frog*) but subject to what was a sort of trust to hold for himself in liferent and his children in fee. This was called the doctrine of the 'fiduciary fee'. One might argue that this was best classified as implied *fideicommissum*. But nobody did. I speak in the past tense, because such conveyances are never now used, but the rule in *Newlands* in fact eventually received statutory blessing and is in substance still law.[235]

10. Resulting trusts and the doctrine of the radical right

A resulting trust arises where the trust's purposes have been exhausted but some trust property remains. In that case the trustees hold on trust for the

That would be like (though not the same as) the English doctrine. However, the language of trust was not used. It is doubtful whether any coherent *ratio* can be found in this decision.

[229] For a valuable study, see Wilson/Duncan (n. 34), ch. 6.
[230] (1735) Mor 4262. The similarity to the English decision—once a leading one—of *Shelley's Case* (1581) Co Rep 93b, 76 ER 206, is striking. [231] (1794) Mor 4289.
[232] The history of *substitutio* in Scots law has yet to be written. [233] (1735) Mor 4262.
[234] Meaning 'only'. [235] Trusts (Scotland) Act 1921, s. 8.

truster, though the doctrine is modified in the case of charitable trusts.[236] A resulting trust seems today to be conceptualized as simply an implied trust purpose. The term is English, and the first use of it I have noticed is a case in 1841.[237] The contingent right of the truster is often called his 'radical right'.[238] According to one theory, the 'radical right' was not an ultimate contingent beneficial right, but rather ownership itself. According to this strange theory, a transfer of ownership failed if intended to create a trust. The truster remained owner, and the trustee acquired a real right less than ownership. This idea was of course contrary to the view of Lord Stair, was hardly reconcilable with conveyancing practice, and suffered from all sorts of internal muddles and inconsistencies, but nevertheless existed as a sort of alternative doctrine for a long period. Its origins can be traced back to a case in 1734.[239] It took vigour from a case of 1801,[240] and reached its high-water mark in *Gilmour* v. *Gilmours* in 1876.[241] But even at that period it was never fully accepted, and it gradually went into decline. Today it is almost, though not quite,[242] forgotten.[243]

11. Executry

The executor is a character who did not exist in Roman law but who became more or less universal in medieval Europe, Scotland included.[244] The executor is obviously like a trustee, in that he holds property for others. Whether an executor actually becomes a fiduciary owner is, however, rather an obscure question, which has attracted surprisingly little discussion. The decree of confirmation issued by the commissary[245] says nothing about ownership. In an example from 1878 the commissary 'give and commit to . . . full power to uplift, receive, administer, and dispose of the said Personal,[246] Estate and

---

[236] Where the English doctrine—with a law-French name—of *cy-près* will mean that new charitable purposes must be found.

[237] *McLeish's Trs* v. *McLeish* (1841) 3 D 914, where Lord Moncreiff quotes it, as an unfamiliar term, from *St Barbe Tregonwell* v. *Sydenham* (1815) 3 Dow 194.

[238] Though this term has also been used in senses unconnected with the law of trusts.

[239] *Snee & Co.* v. *Anderson's Trs* (1734) Mor 1206.

[240] *Campbell of Edderline* (1801) Mor Appendix, 'Adjudication', no. 11.

[241] (1876) 11 M 853.   [242] One sees its ghost in Norrie/Scobbie (n. 150), 35.

[243] The only full study of this curious doctrine is Gretton, 'Radical Rights and Radical Wrongs', [1986] *JR* 51 and 192.

[244] The history of executry in Scotland has been little studied. A valuable article however is A. E. Anton, 'Mediaeval Scottish Executors', (1955) 67 *JR* 129. See also R. Zimmermann, '*Heres Fiduciarius?* Rise and Fall of the Testamentary Executor', in Helmholz/Zimmermann (n. 26), 267 sqq.

[245] The Commissary is the successor of the pre-Reformation Official. See S. Ollivant, *The Court of the Official*, Stair Society, vol. 34, (1982). Today the post is always held by the sheriff.

[246] A curious Anglicism. The meaning is 'moveable'. Until the Succession (Scotland) Act 1964 the executor's role was confined to the moveable property, though he could also be made a trustee of the heritage.

Effects, grant discharges thereof, if needful pursue therefor, and generally every other thing that to the office of Executor nominate is known to belong'.[247] The wording in use today is almost identical.[248] Space does not permit discussion of this complex subject.

One curious feature of Scots law, in a European context, is that an executor is used in both testate and intestate cases. In the former case the term used is executor-nominate, and in the latter, executor-dative. The executor-dative is appointed by the court.

As was mentioned earlier, executry was at one stage thought of as *fideicommissum*.[249] Stair seems not to classify executors as trustees. But once the category of trust was established, it was unsurprising that executry should be subsumed under it, and this had happened by the time of Erskine, who writes[250] that 'the law considers that the executor appointed by the deceased as an *haeres fiducarius*, or trustee, who is to be accountable to the next of kin, creditors, and others having interest in the succession'. Likewise Bell writes[251] that 'where an executor has been confirmed . . . he is trustee for the heirs and legatees and creditors[252] of the deceased'. But executry was not brought into the definition of 'trust' for the purposes of the various Trusts (Scotland) Acts until 1900.[253] This applied to executors-nominate. Executors-dative were included only from 1964.[254] It should perhaps be added that an executor's liability to creditors of the defunct has always been limited to the estate: this is one of the most obvious trust-like features of executry. Despite the views of the institutional writers, Lord President Inglis in 1872[255] said that

[a]n executor is not a trustee in the sense of being a depository. A trustee has to hold as a depository; not so an executor, who has to administer, not to hold . . . An executor is nothing else than a debtor to the legatee or next of kin. He is a debtor to the legatees or next of kin . . . with a limited liability; but he is nothing else than a debtor; and the creditors of the deceased and the legatees who claim against him do so as creditors.

This remark is of course muddled,[256] but it shows that the view of executry as trust had not wholly prevailed. Again, in 1912 Lord Dunedin[257] said of the

---

[247] Edinburgh Commissariot, 27 June 1878, estate of Peter Hepburn. From my collection.
[248] For an example from 1613, which again is silent as to ownership, see P. Goudesbrough, *Formulary of Old Scots Legal Documents*, Stair Society, vol. 36 (1985), 17.
[249] See n. 66 above.   [250] Erskine, III, 9, 5.   [251] Bell, *Commentaries*, II, 80.
[252] This theory eventually did not prevail. The majority view is that the heirs and legatees are trust beneficiaries, but the creditors are simple creditors. But this is a long and complex story which cannot be told here. Incidentally, Bell was keen on this sort of idea. He also argued that any debtor, on becoming insolvent, becomes a trustee for his creditors. This idea too did not establish itself. (For discussion, see *Nordic Travel Ltd* v. *Scotprint Ltd* 1980 SC 1.)
[253] Executors (Scotland) Act 1900, s. 2.   [254] Succession (Scotland) Act 1964, s. 20.
[255] *Jamieson* v. *Clark* 1872 10 M 399.
[256] Both executors and other trustees hold. Both executors and other trustees administer, subject to certain limitations. The claims of legatees and of creditors are quite distinct.
[257] By some considered to be a great judge.

executor that 'emphatically he is not a trustee'.[258] But although such remarks are occasionally still quoted, they do not seem to be taken very seriously. Executry is regarded as trust, but a special sort, to which some special rules apply.[259]

Finally, though lack of space allows only the briefest mention, something must be said of the trust disposition and settlement. This was in effect a testament, whereby the testator conveyed everything to trustees, the legacies being converted into trust purposes. The trustees would be declared executors of the moveables. The deed developed during the eighteenth century, its origins being an *inter vivos* trust having a *mortis causa* purpose.

IV. CURRENT LAW

Compared with some areas of law, such as family law, the law of trusts has not changed very much since the second half of the nineteenth century. Legislation such as the Trusts (Scotland) Act 1921, the Trusts (Scotland) Act 1961, the Trustee Investments Act 1961, and the Law Reform (Miscellaneous Provisions) (Scotland) Act 1990, have been concerned with the adjustment of points of detail. There has been a steady flow of case law, but little of it has been of the first importance. One current issue which certainly is important but which remains uncertain—which has been little studied academically and which awaits a proper treatment by a good court—is the use of trusts as commercial security, the idea being to make the debtor a 'trustee' for the creditor, thereby circumventing all the usual rules about registration, delivery, publicity, and real rights, which public policy has bestowed on conventional rights in security. The point, of course, is that the right of a beneficiary prevails over the creditors of the trustee.[260] Another current issue, which has attracted more academic attention, is that of constructive trusts.[261] But in general one can say that trusts have not attracted as much academic interest as one might have expected. *Wilson & Duncan*[262] is an impressive work, but there has been little in the journals. Such as there has been has often been of an Anglicizing tendency. No one is or has ever been quite sure whether trusts are, in the great

---

[258] *Taylor & Ferguson Ltd* v. *Glass's Trs* 1912 SC 165.
[259] One oddity which cannot be discussed here is that for some, but not all, purposes the executor is deemed to be *eadem persona cum defuncto*.
[260] The main study of this issue is Gretton, 'Using Trusts as Commercial Securities', 1988 *JLSS* 53.
[261] See R. Burgess, 'The Unconstructive Trust?', [1977] *JR* 200, 201; A. Wilson, 'The Constructive Trust in Scots Law', [1993] *JR* 99; Kenneth Norrie, 'Proprietary Rights of Cohabitants', [1995] *JR* 209 (arguing for the use of constructive trusts in sexual relationships, on the lines developed in England, the Commonwealth and the USA); Gretton, (1997) 1 *Edinburgh LR* 281. Though my regard for Professor Norrie is extremely high, I cannot agree with his article. Even the term 'proprietary rights' is to be regretted.   [262] Wilson/Duncan (n. 34).

map of the law, to be assigned to property, or obligations, or persons, or perhaps form a continent of their own. To anyone interested in how the trust can fit in to a system some of whose roots are civilian and which does not know 'equity' Scots law has much to offer, but the truth is that in the Year of Grace 2000 Scots law is still not quite sure how it wants to handle the trust.

Index of Names

Abercromby, David 63
Accursius 19
Adam, William 152
Albany, Murdoch, Duke of 37
Alexander II, king of Scotland 20, 28, 33, 39
Alexander III, king of Scotland 15–16, 32, 33, 36, 38, 41
Alfenus Varus, Publius 455
Alison, Archibald 172
Andreae, Johannes 72
Angell, J. K. 462
Anne I, queen of Great Britain and Ireland 118
Anne, Princess (daughter of James VII) 113, 114
Archibald of Galloway, Lord 49
Ardmillan, Lord 309, 328–9
Areskine, Charles 129
Argyll family 53
Argyll, Archibald, Marquis and 8th Earl of 81, 109, 123
Argyll, John, 2nd Duke of 143
Arthur, John 89
Athole, John, Earl of 383–4
Athole, Marie Ruthven, Countess of 383–4
Auchinleck, Lord 447
Azo 45

Baillie, James 163, 170
Balfour of Pittendreich, Sir James 95, 96, 97, 211, 212, 269, 39–40, 347, 364, 367, 373, 385, 386, 387, 401, 402, 407, 410, 412, 422, 488, 489
Balliol, Edward, king of Scotland 45
Balliol, John, king of Scotland 33, 39, 34, 37
Balmerino, Lord 79
Bankton, Andrew McDouall, Lord 12, 163, 170, 199, 201, 202, 203, 211, 212–13, 217, 222, 223, 228, 229, 236, 237, 238, 239, 241–4 *passim*, 247, 251, 254, 256, 260, 308, 341–2, 348–9, 354–7 *passim*, 357, 367, 368, 391, 392, 414–16, 422–3, 427, 428, 431, 452, 453, 455–6, 466, 469, 506
Bannatyne, Lord 249
Barclay, William 75
Barrow, Geoffrey 32
Bartolus 101, 139, 187, 198, 409
Bayne, Alexander 130, 162, 163

Beaton, David, Cardinal 388
Bell, George Joseph 161, 168, 187, 189, 190, 204–6, 209, 211, 224, 247, 271, 279, 305, 309, 312, 313, 314, 315, 329, 343, 344, 347, 349, 357, 358–60, 406, 418–19, 432, 440, 456, 458, 468, 470, 502, 507, 515
Bell, Montgomerie 207
Bell, Robert 167, 174, 176, 172, 207, 366, 369, 370, 373, 375–6, 391, 392
Bellapertica, Petrus de 45
Benholme, Lord 253
Bisset, Andrew 62
Bisset, Baldred, Official of St Andrews 35
Blackburn J 255
Blackburn, Lord 477
Blackie, John 12, 13
Blackstone, Sir William 466
Blair, Lord President 456
Boece, Arthur 70
Boniface VIII, Pope 19
Bonfante, P. 459
Boswell, James 167
Bracton, Henry de 43, 421, 425
Brash, J. I. 146
Britton 421, 425
Broghill, Lord 104
Brougham, Henry, Lord 145, 252, 255, 475–6
Bruce, Alexander 136–7, 141, 173
Bruce, Sir George 436
Bruce of Annandale, Robert, Lord 20, 33, 34
Bruis, David 488
Bruis, Jonet 488
Bruis, Ninian 488
Buchan, Earl of 72
Buchanan, George 75, 110
Buckland, W. W. 287, 439
Burgess, Robert 486, 490, 491
Burnet, John 172
Burnet, Robert 101, 105
Burns, John 207, 208
Bute, Lord 144

Cairns, Hugh M., Lord 259
Cairns, John 213
Cameron, Lord 266
Campbell, Donald, Abbot of Coupar Angus 388

Campbell, Sir Ilay 151, 356
Campbell, Lord 253
Canning, George 146
Carey Miller, D. L. 245
Carrick, David, Earl of 37
Carrick, John de 40
Carrick, John, Earl of 37
Carrick, Robert Bruce, Earl of 33
Cassilis, Earl of 107
Caven, Gilbert 49
Chadwick, Edwin 472
Chalmer, John 83
Charles I, king of Great Britain and Ireland 79–82, 86, 92, 98, 99, 111, 124
Charles II, king of Scotland and England 74, 105, 106, 120, 122, 124, 125, 494
Cheape, Douglas 167
Chelmsford, Lord 264
Chepman, Walter 64
Cicero 439
Claverhouse, John Graham, 1st Viscount 110, 113
Clement V, Pope 19
Clement VII, Pope 59
Clyde, J. A., Lord President 288, 468
Clyde, J. J., Lord 196, 302, 303
Cocceji, Samuel von 165
Cockburn, Henry Thomas, Lord 145, 146, 177, 255, 475
Coke, Sir Edward 175
Comyn, Alexander, Earl of Buchan 33
Comyn, John, Lord of Badenoch 33
Constantine I (The Great), Roman Emperor 337
Cooper of Culross, Thomas M., Lord 14, 336, 337, 478, 479
Cottenham, Lord 252
Coulsfield, Lord 283, 301
Cowan, John 510
Cowan, Lord 470, 475
Cowell, John 101
Crab, John 45
Craig, James 140, 162, 163, 164, 170, 171
Craig, John 75
Craig, Thomas 12, 75, 78, 94, 96–101 *passim*, 105, 129, 185–6, 187, 191, 194, 198, 199, 223, 226–9 *passim*, 238, 241, 242, 243, 274, 275, 281, 282, 288, 291, 364, 367, 385, 386, 391, 407–8, 422, 423, 427, 430, 431, 436, 443
Craigie, John 207

Crauford, John 487
Crichton, Adam 71
Croft Dickinson, W. 53
Cromwell, Oliver 81–2, 101–5, 124
Cujas, Jacques de (Cujacius) 100, 101, 139, 187, 274
Cuninghame, John 129, 135, 139
Curriehill, Lord 253
Cuthbert, St 369

Dallas, George 388, 390, 391
Dalrymple, Sir David, *see* Hailes
Dalrymple, Sir Hew 173
Dalrymple, Sir James, *see* Stair
Dalrymple, Sir John, *see* Stair
Darandus, G. 45
David I, king of Scotland 15, 19, 20, 21, 23, 24, 28, 33, 34, 37, 38, 44, 97, 369
David II, king of Scotland 37, 38, 39–40, 45, 48, 54
Davidson, Thomas 64–5
Deas, Lord 253, 320, 324, 344
De Groot, *see* Grotius
Dick, Robert 165
Dickson, Janet 492
Dirleton, Sir John Nisbet, Lord 140, 248, 495
Dog, Walter 384
Douglas, Earl of 45, 49
Douglas, Sir William 378–9
Drummond, Alexander 129
Drummond, Walter 63
Duarenus 100, 101
Duff, Alexander 207
Duncan, A. A. M. 17, 43, 45, 369, 370, 377
Duncan, A. G. M. 312, 516
Dundas, Henry, 1st Viscount Melville 145, 150
Dundas, John 137
Dundas, Ralph 394–5
Dunedin, Lord 515–16
Dunpark, Lord 263
Durand, Guillaume (Durandus) 68, 72
Durie, *see* Gibson of Durie

Edgar, English prince, king of Scots 19, 20
Edgar, John 173
Edward I, king of England 33, 34–6, 39
Edward III, king of England 45
Elizabeth I, queen of England 492
Elphinstone, William, Bishop of Aberdeen 63, 69

Index of Names

Emslie, Lord 265, 266, 296
Errol, William, Earl of 400
Erskine, John 163, 170, 198–204 *passim*, 211, 212, 222, 223, 229, 231, 233, 235–9, 242, 243, 244, 247, 251, 252, 254, 255, 256, 260, 277, 283, 305, 309, 311, 315–16, 318, 320, 322, 335, 341–2, 348, 349, 355, 357, 264, 392, 416–19 *passim*, 423, 427, 431, 433, 434, 440, 443, 452, 453, 469, 470, 506, 515

Faber, Antonius 139
Falconer, David 173
Ferguson J. (Sheriff) 475
Ferrarriis, Johannes de 72
Fife, Duncan, Earl of 21, 33
Fife, Robert, Earl of 37, 49
Fife, Malcolm, Earl of 369
Findlater and Seafield, Earl of 117, 391
Fleming, Alexander 39
Fleming, Robert, Lord 60
Fleta 421
Fletcher of Saltoun, Andrew 143
Forbes, William 130, 136, 137, 141, 142, 162, 163, 173
Forester, Alexander 488
Forester, David 488
Forman, Elizabeth 489
Forman, Robert 488–9
Forsyth, Charles 485, 486, 502, 503, 504, 511, 512
Fountainhall, Lord 133, 139, 141, 173
Fraser, William, Bishop of St Andrews 33, 34
Fratcher, W. F. 481
Frederic I, Holy Roman Emperor 433
Frere, William, Archdeacon of Lothian 35–6
Fresell, John 63
Fullerton, Lord 284

Galbraith, Robert 70
George I, king of Great Britain and Ireland 118, 144
George II, king of Great Britain and Ireland 144
George III, king of Great Britain 144
Gibson of Durie, Sir Alexander 101, 492
Gifford, Lord 258
Gillanders, George 388–90
Glanvill, Ranulf de 18, 42–3, 97, 335, 336–7, 420, 421, 423, 425

Glencairn, Earl of 106
Glendonyn, John 488
Glenlee, Lord 456, 464
Gloag, W. M. 205, 245, 333, 361, 406
Gordon, Patrick 487
Gordon, W. M. 138, 245, 275, 276, 292–3, 310, 329, 336
Gothofredus, Aionysius 139
Goudy, Henry 182, 183
Graham, James Maxtone 394–5
Grange, Lord 393–4
Grant of Arnely, James 384
Grant of Fruchie, John 383–4
Gratian 18, 19
Greenshields (episcopalian minister) 117
Gregory IX, Pope 19
Greig, George 388–90
Gretton, George L. 194, 273, 274, 277, 278, 279, 280, 286, 366
Grieve, Lord 266
Grotius, Hugo 6, 12, 136, 165, 234, 319, 391, 427, 430
Gudelinus, P. 12
Guise, Mary of 76, 90

Haakon IV, king of Norway 16
Hailes, Sir David Dalrymple, Lord 162, 175
Hailsham, Quintin Hogg, Lord 441
Haldane, Patrick 147
Hale, Sir Matthew 475, 476
Halliday, J. M. 207, 273, 208, 274
Hamilton, James Douglas, 4th Duke of 115, 117
Hannay, Robert 175–6
Harcarse, Lord 173
Harding, Alan 44
Hardwicke, Philip Yorke, 1st Earl 147
Heineccius, J. G. 165, 256, 327
Heise, A. 511
Henderson, R. C. 205, 406
Henry I, king of England 20
Henry II, king of England 425
Henry VIII, king of England 51
Henry, Prince of Wales 82, 91
Henryson, Edward 90, 95
Henryson, James 70
Heriot, George 493, 510
Holt, Chief Justice 342
Home, Alexander 173
Hope, Charles, Lord President 344
Hope, John, Lord Justice-Clerk 251

Hope, Sir Thomas 211, 278, 340, 385, 386, 408–10, 410, 412, 495–6
Hope of Craighead, David, Lord 295, 296, 297
Horner, Francis 145
Hostiensis 45
Hotman, F. 100
Huber, E. 466
Hugo, Gustav 167
Hume, David (Baron) 159, 166–7, 168, 170, 172, 204–6, 208, 223, 224, 228, 239–42, 244, 271–2, 280, 281–2, 283, 292, 298, 300, 309, 315, 324, 327, 328, 330, 343, 392–3, 432, 434, 440, 449, 453, 456, 458
Hume, David (philosopher) 163–4, 429
Hunter, Robert 375, 377, 380–1, 396–7
Huntingdon, David, Earl of 34
Hutcheson, Francis 163
Hwyme, Alexander 488

Ilay, Archibald, Earl of 143–4, 145, 393
Inglis, John, Lord President 441, 442, 468, 515
Innes, James 163
Innes, Janet 487
Innocentius 45
Ireland, John 52
Irnerius 18
Irvine, J. M. 333, 361

Jagoe, J. 477
James I, king of Scotland 37, 51, 52, 54, 56, 60–1, 65, 66, 74, 95
James II, king of Scotland 51, 54, 65
James III, king of Scotland 16, 50, 51, 62, 66
James IV, king of Scotland 51, 53, 54, 55, 56, 58, 70, 71, 72, 73, 370
James V, king of Scotland 51, 52, 53, 54, 58–9, 63, 64–5, 73, 74
James VI, king of Scotland, I of England 75, 76, 77–8, 79, 90, 91–2, 93, 94, 103, 118, 136, 376, 430, 492, 494
James VII, king of Scotland, II of England 84, 106, 109–10, 111, 113, 124, 127, 131
James the Steward 33
Jauncey, Lord 196, 302, 303
Jeffrey, Francis 145, 146
Jerviswoode, Lord 476
John XXII, Pope 19
Johnston, Archibald 80
Julianus, Salvius 346

Justinian I, emperor 18, 43, 46, 67, 141, 136, 165, 183, 200, 201, 239, 223–4, 229, 230, 235, 426, 466

Kames, Henry Home, Lord 10, 149, 160, 164–5, 166, 167, 169, 170, 173–4, 175, 224, 356, 375, 392, 417–18, 432, 459
Kaser, M. 308, 309, 351
Kennedy, Gilbert, Lord 60
Kennedy, Jane 487
Kennedy, Johnne, Lord 487
Kenneth I, mac Alpin, king of Scots 15
Kent, J. 462
Kilbrandon, Lord 262
King, Alaxander 489
Kinnear, Lord 264, 445
Knox, Andrew James 394–5
Kolbert, C. F. 288, 294
Kyllachy, Lord 261

Lamby, Andro 489
Lauder, William 63
Lauderdale, Earl of 106
Lauer, T. E. 462
Lawson, Richard 72
Le Blanc J. 353
Lennox, David, Earl of 21
Lesley, Walter 63
Lewin, Thomas 503–4, 505, 506
Lindley, Lord 505
Lindores, Abbot of 45
Lokhart, James 487–8
Lokhart, John 487–8
Lorne, *see* Argyll
Louis XIV, king of France 109, 113

McDonald, A. J. 207
Mackay, N. A. M. 288, 294
McKechnie, Hector 61, 478
Mackenzie of Rosehaugh, Sir George 106–7, 126, 128, 133–6, 139, 140, 141–2, 168–9, 198–204 *passim*, 223–4, 229, 235, 239, 242, 349, 380, 423
Mackenzie Stuart, A. 502, 508
Mackie, Charles 130
McLaren, John, Lord 182, 195–6, 263, 264, 505, 507
MacLean, A. J. 123
McLeod, Grant 193, 204
McNair, A. D. 287

Index of Names

McNeill, Duncan, Lord President (later Lord Colonsay) 253, 343, 344
McNeill, Peter G. B. 269
MacQueen, H. L. 8, 30, 32, 62, 424
Macqueen, Robert, Lord Braxfield 355
Mair, John 70
Maitland, F. W. 32, 480, 484
Malcolm III, Canmore, king of Scotland 19
Malcolm IV, king of Scotland 15, 20, 23
Malveisin, Bishop of St Andrews 30
Mansfield, William Murray, 1st Earl 144, 161, 352
Mar, John Erskine, 6th Earl of 118
Marcian 429
Margaret, queen of Scotland 33
Margaret, Princess of Denmark 16
Marjoribanks, Thomas 488
Mary, Queen of Scots 75, 76, 95, 101
Mary II, queen of Great Britain and Ireland 109–11, 113
Maxwell, Eduard 488
Maxwell, Sir John 488
Maxwell, Robert 488
Maxwell, Lord 310
Melfort, Earl of 109
Melville, Andrew 77
Melville, John 377–9
Menochius, Jacobus 477
Menzies, A. J. P. 502
Menzies, Allan 207
Merchant, Alexander Falconer 389
Middleton, Earl of 106
Millar, Andrew 64
Millar, John 159, 161, 165–6, 168
Millar, J. H. 290, 291
Milton, Lord 143, 145
Monboddo, James Burnett, Lord 433, 446, 447
Monck, George, Gen. 82
Moncreiff, James, Lord Justice-Clerk 254, 475
Moncreiff, J. W., Lord 456–7
Monier, R. 429
Monmouth, James, Duke of 108, 109
Monteath, H. H. 277, 279–80
Montesquieu, Charles L., Baron de 164
Moray, Andrew 35
More, J. S. 360
Mortoun, Alexander 488
Mosman, James 489
Mure, Johne 489–90

Muray, Patrik 384
Murray, Lord 265, 477
Murray of Glendook, Sir Thomas 133, 140, 169
Mynsinger, J. 101

Napier, Macvey 207, 290–1
Neaves, Lord 458–9, 470
Newcastle, Thomas Pelham, Duke of 142
Nicholas, B. 346
Nicholson, Ranald 371
Nicolsoune, Patrik 490
Normand, Wilfrid G., Lord 486

Ormidale, Lord 249

Paul(us) 321, 323, 325, 326
Peblis, John de 40
Peel, Robert 146
Peñafort, Raymond de 19
Peregrinus, M. A. 477
Perezius, A. 162
Pernice, Alfred 439
Perth, Earl of 109
Petit, Duncan 49
Pitt (the younger), William 145, 151
Porteous, Oswald 490
Pothier, R. J. 198, 256, 257
Pufendorf, Samuel 229, 351

Queensberry, Duke of 114, 116

Randolph, Sir Thomas 39
Rankine, Sir John 182, 207, 219, 312, 326, 328, 396, 437, 451, 474–5, 476, 477
Redehuch, David 338
Reid, James S. C., Lord 486
Reid, Kenneth 245, 259, 271, 295, 297, 300, 302, 303
Reid, Robert, Bishop of Orkney 90
Reid, Robert, Official of Moray 70
Repgow, Eike von 44
Reygerus, A. 477
Richard III, king of England 51
Robert I, king of Scotland 37, 38, 39, 43, 49, 375
Robert II, king of Scotland 37, 40–1, 42, 399
Robert III, king of Scotland 37, 42, 47
Robert de Brus, *see* Bruce of Annandale
Robert de Kent 377
Robertson, Lord 249, 329

524 *Index of Names*

Rodger, A., Lord 474
Ross, Earl of 45
Ross, Lord 301, 302
Ross, Andrew 509
Ross, Walter 171, 187, 206, 207–8, 285–6, 375, 376, 380, 381
Rothesay and Fife, David, Duke of 37, 47
Roxburghe, Duke of 143
Ruderford, Margret 489–90
Rutherford, Samuel 82
Rutherfurd Clark, Lord 264

St Leonards, Lord 441
Sanderson, Margaret 367–8, 370–1
Sande, F. 466
Sandilands, James 91
Savigny, Friedrich Carl von 167, 177, 511
Schultes, H. 477
Seaforth, Kenneth, Earl of 388–90
Selden, John 430, 431
Sellar, David 14, 194
Senlis, Maud de 20
Seton of Pitmedden, Sir Alexander 136
Shairp, John 86–7
Shand, Lord 257
Shaw, J. 464
Shaw, Patrick 175
Shaw, Thomas, Lord 474, 477
Sinclair, John 70, 72, 73, 213
Skene, John 96, 97, 98, 100, 132, 400, 401, 407
Skene, William 87, 89
Smith, Adam 149–50, 159, 160, 166, 344, 429
Smith, Sidney 145
Smith, Sir Thomas B. 10, 486
Snell, E. H. T. 503–4
Sohm, R. 351
Sophia, Electress of Hanover 113
Spittall, Henry 70
Spottiswoode, John 129, 141
Stair, Sir James Dalrymple, 1st Viscount 12, 107, 109, 111, 130, 134, 137–8, 140, 170–1, 177, 187, 191, 194, 199, 200–6 *passim*, 211, 212, 216, 217, 223, 224–33 *passim*, 235–9 *passim*, 241–4 *passim*, 247, 273, 275–6, 277, 282–3, 288, 290, 293, 295, 298, 299, 308–9, 315, 316, 341, 347–8, 349, 350, 353–4, 355, 365, 368, 369, 374, 380, 386, 391–2, 399, 412–14, 417, 422–3, 427, 431, 433, 443, 452, 453, 466, 482, 486, 489, 491, 494, 495, 506–7, 514, 515

Stair, Sir John Dalrymple, 1st Earl of 113, 124
Stein, P. 43
Steuart of Goodtrees, James 107, 248
Stewart, Charles 445
Stewart, James (Old Pretender) 118
Stewart, Patrick, Earl of Orkney 93
Stewart of Auchmadeis, Sir James 384
Story J 462
Strathanery, Harvey and John of 46
Sutherland, Lord 296–7
Swinton, John, Lord 150–1, 169
Sym, Alexander 90

Tarbet, Viscount 209
Thomson, Lord 262, 298
Trail, Walter, Bishop of St Andrews 49
Trano, Goffredus de 43
Trayner, Lord 333
Tribonian (vs) 141
Troupe, Barbara 489
Tudeschis, Nicholas de (Panormitanus) 72
Turnbull (Bishop of Glasgow) 69
Tweeddale, Marquess of 114
Tytler, Alexander 174, 175

Ulpian 246, 452, 455
Urry, Adam 31

Van Bynkershoek, Cornelis 431
Van der Keessel, A. G. 319
Van der Vyver, J. D. 426
Van Eck, C. 139
Van Groenewegen van der Made, Simon 162, 319
Van Leeuwen, S. 313
Victoria, queen of the United Kingdom of Great Britain and Ireland 178
Vinnius, Arnoldus 12, 455
Voet, Johannes 12, 162, 211, 256, 314, 316, 319, 351
Voet, Paulus 256
Vulteius, H. 477

Walker, David M. 8, 12, 487
Walker, William 60
Wallace, Kathryne 490
Wallace, William 35
Walpole, Sir Robert 143
Wardlaw, Henry, Bishop of St Andrews 69

Index of Names

Watson, Alan 463, 465
Watson, James 169
Watson, William, Lord 195, 437, 476, 507, 508
Wawane, William 63
Weddell, John 70
Welwood, William 89, 90, 94, 97, 98, 430
Westbury, Lord 485, 512
Wiel, S. C. 462
Wilkes, John 144
William I, king of Scotland 20, 21, 25, 27, 28
William II, Rufus, king of England 20
William III, of Orange, king of Great Britain and Ireland 109–11, 113, 186
William of Eaglesham 36
William of Normandy 18, 19
William of Spynie 46
Willock, I. D. 423–4
Wilson, W. A. 301, 516
Wishart, Robert, Bishop of Glasgow 33
Wood, Philip 207
Worral, 505

York, James, Duke of 108–9
Young, Lord 476

Zoesius, Henricus 139

Index of Subjects

Abbey Chartularies 372, 377
Aberdeen 29, 82
   Bishops of 45, 400
   Cathedral Chapter 46
   Society of Advocates 88, 130, 157, 158
Aberdeen University 70
   see also King's College; Marischal College
Abernethy 19, 399
Abolition of Feudal Tenure etc. (Scotland) Act 2000 192, 349
abusus 272, 273, 274
access rights 440, 444, 468
accession 193, 202, 228, 233, 238, 350, 351
   breach of 219
   by building 194, 245–68
'acquired' rights 435
acquittal by compurgation 60
act of will 203
actio aquae pluviae arcendae 458, 469
actio fiduciae 334
actio in rem 346
actio negatoria 469
actio popularis 435
actio utilis 274
Acts of Parliament 60–1, 67–8, 83, 96, 101, 117, 118–19, 131, 132, 135, 152, 360, 424
   regular printing/publishing of 95, 97, 169
   see also Aliens; Revocation; Security; Statutes; Settlement; Supremacy; Union
Acts of Sederunt 131, 133, 147, 152, 153, 169, 179
   admission of advocates (1664) 126
   admission of agents and solicitors (1772) 156–7
   admission on trial by civil law (1688) 127
   creditors (1735/1754) 160–1
   intrant advocates (1619) 87
   lord related to litigant (1594) 85
   Outer House procedure (1693) 121
   possession of properties (1585) 82–3
   procurators (1825) 158
   professorship of laws founding (1619) 90
   written informations: (1596) 85, 99; (1677) 121; (1710) 121
Acts of the Lord Auditors of Causes and Complaints (1466/1494) 338
ad factum praestandum 417, 472

ad manes 436
ad bene placitum appointments 86, 125
ad vitam aut culpam appointments 86
adherence 120
adjudication 205, 414
administration of justice 70, 184
   Commissioners for 102, 103, 104
   justiciar 22, 39
   more professional 93
   Normanization of 24
   royal attempts to interfere with 125
Admiralty, Court of 102, 116, 153, 154
adultery 83
advocates 70, 101, 121, 122, 149, 375
   admission 105, 126–7
   education 128–9
   independence 125–6
   practising before Court of Session 86–7, 89
   search for status 68
   use of canon law/Roman law 99
   see also Faculty of Advocates
Advocates' Library 141, 142, 181
aemulatio vicini 469, 471, 476
aequum et bonum 98
agency 8
agreements:
   bare 349
   hire-purchase 265–6
agri limitati 466
agricultural leases 349, 392
Alba 15
alienation 277, 278, 334, 379, 387, 399
aliens 115
Aliens Act 1705 114
alimentary rights 416
allegiance 118
   changing 41
   oaths of 103, 106, 111
alluvio 439, 466–7
alveus 441, 442, 441–3, 452, 453, 468
   ownership of 466–7
American law 457, 462, 474
Amos's *Law of Fixtures* 256
Amsterdam 161
anchorage 71
Angevin England 32
Angles 15

Index of Subjects

Anglicans 117
Anglo-American approach 462, 481, 482, 483
   common law 463, 474, 475
Anglo-Norman law 10, 186, 340, 353, 423
   feudal 193-4
Anglo-Norman period 21, 29, 32, 47, 343
Anglo-Saxon terms 17-18
animals 234, 246
   ferae naturae 444
animus destinandi 248-9
animus domini 212
Annandale, Lordship of 20, 33, 34, 39
annualrents 200, 400, 414
appeals 35, 113, 125
   encouraged 151
   protestations and 123-4
apprenticeships 88, 89, 128, 130, 157, 206
   regular 158
appropriation 427, 430, 432, 433, 462
   by *occupatio* 436
   prior 451, 458, 461, 463
arbitration 72, 92
Arbroath 25, 55
archbishops 51, 84, 108
Argathelians 143
Argyll 39
   hereditary justiciarship of 148
   and the Isles, Justice-General of 123
arrestment 404-5, 407, 411, 413, 414
Articles 106, 111
assedation 364, 385, 390, 403, 408
assignation 226, 298, 370, 386, 399-419
assimilation 104, 260, 360, 366, 442-3, 474, 475
assizes 27, 28, 48, 62, 65, 122
   prejudiced 60
assythment 53, 402
attorneys 46, 286
'Auld Lawes' 65
Avignon 49, 69
Ayr, River 445, 464-5
Ayrshire 394

bad faith 298, 409
   see also *mala fides*
bail 122, 130
bailies 55, 122-3, 286, 386, 493
   of barony 83
   of regality 83
   surrender of heritable offices 93
ballivi 23, 24

banknotes 417
bankruptcy 131, 160-1, 392, 497
Bankruptcy Act (1772) 161
Bankruptcy (Scotland) Acts (1772/1856/1913/1985) 497
banks 188
baptisms 119
bargains 336
baron courts 24, 54, 103, 148
barons 62, 64, 69, 80, 119, 124
   lost franchise jurisdiction to try serious crimes 148
   small 77
   tenants and 55-6
barony 32, 39, 46, 72, 399, 400
   bailies of 83
   officers of 48
barristers 156
beggars 213
beneficiaries 195, 196, 370, 484, 500
   interest of 481
   right of 482-3, 507, 516
Berne manuscript 42
Berwick 24, 34, 36
bewind 481
bills 85, 121
   of exchange 136, 161, 417
Birgham, Treaty of (1290) 33, 35
birlawmen 18
bishops 29, 59, 107, 109
   Anglican 117
   appointment of commissaries by 120
   commissaries under the authority of 84
   full and general authority to 77
Bishops' Wars (1638/1640) 80, 81
'Black Acts' (1584) 77
Blank Bonds and Trusts Act 1696 496, 498
bloodfeud 89, 92
Bologna 19, 35
bona fides:
   debtors 405, 406, 414, 418, 487
   possession 214, 215, 351, 354, 361
   principals 350
   purchasers 294, 417
   see also good faith
bonds 402, 406, 411
   blank 413, 418
   bottomry 348, 349
   heritable 131, 205, 400
   maintenance 60
   manrent 60

Index of Subjects

moveable 131
respondentia 348, 349
transfer of 413
Boniface VIII, Pope 35
Books of Sederunt 103, 183
see also Acts of Sederunt
border issues 33
Borders:
    landowners 92
    pacification/attempts to pacify 91, 92
Bothwell Brig, battle of (1679) 108
bottomry bonds 348, 349
boundaries 26, 466, 467
Bourges 87, 90
Boyne, battle of (1690) 110
breach of contract 8
Brechin 55, 29
Bretons 20
brieves 29, 32, 59, 74, 478
    de cursu/de gratia 26
    decline of process on 61–2
    de aqueductu 424, 425
    inquest and tutory 26
    non-retourable 26
    pleadable 26, 41, 61, 62, 424
    possessory 423–4
    prohibition 30
    retourable 26, 61, 63
    right 26, 27, 41–2, 61
    royal 58
    royal intervention by 28
    see also novel dissasine
brithem 17
British Empire 442, 474
British Parliament 116, 177
    Commissioners 112–13, 115
    Scottish Office and 178
brocard 349, 456
building societies 188
bureaucracy 49
burgagio tenure 24
burgesses 23, 24, 25, 27, 36, 39, 80
burgh courts 24, 25, 27, 54, 83, 148, 157
    Commissions appointed to examine operation of 120
burghs 22, 23–4, 404
    Chamberlain's loss of authority over 56
    commissioners for 64
    ecclesiastical 55
    free and unfree 55
    prohibition on making bonds in 60
    records 339
    representatives of 38
    royal 55, 158, 281
Burgundy 73
Bute 39

calps 31, 56
'cannon-shot rule' 431
canon law 18, 46, 47, 63, 70, 90, 136, 137, 193, 212, 230
    actio spolii 73
    advocates use of 99
    and ecclesiastical discipline 29–30
    conflict between civil law and 100
    discourse in Latin on text of 86
    exceptio spoli 212
    faculties of 69
    glosses from 67
    jus commune and 376
    land tenure influenced by 366
    quaestio of 87
    rule on the legal presumption of marriage 68
    study of 68, 69
capital 160, 161, 188
Carrick 31, 56
case law 172, 177, 202, 213, 218
    absence of 219
    Anglo-American 207
    mortifications 509
    ownership of land 284
    pledge 342, 343–4
    res communes omnium 431–2
    right of retention 355–6
    servitudes 318, 328
    sharing of 194
    superior/vassal 278
    trusts 499, 503
castle building 21
casual waters 438, 468–71, 479
casus omissus 73
Catholic Church 18
causa 402–3, 487
    of sale 294
causal theory 299
caution 92, 360
Celtic Scotland 18, 21
    institutions 32
    law 17
    people 15
central courts 44, 57, 74, 154–5

Index of Subjects

cessio bonorum 131
chamberlains 24, 36, 57
  ayre 55
  loss of authority over burghs 56
  supervisory jurisdiction 60
Chancery, Court of 116, 503
charitable trusts 511, 514
charters 45
  royal 40, 43, 157, 159
chattels 41
chaudemellee 48
Chief Barons 124, 154
chivalry 47
Chronicle of Lanercost 31
Church 18, 27, 46, 370
  attempt to enforce ecclesiastical discipline 19
  episcopal 77, 143, 117
  land infeudated to 508
  liberties and privileges 40
  national 115
  rejection of ordeal as a mode of proof 31
  revitalized 29
  same in all countries of Europe 375–6
  see also Kirk; Presbyterianism
Church and State 76
Church of England 117
circuit courts 122, 148
  system extended 154
civil causes 160
civil courts 104, 131
  'badge of learning' in 374
  reforms 131
  supreme 59, 82
civil law 1–3, 6, 7, 31, 46, 63, 73, 159, 184, 187, 222, 230
  assignations 412
  attempts to discourage clergy from studying 19
  'breeding' of an intrant educated in 127–8
  common law and 4, 219, 256
  conveyance of property 276
  curriculum 130
  delivery of property 336
  departure from 100–1
  discourse in Latin on text of 86
  dispensation to study 70
  doctrine ultimately founded in 183
  emphyteusis in 366
  faculties of 69
  glosses from 67
  importance of 374
  legitimate use of 136
  lien 350–1
  'naturalised' by being incorporated into practice 167
  pledge of moveables and immoveables 335
  possession 214, 292
  private examination 125, 126, 156
  proof of academic learning by reading lesson on 105
  public examination 125, 126
  quaestio of 87
  respect for 234
  retention 356
  Roman 235
  Scotland's 'affinity' with 138
  Scots law identified as 78
  Scottish customs imitated 139
  status, 'breeding' and 127–8
  'stellionate' assignation 415
  study of 68, 69
  teaching 167, 374
  three-year programme primarily devoted to 129
  'true' law of Scotland 10
  used because so little written law in Scotland 100
  valued as providing illustrations of Smithian natural jurisprudence 165–6
  waters 428, 444, 449
  see also jus commune, Roman Law
civil war 81–2
claims 400, 419, 496–7
  counter 354
Claim of Right 110–11, 113, 123, 125, 131
Clan Act 1715 132
Clan MacDuff, Law of 49, 56
clare constat 495
classification 222, 238
  property rights 427
  rivers 438–65
  rural and urban servitudes 310–14
Clerk of the Registry 64, 96, 133
clerks 46, 108, 121
  advocates' 156, 181
  audit 49
  to the Signet 88, 154
Cliffplant Ltd v. Kinnaird (1981) 262
Clyde, Firth of 442
coastal waters 431, 437

see also littoral rights/proprietors
codification 94, 133, 182–3, 130–5, 190, 312
  English law of sale 194
coinage 115
collateral 337, 415
College of Justice:
  collection of decisions from 173–4
  position consolidated 94
  President 70, 90
  success of 85
  see also Senators
commerce 112, 159–62, 162, 165, 186, 350, 352, 428
commercial law 4, 161, 162
commissaries 84, 120, 514
commissary courts 84, 88, 102, 108, 120, 153, 157, 178
  Commissions appointed to examine the operation of 120
  local 120
Commissioners for Administration of Justice 102, 103, 104
Commissioners of Admiralty of Great Britain 116
Commissioners of Woods and Forests 434
Commissions of Oyer and Terminer 117
Committee of Estates 106
committees:
  ad decisionem judicii 54
  pro articulis advisandis 54
commodatum 351, 353
common carriers 351–2
'common enemy rule' 470–1
common freedoms 443
common interest:
  property 217
  proprietary 451
  riparian 438, 446–8, 450–65, 467–8
common law 1–3, 7, 10, 177, 135, 391
  affirmation of 48–9
  civil law and 256
  codification and legislation 130–5; reason and justice 93–9
  continuing vitality of 41
  courts, legislation, and 168–77
  hypothec 347
  institutions of 118–24
  jus commune and 45–7, 67–8, 99–101, 135–8
  once central and defining area of 180
  pollution 460

reforming 94–5
remedies 471–2
replacement by comprehensive statutory restatement 219
rise of 15–32
rules for regulating rights and obligations 216
Scots law limited to 168
social order and 47–9, 91–3
strength and conservatism of 42
superiority over statute law 177
tidality 445
Common Pleas, Court of 35, 116
commonty 427
Commonwealth and Protectorate (1652–9) 101–5
communis justicia 40
communis lex 40
'community of the realm' 33, 38
Companies Acts 296, 511
Companies Register 350
comparative law 451, 461–2
compear 61
compensation 53, 149, 214, 353, 357, 410, 414, 417
  landlord–tenant 372
competition 404–8 *passim*, 411, 414, 416–19 *passim*
compurgation 27
  acquittal by 60
conductor ad longum tempus 366
Confession of Faith (1560) 76, 109
conjugal rights 416
consent 277, 278, 412
  taking away goods without 213
conservatism and innovation 39–40
consistorial courts 83–4
Constitutio de Regalibus (1158) 426, 432, 433, 440, 477
constitutum possessorium 194
constructive trusts 512
consuetudes 98, 132
Consumer Credit Act 1974 345
consumers 180
contracts 5, 8, 103, 209, 353, 416, 419
  bilateral 372, 378, 380
  debt 357
  gratuitous 351
  law of 180
  marriage 491, 497–8
  mutual 414

contracts (*cont*)
  quasi- 507
  real 341
conventicles 118, 119
conventio 380
Convention of Estates (1575/1598/1689) 92, 94–5, 110
Convention Parliament 111–12
  see also Restoration Parliaments
conveyancing 157, 158–9, 180, 187, 195, 196, 217, 514
  abandonment of sasine in 292
  centrality of the derivative act 293–4
  development of 296
  feudal 274–82, 283, 299
  modern system 292, 294–5
  prominent feature of 188
  rise of 209
  same in all countries of Europe 375
  standard practice 197
  study of 206
  teaching of 159
Conveyancing (Scotland) Act 1924 361
copyhold 368
Copyright Act 1709 142
copyright law 198
corporeal moveables 303, 333, 342
Corpus Juris Civilis 13, 18, 73, 126, 127, 139, 187, 193, 204, 221–2, 231, 236, 240, 242
corruption 124
Council in Parliament 53, 58–9
Council of State for Scotland 104, 105
counsel 122, 159, 181, 259, 475–6, 505–6
coup d'état 38
Coupar Angus Abbey 387–8, 399
court books 89, 94
Court of Appeal 151
Court of Session 104, 120, 123, 144, 179, 260, 402
  admiralty jurisdictions merged with 154
  advocates before 86–7, 89
  agents before 156–7
  annual reports of decisions 175
  causes sent to Jury Court 153
  criticism of 149–51
  decisions 96, 172, 189, 410–11, 412, 418
  division of 151–2, 174
  Exchequer Court merged into 178
  Extra Division 263
  Heriot's Trust and 510
  impact of 82–3
  improving 85–6
  judgments reversed in Parliament 176
  jurisprudentia Romano-Scotica forensis 163
  no appeals to new Parliament 112–13
  practice before 99
  preserved 116
  printing pleadings and other documents 121
  sale of part of an entailed estate 160
  willingness to accept English rules 505
  see also Acts of Sederunt; Inner House; Lords of Council and Session; Outer House
Court of Session Acts (1808/1825/1868) 152, 179
Court of Seven Judges 264
Court of the Four Burghs 24, 55
Court of the Official of Lothian 71
courts 22, 155–6, 474, 503
  ad hoc 102
  commission to improve functioning of 121
  common law 61
  continental, important 100
  dempster 28
  development of 177
  English law and 161–2
  equity 4
  feudal 44
  friends and supporters in 86
  head 26, 160
  important 158
  inferior 116, 120
  intermediate 26
  justiciar 30, 45, 424
  legislation, common law and 168–77
  lords' 28
  lower 64
  Michaelmas, Yule, and Pasch 26
  new, effectiveness of 103–4
  operation of 120–1
  Parliament and 54
  practice of 162
  procedure and 178–9
  reforms of 155–6
  regality 54
  returned to older forms 107
  secular 30, 31, 84, 103
  spiritual 83
  study of decisions of 100
  survival of formal records of proceedings in 74

Index of Subjects

well-structured 150
  see also Admiralty; baron courts; burgh courts; Chancery; circuit courts; civil courts; commissary courts; Common Pleas; consistorial courts; criminal courts; ecclesiastical courts; Exchequer; Jury Court; local courts; ordinary courts; royal courts; sheriff courts; Whole Court; *also under headings above prefixed* 'Court'
Covenanters 80–1, 82, 86, 108
  Parliament 92, 94
craftsmen 91
creditors 132, 258, 284, 338, 399, 408, 414, 488
  assigning claims to one of their number 496–7
  competition with 417
  death of 401
  defraud of 131, 136
  heritable and ordinary 251
  intimation to 401
  limited power to sign leases 418
  possession of property 333
  ranking 161
  real right of security 296, 350
  trust deeds for 195
crimes 92, 97
criminal courts 53
  heritable jurisdictions and 148–9
  reforms 130, 154
criminal justice 93
criminal law 129, 172
Criminal Procedure (Scotland) Act 1887 179
Crofters Acts 180
Crofters Holdings (Scotland) Act 1886 180 n., 396
'Crofters' Wars' (1880s) 180
Cromwellian conquest/occupation 86, 493, 494
crop failures 113
Cruden kirk 400
'culrath' 28
Culross 436
  see also Magistrates of Culross
Cum Universi (papal bull, 1176) 29
Cupar 62
curia regis 22, 28
custodes 33
custody 336, 359, 360
customary law 98, 217, 413
  African 7
  unwritten 72
custom(s) 36, 49, 72, 100, 119, 139, 172, 206, 225, 228, 229, 230, 341, 369
  affirmed 406
  approved 28
  codification of 67
  commission to examine 95, 98
  defective 138
  importance of 218
  laws on 115
  'proper', intimation regarded as 413

Dalriada 15
damage 353
damages 263
Darien 113
de aqueductu (brieve) 424, 425
de deposito 489
death 248, 334, 339, 401, 415
debt 103, 200, 340, 352, 357, 391
  collecting 83
  execution of 234
  land disponed to secure 497
  pledgee entitled to 337
  secured by real rights 410
  see also assignation; creditors; discharge
decisions 167, 172, 175, 176, 407
  evident problems with 132
  full of artificial distinctions 499
  reports of 174
  Scots law founded mainly in 183
  Session 173
  see also Morison's *Dictionary*;
declarators 471
decrees 415, 472
decretals 19
deeds 88, 89, 104–5, 413, 415
  conveyance 294
  subscription of 132
  title 216, 355
  trust 493, 499
defamation 13
default 22, 23, 340
defence 122, 465
delectus personae 278, 416, 417, 418
delict 180, 422, 423
delivery 194, 196, 202, 203, 209, 215, 238
  constructive 344
  formal system of 292
  role of 339–40

delivery (*cont*)
  set in feudal context 288
  symbolical 295
demembration 148, 149
dempster 17, 26, 28
  courts of 28
Department of Trade and Industry 362
depositum 351, 353, 489
deputes 53, 63, 107, 108
derivative acquisition 295, 300
desuetude 61, 134, 169
detention 211
diets 61
Digest 129, 234, 246, 256, 257, 310, 385, 410–11, 452
diligence 161, 343, 347, 348, 356, 413–16 *passim*, 472, 500
  subject to any third party *jus in personam ad rem acquirendam* 494
dioceses 29, 30, 50, 69, 372
discharge 403, 404, 411
  partial 406
disponers/disponees 279, 280, 281–2, 283, 285, 294, 300, 408, 497
  de praesenti dispositive act 295
dispositions 202, 249, 279, 280, 294
  delivery of 296
  ex facie absolute 195
  personal 284
dispossession 212, 213
disputation 128
Disruption (1840s) 117
dissasine 41, 46
  see also novel dissasine
distress 347
dittay 22
divorce 84, 120
  a vinculo matrimonii 83
  move away from 'fault' as ground of 180
doctrine 1–13, 185–219
dominium 193, 198, 272, 307
  waters 427, 435, 436, 483
  see also duplex dominium, ownership
dominium directum 191, 192, 274
dominium utile 187, 191, 192, 273, 274, 275, 277, 280, 443
donation 413
Douglas, Heron & Co. (Ayr Bank) 161
Dumbarton 60
Dumfries 394
Dunbar, battle of (1650) 82
Dunbartonshire 442, 449

'Dundas Despotism' 145
Dundee, University of 207
Dunfermline 25, 55
Dunkeld 29
duplex dominium 187, 191, 192, 508
duties 102, 414
dynasties 33, 51–2, 78, 105–42
Dysart 316

earldoms 21, 39, 42, 51, 52
  powerful 23
East India Company 113
East Linton 444
Ecclesia Scoticana 29
ecclesiastical courts 30, 64, 69–70, 336
  judges 376
  relatively complex procedure of 68
  traditions of practice before 71
ecclesiastical discipline 19
  canon law and 29–30
economic and social factors 463–5
  see also industrialization; urbanization
Edinburgh 24, 71, 105, 108, 110, 143, 206, 214
  Advocates' Library 181
  City Council 493, 510
  commissary courts 84, 120, 153, 178
  criminal court 53
  James VI's departure from 492
  justiciar should remain in 62
  National Library of Scotland 181
  'outed' advocates banished from 125
  pledge 339
  Register House 377, 361
  sheriffdom 153, 378
  Solicitors at Law 157
  water supply 473
  Writers or Clerks to the Signet 88
  see also Court of Session; Leith
Edinburgh Review 145, 146
Edinburgh University 90, 149, 282
  Civil Law 129, 165, 167, 183
  Conveyancing 158–9, 207, 270, 277
  Municipal Law 130
  Roman Law 229
  Scots Law 135, 159, 162, 168, 229, 270, 393
Ednam 369
education 182, 509
  legal 69–70, 71, 86–9, 128–9, 130, 155–9
Education Act 1496 62, 374

Edward I, king of England 186
ejection 212
elders 117
emphyteusis 188, 233, 238, 366, 382
enemies of the state 200
Engagers 81
English law 2, 6, 13, 18, 142, 175, 176, 193–6, 287, 304
  advantages of drawing on 167
  aspects of Scots law compatible with 36
  constructive trust 512
  courts and 161–2
  criterion of tidality 438
  distress 347
  historical links between Scots and 164, 166
  immoveables 335
  influence 177, 183; medieval, water rights 421–3, 425; pledge 337–8, 340; tidality 474; trusts 484–5, 502–6
  land 286–9
  law of Scotland closely akin to 32
  lien 351–3, 357
  main reception of 10
  prior appropriation 461
  rapprochement of Scots and 165
  registration 294
  restatement of 259
  'reunification' of Scots law with 164
  rules and institutions Scots law shares with 8
  Scots law remains different from 183–4
  Scots lawyers' concern with 142
  trusts 481, 484–5, 502–6, 507–8, 512
  waters 448, 450, 460, 462, 471, 473–7
English Navigation Acts 113
English Parliament 35, 80, 102, 113
  hostile 81
English Statute of Frauds 1677 496
Entail Act 1685 393
Entail Amendment (Scotland) Act (1848/1868) 396
Entail Improvement Act 1770 371, 393
entails 160, 180, 189, 393, 396, 513
episcopacy 80, 107
episcopalianism 77, 143, 117
equity 99, 105, 138, 225, 233, 240, 294, 471, 504
  major source of 100
  natural 78
  Roman law usually based on 236
escheats 160

essonzies 61
ethics 155, 175
European Community legislation 473
European Contract Law Commission 8
European Convention on Human Rights 14, 180, 184
European Court of Justice 1, 481
European Union 14, 184
  Council of 1
evidence 130, 265, 449
  interstitial 71
  law of 4
  lawyers' anxieties over adequacy of 130
  new law on 159
  no longer reduced to writing 148
  viva voce 149
  witness 121
  wrongdoing 103
ex adverso 467
examen duelli, aque et ferris caldi 24–5
exceptio doli 351
exceptio non adimpleti contractus 351
exceptio spolii 193
Exchequer, Court of 116, 124
Exchequer Rolls 386
excise 115
executry 83, 84, 514–16
exiles 109
existimatio circumcolentium 449
Extraordinary Lords (Court of Session) 147

Factors Acts 344
facts 27, 284, 404
  future 413
Faculties of Law 182
  see also Aberdeen University; College of Justice; Dundee; Edinburgh University; Glasgow University; Leiden; Leuven; Orléans; Paris; Pavia; St Andrews University; Utrecht
Faculty of Advocates 86, 87, 105, 125, 126–7, 128, 130
  admission 183
  appointment of various collectors of decisions 173
  examinations 156
  Faculty Services 181
  Library 156
  reorganized admission regulations 182
  tensions 155–6
Faculty of Procurators 88, 130, 157

fairness 85, 120
Falkland 37, 51
falsing of dooms 49, 55, 62
family law 180, 516
  see also marriage
favouritism 124
fealty 45, 277
fee 59, 60, 61
fencing 18
feoffees 193
feu 189, 277, 388, 440
feu duty 56, 188, 189, 349, 370, 411
feu farm 160, 364, 369–71, 495
  popularity of 385
  tenure 55–6, 160, 188, 227, 233, 238, 366
feudal rights 291, 298
feudalism 129, 132, 171, 185–92, 195, 201, 203, 270, 272–4
  conveyancing 274–82, 283
  debates over 164
  introduction to Scotland 234
  investiture 205
  jus commune and 478
  justice 28
  land law 160, 225, 234, 239, 241, 289
  leases 376
  origin in Scotland 164–5
  progressive legalization 40
  regalia 427
  Roman law and 191–2, 222, 227, 228–9, 233, 238, 466
  survival of 208–9
  tenures 20–1, 272
  waters 437, 466
feudorum senium 187
feuds 60, 91
feudum militare 508
fideicommissa 139, 233, 485, 510, 513, 515
  and *fideicommissarius* 490
  and *fiduciarius* 482, 490
fiducia 334
fiduciary 434, 513, 514
fiefs 21, 41
Fife 16, 20, 46, 371
  Earls of 32, 56
  King's Comptroller for 386
Figgate burn 447
fire-raising 67–8
firearms control 92
fishing/fisheries 426, 430, 435, 438, 440, 443–6, 448, 463, 476–7

Fithkil 46
fixtures 194, 248, 250–65
Flanders/Flemings 20, 23, 488
'floatability' 449
floating charges 194, 296, 301, 302, 345, 350
Flodden, battle of (1513) 51, 58
fondation 510
foreshore 425, 428, 429, 432–5, 436, 475–6
forfeiture 52, 189, 337, 338, 340, 372
  rejected 341
Forth, River 15, 16, 20, 22, 23, 33, 36, 39, 45, 436
Fortrose 389
'foundation' 510, 511, 512
Fragmenta Collecta 399
France 20, 23, 37, 76, 109
  peace with 145
  universities 128–9
  unpopular wars with 113
  see also French law
franchise 49, 146
fraud 131, 136, 195, 499
free trade 115, 348
freedom of the seas 430
freeholders 64, 69, 77, 147, 260
  of substance 62
French law 2, 3, 129, 135, 348
  Code Napoléon/Civil Code 198, 382, 462
  emphyteutic lease 382
  feudal system abolished 188
  fondation 510
  waters 438, 440, 457, 462, 474
French Revolution 464
fructus 273
fundus 436–8
fungibles 233

Gaelic past 28
gage 339
Galloway 15, 16, 22, 31, 36, 39, 50, 56
  Laws of 49
Garioch 21
General Council 37, 38, 48
'General Jury Book' 154
Genesis 334
geography 15–16
George Heriot's Trust 492–3, 510
German law 2, 3, 135, 315, 382, 474
  Historical School 167
  jus commune 176

Index of Subjects

Stiftung 510
training in 182
see also Pandectists
Germanic law/tribes 216, 376
gifts 303
girth (sanctuary) 53
Glasgow 29, 55, 80, 84
   Faculty of Procurators 88, 130, 157
   water supply 473
Glasgow University 89, 165
   Civil Law 129–30, 162
   Conveyancing 158–9, 207
   Moral Philosophy 163
   Roman Law 229
   Scots Law 229
Glencoe, massacre of (1692) 113
Glenswinton 49
Glossators 273, 274
good faith 197
   see also bona fides
grants 20, 25, 40, 313
   Crown 79, 434
   feudal 21, 466; *cum piscationibus* 443
   heritable 369
   perpetual 366–7
   regalities 39
   royal 42, 386
   secular 377
   unilateral 372, 380–1
grassum 56, 370, 379
grievances 117, 118, 120
   impious and intolerable 119
guardians 33, 35, 37

Haddington 153
haeres fiduciarius 515
Hailes 444
Hamilton v. Edington & Co. (1793) 455, 456, 457
Hamilton v. Western Bank of Scotland (1856) 343, 344
Hamilton v. Wood (1788) 356
hamsocn 17
Hanoverian succession 113, 115
Hawthornden 378
hearings *in praesentia* 174
heirs 62, 248, 259, 261, 262, 264, 370, 376, 400, 495
   of entail 160
   portioner 46, 234
hereditary rights 106
heritable jurisdictions 116, 118–19, 188
   abolition of 102, 147, 148, 149
   and the criminal courts 148–9
Heritable Jurisdictions (Scotland) Act 1747 148, 156
heritable property 186, 189, 201, 227, 247–8, 292, 294
   conveyancing of 299, 466
   derivative acquisition of 295
heritable rights 285, 290, 291, 416, 422
   development of 41–2
heritable securities 195, 247, 249, 261, 264, 265, 302, 355, 356
   early law 335
   wadset 342
heritage 21, 29, 42, 58, 59, 60, 61, 180, 298
   succession to 109, 180
heritors 117
High Commissioner 114, 116
High Court of Justiciary 117, 122–3, 144, 170, 179
   preserved 116
Highlands 32, 108, 110
   clearance 180
   disarming 147
   landowners 92
   pacification of 91, 92, 113
   special commissions of justiciary 123
hire-purchase agreements 265–6
Holland 109, 135
   see also Netherlands
Holyrood Abbey/Palace 24, 37, 51
homage 19, 34, 35, 114
Home Office 142
homicide 31, 36, 47
horning 410, 415, 416
House of Commons 115, 116, 123
House of Lords 115, 117, 148, 151, 196, 317, 442, 460, 505
   controversial role 183
   jurisdictions 123
   mode of electing Scottish representatives to 116
   publication of decisions 176
   Scottish appeals 144, 155
   system that encouraged disgruntled litigants to take appeals to 124
housing 186, 188
Huguenots 109
hypothec 205, 333, 334, 336, 345–50, 359
Hypothec Abolition (Scotland) Act 1880 349, 396

immissio 460
immoveable property 190, 201, 205, 228
  assignations of 407
  incorporeal 408
  lease of 216
  moveable and 247-8, 256, 270
  power to sell 501
  proprietor in possession protected against rectification of errors 215
  study of 206
  unitary treatment 222
  see also heritable property
imperial rights 426
impignoration 335, 348
imprisonment 122
in liberam baroniam (grant) 40
  see also barony
inaedificatio 246, 247, 248, 252, 254
incendium 68
incorporeal rights 408
indictment 22, 122
Indulgence (1669/1672) 108
Industrial Revolution 209, 250-1, 267, 463, 465
industrialization 146, 155
infangthief 25
infeft *cum piscationibus* 443-4
infeftment 132, 189, 276-7, 284, 366, 415
  challenged 72
  charter of 25-6
  ex facie valid 291
  in conjunct fee 205
  liferent 202
  public 495
Infeftment Act 1845 292, 293, 295
inheritance 26, 29, 368
Inner House (Court of Session) 12, 85-6, 104, 125, 153, 343
  cases decided on plurality of the votes of judges 150
  First Division 151, 196, 252, 284, 302, 441, 442
  report of causes to 121
  Second Division 151, 152, 252, 257, 260, 444, 470
innovation 41, 90
  conservatism and 39-40
  consolidation and 82-6
  liturgical, unpopular 79
  technological 146
  worship 80

inquest 30, 33, 83
  prejudiced 42
insolvency 196, 361
institutional writers 220, 221, 223, 297
  see also individuals in Index of Names, e.g. Balfour; Bankton; Bell; Craig; Erskine; Hume; Mackenzie; Stair
insula nata 439
insurance 161-2
intellectual property 210
intention 249-50, 261, 265, 266, 300
  motivating 299
  ownership transferred by 215
interdicts 439, 445, 452, 457, 472
  public law 447
interdictum Salvianum 346
interest 416, 418
interlocutors 85, 86, 152
  scope for review of 150
intermarriage 15
international law 430
interpretation 135-7, 322, 324, 326
intimation 401-11 *passim*, 413-18 *passim*
intransmissability of rights 416, 417
invecta et illata 348
Inverness 54
Ireland 15, 16, 110
  common law 445
irritancy 372
Isles/Islands 50, 51
  attempts to pacify 92
  Northern 93-4
  Western 16
ius insistendi 354
ius retentionis et hypothecae 354
ius retinendi 354

Jacobitism 111, 117, 147
  rebellions (1715/1745) 118, 143, 144, 160
journals 182
judex 17, 28
judges 48, 64, 65, 71, 100, 161
  Court of Session 104
  good 86
  opinions of 174, 175
  ordinary 61, 83
  papal 49
  removed from the bench 124
  temporal 83
judges-delegate 29, 30
Juridical Review 182

Juridical Styles 397
juries 27, 150, 154
jurisdictions 22, 24, 62
   amalgamation of 178
   appellate 84
   baronial 25
   criminal 25, 119, 148, 154
   disciplinary and proprietary 28
   ecclesiastical 29, 30, 99; bishops 107
   franchise 28, 44, 102, 119
   general and local executry 84
   heritable 92
   miscellaneous complaints 54
   rationalization and amalgamation of 153–4
   royal 49
jurisperiti 30
jurisprudence 167, 429, 474, 504
   analytical 168
   natural 156, 159, 165–6
juristic persons 510–11
Jury Court 159
   Lord Chief Commissioner 152
jus civile 18, 126, 372
jus commune 13, 141, 170, 187, 201, 366
   advocates of 128
   attraction of 67–8
   canon law and 376
   civilian heritage derived from 184
   common law and 45–7, 67–8, 99–101, 135–8
   debt to writings of 204
   feudalism and 478
   former centrality of 183
   historical sources of 4
   in practice 138–9
   influence of 376, 426–9
   jus proprium and 71–4
   learning of 162
   legal profession and 70–1
   links with forgotten 171
   litigation and 71–3
   medieval and early modern 7
   moving towards new 2
   Scots law and 140, 162–8
   shift from reliance on 167
   stock definition of 198
   strength of 101
   waters 422, 423, 425, 426–31 *passim*, 438, 443, 451, 454, 462, 473, 476, 477, 478, 483
   works on the procedure 68
jus divinum 98–9
jus feudale 78, 137
jus gentium 98–9, 100, 106, 137–8, 162, 163, 433, 443
jus in re in tem 366, 481
jus in re aliena 307, 308, 481, 483
jus mariti 419
jus municipale 100
jus naturale 106, 136, 137–8, 163, 385
   Roman law binding as 100
   sometimes necessary for human laws to depart from 107
jus piscandi 443
jus proprium 47, 100, 136, 137, 170
   and *jus commune* 71–4
jus retentionis 350
jus Romano-Scoticum 168
jus scriptum 72
jus tollendi 267
justice ayres 25, 60, 62, 92
justices of the peace 93, 103, 108, 119
   granted authority 117
   kept as minor figures 149
justiciars 21–5 *passim*, 27, 28, 30, 32, 39, 41
   hereditary 148
   jurisdiction 62

Katrine, Loch 473
Kelso Abbey 25, 377
'kenkynnol' 31
'kindly' tenants 55, 367, 368–9
King's Bench 35
King's College, Aberdeen 69, 89, 90
King's Council 30, 57, 74
   actions before 60
king's revenue 23, 24
king's sergeants 22
Kingedward 72
kingship 17, 52–3
   central function of 82
   jure divino 106, 118
Kirk 50
   episcopalian establishment 107
   General Assembly 77, 80, 91
   Provincial Council 29
   Reformation of 76–7
   right to appoint ministers 117
   state and 108–9
   teinds for the support of 79
   see also Presbyterianism

540   Index of Subjects

Kirk Sessions 83–4, 92, 103
knights' fees 20–1, 25
knowledge 411, 413
   private 406, 415, 417, 418

lairds 21, 69, 77
Lanark 39
Lanarkshire 394
land 55, 180, 186–7, 208, 251
   agricultural 373
   conflict over 47
   Crown 371
   deeds relating to 215
   duties of an owner 207
   escheated to king or baron 48
   granting out of 21
   neighbouring 469
   ownerless 428
   purchase on credit 188
   registration 194
   riparian 450
   sale and purchase of 209
   security 160
   transfer of 300
Land Register of Scotland 180, 215
   see also Register of Sasines
Land Registration Act 1925 194
land rights 45, 56, 207, 417
landholders 369, 371, 388
landlords 55, 56, 212, 261, 318, 347, 399
   compensation to tenants 372
   expulsion of sitting tenants 381
   hypothec 348
   rental book 367
   statutes affecting tenants and 382–3, 396, 397
   surety 386
   tenants pledging to 346
landowners 79, 92, 149, 445, 463
Largs, battle of (1263) 16
Lateran Councils:
   3rd (1179) 19
   4th (1215) 19, 27, 29
Latin 86, 87, 96, 101, 378
   knowledge of 89
   should no longer be used in writs 103
   study of 157
Law Agents Act 1872 181
law commissions 66–7, 96–8, 152–3
Law Reform (Miscellaneous Provisions) (Scotland) Act (1990) 516

Law Society of Scotland 181–2
Laws of King David 36
Laws of the Burghs 97
lawyers 13, 68–71, 73, 75, 77, 419, 474
   academic 47, 49
   academically trained 40, 63
   access to suitable literature 99
   acting as procurators before local courts 157
   canon 30–1
   classical 439
   comparative 3
   continental 510
   ecclesiastical 35, 46
   English 3, 78
   'enlightened' education for 156
   growth among 155
   increasingly important 89
   Roman 307
   trained in *jus commune* 74
   women 181
   see also legal profession
laymen 30, 58, 71
learned law:
   legal practice and 99–101
   litigation and 45
   rational procedure and 62–3
leases 160, 238, 251, 257, 258, 363–98, 399
   contract of 197
   limiting creditor's power to sign 418
   servitude and 191
   see also tacks
Leases Act 1449 374, 376, 377, 380, 381, 382, 418
Legal Aid and Solicitors (Scotland) Act 1949 181
legal literature 42–5, 385–6, 396–7
   development of Scottish law library 140–2
legal profession 44, 161, 181–2, 498
   appearance of 52
   'common law' 74
   development of 124–30
   emerging 68
   jus commune and 70–1
   legal education and 86–9, 155–9
   recognizable 57
   see also lawyers
Leges inter Brettos et Scotos 36, 39
Leges Quatuor Burgorum 24, 337–8, 339
legislature 177, 183

Index of Subjects 541

legitimacy 120
Leiden 163
Leith 101, 102, 405
leniency 407
Leuven 69
Leven, River 442, 449, 468
lex Anglicana 32
lex scripta 168, 169
liability 217, 218
libel 122
liberty 130–5, 159, 428
libraries 158
Libri Feudorum 47, 187, 426
lien 333, 350–61
  real 205
Lieutenant of the Realm 36, 37, 47
liferents 191, 193, 200, 205, 385, 416, 513
  assignation of 417–18
  organized as trusts 498
  redemptor not bound to 402
Linlithgow 51, 153
liquidation 500
literae humaniores 126
littoral rights/proprietors 420, 426, 433, 434, 436, 475
liturgy 79–80, 117
LL.B. (Bachelor of Laws) degree 182, 183
local courts 83, 120, 148, 154–5
  abolition of 147
  lawyers acting as procurators before 157
  most important 119
Local Government Act 1894 178
locatio conductio 365, 366
Lochnaw case (1873), *see Agnew*
lochs 428, 465–8
  tidal 437
Lombardic law 187
Lomond, Loch 442, 468
London 35, 112, 147, 493
  prominent Scots in 492
Long, Loch 437
Lords Advocate 87, 106, 111, 142, 145, 146, 178
Lord Chancellors 59, 259, 260, 263
Lord of the Isles 56
Lords Auditors of Causes and Complaints 54, 56, 58, 59, 71, 72, 338
Lords Justice-Clerk 53, 107, 122, 152, 154
Lords Justice-General 53, 98, 107, 122, 123, 144, 155
Lords of Congregation 76

Lords of Council and Session 58–9, 61–3 *passim*, 68, 71, 72, 83, 84, 108, 124–30, 139, 148
  admission to practice 87
  appointed as Commissioners of Justiciary 122
  appointments of 81, 107
  jurisdiction over valuation of teinds 116–17
  nominated 111
  Parliament review of actions of 123
  pleaders before 70
  profession under control of 88
  regularly tried to streamline litigation 147
  regulation on qualifications 116
  see also Extraordinary Lords; Lords Ordinary; Lords President Senators (College of Justice)
Lords of the Treasury 142
Lords Ordinary (Court of Session) 85, 86, 252, 263, 297
  permanent 152, 153
Lords President (Court of Session) 154, 155, 224, 295, 323, 356
lordships/lords 24–5, 39, 42, 49, 64, 121, 134–5
  justice 28
  large 23
  of regality 119, 122–3
  spiritual 86
  temporal 79, 86
  territorial 51, 52
  traditions linked with 56
Lothians 15, 16, 20, 36, 39
Lowland Scotland 92

MA (Master of Arts) degree 182
magister 497
magistrates 108, 281
magistri 30
magnates 33, 92, 111–12, 143
  struggle to 'tame' 51–2
  Whig 143
maills 364–5, 370
maintenance 216–17, 218
mairs 17, 21
mala fides 403, 405, 406, 411, 415, 416
  see also bad faith
Man, Lordship of 39
mancipatio 287, 307

mandates 419, 489, 506
  in rem suam 418
manners 166, 167, 172
manrent 91
manuscripts 46–7, 65, 67
  private 64
Mare Clausum 431
marine insurance 161
Marischal College, Aberdeen 89, 158
maritima incrementa 436
maritime law 348
maritime states 430
marriage 19, 20, 160, 419, 491
  antenuptial contracts 497–8
  canon law rule on legal presumption of 68
  'irregular' 119
  nullity of 120
Mearns 16, 20
medicine faculties 69
medieval law 7, 99, 421–3, 425
Mediterranean countries 440
medium filum 467
Melvillians 91
men of law 68
mercantile law 162
merchants 55, 91, 162
  statute of 36
merum imperium 50
Methil 437
Midlothian 21, 441
mill lades 423, 424
minute books 103, 132
missio in bona 497
missives 294, 296
mistake 5
mixed legal systems 3–4
monarchy:
  absolute nature of 107
  hereditary right 106
  limited 74–6
  loss of 82
  multiple 79–80, 112
  Scottish, contractual view of 110
  unlimited 76
money 337, 487–8, 506
  advances of 348
  bankers and 358
  claims to 400
  rent 369
  repayment of 400
  wed 489–90

Montrose, Dukes of 143
'moot' 17
morality 176
Moray 16, 21, 23
mores nostri 139
Morison's *Dictionary of Decisions* 174, 189, 213, 309, 410, 474
mormaers 17, 21
mortancestry 27, 28, 41, 61, 62
mortgages 349
mortification 508–12
Mosaic law 94
mottes 21
Mounth 36
moveable property 186, 190, 192, 201, 205, 212, 225, 228, 234, 241, 252, 258
  bona fide possession 215
  corporeal 303, 333, 342, 419
  dispositions of 202
  immoveable and 247–8, 256, 270
  incorporeal 333
  increased importance of 209
  legislation extending to 290
  ownerless 215–16
  pledge of 216
  power to sell 501
  rights in security over 333–62
  theoretical uncertainty and 419
  unitary treatment 222
moveable rights 412
municipal law 73, 90, 105, 138, 239
  pleadings on 139
murder 48

Nantes, Edict of (1598) 109, 128
Naseby, battle of (1645) 81
National Covenant, *see* Covenanters
national laws 176–7, 183
National Trust for Scotland 511
nationalist sentiment 178
natural justice 168, 352
natural law 82, 98, 100, 129, 137, 164, 225, 229, 233
  not all civil law founded on 235
  rationalist and voluntarist account of 163
  Roman law and 236
Navigation Acts (England and Scotland) 112
navigation/navigability 164, 428–30 *passim*, 435–7 *passim*, 438, 440–6, 448, 449, 452, 463, 468
neighbourhood law 453

Index of Subjects

neighbours 423, 424, 468, 469
Nemo plus ad alium transferre potest quam ipse habet 508
Netherlands 129, 156, 161, 315
   collegia privata 130
   navigability 440
   see also Holland
Newcastle 81
nexus 356, 357
Nicolson v. Melvill (1708) 218, 328
nobile officium 501
nobility 39, 80
   indebted 79
   measures were aimed at authority of 93
   parliamentary 52
   territorial 51
   traditional 77
Normans/Norman law 19–20, 24, 78
norms 26, 99, 140, 428
   customary 21
   legal 175
Norsemen/Norse law 16, 93
North American Empire 161
Northumbria 15
Norway 33, 34
notarial documents 74
notaries 46, 68, 400, 404, 405, 415, 418
   admission 88–9
novel dissasine (brieve) 26–8 *passim*, 61, 212, 421, 423–4
   reform of 41
nudus dominus 482
nuisance 461, 463, 465
   private 421
   public 421, 423
nulla sasina nulla terra 289, 292, 295
nulli res sua servit 317

oaths 88, 109, 496
   allegiance 103, 106, 111
   loyalty 33, 103
   rejecting legality of National Covenant 108
obiter dicta 11, 476
obligations 6, 8, 9, 201, 391
   ad factum praestandum 417
   affirmative 217, 218
   breach of 501
   conjugal 412
   law of 5, 351, 354, 400
   liberation from 355, 357
   maintenance 218
   mutuality of 358
   parental 412
   personal 298, 310
   reciprocal 217, 356
'occupation (*occupatio*)' 193, 202, 216, 228, 233, 436, 444
Officers of State 81
Officials 29
Old Pretender 113
ordeal 27, 31
Ordinance (1654) 102
ordinary courts 57
   common law 63
   failure of 59–61
Orkney 34, 50, 57, 93–4, 277
Orléans 63, 69, 70
Outer House (Court of Session) 85, 86, 104, 152, 153, 266
   academic exercises 87
   statutes regulating procedure of 121
overlords 34, 35, 42
ownership 194–5
   common 467
   defined 198
   description of 205
   divided 216, 508
   foreshore 435
   lochs 466–7
   possession and 210, 269–70
   private 426
   public 439, 448
   registration the only means of acquiring 214
   right of 195, 265, 288
   rivers 426, 441–3, 452, 454, 466
   sectional 216, 219
   several 467
   transfer of 202, 209, 215, 269–304
   vertical 216
   see also dominium
Oxford University 183

Panama, Isthmus of 113
Pandectists 311, 313, 314–15, 325
papal authority 76
Papists 110
pardons 92
parens patriae 428
parental rights 416
Paris 36, 63

Parliament, *see* Acts of Parliament; British Parliament; Commonwealth and Protectorate; Council in Parliament; Covenanters; English Parliament; Restoration Parliaments; Scottish Parliament
partnerships 418
passivity 326–9
pasturage 324
patrimonial injury/loss 451
patrimonial rights 434, 436, 437, 440
patrimony 5, 422
   ordinary and trust 484
patronage 115, 149
   politics of 143–5
Patronage Act 1712 117
Pavia 69
Pawnbrokers Acts (1800/1872) 345
pawnbroking 344–5
payment to the cedent 403–4, 406, 409
Peebleshire 378–9
penalty clauses 5, 390, 396
Penicuik 464
perennitas 438, 440, 446–8, 449
performance 334, 351, 414
   specific 5, 8
perpetua causa 325–6
'perpetual use' 256
personal rights 200, 201, 412, 415
   beneficiaries 482–3
   real rights and 282, 284–5
personality rights 5
Perth 62–3
petitions 121
Picts 15
pignus 334, 335, 336, 340, 341, 346
planning law 188
pleadings 26, 41, 174, 135–9, 167
   oral 126, 153, 179
   written 121–2
pledge 201, 205, 333, 334–45, 346, 359
poinding 341, 347, 410 n.
politics 75, 105–12, 146, 165, 166
   of management 178
   of patronage 143–5
'popery' 109
Popish Plot (1678) 108
possession 83, 193, 201, 203, 204, 210–16, 228, 233, 238, 414
   civil 211
   creditor has 333, 340

   delivery of 284, 286
   interim 214
   natural 211, 285–6
   ownership and 210, 269–70
   prescriptive 434, 443
   real 202
   real right resulting from 357
   recovery of 41
   relative rights to 294
   rightness, in inheritance 368
   security without 340, 344
   symbolic 285–6
   transfer of 489
power of disposal 272, 297
practice 66, 70, 71
   commission to examine 95
   English 183
   rules of 70
   Scots law largely oral in 44
   standard and important areas of 171
   use of sources of *jus commune* in 67
Practicks, see Balfour; Hope; Sinclair *in Index of Names*
practitioner law 197
precedents 12, 176
prejudice 42, 60, 447, 456
prelacy 111
prelocutores/prolocutores 46
prepositus 23, 24
Presbyterianism 77, 109, 116
   counteracting 90
   established 80, 81
   ministers allowed to return to parishes 108
   radical 76, 94
   settlement (1592) 111
Presbyteries 107
prescription 205, 289–92, 475
   acquisitive (positive) 97, 215, 289, 443, 444, 445
   reformed 131
Preston, battle of (1648) 81
primary use (water) 459, 465
primogeniture 21, 34, 186
   male 180
Principal Clerks of Session 125
'Principles of European Trust Law' 8
prior tempore potior jure 415
privileges 24, 88, 104, 205
   ecclesiastical 40, 49, 107
   public 446

university 69
Privy Council 54, 59, 84, 93, 107, 116, 148
    commission to examine the functioning of 120
    indulgences 109
    justices of the peace restored as agents of 119
    Lords of 81
    Scottish 79, 117
Privy Seal 53
    Keeper of 49
procedural law 4
procedure 121
    civil 103, 179
    courts and 178–9
    criminal 27, 179
    early 27
    fairness of 130–1
    familiarity with 46
    oral 63
    proof and 26–7
    proper, emphasis on 41
    rational 62–3
    reforms 62, 177
    Romano-canonical 63–4, 74, 99
    Scots law largely oral in 44
    substantive law and 130–2
procurator in rem suam 401, 412, 413, 416, 417
procurators 46, 68, 70, 71, 87, 88–9, 154, 157, 181, 286
    country 158
    education of 159
    interrupting prohibited 85–6
    prominent bodies of 130
Procurators Act 1865 181
professions 351, 352, 353
    see also legal profession
prolocutor 41
promises 103, 415, 416, 419
    written 418
promissory notes 161
proof 26–7, 31, 449
    Church's rejection of ordeal as a mode of 31
    of trust 496
property 9, 159, 488–9
    acquisition *inter vivos* 293
    bishops' 107
    church 30, 79, 137
    common 195, 455, 456, 467
    corporeal 233, 350
    incorporeal 233

individual 180
liberty and 130–5
protecting 132
public 233, 427, 441
recovery of 73
residual 443
transfer of 298, 483
see also under various headings, e.g.
    accession; heritable property;
    immoveable property; intellectual
    property; moveable property;
    occupation; ownership; possession;
    property law; property rights;
    retention; servitudes; title
property law 6, 256, 269, 270, 283, 294
    death of 208–10
    Romanization of 183, 220–44
    sources and doctrine 185–219
property rights 119, 131, 149, 269, 294
    absolute 441
    classification of 427
proprietary rights 436, 451, 454
prosecution 53, 119
Protectorate, *see* Commonwealth and Protectorate
Protestant religion 101, 109, 110, 114, 116
protestations 113, 125
    and appeals 123–4
protocol books 89
Provenhall's Creditors (1781) 355, 356, 361
public law 447
    interdictum uti priore aestate 455
    regulatory 188
    statutory, on water 472–7
public order 119
public policy 247
public rights:
    fishing 437, 439, 443–6, 448, 468
    foreshore 434, 435
    navigation 437, 442, 448, 468
    of passage 438, 448–50
public trusts 508–12
punishment 52, 53, 409
    of death 149
purpresture 421–3, 478
quasi-owners 196
Quebec law 481
Queen's Bench 116
quod nullius est fit domini regis 437
Quoniam Attachiamenta 44, 46, 65, 66, 95, 97, 386

'quots' 84

'radical right' 195, 515
railways 177
ranking 161, 346
rationalism/rationality 163, 176
real burdens 188, 197, 218, 506
   pecuniary 356, 357
   shift from servitudes to 219, 310, 331
real rights 193, 201, 204, 293, 296–8 *passim*, 303, 308, 350
   by diligence 356
   debts secured by 410
   dispositions of 414
   feudalized 200
   occupancy 382
   personal rights and 282, 284–5
   pledge 337, 341, 342
   registration the only means of acquiring 214
   restricted 307
   resulting from possession 357
   subordinate 205, 216, 360
   unqualified 300
Real Rights Act 1693 132
real securities 189
reason 240
   natural 175–6
reasonableness 450
receivership 351
Record Commission 169
recta ratio 98, 100
Redfearn v. Sommervail (1813) 507 n.
Reform Act 1832 146, 178
Reformation 83, 90, 383
Reformation Parliament (1560) 76, 193, 508–9
reforms 40–2, 99, 164, 350
   commercial law 160–1
   common law 94–5
   constitutional 80
   courts 130, 131, 154, 155–6
   criminal courts, procedural 130
   intended to speed up procedure 62
   law of moveable security 345
   legislative 147–8, 294
   novel dissasine 41
   prescription 131
   procedural 62, 122, 177
   property law 160, 295
   Whigs and 145–6
regalia 35, 452

regalia majora 427, 433, 435, 440, 450
regalia minora 427, 428, 433, 434
regalian rights 56
regalities 49, 83, 119, 122–3
   grants of 39
   heritable 91
   list of 148
   officers of 48
   royal interference in law enforcement in 56
Regiam Majestatem 46–7, 65, 66, 67, 95, 97, 99, 288
   allusion to assignation 399
   debates of the authenticity and authority of 164
   leases, terminology 373
   moveable property 335–7, 338, 339, 340, 346
   water 421–2
Register of Sasines 180, 197, 214, 215, 296, 300, 394, 402, 414
   General and Particular 396
Register of Sasines Act 1693 132
registration 131–2, 180, 293, 294, 296, 300, 390
   creditor's right in security dependent on 349
Registration Act 1617 295
Registration of Leases (Scotland) Act 1857 396
rei vindicatio 351
relief 495
remedies:
   common law 471–2
   Roman public law 452
remeid of law 113, 123, 125
remissions 47–8, 92
   respites (delays) from 53
Removal Terms (Scotland) Act 1886 396
Renfrew 39
rent/rentals 346, 366–8, 369, 371, 379, 384
   assignation of 417
   ecclesiastical 387
   non-payment 372
   security for a loan 399
   sequestration 347, 348
rentallers 55, 367
repossession 42
res communes 429–32, 433, 457
res communes omnium 426, 427, 428, 431–2, 436, 437, 443, 454
res humani juris 427

Index of Subjects

res in commercio 426
res in usu populi 459
res mancipi 307, 312
res nullius 426, 428, 433, 443, 444
res privatae 429
res publicae 426, 427, 428, 429, 432, 433, 438, 439, 452, 468
rescissory act 119
reserved waters 430, 431
resignation 279, 280
    ad favorem 86, 281, 490
respites 53, 92
respondentia bond 348, 349
Restoration 74, 105–8, 118–20 *passim*, 123, 125
    admission of advocates 126
Restoration Parliaments 112
retention 352, 353, 357–60
    right of 215, 351, 355
retour 42
retrocession 402, 408
    unintimated 411
Reversion Act 1469 197, 382, 401–2
reversions 197, 234, 409
    assignation of 400, 401, 402, 415, 416
    legal basis for 407–8
Revocation, Act of (1625) 79
Rhineland 23
right-to-buy legislation 188
riparian issues:
    common interest 438, 446–8, 450–65, 467–8
    proprietors 442, 444, 447, 450, 452
    rights 420, 432, 438, 447, 453, 455, 456, 458, 461–4 *passim*, 477
risk 401
rivers 422, 426, 428, 429, 434, 438–65, 473
    see also navigation; riparian issues
Robertson v. Baxter and Inglis (1897) 344
Roman Catholics 108, 109
Roman-Dutch law 5, 6, 438
    complete transplantation of 7
    guiding criterion in 322
    servitudes 311, 313, 317, 319–20, 324
Roman law 3, 46–7, 71–2, 73, 136–7, 138, 165–8, 192–3, 201, 207, 219
    accession by building 246–7
    advocates' use of 99
    assigned debt 497
    basis of the civilian tradition 7
    beginnings of reception of 187
    claim that calling of advocate was based on 142
    continental tradition of study of 156
    devalued history of reception in Scotland 165
    emphyteusis recognized in 366
    feudal law and 191–2, 222, 227, 228–9, 233, 238, 466
    fideicommissum and 490–1
    guiding criterion in 322
    hypothec 346, 348, 349
    influence on Scots law 366, 374, 407, 410, 412, 451–2
    intimation 409
    leases 372–4, 376, 377
    pledge 334, 345
    possession 211, 212
    property and obligations 183
    property law and 220–44, 275
    Reformers wished to promote academic study of 90
    Scotland bound by 100
    Scots law affinity with 287
    servitudes 307–8, 311, 313, 317, 320, 329
    terminological struggle between Anglo-Norman and 340
    traditional reliance on 126
    valid part of the armoury of every Scots lawyer 135–6
    waters 426, 428, 429, 432, 433, 437, 438–66, 472
    see also civil law, *jus commune*
Roman-Scotch law 6
Romano-canonical procedures 72, 74, 99
Roxburgh/Roxburghshire 24, 40
royal assent 114
royal authority 50
    extending 91–3
    proper exercise of 48
royal courts 24, 29, 68
    upholding of titles 370
royal justice 21–2, 28–9, 47, 55
royal prerogative 106, 111, 120
Royal Secretary 88
royal supremacy 76, 77, 107, 109

St Andrews 29, 50, 55, 60
    Archbishop of 51, 108
St Andrews University 69, 70, 87, 90
    St Mary's College 89

sale:
  causa of 294
  codification of English law of 194
  contract of 351
  delivery completed 286
  express power of 341
  judicial 205
sale of goods 209, 210
Sale of Goods Acts (1893/1979) 194, 215
sasine 42, 189, 276, 282–9, 301, 340, 381
  abandonment in modern conveyancing 292
  de facto/de jure 279
  delivery of 293
  failure to record 293
  heritable rights not perfected by 416
  instruments of 74, 284, 295, 299
  monopoly of the solemn recording of 89
Savoy, Supreme Court 139
scandal 113, 120
Scandinavia 18
Scone 25, 33, 40, 42, 82
Scotia 15, 22
Scotland Act 1979 178
Scots Digest 189
Scots language 378
Scots law 6–8, 182–4
  Anglicization of 395, 442, 448, 475, 508, 516
  as an autonomous national law 175–7
  made by Parliament 116
Scottish Church, *see* Kirk
Scottish Commissions 141
Scottish Company of the Indies 114
Scottish Discount Co. v. Blin (1985) 263, 264, 266, 268
Scottish Education Department 178
Scottish Enlightenment 165–6, 168
Scottish Executive 362
Scottish Grand Committee 178
Scottish Law Commission 194, 219
Scottish Leases Committee 368–9, 393, 394
Scottish National Party 178
Scottish Office 178
Scottish Parliament 14, 48–9, 50, 52, 62, 66, 80–1, 94, 95, 109, 112, 114
  Acts of 197, 376, 381
  chancellors 36, 49
  Charles I's one visit to 79
  Company of Scotland Trading to Africa and the Indies established 113
  Estate of bishops restored to 107
  General Council 38–9, 53
  King's Commissioner to 108–9
  legislation 64
  Lord Clerk Register 89
  Lord High Commissioner 115
  Lords Auditors of Causes and Complaints 54, 56, 58, 59, 71, 72, 338
  measures to promote order and concord 92
  new (1999) 180, 189
  notably submissive 106
  property issues 82–3
  representatives of small barons and freeholders called to 77
  response to litigants' attempts to take cases before 57
  review of actions of Lords of Sessions 123
  Roman rule adopted 67
  royal burghs' representatives to 55
  Scone 33, 40, 42
  survival of formal records of proceedings 74
  see also Reformation Parliament
seals 49, 88, 380
sea/seabed/seashore 425, 426, 428, 429–31, 432, 433, 437
  see also fishing; navigation
secessions 126
secondary use 459, 465
secret ballots 146
Secretaries of State 142
Secretary for Scotland 178
secular law 99
security 191, 193, 200, 284, 391, 400
  commercial 516
  rights of 296, 333–62, 402
  see also collateral; pledge; hypothec; lien; floating charges
Security, Act of (1703) 114
sederunts 63
  see also Acts of Sederunt
sedition 146
seisin, *see* sasine
Senators (College of Justice) 59, 63, 67, 68, 63, 88, 108, 125, 150
  academically trained in law 70
  appointment of 139
  education 71
  tenure 86
  trial of 124

Index of Subjects

sequestration 347, 348, 500
serfdom 55
servants 91
servientes domini Regis 22
servitors 156
servitudes 10, 193, 194, 202, 205, 228, 453
   limitations of 218
   natural 456, 458, 469, 470–1
   praedial 201, 217, 238, 305–32
Session Papers 122
Sessions 57–9
   see also Court of Session
Settlement, Act of (1701) 113, 122
Sheriff-clerks 158
sheriff courts 24, 27, 45, 54, 62–3, 83, 88, 157, 179, 424
   Admiralty jurisdictions merged with 154
   circuits granted jurisdiction to hear appeals from 148
   Commissions appointed to examine the operation of 120
   increasing importance 159
   role as the most important local court 119
sheriffdoms 32, 35, 39, 153, 404
   commissaries amalgamated into 153
   heritable 91, 118
   King's authority to divide, create, and annex 54
   two-thirds held heritably 119
Sheriffmuir, battle of (1715) 118
sheriffs 21, 23, 26, 30, 64, 83, 102, 108, 178
   prejudiced 60
   referring applicants for admission to a group of local procurators 158
   revitalization of the office 149
   surrender of heritable offices of 93
sheriffs depute 118, 148, 154, 156
sheriffs substitute 154, 155
Shetland 57, 93–4, 277
shires 17
show trials 106
Signet 111, 207
   Clerks to 88, 154
   see also seals; Writers to the Signet
signet summons 61, 88, 424
'slains' 17
slaughter 48, 53
social order 47–9, 91–3
Society of Advocates 88, 130, 157, 158
Society of Solicitors at Law 157
Society of Solicitors of the Court of Session and other Supreme Courts of Scotland 157
Society of Writers to His Majesty's Signet 207
   see also Writers to the Signet
Solemn League and Covenant (1643) 81, 108
Solicitors-General 142, 145, 146
Solicitors (Scotland) Act 1933 181
solum maris 436–8
Solway Moss, battle of (1542) 51
South African law 4–9 *passim*, 267, 312, 315, 481
South West Scotland 367
   see also Galloway
Southern Cross (Zimmermann & Visser) 4, 6, 9
sovereignty 75, 77, 100, 114
Spain 135
special practices 31
special registers 89
specification 193, 228, 233
Spey, River 449
Sprouston 40
spuilzie 74, 193, 212–14
Squadrone Secretary for Scotland 143–4
squatters 212
Stair Memorial Encyclopaedia 271, 273, 277, 278, 297
Stair Society 8, 9, 204, 205, 239, 273
stanks 465–9 *passim*
stare decisis 210
status 68, 127–8, 204
statute book 133–4
statutes 36, 53, 89, 100, 230, 235–6, 386
   access to 64, 72
   authority of 169
   commission to examine 95, 98
   comparison of 175
   defective 138
   evident problems with 132
   feu farm 364
   giving increased security to tenants 55
   governing admission as a notary 88
   guns and pistols 92
   homicide 47
   landlord-tenant 382–3, 396, 397
   regulating procedure of Outer House 121
   reliance on 99
   Scots law limited to 168
   superiority of common law over 177

statutes (*cont*)
  tenure 393
  texts of 65
  voting 79
  see also Acts of Parliament
stewarts 83, 108
  depute 148
  surrender of heritable offices 93
  Stiftung 510
stipulations 385, 388
Stirling 16, 24, 51
Stockwerkseigentum 216
Strathclyde 15, 16
Strathearn 386
subinfeudation 20, 186, 188
subletting 372
subrogation 484
substantive law 130–2, 159
substitutio 513
succession 113–16, 194, 248–50, 254, 258
  hereditary 109, 180
  issues decided according to civil law 139
suitors 25–6, 30
suits of 'wrang and unlaw' 27
summary process 154
superiors 409, 423–4
  cooperation of 279
  role of 277–8
  vassals and 188, 189, 191, 274–5, 277, 281, 349, 392, 422
Supremacy, Act of (1669) 108
supreme courts 139, 154, 158
surdit de sergeant 31, 36, 49
surety 28, 386
suspension 472
Synods 107

tacit location 385
tacks 55, 200, 202, 205, 233, 364, 365, 368, 490
  assignation of 414, 415, 417–18
  duration 387, 388
  first serious examination in Scots law 385
  granted to third party 392
  introduced from neighbouring countries 376
  obligation on tenant to pay 390
  oral 391
  ordinarily granted 374–5
  redemptor not bound to 402
  sub- 373

'vitalis' 409
  see also leases
Tarbet kirk 509–10
taxes 77, 79, 84
Tay, River 19, 20
teinds 28, 137, 193, 225, 414
  for support of Kirk 79
  jurisdiction over valuation of 116–77
tenants 22, 45, 146, 148, 188, 253–4, 258, 399
  controlling lords who dissaised 28
  criminal 386
  customary 370
  expulsion of 381
  government between king and 52
  landlord compensation to 372
  pledging to landlords 346
  possession extended to 212
  preserved against unjust recognition 42
  rights 259, 367, 382
  royal willingness to intervene between lords and 41
  sitting 381, 388
  statutes affecting landlords and 382–3, 396, 397
  statutes giving increased security to 55, 382–3
tenants-at-will 55, 368, 369
tenants-in-chief 33–4, 41
tenement, law of the 197, 216–19, 453, 456
tenements 309, 399
  burgage 282
  dominant 308, 311, 312, 313, 317–26 *passim*, 329
  free 41
  inferior 470
  servient 191, 307, 308, 310, 317–21 *passim*, 323, 325, 326
  stream forms a march between 455
  two separately held 317–18
tenure 21
  allodial 201, 272
  blench 160
  burgage 281
  ecclesiastical 508
  feu farm 55–6, 160, 188, 227, 233, 238, 366, 369, 370
  feudal 25, 29, 32, 180, 274, 369–71, 438
  heritable 366, 370
  land 94, 366, 371, 383, 394
  military 40, 149, 160, 188
  other types with similarities to the lease 366

Index of Subjects

security of 381–2
Senators' 86
Tenures Abolition Act 1746 393
terce 21, 26, 68
terminology 211, 232, 356, 337, 340, 354, 429
  civilian 365
  Germanic 272
  leases 364–72
  Roman 342
territorial sea 431, 436
Test Act 1673 109
testaments 84
texts 12, 44, 72, 73, 95, 198–208, 232, 236, 503–4
  extracts from 67
  moving 66
  Roman 19
  statutes 65
thanages/thanes 17, 21, 23
theft 343
Thelluson Act (1800) 504
theology faculties 69
thieves 212, 213
third parties 298
  alienation to 379
  contracts in favour of 5, 8
  debt comprised by 410
  diligence subject to 494
  rights acquired by 508
  tacks granted to 392
thirlage 10, 328
Thomism 98
Three Estates 38–9, 66, 75, 80, 91, 95
'three-mile rule' 431
tidality 438, 441–3, 445, 448, 466, 474, 479
tithes 289
  see also teinds
title 292, 294, 337, 345, 507
  descent of 370
  dispute about 214
  equitable 194
  feudal 291
  formal 195
  legal 194, 195, 196, 502
  tentative 495–6
  unimpeachable 291
  upholding of 370
  void and voidable 300
title deeds 216, 355
Titles to Land Act 1858 295
toieaschdeor 17

toiseach 17
Toleration Act 1712 117
Tories/Toryism 109, 143, 146, 151
tort 2, 421
torture 130
Toulouse 73
Town Councils 146
trade 113, 114, 164, 265, 348
  Dutch 112, 161
  fixtures and 250–7, 258, 259, 264
  laws on 115
traditio 193, 209
tradition 203, 204
  practice before ecclesiastical courts 71
  reconstruction and 44–5
  transfer by 202
transfer:
  bonds 413
  deed of 196
  land 300
  methods of 205
  ownership 202, 209, 215, 269–304
  possession 489
  property 298, 483
Transmission of Moveable Property (Scotland) Act 1862 418
transmission of rights 202, 412, 413, 414, 416, 437
treason 117, 122, 146, 147
treasure 227
Treasury Bonds 499
treatises 42, 47, 161, 182, 431, 503–4
  jus commune 168
  Roman law cited in 182
  specialized 141, 171
tres communitates 38
trespasses 103
trials:
  by battle 27
  by jury 150, 151
  time limits for 122
Trustee Investments Act 1961 516
trusts 194, 196, 333, 480–517
  for administration 195
Trusts (Scotland) Acts 515
  (1867) 501
  (1921) 482, 501, 516
  (1961) 516
tutor populi 428
Tweed, River 15, 32
Tyne, River (Scotland) 444

ultra vires 501
undersea coalmines 436
undue influence 5
Union, Act of (1707) 139, 142, 178, 492
Union of the Crowns (1603) 492
United Kingdom 209, 473
United Nations Convention on Contracts for the International Sale of Goods 1
United States of America 451, 462, 463, 471, 474
universities 69, 128, 129–30
   graduates/degrees in law 49, 182
   legal training/study of law 46, 89–91
   Northern Netherlands, popular for Scots 129
Universities (Scotland) Act 1858 182
unjustified enrichment 214–15, 512
urbanization 146, 188, 322
usages 36, 342
   prescriptive 468
   public 445
use 489–90
usucapio 289
usufruct 187, 193, 200, 274, 456, 498, 513
   right of 187
Usury Acts 344
usus 273, 427
uti priore aestate 447, 451–2, 453, 455, 458
utilitarian views 164
utilitas 319, 321–5, 329, 330
Utrecht 139
utriusque juris 129
utroque jure 70
utrumque jus 19, 47, 67, 87
   secular men with scholarly knowledge of 69

vadimonium 337
vadium 335, 337, 340
valuation cases 261–2
vassals 187, 189, 191, 197, 205, 276, 280, 370
   creating greater legal rights in 42
   de facto primacy 281
   in possession 186
   superiors and 188, 189, 191, 274–5, 277, 281, 349, 392, 422
vera lectio 65

vi et armis 41
vicinitas 318–21
violence 47–8, 92
visibility 431
vitious intromission 131
viva voce 122, 148
void and voidable 300, 501–2

wad 339, 340, 341
wad-wives 338
wadset 200, 205, 284, 339, 341
ward holdings 147, 160, 188
warrandice 384, 413, 418
warrants 291
warranty 390
water law regimes 420–79
wed/wedset 337, 338, 339
weights and measures 115
welfare system 180
Westminster 107
Westminster Confession of Faith (1647) 111
Whigs 109, 117, 151
   and reform 145–6
Whole Court 344, 355
widows 21
witch-hunts 130
witnesses 85, 403, 404, 418
   appending seals before 380
   examination of 63–4, 120–1, 122
Wittenberg 89
Worcester, battle of (1651) 82
Writers to the Signet 88, 103, 125, 130, 156, 375
   apprentice 158
   education of 158–9
   number of 155
   Society of 207
writing chapel 49
writs 33, 35, 103, 424
   Latin should no longer be used in 103
   royal 32
written testimony 63
wrongdoers/wrongdoing 52, 53, 103
wrongs 421

Index compiled by Frank Pert